Lecture Notes in Computer Science 13509

More information about this series at https://link.springer.com/bookseries/558

Yevgeniy Dodis · Thomas Shrimpton (Eds.)

Advances in Cryptology – CRYPTO 2022

42nd Annual International Cryptology Conference, CRYPTO 2022
Santa Barbara, CA, USA, August 15–18, 2022
Proceedings, Part III

Springer

Editors
Yevgeniy Dodis
New York University
New York, NY, USA

Thomas Shrimpton
University of Florida
Gainesville, FL, USA

ISSN 0302-9743   ISSN 1611-3349 (electronic)
Lecture Notes in Computer Science
ISBN 978-3-031-15981-7   ISBN 978-3-031-15982-4 (eBook)
https://doi.org/10.1007/978-3-031-15982-4

This Springer imprint is published by the registered company Springer Nature Switzerland AG
The registered company address is: Gewerbestrasse 11, 6330 Cham, Switzerland

Preface

The 42nd International Cryptology Conference (CRYPTO 2022) was held at the University of California, Santa Barbara, California, USA, during August 15–18, 2022. The conference had a hybrid format, with some presentations made in person, and some delivered virtually. CRYPTO 2022 was sponsored by the International Association for Cryptologic Research (IACR). The conference was preceded by two days of workshops on various topics.

The conference set new records for both submissions and publications: 455 papers were submitted, and 100 were accepted. Two papers were merged into a single joint paper. Three pairs of papers were soft-merged, meaning that they were written separately, but only one paper in each pair was given a presentation slot at the conference. This resulted in 96 presentations, a record by some margin for a non-virtual edition of Crypto. It took a Program Committee of 72 cryptography experts working with 435 external reviewers almost three months to select the accepted papers. We Chairs extend our heartfelt gratitude for the effort and professionalism displayed by the Program Committee; it was our pleasure to be your Chairs.

We experimented with some new policies and mechanisms this year. The most important had to do with the quality of reviewing, author feedback and interaction with the authors.

Shortly after the standard doubly-blind reviewing stage, we assigned a unique discussion leader (DL) to every paper. The DL's job was to make sure the paper received a thorough and fair treatment, and to moderate interactive communication between the reviewers and authors (described below). The DL also prepared a "Reviewers' consensus summary", which provided the authors with a concise summary of the discussion, the decision, and overall trajectory of the paper throughout the process. Many authors expressed gratitude for receiving the Reviewers' consensus summary, in addition to the usual reviews and scores. Overall, feedback on our DL experiment was quite positive, and we recommend it to future chairs to adopt this process as well.

We also experimented with an "interactive rebuttal" process. Traditionally, the rebuttal process has consisted of a single round: the authors were provided with the initial reviews, and had one opportunity to respond prior to the final decision. While better than no opportunity to rebut, our opinion is that the traditional process suffers from several important flaws. First, the authors were left to respond in (say) 750 words to multiple reviews that are, each, much longer. Too often, the authors are left to divine what are the *crucial* points to address; getting this wrong can lead to reviewers feeling that the rebuttal has missed (or dismissed) what mattered to them. In any case, the authors had no idea if their rebuttal was correctly focused, let alone convincing, until the decisions and final reviews were released. In many instances, the final reviews gave no signal that the rebuttal had been thoughtfully considered. In our view, and personal experience, the traditional rebuttal process led to frustration on both sides, with reviewers and authors feeling that their time had been wasted. Moreover, it had unclear benefits in terms of helping the PC to pick the best possible program.

To address this, we created a review form that required reviewers to make explicit what were their core concerns and criticisms; and we allowed for multiple, DL-moderated, rounds of communication between the reviewers and the authors.

Our review form had *exactly one* field visible to the authors during the initial rebuttal round. The field was called "Question/Clarifications for Authors", and reviewers were instructed to include *only* those things that had significant bearing upon the reviewer's accept/reject stance. We gave all reviewers detailed guidance on things that *must* be included. For example, any claimed errors, crucial prior work that was not cited, or other objective weaknesses that appeared in the detailed review comments. In addition, the reviewers were instructed to clearly state less objective concerns that factored into their initial score and disposition towards the paper. Thus, the authors should know exactly what to focus upon in their response. While not perfect, the new rebuttal format was a resounding success. Very strong/weak papers typically had very short rebuttals, allowing the PC to focus their time and energy on papers in need of extensive discussion or additional reviews.

In concert with the new review form and detailed review instructions, we also implemented *interactive discussions* between the reviewers and authors. The traditional rebuttal round became the first round of the interactive discussion. One round was enough for a fraction of the papers (primarily papers that were very strong or very weak), but the evaluation of most submissions benefited from numerous rounds: reviewers were able to sharpen their questions, authors were able to address points directly and in greater detail. The whole review process shifted more towards a collegial technical exchange. We did not encounter any problems that we initially feared, e.g., authors spamming the PC with comment. We believe that having the DLs moderate these interactions was important for keeping emotions and egos in check, and for encouraging reviewers to share any significant new concerns with the authors.

A few minor hiccups notwithstanding, the focused review forms and the "interactive rebuttal" mechanism received a lot of positive feedback, and we strongly encourage future chairs to adopt this tradition.

We also mention several smaller details which worked well. First, our review form included a "Brief Score Justification" field that remained reviewer-visible (only) for the entire process. This was a space for reviewers to speak freely, but concisely, about how they came to their scores. As Chairs, we found this extremely useful for getting a quick view of each paper's reviews. Second, we had an early rejection round roughly in the middle of our reviewing process. This allowed us to reject roughly half of submissions, i.e., those that clearly had no chance of being accepted to the final program. The process generally worked, and we tried to err on the side of caution, keeping papers alive if the PC was unsure of their seemingly negative views. For example, we allowed PC members to tag papers that they wanted to keep alive, even to the point of overturning a preliminary decision to early reject. However, we did feel slightly rushed in finalizing the early reject decisions, as we made them after less than two weeks after the initial reviewing round, and less than a week after the initial rebuttal round. Part of this rush was due to late reviews. Thus, we recommend that future chairs give themselves a bit more slack in the schedule, and perhaps add a second (less) early rejection round. Third, we experimented with allowing PC members to have a variable number of submissions, rather than the usual hard limits (e.g., at most one or two). Concretely, at most 4 papers could be submitted; the first paper was "free", but every subsequent paper submitted by the PC member resulted in this PC member getting roughly three more papers to review, and one additional DL appointment. We adopted this policy to make it easier for experts to accept our invitation to join the PC. (As always, the chairs were not allowed to submit papers.) Despite some unexpected difficulties and complaints about this system, most having to do with the logistic difficulty of assigning DLs to PC members with late initial reviews, many PC members told us that they appreciated the flexibility to submit more papers, especially when students were involved. We found no evidence that our system resulted in more accepted papers that were co-authored by the PC members, or any other biases and irregularities. Hence, we found it to be positive, overall.

The Program Committee recognized three papers and their authors for particularly outstanding work

- "Batch Arguments for NP and More from Standard Bilinear Group Assumptions," by Brent Waters and David Wu
- "Breaking Rainbow Takes a Weekend on a Laptop", by Ward Beullens
- "Some Easy Instances of Ideal-SVP and Implications to the Partial Vandermonde Knapsack Problem", by Katharina Boudgoust, Erell Gachon, and Alice Pellet-Mary

We were very pleased to have Yehuda Lindell as the Invited Speaker at CRYPTO 2022, who spoke about "The MPC journey from theoretical foundations to commercial success: a story of science and business".

We would like to express our sincere gratitude to all the reviewers for volunteering their time and knowledge in order to select a great program for 2022. Additionally, we are grateful to the following people for helping to make CRYPTO 2022 a success: Allison Bishop (General Chair, CRYPTO 2022), Kevin McCurley and Kay McKelly (IACR IT experts), Carmit Hazay (Workshops Chair), and Whitney Morris and her staff at UCSB conference services.

We would also like to thank the generous sponsors, all of the authors of the submissions, the rump session chair, the regular session chairs, and the speakers.

August 2022   Yevgeniy Dodis
                                                                          Thomas Shrimpton

Organization

General Chair

Allison Bishop   Proof Trading and City College, CUNY, USA

Program Committee Chairs

Yevgeniy Dodis   New York University, USA
Thomas Shrimpton   University of Florida, USA

Steering Committee

Helena Handschuh   Rambus Inc., USA
Anna Lysyanskaya   Brown University, USA

Program Committee

Shweta Agarwal	IIT Madras, India
Prabhanjan Ananth	University of California Santa Barbara, USA
Saikrishna Badrinarayanan	Visa Research, USA
Lejla Batina	Radboud University, Netherlands
Carsten Baum	Aarhus University, Denmark
Jeremiah Blocki	Purdue University, USA
Alexandra Boldyreva	Georgia Tech, USA
Elette Boyle	IDC Herzliya and NTT Research, Israel
David Cash	University of Chicago, USA
Itai Dinur	Ben-Gurion University, Israel
François Dupressoir	University of Bristol, UK
Nico Döttling	Helmholtz Center for Information Security (CISPA), Germany
Dario Fiore	IMDEA Software Institute, Spain
Ben Fisch	Stanford, USA
Marc Fischlin	TU Darmstadt, Germany
Rosario Gennaro	City College of New York, USA
Divya Gupta	Microsoft Research, India
Felix Günther	ETH Zurich, Switzerland
Mohammad Hajiabadi	University of Waterloo, Canada
Helena Handschuh	Rambus Inc., USA

Ni Trieu	Arizona State University, USA
Yiannis Tselekounis	Carnegie Mellon University, USA
Mayank Varia	Boston University, USA
Xiao Wang	Northwestern University, USA
Daniel Wichs	Northeastern University and NTT Research, USA
David Wu	UT Austin, USA
Shota Yamada	AIST, Japan
Kan Yasuda	NTT Labs, Japan
Kevin Yeo	Google and Columbia University, USA
Eylon Yogev	Bar-Ilan University, Israel
Vassilis Zikas	Purdue University, USA

Additional Reviewers

Masayuki Abe	Mihir Bellare
Calvin Abou Haidar	Adrien Benamira
Anasuya Acharya	Fabrice Benhamouda
Divesh Aggarwal	Huck Bennett
Shashank Agrawal	Ward Beullens
Gorjan Alagic	Tim Beyne
Navid Alamati	Rishabh Bhadauria
Martin R. Albrecht	Amit Singh Bhati
Nicolas Alhaddad	Ritam Bhaumik
Bar Alon	Sai Lakshmi Bhavana Obbattu
Estuardo Alpirez Bock	Jean-Francois Biasse
Jacob Alprerin-Shreiff	Alexander Bienstock
Joel Alwen	Nina Bindel
Ghous Amjad	Nir Bitansky
Kazumaro Aoki	Olivier Blazy
Gal Arnon	Alexander Block
Rotem Arnon-Friedman	Xavier Bonnetain
Arasu Arun	Jonathan Bootle
Thomas Attema	Katharina Boudgoust
Benedikt Auerbach	Christina Boura
Christian Badertscher	Pedro Branco
David Balbás	Konstantinos Brazitikos
Marco Baldi	Jacqueline Brendel
Gustavo Banegas	Marek Broll
Fabio Banfi	Chris Brzuska
Laaysa Bangalore	Ileana Duhan
James Bartusek	Benedikt Bunz
Andrea Basso	Bin-Bin Cai
Christof Beierle	Federico Canale
Amos Beimel	Ran Canetti

Ignacio Cascudo
Gaëtan Cassiers
Dario Catalano
Pyrros Chaidos
Suvradip Chakraborty
Jeff Champion
Benjamin Chan
Alishah Chator
Shan Chen
Weikeng Chen
Yilei Chen
Yu Long Chen
Nai-Hui Chia
Lukasz Chmielewski
Chongwon Cho
Arka Rai Choudhuri
Miranda Christ
Chitchanok Chuengsatiansup
Peter Chvojka
Michele Ciampi
Benoît Cogliati
Ran Cohen
Alex Cojocaru
Sandro Coretti-Drayton
Arjan Cornelissen
Henry Corrigan-Gibbs
Geoffroy Couteau
Elizabeth Crites
Jan Czajkwoski
Joan Daemen
Quang Dao
Pratish Datta
Bernardo David
Nicolas David
Hannah Davis
Koen de Boer
Leo de Castro
Luca De Feo
Gabrielle De Micheli
Jean Paul Degabriele
Patrick Derbez
Jesus Diaz
Jack Doerner
Jelle Don
Jesko Dujmovic

Sebastien Duval
Ted Eaton
Nadia El Mrabet
Reo Eriguchi
Llorenç Escolà Farràs
Daniel Escudero
Saba Eskandarian
Thomas Espitau
Antonio Faonio
Pooya Farshim
Serge Fehr
Peter Fenteany
Rex Fernando
Rune Fiedler
Matthias Fitzi
Nils Fleischhacker
Danilo Francati
Cody Freitag
Tommaso Gagliardoni
Chaya Ganesh
Rachit Garg
Lydia Garms
Luke Garratt
Adria Gascon
Romain Gay
Peter Gaži
Nicholas Genise
Marios Georgiou
Koustabh Ghosh
Ashrujit Ghoshal
Barbara Gigerl
Niv Gilboa
Emanuele Giunta
Aarushi Goel
Eli Goldin
Junqing Gong
Jesse Goodman
Lorenzo Grassi
Alex Grilo
Alex Bredariol Grilo
Aditya Gulati
Sam Gunn
Aldo Gunsing
Siyao Guo
Yue Guo

Chun Guo
Julie Ha
Ben Hamlin
Ariel Hamlin
Abida Haque
Patrick Harasser
Ben Harsha
Eduard Hauck
Julia Hesse
Clemens Hlauschek
Justin Holmgren
Alexander Hoover
Kai Hu
Yuval Ishai
Muhammad Ishaq
Takanori Isobe
Tetsu Iwata
Hakon Jacobsen
Aayush Jain
Ashwin Jha
Dingding Jia
Zhengzhong Jin
Nathan Ju
Fatih Kaleoglu
Daniel Kales
Simon Kamp
Daniel M. Kane
Dimitris Karakostas
Harish Karthikeyan
Shuichi Katsumata
Marcel Keller
Thomas Kerber
Mustafa Khairallah
Hamidreza Amini Khorasgani
Hamidreza Khoshakhlagh
Dakshita Khurana
Elena Kirshanova
Fuyuki Kitagawa
Susumu Kiyoshima
Dima Kogan
Lisa Kohl
Stefan Kolbl
Dimitris Kolonelos
Ilan Komargodski
Chelsea Komlo

Yashvanth Kondi
Venkata Koppula
Daniel Kuijsters
Mukul Kulkarni
Nishant Kumar
Fukang Liu
Norman Lahr
Russell W. F. Lai
Qiqi Lai
Baptiste Lambin
David Lanzenberger
Philip Lazos
Seunghoon Lee
Jooyoung Lee
Julia Len
Tancrède Lepoint
Gaëtan Leurent
Hanjun Li
Songsong Li
Baiyu Li
Xiao Liang
Yao-Ting Lin
Han-Hsuan Lin
Huijia Lin
Xiaoyuan Liu
Meicheng Liu
Jiahui Liu
Qipeng Liu
Zeyu Liu
Yanyi Liu
Chen-Da Liu-Zhang
Alex Lombardi
Sébastien Lord
Paul Lou
Donghang Lu
George Lu
Yun Lu
Reinhard Lüftenegger
Varun Madathil
Monosij Maitra
Giulio Malavolta
Mary Maller
Jasleen Malvai
Nathan Manohar
Deepak Maram

Lorenzo Martinico
Christian Matt
Sahar Mazloom
Kelsey Melissaris
Nicolas Meloni
Florian Mendel
Rebekah Mercer
Pierre Meyer
Charles Meyer-Hilfiger
Peihan Miao
Brice Minaud
Pratyush Mishra
Tarik Moataz
Victor Mollimard
Andrew Morgan
Tomoyuki Morimae
Travis Morrison
Fabrice Mouhartem
Tamer Mour
Pratyay Mukherjee
Marta Mularczyk
Marcel Nageler
Yusuke Naito
Kohei Nakagawa
Mridul Nandi
Varun Narayanan
Patrick Neumann
Gregory Neven
Samuel Neves
Ngoc Khanh Nguyen
Hai Nguyen
Luca Nizzardo
Ariel Nof
Adam O'Neill
Maciej Obremski
Kazuma Ohara
Miyako Ohkubo
Claudio Orlandi
Michele Orrù
Elisabeth Oswald
Morten Øygarden
Alex Ozdemir
Elena Pagnin
Tapas Pal
Jiaxin Pan

Giorgos Panagiotakos
Omer Paneth
Udaya Parampalli
Anat Paskin-Cherniavsky
Alain Passelègue
Sikhar Patranabis
Chris Peikert
Alice Pellet-Mary
Zachary Pepin
Leo Perrin
Giuseppe Persiano
Edoardo Persichetti
Peter Pessl
Thomas Peters
Stjepan Picek
Maxime Plancon
Bertram Poettering
Christian Porter
Eamonn Postlethwaite
Thomas Prest
Robert Primas
Luowen Qian
Willy Quach
Srinivasan Raghuraman
Samuel Ranellucci
Shahram Rasoolzadeh
Deevashwer Rathee
Mayank Rathee
Divya Ravi
Krijn Reijnders
Doreen Riepel
Peter Rindal
Guilherme Rito
Bhaskar Roberts
Felix Rohrbach
Leah Rosenbloom
Mike Rosulek
Adeline Roux-Langlois
Joe Rowell
Lawrence Roy
Tim Ruffing
Keegan Ryan
Yusuke Sakai
Louis Salvail
Simona Samardjiska

Katerina Samari
Olga Sanina
Amirreza Sarencheh
Pratik Sarkar
Yu Sasaki
Tobias Schmalz
Markus Schofnegger
Peter Scholl
Jan Schoone
Phillipp Schoppmann
André Schrottenloher
Jacob Schuldt
Sven Schäge
Gregor Seiler
Joon Young Seo
Karn Seth
Srinath Setty
Aria Shahverdi
Laura Shea
Yaobin Shen
Emily Shen
Sina Shiehian
Omri Shmueli
Ferdinand Sibleyras
Janno Siim
Jad Silbak
Luisa Siniscalchi
Daniel Slamanig
Yifan Song
Min Jae Song
Fang Song
Nicholas Spooner
Lukas Stennes
Igors Stepanovs
Christoph Striecks
Sathya Subramanian
Adam Suhl
George Sullivan
Mehrdad Tahmasbi
Akira Takahashi
Atsushi Takayasu
Abdul Rahman Taleb
Quan Quan Tan
Ewin Tang
Tianxin Tang

Stefano Tessaro
Justin Thaler
Emmanuel Thome
Søren Eller Thomsen
Mehdi Tibouchi
Radu Titiu
Yosuke Todo
Junichi Tomida
Monika Trimoska
Daniel Tschudi
Ida Tucker
Nirvan Tyagi
Rei Ueno
Dominique Unruh
David Urbanik
Wessel van Woerden
Prashant Vasudevan
Serge Vaudenay
Muthu Venkitasubramaniam
Damien Vergnaud
Thomas Vidick
Mikhail Volkhov
Satyanarayana Vusirikala
Riad Wahby
Roman Walch
Hendrik Waldner
Michael Walter
Qingju Wang
Han Wang
Haoyang Wang
Mingyuan Wang
Zhedong Wang
Geng Wang
Hoeteck Wee
Shiyi Wei
Mor Weiss
Chenkai Weng
Benjamin Wesolowski
Lichao Wu
Keita Xagawa
Jiayu Xu
Anshu Yadav
Sophia Yakoubov
Takashi Yamakawa
Trevor Yap Hong Eng

Xiuyu Ye
Albert Yu
Thomas Zacharias
Michal Zajac
Hadas Zeilberger

Mark Zhandry
Yupeng Zhang
Cong Zhang
Bingsheng Zhang
Dionysis Zindros

Sponsor Logos

Contents – Part III

Cryptanalysis II

Distributed Algorithms

Secure Hash Functions

Post-quantum Cryptography

Symmetric Cryptanalysis

Signatures

PI-Cut-Choo and Friends: Compact Blind Signatures via Parallel Instance Cut-and-Choose and More

Rutchathon Chairattana-Apirom[2], Lucjan Hanzlik[1], Julian Loss[1], Anna Lysyanskaya[2], and Benedikt Wagner[1(✉)]

[1] CISPA Helmholtz Center for Information Security, Saarbrücken, Germany
{hanzlik,loss,benedikt.wagner}@cispa.de
[2] Brown University, Providence, RI 02906, USA
rutchathon_chairattana-apirom@alumni.brown.edu,
anna_lysyanskaya@brown.edu

Abstract. Blind signature schemes are one of the best-studied tools for privacy-preserving authentication. Unfortunately, known constructions of provably secure blind signatures either rely on non-standard hardness assumptions, or require parameters that grow linearly with the number of concurrently issued signatures, or involve prohibitively inefficient general techniques such as general secure two-party computation.

Recently, Katz, Loss and Rosenberg (ASIACRYPT'21) gave a technique that, for the security parameter n, transforms blind signature schemes secure for $O(\log n)$ concurrent executions of the blind signing protocol into ones that are secure for any $\mathsf{poly}(n)$ concurrent executions.

This transform has two drawbacks that we eliminate in this paper: 1) the communication complexity of the resulting blind signing protocol grows linearly with the number of signing interactions; 2) the resulting schemes inherit a very loose security bound from the underlying scheme and, as a result, require impractical parameter sizes.

In this work, we give an improved transform for obtaining a secure blind signing protocol tolerating any $\mathsf{poly}(n)$ concurrent executions from one that is secure for $O(\log n)$ concurrent executions. While preserving the advantages of the original transform, the communication complexity of our new transform only grows logarithmically with the number of interactions. Under the CDH and RSA assumptions, we improve on this generic transform in terms of concrete efficiency and give (1) a BLS-based blind signature scheme over a standard-sized group where signatures are of size roughly 3 KB and communication per signature is roughly 120 KB; and (2) an Okamoto-Guillou-Quisquater-based blind signature scheme with signatures and communication of roughly 9 KB and 8 KB, respectively.

Keywords: Blind Signatures · Standard Assumptions · Random Oracle Model · Cut-and-Choose

© International Association for Cryptologic Research 2022
Y. Dodis and T. Shrimpton (Eds.): CRYPTO 2022, LNCS 13509, pp. 3–31, 2022.
https://doi.org/10.1007/978-3-031-15982-4_1

1 Introduction

In 1982, David Chaum introduced blind signature schemes in the context of electronic cash [9]. A blind signature scheme is a cryptographic primitive in which a signer can interactively sign a message held by a user. Informally, a blind signature scheme must satisfy two security requirements [23,30]. *Blindness:* the signer should not be able to see what message is being signed. *Unforgeability:* The user should only be able to obtain valid signatures by interacting with the signer. Classical applications of blind signature schemes include e-cash [9,28], anonymous credentials [6,7] and e-voting [19]. Recently, blind signatures have also been used to add privacy features to blockchain-based systems [22]. Despite this variety of promising applications, the current state-of-the art is unsatisfactory. This is because even in the random oracle model, schemes with reasonable efficiency are either based on non-standard assumptions [2,4,11] or have parameters that grow linearly in the number of concurrent signing interactions [3,20,25,30]. The main goal of this work is to construct blind signature schemes from well-established assumptions with concurrent security and practically efficient parameter sizes.

State-of-the-Art. Juels, Luby and Ostrovsky showed that blind signature schemes can be built generically from any secure signature scheme using secure two-party computation [23]. Their construction was only shown secure when signatures were issued *sequentially*. However, typically one aims for the stronger notion of concurrent security. Fischlin [10] achieved this by giving universally composable blind signatures from commitment schemes and UC zero-knowledge proofs; but it is not clear how to instantiate these generic constructions efficiently. While it is tempting to instantiate these schemes with efficient signature schemes in the random oracle model, the security implications of such an instantiation are unclear. This is because such an instantiation would imply the use of the random oracle as a circuit, which constitutes a non-standard use of the random oracle model. We refer to the recent work of [1] which discusses these issues in more detail.

In the standard model, a variety of blind signature schemes have been proposed. These schemes are either inefficient as they rely on complexity leveraging [14] or rely on strong q-type or non-interactive assumptions [11,15,16,27].

Unfortunately, even in the random oracle model, the situation does not improve much. While there are simple constructions [2,4,20,21,30], they either require similar non-standard assumptions as their standard model counterparts [2,4] or support only a very small number of signatures per public key [3,20,21,30].

As a first step to overcome these limitations, Katz, Loss, and Rosenberg (KLR) [25] showed how to use a cut-and-choose technique to boost the security of these blind signature schemes in the random oracle model. Their approach is based on an early work by Pointcheval [29]. The resulting schemes support polynomially many concurrent signature interactions and are based on standard assumptions. However, the communication between the signer and the user still grows linearly with the number of signature interactions, which renders the scheme impractical.

We note that relying on the algebraic or generic group model [12,32] yields better composition and efficiency, as recent works [13,24,33] show. However, these models are best avoided as they are non-standard.

Our Goal. In this work, we advance the state of the art by giving the first blind signature schemes in the random oracle model that do not suffer from any of the above drawbacks. Our main research question can be summarized as follows:

Are there practical and concurrently secure blind signatures from well-established hardness assumptions which support polynomially many signatures?

1.1 Starting Point: The Basic Boosting Transform

We answer this question in the affirmative. We propose several new techniques which reduce the size and communication complexity of blind signatures in the random-oracle model.

Before we explain our techniques, we briefly recall the KLR transform [25], which will serve as our starting point. The KLR transform can be applied to a blind signature scheme BS in which the user sends a single message and which supports a logarithmic number of signing sessions. The transformed scheme CCBS supports polynomially many signing sessions and achieves the same notion of blindness as BS. We briefly recall the main ideas of CCBS before explaining our improved version:

- In the Nth signing interaction, the Signer and the User initiate N sessions of the underlying scheme BS. In the ith session, a commitment μ_i of the actual message is signed.
- The User commits to its randomness ρ_i for the ith session using a commitment $com_i = H(\rho_i)$, where H is a hash function (modeled as a random oracle). It sends com_i together with its (only) message in the ith session of BS.
- The Signer picks a session $J \in [N]$ uniformly at random and has the User open the randomness to all commitments $com_i, i \in [N] \setminus \{J\}$.
- If the User cannot open one of these commitments, the Signer aborts. Otherwise, the Signer and User complete the Jth session as in BS.

The proof of one-more unforgeability for CCBS is by reduction to the one-more unforgeability of BS. The reduction's goal is to turn a one-more forgery against CCBS into a one-more forgery against BS. To do so, the reduction must answer all signing queries of the User without knowing the secret key sk of the Signer in BS. It is further restricted by the fact that it may invoke the Signing oracle in the underlying security game for BS only logarithmically many times.

To bypass these restrictions, the reduction heavily relies on its capability of observing the inputs to the random oracle and programming it accordingly. Suppose that the User behaves honestly in Session J, i.e., it uses the randomness in com_J to compute its message in the Jth session of BS. Then the reduction can extract the random coins from the commitments and use random oracle programming to complete this session without knowing sk. If, on the other hand, the User cheats, then the reduction can not use this technique and must ask the Signing oracle in BS for help.

KLR's key observation is that the probability of such a (successful) cheat is at most $1/N$ in the Nth signing session. Thus, the expected number of successful cheats in p interactions is at most $\sum_{N \leq p+1} 1/N < \ln(p+1)$. Using the Chernoff bound, one can show that with overwhelming probability, the number of successful cheats is reasonably close to this expectation. Hence, the signing oracle in the underlying OMUF game of BS needs to be invoked only a logarithmic number of times.

Limitations. Although CCBS exponentially increases the security of the underlying blind signature scheme BS, this comes at a steep price in terms of efficiency: the communication in the resulting scheme grows linearly with the number N of issued signatures. This arguably renders CCBS impractical. In addition, the number of times that the reduction from one-more unforgeability of BS requires invoking the underlying signing oracle behaves as $\ln(1/\epsilon)$. Here, ϵ is the advantage of the adversary in breaking one-more unforgeability of CCBS. For small sizes of ϵ (say, 2^{-128}), this leads to impractical parameter sizes for BS. As an example, if CCBS is applied to the Schnorr blind signature scheme, our calculations show that the resulting scheme will require groups with a 12000 bit representation.

1.2   Our Contribution: Improved Boosting Transforms

As our first contribution, we present a new generic transform to boost the security of blind signature schemes fitting the linear function family framework of Hauck, Kiltz and Loss (HKL) [20]. This is based on three insights, as follows. (1) In the Nth signing session, the User can derive the random coins for the ith instance via $\rho_i := \mathsf{PRF}(k,i)$, where PRF denotes a *puncturable pseudorandom function* [31][1]. The User can now commit to all its randomness as in CCBS. To open the commitments $\mathsf{com}_i, i \in [N] \setminus \{J\}$, the User provides the punctured key k_J. From this key, the Signer can deterministically recompute all the commitments, save for com_J. (2) We use a randomness homomorphic commitment scheme to construct the μ_i as rerandomizations of one initial commitment μ_0 that is sent to the signer. The rerandomization is also determined by PRF, which implies that k_J also reveals μ_i for $i \neq J$ without revealing μ_J. (3) To compress the N messages from the Signer to the User, we use the homomorphic properties of HKL blind signatures and derive N first messages of the underlying blind signature from $\log N$ randomly chosen ones. These insights allow us to lower the communication complexity of the resulting blind signature scheme from linear to logarithmic in the number N of signing sessions[2].

Our results have better blindness guarantees than schemes from the KLR transform. A KLR-transformed blind signature scheme has the same blindness

---

[1] We instantiate PRF efficiently using random oracles [18].

[2] In a different context, namely secure multi-party computation, the combination of puncturable pseudorandom functions and cut-and-choose has been used before.

as its underlying scheme; for many of the schemes underlying it, only so-called *honest signer* blindness was known [20], where the Signer's public key is generated honestly. A much more desirable notion is *malicious signer* blindness, in which the Signer is free to pick his public key adversarially. We show how to achieve this notion using a three step approach. First, we show that the schemes in [20] satisfy a slightly stronger (artificial) notion of blindness without any modification. In this intermediate notion (called *semi-honest signer* blindness), the Signer provides the random coins to generate the public key to the experiment. Next, we show that our improved boosting transform preserves any notion of blindness, including the new one. We then show that by having the signer prove knowledge of the random coins we can transform any scheme that satisfies the intermediate notion into a scheme that satisfies malicious signer blindness.

Practical Schemes from CDH and RSA. Even though our generic transform is an exponential improvement over the state-of-the-art, it still results in schemes that require mega bytes of communication when the number of signatures becomes large (say 2^{30}). On top of this, our generic transform would require large (to the point of being currently impractical) group sizes. To overcome these limitations, we give concrete, 128-bit secure, practical blind signature schemes that satisfy concurrent one-more unforgeability under the CDH and RSA assumptions. We summarize the parameter sizes in Table 1.

Table 1. Concrete efficiency of our schemes supporting a given number of signatures and 128 bit security. Here, communication complexity is given as $a \cdot \log(N) + b$, where N is the number of issued signatures so far. Column Max shows the communication complexity for the maximum N. All sizes are in KiloBytes.

Scheme	Nr. of Signatures	|pk|	|σ|	a	b	Max
BS$_{RSA}$ (Sect. 5)	2^{20}	18.37	7.91	0.02	7.11	7.51
BS$_{RSA}$ (Sect. 5)	2^{30}	18.74	8.66	0.02	7.48	8.08
PIKA$_{CDH}$ (Sect. 4)	2^{20}	3.68	3.16	3.05	26.50	87.50
PIKA$_{CDH}$ (Sect. 4)	2^{30}	3.90	3.16	3.05	26.73	118.20

Our scheme from CDH is statistically malicious signer blind and builds on Boldyreva's blind version of the BLS signature scheme [4] (which is secure under a one-more version of CDH). We observe that by running our boosting transform for several independent keys in parallel, we can ensure that with overwhelming probability, there will be at least one key for which the User is never able to cheat the Signer. We can leverage this into a reduction that embeds the challenge key pk randomly into one of these keys. Then, with high probability, no cheat ever occurs for pk and the reduction can carry out the simulation without having to ever invoke the signing oracle from the underlying one-more unforgeability experiment. This makes it possible to run the scheme with a standard sized group and assuming no more than hardness of the CDH problem. To reduce the size of our resulting signatures, we can use the aggregatability of the BLS scheme.

Overall, our scheme from CDH supports 2^{30} signatures at a size of 3 KB and 120 KB communication per signature.

Our scheme from RSA does not use parallel repetitions to reduce parameter sizes. Instead, we use the trapdoor provided by the RSA system to improve communication complexity of the generic transform. In this way, the Signer can send a single seed from which the User can deterministically derive several values. The Signer, who needs to know the preimages of these values, can then simply use its trapdoor to learn these preimages and proceed with the remainder of the signing protocol. Overall, our scheme from RSA is statistically semi-honest signer blind and supports 2^{30} signatures at a more balanced size of 9 KB per signature and 8 KB communication per signature. To upgrade it to malicious signer blindness we can either rely on generic proof systems, or on more efficient ones based on quadratic residuosity [17] or discrete logarithms [8].[3] We emphasize, however, that using proofs from general complexity assumptions may be sufficiently efficient in our context, as the proofs only have to be generated and verified once upon registering the Signer's public key. Therefore, they do not affect the complexity of the signing protocol or the size of our signatures.

2 Preliminaries

The security parameter is $n \in \mathbb{N}$. All algorithms get 1^n implicitly as input. For a finite set S, we write $x \leftarrow_s S$ if x is sampled uniformly at random from S. For a distribution $\mathcal{D}$, we write $x \leftarrow \mathcal{D}$ if x is sampled according to $\mathcal{D}$. For a (probabilistic) algorithm $\mathcal{A}$, we write $y \leftarrow \mathcal{A}(x)$, if y is output from $\mathcal{A}$ on input x with uniformly sampled random coins. We write $y = \mathcal{A}(x; \rho)$ to make the random coins ρ explicit, and $y \in \mathcal{A}(x)$ means that y is a possible output of $\mathcal{A}(x)$. An algorithm is said to be PPT if its running time can be bounded by a polynomial in its input size. We say that a function $f : \mathbb{N} \to \mathbb{R}_+$ is negligible in its input n, if $f \in n^{-\omega(1)}$. For a security game $\mathbf{G}$, we write $\mathbf{G} \Rightarrow b$ to indicate that $\mathbf{G}$ outputs b. We denote the first K natural numbers by $[K] := \{1, \ldots, K\}$, Euler's totient function by φ and the group of units in $\mathbb{Z}_N$ by $\mathbb{Z}_N^*$.

Next, we introduce the cryptographic primitives that we need. We make use of the well-known computational assumptions CDH and RSA. For the definition of puncturable pseudorandom functions, we follow [31].

Definition 1 (Puncturable Pseudorandom Function). *A puncturable pseudorandom function (PPRF) is defined to be a triple of PPT algorithms* PRF = (Gen, Puncture, Eval) *with the following syntax:*

- Gen$(1^n, 1^{d(n)})$ *takes as input the security parameter* 1^n, *an input length* $1^{d(n)}$ *and outputs a key* k.
- Puncture(k, X) *takes as input a key* k *and a polynomial size set* $\emptyset \neq X \subseteq \mathcal{D} = \{0, 1\}^{d(n)}$ *and outputs a punctured key* k_X.

---

[3] If we rely on these proof systems, our scheme can be proven secure assuming that both the RSA assumption and either of these assumptions hold.

– Eval(k, x) *is deterministic, takes a key k and an element $x \in \mathcal{D}$ as input and outputs an element $r \in \mathcal{R} = \{0, 1\}^{r(n)}$.*

Further, the following security and completeness properties should hold:

– **Completeness of Puncturing.** *For any $d(n) = \mathsf{poly}(n), X \subseteq \{0,1\}^{d(n)}$, any $k \in \mathsf{Gen}(1^n, 1^{d(n)})$, any $k_X \in \mathsf{Puncture}(k, X)$ and any $x' \notin X$ we have $\mathsf{Eval}(k, x') = \mathsf{Eval}(k_X, x')$.*

– **Pseudorandomness.** *For any $d(n) = \mathsf{poly}(n)$ and any PPT algorithm $\mathcal{A}$ the following is negligible:*

$$
\begin{aligned}
\Big| \Pr \left[\mathcal{A}(St, k_X, (r_x)_{x \in X}) = 1 \ \middle| \
\begin{array}{l}
(X, St) \leftarrow \mathcal{A}(1^n), k \leftarrow \mathsf{Gen}(1^n, 1^{d(n)}), \\
k_X \leftarrow \mathsf{Puncture}(k, X), \\
r_x := \mathsf{Eval}(k, x) \ for \ x \in X
\end{array} \right] \\
- \Pr \left[\mathcal{A}(St, k_X, (r_x)_{x \in X}) = 1 \ \middle| \
\begin{array}{l}
(X, St) \leftarrow \mathcal{A}(1^n), k \leftarrow \mathsf{Gen}(1^n, 1^{d(n)}), \\
k_X \leftarrow \mathsf{Puncture}(k, X), \\
r_x \leftarrow_{\$} \{0, 1\}^{r(n)} \ for \ x \in X
\end{array} \right] \Big|.
\end{aligned}
$$

We define a special type of perfectly hiding commitment scheme in which the randomness can be rerandomized publicly. Such commitment schemes can be easily constructed from standard assumptions. For that, we refer to the full version.

Definition 2 (Randomness Homomorphic Commitment Scheme). *A randomness homomorphic commitment scheme is a tuple of PPT algorithms $\mathsf{CMT} = (\mathsf{Gen}, \mathsf{Com}, \mathsf{Translate})$ with the following syntax:*

– $\mathsf{Gen}(1^n)$ *takes as input the security parameter 1^n and outputs a commitment key ck. We assume that ck implicitly defines a message space $\mathcal{M}_{\mathsf{ck}}$ and a randomness space $\mathcal{R}_{\mathsf{ck}}$. Further, we assume that $\mathcal{R}_{\mathsf{ck}}$ is a group with respect to an efficiently computable group operation $+$.*

– $\mathsf{Com}(\mathsf{ck}, x; r)$ *takes as input a key ck, an element $x \in \mathcal{M}_{\mathsf{ck}}$, a randomness $r \in \mathcal{R}_{\mathsf{ck}}$ and outputs a commitment $\mu \in \{0, 1\}^*$.*

– $\mathsf{Translate}(\mathsf{ck}, \mu, r)$ *is deterministic, takes a key ck, a commitment $\mu \in \{0, 1\}^*$, and a randomness $r \in \mathcal{R}_{\mathsf{ck}}$ as input and outputs a commitment μ'.*

Further, the following security and completeness properties should hold:

– **Completeness of Translation.** *For any $\mathsf{ck} \in \mathsf{Gen}(1^n)$, and $x \in \mathcal{M}_{\mathsf{ck}}$ and any $r, r' \in \mathcal{R}_{\mathsf{ck}}$, we have*

$$\mathsf{Translate}(\mathsf{ck}, \mathsf{Com}(\mathsf{ck}, x; r), r') = \mathsf{Com}(\mathsf{ck}, x; r + r').$$

– **Perfectly Hiding.** *For any key ck and any $x_0, x_1 \in \mathcal{M}_{\mathsf{ck}}$, the following distributions are identical:*

$$\{(\mathsf{ck}, x_0, x_1, \mu) \mid r \leftarrow_{\$} \mathcal{R}_{\mathsf{ck}}, \mu := \mathsf{Com}(\mathsf{ck}, x_0; r)\} \ and$$
$$\{(\mathsf{ck}, x_0, x_1, \mu) \mid r \leftarrow_{\$} \mathcal{R}_{\mathsf{ck}}, \mu := \mathsf{Com}(\mathsf{ck}, x_1; r)\}.$$

- **Computationally Binding.** *For any PPT algorithm* $\mathcal{A}$, *the following is negligible:*

$$\Pr\left[\mathsf{Com}(\mathsf{ck}, x_0; r_0) = \mathsf{Com}(\mathsf{ck}, x_1; r_1) \wedge x_0 \neq x_1 \,\middle|\, \begin{array}{l} \mathsf{ck} \leftarrow \mathsf{Gen}(1^n), \\ (x_0, r_0, x_1, r_1) \leftarrow \mathcal{A}(\mathsf{ck}) \end{array}\right].$$

Next, we define the primitive of interest, namely blind signature scheme.

Definition 3 (Blind Signature Scheme). *A blind signature scheme* $\mathsf{BS} = (\mathsf{Gen}, \mathsf{S}, \mathsf{U}, \mathsf{Ver})$ *is a quadruple of PPT algorithms, where*

- $\mathsf{Gen}(1^n)$ *takes as input the security parameter* 1^n *and outputs a pair of keys* $(\mathsf{pk}, \mathsf{sk})$. *We assume that the public key* pk *defines a message space* $\mathcal{M} = \mathcal{M}_{\mathsf{pk}}$ *implicitly.*
- S *and* U *are interactive algorithms, where* S *takes as input a secret key* sk *and* U *takes as input a key* pk *and a message* $\mathsf{m} \in \mathcal{M}$. *After the execution,* U *returns a signature* σ *and we write* $(\bot, \sigma) \leftarrow \langle \mathsf{S}(\mathsf{sk}), \mathsf{U}(\mathsf{pk}, \mathsf{m}) \rangle$.
- $\mathsf{Ver}(\mathsf{pk}, \mathsf{m}, \sigma)$ *is deterministic and takes as input public key* pk, *message* $\mathsf{m} \in \mathcal{M}$, *and a signature* σ, *and returns* $b \in \{0, 1\}$.

We say that BS *is complete if for all* $(\mathsf{pk}, \mathsf{sk}) \in \mathsf{Gen}(1^n)$ *and all* $\mathsf{m} \in \mathcal{M}_{\mathsf{pk}}$ *it holds that*
$$\Pr\left[\mathsf{Ver}(\mathsf{pk}, \mathsf{m}, \sigma) = 1 \mid (\bot, \sigma) \leftarrow \langle \mathsf{S}(\mathsf{sk}), \mathsf{U}(\mathsf{pk}, \mathsf{m}) \rangle\right] = 1.$$

Definition 4 (One-More Unforgeability). *Let* $\mathsf{BS} = (\mathsf{Gen}, \mathsf{S}, \mathsf{U}, \mathsf{Ver})$ *be a blind signature scheme and* $\ell: \mathbb{N} \to \mathbb{N}$. *For an adversary* $\mathcal{A}$, *we consider the following game* $\ell\text{-}\mathbf{OMUF}^{\mathcal{A}}_{\mathsf{BS}}(n)$:

1. *Sample keys* $(\mathsf{pk}, \mathsf{sk}) \leftarrow \mathsf{Gen}(1^n)$.
2. *Let* O *be an interactive oracle simulating* $\mathsf{S}(\mathsf{sk})$. *Run*

$$((\mathsf{m}_1, \sigma_1), \ldots, (\mathsf{m}_k, \sigma_k)) \leftarrow \mathcal{A}^{\mathsf{O}}(\mathsf{pk}),$$

   where $\mathcal{A}$ *can query* O *in an arbitrarily interleaved way and complete at most* $\ell = \ell(n)$ *of the interactions with* O.
3. *Output 1 if and only if all* $\mathsf{m}_i, i \in [k]$ *are distinct,* $\mathcal{A}$ *completed at most* $k - 1$ *interactions with* O *and for each* $i \in [k]$ *it holds that* $\mathsf{Ver}(\mathsf{pk}, \mathsf{m}_i, \sigma_i) = 1$.

We say that BS *is* ℓ-*one-more unforgeable* (ℓ-*OMUF*), *if for every PPT algorithm* $\mathcal{A}$ *the following advantage is negligible:*

$$\Pr\left[\ell - \mathbf{OMUF}^{\mathcal{A}}_{\mathsf{BS}}(n) \Rightarrow 1\right].$$

Further, we say that BS *is one-more unforgeable (OMUF), if it is* ℓ-*OMUF for all polynomial* ℓ.

We note that from a practical perspective, it is sufficient to focus on ℓ-OMUF for some large but a priori bounded ℓ (e.g. $\ell = 2^{30}$), while full OMUF is more of theoretical interest.

Definition 5 (Blindness). *Consider a blind signature scheme* BS = (Gen, S, U, Ver). *For an adversary* $\mathcal{A}$ *and bit* $b \in \{0,1\}$, *consider the following game* $\mathbf{BLIND}_{b,\mathsf{BS}}^{\mathcal{A}}(n)$:

1. *Sample* (pk, sk) ← Gen(1^n) *and run* ($\mathsf{m}_0, \mathsf{m}_1, St$) ← $\mathcal{A}$(pk, sk).
2. *Let* O_0 *be an interactive oracle simulating* U(pk, m_b) *and* O_1 *be an interactive oracle simulating* U(pk, m_{1-b}). *Run* $\mathcal{A}$ *on input* St *with arbitrary interleaved one-time access to each of these oracles, i.e.* $St' ← \mathcal{A}^{\mathsf{O}_0, \mathsf{O}_1}(St)$.
3. *Let* σ_b, σ_{1-b} *be the local outputs of* $\mathsf{O}_0, \mathsf{O}_1$, *respectively. If* $\sigma_0 = \perp$ *or* $\sigma_1 = \perp$, *then run* $b' ← \mathcal{A}(St', \perp, \perp)$. *Else, obtain a bit* b' *from* $\mathcal{A}$ *on input* σ_0, σ_1, *i.e. run* $b' ← \mathcal{A}(St', \sigma_0, \sigma_1)$.
4. *Output* b'.

We say that BS *satisfies honest signer blindness, if for every PPT algorithm* $\mathcal{A}$ *the following advantage is negligible:*

$$\left| \Pr\left[\mathbf{BLIND}_{0,\mathsf{BS}}^{\mathcal{A}}(n) \Rightarrow 1 \right] - \Pr\left[\mathbf{BLIND}_{1,\mathsf{BS}}^{\mathcal{A}}(n) \Rightarrow 1 \right] \right|.$$

We also consider semi-honest and malicious signer blindness, where we modify the game in the following way:

- *For semi-honest signer blindness,* (pk, sk) *is not sampled by the game, but* $\mathcal{A}$ *outputs random coins* ρ *in addition to* $\mathsf{m}_0, \mathsf{m}_1$. *Then, the game defines* (pk, sk) *via* (pk, sk) := Gen(1^n; ρ).
- *For malicious signer blindness,* (pk, sk) *is not sampled by the game, but* $\mathcal{A}$ *outputs* pk *in addition to* $\mathsf{m}_0, \mathsf{m}_1$.

Semi-honest signer blindness is a non-standard notion and lies inbetween honest and malicious signer blindness. We claim that any semi-honest signer blind scheme can be transformed into a malicious signer blind scheme while preserving one-more unforgeability. The high-level idea is to append a non-interactive zero-knowledge proof-of-knowledge to the public key. This proof shows that the signer knows corresponding random coins that generate the key. The rest of the scheme does not change, and thus the transformation is very efficient. For details, we refer to the full version.

We will now introduce linear function families, following [20].

Definition 6 (Linear Function Family). *A linear function family* LF *is a given by a tuple of algorithms* LF = (PGen, F, Ψ) *with the following properties:*

- PGen(1^n) *returns system parameters* par *which define abelian groups* $\mathcal{S}, \mathcal{D}, \mathcal{R}$ *with* $|\mathcal{S}|, |\mathcal{R}| \geq 2^n$ *and there exists scalar multiplication* $\cdot : \mathcal{S} \times \mathcal{D} \to \mathcal{D}$ *with* $s \cdot (x + x') = s \cdot x + s \cdot x'$ *for all* $s \in \mathcal{S}$ *and* $x, x' \in \mathcal{D}$. *The same applies for* $\mathcal{R}$. *Note that it is not necessarily true that* $(s + s') \cdot x = s \cdot x + s' \cdot x$.
- $\mathsf{F}_{\mathsf{par}}(x)$ *is deterministic, takes as input an element* $x \in \mathcal{D}$, *and returns an element in* $y \in \mathcal{R}$. *We require that:*
  - *For all* $s \in \mathcal{S}, x, y \in \mathcal{D}$, $\mathsf{F}_{\mathsf{par}}(s \cdot x + y) = s \cdot \mathsf{F}_{\mathsf{par}}(x) + \mathsf{F}_{\mathsf{par}}(y)$.
  - $\mathsf{F}_{\mathsf{par}}$ *has a pseudo torsion-free element in the kernel, i.e. there exists* $z^* \in \mathcal{D}$ *such that* $\mathsf{F}_{\mathsf{par}}(z^*) = 0$ *and for all distinct* $s, s' \in \mathcal{S}, s \cdot z^* \neq s' \cdot z^*$.

- F_{par} *is smooth, i.e. if* $x \leftarrow \mathcal{D}$ *is sampled uniformly,* $F_{par}(x)$ *has uniform distribution in* $\mathcal{R}$.
- $\Psi_{par}(y, s, s')$ *is deterministic, takes as inputs* $y \in \mathcal{R}$, *and* $s, s' \in \mathcal{S}$, *and returns a value* $x \in \mathcal{D}$. *The function satisfies for all* y *in the range of* F_{par} *and* $s, s' \in \mathcal{S}$,

$$(s + s') \cdot y = s \cdot y + s' \cdot y + F_{par}(\Psi_{par}(y, s, s')).$$

Intuitively, the function Ψ_{par} *corrects for the fact that the group operation in* $\mathcal{S}$ *may not distribute over* $\mathcal{R}$. *When it is clear from the context, we will omit the subscript* par.

As in [25], we define preimage resistance for a linear function family. For the related notion of collision resistance, we refer to the full version and [25].

Definition 7 (Preimage Resistance). *A linear function family* LF *is preimage resistant if for any adversary* $\mathcal{A}$, *the following advantage is negligible:*

$$\Pr\left[F(x) = F(x') \mid x \leftarrow \mathcal{D}, x' \leftarrow \mathcal{A}(par, F(x))\right].$$

3   An Improved Boosting Transform

Hauck, Kiltz, and Loss [20] introduced a generic construction of a three-move blind signature scheme BS[LF] from any linear function family LF and a hash function H modeled as a random-oracle. The main result of [20] is that the linear blind signature scheme BS[LF] is ℓ-one-more unforgeable for $\ell = \mathcal{O}(\log n)$. Building on that, Katz, Loss, and Rosenberg [25] presented a boosting transform CCBS[LF] that turns this logarithmic security into polynomial security. In this section, we introduce an improved boosting transform CCCBS[LF] that eliminates the drawback of linearly growing communication complexity.

3.1   Overview

We recall the main idea of the boosting transform [25] that turns a linear blind signature scheme BS[LF] into a boosted blind signature scheme CCBS[LF].

In the scheme CCBS[LF], at the onset of the Nth interaction, the signer sends the current value of the counter N to the user. Then, user and signer proceed as follows.

1. The user chooses N random strings $ur_j, j \in [N]$ and N random strings $\varphi_j, j \in [N]$. It prepares N commitments $\mu_j = H(m, \varphi_j)$, where H is a random oracle and m is the message to be signed. It also prepares commitments $com_j = H(ur_j, \mu_j)$. Then it sends the commitments com_j to the signer.
2. The user and the signer run N independent sessions of the underlying linear blind signature scheme BS[LF], where the user inputs μ_j, ur_j in the jth session. Recall that the scheme BS[LF] contains three messages R, c, s.

3. Before the signer sends the last message s_j of the underlying scheme, it chooses a cut-and-choose index $J \in [N]$ at random and asks the user to open all commitments com_j with $j \neq J$.
4. Once the signer knows the values μ_j and randomness ur_j, it runs the user algorithm U to check if the user behaved honestly so far, at least for the sessions $j \neq J$. If there is some session for which this check fails, the signer aborts.
5. The signer sends only s_J to the user. That is, signer and user only complete the Jth session. The final signature consists of a signature on μ_J from the underlying scheme BS[LF] as well as the randomness φ_J which binds m to μ_J.

We highlight that the communication now grows linearly with the number of issued signatures.

a) In the second message, the user sends N commitments com_j.
b) In the third message, the signer sends N commitments R_j.
c) In the fourth message, the user sends N challenges c_j.
d) In the sixth message, the user opens $N - 1$ of the commitments com_j.

Our goal is to eliminate these linear dependencies on N and improve them by an at most logarithmic dependency.

First, we eliminate the linear dependency a) by replacing the commitments $com_j = H(ur_j, \mu_j)$ by a single commitment com_r, which commits to (salted) hashes of all ur_j, μ_j at once. By sending all ur_j for $j \neq J$ and the hash of ur_J, the user can still open this commitment without revealing ur_J.

Next, we focus on d). Here, we let the user generate the randomness (ur_j, φ_j) used for each session using the puncturable pseudorandom function PRF. We replace the unstructured commitment with a randomness homomorphic commitment scheme. This allows us to let the user derive the commitments μ_i as rerandomizations $Com(m, \varphi_0 + \varphi_j)$ of one single commitment $\mu_0 = Com(m, \varphi_0)$ with randomness φ_j. The user sends commitment μ_0 together with com_r. Now, the user can open the commitment com_r by sending only a punctured key k_J. Intuitively, this preserves blindness, as the punctured key does not reveal anything about the randomness ur_J, φ_J. Using similar tricks, we eliminate c).

To tackle b), we compute the N values R_i of the underlying linear scheme BS[LF] as subset sums of a logarithmic number of such values. Then, only these basis values have to be sent.

We end up with a scheme with logarithmic communication complexity, for which the ideas that underlie the original boosting transform still apply.

3.2 Blind Signatures from Linear Function Families

We briefly recall the blind signature scheme BS[LF] from a linear function family LF. For more details, we refer the reader to [20] or the full version. For key generation of the blind signature scheme BS[LF], parameters $par \leftarrow LF.PGen(1^n)$ are generated. Then, a secret key and public key are sampled via $sk \leftarrow_\$ \mathcal{D}$ and pk := F(sk), assuming pk implicitly contains par. We present the signature issuing protocol formally in Fig. 1. Signatures $\sigma = (c', s')$ for a message m are verified by checking if $c' = H(m, F(s') - c' \cdot pk)$ holds.

S(sk)		U(pk, m)
$r \leftarrow_\$ \mathcal{D}, R := F(r)$	$\xrightarrow{\quad R \quad}$	$\alpha \leftarrow_\$ \mathcal{D}, \beta \leftarrow_\$ \mathcal{S}, R' := R + F(\alpha) + \beta \cdot pk$
$s := r + c \cdot sk$	$\xleftarrow{\quad c \quad}$	$c' := H(m, R'), c := c' + \beta$
	$\xrightarrow{\quad s \quad}$	if $F(s) \neq R + c \cdot pk$:
		$s' := s + \alpha + \Psi(pk, c, -c')$
		return $\sigma := (c', s')$

Fig. 1. The signature issuing protocol of the linear blind signature scheme BS[LF] for a linear function family LF and a random oracle $H : \{0, 1\}^* \to \mathcal{S}$ [20].

3.3 Construction

In this section, we define our Compact Cut-and-Choose blind signature scheme for a linear function family LF, abbreviated as CCCBS[LF]. To this end, let LF = (PGen, F, Ψ) be a linear function family, CMT be a randomness homomorphic commitment scheme, and PRF be a puncturable pseudorandom function. For efficient instantiations of CMT and PRF, we refer to the full version. Further, let $H: \{0,1\}^* \to \mathcal{S}, H_r: \{0,1\}^* \to \{0,1\}^n, H_x: \{0,1\}^* \to \mathcal{D} \times \mathcal{S} \times \mathcal{R}_{ck} \times \{0,1\}^{n_{PRF}}, H_c: \{0,1\}^* \to \{0,1\}^n$ be random oracles, where $n_{PRF} = \Theta(n)$ is a security parameter used for the pseudorandom function.

Key Generation. Algorithm CCCBS[LF].Gen(1^n) is as follows:

1. Sample ck $\leftarrow$ CMT.Gen(1^n) and par $\leftarrow$ LF.PGen(1^n).
2. Sample sk' $\leftarrow_\$ \mathcal{D}$, and let sk := sk', pk = (par, ck, pk' := F(sk')).
3. Return the public key pk and the secret key sk.

Signature Issuing. The signer and user algorithms S, U are given in Figs. 3 and 2, where the S keeps a state (N, ctr) which is initialized as $N := 2 = 2^2 - 2, ctr := 0$. In each interaction, S atomically increments ctr and, if ctr = N, sets $N := 2N + 2, ctr := 0$.

Verification. Algorithm CCCBS[LF].Ver(pk, m, $\sigma = (c, s, \varphi)$) returns the output of BS[LF].Ver(pk', com(ck, m; φ), (c, s)).

Check(pk, $N, \mu_0, \mathsf{com}_r, \{R_i\}_i, \mathsf{com}_c, J, k_J, c_J, h_J$)

---

1 : **for** $j \in [N] \setminus \{J\}$:

2 : $\quad \mathsf{prer}_j := \mathsf{PRF.Eval}(k_J, j)$, $\mathsf{r}_j := \mathsf{H}_x(\mathsf{prer}_j)$

3 : $\quad$ **parse** $\mathsf{r}_j = (\alpha_j, \beta_j, \varphi_j, \gamma_j) \in \mathcal{D} \times \mathcal{S} \times \mathcal{R}_{\mathsf{ck}} \times \{0,1\}^{n_{\mathsf{PRF}}}$

4 : $\quad \tilde{R}_j := \sum_{i \in S_j} R_j, \quad \mu_j := \mathsf{Translate}(\mathsf{ck}, \mu_0, \varphi_j)$

5 : $\quad c_j := \mathsf{H}(\mu_j, \tilde{R}_j + \mathsf{F}(\alpha_j) + \beta_j \cdot \mathsf{pk}') + \beta_j$

6 : **if** $\mathsf{com}_r \neq \mathsf{H}_r(\mathsf{H}_r(\mathsf{r}_1), \ldots, \mathsf{H}_r(\mathsf{r}_{J-1}), h_J, \mathsf{H}_r(\mathsf{r}_{J+1}), \ldots, \mathsf{H}_r(\mathsf{r}_N))$: **return** 0

7 : **if** $\mathsf{com}_c \neq \mathsf{H}_c(c_1, \ldots, c_N)$: **return** 0

8 : **return** 1

Fig. 2. The algorithm Check used in the issuing protocol of CCCBS[LF], where $\mathsf{H} : \{0,1\}^* \to \mathcal{S}, \mathsf{H}_r, \mathsf{H}_c : \{0,1\}^* \to \{0,1\}^n$, and $\mathsf{H}_x : \{0,1\}^* \to \mathcal{D} \times \mathcal{S} \times \mathcal{R}_{\mathsf{ck}} \times \{0,1\}^{n_{\mathsf{PRF}}}$ are random oracles. The set S_j is defined as $\{i \in [l] : i^{th}\text{-bit of } j \text{ is } 1\}$

3.4 Security Analysis

Completeness of CCCBS[LF] follows by inspection. We show blindness and one-more unforgeability.

Theorem 1. *Let* PRF *be a puncturable pseudorandom function,* LF *be a linear function family, and* CMT *be a randomness homomorphic commitment scheme. Let* $\mathsf{H}_r : \{0,1\}^* \to \{0,1\}^n, \mathsf{H}_x : \{0,1\}^* \to \mathcal{D} \times \mathcal{S} \times \mathcal{R}_{\mathsf{ck}} \times \{0,1\}^{n_{\mathsf{PRF}}}$ *be random oracles. If* BS[LF] *satisfies honest, semi-honest, or malicious signer blindness, then* CCCBS[LF] *satisfies honest, semi-honest, or malicious signer blindness, respectively.*

Concretely, for any adversary that uses N^L *and* N^R *as the counters in its executions with the user, runs in time* t, *has advantage* ϵ *in the blindness game and makes at most* $Q_{\mathsf{H}_x}, Q_{\mathsf{H}_r}$ *queries to* $\mathsf{H}_x, \mathsf{H}_r$ *respectively, there exists an adversary against blindness of* BS[LF] *running in time* t *with advantage* $\epsilon_{\mathsf{BS[LF]}}$ *such that*

$$\epsilon \leq N^L N^R \left(\frac{4(Q_{\mathsf{H}_x} + Q_{\mathsf{H}_r})}{2^{n_{\mathsf{PRF}}}} + 4\epsilon_{\mathsf{PRF}} + \epsilon_{\mathsf{BS[LF]}} \right),$$

where ϵ_{PRF} *is the advantage of an adversary against the security of* PRF *with input length* $\max\{\log(N^L), \log(N^R)\}$ *puncturing at one point.*

We give a intuition of the proof and postpone details to the full version. The strategy is to apply a sequence of changes to the user oracles, such that final game is independent of bit b. In a first step, we guess the cut-and-choose index J. Then, we compute the commitment μ_J directly instead of deriving it from the commitment μ_0. Next, we use the security of PRF and generate r_J for session J at random instead of using the key k. Now, we observe that the randomness

$\underline{S(\mathsf{sk} = \mathsf{sk}'); \text{ state } N, \mathsf{ctr}}$ $\qquad\qquad\qquad$ $\underline{U(\mathsf{pk} = (\mathsf{par}, \mathsf{ck}, \mathsf{pk}'), m)}$

$\mathsf{ctr} := \mathsf{ctr} + 1$

$\mathbf{if}\ \mathsf{ctr} = N:$

$\quad N := 2N + 2, \mathsf{ctr} := 0$ $\qquad\qquad\qquad\qquad$ $\varphi_0 \leftarrow_\$ \mathcal{R}_{\mathsf{ck}}, \mu_0 := \mathsf{Com}(\mathsf{ck}, m; \varphi_0)$

$\quad l := \log(N + 2)$ $\quad\xrightarrow{\quad N \quad}\quad$ $k \leftarrow \mathsf{PRF.Gen}(1^{n_{\mathsf{PRF}}}, 1^{\log(N)})$

$\qquad\qquad\qquad\qquad\qquad\qquad\qquad\qquad$ $\mathbf{for}\ j \in [N]:$

$\qquad\qquad\qquad\qquad\qquad\qquad\qquad\qquad\quad$ $\mathsf{prer}_j := \mathsf{PRF.Eval}(k, j)$

$\qquad\qquad\qquad\qquad\qquad\qquad\qquad\qquad\quad$ $r_j := \mathsf{H}_x(\mathsf{prer}_j)$

$\qquad\qquad\qquad\qquad\qquad\qquad\qquad\qquad\quad$ $\mathbf{parse}\ r_j = (\alpha_j, \beta_j, \varphi_j, \gamma_j)$

$\qquad\qquad\qquad\qquad\qquad\qquad\qquad\qquad\quad$ $\mu_j := \mathsf{Translate}(\mathsf{ck}, \mu_0, \varphi_j)$

$\qquad\qquad\qquad\qquad\qquad\qquad\qquad\qquad\quad$ $h_j := \mathsf{H}_r(r_j)$

$\mathbf{for}\ i \in [l]:$ $\quad\xleftarrow{\ \mathsf{com}_r, \mu_0\ }\quad$ $\mathsf{com}_r := \mathsf{H}_r(h_1, \ldots, h_N)$

$\quad r_i \leftarrow_\$ \mathcal{D}, R_i := \mathsf{F}(r_i)$ $\quad\xrightarrow{\ R_1, \ldots, R_l\ }\quad$ $\mathbf{for}\ j \in [N]:$

$\qquad\qquad\qquad\qquad\qquad\qquad\qquad\qquad\quad$ $\displaystyle \tilde{R}_j := \sum_{i \in S_j} R_i$

$\qquad\qquad\qquad\qquad\qquad\qquad\qquad\qquad\quad$ $\tilde{R}'_j := \tilde{R}_j + \mathsf{F}(\alpha_j) + \beta_j \cdot \mathsf{pk}'$

$\qquad\qquad\qquad\qquad\qquad\qquad\qquad\qquad\quad$ $c'_j := \mathsf{H}(\mu_j, \tilde{R}'_j), \quad c_j := c'_j + \beta_j$

$\qquad\qquad\qquad\qquad\xleftarrow{\ \mathsf{com}_c\ }\qquad$ $\mathsf{com}_c := \mathsf{H}_c(c_1, \ldots, c_N)$

$J \leftarrow_\$ [N]$ $\qquad\xrightarrow{\qquad J \qquad}\qquad$ $k_J \leftarrow \mathsf{PRF.Puncture}(k, J)$

$\mathbf{if}\ \mathsf{Check} = 0 : \mathbf{abort}$ $\quad\xleftarrow{\ k_J, c_J, h_J\ }\quad$

$\displaystyle s_J := \sum_{i \in S_J} r_i + c_J \cdot \mathsf{sk}'$ $\quad\xrightarrow{\qquad s_J \qquad}\quad$ $s'_J := s_J + \alpha_J + \Psi(\mathsf{pk}, c_J, -c'_J)$

$\qquad\qquad\qquad\qquad\qquad\qquad\qquad\qquad$ $\mathbf{return}\ \sigma = (c'_J, s'_J, \varphi_0 + \varphi_J)$

Fig. 3. The signature issuing protocol of the blind signature scheme CCCBS[LF], where $\mathsf{H} \colon \{0,1\}^* \to \mathcal{S}, \mathsf{H}_r, \mathsf{H}_c \colon \{0,1\}^* \to \{0,1\}^n, \mathsf{H}_x \colon \{0,1\}^* \to \mathcal{D} \times \mathcal{S} \times \mathcal{R}_{\mathsf{ck}} \times \{0,1\}^{n_{\mathsf{PRF}}}$ are random oracles. The algorithm Check is defined in Fig. 2. The set S_j is defined as $\{i \in [l] : i^{th}\text{-bit of } j \text{ is } 1\}$. The states ctr and N are incremented atomically

φ_0 is hidden in the final signature, and we can switch μ_0 to a commitment of a random message. Finally, we see that the only dependency on the message is in session J and we can reduce from the blindness of BS[LF].

Theorem 2. *Let* PRF *be a puncturable pseudorandom function,* LF *be a linear function family, and* CMT *be a randomness homomorphic commitment scheme. Let* $\mathsf{H} \colon \{0,1\}^* \to \mathcal{S}, \mathsf{H}_r, \mathsf{H}_c \colon \{0,1\}^* \to \{0,1\}^n$ *be random oracles. If* BS[LF] *sat-*

isfies ℓ-one-more unforgeability for any $\ell = O(\log(n))$, then CCCBS[LF] satisfies ℓ-one-more unforgeability for any $\ell = \mathsf{poly}(n)$.

Concretely, suppose there exists an adversary with advantage ϵ against the ℓ-one-more unforgeability of CCCBS[LF], that runs in time t, starts at most p interactions with his signer oracle, and makes at most Q_H, Q_{H_r}, Q_{H_c} queries to H, H_r, H_c respectively. Then, there exists an adversary against the λ-one-more unforegability BS[LF], where $\lambda = 3\lceil \log p \rceil + \log(2/\epsilon)$, that runs in time t, starts at most p interactions with his signer oracle, makes at most Q_H queries to H, and has advantage $\epsilon_{BS[LF]}$, such that

$$\epsilon \leq 2 \left(\epsilon_{BS[LF]} + p \cdot \epsilon_{LF} + \epsilon_{CMT} + \frac{Q_{H_r}^2 + Q_{H_c}^2 + pQ_{H_r} + pQ_{H_c}}{2^n} + \frac{p^2(p^2 + Q_H)}{|\mathcal{R}|} \right),$$

where ϵ_{LF} is the advantage of an adversary with running time t against the preimage resistance of LF and ϵ_{CMT} is the advantage of an adversary with running time t against the binding property of CMT.

The proof is very similar to the proof for the original boosting transform [25] and can be found in the full version.

Remark 1. As an asymptotic result, we are satisfied with our improved boosting transform with logarithmic communication complexity. However, similar to the original boosting transform, we rely on the very loose security bound of the underlying linear blind signature scheme BS[LF]. For concrete efficiency, this is prohibitive, as we require that BS[LF] supports a non-trivial number λ of signatures. Also, the logarithmic term of the communication complexity depends on computational assumptions. Thus, the loose bound will also have a negative impact on communication complexity.

To highlight this, we computed the parameter sizes for the instantiations of the boosting transform based on the discrete logarithm problem. Our calculations show that in order to support 2^{30} signatures, the scheme requires a 12035 bit group. It is apparent that this group size is impractical, and no standardized elliptic curve groups of this size exist. We remark that Katz et al. [25] also provide a parameter estimate, but this holds only for a very specific choice of signing queries, random oracle queries and advantage. A detailed explanation of our calculations can be found in the full version.

In the following, we will see how to augment the ideas of this section to construct schemes which eliminate aforementioned drawbacks and come with practical concrete parameters.

4 A Concrete Scheme Based on CDH

Here, we construct a concrete blind signature scheme PIKA$_{CDH}$ based on the CDHassumption. While the construction in the previous section was generic, we aim for a scheme with concrete efficiency in this section.

4.1 Overview

As discussed in Remark 1, our improved boosting transform inherits the loose security bound of the underlying linear blind signature scheme. To see how we can circumvent this, let us first recall the reduction idea of the boosting transform. The main challenge is that the underlying scheme BS[LF] allows for a logarithmic number of signing interactions, while the reduction has to simulate an arbitrary polynomial number of signing interactions for the adversary. This is solved as follows. First, note that whenever the adversary honestly commits to ur_j, μ_j, the reduction can extract these values from the commitments com_r by observing the random oracle queries. Then, an important property of linear blind signature schemes comes into play: If one knows the randomness and the message that is input into the user algorithm BS[LF].U and controls the random oracle, one can simulate the signer algorithm without knowing the secret key. Thus, the reduction only needs to access the signer oracle of BS[LF] if the adversary *cheats* (i.e., it malforms the commitment for the Jth session in the first step and is not caught). Fortunately, the probability of such a (successful) cheat is at most $1/N$ in the Nth signing session. Thus, the expected number of successful cheats in p interactions is at most logarithmic in p. Using the Chernoff bound, one can show that with overwhelming probability, the number of successful cheats is reasonably close to this expectation.

We observe that by letting the cut-and-choose parameter grow slightly faster than before and scaling appropriately, the expected number of successful cheats can be bounded to be less than 1. Unfortunately, we can not just use the Chernoff bound, if we want to argue that this also holds with overwhelming probability. We can, however, use the Chernoff bound to show that exceeding a single cheat happens with some constant probability less than 1. Then, we play our next card, which is parallel repetition. Namely, we run K independent instances of our scheme so far, where each instance is relative to a separate key pair. We show that with high probability, in one randomly chosen instance, there is *no cheat at all*. Using this observation, we can give a reduction from the key-only security of the underlying blind signature scheme to finish our proof.

We do not apply this overall strategy to a linear blind signature scheme, but instead to the BLS blind signature scheme [4]. We notice that the approach also works for this scheme and observe additional benefits: First, the BLS scheme allows to aggregate signatures. Hence, it is easy to merge the resulting signatures from the K instances for a significant efficiency improvement. Second, the scheme has two rounds and thus the logarithmic term in the communication complexity is independent of computational assumptions (cf. Remark 1). We emphasize that the original BLS blind signature scheme is secure under a one-more variant of the CDHassumption. Fortunately, we only need key-only security here, which is implied by CDH. Also, the concrete security loss of our scheme is as for the standard BLS digital signature scheme [5], which means that it can be used over the same groups as BLS.

Finally, we introduce further minor optimizations such as making the signer commit to its cut-and-choose indices in its message. In this way, the reduction in the blindness proof can extract these indices rather than guessing them. This leads to more efficient statistical security parameters[4].

4.2   Construction

Let $\mathsf{PGGen}(1^n)$ be a bilinear group generation algorithm that outputs a cyclic group $\mathbb{G}$ of prime order p with generator g, and a pairing $e : \mathbb{G} \times \mathbb{G} \to \mathbb{G}_T$ into some target group $\mathbb{G}_T$. We assume that these system parameters are known to all algorithms. Note that their correctness can be verified efficiently. Our scheme makes use of a randomness homomorphic commitment scheme CMT with randomness space $\mathcal{R}_{\mathsf{ck}}$ and a puncturable pseudorandom function PRF. We can instantiate PRF using random oracles and CMT tightly based on the DLOG assumption. We also need random oracles $\mathsf{H}\colon \{0,1\}^* \to \mathbb{Z}_p, \mathsf{H}'\colon \{0,1\}^* \to \{0,1\}^n$ and $\mathsf{H}_r, \mathsf{H}_c\colon \{0,1\}^* \to \{0,1\}^n, \mathsf{H}_x\colon \{0,1\}^* \to \mathbb{Z}_p \times \mathcal{R}_{\mathsf{ck}} \times \{0,1\}^{n_{\mathsf{PRF}}}$, where n_{PRF} is a security parameter used for PRF.

Our scheme makes use of a parameter $K \in \mathbb{N}$, which defines how many instances of the underlying boosting transform are executed in parallel, and a function $f\colon \mathbb{N} \to \mathbb{N}$, which determines how fast the cut-and-choose parameter N grows. We give a detailed explanation and Python scripts computing all parameters in the full version of our paper.

Key Generation. To generate keys algorithm $\mathsf{PIKA}_{\mathsf{CDH}}.\mathsf{Gen}(1^n)$ does the following:

1. For each instance $i \in [K]$, sample $\mathsf{sk}_i \leftarrow_\$ \mathbb{Z}_p$ and set $\mathsf{pk}_i := g^{\mathsf{sk}_i}$.
2. Sample a commitment key $\mathsf{ck} \leftarrow \mathsf{CMT}.\mathsf{Gen}(1^n)$.
3. Return public key $\mathsf{pk} := (\mathsf{pk}_1, \ldots, \mathsf{pk}_K, \mathsf{ck})$ and secret key $\mathsf{sk} := (\mathsf{sk}_1, \ldots, \mathsf{sk}_K)$.

Signature Issuing. The algorithms S, U and their interaction are formally given in Figs. 4 and 5. Here, S keeps a state ctr, which is inititalized as $\mathsf{ctr} := 1$ and incremented in every interaction.

Verification. The resulting signature $\sigma = (\bar{\sigma}, \varphi_1, \ldots, \varphi_K)$ for a message m is verified by algorithm $\mathsf{PIKA}_{\mathsf{CDH}}.\mathsf{Ver}(\mathsf{pk}, \mathsf{m}, \sigma)$ as follows:

1. For each instance $i \in [K]$, compute the commitment $\mu_i := \mathsf{Com}(\mathsf{ck}, \mathsf{m}; \varphi_i)$.
2. Return 1 if and only if

$$e\,(\bar{\sigma}, g) = \prod_{i=1}^{K} e\,(\mathsf{H}(\mathsf{pk}_i, \mu_i), \mathsf{pk}_i)\,.$$

---

[4] Note that without this optimization, the security loss would be exponential in K.

Check(pk, $N, \mu_0,$ com$_r$, com$_c$, seed$_J, k_J, \{c_{i,J_i}\}_i, \{\eta_i\}_i$)

---

1 : $\mathbf{J} = (H'(\text{seed}_J, 1), \ldots, H'(\text{seed}_J, K)) \in [N]^K$

2 :   **for** $i \in [K]$:

3 :   **for** $j \in [N] \setminus \{J_i\}$:

4 : $\text{prer}_{i,j} := \text{PRF.Eval}(k_J, (i,j)), \; r_{i,j} := H_x(\text{prer}_{i,j})$

5 :   **parse** $r_{i,j} = (\alpha_{i,j}, \varphi_{i,j}, \gamma_{i,j}) \in \mathbb{Z}_p \times \mathcal{R}_{ck} \times \{0,1\}^n$

6 : $\mu_{i,j} := \text{Translate}(\text{ck}, \mu_0, \varphi_{i,j})$

7 : $c_{i,j} := H(\text{pk}_i, \mu_{i,j}) \cdot g^{\alpha_{i,j}}$

8 :   com$_{r,i} := H_r(H_r(r_{i,1}), \ldots, H_r(r_{i,J_i-1}), \eta_i, H_r(r_{i,J_i+1}), \ldots, H_r(r_{i,N}))$

9 :   **if** com$_r \neq H_r(\text{com}_{r,1}, \ldots, \text{com}_{r,K})$: **return** 0

10 : **if** com$_c \neq H_c(c_{1,1}, \ldots, c_{K,N})$: **return** 0

11 : **return** 1

Fig. 4. The algorithm Check used in the issuing protocol of blind signature scheme PIKA$_{CDH}$, where $H: \{0,1\}^* \to \mathbb{G}, H': \{0,1\}^* \to \{0,1\}^n$ and $H_r, H_c: \{0,1\}^* \to \{0,1\}^n, H_x: \{0,1\}^* \to \mathbb{Z}_p \times \mathcal{R}_{ck} \times \{0,1\}^{n_{PRF}}$ are random oracles.

4.3 Security Analysis

Completeness of the scheme follows by inspection. We show blindness and one-more unforgeability. For one-more unforgeability, we show q_{max}-OMUF, where q_{max} is a parameter that can be set freely (e.g. $q_{max} = 2^{30}$) and has influence the function f. We note that making f grow quadratically, one could show full OMUF using a similar proof.

Theorem 3. *Let* PRF *be a puncturable pseudorandom function and* CMT *be a randomness homomorphic commitment scheme. Let* $H': \{0,1\}^* \to \{0,1\}^n$ *and* $H_r: \{0,1\}^* \to \{0,1\}^n, H_x: \{0,1\}^* \to \mathbb{Z}_p \times \mathcal{R}_{ck} \times \{0,1\}^{n_{PRF}}$ *be random oracles. Then* PIKA$_{CDH}$ *satisfies malicious signer blindness.*

In particular, for any adversary who uses N^L *and* N^R *as the counters in its executions with the user and queries* H', H_r, H_x *at most* $Q_{H'}, Q_{H_r}, Q_{H_x}$ *times, respectively, the malicious signer blindness advantage can be bounded by*

$$4\epsilon_{PRF} + \frac{Q_{H'}^2}{2^{n-1}} + \frac{Q_{H'}}{2^{n-2}} + \frac{KQ_{H_x}}{2^{n_{PRF}-2}} + \frac{KQ_{H_r}}{2^{n_{PRF}-2}},$$

where ϵ_{PRF} *is the advantage of an adversary against the security of* PRF *with input length* $\max\{\log(N^L), \log(N^R)\}$ *when puncturing at* K *points.*

Due to space limitation, we postpone the proof to the full version.

Theorem 4. *Let* CMT *be a randomness homomorphic commitment scheme and* PRF *be a puncturable pseudorandom function. Let* PGGen(1^n) *be a bilinear group generation algorithm. Further, let* $H: \{0,1\}^* \to \mathbb{Z}_p, H': \{0,1\}^* \to \{0,1\}^n$ *and*

$\underline{\mathsf{S}(\mathsf{sk})}$; state ctr

$\mathsf{ctr} := \mathsf{ctr} + 1, N := f(\mathsf{ctr})$

$\mathsf{seed_J}, \mathsf{salt} \leftarrow\!\!\$\ \{0,1\}^n$

$\mathsf{com_J} := \mathsf{H}'(\mathsf{seed_J}, \mathsf{salt})$ $\xrightarrow{\quad N, \mathsf{com_J} \quad}$

$\underline{\mathsf{U}(\mathsf{pk}, \mathsf{m})}$

$k \leftarrow \mathsf{PRF.Gen}(1^{n_{\mathsf{PRF}}}, 1^{\log(KN)})$

$\varphi_0 \leftarrow\!\!\$\ \mathcal{R}_{\mathsf{ck}}, \mu_0 := \mathsf{Com}(\mathsf{ck}, \mathsf{m}; \varphi_0)$

for $(i,j) \in [K] \times [N]$:

   $\mathsf{prer}_{i,j} := \mathsf{PRF.Eval}(k, (i,j))$

   $\mathsf{r}_{i,j} := \mathsf{H}_x(\mathsf{prer}_{i,j})$

   parse $\mathsf{r}_{i,j} = (\alpha_{i,j}, \varphi_{i,j}, \gamma_{i,j})$

   $\mu_{i,j} := \mathsf{Translate}(\mathsf{ck}, \mu_0, \varphi_{i,j})$

   $c_{i,j} := \mathsf{H}(\mathsf{pk}_i, \mu_{i,j}) \cdot g^{\alpha_{i,j}}$

for $i \in [K]$:

   $\mathsf{com}_{r,i} := \mathsf{H}_r(\mathsf{H}_r(\mathsf{r}_{i,1}), \ldots, \mathsf{H}_r(\mathsf{r}_{i,N}))$

$\mathsf{com}_r := \mathsf{H}_r(\mathsf{com}_{r,1}, \ldots, \mathsf{com}_{r,K})$

$\xleftarrow{\ \mu_0, \mathsf{com}_r, \mathsf{com}_c\ }$ $\mathsf{com}_c := \mathsf{H}_c(c_{1,1}, \ldots, c_{K,N})$

$\xrightarrow{\quad \mathsf{seed_J}, \mathsf{salt} \quad}$ **if** $\mathsf{com_J} \neq \mathsf{H}'(\mathsf{seed_J}, \mathsf{salt})$: **abort**

for $i \in [K]$:

   $\mathsf{J}_i := \mathsf{H}'(\mathsf{seed_J}, i)$

$\mathbf{J} = (\mathsf{J}_1, \ldots, \mathsf{J}_K)$

if $\mathsf{Check} = 0$: **abort**

for $i \in [K]$:

   for $i \in [K]$: $\mathsf{J}_i := \mathsf{H}'(\mathsf{seed_J}, i)$

   $\mathbf{J} = (\mathsf{J}_1, \ldots, \mathsf{J}_K)$

   $\mathcal{J} := \{(i, \mathsf{J}_i) \mid i \in [K]\}$

   $k_\mathsf{J} \leftarrow \mathsf{PRF.Puncture}(k, \mathcal{J})$

$\xleftarrow{\ k_\mathsf{J}, \{c_{i,\mathsf{J}_i}, \eta_i\}_i\ }$ **for** $i \in [K]$: $\eta_i := \mathsf{H}_r(\mathsf{r}_{i,\mathsf{J}_i})$

for $i \in [K]$: $s_{i,\mathsf{J}_i} := c_{i,\mathsf{J}_i}^{\mathsf{sk}_i}$

$\bar{s} := \prod\limits_{i=1}^{K} s_{i,\mathsf{J}_i}$ $\xrightarrow{\quad \bar{s} \quad}$ $\bar{\sigma} := \bar{s} \cdot \prod\limits_{i=1}^{K} \mathsf{pk}_i^{-\alpha_{i,\mathsf{J}_i}}$

$$\text{\bf if } \prod_{i=1}^{K} e\left(\mathsf{H}(\mathsf{pk}_i, \mu_{i,\mathsf{J}_i}), \mathsf{pk}_i\right)$$

$$\neq e(\bar{\sigma}, g): \quad \textbf{abort}$$

for $i \in [K]$: $\varphi_i := \varphi_0 + \varphi_{i,\mathsf{J}_i}$

return $\sigma := (\bar{\sigma}, \varphi_1, \ldots, \varphi_K)$

Fig. 5. The signature issuing protocol of the blind signature scheme $\mathsf{PIKA}_{\mathsf{CDH}}$, where $\mathsf{H} \colon \{0,1\}^* \to \mathbb{Z}_p, \mathsf{H}' \colon \{0,1\}^* \to \{0,1\}^n$ and $\mathsf{H}_r, \mathsf{H}_c \colon \{0,1\}^* \to \{0,1\}^n, \mathsf{H}_x \colon \{0,1\}^* \to \mathbb{Z}_p \times \mathcal{R}_{\mathsf{ck}} \times \{0,1\}^{n_{\mathsf{PRF}}}$ are random oracles. The algorithm Check is defined in Fig. 4. The state ctr of S is incremented atomically

$H_r, H_c \colon \{0,1\}^* \to \{0,1\}^n$ be random oracles. Also, assume that there is a $\vartheta > 0$ and f is such that

$$f(\mathsf{ctr}) = \lceil 3\vartheta \ln(q_{\max} + 1) \cdot \mathsf{ctr} \rceil.$$

Then PIKA_{CDH} satisfies $q_{\max}$-one-more unforgeability, under the CDH assumption relative to PGGen.

Specifically, assume the existence of an adversary against the OMUF security of PIKA_{CDH} that has advantage ϵ, runs in time t, makes at most $Q_{H_r}, Q_{H_c}, Q_{H'}, Q_H$ queries to oracles H_r, H_c, H', H, respectively, and starts at most $q \leq q_{\max}$ interactions with his signer oracle. Let $\delta > 0$ such that $(1 - \delta)\vartheta > 1$. Then there exists an adversary against the CDH problem relative to PGGen with advantage ϵ_{CDH} and running time t and an adversary against the binding property of CMT with advantage ϵ_{CMT} and running time t such that

$$\epsilon - e^{-\delta K} \leq \epsilon_{CMT} + \frac{K}{p} + 4qK\epsilon_{CDH} + \mathsf{stat}$$

where

$$\mathsf{stat} = \frac{Q_{H_r}^2}{2^n} + \frac{Q_{H_c}^2}{2^n} + \frac{qQ_{H_r}}{2^n} + \frac{qKQ_{H_r}}{2^n} + \frac{qQ_{H_c}}{2^n} + \frac{qQ_{H'}}{2^{n-1}}.$$

Proof. Set $\mathsf{BS} := \mathsf{PIKA}_{CDH}$. Let $\mathcal{A}$ be an adversary against the OMUF security of BS. We prove the statement via a sequence of games.

Game $\mathbf{G}_0$: We start with game $\mathbf{G}_0 := q_{\max}\text{-}\mathbf{OMUF}_{\mathsf{BS}}^{\mathcal{A}}$, which is the one-more unforgeability game. We briefly recall this game. A key pair $(\mathsf{pk}, \mathsf{sk}) \leftarrow \mathsf{Gen}(1^n)$ is sampled, $\mathcal{A}$ is run with concurrent access to an interactive oracle O simulating the signer $\mathsf{S}(\mathsf{sk})$. Assume that $\mathcal{A}$ completes ℓ interactions with O. Further, $\mathcal{A}$ gets access to random oracles H, H', H_r and H_c, which are provided by the game in the standard lazy manner. When $\mathcal{A}$ finishes its execution, it outputs tuples $(\mathsf{m}_1, \sigma_1), \ldots, (\mathsf{m}_k, \sigma_k)$ and wins, if all m_i are distinct, $k > \ell$ and all signatures σ_i verify with respect to pk and m_i.

Game $\mathbf{G}_1$: In game $\mathbf{G}_1$, we add an additional abort. The game aborts if in the end $\mathcal{A}$'s output contains two pairs $(\mathsf{m}^{(0)}, \sigma^{(0)}), (\mathsf{m}^{(1)}, \sigma^{(1)})$ such that $\mathsf{m}^{(0)} \neq \mathsf{m}^{(1)}$ but there exists $i^{(0)}, i^{(1)} \in [K]$ such that

$$\mathsf{Com}(\mathsf{ck}, \mathsf{m}^{(0)}; \varphi_{i^{(0)}}^{(0)}) = \mathsf{Com}(\mathsf{ck}, \mathsf{m}^{(1)}; \varphi_{i^{(1)}}^{(1)}).$$

As CMT is computationally binding, a straight-forward reduction with advantage ϵ_{CMT} and running time t shows that

$$|\Pr[\mathbf{G}_0 \Rightarrow 1] - \Pr[\mathbf{G}_1 \Rightarrow 1]| \leq \epsilon_{CMT}.$$

Game $\mathbf{G}_2$: This game is as $\mathbf{G}_1$, but we rule out collisions for oracles $H_t, t \in \{r, c\}$. To be more precise, we change the simulation of oracles $H_t, t \in \{r, c\}$ in the following way. If $\mathcal{A}$ queries $H_t(x)$ and this value is not yet defined, the game samples an image $y \leftarrow_{\$} \{0,1\}^n$. However, if there exists an $x' \neq x$ with $H_t(x') = y$, the game returns $\bot$. Otherwise it behaves as before. Note that $\mathcal{A}$ can only distinguish between $\mathbf{G}_1$ and $\mathbf{G}_2$ if such a collision happens, i.e. H_t returns $\bot$. We can apply a union bound over all $Q_{H_t}^2$ pairs of random oracle queries and obtain

$$|\Pr[\mathbf{G}_1 \Rightarrow 1] - \Pr[\mathbf{G}_2 \Rightarrow 1]| \leq \frac{Q_{H_r}^2}{2^n} + \frac{Q_{H_c}^2}{2^n}.$$

Note that the change in $\mathbf{G}_2$ implies that at each point of the execution of the game and for each image $y \in \{0,1\}^n$, there is at most one preimage $H_t^{-1}(y)$ under H_t. By looking at the random oracle queries of $\mathcal{A}$, the game can extract preimages of given images y, and we know that for each y at most one preimage can be extracted. We will make use of such an extraction in the following games.

Game $\mathbf{G}_3$: We change the way the signer oracle is executed. In particular, when $\mathcal{A}$ sends $\mu_0, \text{com}_r, \text{com}_c$ as its first message, the game tries to extract values $\overline{\text{com}}_{r,i}$ such that $\text{com}_r = H_r(\overline{\text{com}}_{r,1}, \ldots, \overline{\text{com}}_{r,K})$ by searching through random oracle queries. If the game can not extract such a preimage, we write $\overline{\text{com}}_{r,i} = \bot$ for all $i \in [K]$. Then, the game aborts if it can not extract such a preimage , i.e. $\overline{\text{com}}_{r,i} = \bot$, but later algorithm Check outputs 1. Recall that algorithm Check verifies that

$$\text{com}_r = H_r(\text{com}_{r,1}, \ldots, \text{com}_{r,K}).$$

Thus, for every fixed interaction, we can bound the probability of such an abort by $Q_{H_r}/2^n$. Indeed, once com_r is sent by $\mathcal{A}$ and thus fixed, and the game can not extract, we know that there is no bitstring x such that $H_r(x) = \text{com}_r$. Also, if algorithm Check outputs 1, we know that $\mathcal{A}$ was able to find a preimage of com_r after this was fixed. This can happen with probability at most $1/2^n$ for each random oracle query. Using a union bound over all interactions we obtain

$$|\Pr[\mathbf{G}_3 \Rightarrow 1] - \Pr[\mathbf{G}_4 \Rightarrow 1]| \leq \frac{qQ_{H_r}}{2^n}.$$

Game $\mathbf{G}_4$: We introduce another abort in the signer oracle. In this game, after the extraction of $(\overline{\text{com}}_{r,1}, \ldots, \overline{\text{com}}_{r,K})$ from com_r we introduced before, the game extracts $(\overline{r}_{i,1}, \ldots, \overline{r}_{i,N})$ from $\overline{\text{com}}_{r,i}$ for every $i \in [K]$ for which $\overline{\text{com}}_{r,i} \neq \bot$, such that

$$\overline{\text{com}}_{r,i} = H_r(H_r(\overline{r}_{i,1}), \ldots, H_r(\overline{r}_{i,N})).$$

Again, the game does this by looking at the random oracle queries of $\mathcal{A}$ and we write $\overline{r}_{i,j} = \bot$ if the game can not extract the value $\overline{r}_{i,j}$. If there is an instance $i \in [K]$ and a session $j \in [N]$ such that $\overline{\text{com}}_{r,i} \neq \bot$ but $\overline{r}_{i,j} = \bot$ and later in that execution $\mathbf{J}_i \neq j$ but algorithm Check outputs 1, the game aborts.

To analyze the probability of this abort, fix an interaction and an instance $i \in [K]$. Assume that $\overline{\text{com}}_{r,i} \neq \bot$ and there is a session $j \in [N]$ such that $\overline{r}_{i,j} = \bot$ and later in that interaction $\mathbf{J}_i \neq j$. Then, after $\overline{\text{com}}_{r,i}$ is fixed, we consider two cases. In the first case, the game could not extract $h_1, \ldots, h_N$ such that $\overline{\text{com}}_{r,i} = \mathsf{H}_r(h_1, \ldots, h_N)$. Clearly, once $\overline{\text{com}}_{r,i}$, the probability that one of the hash queries of $\mathcal{A}$ evaluates to $\overline{\text{com}}_{r,i}$ is at most $1/2^n$. Thus, the probability that Check outputs 1, i.e. $\mathcal{A}$ is able to open $\overline{\text{com}}_{r,i}$ in this case, is at most $Q_{\mathsf{H}_r}/2^n$. Similarly, in the case where the game could extract $h_1, \ldots, h_N$, but could not extract $\overline{r}_{i,j}$ such that $\mathsf{H}_r(\overline{r}_{i,j}) = h_j$, the probability that one of $\mathcal{A}$'s hash queries evaluates to h_j is at most $1/2^n$. Thus, the probability that Check outputs 1, i.e. $\mathcal{A}$ is able to open h_j in this case, is at most $Q_{\mathsf{H}_r}/2^n$. Note that here we needed that $j \neq \mathbf{J}_i$, as the definition of Check does not require $\mathcal{A}$ to open $h_{\mathbf{J}_i}$.

Applying a union bound over the interactions and instances we get

$$|\Pr[\mathbf{G}_3 \Rightarrow 1] - \Pr[\mathbf{G}_4 \Rightarrow 1]| \leq \frac{qKQ_{\mathsf{H}_r}}{2^n}.$$

Game $\mathbf{G}_5$: We introduce another abort: Whenever $\mathcal{A}$ sends $\mu_0, \text{com}_r, \text{com}_c$ as its first message, the game behaves as before, but additionally the game extracts values $\overline{c}_{1,1}, \ldots, \overline{c}_{K,N}$ from com_c such that

$$\text{com}_c = \mathsf{H}_c(\overline{c}_{1,1}, \ldots, \overline{c}_{K,N}).$$

If the game can not extract, but later algorithm Check outputs 1, the game aborts. Note that algorithm Check internally checks if

$$\text{com}_c = \mathsf{H}_c(c_{1,1}, \ldots, c_{K,N}).$$

Thus, for each fixed interaction it is possible to argue as in the previous games to bound the probability of such an abort and hence we obtain

$$|\Pr[\mathbf{G}_4 \Rightarrow 1] - \Pr[\mathbf{G}_5 \Rightarrow 1]| \leq \frac{qQ_{\mathsf{H}_c}}{2^n}.$$

Game $\mathbf{G}_6$: In $\mathbf{G}_6$, the signer oracle sends a random $\text{com}_\mathbf{J}$ in the beginning of each interaction. Later, before it has to send $\text{seed}_\mathbf{J}, \text{salt}$, it samples $\text{salt} \leftarrow_\$ \{0,1\}^n$ and aborts if $\mathsf{H}'(\text{seed}_\mathbf{J}, \text{salt})$ is already defined. If it is not yet defined, it defines it as $\mathsf{H}'(\text{seed}_\mathbf{J}, \text{salt}) := \text{com}_\mathbf{J}$. The adversary $\mathcal{A}$ can only distinguish between $\mathbf{G}_5$ and $\mathbf{G}_6$ if $\mathsf{H}'(\text{seed}_\mathbf{J}, \text{salt})$ is already defined. By a union bound over all $Q_{\mathsf{H}'}$ hash queries and q interactions we obtain

$$|\Pr[\mathbf{G}_5 \Rightarrow 1] - \Pr[\mathbf{G}_6 \Rightarrow 1]| \leq \frac{qQ_{\mathsf{H}'}}{2^n}.$$

Game $\mathbf{G}_7$: In $\mathbf{G}_7$, the game aborts if in some interaction there exists an $i \in [K]$ such that $\mathsf{H}'(\text{seed}_\mathbf{J}, i)$ has already been queried before the signing oracle sends $\text{seed}_\mathbf{J}$ to $\mathcal{A}$. Clearly, $\mathcal{A}$ obtains no information about $\text{seed}_\mathbf{J}$ before the potential abort, see $\mathbf{G}_6$. Further, $\text{seed}_\mathbf{J}$ is sampled uniformly at random. A union bound over all $Q_{\mathsf{H}'}$ queries and q interactions shows that

$$|\Pr[\mathbf{G}_6 \Rightarrow 1] - \Pr[\mathbf{G}_7 \Rightarrow 1]| \leq \frac{qQ_{\mathsf{H}'}}{2^n}.$$

Now, fix an interaction in $\mathbf{G}_7$ and assume that Check returns 1 and the game does not abort due to any of the reasons we introduced so far. Note that this means that for all instances $i \in [K]$ the value $\mathrm{c\bar{o}m}_{r,i}$ could be extracted. Furthermore, this means that if there exists $i \in [K], j_0 \in [N]$ such that $\bar{r}_{i,j_0} = \bot$ then later $\mathbf{J}_i = j_0$. Also, note that if Check does not abort, then we have $\mathrm{c\bar{o}m}_{r,i} = \mathrm{com}_{r,i}, \bar{r}_{i,j} = r_{i,j}$ and $\bar{c}_{i,j} = c_{i,j}$ for all $(i,j) \in [K] \times [N]$ for which these values are defined. This is because we ruled out collisions for oracles $\mathsf{H}_r, \mathsf{H}_c$. Now, we define an indicator random variable $\mathrm{cheat}_{i,\mathrm{ctr}}$ for the event that in the ctr^{th} interaction, the signer oracle does not abort and there exists $i \in [K], j \in [N]$ such that $\bar{r}_{i,j} = \bot$ or $\bar{r}_{i,j} = (\alpha, \varphi, \gamma)$ such that

$$c_{i,j} \neq \mathsf{H}(\mathsf{pk}_i, \mathsf{Translate}(\mathsf{ck}, \mu_0, \varphi)) \cdot g^\alpha.$$

We say that $\mathcal{A}$ successfully cheats in instance $i \in [K]$ and interaction ctr if $\mathrm{cheat}_{i,\mathrm{ctr}} = 1$. We also define the number of interactions in which $\mathcal{A}$ successfully cheats in instance i as $\mathrm{cheat}_i^* := \sum_{\mathrm{ctr}=2}^{q+1} \mathrm{cheat}_{i,\mathrm{ctr}}$.

By the above discussion, we have that $\mathrm{cheat}_{i,\mathrm{ctr}} = 1$ implies that $\mathbf{J}_i = j_0$ and thus

$$\Pr\left[\mathrm{cheat}_{i,\mathrm{ctr}} = 1\right] \leq \frac{1}{N}.$$

Therefore, we can bound the expectation of cheat_i^* using

$$\mathbb{E}[\mathrm{cheat}_i^*] \leq \frac{1}{3\vartheta \ln(q_{\max}+1)} \sum_{\mathrm{ctr}=2}^{q+1} \frac{1}{\mathrm{ctr}} \leq \frac{\ln(q+1)}{3\vartheta \ln(q_{\max}+1)} \leq \frac{1}{3\vartheta}.$$

Now, if we plug $X := \mathrm{cheat}_i^*$ and $s := 3\mathbb{E}[\mathrm{cheat}_i^*] + \delta = 1/\vartheta + \delta$ into the Chernoff bound (see the full version), we get that for all $i \in [K]$

$$\Pr\left[\mathrm{cheat}_i^* \geq \frac{1}{\vartheta} + \delta\right] \leq e^{-\delta}.$$

We note that the entire calculation of this probability also holds if we fix the random coins of the adversary.

Game $\mathbf{G}_8$: Game $\mathbf{G}_8$ is defined as $\mathbf{G}_7$, but additionally aborts if for all $i \in [K]$ we have $\mathrm{cheat}_i^* \geq \delta + 1/\vartheta$. In particular, if $\mathbf{G}_8$ does not abort, then there is some instance i for which $\mathcal{A}$ does not successfully cheat at all, which follows from the assumption $(1 - \delta)\vartheta > 1$.

We can now bound the distinguishing advantage of $\mathcal{A}$ between $\mathbf{G}_7$ and $\mathbf{G}_8$ as follows. We denote the random coins of $\mathcal{A}$ by $\rho_\mathcal{A}$ and the random coins of the experiment (excluding $\rho_\mathcal{A}$) by ρ. Let bad be the event that for all $i \in [K]$ we have $\mathrm{cheat}_i^* \geq \delta + 1/\vartheta$. We note that the coins ρ that the experiment uses for the K instances are independent. Thus we have

$$\Pr_{\rho,\rho_A}[\mathsf{bad}] = \sum_{\bar\rho_A} \Pr_{\rho_A}[\rho_A = \bar\rho_A] \cdot \Pr_{\rho,\rho_A}[\mathsf{bad} \mid \rho_A = \bar\rho_A]$$

$$= \sum_{\bar\rho_A} \Pr_{\rho_A}[\rho_A = \bar\rho_A] \cdot \prod_{i \in [K]} \Pr_{\rho,\rho_A}\left[\mathsf{cheat}_i^* \geq \frac{1}{\vartheta} + \delta \;\middle|\; \rho_A = \bar\rho_A\right]$$

$$\leq \sum_{\bar\rho_A} \Pr_{\rho_A}[\rho_A = \bar\rho_A] \cdot e^{-\delta K} = e^{-\delta K},$$

which implies

$$|\Pr[\mathbf{G}_7 \Rightarrow 1] - \Pr[\mathbf{G}_8 \Rightarrow 1]| \leq \Pr_{\rho,\rho_A}[\mathsf{bad}] \leq e^{-\delta K}.$$

Game $\mathbf{G}_9$: In game $\mathbf{G}_9$, we sample a random instance $i^* \leftarrow_\$ [K]$ at the beginning of the game. In the end, the game aborts if $\mathsf{cheat}_{i^*}^* \geq \delta + 1/\vartheta$. In particular, if this game does not abort, then $\mathcal{A}$ does not successfully cheat in instance i^* at all. As $\mathcal{A}$'s view is independent from i^*, we have

$$\Pr[\mathbf{G}_9 \Rightarrow 1] = \Pr\left[\mathbf{G}_8 \Rightarrow 1 \wedge \mathsf{cheat}_{i^*}^* < \frac{1}{\vartheta} + \delta\right]$$

$$= \Pr[\mathbf{G}_8 \Rightarrow 1] \cdot \Pr\left[\mathsf{cheat}_{i^*}^* < \frac{1}{\vartheta} + \delta \;\middle|\; \mathbf{G}_8 \Rightarrow 1\right]$$

$$\geq \Pr[\mathbf{G}_8 \Rightarrow 1] \cdot \Pr\left[\mathsf{cheat}_{i^*}^* < \frac{1}{\vartheta} + \delta \;\middle|\; \exists i \in [K] : \mathsf{cheat}_i^* < \frac{1}{\vartheta} + \delta\right]$$

$$\geq \Pr[\mathbf{G}_8 \Rightarrow 1] \cdot \frac{1}{K},$$

where the first inequality follows from the fact that the event $\mathbf{G}_8 \Rightarrow 1$ implies the event $\exists i \in [K] : \mathsf{cheat}_i^* < \delta + 1/\vartheta$.

We note that from now on, our proof follows the proof strategy of the BLS signature scheme [5].

Game $\mathbf{G}_{10}$: In game $\mathbf{G}_{10}$, we introduce an initially empty set $\mathcal{L}$ and a new abort. We highlight that we treat $\mathcal{L}$ as a set and therefore every bitstring is in $\mathcal{L}$ only once. Recall that when $\mathcal{A}$ sends $\mu_0, \mathsf{com}_r, \mathsf{com}_c$ to the signer oracle, the game tries to extract values $\bar{r}_{i,j}$ for $(i,j) \in [K] \times [N]$. Then the game samples $\mathsf{seed}_\mathbf{J}$ and computes $\mathbf{J}$ accordingly. In particular, due to the changes in the previous games we know that the game extracts $\bar{r}_{i^*,\mathbf{J}_{i^*}} = (\alpha, \varphi, \gamma)$ unless the experiment will abort anyways. Then, in game $\mathbf{G}_{10}$, the game will insert $\mathsf{Translate}(\mathsf{ck}, \mu_0, \varphi)$ into $\mathcal{L}$.

Fix the first pair (m, σ) in $\mathcal{A}$'s final output such that for $\sigma = (\bar\sigma, \varphi_1, \ldots, \varphi_K)$ and $\mu^* := \mathsf{Com}(\mathsf{ck}, \mathsf{m}; \varphi_{i^*})$ we have $\mu^* \notin \mathcal{L}$. Such a pair must exists if $\mathcal{A}$ is successful, see game $\mathbf{G}_1$. Then game $\mathbf{G}_{10}$ aborts if $\mathsf{H}(\mathsf{pk}_{i^*}, \mu^*)$ is not defined yet. Note that $\mathcal{A}$'s success probability in such a case can be at most $1/p$ and hence

$$|\Pr[\mathbf{G}_9 \Rightarrow 1] - \Pr[\mathbf{G}_{10} \Rightarrow 1]| \leq \frac{1}{p}.$$

Game G_{11}: In game G_{11}, we change how the random oracle H is simulated and add a new abort. For every query of the form $H(pk_{i^*}, \mu)$ the game independently samples a bit $b[\mu] \in \{0, 1\}$ such that the probability that $b[\mu] = 1$ is $1/(q + 1)$. Whenever the game adds a value μ to the set $\mathcal{L}$, it aborts if $b[\mu] = 1$. Then, after $\mathcal{A}$ returns its final output, the game determines μ^* as in G_{10}, adds arbitrary values to $\mathcal{L}$ such that all values in $\mathcal{L} \cup \{\mu^*\}$ are distinct and $|\mathcal{L}| = q$ and aborts if $b[\mu^*] = 0$ or there is a $\mu \in \mathcal{L}$ such that $b[\mu] = 1$. Otherwise it continues as before. Note that unless the game aborts, $\mathcal{A}$'s view does not change. As all bits $b[\mu]$ are independent, we derive

$$\Pr[G_{11} \Rightarrow 1] = \Pr[G_{10} \Rightarrow 1] \cdot \Pr[b[\mu^*] = 1 \wedge \forall \mu \in \mathcal{L} : b[\mu] = 0]$$

$$= \Pr[G_{10} \Rightarrow 1] \cdot \frac{1}{q+1} \left(1 - \frac{1}{q+1}\right)^q$$

$$= \Pr[G_{10} \Rightarrow 1] \cdot \frac{1}{q} \left(1 - \frac{1}{q+1}\right)^{q+1}$$

$$\geq \Pr[G_{10} \Rightarrow 1] \cdot \frac{1}{4q},$$

where the last inequality follows from $(1 - 1/x)^x \geq 1/4$ for all $x \geq 2$.

Finally, we construct a reduction $\mathcal{B}$ that solves CDH with running time t and advantage ϵ_{CDH} such that

$$\Pr[G_{11} \Rightarrow 1] \leq \epsilon_{CDH}.$$

Then, the statement follows by an easy calculation. Reduction $\mathcal{B}$ works as follows:

- $\mathcal{B}$ gets as input bilinear group parameters $\mathbb{G}, g, p, e$ and group elements $X = g^x, Y = g^y$. The goal of $\mathcal{B}$ is to compute g^{xy}. First, $\mathcal{B}$ samples $i^* \leftarrow_s [K]$. Then, it defines $pk_{i^*} := X$ (which implicitly defines $sk_{i^*} := x$) and $sk_i \leftarrow_s \mathbb{Z}_p, pk_i := g^{sk_i}$ for $i \subset [K] \setminus \{i^*\}$.
- $\mathcal{B}$ runs adversary $\mathcal{A}$ on input $\mathbb{G}, g, p, e, pk := (pk_1, \ldots, pk_K, ck)$ with oracle access to a signer oracle and random oracles H, H_r, H_c, H'. To do so, it simulates oracles H_r, H_c, H' exactly as in G_{11}. The other oracles are provided as follows:
  - For a query of the form $H(pk_{i^*}, \mu)$ for which the hash value is not yet defined, it samples a bit $b[\mu] \in \{0, 1\}$ such that the probability that $b[\mu] = 1$ is $1/(q+1)$. Then, it defines the hash value as $Y^{b[\mu]} \cdot g^{t[i^*, \mu]}$ for a randomly sampled $t[i^*, \mu] \leftarrow_s \mathbb{Z}_p$. For a query of the form $H(pk_i, \mu), i \neq i^*$ for which the hash value is not yet defined it defines the hash value as $g^{t[i, \mu]}$ for a randomly sampled $t[i, \mu] \leftarrow_s \mathbb{Z}_p$. For all other queries it simulates H honestly.
  - When $\mathcal{A}$ starts an interaction with the signer oracle, $\mathcal{B}$ sends N to $\mathcal{B}$ as in the protocol. When $\mathcal{B}$ sends its first message μ_0, com_r, com_c as its first message, $\mathcal{B}$ behaves as G_{11}. In particular, it tries to extract $\bar{r}_{i,j}, \bar{c}_{i,j}$ for $(i, j) \in [K] \times [N]$. It then sends $seed_J$ to $\mathcal{A}$.

- When $\mathcal{A}$ sends its second message $k_{\mathbf{J}}, \{c_{i,\mathbf{J}_i}, \eta_i\}_{i \in [K]}$, $\mathcal{B}$ aborts under the same conditions as $\mathbf{G}_{11}$ does. In particular, if $\mathcal{B}$ does not abort and the signer oracle does not abort then $\bar{r}_{i^*,\mathbf{J}_{i^*}} = (\alpha, \varphi, \gamma)$ is defined and $\mathcal{B}$ for $\mu := \mathsf{Translate}(\mathsf{ck}, \mu_0, \varphi)$, $\mathcal{B}$ sets $s_{i^*,\mathbf{J}_{i^*}} := X^{t[i^*,\mu]+\alpha}$. As defined in $\mathbf{G}_{11}$, $\mathcal{B}$ also inserts μ into the set $\mathcal{L}$. It computes $s_{i,\mathbf{J}_i}$ for $i \neq i^*$ as game $\mathbf{G}_{11}$ does, which is possible as $\mathcal{B}$ holds the corresponding sk_i. Then, $\mathcal{B}$ sends $\bar{s} := \prod_{i=1}^{K} s_{i,\mathbf{J}_i}$ to $\mathcal{A}$.
- When $\mathcal{A}$ returns its final output, $\mathcal{B}$ performs all verification steps in $\mathbf{G}_{11}$. In particular, it searches for the first pair (m, σ) in $\mathcal{A}$'s final output such that for $\sigma = (\bar{\sigma}, \varphi_1, \ldots, \varphi_K)$ and $\mu^* := \mathsf{Com}(\mathsf{ck}, \mathsf{m}; \varphi_{i^*})$ we have $\mu^* \notin \mathcal{L}$. As defined in $\mathbf{G}_{11}$, $\mathcal{B}$ aborts if $b[\mu^*] = 0$. Finally, $\mathcal{B}$ defines $\mu_i := \mathsf{Com}(\mathsf{ck}, \mathsf{m}; \varphi_i)$ and returns

$$Z := \bar{\sigma} \cdot X^{-t[i^*,\mu^*]} \cdot g^{-\sum_{i \in [K] \setminus \{i^*\}} t[i,\mu_i]\mathsf{sk}_i}$$

to its challenger.

We first argue that $\mathcal{B}$ perfectly simulates $\mathbf{G}_{11}$ for $\mathcal{A}$. To see that, note that as the $t[i, \mu]$ are sampled uniformly at random, the random oracle is simulated perfectly. To see that $s_{i^*,\mathbf{J}_{i^*}}$ is distributed correctly, note that if the signing oracle and $\mathbf{G}_{11}$ do not abort, then we have

$$c_{i^*,\mathbf{J}_{i^*}}^{\mathsf{sk}_{i^*}} = (\mathsf{H}(\mathsf{pk}_{i^*}, \mu) \cdot g^{\alpha})^{\mathsf{sk}_{i^*}} = \left(Y^{b[\mu]} \cdot g^{t[i^*,\mu]} \cdot g^{\alpha}\right)^x = X^{t[i^*,\mu]+\alpha},$$

where the last equality follows from $b[\mu] = 0$, as otherwise $\mathbf{G}_{11}$ would have aborted.

It remains to show that if $\mathbf{G}_{11}$ outputs 1, then we have $Z = g^{xy}$. This follows directly from the verification equation and $b[\mu^*] = 1$. To see this, note that

$$\prod_{i=1}^{K} e\left(\mathsf{H}(\mathsf{pk}_i, \mu_i), \mathsf{pk}_i\right) = e\left(Y^{b[\mu^*]} \cdot g^{t[i^*,\mu^*]}, X\right) \cdot \prod_{i \in [K] \setminus \{i^*\}} e\left(g^{t[i,\mu_i]}, g^{\mathsf{sk}_i}\right)$$

$$= e(g,g)^{xy+t[i^*,\mu^*]x} \cdot e(g,g)^{\sum_{i \in [K] \setminus \{i^*\}} t[i,\mu_i]\mathsf{sk}_i}.$$

Using the verification equation, this implies that

$$g^{xy} = \bar{\sigma} \cdot g^{-\left(t[i^*,\mu^*]x + \sum_{i \in [K] \setminus \{i^*\}} t[i,\mu_i]\mathsf{sk}_i\right)}$$

Concluded.   □

We note that instead of giving games $\mathbf{G}_{10}, \mathbf{G}_{11}$ and the reduction from CDH explicitly, one can also directly reduce from the security of the BLS signature scheme to $\mathbf{G}_9$, leading to the very same bound in total. This tells us that one can use (up to losing $\log(K)$ bits[5] of security) the same curves as for BLS.

Corollary 1 (Informal). *Under the same conditions as in Theorem 4, the scheme* PIKA_{CDH} *satisfies* $q_{\max}$-*one-more unforgeability, if the BLS signature scheme [5] is unforgeable under chosen message attacks relative to* PGGen, *where the concrete security loss is (up to statistically negligible terms) given by* K.

---

[5] In our concrete instantiation, $\log(K) \approx 6.5$.

5 A Concrete Scheme Based on RSA

In addition to our concrete scheme from CDH, we also construct a concrete scheme BS_{RSA} based on the RSAassumption. We postpone the details to the full version and only give a short overview here.

Our scheme is based on the Okamoto-Guillou-Quisquater (OGQ) [26] linear function. That is, we start with this function in our generic transformation from Sect. 3. Informally, the function has domain $\mathcal{D} := \mathbb{Z}_\lambda \times \mathbb{Z}_N^*$, scalar space $\mathcal{S} := \mathbb{Z}_\lambda$ and range $\mathbb{Z}_N^*$, where N is an RSAmodulus and λ is a prime with $\gcd(N, \lambda) = \gcd(\varphi(N), \lambda) = 1$. As we can not aggregate signatures efficiently, we can not mimic the K-repetition technique from our CDH-based scheme. Thus, we still rely on the loose bound of the underlying linear blind signature scheme. To solve this issue and obtain practical parameter sizes, we note that the bound becomes acceptable, once we increase the parameter λ. Our insight is that this can be done independently from the modulus N.

Although this improves the bound and thus concrete parameters, we still have a rather large communication complexity, due to the logarithmic number of $R_i \in \mathbb{Z}_N^*$ that are sent in our generic transformation. Here, our solution is to send a short random seed (e.g. 128 bit) and derive the values R_i using a random oracle. Now, the signer has to recover the preimages of the R_i to continue the protocol. We show that the OGQ linear function admits a trapdoor that allows to sample preimages, solving this problem as well.

References

1. Agrawal, S., Kirshanova, E., Stehlé, D., Yadav, A.: Can round-optimal lattice-based blind signatures be practical? Cryptology ePrint Archive, Report 2021/1565 (2021). https://eprint.iacr.org/2021/1565
2. Bellare, M., Namprempre, C., Pointcheval, D., Semanko, M.: The one-more-RSA-inversion problems and the security of Chaum's blind signature scheme. J. Cryptol. **16**(3), 185–215 (2003)
3. Benhamouda, F., Lepoint, T., Loss, J., Orrù, M., Raykova, M.: On the (in)security of ROS. In: Canteaut, A., Standaert, F.-X. (eds.) EUROCRYPT 2021, Part I. LNCS, vol. 12696, pp. 33–53. Springer, Cham (2021). https://doi.org/10.1007/978-3-030-77870-5_2
4. Boldyreva, A.: Threshold signatures, multisignatures and blind signatures based on the gap-Diffie-Hellman-group signature scheme. In: Desmedt, Y.G. (ed.) PKC 2003. LNCS, vol. 2567, pp. 31–46. Springer, Heidelberg (2003). https://doi.org/10.1007/3-540-36288-6_3
5. Boneh, D., Lynn, B., Shacham, H.: Short signatures from the Weil pairing. In: Boyd, C. (ed.) ASIACRYPT 2001. LNCS, vol. 2248, pp. 514–532. Springer, Heidelberg (2001). https://doi.org/10.1007/3-540-45682-1_30
6. Camenisch, J., Groß, T.: Efficient attributes for anonymous credentials. In: Ning, P., Syverson, P.F., Jha, S. (eds.) ACM CCS 2008: 15th Conference on Computer and Communications Security, Alexandria, Virginia, USA, 27–31 October 2008, pp. 345–356. ACM Press (2008)

7. Camenisch, J., Lysyanskaya, A.: An efficient system for non-transferable anonymous credentials with optional anonymity revocation. In: Pfitzmann, B. (ed.) EUROCRYPT 2001. LNCS, vol. 2045, pp. 93–118. Springer, Heidelberg (2001). https://doi.org/10.1007/3-540-44987-6_7

8. Camenisch, J., Michels, M.: Proving in zero-knowledge that a number is the product of two safe primes. In: Stern, J. (ed.) EUROCRYPT 1999. LNCS, vol. 1592, pp. 107–122. Springer, Heidelberg (1999). https://doi.org/10.1007/3-540-48910-X_8

9. Chaum, D.: Blind signatures for untraceable payments. In: Chaum, D., Rivest, R.L., Sherman, A.T. (eds.) Advances in Cryptology - CRYPTO 1982, Santa Barbara, CA, USA, pp. 199–203. Plenum Press, New York (1982)

10. Fischlin, M.: Round-optimal composable blind signatures in the common reference string model. In: Dwork, C. (ed.) CRYPTO 2006. LNCS, vol. 4117, pp. 60–77. Springer, Heidelberg (2006). https://doi.org/10.1007/11818175_4

11. Fuchsbauer, G., Hanser, C., Slamanig, D.: Practical round-optimal blind signatures in the standard model. In: Gennaro, R., Robshaw, M.J.B. (eds.) CRYPTO 2015, Part II. LNCS, vol. 9216, pp. 233–253. Springer, Heidelberg (2015). https://doi.org/10.1007/978-3-662-48000-7_12

12. Fuchsbauer, G., Kiltz, E., Loss, J.: The algebraic group model and its applications. In: Shacham, H., Boldyreva, A. (eds.) CRYPTO 2018, Part II. LNCS, vol. 10992, pp. 33–62. Springer, Cham (2018). https://doi.org/10.1007/978-3-319-96881-0_2

13. Fuchsbauer, G., Plouviez, A., Seurin, Y.: Blind Schnorr signatures and signed ElGamal encryption in the algebraic group model. In: Canteaut, A., Ishai, Y. (eds.) EUROCRYPT 2020, Part II. LNCS, vol. 12106, pp. 63–95. Springer, Cham (2020). https://doi.org/10.1007/978-3-030-45724-2_3

14. Garg, S., Gupta, D.: Efficient round optimal blind signatures. In: Nguyen, P.Q., Oswald, E. (eds.) EUROCRYPT 2014. LNCS, vol. 8441, pp. 477–495. Springer, Heidelberg (2014). https://doi.org/10.1007/978-3-642-55220-5_27

15. Garg, S., Rao, V., Sahai, A., Schröder, D., Unruh, D.: Round optimal blind signatures. In: Rogaway, P. (ed.) CRYPTO 2011. LNCS, vol. 6841, pp. 630–648. Springer, Heidelberg (2011). https://doi.org/10.1007/978-3-642-22792-9_36

16. Ghadafi, E.: Efficient round-optimal blind signatures in the standard model. In: Kiayias, A. (ed.) FC 2017. LNCS, vol. 10322, pp. 455–473. Springer, Cham (2017). https://doi.org/10.1007/978-3-319-70972-7_26

17. Goldberg, S., Reyzin, L., Sagga, O., Baldimtsi, F.: Efficient noninteractive certification of RSA moduli and beyond. In: Galbraith, S.D., Moriai, S. (eds.) ASIACRYPT 2019, Part III. LNCS, vol. 11923, pp. 700–727. Springer, Cham (2019). https://doi.org/10.1007/978-3-030-34618-8_24

18. Goldreich, O., Goldwasser, S., Micali, S.: How to construct random functions (extended abstract). In: 25th Annual Symposium on Foundations of Computer Science, Singer Island, Florida, 24–26 October 1984, pp. 464–479. IEEE Computer Society Press (1984)

19. Grontas, P., Pagourtzis, A., Zacharakis, A., Zhang, B.: Towards everlasting privacy and efficient coercion resistance in remote electronic voting. In: Zohar, A., et al. (eds.) FC 2018. LNCS, vol. 10958, pp. 210–231. Springer, Heidelberg (2019). https://doi.org/10.1007/978-3-662-58820-8_15

20. Hauck, E., Kiltz, E., Loss, J.: A modular treatment of blind signatures from identification schemes. In: Ishai, Y., Rijmen, V. (eds.) EUROCRYPT 2019, Part III. LNCS, vol. 11478, pp. 345–375. Springer, Cham (2019). https://doi.org/10.1007/978-3-030-17659-4_12

21. Hauck, E., Kiltz, E., Loss, J., Nguyen, N.K.: Lattice-based blind signatures, revisited. In: Micciancio, D., Ristenpart, T. (eds.) CRYPTO 2020, Part III. LNCS, vol. 12171, pp. 500–529. Springer, Cham (2020). https://doi.org/10.1007/978-3-030-56880-1_18

22. Heilman, E., Baldimtsi, F., Goldberg, S.: Blindly signed contracts: anonymous on-blockchain and off-blockchain bitcoin transactions. In: Clark, J., Meiklejohn, S., Ryan, P.Y.A., Wallach, D., Brenner, M., Rohloff, K. (eds.) FC 2016. LNCS, vol. 9604, pp. 43–60. Springer, Heidelberg (2016). https://doi.org/10.1007/978-3-662-53357-4_4

23. Juels, A., Luby, M., Ostrovsky, R.: Security of blind digital signatures. In: Kaliski, B.S. (ed.) CRYPTO 1997. LNCS, vol. 1294, pp. 150–164. Springer, Heidelberg (1997). https://doi.org/10.1007/BFb0052233

24. Kastner, J., Loss, J., Xu, J.: On pairing-free blind signature schemes in the algebraic group model. In: PKC 2022. LNCS. Springer, Heidelberg (2022, to appear)

25. Katz, J., Loss, J., Rosenberg, M.: Boosting the security of blind signature schemes. In: Tibouchi, M., Wang, H. (eds.) ASIACRYPT 2021. LNCS, vol. 13093, pp. 468–492. Springer, Cham (2021). https://doi.org/10.1007/978-3-030-92068-5_16

26. Okamoto, T.: Provably secure and practical identification schemes and corresponding signature schemes. In: Brickell, E.F. (ed.) CRYPTO 1992. LNCS, vol. 740, pp. 31–53. Springer, Heidelberg (1993). https://doi.org/10.1007/3-540-48071-4_3

27. Okamoto, T.: Efficient blind and partially blind signatures without random oracles. In: Halevi, S., Rabin, T. (eds.) TCC 2006. LNCS, vol. 3876, pp. 80–99. Springer, Heidelberg (2006). https://doi.org/10.1007/11681878_5

28. Okamoto, T., Ohta, K.: Universal electronic cash. In: Feigenbaum, J. (ed.) CRYPTO 1991. LNCS, vol. 576, pp. 324–337. Springer, Heidelberg (1992). https://doi.org/10.1007/3-540-46766-1_27

29. Pointcheval, D.: Strengthened security for blind signatures. In: Nyberg, K. (ed.) EUROCRYPT 1998. LNCS, vol. 1403, pp. 391–405. Springer, Heidelberg (1998). https://doi.org/10.1007/BFb0054141

30. Pointcheval, D., Stern, J.: Security arguments for digital signatures and blind signatures. J. Cryptol. **13**(3), 361–396 (2000)

31. Sahai, A., Waters, B.: How to use indistinguishability obfuscation: deniable encryption, and more. In: Shmoys, D.B. (ed.) 46th Annual ACM Symposium on Theory of Computing, New York, NY, USA, 31 May–3 June 2014, pp. 475–484. ACM Press (2014)

32. Shoup, V.: Lower bounds for discrete logarithms and related problems. In: Fumy, W. (ed.) EUROCRYPT 1997. LNCS, vol. 1233, pp. 256–266. Springer, Heidelberg (1997). https://doi.org/10.1007/3-540-69053-0_18

33. Tessaro, S., Zhu, C.: Short pairing-free blind signatures with exponential security. Cryptology ePrint Archive, Report 2022/047 (2022). https://eprint.iacr.org/2022/047

Idealized Models

Augmented Random Oracles

Mark Zhandry[1,2]([✉])

[1] NTT Research, Sunnyvale, USA
mark.zhandry@ntt-research.com
[2] Princeton University, Princeton, USA

Abstract. We propose a new paradigm for justifying the security of random oracle-based protocols, which we call the Augmented Random Oracle Model (AROM). We show that the AROM captures a wide range of important random oracle impossibility results. Thus a proof in the AROM implies some resiliency to such impossibilities. We then consider three ROM transforms which are subject to impossibilities: Fiat-Shamir (FS), Fujisaki-Okamoto (FO), and Encrypt-with-Hash (EwH). We show in each case how to obtain security in the AROM by strengthening the building blocks or modifying the transform.

Along the way, we give a couple other results. We improve the assumptions needed for the FO and EwH impossibilities from indistinguishability obfuscation to circularly secure LWE; we argue that our AROM still captures this improved impossibility. We also demonstrate that there is no "best possible" hash function, by giving a pair of security properties, both of which can be instantiated in the standard model separately, which cannot be simultaneously satisfied by a single hash function.

1 Introduction

The random oracle model (ROM) [BR93] treats a cryptographic hash function as a random function, and is a crucial tool for analyzing the security of cryptosystems that otherwise lack a "standard model" security proof. This model captures most practical cryptographic techniques and attacks involving hash functions. Constructions with ROM proofs are often far more efficient than their standard-model counterparts, and numerous applied cryptosystems utilize this model.

Unfortunately, there are numerous examples of ROM failures, schemes that have been proven secure in the ROM but are insecure when the hash function is instantiated. Starting with [CGH98], the most problematic such failures are *uninstantiability* results, where the protocol is insecure under *any* instantiation of the hash function. This makes it challenging to understand the meaning of a ROM proof, and has lead to significant debate (see e.g. [Gol06,KM15]). Nevertheless, due to their efficiency, schemes with only ROM proofs remain widely deployed.

This practice is often justified by observing that ROM uninstantiabilities are typically contrived, deviating from standard cryptographic design. However,

Y. Dodis and T. Shrimpton (Eds.): CRYPTO 2022, LNCS 13509, pp. 35–65, 2022.
https://doi.org/10.1007/978-3-031-15982-4_2

there are also examples of *natural* uninstantiabilities, even those for design structures widely used in practice, though this has never lead to actual real-world attacks. We will discuss several examples later in this work. In light of this state-of-affairs, it is important to further understand the security of ROM protocols.

Techniques for uninstantiability results. Digging deeper, all known ROM uninstantiability results make essential use of *non-black-box* techniques. They use that real hash functions have code which can be plugged into tools like proof systems, fully homomorphic encryption, program obfuscation, etc. Random oracles, by contrast, cannot be plugged into such tools as they have no code. The ROM uninstantiabilities therefore embed a trigger that can only be accessed by feeding the hash function code into such a tool; this trigger completely breaks security.

More generally, even when considering non-black box tools, essentially all cryptographic techniques use the component systems as black boxes. Even though non-black box tools take programs as input, the programs themselves only treat the component as a black box. The application of these tools does not care about the actual code of components, other than the fact that it has code in the first place. Of course, the implementation of the non-black-box tool will operate on the actual code at the gate or instruction level, but the tool abstracts all this away. The application of the tool only cares that the code exists.

1.1 Augmented Random Oracles

In this work, with the goal of eliminating uninstantiability results, we propose a new paradigm for studying ROM constructions that we call the *Augmented Random Oracle Model* (AROM). In addition to a random oracle O, we add a second oracle M, which will model the various non-black-box tools that ROM impossibilities may try to employ. Like O, M will be a function sampled from a distribution[1]. However, to model tools that can be applied to the code of concrete hash function (which is now an oracle), we will have M be *oracle aided*, meaning it can make queries to O. Making queries is the only way M can learn information from O. Looking ahead, we will often have M take as input programs that themselves query O; M can then evaluate such programs by making queries to O. In this way, we can treat O as having code—namely the instruction to make a query—while still representing O as an oracle, thus capturing the aforementioned non-black-box techniques within our idealized model.

Asharov and Segev [AS15] consider a similar model, but for an entirely different purpose. They propose a model for indistinguishability obfuscation (iO), where M obfuscates programs that can make queries to O. Such M accepts obfuscate queries, which take as input the description of an (oracle-aided) program P^O, and outputs a string $\tilde{P}$, derived via a private random permutation.

---

[1] Once M is sampled, it is fixed an immutable, keeping no state. Though M is stateless, it can still implement potentially stateful cryptographic objects, by having any state be an explicit input and output of M. Modeling M as stateless reflects the real world, where the specification of a cryptographic primitive does not change over time.

M also accepts `evaluate` queries, which take $\tilde{P}$ and an input x, and compute $P^O(x)$. Note that M must make queries to O in order to implement `evaluate` queries. The authors argue that this model captures many of the techniques for using iO. [AS15] use this model to reason about the limits of iO.

As this oracle captures many techniques based on iO, setting M in this way would capture many uninstantiability results based on iO, such as [BFM15] as discussed below. However, we do not want to commit to a single tool. This is for several reasons. The Asharov-Segev model, for example, makes specific choices, such as the fact that M does not apply to programs that themselves can make M queries, or that M operates on oracle-aided *circuits* as opposed to Turing machines. There are also many other non-black-box tools such as proof systems, garbled circuits, fully homomorphic encryption, etc. Asharov and Segev specifically mention the case of NIZKs, as many iO applications involve NIZKs but are not captured in their model. Worse, new non-black-box tools may arise, necessitating new models. We therefore allow M to be *any* oracle, which automatically captures any tool of this nature and any modeling that may arise. In this sense, we can think of M *adversarially*. We will make one important restriction, however: M can only make a polynomial number of queries to O, corresponding to the tool being efficient.

On the other hand, we do not want to rely these black-box tools when designing cryptosystems. First, they are computationally expensive. Moreover, since M is essentially adversarial, we do not want to have to assume any particular structure of M; M could always output 0. We will therefore insist that the system we design, and hence also the security game, only makes queries to O but not M. Thus we only consider constructions that make sense in the plain random oracle model, but we hope that the new model will better capture their security. A visualization of the plain and augmented models are given in Fig. 1.

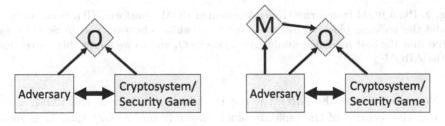

Fig. 1. The plain ROM (L) vs the Augmented ROM (R).

So far, the AROM appears rather useless: by having the adversary simulate M for itself, the AROM collapses to the standard ROM. We will now see an important setting where the AROM is meaningful.

AROM for Transforms. In a ROM *transform*, a building block Π (or potentially multiple building blocks) is transformed into a different cryptosystem Γ using a random oracle. We note ROM transforms are widespread, and even schemes that appear to be direct constructions can often be phrased as transforms from appropriate abstractions. Examples include RSA (trapdoor permutations) or

Diffie-Hellman (cryptographic groups). Moreover, uninstantiability results such as [CGH98] are most often phrased as transforms from the appropriate building blocks (e.g. CS proofs [Mic94] and signatures in the case of [CGH98]). In fact, phrasing a construction as a transform is generally the *preferred* way to model constructions, as it allows for utilizing abstractions, resulting in a better conceptual understanding of the results and more general security proofs.

Well-known uninstantiabilities for ROM transforms include Fiat-Shamir (FS) [FS87] as proved by [GK03], and Encrypt-with-Hash (EwH) [BBO07] and Fujisaki-Okamoto (FO) [FO99], as shown by [BFM15]. These ROM failures for transforms are notable for being for *natural* and even widely deployed.

For transforms, the picture in Fig. 1 changes. Recall that a transform must result in a secure Γ, regardless of the instantiation of the building block Π, as long as Π satisfies the prescribed security property. Since the security of the transform quantifies over all Π, we can think of Π itself as adversarial. ROM transform uninstantiabilities work exactly by designing a contrived Π that makes the transform fail. In the plain ROM, this gives Fig. 2 (L). In the AROM, the transform still only queries O, but now Π may use M to employ non-black box techniques. Therefore, Π makes queries to M, as in Fig. 2 (R).

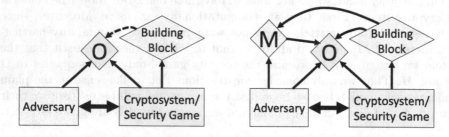

Fig. 2. Plain ROM transforms (L) vs Augmented ROM transforms (R). Some authors model the building block as having access to O while others do not; in Sect. 1.4 we argue that the best modeling would give access to O, and so we adopt this convention in the AROM

Now we see that the AROM is not trivially equivalent to the ROM. Concretely, the security of the building block may rely on the fact that M is sampled from a distribution. For example, the M above for implementing iO is only secure because the obfuscator utilizes a private random permutation. In order to maintain security, this permutation must be hidden from the adversary. Therefore, there is no way for the adversary to simulate the M on its own. Indeed, we will argue that the AROM captures all existing uninstantiability results for ROM transforms, by having M model the appropriate non-black box techniques. This does not mean that the AROM is not subject to uninstantiability results, since it is equivalent to the ROM for direct constructions. More generally, one can take any uninstantiability result, even for transforms, and instantiate the building blocks with particular constructions from the literature, arriving at a direct ROM uninstantiability result, which would then also be an AROM uninstantiability.

However, suppose we have a transform that is *fully abstracted*, in the sense that any cryptography being performed is abstracted underneath an appropriate building block that is input to the transform[2]. Then we argue that all known uninstantiability results for random oracles are captured by the AROM, in the sense that, if fully abstracted, the transform would be correctly labeled as insecure in the AROM. This is because, for any such result, there will be an M which can securely provide all the necessary building blocks, but also the non-black box techniques used, where we replace any time the code of the hash function is used with the instruction to query O. This includes [CGH98] and also the uninstantiability for FS [GK03], where M implements CS proofs on programs that can query O. It also includes the uninstantiability of EwH and FO [BFM15], where M implements an indistinguishability obfuscator. In fact, for any known uninstantiability of the random oracle, when fully abstracted, there is an appropriate M that models the building blocks, resulting in an insecure protocol in the AROM. See Sect. 4.3, where we work through the case of EwH.

Thus, for any fully abstracted protocol, security in the AROM demonstrates immunity to known uninstantiability techniques, and offers the most compelling evidence known for real-world security. Of course, this does not actually prove security in the standard model or completely rule out uninstantiability results, but it implies that brand new techniques would be needed to invalidate security.

1.2   Best Possible Hash Functions?

A quick detour before getting to our results. There have been numerous works on circumventing ROM impossibilities, or at least making ROM proofs more believable. Here, we discuss one, initiated by Canetti [Can97], which seeks to identify and instantiate random oracle security properties using concrete, usually algebraic, hash functions. Examples include oracle hashing [Can97], non-malleable point obfuscation [KY18,BMZ19], various forms of correlation resistance [CCR16,GOR11], and Full Domain Hash [HSW14], to name a few.

A major downside of these results is efficiency. In essentially all cases, the construction is far less efficient than standard hash functions such as SHA2, sometimes being entirely impractical. In addition, the computational assumptions underlying these ROM-free constructions can be quite strong, and it is not clear if the standard model result is actually "more secure."

In light of these downsides, a standard-model instantiation of a ROM protocol may be considered a *proof of concept*, showing that such an application is likely to exist. This could be seen as additional justification for the security (or at

---

[2] We do not attempt formalize *full abstracted* here, as it appears challenging. Do information-theoretic objects, such as even a simple XOR, count? We instead leave the notion as a general intuitive property, and we expect that whether or not a given protocol is fully abstracted will usually be clear. All the transforms we consider in this work are certainly fully abstracted.

least, lack of impossibility) for the more efficient ROM protocol. Implicit in this interpretation is the following assumption: if a security property holds for *some* hash function, then it also holds for a sufficiently well-designed hash function, perhaps SHA2. That is, SHA2 is a "best possible" hash function, in that any security property which holds for *some* hash function will hold for SHA2[3]. This sounds plausible, even in light of the various ROM impossibility results, as no poly-time attacks have been found on SHA2 that does not also apply to all hash functions. We ask, *is such an interpretation reasonable?*

1.3   Our Results

- In Sect. 3 we formally define the AROM.
- We then use the EwH transform as a case study to demonstrate the power of the AROM. In Sect. 4.3, we explain how the AROM captures the uninstantiability of EwH, in the sense that the transform is *insecure* in the AROM, like in the real world.
- In Sect. 4.4, we show the EwH uninstantiability result can be generalized to work under a circular security assumption on LWE, as opposed to needing the full power of indistinguishability obfuscation. Concretely, our impossibility uses fully homomorphic encryption and obfuscation for compute-and-compare programs [GKW17,WZ17]. The improvement also readily adapts to the FO transform. This further demonstrates the need for a model which captures a variety of non-black-box tools.
- In Sect. 4.6, we show that EwH *is* secure in the AROM, if the underlying encryption scheme is strengthened to be *lossy* [BHY09]. Lossy encryption can still be constructed efficiently from most standard tools. We note that the security we prove likely cannot be proven secure in the standard model [Wic13], so some form of idealized model is inherent. Our proof offers the strongest justification yet for security.
- In the Full Version [Zha22], we additionally study the FO and FS transformations, demonstrating that both are insecure in the AROM, again capturing the known uninstantiabilities. For FS, we show that it is sound in the AROM if the underlying proof has statistical soundness. Like EwH, FS even for such proofs likely cannot be proven secure in the standard model [BDG+13], necessitating some idealized model. Our proof offers the strongest justification yet for security in this case. We note that zero knowledge of plain Fiat-Shamir cannot be proved, since this would give NIZKs without a CRS. We explore several ways of obtaining zero knowledge by introducing a CRS.
  For FO, we observe that it is *not* secure in the AROM, even if the underlying encryption scheme is lossy. We therefore propose (Sect. 5.1) a new encryption scheme, which can be seen as a variant of the CCA-secure scheme of Dolev, Dwork, and Naor [DDN91], but with the zero knowledge proof replaced by an EwH-style structure. We prove CCA security of our scheme

---

[3] There will always be *functionalities* that SHA2 or other hash functions cannot achieve. This assumption is only about *security properties* that apply to any hash function.

under the assumed lossiness of the underlying encryption scheme; CCA security is not known to follow from lossy encryption in the standard model. Our results for FO and FS are sketched in Sects. 5 and 6, with the details deferred to the Full Version [Zha22].

– In Sect. 7, we provide a pair of natural security properties for hash functions, namely auxiliary input one-wayness and something we call *anti-lossiness*. These properties can be satisfied by standard-model constructions, and are both trivially satisfied by random oracles. However, we show that these properties *cannot* both be satisfied simultaneously by any real hash function, assuming virtual grey box (VGB) obfuscation [BCKP14]. This implies that SHA2 (or any hash for that matter) cannot be a "best possible" hash. In the AROM, only one of the two properties—namely anti-lossiness—hold for O, consistent with the standard model. This gives further support to the utility of our model, and also indicates that SHA2 (or any hash function plausibly modeled as a random oracle) is likely not auxiliary input one-way.

1.4 A Classification of ROM Failures

Besides uninstantiability results, there are a number of other known ROM failures. Here, we broadly organize known ROM failures into five types, and discuss what they mean and their relevance to the AROM.

Type 1 ($\exists\exists$). Here, there exists a specific protocol with a ROM proof and also a specific hash function H, such that setting $O = H$ makes the protocol insecure.

A well-known example is the length-extension attack when using Merkle-Damgård as MACs without appropriate padding. Another example is the circularly secure encryption scheme $\mathsf{Enc}(k, m) = (r, O(k, r) \oplus m)$, which was proven in the ROM [BRS03], but is insecure when O is replaced with Davies-Meyer [HK07].

For Type 1 failures, the insecurity may point to an issue with the protocol, the hash, or both. However, we observe that in most cases, the particular hash function is not *indifferentiable* [MRH04] from a random oracle (see [CDMP05] for Merkle-Damgård, [KM07] for Davies-Meyer). Indifferentiability has become an important consideration for hash functions, and so an indifferentiability failure should be interpreted as a weakness of the hash function. In particular, using an indifferentiable hash function seems to solve the problem.

More generally, any Type 1 failure will point to a hash function design structure that, if avoided, would block the attack. Such a design structure may then be considered sub-optimal from a security standpoint.

Type 2 ($\forall\exists$). Here, for *any* possible hash function H, there exists a protocol with a ROM proof such that setting $O = H$ makes the protocol insecure.

Type 2 failures were already pointed out by [BR93]. For a typical example, consider the Encrypt-with-Hash (EwH) transform $\mathsf{Enc}'(\mathsf{pk}, m) = \mathsf{Enc}(\mathsf{pk}, m; O(\mathsf{pk}, m))$ which converts a randomized public key encryption scheme into a deterministic one by setting the random coins to $O(\mathsf{pk}, m)$ [BBO07]. For any concrete hash function H, there is an Enc that renders the transform trivially insecure when $O = H$: Enc(pk, m; r) checks if $r = O(\text{pk}, m)$ and if so outputs m in the clear.

For Type 2 failures, we observe that the ROM security is an artifact of the ROM modeling: concretely, when [BBO07] prove ROM security, they assume that Enc cannot make queries to O. But certainly a real-world encryption scheme may evaluate a given hash function. In fact, since there are a limited number of standardized hash functions, it is even expected that different components of a cryptosystem may use the same hash. So a better modeling would allow Enc to query O, in which case EwH is trivially insecure in the ROM for the same reasons as in the standard model. Therefore, Type 2 failures can be seen as demonstrating an issue with the particular protocol design, but not the random oracle itself if properly modeled. Instead, it shows that the scheme should never have been considered to have a ROM proof in the first place.

We observe that our AROM *always* allows the building block to query O (since M may implement a query-forwarding functionality), so failures of this sort are captured by the AROM, in the sense that such protocols will not have AROM proofs. We note that a tweaked EwH, namely Enc$'$(pk$'$, m) = Enc(pk, m; $O(s, m)$) for pk$'$ = (pk, s) and a uniformly random s *would* be secure in the ROM, even if Enc can make random oracle queries. The reason, essentially, is that the random s enforces domain separation, since Enc would almost certainly never evaluate O on inputs of the form (s, m). Nevertheless, the impossibility of [BFM15] still applies to the tweaked EwH.

Type 3 ($\exists\forall$). Here, there exists a protocol with a ROM proof that is insecure under *any* possible instantiation of the hash function.

These are the uninstantiability results motivating our AROM. As observed above, for fully abstracted transforms, no known Type 3 failures apply to the AROM.

Type 4 (**Simulation-based**). Here, security is defined via a simulator, and in the ROM the simulator is allowed to program the random oracle.

Examples include non-interactive zero knowledge without a CRS [Pas03] and non-interactive non-committing encryption [Nie02], both of which exist in the ROM under this modeling of simulators, but not in the real world. The intuition for these failures is that, in the standard model, the simulator is usually required to have extra power relative to the adversary—such as being able to program a CRS or generate transcript messages out of order—in order to not be trivially impossible. Since the adversary cannot program the random oracle, allowing the simulator such programming ability is another form of extra power, allowing it to circumvent standard-model impossibilities without having to resort to CRS's or out-of-order transcript generation. This allows for attainable simulation-based definitions that are impossible in the standard model.

One problem with Type 4 failures is that the random oracle is baked into the security definition since the definition must model the simulator's ability to program the random oracle. This makes the ROM definition actually distinct from the standard model definition. Failures of this type are typically easily avoided by better modeling of the ROM: allow the simulator to make random oracle queries, and even see the adversary's queries, but *do not* allow the simulator to actually program the random oracle. The resulting definition then closely mirrors the standard model, and the only options available to give the simulator the needed extra power are generally the same strategies as in the standard model. For these reasons, we advocate similar modeling of simulators in the AROM.

Type 5 (**Proof impossibilities**). Here, it is proved that, for some protocol with a ROM proof, there cannot be any standard-model proof relative to any hash function, at least with respect to certain classes of constructions, proof strategies, and/or underlying computational assumptions.

A well-known example is Full-Domain Hash (FDH), where [DOP05] show that there is no proof of security in the standard model that makes fully black box use of the trapdoor permutation. A wide class of examples of this type are impossibilities of security proofs relative to "falsifiable" assumptions. Examples include Fiat-Shamir *even when restricted to statistically sound proofs*[4] [BDG+13], succinct non-interactive arguments (SNARGs) [GW11], and correlated input security [Wic13]. We note that correlated input security is in particular implied by the notion of security we prove in the AROM for EwH.

With Type 5 examples, no actual insecurity is shown, just a barrier to proving security. It could therefore be that the examples are in fact secure, but just cannot be demonstrated secure by standard model arguments. An optimistic interpretation is that such examples are actually demonstrating limits of the usual paradigm for provable security, with the ROM offering a way to plausibly justify the security of such protocols. However, in light of Type 3 failures, a pessimistic interpretation could simply be that Type 5 examples are simply insecure. The right answer probably lies somewhere between.

Nevertheless, protocol designs subject to Type 5 failures have been confidently used in practice, such as Fiat-Shamir (not to mention FDH and SNARGs). It is therefore important to try to justify their security despite such Type 5 failures. We can therefore view the AROM as offering additional support for the security of such schemes. This is particularly relevant for our AROM proofs of EwH and Fiat-Shamir for statistically sound proofs, as a standard-model security justification is infeasible.

1.5   Discussion: Do We Really Need Another ROM Variant?

There have been many attempts to rectify the issues with the ROM, each with their own advantages as disadvantages. Numerous works remove the random oracle entirely from a cryptosystem, such as Boneh and Boyen [BB04] for IBE. But such results typically lose significant efficiency, and sometimes require stronger assumptions as well. The aforementioned program initiated by Canetti [Can97] shows how to instantiate certain ROM properties, but likewise results in inefficient hash functions and often requires strong assumptions. One might be

---

[4] The Type 3 counterexample of [GK03] uses computationally sound protocols.

tempted to use such results as proofs of concept and then just use SHA2 to instead, but our results on incompatible security properties show that this is unsound in general.

Both programs also suffer from the fact that they cannot bypass certain limitations of the standard-model, such as the Type 5 ROM failures discussed above. In order to justify the security of these examples, *something* is needed beyond the standard model.

Another approach is to identify a broad class of standard-model security notions, and posit that a hash function simultaneously satisfies the entire class. One example are universal computational extractors (UCEs) [BHK13]. However, it appears challenging to define a natural broad class of security notions that are exempted from ROM failures. In particular, the UCE assumption of [BHK13] is subject to the Type 3 failure from EwH.

This leaves other refinements to the ROM. The *non-programmable* ROM (npROM) [Nie02,FLR+10] prevents the reduction from programming O in any way, but can still allows it to see the adversary's queries. The hope is that this more closely captures standard-model hash functions "behaving like" random functions, since standard-model functions cannot be programmed. A complementary model due to Ananth and Bhaskar [AB12] is the *non-observable* ROM (noROM), where the adversary can adaptively program but cannot observe. They also consider the intersection of the two models, the nonpROM.

These refinements are intuitively appealing. But there is little theoretical justification for preferring them over the plain ROM. Type 3 failures also still apply: the CPA security of EwH [BBO07] can be proven in the nonpROM, and yet we know the transform is insecure in general[5].

Our model, by contrast, is specifically shown to circumvent all known Types 2, 3, and 4 failures for fully abstracted transforms, and the other failures can be handled by using a sufficiently well-designed hash function and making optimistic-yet-plausible assumptions. We thus obtain some of the most compelling justifications known for several cryptosystems.

2   Preliminaries

2.1   Cryptosystems and Games

A cryptosystem is a tuple of stateless deterministic algorithms Π. A *specification* for a cryptosystem is a collection $\mathcal{G}$ of game/probability pairs (G, p), where G take a security parameter 1^λ as input and outputs a bit b, and p takes a security parameter 1^λ as input and outputs a real number in $[0, 1]$. Each G interacts with a cryptosystem Π and adversary $\mathcal{A}$. We also assume G indicates whether adversaries are computationally bounded or unbounded. We will write $b \leftarrow (\mathcal{A} \leftrightarrow G^\Pi)(1^\lambda)$ to denote the interaction. The *advantage* of $\mathcal{A}$ when interacting with

---

[5] Bellare et al. [BBO07] do not claim either noROM or npROM. Yet the proof in the CPA case can be verified to work in both models by inspection.

G^Π is a function of λ defined as $\mathsf{Adv}_{\mathcal{A},G^\Pi}(\lambda) := \Pr[1 \leftarrow (\mathcal{A} \leftrightarrow G^\Pi)(1^\lambda)] - p(\lambda)$. Games model both security properties and correctness properties.

Many cryptosystems will use random coins, which we model as an explicit input. Games will be responsible for choosing the random coins. We will often distinguish random coins from other inputs by separating them with a semicolon, e.g. $\Pi(x; r)$. We will write $\Pi(x)$ to be the distribution $\Pi(x; r)$ for uniform r. A function is *negligible* if it is asymptotically smaller than any inverse polynomial.

Definition 2.1. *A cryptosystem Π securely implements a specification $\mathcal{G}$ if, for all $(G, p) \in \mathcal{G}$ and for all adversaries $\mathcal{A}$, there exists a negligible function* negl *such that* $\mathsf{Adv}_{\mathcal{A},G^\Pi}(\lambda) \leq \mathsf{negl}(\lambda)$.

Transforms. A transform is a method T of compiling a cryptosystem Π securely implementing a specification $\mathcal{G}$ into another cryptosystem Γ securely implementing a specification $\mathcal{H}$. We write $\Gamma = T^\Pi$.

Definition 2.2. *A transform T from $\mathcal{G}$ to $\mathcal{H}$ is secure if, for all Π which securely implement $\mathcal{G}$, T^Π securely implements $\mathcal{H}$.*

Single-stage games. Usually, $\mathcal{A}$ is a single adversary that can keep arbitrary state throughout its interaction with $\mathcal{G}$. We will call these single-stage games. Some games place restrictions on the state $\mathcal{A}$ can keep. We call such games *multi-stage*.

2.2 Cryptographic Definitions

An $\ell = \ell(\lambda)$-source is a distribution is a family of efficiently sampleable distributions $D(1^\lambda)$ over tuples $(x_1, \dots, x_\ell, \mathsf{aux})$.

Definition 2.3 (Unpredictability). *A 1-source $(x, \mathsf{aux}) \leftarrow D(1^\lambda)$ is computationally (resp. statistically) unpredictable if, for all polynomial time (resp. unbounded) $\mathcal{A}$,* $\Pr[\mathcal{A}(\mathsf{aux}) = x : (x, \mathsf{aux}) \leftarrow D(1^\lambda)]$ *is negligible.*

An ℓ-source $(\ell > 1)$ is computationally (resp. statistically) unpredictable (1) if each marginal distribution (x_i, aux) for $i \in [\ell]$ is computationally unpredictable, and (2) except with negligible probability the x_i are all distinct.

Definition 2.4 (Anti-lossiness). *A keyed function $H : \{0,1\}^\lambda \times \{0,1\}^{m(\lambda)} \to \{0,1\}^{n(\lambda)}$ is anti-lossy if, for all sequences $(k_\lambda)_\lambda$ for $k_\lambda \in \{0,1\}^\lambda$, the 1-source $(H(k_\lambda, x), \mathsf{aux} = \{\})$ where $x \leftarrow \{0,1\}^{m(\lambda)}$ is statistically unpredictable. In other words, there are no keys which make H lose too much information.*

Definition 2.5 (One-wayness with correlated inputs). *A keyed function $H : \{0,1\}^\lambda \times \{0,1\}^{m(\lambda)} \to \{0,1\}^{n(\lambda)}$ is one-way against correlated inputs if, for all computationally unpredictable ℓ-sources D and all polynomial-time $\mathcal{A}$,*

$$\Pr\left[\exists i, H(k, x') = y_i : \begin{array}{c} k \leftarrow \{0,1\}^\lambda \\ (x_1, \dots, x_\ell, \mathsf{aux}) \leftarrow D \\ x' \leftarrow \mathcal{A}(k, y_1 = H(k, x_1), \dots, y_\ell = H(k, x_\ell), \mathsf{aux}) \end{array}\right] < \mathsf{negl}(\lambda) .$$

That is, given aux and all the $y_i = H(k, x_i)$, it is intractable to invert any of the y_i. H is one-way against auxiliary input if the above holds only for 1-sources.

Definition 2.6 (Pseudorandomness with correlated inputs). *A keyed function* $H : \{0,1\}^\lambda \times \{0,1\}^{m(\lambda)} \to \{0,1\}^{n(\lambda)}$ *is pseudorandom against correlated inputs if, for all computationally unpredictable ℓ-sources and all polynomial-time $\mathcal{A}$,*

$$\left| \Pr\left[b' = b : \begin{array}{c} b \leftarrow \{0,1\}, k \leftarrow \{0,1\}^\lambda \\ (x_1, \dots, x_\ell, \mathsf{aux}) \leftarrow D \\ y_{i,0} \leftarrow H(k, x_i), y_{i,1} \leftarrow \{0,1\}^{n(\lambda)} \forall i \\ b' \leftarrow \mathcal{A}(k, y_{1,b}, \dots, y_{\ell,b}, \mathsf{aux}) \end{array} \right] - 1/2 \right| < \mathsf{negl}(\lambda) \ .$$

In other words, the vector of $y_i = H(k, x_i)$ is pseudorandom, even though the x_i are correlated and aux *is given. H is* pseudorandom against auxiliary input *if the above holds only for 1-sources.*

Public key encryption (PKE). A PKE scheme is a triple $\Pi = (\mathsf{Gen}, \mathsf{Dec}, \mathsf{Enc})$ such that $(\mathsf{pk}, \mathsf{sk}) \leftarrow \mathsf{Gen}(1^\lambda) = \mathsf{Gen}(1^\lambda; r)$, $c \leftarrow \mathsf{Enc}(\mathsf{pk}, m) = \mathsf{Enc}(\mathsf{pk}, m; r)$ and $m' \leftarrow \mathsf{Dec}(\mathsf{sk}, c)$. We require *correctness*, which insists that for every message m, $\Pr[\mathsf{Dec}(\mathsf{sk}, \mathsf{Enc}(\mathsf{pk}, m)) = m : (\mathsf{pk}, \mathsf{sk}) \leftarrow \mathsf{Gen}(1^\lambda)] \geq 1 - \mathsf{negl}(\lambda)$.

Definition 2.7 (CPA and CCA security). *A PKE scheme Π is* CCA secure *if all polynomial time $\mathcal{A}$ have negligible advantage in the following game:*

- *On input 1^λ, the game samples $(\mathsf{pk}, \mathsf{sk}) \leftarrow \mathsf{Gen}(1^\lambda)$ and sends* pk *to $\mathcal{A}$.*
- *$\mathcal{A}$ makes CCA queries on ciphertexts c, and receives $m \leftarrow \mathsf{Dec}(\mathsf{sk}, c)$.*
- *At some point, $\mathcal{A}$ produces two messages $m_0^*, m_1^* \in \{0,1\}^*$ of equal length.*
- *The game samples a random bit b and replies with $c^* \leftarrow \mathsf{Enc}(\mathsf{pk}, m_b^*)$.*
- *$\mathcal{A}$ can continue making CCA queries, as long as $c \neq c^*$.*
- *$\mathcal{A}$ finally sends a guess b' for b. The advantage of $\mathcal{A}$ is $|\Pr[b' = b] - 1/2|$.*

Π is CPA secure *if the above only holds against $\mathcal{A}$ that cannot make CCA queries.*

Definition 2.8 (Lossy Encryption [BHY09]). *A PKE scheme Π is* lossy *if there is an additional algorithm* pk $\leftarrow \mathsf{GenLossy}(1^\lambda)$ *such that:*

- pk $\leftarrow \mathsf{GenLossy}(1^\lambda)$ *is comp. indist. from* pk *where $(\mathsf{pk}, \mathsf{sk}) \leftarrow \mathsf{Gen}(1^\lambda)$.*
- *Let D_m be the distribution $(\mathsf{pk}, \mathsf{Enc}(\mathsf{pk}, m))$ where* pk $\leftarrow \mathsf{GenLossy}(1^\lambda)$. *Then for any messages m, m' of the same length, $D_m, D_{m'}$ are statistically close.*

Definition 2.9 (Fully Homomorphic Encryption). *A PKE scheme Π is* fully homomorphic *if there is an additional algorithm* $\mathsf{Eval}(\mathsf{pk}, c, f)$ *that outputs ciphertexts, such that for all m and all functions f represented as circuits, the following hold:*

$$\mathsf{length}(\ \mathsf{Eval}(\mathsf{pk}, \mathsf{Enc}(\mathsf{pk}, m), f)\ ) = \mathsf{length}(\ \mathsf{Enc}(\mathsf{pk}, f(m))\ ), \ and$$

$$\Pr\left[\mathsf{Dec}(\mathsf{sk}, c') = f(m) : \begin{array}{c} (\mathsf{pk}, \mathsf{sk}) \leftarrow \mathsf{Gen}(1^\lambda) \\ c \leftarrow \mathsf{Enc}(\mathsf{pk}, m) \\ c' \leftarrow \mathsf{Eval}(\mathsf{pk}, c, f) \end{array} \right] \geq 1 - \mathsf{negl}(\lambda) \ .$$

Deterministic Encryption. A deterministic PKE scheme is plain PKE, except that Enc is deterministic. Deterministic PKE can only be secure for unpredictable messages, formalized by PRIV security [BBO07]:

Definition 2.10 (PRIV-CPA and PRIV-CCA). *A det. PKE scheme Π is strongly (resp. weakly[6]) PRIV CCA secure if for all computationally (resp. statistically) unpred. ℓ-sources D, all polynomial time A have negligible advantage in the following game:*

- *On input 1^λ, the game samples $(\mathsf{pk}, \mathsf{sk}) \leftarrow \mathsf{Gen}(1^\lambda)$ and sends pk to A.*
- *It samples $(m^*_{1,0}, \ldots, m^*_{\ell,0}) \leftarrow D$ and random distinct $m^*_{1,1}, \ldots, m^*_{\ell,1}$.*
- *It samples a random bit b, and sends $c^*_1, \ldots, c^*_\ell$ where $c^*_i \leftarrow \mathsf{Enc}(\mathsf{pk}, m^*_{i,b})$.*
- *A makes CCA queries on $c \notin \{c^*_1, \ldots, c^*_\ell\}$; it receives $m \leftarrow \mathsf{Dec}(\mathsf{sk}, c)$.*
- *A finally sends guess b' for b. The advantage of A is $|\Pr[b' = b] - 1/2|$.*

Π is strongly/weakly PRIV-CPA secure if A cannot make CCA queries.

Obfuscation. An obfuscator $\mathsf{Obf}(1^\lambda, C)$ is an efficient randomized function which maps circuits to circuits[7]. For correctness, we require that $\mathsf{Obf}(1^\lambda, C)(x) = C(x)$ for all λ, x. We will also consider obfuscators that only work on circuits of a particular format. We now discuss two notions of security.

Definition 2.11 (VGB [BCKP14]). *Obf is VGB secure if, for all polynomial-time A, all polynomials s, and all inverse polynomials p, there exists a simulator S that is computationally unbounded but which can only make a polynomial number of queries, such that for all circuits C of size at most $s(\lambda)$, $|\Pr[1 \leftarrow A(1^\lambda, \mathsf{Obf}(1^\lambda, C))] - \Pr[1 \leftarrow S^C(1^\lambda)]| < p(\lambda)$.*

VGB obfuscation is not known under standard assumptions, but it appears plausible that many existing iO constructions satisfy it. Regardless, ruling out VGB obfuscation appears challenging. As we only use VGB for an impossibility, it is still meaningful even if none of the existing candidates are secure. A weakening of VGB obfuscation is *indistinguishability* obfuscation (iO), which is identical except that S can also be query unbounded. An equivalent formulation of iO is that the obfuscations of *equivalent* programs are computationally indistinguishable.

Definition 2.12 (CC security [GKW17, WZ17]). *For a polynomial s, consider the class of binary circuits of the form "Output 1 on input x if and only if $C(x) = y$" where $y \in \{0,1\}^\lambda$ and C has size s. Call this circuit $\mathsf{CC}_{C,y}(x)$. An obfuscator Obf is a compute-and-compare (CC) obfuscator if it is correct for this class of circuits, and satisfies the following security definition: there exists an efficient simulator S such that for all C and all efficient A,*

$$\left| \Pr\left[1 \leftarrow A(\tilde{C}) : \begin{smallmatrix} y \leftarrow \{0,1\}^\lambda \\ \tilde{C} \leftarrow \mathsf{Obf}(1^\lambda, \mathsf{CC}_{C,y}) \end{smallmatrix}\right] - \Pr[1 \leftarrow A(S(1^\lambda, 1^s))] \right| < \mathsf{negl}(\lambda) .$$

That is, if y is random, the obfuscated program can be simulated without knowing C or y at all. [GKW17, WZ17] construct CC-secure obfuscation from LWE.

---

[6] The original PRIV notion corresponds to the weak version.

[7] We can also consider obfuscators for uniform computational models, but we will not need to for this work.

3   The Augmented Random Oracle Model

3.1   The Plain ROM

In the plain ROM, there is a function $O : \{0,1\}^* \to \{0,1\}^\ell$, where the output of O on any input is chosen uniformly at random. All parties can make queries to O. We call this distribution over oracles $\mathcal{O}^8$.

Complexity Metrics. A query x to O has cost $|x|$. The *query complexity* of an algorithm is the total cost of all its queries. The *computational complexity* is the sum of its query complexity and running time. Both the query and computational complexities of an algorithm can be input-specific. Note the cost must increase with input size to yield correct query complexity results for variable-length O.

Secure cryptosystems in the ROM. Specifications remain oracle-free, but now the cryptosystem Π and adversary $\mathcal{A}$ can query O. We denote the interaction $b \leftarrow (\mathcal{A}^O \leftrightarrow G^{\Pi^O})$. $\mathcal{A}$'s advantage is defined as in the standard model, except that the probability is over the choice of $O \leftarrow \mathcal{O}$. Oracle-free specifications means simulators in simulation-based definitions cannot program O, departing from [BR93]. This modeling, however, automatically captures Type 4 failures [Nie02, Pas03].

Definition 3.1. *An oracle-aided cryptosystem Π^O securely implements a specification $\mathcal{G}$ in the ROM if, for all $(G,p) \in \mathcal{G}$ and for all oracle-aided adversaries $\mathcal{A}^O$, there is a negligible* negl *such that* $\mathsf{Adv}_{\mathcal{A}^O, G^{\Pi^O}}(\lambda) \leq \mathsf{negl}(\lambda)$.

Transforms in the ROM. Transforms in the ROM use random oracles. Often in the literature, the underlying building block is prevented from making oracle queries; we will make no such restriction. This models the real world, where the building blocks could have themselves been built using hash functions.

Definition 3.2. *An oracle-aided transform T between from $\mathcal{G}$ to $\mathcal{H}$ is secure in the ROM if, for all oracle-aided cryptosystems Π^O which securely implement $\mathcal{G}$ in the ROM, $\Gamma^O = T^{O,\Pi^O}$ securely implements $\mathcal{H}$ in the ROM.*

3.2   Augmented Random Oracles

In an augmented random oracle, first a function $O \leftarrow \mathcal{O}$ is sampled. Additionally, there is a distribution $\mathcal{M}$ over oracle-aided functions from which $M \leftarrow \mathcal{M}$ is sampled. O and M are sampled independently. Then, parties are provided with the oracles O and M^O; that is, M's own oracle is set to O. Once O, M are sampled, they are deterministic and stateless. Looking ahead, M will provide one or more abstract cryptosystems. M can still model stateful cryptosystems by having the

---

[8] Note that the choice of ℓ is arbitrary: one can obtain an O with ℓ-bit outputs from an O' with 1-bit outputs by setting $O(x)_i = O(x||i)$. One can even obtain O with infinite outputs in this way. Thus, all random oracles are equivalent.

state be an additional input and output. M itself being stateless corresponds to the typical real-world demand that abstract cryptosystem specifications do not change over time. Note that the restriction to deterministic M is without loss of generality, since any random coins can be provided as an additional input.

Query Complexity. We will treat M as outputting both the output, as well as an arbitrary cost for the query, which may or may not depend on in the input-size or complexity of answering the query. The query complexity of an algorithm making queries to M, O will be the total cost of all *direct* queries, excluding those M makes to O.

Complexity preserving. M is *complexity preserving* if the cost it outputs is at least the query complexity of M when answering that query. In this case, the query complexity of an algorithm is lower bounded by the total cost of *all* queries made to O, including those made by M. There is no cost upper bound.

Simulatable. $\mathcal{M}$ is *simulatable* if, for any distinguisher D, there is an *efficient but stateful* oracle-aided algorithm S^O such that D cannot distinguish the oracles (O, M^O) and (O, S^O) except with negligible probability. Note that many oracles are simulatable via lazy sampling, such as random oracles and generic groups.

Secure cryptosystems in the AROM. Specifications themselves still remain oracle-free. Cryptosystems Π are allowed to make queries to O and M, which we denote by Π^{O,M^O}. We denote the interaction $b \leftarrow (\mathcal{A}^{O,M^O} \leftrightarrow G^{\Pi^{O,M^O}})$. The advantage of $\mathcal{A}$ is defined similarly to the standard model, except that the probability is additionally over the choice of $O \leftarrow \mathcal{O}$ and $M \leftarrow \mathcal{M}$.

Definition 3.3. *An oracle-aided cryptosystem Π^{O,M^O} securely implements a specification $\mathcal{G}$ in the $\mathcal{M}$-AROM if, for all $(G,p) \in \mathcal{G}$ and for all oracle-aided adversaries $\mathcal{A}^{O,M^O}$, there exists a negligible function negl such that the advantage of $\mathcal{A}^{O,M^O}$ when interacting with $G^{\Pi^{O,M^O}}$ is at most negl.*

Looking ahead, when actually designing cryptosystems, we generally do not want Π to make queries to M. This is because M will model non-black-box techniques, which are generally inefficient in practice. We denote such a protocol by Π^O. In this case, we can quantify over all M, giving the unquantified AROM. Here we do make restrictions on M: namely we require M to be complexity preserving and simulatable.

Definition 3.4. *An oracle-aided cryptosystem Π^O (making no queries to M) securely implements $\mathcal{G}$ in the AROM (no quantification by $\mathcal{M}$) if it securely implements $\mathcal{G}$ in the $\mathcal{M}$-ROM for all complexity preserving simulatable $\mathcal{M}$.*

Transforms in the ROM. Transforms in the (unquantified) AROM make use of O, but not M, for the same reasons as for cryptosystems. But we always allow the *input* cryptosystems to query M. This will model transform failures, which design input systems employing non-black-box techniques.

Definition 3.5. *An oracle-aided transform $T^{O,\Pi}$ from $\mathcal{G}$ to $\mathcal{H}$ is secure in the AROM if, for all complexity preserving simulatable $\mathcal{M}$, and all oracle-aided Π^{O,M^O} which securely implement $\mathcal{G}$ in the $\mathcal{M}$-AROM, $\Gamma^{O,M^O} = T^{O,\Pi^{O,M^O}}$ securely implements $\mathcal{H}$ in the $\mathcal{M}$-AROM.*

3.3 Some Basic Results

We show that for direct cryptosystems (not transforms), the AROM and ROM are equivalent for single-stage games:

Theorem 3.6. *If all games in $\mathcal{G}$ are single stage, then Π^O securely implements a specification $\mathcal{G}$ in the AROM if and only if it securely implements $\mathcal{G}$ in the plain ROM.*

An immediate corollary of Theorem 3.6 is that most standard-model properties one assumes of hash functions hold for O in the AROM; for example:

Corollary 3.7. *In the AROM, O is one-way, collision resistant, a pseudorandom generator, and anti-lossy.*

Note, however, that Theorem 3.6 does *not* apply to one-wayness against auxiliary input, since that security definition is not single-stage. As we demonstrate in Sect. 7, anti-lossiness and auxiliary input one-wayness are incompatible in the standard model, and this incompatibility extends to the AROM. As such, O is *not* auxiliary input one-way in the AROM. We now prove Theorem 3.6.

Proof. Setting $\mathcal{M}$ to always outputs 0, we see that AROM security readily implies ROM security. In the other direction, consider any oracle distribution $\mathcal{M}$ and adversary $\mathcal{A}$ in the AROM. We replace $\mathcal{M}$ with S^H, only negligibly affecting the advantage of $\mathcal{A}$. Now we merge S and $\mathcal{A}$ into a single adversary $\mathcal{A}'$ for Π in the plain ROM. $\mathcal{A}'$ is therefore still an adversary, provided the game is single-stage since it must remember the state of S. The complexity of $\mathcal{A}'$ is polynomially larger than the query complexity of $\mathcal{A}$ (since $\mathcal{M}$ is complexity preserving). Therefore, the overall computational complexity of $\mathcal{A}'$ is only polynomially larger than that of $\mathcal{A}$ in the AROM. Its success probability is negligibly close to that of $\mathcal{A}$. □

Note that, unlike or cryptosystems, Theorem 3.6 does *not* hold for transforms because there is no way to simulate Π's queries to $\mathcal{M}$.

4 A Case Study: Encrypt-with-Hash

Here, we use the Encrypt-with-Hash (EwH) transform [BBO07] as a case study. We will see how the uninstantiability result of [BFM15] works, how it the uninstantiability is captured by the AROM, and how to circumvent it. Along the way, we will also see how the assumptions necessary to obtain the uninstantiability can be improved, and how this improvement too is captured by the AROM.

4.1 The (Tweaked) EwH Transform

We first give the Encrypt-with-Hash transform.

Construction 4.1 (Tweaked Encrypt-with-Hash [BBO07]). *Let* $\Pi_{PKE} =$ (Gen$_{PKE}$, Enc$_{PKE}$, Dec$_{PKE}$) *be a public key encryption scheme. Define* $\Pi_{EWH} =$ (Gen$_{EWH}{}^O$, Enc$_{EWH}{}^O$, Dec$_{EWH}{}^O$), *where*

- Gen$_{EWH}(1^\lambda)$: *Run* (pk$_{PKE}$, sk$_{PKE}$) $\leftarrow$ Gen$_{PKE}(1^\lambda)$, *sample* $s \leftarrow \{0,1\}^\lambda$, *and output* (pk$_{EWH}$ = (pk$_{PKE}$, s), sk$_{EWH}$ = (sk$_{PKE}$, pk$_{EWH}$)).
- Enc$_{EWH}$(pk$_{EWH}$, m) = Enc$_{PKE}$(pk$_{PKE}$, m; $O(s,m)$)
- Dec$_{EWH}$(sk$_{EWH}$, c) = Dec$_{PKE}$(sk$_{PKE}$, c).

As discussed in Sect. 1.4, the original EwH transform did not have s, replacing $O(s,m)$ with $O(\text{pk}_{PKE}, m)$. However, such a construction gives rise to a much simpler Type 3 failure. The problem is that the original transform is only secure in the ROM if Π_{PKE} is not allowed to query O; if we model the random oracle model as allowing Π_{PKE} to query O, then the transform is insecure. In order to avoid that failure, we introduce the tweaked EwH transform given in Construction 4.1, which is secure in the ROM, even when Π_{PKE} can query O.

4.2 Uninstantiability of EwH

Now we explain the uninstantiability result of [BFM15], and how it can be readily be captured in the AROM. Let Π'_{PKE} be any public key encryption scheme, G be a pseudorandom generator, and Obf an obfuscator that is iO secure. [BFM15] use Π'_{PKE} to build a new secure public key encryption scheme Π_{PKE}, such that when Π_{PKE} is plugged into Construction 4.1, the resulting Π_{EWH} is insecure, thus invalidating the transform in the standard model.

Construction 4.2 (EwH Uninstantiability). Π_{PKE} *is constructed as follows:*

- Gen = Gen$'$
- Enc(pk$_{PKE}$, m; $r = (r_0, r_1)$): *Let* $y = G(r_0)$ *and run* $c' \leftarrow$ Enc$'$(pk$_{PKE}$, m; y). *Then run* $\tilde{P} \leftarrow$ Obf(1^λ, $P_{m,y}$; r_1) *where* $P_{m,y}(f)$ *takes as input the code* f *for some function, and checks if* $G(f(m)) = y$; *if so* $P_{m,y}$ *outputs* m, *otherwise it outputs* $\perp$. *Finally output* $c = (c', \tilde{P})$.
- Dec(sk, $c = (c', \tilde{P})$): *run* Dec$'$(sk, c').

[BFM15] prove the following, paraphrased into our terminology:

Theorem 4.3. *If Construction 4.1 is applied to* Π_{PKE} *from Construction 4.2, then the resulting* Π_{EWH} *is not weakly CPA-PRIV in the standard model, even against 1-sources, regardless of the hash function used to instantiate* O.

We sketch the proof. When Π_{PKE} is plugged into Construction 4.1, the resulting cryptosystem is completely broken when the random oracle O is replaced by any concrete hash function H. An adversary, given pk$_{EWH}$ = (pk$_{PKE}$, s) and $(c', \tilde{P}) \leftarrow$

$Enc_{EWH}(pk_{EWH}, m) = Enc_{PKE}(pk_{PKE}, m; H(s, m))$, constructs the code of the function $f(m')$ which outputs r_0 computed from $(r_0, r_1) \leftarrow H(s, m')$. Then it runs $\tilde{P}(f)$. Recall that $\tilde{P}$ is an obfuscation of $P_{m, G(r_0)}$, and $P_{m, G(r_0)}(f)$ evaluates $G(f(m))$, which for our f is exactly $G(f(m)) = y$, $\tilde{P}(f)$ outputs m.

It remains to show that Π_{PKE} is a secure public key encryption scheme. We briefly sketch the argument. By pseudorandomness of G, the first step is to replace y with uniformly random bits. At this point, since the image of G is sparse, y is outside the image except with negligible probability. In such a case, the function $P_{m,y}$ is actually equivalent to the function that outputs $\bot$ on all inputs. So by the security of the obfuscator (namely indistinguishability obfuscation, iO), $\tilde{P}$ can be replaced by an obfuscation of the program that outputs $\bot$ everywhere. At this point, $\tilde{P}$ contains no information about m or y, so m is hidden by the assumed security of Π'_{PKE}.

4.3   Translation to the AROM

We now explain how the above is readily captured by the AROM. Concretely, we will prove the following:

Theorem 4.4. *For general CPA secure Π_{PKE}, the (tweaked) EwH is not weakly CPA-PRIV in the AROM, even when restricting to 1-sources.*

Proof. M will be the combination of three different M's: M_{PKE} which implements a public key encryption scheme (in order to obtain Π'_{PKE}), M_G which implements a pseudorandom generator (to obtain G), and M_{Obf}, which implements an obfuscation scheme (in order to obtain iO).

M_{PKE}. Here, we model an ideal public key encryption scheme, following [ZZ20]. Let K, E be random injections. We assume the inverse of an injection outputs $\bot$ if evaluated on a point not in the image. M_{PKE} offers three kinds of queries:

- gen queries: takes as input a string sk, and returns $pk = K(sk)$.
- enc queries: takes as input pk, m, r, and returns $E(pk, m, r)$
- dec queries: takes as input sk, c. Compute $d = I^{-1}(c)$. If $d \neq \bot$, then parse $d = (pk, m, r)$. If $pk = K(sk)$, then return m. Otherwise return $\bot$.

Relative to M_{PKE}, a public key encryption scheme Π'_{PKE} unconditionally exists: Gen' simply sets sk to be its random coins, and computes and outputs $pk = K(sk)$ by making a gen query. Then $Enc'(pk, m; r) = E(pk, m, r)$ using an enc query, and $Dec'(sk, c)$ makes a dec query on sk, c to produce m. As explained by [ZZ20], the resulting scheme is readily shown to be CPA secure (and much more) against query-bounded adversaries.

M_G. This is just an *expanding* random oracle. Namely, M_G will just be an expanding random oracle G, independent of K, E. Expanding random oracles are trivially pseudorandom generators.

M_{Obf}. This is the obfuscation model proposed by Asharov and Segev [AS15], except extended to allow programs that also query M_{G}. Let I be a random injection. Then M_{Obf} will offer two kinds of queries:

- obfuscate queries: takes as input the description of a program P and random coins r; it returns $\tilde{P} = I(P, r)$.
- eval queries: takes as input a string $\tilde{P}$ and input x. Compute $d \leftarrow I^{-1}(\tilde{P})$. If $d \neq \perp$, then parse d as P, r and output $P(x)$. Otherwise output $\perp$.

Importantly, we will allow the inputs P to obfuscate to be *oracle-aided* programs, making queries to G and more importantly to O. During the computation of $P(x)$ in an eval query, M_{Obf} will forward queries to G to M_{G} and queries to O to the random oracle O. We can then have $\mathsf{Obf}(P; r)$ simply make an obfuscate query on (P, r). It is straightforward that Obf is iO secure for such oracle-aided programs, and even VGB secure. In fact, it is even virtual *black* box (VBB) secure, which is known to be impossible in the standard model. However, we only need that it is iO. In fact, we could replace M_{Obf} with any model that implements obfuscation, so long as (1) the obfuscator was iO secure, and (2) the input programs could query G and O.

The final M is just the combination $(M_{\mathsf{PKE}}, M_{\mathsf{G}}, M_{\mathsf{Obf}})$. At this point, the proof of Theorem 4.4 proceeds almost identically to Sect. 4.2, with Π'_{PKE} instantiated by M_{PKE}, G instantiated by M_{G}, and Obf instantiated by M_{Obf}. The main difference is that we need f to be oracle-aided, making queries to O. In turn, this means $P_{m,y}$ must also be oracle-aided, now making queries to both O and G. Fortunately, M_{Obf} acts on such oracle-aided programs. We derive Π_{PKE} as in Construction 4.2, and security of Π_{PKE}, relative to M, follows by an identical argument relying on the security of Π'_{PKE}, G, and Obf.

The attack is also quite similar. An adversary, given $\mathsf{pk}_{\mathsf{EWH}} = (\mathsf{pk}_{\mathsf{PKE}}, s)$ and $(c', \tilde{P}) \leftarrow \mathsf{Enc}_{\mathsf{EWH}}(\mathsf{pk}_{\mathsf{EWH}}, m) = \mathsf{Enc}_{\mathsf{PKE}}(\mathsf{pk}_{\mathsf{PKE}}, m; O(s, m))$, constructs the (oracle-aided) code of the function $f(m')$ with s hardcoded, which outputs r_0 computed from $(r_0, r_1) \leftarrow O(s, m')$. This f makes queries to O.

Then it computes $\tilde{P}(f)$ by making an eval query on (P, f). M_{Obf} will respond by computing $P_{m,y}(f)$ where $y = G(r_0)$. $P_{m,y}(f)$ evaluates $G(f(m))$, which for our f is exactly y. Since $G(f(m)) = y$, the eval query outputs m in the clear. This completes the proof of Theorem 4.4. $\qquad\qquad\square$

4.4 An Improved Uninstantiability

Here, we improve the computational assumptions needed for the uninstantiability of EwH. While a potentially interesting fact on its own, our improvement also illustrates the need for flexibility in M in order for the AROM to capture a wide variety of uninstantiability results.

Concretely, we show that it suffices to assume compute-and-compare obfuscation and fully homomorphic encryption, both of which can be instantiated under circularly-secure LWE.

Construction 4.5 (Impossibility). *Let* $\Pi = (\text{Gen}, \text{Enc}, \text{Dec})$ *be any public key encryption scheme,* $\Pi_{\text{fhe}} = (\text{Gen}_{\text{fhe}}, \text{Enc}_{\text{fhe}}, \text{Dec}_{\text{fhe}}, \text{Eval}_{\text{fhe}})$ *be any FHE scheme, and* Obf *a compute-and-compare obfuscator. Let G be a PRG. Define* $\Pi_{\text{PKE}} = (\text{Gen}_{\text{PKE}}, \text{Enc}_{\text{PKE}}, \text{Dec}_{\text{PKE}})$ *to be the following*

- $\text{Gen}_{\text{PKE}}(1^\lambda) = \text{Gen}(1^\lambda)$.
- $\text{Enc}_{\text{PKE}}(\text{pk}, m)$: *choose a random r and compute* $c \leftarrow \text{Enc}(\text{pk}, m; r)$. *Sample* $(\text{pk}_{\text{fhe}}, \text{sk}_{\text{fhe}}) \leftarrow \text{Gen}_{\text{fhe}}(1^\lambda)$ *and compute* $d \leftarrow \text{Enc}_{\text{fhe}}(\text{pk}_{\text{fhe}}, m)$. *Let* $y_0 = G(r)$ *and* y_1 *be uniformly random. Let b the first bit of m. Finally let* $\tilde{P} \leftarrow \text{Obf}(1^\lambda, \text{CC}_{G(\text{Dec}_{\text{fhe}}(\text{sk}_{\text{fhe}}, \cdot)), y_b})$ [9]. *Output* $(c, \text{pk}_{\text{fhe}}, d, \tilde{P})$.
- $\text{Dec}_{\text{PKE}}(\text{sk}, (c, \text{pk}_{\text{fhe}}, d, \tilde{P}))$: *Output* $\text{Dec}(\text{sk}, c)$.

The following theorems prove the uninstantiability result; due to lack of space we defer the proofs to the Full Version [Zha22].

Theorem 4.6. *If Construction 4.1 is applied to* Π_{PKE} *from Construction 4.5, then the resulting* Π_{EWH} *is not weakly CPA-PRIV in the standard model, even against 1-sources, regardless of the hash function used to instantiate O.*

Theorem 4.7. *If* Π *is sub-exponentially CPA secure,* Π_{fhe}, Obf *are polynomially secure, and G is pseudorandom against sub-exponentially hard computationally unpredictable sources, then* Π_{PKE} *is CPA secure.*

Note that the necessary G can be constructed from sub-exponentially hard LWE, following ideas from Brakerski and Segev [BS11] and Zhandry [Zha16].

4.5 Other Possible Oracles

Our improved uninstantiability result shows that it is also important to consider oracles other than M_{Obf}, to adequately capture all the non-black-box techniques that may be used. It is not difficult to come up with oracles M_{FHE} that implement fully homomorphic encryption, where the homomorphic operations may include O gates. This allows the AROM to capture our improved uninstantiability above. Another limitation of M_{Obf} pointed out by Asharov and Segev [AS15] is that it fails to capture NIZKs, another common tool in constructions using iO. In the AROM, we can easily create an oracle M_{NIZK} that provides a NIZK proof functionality for statements that involve queries to O. We can similarly define oracles for any other non-black box tool applied to circuits that involve O queries, and even oracles combining all of the above. Thus, as long as the non-black-box techniques are simply using that the hash function has code that can be run—but not using any particular features of that code—it seems that all such techniques are captured by the AROM. Hence, AROM security provides compelling resiliency to such techniques. This will be the focus of Sect. 4.6.

---

[9] Recall $\text{CC}_{G(\text{Dec}_{\text{fhe}}(\text{sk}_{\text{fhe}}, \cdot)), y_b}$ is the program $x \mapsto G(\text{Dec}_{\text{fhe}}(\text{sk}_{\text{fhe}}, x)) == y_b$.

Non-examples. There are oracles that are non-examples. Most prominently would be Simon's oracle [Sim98], which finds collisions in functions without violating one-wayness. This oracle makes exponentially-many queries to the random oracle, thereby learning its entire truth table, and also cannot be efficiently simulated in any way. More generally, Simon's oracle is an example of the common "two oracle trick" in black box separations, where one oracle implements a cryptosystem $\mathcal{B}$, but another oracle is designed to break any instantiation of $\mathcal{C}$.

4.6   Overcoming ROM Failures for EwH

We now explain how to achieve deterministic encryption in the AROM, despite known uninstantiability results for EwH working in the AROM.

At first glance, proving security in the AROM appears non-trivial: how do you reason about *any* possible oracle M, which may implement arbitrarily complex functionalities? Imagine, for example, that M directly provides oracles implementing a cryptosystem Π as in M_{PKE}. But M knows the injections being used to define the cryptosystem, meaning M itself can internally invert this injection, learning the secret key for any public key. For a given transform T, one could plausibly augment this M with a `break` functionality, that breaks Π whenever it is used inside T, but leaves Π as secure when used "honestly." Any security proof would have to rule out such a M.

Now, the obvious solution is a reduction: showing that any adversary for T^{Π} can be converted into an attacker for Π. Thus, if M provided a mechanism to break T^{Π}, it would contradict that Π is secure. This is the approach we follow. But in the AROM, devising a reduction is nevertheless non-trivial. If the reduction could be performed exactly as it would in the standard model, there is no need to work in the ROM or AROM in the first place. So for the transforms we consider, the reduction will be making non-trivial use of the random oracle O. But it also cannot just freely program the random oracle seen by the adversary as in typical ROM proofs: the reduction must result in an adversary for Π, which makes queries to M (since that is how Π was constructed) which in turn makes queries to O. Thus if we try re-programming O, it will be inconsistent with the "true" O. Since the adversary has indirect access to the true O, this re-programming could plausibly be detected, causing the adversary to abort. How do we structure the proof in such a way that this detection is not possible, *regardless* of the structure of M?

Looking ahead, our solution will first use the security property of Π to move to a hybrid; this step is a standard reduction and does not make any particular use of the random oracle. Then in the hybrid, a *statistical* property will hold. This statistical property allows us to establish some security against M itself, which we then use to carefully program the random oracle, etc.

We now explore how to implement this vague idea in the case of EwH (Construction 4.1) in order to make it secure. In particular, we consider strengthening Π to being *lossy* (Definition 2.8). Observe that the uninstantiability of [BFM15] detailed in Sect. 4.2 uses a non-lossy public key encryption scheme. Afer all, the program $\tilde{P}$ is an obfuscation of $P_{m,y}$, which has the message m hard-coded.

While m is presumably hidden computationally, m determines the program's behavior and therefore is information-theoretically determined by $\tilde{P}$. Thus, even if, say, the original encryption scheme Π'_{PKE} were lossy, the resulting scheme in Construction 4.2 will never be lossy.

We show that this limitation of [BFM15] is inherent: that EwH is weakly CPA-PRIV in the AROM if using a lossy encryption scheme[10]. Since the techniques of [BFM15] are captured by the AROM, we thus show that the techniques cannot extend to EwH when using lossy encryption. We note that weak CPA-PRIV implies correlated-input secure one-way functions, which Wichs [Wic13] shows cannot be proved secure using black-box reductions to any falsifiable assumption. This means some idealized model is necessary for security of EwH.

Theorem 4.8. *If* Π_{PKE} *is lossy, then* Π_{EWH} *is weakly CPA-PRIV in the AROM.*

Proof. Consider a distribution $\mathcal{M}$ over oracles M, and some lossy encryption scheme $\Pi_{\mathsf{PKE}} = (\mathsf{Gen}_{\mathsf{PKE}}{}^{O,M^O}, \mathsf{Enc}_{\mathsf{PKE}}{}^{O,M^O}, \mathsf{Dec}_{\mathsf{PKE}}{}^{O,M^O}, \mathsf{GenLossy}_{\mathsf{PKE}}{}^{O,M^O})$ in the $\mathcal{M}$-AROM. Let $\Pi_{\mathsf{EWH}}{}^{O,M^O}$ be the result of applying EwH to Π_{PKE}.

Consider an ℓ-source D^{O,M^O}, which we assume to be statistically unpredictable in the $\mathcal{M}$-AROM. Let $\mathcal{A}^{O,M^O}$ be a CPA-PRIV adversary with advantage ϵ. We now define hybrids:

Hybrid 0. Here, $\mathcal{A}$ plays the CPA-PRIV game against Γ and D, with $b = 0$. This means $\mathcal{A}$ receives aux and encryptions of $m^*_{i,0}$, where $(m^*_{1,0}, \ldots, m^*_{\ell,0}, \mathsf{aux}) \leftarrow D^{O,M^O}(1^\lambda)$. Let p_0 be the probability $\mathcal{A}$ outputs 1.

Hybrid 1. Here, we switch $\mathsf{pk}_{\mathsf{PKE}}$ to be generated by $\mathsf{pk}_{\mathsf{PKE}} \leftarrow \mathsf{GenLossy}_{\mathsf{PKE}}(1^\lambda)$. Let p_1 be the probability $\mathcal{A}$ outputs 1. By the assumed lossiness of Π_{PKE} in the $\mathcal{M}$-AROM, we must have $|p_1 - p_0|$ is negligible.

Hybrid 2. This is identical to Hybrid 1, except that the experiment immediately aborts if $\mathsf{GenLossy}$ or D (when being run by the experiment) ever make a query $O(s, m^*_{i,b})$ for some $i \in [\ell], b \in \{0, 1\}$, or if they make a query to M that triggers such a query to O. Here, $m^*_{i,1}$ are sampled as uniformly random distinct messages. Let p_2 be the probability $\mathcal{A}$ outputs 1. Notice that $\mathsf{GenLossy}$ and D only receive 1^λ as input, and so are independent of s. Since $\mathcal{M}$ is complexity preserving and $\mathsf{GenLossy}, D$ are efficient, they can only trigger a polynomial number of queries each, so the probability of such a query is negligible. Hence $|p_2 - p_1|$ is negligible.

Observe that in Hybrid 2, the very first queries to $O(s, m^*_{i,0})$ for any $i \in [\ell]$ are when running $\mathsf{Enc}_{\mathsf{EWH}}(\mathsf{pk}_{\mathsf{EWH}}, m^*_{i,b}) = \mathsf{Enc}_{\mathsf{PKE}}(\mathsf{pk}_{\mathsf{PKE}}, m^*_{i,0}; O(s, m^*_{i,0}))$. Note that each of the $m^*_{i,0}$ are distinct, so all such first queries are distinct.

Hybrid 3. This is the same as Hybrid 2, except that the experiment aborts if there are any queries to $O(s, m^*_{i,b})$ occurring *after* those by $\mathsf{Enc}_{\mathsf{EWH}}(\mathsf{pk}_{\mathsf{EWH}}, m^*_{i,0})$. Let p_3 be the probability $\mathcal{A}$ outputs 1. We will prove $|p_3 - p_2|$ is negligible shortly.

---

[10] We do not know how to prove CCA-PRIV or strong security for this construction.

In Hybrid 3, since $O(s, m_{i,0}^*)$ is only ever answered once, namely inside $\mathsf{Enc}_{\mathsf{EWH}}(\mathsf{pk}_{\mathsf{EWH}}, m_{i,0}^*)$, the random coins generated in each call to $\mathsf{Enc}_{\mathsf{EWH}}$ are random and independent of the rest of the experiment. Thus, Hybrid 3 is equivalent to giving $\mathcal{A}$ the ciphertexts $\mathsf{Enc}_{\mathsf{PKE}}(\mathsf{pk}_{\mathsf{PKE}}, m_{i,0}^*)$ for fresh random coins.

Hybrid 4. This is the same as Hybrid 3, except that we switch the ciphertexts given to $\mathcal{A}$ to be $\mathsf{Enc}_{\mathsf{EWH}}(\mathsf{pk}_{\mathsf{EWH}}, m_{i,1}^*)$ for uniformly random $m_{i,1}^*$. Let p_4 be the probability $\mathcal{A}$ outputs 1. As in Hybrid 3, the experiment is equivalent to the ciphertexts being $\mathsf{Enc}_{\mathsf{PKE}}(\mathsf{pk}_{\mathsf{PKE}}, m_{i,1}^*)$ for fresh random coins. By the lossiness of $\mathsf{Enc}_{\mathsf{PKE}}$, $|p_4 - p_3|$ is negligible.

We now prove $|p_3 - p_2|$ negligible. First, since $m_{i,1}^*$ are random distinct messages that are independent of the view of the experiment in Hybrid 2, the probability of querying on $O(s, m_{i,1}^*)$ is negligible. Now we consider the first query of the form $O(s, m_{i,0}^*)$ triggered after $\mathsf{Enc}_{\mathsf{EWH}}$ in Hybrid 2. Up until this point, Hybrids 2, 3, and 4 is statistically close. But in Hybrid 4, prior to any $O(s, m_{i,0}^*)$ query, the experiment only uses $m_{i,1}^*$, and not the $m_{i,0}^*$. Hence, the $m_{i,0}^*$ remains statistically independent of the view of the experiment up until this point. Making a query on $m_{i,0}^*$ would thus violate the statistical unpredictability of D, and hence can only occur with negligible probability.

Hybrids 5,6, and 7. These are the same as Hybrids 2,1, and 0, respectively, except that the messages being encrypted are $m_{i,1}^*$. Let p_5, p_6, p_7 be the probabilities of outputting 1. By analogous arguments, we have that $|p_5 - p_4|, |p_6 - p_5|, |p_7 - p_6|$ are all negligible. Hence $|p_7 - p_0|$ is negligible. But notice that Hybrid 7 is exactly the CPA-PRIV game with $b = 1$, and so $|p_7 - p_0| = \epsilon$ is the advantage of $\mathcal{A}$. This completes the proof. $\qquad\square$

5 Fujisaki-Okamoto in the AROM

Here, we explore the insecurity of the Fujisaki-Okamoto (FO) transform [FO99] in the AROM. Recall that FO starts with $\Pi_{\mathsf{PKE}} = (\mathsf{Gen}_{\mathsf{PKE}}, \mathsf{Enc}_{\mathsf{PKE}}, \mathsf{Dec}_{\mathsf{PKE}})$ and $\Pi_{\mathsf{SKE}} = (\mathsf{Enc}_{\mathsf{SKE}}, \mathsf{Dec}_{\mathsf{SKE}})$, which are public key and secret key encryption schemes. Ciphertexts are then

$$(\, c := \mathsf{Enc}_{\mathsf{PKE}}(\mathsf{pk}, \delta; \, O(0, \delta, d) \,) \,, \, d := \mathsf{Enc}_{\mathsf{SKE}}(\, O(1, \delta) \,, m) \,) \, .$$

Note that, because $\mathsf{Enc}_{\mathsf{PKE}}$ never "sees" d, the Type 2 impossibility of the untweaked EwH does not seem to apply. For simplicity, we therefore stick with the usual description of FO; we could also define a tweaked version with an s as in Sect. 4.1, and everything we say below will still apply.

That FO is insecure for general PKE already follows from [BFM15] following a similar proof as the EwH setting, and the insecurity readily carries over to the AROM following a very similar outline as in Sect. 4.3. In fact, unlike EwH, FO remains insecure in the AROM, even if Π_{PKE} is lossy:

Theorem 5.1. *For general lossy Π_{PKE} and even perfectly secure Π_{SKE}, FO is not secure in the AROM.*

Proof. We start with an oracle M^O which contains families of private random permutations P, Q, and answers the following queries:

- (Gen, $1^\lambda, s$): Output (pk $= P(s, 0)$, sk $= s$).
- (GenLossy, $1^\lambda, s$): Output pk $= P(s, 1)$.
- (Enc, pk, m, r): If P^{-1}(pk) $= $ (sk, 0) for some sk, output $c = Q$(pk, m, r). Otherwise output $c = Q$(pk, 0, r).
- (Dec, sk, c): Compute (pk, m, r) $= Q^{-1}(c)$. If pk $= P$(sk, 0), output m. Otherwise output $\perp$.
- (Forward, x): Output $O(x)$.

M clearly can be used to realize a lossy encryption scheme Π_{PKE}. We instantiate $\mathsf{Enc}_{\mathsf{SKE}}$ with the one-time pad. Let $\Pi_{\mathsf{FO}} = (\mathsf{Gen}_{\mathsf{FO}}{}^{O, M^O}, \mathsf{Enc}_{\mathsf{FO}}{}^{O, M^O}, \mathsf{Dec}_{\mathsf{FO}}{}^{O, M^O})$ be the result of applying the FO transformation to this lossy encryption scheme. Under M as is, Π_{FO} actually will be CCA-secure. We now add two more types of queries to M, which make use of another private random oracle R.

- (EncRand, pk): Compute $(m, r) = R$(pk) and output $c \leftarrow \mathsf{Enc}_{\mathsf{FO}}{}^{O, M^O}$(pk, $m; r$)
- (Break, pk, m): Compute $(m', r) = R$(pk) and (sk, b) $\leftarrow P^{-1}$(pk). If $m = m'$, output sk.

We claim that the addition of these queries preserves the lossiness of Π_{PKE}. Indeed, suppose an adversary is trying to distinguish pk being lossy from regular. An EncRand query on pk does not help: it is just an encryption of a random ciphertext under FO, which the adversary could simulate for itself. On the other hand, suppose it makes a Break query on (pk, m) that causes it to output sk. Consider the first such query. In this case, the adversary must have been able to previously learn the plaintext encrypted in the EncRand query. Since the query was just a random ciphertext, such an adversary can be turned into an adversary against the CPA-security for Π_{FO} in the setting of only Gen, GenLossy, Enc, Dec queries, which we already know is impossible.

However, these queries clearly allow for for CCA attacks on Π_{FO}: simply make an EncRand query on the public key, and then make a CCA query on the resulting ciphertext. Then feed the result into a Break query, revealing the secret key. $\square$

The above "attack" is quite general: it is not clear that it used any particular structure of Π_{FO}. In the following subsection, we will nevertheless show how to modify the construction to achieve CCA security. Very roughly, the way we get around the issue above is by having a public key comprise of several public keys for Π_{PKE}. What we will see is that this lets us simulate CCA queries by ourselves. Then the ability to perform EncRand and Break queries will directly allow us to break the security of the underlying encryption scheme. Note that our proof will be much more general, applying to any oracle M.

5.1   Our CCA-secure Construction

Construction 5.2 (CCA-Secure PKE in the AROM). *Let* $\Pi_{\mathsf{PKE}} = (\mathsf{Gen}_{\mathsf{PKE}}, \mathsf{Enc}_{\mathsf{PKE}}, \mathsf{Dec}_{\mathsf{PKE}})$ *and* $\Pi_{\mathsf{SKE}} = (\mathsf{Enc}_{\mathsf{SKE}}, \mathsf{Dec}_{\mathsf{SKE}})$ *be public key and secret key encryption schemes, respectively. Let* $\Pi_{\mathsf{Sig}} = (\mathsf{Gen}_{\mathsf{Sig}}, \mathsf{Sign}_{\mathsf{Sig}}, \mathsf{Ver}_{\mathsf{Sig}})$ *be a signature scheme. Define* $\Pi_{\mathsf{CCA}} = (\mathsf{Gen}_{\mathsf{CCA}}{}^O, \mathsf{Enc}_{\mathsf{CCA}}{}^O, \mathsf{Dec}_{\mathsf{CCA}}{}^O)$, *where*

- $\mathsf{Gen}_{\mathsf{CCA}}{}^O(1^\lambda)$: *Let* ℓ *be the bit-length of* vk *generated by* $\mathsf{Gen}_{\mathsf{Sig}}(1^\lambda)$. *For* $i \in [\ell], b \in \{0,1\}$, *run* $(\mathsf{pk}_{\mathsf{PKE}}{}^{(i,b)}, \mathsf{sk}_{\mathsf{PKE}}{}^{(i,b)}) \leftarrow \mathsf{Gen}_{\mathsf{PKE}}(1^\lambda)$. *Output* $\mathsf{pk}_{\mathsf{CCA}} = (\mathsf{pk}_{\mathsf{PKE}}{}^{(i,b)})_{i,b}$ *and* $\mathsf{sk}_{\mathsf{CCA}} = ((\mathsf{sk}_{\mathsf{PKE}}{}^{(i,b)})_{i,b}, \mathsf{pk}_{\mathsf{CCA}})$.
- $\mathsf{Enc}_{\mathsf{CCA}}{}^O(\mathsf{pk}_{\mathsf{CCA}}, m)$: *Sample* $(\mathsf{vk}, \mathsf{sk}_{\mathsf{Sig}}) \leftarrow \mathsf{Gen}_{\mathsf{Sig}}(1^\lambda)$. *Sample* $\delta \leftarrow \{0,1\}^\lambda$. *Run* $d \leftarrow \mathsf{Enc}_{\mathsf{SKE}}(O(\mathsf{vk}, \delta)$, $m)$, $c_i \leftarrow \mathsf{Enc}_{\mathsf{PKE}}(\mathsf{pk}_{\mathsf{PKE}}{}^{(i,\mathsf{vk}_i)}, \delta; O(\delta, i, d, \mathsf{vk})$) *for* $i \in [\ell]$. *Finally compute* $\sigma \leftarrow \mathsf{Sign}_{\mathsf{Sig}}(\mathsf{sk}_{\mathsf{Sig}}, ((c_i)_i, d)$). *Output* $c = (\mathsf{vk}, (c_i)_i, d, \sigma)$.
- $\mathsf{Dec}_{\mathsf{CCA}}{}^O(\mathsf{sk}_{\mathsf{CCA}}, c)$: *First run* $\mathsf{Ver}_{\mathsf{Sig}}(\mathsf{vk}, ((c_i)_i, d)$, $\sigma)$; *if it rejects immediately abort and output* $\bot$. *Otherwise run* $\delta \leftarrow \mathsf{Dec}_{\mathsf{PKE}}(\mathsf{sk}_{\mathsf{PKE}}{}^{(1,\mathsf{vk}_1)}, c_1)$. *For each* $i > 1$, *check that* $c_i = \mathsf{Enc}_{\mathsf{PKE}}(\mathsf{pk}_{\mathsf{PKE}}{}^{(i,\mathsf{vk}_i)}, \delta; O(\delta, i, d, \mathsf{vk})$); *if any of the checks fail immediately abort and output* $\bot$. *Finally, output* $m \leftarrow \mathsf{Dec}_{\mathsf{SKE}}(O(\mathsf{vk}, \delta)$, $d)$.

Correctness is immediate from the correctness of the underlying protocols. We now state the security theorem:

Theorem 5.3. *If* Π_{PKE} *is lossy,* Π_{SKE} *is one-time secure, and* Π_{Sig} *is strongly one-time secure, then* Π_{CCA} *is CCA secure in the AROM.*

Due to lack of space, we defer the proof to the Full Version [Zha22]. The idea is to change some of the public keys to be lossy, so that the challenge query invokes only lossy keys but all CCA queries invoke at least one non-lossy key. This allows us to decrypt all CCA queries, while being able to leverage an argument similar to Theorem 4.8 for EwH to show that the challenge message remains hidden.

6   Fiat-Shamir in the AROM

Fiat-Shamir (FS) [FS87] reduces interactive public coin protocols into a single message. There are two variants: interactive into non-interactive arguments, and identification protocols into signatures. We will focus on argument systems.

Let $P(x, w) \leftrightarrow V(x)$ be a proof system for an NP language L, where x is an instance and w a witness. The system is a sound *proof* if, for any $x \notin L$ and any potentially unbounded cheating prover $P^*(x)$, $P^*(x) \leftrightarrow V(x)$ causes V to accept with only negligible probability. The system is a sound *argument* if the above holds for only computationally efficient P^*. The system is *public coin* if V's messages are uniform random strings.

Consider a 3-message public coin proof system, where the prover goes first. Let (a, c, r) be the three messages. The Fiat-Shamir transform compiles such a system into a non-interactive proof, by running $P(x, w)$ but where the verifier's message c is set to $O(s, a)$, resulting in $(a, c = O(s, a), r)$. Here, s is a common reference string (CRS), and is needed to enforce domain separation to avoid trivial Type 2 impossibilities if the underlying proof system can query O. The verifier then just checks the validity of the transcript (a, c, r), and also that $c = O(s, a)$.

Heuristically, one may expect the resulting system to be sound, since the soundness of P, V relied on the un-predictability of c, which seems to hold when deriving c from a good hash function. In the ROM, one can prove this intuition, as shown by [BR93]. Unfortunately, Goldwasser and Kalai [GK03] show that this is not the case in the standard model for general arguments. Following similar ideas to the EwH and FO cases, in the Full Version [Zha22], we show the following:

Theorem 6.1. *For general arguments, FS is* not *secure in the AROM.*

On the other hand, we show that if the proof system is an actual proof (that is, it has statistical soundness), then Fiat-Shamir *is* secure:

Theorem 6.2. *FS is secure in the AROM for statistically sound proofs, assuming $|s| \geq |a| + |r| + \omega(\log \lambda)$.*

The security of FS for proofs has been explicit conjectured by [BLV03], but a Type 5 impossibility was shown by [BDG+13], showing that FS cannot be proved in the standard model relative to standard assumptions. Thus, an idealized model seems inherent in any justification for security. The proof of Theorem 6.2 is given in the Full Version. The idea is that we can turn any adversary for FS in the AROM into a computationally *unbounded* adversary for the underlying proof system. The proof system adversary will essentially brute force the entire oracles O and M, and then use this knowledge to undetectably simulate a re-programmed oracle to the FS adversary.

Remark 6.3. The FS transform is not zero knowledge in the AROM, as the usual zero knowledge proof requires the simulator to be able to program the random oracle, which we disallow due to concerns about Type 4 impossibilities. One option is to use Lindell's transformation [Lin15], which includes a dual-mode commitment that provides a trapdoor for simulation. Another simpler option is to change the way c is computed to $c_i = O(i, s_i, a)$, where c_i is the i-th bit of c, and the CRS is $s = (s_i)_i$ where each s_i is $|a| + |r| + \omega(\log \lambda)$ bits. Now zero knowledge follows from the honest-verifier zero knowledge of (Prov, Ver): first simulate (a, c, r) for (Prov, Ver), and then choose random s_i such that $c_i = O(i, s_i, a)$.

Remark 6.4. Our proof above is not amenable to the case of signatures, as we would need a way to answer signing queries without knowing the witness. This is usually accomplished via random oracle programming. Our techniques only allow for programming using an inefficient reduction. But it seems when programming the oracle to answer signing queries, we need the reduction to remain efficient, since an inefficient reduction could have brute-forced the signatures by itself. We therefore leave the signature case as an interesting open question.

7 On Best Possible Hashing

In this section we identify two security properties that are trivially satisfied by random oracles, and each have standard-model instantiations with *different* hash functions. Yet no *single* hash function can satisfy both properties.

The two properties are anti-lossiness (Definition 2.4) and one-wayness against auxiliary input (Definition 2.5).

Anti-lossiness. Recall that anti-lossiness asks that there is no hashing key that makes the function so lossy so as to have predictable outputs when the input is random. Anti-lossiness is a natural property of hash functions, and is likely satisfied by efficient hash functions such as SHA2, where we turn SHA2 into a keyed hash function by simply concatenating the key with the input. After all, the existence of keys/prefixes that allow the output of SHA2 to be predicted would be considered a major weakness of the hash function. It is also easy to construct anti-lossy hash functions information-theoretically, and using public key tools we can even construct collision resistant anti-lossy functions. For example, for key $k = (g, h)$, the map $(x, y) \to g^x h^y$ is collision resistant (assuming discrete log) and anti-lossy. If we treat a random oracle as a keyed function by concatenating the key to the input, random oracles are also trivially anti-lossy.

One-wayness against auxiliary input. Recall that one-wayness against auxiliary input requires that the function remains one-way even against all computationally unpredictable 1-sources. Zhandry [Zha16] constructs such functions under the assumed *exponential* hardness of DDH. A random oracle (treating it as keyed by concatenating the key to the input) also trivially satisfies this notion in the plain ROM: this is just a simple consequence of random oracles being universal computational extractors [BHK13].

7.1 Incompatibility of the Definitions

Theorem 7.1. *Assuming VGB obfuscation, there is no hash function H that is both anti-lossy and auxiliary input one-way.*

Proof. The proof is closely related to the insecurity auxiliary input DDH, as shown by [BST16]. Our insight is to identify anti-lossiness as the specific property off DDH that facilitates the proof [BST16]. Let H be any hash function. Our distribution $D(1^\lambda)$ samples a uniformly random x. It then lets $P_x(k, y)$ be the program with x hard-coded, which outputs x if and only if $H(k, x) = y$; otherwise it outputs 0. D then outputs $(x, \mathsf{aux} = \mathsf{Obf}(1^\lambda, P_x))$. □

Lemma 7.2. *If H is anti-lossy, then D is computationally unpredictable.*

Proof. Suppose towards contradiction that there is an adversary $\mathcal{A}$ for the unpredictability of D. In other words, $\mathcal{A}$ learns x from $\mathsf{Obf}(1^\lambda, P_x)$, for a uniform choice of x. By VGB security, there must therefore be an *inefficient* but query-bounded simulator S such that $S^{P_x}(1^\lambda)$ outputs x with non-negligible probability. Consider any query (k, y) that S makes to P_x. By statistical unpredictability, with overwhelming probability $H(k, x) \neq y$, and so the query response is 0. By a simple hybrid over all queries, with overwhelming probability the answers to all queries are 0, in which case the view of S is independent of x. Hence S cannot output x except with negligible probability, a contradiction.   □

We now finish the proof of Theorem 7.1. If given $k, y = H(k, x)$ and aux, we can simply run the program aux on k, y; the result is $P_x(k, y)$, which outputs x since $y = H(k, x)$. Hence, H cannot be one-way against the source D.   □

Note that, if H is *not* anti-lossy, then D may be computationally predictable. This is exactly what happens with Zhandry's ELFs. Thus, even though H is not one-way against D, there is no contradiction since D is not a valid source.

We now explain that Theorem 7.1 easily translates to the AROM:

Theorem 7.3. *There is no hash function in the AROM that is both anti-lossy and auxiliary input one-way.*

We sketch the proof due to lack of space. In the AROM, we simply use the obfuscation oracle M_{Obf} from Sect. 4.3 to implement Obf (M_{Obf} is not only iO, but trivially VGB and even VBB). The rest of the proof of Theorem 7.1 is readily adapted to use M_{Obf} instead of Obf.

By Corollary 3.7, we know that O is anti-lossy in the AROM. Thus, we conclude O is *not* auxiliary input one-way in the AROM. We note that this does not contradict Theorem 3.6, as auxiliary input one-wayness is not single-stage owing to D and $\mathcal{A}$ being isolated adversaries, and hence the AROM and ROM are not equivalent for this security property. Thus, we see that the AROM appears to reflect the security of standard hash functions such as SHA2.

References

[AB12] Ananth, P., Bhaskarnnn, R.: Non observability in the random oracle model. Cryptology ePrint Archive, Report 2012/710 (2012). https://eprint.iacr.org/2012/710

[AS15] Asharov, G., Segev, G.: Limits on the power of indistinguishability obfuscation and functional encryption. In: Guruswami, V. (ed.) 56th FOCS, pp. 191–209. IEEE Computer Society Press (2015)

[BB04] Boneh, D., Boyen, X.: Secure identity based encryption without random oracles. In: Franklin, M. (ed.) CRYPTO 2004. LNCS, vol. 3152, pp. 443–459. Springer, Heidelberg (2004). https://doi.org/10.1007/978-3-540-28628-8_27

[BBO07] Bellare, M., Boldyreva, A., O'Neill, A.: Deterministic and efficiently searchable encryption. In: Menezes, A. (ed.) CRYPTO 2007. LNCS, vol. 4622, pp. 535–552. Springer, Heidelberg (2007). https://doi.org/10.1007/978-3-540-74143-5_30

[BCKP14] Bitansky, N., Canetti, R., Kalai, Y.T., Paneth, O.: On virtual grey box obfuscation for general circuits. In: Garay, J.A., Gennaro, R. (eds.) CRYPTO 2014. LNCS, vol. 8617, pp. 108–125. Springer, Heidelberg (2014). https://doi.org/10.1007/978-3-662-44381-1_7

[BDG+13] Bitansky, N., Dachman-Soled, D., Garg, S., Jain, A., Kalai, Y.T., López-Alt, A., Wichs, D.: Why "Fiat-Shamir for proof" lacks a proof. In: Sahai, A. (ed.) TCC 2013. LNCS, vol. 7785, pp. 182–201. Springer, Heidelberg (2013). https://doi.org/10.1007/978-3-642-36594-2_11

[BFM15] Brzuska, C., Farshim, P., Mittelbach, A.: Random-oracle uninstantiability from indistinguishability obfuscation. In: Dodis, Y., Nielsen, J.B. (eds.) TCC 2015. LNCS, vol. 9015, pp. 428–455. Springer, Heidelberg (2015). https://doi.org/10.1007/978-3-662-46497-7_17

[BHK13] Bellare, M., Hoang, V.T., Keelveedhi, S.: Instantiating random oracles via UCEs. In: Canetti, R., Garay, J.A. (eds.) CRYPTO 2013. LNCS, vol. 8043, pp. 398–415. Springer, Heidelberg (2013). https://doi.org/10.1007/978-3-642-40084-1_23

[BHY09] Bellare, M., Hofheinz, D., Yilek, S.: Possibility and impossibility results for encryption and commitment secure under selective opening. In: Joux, A. (ed.) EUROCRYPT 2009. LNCS, vol. 5479, pp. 1–35. Springer, Heidelberg (2009). https://doi.org/10.1007/978-3-642-01001-9_1

[BLV03] Barak, B., Lindell, Y., Vadhan, S.P.: Lower bounds for non-black-box zero knowledge. In: 44th FOCS, pp. 384–393. IEEE Computer Society Press (2003)

[BMZ19] Bartusek, J., Ma, F., Zhandry, M.: The distinction between fixed and random generators in group-based assumptions. In: Boldyreva, A., Micciancio, D. (eds.) CRYPTO 2019. LNCS, vol. 11693, pp. 801–830. Springer, Cham (2019). https://doi.org/10.1007/978-3-030-26951-7_27

[BR93] Bellare, M., Rogaway, P.: Random oracles are practical: a paradigm for designing efficient protocols. In: Denning, D.E., Pyle, R., Ganesan, R., Sandhu, R.S., Ashby, V. (eds.) ACM CCS 93, pp. 62–73. ACM Press (1993)

[BRS03] Black, J., Rogaway, P., Shrimpton, T.: Encryption-scheme security in the presence of key-dependent messages. In: Nyberg, K., Heys, H. (eds.) SAC 2002. LNCS, vol. 2595, pp. 62–75. Springer, Heidelberg (2003). https://doi.org/10.1007/3-540-36492-7_6

[BS11] Brakerski, Z., Segev, G.: Better security for deterministic public-key encryption: the auxiliary-input setting. In: Rogaway, P. (ed.) CRYPTO 2011. LNCS, vol. 6841, pp. 543–560. Springer, Heidelberg (2011). https://doi.org/10.1007/978-3-642-22792-9_31

[BST16] Bellare, M., Stepanovs, I., Tessaro, S.: Contention in cryptoland: obfuscation, leakage and UCE. In: Kushilevitz, E., Malkin, T. (eds.) TCC 2016. LNCS, vol. 9563, pp. 542–564. Springer, Heidelberg (2016). https://doi.org/10.1007/978-3-662-49099-0_20

[Can97] Canetti, R.: Towards realizing random oracles: Hash functions that hide all partial information. In: Kaliski, B.S. (ed.) CRYPTO 1997. LNCS, vol. 1294, pp. 455–469. Springer, Heidelberg (1997). https://doi.org/10.1007/BFb0052255

[CCR16] Canetti, R., Chen, Y., Reyzin, L.: On the correlation intractability of obfuscated pseudorandom functions. In: Kushilevitz, E., Malkin, T. (eds.) TCC 2016. LNCS, vol. 9562, pp. 389–415. Springer, Heidelberg (2016). https://doi.org/10.1007/978-3-662-49096-9_17

[CDMP05] Coron, J.-S., Dodis, Y., Malinaud, C., Puniya, P.: Merkle-Damgård revisited: how to construct a hash function. In: Shoup, V. (ed.) CRYPTO 2005. LNCS, vol. 3621, pp. 430–448. Springer, Heidelberg (2005). https://doi.org/10.1007/11535218_26

[CGH98] Cannetti, R., Goldreich, O., Halevi, S.: The random oracle methodology, revisited (preliminary version). In: 30th ACM STOC, pp. 209–218. ACM Press (1998)

[DDN91] Dolev, D., Dwork, C., Naor, M.: Non-malleable cryptography (extended abstract). In: 23rd ACM STOC, pp. 542–552. ACM Press (1991)

[DOP05] Dodis, Y., Oliveira, R., Pietrzak, K.: On the generic insecurity of the full domain hash. In: Shoup, V. (ed.) CRYPTO 2005. LNCS, vol. 3621, pp. 449–466. Springer, Heidelberg (2005). https://doi.org/10.1007/11535218_27

[FLR+10] Fischlin, M., Lehmann, A., Ristenpart, T., Shrimpton, T., Stam, M., Tessaro, S.: Random oracles with(out) programmability. In: Abe, M. (ed.) ASIACRYPT 2010. LNCS, vol. 6477, pp. 303–320. Springer, Heidelberg (2010). https://doi.org/10.1007/978-3-642-17373-8_18

[FO99] Fujisaki, E., Okamoto, T.: Secure integration of asymmetric and symmetric encryption schemes. In: Wiener, M. (ed.) CRYPTO 1999. LNCS, vol. 1666, pp. 537–554. Springer, Heidelberg (1999). https://doi.org/10.1007/3-540-48405-1_34

[FS87] Fiat, A., Shamir, A.: How to prove yourself: practical solutions to identification and signature problems. In: Odlyzko, A.M. (ed.) CRYPTO 1986. LNCS, vol. 263, pp. 186–194. Springer, Heidelberg (1987). https://doi.org/10.1007/3-540-47721-7_12

[GK03] Goldwasser, S., Kalai, Y.T.: On the (in)security of the fiat-shamir paradigm. In: 44th FOCS, pp. 102–115. IEEE Computer Society Press (2003)

[GKW17] Goyal, R., Koppula, V., Waters, B.: Lockable obfuscation. In: Umans, C. (ed.), 58th FOCS, pp. 612–621. IEEE Computer Society Press (2017)

[Gol06] Goldreich, O.: On post-modern cryptography. Cryptology ePrint Archive, Report 2006/461 (2006). https://eprint.iacr.org/2006/461

[GOR11] Goyal, V., O'Neill, A., Rao, V.: Correlated-input secure hash functions. In: Ishai, Y. (ed.) TCC 2011. LNCS, vol. 6597, pp. 182–200. Springer, Heidelberg (2011). https://doi.org/10.1007/978-3-642-19571-6_12

[GW11] Gentry, C., Wichs, D.: Separating succinct non-interactive arguments from all falsifiable assumptions. In: Fortnow, L., Vadhan, S.P. (eds.) 43rd ACM STOC, pp. 99–108. ACM Press (2011)

[HK07] Halevi, S., Krawczyk, H.: Security under key-dependent inputs. In: Ning, P., di Vimercati, S.D.C., Syverson, P.F. (eds.) ACM CCS 2007, pp. 466–475. ACM Press (2007)

[HSW14] Hohenberger, S., Sahai, A., Waters, B.: Replacing a random oracle: full domain hash from indistinguishability obfuscation. In: Nguyen, P.Q., Oswald, E. (eds.) EUROCRYPT 2014. LNCS, vol. 8441, pp. 201–220. Springer, Heidelberg (2014). https://doi.org/10.1007/978-3-642-55220-5_12

[KM07] Kuwakado, H., Morii, M.: Indifferentiability of single-block-length and rate-1 compression functions. IEICE Trans. Fundam. Electron. Commun. Comput. Sci. E90-A(10), 2301–2308 (2007)

[KM15] Koblitz, N., Menezes, A.J.: The random oracle model: a twenty-year retrospective. Des. Codes Cryptogr. 77(2), 587–610 (2015). https://doi.org/10.1007/s10623-015-0094-2

[KY18] Komargodski, I., Yogev, E.: Another step towards realizing random oracles: non-malleable point obfuscation. In: Nielsen, J.B., Rijmen, V. (eds.) EUROCRYPT 2018. LNCS, vol. 10820, pp. 259–279. Springer, Cham (2018). https://doi.org/10.1007/978-3-319-78381-9_10

[Lin15] Lindell, Y.: An efficient transform from sigma protocols to NIZK with a CRS and non-programmable random oracle. In: Dodis, Y., Nielsen, J.B. (eds.) TCC 2015. LNCS, vol. 9014, pp. 93–109. Springer, Heidelberg (2015). https://doi.org/10.1007/978-3-662-46494-6_5

[Mic94] Micali, S.: CS proofs (extended abstracts). In: 35th FOCS, pp. 436–453. IEEE Computer Society Press (1994)

[MRH04] Maurer, U., Renner, R., Holenstein, C.: Indifferentiability, impossibility results on reductions, and applications to the random oracle methodology. In: Naor, M. (ed.) TCC 2004. LNCS, vol. 2951, pp. 21–39. Springer, Heidelberg (2004). https://doi.org/10.1007/978-3-540-24638-1_2

[Nie02] Nielsen, J.B.: Separating random oracle proofs from complexity theoretic proofs: the non-committing encryption case. In: Yung, M. (ed.) CRYPTO 2002. LNCS, vol. 2442, pp. 111–126. Springer, Heidelberg (2002). https://doi.org/10.1007/3-540-45708-9_8

[Pas03] Pass, R.: On deniability in the common reference string and random oracle model. In: Boneh, D. (ed.) CRYPTO 2003. LNCS, vol. 2729, pp. 316–337. Springer, Heidelberg (2003). https://doi.org/10.1007/978-3-540-45146-4_19

[Sim98] Simon, D.R.: Finding collisions on a one-way street: can secure hash functions be based on general assumptions? In: Nyberg, K. (ed.) EUROCRYPT 1998. LNCS, vol. 1403, pp. 334–345. Springer, Heidelberg (1998). https://doi.org/10.1007/BFb0054137

[Wic13] Wichs, D.: Barriers in cryptography with weak, correlated and leaky sources. In: Kleinberg, R.D. (ed.) ITCS 2013, pp. 111–126. ACM (2013)

[WZ17] Wichs, D., Zirdelis, G.: Obfuscating compute-and-compare programs under LWE. In: Umans, C. (ed.) 58th FOCS, pp. 600–611. IEEE Computer Society Press (2017)

[Zha16] Zhandry, M.: The magic of ELFs. In: Robshaw, M., Katz, J. (eds.) CRYPTO 2016. LNCS, vol. 9814, pp. 479–508. Springer, Heidelberg (2016). https://doi.org/10.1007/978-3-662-53018-4_18

[Zha22] Zhandry, M.: Augmented random oracles. Available at the IACR ePrint Archive (2022). https://eprint.iacr.org/2022/783/

[ZZ20] Zhandry, M., Zhang, C.: Indifferentiability for public key cryptosystems. In: Micciancio, D., Ristenpart, T. (eds.) CRYPTO 2020. LNCS, vol. 12170, pp. 63–93. Springer, Cham (2020). https://doi.org/10.1007/978-3-030-56784-2_3

To Label, or Not To Label (in Generic Groups)

Mark Zhandry[1,2]([✉])

[1] NTT Research, Sunnyvale, USA
mark.zhandry@ntt-research.com
[2] Princeton University, Princeton, USA

Abstract. Generic groups are an important tool for analyzing the feasibility and in-feasibility of group-based cryptosystems. There are two distinct wide-spread versions of generic groups, Shoup's and Maurer's, the main difference being whether or not group elements are given explicit labels. The two models are often treated as equivalent. In this work, however, we demonstrate that the models are in fact quite different, and care is needed when stating generic group results:
- We show that numerous textbook constructions are *not* captured by Maurer, but are captured by Shoup. In the other direction, any construction captured by Maurer *is* captured by Shoup.
- For constructions that exist in both models, we show that security is equivalent for "single stage" games, but Shoup security is strictly stronger than Maurer security for some "multi-stage" games.
- The existing generic group un-instantiability results do not apply to Maurer. We fill this gap with a new un-instantiability result.
- We explain how the known black box separations between generic groups and identity-based encryption do not fully apply to Shoup, and resolve this by providing such a separation.
- We give a new un-instantiability result for the *algebraic* group model.

1 Introduction

Generic groups [Nec94, Sho97, Mau05] are idealized cryptographic groups where group operations are carried out by making queries to a group oracle, each query incurring unit cost. For both adversaries and constructions, generic groups capture natural *generic* algorithms which do not make any use of the particular features of the group in question, and instead only perform legal group operations.

There are plenty of valid criticisms of generic groups (e.g. [Fis00, KM06]), and like random oracles, generic groups cannot exist in the real world [Den02]. Nevertheless, cryptographic groups are one of the core cryptographic building blocks, and generic groups are critical to our understanding of the feasibility and infeasibility of group-based cryptosystems. The best *practical* attacks on many cryptosystems built from appropriate cryptographic groups are often generic. What's more, many of the most efficient schemes have only generic group proofs. As just one example, adaptive security is usually straightforward with generic groups. In contrast, standard model proofs of adaptive security often require

© International Association for Cryptologic Research 2022
Y. Dodis and T. Shrimpton (Eds.): CRYPTO 2022, LNCS 13509, pp. 66–96, 2022.
https://doi.org/10.1007/978-3-031-15982-4_3

more complex and less-efficient cryptosystems, such as the dual system methodology [Wat09]. Additionally, even cryptosystems with a standard-model security proof rely on computational assumptions, and for groups, there are many. When new such assumptions are made, they are often accompanied by a generic group proof of hardness, which at least demonstrates the lack of obvious flaws.

Moreover, generic groups are critical for black box separations, showing barriers to achieving various cryptographic objects from groups. Such barriers are important for the design of cryptosystems, even if one objects to using generic groups in security proofs. Examples of objects separated from generic groups include identity-based encryption [PRV12, SGS21], order revealing encryption [ZZ18], types of delay functions [RSS20], and accumulators [SGS20]. An impossibility relative to generic groups helps guide protocol design by showing what kinds of techniques will be required. While non-black box techniques can sometimes overcome such impossibilities—famously, IBE from the Diffie-Hellman assumption [DG17], for example—the use of such techniques almost always makes the results impractical. Thus, generic group impossibilities most likely rule out any practical protocol based on cryptographic groups.

Two Different Generic Groups. Since first proposed by Nechaev [Nec94], two different flavors of generic groups have emerged. The first is Shoup's [Sho97], where the group is modeled as a random embedding of the additive group $\mathbb{Z}_p$ into bit strings, with the group operations carried out by making oracle queries.

Later, Maurer [Mau05] proposed a different model that uses pointers instead of a random representation. The oracle initializes a table with various values in $\mathbb{Z}_p$, representing exponents in the group. The adversary cannot access the values directly, but just knows their line numbers in the table. The adversary then outsources linear computations on the table to the oracle.

Shoup and Maurer are the main approaches used in the literature. Numerous works (e.g. [BFF14, BCFG17, AY20, CL20, CH20]) actually treat the models as identical, simply referring to both as *the* generic group model. Some of these works justify this lack of distinction by pointing to a result of Jager and Schwenk [JS08], which provides some sort of equivalence between Shoup and Maurer. But Maurer, Portmann, and Zhu [MPZ20] find that Maurer's model allows for stronger hardness proofs, seemingly contradicting [JS08]. Recent works of Schul-Ganz and Segev [SGS20, SGS21] briefly argue that the equivalence only applies to problems that are defined "independent of the representation" of the group, and more generally the models are *incomparable*. The relationship between the models is not further explored, and it is not clarified what "independent of the representation" means. But the purpose of the generic group models is precisely to capture algorithms that work in any group, regardless of representation!

The above state of affairs makes it hard to interpret and compare the various positive and negative results using generic groups.

1.1   Overview of Results

In this work, we address the important questions above by giving a detailed comparison between the models.

The Type-Safe Model. First, we point that many works, primarily those proving black box separations, claiming to use Maurer's model actually do not operate in the model Maurer originally defined. Whereas Maurer's original model has algorithms outsourcing their group computations to a stateful table, many works instead have the algorithms perform the operations locally, but constrain the algorithms to performing only legal group operations through a simple type system. We argue that this is technically a different model than Maurer's original model. However, we observe that Maurer's model is actually poorly suited for the setting of general cryptosystems[1], and that the type-system based model implicitly used in many works is in fact the more appropriate model. We therefore formalize this model, which we call the *Type-Safe* (TS) generic group model.

Likewise, throughout this work, we will refer to Shoup's model as the *Random Representation* (RR) model, to give it a more descriptive name.

From TS/Maurer to RR/Shoup for Cryptosystems (Section 3). For now we ignore security, and just discuss whether group-based cryptosystems exist in one model or the other. We generalize one direction of the proof of Jager and Schwenk [JS08] from algorithms to general cryptosystems, showing that:

Theorem 1.1 (Informal). *Any cryptosystem in the TS/Maurer model also exists in the RR/Shoup model.*

Separations for Cryptosystems (Section 4). We then observe that the converse does not hold. Concrete cryptosystems that do not work in the TS model include the Blum-Micali PRG [BM82] and the Goldreich-Goldwasser-Micali PRF [GGM84]. Worse, we show that several primitives are simply impossible:

Theorem 1.2 (Informal). *Pseudorandom permutations, domain extension for collision resistant hashing, and encryption with additive ciphertext size overhead are each impossible in the TS/Maurer model.*

The applications excluded by Theorem 1.2 follow from textbook techniques that are taught in many introductory cryptography courses. These techniques work in the standard, RR/Shoup, and even random oracle models, the last often being treated as weaker than generic groups.

Remark 1.3. The recent works of [RSS20] and [DHH21] already, perhaps unintentionally, provide separations. [RSS20] proves delay functions impossible in the TS/Maurer model and [DHH21] proves signatures impossible. However, the

---

[1] It appears it was never meant to be: Maurer discusses several classes of problems to consider in his model, capturing discrete log, DDH, and more exotic variants. But general cryptosystems are not covered by the classes of problems.

RR/Shoup model implies random oracles [ZZ21], and both delay functions and signatures can readily be constructed assuming random oracles. Signatures can even be constructed from cryptographic groups in the *standard* model [Rom90]. We note that the purpose of these works was not to demonstrate limitations of the TS/Maurer model relative to RR/Shoup: [RSS20] argues for the difficulty of constructing group-based VDFs and time-lock puzzles, and [DHH21] seeks to explain challenges in efficient group-based signatures. Nevertheless, a separation was a perhaps unintended consequence of their results. Our results show that the case of delay functions and signatures were not isolated incidents, and the inability of cryptosystems to work in the TS/Maurer model is in fact wide-spread.

Remark 1.4. The above results (including those of [RSS20] and [DHH21]) show that the TS/Maurer model is actually *incomparable* to the random oracle model (ROM): public key encryption exists in the TS/Maurer model but not in the ROM [IR89], while the above results give examples that exist in the ROM but not TS/Maurer. This is in contrast to the RR/Shoup model, which is known to be *strictly stronger* than random oracles [ZZ21].

Security in RR/Shoup vs TS/Maurer (Section 5). We next turn to discussing whether schemes are *secure* in the models. We give two theorems, which are adaptations of the two directions of the proof of [JS08]:

Theorem 1.5 (Informal). *Amongst cryptosystems in TS/Maurer (and hence also RR/Shoup), security in RR/Shoup implies security in TS/Maurer.*

Theorem 1.6 (Informal). *Amongst cryptosystems in TS/Maurer, if the security experiment is* **single-stage***, then security in TS/Maurer implies security in RR/Shoup.*

Single-stage means there is a single adversary party; such games capture most of the basic security properties, from one-way functions to public key encryption and more. This is in contrast to *multi-stage* games, which communicate with multiple adversaries that have restricted communication. Multi-stage games include deterministic public key encryption (the message distribution is an additional adversary) and leakage resilience (the leakage function is an adversary).

We complement the above theorems by showing that, in the multi-stage setting, TS/Maurer security does *not* imply RR/Shoup security. Concretely:

Theorem 1.7 (Informal). *There exists a deterministic PKE in TS/Maurer (and therefore also in RR/Shoup), which is secure in TS/Maurer, but is insecure in RR/Shoup and insecure in any standard-model instantiation.*

Thus TS/Maurer and RR/Shoup are equivalent for single-stage games (provided the game works in TS/Maurer), but TS/Maurer is strictly less sound than RR/Shoup in the multi-stage setting.

On the Un-instantiability of Generic Groups (Section 6). Next, we consider the well-known criticism of generic groups that there are (contrived) schemes secure in the generic group model that cannot be securely instantiated under any group. This was proved by Dent [Den02] by adapting similar results for random oracles due to Canetti, Goldreich, and Halevi [CGH98]. There are now numerous ways to achieve the same result [Nie02, GK03, BBP04, BFM15]. These results typically work by having a branch in the honest algorithms that is completely insecure, say by outputting the secret key in the clear. These branches cannot be triggered in the ideal model, but can be triggered under any instantiation of the group.

However, we observe that the vast majority of these results only apply in RR/Shoup: basically the trigger is detected using the bit representation of group elements. In fact, we show that the paradigm of correlation intractability underlying many of these results cannot be used in TS/Maurer. Existing un-instantiability results that apply in TS/Maurer [BCPR14] correspond to a multi-stage game (extractable OWFs), and require indistinguishability obfuscation, a strong tool not known to be implied by any assumption on groups. Our deterministic PKE scheme is unconditional, though still multi-stage. The prior work therefore leaves open the tantalizing possibility of a standard model group which securely instantiates any single-stage TS/Maurer game. We refute this:

Theorem 1.8. *There exists a plain public key encryption (PKE) scheme and one-time message authentication code (MAC)[2] in the TS/Maurer model (and therefore also RR/Shoup) which are unconditionally secure in both models, but insecure under any instantiation of the group.*

Our schemes readily adapt to give private-key encryption and MACs in the random oracle model that are insecure under any instantiation, replicating the result of [CGH98]. Our constructions, however, use different ideas, far simpler tools, and are entirely self-contained. Our PKE scheme may also be qualitatively less contrived: as pointed out by [KM06], the prior approach of inserting a branch that causes insecure behavior goes against reasonable cryptographic practice. Our scheme, by contrast, is just ElGamal applied bit-by-bit, together with a single bit of leakage. Our leakage function itself is contrived, but leakage is usually modeled adversarially. An adversary could very well choose a contrived leakage.

The Impossibility of IBE from Generic Groups (Section 7). The literature contains two impossibilities for identity-based encryption (IBE) from generic groups: Schul-Ganz and Segev [SGS21] prove a separation in the TS/Maurer model, whereas the original separation due to Papakonstantinou, Rackoff, and Vahlis [PRV12] claims to prove a separation RR/Shoup. However, we observe that the definition of generic groups used in the latter work actually is somewhere between the TS/Maurer and RR/Shoup models. In particular, they make a TS/Maurer-style restriction where algorithms get explicit group elements as input, and are only allowed to make queries on those elements or elements derived from them. This

---

[2] Plain PKE and MAC security are single-stage games.

restriction is used at a critical step in their proof, where they show how to eliminate the explicit group elements from a user's secret key.

Restricting algorithms to operating only on explicitly provided group elements makes sense for individual algorithms trying to solve non-interactive problems such as discrete log. But for cryptosystems comprising multiple communicating parts, group elements can easily be transmitted implicitly. One could simply flip all the bits of a group element, and then recover the element by flipping them back. Alternatively, one can secret share a group element into different shares.

We note the close relationship between IBE and signatures, with IBE immediately giving signatures by re-interpreting user secret keys as signatures. What's more, a crucial part of [PRV12] can be seen as running the verification algorithm of the derived signature scheme. Given the close relationship, and the fact that signatures are possible in RR/Shoup, but impossible after making TS/Maurer restrictions, it is important to understand whether [PRV12] can be overcome in the full RR/Shoup model. We fill in this gap, showing that this is not possible:

Theorem 1.9. *IBE does not exist in the RR/Shoup model.*

The Soundness of the Algebraic Group Model (Section 8). Fuchsbauer, Kiltz, and Loss [FKL18] propose the Algebraic Group Model (AGM) as a model that lies between the standard model and generic groups. Here, adversaries can see the actual standard-model group elements, but must be able to "explain" any group element it outputs as a linear combination of its input elements.

We first point out some definitional ambiguities in the literature needed to avoid trivially invalidating the model. We argue that the model envisioned by [FKL18] allows exactly the security games which exist in the TS/Maurer model. This means the model inherits the limitations of the TS/Maurer model. The AGM is therefore actually *incomparable* to the RR/Shoup model, and it cannot reason about many textbook techniques[3]. We also resolve an open question raised by [FKL18], showing an un-instantiability result for the AGM:

Theorem 1.10. *There exists a one-time message authentication code that is secure in the AGM but insecure in any standard-model instantiation of the group.*

We also take a closer look at the comparison between the AGM and the TS/Mauer model. We do not give any formal results, but argue that the claimed advantages of the AGM are not always supported by existing evidence.

1.2 Takeaways

Our work shows that extreme care must be taken when proving security or separations for generic groups. Our equivalence for single-stage *security* justifies the common practice of treating the models as equivalent for positive results in

---

[3] Note that many works in the AGM starting from [FKL18] sometimes additionally add a random oracle, and these techniques *can* be used on the random oracle.

many settings, though the distinction is critical in the multi-stage setting. On the other hand, our separations for *constructions* show that impossibilities in the RR/Shoup vs TS/Maurer models must be interpreted very differently.

We also believe that our work points to significant limitations of black box impossibilities in the TS/Maurer model, as the model excludes numerous textbook (and black-box!) cryptographic techniques, ones that even work for the seemingly weaker random oracle model. On the other hand, these techniques seem to be all captured by RR/Shoup. This shows that impossibilities in RR/Shoup very closely reflect the available black box techniques for groups, whereas TS/Maurer does not. Nevertheless, TS/Maurer impossibilities may still be useful for guiding cryptosystem design, by showing that non-algebraic (but potentially still generic) techniques making use of the group labels would be necessary.

Our work fills in some important gaps in the literature, showing (1) that IBE is impossible in the fully general RR/Shoup model, and (2) that TS/Maurer is impossible to instantiate in general in the standard model. For (2), we give a new, relatively simple, approach to achieving un-instantiability results. We hope that our result sheds additional light on the plausibility of generic groups.

Finally, we shed some additional light on the algebraic group model, by showing that it is incomparable to the RR/Shoup model and is nevertheless un-instantiable, despite being closer to the standard model.

1.3 Organization

Due to limited space and having several different results, we omit a separate detailed technical overview of our results, instead having a brief overview at the beginning of each of our technical sections. Section 2 defines our basic notation. Section 3 defines the TS/Maurer and RR/Shoup models, plus shows when the two can be treated equivalently. Section 4 demonstrates applications which exist in RR/Shoup but not TS/Maurer. Section 5 shows the inequivalence of security for multi-stage games. Section 6 gives our new un-instantiability result for TS/-Maurer. Section 7 gives our new impossibility for IBE in the RR/Shoup model. Finally, Sect. 8 discusses the algebraic group model.

2 Preliminaries and Notation

We will use a non-uniform circuit model of computation, though all of our models and results can be translated into the Turing machine setting.

Throughout, let $\lambda > 0$ be a security parameter. An algorithm is therefore a list of circuits $\mathcal{C} = \{C_\lambda\}_{\lambda \in \mathbb{Z}}$, with domains $\mathcal{D}_\lambda$ and range $\mathcal{E}_\lambda$. The circuits comprising an algorithm can either be deterministic or probabilistic. In the later case, there are random coin gates, which generate a random bit.

For interactive algorithms, each circuit C_λ is replaced by a sequence of circuits $C_\lambda^{(1)}, C_\lambda^{(2)}, \ldots$. The domain of $C_\lambda^{(i)}$ is denoted $\mathcal{S}_\lambda^{(i)} \times \mathcal{I}_\lambda^{(i-1)}$ and the range is $\mathcal{S}_\lambda^{(i+1)} \times \mathcal{O}_\lambda^{(i)}$. Here, $\mathcal{S}_\lambda^{(i)}$ is the space of states that $C_\lambda^{(i)}$ passes to $C_\lambda^{(i+1)}$, $\mathcal{O}_\lambda^{(i)}$ is the space of outgoing messages that the algorithm sends in the ith step, and $\mathcal{I}_\lambda^{(i)}$

is the space of incoming messages. For convenience, we will generally suppress the security parameter.

We next consider *complete sets* of interacting algorithms. Each algorithm in the set is an interactive algorithm, sharing the same security parameter. There is a one-to-one correspondence between outgoing and incoming messages. Therefore, a complete set of interacting algorithms taken together yields a single non-interactive algorithm, which maps the initial inputs of each algorithm to the set of algorithms to the set of outputs. We can also consider a subset of a complete set of interacting algorithms, which we call an *incomplete* set. In this case, some of the messages are *internal*, sent amongst algorithms in the set, while other messages are *external*, and sent to and received from outside the set. An incomplete set of interacting corresponds to a single interactive algorithm, whose incoming and outgoing messages are the external messages.

2.1 Games and Cryptosystems

A game is given by a probabilistic interactive algorithm Ch, called a challenger, and a function $t : \mathbb{Z}^+ \rightarrow [0,1]$. The challenger is given as input a security parameter $\lambda \in \mathbb{Z}^+$, and interacts with k non-communicating parties $\mathsf{A}_1, \ldots, \mathsf{A}_k$. In other words, $(\mathsf{Ch}, \mathsf{A}_1, \ldots, \mathsf{A}_k)$ forms a complete set of interacting algorithms, and $\mathsf{A}_1, \ldots, \mathsf{A}_k$ forms an incomplete set where all messages are external. Collectively, $\mathsf{A} = (\mathsf{A}_1, \ldots, \mathsf{A}_k)$ is called the *adversary*. After the interaction, Ch outputs a bit b; this interaction is denoted $b \leftarrow (\mathsf{A} \rightleftarrows \mathsf{Ch})(\lambda)$. If $b = 1$ we say the adversary wins, and if $b = 0$ we say the adversary looses. In the case $k = 1$, we call (Ch, t) a *single-stage* game. If $k > 1$, we call (Ch, t) a *multi-stage* game.

Let $\mathcal{A}$ be a class of adversaries. A game (Ch, t) is *hard* for $\mathcal{A}$ if, for all $\mathsf{A} \in \mathcal{A}$, there exists a negligible ϵ such that $\Pr[1 \leftarrow (\mathsf{A} \rightleftarrows \mathsf{Ch})(\lambda)] \leq t(\lambda) + \epsilon(\lambda)$. Typical examples of adversary classes are (1) all algorithms, (2) all polynomial-time (in λ) algorithms, or (3) all query algorithms making a polynomial number (in λ) of queries to some oracle. (1) is often referred to as statistical or information-theoretic security, whereas (2) is typically called computational security. For (3), if the algorithms are not restricted, we will call the adversary *query bounded*.

Cryptosystems. Abstractly, a cryptosystem is just a set of algorithms. Typically these algorithms will be non-interactive, though their incoming and outgoing messages may contain multiple components that would be sent to different users.

The security of a cryptosystem is usually defined by a game. In the case where the security experiment makes black-box use of the cryptosystem, the game itself is an incomplete set of interacting algorithms: one of these interacting algorithms is a *coordinator*, and the remaining algorithms are all instances of the cryptosystem components. The various instances of the cryptosystem components receive and send messages from the coordinator, who also sends and receives external messages to the one or more adversaries. The game together with the adversaries then forms a complete set of interacting algorithms.

For example, consider the case of one-way functions: the coordinator chooses a random x, and sends x to one instance of the function F to get y. Then the coordinator sends y externally to the adversary, and receives x' in response. It then sends x' to a second instance of F to get y', and then checks $y = y'$.

2.2   Groups

We will write groups multiplicatively, writing $g \times h$ or simply gh to denote group multiplication. We will always assume cyclic groups of prime order p. Given a group element $g \in \mathbb{G}$, a matrix of group elements $\mathbf{G} \in \mathbb{G}^{n \times m}$ and matrices $\mathbf{A} \in \mathbb{Z}_p^{m \times r}, \mathbf{B} \in \mathbb{Z}_p^{s \times n}$, let $g^{\mathbf{A}} \in \mathbb{G}^{m \times r}$, $\mathbf{G}^{\mathbf{A}} \in \mathbb{G}^{n \times r}$ and ${}^{\mathbf{B}}\mathbf{G} \in \mathbb{G}^{s \times m}$ be the matrices defined as:

$$(g^{\mathbf{A}})_{i,j} = g^{\mathbf{A}_{i,j}} \qquad \left(\mathbf{G}^{\mathbf{A}}\right)_{i,j} = \prod_{k=1}^{m} \mathbf{G}_{i,k}^{\mathbf{A}_{k,j}} \qquad \left({}^{\mathbf{B}}\mathbf{G}\right)_{i,j} = \prod_{k=1}^{n} \mathbf{G}_{k,j}^{\mathbf{B}_{i,k}} .$$

Observe that for any appropriately-sized matrices $\mathbf{A}, \mathbf{B}$, $g^{\mathbf{A} \cdot \mathbf{B}} = (g^{\mathbf{A}})^{\mathbf{B}} = {}^{\mathbf{B}}(g^{\mathbf{A}})$.

3   Different Generic Group Models

Here, we recall Shoup's [Sho97] (which we will also call the *random representation* model) and Maurer's [Mau05] generic group models, as well as propose a *Type Safe* model, formalizing a model implicit in prior work.

3.1   Random Representation (RR)/Shoup Model [Sho97]

Let $p \in \mathbb{Z}$ be a positive integer, and let $S \subseteq \{0,1\}^*$ be a set of strings of cardinality at least p. We will assume an upper bound is known on the length of strings in S. A *random* injection $L : \mathbb{Z}_p \to S$ is chosen, which we will call the *labeling function*. We will think of $L(x)$ as corresponding to g^x, where g is a fixed generator of the group. All parties—including the adversary, the cryptosystem, and the challenger—are able to make the following queries:

- **Labeling queries.** The party submits $x \in \mathbb{Z}_p$, and receives $L(x)$.
- **Group operations.** The party submits $(\ell_1, \ell_2, a_1, a_2) \in S^2 \times \mathbb{Z}_p^2$. If there exists $x_1, x_2 \in \mathbb{Z}_p$ such that $L(x_1) = \ell_1$ and $L(x_2) = \ell_2$, then the party receives $L(a_1 x_1 + a_2 x_2)$. Otherwise, the party receives $\perp$.

All queries incur unit cost. We denote the oracles together as $\mathbb{G}_{\mathrm{RR}}$. For an algorithm A that makes queries to $\mathbb{G}_{\mathrm{RR}}$, we write $A^{\mathbb{G}_{\mathrm{RR}}}$. A game (Ch, t) in the RR model allows all parties (the challenger and one or more adversaries) to make queries to the generic group. We say that (Ch, t) is hard in the RR model if it is hard for the class of adversaries whose cost is polynomial in $\log p$.

We will think of $L(x)$ as corresponding to g^x, for some fixed generator g of the group. Therefore, if ℓ_1, ℓ_2 correspond to g^{x_1}, g^{x_2}, the group operation query computes $g^{a_1 x_1 + a_2 x_2} = (g^{x_1})^{a_1} \times (g^{x_2})^{a_2}$.

3.2 Maurer's Model [Mau05]

Again let $p \in \mathbb{Z}$ be a positive integer. An empty table T is initialized. Then all parties are able to make the following queries:

- Labeling queries. The party submits $(x, i) \in \mathbb{Z}_p \times \mathbb{Z}$. Row i of T is then set to x, potentially overwriting any contents at row i. No response is given.
- Group operations. The party submits $(i_1, i_2, i_3, a_1, a_2) \in \mathbb{Z}^2 \times \mathbb{Z}_p^2$. If there are entries x_1, x_2 in rows i_1, i_2, respectively, of T, then row i_3 is set to $a_1 x_1 + a_2 x_2$, potentially overwriting any contents at row i_3. If the contents of i_1 or i_2 are empty, then nothing is written. No response is given.
- Equality queries. The party submits $(i_1, i_2) \in \mathbb{Z}^2$. If there are entries x_1, x_2 in rows i_1, i_2, respectively, of T, then the party receives 1 if $x_1 = x_2$, and 0 otherwise. If the contents of i_1 or i_2 are empty, then the party receives $\perp$.

All non-equality queries incur unit cost, and we define hardness analogously to the RR model. We denote the oracles together as $\mathbb{G}_{\mathrm{Ma}}$. For an algorithm A that makes queries to $\mathbb{G}_{\mathrm{Ma}}$, we write $A^{\mathbb{G}_{\mathrm{Ma}}}$. As in the RR model, we will imagine there is a fixed generator g, and a row containing x will correspond to the group element g^x. The group operation queries therefore take the group elements in two positions, and write the desired combination of them to the third position.

Remark 3.1. Our convention of zero-cost equality queries follows Maurer, and better reflects reality: it is easy to show a lower bound of $\Omega(p)$ cost for discrete logarithms when counting equality queries. Yet baby-step-giant-step only takes $\Theta(\sqrt{p})$ cost in the standard and RR/Shoup models, using a data structure that cannot be simulated with just equality queries. With free equality queries, the cost in Maurer's model is the correct $\Theta(\sqrt{p})$. [MPZ20] takes a different approach, refining Maurer's model to allow more sophisticated queries that can implement the required data structure with $\Theta(\sqrt{p})$ queries. Regardless, the number of possible equality queries is at most quadratic in the number of wires, so this convention only makes a polynomial difference, which does not effect our results.

Challenges of Maurer's Model. Maurer's model makes sense for reasoning about computational problems, such as discrete logarithms or Diffie-Hellman. Here, the table is initialized to contain the problem instance in the first several rows, with the rest of the table as scratch space for performing computations.

However, the model is potentially problematic when reasoning about cryptosystems, where different components of the cryptosystem (or even the same component run multiple times) are using the group. Since the oracle is stateful, this can cause bad behavior of the algorithms. For example, the security experiment for one-wayness runs the function twice, once to generate the adversary's input, and once to check its output. If running the function causes the table values to change, then the outputs of the function is not deterministic. Worse, the adversary may influence the outputs by writing values to the table, which could make inversion easier. Of course this is not an issue in the real world, but it demonstrates an issue when trying to apply Maurer's model to cryptosystems.

3.3   The Type Safe (TS) Model

Here we offer a model that tries to capture the intuitive properties of Maurer's model, while also having a stateless oracle to avoid the issues above. This model is, in fact, implicit in many works claiming to use Maurer's model [RSS20, SGS20, SGS21, DHH21], but has not to our knowledge been formally written down.

Let $p \in \mathbb{Z}$ be a positive integer. An algorithm A will be given as a circuit. Unlike a standard binary circuit, the circuit for A will have the following features:

- There will be two kinds of wires, *bit* wires and *element* wires. Bit wires take values in $\{0, 1\}$, whereas element wires take values in $\mathbb{Z}_p \cup \{\perp\}$.
- There will be "bit gates" that map bits to bits. These gates *cannot* take element wires as input. Any universal gate set is allowed for the bit gates.
- Additionally, there will be a few special "element gates", whose inputs and/or outputs include element wires:
  - **Labeling Gate.** This takes as input $\lceil \log_2(p) \rceil$ bit wires, and interprets them as $x \in \mathbb{Z}_p$. Its output is an element wire, containing x. This element wire will be thought of as corresponding to the value g^x. If the input wires do not correspond to an $x \in \mathbb{Z}_p$, the output wire will contain $\perp$.
  - **Group Operation Gate.** This takes as input $2 \times \lceil \log_2(p) \rceil$ bit wires and 2 element wires. The bit wires are interpreted as $a_1, a_2 \in \mathbb{Z}_p$. Let x_1, x_2 be the contents of the element wires. The output wire is an element wire, set to $a_1 x_1 + a_2 x_2$. If any of the bit or element input wires do not correspond to elements of $\mathbb{Z}_p$, then the output wire is set to $\perp$.
  - **Equality Gate.** This takes as input two element wires, and outputs a bit wire. If the input wires both contain the same $x \in \mathbb{Z}_p$, the output wire is set to 1. In all other cases (including $\perp$ inputs) the output is 0.

We somewhat abuse notation, and for an algorithm A in the type safe model, we write $A^{\mathbb{G}_{\mathrm{TS}}}$. Our cost metric for circuits in the TS model will count only labeling and group operation gates, with bit and equality gates being free. Free bit gates corresponds to the other generic group models, where queries are bounded but computation outside of queries is free. Free equality gates are used for the same reason as equality queries in Maurer's model.

A game (Ch, t) in the TS model allows all parties (the challenger and one or more adversaries) to use labeling and group operation gates, and send both bit and element wires to each other. We define hardness as in the previous models.

In the TS model, we will think of element wires as containing $\log_2 p$ bits. Therefore, if an algorithm has k_1 element wires as input and k_2 bit wires, its overall input size will be $k_1 \log_2 p + k_2$.

3.4   Examples

We now discuss several examples of cryptosystems based on groups, to illustrate the differences between the TS and RR models.

One-Way Functions. Discrete logs give a simple one-way function $f(x) = g^x$. This function easily maps to the RR model as $f(x) = L(x)$, which is evaluated by a single labeling query. The function *also* maps to the Type Safe model, but with some caveats. Namely, $f(x)$ is simply a labeling gate, which outputs an element wire. Thus, in the TS model, $f(x)$ does not map bits to bits, but rather maps bits to *elements*. This makes sense, but it means that the outputs of f cannot be operated on at the bit level, and in particular cannot be fed back into f.

Pseudorandom Generators. Consider the Blum-Micali [BM82] PRG: on input x, let $x_0 = x$. Then define $x_i = g^{x_{i-1}}$ for $i = 1, \ldots, n$, where n is the number of desired outputs. Then for each i, output a hardcore bit b_i extracted from x_i.

Blum-Micali easily translates to the RR model: just let $x_i = L(x_{i-1})$. The only caveat is that the set of labels must be $\log p$ bits so the domain and range of $x \mapsto g^x$ are essentially identical. On the other hand, Blum-Micali does *not* work in the Type Safe model: x_1 is an element wire, and so it cannot be fed into another labeling gate in order to derive x_2.

Other standard PRGs work in the TS model. Consider $G(x, y) = (g^x, g^y, g^{xy})$, which is secure under the decisional Diffie-Hellman assumption. To evaluate, compute xy over $\mathbb{Z}_p$ using standard circuit gates, and then apply labeling gates to x, y, and xy. It is straightforward to generalize G to obtain arbitrary stretch.

Pseudorandom Functions. Once we have a pseudorandom generator like $G(x, y)$ above, we may hope to build a pseudorandom *function* following Goldreich, Goldwasser, and Micali [GGM84]. This construction takes any length-doubling PRG $G : \{0,1\}^n \rightarrow \{0,1\}^{2n}$, and constructs a PRF as follows. Define G_0 to be the first n bits of the output of G, and G_1 to be the second n bits. For a key $k \in \{0,1\}^n$ and input $x \in \{0,1\}^m$, define $F(k, x) = G_{x_m}(G_{x_{m-1}}(\ldots G_{x_1}(k) \ldots))$.

For a PRG G in the RR model, the PRF of [GGM84] readily also translates to the RR model. However, the same is not true for the Type Safe model. For example, our G from above takes bits as input but outputs *element* wires, and so the outputs cannot be fed back into G as in [GGM84].

Nevertheless, there are PRGs in the TS model, namely Naor-Reingold [NR97]. The secret key consists of $\alpha_0, \ldots, \alpha_m$, and $F(k, x) = g^{\alpha_0 \prod_{i=1}^m \alpha_i^{x_i}}$. To evaluate in the TS model, simply compute $\alpha_0 \prod_{i=1}^m \alpha_i^{x_i}$ and then apply a labeling gate.

Preprocessing Attacks. Several works [CK18,BL22] have studied pre-processing attacks on groups, where an expensive pre-processing stage stores information about the labeling function of the group. These attacks make sense in the RR model, but do not appear to have any meaning in the TS model.

The above examples already begin to show that the Type Safe model does not capture all common cryptographic techniques one may apply to groups. In Sect. 4, we strengthen these observations to show some concepts that are simply impossible in the TS model, despite there being standard-model constructions from groups. On the other hand, the Random Representation model seems to capture known black-box techniques, and does not suffer from these limitations.

Next, we prove certain positive relationships between the TS and RR model. These results are analogous to the theorem of [JS08], which is often cited as proving the equivalence between Shoup's and Maurer's generic group models. Our results below formalize what this equivalence means, and where it falls short.

3.5   Compiling TS to RR

Here we show that any algorithm which exists in the TS model also exists in the RR model. By applying this to cryptosystems and games, we see that any technique which is captured by the TS model is also captured by the RR model. By applying this to adversaries, we see that security in the RR model implies security in the TS model, amongst games the TS model (and hence in both models). These results are an adaptation of one direction of the proof of [JS08].

In more detail, we show that there is a *canonical translation* of any algorithm (or set of interacting algorithms) into the RR model.

Definition 3.2. *Let $A^{\mathbb{G}_{TS}}$ be an algorithm in the TS model. We then define the canonical translation of $A^{\mathbb{G}_{TS}}$ into the RR model, which we will denote as $A^{\mathbb{G}_{RR}}$, which is identical to $A^{\mathbb{G}_{TS}}$ except that:*

– *All element wires are replaced by collections of bit wires, which together are interpreted as labels.*
– *Labeling and group operation gates are replaced with the corresponding labeling and group operation queries.*
– *Equality gates are replaced by string comparison sub-routines.*

For a set of interactive algorithms $A^{\mathbb{G}_{TS}} = (A_1^{\mathbb{G}_{TS}}, ... A_k^{\mathbb{G}_{TS}})$ in the TS model, we define the canonical translation as $A^{\mathbb{G}_{RR}} = (A_1^{\mathbb{G}_{RR}}, ..., A_k^{\mathbb{G}_{RR}})$.

Theorem 3.3. *Let $A^{\mathbb{G}_{TS}}$ be a complete set of interactive algorithms in the TS model, whose final output is a set of bit wires. Let $A^{\mathbb{G}_{RR}}$ be its canonical translation. Then the output distributions of $A^{\mathbb{G}_{TS}}$ and $A^{\mathbb{G}_{RR}}$ are identical.*

Proof. To see that the distributions of outputs are identical between $A^{\mathbb{G}_{TS}}$ and $A^{\mathbb{G}_{RR}}$, we observe that, in the TS model, it is equivalent to consider the element wires as containing $L(x)$ instead of x. Each algorithm in $A^{\mathbb{G}_{RR}}$ then simply replaces each element wire with bit wires, but still containing $L(x)$, and evaluates the equality gates for itself using string comparison.   □

Now let Π be a protocol and (Ch, t) an associated security game in the TS model. Let $\Pi', (\mathsf{Ch}', t)$ be the canonical translation into the RR model.

Theorem 3.4. *If (Ch', t) is hard in the RR model, then (Ch, t) is hard the TS model. This holds whether or not $\mathsf{Ch}, \mathsf{Ch}'$ are single-stage games.*

Proof. Toward contradiction, let $A = (A_1, \ldots, A_k)$ be an adversary playing the game Ch in the TS model, and winning with probability q, which is non-negligibly greater than t. Let A' be the canonical translation of A. Then (A', Ch') is the canonical translation of (A, Ch), which are complete sets of interacting algorithms. By Theorem 3.3, the output distribution is identical, which contradicts the hardness of (Ch', t). $\square$

3.6 From TS Security to RR Security for Single-Stage Games

Now, we visit the other direction of the equivalence claimed in [JS08], showing that TS security implies RR security *sometimes*, namely in single-stage games.

Theorem 3.5. *If* Ch *is a* single-stage *game and* Π *is* (Ch, t)-*secure in the TS model, then* Π' *is* (Ch', t)-*secure in the RR model, where* (Ch', t) *is the canonical translation of* (Ch, t).

The proof is given in the Full Version [Zha22]. The intuition is that an adversary A' for Π' is compiled into an adversary A for Π, where A lazily simulates the RR labeling function with a table T, using its TS gates to ensure consistency.

   Note that Theorem 3.5 only applies to single-stage games. If we try applying the proof to a multi-stage adversary, our new adversary has to maintain the table T, which must be shared across all the adversaries to maintain consistency. Thus, we actually obtain a single-stage adversary, violating the requirements of the game. Section 5 demonstrates that this limitation is inherent, giving a multi-stage cryptosystem that is secure in the TS model but not in the RR model.

4   Further Impossibilities in the Type Safe Model

Here, we give impossibility results in the Type-Safe (TS) generic group model, which nevertheless have standard-model constructions from cryptographic groups and moreover translate to and have security in the Random Representation/Shoup model. These impossibilities are for textbook cryptographic applications, showing a significant weakness for the TS model.

   We first state the following lemma, which is implicit in numerous works, and is the main justification for the Algebraic Group Model [FKL18] being implied by the generic group model. The lemma is proved in the Full Version [Zha22].

Lemma 4.1. *Consider any deterministic algorithm* $A(\mathbf{h}, x)$ *in the TS model whose input contains a vector* $\mathbf{h}$ *of* n *group elements and which outputs a single group element. Then there is another deterministic algorithm* $E(\mathbf{h}, x)$ *whose runtime and query complexity is linearly related to* A, *such that* $E(x)$ *outputs a vector* $\mathbf{v} \in \mathbb{Z}_p^{n+1}$ *satisfying* $A(\mathbf{h}, x) = (q, \mathbf{h})^{\mathbf{v}}$.

Note that, while Lemma 4.1 discusses deterministic algorithms, it can readily be applied to randomized algorithms by supplying the same random coins to A and E, making them deterministic functions of the random coins.

As is typical in the generic group literature, we will also observe that any equality gate can be thought of as a linear test on $(g, \mathbf{h})$: let $\mathbf{v}_1, \mathbf{v}_2$ be the vectors guaranteed by Lemma 4.1 for the two gate inputs. Then the equality gate tests whether $(g, \mathbf{h})^{\mathbf{v}_1 - \mathbf{v}_2} = 1$. We call the linear test *trivial* if $\mathbf{v}_1 = \mathbf{v}_2$, and *non-trivial* if $\mathbf{v}_1 \neq \mathbf{v}_2$. Note that trivial tests will always output 1 (denoting equal), whereas the result of non-trivial tests will depend on the elements in $\mathbf{h}$.

4.1 Collision Resistant Domain Extension

Here, we will prove that any hash function H in the TS model must have somewhat large hashing keys. This is in contrast to the standard model, where domain extension allows for constant-sized keys. Intuitively, domain extension typically operates on outputs of H (say, by feeding them back in as inputs), which may be group elements protected by the type system.

Theorem 4.2. *Let H be a collision resistant hash function in the TS model with key length k, input length n, and output length m. Let p be the group order. Then $n \leq 1 + m \times (k + \log p)$.*

Proof. Suppose H has key space $\mathbb{G}^{k_1} \times \{0,1\}^{k_2}$, domain $\mathbb{G}^{n_1} \times \{0,1\}^{n_2}$, and range $\mathbb{G}^{m_1} \times \{0,1\}^{m_2}$. We assume for simplicity that p is a power of 2; the general case follows from the same arguments, but more care is needed to track parameter sizes. Then $k = k_2 + k_1 \log p$, $n = n_2 + n_1 \log p$, and $m = m_2 + m_1 \log p$. Then our goal is to show that $n \leq 2 + m \times (k + \log p)$. We will prove a stronger statement, namely that: $n \leq 1 + m(k_1 + 1) \log p$.

We first make two simplifying assumption, which we argue are wlog.

Simplifying Assumption 4.3. $n_1 = 0$, *meaning* $n = n_2$.

In other words, the input consists entirely of bits and no group elements.

Lemma 4.4. *For any H, there exists a new collision resistant hash function H' with the same domain, range, and key size as H, but which satisfies Simplifying Assumption 4.3.*

Proof. H' is defined as $H(k, (\alpha_1, \ldots, \alpha_{n_1}, x)) = H'(k, (g^{\alpha_1}, \ldots, g^{\alpha_{n_1}}, x))$; H' uses the same key sampling algorithm Gen as H. Clearly, any collision for H' can be converted into a collision for H, so if H is collision resistant, then so is H'. Moreover, this change from H to H' preserves $n = n_2 + n_1 \log p$. □

Let $K_2 \in \{0,1\}^{k_2}$ be the bits of the key, and $K_1 \in \mathbb{G}^{k_1}$ be the group elements. For a key (K_1, K_2), we say that an input x is "good" if all the non-trivial linear equations over K_1 queried during evaluating $H(x)$ evaluate to non-zero. We will pick an inverse polynomial δ (in fact, a constant), to be specified later.

Simplifying Assumption 4.5. *Except with negligible probability over the choice of key $(K_1, K_2) \leftarrow$ Gen(), a $1 - \delta$ fraction of x in the domain are good.*

Lemma 4.6. *For any H satisfying Simplifying Assumption 4.3, there exists H' satisfying Simplifying Assumptions 4.3 and 4.5, with $n' = n, m' = m, k'_1 \leq k_1$.*

Lemma 4.6 is proved in the Full Version [Zha22]. The idea is that "bad" inputs yield a linear equation over the exponents of the key. By solving the linear system, one can solve for one element of the hashing key in terms of others, compiling H into a new hash function with fewer bad inputs. One can iterate this process until the fraction of bad inputs becomes sufficiently small. This process expands the bit part of the hashing key (k_2), but this is fine since it is independent of the stronger bound $n \leq 1 + m(k_1 + 1) \log p$ that we will prove.

With our simplifying assumptions, we can now finish the proof, which is given in detail in the Full Version [Zha22]. The idea is that for good x, we can write the output $(O_1, O_2) \in \mathbb{G}^{m_1} \times \{0,1\}^{m_2}$ as $O_1 = {}^{\mathbf{A}(K_2, x)}(g, K_1)$ $O_2 = F(K_2, x)$ for $\mathbf{A} : \{0,1\}^{k_2} \times \{0,1\}^n \to \mathbb{Z}_p^{m_1 \times (k_1 + 1)}$ and $F : \{0,1\}^{k_2} \times \{0,1\}^n \to \{0,1\}^{m_2}$. Recall that a left superscript means left multiplication in the exponent. A collision amongst good x for the map $x \mapsto (\mathbf{A}(K_2, x), F(K_2, x))$ therefore yields a collision for the hash function. This means that $(\mathbf{A}(K_2, x), F(K_2, x))$ must be injective for good x, since otherwise a collision can be computed inefficiently without making any queries. Since a $1 - \delta$ fraction of x are good, this allows us to lower bound the output length of $(\mathbf{A}(K_2, x), F(K_2, x))$, thereby giving our bound. $\square$

4.2   Pseudorandom Permutations

Theorem 4.7. *Let F, F^{-1} be an efficient keyed permutation pair in the TS model. Then it is not a secure PRP.*

Theorem 4.7 will be the immediate consequence of the following three lemmas:

Lemma 4.8. *Let F be an efficient keyed function in the TS model, such that the output contains at least one bit. Then F is not a secure PRF.*

Lemma 4.9. *Let F be an efficient keyed function in the TS model, such that the input contains at least one group element. Then F is not a secure PRF.*

Lemma 4.10. *Let F, F^{-1} be an efficient keyed permutation pair in the TS model. Then the number of group elements in the domain and range must be equal.*

Lemmas 4.9, 4.8, and 4.10 are proved in the Full Version [Zha22]; here we sketch the high-level idea. For Lemma 4.8, the idea is to first ignore all the group element outputs and just focus on the bit output. As with Simplifying Assumption 4.3, we can replace all key element wires with bit wires. Then we argue that the resulting function can be computed without element gates at all, and hence insecure against computationally unbounded (but element gate-bounded) adversaries.

For Lemma 4.9, the idea is that any function with group element inputs must be linear in those inputs. But linear functions cannot be pseudorandom.

Finally, for Lemma 4.10, suppose the number of group elements were not equal. By potentially exchanging the roles of F, F^{-1}, we assume F has fewer group element outputs than it's inputs. Now consider running F on a random input. Since F is a permutation, the output must information-theoretically encode the input. But since there are now fewer group elements, this means some information about the exponents of the input must now be present in the bit wires of the output. We show how to embed a discrete log challenge into the input, and then extract this information from the bit wires using F^{-1} and Lemma 4.1, resulting in computing the discrete log. But discrete logs are intractable in the TS model.

4.3   Efficient CPA-Secure Encryption for Message Strings

We now prove that any CPA-secure encryption scheme in the TS model, whose domain is bits (as opposed to group elements), must have the number of group elements in the ciphertext be approximately at least the bit-length of the message. As group elements are $\log p$ bits, ciphertexts are a $\log p$ factor larger than messages.

Definition 4.11. *A CPA-secure encryption scheme consists of a pair of efficient probabilistic algorithms* $\mathsf{Enc} : \mathcal{K} \times \mathcal{M} \to \mathcal{C}, \mathsf{Dec} : \mathcal{K} \times \mathcal{C} \to \mathcal{M}$ *satisfying:*

- **Correctness:** $\forall K \in \mathcal{K}, M \in \mathcal{M}$, $\Pr[\mathsf{Dec}(K, \mathsf{Enc}(K, M)) = M] \geq 1 - \mathsf{negl}$.
- **Chosen Plaintext Security:** *Consider an adversary* A *playing the following game with a challenger. The challenger first chooses a random* $K \leftarrow \mathcal{K}$, *and chooses a random bit* $b \in \{0, 1\}$. *Then* A *makes queries on message pairs* (M_0, M_1), *and receives* $\mathsf{Enc}(k, M_b)$. *The adversary outputs a guess* b' *for* b. *We require that, for any efficient* A, $\Pr[b' = b] \leq 1/2 + \mathsf{negl}$.

Theorem 4.12. *Let* $\mathsf{Enc}, \mathsf{Dec}$ *be a CPA-secure encryption scheme which compiles in the TS model. Suppose the message space is bit-strings* $\{0, 1\}^n$. *If the ciphertext space is* $\mathbb{G}^{m_1} \times \{0, 1\}^{m_2}$, *then* $m_1 \geq \Omega(n/\log \lambda)$.

Proof. Let $\mathsf{Enc}, \mathsf{Dec}$ be a CPA-secure encryption scheme in the TS model. Note that we can consider the bit portion of the ciphertexts alone as an encryption scheme; there is no correctness, but we can still consider security which is implied by the security of the full $(\mathsf{Enc}, \mathsf{Dec})$. Now suppose the bit portion was not statistically independent of the message conditioned on the secret key K. Then by the standard impossibility of statistically secure CPA-secure encryption in the standard model, there is an inefficient query-less attacker that would break CPA-security, thus violating the security of $(\mathsf{Enc}, \mathsf{Dec})$. Therefore we know that the bit portion must be statistically independent of the message.

Now consider decrypting a ciphertext $c \in \mathbb{G}^{m_1}$. Dec will make a polynomial number T of equation queries over $(1, c)$. The message outputted will be some function of the results and the bit portion of the ciphertext. We can assume without loss of generality that Dec never makes a query that is linearly dependent on previous queries which returned 0. Indeed, Dec can correctly predict the output of the query will be 0. Therefore, there will be at most m_1 queries that will result in zero, since the dimension of the zero queries is m_1.

This means there is $\ll 1$ bit of information about the message in the bit-portion of the ciphertext, and only $\log_2 \binom{T}{m_1} \leq m_1 \log_2 T$ bits of information in the queries, and therefore the message length n is at most this quantity. Hence, $m_1 \geq n/\log_2 T$. Since T is polynomial in the security parameter, this gives the desired lower-bound on the ciphertext size.   □

5   On the Insecurity of the Type-Safe Model for Multi-stage Games

Here, we show that security in the TS model does *not* imply security in the RR model. We first define deterministic public key encryption, following [BBO07].

Definition 5.1. *A deterministic encryption scheme is a triple of efficient algorithms* (Gen, Enc, Dec) *where* Enc, Dec *are deterministic such that:*

- **Correctness:** *For all* m, $\Pr[\text{Dec}(\text{sk}, c) = m : {}^{(\text{sk},\text{pk}) \leftarrow \text{Gen}()}_{c \leftarrow \text{Enc}(\text{pk},m)}] \geq 1 - \text{negl}.$
- **ℓ-Security:** *For any two distributions* D_0, D_1 *with min-entropy at least* ℓ, *and for any efficient probabilistic adversary* A, $| \Pr[A(\text{pk}, \text{Enc}(\text{pk}, D_0)) = 1] - \Pr[A(\text{pk}, \text{Enc}(\text{pk}, D_1)) = 1] | \leq \text{negl}$, *where* $(\text{pk}, \text{sk}) \leftarrow \text{Gen}()$.

Here, the min-entropy of a distribution D is $H_\infty(D) = \min \log_2 \Pr[x \leftarrow D]^{-1}$. Since Enc is deterministic, for security to be possible at all, we require $\ell = \omega(\log \lambda)$. For security to be non-trivial, we usually ask that $\ell \ll |m|$.

Note that ℓ-security is *not* single-stage, since the definition quantifies over D_0, D_1 and A, and A cannot see the random coins of D_0, D_1.

Construction 5.2. *Let* (Gen, Enc, Dec) *be the following deterministic encryption scheme for messages in* $\mathbb{Z}_p$:

- $\text{Gen}^{\mathbb{G}_{TS}}()$: *run* $a_1, \ldots, a_n \leftarrow \mathbb{Z}_p$, *and output* $\text{sk} = (a_1, \ldots, a_n), \text{pk} = (h_1 = g^{a_1}, \ldots, h_n = g^{a_n})$.
- $\text{Enc}^{\mathbb{G}_{TS}}(\text{pk}, m)$: *run* $c_0 \leftarrow g^m$ *and* $c_i = h_i^m g^{m_i}$ *for* $i = 1, \ldots, n$.
- $\text{Dec}^{\mathbb{G}_{TS}}(\text{sk}, c)$: *for* $i = 1, \ldots, n$, *compute* $u_i = c_0^{a_i}$. *If* $c_i = u_i$, *set* $m_i = 0$; *otherwise set* $m_i = 1$.

It is straightforward that Construction 5.2 is correct: $u_i = g^{m a_i} = h_i^m$. Therefore $c_i = u_i$ if and only if $m_i = 0$.

Theorem 5.3. *Construction 5.2 is an ℓ-secure deterministic encryption scheme in the TS model for $\ell = \log_2 p - 2$, but is insecure in the RR model or in any standard-model instantiation of the group.*

The proof is given in the Full Version [Zha22]. For *insecurity* in the RR and standard models, the idea is to have D_0, D_1 be random messages conditioned on, say, the first bit of g^m being 0 and 1, respectively. These have high min-entropy, but also allow the adversary to trivially distinguish the two cases by looking at the first bit of c_0. For *security* in the TS model, we first note that this bit fixing strategy does not apply since the distribution cannot have direct access to the bits of g^m. We give a simple proof that *no* distinguishing strategy is possible.

6 TS Un-instantiability

Here, we give an example of a protocol in the TS model that is secure under a single-stage game (and hence also in the RR model, by Theorem 3.5) and yet is insecure under any standard-model instantiation of the group.

6.1 Overview

We first explain limitations of the existing works on the un-instantiability of idealized models, as well as sketch our solution. The first such un-instantiability result was for random oracles (RO), a predecessor of generic groups, where one models an hash function as a truly random function. Canetti, Goldreich, and Halevi [CGH98] give contrived schemes that are secure in the random oracle model, but which are insecure under any instantiation of the oracle by a concrete hash function. Their impossibility works by identifying a security property of a hash function H called *correlation intractability*, which requires that for any "sparse" relation over input/output pairs, it is computationally infeasible to find an input x such that $(x, H(x))$ satisfies the relation. Correlation intractability is trivially satisfied by random oracles, but [CGH98] show that it is impossible (in certain parameter regimes) for standard-model hash functions. They then build contrived cryptosystems where an input/output pair satisfying the relation causes some clearly insecure behavior: e.g. the secret key holder completely reveals their key, or the encrypter encrypts uses the identity function. In the random oracle model, this will never happen and the system will remain secure. But in the standard model, the attacker simply uses the impossibility for correlation intractability to find such an input. triggering a complete break of the system.

This idea was translated to generic groups by Dent [Den02], who uses similar ideas but where the hash function is replaced by the group labeling function. Another way to obtain a separation is through the recent work of Zhandry and Zhang [ZZ21], who show that the labeling function of a generic group, when properly truncated, gives a random oracle, which in turn is impossible.

However, both of these results crucially rely on the labeling function; that is, they only work in the RR/Shoup model. There are at least a couple reasons why the un-instantiability result appears to not generalize to the TS model. First, [CGH98, Den02] use a random oracle to instantiate Micali's CS proofs [Mic94], which in turn requires a domain-extending Merkle tree; we already showed (Sect. 4) that domain extension is impossible in the TS model.

More fundamentally, we show in the Full Version [Zha22] that correlation intractability *cannot* separate the TS and standard model, regardless of the construction. Concretely, we give a simple hash function which is correlation intractable (in the standard model) with respect to every evasive relation that exists in the TS model. We note that, the cryptosystems derived from correlation intractability [CGH98] must execute the relation, and therefore the relation must exist in the TS model if we want to use it for an un-instantiability result.

Other un-instantiability results [Nie02, GK03, BBP04, BFM15] have similar issues to the above. Meanwhile, [BCPR14] give an un-instantiability result that works in the TS model, but it is a multi-stage game and requires strong computational assumptions, namely indistinguishability obfuscation.

We fill in this gap, showing that the single-stage TS model is unconditionally un-instantiable, albeit via very different, and arguably simpler, techniques. We start with ElGamal, but where message bits are encrypted bit by bit. This is easily proved secure in the standard model. We then modify the scheme to append a single bit, which is a contrived leakage function of the message and randomness.

In either the TS or RR model, we show this leakage offers minimal advantage to breaking the cryptosystem. However, in the standard model, we show that by encrypting the description of (that is, the code) of the group, the ciphertext, leakage included, easily reveals one bit about the message. This breaks security.

The main challenges are two-fold. First we must make sure the encryption scheme can actually be decrypted in the TS model, which we showed is not trivial in Sect. 4. A more difficult problem is to maintain security in the generic group models. This is challenging because our leakage function interprets the message as arbitrary code and runs it on some inputs. Without care, this arbitrary code could already break security without having anything to do with the generic group. For example, the code could just be a constant function, in which case the leakage reveals which constant. We give our solution in Sect. 6.2. In Sect. 8 we give another un-instantiability result for one-time MACs in the context of the Algebraic Group Model (AGM), which also applies to the TS model.

6.2   Our Un-instantiable Construction

Construction 6.1. *Let* $(\mathsf{Gen}^{\mathbb{G}_{TS}}, \mathsf{Enc}^{\mathbb{G}_{TS}}, \mathsf{Dec}^{\mathbb{G}_{TS}})$ *be the following:*

- $\mathsf{Gen}^{\mathbb{G}_{TS}}(1^\lambda)$: *sample* $\alpha \leftarrow \mathbb{Z}_p \setminus \{0\}$, *and let* $\mathsf{pk} = (g, h = g^\alpha, \lambda)$ *and* $\mathsf{sk} = \alpha$.
- $\mathsf{Enc}^{\mathbb{G}_{TS}}(\mathsf{pk}, m)$: *Let* n *be the bit-length of* m. *For each* $i \in [n]$, *sample* $r_i \leftarrow \mathbb{Z}_p$ *and let* $c_i = g^{r_i}, d_i = h^{r_i + m_i}$, *where* $m_i \in \{0, 1\}$ *is the ith bit of* m. *Let* $e \leftarrow L(m, \{r_i\}_i$ *where* L *is defined below. Output output* $c = (\{c_i, d_i\}_{i \in [n]}, e)$.
- $\mathsf{Dec}^{\mathbb{G}_{TS}}(\mathsf{sk}, c)$: *for each* $i \in [n]$, *compute* $d_i' = c_i^\alpha$. *If* $d_i' = d_i$, *set* $m_i = 0$; *otherwise set* $m_i = 1$. *Output* $m = m_1 m_2 \cdots m_n$.

$L(m, \{r_i\}_i)$ *works as follows: interpret the last* $n - \lambda$ *bits of* m *as the description of a function* $H : \mathbb{Z}_p \to \{0, 1\}$ *in some canonical way. Then:*

- *Test if* H *is "balanced" by sampling* $k = 32\lambda$ *random* $s_j \leftarrow \mathbb{Z}_p, j = 1, \ldots, k$, *computing* $b_i \leftarrow H(s_i)$, *and checking that* $\sum_{j=1}^k s_i \in (3k/8, 5k/8)$.
- *If* H *is not balanced, sample a random bit* $e \leftarrow \{0, 1\}$. *Otherwise, let* $e = H(r_1) \oplus H(r_2) \oplus \cdots \oplus H(r_\lambda)$. *Output* e.

Theorem 6.2. *Construction 6.1 is a secure public key encryption scheme in the TS generic group model (and hence also in the RR model, by Theorem 3.5). However, Construction 6.1 is insecure in the standard model.*

Proof. We first show that the construction is correct and secure. Correctness is a straightforward adaptation of the correctness of ElGamal: $d_i = h^{r_i+m_i} = g^{\alpha r_i+\alpha m_i} = c_i^\alpha h^{m_i}$. Therefore $d_i = c_i^\alpha$ if and only if $m_i = 0$.

For security, we first show the following in the Full Version [Zha22]:

Lemma 6.3. *For any message m, the bit e is statistically close to a uniform random bit. Concretely,* $|\Pr[e = 0] - 1/2| \le 2^{-\lambda}$.

The proof idea is e is the XOR of many independent samples from the not-too-biased outputs of H. Lemma 6.3 above shows that an adversary cannot break Construction 6.1 just by looking at the bit e. We now expand this to consider general adversaries which also get c_i, d_i:

Lemma 6.4. *Construction 6.1 is secure in the TS generic group model.*

Lemma 6.4 is proved in the Full Version [Zha22]. There we give a simple proof that a TS model adversary essentially must break either the c_i, d_i, or the bit e, but gains no advantage by considering both together. c_i, d_i is just plain ElGamal, which hides the message; Lemma 6.3 shows that e hides the message as well.

Finally, we show that no matter how the group is instantiated, Construction 6.1 is insecure in the standard model

Lemma 6.5. *For any standard-model group, Construction 6.1 is insecure.*

Proof. Consider instantiating Construction 6.1 with an arbitrary standard model group scheme. Then consider the following adversary A.

- On input $\mathsf{pk} = (g, h)$, let ℓ be the bit-length of group elements.
- Choose a random $t \in \{0,1\}^\ell$, and construct the circuit $H(s) = \langle t, h^s \rangle$, where $\langle \cdot, \cdot \rangle$ denotes the inner product mod 2 of the bit string inputs.
- Send to the challenger the challenge messages $(m_0 = (0^\lambda, H), m_1 = (1^\lambda, H))$. Receive the ciphertext $c = (\{c_i, d_i\}_i, e)$.
- Output $e \oplus \langle t, d_1 \oplus \cdots \oplus d_\lambda \rangle$.

We now analyze A. First, since inner products are good extractors, H is balanced with overwhelming probability. Thus $e = H(r_1) \oplus H(r_2) \oplus \cdot \oplus H(r_\lambda)$.

Suppose c is an encryption of m_0. Then $\langle t, d_i \rangle = \langle t, h^{r_i} \rangle = H(r_i)$. Hence, with overwhelming probability, the output of A is exactly 0. Next suppose c is an encryption of m_1. Then $\langle t, d_i \rangle = \langle t, h^{r_i+1} \rangle$. Hence, if we define $W = (h^{r_1} \oplus h^{r_1+1}) \oplus \cdot \oplus (h^{r_\lambda} \oplus h^{r_\lambda+1})$, the output is equal to $\langle t, W \rangle$. The following is proved in the Full Version [Zha22]:

Lemma 6.6. $\Pr[W = 0] \le 1/2$.

Notice that t is independent from the r_i, and hence W. Hence, if $W \neq 0$, $\langle t, W \rangle$ is a uniform random bit. Therefore the output of A on m_1 is 1 with probability at least $1/4$, giving it a non-negligible advantage. $\square$

Putting together Lemmas 6.4 and 6.5 proves Theorem 6.2. $\square$

7 Impossibility of IBE from Generic Groups

Papakonstantinou, Rackoff, and Vahlis [PRV12] give an impossibility of identity-based encryption (IBE) from generic groups. The authors cite Shoup's model, and like Shoup they define the generic group model as a random mapping from $\mathbb{Z}_p$ into bit strings. However, we argue that their definitions and proofs actually lie somewhere between Shoup's and the Maurer/TS model. For example, consider their definition of a *generic algorithm* ([PRV12], page 6):

> A generic algorithm A is a probabilistic algorithm (or with randomness in its input) that takes inputs and produces outputs of the form $(w, g_1, \ldots, g_k) \in (\{0,1\}^* \times \mathbb{G}^k)$ for an arbitrary $k \in \mathbb{N}$. A is given oracle access to $\mathcal{O}$ restricted to sums that have non-zero coefficients only for the elements $g_1, \ldots, \gamma_k$.

Above, $\mathcal{O}$ is their notation for the oracle implementing the generic group. Requiring an algorithm to be explicitly given group elements as input, and then only allowing queries on linear combinations of those explicit group elements, is a TS-style restriction that is not present in the RR/Shoup model. Since all algorithms must declare the type of inputs they work on, this also means that the components of any cryptosystem (public keys, secret keys, ciphertexts, etc.) must explicitly delineate between group elements and bits, just as in the TS model.

This restriction on algorithms plays an important role in the impossibility proof. The proof of [PRV12] proceeds in two steps, where in the first step they compile a generic group IBE scheme into one where user secret keys do not contain any group elements. The second step is to show that such a restricted IBE cannot exist in the generic group model. Unfortunately, the distinction between user keys containing group elements or not, is only well-defined if the group elements of secret keys are explicitly labeled, as in the TS model. In the RR model, one could imagine trivially hiding group elements by, say, XORing them with an arbitrary string, or secret sharing into different pieces.

Digging deeper, the impossibility proof does the following many times: compute an encryption of a random message, and then promptly decrypt it, collecting all the queries made during the process. We observe that this process is *exactly* how verification works when compiling IBE to a signature scheme in the usual way. However, signatures were shown *impossible* in the TS model by [DHH21], who also runs the verification procedure many times to collect queries. But we know that signatures *are* possible in the RR model, so the impossibility of [DHH21] *only* applies in the TS model. Given these similarities between the impossibility proofs, together with the fact that [PRV12] imposes TS-like restrictions, it is unclear whether the IBE impossibility should extend to the full RR model.

A Full Impossibility. Here, we prove a full impossibility of IBE in the RR generic group model, resolving this gap. We first define IBE; we use a key encapsulation variant for simplicity, which is equivalent to the standard notion.

Definition 7.1. *An identity-based encryption (IBE) scheme consists of a tuple of efficient probabilistic algorithms* (Gen, Extract, Enc, Dec) *satisfying:*

- **Correctness:** *For all identities* id,
$$\Pr\left[\mathsf{Dec}(\mathsf{sk_{id}}, c) = k : \begin{smallmatrix}(\mathsf{msk},\mathsf{mpk})\leftarrow\mathsf{Gen}()\\ \mathsf{sk_{id}}\leftarrow\mathsf{Extract}(\mathsf{msk},\mathsf{id})\\ (c,k)\leftarrow\mathsf{Enc}(\mathsf{mpk},\mathsf{id})\end{smallmatrix}\right] \geq 1 - \mathsf{negl}.$$

- **Random Identity Security:** *Consider an adversary* A *playing the following game. The challenger first chooses a random* (msk, mpk) ← Gen(), *and chooses a random bit* $b \in \{0, 1\}$. *The challenger samples* $q + 1$ *random identities* $\mathsf{id}_1, \ldots, \mathsf{id}_q, \mathsf{id}^*$. *For* $i = 1, \ldots, q$, *is compute* $\mathsf{sk_{id}}_i \leftarrow \mathsf{Extract}(\mathsf{msk}, \mathsf{id}_i)$. *It also computes* $(c^*, k_0^*) \leftarrow \mathsf{Enc}(\mathsf{mpk}, \mathsf{id}^*)$ *and samples a uniform* k_1^*. *It sends* $\{\mathsf{id}_i, \mathsf{sk_{id}}_i\}_{i \in [q]}, c^*, k_b^*$ *to* A, *which outputs a guess* b' *for* b. *We require that, for all efficient* A *and polynomial* q, $\Pr[b' = b] \leq 1 + \mathsf{negl}$.

Theorem 7.2. *There is no random identity-secure IBE scheme in the RR model.*

Proof. Our proof, while different than [PRV12], will follow the same basic outline, though it will replace "secret keys contain no group elements" with a related restriction that is well-defined in the RR model. It will also clarify what about IBE makes it impossible in the RR model, where signatures are possible.

Concretely, we will define a type of *signature* scheme, where generic group queries during verification are independent of the signature (but dependent on the message and public key). Such a signature scheme is rather easily shown to be impossible, in *any* idealized model. This replaces the second part of the proof of [PRV12]. By using a simpler object (signatures instead of IBE) we are able to significantly simplify this part of the proof of [PRV12]. It also offers a clear explanation for the gap between general signatures and IBE in the generic group model, since general signatures will not have the special structure.

The bulk of the proof of Theorem 7.2 is showing that any IBE in the RR model can be compiled into such a restricted signature scheme. The idea is to view the IBE as a signature scheme, which is already well-known. However, the resulting signature scheme has a special structure: a first phase that is independent of the signature, and then a second phase that depends on the signature. Importantly, the second phase is decrypting a ciphertext produced in the first phase. We use the correctness of the IBE to argue we can compile out the queries made in the second phase; this compiling-out step crucially uses the linear structure of groups.

We now give the proof. We first define a *restricted signature scheme*:

Definition 7.3. *An restricted signature scheme (R-Sig) relative to an oracle* $\mathcal{O}$ *consists of a tuple of oracle algorithms* $(\mathsf{Gen}^{\mathcal{O}}, \mathsf{Sign}^{\mathcal{O}}, \mathsf{Ver}^{\mathcal{O}})$ *such that:*

- δ-**Correctness:** $\Pr\left[\mathsf{Ver}^{\mathcal{O}}(\mathsf{PK}, \sigma) = 1 : \begin{smallmatrix}M\leftarrow\$\\ (\mathsf{SK},\mathsf{PK})\leftarrow\mathsf{Gen}^{\mathcal{O}}()\\ \sigma\leftarrow\mathsf{Sign}^{\mathcal{O}}(\mathsf{SK},M)\end{smallmatrix}\right] \geq \delta.$

- **Restricted Structure:** $\text{Ver}^{\mathcal{O}}(\text{PK}, M, \sigma) = \text{Ver1}(\text{Ver0}^{\mathcal{O}}(\text{PK}, M), \sigma)$, where Ver1 is independent of $\mathcal{O}$, but Ver0 is independent of σ.
- **0-random message security:** For any query-bounded adversary A,

$$\Pr[\text{Ver}^{\mathcal{O}}(\text{PK}, M, \sigma) = 1 : \begin{array}{c} (\text{SK}, \text{PK}) \leftarrow \text{Gen}^{\mathcal{O}}() \\ M \leftarrow \$ \\ \sigma \leftarrow A^{\mathcal{O}}(\text{PK}, M) \end{array}] \text{ is negligible.}$$

Lemma 7.4. For any oracle $\mathcal{O}$ and any constant $\delta > 0$, R-Sigs do not exist.

Proof. Consider choosing an oracle $\mathcal{O}$, a random M, and $(\text{SK}, \text{PK}) \leftarrow \text{Gen}^{\mathcal{O}}()$, and then fixing them. We will say that σ is "good" if $\Pr[\text{Ver}^{\mathcal{O}}(\text{PK}, M, \sigma) = 1] \geq \delta/2$, where the probability is taken over the random coins of Ver. By correctness, with probability at least $\delta/2$ over $\mathcal{O}, M, \text{SK}, \text{PK}$, there will exist at least one good σ, namely the output of $\text{Sign}^{\mathcal{O}}(\text{SK}, M)$.

Suppose Ver0 was deterministic. Then we could compute $v \leftarrow \text{Ver0}^{\mathcal{O}}(\text{PK}, M)$, and consider the oracle-free probabilistic circuit $C(\sigma) = \text{Ver1}(v, \sigma)$. Then an input σ is good if and only if $C(\sigma)$ accepts with probability at least $\delta/2$. Since C is oracle-free, we can brute-force search for such a σ, finding it with probability at least $\delta/2$. The forgery will then be (M, σ), which is accepted by the challenger with probability $\delta/2$, giving an overall advantage $\delta^2/4$.

For a potentially randomized Ver1, we have to work slightly harder. For a good σ, we have that $\Pr_{v \leftarrow \text{Ver0}^{\mathcal{O}}(\text{PK},M)}[\Pr[\text{Ver1}(v, \sigma) = 1] \geq \delta/4] \geq \delta/4$. Meanwhile, we will call a σ "bad" if $\Pr_{v \leftarrow \text{Ver0}^{\mathcal{O}}(\text{PK},M)}[\Pr[\text{Ver1}(v, \sigma) = 1] \geq \delta/4] \leq \delta/8$.

For a parameter t chosen momentarily, we let $v_1, \ldots, v_t \leftarrow \text{Ver0}^{\mathcal{O}}(\text{PK}, M)$, and construct circuits $C_i(\sigma) = \text{Ver1}(v_i, \sigma)$. We then brute-force search for a σ such that $\Pr_{i \leftarrow [t]}[\Pr[C_i(\sigma) = 1] \geq \delta/4] \geq 3\delta/8$. By Hoeffding's inequality, any good σ will be a solution with probability $1 - 2^{\Omega(\delta^2 t)}$. Meanwhile, any bad σ will be a solution with probability $2^{-\Omega(\delta^2 t)}$. By setting t such that t/δ^2 is sufficiently longer than the bit-length of signatures, we can union bound over all bad σ, showing that there will be no bad solutions except with negligible probability. We will therefore find a not-bad solution with probability at least $\delta/2 - \text{negl} \geq \delta/3$. In this case, with probability at least $\delta/8$ over the choice of v by the verifier, $\Pr[\text{Ver1}(v, \sigma) = 1] \geq \delta/4$. Hence, the overall success probability is at least $(\delta/3) \times (\delta/8) \times (\delta/4) \geq \delta^3/100$. $\qquad\square$

Lemma 7.5. If there is an IBE scheme in the RR generic group model, then for any constant δ there exists a restricted signature scheme in the same model.

Proof. Let $(\text{Gen}^{\text{GRR}}, \text{Extract}^{\text{GRR}}, \text{Enc}^{\text{GRR}}, \text{Ver}^{\text{GRR}})$ be a supposed IBE scheme in the RR model. Now consider the following standard way of constructing a signature scheme from an IBE scheme:

- Key generation is simply Gen^{GRR}, with $\text{PK} = \text{mpk}$ and $\text{SK} = \text{msk}$.
- $\text{Sign}^{\text{GRR}}(\text{SK}, M) = \text{Extract}^{\text{GRR}}(\text{SK}, M)$, where M is interpreted as an identity.
- $\text{Ver}^{\text{GRR}}(\text{PK}, M, \sigma)$: Run $(c, k) \leftarrow \text{Enc}^{\text{GRR}}(\text{PK}, M)$, where again M is interpreted as an identity, and output 1 if and only if $\text{Dec}^{\text{GRR}}(\sigma, c) = k$.

Notice that (Gen, Sign, Ver) almost already is restricted: $\text{Ver}^{\mathbb{G}_{\text{RR}}}(\text{PK}, M, \sigma) = \text{Ver1}^{\mathbb{G}_{\text{RR}}}(\text{Ver0}^{\mathbb{G}_{\text{RR}}}(\text{PK}, M), \sigma)$ where $\text{Ver0}^{\mathbb{G}_{\text{RR}}}(\text{PK}, M)$ outputs $v = (c, k) \leftarrow \text{Enc}(\text{PK}, \text{id})$ while $\text{Ver1}^{\mathbb{G}_{\text{RR}}}(v, \sigma)$ checks that $\text{Dec}^{\mathbb{G}_{\text{RR}}}(\sigma, c) = k$.

The problem, of course, is that Ver1 likely makes queries to $\mathbb{G}_{\text{RR}}$, so does not have the required structure. We will therefore need to show how to compile out $\mathbb{G}_{\text{RR}}$ from Ver1, which we do in the Full Version [Zha22]. The idea is to provide Ver1 some extra hints (through both v and PK) to help it answer the queries. First, any query made during Ver0 is provided in v. Second, during setup, we choose many random messages, which we sign and verify, collecting all queries made during the verification process (both Ver0 and Ver1). We provide these queries in PK. Then Ver1 answers its queries by seeing if the query is in the span of the various queries it has available through v and PK. If so, it knows how to correctly answer the query. If not, it answers with a random label.

By standard arguments, we show that the only way Ver1 can answer incorrectly is if a query corresponds to a "new" equation over labels seen during Gen. By increasing the number of sign/verify trials during setup, we expand the span of queries provided in PK. Since there are only a polynomial number of queries during Gen, we can set the number of trials large enough to ensure any arbitrarily small inverse polynomial correctness error. □

Combining Lemmas 7.4 and 7.5, we therefore prove Theorem 7.2. □

8   On the Algebraic Group Model

Here, we discuss the Algebraic Group Model (AGM) of Fuchsbauer, Kiltz, and Loss [FKL18]. The AGM is proposed as a model lying between the standard and generic group models, striking a compromise between the wide applicability of generic groups and the security conferred by a standard-model proof. For these reasons, the AGM has become a popular model for proving security (e.g. [GRWZ20, BFL20, KLX20, BDFG20, GT21]).

In the AGM, adversaries can see the actual standard model group representation without any type-system constraints. They can therefore perform arbitrary standard-model computations on these elements. However, any time the adversary outputs a group element h, it must "explain" that element, by outputting a vector $\mathbf{a}$ such that $h = \prod_i g_i^{a_i}$, where g_i are the input group elements. Because the adversary has unfettered access to the group representation, security cannot hold unconditionally; instead, security is proven by a reduction transforming an algebraic adversary into an algorithm for a hard problem, typically discrete log.

8.1   Allowed Games in the AGM

One wrinkle discussed in [FKL18] is that, without further constraints, the model is trivially invalid. Suppose the experiment provides the adversary a group element h, but implicitly encoded as a string s by, say, by flipping every bit in the representation of h. Then the adversary can turn around and output h (by flipping all the bits back), but it would have no way of producing a representation of h without solving the discrete log of h. [FKL18] suggest the following resolution:

> We therefore demand that non-group-element inputs must not depend on group elements.

This demand, however, is never formalized. Fortunately, we can see that the Type Safe mode readily captures the desired intuition. After all, the TS model distinguishes between group and non-group elements, and the type safety guarantee means that once a group element is obtained, nothing can be done with it except for generating new group elements and equality gates. Since equality gates do not depend on the group element itself but just the exponent, no information about the group element can be extracted into bit wires.

We therefore propose that the AGM is restricted to TS model games. In the Full Version [Zha22], we offer a formal definition of the AGM.

8.2 AGM Un-instantiability

We now give an construction of a one-time MAC that is secure in the AGM, but insecure in the standard model, resolving an open question from [FKL18]. This result also gives an un-instantiability result for the TS model, which is simpler but somewhat more contrived. We note that our PKE scheme from Sect. 6 does *not* demonstrate anything about the AGM, since the adversary is not asked to produce any group elements. As such, for the PKE scheme, the AGM is actually *equivalent* to the standard model and hence the scheme is insecure in the AGM.

Definition 8.1. *A one-time message authentication code (MAC) is a triple of PPT algorithms* (Gen, MAC, Ver) *where:*

- **Correctness:** $\forall m,\ \Pr[\mathsf{Ver}(k, m, \sigma) = 1 : \substack{k \leftarrow \mathsf{Gen}() \\ \sigma \leftarrow \mathsf{MAC}(k,m)}] \geq 1 - \mathsf{negl}$
- **Security:** *For any adversary* A, *there exists a negligible* negl *such that* A *wins the following game with probability at most* negl: *First* A *produces a message m; in response it receives $\sigma \leftarrow \mathsf{MAC}(k, m)$ for a random key k; finally it outputs $m^* \neq m$ and σ^*. It wins if* $\mathsf{Ver}(k, m^*, \sigma^*) = 1$.

Note we require MACs for *unbounded-length* messages. Such one-time MACs can readily be built unconditionally. We now give our counter-example:

Construction 8.2. *Let* (Gen', MAC', Ver') *be an unconditional one-time MAC. We construct a new MAC* (Gen, MAC, Ver) *using a group* $\mathbb{G}$. *We assume elements in* $\mathbb{G}$ *have bit-length* $\log_2 p$; *we can easily extend to general* $\mathbb{G}$. *We will assume* $\mathbb{G}$ *comes with two generators* g, h, *with the discrete log between them unknown[4].*

---

[4] g, h could be created by Gen, but we would need to get g, h to the adversary before the first query. We could consider a 1-time signature, where g, h would be included in the public key. Alternatively, we could consider a 2-time MAC, which includes g, h as part of each MAC, giving the adversary g, h in time for the second query.

- Gen(): *run* $k' \leftarrow$ Gen'() *and sample* $\gamma, \delta \leftarrow \mathbb{Z}_p$. *Output* $k = (k', \gamma, \delta)$.
- MAC(k, m): *first run* $\sigma' \leftarrow$ MAC'(k', m). *Then interpret* m *as a function* H *whose output length is* $\log_2 p$ *bits. Compute* $u = H(\gamma, \delta)$. *Output* $\sigma = (\sigma', u, g)$.
- Ver(k, m, σ): *First run* Ver(k', m, σ'). *If it accepts, also accept. Otherwise, write* $\sigma = (\sigma', u, w)$. *Check if* $w = g^\gamma h^\delta$. *If so, accept. Otherwise, reject.*

Theorem 8.3. *Construction 8.2 is a secure one-time MAC in the AGM under the discrete log assumption, but insecure under any instantiation of the group.*

Proof. We start with standard-model insecurity. We query on the m which will be interpreted as the function $H(\gamma, \delta) = g^\gamma h^\delta$. In the resulting signature, u therefore gives $g^\gamma h^\delta$. It can then sign any message with the signature $(*, *, u)$.

For AGM security, consider an adversary A breaking security in the AGM. Let m^* be the message it forges, and $\sigma^* = (\sigma', u^*, w^*)$ be the forgery. By the one-time security of (Gen', MAC', Ver'), we know that the only way for this signature to pass verification is for $w^* = g^\gamma h^\delta$. Since A is algebraic, and only previously received two group elements g, h (u was provided as bits), it must therefore explain w^* by producing α, β such that $w^* = g^\alpha h^\beta$. There are two cases:

- $(\alpha, \beta) \neq (\gamma, \delta)$. Then we can use the adversary to solve the discrete log of h relative to g, contradicting the assumed hardness of discrete logarithms.
- $(\alpha, \beta) = (\gamma, \delta)$. But γ, δ are random strings of total length $2\log_2 p$, and the adversary only gets at most $\log_2 p$ bits of information about them, namely the output of H. And yet the adversary is somehow able to recover all $2\log_2 p$ bits. This violates the incompressibility of random strings.

$\square$

8.3   Is the AGM Superior to Generic Groups?

Since the AGM requires TS games, it is in some ways inferior to the RR model. From now on, we will therefore compare to the TS model. We now argue, however, that even though the AGM is "between" the standard and TS models, this does not necessarily demonstrate the AGM to be advantageous to generic groups. We consider two possible perspectives in which to compare the models.

Attack-Oriented Perspective. From an "attack-oriented" perspective, the AGM captures a wider class of attacks than generic groups. In this sense, the model offers a clear advantage when applied to the multiplicative groups over finite fields. The best attacks on such groups are index calculus attacks, which are captured by the AGM but not generic groups.

However, we note that some groups are not susceptible to index calculus attacks. Concretely, elliptic curves without efficient pairings are not, and this is exactly the reason why these curves are often conjectured to have optimal 128-bit security with groups of size 2^{256}. In fact, essentially the only known attacks on elliptic curves are either generic, rely on a pairing, or the contrived counter-examples to generic groups such as [Den02]. For these groups, there are no known algebraic-but-non-generic adversaries, so it is not obvious that the AGM captures a wider class of adversaries. Thus while not worse than the TS generic group model, it seems that the AGM does not offer significant advantages for pairing-free elliptic curves for this perspective either.

Security Prediction Perspective. Another perspective is that a model is about making predictions about security. For any game (p, Ch) and group $\mathbb{G}$, the standard, algebraic, and TS models will each make a decision about whether the game is hard. The standard model is the ground truth, but it may be infeasible to actually know if a game is secure or not in this model. The algebraic and TS models can be seen as predictions about this ground truth that are easier to reason about by giving more power to the prover, but they will have false-positives.

   We now argue that existing work does not demonstrate any benefits of the AGM from this perspective. Concretely, looking at the AGM literature, we can break the known games into two cases:

– Those in which the AGM is trivially equivalent to the standard model. These are cases like public key encryption where the game does not ask for any group elements from the adversary and so the AGM imposes no restrictions over the standard model.
– Those in which the security holds in the AGM if and only if it also holds in the TS model. These include Construction 8.2 and all the positive results about the AGM, as well as trivially easy games in the TS model.

Thus, amongst known games, the AGM offers little predictive power for which games should be secure: in the first case we just stick with the standard model, and in the second case we can just stick with the TS model. So despite having fewer false positives, once we condition on the game, the known examples do not demonstrate any predictive advantages of the AGM over the existing models.

   Note that this does not mean the AGM does not offer any predictive advantages, just that the current evidence does not support advantages from this perspective. We leave demonstrating such an advantage, or proving that one cannot exist, as an interesting question for future work.

References

[AY20]   Agrawal, S., Yamada, S.: Optimal Broadcast Encryption from Pairings and LWE. In: Canteaut, A., Ishai, Y. (eds.) EUROCRYPT 2020, Part I. LNCS, vol. 12105, pp. 13–43. Springer, Cham (2020). https://doi.org/10.1007/978-3-030-45721-1_2
[BBO07] Bellare, M., Boldyreva, A., O'Neill, A.: Deterministic and efficiently searchable encryption. In: Menezes, A. (ed.) CRYPTO 2007. LNCS, vol. 4622, pp. 535–552. Springer, Heidelberg (2007). https://doi.org/10.1007/978-3-540-74143-5_30
[BBP04] Bellare, M., Boldyreva, A., Palacio, A.: An uninstantiable random-oracle-model scheme for a hybrid-encryption problem. In: Cachin, C., Camenisch, J.L. (eds.) EUROCRYPT 2004. LNCS, vol. 3027, pp. 171–188. Springer, Heidelberg (2004). https://doi.org/10.1007/978-3-540-24676-3_11

[BCFG17] Baltico, C.E.Z., Catalano, D., Fiore, D., Gay, R.: Practical functional encryption for quadratic functions with applications to predicate encryption. In: Katz, J., Shacham, H. (eds.) CRYPTO 2017, Part I. LNCS, vol. 10401, pp. 67–98. Springer, Cham (2017). https://doi.org/10.1007/978-3-319-63688-7_3

[BCPR14] Bitansky, N., Canetti, R., Paneth, O., Rosen, A.: On the existence of extractable one-way functions. In: Shmoys, D.B. (ed.) 46th ACM STOC, pp. 505–514. ACM Press (2014)

[BDFG20] Boneh, D., Drake, J., Fisch, B., Gabizon, A.: Efficient polynomial commitment schemes for multiple points and polynomials. Cryptology ePrint Archive, Report 2020/081 (2020). https://eprint.iacr.org/2020/081

[BFF14] Barthe, G., Fagerholm, E., Fiore, D., Mitchell, J., Scedrov, A., Schmidt, B.: Automated analysis of cryptographic assumptions in generic group models. In: Garay, J.A., Gennaro, R. (eds.) CRYPTO 2014, Part I. LNCS, vol. 8616, pp. 95–112. Springer, Heidelberg (2014). https://doi.org/10.1007/978-3-662-44371-2_6

[BFL20] Bauer, B., Fuchsbauer, G., Loss, J.: A classification of computational assumptions in the algebraic group model. In: Micciancio, D., Ristenpart, T. (eds.) CRYPTO 2020, Part II. LNCS, vol. 12171, pp. 121–151. Springer, Cham (2020). https://doi.org/10.1007/978-3-030-56880-1_5

[BFM15] Brzuska, C., Farshim, P., Mittelbach, A.: Random-oracle uninstantiability from indistinguishability obfuscation. In: Dodis, Y., Nielsen, J.B. (eds.) TCC 2015, Part II. LNCS, vol. 9015, pp. 428–455. Springer, Heidelberg (2015). https://doi.org/10.1007/978-3-662-46497-7_17

[BL22] Blocki, J., Lee, S.: On the multi-user security of short Schnorr signatures with preprocessing. In: Dunkelman, O., Dziembowski, S. (eds.) EUROCRYPT 2022, Part II, volume 13276 of LNCS, pp. 614–643. Springer, Heidelberg (2022)

[BM82] Blum, M., Micali, S.: How to generate cryptographically strong sequences of pseudo random bits. In: 23rd FOCS, pp. 112–117. IEEE Computer Society Press (1982)

[CGH98] Canetti, R., Goldreich, O., Halevi, S.: The random oracle methodology, revisited (preliminary version). In: 30th ACM STOC, pp. 209–218. ACM Press (1998)

[CH20] Couteau, G., Hartmann, D.: Shorter non-interactive zero-knowledge arguments and ZAPs for algebraic languages. In: Micciancio, D., Ristenpart, T. (eds.) CRYPTO 2020, Part III. LNCS, vol. 12172, pp. 768–798. Springer, Cham (2020). https://doi.org/10.1007/978-3-030-56877-1_27

[CK18] Corrigan-Gibbs, H., Kogan, D.: The discrete-logarithm problem with preprocessing. In: Nielsen, J.B., Rijmen, V. (eds.) EUROCRYPT 2018, Part II. LNCS, vol. 10821, pp. 415–447. Springer, Cham (2018). https://doi.org/10.1007/978-3-319-78375-8_14

[CL20] Chiesa, A., Liu, S.: On the impossibility of probabilistic proofs in relativized worlds. In: Vidick, T. (ed.) ITCS 2020, vol. 151, pp. 57:1–57:30; LIPIcs (2020)

[Den02] Dent, A.W.: Adapting the weaknesses of the random oracle model to the generic group model. In: Zheng, Y. (ed.) ASIACRYPT 2002. LNCS, vol. 2501, pp. 100–109. Springer, Heidelberg (2002). https://doi.org/10.1007/3-540-36178-2_6

[DG17]   Döttling, N., Garg, S.: Identity-based encryption from the Diffie-Hellman assumption. In: Katz, J., Shacham, H. (eds.) CRYPTO 2017, Part I. LNCS, vol. 10401, pp. 537–569. Springer, Cham (2017). https://doi.org/10.1007/978-3-319-63688-7_18

[DHH21] Döttling, N., Hartmann, D., Hofheinz, D., Kiltz, E., Schäge, S., Ursu, B.: On the impossibility of purely algebraic signatures. Cryptology ePrint Archive, Report 2021/738 (2021). https://eprint.iacr.org/2021/738

[Fis00] Fischlin, M.: A note on security proofs in the generic model. In: Okamoto, T. (ed.) ASIACRYPT 2000. LNCS, vol. 1976, pp. 458–469. Springer, Heidelberg (2000). https://doi.org/10.1007/3-540-44448-3_35

[FKL18] Fuchsbauer, G., Kiltz, E., Loss, J.: The algebraic group model and its applications. In: Shacham, H., Boldyreva, A. (eds.) CRYPTO 2018. Part II, LNCS, vol. 10992, pp. 33–62. Springer, Cham (2018). https://doi.org/10.1007/978-3-319-96881-0_2

[GGM84] Goldreich, O., Goldwasser, S., Micali, S.: How to construct random functions (extended abstract). In: 25th FOCS, pp. 464–479. IEEE Computer Society Press (1984)

[GK03]   Goldwasser, S., Kalai, Y.T.: On the (in)security of the Fiat-Shamir paradigm. In: 44th FOCS, pp. 102–115. IEEE Computer Society Press (2003)

[GRWZ20] Gorbunov, S., Reyzin, L., Wee, H., Zhang, Z.: Pointproofs: aggregating proofs for multiple vector commitments. In: Ligatti, J., Ou, X., Katz, J., Vigna, G. (eds.) ACM CCS 2020, pp. 2007–2023. ACM Press (2020)

[GT21]   Ghoshal, A., Tessaro, S.: Tight state-restoration soundness in the algebraic group model. In: Malkin, T., Peikert, C. (eds.) CRYPTO 2021, Part III. LNCS, vol. 12827, pp. 64–93. Springer, Cham (2021). https://doi.org/10.1007/978-3-030-84252-9_3

[IR89]   Impagliazzo, R., Rudich, S.: Limits on the provable consequences of one-way permutations. In: 21st ACM STOC, pp. 44–61. ACM Press (1989)

[JS08]   Jager, T., Schwenk, J.: On the equivalence of generic group models. In: Baek, J., Bao, F., Chen, K., Lai, X. (eds.) ProvSec 2008. LNCS, vol. 5324, pp. 200–209. Springer, Heidelberg (2008). https://doi.org/10.1007/978-3-540-88733-1_14

[KLX20] Katz, J., Loss, J., Xu, J.: On the security of time-lock puzzles and timed commitments. In: Pass, R., Pietrzak, K. (eds.) TCC 2020, Part III. LNCS, vol. 12552, pp. 390–413. Springer, Cham (2020). https://doi.org/10.1007/978-3-030-64381-2_14

[KM06]   Koblitz, N., Menezes, A.: Another look at generic groups. Cryptology ePrint Archive, Report 2006/230 (2006). https://eprint.iacr.org/2006/230

[Mau05] Maurer, U.: Abstract models of computation in cryptography. In: Smart, N.P. (ed.) Cryptography and Coding 2005. LNCS, vol. 3796, pp. 1–12. Springer, Heidelberg (2005). https://doi.org/10.1007/11586821_1

[Mic94] Micali, S.: CS proofs (extended abstracts). In: 35th FOCS, pp. 436–453. IEEE Computer Society Press (1994)

[MPZ20] Maurer, U., Portmann, C., Zhu, J.: Unifying generic group models. Cryptology ePrint Archive, Report 2020/996 (2020). https://eprint.iacr.org/2020/996

[Nec94] Nechaev, V.I.: Complexity of a determinate algorithm for the discrete logarithm. Math. Notes 55(2), 165–172 (1994)

[Nie02] Nielsen, J.B.: Separating random oracle proofs from complexity theoretic proofs: the non-committing encryption case. In: Yung, M. (ed.) CRYPTO 2002. LNCS, vol. 2442, pp. 111–126. Springer, Heidelberg (2002). https://doi.org/10.1007/3-540-45708-9_8

[NR97] Naor, M., Reingold, O.: Number-theoretic constructions of efficient pseudo-random functions. In: 38th FOCS, pp. 458–467. IEEE Computer Society Press (1997)

[PRV12] Papakonstantinou, P.A., Rackoff, C.W., Vahlis, Y.: How powerful are the DDH hard groups? Cryptology ePrint Archive, Report 2012/653 (2012). https://eprint.iacr.org/2012/653

[Rom90] Rompel, J.: One-way functions are necessary and sufficient for secure signatures. In: 22nd ACM STOC, pp. 387–394. ACM Press (1990)

[RSS20] Rotem, L., Segev, G., Shahaf, I.: Generic-group delay functions require hidden-order groups. In: Canteaut, A., Ishai, Y. (eds.) EUROCRYPT 2020, Part III. LNCS, vol. 12107, pp. 155–180. Springer, Cham (2020). https://doi.org/10.1007/978-3-030-45727-3_6

[SGS20] Schul-Ganz, G., Segev, G.: Accumulators in (and beyond) generic groups: non-trivial batch verification requires interaction. In: Pass, R., Pietrzak, K. (eds.) TCC 2020, Part II. LNCS, vol. 12551, pp. 77–107. Springer, Cham (2020). https://doi.org/10.1007/978-3-030-64378-2_4

[SGS21] Schul-Ganz, G., Segev, G.: Generic-group identity-based encryption: a tight impossibility result. In: Information Theoretic Cryptography (2021)

[Sho97] Shoup, V.: Lower bounds for discrete logarithms and related problems. In: Fumy, W. (ed.) EUROCRYPT 1997. LNCS, vol. 1233, pp. 256–266. Springer, Heidelberg (1997). https://doi.org/10.1007/3-540-69053-0_18

[Wat09] Waters, B.: Dual system encryption: realizing fully secure IBE and HIBE under simple assumptions. In: Halevi, S. (ed.) CRYPTO 2009. LNCS, vol. 5677, pp. 619–636. Springer, Heidelberg (2009). https://doi.org/10.1007/978-3-642-03356-8_36

[Zha22] Zhandry, M.: To label, or not to label (in generic groups). Cryptology ePrint Archive, Report 2022/226 (2022). https://eprint.iacr.org/2022/226

[ZZ18] Zhandry, M., Zhang, C.: Impossibility of order-revealing encryption in idealized models. In: Beimel, A., Dziembowski, S. (eds.) TCC 2018, Part II. LNCS, vol. 11240, pp. 129–158. Springer, Cham (2018). https://doi.org/10.1007/978-3-030-03810-6_5

[ZZ21] Zhandry, M., Zhang, C.: The relationship between idealized models under computationally bounded adversaries. Cryptology ePrint Archive, Report 2021/240 (2021). https://ia.cr/2021/240

Lower Bound on SNARGs in the Random Oracle Model

Iftach Haitner[1], Daniel Nukrai[1], and Eylon Yogev[2]($\boxtimes$)

[1] Tel-Aviv University, Tel Aviv, Israel
iftachh@tauex.tau.ac.il, daniel.nukrai@cs.tau.ac.il
[2] Bar-Ilan University, Ramat Gan, Israel
eylon.yogev@biu.ac.il

Abstract. Succinct non-interactive arguments (SNARGs) have become a fundamental primitive in the cryptographic community. The focus of this work is constructions of SNARGs in the Random Oracle Model (ROM). Such SNARGs enjoy post-quantum security and can be deployed using lightweight cryptography to heuristically instantiate the random oracle. A ROM-SNARG is (t, ε)-*sound* if no t-query malicious prover can convince the verifier to accept a false statement with probability larger than ε. Recently, Chiesa-Yogev (CRYPTO '21) presented a ROM-SNARG of length $\Theta(\log(t/\varepsilon) \cdot \log t)$ (ignoring $\log n$ factors, for n being the instance size). This improvement, however, is still far from the (folklore) lower bound of $\Omega(\log(t/\varepsilon))$.

Assuming the *randomized exponential-time hypothesis*, we prove a tight lower bound of $\Omega(\log(t/\varepsilon) \cdot \log t)$ for the length of (t, ε)-sound ROM-SNARGs. Our lower bound holds for constructions with non-adaptive verifiers and strong soundness notion called *salted soundness*, restrictions that hold for *all* known constructions (ignoring contrived counterexamples). We prove our lower bound by transforming any short ROM-SNARG (of the considered family) into a same length ROM-SNARG in which the verifier asks only a *few* oracles queries, and then apply the recent lower bound of Chiesa-Yogev (TCC '20) for such SNARGs.

Keywords: Random oracle · SNARGs · high-entropy sets · lower bound

1 Introduction

Constructions in the *random oracle model* (ROM) have shaped our understanding of the cryptographic world. Being a simple information-theoretic model, the ROM was found to be a very useful framework for understanting what can be done (sometimes only heuristically), and what is unlikely to be achieved using (merely) *symmetric-key* cryptography. A notable example for the above is *key-agreement* protocols. Merkle [Mer82] has constructed a key-agreement protocol in the ROM with a quadratic gap between the query complexity of the players and the eavesdropper. Barak and Mahmoody-Ghidary [BM17], building on the

© International Association for Cryptologic Research 2022
Y. Dodis and T. Shrimpton (Eds.): CRYPTO 2022, LNCS 13509, pp. 97–127, 2022.
https://doi.org/10.1007/978-3-031-15982-4_4

seminal work of Impagliazzo and Rudich [IR89], proved that the quadratic gap achieved by [Mer82] is optimal, and Haitner, Mazor, Oshman, Reingold, and Yehudayoff [HMORY19], showed that for a large family of constructions, the communication complexity of [Mer82] is optimal.

Another primitive whose constructions in the ROM have high impact is *Succinct Non-interactive Argument systems* (SNARGs): non-interactive computationally sound proofs (arguments) for NP of *succinct* proof length (sublinear in the instance length). The first construction of SNARGs was given by Micali [Mic00] in the ROM. This feasibility result turned out to be very influential both theoretically and practically. In theory, it was shown how to instantiate SNARGs in the *standard model* for many languages of interest by instantiating the Fiat and Shamir [FS86] paradigm with a specific family of hash functions [CCHLRR18]. In practice, the succinctness of the proof is imperative in applications such as cryptocurrency and blockchain, where proofs are broadcast in a peer-to-peer network and (redundantly) stored at every network node, c.f., [BCGGMTV14, Zc14]. As such, improving the concrete efficiency of SNARGs is the focus of long line of work c.f., [Gro16, ZGKPP17, AHIV17, BBHR19, WTSTW18, BBBPWM18, BCRSVW19, CHMMVW20, BFS20, COS20, Sta18, LSTW21, CY21b, CY21a, GNS21].

ROM-SNARGs, like the one of [Mic00], have several attractive features. First, to date, they are the most efficient approach for post-quantum security with public verification (i.e., the verifier has no secrets). Moreover, from a practical perspective, one can heuristically instantiate the random oracle with a suitable cryptographic hash function. The result is a SNARG that uses lightweight cryptography (no need for public-key primitives), is easy to deploy (users only need to agree on a hash function), and has no trusted setup. The best ROM-SNARG appeared in the recent work of Chiesa and Yogev [CY21a], who constructed a (t, ε)-sound ROM-SNARG of proof length of $O(\log(t/\varepsilon) \cdot \log t \cdot \log n)$, where n is the instance length. A ROM-SNARG is (t, ε)-*sound* if no t-queries (malicious) prover can convince the verifier to accept a false statement with probability larger than ε.[1]

Interestingly, and in contrast to other important primitives such as key-agreement protocols [IR89, HMORY19] and digital signatures [GGKT05, BMG07], we are lacking crucial lower bounds on the length of SNARGs in the ROM. Apart from the weak (folklore) lower bound of $\Omega(\log(t/\varepsilon))$ (which appears in the full version of the paper), the only exception is the recent bound of Chiesa and Yogev [CY20], who proved that the verifier query complexity of SNARGs cannot be too small. However, their bound does not rule out short ROM-SNARGs with verifier query complexity $\Omega(\log 1/\varepsilon)$, which is common for SNARG constructions.

This state-of-affairs naturally leads to the question of finding the shortest ROM-SNARG. Is it $O(\log(t/\varepsilon) \cdot \log t \cdot \log n)$, as the best-known construction achieve, or is it as short as $O(\log(t/\varepsilon) \cdot \log n)$, as achieved in other security

---

[1] We focus on the *bare* ROM— no computational assumptions are made beyond bounding the query complexity to the oracle.

models (see Sect. 1.2.2). In this work, we advance our understanding about the existence of short ROM-SNARGs (with *arbitrary* verifier query complexity).

1.1 Our Results

Assuming the *(randomized) exponential time hypothesis (rETH)*, see details below, we prove that for a large family of constructions, the current state-of-the art ROM-SNARG is (essentially) *optimal*. Specifically, we show that, for this family of constructions, a proof of 3SAT over n variables is of length $\tilde{\Omega}(\log(t/\varepsilon) \cdot \log t)$ (hiding $\log n$ factors). Matching (up to $\log n$ factors) the construction of the [CY21a]. The family of constructions we consider includes all constructions that have: (i) *non-adaptive* verifier and (ii) *salted soundness*. This includes *all types of constructions* we are aware of [Mic00, BCS16, CY21b, CY21a]). See details below.

- **Exponential time hypothesis.** The (randomized) Exponential Time Hypothesis (rETH) is a stronger version $P \neq NP$ that states that solving 3SAT on n variables takes (randomized) time $2^{\Omega(n)}$. Note that some complexity assumption is inevitable for proving lower bounds on a SNARGs length.[2]
- **Non-adaptive verifier.** The oracle queries are asked by a non-adaptive (deterministic[3]) verifier. That is, the queries are a function of the proof and are *independent* of the answers to other queries.[4]
- **Salted soundness.** This is a natural strengthening of the standard soundness of SNARG, which was introduced in Chiesa and Yogev [CY20]. A (t, ε)-salted-soundness ROM-SNARG allows a cheating prover to request the random oracle to re-sample the answer for a chosen query (similar to changing a "salt" for this query). Each re-sampling costs a unit from the total t query budget allowed. The cheating prover can also return to previously sampled query answers at no cost.[5]
  While one can easily construct contrived ROM-SNARGs for which salted soundness does not hold, we are not aware of any ROM-SNARG that exploits the fact that the prover cannot resample some of the oracle answers in a meaningful way. All constructions we are aware of satisfy salted soundness.[6]

---

[2] This follows since $P = NP$ yields trivial SNARGs for all NP.

[3] If the verifier is "public-coin" then it can be made deterministic by extracting randomness from the random oracle. However, this makes the verifier *adaptive* and thus cannot be used for our lower bound.

[4] We mention that SNARGs resulting from applying the Fiat and Shamir [FS86] paradigm on interactive proofs do *not* require an adaptive verifier, as the queries added by the compilation are determined by the proof (i.e., transcript) sent by the non-adaptive prover.

[5] Our notion of salted soundness is a strengthening of the salted-soundness notion considered in Chiesa and Yogev [CY20]. There, the cheating prover has to decide on a salt for a specific query *before* moving to the next one. See details in Sect. 3.5.1.

[6] See the analysis given in [CY21b] and in [CY21a], which explicitly allowed the adversary to choose a salt for each query in the construction (e.g., see remark 3.2 in [CY21b]).

With these notions, we are ready to state our main result.(The precise statements of the following results are given in the main body of the paper, see Paper Organization for references.)

Theorem 1 (Conditional lower bound on ROM-SNARG length. Informal). *Let* $\mathsf{ARG} = (\mathsf{P},\mathsf{V})$ *be an* s*-length ROM-SNARG for* n*-variable 3SAT, with* (t,ε)*-salted-soundness, perfect completeness, and (deterministic) non-adaptive verifier. Let* $\mathsf{q_P}$ *and* $\mathsf{q_V}$ *be the query complexity of* P *and* V*, respectively, and let* λ *denote the random oracle input and output length.*

Assuming rETH, if $\mathsf{q_V} \cdot \lambda \in o(n)$*, and* $\log^2(t/\varepsilon) \cdot \log^{-1}\mathsf{q_P} \in o(n)$ *then* $\mathsf{s} \geq c \cdot \log t \cdot \log \frac{t}{\varepsilon} \cdot \log^{-1}\mathsf{q_P}$*, for some universal constant* $c > 0$.

We argue that the assumptions on the parameters regime in our theorem are reasonable and consider the most interesting settings (see Theorem 13 for the precise list of requirements). The goal of a SNARG is to have the proof length and the verifier complexity be much smaller than the instance size n. Usually, proportional to $\mathrm{poly}(\lambda, \log n)$. Thus, our assumption that $\mathsf{q_V} \cdot \lambda$, and $\log t \cdot \log \frac{t}{\varepsilon}/\log \mathsf{q_P}$ are of order $o(n)$ is rather mild. The third requirement of $\mathsf{q_V} \leq t^{1/10}$ is almost trivial. It says that the query complexity of the verifier is much smaller than the query bound t of the *adversary*, which is very much expected from any reasonable SNARG.

The proof of Theorem 1 immediately follows by combing the following lemma with the recent lower bound of Chiesa and Yogev [CY20] on the length ROM-SNARG with low query-complexity verifiers.

Lemma 1 (Short ROM-SNARG → low query ROM-SNARG. Informal). *Let* $\mathsf{ARG} = (\mathsf{P},\mathsf{V})$ *be a ROM-SNARG for a language* $\mathcal{L}$ *with a deterministic non-adaptive verifier and* (t,ε)*-salted-soundness, perfect completeness, proof length* s*, and verifier query complexity* $\mathsf{q_V}$*. Then there exists a verifier* V' *of query complexity* $\mathsf{s}/\log t$*, running time* $2^{\mathsf{q_V} \cdot \log t}$ *times that of* V*, such that* (P,V') *is a ROM-SNARG for* $\mathcal{L}$ *with* (t,ε)*-soundness and completeness* $\omega(\varepsilon)$.

That is, the larger the salted-soundness of ARG, the smaller the number of queries made by V', and the better the completeness. While the completeness and verifier running time of the resulting scheme are rather poor, and we do not encourage to use it as an actual proof system, it is still non-trivial for the parameters in consideration: V' running time is $2^{o(n)}$, for n being the instance length, and the completeness is larger than the soundness error. By [CY20], the existence of such ROM-SNARG for 3SAT contradicts rETH.

Using similar means, we can compile ARG into $(\mathsf{P}',\mathsf{V}')$, with (almost) perfect completeness, but with inefficient prover and slightly longer proof (see details in Sect. 2). Since this transformation does not yield better lower bounds, and the resulting scheme is impractical, we present the simpler transformation above.

Lower bound on the length of ROM subvector commitments. A *subvector commitment* (SVC) [LM19] allows to succinctly commit to a sequence of values, and later open the commitment for a *subset* of positions (an adversary cannot open any location into two different values). Ideally, the commitment string and the opening size of the SVC are *independent* (or at least not strongly related) of the length of the committed vector and the number of positions to open. This generalization of *vector commitments* [CF13] has a variety of applications, including SNARGs, *verifiable databases with efficient updates, updatable zero-knowledge databases, universal dynamic accumulators*, and more. Since SVCs in the (bare) ROM are the main building blocks in all ROM-SNARGs constructions, finding shorter ROM-SVCs is the obvious approach towards construction shorter ROM-SNARGs. For this very reason, Theorem 1 yields a lower bound on ROM-SVCs for an analog family of constructions: non-adapter receiver and salted-binding (i.e., the sender can resample the oracle outputs).

Theorem 2 (Conditional lower bound on the length of ROM subvector commitments. Informal). *Let* CM *be a* (t, ε)-*salted-sound, non-adaptive (deterministic) verification ROM-SVC for vectors of length* n. *Let* $\mathsf{q_S}$ *and* $\mathsf{q_R}$ *be the query complexity of the sender and receiver, respectively. Let* α *denote the commitment length, and* $\beta(\ell)$ *denote the opening length for subsets of size* ℓ.

Assuming rETH, if $\mathsf{q_R} \cdot \lambda \in o(n)$, *and* $\log^2(t/\varepsilon) \cdot \log^{-1} \mathsf{q_S} \in o(n)$, *then* $\alpha + \beta(\log \frac{t}{\varepsilon}) \in \Omega(\log t \cdot \log \frac{t}{\varepsilon} / \log n)$.

That is, unless the commitment itself is large, the opening of subsets of size $\log \frac{t}{\varepsilon}$ must be large: about $\log t / \log n$ bits per element. SVCs are relatively a strong primitive as they imply SNARGs for NP via the Micali construction (the other direction is not known to hold). However, we only know how to derive lower bounds for them by a reduction to SNARGs. An interesting open question is to directly get lower bounds for SVC, presumably for a larger class of constructions. Moreover, we can hope to get a lower bound for SVCs (in the ROM) without assuming rETH (or any complexity assumption). Indeed, even P = NP is not known to yield trivial SVCs in the ROM (which is not the case for SNARGs).

1.1.1 Hitting High-Entropy Distributions

The crux of Lemma 1 proof is analyzing the completeness of the resulting low verifier query scheme. We manage to translate this challenge into the following task of hitting high-entropy distributions.

Let $X = (X_1, \ldots, X_m)$ be a random variable uniformly distributed over $(\{0, 1\}^\lambda)^m$, let W be an event, and consider the random variable $X|_W$, i.e., X conditioned on W. It is instructive to think of this question as *"How does X appear to an adversary who received* $\log(1/\Pr[W])$ *bits of information about X?"* A long sequence of works have studied the question of how "close" $X|_W$ is to the uniformly distributed (unconditioned) X. In particular, these works considered the question of *indistinguishability*: showing that parts of $X|_W$ are close to being uniform. Some works, see [EIRS01, Raz98, SV10] to name a few, proved that the distribution of $(X|_W)_i$ is close in statistical distance to the uniform one, apart from a size $\log(1/\Pr[W])$ set of bad i's. Other works extended the above to bounded-query adversaries [Unr07, DGK17, CDGS18, GSV18, GLLZ20].

Unlike the above works, the focus of our result is *forgeability*: can we hit/sample from the conditional distribution $X|_W$ using a simple distribution? We show that after putting aside some bad indices, one can hit the support of $X|_W$, conditioned on its value in these bad indices, using a large enough product distribution. Like some of the above works, we state our result for high-entropy distributions, and not only for the uniform distribution conditioned on a high probability event.[7]

Theorem 3 (Hitting high-entropy distributions using product sets, informal). *Let* $X = (X_1, \ldots, X_m)$ *be a random variable over the product set* $(\{0,1\}^\lambda)^m$ *with* $H(X) \geq \lambda m - \ell$, *and let* $\lceil \log m \rceil \leq \gamma \leq \lambda$. *Then with probability at least* $1/2$ *over* $x \leftarrow X$, *there exists an* $O(\ell/\gamma)$-*size set* $\mathcal{B} \subseteq [m]$ *(of bad indices) such that*

$$\Pr\nolimits_{S \leftarrow (\{0,1\}^\lambda)^{m-|\mathcal{B}|}} \left[S \cap \mathsf{Supp}\big(X_{[m]\backslash\mathcal{B}} \mid X_\mathcal{B} = x_\mathcal{B}\big) \neq \emptyset \right] \in \Omega(1/\lambda m).$$

Letting H be the Shannon entropy function, and $v_\mathcal{I}$, for a vector v, denote the ordered vector $(v_i)_{i \in \mathcal{I}}$. That is, with high probability over $x \leftarrow X$, and after a few "bad" locations (indexed by $\mathcal{B}$) are exposed, one can hit (i.e., forge a sample from) the conditional distribution $X_{[m]\backslash\mathcal{B}} \mid X_\mathcal{B} = x_\mathcal{B}$ by sampling a *tiny*, in relative terms, product set.

Note that Theorem 3 does *not* state that $X_{[m]\backslash\mathcal{B}} \mid X_\mathcal{B} = x_\mathcal{B}$ is close to the uniform distribution. Actually, it might be very far from that, e.g., for $X = (U_1, \ldots, U_m) \mid \bigoplus U_i = 0^\lambda$ where the U_i's are uniform and independent random variables over $\{0,1\}^\lambda$, there is no choice of $\mathcal{B}$, apart from the trivial one of $\mathcal{B} = [m]$, that makes $X_{[m]\backslash\mathcal{B}} \mid X_\mathcal{B} = x_\mathcal{B}$ being close to uniform. (And this example demonstrates why the "pre-sampling" approach and alike, c.f., [Unr07], do not seem to be relevant for proving bounds of the type stated in the theorem.)It is also worth mentioning that one cannot prove Theorem 3 using the simple observation that after fixing some bad indices, the projection of $X' \overset{\text{def}}{=} (X \mid X_\mathcal{B} = x_\mathcal{B})$ on all other coordinates has large support. While the latter guarantees that, with high probability, each random subset $S_i \leftarrow \{0,1\}^\gamma$ intersects the support of X'_i, appending these samples together does not necessarily form an element in X'. Rather, we prove the theorem by showing that the number of points in $S \cap \mathsf{Supp}(X'_{[m]\backslash\mathcal{B}})$ is well-concentrated around its mean.

In our application of Theorem 3, the event W is the proof sent by P being a fixed ℓ-bit value π, and the size of the bad set $\mathcal{B}$ translates to the query complexity of the new verier V'. The theorem yields, see Sect. 2, that if V' makes all queries is $\mathcal{B}$, and samples the potential answers for the other queries by itself, then it will accept (i.e., hitting the support of the accepting distribution) with good probability.

1.2   Related Work

1.2.1   SNARGs in the Random Oracle Model

There are several approaches to construct ROM-SNARGs. Micali [Mic00] (building on [Kil92,FS86]) showed a transformation that compiles a *probabilistically*

---

[7] This is a generalization since for uniformly distributed X it holds that $H(X \mid W) \geq \lambda m - \log 1/\Pr[W]$.

checkable proof (PCP) and a commitment scheme into ROM-SNARG. Using the best know PCPs, the proof length of Micali's construction, to get (t, ε)-soundness, is $O((\log(t/\varepsilon))^2 \cdot \log n)$, where n is the instance size. Even when using the best-conjectured parameters for PCPs, known as the *Sliding Scale Conjecture* [BGLR93], the proof length remains the same up to the $\log n$ factors (see [CY21b] for a tight analysis of the Micali construction). Ben-Sasson, Chiesa, and Spooner [BCS16] (hereon BCS) transformed a public-coin *interactive oracle proofs* (IOPs) into ROM-SNARG. The benefit of their is approach is that we are much better at constructing IOPs, with good parameters, than PCPs. Still, even when using the best known (or conjectured) IOP, the proof length of the BCS construction remains $O((\log(t/\varepsilon))^2 \cdot \log n)$.

Recently, Chiesa and Yogev [CY21a] have constructed a ROM-SNARG of proof length of $O(\log(t/\varepsilon) \cdot \log t \cdot \log n)$, and hence slightly overcome the above "quadratic" barrier. Yet, the proof length of their construction is still far from the only (folklore) lower bound of $\Omega(\log(t/\varepsilon))$. Thus, the question of how to close this gap remains a major open question in this area.

1.2.2   SNARGs in Other Models

The security of SNARGs is unlikely to be proven in a non-idealized model (using falsifiable assumptions) Gentry and Wichs [GW11], but if one is willing to rely on "more structured" non-falsifiable assumptions (in addition or instead of the random oracle), much shorter SNARGs become feasible. Treating t as the running time of the adversary, constructions that use *group-based and pairing-based assumptions* achieve the optimal length (or close to optimal) of $O(\log(t/\varepsilon))$ (c.f., [Gro10, GGPR13, BCIOP13, BCCGP16, BBBPWM18, BFS20, PGHR13, MBKM19, CHMMVW20, Set19]). These constructions are *insecure* against quantum adversaries. Lattice based constructions, which are plausibly post-quantum, either achieve *private-verifiability* [BISW17, BISW18, GMNO18, ISW21, Nit19], or are public-verifiable, but with large proof length in practice (moreover, they typically use a random oracle as an additional assumption) [BBCPGL18, BLNS20, BCS21, CMSZ21]. (All of the above works assume a common random or reference string.)

To date, relying on the ROM is the best way to construct SNARGs that overcome all of the drawbacks mentioned above (alas, at the price of larger proofs).

Paper Organization

In Sect. 2, we give a high-level overview of the techniques for proving Lemma 1 (from short ROM-SNARGs to short ROM-SNARGs with low verifier query complexity). A formal definition of our notion of salted soundness, along with notations, definitions, and general statements used throughout the paper are given in Sect. 3. Theorem 3 (hitting high-entropy events using product sets) is proved in Sect. 4. Theorem 1 (lower bound on the length of ROM-SNARGs) and its accompanied Lemma 1 are proved in Sect. 5, and Theorem 2 (lower bound on the length of ROM subvector commitments) is proved in the full version of the paper.

2   Techniques

In this section, we give a high-level overview of our proof for Lemma 1, explaining how to transform a short salted-soundness, perfect completeness, deterministic non-adaptive verifier ROM-SNARG into a low verifier query ROM-SNARG for the same language.

Fix a deterministic non-adaptive ROM-SNARG $\mathsf{ARG} = (\mathsf{P}, \mathsf{V})$ for a language $\mathcal{L}$ with (t, ε)-slated-soundness and perfect completeness. Let s denote the proof length ARG, and let $\mathsf{q_P}$ and $\mathsf{q_V}$ denote the query complexity of P and V, respectively.

2.1   Warmup

As a warmup, assume that the honestly generated proof π, sent by P, only contains information about outputs of k ("important") queries, whose identity is independent of the oracle. (The proof might contain additional information depending only on the instance x and the witness w.) For this simple scenario, the construction of a k-query V' is rather straightforward:

Algorithm 4 (Low-query verifier V'. Warmup).
Oracle: $\zeta \colon \{0,1\}^\lambda \mapsto \{0,1\}^\lambda$.
Input: Instance x and a proof π.
Operation:

1. Emulate $\mathsf{V}(\mathrm{x}, \pi)$ till it produces a list of oracle queries $(w_1, \ldots, w_{\mathsf{q_V}})$. (Recall that V is non-adaptive.)
2. Sample a random k-size subset $\mathcal{J} \subseteq [\mathsf{q_V}]$.
3. For $i = 1, \ldots, \mathsf{q_V}$:
    If $i \in \mathcal{J}$, set $y_i = \zeta(w_i)$.
    Otherwise, sample $y_i \leftarrow \{0,1\}^\lambda$.
4. Accept if V accepts on the emulation with $(y_1, \ldots, y_{\mathsf{q_V}})$ as the answers to its oracle queries

Namely, V' guesses the identity of the important queries, and then uses the oracle ζ to answer them. It samples the answers to the other queries uniformly at random. The query complexity of V' is small if the number of important queries is small. Let us quickly argue about the completeness and soundness of $\mathsf{ARG}' = (\mathsf{P}, \mathsf{V}')$.

– Completeness. If the set $\mathcal{J}$ happens to contain all important queries, then the given proof π, the instance x, and the witness w, the oracle answers provided to the emulated V have *exactly* the same distribution as in its non-emulated execution. Since we assume ARG has perfect completeness, the completeness of ARG' is at least $1 / |\binom{\mathsf{q_V}}{k}|$—the probability that $\mathcal{J}$ contains all important queries.

- Soundness: Here we rely on the salted soundness of the original SNARG scheme. Assume there exists a $(t - q_V)$-query cheating prover P' that makes V' accept $x \notin \mathcal{L}$ with probability ε. Consider the following t-query cheating prover P for violating the salted-soundness of ARG.[8]

1. Run $\widetilde{\mathsf{P}}'^{\zeta}$ to generate a proof π.
   Emulate $\mathsf{V}(x, \pi)$ till it produces a list of oracle queries $(w_1, \ldots, w_{q_V})$.
2. For $i = 1, \ldots, q_V$:
   Query ζ on w_i with a fresh salt. Set $S_i = \{y_i\}$ for y_i be the query answer.
   If w_i was asked by $\widetilde{\mathsf{P}}'$ in Step 1, add the retrieved answer to S_i.
3. If there exists $(y_1, \ldots, y_{q_V}) \in S_1 \times \ldots \times S_{q_V}$ that would make V accept (x, π) with $(y_1, \ldots, y_{q_V})$ as the answers to its oracle queries, program $\zeta(w_i) = y_i$ for each $i \in [q_V]$ (this programming is allowed by the salted soundness security game).
4. Output π.

By definition, if $\widetilde{\mathsf{P}}$ outputs a proof π then V accepts π on the programmed oracle. In addition, the probability that $\widetilde{\mathsf{P}}$ outputs the proof π generated in Step 1, is at least as large as the probability that V' accepts π on the non-programmed oracle: $\widetilde{\mathsf{P}}$ considers for each query the original output of the oracle, as seen by V' on queries in $\mathcal{J}$, and a uniform output, as sampled by V' on inputs not in $\mathcal{J}$.

2.2 Actual Scenario

Things get way more challenging when the proof π depends on the queries made by P, even in a slightly more complicated way. For instance, suppose π contains the XOR of some k queries, and V verifies that the XOR of these queries is consistent with π. Since k might be arbitrarily large, i.e., much larger than π, there is no low-query verifier that makes all those queries. So the challenge is to design a verifier that does not make all queries that effect the value of π, but still has non-trivial soundness and completeness.

The key observation is that for the general case, where π depends *arbitrarily* on all oracle answers, we can modify the verifier so that the completeness and soundness are not that different from the naïve example considered in the warmup. Very informally, with high probability over the value of π and apart from $k = s/\gamma$ "important" queries, the verification verdict does not depend "too much" on the answer to all other "non-important" queries. That is, there are many possible answers for the non-important queries that lead to acceptance (compared with *all* possible answers in the warmup case). See Sect. 2.3 for

---

[8] Recall that the salted-soundness game allows a cheating prover to *resample* (many times) the output of the random oracle on a query. Each resampling costs the cheating prover a single query call from its query budget. The prover can role-back the oracle on certain queries, to set their answers to a previously answered values. See Sect. 3.5.1 for exact definition.

details. It follows that the answers for the non-important queries can be emulated by the verifier (without querying the oracle). Equipped with this understanding, the low query V′ is defined as follows:

Algorithm 5 (Low-query verifier V′).
Oracle: $\zeta \colon \{0,1\}^{\lambda} \mapsto \{0,1\}^{\lambda}$.
Paramters: $\gamma < \lambda$.
Input: Instance x and a proof π.
Operation:

1. Emulate $V(x, \pi)$ till it produces a list of oracle queries $(w_1, \ldots, w_{qv})$. (Recall that V is non-adaptive.)
2. Sample $k' \in [k]$ at random and sample, a random $k' = \lceil s/\gamma \rceil$-size subset $\mathcal{J} \subseteq [qv]$.
3. For $i = 1, \ldots, qv$:
   If $i \in \mathcal{J}$, set $S_i = \{\zeta(w_i)\}$.
   Otherwise, let S_i be a 2^{γ}-size *random* subset of $\{0,1\}^{\lambda}$.
4. Accept if there exists $(y_1, \ldots, y_{qv}) \in S_1 \times \ldots \times S_{qv}$ that make V accepts on the emulation, with $(y_1, \ldots, y_{qv})$ as the answers to its oracle queries

That is, similar to the warmup scenario, V′ only uses the oracle to answer the $k = \lceil s/\gamma \rceil$ queries in the guessed set $\mathcal{J}$. For each other query, V′ samples 2^{γ} candidates answers. It accepts if there is a choice from the candidate answers that jointly with the oracle answers to the queries in $\mathcal{J}$, leads to acceptance. The running-time of V′ is (roughly) $2^{qv \cdot \gamma}$, and the following claim states the completeness and soundness of $\mathsf{ARG}' = (\mathsf{P}, \mathsf{V}')$:

Claim (Informal). ARG′ has $\left(\lambda \cdot q_P \cdot k \cdot \binom{qv}{s/\gamma}\right)^{-1}$-completeness and $(t - q_V \cdot 2^{\gamma}, \varepsilon)$-soundness.

We argue completeness in Sect. 2.3, using the observation we made above regarding the small number of important queries, and argue soundness in Sect. 2.4, by extending the approach we took for proving soundness in the warmup case.

2.3 Completeness

Let Π and $Y = (Y_1, \ldots, Y_{q_P})$ denote the proof and the random oracle answers to honest prover P queries on instance x and witness w, respectively. Since the Y_i's are independent uniform values in $\{0,1\}^{\lambda}$, it holds that

$$H(Y) = q_P \cdot \lambda \tag{1}$$

where $H(Y)$ is the Shannon entropy of Y. A standard entropy argument yields that with probability at least $1/2$ over $\pi \leftarrow \Pi$:

$$H(Y \mid \Pi = \pi) \geq q_P \cdot \lambda - 2|\pi| \tag{2}$$

In the following, fix $\pi \in \mathsf{Supp}(\Pi)$ for which Equation (2) holds. Applying Theorem 3 with respect to $Y|_{\Pi=\pi}$ and $\ell = 2|\pi|$, yields that with probability $1/2$ over the value of $(y_1, \ldots, y_{\mathsf{q_P}}) \leftarrow Y|_{\Pi=\pi}$, there exists a set $\mathcal{B} \subseteq [\mathsf{q_P}]$ of size ℓ/γ (omitting constant factors) such that

$$\Pr\left[(S_1 \times \cdots \times S_{\mathsf{q_P} - |\mathcal{B}|}) \cap \mathsf{Supp}(Y'_{[\mathsf{q_P}]\setminus\mathcal{B}}) \neq \emptyset \right] \in \Omega(1/\lambda \cdot \mathsf{q_P}) \qquad (3)$$

where each of the S_i's is an independent 2^γ-size subset of $\{0,1\}^\lambda$, $Y' \stackrel{\mathsf{def}}{=} Y|_{Y_\mathcal{B}=y_\mathcal{B}, \Pi=\pi}$, and $Y'_{\mathcal{I}}$ is the ordered vector $(Y'_i)_{i\in\mathcal{I}}$.

Assume for simplicity that V and P make exactly the same queries. By Equation (3), if the random set $\mathcal{J}$ (sampled by V') is exactly $\mathcal{B} = \mathcal{B}(\pi)$, then with probability $\Omega(1/\lambda \cdot \mathsf{q_P})$ over the choice of the sets S_i's sampled by V', exit answers $\{y_j \in S_j\}_{j\notin\mathcal{J}}$ that when combined with the oracle answers $\{y_j \in S_j\}_{j\in\mathcal{J}}$, it holds that $y = (y_1, \ldots, y_{\mathsf{q_P}}) \in \mathsf{Supp}(Y|_{\Pi=\pi})$. Since such a vector y is *possible* to occur as random oracle answers in an honest execution of P that results in π, the perfect completeness of ARG yields that V accepts on (the answers in) y with probability one. We conclude that V' accepts with probability $\Omega(1/\lambda \cdot \mathsf{q_P})$ times $\Pr[\mathcal{J} = \mathcal{B}] \geq 1/k \cdot 1/\binom{\mathsf{q_V}}{s/\gamma}$.

Remark 1 (Improved completeness). We note that one could slightly modify the transformation to improve the completeness significantly (at the cost of proof length and prover running time). However, as this does not improve our lower bound, we only sketch the idea here. Instead of having the verifier guess the set $\mathcal{J}$, let the prover find $\mathcal{J}$, and send its description to the verifier. The completeness error now would come only from the error in Equation (2) (i.e., an error of $(\lambda \cdot \mathsf{q_P})^{-1}$), and not from the probability of choosing the right set $\mathcal{J}$. The proof would be slightly larger (as it needs to contain the description of $\mathcal{J}$), and the running-time of the honest prover would increase, as it needs to find the right set $\mathcal{J}$ (query complexity will stay the same). Even more so, using a prefix salt for all queries (included in the proof), one can make the completeness error exponentially small.

2.4 Soundness

Assume there exists a $(t - \mathsf{q_V} \cdot 2^\gamma)$-query cheating prover $\widetilde{\mathsf{P}}'$ that makes V' accepts $\mathrm{x} \notin \mathcal{L}$ with probability ε, and consider the following t-query cheating prover $\widetilde{\mathsf{P}}$ for violating the salted-soundness of ARG.

Algorithm 6 ($\widetilde{\mathsf{P}}$).
Oracle: $\zeta \colon \{0,1\}^\lambda \mapsto \{0,1\}^\lambda$.
Input: Instance x.

1. Run $\widetilde{\mathsf{P}}'^\zeta(\mathrm{x})$ to generate a proof π.
2. Emulate V on (x, π) to determine its list of oracle queries $(w_1, \ldots, w_{\mathsf{q_V}})$.
3. For $i = 1, \ldots, \mathsf{q_V}$:

(a) Query ζ on w_i for 2^γ times. Let S_i be the set of answers.

(b) If w_i was asked by $\widetilde{\mathsf{P}}'$ in Step 1, add the retrieved answer to S_i.

4. If there exists $(y_1, \ldots, y_{\mathsf{qv}}) \in S_1 \times \ldots \times S_{\mathsf{qv}}$ that make V accept (x, π) with $(y_1, \ldots, y_{\mathsf{qv}})$ as the answers to its oracle queries, program $\zeta(w_i) = y_i$ for each $i \in [\mathsf{qv}]$.

5. Output π.

The cheating probability of $\widetilde{\mathsf{P}}$ it as least as high as that of $\widetilde{\mathsf{P}}'$. This is shown via a coupling argument, and the precise details are given in Sect. 5.2.2.

3   Preliminaries

3.1   Notations

We use calligraphic letters to denote sets, uppercase for random variables, and lowercase for values and functions. Let poly stand for the set of all polynomials. Throughout the paper, log is the base 2 logarithm. For $n \in \mathbb{N}$, let $[n] = \{1, \ldots, n\}$. Given a vector $v \in \Sigma^n$, let v_i denote its ith entry. Similarly, for a set $\mathcal{I} \subseteq [n]$, let $v_{\mathcal{I}}$ be the *ordered sequence* $(v_i)_{i \in \mathcal{I}}$, let $v_{-\mathcal{I}} \stackrel{\text{def}}{=} v_{[n] \setminus \mathcal{I}}$. For a set $\mathcal{S}$ and $k \in \mathbb{N}$, let $\mathcal{P}_k(\mathcal{S})$ denote all k-size subsets of $\mathcal{S}$. The *support* of a random variable X, denoted $\mathsf{Supp}(X)$, is defined as $\{x \colon \Pr[X = x] > 0\}$. For an event E, we write $X|_E$ to denote the random variable X conditioned on E.

The language 3SAT over n variables is the set of all satisfiable formulas in conjunctive normal form where each clause is limited to at most three literals. The class BPTIME$[T]$ refers to all languages that can be decided by a probabilistic TM that runs in time $T(n)$, on inputs of length n.

Some basic inequalities. We use the following well-known facts:

Fact 7. $\log(1-x) \le -x$ *for* $x \in [0, 1]$, *and* $\log(1-x) \ge -2x$, *for any* $x \in [0, 1/2]$.

Theorem 8 (Paley-Zygmund inequality). *For any finite non-negative random variable X it holds that* $\Pr[X > 0] \ge \mathrm{E}[X]^2 / \mathrm{E}[X^2]$.

3.2   Entropy Measures

We refer to several measures of entropy. The relation and motivation of these measures are best understood by considering a notion that we will refer to as the sample-entropy: for a random variable X and $x \in \mathsf{Supp}(X)$, the *sample-entropy* of x with respect to X is the quantity

$$H_X(x) \stackrel{\text{def}}{=} \log \tfrac{1}{\Pr[X=x]},$$

letting $H_X(x) = \infty$ for $x \notin \mathsf{Supp}(X)$, and $2^{-\infty} = 0$.

The sample-entropy measures the amount of "randomness" or "surprise" in the specific sample x, assuming that x has been generated according to X. Using this notion, we can define the *Shannon entropy* $H(X)$ and *min-entropy* $H_\infty(X)$ as follows:

$$H(X) \overset{\text{def}}{=} E_{x \leftarrow X} [H_X(x)], \quad H_\infty(X) \overset{\text{def}}{=} \min_{x \in \mathsf{Supp}(X)} H_X(x).$$

We will also discuss the *max-entropy* $H_0(X) \overset{\text{def}}{=} \log |\mathsf{Supp}(X)|$. The term "max-entropy" and its relation to the sample-entropy will be made apparent below.

It can be shown that $H_\infty(X) \leq H(X) \leq H_0(X)$ with each inequality being an equality if and only if X is flat (uniform on its support). Thus, saying that $H_\infty(X) \geq k$ is a strong way of saying that X has "high entropy" and $H_0(X) \leq k$ a strong way of saying that X has "low entropy".

Conditional entropies. We will also be interested in conditional versions of entropy. For jointly distributed random variables (X, Y) and $(x, y) \in \mathsf{Supp}(X, Y)$, we define the *conditional sample-entropy* to be $H_{X|Y}(x|y) = \log \frac{1}{\Pr_{X|Y}[x|y]} = \log \frac{1}{\Pr[X=x|Y=y]}$. Then the standard *conditional Shannon entropy* can be written as

$$H(X \mid Y) = E_{(x,y) \leftarrow (X,Y)} [H_{X|Y}(x \mid y)] = E_{y \leftarrow Y} [H(X|_{Y=y})] = H(X,Y) - H(Y).$$

The following fact gives a bound on the amount of entropy that is reduced when conditioning on an event for uniformly distributed random variables.

Fact 9. *Let X be a random variable uniform over a set $\mathcal{S}$ and let W be an event. Then $H(X \mid W) \geq \log(|\mathcal{S}|) - \log 1/\Pr[W]$.*

3.3 Randomized Exponential Time Hypothesis

Definition 1 (rETH; [DHMTW14]). *The randomized Exponential Time Hypothesis (rETH) states that there exist $\varepsilon > 0$ and $c > 1$ such that 3SAT on n variables and with $c \cdot n$ clauses cannot be solved by probabilistic algorithms that run in time $2^{\varepsilon \cdot n}$.*

3.4 Random Oracles

We denote by $\mathcal{U}(\lambda)$ the uniform distribution over all functions $\zeta \colon \{0,1\}^* \to \{0,1\}^\lambda$. Given an oracle algorithm A and an oracle $\zeta \in \mathcal{U}(\lambda)$, $\mathsf{queries}(A, \zeta)$ is the set of oracle queries that A^ζ makes. We say that A is t-*query* if $|\mathsf{queries}(A, \zeta)| \leq t$ for every $\zeta \in \mathcal{U}(\lambda)$. We say that A is *non-adaptive* if its queries do not depend on the responses of the random oracle to previous queries. Finally, we consider the length of oracle queries, i.e., the number of bits used to specify the query: we say that A has queries of length λ if for every $\zeta \in \mathcal{U}(\lambda)$ and $x \in \mathsf{queries}(A, \zeta)$ it holds that $|x| \leq \lambda$.

3.5 Non-interactive Arguments in the ROM

We consider non-interactive arguments in the ROM, where security holds against query-bounded, yet possibly computationally-unbounded, adversaries. Recall that a non-interactive argument typically consists of a prover algorithm and a verifier algorithm that prove and validate statements for a binary relation, which represents the valid instance-witness pairs.

A pair of polynomial-time oracle algorithms $\mathsf{ARG} = (\mathsf{P}, \mathsf{V})$ is a ROM-SNARG with α-completeness and (t, ϵ)-soundness, for a relation $\mathcal{R}$, if the following holds.

– **Completeness.** For every $\lambda \in \mathbb{N}$ and $(\mathrm{x}, \mathrm{w}) \in \mathcal{R}$:

$$\Pr_{\substack{\zeta \leftarrow \mathcal{U}(\lambda) \\ \pi \leftarrow \mathsf{P}^\zeta(\mathrm{x}, \mathrm{w})}} \left[\mathsf{V}^\zeta(\mathrm{x}, \pi) = 1 \right] \geq \alpha(|\mathrm{x}|, \lambda) \ .$$

– **Soundness.**[9] For every $\lambda \in \mathbb{N}$, t-query $\widetilde{\mathsf{P}}$ and $\mathrm{x} \notin \mathcal{L}(\mathcal{R})$:

$$\Pr_{\substack{\zeta \leftarrow \mathcal{U}(\lambda) \\ \pi \leftarrow \widetilde{\mathsf{P}}^\zeta}} \left[\mathsf{V}^\zeta(\mathrm{x}, \pi) = 1 \right] \geq \epsilon(|\mathrm{x}|, \lambda, t) \ .$$

Complexity measures. We consider several complexity measures beyond soundness error. All of these complexity measures are, implicitly, functions of x and the security parameter λ.

– *argument length*: $\mathsf{s} := |\pi|$.
– *times*: the prover P runs in time pt; the verifier V runs in time vt.
– *queries*: the prover P is a $\mathsf{q_P}$-query algorithm the verifier V is a $\mathsf{q_V}$-query algorithm.

3.5.1 Salted Soundness

Chiesa and Yogev [CY20] introduced a stronger notion of soundness for ROM-SNARG that they named salted soundness. This notion requires soundness to hold also against a malicious prover that has limited ability to *program* the oracle: it can obtain a set of random, independent strings as candidates for random oracle answers to a specific query. After obtaining such sets to the queries of his choice, the malicious prover can pick an answer of his desire from each set to be the random oracle answer.[10] This notion is formalized via the following *salted soundness game* defined as follows:

Game 10 ($\mathsf{SaltedSoundess}_{\mathsf{V}, \lambda, t}(\mathsf{A}, \mathrm{x})$).
Parameters: Algorithm V and $\lambda, t \in \mathbb{N}$.

---

[9] This notion, where x is set before the oracle, is sometimes refereed to as *non-adaptive soundness*. Clearly, lower bounds on this weaker notion , as we do in this work, apply also for its adaptive variant (where the cheating prover is allowed to choose x as a function of the oracle).

[10] Our notion slightly strengthens the notion of Chiesa and Yogev [CY20], in which the prover cannot roll back the oracle answer to a previously seen answer.

Input: $\mathrm{x} \in \{0,1\}^*$
Player: A.
Operation:

1. Initialize keyed-map S of lists (each entry is initialized with the empty list).
2. Repeat the following t times:
   (a) A sends a query $x \in \{0,1\}^*$.
   (b) Send $y \leftarrow \{0,1\}^\lambda$ to A, and add it to the list $S[x]$.
3. A outputs a proof string π and query-answer list $\sigma = [(x_1, y_1), \ldots, (x_n, y_n)]$.
4. Abort if $y_i \notin S[x_i]$ for some $i \in [n]$.
5. Output $\mathsf{V}^{\zeta_\sigma}(\mathrm{x}, \pi)$.

Definition 2 (Salted soundness). *We say that ROM-SNARG* (P, V) *has* (t, ε)*-salted-soundness for a language* $\mathcal{L}$*, if for any* λ*,* $\mathrm{x} \notin \mathcal{L}$ *and* $\widetilde{\mathsf{P}}$ *it holds that* $\mathrm{Pr}\left[\mathsf{SaltedSoundess}_{\mathsf{V},\lambda,t}(\widetilde{\mathsf{P}}, \mathrm{x}) = 1\right] \leq \varepsilon(|\mathrm{x}|, \lambda, t)$.

Remark 2 (Known constructions satisfy salted soundness). Known constructions of ROM-SNARGs are usually proven to have standard soundness (as opposed to salted soundness). However, we observe that the constructions of [Mic00, BCS16, CY21b, CY21a] actually achieve this stronger notion of security. In particular, the tight analysis given in [CY21b] and in [CY21a] explicitly allowed the adversary to choose a salt for each query in the construction (e.g., see remark 3.2 in [CY21b]).

Amplification. It turns out that salted soundness can be easily amplified (at the expense of the query complexity). The proof of Lemma 2 is proved in the full version of the paper.

Lemma 2. *Let* ARG *be an ROM-SNARG for a language* $\mathcal{L}$ *with* (t, ε)*-salted-soundness for* $\varepsilon \leq 1/4$*. Then* ARG *has* $(t/k, 2\varepsilon/k)$*-salted-soundness for any* $k \in \mathbb{N}$.

4   Hitting High-Entropy Distribution Using Product Sets

In this section we formally state and prove Theorem 3. Recall that for a set $\mathcal{S}$ and $k \in \mathbb{N}$, we let $\mathcal{P}_k(\mathcal{S})$ denote all k-size subsets of $\mathcal{S}$. Thus, a uniform sample from $(\mathcal{P}_{2^\gamma}(\{0,1\}^\lambda))^{m-|\mathcal{B}|}$ is a random product in $(\{0,1\}^\lambda)^{m-|\mathcal{B}|}$ of width 2^γ.

Theorem 11 (Hitting high-entropy distributions using product sets, restatement of Theorem 3). *Let* $\gamma \leq \lambda \in \mathbb{N}$*, and let* $X = (X_1, \ldots, X_m)$ *be a random variable over* $(\{0,1\}^\lambda)^m$*. If* $H(X) > \lambda m - \ell$ *and* $\gamma > 4\lceil \log m \rceil + 4$*, then with probability at least* $1/2$ *over* $x \leftarrow X$*, then there exists a set* $\mathcal{B} \subseteq [m]$ *of size at most* $8\ell/\gamma + 4$ *such that*

$$\mathrm{Pr}_{S \leftarrow (\mathcal{P}_{2^\gamma}(\{0,1\}^\lambda))^{m-|\mathcal{B}|}} \left[S \cap \mathsf{Supp}(X_{[m]\setminus\mathcal{B}} \mid X_\mathcal{B} = x_\mathcal{B}) \neq \emptyset\right] \geq 1/32\lambda m.$$

Remark 3 (Tightness of Theorem 11). The size of $\mathcal{B}$ in Theorem 11 is tight up to a constant: Let $m, \lambda, \gamma \in \mathbb{N}$ be as in Theorem 11, let $X = (X_1, \ldots, X_m)$ be uniform over $(\{0,1\}^\lambda)^m$ and let W be the event that $X_1 = \ldots = X_t = 0^\lambda$, for some $t \in [m]$. Clearly, $H(X|_W) = (m - t)\lambda$. It is also clear that for every x and every set $\mathcal{B} \subseteq [m]$ of size $t' < t$, it holds that

$$\Pr_{S \leftarrow (\mathcal{P}_{2\gamma}(\{0,1\}^\lambda))^{m-t'}} \left[S \cap \mathsf{Supp}(X_{[m]\setminus\mathcal{B}} \,|_{X_\mathcal{B}=x_\mathcal{B}}) \neq \emptyset \right] \leq 2^{\gamma-\lambda},$$

which is negligible for sufficiently small γ, e.g., $\gamma = \lambda/2$. This matches, up to a constant, Theorem 11, which states that with high probability over $x \leftarrow X \,|_W$, there exists a set $\mathcal{B}$ of size at most $16t + 4$ for which that the above event occurs with probability at least $1/32\lambda m$.

Proving Theorem 11. We start with describing the high-level approach of the proof. We need to prove that with high probability over $x \leftarrow X$, there exists a small (i.e., with size at most $8\ell/\gamma + 4$) subset $\mathcal{B} \subseteq [m]$ such that

$$\Pr_{S \leftarrow (\mathcal{P}_{2\gamma}(\{0,1\}^\lambda))^{\widehat{m}}} \left[S \cap \mathsf{Supp}(\widehat{X}) \neq \emptyset \right] \geq 1/32\lambda m,$$

for $\widehat{X} = X_{[m]\setminus\mathcal{B}} \,|_{X_\mathcal{B}=x_\mathcal{B}}$ and $\widehat{m} = m - |\mathcal{B}|$. We assume, without loss of generality, that the elements of each S_i are chosen in a uniform order, and denote the jth element of S_i, according to this order, by $S_i[j]$. For $y = (y_1, \ldots, y_{\widehat{m}}) \in [2^\gamma]^{\widehat{m}}$, let $S^y \in \{0,1\}^{\lambda \times \widehat{m}}$ be the random variable defined by $(S^y)_i = S_i[y_i]$. Let Z^y be the indicator for the event $S^y \in \mathsf{Supp}(\widehat{X})$, and let $Z \stackrel{\text{def}}{=} \sum_{y \in [2^\gamma]^{\widehat{m}}} Z^y$. That is, Z^y is event that the yth element of S is in $\mathsf{Supp}(\widehat{X})$. Given this notation, we need to prove that $\Pr[Z > 0] \geq 1/32\lambda m$. We start by proving that the expected value of Z is large. By linearity of expectation,

$$\mathrm{E}[Z] = \sum_{y \in [2^\gamma]^{\widehat{m}}} \mathrm{E}[Z^y] = 2^{\gamma\widehat{m}} \cdot |\mathsf{Supp}(\widehat{X})|/2^{\widehat{m}\lambda} = 2^{(\gamma-\lambda)\widehat{m}} \cdot |\mathsf{Supp}(\widehat{X})| \quad (4)$$

To guarantee that $\mathrm{E}[Z]$ is at least one, we chose $\mathcal{B}$ to be a *maximal* subset of $[m]$ with

$$H_{X_\mathcal{B}}(x_\mathcal{B}) \leq (\lambda - \gamma) \cdot |\mathcal{B}| \quad (5)$$

for $H_Y(y)$ be the *sample entropy of y according to Y* (see Sect. 3.2). It is rather straightforward to show that with respect to this choice of $\mathcal{B}$, the expected value of Z is indeed at least one. Furthermore, since, by assumption, X has high entropy, the expected size of $\mathcal{B}$, as a function of x, is small, and therefore, with high probability over x the size of $\mathcal{B}$ is also small. (See proof in Lemma 3).

The above would suffice for lower-bounding $\Pr[Z > 0]$, if the random variables $\{Z^y\}$ would have been independent. This, however, is clearly not the case since most Z^y are not even pairwise independent: for a pair $y, y' \in [2^\gamma]^{\widehat{m}}$ with $y_\mathcal{I} = y'_\mathcal{I}$ for some $\mathcal{I} \subseteq [\widehat{m}]$, the event $Z^y = 1$, implying $(S^{y'})_\mathcal{I} \in \mathsf{Supp}(\widehat{X}_\mathcal{I})$, is likely to increase the probability of $Z^{y'} = 1$. Yet, we manage to show that the expected value of Z^2 is small enough, implying that Z is well concentrated around its mean, and therefore $\Pr[Z > 0]$ is large. To do that, we notice that for the maximal set $\mathcal{B}$ defined above, it holds that

$$H_{X_{\mathcal{I}}|X_{\mathcal{B}}=x_{\mathcal{B}}}(x_{\mathcal{I}}) > (\lambda - \gamma) \cdot |\mathcal{I}| \tag{6}$$

for *every* $\mathcal{I} \subseteq [m] \setminus \mathcal{B}$. This condition implies that for every y, y' with $y_{\mathcal{I}} = y'_{\mathcal{I}}$, the probability of $Z^y \wedge Z^{y'}$ is sufficiently small (quantified by the size of $\mathcal{I}$), implying that $\mathrm{E}[Z^2]$ is small.

Moving to the formal proof, Theorem 11 is an immediate corollary of the following two lemmata: Lemma 3 states that with high probability over x, there exists a small set $\mathcal{B}$ for which Equation (6) holds, and Lemma 4 completes the job by proving the conclusion of the theorem for the random variable $X_{[m]\setminus\mathcal{B}}|X_{\mathcal{B}}=x_{\mathcal{B}}$.

Lemma 3 (High-entropy events have an almost full-entropy large projection). *Let $\gamma \leq \lambda \in \mathbb{N}$, and let $X = (X_1, \ldots, X_m)$ be a random variable over $(\{0,1\}^{\lambda})^m$. If $H(X) \geq \lambda \cdot m - \ell$ and $\gamma \geq 2 \cdot \lceil \log m \rceil + 2$, then with probability at least $1/2$ over $x \leftarrow X$, exists a set $\mathcal{B} \subseteq [m]$ of size at most $4\ell/\gamma + 4$ such that for every $\mathcal{I} \subseteq [m] \setminus \mathcal{B}$:*

$$H_{X_{\mathcal{I}}|X_{\mathcal{B}}=x_{\mathcal{B}}}(x_{\mathcal{I}}) \geq (\lambda - \gamma)|\mathcal{I}|.$$

Lemma 4 (Hitting almost full-entropy events using product sets). *Let $\gamma \leq \lambda \in \mathbb{N}$, let $X = (X_1, \ldots, X_m)$ be a random variable over $(\{0,1\}^{\lambda})^m$. Assume $\gamma \geq 2 \cdot \lceil \log m \rceil + 3$, and that for every $x \in \mathsf{Supp}(X)$ and $\mathcal{I} \subseteq [m]$, it holds that $H_{X_{\mathcal{I}}}(x_{\mathcal{I}}) \geq (\lambda - \gamma/2) \cdot |\mathcal{I}|$. Then*

$$\Pr_{S \leftarrow (\mathcal{P}_{2^{\gamma}}(\{0,1\}^{\lambda}))^m}[S \cap \mathsf{Supp}(X) \neq \emptyset] \geq 1/32\lambda m.$$

We prove Lemmas 3 and 4 in Sects. 4.1 and 4.2, receptively, but first use them for proving Theorem 11.

Proof of Theorem 11: Let $t \overset{\text{def}}{=} 8\ell/\gamma + 4$, and let

$$\mathcal{T} \overset{\text{def}}{=} \{x \in \mathsf{Supp}(X) : \exists \mathcal{B} \subseteq [m], |\mathcal{B}| \leq t : \forall \mathcal{I} \subseteq [m] \setminus \mathcal{B}, H_{X_{\mathcal{I}}|X_{\mathcal{B}}=x_{\mathcal{B}}}(x_{\mathcal{I}}) \geq (\lambda - \gamma/2) \cdot |\mathcal{I}|\}.$$

Since, by assumption, $\gamma/2 \geq 2 \lceil \log m \rceil + 2$, Lemma 3 yields that

$$\Pr[X \in \mathcal{T}] \geq 1/2. \tag{7}$$

Fix $x \in \mathcal{T}$, let $\mathcal{B}$ be the set guaranteed by the definition of $\mathcal{T}$ (choose an arbitrary one, if there is more than one), and let $X' \overset{\text{def}}{=} X_{[m]\setminus\mathcal{B}}|X_{\mathcal{B}}=x_{\mathcal{B}}$, and let $m' \overset{\text{def}}{=} m - |\mathcal{B}|$. By Lemma 4

$$\Pr_{S \leftarrow (\mathcal{P}_{2^{\gamma}}(\{0,1\}^{\lambda}))^{m'}}[S \cap \mathsf{Supp}(X') \neq \emptyset] \geq 1/32\lambda m' \geq 1/32\lambda m. \tag{8}$$

Combining Equations (7) and (8), concludes the proof. $\square$

4.1 High-Entropy Distributions Have an (Almost) Uniform Large Projection, Proving Lemma 3

Proof of Lemma 3. Let m, λ, γ and X be as in Lemma 3. For $x \in \mathsf{Supp}(X)$, let $\mathcal{B}^x$ be the (lex. first) *maximal*[11] subset of $[m]$ with

$$H_{X_{\mathcal{B}^x}}(x_{\mathcal{B}^x}) \leq (\lambda - \gamma)|\mathcal{B}^x| \tag{9}$$

Since Equation (9) holds for the empty set, $\mathcal{B}^x$ is always defined. We prove Lemma 3 using the following two claims, proven below.

Claim. For every $x \in \mathsf{Supp}(X)$ and $\mathcal{I} \subseteq [m] \setminus \mathcal{B}^x$, it holds that $H_{X_{\mathcal{I}}|X_{\mathcal{B}^x}=x_{\mathcal{B}^x}}(x_I) \geq (\lambda - \gamma) \cdot |\mathcal{I}|$.

Claim. If $H(X) \geq \lambda \cdot m - \ell$, then for every random variable $I \subseteq [m]$ it holds that $H(X_I \mid I) \geq (\lambda - \lceil \log m \rceil) \cdot \mathrm{E}[|I|] - \ell - \lceil \log m \rceil$.

By Sect. 4.1, for every $x \in \mathsf{Supp}(X)$ and $\mathcal{I} \subseteq [m] \setminus \mathcal{B}^x$, it holds that

$$H_{X_{\mathcal{I}}|X_{\mathcal{B}^x}=x_{\mathcal{B}^x}}(x_I) \geq (\lambda - \gamma)|\mathcal{I}| \tag{10}$$

Hence, to conclude the proof, it is left to argue that with high probability over $x \leftarrow X$, the size of $\mathcal{B}^x$ is small. For $\mathcal{I} \subseteq [m]$, let $f_{\mathcal{I}}(x) = x_{\mathcal{I}}$ if $\mathcal{B}^x = \mathcal{I}$, and $f_{\mathcal{I}}(x) = \perp$ otherwise, and let $p_{\mathcal{I}} = \Pr[f_{\mathcal{I}}(X) = \perp]$. Compute

$$H(X_{\mathcal{B}^X} \mid \mathcal{B}^X) = \mathrm{E}_{\mathcal{B} \leftarrow \mathcal{B}^x}\left[H(X_{\mathcal{B}} \mid \mathcal{B}^X = \mathcal{B})\right] \tag{11}$$

$$= \mathrm{E}_{\mathcal{B} \leftarrow \mathcal{B}^x}\left[H(f_{\mathcal{B}}(X) \mid \mathcal{B}^X = \mathcal{B})\right] \leq \sum_{\mathcal{I}} \mathrm{E}_{\mathcal{B} \leftarrow \mathcal{B}^x}\left[H(f_{\mathcal{I}}(X) \mid \mathcal{B}^X = \mathcal{B})\right]$$

$$= \sum_{\mathcal{I}} H(f_{\mathcal{I}}(X) \mid \mathcal{B}^X) \leq \sum_{\mathcal{I}} H(f_{\mathcal{I}}(X))$$

$$= \sum_{\mathcal{I}}\left(\sum_{x:\, \mathcal{B}^x = \mathcal{I}} \Pr[X = x] \cdot H_{X_{\mathcal{I}}}(x_{\mathcal{I}})\right) + p_{\mathcal{I}} \cdot \log(1/p_{\mathcal{I}})$$

$$\leq \sum_{\mathcal{I}} \Pr[\mathcal{B}^X = \mathcal{I}] \cdot (\lambda - \gamma) \cdot |\mathcal{I}| + p_{\mathcal{I}} \cdot \log(1/p_{\mathcal{I}}) \tag{12}$$

$$= (\lambda - \gamma)\mathrm{E}\left[|\mathcal{B}^X|\right] + \sum_{\mathcal{I}} p_{\mathcal{I}} \cdot \log(1/p_{\mathcal{I}})$$

$$\leq (\lambda - \gamma)\mathrm{E}\left[|\mathcal{B}^X|\right] + 1 + \sum_{\mathcal{I}, p_{\mathcal{I}} \geq 1/2} -p_{\mathcal{I}} \cdot \log(p_{\mathcal{I}})$$

$$\leq (\lambda - \gamma)\mathrm{E}\left[|\mathcal{B}^X|\right] + 1 + \sum_{\mathcal{I}, p_{\mathcal{I}} \geq 1/2} p_{\mathcal{I}} \cdot 2(1 - p_{\mathcal{I}}) \tag{13}$$

$$= (\lambda - \gamma)\mathrm{E}\left[|\mathcal{B}^X|\right] + 1 + 2 \cdot \sum_{\mathcal{I}, p_{\mathcal{I}} \geq 1/2} p_{\mathcal{I}} \cdot \Pr[\mathcal{B}^X = \mathcal{I}]$$

$$\leq (\lambda - \gamma)\mathrm{E}\left[|\mathcal{B}^X|\right] + 3.$$

---

[11] Maximal means relative to inclusion—there is no $\mathcal{I}$ strictly containing $\mathcal{B}^x$ with $H_{X_{\mathcal{I}}}(x_{\mathcal{I}}) \leq (\lambda - \gamma) \cdot |\mathcal{I}|$.

Inequality 12 holds by the definition of $\mathcal{B}^x$, and Inequality 13 holds since $\log(1-x) \geq -2x$ for $x \in [0, 1/2]$.

On the other hand since, by assumption, $H(X) \geq \lambda \cdot m - \ell$, Sect. 4.1 yields that

$$H(X_{\mathcal{B}^X} \mid \mathcal{B}^X) \geq (\lambda - \lceil \log m \rceil) \cdot \mathrm{E}\left[|\mathcal{B}^X|\right] - \ell - \lceil \log m \rceil \tag{14}$$

Combining Equations (11) and (14), we conclude that $\mathrm{E}\left[|\mathcal{B}^X|\right] \leq \frac{\ell + \lceil \log m \rceil + 3}{\gamma - \lceil \log m \rceil} \leq 2\ell/\gamma + 2$, where the 2nd inequality follows from the fact that $\gamma \geq 2 \cdot \lceil \log m \rceil + 3$. The proof follows by Markov inequality. $\qquad\square$

Proving Section 4.1.

Proof of Section 4.1. Let $\mathcal{B} = \mathcal{B}^x$. Since for every disjoint sets $\mathcal{A}, \mathcal{C} \subseteq [m]$ and $x \in \mathsf{Supp}(X)$

$$\Pr[X_{\mathcal{A}} = x_{\mathcal{A}}] \cdot \Pr[X_{\mathcal{C}} = x_{\mathcal{C}} \mid X_{\mathcal{A}} = x_{\mathcal{A}}] = \Pr[X_{\mathcal{A} \cup \mathcal{C}} = x_{\mathcal{A} \cup \mathcal{C}}],$$

for every $\mathcal{I} \subseteq [m] \setminus \mathcal{B}$

$$H_{X_{\mathcal{B}}}(x_{\mathcal{B}}) + H_{X_{\mathcal{I}} \mid X_{\mathcal{B}} = x_{\mathcal{B}}}(x_{\mathcal{I}}) = H_{X_{\mathcal{I} \cup \mathcal{B}}}(x_{\mathcal{I} \cup \mathcal{B}}).$$

Assume towards a contradiction that $H_{X_{\mathcal{I}} \mid X_{\mathcal{B}} = x_{\mathcal{B}}}(x_{\mathcal{I}}) < (\lambda - \gamma)\,|\mathcal{I}|$. Since, by definition, $H_{X_{\mathcal{B}}}(x_{\mathcal{B}}) \leq (\lambda - \gamma)\,|\mathcal{B}|$, it follows that

$$H_{X_{\mathcal{I} \cup \mathcal{B}}}(x_{\mathcal{I} \cup \mathcal{B}}) < (\lambda - \gamma) \cdot (|\mathcal{B}| + |\mathcal{I}|) = (\lambda - \gamma) \cdot |\mathcal{B} \cup \mathcal{I}|,$$

in contradiction to the maximality of $\mathcal{B}$. $\qquad\square$

Proving Section 4.1.

Proof. Since, by assumption, $H(X) \geq \lambda m - \ell$, and since

$$H(I) = H(I, |I|) \leq \lceil \log m \rceil + H(I \mid |I|) \leq \lceil \log m \rceil + \mathrm{E}\left[|I|\right] \cdot \lceil \log m \rceil = \lceil \log m \rceil\,(\mathrm{E}\left[|I|\right] + 1),$$

we conclude that

$$H(X \mid I) \geq \lambda m - \ell - (\mathrm{E}_{x \leftarrow X}\left[|I|\right] + 1) \lceil \log m \rceil \tag{15}$$

Therefore,

$$H(X \mid I) = H(X_I, X_{[m] \setminus I} \mid I) \leq H(X_I \mid I) + H(X_{[m] \setminus I} \mid I) \tag{16}$$

Finally, since $H(X_{[m] \setminus I} \mid I) \leq H_0(X_{[m] \setminus I}) \mid I) \leq \lambda \cdot (m - \mathrm{E}_{x \leftarrow X}\left[|I|\right])$, we conclude that

$$\begin{aligned}
H(X_I \mid I) \geq &\, \lambda \cdot m - \ell - \lceil \log m \rceil\,(\mathrm{E}\left[|I|\right] + 1) - \lambda \cdot (m - \mathrm{E}\left[|I|\right]) \\
= &\, (\lambda - \lceil \log m \rceil) \cdot \mathrm{E}\left[|I|\right] - \ell - \lceil \log m \rceil.
\end{aligned}$$

$\qquad\square$

4.2 Hitting Almost Full-Entropy Distributions Using Product Set, Proving Lemma 4

We start by proving the following variant of Lemma 4, stated for *flat* distributions, i.e., X is uniform over a set. In Sect. 4.2.1, we use this variant for proving Lemma 4.

Lemma 5 (Hitting flat distributions). *Let $m, \gamma \leq \lambda \in \mathbb{N}$ be such that $\gamma \geq 2 \cdot \lceil \log m \rceil + 2$, let $\delta > 0$, and let $\mathcal{T} \subseteq \{0,1\}^{\lambda \cdot m}$ be a non empty set. If for all $\mathcal{I} \subseteq [m]$ and $a \in \{0,1\}^{\lambda \cdot |\mathcal{I}|}$, it holds that*

$$|\{x \in \mathcal{T} : x_{\mathcal{I}} = a\}| \leq |\mathcal{T}| \cdot 2^{(\gamma/2 - \lambda)|\mathcal{I}|}/\delta , \tag{17}$$

then

$$\Pr_{S \leftarrow (\mathcal{P}_{2^\gamma}(\{0,1\}^\lambda))^m} [S \cap \mathcal{T} \neq \emptyset] \geq \delta/2 .$$

Proof. Let $S = (S_1, \ldots, S_m)$ be as in the lemma statement, i.e., uniformly distributed over $\left(\mathcal{P}_{2^\gamma}(\{0,1\}^\lambda)\right)^m$. We assume, without loss of generality, that the elements of each S_i are chosen in a uniform order and denote the jth element of S_i, according to this order, by $S_i[j]$. For $y = (y_1, \ldots, y_m) \in [2^\gamma]^m$, let $S^y \in \{0,1\}^{\lambda \times m}$ be the random variable defined by $(S^y)_i \overset{\text{def}}{=} S_i[y_i]$. Let Z^y be the indicator for the event $S^y \in \mathcal{T}$, and let $Z \overset{\text{def}}{=} \sum_{y \in [2^\gamma]^m} Z^y$. By the Paley-Zygmund inequality, Theorem 8, it holds that

$$\Pr_{S \leftarrow (\mathcal{P}_{2^\gamma}(\{0,1\}^\lambda))^m} [S \cap \mathcal{T} \neq \emptyset] = \Pr[Z > 0] \geq \mathrm{E}[Z]^2/\mathrm{E}[Z^2] . \tag{18}$$

Thus, we prove Lemma 5 by properly bounding $\mathrm{E}[Z]$ and $\mathrm{E}[Z^2]$. Let $\rho \overset{\text{def}}{=} \frac{|\mathcal{T}|}{2^{m\lambda}}$. Since we associate a random order with the elements of each S_i, for every $y \in [2^\gamma]^m$ it holds that $\mathrm{E}[Z^y] = \rho$. Hence,

$$\mathrm{E}[Z] = \sum_{y \in [2^\gamma]^m} \mathrm{E}[Z^y] = 2^{\gamma m}\rho . \tag{19}$$

For upper bounding $\mathrm{E}[Z^2]$, we use the following claim (proved in Sect. 4.2). In the following for $y, y' \in [2^\gamma]^m$, let $\mathcal{K}_{y,y'} \overset{\text{def}}{=} \{i \in [m] : y_i = y_i'\}$.

Claim 12. *For every $y, y' \in [2^\gamma]^m$ it holds that $\Pr[Z^y \wedge Z^{y'}] \leq 2^{\gamma \cdot |\mathcal{K}_{y,y'}|/2} \cdot \rho^2/\delta$.*

For $\mathcal{K} \subseteq [m]$, let $\mathcal{A}_\mathcal{K} \overset{\text{def}}{=} \{(y, y') \in [2^\gamma]^m : \mathcal{K}_{y,y'} = \mathcal{K}\}$. Using Claim 12, we deuce that

$$\mathrm{E}\left[Z^2\right] = \sum_{y,y' \in [2^\gamma]^m} \Pr[Z^y \wedge Z^{y'}] \tag{20}$$

$$= \sum_{\mathcal{K} \subseteq [m]} \sum_{y,y' \in \mathcal{A}_\mathcal{K}} \Pr[Z^y \wedge Z^{y'}]$$

$$\leq \sum_{\mathcal{K} \subseteq [m]} \sum_{y,y' \in \mathcal{A}_\mathcal{K}} 2^{\gamma|\mathcal{K}|/2} \cdot \rho^2/\delta$$

$$\leq \frac{\rho^2}{\delta} \cdot \sum_{k=0}^{m} \sum_{\mathcal{K} \subseteq [m], |\mathcal{K}|=k} 2^{\gamma k} \cdot (2^{2\gamma})^{m-k} \cdot 2^{\gamma k/2}$$

$$= \frac{\rho^2}{\delta} \cdot 2^{2\gamma m} \cdot \sum_{k=0}^{m} \binom{m}{k} \cdot 2^{-\gamma k/2}$$

$$\leq \frac{\rho^2}{\delta} \cdot 2^{2\gamma m} \cdot \sum_{k=0}^{m} 2^{-k \cdot (\gamma/2 - \log m)} \leq 2 \cdot \frac{\rho^2}{\delta} \cdot 2^{2\gamma m}.$$

The first inequality holds by Claim 12, and the last one by holds since, by assumption, $\gamma \geq 2 \cdot \lceil \log m \rceil + 2$. Combining Equations (18) to (20), prove the lemma by deducing that

$$\Pr[Z > 0] \geq \frac{\mathrm{E}[Z]^2}{\mathrm{E}[Z^2]} \geq \frac{(2^{\gamma m} \cdot \rho)^2}{2 \cdot \frac{\rho^2}{\delta} \cdot 2^{2\gamma m}} = \delta/2.$$

$\square$

Proving Claim 12.

Proof. Let $\mathcal{K} = \mathcal{K}_{y,y'}$, and for $a \in \{0,1\}^{\lambda|\mathcal{K}|}$ let $\mathcal{T}_a = \{x \in \mathcal{T} : x_\mathcal{K} = a\}$. Compute

$$\Pr\left[Z^y \wedge Z^{y'}\right] = \sum_{a \in \{0,1\}^{\lambda \cdot |\mathcal{K}|}} \Pr[S^y_\mathcal{K} = a] \cdot \Pr\left[Z^y \wedge Z^{y'} \mid S^y_\mathcal{K} = a\right]$$

$$= \sum_{a \in \{0,1\}^{\lambda \cdot |\mathcal{K}|}} \Pr[S^y_\mathcal{K} = a] \cdot \left(\frac{|\mathcal{T}_a| \cdot (|\mathcal{T}_a| - 1)}{2^{2\lambda(m-|\mathcal{K}|)}}\right)$$

$$\leq \sum_{a \in \{0,1\}^{\lambda \cdot |\mathcal{K}|}} 2^{-\lambda|\mathcal{K}|} \cdot \left(\frac{|\mathcal{T}|}{2^{\lambda(m-|\mathcal{K}|)}}\right)^2 \cdot \left(\frac{|\mathcal{T}_a|}{|\mathcal{T}|}\right)^2$$

$$\leq \sum_{a \in \{0,1\}^{\lambda|\mathcal{K}|}} 2^{-\lambda|\mathcal{K}|} \cdot \left(\frac{|\mathcal{T}|}{2^{\lambda(m-|\mathcal{K}|)}}\right)^2 \cdot \frac{|\mathcal{T}_a|}{|\mathcal{T}|} \cdot 2^{(\gamma/2-\lambda)\cdot|\mathcal{K}|}/\delta$$

$$= \frac{1}{\delta} \cdot \left(\frac{|\mathcal{T}|}{2^{\lambda m}}\right)^2 \cdot 2^{\gamma|\mathcal{K}|/2} \cdot \sum_{a \in \{0,1\}^{\lambda|\mathcal{K}|}} \frac{|\mathcal{T}_a|}{|\mathcal{T}|} = \frac{1}{\delta} \cdot \rho^2 \cdot 2^{\gamma|\mathcal{K}|/2}.$$

The second inequality holds by the assumption of the lemma (Equation (17)). $\square$

4.2.1   Proving Lemma 4

Proof of Lemma 4. Define

$$T \stackrel{\text{def}}{=} \{x \in \mathsf{Supp}(X) \colon \forall \mathcal{I} \subseteq [m], H_{X_\mathcal{I}}(x_\mathcal{I}) \geq (\lambda - \gamma/2) \cdot |\mathcal{I}|\}$$

We partition the set T into $2\lambda m$ subsets, such that the elements of each part have roughly the same probability under X. Specifically, for $i \in [2\lambda m]$ let

$$T^i \stackrel{\text{def}}{=} \{x \in T \colon H_X(x) \in [i-1, i)\},$$

and let $T^0 \stackrel{\text{def}}{=} \{x \in T \colon H_X(x) \geq 2\lambda m\}$. By definition,

$$\Pr[X \in T^0] = \sum_{x \in T^0} \Pr[X = x] \leq 2^{\lambda \cdot m} \cdot 2^{-2 \cdot \lambda \cdot m} = 2^{-\lambda \cdot m},$$

and therefore $2^{-\lambda \cdot m} + \sum_{i \in [2 \cdot \lambda \cdot m]} \Pr[X \in T^i] \geq 1$. Hence, by averaging argument, exists $i \in [2\lambda m]$ such that

$$\Pr[X \in T^i] \geq \frac{1 - 2^{-\lambda \cdot m}}{2\lambda m} \geq \frac{1}{4\lambda m} \tag{21}$$

The second inequality hold since, by assumption, $\lambda \geq \gamma \geq 2$. In the rest of the proof we use Lemma 5 to prove that $\Pr_{S \leftarrow \mathcal{P}_{2\gamma}(\{0,1\}^\lambda)}[S \cap T^i \neq \emptyset]$. Let $X^i = X|_{X \in T^i}$, and for $\mathcal{I} \subseteq [m]$ and $a \in \mathsf{Supp}(X_\mathcal{I}^i)$, let $T_{\mathcal{I},a}^i \stackrel{\text{def}}{=} \{x \in T^i \colon x_\mathcal{I} = a\}$. Since X^i is almost flat, for every $a \in \mathsf{Supp}(X_\mathcal{I}^i)$ and $x \in T_{\mathcal{I},a}^i$:

$$\Pr[X_\mathcal{I}^i = a] = \sum_{x' \in T_{\mathcal{I},a}^i} \Pr[X^i = x'] \geq |T_{\mathcal{I},a}^i| \cdot \Pr[X^i = x]/2.$$

Similarly,

$$1 = \sum_{a \in \mathsf{Supp}(X_\mathcal{I}^i)} \Pr[X_\mathcal{I}^i = a] = \sum_{a \in \mathsf{Supp}(X_\mathcal{I}^i)} \sum_{x' \in T_{\mathcal{I},a}^i} \Pr[X^i = x']$$

$$\leq \sum_{a \in \mathsf{Supp}(X_\mathcal{I}^i)} |T_{\mathcal{I},a}^i| \cdot 2 \cdot \Pr[X^i = x] = 2 \cdot |T^i| \cdot \Pr[X^i = x].$$

Combing the above two inequalities, we get that

$$\Pr[X_\mathcal{I}^i = a] \geq \frac{1/2 \cdot |T_{\mathcal{I},a}^i| \cdot \Pr[X^i = x]}{2 \cdot |T^i| \cdot \Pr[X^i = x]} = \frac{|T_{\mathcal{I},a}^i|}{4 \cdot |T^i|} \tag{22}$$

By assumption, for every $x \in T$ and $\mathcal{I} \subseteq [m]$:

$$\Pr[X_\mathcal{I} = x_\mathcal{I}] \leq 2^{(\gamma/2 - \lambda)|\mathcal{I}|} \tag{23}$$

Therefore, for every $a \in \mathsf{Supp}(X_\mathcal{I}^i)$:

$$\frac{|T_{\mathcal{I},a}^i|}{|T^i|} \leq 4 \cdot \Pr[X_\mathcal{I}^i = a] \leq 4 \cdot \frac{\Pr[X_\mathcal{I} = a]}{\Pr[X \in T^i]} \leq 16\lambda m \cdot 2^{(\gamma/2 - \lambda)|\mathcal{I}|} \tag{24}$$

The first inequality holds by Equation (22), and the third by Equation (23). Applying Lemma 5 for the set $\mathcal{T}^i$ with parameter $\delta = 1/16\lambda m$, yields that

$$\Pr_{S \leftarrow \mathcal{P}_{2\gamma}(\{0,1\}^\lambda)} \left[S \cap \mathcal{T}^i \neq \emptyset \right] \geq \frac{1}{32\lambda m},$$

and we deduce that $\Pr_{S \leftarrow \mathcal{P}_{2\gamma}(\{0,1\}^\lambda)} \left[S \cap \mathsf{Supp}(X) \neq \emptyset \right] \geq \frac{1}{32\lambda m}$.   □

5   Lower Bound on the Length of ROM-SNARGs

In this section, we present our lower bound on the proof length of ROM-SNARGs, formally stated below (see Definition 1 for the formal definition of rETH, and Sect. 3.5 for that of salted-soundness ROM-SNARGs).

Theorem 13 (Conditional lower bound on ROMSNARGs length). *Let* $\mathsf{ARG} = (\mathsf{P}, \mathsf{V})$ *be an* s-*length ROM-SNARG for* n-*variable 3SAT, with* (t, ε)-*salted-soundness, perfect completeness, and deterministic non-adaptive verifier. Let* $\mathsf{q_P}$ *and* $\mathsf{q_V}$ *be the query complexity of* P *and* V, *respectively, let* v *denotes* V's *running time, and let* λ *denote the random oracle input and output length. Assuming rETH, if*

1. $\varepsilon \leq 1/4$;
2. $\mathsf{q_V} \cdot \lambda \in o(n)$, $\mathsf{q_V} + \lambda \leq t^{1/10}$;
3. $\log^2(t/\varepsilon) \cdot \log^{-1} \mathsf{q_P} \in o(n)$; *and*
4. $v \in 2^{o(n)}$,

then $\mathsf{s} \geq 2^{-15} \cdot \log t \cdot \log \frac{t}{\varepsilon} / \log \mathsf{q_P}$.

Theorem 13 is proved using the following two lemmata. Lemma 6 states that the verifier query complexity of a short ROM-SNARG can be significantly reduced, and Lemma 7, taken from [CY20], states that the existence of a low verifier query complexity ROM-SNARGs contradicts rETH.

Lemma 6 (Short ROMSNARGs → Low Query ROMSNARGs). *Let* $\mathsf{ARG} = (\mathsf{P}, \mathsf{V})$ *be as in Theorem 13, then for any* $\gamma \in \mathbb{N}$, *there exists a verifier* V' *such that* $\mathsf{ARG}' \overset{\text{def}}{=} (\mathsf{P}, \mathsf{V}')$ *is a ROM-SNARG for* $\mathcal{L}$ *with the following properties:*

1. *completeness* $\left(\lambda \cdot \mathsf{q_P} \cdot \mathsf{q_V}^{20 \cdot \lceil s/\gamma \rceil}\right)^{-1}$;
2. $(t - \mathsf{q_V} \cdot 2^\gamma, \varepsilon)$-*soundness*;
3. *verifier query complexity* $20 \cdot \lceil s/\gamma \rceil$; *and*
4. *verifier running time* $O(2^{\mathsf{q_V} \cdot \log t} \cdot v)$.

Furthermore, the transformation from V *to* V' *is efficient (in the description length of* V).*

In words, Lemma 6 states that there exists a generic transformation from short ROM-SNARGs into the same length ROM-SNARGs with low verifier query complexity (but worse completeness and soundness). Lemma 6 is proven in Sect. 5.2.

While not explicit in their work, the following lemma follows by similar arguments to the main proof in [CY20]. A formal proof is given in the full version of the paper.

Lemma 7 (Follows from [CY20]). *Let* $\mathsf{ARG} = (\mathsf{P}, \mathsf{V})$ *be a* (t, ε)*-sound ROM-SNARG for n-variable 3SAT with random oracle (input and output) length* λ*, argument length* s*, and let* $\mathsf{q_V}$ *and* $\mathsf{q_P}$ *denote* P*'s and* V*'s query complexity, respectively. Assume*

1. $\mathsf{s} + \lambda \cdot \mathsf{q_V} \in o(n)$;
2. $\mathsf{q_V} \le 1/4 \cdot \log(1/\varepsilon) \cdot \log^{-1} \mathsf{q_P}$;
3. *completeness* $\ge \varepsilon^{2/3}$;
4. $\log^2(1/\varepsilon) \cdot \log^{-1} \mathsf{q_P} \le o(n)$; *and*
5. V*'s running time* $2^{o(n)}$,

then $3SAT \in BPTIME[2^{o(n)}]$.

Note that Lemma 7 does not require V to be deterministic or non adaptive.

5.1   Proof of Theorem 13

Proof of Theorem 13. Suppose we are given a SNARG ARG for 3SAT that satisfies the conditions of the theorem, and assume without loss of generality that $\mathsf{q_P} \le t^{1/10}$. (Otherwise, for $\mathsf{q_P} > t^{1/10}$, the lower bound we need to prove can be written as $\mathsf{s} \ge 2^{-15} \cdot \log \frac{t}{\varepsilon}$, which follows by the folklore lower bound[12]). Assume towards contradiction that $\mathsf{s} \le 2^{-15} \cdot \log t \cdot \log \frac{t}{\varepsilon} / \log \mathsf{q_P}$. Theorem 13 is proved via the following steps:

1. Apply Lemma 2 with parameter $k = t^{0.5}$ which yields a scheme ARG that has (t', ε')-salted-soundness, where $t' = t^{1/2}$, and $\varepsilon' = 2\varepsilon/t^{1/2}$.
2. Apply Lemma 6 with $\gamma = 1/10 \cdot \log t$, to get a ROM-SNARG ARG' for 3SAT with the following parameters:
   (a) completeness $\left(\lambda \cdot \mathsf{q_P} \cdot \mathsf{q_V}^{20 \cdot \lceil \mathsf{s}/\gamma \rceil}\right)^{-1}$;
   (b) $(t' - \mathsf{q_V} \cdot 2^\gamma, \varepsilon')$-soundness.
   (c) verifier query complexity $\mathsf{q_{V}'} = 20 \cdot \lceil \mathsf{s}/\gamma \rceil$; and
   (d) verifier running time $v' = O(2^{\mathsf{q_V} \cdot \log t} \cdot v)$.
3. Apply Lemma 7 on ARG' to contradict rETH. For this, we need to verify that all five conditions of the lemma apply. Indeed,
   (i) $\mathsf{s} + \lambda \cdot \mathsf{q_{V}'} \in o(n)$: First, observe that $\mathsf{s} \le 2^{-15} \cdot \log t \cdot \log \frac{t}{\varepsilon} / \log \mathsf{q_P} \in o(n)$. Then, since $\lambda \cdot \mathsf{q_V} \in o(n)$, we get that $\lambda \cdot \mathsf{q_{V}'} = O(\lambda \cdot \mathsf{s}/\gamma) = O(\log t \cdot \mathsf{s}/\log t) = o(n)$. Together, we have that $\mathsf{s} + \lambda \cdot \mathsf{q_{V}'} \le o(n) + o(n) = o(n)$:

---

[12] The proof of the folklore lower bound appears in the full version of the paper.

(ii) $q_{V'} \leq 1/4 \cdot \log(1/\varepsilon') \cdot \log^{-1} q_P$: the query complexity of the verifier of ARG' is

$$q_{V'} \leq 20 \cdot \lceil s/\gamma \rceil \leq 20 \cdot \left\lceil \frac{2^{-15} \cdot \log t \cdot \log \frac{t}{\varepsilon} / \log q_P}{1/10 \cdot \log t} \right\rceil \leq 1/8 \cdot \log \frac{t}{\varepsilon} \cdot \log^{-1} q_P$$

$$\leq 1/4 \cdot \log \frac{t^{1/2}}{2\varepsilon} \cdot \log^{-1} q_P = 1/4 \cdot \log \frac{1}{\varepsilon'} \cdot \log^{-1} q_P \ .$$

(iii) completeness $\geq \varepsilon'^{2/3}$: Observe that $20 \lceil s/\gamma \rceil \leq 2^{-10} \cdot \log(t/\varepsilon) \cdot \log^{-1} q_P$. Thus, the completeness of our scheme satisfies:

$$\left(\lambda \cdot q_P \cdot q_V{}^{20 \cdot \lceil s/\gamma \rceil} \right)^{-1} \geq \left(t^{1/10} \cdot t^{1/10} \cdot q_V{}^{2^{-10} \cdot \log(t/\varepsilon) \cdot \log^{-1} q_P} \right)^{-1}$$

$$\geq 2^{-2/10 \log t - 2^{-10} \cdot \log(t/\varepsilon)} \geq 2^{-2/10 \log t - 2^{-9} \cdot \log(t^{1/2}/2\varepsilon)}$$

$$\geq 2^{-3/10 \cdot \log(t^{1/2}/2\varepsilon)} = 2^{3/10 \cdot \log(\varepsilon')} \geq \varepsilon'^{2/3} \ .$$

(iv) $\log^2(1/\varepsilon') \cdot \log^{-1} q_P \leq o(n)$: By the definition of ε' and the conditions of the theorem we get that $\log^2(1/\varepsilon') \cdot \log^{-1} q_P = O(\log^2(t/\varepsilon) \cdot \log^{-1} q_P) = o(n)$.

(v) V's running time $2^{o(n)}$: The verifier running time of the scheme is $O(2^{q_V \cdot \log t} \cdot v)$. Since $q_V \cdot \log t = o(n)$ and $v = 2^{o(n)}$, its total running time is $2^{o(n)}$.

4. We conclude that $3SAT \in BPTIME[2^{o(n)}]$, contradicting rETH.

$\square$

5.2 Short ROM-SNARGs to Low Query ROM-SNARGs, Proving Lemma 6

In this section, we prove Lemma 6 (see Sect. 2 for a high-level overview of the proof). Let $ARG = (P, V)$ be ROM-SNARG with (t, ε)-salted soundness, random oracle of length λ, a non-adaptive deterministic verifier, prover query complexity q_P, and verifier query complexity q_V. The low query verifier V' is defined as follows:

Algorithm 14 (Low-query verifier V').
Oracle: $\zeta \colon \{0,1\}^\lambda \mapsto \{0,1\}^\lambda$.
Parameter: $\gamma \leq \lambda$. Let $k = 20 \lceil s/\gamma \rceil$.
Input: Instance $\mathbb{x}$ and proof π.
Operation:

1. Emulate V on $(\mathbb{x}, \pi)$ to get a list of queries $w = (w_1, \ldots, w_{q_V})$.
2. Sample $k' \in [k]$, uniformly at random and uniformly sample a k'-size subset $\mathcal{J} \subseteq [q_V]$.

3. For each $i \in [q_V]$:
   If $i \in \mathcal{J}$, set $S_i = \{\zeta(w_i)\}$.
   Otherwise, let S_i be a 2^γ-size *random* subset of $\{0,1\}^\lambda$.
4. Accept if there exists $(y_1, \ldots, y_{q_V}) \in S_1 \times \ldots \times S_{q_V}$ that make V accepts given $(y_1, \ldots, y_{q_V})$ as answers to its oracle queries.

It is easy to observe that V' has the desired query complexity and running time. Thus, it is left to prove that $\mathsf{ARG}' = (\mathsf{P}, \mathsf{V}')$ has the desired completeness and soundness. The completeness of ARG' is analyzed in Sect. 5.2.1 and its soundness in Sect. 5.2.2. We put things together in Sect. 5.2.3.

5.2.1   Completeness

We prove the following lower bound on the completeness of ARG'.

Claim. ARG' has completeness $\geq \left(\lambda \cdot q_P \cdot q_V{}^{20 \cdot \lceil s/\gamma \rceil}\right)^{-1}$.

In the following, we assume for simplicity that the V's queries are (always) a subset of the P's queries. (The proof without this assumption follows very similar lines, though with more complicated notation. Also, one could always modify the honest prover to perform all the verifier's queries, this comes with a negligible cost that has no effect on our results.)

Proof. We associate the following random variable with the probability space defined by the choice of ζ over the (honest) execution of $(\mathsf{P}^\zeta(\mathsf{w}), \mathsf{V}'^\zeta)(\mathsf{x})$: denote P's queries by $X = (X_1, \ldots, X_{q_P})$, define $Z = (Z_1, \ldots, Z_{q_P})$ by $Z_i = \zeta(X_i)$, and let Π denote the proof sent by P. We assume for ease of notation that the queries that V would have made on the proof Π are just $X_1, \ldots, X_{q_V}$.

The length of Π is s, thus a standard argument yields that $H(\Pi) \leq H_0(\Pi) \leq$ s. Since each Z_i is a bit string of length λ (recall that λ is the output length of ζ), it holds that $H(Z \mid \Pi) \geq H(Z) - H(\Pi) \geq \lambda \cdot q_P - $ s.

Since (by definition) $H(Z \mid \Pi) = \mathrm{E}_{\pi \leftarrow \Pi}[H(Z \mid \Pi = \pi)]$, with probability at least $1/2$ over $\pi \leftarrow \Pi$, it holds that $H(Z \mid \Pi = \pi) \geq \lambda \cdot q_P - 2 \cdot $ s. Fix any such proof π, and let $Y = (Y_1, \ldots, Y_{q_P}) = Z \mid_{\Pi=\pi}$. For $\ell = 2 \cdot $ s, it holds that $H(Y) \geq \lambda \cdot q_P - \ell$. Applying Theorem 11 on Y yields that with probability $1/2$ over $y \leftarrow Y$ there exists a subset $\mathcal{B} \subseteq [q_P]$ with $|\mathcal{B}| \leq \lfloor 8\ell/\gamma \rfloor + 4$ such that:

$$\Pr_{S \leftarrow (\mathcal{P}_{2\gamma}(\{0,1\}^\lambda))^{q_P - |\mathcal{B}|}} [S \cap \mathsf{Supp}(Y \mid_{Y_\mathcal{B}=y_\mathcal{B}}) \neq \emptyset] \geq \frac{1}{32 \cdot \lambda \cdot q_P} \ . \qquad (25)$$

An immediate corollary of Equation (25) is that with probability at least $1/2$ over the choice of $y \leftarrow Y$, the following process outputs 1 with probability $\frac{1}{32 \cdot \lambda \cdot q_P}$:

1. For each $i \in [q_V]$:
   If $i \in \mathcal{B}$, set $S_i = \{y_i\}$.
   Otherwise, let S_i be a 2^γ-size *random* subset of $\{0,1\}^\lambda$.
2. Output 1 if $(S_1 \times \ldots \times S_{q_V}) \cap \mathsf{Supp}((Y \mid_{Y_\mathcal{B}=y_\mathcal{B}})_{[q_V]}) \neq \emptyset$.

The perfect completeness of the argument scheme ARG yields that for any $\pi \in \mathsf{Supp}(\Pi)$, it holds that $\mathsf{V}(\mathbf{x}, \pi)$ accepts on any value of $z \in \mathsf{Supp}((Y = Z|_{\Pi=\pi})_{[\mathsf{qv}]})$ given as oracle answers. Thus, it accepts any value of $z \in \mathsf{Supp}((Y|_{Y_B=y_B})_{[\mathsf{qv}]})$ for any $y \in \mathsf{Supp}(Y)$.

We deduce that V' accepts with this probability, assuming that $\mathcal{J} = \mathcal{B} \cap [\mathsf{qv}]$. Noting that $|\mathcal{B}| \leq \lfloor 8\ell/\gamma \rfloor + 4 = \lfloor 16s/\gamma \rfloor + 4 \leq 20\lceil s/\gamma \rceil = k$, the latter happens with probability at least $k^{-1} \cdot \binom{\mathsf{qv}}{k}^{-1}$. We conclude that V' accepts with probability at least

$$\frac{1}{2} \cdot \frac{1}{2} \cdot \frac{1}{32 \cdot \lambda \cdot \mathsf{qp}} \cdot \frac{1}{k} \cdot \frac{1}{\binom{\mathsf{qv}}{k}} \geq \frac{1}{128 \cdot \lambda \cdot \mathsf{qp}} \cdot \frac{1}{k} \cdot \frac{(k/e)^k}{\mathsf{qv}^k}$$

$$\geq \frac{1}{e \cdot 128 \cdot \lambda \cdot \mathsf{qp}} \frac{(k/e)^{k-1}}{\mathsf{qv}^k} \geq \frac{1}{e \cdot 128 \cdot \lambda \cdot \mathsf{qp}} \frac{(20/e)^{19}}{\mathsf{qv}^k} \geq \frac{1}{\lambda \cdot \mathsf{qp} \cdot \mathsf{qv}^k} \ .$$

$\square$

5.2.2 Soundness

We prove the following upper bound on the soundness error of ARG'.

Claim. ARG' has $(t - \mathsf{qv} \cdot 2^\gamma, \varepsilon)$-soundness.

Proof. Let $\widetilde{\mathsf{P}}'$ be a $t' := t - \mathsf{qv} \cdot 2^\gamma$-query cheating prover such that $\Pr\left[\langle \widetilde{\mathsf{P}}', \mathsf{V}'(\mathbf{x})\rangle = 1\right] > \varepsilon$, for some $\mathbf{x} \notin \mathcal{L}$. We show how to use $\widetilde{\mathsf{P}}$ to construct the following t-query cheating prover $\widetilde{\mathsf{P}}$ such that $\Pr\left[\mathsf{SaltedSoundness}_{\mathsf{V},\lambda,t'}(\widetilde{\mathsf{P}}, \mathbf{x}) = 1\right] > \varepsilon$, violating the assumed salted-soundness of (P, V).

We assume without loss of generality that $\widetilde{\mathsf{P}}'$ is deterministic. Indeed, since $\widetilde{\mathsf{P}}$ is computationally unbounded (it is only bounded by its query complexity to the random oracle), it has sufficient time to enumerate all random strings and choose the best one.

Algorithm 15. $(\widetilde{\mathsf{P}})$.
Oracle: $\zeta \colon \{0,1\}^\lambda \mapsto \{0,1\}^\lambda$. Input: Instance $\mathbf{x}$.

1. Run $\widetilde{\mathsf{P}}'^\zeta(\mathbf{x})$ to generate a proof π.
2. Emulate V on $(\mathbf{x}, \pi)$ to determine its list of oracle queries $(w_1, \ldots, w_{\mathsf{qv}})$.
3. For $i = 1, \ldots, \mathsf{qv}$:
   (a) Iterate in the salted soundness loop with query w_i for 2^γ times. Let $\widetilde{S}_i$ be the set of obtained answers.
   (b) If w_i was asked by $\widetilde{\mathsf{P}}'$ in Step 1, add the retrieved answer to $\widetilde{S}_i$.
4. If there exists $(y_1, \ldots, y_{\mathsf{qv}}) \in \widetilde{S}_1 \times \ldots \times \widetilde{S}_{\mathsf{qv}}$ that make V accept $(\mathbf{x}, \pi)$ with $(y_1, \ldots, y_{\mathsf{qv}})$ as the answers to its oracle queries, output $(\pi, \sigma = [(w_1, y_1), \ldots, (w_{\mathsf{qv}}, y_{\mathsf{qv}})])$.

Recall that for $i \in \mathcal{J}$, the verifier V' sets S_i to be the output of a single call to the oracle, and for $i \notin \mathcal{J}$, it sets S_i to 2^γ random strings in $\{0,1\}^\lambda$. Hence, for every choice of ζ, there exists a coupling between the sets S_i sampled by V' to the sets $\widetilde{S}_i$ sampled by $\widetilde{\mathsf{P}}$ with $\widetilde{S}_i \supseteq S_i$ for every i. It follows that the probability that $\widetilde{\mathsf{P}}$ makes V accept $\mathbf{x}$ is at least as high as the probability that $\widetilde{\mathsf{P}}'$ makes P' accept $\mathbf{x}$, which by assumption is at least ε. This concludes the proof since by construction, $\widetilde{\mathsf{P}}'$ makes t' queries. $\qquad\square$

5.2.3 Putting It Together

Proof of Lemma 6. Immediately follows by Sects. 5.2.1 and 5.2.2. $\qquad\square$

References

[AHIV17] Ames, S., Hazay, C., Ishai, Y., Venkitasubramaniam, M.: Ligero: lightweight sublinear arguments without a trusted setup. In: CCS 2017 (2017)

[BBBPWM18] Bünz, B., Bootle, J., Boneh, D., Poelstra, A., Wuille, P., Maxwell, G.: Bulletproofs: short proofs for confidential transactions and more. In: S&P 2018 (2018)

[BBCPGL18] Baum, C., Bootle, J., Cerulli, A., del Pino, R., Groth, J., Lyubashevsky, V.: Sub-linear lattice-based zero-knowledge arguments for arithmetic circuits. In: Shacham, H., Boldyreva, A. (eds.) CRYPTO 2018. LNCS, vol. 10992, pp. 669–699. Springer, Cham (2018). https://doi.org/10.1007/978-3-319-96881-0_23

[BBHR19] Ben-Sasson, E., Bentov, I., Horesh, Y., Riabzev, M.: Scalable zero knowledge with no trusted setup. In: Boldyreva, A., Micciancio, D. (eds.) CRYPTO 2019. LNCS, vol. 11694, pp. 701–732. Springer, Cham (2019). https://doi.org/10.1007/978-3-030-26954-8_23

[BCCGP16] Bootle, J., Cerulli, A., Chaidos, P., Groth, J., Petit, C.: Efficient zero-knowledge arguments for arithmetic circuits in the discrete log setting. In: Fischlin, M., Coron, J.-S. (eds.) EUROCRYPT 2016. LNCS, vol. 9666, pp. 327–357. Springer, Heidelberg (2016). https://doi.org/10.1007/978-3-662-49896-5_12

[BCGGMTV14] Ben-Sasson, E., et al.: Zerocash: decentralized anonymous payments from bitcoin. In: SP 2014 (2014)

[BCIOP13] Bitansky, N., Chiesa, A., Ishai, Y., Ostrovsky, R., Paneth, O.: Succinct non-interactive arguments via linear interactive proofs. In: TCC 2013 (2013)

[BCRSVW19] Ben-Sasson, E., Chiesa, A., Riabzev, M., Spooner, N., Virza, M., Ward, N.P.: Aurora: transparent succinct arguments for R1CS. In: Ishai, Y., Rijmen, V. (eds.) EUROCRYPT 2019. LNCS, vol. 11476, pp. 103–128. Springer, Cham (2019). https://doi.org/10.1007/978-3-030-17653-2_4

[BCS16] Ben-Sasson, E., Chiesa, A., Spooner, N.: Interactive oracle proofs. In: Hirt, M., Smith, A. (eds.) TCC 2016. LNCS, vol. 9986, pp. 31–60. Springer, Heidelberg (2016). https://doi.org/10.1007/978-3-662-53644-5_2

[BCS21] Bootle, J., Chiesa, A., Sotiraki, K.: Sumcheck arguments and their applications. In: Malkin, T., Peikert, C. (eds.) CRYPTO 2021. LNCS, vol. 12825, pp. 742–773. Springer, Cham (2021). https://doi.org/10.1007/978-3-030-84242-0_26

[BFS20] Bünz, B., Fisch, B., Szepieniec, A.: Transparent SNARKs from DARK compilers. In: Canteaut, A., Ishai, Y. (eds.) EUROCRYPT 2020. LNCS, vol. 12105, pp. 677–706. Springer, Cham (2020). https://doi. org/10.1007/978-3-030-45721-1_24

[BGLR93] Bellare, M., Goldwasser, S., Lund, C., Russell, A.: Efficient probabilistically checkable proofs and applications to approximations. In: STOC 1993 (1993)

[BISW17] Boneh, D., Ishai, Y., Sahai, A., Wu, D.J.: Lattice-based SNARGs and their application to more efficient obfuscation. In: Coron, J.-S., Nielsen, J.B. (eds.) EUROCRYPT 2017. LNCS, vol. 10212, pp. 247–277. Springer, Cham (2017). https://doi.org/10.1007/978-3-319-56617-7_9

[BISW18] Boneh, D., Ishai, Y., Sahai, A., Wu, D.J.: Quasi-optimal SNARGs via linear multi-prover interactive proofs. In: Nielsen, J.B., Rijmen, V. (eds.) EUROCRYPT 2018. LNCS, vol. 10822, pp. 222–255. Springer, Cham (2018). https://doi.org/10.1007/978-3-319-78372-7_8

[BLNS20] Bootle, J., Lyubashevsky, V., Nguyen, N.K., Seiler, G.: A non-PCP approach to succinct quantum-safe zero-knowledge. In: Micciancio, D., Ristenpart, T. (eds.) CRYPTO 2020. LNCS, vol. 12171, pp. 441–469. Springer, Cham (2020). https://doi.org/10.1007/978-3-030-56880-1_16

[BM17] Barak, B., Mahmoody-Ghidary, M.: Merkle's key agreement protocol is optimal: an $O(n^2)$ attack on any key agreement from random oracles. J. Cryptol. **30**(3), 699–734 (2017)

[BMG07] Barak, B., Mahmoody-Ghidary, M.: Lower bounds on signatures from symmetric primitives (2007)

[CCHLRR18] Canetti, R., Chen, Y., Holmgren, J., Lombardi, A., Rothblum, G.N., Rothblum, R.D.: Fiat–Shamir from simpler assumptions. Cryptology ePrint Archive, Report 2018/1004

[CDGS18] Coretti, S., Dodis, Y., Guo, S., Steinberger, J.: Random oracles and non-uniformity. In: Nielsen, J.B., Rijmen, V. (eds.) EUROCRYPT 2018. LNCS, vol. 10820, pp. 227–258. Springer, Cham (2018). https:// doi.org/10.1007/978-3-319-78381-9_9

[CF13] Catalano, D., Fiore, D.: Vector commitments and their applications. In: Kurosawa, K., Hanaoka, G. (eds.) PKC 2013. LNCS, vol. 7778, pp. 55–72. Springer, Heidelberg (2013). https://doi.org/10.1007/978-3-642-36362-7_5

[CHMMVW20] Chiesa, A., Hu, Y., Maller, M., Mishra, P., Vesely, N., Ward, N.: Marlin: preprocessing zkSNARKs with universal and updatable SRS. In: Canteaut, A., Ishai, Y. (eds.) EUROCRYPT 2020. LNCS, vol. 12105, pp. 738–768. Springer, Cham (2020). https://doi.org/10.1007/978-3-030-45721-1_26

[CMSZ21] Chiesa, A., Ma, F., Spooner, N., Zhandry, M.: Post-quantum succinct arguments. In: IACR Cryptol. ePrint Arch (2021)

[COS20] Chiesa, A., Ojha, D., Spooner, N.: FRACTAL: post-quantum and transparent recursive proofs from holography. In: Canteaut, A., Ishai, Y. (eds.) EUROCRYPT 2020. LNCS, vol. 12105, pp. 769–793. Springer, Cham (2020). https://doi.org/10.1007/978-3-030-45721-1_27

[CY20] Chiesa, A., Yogev, E.: Barriers for succinct arguments in the random oracle model. In: Pass, R., Pietrzak, K. (eds.) TCC 2020. LNCS, vol. 12551, pp. 47–76. Springer, Cham (2020). https://doi.org/10.1007/978-3-030-64378-2_3

[CY21a] Chiesa, A., Yogev, E.: Subquadratic SNARGs in the random oracle model. In: Malkin, T., Peikert, C. (eds.) CRYPTO 2021. LNCS, vol. 12825, pp. 711–741. Springer, Cham (2021). https://doi.org/10.1007/978-3-030-84242-0_25

[CY21b] Chiesa, A., Yogev, E.: Tight security bounds for Micali's SNARGs. In: Nissim, K., Waters, B. (eds.) TCC 2021. LNCS, vol. 13042, pp. 401–434. Springer, Cham (2021). https://doi.org/10.1007/978-3-030-90459-3_14

[DGK17] Dodis, Y., Guo, S., Katz, J.: Fixing cracks in the concrete: random oracles with auxiliary input, revisited. In: Coron, J.-S., Nielsen, J.B. (eds.) EUROCRYPT 2017. LNCS, vol. 10211, pp. 473–495. Springer, Cham (2017). https://doi.org/10.1007/978-3-319-56614-6_16

[DHMTW14] Dell, H., Husfeldt, T., Wahlén, M.: Exponential time complexity of the permanent and the Tutte polynomial. In: Abramsky, S., Gavoille, C., Kirchner, C., Meyer auf der Heide, F., Spirakis, P.G. (eds.) ICALP 2010. LNCS, vol. 6198, pp. 426–437. Springer, Heidelberg (2010). https://doi.org/10.1007/978-3-642-14165-2_37

[EIRS01] Edmonds, J., Impagliazzo, R., Rudich, S., Sgall, J.: Communication complexity towards lower bounds on circuit depth. Comput. Complex. **10**, 210–246 (2001)

[FS86] Fiat, A., Shamir, A.: How to prove yourself: practical solutions to identification and signature problems. In: Odlyzko, A.M. (ed.) CRYPTO 1986. LNCS, vol. 263, pp. 186–194. Springer, Heidelberg (1987). https://doi.org/10.1007/3-540-47721-7_12

[GGKT05] Gennaro, R., Gertner, Y., Katz, J., Trevisan, L.: Bounds on the efficiency of generic cryptographic constructions. In: SICOMP (2005)

[GGPR13] Gennaro, R., Gentry, C., Parno, B., Raykova, M.: Quadratic span programs and Succinct NIZKs without PCPs. In: Johansson, T., Nguyen, P.Q. (eds.) EUROCRYPT 2013. LNCS, vol. 7881, pp. 626–645. Springer, Heidelberg (2013). https://doi.org/10.1007/978-3-642-38348-9_37

[GLLZ20] Guo, S., Li, Q., Liu, Q., Zhang, J.: Unifying presampling via concentration bounds. In: Nissim, K., Waters, B. (eds.) TCC 2021. LNCS, vol. 13042, pp. 177–208. Springer, Cham (2021). https://doi.org/10.1007/978-3-030-90459-3_7

[GMNO18] Gennaro, R., Minelli, M., Nitulescu, A., Orrù, M.: Lattice-based zk-SNARKs from square span programs. In: CCS 2018 (2018)

[GNS21] Ganesh, C., Nitulescu, A., Soria-Vazquez, E.: Rinocchio: SNARKs for ring arithmetic. In: IACR Cryptol. ePrint Arch (2021)

[Gro10] Groth, J.: Short pairing-based non-interactive zero-knowledge arguments. In: Abe, M. (ed.) ASIACRYPT 2010. LNCS, vol. 6477, pp. 321–340. Springer, Heidelberg (2010). https://doi.org/10.1007/978-3-642-17373-8_19

[Gro16] Groth, J.: On the size of pairing-based non-interactive arguments. In: Fischlin, M., Coron, J.-S. (eds.) EUROCRYPT 2016. LNCS, vol. 9666, pp. 305–326. Springer, Heidelberg (2016). https://doi.org/10.1007/978-3-662-49896-5_11

[GSV18]   Grinberg, A., Shaltiel, R., Viola, E.: Indistinguishability by adaptive procedures with advice, and lower bounds on hardness amplification proofs (2018)

[GW11]   Gentry, C., Wichs, D.: Separating succinct non-interactive arguments from all falsifiable assumptions. In: STOC 2011 (2011)

[HMORY19]   Haitner, I., Mazor, N., Oshman, R., Reingold, O., . Yehudayoff, A: On the communication complexity of key-agreement protocols (2018)

[IR89]   Impagliazzo, R., Rudich, S.: Limits on the provable consequences of one-way permutations (1989)

[ISW21]   Ishai, Y., Su, H., Wu, D.J.: Shorter and faster post-quantum designated-verifier zkSNARKs from lattices (2021)

[Kil92]   Kilian, J.: A note on efficient zero-knowledge proofs and arguments. In: STOC 1992 (1992)

[LM19]   Lai, R.W.F., Malavolta, G.: Subvector commitments with application to succinct arguments. In: Boldyreva, A., Micciancio, D. (eds.) CRYPTO 2019. LNCS, vol. 11692, pp. 530–560. Springer, Cham (2019). https://doi.org/10.1007/978-3-030-26948-7_19

[LSTW21]   Lee, J., Setty, S.T.V., Thaler, J., Wahby, R.S.: Linear-time zero-knowledge SNARKs for R1CS. In: IACR Cryptol. ePrint Arch (2021)

[MBKM19]   Maller, M., Bowe, S., Kohlweiss, M., Meiklejohn, S.: Sonic: zero-knowledge SNARKs from linear-size universal and updatable structured reference strings (2019)

[Mer82]   Merkle, R.C.: Secure communications over insecure channels. Commun. ACM 21(4), 294–299 (1978)

[Mic00]   Micali, S.: Computationally sound proofs. SIAM J. Comput. (2000); Preliminary version appeared in FOCS 1994

[Nit19]   Nitulescu, A.: Lattice-based zero-knowledge SNARGs for arithmetic circuits. In: Schwabe, P., Thériault, N. (eds.) LATINCRYPT 2019. LNCS, vol. 11774, pp. 217–236. Springer, Cham (2019). https://doi.org/10.1007/978-3-030-30530-7_11

[PGHR13]   Parno, B., Gentry, C., Howell, J., Raykova, M.: Pinocchio: nearly practical verifiable computation. In: Oakland 2013 (2013)

[Raz98]   Raz, R.: A parallel repetition theorem. SIAM J. Comput. 27(3), 769–803 (1998)

[Set19]   Setty, S.: Spartan: efficient and general-purpose zkSNARKs without trusted setup. Cryptology ePrint Archive, Report 2019/550

[Sta18]   libstark. libstark: a C++ library for zkSTARK systems (2018). https://github.com/elibensasson/libSTARK

[SV10]   Shaltiel, R., Viola, E.: Hardness amplification proofs require majority. SIAM J. Comput. 39, 3122–3154 (2010)

[Unr07]   Unruh, D.: Random oracles and auxiliary input. In: Menezes, A. (ed.) CRYPTO 2007. LNCS, vol. 4622, pp. 205–223. Springer, Heidelberg (2007). https://doi.org/10.1007/978-3-540-74143-5_12

[WTSTW18]   Wahby, R.S., Tzialla, I., Shelat, A., Thaler, J., Walfish, M.: Doubly-efficient zkSNARKs without trusted setup (2018)

[Zc14]   Electric Coin Company: Zcash Cryptocurrency. https://z.cash/

[ZGKPP17]   Zhang, Y., Genkin, D., Katz, J., Papadopoulos, D., Papamanthou, C.: A zero-knowledge version of vSQL. Cryptology ePrint Archive, Report 2017/1146

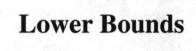

Lower Bounds

Lower Bounds

Time-Space Tradeoffs for Sponge Hashing: Attacks and Limitations for Short Collisions

Cody Freitag[1] , Ashrujit Ghoshal[2]([✉]) , and Ilan Komargodski[3,4]

[1] Cornell Tech, New York, USA
cfreitag@cs.cornell.edu
[2] Paul G. Allen School of Computer Science & Engineering,
University of Washington, Seattle, Washington, USA
ashrujit@cs.washington.edu
[3] School of Computer Science and Engineering,
Hebrew University of Jerusalem, 91904 Jerusalem, Israel
ilank@cs.huji.ac.il
[4] NTT Research, Sunnyvale, USA

Abstract. Sponge hashing is a novel alternative to the popular Merkle-Damgård hashing design. The sponge construction has become increasingly popular in various applications, perhaps most notably, it underlies the SHA-3 hashing standard. Sponge hashing is parametrized by two numbers, r and c (bitrate and capacity, respectively), and by a fixed-size permutation on $r + c$ bits. In this work, we study the collision resistance of sponge hashing instantiated with a random permutation by adversaries with arbitrary S-bit auxiliary advice input about the random permutation that make T online queries. Recent work by Coretti et al. (CRYPTO '18) showed that such adversaries can find collisions (with respect to a random c-bit initialization vector) with advantage $\Theta(ST^2/2^c + T^2/2^r)$.

Although the above attack formally breaks collision resistance in some range of parameters, its practical relevance is limited since the resulting collision is very long (on the order of T blocks). Focusing on the task of finding *short* collisions, we study the complexity of finding a B-block collision for a given parameter $B \geq 1$. We give several new attacks and limitations. Most notably, we give a new attack that results in a single-block collision and has advantage

$$\Omega\left(\left(\frac{S^2 T}{2^{2c}} \right)^{2/3} + \frac{T^2}{2^r} \right).$$

In certain range of parameters (e.g., $ST^2 > 2^c$), our attack outperforms the previously-known best attack. To the best of our knowledge, this is the first natural application for which sponge hashing is *provably less secure* than the corresponding instance of Merkle-Damgård hashing. Our attack relies on a novel connection between single-block collision finding in sponge hashing and the well-studied function inversion problem. We also give a general attack that works for any $B \geq 2$ and has advantage $\Omega(STB/2^c + T^2/2^{\min\{r,c\}})$, adapting an idea of Akshima et al. (CRYPTO '20).

© International Association for Cryptologic Research 2022
Y. Dodis and T. Shrimpton (Eds.): CRYPTO 2022, LNCS 13509, pp. 131–160, 2022.
https://doi.org/10.1007/978-3-031-15982-4_5

We complement the above attacks with bounds on the best possible attacks. Specifically, we prove that there is a qualitative jump in the advantage of best possible attacks for finding unbounded-length collisions and those for finding very short collisions. Most notably, we prove (via a highly non-trivial compression argument) that the above attack is optimal for $B = 2$ in some range of parameters.

1 Introduction

Due to a series of successful attacks on widely used hash functions such as MD5, SHA-0, and SHA-1, in 2006 the National Institute of Standards and Technology (NIST) organized a competition to create a new hash standard. At that time, the existing hash functions were all based on the well-known Merkle-Damgård hash function construction [14,24–26]. The goal of the competition was to find an alternative, dissimilar cryptographic hashing design. It took almost a decade until the winner, a family of cryptographic functions called Keccak, become a hashing standard called SHA-3. The Keccak family is based on the *sponge construction* [7,8] which was a novel alternative to the popular Merkle-Damgård design. By now, the sponge paradigm is used for building collision resistant hash functions, message authentication codes (MACs), pseudorandom functions (PRFs) [9], key derivation functions [19], and more.

A sponge function $\mathsf{Sp}: \{0,1\}^* \to \{0,1\}^r$ is defined via three parameters: (1) two natural numbers r (for bitrate) and c (for capacity) so that $n = c + r$, (2) an initial state $\sigma^{(0)} = (\sigma_r^{(0)}, \sigma_c^{(0)}) \in \{0,1\}^r \times \{0,1\}^c$, and (3) a function $\Pi : \{0,1\}^n \to \{0,1\}^n$ which is usually thought of as a (public) pseudorandom permutation. The hashing operation (a.k.a. absorbing) is defined by iterating the state by computing a *round function*. Specifically, given a sequence of r-bit blocks $(m_1, m_2, \ldots, m_\ell)$, $\mathsf{Sp}(m_1, m_2, \ldots, m_\ell)$ is defined as:[1]

1. For $i = 1, \ldots, \ell$, do:
   (a) Compute the round function $\Pi((\sigma_r^{(i-1)} \oplus m_i) \| \sigma_c^{(i-1)})$ and let $\sigma^{(i)}$ denote the output.
   (b) Parse $\sigma^{(i)}$ as $(\sigma_r^{(i)}, \sigma_c^{(i)}) \in \{0,1\}^r \times \{0,1\}^c$.
2. Output the first r bits of $\sigma^{(\ell)}$, namely, $\sigma_r^{(\ell)}$.

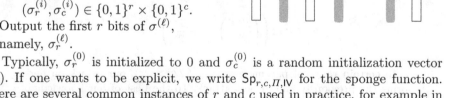

Typically, $\sigma_r^{(0)}$ is initialized to 0 and $\sigma_c^{(0)}$ is a random initialization vector (IV). If one wants to be explicit, we write $\mathsf{Sp}_{r,c,\Pi,\mathsf{IV}}$ for the sponge function. There are several common instances of r and c used in practice, for example in SHA-3-256 $c = 512$ and $r = 1088$, and in SHA-3-512 $c = 1024$ and $r = 576$. These instance are particularly useful since they were designed to be used as drop-in replacements for the corresponding SHA-2 instances, and as such they were intended to have identical (or better) security properties.

---

[1] For simplicity, we do not consider padding of the input.

Sponge in the Random Permutation Model. The concrete permutations Π that are used in real-life do not have solid theoretical foundations from the perspective of provable security. Therefore, when coming to analyze the security of the sponge construction, we model the permutation Π as a completely random one. That is, the permutation is randomly chosen, and all parties are given (black-box) access to it and its inverse.[2] This is called the *random permutation model* (RPM). Such bounds are used as an approximation to the best possible security level that can be achieved by the corresponding construction in the real-life implementation. This heuristic has been extensively and successfully used in the past several decades, with exceptions (i.e., examples where the real-life implementation and the ideal world construction are separated) being somewhat contrived and artificial. For "natural" applications it is widely believed that the concrete security proven in the RPM is the right bound even in the real-world, assuming the "best possible" instantiation for the idealized permutation is chosen.

As mentioned, the sponge construction was introduced by Bertoni et al. [8] and its security was analyzed in a follow-up work [7] assuming that the underlying hash function is an invertible random permutation. The latter work showed a strong property called *indifferentiability* from a random oracle, which directly implies many other properties such as collision resistance, pseudorandomness, and more.

For instance, the following is known about Sponge's collision resistance (which is perhaps the most widely used property). For fixed c, r, the collision resistance game is defined as follows: a challenger sends a uniformly random IV to the adversary. The adversary "wins" if it is able to come up with distinct $m, m' \in \{0,1\}^*$ for which $\mathsf{Sp}_{r,c,\Pi,\mathsf{IV}}(m) = \mathsf{Sp}_{r,c,\Pi,\mathsf{IV}}(m')$. There is a well-known attack due to the original works of Bertoni et al. [7,8]: the adversary is given an IV and it merely queries the permutation oracle on inputs of the form $(m\|\mathsf{IV})$, where the m's are chosen uniformly at random. If a collision was observed (i.e., the adversary finds distinct m_1, m_2 such that the first r bits of $\Pi(m_1\|\mathsf{IV})$, $\Pi(m_2\|\mathsf{IV})$ are the same), then the adversary wins. By the well-known birthday bound, the success probability of this event is $\Omega(T^2/2^r)$. Alternatively, if two messages m_1, m_2 such that the query returned a state with the same last c bits (i.e., $\Pi(m_1\|\mathsf{IV}) = a_1\|b$ and $\Pi(m_2\|\mathsf{IV}) = a_2\|b$, then $m_1 \| a_1$ and $m_2 \| a_2$ form a collision. The success probability of this event is $\Omega(T^2/2^c)$. Overall, the attacker wins with probability $\Omega(T^2/2^{\min\{c,r\}})$. This is known to be the best possible attack due to the indifferentiability result of [7].

Non-uniformity/Preprocessing Attacks. The above discussion assumes that the adversary is uniform in the sense that it starts off with no knowledge about Π, as if it did not exist before it was invoked. However, this does not capture real life attack scenarios where an attacker can invest a significant

---

[2] In typical permutation designs, including the permutations underlying the Keccak family, if you have the entire state, you can apply the inverse permutation to go backward to the previous state. This is why we also give free access to the inverse of the permutation as part of the model.

amount of preprocessing on the public permutation Π to speed up the actual attack whenever the IV is chosen. This is why most works (at least in theoretical cryptography) model attackers as non-uniform machines, where the attacker could obtain arbitrary but bounded-length advice, before attacking the system. The advice generation phase is called *the offline phase* and the "attack" given the advice and the challenge is called *the online phase*. The output size of the offline phase (i.e., the size of the advice) is denoted S and the number of queries allowed in the online phase is denoted T; computation is free of charge in both phases. This model, being an extension of the RPM where the online adversary may know a bounded-length hint about the permutation, is called the auxiliary-input RPM, or AI-RPM in short. This model was first explicitly put forward by Coretti, Dodis, and Guo [10], naturally extending the influential auxiliary-input random oracle model (AI-ROM) from the seminal work of Unruh [31] (which in turn is an explicit version of the model studied by Hellman [23], Yao [33], and Fiat-Naor [17]). Bounds on the power of "auxiliary-input" adversaries are also referred to as "time-space" trade-offs.

Although the sponge paradigm is becoming widespread, very little is known about its formal security guarantees against such attackers that may have a short preprocessed hint about the permutation computed in an offline phase. In fact, there is an attack that utilizes this extra power to achieve advantage $\Omega(ST^2/2^c + T^2/2^r)$ (notice the extra multiplicative S term).[3] The attack is based on a combination of a birthday-style attack, as above, together with a variant of an attack by Hellman [23] which is nowadays referred to as rainbow tables (due to Oechslin [29]). While this attack uses known techniques, we were not able to find an explicit description of it in the literature and so for completeness, we give the attack and its analysis in Sect. 4.1.[4,5] Only very recently, in the beautiful work of Coretti et al. [10] (henceforth CDG) it was shown that this attack is optimal; that is, no S-space T-query attackers can find a collision with probability better than $\Omega(ST^2/2^c + T^2/2^r)$.

It turns out that the above attack results in a very long collision. Specifically, for parameters S and T as above, the above attack results in a collision of length $\approx T$. While this formally breaks collision resistance, it is hard to imagine a natural application where such a collision would be helpful in an attack. Say we have a system that uses a sponge-based hash with an output of size 256 bits. Running the above attack with $S = T = 2^{60}$ would result in a collision of several petabytes long, which is likely to be practically useless for any natural attack scenario. Therefore, we ask whether there exist attacks that find shorter collisions and what is their success probability. Specifically, we introduce an

---

[3] Throughout the introduction, for easy of notation, we supress poly-logarithmic (i.e., $\mathsf{poly}(c, r)$ terms inside the big "O/Ω" notation. The formal theorems state the precise bounds.

[4] More precisely, we give a generalization of this attack which finds collisions of length $B \geq 2$, and this particular attack follows by setting $B = T$.

[5] A related bound is stated in CDG [10, Table 1] but after communication with an author, they confirmed that the attack was never worked out.

additional parameter B (for blocks) and require an attacker, on a random IV, to come up with two $\leq B$-block messages that collide. The main question studied in this work is:

What is the complexity of a preprocessing attacker in finding a B block collision in a Sponge hash function, assuming the underlying permutation is modeled as random?

1.1   Detour: The Case of Merkle-Damgård

Except being a fundamental problem with theoretical and practical importance, another motivation to study the above question comes from the recent work of Akshima et al. [3] (henceforth ACDW), who studied a similar question in the context of Merkle-Damgård hashing (henceforth MD). Recall that sponge hashing was designed to be used as a drop-in replacement for Merkle-Damgård-based hash functions, and as such, it is essential to compare their security guarantees in this natural model that allows attackers to perform preprocessing.

Recall that a Merkle-Damgård hash is defined relative to a *compression* function $h\colon [N] \times [M] \to [N]$. Hashing is performed by breaking the input message into blocks from $[M]$, and processing them one at a time with the compression function, each time combining a block of the input with the output of the previous round, where the 0th round value is the IV.[6] To obtain provable-security guarantees, the analysis models the underlying compression function h as a completely random one. Preprocessing attackers are captured by considering the AI-ROM [10,11,17,23,31,33] which models attackers as two-stage algorithms $(\mathcal{A}_1, \mathcal{A}_2)$. The first algorithm $\mathcal{A}_1$ is unbounded except that it generates an S-bit "advice". The second algorithm $\mathcal{A}_2$ gets the advice and makes T queries to the oracle.

Coretti et al. [11] fully characterize the collision resistance of salted-MD hashing: there exists an attack with advantage $\Omega(ST^2/N + T^2/N)$ (loosely based on the idea of rainbow tables [23,29]), and this is the best possible attack, as shown using the "bit-fixing" technique [31]. As in the case of sponge hashing, this attack results in a very long collision, on the order of T blocks. Motivated by this observation, ACDW [3] ask whether it is strictly harder to find shorter collisions. They have two main results. The first is an extension of the above simple attack to result in B-block collisions with advantage $\Omega(STB/N + T^2/N)$. The second result is an upper bound on the advantage for $B = 2$ of $O(ST/N + T^2/N)$, showing that the above attack is tight. For $B = 1$, the problem is equivalent to finding collisions in a compressing random function, and the advantage is precisely $\Theta(S/N + T^2/N)$ [16].

ACDW [3] could not prove or disprove that their $\Omega(STB/N + T^2/N)$ attack is optimal for any other value of B (except $B = 2$ and $B \in \Omega(T)$). They conjectured that it is optimal and formulated it as *the STB conjecture*. In very recent works, Akshima, Guo, and Liu [4] and Ghoshal and Komargodski [21] proved

---

[6] All of the results directly extend to the padded version, but we ignore it for simplicity.

new bounds for this problem (almost resolving the conjecture). Can we prove similar bounds for sponge hashing? Should we believe an analogous conjecture?

1.2   Our Results

We initiate the study of time-space tradeoffs for *bounded length collisions in sponge hashing*. First, the known best attack that gives a single-block collision has advantage

$$\Omega \left(\frac{S}{2^c} + \frac{T^2}{2^r} \right). \tag{1}$$

In this attack, the preprocessing is used to "remember" a collision for S different IVs. If the challenge IV is in the set of remembered IVs, then the attack succeeds (this happens with probability $S/2^c$); otherwise, we run a birthday-style attack which succeeds with probability $\Omega(T^2/2^r)$. For MD hashing, the analogous bound for $B = 1$ is known to be tight. Second, there is an attack (loosely based on rainbow tables) that has advantage $\Omega(ST^2/2^c + T^2/2^r)$ and results with a $\Omega(T)$-blocks collision [10].

At this point, if one were to speculate that sponge's security guarantees are at least as good as MD's, one would guess that the above attacks should be tight, at least for $B \in \{1, 2\}$. With some luck and labor, we may even be able to prove it. This is where the situation gets interesting. We show that the above speculation is **false** for $B = 1$ and in some natural settings of parameters, **sponge is strictly less secure than MD** for this task. On the other hand, for $B = 2$ we can only prove tightness for a certain range of parameters.

In what follows, we elaborate on our results. We design two new attacks, one designed for any $B \geq 2$ and the other specifically for $B = 1$. We complement our attacks with "lower bounds", which are actually upper bounds on the best possible advantage. Specifically, we prove that there is a qualitative jump in the advantage of best possible attacks for finding unbounded-length collisions and those for finding very short collisions (i.e., $B \leq 2$).

Attacks

We give two new attacks, one for any $B \geq 2$ and the other is specialized for $B = 1$. The generic attack is the first to result with an arbitrary block length collision while the one specialized to $B = 1$ beats the previously known best attack, at least in some range of parameters. By the latter, to the best of our knowledge, we show the first natural application for which sponge hashing is less secure than MD.

A New Attack for $B \geq 2$. The above-mentioned attack on sponge hashing that has advantage $\Omega(ST^2/2^c + T^2/2^r)$ can be modified to result with a B-block collision for $B \geq 2$ and with advantage

$$\Omega \left(\frac{STB}{2^c} + \frac{T^2}{2^{\min\{c,r\}}} \right). \tag{2}$$

The attack follows a similar observation of ACDW [3] regarding MD hashing. Given the upper bound of CDG [10] mentioned earlier, this attack is optimal for $B \in \Omega(T)$. For MD hashing, the analogous bound is known to be tight for $B = 2$ and $B \in \Omega(T)$.

A New Attack for $B = 1$. We design a new attack for sponge hashing that results with a a single-block collision. Specifically, we show that if $ST^2 > 2^c$, then there is an attack with advantage

$$\Omega \left(\left(\frac{S^2 T}{2^{2c}} \right)^{2/3} + \frac{T^2}{2^r} \right).$$

To see why this attack is superior to the previously known one (Eq. 1), we give a setting of parameters where it achieves a significantly higher advantage. Consider $r = c$, $S = 2^{4c/5}$, and $T = 2^{2c/5}$. Indeed, $ST^2 > 2^c$ and therefore we can apply the attack. The previously known best attack (Eq. 1) has advantage

$$\Omega \left(\frac{S + T^2}{2^c} \right) = \Omega \left(\frac{1}{2^{c/5}} \right).$$

This attack is the analog of the *provably* best attack for MD. On the other hand, our new attack has strictly better advantage

$$\Omega \left(\left(\frac{S^2 T}{2^{2c}} \right)^{2/3} + \frac{T^2}{2^c} \right) = \Omega \left(\left(\frac{2^{8c/5} 2^{2c/5}}{2^{2c}} \right)^{2/3} + \frac{1}{2^{c/5}} \right) = \Omega (1).$$

Thus, at least in this range of parameters, we beat the state-of-the-art attack and show that sponge is *less secure than MD*. In the example above, we chose a setting of parameters where the gap between the attacks is the largest (our attack succeeds with *constant* probability, while the previously known one succeeds with exponentially small probability). However, there are many more concrete settings where our attack is superior, although the gap could be less dramatic. We note that our bounds in this section and the technical overview are simplified for ease of parsing and refer the reader to the technical sections for the exact bounds.

Conceptual novelty: Our attack for $B = 1$ use the famous time-space tradeoffs for function inversion of Hellman [23] and its extension by Fiat-Naor [17]. We leverage the possibility of inverse queries to the underlying permutation Π in the random-permutation model. This is in contrast to Merkle-Damgård construction which is analyzed in the random-oracle model that does not permit inverse queries. At a very high level, we use time-space tradeoffs for function inversion to "invert" the function Π^{-1} on a restricted domain. We view this conceptual connection between time-space tradeoffs for collision resistance of sponge hashing and function inversion as novel and hope that it will lead to better designs and additional attacks in the future.

Lower Bounds

We complement the picture by showing "lower bounds", namely impossibility results for better attacks. (In other words, these are upper bounds on the best possible advantage of any attacker.) We prove two such lower bounds, one for the case where $B = 1$ and the other is for $B = 2$, corresponding to our attacks.

On Optimal Attacks for $B = 2$. We show that any attack for $B = 2$ must have advantage

$$O\left(\frac{ST}{2^c} + \frac{S^2T^4}{2^{2c}} + \frac{T^2}{2^{\min\{c,r\}}}\right).$$

We note that this bound is tight with the best known attacks for a large range of parameters, but there still may be a gap otherwise. Specifically, if $ST^3 \leq 2^c$, then the above bound simplifies to $O(ST/2^c + T^2/2^{\min\{c,r\}})$ which matches the attack from Eq. (2). Thus, any improvement on the generic attack from Eq. (2) must take advantage of the regime where $ST^3 > 2^c$.

The proof of this result *provably* cannot be obtained via the bit-fixing method. Rather, we obtain the result via a compression argument. In such arguments, an imaginary adversary that is successful too often is used to compress a uniformly random string, a task which is (information-theoretically) impossible. The compression technique has been instrumental in proving lower bounds in computer science (see the survey of Morin et al. [28]). It has become useful in the context of cryptographic constructions and primitives, starting with the work of Gennaro and Trevisan [20]. Unfortunately, one common "feature" of such proofs is that they tend to be extremely technical and involved. Our proof is no different; in fact, it is even much more complicated than the analogous result for $B = 2$ of ACDW [3] since we work in the RPM and need to handle inverse queries.

On Optimal Attacks for $B = 1$. We show that any attack for $B = 1$ must have an advantage

$$O\left(\frac{ST}{2^c} + \frac{T^2}{2^r}\right).$$

The proof of this result is relatively straightforward by using an optimized version of the remarkable bit-fixing (or presampling) method [10,11,31]. The main point of distinction of our proof from most previous ones is that we need to apply this technique in the RPM context, so our argument needs to handle inverse queries. (This result might have been known before, but we could not find such a statement, so we give it for completeness.)

We summarize our main results as well as the known best bounds in Fig. 1.

1.3   Future Directions

Our work is the first to address the question of characterizing the complexity of a preprocessing attacker in finding a B-block collision in a Sponge hash function.

	Best Attack	Advantage Upper Bound
$B = 1$	$\min\left(\dfrac{S^2T^2}{2^{2c}}, \left(\dfrac{S^2T}{2^{2c}}\right)^{2/3}\right) + \dfrac{S}{2^c} + \dfrac{T^2}{2^r}$ [Thm 2]	$\dfrac{ST}{2^c} + \dfrac{T^2}{2^r}$ [Thm 4]
$B = 2$	$\dfrac{ST}{2^c} + \dfrac{T^2}{2^{\min\{c,r\}}}$ [Thm 1]	$\dfrac{ST}{2^c} + \dfrac{S^2T^4}{2^{2c}} + \dfrac{T^2}{2^{\min(c,r)}}$ [Thm 5]
$B \geq 3$	$\dfrac{STB}{2^c} + \dfrac{T^2}{2^{\min\{c,r\}}}$ [Thm 1]	$\dfrac{ST^2}{2^c} + \dfrac{T^2}{2^r}$ [10]

Fig. 1. A summary of the attacks and advantage upper bounds for finding B-block collisions for the Sponge hash function. All bounds are given ignoring poly(c, r) terms. We note that the attack for $B = T$ is implicitly claimed in [10] based on [11].

Our results raise many natural open problems on both the attacks side and lower bounds side. Regarding attacks, we have shown, somewhat surprisingly, that there is a non-trivial attack for $B = 1$ that takes advantage of inverse queries in a novel way. We hope that these ideas can be pushed forward to obtain even better attacks for $B = 1$ or beyond. Specifically, is it possible to beat the $ST/2^c$ attack for $B = 2$ in some range of parameters? In ruling out possible attacks, it would be interesting to come up with a tight upper bound on the advantage for $B = 1$ or $B = 2$. Our work suggests that ruling out attacks that use inverse queries may indeed be a complicated task. In fact, for $B = 3$ we are not aware of any upper bound on the advantage that is better than $O(ST^2/2^c + T^2/2^r)$.

1.4 Related Work

Time-space tradeoffs are fundamental to the existence of efficient algorithms. For example, look-up tables (used to avoid "online" recalculations) have been implemented since the very earliest operating systems. In cryptography (or cryptanalysis), they were first used by Hellman [23] in the context of inverting random functions. Hellman's algorithm was subsequently rigorously analyzed by Fiat and Naor [17] where it was also extended to handle *arbitrary* (not necessarily random) functions. Limitations of such algorithms were studied by Yao [33], and by De, Trevisan, and Tulsiani [15] (building on works by Gennaro and Trevisan [20] and Wee [32]). More limitations were proven by Barkan, Biham, and Shamir [5] but for a restricted class of algorithms. Very recently, Corrigan-Gibbs and Kogan [13] showed complexity-theoretic limitations for improving the lower bound of Yao. While these techniques have mostly cryptographic origins, interesting relations were discovered to other classical problems in other fields (e.g., [1,22]). Time-space tradeoffs have been studied for other problems beyond the ones we mentioned (various cryptographic properties of random oracles, function and permutation inversion, and security of common hashing paradigms). For instance, specific modes for block ciphers (e.g., [18] studied the Even-Mansour cipher), and various assumptions related to cyclic groups, such as discrete logarithms and Diffie-Hellman problems [6,10,12,27].

On the Salt. In the theoretical cryptography literature collision resistance is defined with respect to a family of hash functions indexed by a key. This is important to achieve the standard notion of *non-uniform* security. Indeed, no single hash function can be collision-resistant as a non-uniform attacker can just hardwire a collision. In practice, however, a single hash function is considered by fixing an IV. Thus, the relevance of our model could be questioned. However, often applications, the hash function used is salted by prepending a random salt value to the input, for example in password hashing [30]. Salting essentially brings us back to the random-IV/keyed setting, where our results become relevant.

2   Technical Overview

In this section, we provide a high-level overview of our techniques. We first describe the generic attack for finding B-block collisions for $B \geq 2$. This attack is a variant of an analogous attack for MD, given by ACDW [3]. We also recall the known best attack for $B = 1$. Then, we describe our new attack for finding 1-block collisions. In particular, our attack outperforms the optimal analogous attacks for MD for specific regimes of parameter settings. Lastly, we overview the techniques used to prove limitations on the best possible attacks for finding short collisions.

Sponge Notation. A sponge function is a keyed hash function that takes as input an a c-bit initialization vector IV along with an arbitrary size input and outputs an r-bit string: $\mathsf{Sp}: \{0,1\}^c \times \{0,1\}^* \to \{0,1\}^r$. The second input is parsed as a sequence of r-bit blocks, denoted $(m_1, m_2, \ldots)$. On such an input $\mathsf{Sp}(\mathsf{IV}, (m_1, m_2, \ldots))$ is defined as follows. The function Sp is defined relative to a permutation $\Pi: \{0,1\}^{r+c} \to \{0,1\}^{r+c}$. An input to or an output of this permutation, denoted $\sigma \in \{0,1\}^{r+c}$, contains an r-bit block, denoted $\sigma[1]$, and a c-bit block, denoted $\sigma[2]$. We sometimes use $(\sigma[1], \sigma[2])$ to mean $\sigma[1] \| \sigma[2] = \sigma$.

On input $m_1, m_2, \ldots, m_\ell$ to Sp, it works as follows:

1. Initialize $\sigma^{(0)} = (\sigma^{(0)}[1], \sigma^{(0)}[2]) = (0, \mathsf{IV})$.
2. For $i = 1, \ldots, \ell$, compute $\sigma^{(i)} = \Pi((\sigma^{(i-1)}[1] \oplus m_i) \| \sigma^{(i-1)}[2])$.
3. Output $\sigma^{(\ell)}[1]$.

2.1   Attacks

Generic Attack for Finding Length B Collisions. In the preprocessing phase the adversary randomly samples $t \approx S$ different IVs $\mathsf{IV}_1, \ldots, \mathsf{IV}_t$ and for $i = 1, \ldots, t$ it does as follows.

1. Compute $\sigma_{i,j}$ for $j \in [B/2 - 1]$ as $\sigma_{i,j} = \Pi(0, \sigma_{i,j-1}[2])$, where $\sigma_{i,0} = (0, \mathsf{IV})$. The sequence $\sigma_{i,0}, \ldots, \sigma_{i,B/2-1}$ forms a "zero-walk" on IV_i.

2. Find m_i, m_i' such that $\Pi(m_i, \sigma_{i,B/2-1}[2])[1] = \Pi(m_i', \sigma_{i,B/2-1}[2])[1]$.

The preprocessing phase outputs $(\sigma_{i,B/2-1}[2], m_i, m_i')_{i=1,\ldots,t}$. In Fig. 2, we depict the preprocessing phase of the attack. In the online phase, the adversary gets

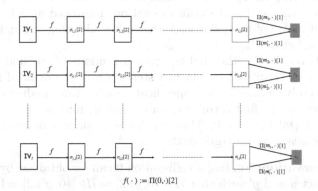

$$f(\cdot) := \Pi(0, \cdot)[2]$$

Fig. 2. An illustration of the preprocessing phase of the generic attack. In red, we depict the components that are part of the output of the preprocessing phase. In blue we see the collisions that will be outputted in the online phase if some chain is hit. Notice that we denote $f(\cdot) := \Pi(0, \cdot)[2]$ (Color figure online)

a challenge IV as input. For $i = 1, \ldots, T/B$, it computes $\mathsf{IV}_i = \Pi(i, \mathsf{IV})[2]$ (for simplicity, we assume that i is in its bit representation). For each of the IV_i's, it does a zero-walk of length $B - 2$. Formally, it sets $\sigma_{i,0} \leftarrow \Pi(i, \mathsf{IV}_i)$ and then for $j = 1, \ldots, B - 1$ it does the following.

1. If there is a tuple of the form $(\sigma_{i,j-1}[2], m, m')$ in the preprocessing output, then return

$$(\sigma_{i,0}[1] \parallel \ldots \sigma_{i,j-1}[1] \parallel m), (\sigma_{i,0}[1] \parallel \ldots \sigma_{i,j-1}[1] \parallel m').$$

2. Set $\sigma_{i,j} \leftarrow \Pi(0, \sigma_{i,j-1}[2])$.

Correctness is easy to verify. We next discuss the success probability of the adversary. Suppose that the online phase of the adversary computes a $\sigma_{i,j}$ during the first half of any of the T/B zero-walks such $\sigma_{i,j}[2]$ matches the last c bits of one of the $\sigma_{i',j'}$'s defined in the preprocessing phase. Then, it is guaranteed to stumble on $\sigma_{i',B/2-1}[2]$ during its zero walk. Hence, in this case, it would output a collision.

Since the adversary encounters roughly $\Omega(SB)$ distinct $\sigma_{i,j}[2]$'s in expectation during the preprocessing phase, this suffices to prove that with probability roughly $\Omega(STB/2^c)$ the online phase will win. The term $\Omega(T^2/2^c + T^2/2^r)$ appears due to birthday-style collisions. We refer the reader to Sect. 4.1 for details.

Attack for $B = 1$. As described in the introduction, the best attack known so far for $B = 1$ has an advantage of $O(S/2^c + T^2/2^r)$. The analogous attack for MD is provably optimal, as mentioned. However, in contrast to the setting in MD where the ideal object is a random function, here the ideal object is a random permutation, which gives us the additional ability to make inverse queries. This is precisely the leverage that we utilize to get our improved attack. We remark that we are not aware of any prior work that takes advantage of making inverse queries in related contexts.

For $B = 1$, recall that the goal is, given a random IV, to find m, m' such that $\Pi(m, \mathsf{IV})[1] = \Pi(m', \mathsf{IV})[1]$. Our first step is a bit counter-intuitive since we actually aim to solve a *harder* task. Specifically, rather than finding an arbitrary collision, we set out to find a collision on 0, that is, find m and m' such that $\Pi(m, \mathsf{IV})[1] = \Pi(m', \mathsf{IV})[1] = 0$. This step helps us since a natural way to use inverse queries arises, as we argue next.

Main observation: Finding a collision on 0 can be obtained by finding distinct y and y' such that $\Pi^{-1}(0, y)[2] = \Pi^{-1}(0, y')[2] = \mathsf{IV}$.

In other words, it suffices to find two pre-images of IV with respect to the function $f_\Pi \colon \{0,1\}^c \to \{0,1\}^c$ where $f_\Pi(x)$ outputs the last c bits of $\Pi^{-1}(0, x)$. In Fig. 3, we show the partite representations of $\Pi(\cdot)$ and $\Pi^{-1}(0, \cdot)$. Note that while $\Pi(\cdot)$ is a perfect matching, the function $f_\Pi(\cdot) = \Pi^{-1}(0, \cdot)$ has several elements in its co-domain with multiple pre-images.

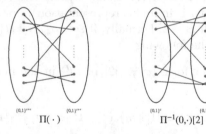

$$\Pi(\cdot) \qquad\qquad\qquad \Pi^{-1}(0, \cdot)[2]$$

Fig. 3. Partite representation of $\Pi(\cdot)$ and $\Pi^{-1}(0, \cdot)$. Notice that Π is a permutation and thus forms a perfect matching while $\Pi^{-1}(0, \cdot)$ is not a permutation and in expectation a random image will have several pre-images

At this point, we made some progress: we reduced the problem of collision finding to a function inversion problem (for the function $f_\Pi \colon \{0,1\}^c \to \{0,1\}^c$). Indeed, preprocessing attacks for function inversion have been well studied since the 80's. Hellman [23] described an algorithm that gets S bits of preprocessing on the random function $f \colon \{0,1\}^a \to \{0,1\}^b$ as input and inverts it at a point in its image making T queries to the function. It was later formally analyzed by Fiat and Naor [17] and shown to have advantage $\epsilon(a, b)$ at inverting $y = f(x)$

for a random $x \leftarrow_\$ \{0,1\}^a$, where

$$\epsilon(a,b) = \Omega\left(\min\left\{1, \frac{ST}{2^{\min(a,b)}}, \left(\frac{S^2T}{2^{2\min(a,b)}}\right)^{1/3}\right\}\right) \quad (3)$$

We are almost done; three technical challenges remain. First, the result of Hellman applies only to random functions. On the other hand, our function is a restriction of a random permutation (which is not a random function). Fiat and Naor [17] showed a clever method to extend Hellman's algorithm to support any function (rather than only random ones), but this improvement is more complicated and comes with a cost in efficiency, which we would like to avoid. To this end, we re-do and adapt the analysis of Hellman to our setting by using the fact that restrictions of permutations are "close enough" to random functions. Our analysis achieves the same parameters as the original one of Hellman, up to constants.

The second problem is that we want to find a pre-image of $\mathsf{IV} \leftarrow_\$ \{0,1\}^c$ under f_Π, but IV may not even have any pre-images under f_Π, let alone two which are required for our attack. Fortunately, as f_Π is at least "close" to a random function, we can show via a balls-into-bins analysis that a constant fraction of the co-domain will have at least two distinct pre-images. Still, could it be the case that Hellman's attack somehow fails on this fraction of the co-domain? Via a closer analysis of Hellman's attack, we show that for any function $f \colon \{0,1\}^a \to \{0,1\}^b$ and fixed element $y \in \{0,1\}^b$, the attack succeeds at finding a pre-image $x' \in f^{-1}(y)$ with probability $\epsilon(a,b)$ where

$$\epsilon(a,b) = \Omega\left(\frac{1}{b}\min\left(1, \frac{ST \cdot |f^{-1}(y)|}{2^a}, \left(\frac{S^2T \cdot |f^{-1}(y)|^2}{2^{2a}}\right)^{1/3}\right)\right) \quad (4)$$

The last problem we face is that we need to find two *distinct* pre-images for IV. However, applying an inversion algorithm in a black box fashion does not guarantee that distinct inverses will be found. Thus, we also prove that Hellman's inversion algorithm finds a uniform pre-image among all possible pre-images for a given element in the co-domain.

After resolving the above technical challenges, we show that if we run Hellman's attack twice independently for the function f_Π on the image IV, if IV has at least two pre-images (which it does with constant probability), then we will find two distinct pre-images with at least $1/2$ probability times the probability that both attacks succeed. Thus, our overall success probability is roughly $\Omega(\epsilon(c,c)^2)$ where ϵ is defined in (4). We refer the reader to Sect. 4.2 for the details.

2.2 Impossibility Results for Best Attacks

When giving new attacks for finding short collisions, the natural question is how far we can go. In other words, what are the best possible attacks? For $B = 1, 2$ in the case of MD, optimal attacks are known. Our goal here is to prove an upper bound on the advantage for the best-possible adversary that has S bits of preprocessing as input and can make T queries to Π, Π^{-1} in finding collisions of length 1 and 2 for the sponge construction.

Impossibility Result for $B = 1$. We use the pre-sampling technique proposed by [31] and later optimized and adapted to the AI-RPM by [10] to get an advantage upper bound of roughly $O(ST/2^c + T^2/2^r)$. However, we note that this bound does not match the best $B = 1$ attacks, so it is open which side can be improved. Ideally, one could use a compression-based technique as done in [16] to get a tight bound for the $B = 1$ case for MD, but it is not clear how to adapt this argument to handle inverse queries in the AI-RPM model, as we shall see below.

Impossibility Result for $B = 2$. The presampling technique of [10,31] *provably* cannot give an advantage upper bound better than $O(ST^2/2^c + T^2/2^r)$ for $B = 2$. Since we can prove this advantage upper bound even for unbounded length collisions, it is natural to ask whether we can prove that 2-block collisions are, in fact, harder to find than collisions of arbitrary length. Aside from presampling techniques, the main technique used to rule out attacks is via a compression argument [20,32], which we turn to for our impossibility result. As a warm up, we first give an overview for the $B = 1$ compression argument for MD from [16] to highlight the key challenges in our setting.

Overview of $B = 1$ Compression Argument for MD. In a compression argument, the main idea is to use an adversary $\mathcal{A}$ that succeeds at some task involving a random object $\mathcal{O}$, to compress $\mathcal{O}$ beyond what is information theoretically possible. This clearly establishes a contradiction, which gives an upper bound in the success probability of $\mathcal{A}$.

Let $h \colon [N] \times [M] \to [N]$ be a hash function that is modeled as a random oracle, and $\mathcal{A} = (\mathcal{A}_1, \mathcal{A}_2)$ be an (S, T) adversary that tries to find a 1-block collision in h. $\mathcal{A}_1$ gets h as input and can output S bits of advice σ. $\mathcal{A}_2$ gets σ along with a random salt $a \in [N]$, can make T queries to h, and tries to output $m, m' \in [M]$ such that $h(a, m) = h(a, m')$ and $m \neq m'$. We show that if $\mathcal{A}$ succeeds at this task for many salts a, then we can describe h with fewer bits than possible.

To encode h, we first compute $\sigma \leftarrow \mathcal{A}_1(h)$. We let $G \subseteq [N]$ be the set of elements for which $\mathcal{A}_2$ succeeds on inputs (σ, a) for all $a \in G$. We run $\mathcal{A}_2$ on (σ, a) for all $a \in G$ in lexicographic order. The hope is that whenever $\mathcal{A}_2$ succeeds in finding a collision, we can use the corresponding queries for the collision it makes to compress the function h.

For example, if $\mathcal{A}_2(\sigma, a)$ outputs a collision (m, m'), then we can assume that $\mathcal{A}_2$ must have queried $h(a, m)$ and $h(a, m')$ at some point (we assume without loss of generality that (a, m) was queried before (a, m')). So whenever it queries $h(a, m')$, rather than encoding the output of h, we write down information to indicate that it's the same output as the query for $h(a, m)$. It is easy to see by a counting argument that at least half of the $a \in G$ cannot be queried by $\mathcal{A}_2$ more than $2T$ times. For all such a, we can refer back to the previous query $h(a, m)$

using $\log 2T$ bits, and we use another $\log 2T$ bits to identify the query $h(a, m')$. Thus, we save $\log N - 2 \log 2T$ bits per each of these a values in G, which gives a non-trivial compression of h if $T^2 < N$.

The Problem with Inverse Queries. As we stated before, the first major roadblock we encounter when adapting this framework to the AI-RPM is the existence of inverse queries. Let's try to adapt the argument above to the setting of Sponge with 1-block collision. Now the preprocessing adversary $\mathcal{A}_1$ is given a random permutation Π and outputs some state σ with $|\sigma| \leq S$. The online adversary $\mathcal{A}_2$ receives σ and a random IV, and tries to find m, m' such that $\Pi(m, \mathsf{IV})[1] = \Pi(m', \mathsf{IV})[1]$.

Now suppose that $\mathcal{A}_2$ outputs a collision (m, m') with respect to the sponge construction. We can no longer even assume that $\mathcal{A}_2$ queries both $\Pi(m, \mathsf{IV})$ and $\Pi(m', \mathsf{IV})$! For example, it may have first queried $\Pi(m, \mathsf{IV}) = (y, u_1)$ and then queried $\Pi^{-1}(y, u_2) = (m', \mathsf{IV})$. At first glance, this doesn't seem like a problem, we can again note that part of the output of query (y, u_2) is the same as the input to the query for (m, IV). So maybe we can use the same trick as before and instead of storing the whole answer of $\Pi^{-1}(y, u')$, store information indicating that the last c bits of the answer is the same as the input of the query $\Pi(m, \mathsf{IV})$. This intuition is misleading. We can no longer do a counting argument to show that this information is short. It is not clear how to identify the query $\Pi^{-1}(y, u')$ with few bits to be able to point back to the $\Pi(m, \mathsf{IV})$ query. For example, the adversary may just query $\Pi^{-1}(y, *)$ many times and hope to hit IV twice. We hope that this example sheds light on why, at a minimum, inverse queries significantly complicate the situation and deserve extra attention.

Compression for $B = 2$ via Multi-instance Games. The above compression approach is not known to generalize to the case of $B \geq 2$ collisions for MD. To overcome this limitation, Akshima et al. [3] propose a beautiful framework that gives non-trivial bounds $B \geq 2$ for the case of MD. Their framework reduces the problem to a related "multi-instance" game. In a multi-instance game, the adversary has an arbitrary size string σ of S-bits hard-coded, and its goal is to find a 2-block collision for a set of $u \approx S$ uniformly random a's. The adversary $\mathcal{A}_2$ can make T queries to h when running on each of the u IVs. The key distinctions in this multi-instance game is that (1) the advice sigma that $\mathcal{A}_2$ receives is *independent* of h, and (2) we only need to analyze $\mathcal{A}_2$'s success probability for a random set of u IVs. The core of the proof is a compression argument to upper bound the advantage of this adversary. This framework unfortunately is not strong enough to deal with $B = 1$, as at best it gives the same bound as bit-fixing. However, we adapt this framework to the setting of random permutations to give a non-trivial bound for $B = 2$.

In our case, we need to build a compression argument to compress Π and a set of u random IVs, $\mathsf{IV}_1, \ldots, \mathsf{IV}_u$, (for $u \approx S$) using an adversary $\mathcal{A}_2$ which has some fixed hard-coded advice. $\mathcal{A}_2$ runs on the IVs one by one and succeeds in finding 2-block collisions for all of them. The encoding avoids storing some of the values of Π explicitly, and instead stores information about the queries of $\mathcal{A}_2$ to Π and Π^{-1} which help during the decoding procedure to recover these particular values of Π.

For $B = 2$ collisions, there are possibly 4 "crucial" queries that the adversary might make that correspond to a 2-block collision (two for each message). We possibly need to consider all combinations of ways that the queries could have been made in either the forward or the reverse direction. For the case of this overview, we zoom in on a single case where inverse queries complicate the situation, and explain how we overcome this.

Suppose on an input IV_j (where $\mathcal{A}_2$ had previously been run on inputs $\mathsf{IV}_1, \ldots, \mathsf{IV}_{j-1}$), $\mathcal{A}_2$ arrives at a collision by making the crucial queries q_1, q_2, q_3, q_4 (not necessarily in that order) such that

1. q_1 was a query to Π on (m_1, IV_j) and returned (x_1, IV'_1)
2. q_2 was a query to Π on (m_2, IV_j) and returned (x_2, IV'_2)
3. q_3 was a query to Π on $(m_3 \oplus x_1, \mathsf{IV}'_1)$ and returned (y, IV'_3)
4. q_4 was a query to Π on $(m_4 \oplus x_2, \mathsf{IV}'_2)$ and returned (y, IV'_4)

Clearly, (m_1, m_3) and (m_2, m_4) hash to the same output and hence are a collision. Now suppose queries q_1 and q_2 were first made during $\mathcal{A}_2(\mathsf{IV}_j)$,[7] while queries q_3 and q_4 were each made previously while running $\mathcal{A}_2$ on an earlier IV_i value. Now, the strategy to compress on the lines of [3] is not to include the last c bits of the answers of q_1, q_2 and the last r bits of the answer of q_4 in the encoding. Instead, we can store the index of the queries q_3, q_4 among all queries (these indices will be in $[uT]$ since there are u IVs and T queries for each of them) and store the indices of the queries q_1, q_2 among the queries made while running $\mathcal{A}_2$ on IV_j (these indices will be in $[T]$). This leads to a saving of roughly $2c + r - 2\log T - 2\log uT$ bits. For reasonable parameters of S, T, c, r, this implies a compression of at least $c - \log uT$ bits, so if $uT \approx ST < 2^c$, this gives non-trivial compression. This implies an upper bound of $ST/2^c$ on the advantage for this case.

However, with inverse queries allowed, things get more complicated. Suppose instead that queries q_3 and q_4 were made in the reverse direction, so $\mathcal{A}_2$ queries $\Pi^{-1}(y, \mathsf{IV}'_3)$ and $\Pi^{-1}(y, \mathsf{IV}'_4)$ prior to running $\mathcal{A}_2(\mathsf{IV}_j)$. In this case, we can still save the c bits from the answers of q_1, q_2. But there is no clear way to save in storing the answer to query q_4 since its answer $(m_4 \oplus x_2, \mathsf{IV}'_2)$ has seemingly no relation to either the answer or input of q_3. So, in this case, we are only able to save $2c - 2\log T - 2\log uT$ bits, which leads to non-trivial compression only if $u^2 T^4 \approx S^2 T^4 < 2^c$. This implies an upper bound of $S^2 T^4/2^{2c}$ on the attacker's advantage for this case. Note that this is actually *better* than the $ST/2^c$ bound we got when considering only forward queries whenever $ST^3 < 2^c$. However, it is important to note that we still need to consider all possible ways in which the

---

[7] Note that this assumption is easy to remove as otherwise we can achieve compression by not including IV_j in the encoding and recovering it from $\mathcal{A}_2$'s queries during decoding.

attacker may find a collision. We need to show even in the worst case, we can compress Π in order to get an upper bound on the advantage.

The above highlights just one of the several subtleties that inverse queries introduce in the proof. The ability of the adversary to make queries in two directions makes the encoding and decoding procedures significantly more complicated and lengthy. See Sect. 5 for full details.

3 Preliminaries

We let $[N] = \{1, 2, \ldots, N\}$ for $N \in \mathbb{N}$ and for $k \in \mathbb{N}$ such that $k \leq N$, let $\binom{S}{k}$ denote the set of k-sized subsets of S. We use $|X|$ to denote the size of a set X and use X^+ to denote one or more elements of X. The set of all permutations on D is denoted by $\mathsf{Perm}(D)$. We let $*$ denote a wildcard element. For example $(*, z) \in L$ is true if there is an ordered pair in L where z is the second element (the type of the wildcard element shall be clear from the context). For a random variable X we use $\mathbb{E}[X]$ to denote its expected value.

We use $x \leftarrow_\$ \mathcal{D}$ to denote sampling x according to the distribution $\mathcal{D}$. If D is a set, we overload notation and let $x \leftarrow_\$ D$ denote uniformly sampling from the elements of D. For a bit-string s we use $|s|$ to denote the number of bits in s.

All logarithms in this paper are for base 2 unless otherwise specified.

Sponge-Based Hashing. For $c, r \in \mathbb{N}$, let $\Pi : \{0, 1\}^{c+r} \rightarrow \{0, 1\}^{c+r}$ be a permutation. We define sponge-based hashing $\mathsf{Sp}_\Pi : \{0, 1\}^c \times (\{0, 1\}^r)^+ \rightarrow \{0, 1\}^r$ as follows. For $s \in \{0, 1\}^{r+c}$ we use $s[1]$ to denote its first r bits and $s[2]$ to denote its last c bits.

$\underline{\mathsf{Sp}_\Pi(\mathsf{IV}, m = (m_1, \ldots, m_B))}$
$s_0 \leftarrow 0^r \parallel \mathsf{IV}$
For $i = 1, \ldots, B$
$\quad s_i[1] \parallel s_i[2] \leftarrow \Pi((m_i \oplus s_{i-1}[1]) \parallel s_{i-1}[2])$
Return $s_B[1]$

The elements of $\{0, 1\}^r$ shall be referred to as *blocks* and IV refers to the *initialization vector* (also referred to as *salt* in the literature). This is the same abstraction of sponge-based hashing as the one used in [10].

Auxiliary-Input Random Permutation Model (AI-RPM). We use the Auxiliary-Input Random Permutation Model (AI-RPM) introduced by Coretti, Dodis and Guo [10] to study non-uniform adversaries in the Random Permutation Model (this was a natural extension of the AI-ROM model proposed by Unruh in [31]). This model is parameterized by two non-negative integers S and T and an adversary $\mathcal{A}$ is divided into two stages $(\mathcal{A}_1, \mathcal{A}_2)$. Adversary $\mathcal{A}_1$, referred to as the preprocessing phase of $\mathcal{A}$ has unbounded access to the random permutation Π and it outputs an S-bit auxiliary input σ. Adversary $\mathcal{A}_2$, referred to as the online phase, gets σ as input and can make a total of T queries to Π, Π^{-1}, and attempts to accomplish some goal involving Π. Formally, we say that $\mathcal{A} = (\mathcal{A}_1, \mathcal{A}_2)$ is an (S, T)-AI adversary if $\mathcal{A}_1$ outputs S bits and $\mathcal{A}_2$ issues T

Game $\mathsf{G}^{\text{ai-cr}}_{c,r,B}(\mathcal{A} = (\mathcal{A}_1, \mathcal{A}_2))$	Subroutine AI-CR$_{\Pi,\text{IV}}(\mathcal{A} = (\mathcal{A}_1, \mathcal{A}_2))$

1. $\Pi \leftarrow\!\!{}^{\$} \mathsf{Perm}(\{0,1\}^{c+r})$
 2. $\text{IV} \leftarrow\!\!{}^{\$} \{0,1\}^c$
 3. Return AI-CR$_{\Pi,\text{IV}}(\mathcal{A})$
	1. $\sigma \leftarrow\!\!{}^{\$} \mathcal{A}_1(\Pi)$
	 2. $(\alpha, \alpha') \leftarrow\!\!{}^{\$} \mathcal{A}_2^{\Pi, \Pi^{-1}}(\sigma, \text{IV})$
	 3. Return true if:
	    (a) $\alpha \neq \alpha'$,
	    (b) $|\alpha|, |\alpha'|$ are at most B blocks long and
	    (c) $\mathsf{Sp}_\Pi(\text{IV}, \alpha) = \mathsf{Sp}_\Pi(\text{IV}, \alpha')$
	 4. Else, return false

Fig. 4. The bounded-length collision resistance game of salted sponge based hash in the AI-RPM, denoted $\mathsf{G}^{\text{ai-cr}}_{c,r,B}$.

queries to its oracles. We next formalize the collision resistance of sponge-based hash functions in AI-RPM.

Short Collision Resistance of Sponge-Based Hashing in AI-RPM. We formalize the hardness of bounded-length collision resistance of sponge-based hash functions in the AI-RPM. The game is parameterized by c, r. The game first samples a permutation Π uniformly at random from $\mathsf{Perm}(\{0,1\}^{c+r})$ and IV uniformly at random from $\{0,1\}^c$. Then, $\mathcal{A}_1$ is given unbounded access to Π, and it outputs σ. At this time, $\mathcal{A}_2$ gets σ and IV as input and has oracle access to Π, Π^{-1}. It needs to find $\alpha \neq \alpha'$ such that (1) $\mathsf{Sp}_\Pi(\text{IV}, \alpha) = \mathsf{Sp}_\Pi(\text{IV}, \alpha')$ and (2) α, α' consist of $\leq B$ blocks from $\{0,1\}^r$. This game, denoted $\mathsf{G}^{\text{ai-cr}}_{c,r,B}$, is explicitly written in Fig. 4. In Fig. 4, we write the adversary's execution in its own subroutine only for syntactical purposes (as we shall use it later).

Definition 1 (AI-CR Advantage). *For parameters $c, r, B \in \mathbb{N}$, the advantage of an adversary $\mathcal{A}$ against the bounded-length collision resistance of sponge in the AI-RPM is*

$$\mathsf{Adv}^{\text{ai-cr}}_{\mathsf{Sp},c,r,B}(\mathcal{A}) = \Pr\left[\mathsf{G}^{\text{ai-cr}}_{c,r,B}(\mathcal{A}) = \text{true}\right]$$

For parameters $S, T \in \mathbb{N}$, we overload notation and denote

$$\mathsf{Adv}^{\text{ai-cr}}_{\mathsf{Sp},c,r,B}(S,T) = \max_{\mathcal{A}}\left\{\mathsf{Adv}^{\text{ai-cr}}_{\mathsf{Sp},c,r,B}(\mathcal{A})\right\},$$

where the maximum is over all (S, T)-AI adversaries.

The Compression Lemma. Our proof of the impossibility result for $B = 2$ uses the well-known technique of finding an "impossible compression". The main idea, formalized in the following proposition, is that it is impossible to compress a random element in set $\mathcal{X}$ to a string shorter than $\log |\mathcal{X}|$ bits long, even relative to a random string.

Proposition 1 (E.g., [15]) *Let* Encode *be a randomized map from* $\mathcal{X}$ *to* $\mathcal{Y}$ *and let* Decode *be a randomized map from* $\mathcal{Y}$ *to* $\mathcal{X}$ *such that*

$$\Pr_{x \xleftarrow{\$} \mathcal{X}} [\mathsf{Decode}(\mathsf{Encode}(x)) = x] \geq \epsilon.$$

Then, $\log |\mathcal{Y}| \geq \log |\mathcal{X}| - \log(1/\epsilon)$.

4 Attacks

In this section, we first provide the generic attack for finding B-block collisions inspired by the analogous attack for MD in [3]. We then provide our new AI-RPM attack for finding 1-block collision (Sect. 4.2). Additionally, in Sect. 4.3, we prove the key lemma for our attack. The key lemma is a preprocessing attack for inverting a function f which is a restricted random permutation. The attack is closely related to that of Hellman [23], but we provide rigorous analysis for our specific application for completeness.

4.1 Generic Attack for B-Block Collisions

We give a (S,T) adversary $\mathcal{A}$ that has advantage $O(STB/2^c + T^2/2^c + T^2/2^r)$ against $\mathsf{G}^{\mathsf{ai\text{-}cr}}_{c,r,B}$. The main idea for this attack is similar to the zero-walk attack for finding B-block collisions in the Merkle-Damgård construction introduced in [3] which was in turn inspired by an attack in [11].

High Level Idea. In the preprocessing phase the adversary randomly samples $t \approx S$ different IVs $\mathsf{IV}_1, \ldots, \mathsf{IV}_t$ and for each of them computes $\sigma_{i,j}$ for $j \in [B/2 - 1]$ as $\sigma_{i,j} = \Pi(0, \sigma_{i,j-1}[2])$, where $\sigma_{i,0} = (0, \mathsf{IV})$. The sequence $\sigma_{i,0}, \ldots, \sigma_{i,B/2-1}$ forms a "zero-walk" on IV_i. It then finds m_i, m_i' such that $\Pi(m_i, \sigma_{i,B/2-1}[2])[1] = \Pi(m_i', \sigma_{i,B/2-1}[2])[1]$ for $i = 1, \ldots, t$. It outputs

$$(\sigma_{i,B/2-1}[2], m_i, m_i')_{i=1,\ldots,t} .$$

In the online phase, the adversary gets a challenge IV as input. For $i = 1, \ldots, T/B$, it computes $\mathsf{IV}_i = \Pi(i, \mathsf{IV})[2]$. For each of the IV_i's, it does a zero-walk of length $B - 2$. If on any of the walks it hits an IV that the preprocessing phase output then it outputs a collision. The reason this attack achieves an advantage of $\Omega(STB/2^c)$ is because in the preprocessing phase the adversary roughly hits $\Omega(SB)$ distinct IVs and in the online phase if it hits any of these IV's in the first half of its T/B (i.e., in roughly $T/2$ of the queries) walks it finds a collision.

We formally state our result below.

Theorem 1. *Let* $S, T, B, c, r \in \mathbb{N}$ *such that* $SB \leq 2^{c-1}$, $T \leq \min\{(2^{c-1}, 2^{r-1})\}$, $T \geq 2B$. *There exists an* (S,T) *adversary* $\mathcal{A} = (\mathcal{A}_1, \mathcal{A}_2)$ *such that*

$$\mathsf{Adv}^{\mathsf{ai\text{-}cr}}_{\mathsf{Sp},c,r,B}(\mathcal{A}) \geq \left\lfloor \frac{S}{c+2r} \right\rfloor \left\lfloor \frac{B}{2} - 1 \right\rfloor \frac{T}{2^{c+3}} + \frac{(T-B)(T-B-1)}{2^{c+1}}$$

$$+ \frac{3(T-B)(T-B-1)}{2^{r+3}} - \frac{S}{e^{(2^r-1)}} .$$

We defer the proof of this theorem to the full version.

4.2 Preprocessing Attack for $B = 1$

We give a new AI-RPM attack for finding 1-block collisions in the Sponge construction. The key ingredient in our attack is an (S, T) adversary for a function f finds two distinct pre-images of a random element of the co-domain under f. We construct this adversary in Lemma 1 based on the adversary from Lemma 2 that finds a single pre-image of a random element of the co-domain under f.

Theorem 2. *Let* $c, r \in \mathbb{N}$. *For any* $S, T \in \mathbb{N}$ *such that* $S \geq 24c$, $2^c \geq 24S$, *and* $2^c \geq (S/(T-2)) \cdot 24^3$, *there exists an* (S, T) *attacker* $\mathcal{A} = (\mathcal{A}_1, \mathcal{A}_2)$ *that on input* $\{0, 1\}^c$ *outputs a valid 1-block collision with probability* ϵ, *where*

$$\epsilon \geq \left(\frac{1}{20 \cdot 288^2 \cdot c^2} \right) \cdot \min \left(1, \frac{S^2(T-2)^2}{2^{2c+2}}, \left(\frac{S^2(T-2)}{2^{2c+1}} \right)^{2/3} \right).$$

Proof. Let $\Pi \colon \{0, 1\}^{c+r} \to \{0, 1\}^{c+r}$ be a random permutation. Define the function $f_\Pi \colon \{0, 1\}^c \to \{0, 1\}^c$ as $f_\Pi(x) = \Pi^{-1}(0^r \| x)[2]$. Note that f_Π is equivalent to the function that outputs the first c bits of the permutation $\Pi'(x \| 0^r)$, where $\Pi'(x \| y)$ for $x \in \{0, 1\}^c, y \in \{0, 1\}^r$ computes $\Pi^{-1}(y \| x)$ and shifts the first r bits of the output to the end of its output. Thus, we can invoke Lemma 1 for the function f_Π, which implies an $(S, T - 2)$ attacker $\mathcal{B} = (\mathcal{B}_1, \mathcal{B}_2)$ for finding two distinct pre-images of a random $y \leftarrow_\$ \{0, 1\}^c$. The attacker $\mathcal{A} = (\mathcal{A}_1, \mathcal{A}_2)$ is defined as follows.

- $\mathcal{A}_1(\Pi)$:
    1. Output $\sigma \leftarrow \mathcal{B}_1(f_\Pi)$.
- $\mathcal{A}_2(\mathsf{IV}, \sigma)$:
    1. Compute $(x_1, x_2) \leftarrow \mathcal{B}_1(\mathsf{IV}, \sigma)$.
    2. If $f_\Pi(x_1) = f_\Pi(x_2) = \mathsf{IV}$ and $x_1 \neq x_2$, compute $m_1 \| \mathsf{IV} = \Pi^{-1}(0^r \| x_1)$ and $m_2 \| \mathsf{IV} = \Pi^{-1}(0^r \| x_2)$ and output (m_1, m_2).
    3. Otherwise, output $\perp$.

For correctness, we note that if $\mathcal{A}_2$ outputs a non-$\perp$ value, then $\mathcal{A}_2$ succeeds in finding a 1-block collision. Recall that $\mathsf{Sp}_\Pi(\mathsf{IV}, m_1) = \Pi(m_1 \| \mathsf{IV})[1]$ and $\mathsf{Sp}_\Pi(\mathsf{IV}, m_2) = \Pi(m_2 \| \mathsf{IV})[1]$. By construction, $f_\Pi(x_1) = f_\Pi(x_2) = \mathsf{IV}$ implies $m_1 \| \mathsf{IV} = \Pi^{-1}(0^r \| x_1)$ and $m_2 \| \mathsf{IV} = \Pi^{-1}(0^r \| x_2)$ for some $m_1, m_2 \in \{0, 1\}^r$. But this in turn implies that $\Pi(m_1 \| \mathsf{IV})[1] = \Pi(m_2 \| \mathsf{IV})[1] = 0^r$. Since Π is a permutation and $x_1 \neq x_2$, it must be the case that $m_1 \neq m_2$, so (m_1, m_2) is a valid 1-block collision, as required.

Whenever $\mathcal{B}$ succeeds, $\mathcal{A}$ succeeds, so the success probability follows immediately from Lemma 1. ∎

Lemma 1. *Let* $n \geq 1$, $a \leq n - 3$ *and* Π *be a random permutation over* $\{0, 1\}^n$. *Let* $f \colon \{0, 1\}^a \to \{0, 1\}^a$ *such that* $f(x)$ *consists of the first* a *bits output by* $\Pi(x \| 0^{n-a})$. *For any* $S, T \in \mathbb{N}$ *such that* $S \geq 24a$, $2^a \geq 24S$, *and* $2^a \geq (S/T) \cdot$

24^3, there exists an (S,T) attacker $\mathcal{A} = (\mathcal{A}_1, \mathcal{A}_2)$ that on input $y \leftarrow_\$ \{0,1\}^a$ outputs x_1, x_2 such that $f(x_1) = f(x_2) = y$ and $x_1 \neq x_2$ with probability ϵ, where

$$\epsilon \geq \left(\frac{1}{20 \cdot 288^2 \cdot a^2} \right) \cdot \min \left(1, \frac{S^2 T^2}{2^{2a+2}}, \left(\frac{S^2 T}{2^{2a+1}} \right)^{2/3} \right).$$

Proof. Let $\mathcal{B} = (\mathcal{B}_1, \mathcal{B}_2)$ be an $(S/2, T/2)$ adversary from Lemma 2. In the offline phase, $\mathcal{A}_1$ on input the function f runs $\mathcal{B}_1(f)$ twice and gets σ_1, σ_2. $\mathcal{A}_1$ outputs $\sigma = (\sigma_1, \sigma_2)$. In the online phase, $\mathcal{A}_2$ on input σ and $y = f(x)$ for $x \leftarrow_\$ \{0,1\}^a$, computes $x_1 = \mathcal{B}_2(y, \sigma_1)$ and $x_2 = \mathcal{B}_2(y, \sigma_2)$. If $f(x_1) = f(x_2) = y$ and $x_1 \neq x_2$, $\mathcal{A}_2$ outputs (x_1, x_2) and otherwise outputs $\perp$. It directly follows that $\mathcal{A}$ uses space $|\sigma| = |\sigma_1| + |\sigma_2| \leq S$ and makes at most $2 \cdot (T/2) = T$ queries. So it remains to analyze the advantage of $\mathcal{A}$.

We define the following events that are relevant to the analysis. Let $\mathsf{Success}_1$, $\mathsf{Success}_2$ be the events that $\mathcal{B}_1(f, \sigma_1)$ and $\mathcal{B}_1(f, \sigma_2)$ output a valid pre-image, respectively. Let $\mathsf{Inverse}$ be the event that $|f^{-1}(y)| \geq 2$ for the challenge $y \leftarrow_\$ \{0,1\}^a$. Let $\mathsf{Distinct}$ be the event that the outputs x_1 and x_2 are distinct. Thus, the probability of success is given by

$$\epsilon = \Pr[\mathsf{Success}_1 \wedge \mathsf{Success}_2 \wedge \mathsf{Inverse} \wedge \mathsf{Distinct}].$$

Note that $\mathsf{Success}_1$ and $\mathsf{Success}_2$ are identical and independently distributed given a fixed value for y. Thus, we can rewrite the success probability as

$$\epsilon = \Pr[\mathsf{Inverse}] \cdot \Pr[\mathsf{Success}_1 \mid \mathsf{Inverse}] \cdot \Pr[\mathsf{Success}_2 \mid \mathsf{Inverse}]$$
$$\cdot \Pr[\mathsf{Distinct} \mid \mathsf{Success}_1 \wedge \mathsf{Success}_2 \wedge \mathsf{Inverse}].$$
$$= \Pr[\mathsf{Inverse}] \cdot \Pr[\mathsf{Success}_1 \mid \mathsf{Inverse}]^2$$
$$\cdot \Pr[\mathsf{Distinct} \mid \mathsf{Success}_1 \wedge \mathsf{Success}_2 \wedge \mathsf{Inverse}].$$

We analyze each of these terms separately.

In Claim 3, we show that $\Pr[\mathsf{Inverse}] \geq 1/10$ as long as $a \leq n-3$. $\Pr[\mathsf{Success}_1 \mid \mathsf{Inverse}]$ is given in Lemma 2 using $S' = S/2$ and $T' = T/2$. As $|f^{-1}(y)| \geq 2$ by assumption, it holds that

$$\Pr[\mathsf{Success}_1 \mid \mathsf{Inverse}] \geq \left(\frac{1}{288 \cdot a} \right) \cdot \min \left(1, \frac{ST}{2^{a+1}}, \left(\frac{S^2 T}{2^{2a+1}} \right)^{1/3} \right).$$

For the event $\mathsf{Distinct}$, note that in the worst case $|f^{-1}(y)| = 2$. In this case, it is equally as likely that $x_1 = x_2$ compared to $x_1 \neq x_2$ since there are only two equally likely values for x_1, x_2. Thus,

$$\Pr[\mathsf{Distinct} \mid \mathsf{Success}_1 \wedge \mathsf{Success}_2 \wedge \mathsf{Inverse}] = 1/2.$$

Combining the above, we conclude that the attackers probability of success is at least

$$\epsilon \geq \frac{1}{2} \cdot \frac{1}{10} \cdot \left(\frac{1}{288^2 \cdot a^2} \right) \cdot \min \left(1, \frac{S^2 T^2}{2^{2a+2}}, \left(\frac{S^2 T}{2^{2a+1}} \right)^{2/3} \right),$$

as required. ∎

Claim 3. *Let $n \geq 1$, $a \leq n - 3$ and Π be a random permutation over $\{0,1\}^n$. Let $f \colon \{0,1\}^a \to \{0,1\}^a$ such that $f(x)$ consists of the first a bits output by $\Pi(x \| 0^{n-a})$. Then, $\Pr[y \leftarrow_\$ \{0,1\}^a : |f^{-1}(y)| \geq 2] \geq 1/10$.*

We provide the proof of this claim in the full version due to lack of space.

4.3   Time-Space Tradeoffs for Inverting a Restricted Permutation

In this section, we prove a time-space tradeoff for inverting a restricted permutation. Let $n \in \mathbb{N}$, $a, b < n$, and let $\Pi \leftarrow \mathsf{Perm}(n)$ be a randomly chosen permutation. Consider the function $f \colon \{0,1\}^a \to \{0,1\}^b$ defined such that $f(x)$ outputs the first b bits of $\Pi(x \| 0^{n-a})$. We show that there exists an (S,T) adversary $\mathcal{A}$ that inverts f with advantage roughly $\Omega(\min(1, ST/2^{\min(a,b)}, (S^2 T/2^{2\min(a,b)})^{1/3}))$. Additionally, we show that on input $y = f(x)$ for a random $x \leftarrow_\$ \{0,1\}^a$, $\mathcal{A}$ outputs a uniformly random pre-image $x' \in f^{-1}(y)$ if it succeeds.

We note that our attack closely follows the approach of Hellman [23] and its extension from Fiat and Naor [17]. We provide the full details of the attack and analysis for completeness. We emphasize that our analysis differs from Hellman's analysis since our function f is not quite a random function. Still, we do not need the full generality of the result of Fiat and Naor that works for arbitrary functions. We also note that we show how to instantiate and analyze the "g" functions (see the proof for full details) used in Hellman's attack using only pairwise independence, whereas Fiat and Naor's result for arbitrary functions required k-wise independence for $k \approx T$.

Lemma 2. *Let $n \geq 1$, $a, b \leq n$ and Π be a random permutation over $\{0,1\}^n$. Let $f \colon \{0,1\}^a \to \{0,1\}^b$ such that $f(x)$ consists of the first b bits output by $\Pi(x \| 0^{n-a})$. For any $S, T \in \mathbb{N}$ such that $S \geq 24 \max(a,b)$, $2^{\min(a,b)} \geq 24S$, and $2^{\min(a,b)} \geq (S/T) \cdot 24^3$, there exists an (S,T) attacker $\mathcal{A} = (\mathcal{A}_1, \mathcal{A}_2)$ that succeeds in inverting f on input $y = f(x)$ for $x \leftarrow_\$ \{0,1\}^a$ with probability ϵ, where*

$$\epsilon \geq \left(\frac{1}{288 \cdot b}\right) \cdot \min\left(1, \frac{ST}{2^{\min(a,b)}}, \left(\frac{S^2 T}{2^{2\min(a,b)}}\right)^{1/3}\right).$$

Additionally, the following hold:

- *If the attacker $\mathcal{A} = (\mathcal{A}_1, \mathcal{A}_2)$ succeeds at inverting $y = f(x)$, it outputs a uniform pre-image $x' \in f^{-1}(y)$ over the randomness of $\mathcal{A}_1$ and $\mathcal{A}_2$.*
- *For any fixed $x \in \{0,1\}^a$ and $y = f(x)$, the attack succeeds with probability at least*

$$\epsilon \geq \left(\frac{1}{288 \cdot b}\right) \cdot \min\left(1, \frac{ST \cdot |f^{-1}(y)|}{2^a}, \left(\frac{S^2 T |f^{-1}(y)|^2}{2^{2a}}\right)^{1/3}\right).$$

Due to a lack of space, we defer the proof of this lemma to the full version.

5   Impossibility Results

We next give impossibility results for attacks for 1-block and 2-block collisions for sponge hashing. This consists of upper bounding the best possible advantage of any (S, T) adversary.

5.1   Advantage Upper Bound for B=1

We prove an upper bound for the advantage of an adversary in finding a 1-block collision for the sponge construction. Formally, we prove the following theorem.

Theorem 4. *For all* $S, T, c, r \in \mathbb{N}$

$$\mathsf{Adv}^{\mathsf{ai\text{-}cr}}_{\mathsf{Sp}, c, r, 1}(S, T) \leq \frac{2(S + c)T + 1}{2^c} + \frac{T^2}{2^r} .$$

To prove this theorem, we use the result of [10] which relates the advantage upper bound of an adversary in the AI-RPM to that in BF-RPM (bit-fixing RPM). Due to lack of space we defer the preliminaries for BF-RPM, the proof of Theorem 4 and the argument why the bit-fixing technique cannot be used to prove an advantage upper bound for $B = 2$ better than $O(ST^2/2^c)$ to the full version.

5.2   Advantage Upper Bound for $B = 2$

In this section we prove an upper-bound the advantage of an adversary in finding a 2-block collision for the sponge construction in the AI-RPM, according to the game $\mathsf{G}^{\mathsf{ai\text{-}cr}}_{c, r, B}$ described in Fig. 4. First, without loss of generality, in what follows we assume that the adversary is deterministic. This is because we can transform any probabilistic attacker into a deterministic one by hard-wiring the best randomness (see Adleman [2]).

We reduce the task of bounding the advantage of an attacker in finding a 2-block collision in the sponge construction, to a "multi-instance" game where the adversary does not have a preprocessing phase but rather only has non-uniform auxiliary input, chosen *before* the random permutation Π. The latter game is easier to analyze. This is in line with the work of Akshima et al. [3].

We define the following "multi-instance" game $\mathsf{G}^{\mathsf{mi\text{-}cr}}_{c, r, B, u}(\sigma, \mathcal{A}_2)$, where the preprocessing part of the adversary $\mathcal{A}_1$ is degenerate and outputs the fixed string σ. More precisely, the game has the following steps:

1. $\Pi \leftarrow_\$ \mathsf{Perm}(\{0, 1\}^{c+r})$
2. $U \leftarrow_\$ \binom{\{0,1\}^c}{u}$
3. Define $\mathcal{A}_1$ to be the algorithm that always outputs the string σ.
4. Return true if AI-CR$_{\Pi, \mathsf{IV}}(\mathcal{A} = (\mathcal{A}_1, \mathcal{A}_2)) = $ true for every $\mathsf{IV} \in U$. Otherwise, return false.

For a string σ and an adversary $\mathcal{A}_2$, define

$$\mathsf{Adv}^{\mathsf{mi\text{-}cr}}_{\mathsf{Sp},c,r,B,u}(\sigma, \mathcal{A}_2) = \Pr\left[\mathsf{G}^{\mathsf{mi\text{-}cr}}_{c,r,B,u}(\sigma, \mathcal{A}_2)\right].$$

Lemma 3 (Reducing the problem to the multi-instance game). *Fix* $c, r, B, S, T, u \in \mathbb{N}$. *Then,*

$$\mathsf{Adv}^{\mathsf{ai\text{-}cr}}_{\mathsf{Sp},c,r,B}(S, T) \leq 6 \cdot \left(\max_{\sigma, \mathcal{A}_2}\left\{\mathsf{Adv}^{\mathsf{mi\text{-}cr}}_{\mathsf{Sp},c,r,B,u}(\sigma, \mathcal{A}_2)\right\}\right)^{\frac{1}{u}} + 2^{S-u},$$

where the maximum is taken over all $\sigma \in \{0,1\}^S$ *and* T*-query algorithms* $\mathcal{A}_2$.

We refer the reader to [21] for a proof.

We next prove an upper bound on the advantage of any auxiliary-input adversary in finding a 2-block collision for the sponge construction. The main theorem is stated next.

Theorem 5. *For any* $c, r, S, T \in \mathbb{N}$ *and fixing* $\hat{S} := S + c$, *it holds that*

$$\mathsf{Adv}^{\mathsf{ai\text{-}cr}}_{\mathsf{Sp},c,r,2}(S, T) \leq \left(2^7 e \cdot \max\left\{\frac{T^2}{2^{c-1}}, \frac{T^2}{2^{r-1}}, \frac{\hat{S}T}{2^{c-3}}, \frac{\hat{S}^2 T^4}{2^{2c-2}}\right\}\right) + \frac{1}{2^c}.$$

Theorem 5 follows as a direct corollary of Lemma 3 together with the following lemma, setting $u = S + c$ and observing that **(1)** the lemma holds trivially when $\frac{T^2}{2^{r-1}} > 1$ and **(2)** $\frac{uT^3}{2^{c+r-2}} \leq \frac{uT}{2^{c-1}}$ whenever $\frac{T^2}{2^{r-1}} \leq 1$.

Lemma 4 (Hardness of the multi-instance game). *Fix* c, r, T, $u \in \mathbb{N}$ *and* $\sigma \in \{0,1\}^S$. *Then, for any* $\mathcal{A}_2$ *that makes at most* T *queries to its oracle, it holds that*

$$\mathsf{Adv}^{\mathsf{mi\text{-}cr}}_{\mathsf{Sp},c,r,2,u}(\sigma, \mathcal{A}_2) \leq \left(2^7 \cdot e \cdot \max\left\{\frac{T^2}{2^{c-1}}, \frac{T^2}{2^{r-1}}, \frac{uT}{2^{c-3}}, \frac{uT^3}{2^{c+r-2}}, \frac{u^2 T^4}{2^{2c-2}}\right\}\right)^u.$$

The rest of this section is devoted to the proof of Lemma 4.

We are interested in bounding the advantage of the best strategy, i.e., a pair $(\sigma, \mathcal{A}_2)$ where $\sigma \in \{0,1\}^S$ is a fixed string and $\mathcal{A}_2$ is a T-query algorithm, of finding collisions of length 2 in a sponge with respect to the game $\mathsf{G}^{\mathsf{mi\text{-}cr}}_{c,r,2,u}(\sigma, \mathcal{A}_2)$. Recall that in this game $\mathcal{A}_2$ needs to find proper collisions for u randomly chosen IVs, denoted U. The main idea in the proof is to use any such adversary $(\sigma, \mathcal{A}_2)$ in order to represent the permutation Π *as well as* the set of random IVs U with as few bits as possible. If the adversary is "too good to be true" we will get an impossible representation, contradicting Proposition 1.

Setup. Denote

$$\zeta^* := \log\left(\left(2^5 \cdot 4e \cdot \max\left\{\frac{T^2}{2^{c-1}}, \frac{T^2}{2^{r-1}}, \frac{uT}{2^{c-3}}, \frac{uT^3}{2^{c+r-2}}, \frac{u^2 T^4}{2^{2c-2}}\right\}\right)^u \cdot \binom{2^c}{u} \cdot (2^{c+r})!\right).$$

Assume the existence of an adversary $\mathcal{A} = (\sigma, \mathcal{A}_2)$, where $\sigma \in \{0,1\}^S$ is a string and $\mathcal{A}_2$ is a T-query adversary, that contradict the inequality stated in the lemma. That is, there is $\zeta > \zeta^*$ such that

$$\mathsf{Adv}^{\mathsf{mi\text{-}cr}}_{\mathsf{Sp},c,r,2,u}(\mathcal{A}) := \zeta > \zeta^*. \tag{5}$$

Define $\mathcal{G}$ to be the set of permutations-sets of IV pairs for which the attacker succeeds in winning the game for every IV in the set relative to the permutation, That is,

$$\mathcal{G} = \left\{ (U, \Pi) \;\middle|\; \begin{array}{l} U \in \binom{\{0,1\}^c}{u}, \\ \Pi \in \mathsf{Perm}(\{0,1\}^{c+r}), \end{array} \forall \mathsf{IV} \in U : \mathsf{AI\text{-}CR}_{\Pi,\mathsf{IV}}(\mathcal{A}) = \mathsf{true} \right\}.$$

Recall that ζ is defined to be the advantage of $\mathcal{A}$ in the game $\mathsf{G}^{\mathsf{mi\text{-}cr}}_{c,r,2,u}(\mathcal{A})$ in which Π and U are chosen uniformly, and then $\mathcal{A}$ needs to find a collision with respect to every one of the u IVs in U. Therefore,

$$|\mathcal{G}| = \zeta \cdot \binom{2^c}{u} \cdot (2^{c+r})!.$$

In what follows we define an encoding and a decoding procedure such that the encoding procedure gets as input U, Π such that $U \in \binom{\{0,1\}^c}{u}$ and $\Pi \in \mathsf{Perm}(\{0,1\}^{c+r})$, and it outputs an L bit string, where $L = \log\left(\zeta^* \cdot \binom{2^c}{u} \cdot (2^{c+r})!\right)$. The decoding procedure takes as input the string L and outputs U^*, Π^*. It will hold that $U^* = U$ and $\Pi^* = \Pi$ with probability ζ.[8] Using Proposition 1, this would give us that

$$\log \zeta \leq L - \log\left(\binom{2^c}{u} \cdot (2^{c+r})!\right) \Longrightarrow \zeta \leq \zeta^*$$

which is a contradiction to the assumption (see (5)).

Using $\mathcal{A}$, we shall define procedures $\mathsf{Encode}, \mathsf{Decode}$ such that for every $(U, \Pi) \in \mathcal{G}$, $\mathsf{Decode}(\mathsf{Encode}(U, \Pi)) = (U, \Pi)$ and the size of the output of $\mathsf{Encode}(U, \Pi)$ is at most L bits where

$$L = \log\left(\left(2^5 \cdot 4e \cdot \max\left\{ \frac{T^2}{2^{c-1}}, \frac{T^2}{2^{r-1}}, \frac{uT}{2^{c-3}}, \frac{uT^3}{2^{c+r-2}}, \frac{u^2T^4}{2^{2c-2}} \right\} \right)^u \cdot \binom{2^c}{u} \cdot (2^{c+r})! \right).$$

Using Proposition 1, this would give us that

$$\epsilon \leq \left(2^7 \cdot e \cdot \max\left\{ \frac{T^2}{2^{c-1}}, \frac{T^2}{2^{r-1}}, \frac{uT}{2^{c-3}}, \frac{uT^3}{2^{c+r-2}}, \frac{u^2T^4}{2^{2c-2}} \right\} \right)^u.$$

This immediately gives the bound claimed in the statement of the lemma. The rest of the proof of the lemma would define $\mathsf{Encode}, \mathsf{Decode}$, show an upper bound

---

[8] Essentially, we will show that for all $(U, \Pi) \in |\mathcal{G}|$, if the encoding procedure produces output L, then the decoding procedure on input L outputs U^*, Π^* such that $U^* = U$ and $\Pi^* = \Pi$.

on the size of the output of Encode and that $\mathsf{Decode}(\mathsf{Encode}(U, \Pi)) = (U, \Pi)$ for all $(U, \Pi) \in \mathcal{G}$.

Notation and Definitions. Fix $(U, \Pi) \in \mathcal{G}$. Let $U = \{\mathsf{IV}_1, \dots, \mathsf{IV}_u\}$ where the IV_i's are ordered lexicographically. Let $\mathsf{Qrs}(\mathsf{IV}) \in (\{0, 1\}^{r+c})^T$ be the list of queries that $\mathcal{A}_2$ makes to Π or Π^{-1} when executed with input (σ, IV). Namely, for $\mathsf{IV} \in \{0, 1\}^c$,

$$\mathsf{Qrs}(\mathsf{IV}) = \left\{ s \in \{0, 1\}^{c+r} \mid \mathcal{A}_2(\sigma, \mathsf{IV}) \text{ queries } \Pi \text{ or } \Pi^{-1} \text{ on } s \right\}$$

Note that $\mathsf{Qrs}(\mathsf{IV})$ is indeed a set as we can assume (without loss of generality) that $\mathcal{A}_2$ never repeats queries in a single execution (since $\mathcal{A}_2$ can just remember all of its past queries).

Let $\mathsf{Ans}(\mathsf{IV}) \in (\{0, 1\}^{r+c})^T$ be the list of answers to the queries of that $\mathcal{A}_2$ to Π or Π^{-1} when executed with input (σ, IV). Namely, for $\mathsf{IV} \in \{0, 1\}^c$,

$$\mathsf{Ans}(\mathsf{IV}) = \left\{ s \in \{0, 1\}^{c+r} \mid \mathcal{A}_2(\sigma, \mathsf{IV}) \text{ queries } \Pi \text{ or } \Pi^{-1} \text{ on } s \right\}$$

We say that $\mathsf{IV}' \in \mathsf{SIVs}(\mathsf{IV})$ if there is some $s[2] \in \{0, 1\}^r$ such that $s[2] \| \mathsf{IV}'$ is an entry in $\mathsf{Qrs}(\mathsf{IV})$ or $\mathsf{Ans}(\mathsf{IV})$. Namely, for $\mathsf{IV}, \mathsf{IV}' \in \{0, 1\}^c$,

$$\mathsf{IV}' \in \mathsf{SIVs}(\mathsf{IV}) \iff \exists s[2] \in \{0, 1\}^r \text{ s.t. } s[2] \| \mathsf{IV}' \in \mathsf{Qrs}(\mathsf{IV}) \cup \mathsf{Ans}(\mathsf{IV}).$$

We define the set of *fresh* IVs in U. An IV IV_i for $i \in [u]$ is called fresh if it was never an IV in either input or output of any query performed by $\mathcal{A}_2$ while being executed on IV_j for $j \leq i - 1$ which are fresh. The first IV IV_1 is always fresh. An IV IV_i for $i \geq 2$ is fresh if for any fresh IV_j for $j \leq i - 1$, $\mathsf{IV}_i \notin \mathsf{SIVs}(\mathsf{IV}_j)$. Namely, denoting the set of fresh IVs by U_{fresh}, we have the following inductive (on $i \in [u]$) definition:

$$\mathsf{IV}_i \in U_{\mathsf{fresh}} \iff \forall j \leq i - 1, \mathsf{IV}_j \in U_{\mathsf{fresh}} : \mathsf{IV}_i \notin \mathsf{SIVs}(\mathsf{IV}_j).$$

Looking ahead, we define U_{fresh} like this because we run $\mathcal{A}_2$ on the IVs in U_{fresh} in lexicographical order, and this definition ensures that each IV that $\mathcal{A}_2$ is executed on was not queried by it previously. Denote

$$F := |U_{\mathsf{fresh}}| \quad \text{and} \quad U_{\mathsf{fresh}} = \{\mathsf{IV}'_1, \dots, \mathsf{IV}'_F\} \text{ (ordered lexicographically)}.$$

Denote

$$\forall i \in [F] : \mathsf{Q}_i := \mathsf{Qrs}(\mathsf{IV}'_i) \quad \text{and} \quad \mathsf{Q}_{\mathsf{fresh}} := \mathsf{Q}_1 \| \mathsf{Q}_2 \| \dots \| \mathsf{Q}_F,$$

where $\|$ is the concatenation operator. Let $\mathsf{Q}_{\mathsf{fresh}}[r]$ be the rth query in the list $\mathsf{Q}_{\mathsf{fresh}}$. Note that $r \in [F \cdot T]$. For every $\mathsf{IV} \in U \setminus U_{\mathsf{fresh}}$, let t_{IV} be the minimum value such that $\mathsf{Q}_{\mathsf{fresh}}[t_{\mathsf{IV}}]$ is a query either with input or output of the form $(*, \mathsf{IV})$. Let $b_{\mathsf{IV}} = 0$ if input of $\mathsf{Q}_{\mathsf{fresh}}[t_{\mathsf{IV}}]$ was of the form $(*, \mathsf{IV})$ and 1 otherwise. Define the set of *prediction* queries as

$$\mathsf{P} := \{2t_{\mathsf{IV}} - b_{\mathsf{IV}} \mid \mathsf{IV} \in U \setminus U_{\mathsf{fresh}}\}.$$

The encoding algorithm will output $U_{\mathsf{fresh}}, \mathsf{P}$, which suffices to recover the set U by running $\mathcal{A}_2$.

Structure of Collisions. Since adversary $\mathcal{A}_2$ succeeds on all of the IVs in U, it holds that for every $j \in [F]$, the output of the adversary is (α_j, α_j') such that $\alpha_j \neq \alpha_j'$, $\mathsf{Sp}_\Pi(\mathsf{IV}_j', \alpha_j) = \mathsf{Sp}_\Pi(\mathsf{IV}_j', \alpha_j')$ and both $\alpha_j \neq \alpha_j'$. We can assume without loss of generality that the last blocks of α_j and α_j' are distinct (because otherwise we can trim α_j, α_j' to obtain a shorter collision).

Definition 2 (Crucial queries). *The queries to Π, Π^{-1} in Q_j include a subset of queries that we call the* crucial queries. *The subset consists of earliest appearing queries in Q_j that are required to compute $\mathsf{Sp}_\Pi(\mathsf{IV}_j', \alpha_j)$ and $\mathsf{Sp}_\Pi(\mathsf{IV}_j', \alpha_j')$. It follows that for 2-block collisions, this subset consists of at most four queries.*

We say that a query made by running while running on (σ, IV_j') is NEW if either of the following hold.

- the query is $\Pi(m, \mathsf{IV})$ with answer (m', IV') and neither $\Pi(m, \mathsf{IV})$ or $\Pi^{-1}(m', \mathsf{IV}')$ had been queried by $\mathcal{A}_2$ while running on $\mathsf{IV}_1', \ldots, \mathsf{IV}_{j-1}'$.
- the query is $\Pi^{-1}(m, \mathsf{IV})$ with answer (m', IV') and neither $\Pi^{-1}(m, \mathsf{IV})$ or $\Pi(m', \mathsf{IV}')$ had been queried by $\mathcal{A}_2$ while running on $\mathsf{IV}_1', \ldots, \mathsf{IV}_{j-1}'$.

If a query is not NEW we classify it into one of 2 types: REPEATEDUSED, and REPEATEDUNUSED. A REPEATEDUSED query is one such that it was a crucial query for IV_i' where $i < j$. A REPEATEDUNUSED query is one such that it is not a NEW or a REPEATEDUSED query.

Our goal is to compress (U, Π) and we are going to achieve this by using our collision finding adversary $\mathcal{A}_2$. The encoding procedure shall output the set U_{fresh}, the set P, the list $\tilde{\Pi}$ with some entries removed and some additional lists and sets. We will be describing the details of these lists and sets below and which entries we remove from $\tilde{\Pi}$. Our main goal is to show that when we remove entries of $\tilde{\Pi}$ and instead using additional lists and set, we are actually compressing. Our ways to compress will depend on the crucial queries in each Q_j for $j \in [F]$.

We classify the IV_j'th for each $j \in [F]$ into the first of the following cases it satisfies, e.g., if the crucial queries for IV_j' satisfies both cases 1 and 2, we categorize it into 1.

1. One of the crucial queries for IV_j' is a query such that the last c bits of the answer is IV_j'
2. All of the crucial queries to are NEW.
3. At least one of the crucial queries is REPEATEDUSED.
4. There is exactly one REPEATEDUNUSED crucial query.
5. There are exactly two REPEATEDUNUSED crucial queries.

Claim 6 *We claim that each IV_j' will be categorized into one of the above cases.*

Proof To begin with, observe that given how we define *fresh* IV_j', there will have to be a NEW crucial query such that either it is a query to Π with input of the form $(*, \mathsf{IV}'_j)$ or it is a query to Π^{-1} with answer of the form $(*, \mathsf{IV}'_j)$, because we have assumed without loss of generality that $\mathcal{A}_2$ makes all the queries while running on IV'_j required to find the collision. If there is a NEW crucial query to Π^{-1} with answer of the form $(*, \mathsf{IV}'_j)$ then case 1 is satisfied. Also observe that there are at most two crucial queries that are not NEW since we are looking at 2-block collisions because any query whose input or output is of the form $(*, \mathsf{IV}'_j)$ is NEW for all IV'_j as they are fresh. So it follows if IV'_j is not categorized into 1, it will either have all NEW crucial queries (case 2) or have at least one REPEATEDUSED query (case 3) or have one (case 4) or two REPEATEDUNUSED (case 5) queries. This proves the claim.   ■

Due to a lack of space, we defer all the details of how we handle each of the cases, and achieve the required amount of compression to the full version.

Acknowledgments. Ilan Komargodski is supported in part by an Alon Young Faculty Fellowship, by a JPM Faculty Research Award, by a grant from the Israel Science Foundation (ISF Grant No. 1774/20), and by a grant from the US-Israel Binational Science Foundation and the US National Science Foundation (BSF-NSF Grant No. 2020643). Part of Ashrujit Ghoshal's and Cody Freitag's work was done during an internship at NTT Research. Cody Freitag is also supported in part by the National Science Foundation Graduate Research Fellowship under Grant No. DGE-2139899 and DARPA Award HR00110C0086. Any opinion, findings, and conclusions or recommendations expressed in this material are those of the authors and do not necessarily reflect the views of the National Science Foundation or the Defense Advanced Research Projects Agency (DARPA).

References

1. Abusalah, H., Alwen, J., Cohen, B., Khilko, D., Pietrzak, K., Reyzin, L.: Beyond Hellman's time-memory trade-offs with applications to proofs of space. In: Takagi, T., Peyrin, T. (eds.) ASIACRYPT 2017, Part II. LNCS, vol. 10625, pp. 357–379. Springer, Cham (2017). https://doi.org/10.1007/978-3-319-70697-9_13
2. Adleman, L.: Two theorems on random polynomial time. In: 19th Annual Symposium on Foundations of Computer Science (SDCS 1978), pp. 75–83 (1978)
3. Akshima, X., Cash, D., Drucker, A., Wee, H.: Time-space tradeoffs and short collisions in Merkle-Damgård hash functions. In: Micciancio, D., Ristenpart, T. (eds.) CRYPTO 2020. LNCS, vol. 12170, pp. 157–186. Springer, Cham (2020). https://doi.org/10.1007/978-3-030-56784-2_6
4. Akshima, Guo, S., Liu, Q.: Time-space lower bounds for finding collisions in Merkle-Damgård hash functions. In: Dodis, Y., Shrimpton, T. (eds.) CRYPTO 2022, LNCS 13509, pp. 192–221 (2022)
5. Barkan, E., Biham, E., Shamir, A.: Rigorous bounds on cryptanalytic time/memory tradeoffs. In: Dwork, C. (ed.) CRYPTO 2006. LNCS, vol. 4117, pp. 1–21. Springer, Heidelberg (2006). https://doi.org/10.1007/11818175_1
6. Bernstein, D.J., Lange, T.: Non-uniform cracks in the concrete: the power of free precomputation. In: Sako, K., Sarkar, P. (eds.) ASIACRYPT 2013, Part II. LNCS, vol. 8270, pp. 321–340. Springer, Heidelberg (2013). https://doi.org/10.1007/978-3-642-42045-0_17

7. Bertoni, G., Daemen, J., Peeters, M., Van Assche, G.: On the indifferentiability of the sponge construction. In: Smart, N. (ed.) EUROCRYPT 2008. LNCS, vol. 4965, pp. 181–197. Springer, Heidelberg (2008). https://doi.org/10.1007/978-3-540-78967-3_11
8. Bertoni, G., Daemen, J., Peeters, M., Van Assche, G.: Sponge functions. In: ECRYPT Hash Workshop. Citeseer (2007)
9. Bertoni, G., Daemen, J., Peeters, M., Van Assche, G.: On the security of the keyed sponge construction. In: Symmetric Key Encryption Workshop (2011)
10. Coretti, S., Dodis, Y., Guo, S.: Non-uniform bounds in the random-permutation, ideal-cipher, and generic-group models. In: Shacham, H., Boldyreva, A. (eds.) CRYPTO 2018, Part I. LNCS, vol. 10991, pp. 693–721. Springer, Cham (2018). https://doi.org/10.1007/978-3-319-96884-1_23
11. Coretti, S., Dodis, Y., Guo, S., Steinberger, J.: Random oracles and non-uniformity. In: Nielsen, J.B., Rijmen, V. (eds.) EUROCRYPT 2018, Part I. LNCS, vol. 10820, pp. 227–258. Springer, Cham (2018). https://doi.org/10.1007/978-3-319-78381-9_9
12. Corrigan-Gibbs, H., Kogan, D.: The discrete-logarithm problem with preprocessing. In: Nielsen, J.B., Rijmen, V. (eds.) EUROCRYPT 2018, Part II. LNCS, vol. 10821, pp. 415–447. Springer, Cham (2018). https://doi.org/10.1007/978-3-319-78375-8_14
13. Corrigan-Gibbs, H., Kogan, D.: The function-inversion problem: barriers and opportunities. In: Hofheinz, D., Rosen, A. (eds.) TCC 2019, Part I. LNCS, vol. 11891, pp. 393–421. Springer, Cham (2019). https://doi.org/10.1007/978-3-030-36030-6_16
14. Damgård, I.B.: Collision free hash functions and public key signature schemes. In: Chaum, D., Price, W.L. (eds.) EUROCRYPT 1987. LNCS, vol. 304, pp. 203–216. Springer, Heidelberg (1988). https://doi.org/10.1007/3-540-39118-5_19
15. De, A., Trevisan, L., Tulsiani, M.: Time space tradeoffs for attacks against one-way functions and PRGs. In: Rabin, T. (ed.) CRYPTO 2010. LNCS, vol. 6223, pp. 649–665. Springer, Heidelberg (2010). https://doi.org/10.1007/978-3-642-14623-7_35
16. Dodis, Y., Guo, S., Katz, J.: Fixing cracks in the concrete: random oracles with auxiliary input, revisited. In: Coron, J.-S., Nielsen, J.B. (eds.) EUROCRYPT 2017, Part II. LNCS, vol. 10211, pp. 473–495. Springer, Cham (2017). https://doi.org/10.1007/978-3-319-56614-6_16
17. Fiat, A., Naor, M.: Rigorous time/space trade-offs for inverting functions. SIAM J. Comput. 29(3), 790–803 (1999)
18. Fouque, P.-A., Joux, A., Mavromati, C.: Multi-user collisions: applications to discrete logarithm, Even-Mansour and PRINCE. In: Sarkar, P., Iwata, T. (eds.) ASIACRYPT 2014, Part I. LNCS, vol. 8873, pp. 420–438. Springer, Heidelberg (2014). https://doi.org/10.1007/978-3-662-45611-8_22
19. Gaži, P., Tessaro, S.: Provably robust sponge-based PRNGs and KDFs. In: Fischlin, M., Coron, J.-S. (eds.) EUROCRYPT 2016, Part I. LNCS, vol. 9665, pp. 87–116. Springer, Heidelberg (2016). https://doi.org/10.1007/978-3-662-49890-3_4
20. Gennaro, R., Trevisan, L.: Lower bounds on the efficiency of generic cryptographic constructions. In: 41st Annual Symposium on Foundations of Computer Science, FOCS, pp. 305–313. IEEE Computer Society (2000)
21. Ghoshal, A., Komargodski, I.: On time-space tradeoffs for bounded-length collisions in Merkle-Damgård hashing (2022)
22. Golovnev, A., Guo, S., Horel, T., Park, S., Vaikuntanathan, V.: Data structures meet cryptography: 3SUM with preprocessing. In: 52nd Annual ACM SIGACT Symposium on Theory of Computing, STOC, pp. 294–307 (2020)

160   C. Freitag et al.

23. Hellman, M.E.: A cryptanalytic time-memory trade-off. IEEE Trans. Inf. Theory **26**(4), 401–406 (1980)
24. Merkle, R.C.: Secrecy, authentication and public key systems. Ph.D. thesis, UMI Research Press, Ann Arbor, Michigan (1982)
25. Merkle, R.C.: A digital signature based on a conventional encryption function. In: Pomerance, C. (ed.) CRYPTO 1987. LNCS, vol. 293, pp. 369–378. Springer, Heidelberg (1988). https://doi.org/10.1007/3-540-48184-2_32
26. Merkle, R.C.: A certified digital signature. In: Brassard, G. (ed.) CRYPTO 1989. LNCS, vol. 435, pp. 218–238. Springer, New York (1990). https://doi.org/10.1007/0-387-34805-0_21
27. Mihalcik, J.: An analysis of algorithms for solving discrete logarithms in fixed groups. Technical report, Naval Postgraduate School, Monterey, CA (2010)
28. Morin, P., Mulzer, W., Reddad, T.: Encoding arguments. ACM Comput. Surv. **50**(3), 46:1-46:36 (2017)
29. Oechslin, P.: Making a faster cryptanalytic time-memory trade-off. In: Boneh, D. (ed.) CRYPTO 2003. LNCS, vol. 2729, pp. 617–630. Springer, Heidelberg (2003). https://doi.org/10.1007/978-3-540-45146-4_36
30. Morris, R., Thompson, K.: Password security - a case history. Commun. ACM **22**(11), 594–597 (1979)
31. Unruh, D.: Random oracles and auxiliary input. In: Menezes, A. (ed.) CRYPTO 2007. LNCS, vol. 4622, pp. 205–223. Springer, Heidelberg (2007). https://doi.org/10.1007/978-3-540-74143-5_12
32. Wee, H.: On obfuscating point functions. In: 37th Annual ACM Symposium on Theory of Computing, STOC, pp. 523–532 (2005)
33. Yao, A.C.: Coherent functions and program checkers (extended abstract). In: STOC, pp. 84–94 (1990)

On Time-Space Tradeoffs for Bounded-Length Collisions in Merkle-Damgård Hashing

Ashrujit Ghoshal[1]([✉]) [iD] and Ilan Komargodski[2,3] [iD]

[1] Paul G. Allen School of Computer Science & Engineering,
University of Washington, Seattle, WA, USA
ashrujit@cs.washington.edu
[2] School of Computer Science and Engineering,
Hebrew University of Jerusalem, 91904 Jerusalem, Israel
ilank@cs.huji.ac.il
[3] NTT Research, Sunnyvale, USA

Abstract. We study the power of preprocessing adversaries in finding bounded-length collisions in the widely used Merkle-Damgård (MD) hashing in the random oracle model. Specifically, we consider adversaries with arbitrary S-bit advice about the random oracle and can make at most T queries to it. Our goal is to characterize the advantage of such adversaries in finding a B-block collision in an MD hash function constructed using the random oracle with range size N as the compression function (given a random salt).

The answer to this question is completely understood for very large values of B (essentially $\Omega(T)$) as well as for $B = 1, 2$. For $B \approx T$, Coretti et al. (EUROCRYPT '18) gave matching upper and lower bounds of $\tilde{\Theta}(ST^2/N)$. Akshima et al. (CRYPTO '20) observed that the attack of Coretti et al. could be adapted to work for any value of $B > 1$, giving an attack with advantage $\tilde{\Omega}(STB/N + T^2/N)$. Unfortunately, they could only prove that this attack is optimal for $B = 2$. Their proof involves a compression argument with exhaustive case analysis and, as they claim, a naive attempt to generalize their bound to larger values of B (even for $B = 3$) would lead to an explosion in the number of cases needed to be analyzed, making it unmanageable. With the lack of a more general upper bound, they formulated the *STB conjecture*, stating that the best-possible advantage is $\tilde{O}(STB/N + T^2/N)$ for any $B > 1$.

In this work, we confirm the STB conjecture in many new parameter settings. For instance, in one result, we show that the conjecture holds for all constant values of B. Further, using combinatorial properties of graphs, we are able to confirm the conjecture even for super constant values of B, as long as some restriction is made on S. For instance, we confirm the conjecture for all $B \leqslant T^{1/4}$ as long as $S \leqslant T^{1/8}$. Technically, we develop structural characterizations for bounded-length collisions in MD hashing that allow us to give a compression argument in which the number of cases needed to be handled does not explode.

1 Introduction

Starting from the seminal work of Hellman [21], there have been significant efforts to understand the power of preprocessing attacks in various applications

© International Association for Cryptologic Research 2022
Y. Dodis and T. Shrimpton (Eds.): CRYPTO 2022, LNCS 13509, pp. 161–191, 2022.
https://doi.org/10.1007/978-3-031-15982-4_6

and constructions (e.g., [1,3,5,6,8,9,11,13,15,16,28,30,31]). Preprocessing attacks, i.e., ones that utilize a bounded amount of auxiliary information, capture the standard modeling of attackers as *non-uniform*, allowing them to obtain some arbitrary (but bounded length) "advice" before attacking the system. In this work, we continue the recent line of works studying the power of preprocessing adversaries in the context of finding collisions in the widely used Merkle-Damgård (MD) design.

Collision Resistance of Salted MD. The Merkle-Damgård hash function construction [12,24–26] is a popular design for building an arbitrary-size-input compression function from a fixed-size-input compression function. This design is not only extremely fundamental in cryptographic theory, but it also underlies popular hash functions used in practice, most notably MD5, SHA-1, and SHA-2.

The MD construction is defined relative to a compressing function $h\colon [N] \times [M] \to [N]$[1], modeled as a random oracle, as follows. First, for $a \in [N]$ and $\alpha \in [M]$, let $\mathsf{MD}_h(a, \alpha) = h(a, \alpha)$. Then, define recursively

$$\mathsf{MD}_h(a, (\alpha_1, \ldots, \alpha_B)) = h(\mathsf{MD}_h(a, (\alpha_1, \ldots, \alpha_{B-1})), \alpha_B)$$

for $a \in [N]$ and $\alpha_1, \ldots, \alpha_B \in [M]$. The a is referred to as *salt* (sometimes also called IV) and each of the following B elements are referred to as *blocks*.

Due to the ubiquitous influence of this hashing paradigm, both in theory and practice, characterizing the complexity of finding collisions in MD_h (on a random salt) is a fundamental problem. The well-known birthday attack gives a T-query attacker with $\Theta(T^2/N)$ advantage. However, this attack is very generic: it neither takes advantage of the structure of MD_h nor does it utilize the fact that the attacker may have access to some limited amount of "advice" about h due to a long preprocessing phase. But, there is a good reason that security against non-uniform attackers has become the standard notion of security in the cryptographic literature: it captures the natural idea that an adversary may have been designed to attack specific instances, guaranteeing security against an expensive preprocessing stage, or even unknown future attacks. On the whole, it is widely believed by the theoretical community that non-uniformity is the right cryptographic modeling of attackers, despite being overly conservative and including potentially unrealistic attackers. Therefore, understanding the complexity of finding collisions in MD, allowing preprocessing, is a fundamental problem.

The Auxiliary-Input Random Oracle Model. The concrete hash functions h used in real-life do not have solid theoretical foundations from the perspective of provable security. Therefore, when analyzing the security of the MD construction, the function h is typically modeled as a completely random one, i.e., a random oracle. We follow the standard approach and model preprocessing adversaries using the influential extension of the random oracle model termed *auxiliary-input random oracle model* (AI-ROM). This model was (implicitly) used, for example, in the classical works of Yao [31] and Fiat and Naor [16],

---

[1] We use the notation $[N]$ to denote the set $\{1, 2, \ldots, N\}$ for a natural number N.

and formally defined in the influential work of Unruh [30] which was recently revisited by Dodis, Guo, and Katz [15] and Coretti et al. [9].

The AI-ROM models preprocessing adversaries as two-stage algorithms ($\mathcal{A}_1$, $\mathcal{A}_2$) parametrized by S (for "space") and T (for "time"). The first part $\mathcal{A}_1$ has unbounded access to the random oracle h, and its goal is to compute an S-bit "advice" σ for $\mathcal{A}_2$. The second part $\mathcal{A}_2$ gets the advice σ, can make at most T queries to the random oracle, and attempts to accomplish some task involving h. In our case, $\mathcal{A}_2$ gets a random salt a as a challenge and its goal is to come up with a collision in $\mathsf{MD}_h(a, \cdot)$. Both $\mathcal{A}_1$ and $\mathcal{A}_2$ are unbounded in running time.

Known Results. Collision resistance of salted MD hash functions in the AI-ROM was first studied by Coretti, Dodis, Guo, and Steinberger [9]. Among other results, they showed an attack, loosely based on the idea of rainbow tables [21,28], with advantage $\tilde{\Omega}(ST^2/N)$.[2][3] They further showed that this attack is optimal. Namely, no attack can have an advantage better than $\tilde{O}(ST^2/N)$. (Notice that this attack beats the naive birthday attack mentioned above for typical values of S.) In a more recent work of Akshima, Cash, Drucker, and Wee [3] observed that the attack of Coretti et al. [9] results in very long collisions, of the order of T blocks, which may limit their practical usefulness. While formally, a length T collision does violate collision resistance, it is hard to imagine a natural application where it is useful. Indeed, for reasonable values of T, say $T = 2^{60}$, it is unlikely that such a collision, which is several petabytes long, could damage any widely-used application.

Akshima et al. [3] therefore raise the very natural question of what is the complexity of finding *short* collisions.

What is the complexity, as a function of S and T (the allowed space and query bounds, respectively),
of finding a B-block collision in salted MD?

Although this question is very natural and clean, as mentioned, a complete answer is known only in the extreme cases, either when $B = 2$ or when $B = \tilde{\Omega}(T)$. Indeed, when B is very close to T, the result above of Coretti et al. [9] implies that the advantage is $\tilde{\Theta}(ST^2/N)$. The case of $B = 2$ was resolved by Akshima et al. [3] who showed that the advantage is $\tilde{\Theta}(ST/N + T^2/N)$. Even for $B = 3$, a complete answer is not known: The analysis of Akshima et al. [3] consists of an elaborate case analysis tailored to the $B = 2$ case, and they claim that even for $B = 3$ the proof of their lower bound "... *would be too long and complex to write down*".[4]

The STB Conjecture. In terms of upper bounds, Akshima et al. [3] showed that a variant of Coretti et al.'s (rainbow tables inspired) attack could be generalized to get a B-block collision with advantage $\tilde{\Omega}(STB/N)$. This attack generalized the attack of Coretti et al. [9] which gives an $O(T)$-block collision with probability $\tilde{\Omega}(ST^2/N)$. With the lack of better bounds on the best possible

---

[2] Throughout the paper, the ˜ notation suppresses poly-logarithmic terms in N.

[3] By "advantage" we mean the probability of finding a collision.

[4] For $B = 1$ a tight bound of $\Theta(S/N + T^2/N)$ is known [15].

attack for a wide range of B's (anywhere between $B = 3$ and $B \ll T$), Akshima et al. [3] put forward the *"STB conjecture"* which posits that the optimal attack for finding length B collisions has advantage $\tilde{\Theta}(STB/N + T^2/N)$ (i.e., the better between their attack and the generic birthday attack).

We believe that our current understanding of the exact security that MD-style constructions could ideally achieve is insufficient. Therefore, given how widespread MD-based hash functions are, progress towards resolving the conjecture is highly important.

1.1 Our Results

Our main result confirms the STB conjecture in many new parameter settings. Specifically, we prove two new upper bounds on the advantage of the best attack for finding short collisions in salted MD hash functions in the AI-ROM. The first bound confirms the STB conjecture for all constant values of B. The second result confirms the STB conjecture even for super constant values of B but only for moderately large values of S compared to T.

STB Conjecture is True for all Constant B. We show that for any $B \in O(1)$, the advantage of any S-space T-query attacker in finding a length B collision is bounded by $\tilde{O}(ST/N + T^2/N)$, matching the known attack up to poly-logarithmic factors.

Theorem 1.1 (Informal; See Theorem 5.1). *For every constant B, the STB conjecture is true.*

This theorem is obtained as a special case of a more general bound on the advantage of any S-space T-query attacker in finding a length B collision of the form

$$\tilde{O}\left(\frac{STB^2(\log^2 S)^{B-2}}{N} + \frac{T^2}{N}\right).$$

Note that this bound is meaningful when B is a constant (or slightly bigger) but becomes vacuous when say, $B = \log N$.

STB Conjecture is True for all $SB \ll T$. We show that as long as $S, B \ll T$, the conjecture is true again. Specifically, we show that whenever $S^4 B^2 \in \tilde{O}(T)$, the maximal advantage of any S-space T-query attacker in finding a length B collision is obtained by the birthday attack, up to poly-logarithmic factors. For example, when $SB \leqslant T^{1/4}$, the maximal advantage is $O(T^2/N)$, and therefore the STB conjecture holds.

Theorem 1.2 (Informal; See Theorem 6.1). *For every $S^4 B^2 \in \tilde{O}(T)$, the STB conjecture is true. For instance, the conjecture holds if either*

- $B \in \mathsf{poly} \log N$ *and* $S \in \tilde{O}(T^{1/4})$, *or*
- $B \in \tilde{O}(T^{1/4})$ *and* $S \in \tilde{O}(T^{1/8})$.

This theorem is obtained as a special case of a more general bound on the advantage of any S-space T-query attacker in finding a length B collision of the form

$$\tilde{O}\left(\frac{S^4 T B^2}{N} + \frac{T^2}{N}\right).$$

A Concrete Comparison Between the Results. The two bounds are generally incomparable. While the bound from Theorem 1.1 is asymptotically tight whenever B is constant (independent of S, T), it becomes vacuous for say $B = \log N$. On the other hand, the bound from Theorem 1.2 is meaningful for all $B \in o(N^{1/2})$, as long as $S^4 \cdot B^2 \ll N$. For instance, assume that $S = N^{1/16}$ and $B \in \Theta(N^\epsilon)$ (for $0 < \epsilon < 1/8$). In this setting, the bound from Theorem 1.1 is trivial. On the other hand, the bound from Theorem 1.2 gives that any successful attack must satisfy $T \in \tilde{\Omega}(N^{1/2})$ which is strictly better than what the generic $\tilde{O}(ST^2/N)$ bound gives (it only gives $T \in \tilde{\Omega}(N^{15/32})$).

Technical Highlight. The main technical component in both of our bounds is a compression argument that uses a "too-good-to-be-true" attacker to non-trivially compress a uniformly random sequence of bits, thereby getting a contradiction. The setup is somewhat similar to the one of Akshima et al. [3] (although slightly more modular), but our compression argument deviates from theirs significantly. Their argument inherently relied on the fact that there are at most two blocks in the collision, therefore greatly simplifying the possible structures to consider. In contrast, we consider arbitrary length collisions, and thus we have to deal with all possible structures of collisions. Our proof identifies and analyzes a general structure for MD collisions and unveils a natural combinatorial problem that influences the resulting upper bound on the advantage of preprocessing adversaries. Specifically, it turns out that the "dominant extra" terms in both of our bounds $((\log^2 S)^{B-2}$ in the first bound and S^3 in the second) emerge due to the need to encode a *reverse path* in a general (fan-out 1, but possibly large fan-in) directed graph, where the graph is the one induced by the queries that the adversary makes to the random oracle. Any improvement on this encoding would immediately imply a better upper bound, a fact that we hope will lead to better bounds in the future.

1.2 Discussion

As mentioned, the MD paradigm underlies numerous hash function constructions that are central building blocks in many applications. There are several popular variants of the MD paradigm implemented in practice. In this work, we follow previous works and focus on the cleanest variant for concreteness. One prominent variant withstands length extension attacks by padding the input message with its length. (In fact, this is the version suggested by Merkle and Damgård.) We remark that our results directly apply to this padded variant. Specifically, the "STB" attack finds a collision with the same number of blocks, so it readily extends to this padded variant. Our bounds on the best possible attacks also extend to this setting since the argument did not use any specific property on the collision blocks. It is interesting to study other practically used variants and understand if similar results can be obtained. To this end, we hope that the techniques we develop in this work will be helpful.

From a theoretical perspective, no single function can be collision-resistant (in the plain model), as a non-uniform attacker can trivially hardwire a collision. This is why collision resistance is considered with respect to a family of hash functions indexed by a key called *salt*. The salt is chosen after the attacker is fixed (and so is the non-uniform advice about the family of functions). Still, in practice, a single hash function is typically defined by fixing an IV, making it insecure against non-uniform attackers. This contrasts with how we define the collision resistance game, where the IV is chosen randomly after the prepro-cessing phase. Thus, it may seem that the expensive preprocessing needed for attacks in our model does not represent real-life scenarios. However, often the hash function used in a particular application (relying on collision-resistance) is *salted* by prepending a random salt value to the input. One such well-known application is *password hashing* [29]. Such salting essentially corresponds to the random-IV setting considered here, and, therefore, the attack becomes relevant again.

The primary motivation for our work is to make progress towards the STB conjecture, which we view as a fundamental problem. To this end, we focused on asymptotic bounds as a function of S, T, and B. We hope that the concrete bounds could be improved in future works, affecting design choices of real-life hash functions.

Follow Up Work. A recent work of Akshima, Guo, and Liu [4] proved a new bound on the maximal possible advantage in finding B-block collisions. Their bound is overall incomparable to ours: it is better than our Theorem 1.2 but worse than Theorem 1.1. Also, Freitag et al. [17] studied related problems in the context of sponge hashing, an alternative to the Merkle-Damgård paradigm that underlies (for instance) the SHA-3 standard.

2 Our Techniques

In this section, we provide a high-level overview of our techniques. Both of our results follow a similar high-level rationale, and thus throughout this overview, we mainly focus on the techniques for proving the STB conjecture whenever $B \in O(1)$ (Theorem 1.1). Towards the end, we describe the additional ideas needed to obtain the result for $SB \ll T$ (Theorem 1.2).

Before explaining the ideas, let us describe the challenge more precisely. We are given a compressing function $h : [N] \times [M] \to [N]$, modeled as a random oracle, and we want to upper bound the probability of a non-uniform attacker in finding a collision in an MD_h instance with a random salt. We model non-uniform attackers by thinking of them as two-stage adversaries $\mathcal{A} = (\mathcal{A}_1, \mathcal{A}_2)$. The offline part $\mathcal{A}_1$ is unbounded in running time, and its only restriction is that it can output only S bits. This output is the non-uniform advice given to the online part $\mathcal{A}_2$ which is then allowed to make up to T queries after which it must output a B-block collision for MD_h and terminate. We assume unbounded running time for both parts $\mathcal{A}_1$ and $\mathcal{A}_2$ and only restrict the output-size for $\mathcal{A}_1$ and the number of queries for $\mathcal{A}_2$. We refer to such a two-stage adversary $(\mathcal{A}_1, \mathcal{A}_2)$ as a (S,T)-adversary. In the context of length-B collisions in MD_h, the game is as follows:

- $\mathcal{A}_1$ has unbounded access to h and it outputs $\sigma \in \{0,1\}^S$.
- $\mathcal{A}_2$ gets σ as input along with a random salt $a \in [N]$.
- $\mathcal{A}_2$ outputs α, α'.
- $\mathcal{A}$ wins if $\alpha \neq \alpha'$, α, α' consist of $\leqslant B$ blocks, and $\mathsf{MD}_h(a, \alpha) = \mathsf{MD}_h(a, \alpha')$.

There are essentially two main generic approaches known in the literature for proving bounds of this sort. The first is the so-called *pre-sampling* technique, originally due to Unruh [30], and the second is a compression argument. The first technique reduces the problem from considering general hash functions and adversaries $(\mathcal{A}_1, \mathcal{A}_2)$ as above to a simpler model (and associated attacker) called the *bit-fixing* model. The advantage of the latter model is that it is typically easier to analyze and results in clean proofs. The second technique is based on a simple information-theoretic idea that *random bits cannot be compressed.*[5] Thus, an attacker that succeeds in finding collisions is used to compress some random information that is used in the game, and thereby contradiction is reached. This technique, while being extremely influential in many fields and problems in computer science (e.g., "Algorithmic Lovász Local Lemma" [27], lower bounds on cryptographic constructions [13,18,20], analyzing hardness of problems in the non-uniform setting [10,15] and time-space tradeoffs for quantum algorithms [7]), often results in technical and complex proofs.

It would have been convenient if any non-trivial bound on our problem could be obtained using the bit-fixing technique. Unfortunately, Akshima et al. [3] observed that finding short collisions is relatively easy in the bit-fixing model. Hence, the only remaining potentially helpful technique is based on compression. Indeed, Akshima et al. [3], as their primary technical contribution, managed to carry out such an argument for the particular case of $B = 2$, and already then their proof is highly non-trivial and consists of a tedious case analysis. We distill some of the main ideas underlying their general framework approach[6] next—this will be useful for us, as well.

The Framework. We reduce the task of handling arbitrary (S,T)-adversaries to the problem of handling (S,T)-adversaries, where the preprocessing part $\mathcal{A}_1$ is degenerate and outputs a fixed string σ, independent of h. Specifically, we define a game, parameterized by $u \in \mathbb{N}_{>0}$, where $\mathcal{A}_2$ has an arbitrary size S string σ hard-coded, and its goal is to find a collision relative to a given salt. $\mathcal{A}_2$ wins the game if it succeeds in finding a collision when executed with *every one* of u uniformly random salts (there is no $\mathcal{A}_1$ in this game). The reduction shows that

---

[5] Specifically, it is impossible to save w bits of information about a random string, except with probability 2^{-w}.

[6] We note that [7] introduced an equivalent framework in independent work.

if $\mathcal{A}_2$ has advantage ϵ in the modified game, then the best advantage of an (S, T)-adversary in the original game is (roughly) $O(\epsilon^{1/u})$ for $u \approx S$. This reduction, formalized in Lemma 4.1, is adapted from Akshima et al. [3] and it uses the beautiful "constructive Chernoff bound" of Impagliazzo and Kabanets [22].[7]

The advantage of considering the new game is that there is no $\mathcal{A}_1$, so it is easier to handle. But, to obtain a meaningful result for the original (S, T) game, say an upper bound of ϵ, we need to prove a somewhat stronger upper bound for the new game, that is, roughly ϵ^u. This means, in other words, that we need to show how to compress about $\log(1/\epsilon)$ bits *per each one of the u salts*. (Actually, keep in mind that it suffices to achieve this on average!) For our target ϵ, we therefore have the following goal.

Main challenge: For every one of the u salts, we need to "save/compress" (on average) roughly the following number of bits:

$$\log\left(\min\left\{\frac{N}{uT(\log u)^{2(B-2)}B^2}, \frac{N}{T^2}\right\}\right).$$

By impossibility of non-trivial compression, this would imply that $\mathcal{A}_2$ must succeed with probability at most

$$\epsilon \leqslant O\left(\left(\frac{uT(\log u)^{2(B-2)}B^2}{N} + \frac{T^2}{N}\right)^u\right),$$

which would give our result when plugged into the framework.

The Compression Argument. The random string that we shall compress consists of the set of salts denoted U, as well as the function h. We give encoding and decoding algorithms that use $\mathcal{A}_2$ first to encode the pair (U, h) and then use the result to fully decode them whenever $\mathcal{A}_2$ wins the game. If $\mathcal{A}_2$ wins with good enough probability, the output of the encoding procedure will be non-trivially short with good probability, which is a contradiction.

Remark 1 Akshima et al. [3] used the same approach for $B = 2$, but their proof does not seem to scale for larger values of B. Specifically, their proof involves an exhaustive case analysis. It seems like a naive attempt to generalize their bound to larger values of B would proliferate the number of cases needed to be analyzed, making it unmanageable. One of our key conceptual insights is a structural characterization of collisions in MD_h that prevents this explosion in the number of cases needed to be handled. While our analysis applies to any B, the number of total cases we consider is roughly the same as Akshima et al.

A First Attempt and a Glimpse at the Challenge. Let us make a strong (and typically false) assumption: *the adversary $\mathcal{A}_2$ never repeats any query to h*

---

[7] The use of this reduction is the main (and perhaps only) point of similarity between our proof and [3]'s.

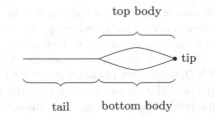

Fig. 1. A mouse structure. For ease of visual representation we do not draw the nodes and edges of the graph, instead represent it as a continuous structure.

across all the u runs.[8] Since we can assume (w.l.o.g) that if $\mathcal{A}_2$ outputs (α, α') when run on salt a, it has queried h at all values needed to compute $\mathsf{MD}_h(a, \alpha)$ and $\mathsf{MD}_h(a, \alpha')$, we are guaranteed that for each of the salts $u \in U$ there are at least two *distinct* queries which have the same answer, i.e., a collision. The indices of these queries reside in $[T]$ as this is the query complexity of $\mathcal{A}_2$ when executed on the particular salt a. Thus, we could avoid encoding the answer of the second query and instead encode these two indices in T and remove the answer of the second query from evaluations of h. This saves us $\log(N/T^2)$ bits for every salt, giving us even more savings than what we are aiming for. Such compression, in turn, would imply that the birthday attack is optimal, no matter what B is (which makes sense given our assumption but is clearly false for general attackers).

A naive way to get rid of the assumption (that queries never repeat across different u runs) would be to encode the index of the other query among all uT queries made (instead of T). But, this would eventually result in another multiplicative S term in our bound. Namely, we would only be able to save $\log(N/(ST^2))$ bits per salt which is too little for us (as it leads to a trivial upper bound). This motivates us to look more closely at how MD collisions are formed, what kind of queries could be involved, and how we could leverage the fact that collisions are short to get more efficient encoding.

The Mouse Structure and Query Types. We consider the graph implicitly formed through the queries made by $\mathcal{A}_2$ when running on salts $a_1, \ldots, a_u \in U$. The nodes of the graph are the possible salts and there is a directed edge from salt a to a' with label α if $h(a, \alpha) = a'$ and this query was made by $\mathcal{A}_2$.

Suppose that $\mathcal{A}_2$, when run on salt a_i, outputs (α, α'). Since $\mathcal{A}_2$ wins on every salt in U, its output on salt a_i, denoted α, α' must satisfy: (1) $\mathsf{MD}_h(a_i, \alpha) = \mathsf{MD}_h(a_i, \alpha')$, (2) $\alpha \neq \alpha'$, and (3) α, α' are at most B blocks long. Without loss of generality we can assume that the adversary $\mathcal{A}_2$ outputs a "minimal" collision, i.e., one that does not contain a prefix which is a collision by itself.

---

[8] While we can assume without loss of generality that $\mathcal{A}_2$ does not repeat queries within a single execution (since it is not memory-bounded), it is not very reasonable to assume that it will never repeat queries across different executions on different salts.

For instance, say the collision is $x_1, x_2, x_3, x_4, x_5, x_6$ and $y_1, y_2, y_3, y_4, y_5, y_6$ (wrt salt a) and it happens that x_1, x_2, x_3, x_4 and y_1, y_2, y_3, y_4 already collide (wrt same salt a), we can simply ignore x_5, x_6, y_5, y_6. Considering the *core* sub-graph of the query graph that is induced by queries made by $\mathcal{A}_2$ that are *required* to evaluate $\mathsf{MD}_h(a, \alpha)$ and $\mathsf{MD}_h(a, \alpha')$, we obtain a structure that we call a **mouse structure**. Important parts of the mouse structure are the tail, top and bottom body, and the tip, as depicted in Fig. 1. Our entire approach is based on studying these mouse structures to come up with encoding strategies.

Given the concept of a mouse structure and our discussion from above about the adversary, possibly repeating queries motivates us to classify each query into one of three types. The first is called NEW and refers to queries made for the first time. The rest of the queries are called *repeated*, and they are further classified into two types, depending on whether they previously appeared in some mouse structure or not. Specifically, a repeated query is called REPEATEDMOUSE if the same query was already made by $\mathcal{A}_2$ when executed on a previous salt, and otherwise, a repeated query is called REPEATEDNONMOUSE.

Intuitively, we want to save bits when the answer of a NEW query was the input salt of a repeated query. A REPEATEDMOUSE query facilitates such savings since we can encode the answer to the query by storing its index along with the index of the previous query and the corresponding index within the mouse structure—a total of $\approx \log(uTB)$ bits instead of $\log N$—which eventually turns into an STB/N term in the upper bound, as conjectured. The problem is with encoding REPEATEDNONMOUSE queries—there seems to be no trivial way to write the index of the previously-made query with less than $\log(uT^2)$ bits, which is too much (since it will eventually turn into a ST^2/N term in the upper bound).

Some "Easy" Mouse Structures. We observe that some cases of mouse structures readily give us a way to have efficient encoding and save sufficiently many bits. We offer three examples to convey intuition on how our analysis is done. Throughout, let us assume that every mouse structure contains at least one NEW query—otherwise, we will ignore this mouse structure altogether.[9]

As a first example, if two NEW queries form the tip of the mouse structure of salt a_j, we can simply encode the index of these queries within the queries made while handling this salt—this uses $2 \log T$ bits instead of $\log N$ bits which is sufficient. As another example, if a self-loop forms the body of the mouse structure and the self loop query is NEW or REPEATEDNONMOUSE, we can simply encode the index of the self loop query in the list of queries used to handle this salt and avoid encoding the answer of the query—this uses $\log(uT)$ bits instead of $\log N$ which is again sufficient. As the last example, suppose the answer to a NEW query is a salt that appeared in some earlier mouse structure. In this case, we can avoid encoding the answer of the NEW query and instead encode

---

[9] In the technical section, we refer to salts a_j in U that were not the input salt of a query when running $\mathcal{A}_2$ on a_i for $i < j$ as *fresh*. It follows that mouse structures for fresh salts will always have a NEW query. For salts that are not fresh, it is relatively straightforward to achieve some compression by avoiding storing these salts in the encoding of U. For now, the reader can imagine that all salts are fresh for simplicity.

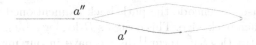

Fig. 2. An example of a "hard" mouse structure. The NEW queries are drawn in red, REPEATEDMOUSE queries are drawn in blue and the REPEATEDNONMOUSE queries are drawn in green. (Color figure online)

the index of the query and which of the salts in the previous mouse structures is the answer—this uses $\log(2uB)$ bits (because there are at most $2B$ salts in mouse structures and at most u mouse structures) instead of $\log N$ which is also sufficient.

Some "Hard" Mouse Structures. The aforementioned easy cases give rise to a relatively easy encoding that results in an optimal STB/N term. Next, we focus on the more complex cases, which cause our bound to have the extra $\approx B \cdot (\log S)^B$ factor.

Assume that there is a mouse structure where there are two salts a' and a'' such that a' is the input salt to a REPEATEDMOUSE query, a'' is the answer to a NEW query, and the path from a'' to a' in the mouse structure consists of only REPEATEDNONMOUSE queries (as shown in Fig. 2). By definition, the distance between a' and a'' is at most B.[10] Potential savings could be achieved by not encoding a'', the answer of the NEW query, as it can essentially be extracted from already-observed queries. We can easily encode the appropriate index of the query in the mouse structure and the salt a' using roughly $\log(uB)$ bits, but how can we encode the information about the path back from a' to a''?

The non-triviality is that for each node on this path, there might be many possible ways to reach it among all the different queries that have been already made, i.e., if each node on this path has fan-in m, namely an m-multi-collision, then the natural encoding of the path back would cost at most $\log(m^B)$ bits, specifying which back edge to take for every node. Here, m could be very large, e.g., as large as S or even larger, making the whole result meaningless for most reasonable parameters settings. (We also need to encode the length of the path, which would lead to the additional multiplicative B factor, but we ignore it in the discussion here.)

We get around this problem of m potentially being very large by observing that one of the following two cases holds:

- *Many small multi-collisions:* either the fan-in of every node along the path (i.e., the number of previously-made queries whose result is a node on this path) is smaller than $\log u$, or
- *One large multi-collision:* there is (at least one) node on the path where the fan-in is at least $\log u$.

---

[10] By being slightly more careful, we can show that the distance is $B-2$ but we ignore this fact for the overview.

In the earlier case, we encode the path back as mentioned above, where we write the index of each back edge. This costs us $B \cdot \log \log u$ bits, which eventually translates to an extra $(\log S)^B$ term,[11] as we have in our main theorem. The question is, what do we do when the second case occurs.

The idea is to leverage the fact that there is a large multi-collision and obtain our savings from a completely different place. Specifically, we remember the index of all the queries involved in the multi-collision and the common answer. A calculation reveals that if the collision consists of $\approx \log u$ edges, we can already save enough. One subtlety is that the same multi-collision might repeat throughout many different mouse structures, and we need to make sure not to double count the savings from a single multi-collision more than what we get. The reason why we do not double count is that a single large-enough (i.e., with $\log u$ edges) multi-collision saves us enough bits for about $\log u$ different structures, and at the same time, such a multi-collision can appear in at most $\log u$ mouse structures.[12]

Let us finally remark that while the above description conveys the main idea underlying our compression strategy, it is somewhat simplified and glossed over many technicalities and the complete specification of all possible cases that our full proof covers. We refer to Sect. 5 for full details.

Proving the STB Conjecture for $S \cdot B \ll T$. The proof of our second upper bound follows the same overall structure. The only difference is, naturally, in the way we encode reverse paths in mouse structures that have nodes corresponding to REPEATEDNONMOUSE queries between the output a'' of a NEW query and a node a' corresponding to a REPEATEDMOUSE query.

In the earlier proof, when we needed to locate the salt a'' from salt a', we encoded the number of edges in between and all the edges on the path. Here, we prove a purely graph-theoretic lemma saying that if for salt a' there are more than $\approx u^2$ salts a'' such that there are $d > 0$ edges on the shortest path back from a' to a'' in the query graph, then there must be $t \geqslant 1$ multi-collisions in the graph, such that the total number of edges involved in the t multi-collisions is at least $\approx u^2$. While the proof of this lemma is a simple inductive argument, it turns out to be extremely helpful for us. Specifically, if there are $t \geqslant 1$ different multi-collisions such that a total of at least $\approx u^2$ different queries are involved in the t multi-collisions, *we can save enough by only encoding these multi-collisions and nothing else*. To prove this fact, we consider the minimum savings we can get from encoding these t multi-collisions. We show using some elementary calculus that if there are $\approx u^2$ queries involved in t different multi-collisions, the minimum saving is more than the total amount of savings we need.

Equipped with this fact, we split our analysis into the two following scenarios.

---

[11] Remember that the actual term is $(\log S)^{B-2}$ and that is why the proof of Akshima et al. [3], in which it was assumed that $B = 2$, did not have an extra term that depends on S.

[12] We mention that multi-collisions in hash functions have been studied on their own right (e.g., [14,23]), but our context is totally different.

Game $\mathsf{G}_{N,M,B}^{\text{ai-cr}}(\mathcal{A} = (\mathcal{A}_1, \mathcal{A}_2))$	Subroutine $\mathsf{AI\text{-}CR}_{h,a}(\mathcal{A} = (\mathcal{A}_1, \mathcal{A}_2))$
1. $h \leftarrow_{\$} \mathsf{Fcs}([N] \times [M], [N])$	1. $\sigma \leftarrow_{\$} \mathcal{A}_1(h)$
2. $a \leftarrow_{\$} [N]$	2. $(\alpha, \alpha') \leftarrow_{\$} \mathcal{A}_2^h(\sigma, a)$
3. Return $\mathsf{AI\text{-}CR}_{h,a}(\mathcal{A})$	3. Return true if:
	(a) $\alpha \neq \alpha'$,
	(b) α, α' consist of $\leqslant B$ blocks from $[M]$,
	(c) $\mathsf{MD}_h(a, \alpha) = \mathsf{MD}_h(a, \alpha')$
	4. Else, return false

Fig. 3. The bounded-length collision resistance game of salted MD hash in the AI-ROM, denoted $\mathsf{G}_{N,M,B}^{\text{ai-cr}}$.

1. The first is where for each case where we need to encode the location of a'' from a' at a distance d, there are at most $\approx u^2$ salts – here we simply encode the index of the "right" a'' using $\approx \log u^2$ bits.
2. The other scenario is when for at least one case, there are more than $\approx u^2$ salts. Here we can save enough by encoding the t multi-collisions involving at least $\approx \log u^2$ that the graph-theoretic lemma guarantees us. We get enough savings by only encoding these t multi-collisions.

The u^2 term from the first scenario above turns into an additional factor of the form S^2 in the final bound. Due to additional technicalities that we glossed over during this overview, we suffer another multiplicative factor S in our bound, which amounts to having an S^4 term. Full details appear in Sect. 6.

3 Preliminaries

For a positive integer $N \in \mathbb{N}_{>0}$, let $[N] = \{1, 2, \ldots, N\}$ and for $k \in \mathbb{N}$ such that $k \leqslant N$, let $\binom{[N]}{k}$ denote the set of k-sized subsets of $[N]$. For a set X, let $|X|$ be its size and X^+ denote one or more elements of X. We denote $\mathsf{Fcs}(D, R)$ the set of all functions mapping elements in D to the elements of R. We let $x \leftarrow_{\$} \mathcal{D}$ denote sampling x according to the distribution $\mathcal{D}$. We let $*$ denote a wildcard element. For example $(*, z) \in L$ is true if there is an ordered pair in L where z is the second element (the type of the wildcard element shall be clear from the context). If D is a set, we overload notation and let $x \leftarrow_{\$} D$ denote uniformly sampling from the elements of D. For a bit-string s we use $|s|$ to denote the number of bits in s.

When referring to directed graphs in this paper, we mean directed multi-graphs, i.e., these directed graphs might have parallel edges. All logarithms in this paper are for base 2 unless otherwise stated.

Auxiliary-Input Random Oracle Model (AI-ROM). We use the Auxiliary-Input Random Oracle Model (AI-ROM) introduced by Unruh [30] to study non-uniform adversaries in the Random Oracle Model. This model is parameterized by two non-negative integers S and T and an adversary $\mathcal{A}$ is divided into two stages $(\mathcal{A}_1, \mathcal{A}_2)$. Adversary $\mathcal{A}_1$, referred to as the preprocessing phase of $\mathcal{A}$, has unbounded access to the random oracle h and outputs an S-bit auxiliary input σ. Adversary $\mathcal{A}_2$, referred to as the online phase, gets σ as input and can make T queries to h, attempting to accomplish some goal involving the function h. Formally, we say that $\mathcal{A} = (\mathcal{A}_1, \mathcal{A}_2)$ is an (S, T)-AI adversary if $\mathcal{A}_1$ outputs S bits and $\mathcal{A}_2$ issues T queries to its oracle. We next formalize the salted-collision resistance of MD hash functions in AI-ROM.

Salted Short Collision Resistance of MD in AI-ROM. We formalize the hardness of bounded-length collision resistance of salted MD hash functions in the AI-ROM. The game is parametrized by N, M, and B. The game first samples a function h uniformly at random from $\mathsf{Fcs}([N] \times [M], [N])$ and a salt a uniformly at random from $[N]$. Then, $\mathcal{A}_1$ is given unbounded access to h, and it outputs σ. At this time, $\mathcal{A}_2$ is given the auxiliary input σ, a salt a, as well as oracle access to h, and it needs to find $\alpha \neq \alpha'$ such that (1) $|\alpha|, |\alpha'| \leqslant B \cdot M$, and (2) $\mathsf{MD}_h(a, \alpha) = \mathsf{MD}_h(a, \alpha')$. This game, denoted $\mathsf{G}^{\mathsf{ai\text{-}cr}}_{N,M,B}$, is explicitly written in Fig. 3. In Fig. 3, we write the adversary's execution in its own subroutine only for syntactical purposes (as we shall use it later in our proof).

Definition 1 (AI-CR Advantage). *For parameters $N, M, B \in \mathbb{N}$, the advantage of an adversary $\mathcal{A}$ against the bounded-length collision resistance of salted MD in the AI-ROM is*

$$\mathsf{Adv}^{\mathsf{ai\text{-}cr}}_{\mathsf{MD},N,M,B}(\mathcal{A}) = \Pr\left[\mathsf{G}^{\mathsf{ai\text{-}cr}}_{N,M,B}(\mathcal{A}) = \mathsf{true}\right]$$

For parameters $S, T \in \mathbb{N}$, we overload notation and denote

$$\mathsf{Adv}^{\mathsf{ai\text{-}cr}}_{\mathsf{MD},N,M,B}(S,T) = \max_{\mathcal{A}}\left\{\mathsf{Adv}^{\mathsf{ai\text{-}cr}}_{\mathsf{MD},N,M,B}(\mathcal{A})\right\},$$

where the maximum is over all (S, T)-AI adversaries.

The Compression Lemma. Our proof uses the well-known technique of finding an "impossible compression". The main idea, formalized in the following proposition, is that it is impossible to compress a random element in set $\mathcal{X}$ to a string shorter than $\log |\mathcal{X}|$ bits long, even relative to a random string.

Proposition 1 (E.g., [13]). *Let Encode be a randomized map from $\mathcal{X}$ to $\mathcal{Y}$ and let Decode be a randomized map from $\mathcal{Y}$ to $\mathcal{X}$ such that*

$$\Pr_{x \overset{\$}{\leftarrow} \mathcal{X}}[\mathsf{Decode}(\mathsf{Encode}(x)) = x] \geqslant \epsilon.$$

Then, $\log |\mathcal{Y}| \geqslant \log |\mathcal{X}| - \log(1/\epsilon)$.

4 The Framework: Reducing the Problem to a Multi-instance Collision Finder

Our task here is to upper-bound the advantage of an adversary in finding a short collision in a salted MD, according to the game $\mathsf{G}^{\mathsf{ai\text{-}cr}}_{N,M,B}$ described in Fig. 3.

First, without loss of generality, in what follows, we assume that the adversary is deterministic. This follows since we can transform any probabilistic attacker into a deterministic one by hard-wiring the best randomness (see Adleman [2]).

We reduce the task of bounding the advantage of an attacker in finding a short collision in a salted MD, according to the game $\mathsf{G}^{\text{ai-cr}}_{N,M,B}$, to a "multi-instance" game where the adversary does not have a preprocessing phase but instead only has a non-uniform auxiliary input, chosen *before* the random oracle h. The latter game is easier to analyze. Although the statement and reduction below were implicit in the work of Akshima et al. [3], we make it formal and hopefully useful for future works.

We define the following "multi-instance" game $\mathsf{G}^{\text{mi-cr}}_{N,M,B,u}(\sigma, \mathcal{A}_2)$, where the preprocessing part of the adversary $\mathcal{A}_1$ is degenerate and outputs the fixed string σ. More precisely, the game has the following steps:

1. $h \leftarrow_\$ \mathsf{Fcs}([N] \times [M], [N])$
2. $U \leftarrow_\$ \binom{[N]}{u}$
3. Define $\mathcal{A}_1$ to be the algorithm that always outputs the string σ.
4. Return true if $\mathsf{AI\text{-}CR}_{h,a}(\mathcal{A} = (\mathcal{A}_1, \mathcal{A}_2)) = \mathsf{true}$ for every $a \in U$. Otherwise, return false.

For a string σ and an adversary $\mathcal{A}_2$, define

$$\mathsf{Adv}^{\text{mi-cr}}_{\mathsf{MD},N,M,B,u}(\sigma, \mathcal{A}_2) = \Pr\left[\mathsf{G}^{\text{mi-cr}}_{N,M,B,u}(\sigma, \mathcal{A}_2)\right].$$

Lemma 4.1. *Fix* $N, M, B, S, T, u \in \mathbb{N}_{>0}$. *Then,*

$$\mathsf{Adv}^{\text{ai-cr}}_{\mathsf{MD},N,M,B}(S,T) \leqslant 6 \cdot \left(\max_{\sigma, \mathcal{A}_2}\left\{\mathsf{Adv}^{\text{mi-cr}}_{\mathsf{MD},N,M,B,u}(\sigma, \mathcal{A}_2)\right\}\right)^{\frac{1}{u}} + 2^{S-u},$$

where the maximum is taken over all $\sigma \in \{0,1\}^S$ *and* T-*query algorithms* $\mathcal{A}_2$.

The proof of this lemma is similar to a proof that appears in [3]. For completeness, we provide the full details in the full version [19].

5   Proving the STB Conjecture for $B \in O(1)$

This section proves an upper bound on the advantage of any auxiliary-input adversary in the bounded-length collision resistance game of salted MD hash in the AI-ROM. The main theorem is stated next.

Theorem 5.1. *Let* $C = 2^{16} \cdot 6 \cdot e^2$. *For any* $N, M, B, S, T \in \mathbb{N}_{>0}$ *and fixing* $\hat{S} := S + \log N$, *it holds that*

$$\mathsf{Adv}^{\text{ai-cr}}_{\mathsf{MD},N,M,B}(S,T) \leqslant C \cdot \max\left\{\left(\frac{\hat{S}TB^2\left(\frac{3e\log\hat{S}}{\log\log\hat{S}}\right)^{2(B-2)}}{N}\right), \left(\frac{T^2}{N}\right)\right\} + \frac{1}{N} \cdot$$

Theorem 5.1 follows as a direct corollary of Lemma 4.1 together with the following lemma and setting $u = S + \log N$.

Lemma 5.1 (Hardness for a multi-instance collision finder). *Fix N, M, B, S, T, $u \in \mathbb{N}_{>0}$ and $\sigma \in \{0,1\}^S$. Then, for any $\mathcal{A}_2$ that makes at most T queries to its oracle, it holds that*

$$\mathsf{Adv}^{\mathsf{mi\text{-}cr}}_{\mathsf{MD},N,M,B,u}(\sigma, \mathcal{A}_2) \leqslant$$

$$\left(2^{16} e^2 \cdot \max\left\{ \left(\frac{uTB^2(3e \log u / \log \log u)^{2(B-2)}}{N} \right), \left(\frac{T^2}{N} \right) \right\} \right)^u.$$

The rest of this section is devoted to the proof of Lemma 5.1. Unlike the proof of Lemma 4.1, the proof of this lemma is novel and differs completely from that of Akshima et al. [3]. The key conceptual insight is a structural characterization of collisions in MD_h that prevents the explosion in the number of cases that [3] faced during the case analysis.

We are interested in bounding the advantage of the best strategy, i.e., a pair $(\sigma, \mathcal{A}_2)$ where $\sigma \in \{0,1\}^S$ is a fixed string and $\mathcal{A}_2$ is a T-query algorithm, of finding bounded-length collisions in a salted MD with respect to the game $\mathsf{G}^{\mathsf{mi\text{-}cr}}_{N,M,B,u}(\sigma, \mathcal{A}_2)$. Recall that in this game, $\mathcal{A}_2$ needs to find proper collisions for u randomly chosen salts, denoted U. The main idea in the proof is to use any such adversary $(\sigma, \mathcal{A}_2)$ to represent the function h *as well as* the set of random salts U with as few bits as possible. If the adversary is "too good to be true," we will get an impossible representation, contradicting Proposition 1.

Non-trivial Range. If either

$$\frac{T^2}{N} > 1 \quad \text{or} \quad \frac{uTB^2(3e \log u / \log \log u)^{2(B-2)}}{N} > 1,$$

then Lemma 5.1 is trivially true. Hence, from now on we assume that both of the above left hand side terms are upper bounded by 1.

Setup. Denote

$$\zeta^* := \left(2^{16} e^2 \cdot \max\left\{ \left(\frac{uTB^2(3e \log u / \log \log u)^{2(B-2)}}{N} \right), \left(\frac{T^2}{N} \right) \right\} \right)^u.$$

Assume the existence of an adversary $\mathcal{A} = (\sigma, \mathcal{A}_2)$, where $\sigma \in \{0,1\}^S$ is a string and $\mathcal{A}_2$ is a T-query adversary, that contradict the inequality stated in the lemma. That is, there is $\zeta > \zeta^*$ such that

$$\mathsf{Adv}^{\mathsf{mi\text{-}cr}}_{\mathsf{MD},N,M,B,u}(\mathcal{A}) := \zeta > \zeta^*. \tag{1}$$

Define $\mathcal{G}$ to be the set of functions-sets of salts pairs for which the attacker succeeds in winning the game for every salt in the set relative to the function, That is,

$$\mathcal{G} = \left\{ (U, h) \,\middle|\, \begin{array}{l} U \in \binom{[N]}{u}, \\ h \in \mathsf{Fcs}([N] \times [M], [N]), \end{array} \forall a \in U : \mathsf{AI\text{-}CR}_{h,a}(\mathcal{A}) = \mathsf{true} \right\}.$$

Recall that ζ is defined to be the advantage of $\mathcal{A}$ in the game $\mathsf{G}^{\mathsf{mi\text{-}cr}}_{N,M,B,u}(\mathcal{A})$ in which h and U are chosen uniformly, and then $\mathcal{A}$ needs to find a collision with respect to every one of the u salts in U. Therefore,

$$|\mathcal{G}| = \zeta \cdot \binom{N}{u} \cdot N^{MN}.$$

In what follows we define an encoding and a decoding procedure such that the encoding procedure gets as input U, h such that $U \in \binom{[N]}{u}$ and $h \in \mathsf{Fcs}([N] \times [M], [N])$, and it outputs an L bit string, where $L = \log\left(\zeta^* \cdot \binom{N}{u} \cdot N^{MN}\right)$. The decoding procedure takes as input the string L and outputs U^*, h^*. It will hold that $U^* = U$ and $h^* = h$ with probability ζ.[13] Using Proposition 1, this would give us that

$$\log \zeta \leqslant L - \log\left(\binom{N}{u} \cdot N^{MN}\right) \Longrightarrow \zeta \leqslant \zeta^*$$

which is a contradiction to the assumption (see (1)).

Notation and Definitions. Fix $(U, h) \in \mathcal{G}$. Let $U = \{a_1, \ldots, a_u\}$ where the a_i's are ordered lexicographically. Let $\mathsf{Qrs}(a) \in ([N] \times [M])^T$ be the list of queries that $\mathcal{A}_2$ makes to h when executed with input (σ, a). Namely, for $a \in [N]$,

$$\mathsf{Qrs}(a) = \{(a', \alpha') \in [N] \times [M] \mid \mathcal{A}_2(\sigma, a) \text{ queries } h \text{ on } (a', \alpha')\}.$$

Note that $\mathsf{Qrs}(a)$ is indeed a set as we can assume (without loss of generality) that $\mathcal{A}_2$ never repeats queries in a single execution (since $\mathcal{A}_2$ can just store all of its past queries).

We say that $a' \in \mathsf{Slts}(a)$ if there is some $\alpha' \in [M]$ such that (a', α') is an entry in $\mathsf{Qrs}(a)$. Namely, for $a, a' \in [N]$,

$$a' \in \mathsf{Slts}(a) \Longleftrightarrow \exists \alpha' \in [M] \text{ s.t. } (a', \alpha') \in \mathsf{Qrs}(a).$$

We define the set of *fresh* salts in U. A salt a_i for $i \in [u]$ is called fresh if it was never used as the salt in any query performed by $\mathcal{A}_2$ while being executed on salts a_j for $j \leqslant i-1$ which are fresh. The first salt a_1 is always fresh. A salt a_i for $i \geqslant 2$ is fresh if for any fresh a_j for $j \leqslant i-1$, $a_i \notin \mathsf{Slts}(a_j)$. Namely, denoting the set of fresh salts by U_{fresh}, we have the following inductive (on $i \in [u]$) definition:

$$a_i \in U_{\mathsf{fresh}} \Longleftrightarrow \forall j \leqslant i-1, a_j \in U_{\mathsf{fresh}}: a_i \notin \mathsf{Slts}(a_j).$$

Looking ahead, we define U_{fresh} like this because we run $\mathcal{A}_2$ on the salts in U_{fresh} in lexicographical order, and this definition ensures that each salt that $\mathcal{A}_2$ is executed on was not queried by it previously. Denote

$$F := |U_{\mathsf{fresh}}| \quad \text{and} \quad U_{\mathsf{fresh}} = \{a'_1, \ldots, a'_F\} \text{ (ordered lexicographically)}.$$

---

[13] Essentially, we will show that for all $(U, h) \in |\mathcal{G}|$, if the encoding procedure produces output L, then the decoding procedure on input L outputs U^*, h^* such that $U^* = U$ and $h^* = h$.

Denote

$$\forall i \in [F]: \mathsf{Q}_i := \mathsf{Qrs}(a_i') \quad \text{and} \quad \mathsf{Q}_{\mathsf{fresh}} := \mathsf{Q}_1 \,\|\, \dots \,\|\, \mathsf{Q}_F,$$

where $\|$ is the concatenation operator. Let $\mathsf{Q}_{\mathsf{fresh}}[r]$ be the rth query in the list $\mathsf{Q}_{\mathsf{fresh}}$. Note that $r \in [F \cdot T]$. For every $a \in U \setminus U_{\mathsf{fresh}}$, let t_a be the minimum value such that $\mathsf{Q}_{\mathsf{fresh}}[t_a]$ is a query with salt a. Define the set of *prediction* queries as

$$\mathsf{P} := \{t_a \mid a \in U \setminus U_{\mathsf{fresh}}\}.$$

The encoding algorithm will output $U_{\mathsf{fresh}}, \mathsf{P}$, which suffices to recover the set U by running $\mathcal{A}_2$.

We let $\tilde{h}$ be the list of $h(a, \alpha)$ values when executed on distinct queries in $\mathsf{Q}_{\mathsf{fresh}}$, in the same order as they appear in $\mathsf{Q}_{\mathsf{fresh}}$, followed by the evaluation of h on the following values in lexicographical order of the inputs.

$$\{(a, \alpha) : a \in [N], \alpha \in [M]\} \setminus \mathsf{Q}_{\mathsf{fresh}}.$$

Therefore, $\tilde{h}$ is initialized to contain the evaluation of h at all points in its domain. Looking ahead, in the encoding procedure, we will remove elements from $\tilde{h}$ as needed to compress h.

Function and Query Graphs. A notion that will be useful is that of a "function graph".

Definition 2 (Function graph). *For a function $h : [N] \times [M] \to [N]$, consider the following directed graph: it has N nodes labelled with elements of $[N]$ and each node has exactly M outgoing edges, each labelled with elements of $[M]$. There is an edge from node a_i to a_j labelled α if and only if $h(a_i, \alpha) = a_j$.*

We define the notion of query graph for an adversary as follows.

Definition 3 (Query graph). *Execution of an adversary $\mathcal{A}_2$ on salts $a_1', \dots, a_F'$ defines a query graph as follows. Initially the graph is empty. Whenever $\mathcal{A}_2$ queries (a, α) to h, we add a node with label a if not already present and add an edge $(a, h(a, \alpha))$ with label α if not already present.*

Fact 5.2. *The query graph is always a sub-graph of the function graph of h.*

Structure of Collisions: The Mouse Structure. Since adversary $\mathcal{A}_2$ succeeds on all of the salts in U, it holds that for every $j \in [F]$, the output of the adversary is (α_j, α_j') such that $\alpha_j \neq \alpha_j'$, $\mathsf{MD}_h(a_j, \alpha_j) = \mathsf{MD}_h(a_j, \alpha_j')$ and both α_j, α_j' are at most B blocks long. We can assume without loss of generality that the colliding messages α_j and α_j' are "minimal" (because otherwise, we can trim α_j, α_j' to obtain a shorter collision). The evaluations of h in order to compute $\mathsf{MD}_h(a_j', \alpha_j)$ and $\mathsf{MD}_h(a_j', \alpha_j')$ induce a structure that we call a *mouse structure* as shown in Fig. 4. More explicitly, suppose the output of the $\mathcal{A}_2$ is $(\alpha_j = (\alpha_{j,1}, \dots, \alpha_{j,B_1}), \alpha_j' = (\alpha_{j,1}', \dots, \alpha_{j,B_2}'))$ for $B_1, B_2 \leqslant B$ such that $\alpha_{j,i} = \alpha_{j,i}'$

for all $1 \leqslant i \leqslant k$ where $k \geqslant 0$. Define $(x_1, \ldots, x_k, y_1, \ldots, y_{k'}, z_1, \ldots, z_{k''})$ where $k' = B_1 - k, k'' = B_2 - k$ as follows.

$$x_1 = h(a_j', \alpha_{j,1}) \ , \ x_i = h(x_{i-1}, \alpha_{j,i}) \text{ for } 1 < i \leqslant k$$

$$y_1 = \begin{cases} h(a_j', \alpha_{j,1}) & \text{if } k = 0 \\ h(x_k, \alpha_{j,k+1}) & \text{otherwise} \end{cases} , \ y_i = h(y_{i-1}, \alpha_{j,i+k}) \text{ for } 1 < i \leqslant B_1 - k$$

$$z_1 = \begin{cases} h(a_j', \alpha_{j,1}') & \text{if } k = 0 \\ h(x_k, \alpha_{j,k+1}') & \text{otherwise} \end{cases} , \ z_i = h(z_{i-1}, \alpha_{j,i+k}') \text{ for } 1 < i \leqslant B_2 - k$$

Then $(x_1, \ldots, x_k, y_1, \ldots, y_{k'}, z_1, \ldots, z_{k''})$ form a mouse structure as specified in

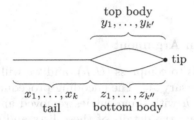

Fig. 4. A mouse structure. For ease of visual representation we do not draw the nodes and edges of the graph, instead represent it as a continuous structure.

Fig. 4. Without loss of generality, we can assume that the mouse structure is present in the query graph of $\mathcal{A}_2$ before it outputs the answer for salt a_j'. We refer to this structure as the mouse structure for salt a_j'.

We define $\mathsf{MouseQrs}_j$ to be the set of queries in the mouse structure. Similarly, we define $\mathsf{MouseSlts}_j$ as the set of salts that comprise the mouse structure. By definition, $1 \leqslant |\mathsf{MouseQrs}_j|, |\mathsf{MouseSlts}_j| \leqslant 2B$.

Classifying Queries. We classify every one of the queries in $\mathsf{Q}_{\mathsf{fresh}}$ into one of 3 types by scanning through them in order. Recall that $\mathsf{Q}_{\mathsf{fresh}}$ consists of F blocks, each consisting of T queries. Each block contains a mouse structure as in Fig. 4. The first type of query is called NEW. A NEW query did not appear in any previous block. Non-NEW queries are called *repeated* and they are classified further into one of 2 types: REPEATEDMOUSE, and REPEATEDNONMOUSE. A query (a, α) would be a REPEATEDMOUSE query if it was made as part of a mouse structure during some earlier salt in U_{fresh}. Lastly, a REPEATEDNONMOUSE query is one that was made before but is not part of any mouse structure. That is,

1. NEW: A query with index $r \in [F \cdot T]$ is NEW if there does not exist $r' < r$ such that $\mathsf{Q}_{\mathsf{fresh}}[r'] = \mathsf{Q}_{\mathsf{fresh}}[r]$.
2. A non-NEW queries is called *repeated*. We classify the latter into two subcategories:

(a) REPEATEDMOUSE: A query in Q_j with index $s \in [T]$ such that $h(Q_j[s]) = a$ is REPEATEDMOUSE if it is not NEW and $Q_j[s] \in \mathsf{MouseQrs}_i$ for some $i < j$.

(b) REPEATEDNONMOUSE: A query in Q_j with index $s \in [T]$ such that $h(Q_j[s]) = a$ is REPEATEDNONMOUSE if it is not NEW, $Q_j[s] \notin \mathsf{MouseQrs}_i$ for all $i < j$.

Note that this classification covers all queries made during execution. The following is a simple observation.

Claim 5.3. *Every mouse structure has at least one NEW query.*

Proof. For every $j \in [F]$, the queries in Q_j with salt a'_j are necessarily NEW because we defined U_{fresh} to contain a'_j's that were not queried earlier by $\mathcal{A}_2$ when run on a'_i for $i < j$, and also assumed that $\mathcal{A}_2$ does not repeat queries during a single execution. ∎

5.1 The Compression Argument

As mentioned, our goal is to compress (U, h), and we will achieve this by using our collision finding adversary $\mathcal{A}_2$. The encoding procedure shall output the set U_{fresh}, the set P, the list $\tilde{h}$ with some entries removed and additional lists and sets. We will be describing the details of these lists and sets below and which entries we remove from $\tilde{h}$. Our main goal is to show that we are compressing when we remove entries of $\tilde{h}$ and instead use additional lists and set. Our ways to compress will depend on the induced mouse structure in each Q_j for $j \in [F]$. To this end, we first classify the mouse structures into six broad cases. We classify the jth mouse structure for each $j \in [F]$ into the first of the following six cases it satisfies, e.g., if a mouse structure satisfies both cases 2 and 3, we categorize it into 2.

1. There is a NEW query (a, α) such that $h(a, \alpha) = a$.
2. There are two distinct NEW queries (a_1, α_1), (a_2, α_2) such that $h(a_1, \alpha_1) = h(a_2, \alpha_2)$.
3. There is a NEW query (a, α) such that $h(a, \alpha) = a'$ and $a' \in \mathsf{MouseSlts}_i$ for some $i < j$.
4. There is a REPEATEDNONMOUSE query (a, α) such that $h(a, \alpha) = a$.
5. There is at least one salt a such that $a \in \mathsf{MouseSlts}_i$ for some $i < j$ and there is a path of at most $B - 2$ edges in the mouse structure from a back to a' where a' is an answer to a NEW query.
6. There are no REPEATEDMOUSE queries in the mouse structure.

Note that these cases cover all mouse structures.

Claim 5.4. *Every mouse structure can be categorized into one of the cases 1 to 6.*

Proof. We will show that if a mouse structure does not satisfy case 6, it has to satisfy case 5, which suffices to prove our claim. Since the mouse structure is not in 6, it has a REPEATEDMOUSE query. Let the input salt of this query be a. Moreover, since the first query of the mouse structure has to be new, let the answer salt of this query be a'. Since the longest path in the mouse structure is of length B, it follows that there are at most $B-2$ edges in the mouse structure between a and a'. Hence, case 5 is satisfied. ∎

Compression Budget. Recall that we need to prove that the size of the output of the encoding procedure is

$$L = \log\left(\left(2^{16}e^2 \cdot \max\left\{\left(\frac{uTB^2m_0^{2(B-2)}}{N}\right), \left(\frac{T^2}{N}\right)\right\}\right)^u \cdot \binom{N}{u} \cdot N^{MN}\right)$$

bits, where $m_0 = 3e\log u / \log\log u$. In other words, we need to show that the encoding procedure saves at least

$$u \cdot \log\left(\min\left\{\frac{N}{4T^2}, \frac{N}{4uTB^2m_0^{2(B-2)}}\right\}\right) - 2u\log e - 14u \qquad (2)$$

bits overall.

Required Savings in $\tilde{h}$. As mentioned earlier, the output of the encoding algorithm will consist of $U_{\text{fresh}}, \mathsf{P}, \tilde{h}$, and some additional sets and lists. The lists U_{fresh} and P will suffice to recover the set U. The list $\tilde{h}$ and the additional sets and lists are used to recover h.

Denoting $|U_{\text{fresh}}| = F$ and $|U| = u$, we can describe P using $\binom{FT}{u-F}$ bits. Therefore, U, which is trivially described using $\log\binom{N}{u}$ bits, can be encoded using $\log\left(\binom{FT}{u-F}\binom{N}{F}\right)$ bits. Therefore, the saving in bits in the description of U is at least

$$\log\binom{N}{u} - \log\left(\binom{FT}{u-F}\binom{N}{F}\right) \geq \log\left(\frac{\left(\frac{N}{u}\right)^u}{\left(\frac{eFT}{u-F}\right)^{u-F}\left(\frac{eN}{F}\right)^F}\right)$$

$$= (u-F)\log\left(\frac{N}{FT}\right) - \log\left(e^u\left(\frac{u}{F}\right)^F\left(\frac{u}{u-F}\right)^{u-F}\right)$$

$$\geq (u-F)\log\left(\frac{N}{uT}\right) - u\log 4e. \qquad (3)$$

where the first inequality uses the basic bounds for binomial coefficients $(n/r)^r \leq \binom{n}{r} \leq (en/r)^r$, and the last inequality follows since $\forall x \geq 0 : x \leq 2^x$, and $u \geq F$.

By subtracting (3) (how much we save in U) from (2) (how much we need to save in total), it suffices to show that we save at least

$$u \cdot \log\left(\min\left\{\frac{N}{4T^2}, \frac{N}{4uTB^2 m_0^{2(B-2)}}\right\}\right) - 2u\log e$$
$$- 14u - (u-F)\log\left(\frac{N}{uT}\right) + u\log 4e$$

bits while encoding h. Since $\log(N/uT) \geqslant \log\left(\min\left\{N/4T^2, N/4uTB^2 m_0^{2(B-2)}\right\}\right)$, this is at most the following number of bits.

$$F \cdot \log\left(\min\left\{\frac{N}{4T^2}, \frac{N}{4uTB^2 m_0^{2(B-2)}}\right\}\right) - u\log e - 12u \qquad (4)$$

To show that the compression indeed achieves the savings from (4), we will show that for every salt in U_{fresh}, we can save at least the following number of bits, except for a few cases.

$$\log\left(\min\left\{N/4T^2, N/4uTB^2 m_0^{2(B-2)}\right\}\right) .$$

In the rare cases where we cannot save as much, we will incur a small penalty. We will show that the cumulative penalty we incur is at most $7u + u\log e$ bits. Additionally, we will label each of the salts in F with a few bits that describe its "type" (according to the cases described above – case 5 will have 3 subcategories, and case 6 will have 10 subcategories), and for this 5 bits will suffice. This will cost, in total, another $5u$ bits, and therefore the total size of the encoding will indeed be bounded by the term from (4).

We now describe the details of how we handle each case. Assuming that the mouse structure for salt a'_j satisfies a particular case, we describe the encoding procedure, calculate the amount of compression we get, and then explain how decoding would work. In Sect. 5.2 we handle Cases 1 to 4, in Sect. 5.3, we handle case 5, and lastly in the full version [19], we handle case 6. Here we describe the details such that they are locally verifiable. We do provide the full pseudocode of encoding and decoding in the full version [19].

5.2   Handling Cases 1 to 4

In each of the four cases below, we will be saving more bits than we need, i.e., more bits than $\log\left(\min\left\{N/4T^2, N/4uTB^2 m_0^{2(B-2)}\right\}\right)$.

Case 1. The jth mouse structure contains a NEW query (a, α) such that $h(a, \alpha) = a$, as depicted in Fig. 5a. The encoding procedure stores the index of the query (a, α) in Q_j in a list L_1 and removes the entry $h(a, \alpha)$ from $\tilde{h}$.

In decoding, if the current (jth) salt is categorized as case 1, then it removes the front index in the list L_1, and denote the index by i. It answers the ith h query, denoted (a, α), with a and sets $h(a, \alpha) = a$.

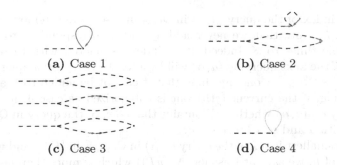

(a) Case 1   (b) Case 2

(c) Case 3   (d) Case 4

Fig. 5. Cases 1 to 4. The NEW queries are drawn in red, the REPEATEDMOUSE queries are drawn in blue, and the REPEATEDNONMOUSE queries are drawn in green. The black dashed lines indicate zero or more queries of any type. (Color figure online)

Since the index of the query (a, α) in Q_j is in $[T]$, and we remove one element of $\tilde{h}$, we save $\log(N/T)$ which is more than what we need to save.

Case 2. The jth mouse structure contains two distinct NEW queries (a_1, α_1), (a_2, α_2) such that $h(a_1, \alpha_1) = h(a_2, \alpha_2)$, and (a_1, α_1) is queried before (a_2, α_2). This is depicted in Fig. 5b. The encoding procedure stores the pair indices of the queries (a_1, α_1), (a_2, α_2) in Q_j in a list L_2 and removes the entry $h(a_2, \alpha_2)$ from $\tilde{h}$.

In decoding, if the current (jth) salt is categorized as case 2, then it removes the front element (i_1, i_2) in the list L_2. Suppose that the i_1th h query while running on salt a'_j is on (a_1, α_1). The decoding procedure gets the answer to this query from $\tilde{h}$. It answers the i_2th h query on (a_2, α_2) with $h(a_1, \alpha_1)$ and sets $h(a_2, \alpha_2) = h(a_1, \alpha_1)$.

Since the pair of indices of the queries $(a_1, \alpha_1), (a_2, \alpha_2)$ in Q_j are in $[T]$, and we remove one element of $\tilde{h}$, we save $\log(N/T^2)$ bits which is more than what we need to save.

Case 3. The jth mouse structure contains a NEW query (a, α) such that $h(a, \alpha) = a'$ and $a' \in \text{MouseSlts}_i$ for some $i < j$. This is depicted in Fig. 5c. The encoding procedure stores the tuple consisting of i, the index of the query (a, α) in Q_j, and the lexicographical order of a' in MouseSlts_i in a list L_3 and removes the entry $h(a, \alpha)$ from $\tilde{h}$.

In decoding, if the current (jth) salt is categorized as case 3, it removes the front element (i_1, i_2, i_3) in the list L_3. Suppose the i_2th h query while running on salt a'_j is on (a, α). It answers the query with a' such that a' is the salt in MouseSlts_{i_1} whose lexicographical order is i_3. It sets $h(a, \alpha) = a'$.

Since $i \in [F]$, $F \leqslant u$, the index of (a, α) in Q_j is in $[T]$, the lexicographical index of a' in MouseSlts_i is in $[2B]$, and we remove one element of $\tilde{h}$, we save $\log(N/(2uTB))$ bits which is more than what we need to save.

Case 4. The jth mouse structure contains a REPEATEDNONMOUSE query (a, α) such that $h(a, \alpha) = a$. This is depicted in Fig. 5d. The encoding procedure stores the smallest index of the query (a, α) in $\mathsf{Q_{fresh}}$ in a set S and removes the entry $h(a, \alpha)$ from $\tilde{h}$. Note that we never add an index corresponding to the same query multiple times to S. Indeed, if an index associated with (a, α) already appears in S, the next query on (a, α) will be a REPEATEDMOUSE query and not a REPEATEDNONMOUSE one, meaning that it cannot be added to S again.

In decoding, if the current (jth) salt is categorized as case 4, it checks for every h query on (a, α) whether S contains the index of the query in $\mathsf{Q_{fresh}}$. If so it answers with a and sets $h(a, \alpha) = a$.

Since the smallest index of the query (a, α) in $\mathsf{Q_{fresh}}$ is in $[FT]$, and we remove one element of $\tilde{h}$, we save at least $\log(N/(uT))$ which is more than necessary.

5.3   Handling Case 5

In this section, we describe our compression strategy in case the jth mouse structure for salt a'_j is categorized as case 5. That is, there is at least one salt d such that $d \in \mathsf{MouseSlts}_i$ for some $i < j$ and there are at most $B - 2$ edges in the mouse structure between d and s where s is an answer to a NEW query. If there are several possible candidate pairs, we choose one where the number of edges is the smallest between the source and the destination salt.

Intuition. We refer to the salt s in the answer to the NEW query as the *source* salt, and the salt that appears in some earlier mouse structure as the *destination*. We are guaranteed that the path in the mouse structure from the source salt to the destination salt consists of at most $B - 2$ edges that are REPEATED-NONMOUSE queries. (There is at least one intermediate edge between the source and the destination because otherwise, the answer of a new query will be the input of a REPEATEDMOUSE query, in which case this scenario would have been classified into case 3. Additionally, all the intermediate edges must be REPEATEDNONMOUSE since we consider the shortest possible path from such source to such destination.)

Let the NEW query, whose answer is s, be (a, α). Suppose the path from the s to the d in the mouse structure consists of REPEATEDNONMOUSE queries $(a_1, \alpha_1), \ldots, (a_p, \alpha_p)$ where $a_1 = s$, $p \leqslant B - 2$. The main idea is to avoid encoding $s = h(a, \alpha)$ and recover it by encoding the lexicographical order of d in $\mathsf{MouseSlts}_i$ and encoding the path required to backtrack from d to s in the query graph at the time (a, α) is queried, i.e., encoding which of the past queries were $(a_p, \alpha_p), \ldots, (a_1, \alpha_1)$ (in this order). The problem is that, in general, the path back from d to s might be too expensive to encode. This depends on the number of "other" edges incident on the nodes on the real path back from t to s. If all nodes on the path have very few edges incident on them, say less than m_0 of them, we encode each back edge using $\log m_0$ bits per node, which requires with at most $\log(B(m_0)^{B-2})$ bits for the whole path back (the term B comes from encoding the length of the path). But, if some node has many adjacent edges, namely a *multi-collision* with more than m_0 edges, we will need to take advantage of this fact to obtain our savings (and not encode the path back from d to s).

Definition 4 (Large multi-collision). *We say that queries $q_1, \cdots, q_m$ form an m-way multi-collision if all the q_i's are distinct and all the $h(q_i)$ are equal. We say that the multi-collision is* large *if $m \geqslant m_0$, where $m_0 := 3e \log u / \log \log u$.*

If any of the queries in $(a_p, \alpha_p), \ldots, (a_1, \alpha_1)$ are involved in a large multi-collision of REPEATEDNONMOUSE queries in the query graph so far, we say we have "encountered a large multi-collision". In what follows, we explain how to obtain the required compression if a large multi-collision was *not* encountered.

Encoding When No Large Multi-collision. Suppose that the NEW query whose answer is the source salt s is (a, α), the destination salt is d and $d \in$ MouseSlts$_i$ for some $i < j$. The path back from d to s contains only nodes that have at most m_0 adjacent edges in the corresponding query graph since we have not encountered a large multi-collision. The encoding procedures constructs a tuple consisting of the index i, the index of query (a, α) in Q_j, the lexicographical index of d in MouseSlts$_i$, and the path back from d to s in the query graph when (a, α) is queried. It stores the tuple in a list L_5. Finally, it removes the entry $h(a, \alpha)$ from $\tilde{h}$.

In decoding, if the current (jth) salt is categorized as case 5 *without a large multi-collision*, it detects the query (a, α) from its index in Q_j, then finds the salt d using the index i and the lexicographical order of d in MouseSlts$_i$, and finally finds s using the path back from d to s. It answers the query with s.

Since $i \in [F]$, the index of (a, α) in Q_j is in $[T]$, the lexicographical index of a' in MouseSlts$_i$ is in $[2B]$, the path back from d to s can be encoded in $\log(B(m_0)^{B-2})$ bits, and we remove one element of $\tilde{h}$, we save at least $\log(N/(2uTB^2(m_0)^{B-2}))$ bits which is more than necessary.

Encoding with Large Multi-collision. Suppose that the NEW query whose answer is the source salt s is (a, α), the destination salt is d and $d \in$ MouseSlts$_i$ for some $i < j$. Suppose further that the path back from d to s contains at least one node that has $m \geqslant m_0$ adjacent edges in the corresponding query graph (i.c., an m-multi-collision) such that these m edges are REPEATEDNONMOUSE queries when running $\mathcal{A}_2$ on a_j. First, observe that the multi-collision does not involve a self-loop. Indeed, if any node in the mouse structure has a REPEATEDNONMOUSE query whose answer is itself, the mouse structure would be classified into case 4, and therefore we will never reach this case.

At this point, we argue that we can record the multi-collision by encoding the indices of all queries associated with the multi-collision and the center, and remove their answers from $\tilde{h}$. To this end, we store $\log N + \log \binom{FT}{m}$ bits and remove $m \log N$ bits. We have that the saving is at least

$$m \log N - \log N - \log \binom{FT}{m} \geqslant \log \left(N^{m-1} \cdot \left(\frac{m}{eFT} \right)^m \right)$$
$$\geqslant \log \left(\left(\frac{N}{uT} \right)^{m-2} \cdot \frac{N}{T^2} \cdot \frac{m^m}{e^m u^2} \right) \geqslant \log \left(\left(\frac{N}{uT} \right)^{m-2} \cdot \frac{N}{T^2} \right) \quad (5)$$

bits, where the first inequality follows by using the binomial inequality $\binom{FT}{m} \leqslant (eFT/m)^m$, the second inequality follows since $F \leqslant u$, and the last inequality follows since for $m \geqslant m_0 = 3e \log u / \log \log u$ it holds that $m^m \geqslant e^m u^2$. Thus,

Claim 5.5. *The number of bits saved is at least*

$$(m-1) \cdot \log \left(\min \left\{ \frac{N}{T^2}, \frac{N}{uTB^2 m_0^{2(B-2)}} \right\} \right).$$

Proof. The claim follows since the minimum between the two terms is always upper bound by $N/(uT)$ and upper bounded by N/T^2.   ∎

Thus, every m-multi-collision we record allows us to save the number of bits corresponding to $m-1$ mouse structures. It is left to argue that we do not over-count, namely, that we do not count the removal of the same element from $\tilde{h}$ twice. Indeed, the same multi-collision may be encountered in several mouse structures. To this end, observe that if a salt in a mouse structure is the center of a large multi-collision which we had recorded earlier, we will be in one of the following two cases:

1. There is a query in this mouse structure whose answer is the center of the multi-collision, and this query was in an earlier mouse structure.
2. There is a query in this mouse structure whose answer is the center of the multi-collision, and this query was not in any earlier mouse structure. (Note that by the structure of collisions, i.e., a mouse structure, there could be either one such query or two.)

Case 1 need not be handled. The reason is that if the condition in it holds, then the multi-collision is, in fact, outside of the (shortest) path from the source to the destination. Therefore the scenario will either be classified as a mouse structure *without* a large multi-collision or a different large multi-collision will be encountered for this mouse structure.

In case 2, first note that when we encounter a multi-collision, we add the relevant queries to the multi-collision if they were not already recorded and only then remove the corresponding entry from $\tilde{h}$. Therefore, we never remove anything twice. The last point we need to argue is that the we get enough savings. Above we showed that we have sufficient saving for $m-1$ mouse structures. Recall that we defined that we encounter a large multi-collision if at least m_0 REPEATEDNONMOUSE queries are involved in a multi-collision on some path we care about. It follows from this that a multi-collision of size m will be relevant in at most $m - m_0$ mouse structures- beyond that, it will no longer be a multi-collision because there will be less than m_0 REPEATEDNONMOUSE queries among the queries of the multi-collision. Since $m_0 \geqslant 1$, savings for $m-1$ mouse structures is sufficient for us.

Overall, as claimed earlier, case 5 has 3 different further categorizations- no multi-collisions and the two cases for multi-collisions.

The general ideas required for handling case 6 are similar to what we have already presented, but there are some subtleties. See full details in the full version [19].

6 Proving the STB Conjecture for $SB \ll T$

This section proves another upper bound on the advantage of any auxiliary-input adversary in the bounded-length collision resistance game of salted MD hash in the AI-ROM. The main theorem is stated next.

Theorem 6.1. *Let* $C = 2^9 \cdot 6 \cdot e^4$. *For any* $N, M, B, S, T \in \mathbb{N}_{>0}$ *and fixing* $\hat{S} := S + \log N$, *it holds that*

$$\mathsf{Adv}^{\mathsf{ai\text{-}cr}}_{\mathsf{MD},N,M,B}(S,T) \leqslant C \cdot \max\left\{\left(\frac{T^2}{N}\right), \left(\frac{\hat{S}^4 T B^2}{N}\right)\right\} + \frac{1}{N}.$$

The proof of this theorem mostly mirrors that of Theorem 5.1, except in the way that few of the cases are handled in the compression argument. Technically, we derive the following Lemma 6.1 (an analogue of Lemma 5.1), and combine it with Lemma 4.1 to get the claimed bound in Theorem 6.1.

Lemma 6.1. *Fix* $N, M, B, S, T, u \in \mathbb{N}_{>0}$, $\sigma \in \{0,1\}^S$. *Then, for any* $\mathcal{A}_2$ *that makes at most* T *queries to its oracle, it holds that*

$$\mathsf{Adv}^{\mathsf{mi\text{-}cr}}_{\mathsf{MD},N,M,B,u}(\sigma, \mathcal{A}_2) \leqslant \left(2^9 e^4 \max\left\{\left(\frac{u^4 T B^2}{N}\right), \left(\frac{T^2}{N}\right)\right\}\right)^u.$$

The proof of this lemma is in the same spirit as the proof of Lemma 5.1 with several key differences. The main difference is how we encode the path back from a given destination node to the associated source node. In Sect. 5, we do this in a somewhat straightforward manner by encoding the length of the path and then the index of every edge to take, where the index might be large if there is a large multi-collision associated with that node. Large-enough multi-collisions were handled separately, so we had a bound $(m_0 \approx \log u / \log \log u)$ for the range of the index of each back-edge. In this section, we encode the source node by just writing its lexicographic index among all possible sources within a given distance in the query graph. Of course, there might be too many possible sources at a given distance, making it too expensive to encode. But, and this is our main technical observation in this section, if there are too many possible sources, then there must be many large multi-collision, and therefore we can save enough bits by taking advantage of it.

We proceed by setting up the graph-theoretic definitions and lemmas. In the lemma below, we show that if in the query graph there is a node v such that there are at least p nodes which have a shortest path of length d to the node v, then there must be at least $p - 1$ edges involved in a multi-collision in the induced sub-graph.

Definition 5 (d-neighborhood of a vertex). *Let* $G = (V, E)$ *be a directed graph. We say that a node* $v_1 \in V$ *is in the* d-*neighborhood of* $v_2 \in V$ *if the shortest directed path from* v_1 *to* v_2 *in* G *consists of (exactly)* d *edges.*

Definition 6 (multi-collision of edges in a graph). *For an edge $e = (a, b)$, we refer to b as the target of the edge. We say that edges $e_1, \cdots, e_m$ form a m-multi-collision if all of them share a common target. We refer to the common target as the center of the multi-collision. We refer to m as the size of the multi-collision.*

Lemma 6.2. *Let $G = (V, E)$ be a directed graph. Let $d \in \mathbb{N}_{>0}$ and $p \in \mathbb{N}_{>0}$ such that $p \geqslant 2$. Suppose that there is a node $v \in V$ such that there are p distinct nodes in its d-neighborhood. Then, there are $t \geqslant 1$ distinct nodes in G, such that each of them have in-degree $\beta_i \geqslant 2$ for $i = 1, \ldots, t$, and $\sum_{i=1}^{t}(\beta_i - 1) \geqslant p - 1$.*

The proof of this lemma is via an inductive argument and appears in the full version [19].

A direct corollary is that in the query graph, if for any salt s there are at least $p + 1$ salts in its d-neighborhood, then there must be p queries involved in multi-collisions on the paths from the nodes in its d-neighborhood to s. We obtain non-trivial compression for large enough p by encoding those multi-collisions.

Non-trivial Encoding for Multiple Multi-collisions. We consider t multi-collisions of sizes $\beta_1, \ldots, \beta_t$. We encode these t multi-collisions by encoding the t centers of the multi-collision, and for each center, we encode the index of the queries in Q_{fresh} that form the multi-collision in a set. Recall that the indices of the queries in Q_{fresh} are in $[FT]$. The total number bits we need to encode is

$$\log\left(\binom{N}{t}\binom{FT}{\beta_1}\cdots\binom{FT - \sum_{i=1}^{t-1}\beta_i}{\beta_t}\right) \leqslant \log\left(\frac{N^t(uT)^{\sum_{i=1}^{t}\beta_i}}{t!\beta_1!\beta_2!\cdots\beta_t!}\right)$$

$$= \log\left(\frac{N^t(u^4T)^{\beta-2t}T^{2t}u^{8t-3\beta}}{t!\beta_1!\beta_2!\cdots\beta_t!}\right), \quad (6)$$

where the inequality follows by using $\binom{n}{r} \leqslant \frac{n^r}{r!}$ and $F \leqslant u$, and the equality follows by letting $\beta = \sum_{i=1}^{t}\beta_i$ and rearranging.

Claim 6.2. *If $\beta \geqslant e^3u^2/2$, then Eq. (6) $\leqslant \log\left(N^t(u^4T)^{\beta-2t}T^{2t}\right)$.*

We defer the proof of this claim to the full version [19]. From this claim it follows that when $\beta \geqslant e^3u^2/2$, by storing the multi-collisions as above, the amount of bits saved is at least

$$\log N^\beta - \log\left(N^t(u^4T)^{\beta-2t}T^{2t}\right) = t\log\left(\frac{N}{T^2}\right) + (\beta - 2t)\log\left(\frac{N}{u^4T}\right)$$

$$\geqslant (\beta - t)\log\left(\min\left\{\frac{N}{T^2}, \frac{N}{u^4T}\right\}\right) \geqslant u\log\left(\min\left\{\frac{N}{T^2}, \frac{N}{u^4T}\right\}\right),$$

where the second inequality follows since $t \leqslant \beta/2$, and $\beta/2 \geqslant e^3u^2/4 \geqslant u^2 \geqslant u$.

For the bound that we want to get in this section, the amount of bits we need to save *per mouse structure* is $\log\left(\min\left\{\frac{N}{T^2}, \frac{N}{u^4TB^2}\right\}\right)$ (see explanation below), and so *we indeed save enough from encoding one such set of multi-collisions.*

The Compression Argument. We encode a source node from a destination node by encoding the distance and which of the nodes at the given distance from the destination node is the source node. If the number of candidate nodes at the specified distance is larger than $e^3 u^2/2$, by Lemma 6.2, we are guaranteed that there exist t multi-collisions of size $\beta_1, \beta_2, \ldots, \beta_t$ such that $\beta \geqslant \sum_{i=1}^{t}(\beta_i - 1) \geqslant e^3 u^2/2$. This implies, by Claim 6.2, that we can already save enough by only encoding this set of multi-collisions. Using this argument we prove Lemma 6.1 which in turn implies Theorem 6.1, as explained above. We defer the proof of Lemma 6.1 to the full version [19].

Acknowledgments. Ilan Komargodski is supported in part by an Alon Young Faculty Fellowship, by a JPM Faculty Research Award, by a grant from the Israel Science Foundation (ISF Grant No. 1774/20), and by a grant from the US-Israel Binational Science Foundation and the US National Science Foundation (BSF-NSF Grant No. 2020643). Part of Ashrujit Ghoshal's work was done during an internship at NTT Research.

References

1. Abusalah, H., Alwen, J., Cohen, B., Khilko, D., Pietrzak, K., Reyzin, L.: Beyond Hellman's time-memory trade-offs with applications to proofs of space. In: Takagi, T., Peyrin, T. (eds.) ASIACRYPT 2017. LNCS, vol. 10625, pp. 357–379. Springer, Cham (2017). https://doi.org/10.1007/978-3-319-70697-9_13
2. Adleman, L.: Two theorems on random polynomial time. In: Symposium on Foundations of Computer Science, SFCS, pp. 75–83 (1978)
3. Akshima, Cash, D., Drucker, A., Wee, H.: Time-space tradeoffs and short collisions in Merkle-Damgård hash functions. In: Micciancio, D., Ristenpart, T. (eds.) CRYPTO 2020. LNCS, vol. 12170, pp. 157–186. Springer, Cham (2020). https://doi.org/10.1007/978-3-030-56784-2_6
4. Akshima, Guo, S., Liu, Q.: Time-space lower bounds for finding collisions in Merkle-Damgård hash functions. In: Dodis, Y., Shrimpton, T. (eds.) CRYPTO 2022. LNCS, vol. 13509, pp. 192–221. Springer, Cham (2022)
5. Barkan, E., Biham, E., Shamir, A.: Rigorous bounds on cryptanalytic time/memory tradeoffs. In: Dwork, C. (ed.) CRYPTO 2006. LNCS, vol. 4117, pp. 1–21. Springer, Heidelberg (2006). https://doi.org/10.1007/11818175_1
6. Chawin, D., Haitner, I., Mazor, N.: Lower bounds on the time/memory tradeoff of function inversion. In: Pass, R., Pietrzak, K. (eds.) TCC 2020. LNCS, vol. 12552, pp. 305–334. Springer, Cham (2020). https://doi.org/10.1007/978-3-030-64381-2_11
7. Chung, K., Guo, S., Liu, Q., Qian, L.: Tight quantum time-space tradeoffs for function inversion. In: FOCS, pp. 673–684 (2020)
8. Coretti, S., Dodis, Y., Guo, S.: Non-uniform bounds in the random-permutation, ideal-cipher, and generic-group models. In: Shacham, H., Boldyreva, A. (eds.) CRYPTO 2018. LNCS, vol. 10991, pp. 693–721. Springer, Cham (2018). https://doi.org/10.1007/978-3-319-96884-1_23

9. Coretti, S., Dodis, Y., Guo, S., Steinberger, J.P.: Random oracles and non-uniformity. In: Nielsen, J.B., Rijmen, V. (eds.) EUROCRYPT 2018. LNCS, vol. 10820, pp. 227–258. Springer, Cham (2018). https://doi.org/10.1007/978-3-319-78381-9_9

10. Corrigan-Gibbs, H., Kogan, D.: The discrete-logarithm problem with preprocessing. In: Nielsen, J.B., Rijmen, V. (eds.) EUROCRYPT 2018. LNCS, vol. 10821, pp. 415–447. Springer, Cham (2018). https://doi.org/10.1007/978-3-319-78375-8_14

11. Corrigan-Gibbs, H., Kogan, D.: The function-inversion problem: barriers and opportunities. In: Hofheinz, D., Rosen, A. (eds.) TCC 2019. LNCS, vol. 11891, pp. 393–421. Springer, Cham (2019). https://doi.org/10.1007/978-3-030-36030-6_16

12. Damgård, I.: Collision free hash functions and public key signature schemes. In: Chaum, D., Price, W.L. (eds.) EUROCRYPT 1987. LNCS, vol. 304, pp. 203–216. Springer, Heidelberg (1988). https://doi.org/10.1007/3-540-39118-5_19

13. De, A., Trevisan, L., Tulsiani, M.: Time space tradeoffs for attacks against one-way functions and PRGs. In: Rabin, T. (ed.) CRYPTO 2010. LNCS, vol. 6223, pp. 649–665. Springer, Heidelberg (2010). https://doi.org/10.1007/978-3-642-14623-7_35

14. Dinur, I.: Tight time-space lower bounds for finding multiple collision pairs and their applications. In: Canteaut, A., Ishai, Y. (eds.) EUROCRYPT 2020. LNCS, vol. 12105, pp. 405–434. Springer, Cham (2020). https://doi.org/10.1007/978-3-030-45721-1_15

15. Dodis, Y., Guo, S., Katz, J.: Fixing cracks in the concrete: random oracles with auxiliary input, revisited. In: Coron, J.-S., Nielsen, J.B. (eds.) EUROCRYPT 2017. LNCS, vol. 10211, pp. 473–495. Springer, Cham (2017). https://doi.org/10.1007/978-3-319-56614-6_16

16. Fiat, A., Naor, M.: Rigorous time/space trade-offs for inverting functions. SIAM J. Comput. **29**(3), 790–803 (1999)

17. Freitag, C., Ghoshal, A., Komargodski, I.: Time-space tradeoffs for sponge hashing: attacks and limitations for short collisions. In: Dodis, Y., Shrimpton, T. (eds.) CRYPTO 2022. LNCS, vol. 13509, pp. 131–160. Springer, Cham (2022)

18. Gennaro, R., Trevisan, L.: Lower bounds on the efficiency of generic cryptographic constructions. In: FOCS, pp. 305–313 (2000)

19. Ghoshal, A., Komargodski, I.: On time-space tradeoffs for bounded-length collisions in Merkle-Damgård hashing. Cryptology ePrint Archive, Paper 2022/309 (2022)

20. Ghoshal, A., Tessaro, S.: On the memory-tightness of hashed ElGamal. In: Canteaut, A., Ishai, Y. (eds.) EUROCRYPT 2020. LNCS, vol. 12106, pp. 33–62. Springer, Cham (2020). https://doi.org/10.1007/978-3-030-45724-2_2

21. Hellman, M.E.: A cryptanalytic time-memory trade-off. IEEE Trans. Inf. Theory **26**(4), 401–406 (1980)

22. Impagliazzo, R., Kabanets, V.: Constructive proofs of concentration bounds. In: Serna, M., Shaltiel, R., Jansen, K., Rolim, J. (eds.) APPROX/RANDOM -2010. LNCS, vol. 6302, pp. 617–631. Springer, Heidelberg (2010). https://doi.org/10.1007/978-3-642-15369-3_46

23. Joux, A.: Multicollisions in iterated hash functions. Application to cascaded constructions. In: Franklin, M. (ed.) CRYPTO 2004. LNCS, vol. 3152, pp. 306–316. Springer, Heidelberg (2004). https://doi.org/10.1007/978-3-540-28628-8_19

24. Merkle, R.C.: Secrecy, authentication and public key systems. Ph.D. thesis, UMI Research Press, Ann Arbor, Michigan (1982)

25. Merkle, R.C.: A digital signature based on a conventional encryption function. In: Pomerance, C. (ed.) CRYPTO 1987. LNCS, vol. 293, pp. 369–378. Springer, Heidelberg (1988). https://doi.org/10.1007/3-540-48184-2_32
26. Merkle, R.C.: A certified digital signature. In: Brassard, G. (ed.) CRYPTO 1989. LNCS, vol. 435, pp. 218–238. Springer, New York (1990). https://doi.org/10.1007/0-387-34805-0_21
27. Moser, R.A., Tardos, G.: A constructive proof of the general lovász local lemma. J. ACM **57**(2), 11:1–11:15 (2010)
28. Oechslin, P.: Making a faster cryptanalytic time-memory trade-off. In: Boneh, D. (ed.) CRYPTO 2003. LNCS, vol. 2729, pp. 617–630. Springer, Heidelberg (2003). https://doi.org/10.1007/978-3-540-45146-4_36
29. Sr, R.H.M., Thompson, K.: Password security - a case history. Commun. ACM **22**(11), 594–597 (1979)
30. Unruh, D.: Random oracles and auxiliary input. In: Menezes, A. (ed.) CRYPTO 2007. LNCS, vol. 4622, pp. 205–223. Springer, Heidelberg (2007). https://doi.org/10.1007/978-3-540-74143-5_12
31. Yao, A.C.: Coherent functions and program checkers (extended abstract). In: STOC, pp. 84–94 (1990)

Time-Space Lower Bounds for Finding Collisions in Merkle-Damgård Hash Functions

Akshima[1(✉)], Siyao Guo[2], and Qipeng Liu[3]

[1] University of Chicago, Chicago, USA
akshima@uchicago.edu
[2] NYU Shanghai, Shanghai, China
[3] Simons Institute for the Theory of Computing, Berkeley, USA

Abstract. We revisit the problem of finding B-block-long collisions in Merkle-Damgård Hash Functions in the auxiliary-input random oracle model, in which an attacker gets a piece of S-bit advice about the random oracle and makes T oracle queries.

Akshima, Cash, Drucker and Wee (CRYPTO 2020), based on the work of Coretti, Dodis, Guo and Steinberger (EUROCRYPT 2018), showed a simple attack for $2 \leq B \leq T$ (with respect to a random salt). The attack achieves advantage $\widetilde{\Omega}(STB/2^n + T^2/2^n)$ where n is the output length of the random oracle. They conjectured that this attack is optimal. However, this so-called STB conjecture was only proved for $B \approx T$ and $B = 2$. Very recently, Ghoshal and Komargodski (CRYPTO 22) confirmed STB conjecture for all constant values of B, and provided an $\widetilde{O}(S^4TB^2/2^n + T^2/2^n)$ bound for all choices of B.

In this work, we prove an $\widetilde{O}((STB/2^n) \cdot \max\{1, ST^2/2^n\} + T^2/2^n)$ bound for every $2 < B < T$. Our bound confirms the STB conjecture for $ST^2 \leq 2^n$, and is optimal up to a factor of S for $ST^2 > 2^n$ (note as T^2 is always at most 2^n, otherwise finding a collision is trivial by the birthday attack). Our result subsumes all previous upper bounds for all ranges of parameters except for $B = \widetilde{O}(1)$ and $ST^2 > 2^n$.

We obtain our results by adopting and refining the technique of Chung, Guo, Liu, and Qian (FOCS 2020). Our approach yields more modular proofs and sheds light on how to bypass the limitations of prior techniques. Along the way, we obtain a considerably simpler and illuminating proof for $B = 2$, recovering the main result of Akshima, Cash, Drucker and Wee.

1 Introduction

Merkle-Damgård paradigm [Mer89, Dam89] is a domain extension technique for extending a compression function $H : [N] \times [M] \to [N]$ (where $N := 2^n$ and $M > N$) with fixed input length into a full-fledged hash function to handle arbitrary long inputs. Specifically, a B-block message $\mathbf{m} = (m_1, \cdots, m_B)$ with

© International Association for Cryptologic Research 2022
Y. Dodis and T. Shrimpton (Eds.): CRYPTO 2022, LNCS 13509, pp. 192–221, 2022.
https://doi.org/10.1007/978-3-031-15982-4_7

$m_i \in [M]$ is hashed into $\mathsf{MD}_H(a, \mathbf{m})$ as follows: $\mathsf{MD}_H^1(a, m_1) = H(a, m_1)$ and

$$\mathsf{MD}_H^\ell(a, (m_1, \cdots, m_\ell)) = H(\mathsf{MD}_H^{\ell-1}(a, (m_1, \cdots, m_{\ell-1})), m_\ell), \text{ for } \ell > 1,$$

where $a \in [N]$ is some random given salt. We say $\mathbf{m} \neq \mathbf{m}'$ is a pair of B-block collision with respect to a salt a if they both have at most B blocks and $\mathsf{MD}_H(a, \mathbf{m}) = \mathsf{MD}_H(a, \mathbf{m}')$.

Merkle-Damgård paradigm is widely used in practice for hash functions, including MD5 and SHA family. The primary requirement of a hash function is collision resistance. In this work, we are interested in the collision resistance property of Merkle-Damgård hash functions against preprocessing attackers, which can have an arbitrary (but bounded) precomputed advice about H to help. The power of preprocessing attacks was first demonstrated by Hellman [Hel80] for inverting functions. Recently, several works [DGK17, CDG18, ACDW20, GK22] set out to understand the power of such attacks for finding collisions. All of them studied this question in the auxiliary-input random oracle model (AI-ROM) proposed by Unruh [Unr07], for dealing with non-uniform and preprocessing attackers. In this ideal model, H is treated as a random function, and an adversary $\mathcal{A}$ consists of a pair of algorithms $(\mathcal{A}_1, \mathcal{A}_2)$. (Computationally unbounded) $\mathcal{A}_1$ precomputes S bits of advice about H in an offline stage, then $\mathcal{A}_2$ takes this advice and makes T oracle queries to H during the attack.

Dodis, Guo, and Katz [DGK17] studied the collision resistance of a salted random function (which also corresponds to the $B = 1$ case for Merkle-Damgård). They proved an $\widetilde{O}(S/N + T^2/N)$ security upper bound (with respect to a random salt) where the notation $\widetilde{O}(\cdot)$ hides lower-order factors that are polynomial in $\log N$. This bound shows the optimality of the naive attack, which precomputes collisions for S distinct salts as the advice (the T^2/N term is tight due to the birthday attack).

Since most practical hash functions are based on the Merkle-Damgård paradigm, Coretti, Dodis, Guo and Steinberger [CDGS18] studied finding collisions for salted Merkle-Damgård hash functions (corresponds to the unbounded B case). Interestingly, unlike the $B = 1$ case, they showed an attack achieving advantage $\widetilde{\Omega}(ST^2/N)$, improving the birthday attack by a factor of S. They also proved that this attack is optimal.

Akshima, Cash, Drucker and Wee [ACDW20] observed that the collision produced by the attack of [CDGS18] is very long, which is not appealing for practical relevance. They, therefore, studied the question of finding short collisions, and put forth the following intriguing conjecture.

STB conjecture [ACDW20]: The best attack with time T and space S for finding collisions of length B in salted MD hash functions built from hash functions with n-bit outputs achieves success probability $\Theta((STB + T^2)/2^n)$.

[ACDW20] showed that, a straightforward modification of the attack of [CDGS18] finds B-block collisions with advantage $\Omega((STB + T^2)/N)$. Unfortunately, they also showed that the lower bound techniques of [CDGS18] can not rule out attacks with success probability $\Omega(ST^2/N)$, even for $B = 2$. They presented new approaches to prove the STB conjecture for $B = 2$ in AI-ROM. Combining with known results for $B = 1$ and $B = T$, this demonstrates qualitative jumps in the optimal attacks for finding length 1, length 2, and unbounded-length collisions. Very recently, Ghoshal and Komargodski [GK22] confirmed STB conjecture for all constant B. However, for other choices of B, there is still a significant gap between the best-known attack [ACDW20] and known security upper bound $\widetilde{O}(S^4TB^2/N + T^2/N)$ by [GK22] or $\widetilde{O}(ST^2/N)$ by [CDGS18]. That motivates us to study the following question in this paper:

Can we further bridge the gap between the security upper and lower bounds, and prove STB conjecture for more choices of parameters?

Since prior techniques are limited or laborious even for $B = 2$, we start by asking:

Can we prove STB conjecture for $B = 2$ in a simpler way?

Looking ahead, we answer both questions affirmatively.

1.1 Our Results

Our main contribution is the following theorem.

Theorem 1 (Informal). *For any $2 < B < T$, the advantage of the best adversary with S-bit advice and T queries for finding B-block collisions in Merkle-Damgård hash functions in the auxiliary-input random oracle model, is*

$$\widetilde{O}\left((STB/N) \cdot \max\{1, ST^2/N\} + T^2/N\right).$$

Our bound confirms the STB conjecture for any $2 < B < T$ for the range of S, T such that $ST^2 \leq N$. For the other range of S, T, as $T^2 \leq N$ (otherwise, finding a collision is trivial by the birthday attack), Our bound is at most $\widetilde{O}(S^2TB/N + T^2/N)$, which is optimal up to a factor of S.

Comparing to the $\widetilde{O}(STB^2(\log^2 S)^{B-2}/N + T^2/N)$ bound by [GK22], our bound works for any $2 < B < T$, while their bound becomes vacuous when $B > \log N$. However, for $B \leq \log N$, unlike our bound, their bound could be tight even when $ST^2 > N$. In particular, their bound confirms STB conjecture for $B = O(1)$.

Our bound strictly improves the $\widetilde{O}(S^4TB^2/N + T^2/N)$ bound by [GK22], and the $\widetilde{O}(S^2T/N)$ bound by [CDGS18] for any $2 < B < T$ and non-trivial choices of S, T (specifically, when STB attack succeeds with at most a constant probability, i.e., $STB = O(N)$). The two bounds by [GK22] only beat [CDGS18] for $B \ll \sqrt{T}$.

As an additional contribution, we give a considerably simpler proof for proving the tight bound for $B = 2$, recovering the main result of [ACDW20].

Theorem 2 (Informal). *The advantage of the best adversary with S-bit advice and T queries for finding 2-block collisions in Merkle-Damgård hash functions in the auxiliary-input random oracle model, is* $\widetilde{O}\left(ST/N + T^2/N\right)$.

A comparison of our results with the prior works is summarized in Table 1. Overall, our results subsume all previous upper bounds except for the range of S, T, B such that $B \leq \log N$ and $ST^2 > N$.

Table 1. Asymptotic security bounds on the security of finding B-block-long collisions in Merkle-Damgård Hash Functions constructed from a random function $H : [N] \times [M] \mapsto [N]$ against (S, T)-algorithms. For simplicity, logarithmic terms and constant factors are omitted.

	Best attacks	Security bounds	Ref.	Proof techniques
$B = 1$	$\frac{S}{N}+\frac{T^2}{N}$	$\frac{S}{N}+\frac{T^2}{N}$	[DGK17]	Compression
$B = 2$	$\frac{ST}{N}+\frac{T^2}{N}$	$\frac{ST}{N}+\frac{T^2}{N}$	[ACDW20]	Multi-instance problems
$B = 2$	$\frac{ST}{N}+\frac{T^2}{N}$	$\frac{ST}{N}+\frac{T^2}{N}$	Theorem 2	Multi-instance games
$2 < B < T$	$\frac{STB}{N}+\frac{T^2}{N}$	$\frac{STB^2(\log^2 S)^{B-2}}{N}+\frac{T^2}{N}$	[GK22]	Multi-instance problems
$2 < B < T$	$\frac{STB}{N}+\frac{T^2}{N}$	$\frac{S^4TB^2}{N}+\frac{T^2}{N}$	[GK22]	Multi-instance problems
$2 < B < T$	$\frac{STB}{N}+\frac{T^2}{N}$	$\frac{STB}{N}\cdot\max\{1,\frac{ST^2}{N}\}+\frac{T^2}{N}$	Theorem 1	Multi-instance games
Unbounded	$\frac{ST^2}{N}$	$\frac{ST^2}{N}$	[CDGS18]	Presampling

1.2 Our Techniques

In this section, we describe our techniques, how to use them to prove our main results, and what makes our techniques different from prior approaches used in [CDGS18, ACDW20, GK22].

Existing Reduction to Sequential Multi-instance Games. Our initial inspiration is the recent framework of Chung, Guo, Liu, Qian [CGLQ20] for establishing tight time-space tradeoffs in the quantum random oracle model. Generally speaking, they reduce proving the security of a problem with S-bit advice to proving the security of multiple random instances of the problem, presented one at a time, *without* advice. Specifically, they observe that[1], if any adversary (with no advice) can solve S instances of the problem "sequentially" with success probability at

---

[1] The framework of Chung, Guo, Liu, Qian [CGLQ20] reduces to analyzing sequential multi-instance security for $S + \log N + 1$ instances instead of S-instances. We slightly improve their parameters and obtain a considerably cleaner version in Theorem 3.

most δ^S, then any adversary with S-bit advice can solve one instance of the problem with success probability at most 2δ.

This idea of reducing the security of a problem with advice to the security of a multi-instance problem without advice was first introduced by Impagliazzo and Kabanets in [IK10]. The idea was also used by later works [ACDW20, GK22]. The difference between [IK10] and the later works, including this work, is that we reduce to a "sequential" multi-instance game as opposed to a "parallel" multi-instance problem. More concretely, in the parallel multi-instance problem, the adversary is presented with all the randomly chosen instances of the challenge problems to solve once at the start. Whereas in the multi-instance game, the adversary gets a new randomly chosen instance of challenge problem one at a time and only after solving all the previous challenges.

Chung et al. [CGLQ20] recently demonstrated a separation between "sequential" multi-instance games and "parallel" multi-instance problems in the context of function inversion in the quantum setting[2]. Guo, Li, Liu and Zhang [GLLZ21] pointed out a connection between "sequential" multi-instance game and the presampling technique (first introduced by Unruh [Unr07], and further optimized by Coretti et al. [CDGS18])—the main technique used by Coretti et al. [CDGS18] for proving the $O(ST^2/N)$ bound. Roughly speaking, all results relying on presampling technique can be reproved using "sequential" multi-instance games. That suggested that "sequential" multi-instance games have the potential to prove stronger results. Therefore we are motivated to adapt and take full advantage of "sequential" multi-instance games in the context of collision finding.

To better illustrate the connection between "sequential" multi-instance games and the presampling technique, we show how to recover the $O(ST^2/N)$ bound by Coretti et al. [CDGS18]. Recall that presampling technique by Coretti et al. [CDGS18] generically reduces security proofs of unpredictability applications (including collision finding) in the AI-ROM to a much simpler P-bit-fixing random-oracle model (BF-ROM), where the attacker can arbitrarily fix the values of the random oracle on some $P := O(ST)$ coordinates, but then the remaining coordinates are chosen at random. Coretti et al. [CDGS18] showed that the security of finding collisions in Merkle-Damågard Hash Functions in the BF-ROM is $O(ST/N)$.

Using "sequential" multi-instance games, it suffices to bound the advantage of any adversary (with no advice) winning a new game, conditioning on winning all previous (up to at most S) ones, by $O(ST^2/N)$. The adversary wins all games with advantage $O(ST^2/N)^S$, which implies the desired security against S-bit advice. The key point is that the adversary (with no advice) made at most ST queries in previous games. Therefore, conditioning on any possible events of earlier games, from the view of the adversary, the random oracle is essentially a

---

[2] In particular, they showed that "sequentially" inverting S random images (with T quantum queries per round to a given random function $f : [N] \rightarrow [N]$) admits security $O(ST/N + T^2/N)^S$, and the corresponding "parallel" multi-instance problems admits an attack with advantage $\Omega(ST^2/N)^S$.

(convex combination of) bit-fixing random oracles (BF-ROM) [CDGS18], where at most ST-positions are known, and the rest remains independent and random. Hence, it suffices to prove the security of a single game in BF-ROM by $O(ST^2/N)$, which has been shown by Coretti et al. [CDGS18] as a necessary step to use the presampling technique.

Barriers of the Above Idea. Akshima et al. [ACDW20] pointed out a barrier to using the vanilla presampling technique towards proving $B = 2$. In particular, one can only hope to achieve $\Omega(ST^2/N)$ in the BF-ROM even for $B = 2$. Recall that, to prove the sequential multi-instance security, it is sufficient to bound the advantage of any adversary that finds a 2-block collision for a fresh salt a, conditioned on it finds 2-block collisions for all the previous random challenge salts $a_1, \cdots, a_S$.

We will call these ST queries made during the first S rounds as offline queries. Among the T queries made for a, we will call the queries that were not made during the first S rounds as online queries. Throughout the discussion, we will focus on the case that the new salt a has never been queried before in offline queries, because the other case happens with probability at most ST/N (so won't affect our conclusion). As a result, all queries starting with the challenge salt a have to be online queries.

It is clear that the adversary learns about the function not only using the online queries but also from the offline queries. The information this algorithm can take advantage of from the offline queries varies by a lot. The followings are two extreme cases:

1. The offline queries consist of exactly one single query for each of ST distinct salts.
2. The offline queries consist of one collision for each of $ST/2$ distinct salts

For the first case, the offline queries can barely help[3]. Whereas, in the second case, as long as an adversary can find a pre-image (starting with the challenge salt a) of any of these $ST/2$ salts, it finds a 2-block collision (Fig. 1). Since there are T online queries, the algorithm achieves advantage at least $ST^2/(2N)$ in the second case.

The vanilla presampling approach works for worst-case offline queries. Given the above example, the best security bound one can hope to achieve in the BF-ROM for $B = 2$ is $\Omega(ST^2/N)$.

Our Main Technical Novelty. Our main insight is that, unlike the presampling technique in which offline queries can be arbitrary, the worst offline queries are not typical and can be tolerated by refining the technique. In the above example, the chance that offline queries form $ST/2$ pairs of collisions is quite unlikely. We define the following "high knowledge gaining" event $\mathbf{E}_1$:

---

[3] We do not prove it rigorously here. Instead, we focus on the more interesting case – offline queries do provide advantages.

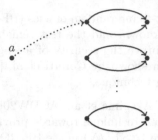

Fig. 1. Nodes indicate salts in $[N]$. An arrow connected two salts means there is a query on the starting salt and a message in $[M]$ such that the output is the other salt. An online query hits an existing collision. Solid lines denote offline queries. The dotted line denotes the online query that forms a 2-block collision.

$\mathbf{E}_1$: By making ST queries, there are more than S distinct salts with 1-block collision.

The name "high knowledge gaining" suggests that whenever this event happens, the online algorithm can behave significantly better than average (following the attack in Fig. 1). If this event $\mathbf{E}_1$ does not happen, the probability that an online algorithm finds a query hitting an existing offline collision is bounded by $O((S/N) \cdot T)$; it is much better compared to the worst case – which is $O(ST^2/N)$. Remember that we have not shown how to prove that $\mathbf{E}_1$ happens with a tiny probability. We will not do that in this section since this is not our main technical novelty.

We then show two more "high knowledge gaining" events, which are all the events we consider. Conditioned on none of them happens, no online algorithms can find 2-block collisions with advantage better than $O(ST/N + T^2/N)$. The second event $\mathbf{E}_2$ is defined as:

$\mathbf{E}_2$: By making ST queries, there are more than S^2 pairs of queries forming collisions.

In Fig. 2a, we denote a multi-collision by a claw. $\mathbf{E}_2$ says that many pair-wise collisions are found among all the offline queries. $\mathbf{E}_1$ only cares about collisions starting with the same salt, whereas $\mathbf{E}_2$ counts every pair of collisions (even starting with distinct salts). If there are many pairs of collisions, as long as an online adversary can hit two queries that form a collision, it finds a 2-block collision. The probability that an online algorithm having two queries hitting one particular existing collision is at most $O(T^2/N^2)$; if $\mathbf{E}_2$ does not happen, by union bound, the advantage of this type of attack is bounded by $O(S^2 \cdot (T^2/N^2))$, again smaller than $O(ST/N)$.

The final event $\mathbf{E}_3$ is very similar to $\mathbf{E}_1$:

$\mathbf{E}_3$: By making ST queries, there are more than S distinct salts with self-loops.

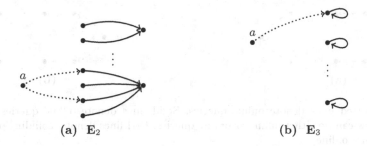

(a) $\mathbf{E}_2$ (b) $\mathbf{E}_3$

Fig. 2. Other two "high knowledge gaining" events and their corresponding attacks.

If an online algorithm hits an offline self-loop, it forms a 2-block collision. Following the same reasoning as $\mathbf{E}_1$, if $\mathbf{E}_3$ does not happen, the probability that an online algorithm finds a query hitting an existing self-loop is bounded by $O((S/N) \cdot T)$.

By identifying the "high knowledge gaining" events and managing to show that they are all unlikely (which is intuitive but non-trivial to prove), we obtain a considerably simpler proof for the $B = 2$ result from [ACDW20] using our approach in Sect. 3 for illustration. More precisely, with all these "high knowledge gaining" events, we show that[4]: (1) these events happen with probability at most $O(N^{-S})$, even conditioned on the adversary winning all the previous rounds; (2) when none of them happens, an online algorithm making T queries can find a 2-block collision with advantage $O(ST/N + T^2/N)$: such a 2-block collision will consist of either hybrid queries (both online and offline queries) or solely online queries; but for both cases, the probability is small.

It is an upside of our technique that it modularises and separates the bad events, making the overall proof more straightforward and intuitive. Following the same structure, we then extend our proof to larger B by identifying a few events, and obtaining our main result.

Applying Our New Techniques to Larger B. As for $B = 2$, we present results for the sequential multi-instance model and use the reduction to prove results in the auxiliary input model. We simplify the sequential multi-instance model into the offline phase and online phase as in the $B = 2$ result and again use our insight that worst offline queries are unlikely and better bounds than $O(ST^2/N)$ can be achieved using a more refined analysis. However, unlike for $B = 2$ analysis, our larger B analysis is not as straightforward and requires some creative case analysis in terms of collision types.

We call offline queries that share an image under H with other offline query/queries as marked queries. We define the following "high knowledge gaining" event:

---

[4] This is not a formal argument but captures the intuition behind our technique. For the formal proofs, please refer to Sect. 3.

Fig. 3. Dotted lines denote online queries. Solid lines denote offline queries. Dash-dotted lines can be either offline or online queries. Red lines denote 'colliding' queries. (Color figure online)

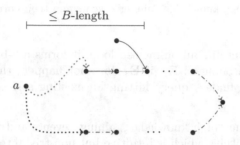

Fig. 4. The B-length collision uses some marked query. The solid red line denotes the *first* marked query along the B-length collisions. The dotted blue line denote the *closest* online query to the red line along the B-length collisions. (Color figure online)

E: By making ST queries, there are more than κ marked queries where $\kappa = S \cdot \max\{1, ST^2/N\}$.

We can show that this event happens with probability at most $O(N^{-S})$, even conditioned on the adversary finding B-length collisions in all the previous rounds. When event E does not happen, there are two possibilities: 1) The B-length collisions found 'use' at least one of these (at most) κ marked queries 2) The B-length collisions found 'use' none of those κ marked queries. For case (1), we will show that some online query should hit one of (at most) $\kappa \cdot B$ offline queries en route to one of κ queries within B steps to succeed, and this happens with probability at most $O(\kappa TB/N)$. For case (2), note that it implies at least one of the two 'colliding' queries among the B-length collisions is a 'new' online query. Then, using this fact along with the structural knowledge of the type of B-length collision, we can show that probability of finding any of these types of B-length collisions is bounded by $O(STB/N + T^2/N)$.

Here, we focus on one type of B-length collisions to reiterate our strategy with more details. Refer to Sect. 4 for the complete proof. Consider the type of B-length collision depicted in Fig. 3a on input salt a.

First, as we have discussed at the beginning of the section, note that the probability that the input salt a has been queried in the offline queries is at most ST/N (as a is randomly and independently sampled). So, it suffices to focus on the case that a has not being queried during offline queries depicted in Fig. 3b. For this case, there should exist some queries (including the queries

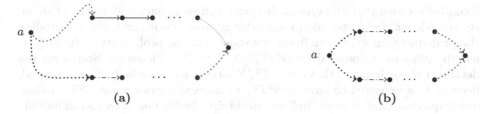

Fig. 5. The B-length collision uses no marked queries. The solid red line (if any) denotes the colliding query made in the offline phase. The dotted blue lines denote the two closest online queries to the colliding queries along the B-length collisions (they can also be colliding queries themselves). (Color figure online)

on a) along with the outputted B-length collisions that are online queries (i.e., made for the first time during the online phase).

In addition, we can also condition on event E not happening as we can show that the probability of event E is at most $O(N^{-S})$, even conditioned on the adversary winning all the previous rounds. Now observe that the queries in any found this type of B-length collisions would satisfy one of the two following possibilities:

1. The B-length collision uses some marked query.
2. None of the offline queries used by B-length collision is a marked query.

We first analyze B-length collisions with queries satisfying (1) above. Refer to Fig. 4 for a pictorial depiction of such collisions. Conditioned on event E not happening, there will be at most κ marked queries. Consider the first such query along the B-length collisions. There is a unique 'chain' consisting of at most B offline queries connecting some online query to this marked query. Thus, the probability of finding B-length collisions satisfying (1) conditioned on event $\overline{E}$ is at most the probability of some online query whose output is one of (the salts of) these κB offline queries, which is at most $O(\kappa TB/N)$.

Note that when queries in the B-length collision satisfy (2) above, it implies at least one of the 'colliding queries' (two queries denoted by red arrows in Fig. 3b) is made for the first time in the online phase.

The probability of both the colliding queries happening for the first time in the online phase (see Fig. 5b) is bounded by $O(T^2/N)$.

In the case exactly one of the colliding queries happens in the offline phase, there are at most ST possibilities for this offline colliding query. There is a unique 'chain' of at most B offline queries from some online query to this query and the output of another online query should be the output of this query (see Fig. 5a). Thus, the probability of finding such B-length collisions is bounded by $O(STB \cdot T/N \cdot T/N) = O(STB/N + T^2/N)$.

For other types of B-length collisions, we can analyze each type in a similar way. Instead of analyzing each type of B-length collisions, we further abstract out

5 conditions such that any type of B-length collisions must satisfy one of them. By considering one more "high knowledge gaining" event, and upper bounding the probability for every condition, we show that the probability of finding B-length collisions is bounded by $O(\kappa TB/N + T^2/N)$. Please see Sect. 4 for the details. It is worth noting that the S^2T^2/N term in κ cannot be further improved, because it is expected to have $\Omega(S^2T^2/N)$ marked queries among ST random oracle queries. Thus, it seems unlikely to obtain a better bound by just improving event E and its analysis.

A Detailed Comparison with Prior Techniques. The similarity between [ACDW20, GK22] and us is that we all adopt the idea of reducing the problem of interest to a multi-instance variant, in which an adversary has to solve multiple copies of the given problem.

Both [ACDW20] and [GK22] directly analyze the probability of solving all instances using the compression paradigm, which typically requires a non-trivial case analysis of the more complicated *multi-instance* problem. These case analyses may be quite laborious and detached from the single-instance problem (thus may not give many insights for the single-instance problem).

Our approach differs significantly from [ACDW20] and [GK22] in two places. First, we focus on analyzing a simple variant of the *single-instance* problem (corresponding to a single round of the sequential multi-instance game conditioning on winning previous games), which is sufficient to establish desired results in multi-instance security. This variant is more similar to the original problem, and may be easier to analyze than the multi-instance problems. The first step (reducing to a variant of the single-instance problem) is somewhat used and captured in the presampling technique (via a different route [CDGS18]). We do think this step is more modular than [ACDW20] and [GK22], but don't consider this as our main technical novelty.

The second place, also our main technical novelty, is that we further introduce "knowledge gaining events" for analyzing the variant of the single-instance problem. These events can be isolated and analyzed on their own, and precisely highlight the correlation in finding collisions given "typical" presampled random oracles. Before this work, all the presampling techniques for time-space trade-offs considered worst-case presampled random oracles. The worst-case presampling may make the existing analyses sub-optimal. Our approach analyzes the "average-case" presampling random oracles and shows that those "worst-case" ones can never happen except with a tiny probability. To our best knowledge, this is the first work that takes advantage of "average-case" presampling and achieves tight bounds.

Overall, we consider our proofs more modular, because we utilize sequential games to focus on variants of the single-instance game (rather than directly compressing multi-instance games used by [ACDW20] and [GK22]). We further introduce "knowledge gaining events" to take advantage of "average-case" presampling (rather than working with worst-case ones used by [CDGS18]).

1.3   Discussions and Open Problems

A Better Attack or Security Bound for $ST^2 > N$? Our main result suggests that the attack by [ACDW20] is optimal when $ST^2 \leq N$, and is potentially suboptimal when $ST^2 > N$. This attack shares many similarities with the Hellman's attack for inverting random functions. Interestingly, Hellman's attack is also known to be optimal when $ST^2 \leq N$, and is potentially sub-optimal when $ST^2 > N$. A better attack for $ST^2 > N$ will be exciting and may give insights for improving Hellman's attack. We think that our framework has the potential to prove a better security bound or even the STB-conjecture, by identifying the right set of "high knowledge gaining" events.

Tight Quantum Time-Space Tradeoffs for Finding Collisions in MD? Motivated by analyzing post-quantum non-uniform security, several recent works [CGLQ20, GLLZ21] studied the same question in the quantum setting, in which the adversary is given S-(qu)bit of advice and T quantum oracle queries. However, unlike the classical setting, no matching bounds are known, even for $B = 2$ and $B = T$. The $\Omega(ST^3/N)$ security bound by [GLLZ21], suggests that the optimal attack may speed up the trivial quantum collision finding by a factor of S. However, the best-known attack achieves $O(ST^2/N + T^3/N)$ for every $2 \leq B \leq T$. Is there a security jump for finding 2-block collisions and unbounded collisions in the quantum setting? Can we leverage our new proof for $B = 2$ to prove a tight security bound in the quantum setting?

Other Related Works. We mention that time-space lower bounds of attacks (or non-uniform security) against other fundamental cryptographic primitives, such as one-way functions, pseudorandom random generators, discrete log, have been investigated in various idealized models [DTT10, CHM20, CGK18, CGK19, GGKL21, DGK17, CDG18, CDGS18].

2   Preliminaries

Notation. For non-negative integers N, k, we write $[N]$ for $\{1, 2, \cdots, N\}$ and $\binom{[N]}{k}$ for the collection of all size-k subsets of $[N]$. For a finite set X, we write X^+ for the set of tuples of 1 or more elements of X. Random variables will be written in bold, and we write $\mathbf{x} \leftarrow_\$ X$ to indicate that $\mathbf{x}$ is a uniform random variable in X.

Chernoff Bound. Suppose $\mathbf{X}_1, \cdots, \mathbf{X}_t$ are independent binary random variables. Let $\mathbf{X}$ denote their sum and $\mu = \mathbb{E}[\mathbf{X}]$. For any $\delta \geq 0$,

$$\Pr[\mathbf{X} \geq (1 + \delta)\mu] \leq \exp\left(-\frac{\delta^2 \mu}{2 + \delta}\right).$$

Random Oracle [BR93]. In random oracle model, we model a hash function as a random function H that is sampled uniformly at random from all functions at the beginning. H is publicly accessible to every entity.

A useful property about random oracle model is that, instead of sampling H uniformly at random, one can assume H is initialized as a function that always outputs $\perp$; which indicates the response has not been sampled. Whenever an input x is queried and $H(x)$ has not been sampled (i.e. $H(x) = \perp$), the random oracle samples y uniformly from the range and $H(x) := y$.

Definition 1 (Lazy Sampling and Databases). *We refer to the table of sampled queries (for those $H(x) \neq \perp$) on H and their responses as the database or the partially sampled random oracle.*

*The set of **offline queries** is the set of distinct queries made in the offline stage. The set of **online queries** is the set of distinct queries made in the online stage and had not been made in the offline stage.*

While dealing with algorithms with both offline and online stages, the table of only the offline queries on H and their responses is referred to as the offline database.

Note that the outputs of the offline and online queries are independent and uniformly distributed.

2.1   Merkle-Damågard Hash Functions (MD)

A hash function usually is required to function over inputs with different lengths. Many practical hash functions are based on the Merkle-Damågard construction (MD). It takes a hash function with fixed length input to a new hash function with arbitrary input lengths.

We treat the underlying hash function as a random oracle $H : [N] \times [M] \to [N]$. We call a message $\mathbf{m}$ is a B-block message if $\mathbf{m}$ can be written as $\mathbf{m} =$

$(m_1, \cdots, m_B)$ where each $m_i \in [M]$. The function $\mathsf{MD}_H(a, \mathbf{m})$ evaluates on a salt $a \in [N]$ and a message $\mathbf{m}$ as the follows:

$$\mathsf{MD}_H(a, \mathbf{m}) = \mathsf{MD}_H^\ell(a, (m_1, \cdots, m_\ell)) = \begin{cases} H(\mathsf{MD}_H^{\ell-1}(a, (m_1, \cdots, m_{\ell-1})), m_\ell) & \ell > 1 \\ H(a, m_1) & \ell = 1 \end{cases}$$

It applies the fixed-length hash function H on the salt a and the first block m_1 to get a new salt a_2; it then applies H again on a_2 and m_2 until finally it outputs a single string in $[N]$.

2.2 Collision-Resistance Against Auxiliary Input (AI)

We start by defining the security game of collision-resistance against auxiliary input adversaries. The adversary is unbounded in the preprocessing stage and leave nothing but a piece of bounded-length advice for the online stage.

Definition 2 ((S, T)-AI algorithm). *A pair of algorithms $\mathcal{A} = (\mathcal{A}_1, \mathcal{A}_2)$ is an $(S, T) - AI adversary$ for MD if*

- *$\mathcal{A}_1^H$ is unbounded (making unbounded number of oracle queries to H) and outputs S bits of advice σ;*
- *$\mathcal{A}_2^H$ takes σ and a salt $a \in [N]$, issues T queries to H and outputs $\mathbf{m}_1, \mathbf{m}_2$.*

We are ready to define the security game of collision-resistance against an (S, T)-AI adversary.

Definition 3 (Auxiliary-Input Collision-Resistance). *We define the following game B-AICR for a fixed random oracle H and a salt $a \in [N]$ in Fig. 6, where B is a function of N (the range size of the random oracle). The game outputs 1 (indicating that the adversary wins) if and only if $\mathcal{A}$ outputs a pair of MD collision with at most $B(N)$ blocks.*

Game B-$\mathsf{AICR}_{H,a}(\mathcal{A})$

$\quad \sigma \leftarrow \mathcal{A}_1^H$

$\quad \mathbf{m}_1, \mathbf{m}_2 \leftarrow \mathcal{A}_2^H(\sigma, a)$

$\quad$ If $\mathbf{m}_1$ or $\mathbf{m}_2$ consists of more than $B(N)$ blocks

$\quad\quad$ Then Return 0

$\quad$ If $\mathbf{m}_1 \neq \mathbf{m}_2$ and $\mathsf{MD}_H(a, \mathbf{m}_1) = \mathsf{MD}_H(a, \mathbf{m}_2)$

$\quad\quad$ Then Return 1

$\quad$ Else Return 0

Fig. 6. B-$\mathsf{AICR}_{H,a}(\mathcal{A})$

For an (S, T)-AI adversary $\mathcal{A} = (\mathcal{A}_1, \mathcal{A}_2)$, we define the advantage of $\mathcal{A}$ as its winning probability in the B-$\mathsf{AICR}_{H,a}$ with uniformly random $H \leftarrow \{f :$

$$
\boxed{
\begin{aligned}
&\text{Game 2-AICR}_{H,a}(\mathcal{A}) \\
&\quad \sigma \leftarrow \mathcal{A}_1^H \\
&\quad \mathbf{m}_1, \mathbf{m}_2 \leftarrow \mathcal{A}_2^H(\sigma, a) \\
&\quad \text{If } \mathbf{m}_1 \text{ or } \mathbf{m}_2 \text{ consists of more than 2 blocks} \\
&\qquad \text{Then Return } 0 \\
&\quad \text{If } \mathbf{m}_1 \neq \mathbf{m}_2 \text{ and } \mathsf{MD}_H(a, \mathbf{m}_1) = \mathsf{MD}_H(a, \mathbf{m}_2) \\
&\qquad \text{Then Return } 1 \\
&\quad \text{Else Return } 0
\end{aligned}
}
$$

Fig. 7. 2-AICR$_{H,a}(\mathcal{A})$

$[N] \times [M] \to [N]\}$ *and random* $a \leftarrow [N]$. *We define the* (S, T, B)-*auxiliary-input collision-resistance of Merkle-Damgård, denoted by* $\mathsf{Adv}_{B\text{-MD}}^{\text{AI-CR}}(S, T)$, *as the maximum of advantage taken over all* (S, T)-*AI adversaries* $\mathcal{A}$.

For convenience, we similarly define $\mathsf{Adv}_{2\text{-MD}}^{\text{AI-CR}}(S, T)$ *as the maximum of advantage of winning the game 2-AICR (see Fig. 7) taken over all* (S, T)-*AI adversaries* $\mathcal{A}$.

Multi-Instance Collision-Resistance (MI). We then define the sequential multi-instance collision-resistance of Merkle-Damgård. As shown by [CGLQ20], the AI-security is closely related to the (sequential) MI-security. Note that in the MI security, an adversary does not take any advice but tries to solve independent instances sequentially.

Definition 4 (Multi-Instance Collision-Resistance). *Fixing functions* B *and* S, *and a random oracle* H, *we define the following game* B-MICR^S *in Fig. 8. In this game,* $\mathcal{A}$ *will receive* S *freshly independent and uniform salts and it needs to find a MD collision with respect to each salt* a_i *of at most* B *blocks, in a sequential order. In other words,* $\mathcal{A}$ *will never see the next challenge salt until it solves the current one.*

$$
\boxed{
\begin{aligned}
&\text{Game } B\text{-MICR}_{H,a}^S(\mathcal{A}) \\
&\quad \text{For } i \in \{1, 2, \cdots, S\}: \\
&\qquad \text{Sample } a_i \leftarrow [N] \\
&\qquad \mathbf{m}_1, \mathbf{m}_2 \leftarrow \mathcal{A}^H(a_i) \\
&\qquad \text{If } \mathbf{m}_1 \text{ or } \mathbf{m}_2 \text{ consists of more than } B \text{ blocks}, \\
&\qquad \text{or } \mathsf{MD}_H(a_i, \mathbf{m}_1) \neq \mathsf{MD}_H(a_i, \mathbf{m}_2) \\
&\qquad\quad \text{Return } 0 \\
&\quad \text{Return } 1
\end{aligned}
}
$$

Fig. 8. Games B-MICR$_{H,a}^S(\mathcal{A})$.

In this security game, $\mathcal{A}$ is a stateful algorithm that maintains its internal state between each stage. We usually consider an (S,T)-MI adversary $\mathcal{A}$ which makes at most T queries in each of these S stages. We similarly define 2-MICR by setting $B = 2$ in B-MICR.

For an (S,T)-MI adversary $\mathcal{A}$, we define the advantage of $\mathcal{A}$ as its winning probability in the B-MICR$_{H,a}^S$ with uniformly random H and $a \leftarrow [N]$.

We define the (S,T,B)-multi-instance collision-resistance of Merkle-Damgård, denoted by $\mathsf{Adv}_{\text{B-MD}}^{\text{MI-CR}}(S,T)$, as the maximum of advantage taken over all (S,T)-MI adversaries $\mathcal{A}$.

For convenience, we similarly define $\mathsf{Adv}_{\text{2-MD}}^{\text{MI-CR}}(S,T)$ as the maximum of advantage of winning the game 2-MICR$_{H,a}^S$ (for random H,a) taken over all (S,T)-MI adversaries $\mathcal{A}$.

The following theorem will be useful for proving the AI collision-resistance of Merkle-Damgård. It says a lower bound for the MI collision-resistance implies a lower bound for the AI security. Therefore, in the rest of the paper, we will focus on the MI collision-resistance of Merkle-Damgård with different lengths B. The theorem is based on the idea of Theorem 4.1 in [CGLQ20], which implies that if $\mathsf{Adv}_{\text{B-MD}}^{\text{MI-CR}}(S + \log N + 1, T) \leq \delta^{S + \log N + 1}$, then $\mathsf{Adv}_{\text{B-MD}}^{\text{AI-CR}}(S,T) \leq 4\delta$. We slightly improve their parameter, and obtain a considerably cleaner statement.

Theorem 3. For any S,T,B and $0 \leq \delta \leq 1$, if $\mathsf{Adv}_{\text{B-MD}}^{\text{MI-CR}}(S,T) \leq \delta^S$, then $\mathsf{Adv}_{\text{B-MD}}^{\text{AI-CR}}(S,T) \leq 2\delta$.

Proof of Theorem 3. We prove by contradiction. Assume there is an (S,T)-AI adversary $\mathcal{A} = (\mathcal{A}_1, \mathcal{A}_2)$ such that

$$\Pr_{H,a}\left[B\text{-AICR}_{H,a}(\mathcal{A}) = 1\right] > 2\delta,$$

Consider the following (S,T)-MI adversary $\mathcal{B}$:

1. $\mathcal{B}$ samples a uniformly random σ of S bits.
2. For each stage $i \in [S]$:
   - $\mathcal{B}$ receives a_i from the challenger.
   - $\mathcal{B}$ runs $\mathcal{A}_2^H(\sigma, a_i)$ to obtain and output $\mathbf{m}_1, \mathbf{m}_2$.

We will show that $\Pr_{H,a_1,\dots,a_S}\left[B\text{-MICR}_H^S(\mathcal{B}) = 1\right] > \delta^S$. For every fixed choice of H, we define

$$\delta_H := \Pr_a\left[B\text{-AICR}_{H,a}(\mathcal{A}) = 1\right].$$

Observe that $\mathbb{E}_H[\delta_H] = \Pr_{H,a}\left[B\text{-AICR}_{H,a}(\mathcal{A}) = 1\right] > 2\delta$. For every fixed choice of H, conditioning on that $\mathcal{B}$ guesses the output of $\mathcal{A}_1^H$ correctly, then $\mathcal{B}$ perfectly simulates $\mathcal{A}$. Therefore,

$$\Pr_{a_1,\dots,a_S}\left[B\text{-MICR}_H(\mathcal{B}) = 1\right] \geq \Pr_{a_1,\dots,a_S}\left[B\text{-MICR}_H(\mathcal{B}) = 1 \mid \sigma = \mathcal{A}_1^H\right] \cdot \Pr[\sigma = \mathcal{A}_1^H] = \delta_H^S/2^S.$$

By averaging over the randomness of H,

$$\Pr_{H,a_1,\dots,a_S}[B\text{-MICR}_{H,a}(\mathcal{B}) = 1] \geq \mathbb{E}_H[\delta_H^S]/2^S \geq \mathbb{E}[\delta_H]^S/2^S > \delta^S ,$$

where the second inequality is by Jensen's inequality, and the last inequality is by $\mathbb{E}_H[\delta_H] > 2\delta$. $\qquad\qquad\qquad\qquad\qquad\qquad\qquad\qquad\qquad\qquad\qquad\qquad$ □

3   Auxiliary Input Collision Resistance for $B = 2$ Merkle-Damgård

In this section we prove the following theorem, which recovers Theorem 7 in [ACDW20].

Theorem 4. *For any S, T and $N \geq 64$,*

$$\mathsf{Adv}_{2\text{-MD}}^{\text{AI-CR}}(S, T) \leq (200 \log^2 N) \cdot \frac{ST + T^2}{N}.$$

By Theorem 3, it suffices to prove the following lemma.

Lemma 1. *For any S, T and $N \geq 64$, $\mathsf{Adv}_{2\text{-MD}}^{\text{MI-CR}}(S, T) \leq \frac{100(ST+T^2)\log^2 N}{N}$.*

The purpose of this section is to show the simplicity of our new framework. The proof will also serve as a stepping stone for a better understanding of our proof for larger B cases.

Proof of Lemma 1. Let H be a random oracle in the game 2-MICR^S and $\mathcal{A}$ be an arbitrary (S, T)-MI adversary. We show that its advantage of succeeding in 2-MICR^S is at most $(100(ST+T^2) \log^2 N/N)^S$. In this proof, we will also assume the random oracle H is lazily sampled by the challenger, which is equivalent to being sampled at the very beginning.

Let $\mathbf{X}_i$ be the indicator variable that $\mathcal{A}$ wins the i-th stage on a uniformly random salt a_i. The advantage of $\mathcal{A}$ can be then written as $\Pr[\mathbf{X}_1 \wedge \cdots \wedge \mathbf{X}_S]$. We additionally define the indicator variable $\mathbf{X}_{<i} = \mathbf{X}_1 \wedge \cdots \wedge \mathbf{X}_{i-1}$, meaning whether $\mathcal{A}$ wins the first $(i - 1)$ stages of the sequential game. Then

$$\Pr[\mathbf{X}_1 \wedge \dots \wedge \mathbf{X}_S] = \prod_{i=1}^{S} \Pr[\mathbf{X}_i | \mathbf{X}_{<i}]. \tag{1}$$

We will bound $\Pr[\mathbf{X}_{<i+1}] < (\delta_S)^i$ for each $i \in \{1, \cdots, S\}$ by induction, where $\delta_S = 100 \cdot \frac{(ST+T^2)\log^2 N}{N}$.

If $\Pr[\mathbf{X}_{<i}]$ is already bounded by $(\delta_S)^i$, then it trivially holds for $\Pr[\mathbf{X}_{<i+1}]$. Otherwise, we assume $\Pr[\mathbf{X}_{<i}] \geq (\delta_S)^i$.

We want to bound $\Pr[\mathbf{X}_i | \mathbf{X}_{<i}] \leq \delta_S$ for any arbitrary $i \in [S]$. In the following proof, we will carefully deal with the conditioning on $\mathbf{X}_{<i}$, since $\mathcal{A}$ learns about the function H not only using the T queries in the i-th stage, but also from

these $(i-1)T$ queries in the early stages. We will call all the queries made in the previous $(i-1)$ stages as "offline" queries and those made in the i-th stage as "online" queries. We also recall the definition for "databases" in Definition 1.

As mention in the introduction, one bad example is that the previous $(i-1)T$ queries consist of $(i-1)T/2$ distinct salts, each has a pair of 1-block collision. An online adversary can use T queries to hit any of these salts and form a 2-block collision with probability roughly iT^2/N. Below, we will show that this event (and other events that give non-trivial advantage to the online adversary) happens with very small probability.

Defining Knowledge-Gaining Events. To bound the knowledge that $\mathcal{A}$ learns in the previous stages, we define the following events: all events are defined for the lazily sampled random oracle right after the first $(i-1)$ stages. We are going to show that these events are the "only events" that $\mathcal{A}$ can learn take advantage of the previous queries but they happen with very small probability.

- Let $\mathbf{E}_1^i$ be the event that 1-block collisions can be found for at least $10i \log N$ distinct salts within $(i-1)T$ queries.
  Formally, in the database, there exist $10i \log N$ salts: for each such salt a, there exists $m \neq m' \in [N]$ satisfying $H(a,m) = H(a,m')$. See Fig. 9a.

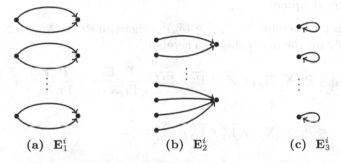

| (a) $\mathbf{E}_1^i$ | (b) $\mathbf{E}_2^i$ | (c) $\mathbf{E}_3^i$ |

Fig. 9. All events $\mathbf{E}_1^i, \mathbf{E}_2^i, \mathbf{E}_i^3$. Nodes indicate salts in $[N]$. An arrow connected two salts means there is a query on the starting salt and a message in $[M]$, and the output is the other salt.

- Let $\mathbf{E}_2^i$ be the event that at least $10i^2 \log^3 N$ pairs of block collisions can be found within $(i-1)T$ queries.
  Formally, in the database, there exist $10i^2 \log^3 N$ pairs of inputs $(a,m) \neq (a',m')$ satisfying $H(a,m) = H(a',m')$. We emphasize that we do not ask a pair of collision to start with distinct salts. See Fig. 9b.
- Let $\mathbf{E}_3^i$ be the event that self loops can be found for at least $10i \log N$ distinct salts within $(i-1)T$ queries.
  Formally, in the database, there exist $10i \log N$ distinct salts: for each such salt a, there exists some $m \in [N]$ satisfying $H(a,m) = a$. See Fig. 9c.

Then

$$\Pr[\mathbf{X}_i | \mathbf{X}_{<i}] \le \Pr[\mathbf{X}_i | \mathbf{X}_{<i} \wedge \overline{\mathbf{E}_1^i} \wedge \overline{\mathbf{E}_2^i} \wedge \overline{\mathbf{E}_3^i}] + \Pr[\mathbf{E}_1^i \vee \mathbf{E}_2^i \vee \mathbf{E}_3^i | \mathbf{X}_{<i}]$$

$$\le \Pr[\mathbf{X}_i | \mathbf{X}_{<i} \wedge \overline{\mathbf{E}_1^i} \wedge \overline{\mathbf{E}_2^i} \wedge \overline{\mathbf{E}_3^i}] + \frac{\Pr[\mathbf{E}_1^i]}{\Pr[\mathbf{X}_{<i}]} + \frac{\Pr[\mathbf{E}_2^i]}{\Pr[\mathbf{X}_{<i}]} + \frac{\Pr[\mathbf{E}_3^i]}{\Pr[\mathbf{X}_{<i}]}.$$

Here we use the fact that $\Pr[\mathbf{A}|\mathbf{B}] \le \Pr[\mathbf{A}]/\Pr[\mathbf{B}]$ for $\Pr[\mathbf{B}] > 0$.

Next, we will show that assuming none of $\mathbf{E}_1^i, \mathbf{E}_2^i, \mathbf{E}_3^i$ happens, an adversary can not take too much advantage of the information from the previous stages. We show that its advantage $\Pr[\mathbf{X}_i | \mathbf{X}_{<i} \wedge \overline{\mathbf{E}_1^i} \wedge \overline{\mathbf{E}_2^i} \wedge \overline{\mathbf{E}_3^i}]$ is bounded by $98 \cdot (ST + T^2) \log^2 N / N$. Secondly, any of these event happens with very small probability. We can safely "assume" these events never happen. In total, the conditional probability is at most $100 \cdot (ST + T^2) \log^2 N / N = \delta_S$.

Claim 1. *For any $i \in [S]$ and $T^2 \le N/2$, $Pr[\mathbf{E}_1^i] \le N^{-10i}$.*

Claim 2. *For any $i \in [S]$, $iT + T^2 < N/2$ and $N \ge 64$, $Pr[\mathbf{E}_2^i] \le 4N^{-2i}$.*

Claim 3. *For any $i \in [S]$, $N \ge 4$ and $T \le N/2$, $Pr[\mathbf{E}_3^i] \le N^{-4i}$.*

The proofs for these lemma are in the full version of the paper. Readers may skip the proofs for all these claims. The proofs are not necessary for understanding the rest of the proof.

Recall that we assume $\Pr[X_{<i}] \ge (\delta_S)^i$, otherwise $\Pr[\mathbf{X}_1 \wedge \ldots \wedge \mathbf{X}_i] \le (\delta_S)^i$ holds trivially for the first i stages. Therefore,

$$\Pr[\mathbf{X}_i | \mathbf{X}_{<i}] \le \Pr[\mathbf{X}_i | \mathbf{X}_{<i} \wedge \overline{\mathbf{E}_1^i} \wedge \overline{\mathbf{E}_2^i} \wedge \overline{\mathbf{E}_3^i}] + \frac{\Pr[\mathbf{E}_1^i]}{\Pr[\mathbf{X}_{<i}]} + \frac{\Pr[\mathbf{E}_2^i]}{\Pr[\mathbf{X}_{<i}]} + \frac{\Pr[\mathbf{E}_3^i]}{\Pr[\mathbf{X}_{<i}]} \tag{2}$$

$$\le \Pr[\mathbf{X}_i | \mathbf{X}_{<i} \wedge \overline{\mathbf{E}_1^i} \wedge \overline{\mathbf{E}_2^i} \wedge \overline{\mathbf{E}_3^i}] + \frac{1}{N}, \tag{3}$$

where the last inequality comes from the fact that $1/\Pr[\mathbf{X}_{<i}] \le N^i$ but $(\Pr[\mathbf{E}_1^i] + \Pr[\mathbf{E}_2^i] + \Pr[\mathbf{E}_3^i]) \le 6N^{-2i}$.

Bounding the Last Term. Finally, we are going to bound $\Pr[\mathbf{X}_i | \mathbf{X}_{<i} \wedge \overline{\mathbf{E}_1^i} \wedge \overline{\mathbf{E}_2^i} \wedge \overline{\mathbf{E}_3^i}]$. In order to do that, we define another event $\mathbf{G}$ as the event that the input salt a_i has been queried among the queries in the previous $(i-1)$ iterations; i.e., for some $m \in [N]$, (a_i, m) is in the lazily sampled hash function. Then it holds that:

$$\Pr\left[\mathbf{X}_i \middle| \mathbf{X}_{<i} \wedge \overline{\mathbf{E}_1^i} \wedge \overline{\mathbf{E}_2^i} \wedge \overline{\mathbf{E}_3^i}\right]$$

$$\le \Pr\left[\mathbf{G} \middle| \mathbf{X}_{<i} \wedge \overline{\mathbf{E}_1^i} \wedge \overline{\mathbf{E}_2^i} \wedge \overline{\mathbf{E}_3^i}\right] + \Pr\left[\mathbf{X}_i \middle| \mathbf{X}_{<i} \wedge \overline{\mathbf{E}_1^i} \wedge \overline{\mathbf{E}_2^i} \wedge \overline{\mathbf{E}_3^i} \wedge \overline{\mathbf{G}}\right]$$

$$\le \frac{(i-1)T}{N} + \Pr\left[\mathbf{X}_i \middle| \mathbf{X}_{<i} \wedge \overline{\mathbf{E}_1^i} \wedge \overline{\mathbf{E}_2^i} \wedge \overline{\mathbf{E}_3^i} \wedge \overline{\mathbf{G}}\right].$$

Now all that remains to bound is $\Pr\left[\mathbf{X}_i \middle| \mathbf{X}_{<i} \wedge \overline{\mathbf{E}_1^i} \wedge \overline{\mathbf{E}_2^i} \wedge \overline{\mathbf{E}_3^i} \wedge \overline{\mathbf{G}}\right]$, which requires collision type-wise analysis. By enumeration, there are total 6 types of 2-block collisions (Fig. 10).

A dashed line origins from a_i. It indicates that the query should be made online, conditioned on $\overline{\mathbf{G}}$. Other queries can be either made online or offline in the previous iterations. The label $\clubsuit, \blacklozenge, \heartsuit$ and $\spadesuit$ will be used later for a better presentation of our proof. By enumerating each solid edge being an online query or a offline query, we show that it is sufficient to consider the cases in Claim 4.

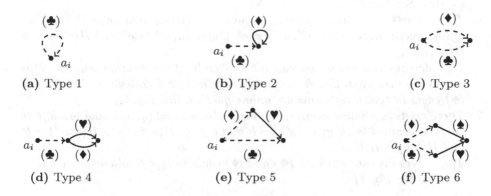

Fig. 10. All types of 2-block collisions.

Claim 4. *For any $i \in [S]$, to find a 2-block collision on a_i conditioned on $\overline{\mathbf{G}}$, the queries should satisfy at least one of the following conditions:*

1. *There exists an online query (i.e., a query among the T queries in the i-th iteration after receiving the challenge input a_i), denoted (a, m) such that $H(a, m) = a$.*
   In other words, a self loop is found among the online queries. This covers the case when ($\clubsuit$) edge in type 1 collisions and the ($\blacklozenge$) edge in type 2 collisions are online queries. See Fig. 11a.
2. *There exists two online queries, denoted (a, m) and (a', m'), such that $(a, m) \neq (a', m')$ and $H(a, m) = H(a', m')$.*
   A collision is found among the online queries. This covers the case when the ($\clubsuit$) and ($\blacklozenge$) edges in Type 3 collisions, the ($\blacklozenge$) and ($\heartsuit$) edges in Type 4 collisions, the ($\clubsuit$) and ($\heartsuit$) edges in Type 5 collisions, the ($\heartsuit$) and ($\spadesuit$) edges in Type 6 collisions are online queries. See Fig. 11b.
3. *There exists an online query, denoted by (a, m), and one offline query, denoted by (a', m'), such that $a \neq a'$, $H(a, m) = a'$ and $H(a', m') = a'$.*
   This denotes an online query hits an existing self loop. This covers the case when the ($\clubsuit$) edge in type 2 collisions is an online query. See Fig. 11c.

4. There exists an online query, denoted by (a, m), and two offline queries, denoted by (a', m') and (a', m''), such that $a \neq a'$, $H(a, m) = a'$ and $H(a', m') = H(a', m'')$.

   This denotes an online query hits an existing collision (starting with the same salt a'). This covers the case when (♣) edge in type 4 collisions is an online query. See Fig. 11d.

5. There exists two online queries, denoted by (a, m) and (a', m'), and an offline query, denoted by (a', m'') such that $a \neq a'$, $H(a, m) = a'$ and $H(a', m') = H(a', m'')$.

   This covers the case when the (♣) and (♦) edges in type 4 collisions are online queries. See Fig. 11e.

6. There exists two online queries, denoted by (a, m) and (a', m'), and an offline query, denoted by (a'', m'') such that $H(a, m) = a'$ and $H(a', m') = H(a'', m'')$.

   This denotes two online queries hit two ends of an existing queries. This covers the case when the (♣) and (♦) edges in type 5 collisions, the (♣) and (♠) edges in type 6 collisions are online queries. See Fig. 11f.

7. There exists two online queries, denoted by (a, m) and (a, m'), and two offline queries, denoted by $(b, y), (b', y')$ such that $b \neq b'$, $H(a, m) = b, H(a, m') = b'$ and $H(b, y) = H(b', y')$.

   This covers the case when the (♣) and (♦) edges in type 6 collisions are online queries. See Fig. 11g.

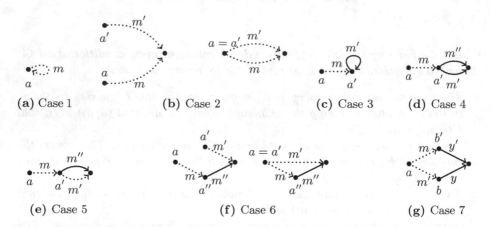

(a) Case 1   (b) Case 2   (c) Case 3   (d) Case 4

(e) Case 5   (f) Case 6   (g) Case 7

Fig. 11. All possible types of collisions. A dotted line denotes an online query. A solid line denotes a offline query.

Proof for Claim 4. We only prove for type 6 collisions. Other five cases are easier and similar.

When both (♥) and (♠) are offline queries, it is Case 7. If only one of the two edges is offline, it is Case 6. If they are all online queries, we can reduce it to Case 2.   □

Finally, we show that for each case in Claim 4, the advantage is bounded by $(98(ST + T^2)\log^2 N)/N$.

Case 1. By making T new queries, each query (a, m) has $1/N$ chance to satisfy $H(a, m) = a$. Therefore, the probability is bounded by T/N.

Case 2. The probability of finding a collision among these T new queries is smaller than T^2/N, by birthday bound.

Case 3. Recall $\mathbf{E}_3^i$: there are at most $10i \log N$ salts that has a self loop in the offline queries. By making T new queries, each query (a, m) has $(10i \log N)/N$ chance to hit any of these salts. Therefore, the probability is bounded by $(10iT \log N)/N$.

Case 4. Recall $\overline{\mathbf{E}_1^i}$: there are at most $10i \log N$ salts that has a collision starting from it in the offline queries. By making T new queries, each query (a, m) has $(10i \log N)/N$ chance to hit any of these salts. Therefore, the probability is bounded by $(10iT \log N)/N$.

Case 5. and **Case 6.** The proofs are identical. Fixing any offline query (a'', m''), by making T queries, the chance of hitting both ends is T^2/N^2. This is because we can enumerate which are the first queries that hit the starting salt a'' and the end $H(a'', m'')$. Each case happens w.p. at most $1/N^2$.

Since there are total $(i - 1)T$ offline queries, by union bound, the advantage is at most $(i - 1)T \cdot T^3/N^2 \leq \frac{iT}{N} \cdot \frac{T^2}{N}$ for both cases.

Case 7. Recall $\overline{\mathbf{E}_2^i}$: there are at most $10i^2 \log^3 N$ pair-wise collisions. For every such collision that start with different salts, the probability of hitting both salts within T queries is T^2/N^2. This is due to the same counting argument in the analysis of Case 5 and Case 6.

By union bound, the advantage is at most $(10i^2T^2 \log^3 N)/N^2$.

We have shown all the cases in Claim 4. Therefore,

$$\Pr[\mathbf{X}_i|\mathbf{X}_{<i} \wedge \overline{\mathbf{E}_1^i} \wedge \overline{\mathbf{E}_2^i} \wedge \overline{\mathbf{E}_3^i}] \leq \frac{98(iT + T^2)\log^2 N}{N}.$$

Combining with Eq. (1) and Eq. (2), we conclude Lemma 1: $\Pr[\mathbf{X}_1 \wedge \ldots \wedge \mathbf{X}_S] \leq (\delta_S)^S$.   □

4   Auxiliary Input Collision Resistance for B Merkle-Damgård

In this section we prove the following theorem.

Theorem 5. *For any functions S, T, B, and $N \geq 64$*

$$\mathsf{Adv}_{\mathsf{B\text{-}MD}}^{\mathsf{AI\text{-}CR}}(S, T) \leq (34 \log^2 N) \cdot \frac{STB}{N} \cdot \max\left\{1, \frac{ST^2}{N}\right\} + 2 \cdot \frac{T^2}{N}.$$

Lemma 2. *For any functions S, T, B, and $N \geq 64$,*

$$\mathsf{Adv}_{\mathsf{B\text{-}MD}}^{\mathsf{MI\text{-}CR}}(S, T) \leq \left(\frac{17\kappa TB \log^2 N + T^2}{N} \right)^S$$

where $\kappa = S \cdot \max\{1, ST^2/N\}$.

As for the case of $B = 2$, we prove an upper bound on the advantage of B-block collision finding adversary in the MI-CR model, which implies an upper bound in the AI-CR model via Theorem 3.

Proof of Lemma 2. We prove this lemma in similar fashion as Lemma 1. Let H be a random oracle (which is lazily sampled) in the game $B\text{-}\mathsf{MICR}^S$ and $\mathcal{A}$ be any (S, T)-MI adversary.

We analogously define $\mathbf{X}_i$ to be the indicator variable that $\mathcal{A}$ finds at most B-length collisions on uniformly random salt a_i given as input in the i-th stage of the game. We also define $\mathbf{X}_{<i} = \mathbf{X}_1 \wedge \cdots \wedge \mathbf{X}_{i-1}$. So, the advantage of $\mathcal{A}$ is

$$\Pr[\mathbf{X}_1 \wedge \ldots \wedge \mathbf{X}_S] = \prod_{i=1}^{S} \Pr[\mathbf{X}_i | \mathbf{X}_{<i}].$$

As in the proof for $B = 2$ case, we will inductively bound $\Pr[\mathbf{X}_{<i+1}]$ for each $i \in [S]$. Here we will bound $\Pr[\mathbf{X}_{<i+1}]$ to $((17\kappa_i TB \log^2 N + T^2)/N)^i$ where $\kappa_i = i \cdot \max\{1, iT^2/N\}$. Recall that we will analogously assume $\Pr[\mathbf{X}_{<i}] \geq ((17\kappa_i TB \log^2 N + T^2)/N)^i$. Otherwise $\Pr[\mathbf{X}_{<i+1}] \leq ((17\kappa_i TB \log^2 N + T^2)/N)^i$ holds trivially.

In order to prove the lemma, it suffices to upper bound $\Pr[\mathbf{X}_i | \mathbf{X}_{<i}]$ by $17\kappa_i TB \log^2 N/N + T^2/N$ for any arbitrary $i \in [S]$. That is because $\Pr[\mathbf{X}_{<i+1}] = \Pr[\mathbf{X}_i | \mathbf{X}_{<i}] \cdot \Pr[\mathbf{X}_{<i}]$ where $\Pr[\mathbf{X}_{<i}] \leq ((17\kappa_i TB \log^2 N + T^2)/N)^{i-1}$ by the inductive hypothesis. In the proof, we will handle the conditioning on $\mathbf{X}_{<i}$ in a similar fashion to our proof for $B = 2$ case.

First we state some useful definitions.

Definition 5. *A list of elements $(a_1, m_1), \ldots, (a_\ell, m_\ell)$ in $[N] \times [M]$ are said to form a chain for H when for every $j \in [\ell - 1]$, $H(a_j, m_j) = a_{j+1}$.*

A chain $(a_1, m_1), \ldots, (a_\ell, m_\ell)$ for H is called a cycle when $H(a_\ell, m_\ell) = a_1$. The length of a cycle is the number of elements in it, ℓ here.

Definition 6. *Two distinct chains $(a_1, m_1), \ldots, (a_\ell, m_\ell)$ and $(a'_1, m'_1), \ldots, (a'_{\ell'}, m'_{\ell'})$ are called colliding chains for H if $H(a_\ell, m_\ell) = H(a'_{\ell'}, m'_{\ell'})$.*

Definition 7. *For any $a \in [N]$, a set of elements $(a_1, m_1), \ldots, (a_\ell, m_\ell)$ in $[N] \times [M]$ are said to form a claw at a under H if $\ell > 1$, $a_1, \ldots, a_\ell$ are distinct and $H(a_1, m_1) = \ldots = H(a_\ell, m_\ell) = a$. We refer to $a_1, \ldots, a_\ell$ as the pre-images of a.*

Next, we define events to illustrate the bound on 'useful' information gained by $\mathcal{A}$ from the prior iterations in the $B\text{-}\mathsf{MICR}$ game. Each of these events are defined over responses from the random oracle in the first $(i - 1)$ iterations.

- Let Y be the set of salts with more than one pre-image on it in the offline database. Then we define $\mathbf{E}_2^i$ to be the event that $\sum_{a \in Y}$ (# pre-images on a) $\geq 16\kappa_i \log^2 N$ after $(i-1)T$ queries where $\kappa_i = \max\left\{i, \frac{i^2 T^2}{N}\right\}$.
- Let $\mathbf{E}_3^i$ be the event that there exists at least $i \log N$ 'special' cycles of length in $[B-1]$ among the $(i-1)T$ offline queries. A cycle $(a_1, m_1), \ldots, (a_\ell, m_\ell)$ is called 'special' if the number of pre-images on a_i is exactly 1 for every $i \in [\ell]$.

Next, we can write

$$\Pr[\mathbf{X}_i | \mathbf{X}_{<i}] = \Pr[\mathbf{X}_i | \mathbf{X}_{<i} \wedge \overline{\mathbf{E}_2^i} \wedge \overline{\mathbf{E}_3^i}] + \Pr[\mathbf{E}_2^i \vee \mathbf{E}_3^i | \mathbf{X}_{<i}]$$

$$\leq \Pr[\mathbf{X}_i | \mathbf{X}_{<i} \wedge \overline{\mathbf{E}_2^i} \wedge \overline{\mathbf{E}_3^i}] + \frac{\Pr[\mathbf{E}_2^i]}{\Pr[\mathbf{X}_{<i}]} + \frac{\Pr[\mathbf{E}_3^i]}{\Pr[\mathbf{X}_{<i}]}$$

$$\leq \Pr[\mathbf{X}_i | \mathbf{X}_{<i} \wedge \overline{\mathbf{E}_2^i} \wedge \overline{\mathbf{E}_3^i}] + \frac{1}{N}$$

where the last inequality holds via Claim 5, Claim 6 (which are stated next) and our assumption that $\Pr[\mathbf{X}_{<i}] \geq ((17\kappa_i TB \log^2 N + T^2)/N)^i$.

Claim 5. *For any $i \in [S]$, $iT + T^2 < N/2$, $2i \log N + 1 \leq N/2$ and $N \geq 64$, $Pr[\mathbf{E}_2^i] \leq \frac{5}{N^{2i}}$.*

Claim 6. *For any $i \in [S]$, $Pr[\mathbf{E}_3^i] \leq \left(\frac{T}{N}\right)^{i \log N}$.*

As before, we will prove Claim 5 and 6 in the full version of the paper. Readers may safely skip the proofs and assume these "knowledge-gaining events" happen with exponentially small probability.

Next, we want to study $\Pr[\mathbf{X}_i | \mathbf{X}_{<i} \wedge \overline{\mathbf{E}_2^i} \wedge \overline{\mathbf{E}_3^i}]$. We define $\mathbf{G}$ to be the event that input salt a_i has been queried among the previous $(i-1)$ iterations or that input salt a_i is the output of some query among the previous $(i-1)$ iterations. So, we can rewrite $\Pr[\mathbf{X}_i | \mathbf{X}_{<i} \wedge \overline{\mathbf{E}_2^i} \wedge \overline{\mathbf{E}_3^i}]$ as follows:

$$\Pr[\mathbf{X}_i | \mathbf{X}_{<i} \wedge \overline{\mathbf{E}_2^i} \wedge \overline{\mathbf{E}_3^i}] \leq \Pr[\mathbf{X}_i | \mathbf{X}_{<i} \wedge \overline{\mathbf{E}_2^i} \wedge \overline{\mathbf{E}_3^i} \wedge \overline{\mathbf{G}}] + \Pr\left[\mathbf{G} \middle| \mathbf{X}_{<i} \wedge \overline{\mathbf{E}_2^i} \wedge \overline{\mathbf{E}_3^i}\right]$$

$$\leq \Pr[\mathbf{X}_i | \mathbf{X}_{<i} \wedge \overline{\mathbf{E}_2^i} \wedge \overline{\mathbf{E}_3^i} \wedge \overline{\mathbf{G}}] + \frac{2(i-1)T}{N}.$$

Note that a_i is chosen uniformly and independently and as queries in the previous iterations could be made on at most $(i-1)T$ distinct salts and can output at most $(i-1)T$ distinct salts in the previous $(i-1)$ iterations, it is easy to bound

$$\Pr\left[\mathbf{G} \middle| \mathbf{X}_{<i} \wedge \overline{\mathbf{E}_2^i} \wedge \overline{\mathbf{E}_3^i}\right] \leq \frac{2(i-1)T}{N}.$$

Finally, we analyze $\Pr[\mathbf{X}_i | \mathbf{X}_{<i} \wedge \overline{\mathbf{E}_2^i} \wedge \overline{\mathbf{E}_3^i} \wedge \overline{\mathbf{G}}]$.

Claim 7. *For any $i \in [S]$,*

$$Pr[\mathbf{X}_i | \mathbf{X}_{<i} \wedge \overline{\mathbf{E}_2^i} \wedge \overline{\mathbf{E}_3^i} \wedge \overline{\mathbf{G}}] \leq \frac{16 \kappa_i T B \log^2 N + T^2}{N}.$$

Proof of Claim 7 requires different analysis for different types of colliding chains which we show in Subsect. 4.1. Before we move onto that subsection, we first show how we obtain the lemma by putting together all the claims.

$$\Pr[\mathbf{X}_i | \mathbf{X}_{<i}] \leq \Pr[\mathbf{X}_i | \mathbf{X}_{<i} \wedge \overline{\mathbf{E}_2^i} \wedge \overline{\mathbf{E}_3^i} \wedge \overline{\mathbf{G}}] + \Pr\left[\mathbf{G} \middle| \mathbf{X}_{<i} \wedge \overline{\mathbf{E}_2^i} \wedge \overline{\mathbf{E}_3^i}\right] + \Pr[\mathbf{E}_2^i \vee \mathbf{E}_3^i | \mathbf{X}_{<i}]$$

$$\leq \frac{16 \kappa_i T B \log^2 N + T^2}{N} + \frac{2(i-1)T}{N} + \frac{1}{N}$$

$$\leq \frac{17 \kappa_i T B \log^2 N}{N} + \frac{T^2}{N}$$

where the last inequality holds from that $\kappa_i = \max\{i, i^2 T^2 / N\}$ and $N \geq 4$.

4.1 Proof of Claim 7

To this end, we state the following claim.

Claim 8. *For any $i \in [S]$, to find a B-length collision on a_i, the queries in the database should satisfy at least one of the following conditions given there exists no query in the offline database that takes a_i as input or outputs a_i:*

1. *There exists an online query (i.e., a query among at most T queries that were made for the first time in the i-th iteration after receiving the challenge input a_i), denoted (a, m) such that $H(a, m) = a_i$.*
2. *There exists two distinct online queries, denoted (a, m) and (a', m') such that $H(a, m) = H(a', m')$.*
   This includes both of the following possibilities: the online queries are such (1) $a = a'$ (and thus m and m' will be distinct); (2) $a \neq a'$.
3. *There exists an online query, denoted (a, m), a chain (recall Definition 5) of offline queries[5], denoted $(b_1, m_1), \ldots, (b_\ell, m_\ell)$ for some $0 < \ell < B$, and an offline query $(b, m') \neq (b_\ell, m_\ell)$ such that $H(a, m) = b_1$, $H(b, m') = H(b_\ell, m_\ell)$ and the number of pre-images for every salt in $\{b_2, \ldots, b_\ell\}$ in the offline database is exactly 1.*

---

[5] The set of **Offline queries** is the set of distinct queries made in the previous $(i-1)$ iterations. So there are at most $(i-1)T$ of these queries and their outputs are independent and uniformly distributed. The set of **Online queries** is the set of distinct queries made in the i-th iteration after receiving the challenge input a_i that had not been made in any of the previous $(i-1)$ iterations. Note that the outputs of online queries are also independent and uniformly distributed.

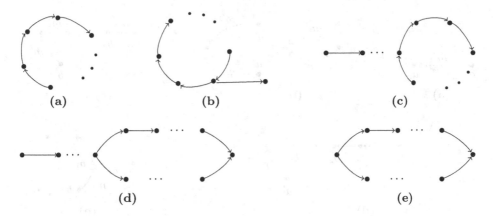

Fig. 12. All types of colliding chains

4. *There exists two online queries, denoted (a, m) and (a', m'), and a chain of offline queries, denoted $(b_1, m_1), \ldots, (b_\ell, m_\ell)$ for some $\ell < B$, such that $H(a, m) = b_1$, $H(a', m') = H(b_\ell, m_\ell)$ and the number of pre-images on every salt in $\{b_2, \ldots, b_\ell\}$ in the offline database is exactly 1.*

5. *There exists an online query, denoted (a, m), and a cycle in the offline database, denoted $(b_1, m_1), \ldots, (b_\ell, m_\ell)$ for some $\ell < B$, such that $H(a, m) = b_1$ and the number of pre-images on every salt in $\{b_1, b_2, \ldots, b_\ell\}$ in the offline database is exactly 1.*

Proof for Claim 8. Figure 12 enumerates all the possible types of colliding chains. Depending on where the queries in the chains are first made for each of the types, we show that the list of conditions in the claim is complete. (Refer to Fig. 13 for a visual representation of the conditions in the claim.)

We know that all the queries with output a_i or of the form $(a_i, \cdot)$ in the colliding chains are online queries. This implies if the colliding chains are of the types in Fig. 12a or 12b, the queries in the database will satisfy condition 1.

For the remaining types of colliding chains (ref Fig. 12c, 12d, 12e), one of the following 3 cases can happen:

1. **Both the 'colliding' queries are online.** In this case, the queries in the database will satisfy condition 2.
2. **Both the 'colliding' queries are offline.** In this case, the queries in the database will satisfy condition 3. Note that b_ℓ can be thought of as the earliest query among the chains that has more than one pre-image in the offline database.
3. **One of the 'colliding' queries is offline and online each.** For the colliding chains of types in Fig. 12d and 12e), the queries in the database will satisfy condition 4. For the colliding chains of type in Fig. 12c, there are two possibilities as shown in Fig. 14. For the possibility in Fig. 14a, the queries

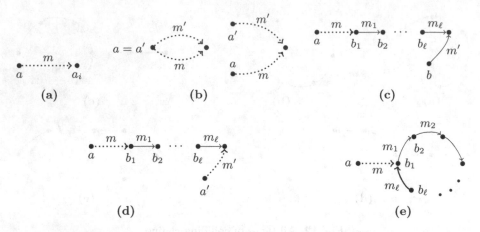

Fig. 13. Pictorial depiction of Conditions 1–5. A dotted line denotes an online query. A solid line denotes an offline query.

Fig. 14. A dotted line denotes an online query. A solid line denotes an offline query.

in the database satisfy condition 4. On the other hand, for the possibility in Fig. 14b, the queries in the database satisfy condition 5.

□

Claim 9. *For $j \in [5]$, let ϵ_j be the advantage in achieving condition j from Claim 8 when $\overline{\mathbf{E}_2^i}$, $\overline{\mathbf{E}_3^i}$ and $\overline{\mathbf{G}}$ hold. Then for any $i \in [S]$, the results summarized in Table 2 on the upper bounds of ϵ_j hold.*

Table 2. Summary of upper bounds on ϵ_j for $j \in [5]$ where $\kappa_i := \max\{i, i^2 T^2/N\}$.

Condition j	1	2	3	4	5
ϵ_j	$\frac{T}{N}$	$\frac{T^2}{N}$	$\frac{16\kappa_i TB \log^2 N}{N}$	$\frac{iT}{N} \cdot \frac{T^2}{N}$	$\frac{iTB \log N}{N}$

We prove the bounds stated in Claim 9 next.

Condition 1. Recall that online queries are 'new' queries, as in they are made for the first time among the T queries in the i-th iteration after receiving a_i. Thus, the output of online queries is independent of output from offline queries and has $1/N$ chance to be a_i under H via lazy sampling. By taking a union bound over at most T online queries, we can bound the probability to T/N.

Condition 2. By birthday bound, it holds that the probability of finding 'colliding' queries among T online queries is at most T^2/N.

Condition 3. Given $\overline{\mathbf{E}_2^i}$ implies that there can be at most $16\kappa_i \log^2 N$ queries in the offline database that are part of some claw. As per the definition of condition 4, there will be a unique chain of length $< B$ in the offline database ending in each of these at most $16\kappa_i \log^2 N$ queries, such that an online query hits the start of this chain. The probability of hitting one of these at most $B \cdot 16\kappa_i \log^2 N$ salts within T queries is at most $16\kappa_i TB \log^2 N/N$.

Condition 4. As per the definition of condition 5, there can be at most iT such chains of length $< B$ in the offline database, such that an online query hits the start of this chain and another online hits the end of this chain. The probability of hitting both the salts within at most T queries is bounded by T^2/N^2. By union bound the advantage is at most iT^3/N^2.

Condition 5. Given $\overline{\mathbf{E}_3^i}$ implies there are at most $i \log N$ 'special' cycles in the offline database, each with at most B queries in it. So, there are at most $iB \log N$ queries in these cycles and the probability of hitting one of the starting salts of these queries within T online queries is bounded by $iB \log N \cdot T/N$.

From Claim 9 it holds that the advantage of achieving any of the conditions in Claim 8 given $\overline{\mathbf{E}_2^i}$, $\overline{\mathbf{E}_3^i}$ and $\overline{\mathbf{G}}$ is bounded by $(16\kappa_i TB \log^2 N + T^2)/N$. Note that for $i \leq S$, when $ST^2 < N$ implies $iT^2 < N$. Hence $\kappa_i = i$ if $\kappa_S = S$.

$\square$

Acknowledgements. We thank CRYPTO reviewers and Xiaoqi Duan for their constructive comments. We thank Ashrujit Ghoshal and Ilan Komargodski for sharing an early draft of their work. Akshima is supported in part by NSF Grant No. 1925288. Siyao Guo is supported by National Natural Science Foundation of China Grant No.62102260, Shanghai Municipal Education Commission (SMEC) Grant No. 0920000169, NYTP Grant No. 20121201 and NYU Shanghai Boost Fund. Qipeng Liu is supported in part by the Simons Institute for the Theory of Computing, through a Quantum Postdoctoral Fellowship and by the DARPA SIEVE-VESPA grant No. HR00112020023. Any opinions, findings and conclusions or recommendations expressed in this material are those of the author(s) and do not necessarily reflect the views of the United States Government or DARPA.

References

[ACDW20] Akshima, Cash, D., Drucker, A., Wee, H.: Time-space tradeoffs and short collisions in Merkle-Damgård hash functions. In: Micciancio, D., Ristenpart, T. (eds.) CRYPTO 2020, Part I. LNCS, vol. 12170, pp. 157–186. Springer, Cham (2020). https://doi.org/10.1007/978-3-030-56784-2_6

[BR93] Bellare, M., Rogaway, P.: Random oracles are practical: a paradigm for designing efficient protocols. In: Proceedings of the 1st ACM Conference on Computer and Communications Security, pp. 62–73 (1993)

[CDG18] Coretti, S., Dodis, Y., Guo, S.: Non-uniform bounds in the random-permutation, ideal-cipher, and generic-group models. In: Shacham, H., Boldyreva, A. (eds.) CRYPTO 2018, Part I. LNCS, vol. 10991, pp. 693–721. Springer, Cham (2018). https://doi.org/10.1007/978-3-319-96884-1_23

[CDGS18] Coretti, S., Dodis, Y., Guo, S., Steinberger, J.: Random oracles and non-uniformity. In: Nielsen, J.B., Rijmen, V. (eds.) EUROCRYPT 2018, Part I. LNCS, vol. 10820, pp. 227–258. Springer, Cham (2018). https://doi.org/10.1007/978-3-319-78381-9_9

[CGK18] Corrigan-Gibbs, H., Kogan, D.: The discrete-logarithm problem with pre-processing. In: Nielsen, J.B., Rijmen, V. (eds.) EUROCRYPT 2018, Part II. LNCS, vol. 10821, pp. 415–447. Springer, Cham (2018). https://doi.org/10.1007/978-3-319-78375-8_14

[CGK19] Corrigan-Gibbs, H., Kogan, D.: The function-inversion problem: barriers and opportunities. In: Hofheinz, D., Rosen, A. (eds.) TCC 2019, Part I. LNCS, vol. 11891, pp. 393–421. Springer, Cham (2019). https://doi.org/10.1007/978-3-030-36030-6_16

[CGLQ20] Chung, K.-M., Guo, S., Liu, Q., Qian, L.: Tight quantum time-space tradeoffs for function inversion. In: Irani, S. (ed.) 61st IEEE Annual Symposium on Foundations of Computer Science, FOCS 2020, Durham, NC, USA, 16–19 November 2020, pp. 673–684. IEEE (2020)

[CHM20] Chawin, D., Haitner, I., Mazor, N.: Lower bounds on the time/memory tradeoff of function inversion. In: Pass, R., Pietrzak, K. (eds.) TCC 2020, Part III. LNCS, vol. 12552, pp. 305–334. Springer, Cham (2020). https://doi.org/10.1007/978-3-030-64381-2_11

[Dam89] Damgård, I.B.: A design principle for hash functions. In: Brassard, G. (ed.) CRYPTO 1989. LNCS, vol. 435, pp. 416–427. Springer, New York (1990). https://doi.org/10.1007/0-387-34805-0_39

[DGK17] Dodis, Y., Guo, S., Katz, J.: Fixing cracks in the concrete: random oracles with auxiliary input, revisited. In: Coron, J.-S., Nielsen, J.B. (eds.) EUROCRYPT 2017, Part II. LNCS, vol. 10211, pp. 473–495. Springer, Cham (2017). https://doi.org/10.1007/978-3-319-56614-6_16

[DTT10] De, A., Trevisan, L., Tulsiani, M.: Time space tradeoffs for attacks against one-way functions and PRGs. In: Rabin, T. (ed.) CRYPTO 2010. LNCS, vol. 6223, pp. 649–665. Springer, Heidelberg (2010). https://doi.org/10.1007/978-3-642-14623-7_35

[GGKL21] Gravin, N., Guo, S., Kwok, T.C., Lu, P.: Concentration bounds for almost k-wise independence with applications to non-uniform security. In: Proceedings of the 2021 ACM-SIAM Symposium on Discrete Algorithms, SODA 2021, Virtual Conference, 10–13 January 2021, pp. 2404–2423 (2021)

[GK22] Ghoshal, A., Komargodski, I.: On time-space tradeoffs for bounded-length collisions in Merkle-Damgård hashing. In: Dodis, Y., Shrimpton, T. (eds.) CRYPTO 2022, LNCS 13509, pp. 161–191 (2022)

[GLLZ21] Guo, S., Li, Q., Liu, Q., Zhang, J.: Unifying presampling via concentration bounds. In: Nissim, K., Waters, B. (eds.) TCC 2021, Part I. LNCS, vol. 13042, pp. 177–208. Springer, Cham (2021). https://doi.org/10.1007/978-3-030-90459-3_7

[Hel80] Hellman, M.E.: A cryptanalytic time-memory trade-off. IEEE Trans. Inf. Theory 26(4), 401–406 (1980)

[IK10] Impagliazzo, R., Kabanets, V.: Constructive proofs of concentration bounds. In: Serna, M., Shaltiel, R., Jansen, K., Rolim, J. (eds.) APPROX/RANDOM -2010. LNCS, vol. 6302, pp. 617–631. Springer, Heidelberg (2010). https://doi.org/10.1007/978-3-642-15369-3_46

[Mer89] Merkle, R.C.: A certified digital signature. In: Brassard, G. (ed.) CRYPTO 1989. LNCS, vol. 435, pp. 218–238. Springer, New York (1990). https://doi.org/10.1007/0-387-34805-0_21

[Unr07] Unruh, D.: Random oracles and auxiliary input. In: Menezes, A. (ed.) CRYPTO 2007. LNCS, vol. 4622, pp. 205–223. Springer, Heidelberg (2007). https://doi.org/10.1007/978-3-540-74143-5_12

Sustained Space and Cumulative Complexity Trade-Offs for Data-Dependent Memory-Hard Functions

Jeremiah Blocki$^{(\boxtimes)}$ and Blake Holman

Purdue University, West Lafayette, IN 47906, USA
{jblocki,holman14}@purdue.edu

Abstract. Memory-hard functions (MHFs) are a useful cryptographic primitive which can be used to design egalitarian proof of work puzzles and to protect low entropy secrets like passwords against brute-force attackers. Intuitively, a memory-hard function is a function whose evaluation costs are dominated by memory costs even if the attacker uses specialized hardware (FPGAs/ASICs), and several cost metrics have been proposed to quantify this intuition. For example, space-time cost looks at the product of running time and the maximum space usage over the entire execution of an algorithm. Alwen and Serbinenko (STOC 2015) observed that the space-time cost of evaluating a function multiple times may not scale linearly in the number of instances being evaluated and introduced the stricter requirement that a memory-hard function has high cumulative memory complexity (CMC) to ensure that an attacker's amortized space-time costs remain large even if the attacker evaluates the function on multiple different inputs in parallel. Alwen et al. (EUROCRYPT 2018) observed that the notion of CMC still gives the attacker undesirable flexibility in selecting space-time tradeoffs e.g., while the MHF Scrypt has maximal CMC $\Omega(N^2)$, an attacker could evaluate the function with constant $O(1)$ memory in time $O(N^2)$. Alwen et al. introduced an even stricter notion of Sustained Space complexity and designed an MHF which has $s = \Omega(N/\log N)$ sustained complexity $t = \Omega(N)$ i.e., any algorithm evaluating the function in the parallel random oracle model must have at least $t = \Omega(N)$ steps where the memory usage is at least $\Omega(N/\log N)$. In this work, we use dynamic pebbling games and dynamic graphs to explore tradeoffs between sustained space complexity and cumulative memory complexity for data-dependent memory-hard functions such as Argon2id and Scrypt. We design our own dynamic graph (dMHF) with the property that *any* dynamic pebbling strategy either (1) has $\Omega(N)$ rounds with $\Omega(N)$ space, or (2) has CMC $\Omega(N^{3-\epsilon})$—substantially larger than N^2. For Argon2id we show that *any* dynamic pebbling strategy either(1) has $\Omega(N)$ rounds with $\Omega(N^{1-\epsilon})$ space, or (2) has CMC $\omega(N^2)$. We also present a dynamic version of DRSample (Alwen et al. 2017) for which *any* dynamic pebbling strategy either (1) has $\Omega(N)$ rounds with $\Omega(N/\log N)$ space, or (2) has CMC $\Omega(N^3/\log N)$.

Keywords: Data-Dependent Memory Hard Function · Dynamic Pebbling Game · Sustained Space Complexity · Cumulative Memory Complexity

© International Association for Cryptologic Research 2022
Y. Dodis and T. Shrimpton (Eds.): CRYPTO 2022, LNCS 13509, pp. 222–251, 2022.
https://doi.org/10.1007/978-3-031-15982-4_8

1   Introduction

Memory-hard functions (MHFs) are an important cryptographic primitive which have been used to design egalitarian proof of work puzzles [16] and to protect low entropy secrets against brute-force attacks e.g., password hashing. Intuitively, a function is "memory-hard" if for *any* algorithm the costs associated with evaluating this function are dominated by memory costs—even if the attacker uses specialized hardware such as Field Programmable Gate Arrays (FPGAs) or Application Specific Integrated Circuits (ASICs). Several complexity measures have been proposed to capture this intuition including space-time complexity, cumulative memory complexity (CMC) [7], and sustained space complexity (SSC) [5].

Intuitively, space-time cost considers the product of running time and the maximum space usage across the entire execution trace. For example, suppose we are given an execution trace $\sigma_1, \ldots, \sigma_t$ where σ_i denotes the state of our program at time i. The space-time costs associated with this execution trace would be $t \cdot \max_{i \leq t} |\sigma_i|$. Alwen and Serbinenko [7] observed that space-time complexity is not well suited in situations where an attacker wants to evaluate the function on multiple different inputs in parallel. In particular, the amortized space-time costs associated with multiple parallel computations can be significantly lower than the space-time costs associated with a single execution. Alwen and Blocki [2] later gave pebbling attacks on practical MHF candidates such as Catena and Argon2i demonstrating that this concern is not merely a theoretical issue. Alwen and Serbinenko [7] proposed the notion of cumulative memory complexity (CMC) to address this concern by modeling amortized space-time complexity. Intuitively, the cumulative memory cost of our execution trace $\sigma_1, \ldots, \sigma_t$ would be given by $\sum_{i=1}^{t} |\sigma_i|$. Observe that the cumulative memory cost is a lower bound for the space-time costs since $\sum_{i=1}^{t} |\sigma_i| \leq t \times \max_{i \leq t} |\sigma_i|$. Thus, requiring that a MHF has high CMC is a strictly stronger requirement than space-time complexity.

If we adopt high CMC as our goal then we want to find a function f which satisfies the requirements that (1) the function can be evaluated in $O(N)$ steps on a sequential machine, and (2) any parallel algorithm evaluating the function has CMC at least $\Omega(N^2)$. We note that because the function can be evaluated in $O(N)$ sequential steps the CMC cannot be larger than $O(N^2)$. In fact, the Scrypt MHF [18] has been shown to satisfy both properties in the parallel random oracle model [6]. However, while Scrypt has maximal CMC the MHF also allows the attacker undesirable flexibility when selecting space-time trade-offs. For example, an attacker could evaluate Scrypt using constant space $O(1)$ in time $O(N^2)$ or the attacker could evaluate the function using space $O(\sqrt{N})$ and time $O(N\sqrt{N})$.

Motivated by this observation, Alwen et al. [5] introduced the stricter requirement of sustained space complexity (SSC). Returning to our example execution trace $\sigma_1, \ldots, \sigma_t$ we would say that this execution trace has s-Sustained Space complexity t' if $|\{i : |\sigma_i| \geq s\}| \geq t'$ i.e., there are at least t' steps where the memory usage exceeds s. We remark that $st' \leq \sum_i |\sigma_i|$ is a lower bound on the cumulative memory costs so the requirement that a MHF have high SSC is even stricter than requiring high CMC.

Broadly speaking there are two types of MHFs: data-independent memory-hard functions (iMHFs) and data-dependent memory-hard functions (dMHFs)[1]. In an iMHF, the memory access pattern induced by evaluating the function is not allowed to depend on the (potentially sensitive) input. By contrast, a dMHF places no restrictions on the memory access pattern. While iMHFs provide natural resistance to side-channel attacks, this comes at the cost of memory hardness. For example, Scrypt is a dMHF with CMC at least $\Omega(N^2)$ while *any* iMHF has CMC *at most* $O(N^2 \log \log N / \log N)$ [2]. In the context of password hashing hybrid "id" modes have been proposed to balance side-channel resistance with memory hardness. For example, the MHF Argon2id runs Argon2i (data-independent mode) for $N/2$ steps before switching to Argon2d (data-dependent mode). Optimistically, if there are no side-channel attacks we achieve stronger memory hardness. In the worst case, if there is a side-channel attack, the security of the hybrid mode (e.g., Argon2id) is downgraded to that of the data-independent mode (e.g., Argon2i).

Alwen et al. [5] gave a construction of an iMHF with $s = \Omega(N/\log N)$-sustained space complexity $\Omega(N)$ i.e., any algorithm evaluating this function in the parallel random oracle model requires at least $t' = \Omega(N)$ steps in which the space usage is at least $s = \Omega(N/\log N)$. We remark that this result is (essentially) optimal due to a pebbling result of Hopcroft [15] showing that any directed acyclic graph with N nodes and constant indegree can be pebbled using space at most $s = O(N/\log N)$. Thus, if $s = \omega(N/\log N)$ we cannot guarantee that there are *any* steps in which the space usage is at least s and this observation can be extended to dMHFs as well. However, the general $O(N/\log N)$-space pebbling strategy of Hopcroft [15] also requires exponential time so the cumulative cost of this pebbling strategy would be exponentially large. While the construction of Alwen et al. [5] was primarily theoretical, Blocki et al. [12] gave a practical iMHF construction with the following trade-off guarantee: any evaluation algorithm either (1) has CMC $\Omega(N^2)$ or (2) has $\Omega(N)$ rounds in which the space usage is at least $\Omega(N/\log N)$ space.

The construction of Blocki et al. [12] achieves (essentially) optimal trade-offs between CMC and SSC. While it is possible that the attacker's $s = \Omega(N/\log N)$ sustained space-complexity is lower than $\Omega(N)$ any such attack would incur a higher penalty on CMC costs. Similarly, general pebbling attacks of Alwen and Blocki [2] against any iMHF simultaneously achieve CMC $O(N^2 \log \log N/\log N)$ and there are also $o(N)$ rounds where the space usage exceeds $O(N \log \log N/\log N)$. However, trade-offs between CMC and SSC have not been explored for dMHFs where the general pebbling attacks of Alwen and Blocki [2] no longer apply. Thus, for a dMHF we might hope to achieve even stronger trade-offs e.g., it may

---

[1] Ameri et al. [9] also introduced the notion of a computationally data-independent memory-hard function where the memory access pattern is allowed to depend on the input, but should be computationally bounded adversary should not be able to detect or exploit this dependence.

be possible to find a dMHF with the property that any evaluation algorithm either (1) has $\Omega(N)$ rounds in which the space usage is at least $\Omega(N)$, or (2) has CMC at least $\omega(N^2)$.

In this paper, our focus will be on understanding and quantifying SSC and CMC trade-offs for data-dependent memory-hard Functions using dynamic graphs and dynamic pebbling games.

1.1   Our Results

Any attempt to solely analyze the SSC of a (dynamic or otherwise) pebbling graph will lead to weaker lower bounds. In fact, any DAG G with N nodes and constant indegree can be pebbled using at most $s = O\left(\frac{N}{\log N}\right)$ pebbles during any pebbling round [5,15]. We observe that the pebbling strategy of Hopcroft [15] easily extends to dynamic graphs. In particular, we can use Hopcroft's strategy [15] to place a pebble on node i using at most $i/\log i$ pebbles. We can then remove pebbles from all nodes except i and repeat this method to pebble node $i+1$ etc. Thus, if $\mathbb{G}$ is a distribution over DAGs G with constant indegree we can't hope to prove that pebbling G requires $\omega\left(\frac{N}{\log N}\right)$ pebbles for some number of steps, since its $\omega\left(\frac{N}{\log N}\right)$-SSC is zero. However, while Hopcroft's general pebbling strategy uses minimal space $O(N/\log N)$ the pebbling also runs in exponential time. Thus, we can still hope to establish stronger CMC/SSC trade-offs for dMHFs.

Ideally, we want to construct a dynamic pebbling graph in which any strategy must sustain $\Omega(N)$ nodes for $\Omega(N)$ steps, or incurs CC $\Omega(N^3)$. This is the best possible trade-off one could hope to achieve for dynamic graphs with constant indegree. To see this we observe that Lengauer and Tarjan [17] gave a general sequential pebbling strategy for any (static) DAG G with maximum indegree $\delta = O(1)$ and any space parameter $S = \Omega(N/\log N)$. In particular, pebbling strategy at most S pebbles and takes time *at most* using time $t \leq S \cdot 2^{2^{c\delta N/S}}$ where δ denotes the indegree of the DAG G and $c > 0$ is some fixed constant. The strategy can be extended to dynamic graphs i.e., once we have place a pebble on node i we can apply the strategy of Lengauer and Tarjan [17] to place a pebble on node $i+1$ using time at most $t_{i+1} \leq S \cdot 2^{2^{c\delta(i+1)/S}} \leq S2^{2^{c\delta N/S}}$. In this way we obtain a dynamic pebbling strategy which uses space *at most* S and the total pebbling time is at most $\sum_i t_i \leq S \cdot N \cdot 2^{2^{c\delta N/S}}$ —the CC is at most $S^2 \cdot N \cdot 2^{2^{c\delta N/S}}$. Assume that $\mathbb{G}$ is a distribution over DAGs with constant indegree ($\delta = O(1)$). Now for any constant $\epsilon > 0$ if we plugin $S = \epsilon N$ then we obtain a dynamic pebbling strategy which uses space at most ϵN and the CC is *at most* $O(N^3)$. Similarly, if we set $S = c\delta N/\log\log N$ then we obtain a pebbling which uses space at most $O(N/\log\log N)$ and the CC is at most $O\left(\frac{N^3 \log N}{(\log\log N)^2}\right)$. See more details in the full version of the paper.

We analyze CMC/SSC tradeoffs for four dMHFs. The first dMHF that we analyze is based on a constant indegree dynamic graph that we construct. While the construction is primarily of theoretical interest it achieves (essentially) optimal CMC/SSC tradeoffs—either there are $\Omega(N)$ steps with $\Omega(N)$ pebbles or the cumulative memory complexity is $\Omega(N^{3-\epsilon})$. The second dMHF that we analyze is based on a family of depth-robust graphs [14] with indegree $O(\log N)$. We introduce dynamic edges and prove that (whp) either there are $\Omega(N)$ steps with $\Omega(N)$ pebbles or the cumulative memory complexity is $\Omega(N^3)$. While the first two dMHFs are primarily of theoretical interest we also analyze CMC/SSC tradeoffs for two practical dMHF candidates including Argon2id [10] (winner of the password hashing competition) and DRSample [3]. Our results are summarized in Table 1 below.

Table 1. Lower Bounds: SSC vs CC Tradeoffs

Dynamic Graph	Space Sustained for $\Omega(N)$ steps	CC
Scrypt [6]	$O(1)$	$O(N^2)$
Dynamic EGS (Sec 4)	$\Omega(N)$	$\Omega(N^3)$
Dynamic DRSample (Sec 5)	$\Omega\left(\frac{N}{\log N}\right)$	$\Omega\left(\frac{N^3}{\log N}\right)$
Argon2id (Sec 6)	$e \leq N$	$\tilde{\Omega}(N^4 e^{-2})$
Argon2id (Example)	$\Omega(N^{1-\epsilon})$	$\tilde{\Omega}(N^{2+2\epsilon})$
Our Construction (Sec 3)	$\Omega(N)$	$\Omega(N^{3-\epsilon})$

Before we elaborate on each of these results, we first describe dynamic pebbling graphs and pebbling strategies in more detail.

1.2   Dynamic Graphs and Dynamic Pebbling Games

Review: Black Pebbling Games and iMHFs. Before introducing dynamic graphs and dynamic pebbling games we first review the parallel black pebbling game for regular (static) graphs. The (parallel) black pebbling game is a powerful abstraction that has been used to analyze the cumulative memory complexity (or sustained space complexity) of iMHFs in the random oracle model. In the parallel black pebbling game we are given a directed acyclic graph (DAG) G which initially contains no pebbles $P_0 = \{\}$ and the goal of the pebbling game is to eventually pebble the sink node(s) of G. A legal black pebbling is a sequence $P_0, \ldots, P_t \subseteq V$ of pebbling configurations such that (0) $P_0 = \{\}$ (1) $V \subseteq \bigcup_i P_i$, and (2) for all $i < t$ and for each $v \in P_{i+1} \setminus P_i$ we have $\mathsf{parents}(v) \doteq \{u : (u,v) \in E\} \subseteq P_i$. Intuitively, each node in G corresponds to an intermediate data label, and placing a pebbling on the graph corresponds to computing the corresponding data label and placing it in memory. We initially start with no data labels in memory (rule 0) and are not finished until we have computed all of the output labels (rule 1). We also cannot compute a new data label unless all of the dependent data labels are already available in memory (rule 2). In the sequential black pebbling game, we also require that we place at most one new pebble on the graph in each round (i.e., $|P_{i+1} \setminus P_i| \leq 1$), while no such constraint applies in the parallel black pebbling game.

An iMHF $f_{G,H}(x)$ can be viewed as a mode of operation over a DAG G and a hash function H (typically modeled as a random oracle). The source label $L_1 = H(x)$ is typically obtained by hashing the input x and the label of a node $v > 1$ is obtained by hashing the labels of v's parents in G e.g., if $\mathsf{parents}(v) = \{v - 1, r(v)\}$ then we might set $L_v = H(L_{v-1}, L_{r(v)})$. The output of the function $f_{G,H}$ is simply the label L_N of the final sink node N—if there are multiple sink nodes the output can be obtained by concatenating all of these labels together. Alwen and Serbinenko [7] proved that in the parallel random oracle model the cumulative memory complexity of the function $f_{G,H}$ is completely captured by the pebbling complexity of the graph G, and Alwen et al. [5] later observed that essentially the same pebbling reduction extends to the notion of sustained space complexity. Here, the cumulative pebbling cost of a pebbling $P = (P_1, \ldots, P_t)$ is $\sum_{i=1}^{t} |P_i|$ and the s-sustained space cost is $|\{i : |P_i| \geq s\}|$ i.e., the number of pebbling rounds with *at least* s pebbles on the graph. The cumulative pebbling complexity (resp. s-sustained space complexity) of a graph G is the minimum cumulative pebbling cost (resp. s-sustained space cost) taken over all legal black pebblings of G.

dMHFs and Dynamic Graphs. For an iMHF $f_{G,H}$ the data-dependency graph G is completely independent of the input x. By contrast, for a dMHF we might get a different data-dependency graph for each different input x. For example, in Scrypt there are $2N$ internal labels and the label for node $N + i$ is computed using the rule $L_{N+i} = H\left(L_{N+i-1} \oplus L_{1+(L_{N+i-1} \bmod N)}\right)$. Thus, the data-dependence graph will contain a directed edge from node $r(N + i) = 1 + (L_{N+i-1} \bmod N)$ to node $N+i$ where the value $r(N+i)$ depends on the label L_{N+i-1} and, by extension, the input x. We call this edge $(r(N + i), N + i)$ a dynamic edge since it is not fixed a priori and the value $r(N + i)$ will remain hidden until label L_{N+i-1} is computed i.e., until we place a pebble on node $N + i - 1$.

In this paper we will use the notion of a dynamic pebbling game to model the complexity of a dMHF. We begin by defining a dynamic pebbling graph following the notation of [9].

Definition 1 (Dynamic Pebbling Graph [9]). *A dynamic pebbling graph* $\mathbb{G}$ *is a distribution over DAGs* $G = (V, E)$ *with nodes* $V = [N]$ *and edges* $E \subseteq \{(i, j) : 1 \leq i < j \leq N\}$. *We say that an edge* (i, j) *is* static *if for all DAGs* $G = (V, E)$ *in the support of* $\mathbb{G}$ *we have* $(i, j) \in E$ *and we let* $E_{\text{static}} \subseteq \{(i, j) : 1 \leq i < j \leq N\}$ *denote the set of all* static *edges. Similarly, we use* $E_{\text{dynamic}} = E \setminus E_{\text{static}}$ *to refer to the set of* dynamic *edges which are not fixed a priori and for each node* $j \in V$ *we use* $E_{\text{dynamic}}^{j} = \{(i, j) : (i, j) \in E_{\text{dynamic}}\}$ *to denote the set of incoming dynamic edges. In the dynamic pebbling game each dynamic edge* $(i, j) \in E_{\text{dynamic}}^{j}$ *is not revealed until node* $j - 1$ *is pebbled.*

All of the dynamic pebbling graphs $\mathbb{G}$ *considered in this paper have the additional property that for each DAG* $G = (V, E)$ *in the support of* $\mathbb{G}$ *and each node* $j \in V$ *we have* $\left|E_{\text{dynamic}}^{j}\right| \leq 1$ *i.e.,* j *has at most* one *incoming dynamic edge.*

Whenever $\left|E^j_{\text{dynamic}}\right| = 1$ *it will be convenient to use* $r(j)$ *to denote the randomly chosen parent of node* j *i.e.,* $E^j_{\text{dynamic}} = \{(r(j), j)\}$.

Strategies for pebbling such graphs can simply be thought of as algorithms, which place pebbles according to some set of instructions, possibly reacting to the dynamic edges as they are discovered. More formally, strategies are functions that output legal pebbling steps when given a partial graph.

Definition 2 (Dynamic Pebbling Strategy). *A dynamic pebbling strategy* $\mathcal{S}$ *is a function that takes as input*

1. *an integer* $i \leq N$,
2. *an initial pebbling configuration* $P^i_0 \subseteq [i]$ *with* $i \in P^i_0$, *and*
3. *a partial graph* $G_{\leq i+1}$,

where the partial graph $G_{\leq i}$ *is the subgraph of* G *induced by the nodes* $1, \ldots, i$. *The output of* $\mathcal{S}(i, P^i_0, G_{\leq i+1})$ *is a legal sequence of pebbling moves* $P^i_1, \ldots, P^i_{r}$ *that will be used in the next phase to place a pebble on node* $i+1$, *so that* $i+1 \in P^i_{r_i} \subseteq [i+1]$. *Given* $G \sim \mathbb{G}$, *we let* $\mathcal{S}(G)$ *denote the sequence of pebbling moves* $\left\langle P^0_1, \ldots, P^0_{r0}, P^1_1, \ldots, P^{N-1}_{r_1}, \ldots, P^{N-1}_{r_{N-1}} \right\rangle$. *Here,* $P^i_1, \ldots, P^i_{r_i} = \mathcal{S}\left(i, P^i_0, G_{\leq i+1}\right)$, $P^i_0 = P^{i-1}_{r_{i-1}}$, *and* $P^0_0 = \emptyset$. *We call* $\mathcal{S}(G)$ *a pebbling (for* G.*)*

We note that even after a the pebbling strategy $\mathcal{S}$ is fixed the final pebbling $\mathcal{S}(G)$ is not determined until the graph $G \sim \mathbb{G}$ has been chosen i.e., all of the dynamic edges have been revealed. In particular, this means that the cumulative (resp. sustained-space) cost associated with $\mathcal{S}$ can also vary depending on which dynamic edges are sampled. However, once $\mathcal{S}$ and G are fixed we can define the cumulative pebbling cost of $P = \mathcal{S}(G) = \langle P_1, \ldots, P_T \rangle$ as $\sum_{i=1}^{T} |P_i|$. Similarly, the s-sustained space cost is $|\{i : |P_i| \geq s\}|$. Our dynamic pebbling dMHF lower-bounds will take the following form for any dynamic pebbling strategy $\mathcal{S}$ with high probability (over the sampling of $G \sim \mathbb{G}$) when $P = (P_1, \ldots, P_T) = \mathcal{S}(G)$ we either have (1) $\sum_{i=1}^{T} |P_i| \geq LB_1(N)$, or (2) $|\{i : |P_i| \geq s\}| \geq LB_2(N)$. Where the value s and the exact functions LB_1 and LB_2 will depend on the particular dMHF we are analyzing.

Open Research Challenge: Dynamic Pebbling Reductions. For iMHFs it is known that, in the parallel random oracle model, the cumulative memory complexity of the function $f_{G,H}$ is fully characterized by the cumulative pebbling cost of the corresponding data-dependency graph G similar for sustained space complexity [5]. By contrast, there is no formal reduction proving that the cumulative memory complexity (resp. sustained space complexity) of a dMHF is captured by the dynamic pebbling game. In this sense a dynamic pebbling lower bound would not absolutely rule out the possibility of a more efficient attack—unless one can establish a dynamic pebbling reduction. Establishing a formal reduction between dynamic pebbling costs and the cumulative memory complexity of the associated dMHF is a major open research challenge. In the meantime, we can still interpret a dynamic pebbling lower bound as ruling out "natural" attacks and providing compelling evidence that the associated dMHF is secure.

1.3   Trade-Offs for dMHFs

Now we elaborate on the results shown in Table 1.

Our Construction. We construct a dMHF (dynamic graph) with constant indegree and prove that for *any* pebbling strategy S that, except with negligible probability over the sampled graph $G \sim \mathbb{G}$, the pebbling $P = (P_1, \ldots, P_T) = S(G)$ satisfies either (1) $|\{i \in [T] : |P_i| \geq c_1 N\}| \geq c_2 N$, or (2) $\sum_{i=1}^{T} |P_i| \geq c_3 N^{3-\epsilon}$. Here, $\epsilon > 0$ can be arbitrary and the constants $c_1, c_2, c_3 > 0$ depend only on ϵ. We remark that the naive sequential pebbling strategy (i.e., set $P_i = \{1, \ldots, i\}$ for each $i = 1, \ldots, N$) has $s = N/2$-sustained space complexity $N/2$ and cumulative memory cost $O(N^2)$. Our results tell us that any pebbling strategy with lower sustained space complexity *must* pay a massive penalty in terms of a higher CMC cost.

Dynamic EGS. The second graph we examine is based on a family of depth-robust graphs constructed by Erdős et al., which we call EGS [14]. While the indegree $O(\log N)$ of these graphs is a bit larger than we might desire, the cumulative pebbling cost of the graph G is $\Omega(N^2)$ [4]. However, the sustained space-complexity of EGS has not been studied previously. We add dynamic edges to EGS to obtain a dynamic graph and show that, for suitable choices of the constants $c_1, c_2, c_3 > 0$, (whp) the pebbling $(P_1, \ldots, P_T) = S(G)$ produced by any dynamic pebbling strategy satisfies either (1) $|\{i : |P_i| \geq c_1 N\}| \geq c_2 N$ or (2) $\sum_{i=1}^{T} |P_i| \geq c_3 N^3$. In particular, either there are $\Omega(N)$ rounds where the space usage is $\Omega(N)$ or the cumulative pebbling cost is massive $\Omega(N^3)$.

Dynamic DRSample. We next consider DRSample, a randomized algorithm that, except with negligible probability, outputs a DAG G with cumulative pebbling cost $\Omega\left(\frac{N^2}{\log N}\right)$ and maximum indegree 2 [3]. Alwen et al. [3] implemented the corresponding iMHF and demonstrated that it is practical i.e., the execution time for a graph on N nodes is equivalent to Argon2i. While the intended use case for DRSample was to generate a static DAG G for an iMHF $f_{G,H}$ we can easily modify the definition to include dynamic (data-dependent) edges. We prove that the dynamic version $\mathbb{G}$ of DRSample achieves the following CMC/SMC trade-offs: for any dynamic pebbling strategy S with high probability (over the selection of $G \sim \mathbb{G}$) the pebbling $(P_1, \ldots, P_T) = S(g)$ either satisfies (1) $|\{i : |P_i| \geq c_1 N/\log N\}| \geq c_2 N$, or (2) $\sum_{i=1}^{T} |P_i| \geq c_3 N^3/\log N$. In particular, either there are $\Omega(N)$ rounds with $\Omega(N/\log N)$ pebbles on the graph or we pay a massive penalty in our cumulative pebbling costs.

Argon2id. Argon2 is a collection MHFs that won the Password Hashing Competition in 2015 [1]. There are three modes of Argon2: Argon2i, Argon2d, and Argon2id. The Argon2 designers initially recommended Argon2i (data-independent mode) for password hashing to protect against side-channel attacks. This recommendation was later changed to Argon2id (hybrid mode) after Alwen and Blocki [2,8] found pebbling attacks on Argon2i which reduced the cumulative memory complexity—the pebbling attacks do no extend to data-dependent modes such as Argon2id. While Argon2i has weaker theoretical guarantees than DRSample [3,13], Argon2 is available in cryptographic libraries such as libsodium and has seen wider use in practice. In particular, the cumulative complexity of Argon2i is at most $O(N^{1.768})$ and at least $\tilde{\Omega}(N^{1.75})$. We are able to establish stronger tradeoffs for Argon2id. In particular, for any parameter e and any pebbling strategy $\mathcal{S}$ we can show that (except with negligible probability over the selection of the graph $G \sim \mathbb{G}$) the pebbling $(P_1, \ldots, P_t) = \mathcal{S}(G)$ satisfies either (1) $|\{i : |P_i| \ge e\}| \ge c_1 N$, or (2) $\sum_{i=1}^{T} |P_i| \ge c_2 N^4 e^{-2} \log^{-c_3} N$ for suitable constants $c_1, c_2, c_3 > 0$. As a concrete example if we set $e = N^{1-\epsilon}$ there are $\Omega(N)$ rounds with at least e pebbles or the cumulative memory cost is at least $\tilde{\Omega}(N^{2+2\epsilon}) = \omega(N^2)$. We remark that one can separately prove an absolute lower bound of $\Omega(N^2)$ for the cumulative pebbling complexity of Argon2id.

1.4 Technical Overview

We develop two techniques for proving CMC/SSC trade-offs for dynamic graphs. The first general technique is to define an indicator random variable $\mathsf{unlucky}_i$ for each dynamic edge $(r(i), i)$. Intuitively, we define $\mathsf{unlucky}_i = 1$ to be the event that either (1) the dynamic pebbling strategy already had a lot of pebbles (say $s = \Omega(N)$) on the graph when the edge $(r(i), i)$ was revealed, or (2) the particular choice edge $(r(i), i)$ will require us to re-pebble a lot of previously pebbled nodes. Our general strategy is to argue that the following:

1. For any sequence of bits $b_1, \ldots, b_{i-1} \in \{0, 1\}$ we have $\Pr[\mathsf{unlucky}_i \mid \forall j < i, \mathsf{unlucky}_j = b_j] \ge p$. While the events $\mathsf{unlucky}_i$ do not need to be independent, the conditional probability that $\mathsf{unlucky}_i$ is always $\ge p$ for any prior outcomes $\mathsf{unlucky}_1, \ldots, \mathsf{unlucky}_{i-1}$.
2. For some suitable constant $c \in (0, 1)$ and any $i \in [cN, N]$ with $\mathsf{unlucky}_i = 1$ either we had $s = \Omega(N)$ pebbles on the graph when $r(i)$ was revealed or the cumulative pebbling cost to place a pebble on node i will be high (say M)
3. We apply generalized concentration bounds to argue that (whp) we have $\sum_{i=cN}^{N} \mathsf{unlucky}_i \ge p(1 - c)N/2$.
4. Assuming there are at least $p(1-c)N/2$ unlucky rounds $i > cN$ we either (1) have $s = \Omega(N)$ pebbles on the graph for $p(1-c)N/4$ pebbling rounds, or (2) we pay CMC cost at least M at least $p(1-c)N/4$ separate times for a total cost of $p(1-c)NM/4$.

To prove our SSC/CMC trade-offs for Argon2id we generalize and a technique introduced in [6] to analyze `Scrypt`. In particular, [6] observed that if we start with e pebbles on a line graph and are challenged to re-pebble a random node $r(i)$ on the line graph then it will take us at least $\frac{N}{4e}$ steps in expectation to place a pebble on a random node $r(i)$. Suppose that $r(i)$ is revealed at time t_1 and a pebble is placed on node $r(i)$ at time $t_2 \geq t_1$. The challenge $r(i)$ is called "easy" if for some $t \leq t_2$ there were fewer than $|P_{t_2-t}| < \frac{N}{8t}$ pebbles on the graph at time $t_2 - t$—in this case even if $r(i)$ had been revealed at time $t_2 - t$ we would have expected that it takes at least $\frac{N}{4\frac{N}{8t}} = 2t$ rounds to place a pebble on node $r(i)$. Thus, there is a good chance (at least $\frac{1}{2}$) that the challenge $r(i)$ is "hard" meaning that $|P_{t_2-t}| \geq \frac{N}{8t}$ for every $t \leq t_2$. Alwen et al. [6] then apply concentration bounds to argue that there are a lot of "hard" rounds which allowed them to prove that (whp) the cumulative pebbling cost for Scrypt is at least $\Omega(N^2)$.

We can generalize the argument of Alwen et al. [6] by exploiting the fact that Argon2i provides stronger (fractional) depth-robustness guarantees than the line graph [13]. In particular, if we start with with e pebbles on Argon2i and are challenged to place a pebble on a random node $r(i)$ we can argue that it will take us at least $\tilde{\Omega}\left((N/e)^3\right)$ steps to re-pebble node $r(i)$ in expectation. With this observation in mind we can redefine "hard" challenges to require that $|P_{t_2-t}| = \tilde{\Omega}((N/t)^3)$ for every $t \leq t_2$—where t_2 is the time when we actually placed a pebble on node $r(i)$. Fixing $e = N^{1-\epsilon}$ we can argue that either (1) there are $\Omega(N)$ rounds with at least e pebbles on the graph, or (2) there are a lot of "hard" rounds where we started with at most e pebbles on the graph. In the second case we can argue that the cumulative pebbling cost is at least $\tilde{\Omega}(N^{2+2\epsilon})$.

Our Construction. We construct a family of dynamic graphs $\mathbb{G}_D^N$ with $O(N)$ nodes and indegree 2 which has essentially optimal CMC/SSC tradeoffs. We rely on several building blocks to construct our dynamic graphs. The first building block is the notion of a maximally ST-robust graph which was recently introduced by Blocki and Cinkoske [11]. Intuitively, a maximally ST-robust graph is a DAG G with has N inputs (sources) and N outputs (sinks) with the following property: for any $k \leq N$ we can delete any subset S of k nodes from the graph and there will remain subsets A of $|A| \geq N - k$ inputs and B of $|B| \geq N - k$ outputs such that *for every pair* $u \in A, v \in B$ the graph $G - S$ still contains a directed path from u to v. Blocki and Cinkoske [11] gave a construction of a maximally ST-robust graph with linear size $O(N)$ and constant indegree. The second building block is a family of depth-robust graphs which we overlay on top of the source nodes of our maximally ST-robust graph. Finally, we add our data-dependent layer such that each dynamic edge $(r(i), i)$ uses a uniformly random output node $r(i)$ from our maximally ST-robust graph. Intuitively, when $r(i)$ is revealed we will get "unlucky" if either we have more than k pebbles on the graph or $r(i) \in B$, which happens with probability at least $1 - k/N$. Then whenever we get unlucky, we either have many pebbles on the graph or we will need to repebble the entire set A of $N - k$ inputs before node $r(i)$ can be pebbled. By overlaying a depth-robust graph over the input nodes we can ensure that either (1) $k = \Omega(N)$, or (2) we get unlucky with constant probability and repebbling A requires cumulative cost $\Omega(N^{2-\epsilon})$. If we get unlucky a linear number of times with respect to N (which happens with overwhelming probability) then we either sustained $\Omega(N)$ pebbles for $\Omega(N)$ steps or incurred CC $\Omega(N^{3-\epsilon})$

Dynamic EGS. To prove our CMC/SSC trade-off for EGS we primarily rely on the known observation that these graphs $G = (V = [N], E)$ satisfy a key property called δ-*local expansion*. If G is a δ-local expander, then for any $S \subseteq [N]$, the graph $G - S$ contains a directed path of length $N - O(|S|)$. Intuitively, if we started with pebbles on S and we were challenged to place a pebble on one of the last cN nodes on this directed path then we would need to repebble $(1 - c)N - O(|S|)$ nodes beforehand. For a suitable constant $0 < c < 1$ if $|S| = o(N)$ we can argue that the cumulative memory cost associated with repebbling $r(i)$ would be at least $\Omega(N^2)$ in this case. Observing that the probability of getting an unlucky challenge is at least $cN/N = c$ it follows that there are at least $\Omega(N)$ unlucky challenges. Thus, we either have $\Omega(N)$ challenge rounds where our initial space usage was $\Omega(N)$ or we have $\Omega(N)$ challenge rounds where we pay CMC cost $\Omega(N^2)$—in the later case our total CMC cost is $\Omega(N^3)$.

Dynamic DRSample. Our argument follows a similar pattern as our dynamic pebbling analysis of EGS. One key difference is that the DRSample graph G is less depth-robust than EGS due to the fact that DRSample has constant indegree. Instead we rely on the notion of a "metagraph" where groups of $O(\log N)$ nodes in DRSample are "merged" into a single metanode. Alwen et al. [3] showed that the metagraph G' for DRSample had $N' = O(N/\log N)$ nodes and satisfied the key-property that for every subset $S' \subseteq [N']$ of metanodes that the graph $G' - S'$ still had a path of length $(1 - \eta)N' - O(|S'|)$ for some suitably small constant $\eta > 0$. A path in the metagraph extrapolates back to a path of length $O(N)$ in the original graph. At this point our argument is similar to EGS with the difference that repebbling the graph will be expensive when we begin the challenge with more than $N' = O(N/\log N)$ pebbles on the graph. Thus, we can argue that either (1) we have $\Omega(N)$ challenge rounds where we start with $\Omega(N/\log N)$ pebbles on the graph or (2) there are at least $\Omega(N)$ challenge rounds where we start with fewer than $O(N/\log N)$ pebbles on the graph and we pay CMC costs $\Omega(N^2/\log N)$ to repebble nodes while responding to the challenge complete the challenge. In the latter case the total CMC cost over all challenge rounds is $\Omega(N^3/\log N)$.

2   Preliminaries

We let $[N] = \{1, 2, \ldots, N\}$ and $[i : j] = \{i, i + 1, \ldots, j - 1, j\}$. For any list $A = \langle a_1, \ldots, a_n \rangle$, we let A_i denote the ith entry of A. For a DAG $G = (V, E)$ and any set S, we let $G - S$ denote the graph $G' = (V', E')$ such that $V' = V \setminus S$ and $E' = \{(u, v) \mid (u, v) \in E, u, v \in V'\}$. We use $\texttt{indeg}(G, v) = |\{u : (u, v) \in E\}|$ to denote the indegree of a node $v \in V$ and $\mathrm{indeg}(G) = \max_{v \in V} |\{u : (u, v) \in E\}|$ to denote the maximum indegree of the DAG. For a dynamic pebbling graph $\mathbb{G}$ we use $\mathrm{indeg}(\mathbb{G}) = \max_{G \in \mathrm{sup}(\mathbb{G})} \mathrm{indeg}(G)$ to denote the maximum indegree of any DAG in the support of $\mathbb{G}$. Whenever we implicitly refer to some $x \in \mathbb{R}$ as an integer, we always mean $\lfloor x \rfloor$. For example, $[x] = \{1, 2, \ldots, \lfloor x \rfloor\}$. For some set S, we use the notation $y \in_R S$ to indicate that y is sampled from S uniformly at random.

2.1 Dynamic Pebbling Notation

We formalize some convenient pebbling notation. Fix some dynamic pebbling strategy $\mathcal{S}$, $G = ([N], E)$, and let $P = \mathcal{S}(G) = \langle P_1, \ldots, P_T \rangle$ be the pebbling that is produced when $G = (V, E) \sim \mathbb{G}$ is sampled. For each $v \in V$ let $\mathrm{parents}_G(i) = \{j \mid (j, i) \in E\}$ denote the parents of node v. When the graph G is clear from context we will omit G from the subscript and simply write $\mathrm{parents}(i)$. For $i \in [N]$ in which there exists a dynamic edge $(r(i), i)$, let $P(i)$ denote the pebbling configuration during the round $s(i)$ when $r(i)$ was first discovered. That is, $P(i) = P_{s(i)}$, where

$$s(i) = \begin{cases} 1 & \text{if } i = 1, \text{ and} \\ \min\{j \in [T] \mid i - 1 \in P_j\} & \text{otherwise.} \end{cases}$$

Similarly, we let $t(i) = \min_{k \geq s(i) \in [T]} \{k \mid r(i) \in P_k\}$ denotes the first round in which $r(i)$ is pebbled after $r(i)$ is revealed in round $s(i)$.

2.2 Generalized Hoeffding Inequality

The pebbling $P = \mathcal{S}(G)$ and its associated costs will depend on the particular graph $G \sim \mathbb{G}$. Thus, when analyzing the cumulative memory complexity and/or sustained space complexity of a dynamic graph we are inherently making a probabilistic claim. In particular, we would like to argue that a particular lower bound on the pebbling cost of $\mathcal{S}(G)$ holds with high probability—over the selection of $\mathcal{G} \sim \mathbb{G}$. We use the Generalized Hoeffding's Inequality to lowerbound these values [6].

Lemma 1 (Generalized Hoeffding's Inequality [6]). *If $V_1, \ldots, V_Q$ are binary random variables such that for any i $(0 \leq i \leq Q)$ and any values $v_1, v_2, \ldots, v_i$,*

$$\Pr[V_{i+1} = 1 \mid V_1 = v_1, \ldots, V_i = v_i] \geq \rho, \tag{1}$$

then for any $\epsilon > 0$, with probability at least $1 - e^{-2\epsilon^2 Q}$, $\sum_{i=1}^{Q} V_i \geq Q(\mu - \epsilon)$.

2.3 Useful Graphs and Their Pebbling Complexity

Naturally, we define notions of measuring the time-space requirements for pebbling dynamic graphs. Cumulative complexity refers to the total number of pebbles used at each step to pebble a graph, while sustained space complexity describes how many steps a certain amount of pebbles were on the graph.

Definition 3 (Pebbling Complexity). *Let $\mathbb{G}$ be a dynamic pebbling graph, G be a graph in the sample space of $\mathbb{G}$, $\mathcal{P}$ be the set of legal pebblings of G, and $\mathcal{S}$ be the set of pebbling strategies for $\mathbb{G}$. We define the cumulative complexity of a*

- *pebbling $P = \langle P_1, \ldots, P_T \rangle \in \mathcal{P}$ as $\mathrm{cc}(P) = \sum_{i=1}^{T} |P_i|$,*
- *a sequence of pebbling moves $\langle P_i, \ldots, P_j \rangle$ as $\mathrm{cc}(P, i, j) = \sum_{k=i}^{j} |P_k|$*
- *graph G as $\mathrm{cc}(G) = \min_{P \in \mathcal{P}} \{\mathrm{cc}(P)\}$, and*
- *dynamic pebbling graph $\mathbb{G}$ as $\mathrm{cc}(G) \min_{S \in \mathcal{S}} \{\mathbb{E}_{G \sim \mathbb{G}}[\mathrm{cc}(S(G))]\}$.*

Likewise, we define the s-sustained space complexity of a

- *pebbling P as $\mathrm{ss}(P, s) = |\{i \mid |P_i| \geq s, i \in [T]\}|$,*
- *graph G as $\mathrm{ss}(G, s) = \min_{P \in \mathcal{P}} \{\mathrm{ss}(P, s)\}$, and*
- *dynamic pebbling graph $\mathbb{G}$ as $\min_{S \in \mathcal{S}} \{\mathbb{E}_{G \sim \mathbb{G}}[\mathrm{ss}(S(G), s)]\}$.*

For notational purposes, we also define the opposite of s-sustained space complexity called (p, ℓ)-low memory.

Definition 4 (Low Memory Pebbling). *Let S be a pebbling strategy for a graph distribution $\mathbb{G}$ and G be any graph in the sample space of $\mathbb{G}$. We say that $P = S(G)$ is a (p, ℓ)-low memory pebbling for G if*

1. *there exists $A \subseteq [T]$ such that $|A| \leq \ell N$, and*
2. *for all $i \in A \setminus [T]$ we have $|P_i| \leq pN$.*

The cumulative complexity of a graph is tightly correlated with the notion of depth robustness, the property of a graph having long paths even when many nodes are removed from the graph.

Definition 5 (Depth Robustness). *A DAG $G = (V, E)$ is (e, d)-depth robust if for any $S \subseteq V$ of size at most e, there exists a path of length d in $G - S$.*

Throughout this paper we make use of the following remark on node-deletion.

Remark 1 (of [4]). Let G be an (e, d)-depth robust graph. Then for any $S \subseteq V(G)$ of size $k \leq e$, the graph $G - S$ is $(e - k, d)$-depth robust.

We rely heavily on a lowerbound for the cumulative complexity of graphs according to their depth-robustness.

Theorem 1 (of [4]). *Let G be an (e, d)-depth-robust DAG, then $\mathrm{cc}(G) > ed$.*

3   A Theoretical MHF with Ideal Trade-Off

In this section we use an $(e = \Omega(N), d)$-depth robust graph D with constant indegree and a maximally ST-robust graph to construct a dynamic graph $\mathbb{G}_D^N$ with the property that for any pebbling strategy $\mathcal{S}$ with high probability either there are at least $\Omega(N)$ rounds with at least $\Omega(N)$ pebbles on the graph) or $\mathsf{cc}(\mathcal{S}(G)) \geq \Omega(N^2 d)$. Furthermore, if D has constant indegree than any graph G in the support of $\mathbb{G}_D^N$ also has constant indegree.

Theorem 2. *Let D be an $(e = 2pN, d)$-depth robust graph. There exist constants $0 < c, c_1, p, \ell < 1$, such that for any strategy $\mathcal{S}$, except with probability at most $\exp(-2(1 - p - c_1)^2 N)$, either $\mathsf{ss}(\mathcal{S}(G), pN) > \ell N$ or $\mathsf{cc}(\mathcal{S}(G)) \geq cN^2 d$, where the probability is taken over the choice of $G \sim \mathbb{G}_D^N$.*

For every constant $\epsilon > 0$ and every $N \geq 1$ Schnitger [19] gave a construction of a DAG $\mathsf{Grates}_{N,\epsilon}$ which is $(\Omega(N), \Omega(N^{1-\epsilon}))$-depth robust and has constant indegree. Specifically, for all $\epsilon > 0$, there exist constants $\gamma, c > 0$, depending only on ϵ such that the graph $\mathsf{Grates}_{N,\epsilon}$ on N nodes is $(\gamma N, cN^{1-\epsilon})$-depth robust and has constant indegree.

In our construction $\mathbb{G}_D^N$ if we instantiate $D = \mathsf{Grates}_{N,\epsilon}$ using $\mathsf{Grates}_{N,\epsilon}$ (or any other $(\Omega(N), \Omega(N^{1-\epsilon}))$-depth robust graph) we obtain the Corollary 1 which says that (whp) either our cc cost is at least $\Omega(N^{3-\epsilon})$ or we will have $\Omega(N)$ rounds with $\Omega(N)$ pebbles.

Corollary 1 (of Theorem 2). *For any $\epsilon > 0$, there exist constants $0 < c, c', c'', p, \ell < 1$ such that for any strategy $\mathcal{S}$, except with probability at most $\exp(-2(1 - p - c')^2 N)$, either $\mathsf{ss}(\mathcal{S}(P), pN) > \ell N$ or $\mathsf{cc}(P) \geq c'' N^{3-\epsilon}$, where the probability is taken over the choice of $G \sim \mathbb{G}_{\mathsf{Grates}_{N,\epsilon}}^N$.*

We remark it is better to instantiate $\mathbb{G}_D^N$ with $D = \mathsf{Grates}_{N,\epsilon}$ instead of another depth-robust graph like DRSample [3] is $(\Omega(N/\log N), \Omega(N))$-depth robust. This is an interesting observation because if we considered these DAGs as a standalone iMHF then we would prefer to use DRSample. In particular, DRSample has $\mathsf{cc} = \Omega(N^2/\log N)$ in comparison to $\mathsf{cc} = \Omega(N^{2-\epsilon})$ for grates. The reason why DRSample is not suitable is that we do not have any guarantees that the graph is (e, d)-depth robust when $e = \Omega(N)$. The graph $\mathsf{Grates}_{N,\epsilon}$ is ideal for instantiating D in our construction, as it is $(\Omega(N), \Omega(N^{1-\epsilon}))$-depth robust.

3.1   The Construction

The dynamic graph $\mathbb{G}_D^N$ consists of three components. A maximally ST robust graph with input and output sets of size N, a highly depth-robust graph overlayed on the input set as seen in Fig. 1, and a line graph with each node having a dynamic edge from a node sampled uniformly at random from the output set of our ST robust graph. A visualization of the complete construction of $\mathbb{G}_D^N$ is shown in Fig. 2. We elaborate on each component in further detail below.

ST-robust graphs play an integral role in our construction [11]. ST-robust graphs are DAGs that have a high connectivity between the sources and sinks even when many nodes are removed. We use ST-robust graphs of the strongest variety—ones that have the maximum possible paths from the inputs to the outputs given arbitrary node deletion.

Definition 6 (ST-Robustness [11]). *Let $G = (V, E)$ be a DAG with n inputs denoted by set I and n outputs denoted by set O. Then G is (k_1, k_2)-ST robust if for all $D \subset V(G)$ with $|D| \leq k_1$ there exists a subgraph H of $G - D$ with $|I \cap V(H)| \geq k_2$ and $|O \cap V(H)| \geq k_2$ such that for all $s \in I \cap V(H)$ and $t \in O \cap V(H)$, there exists a path from s to t in H. The graph G is maximally ST-robust if G is $(k, n - k)$-ST robust for all $0 \leq k \leq n$.*

In particular, Blocki et al. [11] prove the existence of a family of maximally ST-robust graphs with size linear with respect to the size of the input and output sets.

Theorem 3 (of [4]). *For all $N > 0$, there exist maximally ST-Robust graphs on N inputs and N outputs on $O(N)$ nodes and constant indegree.*

Intuitively, suppose that when the challenge $r(L_i)$ is revealed we had pebbles on nodes S. By ST-robustness there exists a subset of $|A| \geq N - |S|$ input nodes and $|B| \geq N - |S|$ output nodes such that every $a \in A$ and $b \in B$ there is a directed path from a to b which avoids the set S entirely. In particular, this means that if the challenge $r(L_i) \in B$ is in the set B (which happens with probability at least $|B|/N \geq 1 - |S|/N$) then we will need to repebble *every* node in the set A before we can pebble node $r(L_i)$.

Lastly, we define a function overlay, shown in Fig. 1, which we use to combine graphs as part of our construction. Intuitively, we overlay a depth-robust graph on top of the inputs of our ST-robust graph to ensure that, unless $|S|$ is sufficiently large, it will be expensive to repebble the entire set A above.

Definition 7 (Overlay). *Let $G = (V = [n], E)$ and $G' = (V' = [m], E')$ for $m > 2n$ with sources $[n]$ and sinks $[m - n + 1 : m]$. Then $\mathsf{overlay}(G, G') = (V', E \cup E')$.*

Definition 8 (The Dynamic Graph $\mathbb{G}_D^N$). *Let D be an (e_N, d_N)-depth robust graph on N nodes and ST be a maximally ST-robust graph with N inputs $\mathrm{ST}^{\mathsf{in}}$ and N outputs $\mathrm{ST}^{\mathsf{out}}$. Next let $G = \mathsf{overlay}(D, \mathrm{ST})$ on M nodes. Let $L = \langle M + 1, \ldots, M + N \rangle$ and $G' = (V, E)$ such that $V = V(G) \cup L$ and $E = E(G) \cup \{(M + i - 1, M + i) \mid i \in [1 : N]\}$. Finally, let $\mathbb{G}_D^N$ be the distribution over the set of all G' with additional edges $\{(r(L_i), L_i) \mid i \in [N]\}$, where $r(L_i)$ maps L_i to some $j \in \mathrm{ST}^{\mathsf{out}}$ chosen uniformly at random.*

For each P_i, let ST_{P_i} denote a subgraph of $G - L - P_i$ with paths from at least $N - |P_i|$ inputs $\mathrm{ST}_{P_i}^{\mathsf{in}}$ to at least $N - |P_i|$ outputs $\mathrm{ST}_{P_i}^{\mathsf{out}}$. Intuitively, if a strategy keeps a small number of pebbles on the graph for a large number of steps, then, upon the discovery of a dynamic edge, a large amount of inputs will likely need to be repebbled, which is expensive due to its depth robustness.

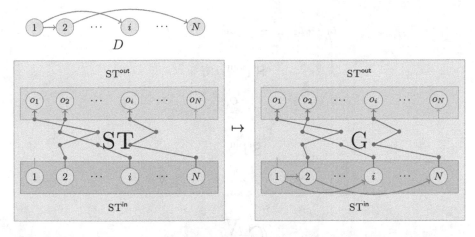

Fig. 1. Above is the visualization of the mapping overlay applied to D and ST to get the graph G. The result is an ST-robust graph with a highly depth robust input set. The red edges from ST^{in} to ST^{out} represent the high connectivity between the sets due to the maximal ST-robustness. (Color figure online)

3.2 Lowerbounding Costly Edges

The first step in describing the trade-off between sustained space and cumulative complexity of $\mathbb{G}_D^N$ is describing how often a low-memory pebbling encounters a costly edge, one that requires a large amount of repebbling. Even if a pebbling keeps only a small number of pebbles on the graph, it's possible that it gets "lucky" and avoids costly edges. In this section we show that a pebbling can't get lucky many times, except with negligible probability.

Fix some parameters $0 < \ell < 1 - p < 1$. Let $\text{unlucky}_1, \ldots, \text{unlucky}_N$ be random variables such that $\text{unlucky}_i = 1$ if $|P(L_i)| > pN$ or $r(L_i) \in \text{ST}^{\text{out}}_{P(L_i)}$ i.e., we have at most pN pebbles on the graph when the challenge edge $r(L_i)$ is revealed or we will need to repebble the entire set $\text{ST}^{\text{in}}_{P(L_i)}$ since $r(L_i) \in \text{ST}^{\text{out}}_{P(L_i)}$. Let $\text{unlucky} = \sum_{i \in [N]} \text{unlucky}_i$. Getting "lucky" during a round in which some $r(L_i)$ is discovered refers to the event that there are a small amount of pebbles on the graph, yet $r(L_i) \notin \text{ST}^{\text{out}}_{P(L_i)}$ and isn't guaranteed to be costly. Intuitively, the challenge $r(L_i)$ is guaranteed to be costly if it happens to be in $\text{ST}^{\text{out}}_{P(L_i)}$. The exact penalty for being unlucky will be described later. Here, we find that the probability of getting lucky is simply upperbounded by p, since there are at most pN nodes of ST^{out} that are not in $\text{ST}^{\text{in}}_{P(L_i)}$.

Lemma 2. *Let $\mathcal{S}$ be any strategy and let $P = \langle P_1, \ldots, P_T \rangle = \mathcal{S}(G)$, where $G \sim \mathbb{G}_D^N$. Then for any fixed $b_1, \ldots, b_{i-1} \in \{0, 1\}$ we have*

$$q := \Pr\left[\text{unlucky}_i \,\middle|\, \bigwedge_{j \in [i-1]} \text{unlucky}_j = b_j\right] \geq 1 - p,$$

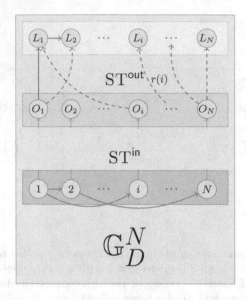

Fig. 2. Above is the final construction of $\mathbb{G}_D^N$, which combines overlay(D, ST) with a line graph on nodes L. For each L_i there is a dynamic edge from $r(L_i) \in_R \mathrm{ST}^{\mathrm{out}}$.

where the probability is taken over the selection of $G \sim \mathbb{G}_D^N$.

Proof. If $|P(L_i)| > pN$, then by definition $\mathsf{unlucky}_i = 1$. If $|P(L_i)| \leq pN$. Then regardless of any prior pebbling steps, we have that there are at most pN nodes in $\mathrm{ST}^{\mathrm{out}} \setminus \mathrm{ST}^{\mathrm{out}}_{P(L_i)}$ by construction. Since $r(L_i)$ is chosen uniformly at random, it follows by Theorem 1 that $r(L_i) \notin \mathrm{ST}^{\mathrm{out}}_{P(L_i)}$ with probability at most

$$\frac{\left| \mathrm{ST}^{\mathrm{out}} \setminus \mathrm{ST}^{\mathrm{out}}_{P(L_i)} \right|}{N} \leq p,$$

so $q \geq 1 - p$.

Ultimately, our goal is to show that, with overwhelming probability, any low-memory pebbling gets unlucky so often that it incurs an unreasonable time cost, because each time the pebbling gets unlucky it incurs a high cost while repebbling $r(L_i)$. So, we must show that it's very unlikely that such pebblings get unlucky only a relatively few amount of times. From Lemmas 1 and 2, Lemma 3 immediately follows, and so the proof is left to the full version of this paper.

Lemma 3. *Let $\mathcal{S}$ be any pebbling strategy, and let $P = S(G)$ for $G \sim \mathbb{G}_D^N$. Then for all $\epsilon > 0$ $\Pr\left[\sum_{i \in [N]} \mathsf{unlucky}_i < N(1 - p - \epsilon)\right] \leq \exp(-2\epsilon^2 N)$*

3.3 The Trade-Off Between Sustained Space and Cumulative Complexity

We now argue that whenever $\mathsf{unlucky}_i = 1$ and we have at most $|P(L_i)| \leq pN$ pebbles on the graph when the challenge $r(L_i)$ is revealed that the cumulative pebbling cost incurred between rounds $s(L_i)$ (when the challenge $r(L_i)$ is revealed) and $t(L_i)$ (when we place a pebble on node $r(L_i)$) is at least $\mathsf{cc}(P, s(L_i), t(L_i)) \geq pNd$. We conclude with the proof of our main result from this section.

If few pebbles are on the graph at step $s(L_i)$, then the pebbling can get lucky in the sense that $r(L_i)$ isn't expensive to pebble; otherwise, the configuration necessitates some costly pebbling moves from step $s(L_i)$ to step $t(L_i)$. More concretely, if $\mathsf{unlucky}_i = 1$ and $|P(L_i)| \leq pN$ then $r(L_i)$ is in $\mathrm{ST}^{\mathrm{out}}_{P(i)}$ and pebbling $r(L_i)$ requires pebbling at least $N(1-p)$ nodes of $\mathrm{ST}^{\mathrm{in}}_{P(i)}$, which is $(e - pN, d)$-depth robust by Remark 1.

Lemma 4. *For any pebbling strategy $\mathcal{S}$ and $P = S(G)$ for $G \sim \mathbb{G}^N_D$. If $\mathsf{unlucky}_i = 1$, $|P(L_i)| \leq pN$, and D is $(2pN, d)$-depth robust, then $\mathsf{cc}(P, s(L_i), t(L_i)) \geq pNd$. We call such $(r(L_i), L_i)$ costly edges.*

Proof. If $\mathsf{unlucky}_i = 1$, and $|P(L_i)| \leq pN$ then $r(L_i) \in \mathrm{ST}^{\mathrm{out}}_{P(L_i)}$. Since $\mathrm{ST}_{P(L_i)}$ is maximally ST-robust, there are paths from at least $N(1-p)$ inputs to $r(L_i)$. That is, $\mathrm{ST}^{\mathrm{in}}_{P(L_i)}$ must be pebbled by round $t(L_i)$. Since $\mathrm{ST}^{\mathrm{in}}$ is $(2pN, d)$-depth robust, $\mathrm{ST}^{\mathrm{in}}_{P(L_i)}$ is (pN, d)-depth robust by Remark 1. It follows that

$$\mathsf{cc}(P, s(L_i), t(L_i)) \geq \mathsf{cc}\left(\mathrm{ST}^{\mathrm{in}}_{P(L_i)}\right) \geq pNd.$$

Now we have the tools to prove Theorem 2, which is a straight-forward consequence of Lemmas 3 and 4.

Proof (of Theorem 2). If P is not (p, ℓ)-low memory, then $\mathsf{ss}(P, pN) > \ell N$. Suppose P is (p, ℓ)-low memory. By Lemma 3, except with probability at most $e^{-2(1-p-c_1)^2 N}$ (for $\ell < c_1 < 1 - p$), there are at least $c_1 N$ pebbling moves in which either $|P(L_i)| > pN$ or $r(L_i) \in \mathrm{ST}^{\mathrm{out}}_{P(L_i)}$, so for $c_2 = c_1 - \ell$, there are nodes $i_1, \ldots i_{c_2 N}$ in which $\mathsf{unlucky}_{i_j} = 1$ and $|P(L_{i_j})| \leq pN$. It follows by Lemma 4 that $\mathsf{cc}(P) \geq \sum_{j \in [c_2 N]} \mathsf{cc}\left(P, s(L_{i_j}), t(L_{i_j})\right) \geq c_2 pN^2 d$.

4   Dynamic EGS

The next graph family we hybridize is a construction by Erdős et al., which we will call EGS. EGS achieves the maximum possible cumulative complexity of $\Omega(N^2)$ [14]. While EGS achieves the highest possible cumulative complexity, it is the least practical of the graphs we're considering, as it has indegree $\Omega(\log N)$ [14]. In this section we construct a simple, dynamic version of this graph and show that it achieves the maximal sustained space and cumulative memory trade-off. The precise details of this construction are unnecessary, as we rely only on the fact that the graph satisfies the properties of local expansion.

Definition 9 (Local Expansion [5]). *Let I_r and I^*_r be defined such that $I_r(x) = \{x - r - 1, \ldots, x\}$ and $I^*_r(x) = \{x + 1, \ldots, x + r\}$. We say that a DAG $G = (V = [N], E)$ is a δ-local expander if for all $i \in V$, $r \leq i, N - i$, and $A \subseteq I^*_r(x)$ and $B \subseteq I_r(x)$ each of size at least δr, there exists an edge from A to B.*

Local expansion naturally gives guarantees on connectivity and depth-robustness after arbitrary node deletion and is a key property of EGS.

Theorem 4 (of [5,14]). *For any $0 < \delta < 1$, there exists a family of graphs $\{EGS_N^\delta\}_{N=1}^\infty$ such that EGS_N^δ is a δ-local expander on N nodes. For some constants $c, \eta, \eta' > 0$, depending only on δ, each EGS_N^δ has indegree $c \log N$ and is $(\eta N, \eta' N)$-depth robust. Furthermore, for each $i \in [N]$, $EGS_N^\delta([i])$ is $(\eta i, \eta' i)$-depth robust.*

In constructing a hybrid extension of EGS, we want to add dynamic edges that require the adversary to repebble many nodes. For each node, we simply select an incoming edge from a prior node chosen uniformly at random. We'll show that if an adversary doesn't keep sufficiently many pebbles on the graph, then it will have to repebble maximally depth-robust subgraphs of EGS many times.

Definition 10 (Dynamic EGS). *The dynamic pebbling graph $DEGS_N^\delta$ is the graph EGS_N^δ with additional dynamic edges $\{(r(i), i) \mid i \in [3 : N]\}$ with $r(i) \in_R [i - 2]$.*

We'll show that with overwhelming probability, any dynamic pebbling strategy either maintains pN nodes on the graph for more than ℓN steps, or has cumulative complexity $\Omega(N^3)$.

Theorem 5. *There exist constants $0 < c, c', c_1, \rho, p, \ell < 1$ such that for any strategy S, except with probability at most $\exp(-2 \left(\rho - \frac{c}{1-c_1} \right)^2 (1 - c_1)N)$, we either have $ss(S(G), pN) > \ell N$ or $cc(S(G)) \geq c' N^3$ where the probability is taken over the selection of $G \sim DEGS_N^\delta$.*

The last tool we'll use to prove Theorem 5 are good nodes. If a pebbling strategy has pebbles S on a graph, then it's useful to know whether a given node is surrounded by only relatively few pebbles, since that way the node is more likely to be a part of a long path.

Definition 11 (Good Nodes [3]). *Let $\gamma > 0$, $G = ([N], E)$ be a DAG, and $S \subseteq V$. The node $i \in [N]$ is γ-good with respect to S if (1) for all $r \in [i]$ $|I_r(i) \cap S| \leq \gamma r$ and (2) for all $r \in [m - i + 1]$ $|I_r^*(i) \cap S| \leq \gamma r$.*

We first show that if a strategy keeps some sufficiently small amount of pebbles on the graph, then there will be large paths in the remaining graph. The good nodes form such paths.

Lemma 5 (Lemma 5 of [5]). *Let $G = ([N], E)$ be a δ-local expander and $x < y \in [N]$. For any $S \subseteq [N]$ and γ such that $\delta < \min\{\gamma/2, 1/4\}$, the graph $G - S$ contains a directed path through all nodes in G which are γ-good with respect to S.*

Prior work gave a lowerbound on the number good nodes in arbitrary DAGs with respect to an arbitrarily-sized subset of nodes. This immediately allows us to lowerbound the probability that $r(i)$ is a good node.

Lemma 6 (Lemma 6 of [5]). *For any DAG $G = ([N], E)$, $\gamma > 0$, and $S \subseteq [N]$, there are at least $N - \frac{1+\gamma}{1-\gamma}|S|$ nodes in G which are γ-good with respect to S.*

4.1   Lowerbounds on Getting Unlucky

We define events that are costly for strategies that employ low-memory pebblings and show that they happen with reasonably large probability. First, we must characterize events that may lead to high cumulative cost if an adversary has relatively few pebbles on the graph upon discovering $r(i)$. We know by Lemma 5, there's a good chance that $r(i)$ is a γ-good node. If that's the case, then there's a long path that includes $r(i)$. Eventually, we show that if $r(i)$ is good and sufficiently large, then the subgraph of good nodes prior to $r(i)$ is highly depth robust and must be repebbled.

To quantify what it means for i and $r(i)$ to be "large" enough that pebbling the subgraph of good nodes is sufficiently costly, we require the assignment of several constants with various constraints in agreement with Lemma 7.

Lemma 7. *Fix any $0 < \eta < 1$ according to Theorem 4. There exists an assignment of p, ℓ, c_1, c_2, and c_3 such that for all $0 < \gamma < 1$,*

*1. $1 - \eta < c_3 < c_2 = c_1 \left(1 - p\frac{1+\gamma}{1-\gamma}\right)$,   2. $0 < \ell < c_2(c_2 - c_3)(1 - c_1)$, and
3. $0 < c_2 < c_1 < 1 - \ell$.*

Proof. To satisfy $1 - \eta < c_2 < 1$, we first pick $0 < p < \frac{\eta(1-\gamma)}{1+\gamma}$. Since $c_2 = c_1(1 - p\frac{1-\gamma}{1+\gamma})$, it follows that $c_2 < c_1$. Fix ℓ such that $0 < \ell < c_2(c_2 - c_3)(1 - c_1)$. Then (3) is satisfied by the fact that $0 < c_1, c_2, c_3 < 1$. Finally, fix any c_3 such that $1 - \eta < c_3 < c_2$.

Let $0 < \delta < 1$, assign $0 < \gamma < 1$ satisfying Lemma 5, and fix p, ℓ, c_1, c_2, and c_3 according to Lemma 7. Let $\mathcal{S}$ be any pebbling strategy for $G \sim \text{DEGS}_N^\delta$ and $P = \mathcal{S}(P)$. Next we define an indicator random variable for the whether or not $r(i)$ is good. Let good_i be the random variable such that $\text{good}_i = 1$ if $r(i)$ is γ-good with respect to $P(i)$ and $\text{good}_i = 0$ otherwise. The function rank_i determines how far $r(i)$ is along the path of good nodes. The higher the value of $\text{rank}_i(r(i))$, the more expensive it will be to pebble $r(i)$. More formally, $\text{rank}_i(v) = j$ if v is topologically the jth γ-good node respect to $P(i)$, and $\text{rank}_i(v) = 0$ otherwise.

Finally we say that an adversary is unlucky at a step $s(i)$ if $r(i)$ is good and sufficiently far along the path of good nodes. For $i \geq c_1 N + 2$, let unlucky_i be the random variable such that $\text{unlucky}_i = 0$ if $P(i) \leq pN$ and either $\text{good}_i = 0$ or $\text{rank}_i(v) < c_3 N$ and $\text{unlucky}_i = 0$ otherwise. Let $\text{unlucky} = \sum_{i \in [c_1 N + 2, N]} \text{unlucky}_i$.

Intuitively, an adversary that has few pebbles on the graph at step $s(i)$ is unlucky if $r(i)$ is a γ-good node with respect to $P(i)$ and of large depth. We show that any strategy gets unlucky at step $s(i)$ with some constant probability.

Lemma 8. *There exists a constant $\rho > 0$ such that for each for each $i \in [c_1 N + 2 : N]$ and $b_{c_1 N+2}, \ldots, b_{i-1} \in \{0, 1\}$.*

$$\Pr\left[\text{unlucky}_i \middle| \bigwedge_{j \in [c_1 N + 2 : i - 1]} \text{unlucky}_j = b_j\right] \geq \rho.$$

Proof. If $|P(i)| > pN$ then $\text{unlucky}_i = 1$, so assume $|P(i)| \le pN$. Then $G([i-2])$ is a δ-local expander on at least $c_1 N$ nodes, and there are at least $c_2 N = c_1 N - c_1 p N \frac{1+\gamma}{1-\gamma}$ γ-good nodes with respect to $P(i)$ in $G([i-2])$ by Theorem 6. So, the probability that $\text{good}_i = 1$ is at least $\frac{c_2 N}{i-2} \ge \frac{c_2 N}{N} = c_2$

For c_3 assigned according to Lemma 7, we have

$$\Pr[\text{rank}_i(r(i)) \ge c_3 N \mid \text{good}_i] \ge c_2 - c_3,$$

then by conditional probability $\Pr[\text{rank}_i(r(i)) \ge c_3 N] \ge c_2(c_2 - c_3)$. Then for $\rho = c_2(c_2 - c_3)$, $\Pr\left[\text{unlucky}_i \Big| \bigwedge_{j \in [c_1 N + 2:i-1]} \text{unlucky}_j = b_j\right] \ge \rho$.

Just as before, combining Lemmas 1 and 8 immediately implies Lemma 9.

Lemma 9. *For some constant $c > 0$,*

$$\Pr[\text{unlucky} < cN] \le \exp\left(-2\left(\rho - \frac{c}{1-c_1}\right)^2 (1-c_1)N\right).$$

4.2   The Cost of Getting Unlucky

Next we examine the cost associated with unlucky_i. Theorem 4 implies that being unlucky results in high cumulative cost from step $s(i)$ to step $t(i)$.

Lemma 10. *If $\text{unlucky}_i = 1$ and $|P(i)| < pN$ then $\text{cc}(P, s(i), t(i)) \ge c_5 N^2$ for some constant $c_5 > 0$.*

Proof. If $\text{unlucky}_i = 1$ and $|P(i)| < pN$, then all of the γ-good nodes of $G([r(i)])$ with respect to $P(i)$ must be repebbled before or on step $t(i)$. It follows by Theorem 4 that this subgraph is $(\eta c_3 N, \eta' c_3 N)$-depth robust for some constants $\eta, \eta' > 0$. Since by Lemma 7 $c_3 > 1 - \eta$, we can apply Theorem 1 to get

$$\text{cc}(i, s(i), t(i)) \ge (c_3 + \eta - 1)\eta' c_3 N^2$$
$$\ge (c_3 + \eta - 1)\eta' c_3 N^2$$
$$= c_5 N^2,$$

for $c_5 = (c_3 + \eta - 1)\eta' c_3$

As with Theorem 2, Theorem 5 directly follows from Lemma 10. This is because Lemma 9 implies that, except with negligible probability, there are $\Omega(N)$ steps in which $\text{unlucky}_i = 1$ and $|P(i)| \le pN$. Then Lemma 10 implies that such a strategy incurs CC $\Omega(N^2)$ for each of these incidences, resulting in a total CC of $\Omega(N^3)$.

5 Dynamic DRSample

DRSample is a randomized algorithm that, except with negligible probability, outputs an $\left(\Omega\left(\frac{N}{\log N}\right), \Omega(N)\right)$-depth robust graph on N nodes [3]. While losing a $\log N$ factor in depth robustness, output graphs of DRSample contrast EGS by having indegree 2 and being practical for common applications of MHFs. To prove this section's main result, Theorem 6, we use a stronger version of depth-robustness, where we are guaranteed sufficiently long paths even after the deletion of blocks of consecutive nodes.

Definition 12 (Block-Depth Robust [3]). *Let $N \in \mathbb{N}$ and $G = (V = [n], E)$ be a DAG. For a node v, let $N(v, b) = \{v - b + 1, \ldots, v\}$, and for $S \subseteq V$, let $N(S, b) = \bigcup_{v \in S} N(v, b)$. The graph G is (e, d, b)-block-depth robust if for every set $S \subseteq V$ of size at most e, there exists a path of length d in $G - N(S, b)$.*

We also use a more general form of local expansion, which implies high connectivity between the nodes after node deletion.

Definition 13 (Local Expansion Node [3]). *For a graph $G = (V = [N], E)$, $c > 0$ and $r^* \in \mathbb{Z}^+$, we say that a node $v \in V$ is a (c, r^*)-local expander if for all $r \geq r^*$ we have*

- *for all $A \subset I_v^*(r)$ and $B \subseteq I_{v+r}^*(r)$ of size $|A|, |B| \geq cr$ there exists an edge from A to B, and*
- *for all subsets $A \subseteq I_v(r)$ and $B \subseteq I_{v-r}^*(r)$ of size $|A|, |B| \geq cr$, there exists an edge from A to B.*

In our analysis of Dynamic DRSample, we will often examine its metagraph. The metagraph of a DAG $G = ([N], E)$ with parameter m simply maps each block $[mi + 1 : m(i + 1)]$ to a node. Two nodes of the metagraph u and v are connected if in the original graph there's an edge from the "last part" of the u block to the "first part" of the v block.

Definition 14 (Metagraph [3]). *For a graph $G = ([N], E)$ and $m > 0$, we define the metagraph $G_m = (V_m, E_m)$ as follows. Let $N' = \lfloor N/m \rfloor$ and $V_m = [N']$. Let*

- $M_i = [(i - 1)m + 1 : im]$,
- $M_i^F = \left[(i - 1)m + 1 : (i - 1)m + \left\lfloor m\frac{1 - 1/10}{2} \right\rfloor\right]$, *and*
- $M_i^L = \left[(i - 1)m + 1 + \left\lceil m\frac{1 + 1/10}{2} \right\rceil : im\right]$.

Then $E_m = \{(i, j) \mid M_i^L \times M_j^F \cap E \neq \emptyset\}$.

There is a natural correspondence between the depth-robustness and block-depth robustness of graphs and metagraphs.

Remark 2 (Claim 1 of [3]). Let G be a DAG. If G_m is (e, d)-depth robust, then G is $(e/2, md/10, m)$-block depth robust.

DRSample has a number of tunable parameters. We exclusively refer to DRSample with the recommended parameters from [3].

Definition 15 (DRSample [3]). *The randomized algorithm* DRSample *on input* N *outputs a graph* DR $= (V, E)$ *on* N *nodes with the following properties. Fix any* $0 < p, \epsilon < 1$ *and let*

- $a = 160$
- $m = a \log N$,
- $N' = \lfloor N/m \rfloor$
- $\gamma = 0.1$,

- $\sigma = 0.125$
- $x = 0.00861$,
- $\alpha = 0.2916$,
- $r^* = 8$,

- $c_{10} = 1 - \frac{2p}{\sigma} - x - \epsilon$,
- $\eta = 0.038945$, *and*
- $\eta' = 0.3$.

Except with negligible probability $\mu(N)$, *for any subset of metanodes* S *of size at most* pN', $DR_m - S$ *contains at least* $c_{10}N'$ (α, r^*)-*local expanders that are* γ-*good with respect to* S. *Each of the these nodes are connected, and the metagraph* DR_m *is* $(\eta N', \eta' N')$-*depth robust.*

Next we hybridize DRSample by adding dynamic edges for each node. Here, we make the block parameter m inherent in the construction, as each node has a random edge to the "end" of a random metanode. For the ease of notation, we let FromMeta be the function mapping metanodes to nodes in the original graph, meaning FromMeta$(i) = (i - 1)m + 1$. Likewise, for $v \in V$, we let ToMeta$(v) = \lfloor (v - 1)/m \rfloor + 1$.

Definition 16 (Dynamic DRSample). *Dynamic DRSample is the dynamic pebbling graph* DDR_N^m, *constructed as follows. Let* DR $= (V, E) \leftarrow$ DRSample(N). *Then* DDR_N^m *is* DR *with additional dynamic edges* $\{(r(i), i) \mid i \in [$FromMeta$(3) : N]\}$, *where* $r(i)$ *is chosen from* $\{km \mid 1 \leq k \leq$ ToMeta$(i) - 2\}$ *uniformly at random. That is, for each node* $i \geq 2m + 1$ *of* DDR_N^m, *there's a dynamic edge to* i *from the end of a random metanode.*

The main result of this section is that any pebbling strategy, except with negligible probability, either sustains $p\frac{N}{a \log N}$ pebbles for ℓN steps, or has cumulative complexity $\Omega\left(\frac{N^3}{\log N}\right)$.

Theorem 6. *There exists constants* $0 < p, \ell, a, c_{13}, c_{14} < 1$ *and negligible function* μ, *such that for* $m = a \log N$, *any strategy* $\mathcal{S}$, *except with probability at most* $\mu(N)$, *we have either* $ss\left(\mathcal{S}(G), \frac{pN}{a \log N}\right) > \ell N$ *or* $cc(\mathcal{S}(G)) \geq \frac{c_{14}N^3}{\log N}$, *where the probability is taken over the selection of* $G \sim DDR_N^m$.

Before we begin proving Theorem 6, we need to setup some useful variables and notation. Let $G \sim DDR_N^m$, $\mathcal{S}$ be any strategy, and $P = \mathcal{S}(G)$, and assign a, m, N', γ, α, r^*, c_{10}, η, and η' according to Definition 15. Let $r_m(i) =$ ToMeta$(r(i))$ and $P_m(i) =$ ToMeta$(P(i))$. When i and P are known, we say that v is a *good expander* when v is γ-good with respect to $P_m(i)$ in G_m and is a (δ, r^*)-local expander in G_m. We'll heavily use fact from Definition 15 that all good expanders are connected.

We'll want to show that for some chosen $0 < c_{11} < 1$ and $i \geq c_{11}N + 2$, if $|P_m(i)| \leq pN'$ then the subgraph induced by the good expanders less than $i - 1$ is still $\left(\Omega\left(\frac{N}{\log N}, N\right), \Omega(N)\right)$-depth robust. While there are $c_{10}N'$ good expanders in $G_m - P_m(i)$, there could be as many as $(1 - c_{11})N'$ good expanders that have never been pebbled (and thus are not candidates for $r_m(i)$). So, we need to show that c_{10} can take values greater than $1 - \eta + (1 - c_{11})$, yet still be less than 1. Recall from Definition 15 that c_{10} is an implicit function of p, so we can only achieve this by assigning p and c_{11} the appropriate values. Namely, we need

$$\eta - (1 - c_{10}) - (1 - c_{11}) > 0. \tag{2}$$

It suffices for $c_{11} = 0.97$, $p = 2 \times 10^{-5}$, and $c_{10} = 0.99106$.

Until the proof of Theorem 6, we assume that G is $(\eta N', \eta' N')$-depth robust, and for any set S of size at most pN', $G - S$ contains at least $c_{10}N'$ good expanders.

5.1   Lowerbounds on Getting Unlucky

We want to determine the number of times an adversary could be "unlucky." For a step to be unlucky, we need it to be sufficiently large, so that it may be costly to rectify. Specifically, we want the metanode corresponding to this step to be at least $c_{11}N' + 2$. Moreover, if $|P(i)| \leq pN'$, we say the adversary is unlucky if $r(i)$ is a good expander and large. As before, let $\mathsf{rank}_i(v) = j$ when v is topologically the jth good expander in G.

These trials consist of the nodes starting from $\mathsf{FromMeta}(c_{11}N' + 2)$ to N. There are $K \geq N - \mathsf{FromMeta}(c_{11}N' + 2) \geq N(1 - c_{11}) + m - 2$ such nodes. We'll assume that $N > 200$ and fix $\kappa = 1 - c_{11} - \frac{1}{100}$ so that $0 < \kappa N \leq K$. For $i \in [(1 - \kappa)N : N]$, we define the random variable $\mathsf{unlucky}_i$ such that

$$\mathsf{unlucky}_i = \begin{cases} 0 & \text{if } |P(i)| \leq p, \text{ but either } r_m(i) \text{ isn't a good expander} \\ & \text{or } \mathsf{rank}_i(r_m(i)) < c_{12}N', \text{ and} \\ 1 & \text{otherwise,} \end{cases}$$

for some constant c_{12} such that

$$1 - \eta < c_{12} < c_{10} - (1 - c_{11}). \tag{3}$$

See that c_{12} can take such values since c_{10} and c_{11} satisfy Equation 2. Then when we take out all nodes but the $c_{12}N'$ good expanders that must be repebbled, G will still be adequately depth-robust since the $c_{12}N'$ good expanders account for almost all nodes of G. Finally, let $\mathsf{unlucky} = \sum_{i \in [(1-\kappa)N:N]} \mathsf{unlucky}_i$. We show that such steps are unlucky with constant probability.

Lemma 11. *For any* $i \in [(1 - \kappa)N \cdot N]$ *and* $b_1, \ldots, b_{i-1} \in \{0, 1\}$,

$$\Pr\left[\mathsf{unlucky}_i \,\middle|\, \bigwedge_{j \in [i-1]} \mathsf{unlucky}_j = b_j\right] \geq \rho,$$

for some constant $\rho > 0$.

Proof. If $|P_m(i)| > pN'$ then $\mathsf{unlucky}_i = 1$, so assume otherwise. There are at least $(c_{10} - (1 - c_{11}))N'$ good expanders in $G_m([i - 2])$, so the probability that $r_m(i)$ is a good expander out of at most N' total nodes is at least $c_{10} - (1 - c_{11})$.

If $r_m(i)$ is a good expander, then $\mathsf{rank}_i(r_m(i)) \geq c_{12}N'$ with probability at least $1 - c_{12}$, so by conditional probability, $r_m(i)$ is a good expander and the $c_{12}N'$th or higher good expander with probability at least $\rho = (c_{10} - (1 - c_{11}))(1 - c_{12})$. Finally, $\rho > 0$ since $c_{10} > 1 - \eta + (1 - c_{11})$ by Equation 2.

5.2   The Cost of Being Unlucky

Intuitively, we want to show that a costly node requires high cumulative cost to repebble since all of the good expanders are connected.

Lemma 12. *If* $\mathsf{unlucky}_i = 1$ *and* $|P(i)| < pN'$, *then* $\mathsf{cc}(P, s(i), t(i)) \geq \frac{c_{15}N^2}{\log N}$ *for some* $c_{15} > 0$.

Proof. First we have $|P_m(i)| \leq |P(i)| \leq pN'$. Let $i_m = \mathsf{ToMeta}(i) - 2$. If the above assumptions hold, then $i_m \geq c_{11}N'$ and $r_m(i)$ is a good expander with $\mathsf{rank}_i(r_m(i)) \geq c_{12}N'$. Then there are nodes $v_1, \ldots, v_{c_{12}N'}$ which are good expanders and connected in $G_m[i - 2] - P_m(i)$. Since c_{12} and c_{11} satisfy Equation 3, $c_{12} > 1 - \eta + (1 - c_{11})$ it follows that the subgraph $G_m(\{v_1, \ldots, v_{c_{12}N'}\})$ is $((\eta + c_{12} - 1)N', \eta'N')$-depth robust. To pebble $r(i)$, all of the nodes that comprise each metanode v_j must be pebbled. By Remarks 1 and 2, $G\left(\bigcup_{j \in [c_{12}N']} I_m^*(\mathsf{FromMeta}(v_j))\right)$ is

$$\left(\frac{(\eta + c_{12} - 1)N'}{2}, c_{11}\eta'N/10, m\right)\text{-block depth robust.}$$

Since this subgraph has no pebbles on it on step $s(i)$ and must be repebbled by step $t(i)$, we have $\mathsf{cc}(P, s(i), t(i)) \geq \frac{c_{15}N^2}{\log(N)}$ for $c_{15} = \frac{\eta + c_{12} - 1}{20}c_{11}\eta'$.

The proof of Theorem 6 closely follows the proof of Theorem 2, and a formal proof is deferred to the full version of this paperThe main difference has to do with arguments on the metagraph G_m, which is covered by the proof of Lemma 16. More closely, if $\mathsf{ss}\left(\mathcal{S}(G), \frac{pN}{a \log N}\right) \leq \ell N$ then with overwhelming probability there are $c_{13}N$ nodes in which $\mathsf{unlucky}_j = 1$ for $\ell < c_{13} < \kappa\rho$. Then there are nodes $i_1, \ldots, i_{(c_{13} - \ell)N}$ in which $\mathsf{unlucky}_{i_j} = 1$ *and* $|P(i_j)| \leq pN'$. Then by Lemma 16, it follows that $\mathsf{cc}(\mathcal{S}(G)) = \Omega\left(\frac{N^3}{\log N}\right)$.

6   Argon2id

Argon2id is a hybrid MHF that's currently deployed in several cryptographic libraries, so it is necessary to understand its sustained space guarantees [10]. The first half of the evaluation is data-independent, while the second half is data-dependent. In the pebbling model, this corresponds to the first half of the nodes having fixed edges that are known at the start of Argon2id's evaluation, while the random edges in the second half are dynamic. Intuitively, the data-dependent phase induces high cumulative cost, while the data-independent phase has weaker, yet still significant, cumulative cost to fall back on in the presence of a side-channel attack.

Definition 17 (Argon2id [10]). *The dynamic pebbling graph* $\mathsf{Argon2id}_N$ *consists of the vertex set* $V = [2N]$ *and edge set*

$$E = \{(i, i + 1) \mid i \in [2N - 1]\} \cup \{(r(i), i) \mid i \in [2N]\},$$

where $r(i)$ *is a random value distributed as follows:*

$$Pr[r(i) = j] = \Pr_{x \in_R [M]} \left[i \left(1 - \frac{x^2}{M^2} \right) \in (j - 1, j] \right]$$

for some $M \gg N$. *The edges* $(r(i), i)$ *are only dynamic when* $i > N$. *When* $i \leq N$, $(r(i), i)$ *is static and known prior to pebbling.*

In particular, we show the following results.

Theorem 7. *There exists some constants* $\delta, \gamma < 0 < f, u, \ell, \delta', \gamma' < 1$ *such that for any pebbling strategy* $\mathcal{S}$, *with high probability, either* $\mathsf{ss}(\mathcal{S}(G), \delta' \log^\delta Ne) > \ell N$ *or* $\mathsf{cc}(\mathcal{S}(G)) \geq \gamma' N^4 e^{-2} \log^\gamma N$, *where the probability is taken over the choice of* $G \sim \mathsf{Argon2id}_N$.

Corollary 2. *Let* $\mathcal{S}$ *be any strategy and* $G \sim \mathsf{Argon2id}_N$. *Then there exists constants* $\delta, \gamma < 0 < f, u, \ell, \delta', \gamma' < 1$ *such that for all* $\epsilon > 0$ *and with high probability, either* $\mathsf{ss}(\mathcal{S}(G), \delta' N^{1-\epsilon} \log^\delta N) > \ell N$ *or* $\mathsf{cc}(\mathcal{S}(G)) = \gamma' N^{2+2\epsilon} \log^\gamma N$.

The techniques used to prove Theorem 7 are completely different than the other three trade-off proofs in this paper. We start by arguing if an strategy has e pebbles on the graph on step $s(i)$, then with some reasonably large probability the depth of $r(i)$ is $d = \tilde{\Omega}(N^3/e^3)$. For this argument, we use a new graph property called fractional-depth robustness, which says that if a limited amount of nodes are deleted from the graph, then there are some fraction of nodes still with large depth. From then on, the proof of Theorem 7 uses techniques from the proof that the dynamic pebbling graph Scrypt_N has CC $\Omega(N^2)$ [6]. Specifically, if $r(i)$ has depth d in $G - P(i)$, then the minimum required steps to pebble $r(i)$ is d. For this to happen, e must have been sufficiently large (otherwise d would necessarily be larger). The argument is repeated for all steps between $s(i-1)+1$ and $s(i)$ to lowerbound its CC.

6.1 The Trade-Off and Cumulative Complexity

We prove the CC penalty for low-memory pebblings using a graph property called fractional depth-robustness.

Definition 18 (Fractional Depth-Robustness [13]**).** *For a vertex v in a graph G, let* depth(v, G) *denote the longest path to v in G. A DAG $G = (V = [N], E)$ (e, d, f)-fractionally depth robust if for all $S \subseteq V$ with $|S| \leq e$, we have $|\{v \mid, v \in V, $ depth$(v, G) \geq d\}| \geq fN$.*

Next we'll use the following facts about the graph underlying Argon2id.

Lemma 13 (of [13]**).** *Let $G \sim$ Argon2id$_N$. There exists $0 < \alpha', f < 1$ and $\alpha \leq 0$ such that, with probability $1 - o\left(\frac{1}{N}\right)$, $G([N])$ is $\left(e, \frac{\alpha' N^3 \log^\alpha N}{e^3}, f\right)$-fractionally depth robust.*

Let S be a pebbling strategy, $G \sim$ Argon2id$_N$, and $P = S(G)$. For the ease of notation, $e_i = |P_i|$ and d_i denote the minimum required steps from $s(i)$ to pebble $r(i)$. For now we'll assume from Lemma 13 that G is $\left(e, \frac{\alpha' N^3 \log^\alpha N}{e^3}, f\right)$-fractionally depth-robust for some $0 < \alpha', f < 1$ and $\alpha \leq 0$. Immediately, this says that if $|P(i)| \leq e$ then there are fN nodes of depth at least $\frac{\alpha' N^3 \log^\alpha N}{e^3}$ in $G - P(i)$. By Definition 17 $r(i)$ is not chosen uniformly at random, as the distribution slightly shifts probability mass to nodes closer to i. However, this shift isn't significant enough for our arguments. This is formalized by Lemma 14. This claim is inherent by the work of [13], but we include a proof in the full version of this paper.

Lemma 14 (of [13]**).** *Let $G \sim$ Argon2id$_N$, $i > N$, and $j \leq N$. Then*
$\Pr[r(i) = j] \geq \frac{1}{8N}$.

Immediately from Lemma 14, we have

$$\Pr\left[d_i \geq \frac{\alpha' N^3 \log^\alpha N}{e^3_{s(i)}}\right] \geq f/8. \tag{4}$$

This is the probability that the adversary, upon discovering $r(i)$ at step $s(i)$, must take at least $\frac{\alpha' N^3 \log^\alpha N}{e^3_{s(i)}}$ steps to pebble $r(i)$. From any $j \leq s(i)$, the minimum required steps to pebble $r(i)$ is at least $s(i) - j + d_i$. Then even if the adversary knew $r(i)$ on step $s(i) - j$, it would have to take at least $d_i + j \geq \frac{\alpha' N^3 \log^\alpha N}{e^3_{s(i)-j}}$ steps with probability at least $f/8$. Intuitively, this is because each $r(i)$ is independent of the strategy employed by S, meaning we can take $r(i)$ to be chosen before the pebbling begins. Then even if $f(i)$ was discovered on step $s(i) - j$, Equation 4 applies. Let $s(i) - h_i$ be a step that maximizes this bound on d_i. Then for all $k \leq s(i)$, $d_i \geq \frac{\alpha' N^3 \log^\alpha N}{e^3_{s(i)-h_i}} - h_i \geq \frac{\alpha' N^3 \log^\alpha N}{e^3_{s(i)-k}} - k$, so $e_{s(i)-k} \geq \frac{\alpha'^{1/3} N \log^{\alpha/3} N}{(d_i+k)^{1/3}}$ by the construction of h_i. For $i \in [N+1 : 2N]$, we define the random variables hard$_i = 1$ if $d_i \geq \frac{\alpha' N^3 \log^\alpha N}{e^3_{s(i)-h_i}} - h_i$, and hard$_i = 0$ otherwise. If hard$_i = 1$, then for all $k \leq s(i)$, $e_{s(i)-k} \geq \frac{\alpha'^{1/3} N \log^{\alpha/3} N}{(d_i+k)^{1/3}}$ by the construction of h_i. This allows us to lowerbound the cumulative cost associated with steps $s(i-1)+1$ to $s(i)$. Next we define the random variables

$$\mathsf{unlucky}_i^e = \begin{cases} 1 & \text{if either } e_{s(i)} > e \text{ or both } e_{s(i)} \le e \text{ and } \mathsf{hard}_i = 1, \text{ and} \\ 0 & \text{otherwise.} \end{cases}$$

Lemma 15. *For any* $b_1, \ldots, b_{i-1} \in \{0, 1\}$, $\Pr\left[\mathsf{unlucky}_i^e \Big| \bigwedge_{j \in [i-1]} \mathsf{unlucky}_j^e = b_j\right] \ge f/8$.

Proof. If $e_i > e$, then $\mathsf{unlucky}_i^e = 1$, so assume otherwise. By the fractional-depth robustness of Argon2id, even if $r(i)$ was discovered on round $s(i) - h_i$, $r(i)$ has depth at least $\frac{\alpha' N^3 \log^\alpha N}{e_{s(i)-h_i}^3 - (s(i)-h_i)}$ with probability at least $f/8$ by Equation 4.

Next we show that there is high cost associated with being unlucky. This argument closely follows Claim 8 of [6].

Lemma 16. *If* $\mathsf{unlucky}_i^e = \mathsf{unlucky}_j^e = 1$ *and* $|P(i)|, |P(j)| \le pe$ *for some* $j < i$, *then* $\mathsf{cc}(s(j)+1, s(i)) \ge \beta' N^3 e^{-2} \log^\beta N$ *for some* $0 < \beta' < 1$ *and* $\beta \le 0$.

Proof. We have

$$\mathsf{cc}(s(j)+1, s(i)) \ge \mathsf{cc}(s(i) - d_j + 1, s(i))$$

$$= \sum_{k=0}^{d_j - 1} e_{i-k}$$

$$= \sum_{k=0}^{d_j - 1} \frac{\alpha'^{1/3} N \log^{\alpha/3} N}{(d_i + k)^{1/3}} \qquad \mathsf{hard}_i = 1$$

$$\ge \alpha'^{1/3} N \log^{\alpha/3} N \int_{d_i}^{d_i + d_{j_i - 1}} \frac{1}{x^{1/3}} dx$$

$$= 3\alpha'^{1/3} N \log^{\alpha/3} N / 2((d_i + d_j)^{2/3} - d_i^{2/3})$$

$$\ge \beta' N^3 e^{-2} \log^\beta N \tag{5}$$

for some $0 < \beta' < 1$ and $\beta \ge 0$. Step 5 follows from a simple argument, which is detailed in the full version of this paper.

Just as with Theorems 5 and 6, Theorem 7 directly follows from Lemma 16, so the proof has been deferred to the full version of this paper. Corollary 2 directly follows.

7 Open Problems

We conclude with several open question for future work. The most pressing question is whether or not there exists a dynamic pebbling reduction for dMHFs in an idealized model of computation—similar to the pebbling reduction for iMHFs in parallel random oracle model [7]. Such a pebbling reduction would greatly simplify the design and analysis of future dMHFs. Another interesting direction would be to try to find direct proofs of CMC/SSC trade-offs for one or more of the dMHFs considered in this paper. For example, while [6] used dynamic pebbling to build intuition about the cumulative memory complexity of Scrypt the final security proof was direct and did not rely on pebbling arguments. Another natural question is the development of dynamic pebbling attacks. For example, fixing $s = o(N/\log N)$ we could ask what is the minimum cc pebbling strategy which is guaranteed to have s-sustained space complexity $o(N)$.

Acknowledgements. We would like to thank anonymous reviewers for providing constructive feedback. Jeremiah Blocki was supported in part by the National Science Foundation under NSF CAREER Award CNS-2047272. Blake Holman was supported by a Ross Fellowship at Purdue University.

References

1. Password hashing competition (2015). https://www.password-hashing.net/
2. Alwen, J., Blocki, J.: Efficiently computing data-independent memory-hard functions. In: Robshaw, M., Katz, J. (eds.) CRYPTO 2016, Part II. LNCS, vol. 9815, pp. 241–271. Springer, Heidelberg (2016). https://doi.org/10.1007/978-3-662-53008-5_9
3. Alwen, J., Blocki, J., Harsha, B.: Practical graphs for optimal side-channel resistant memory-hard functions. In: Thuraisingham, B.M., Evans, D., Malkin, T., Xu, D. (eds.) ACM CCS 2017: 24th Conference on Computer and Communications Security, 31 October–2 November 2017, pp. 1001–1017. ACM Press (2017)
4. Alwen, J., Blocki, J., Pietrzak, K.: Depth-robust graphs and their cumulative memory complexity. In: Coron, J.-S., Nielsen, J.B. (eds.) EUROCRYPT 2017, Part III. LNCS, vol. 10212, pp. 3–32. Springer, Cham (2017). https://doi.org/10.1007/978-3-319-56617-7_1
5. Alwen, J., Blocki, J., Pietrzak, K.: Sustained space complexity. In: Nielsen, J.B., Rijmen, V. (eds.) EUROCRYPT 2018, Part II. LNCS, vol. 10821, pp. 99–130. Springer, Cham (2018). https://doi.org/10.1007/978-3-319-78375-8_4
6. Alwen, J., Chen, B., Pietrzak, K., Reyzin, L., Tessaro, S.: Scrypt is maximally memory-hard. In: Coron, J.-S., Nielsen, J.B. (eds.) EUROCRYPT 2017, Part III. LNCS, vol. 10212, pp. 33–62. Springer, Cham (2017). https://doi.org/10.1007/978-3-319-56617-7_2
7. Alwen, J., Serbinenko, V.: High parallel complexity graphs and memory-hard functions. In: Servedio, R.A., Rubinfeld, R. (eds.) 47th Annual ACM Symposium on Theory of Computing, 14–17 June 2015, pp. 595–603. ACM Press (2015)
8. Alwen, J., Blocki, J.: Towards practical attacks on argon2i and balloon hashing. In: 2017 IEEE European Symposium on Security and Privacy (EuroS P), pp. 142–157 (2017). https://doi.org/10.1109/EuroSP.2017.47
9. Ameri, M.H., Blocki, J., Zhou, S.: Computationally data-independent memory hard functions. In: Vidick, T. (ed.) ITCS 2020: 11th Innovations in Theoretical Computer Science Conference, 12–14 January 2020, vol. 151, pp. 36:1–36:28. LIPIcs (2020)

10. Biryukov, A., Dinu, D., Khovratovich, D.: Argon2: new generation of memory-hard functions for password hashing and other applications. In: 2016 IEEE European Symposium on Security and Privacy (EuroS&P), pp. 292–302. IEEE (2016)
11. Blocki, J., Cinkoske, M.: A new connection between node and edge depth robust graphs. In: Lee, J.R. (ed.) ITCS 2021: 12th Innovations in Theoretical Computer Science Conference, 6–8 January 2021, vol. 185, pp. 64:1–64:18. LIPIcs (2021)
12. Blocki, J., Harsha, B., Kang, S., Lee, S., Xing, L., Zhou, S.: Data-independent memory hard functions: new attacks and stronger constructions. In: Boldyreva, A., Micciancio, D. (eds.) CRYPTO 2019, Part II. LNCS, vol. 11693, pp. 573–607. Springer, Cham (2019). https://doi.org/10.1007/978-3-030-26951-7_20
13. Blocki, J., Zhou, S.: On the depth-robustness and cumulative pebbling cost of Argon2i. In: Kalai, Y., Reyzin, L. (eds.) TCC 2017, Part I. LNCS, vol. 10677, pp. 445–465. Springer, Cham (2017). https://doi.org/10.1007/978-3-319-70500-2_15
14. Erdös, P., Graham, R.L., Szemerédi, E.: On sparse graphs with dense long paths. Comput. Math. Appl. 1(3–4), 365–369 (1975)
15. Hopcroft, J., Paul, W., Valiant, L.: On time versus space. J. ACM (JACM) 24(2), 332–337 (1977)
16. Lee, C.: Litecoin (2011)
17. Lengauer, T., Tarjan, R.E.: Upper and lower bounds on time-space tradeoffs. In: Proceedings of the Eleventh Annual ACM Symposium on Theory of Computing, STOC 1979, New York, NY, USA, pp. 262–277. Association for Computing Machinery (1979). https://doi.org/10.1145/800135.804420
18. Percival, C.: Stronger key derivation via sequential memory-hard functions, January 2009
19. Schnitger, G.: On depth-reduction and grates. In: 24th Annual Symposium on Foundations of Computer Science, 7–9 November 1983, pp. 323–328. IEEE Computer Society Press (1983)

Low Communication Complexity Protocols, Collision Resistant Hash Functions and Secret Key-Agreement Protocols

Shahar P. Cohen and Moni Naor[✉]

Department of Computer Science and Applied Mathematics,
Weizmann Institute of Science, Rehovot, Israel
{shahar.cohen,moni.naor}@weizmann.ac.il

Abstract. We study communication complexity in computational settings where bad inputs may exist, but they should be hard to find for any computationally bounded adversary.

We define a model where there is a source of public randomness but the inputs are chosen by a computationally bounded adversarial participant *after seeing the public randomness*. We show that breaking the known communication lower bounds of the private coins model in this setting is closely connected to known cryptographic assumptions. We consider the simultaneous messages model and the interactive communication model and show that for any non trivial predicate (with no redundant rows, such as equality):

1. Breaking the $\Omega(\sqrt{n})$ bound in the simultaneous message case or the $\Omega(\log n)$ bound in the interactive communication case, implies the existence of distributional collision-resistant hash functions (dCRH). This is shown using techniques from Babai and Kimmel [BK97]. Note that with a CRH the lower bounds can be broken.
2. There are no protocols of constant communication in this preset randomness settings (unlike the plain public randomness model).

The other model we study is that of a stateful "free talk", where participants can communicate freely *before* the inputs are chosen and may maintain a state, and the communication complexity is measured only afterwards. We show that efficient protocols for equality in this model imply secret key-agreement protocols in a constructive manner. On the other hand, secret key-agreement protocols imply optimal (in terms of error) protocols for equality.

1 Introduction

What does a lower bound mean if it is not feasible to find the bad inputs? In other words, can we bypass it, if we assume that the choice of inputs is done by

Research supported in part by grants from the Israel Science Foundation (no. 2686/20) and by the Simons Foundation Collaboration on the Theory of Algorithmic Fairness. The second author is incumbent of the Judith Kleeman Professorial Chair.
The full version of this paper is available at ia.cr/2022/312.

Y. Dodis and T. Shrimpton (Eds.): CRYPTO 2022, LNCS 13509, pp. 252–281, 2022.
https://doi.org/10.1007/978-3-031-15982-4_9

a process that is computationally limited? In this work we study this issue in the setting of communication complexity.

The study of communication complexity deals with proving bounds on the amount of communication that is required to perform certain tasks when the input is separated: two parties, Alice and Bob, have as inputs $x \in X$ and $y \in Y$ respectively; how many bits do they have to send each other (as a function of $|X|$ and $|Y|$) for computing the value of a function $f(x, y)$? An answer for such a question depends, of course, on the exact model details: Do Alice and Bob have any limitation in the communication? Do they communicate directly or through a third party? What predicates f are they trying to compute? See Kushilevitz and Nisan [KN96] and Rao and Yehudayoff [RY20] for extensive background on communication complexity.

There are several models of communication that differ mainly on two properties: whether the strategy of the participants can be probabilistic and the exact communication settings (network layout). The participants of those models do not have a bound on their running time, however, they are required to be correct[1] for every input in the space.

When the participants are allowed to be probabilistic there is an important distinction: whether they share common random bits (public coins) or not (private coins). It is important to note that the random bits (in both options) and the problem's inputs (x and y) are *independent*. This can be seen as uniform random bits that are chosen *after* the (worst-case) input was chosen.

By definition, the private coins model is no stronger than the public coins model and indeed some tasks can be done in the latter but cannot be done in the former with the same communication complexity (see below). On the other hand, the private coins model may be considered more *realistic*, where there is no assumption of *independent* public random string.

However, both the public and private coins models are known to be 'better' than the deterministic model in the sense that they have more efficient protocols in terms of the communication complexity: for instance, as proved by Yao, the deterministic communication complexity of many predicates is $\Omega(n)$ (Alice and Bob can do nothing better than just sending their full inputs), while in the probabilistic world there is quite a lot to be done. Equality is a prominent example, with complexity of $\Theta(\log n)$ for the private coins model and $\Theta(1)$ for the public coins model.

We examine another relaxation that can help us: limiting all parties, including the one who selects the inputs (the adversary), to a computationally bounded world. We will not require that Alice and Bob be correct for every input in the space, but only on inputs that are chosen by a computationally bounded adversary. Note that the new definition is by nature relevant only to probabilistic algorithms.

Considering a polynomially bounded adversary raises the question of whether there are benefits from different computational hardness assumptions: *can we re-*

---

[1] For the probabilistic version they are required to succeed with constant high probability.

duce the communication complexity of protocols by assuming that certain tasks cannot be performed efficiently? That is, given that Alice and Bob in our new definition do not have to be correct for every input in the input space, a computational hardness assumption can be used for proving that no efficient adversary can find bad inputs with non-negligible probability.

Back to the relationship between the public and private coins models: we propose a new model that is, in general, more powerful than the private coins but still realistic. Also, in contrast to the above mentioned models, our model is *computational* – the participants' running time is bounded by some $\text{poly}(\lambda)$ where λ is the security parameter. In our model, there is a public random string but there is an additional adversarial participant that *chooses the inputs depending on the public random string*, it can be seen as a public random string that is 'fixed' in advance and therefore we called it *preset public coins* model. See Definition 2.7 for formal specification.

The two communication patterns we consider are:

Simultaneous Messages Model (SM). Alice and Bob are given x and y respectively and should compute a function $f(x,y)$ but *without communicating with each other*. Instead, each one sends a message to a third party (a referee) who calculates $f(x,y)$ given the messages from Alice and Bob.

Interactive Communication Model. Alice and Bob get their inputs x and y respectively and can communicate with each other without any limitations on the number of rounds.

In both settings, the communication complexity measure is the total length of the messages sent by Alice and Bob.

Stateful Preprocessing Communication. The second type of model we consider is where the communication complexity matters *only at some critical period* and the question is whether we can get very succinct protocols. The two parties can talk freely beforehand. At some point the action starts, they receive their inputs and need to decide with little communication the result.

In the SM model we consider a variation that differs by two properties:

Free talk. A protocol with *free talk* is one where Alice and Bob communicate also before getting their inputs. The messages during the free talk phase (before the inputs are chosen) do not count in the communication complexity of the protocol. Alice and Bob maintain (secret) states afterwards. However the adversary sees the whole communication and can use it when choosing the inputs.

Rushing adversary. The inputs are chosen by a computationally bounded adversary depending on the public discussion it witnesses in the preprocessing phase. A rushing adversary can choose Bob's input at the 'last moment': The adversary first chooses the input of Alice depending on the public random string and *after* Alice sends her message to the referee the adversary chooses the input of Bob depending on both the preprocessing transcript and on *and Alice's message.*

Note: while allowing "rushing" gives the adversary more power, it is not an unreasonable model, e.g. in a sketching environment, when the adversary sees how one party 'sketched' its input and may then select the inputs to the other one. We do not know whether we need this power in order to get the result that very succinct protocols imply secret key agreement.

1.1 Cryptographic Primitives

We discuss a computationally bounded world. We assume that all parties have limited resources (especially at runtime). A way to express those limits is by cryptographic primitives (see the next examples).

Necessity of Primitives. One of the aims of research in foundations of cryptography is to find out which cryptographic primitives are essential and sufficient for which tasks. Similarly, it is valuable to know whether certain primitives on their own *cannot* help us achieve a certain goal.

In this paper we prove several implications of the form that the existence of communication protocols with certain properties entails the existence of certain primitives. In other words, in order to design succinct protocols in those models we must be using somewhere in the protocol primitives of a certain kind.

1.2 Cryptographic Hash Functions

A hash function is one that maps values from a large domain to a smaller range. One of the most basic cryptographic objects is a hash function with some hardness property. For instance, a family of hash functions $\mathcal{H}$, is collision resistant if for a random $h \in_R H$ it is hard to find two inputs $x \neq y$ that collide $(h(x) = h(y))$.

For such a function, for any two inputs that were chosen by a computationally bounded adversary, we know that w.h.p., $h(x) = h(y) \implies x = y$. This means that the function *preserves* some relation between its inputs: The equality predicate is (w.h.p.) preserved also after the values were compressed by h. Moreover, since the function is collision resistant, that property holds for any (x, y) chosen by a computationally bounded adversary knowing h.

This notion can be generalized in several directions:

1. More relaxed hardness requirements can be defined. The weaker the definition the more hope we have to construct it from minimal assumptions.
2. We can extend the definitions to include random algorithms: functions that get also random bits and output correct values w.h.p.[2].
3. We can extend the definitions to hash functions that preserve more properties and not just the equality predicate.

We discuss the last two points in the section below.

---

[2] The probability is over the choices of the random bits.

1.3   Adversarially Robust Property-Preserving Hash Functions

Consider a predicate $P : U \times U \rightarrow \{0,1\}$ for a universe $U = \{0,1\}^n$. Let $x, y \in U$ and we want to compute $P(x,y)$, but we cannot have both x, y on the same machine (say, for some storage reasons). A natural approach for this issue is using *sketching*: By using sketches we get shorter strings and it is easier to get both (sketched) values on the same machine. Of course, computing P on sketched values may be impossible in terms of information, so we relax the correctness requirement: the process may fail (compute a wrong value) with at most a negligible probability[3].

Hash functions as above, that allow us to compute a predicate given the hashed values, are called *property-preserving* hash functions (hereafter PPH). We examine PPH in an *adversarial* environment, that is, the predicate should be computed correctly w.h.p. also for values chosen by an adversary. Such hash functions are called *adversarially robust* PPH. The more access to the hash function given to the adversary the more robust the PPH is.

The study of adversarially robust property-preserving hash functions was initiated by Boyle et al. [BLV18]. It can be seen as a special case of the model introduced by Mironov et al. [MNS11] who initiated the study of the *adversarial sketch model* (here the participants also get the input *online*). That notion is similar to the SM model except for the differences:

1. The allowed error probability in communication complexity is a (small) constant instead of negligible in PPHs.
2. The parties in the SM model are allowed to be randomized.
3. The PPHs model is computational.

Our model bridges some of the gaps and we will show the connection between the models. Note that the preset public coins SM model is a generalization of the PPHs model in the sense that the participants are allowed to be randomized. In this regards it is closer to the model of Mironov et al. [MNS11].

1.4   Secret Key Agreement

A secret key agreement (SKA) is a protocol where two parties with no prior common information agree on a secret key. The key has to be secret in the sense that no probabilistic polynomial time adversary given the full transcript of the communication between Alice and Bob can compute it with non-negligible probability (more accurately, distinguish it from a random string). That notion is defined formally in Definition 2.19.

We will show that certain low communication protocols imply the existence of SKA by showing a construction of SKA from those protocols.

---

[3] The probabilities are over the sampling of a hash function among the functions family.

1.5   Our Results

We consider preset public coins communication complexity models and prove that the lower bounds proved for the private coins model cannot be broken in our computational model without assuming the existence of distributional CRHs (dCRH is a hash function where uniformly random collisions cannot be found by a bounded adversary w.h.p., see Definition 2.16) It is known that dCRHs exist only if one-way functions exist and there is an oracle separation between them (i.e. there are no black-box constructions of dCRHs from one-way functions).

A non-trivial predicate is one with no redundant rows and columns (see Definition 2.1)

Theorem (informal, see Theorems 3.2 *and* 3.14). In the preset public coins Simultaneous Message model: for any non-trivial predicate, protocols with communication complexity $o(\sqrt{n})$ imply the existence of dCRHs (in the sense that a dCRH can be constructed from the protocol).

In the interactive model: The same is true for $c(n) = o(\log n)$.

Gap from Upper Bound. We note that such succinct protocols are achievable using a CRH. Closing the gap between CRH and dCRH is left as an open problem (see conclusions).

Consider the free talk model, where two parties communicate and may have a secret state as a result, *before* the inputs are chosen based on an eavesdropper adversary who has access to the communication but not to the secret states. If secret key agreement protocols exist, then we can get the power of the public coins model: we can construct a protocol for the equality predicate with error probability bounded by 2^{-c} where c is the communication complexity.

In the other direction, nearly optimal protocols imply a secret key agreement:

Theorem (informal, see Theorem 5.2). In the stateful free talk model, the existence of a protocol of complexity $c(n)$ for equality with failure probability bounded by $\varepsilon \leq 2^{-0.7c}$ against a rushing adversary implies the existence of a secret key agreement protocol.

Again here there are gaps between the possibility and impossibility results. For the implication we do need a low error protocol (with respect to the communication complexity) and also we do not know whether a rushing adversary is essential.

The various implications we showed are summarized in Table 1.

On the other hand, regardless of assumptions, constant communication protocols cannot exist in our model. This is in contrast to the public coins model, where there are protocols of $O(1)$ communication even in the SM model (e.g. for the equality predicate).

Theorem (informal, see Theorem 4.1). In the interactive communication model, protocols for any non trivial predicate, of communication complexity $O(\log \log n)$ bits are not secure against an adversary with running time poly(n).

Table 1. Summary of Implications and Results

		Information-Theoretic Lower Bound	Comput. Bounded World: Breaking The Bound	
			Possible Using	Implies
Stateless	SM	$\Omega(\sqrt{n})$	CRH	dCRH
	Interactive	$\Omega(\log n)$	CRH	dCRH
Stateful (Rushing $\mathcal{A}$dv)	SM	$\Omega(n)$	SKA	For Equality: SKA*

* Holds only for near optimal protocols.

1.6   Related Work

Communication Complexity

The study of communication complexity was initiated by Yao [Yao79] who introduced the SM private coins model and asked what is the complexity of the equality predicate in this model. The problem was solved by Newman and Szegedy [NS96] who provided the $\Omega(\sqrt{n})$ tight lower bound. It was also solved, using different and simpler techniques, by Babai and Kimmel [BK97][4] using a combinatorial proof, and by Bottesch et al. [BGK15] using information theory[5].

Babai and Kimmels's result is more general and they actually proved the lower bound not only to the equality predicate but to any non-redundant predicate (see Definition 2.1). Moreover, their technique proved to be useful in more models: Ben-Sasson and Maor [BM15] applied this technique also for the interactive model and proved that for any non redundant function, any private coins protocol requires communication complexity of at least $\Omega(\log n)$ (see proof for the equality predicate in Kushilevitz and Nisan [KN96]).

Although the above mentioned results are in the information-theoretic world (can be seen as an unbounded adversary), Naor and Rothblum [NR09] introduced and studied a computational model in order to study online memory checking algorithms: The consecutive messages model where the public coins are chosen *after* the adversary chooses x (the input for Alice). They adapted this technique and showed that breaking the mentioned information-theoretic $\Omega(\sqrt{n})$ lower bound in their computational model is possible if and only if one-way functions exist. At first glance one can think that their model is very close to our preset public coins SM model. However, important details differ: For instance, the fact that x (Alice's input) does not depend on the public random string.

Public Coins vs. Private Coins. In certain ways our model lies between the public and private coins ones. Therefore, it is worth pointing out the possible

---

[4] See in [BK97] also the similar proof of Bourgain and Wigderson.

[5] Bottesch et al. actually discuss quantum variants of the SM model and give the simpler proof for our classical case as a warm-up.

gap between them. For the interactive communication settings, Newman [New91] proved that the gap can be at most $O(\log n)$ additively. It is tight, since the equality predicate can be computed by protocols of $O(1)$ communication in the public coins model but requires $\Theta(\log n)$ bits in the private coins model.

In the SM model, as mentioned, the gap may be much larger: the equality predicate can be computed using $O(1)$ bits in the public coins model, but in the private coins model $\Omega(\sqrt{n})$ bits are required.

Settings Where Worst-Case Inputs are Hard to Find

One area where computationally bounded choices of inputs was considered is error correcting codes. Here assuming the channel is computationally bounded may help and better rates than those achievable by codes for worst-case errors are possible. Such works were done by Lipton [Lip94] and Micali et al. [MPSW10]. These constructions required a trusted setup with a key that should not leak. Grossman et al. [GHY20] suggested "good" uniquely decodable codes for the computationally bounded channel with transparent setup. Grossman et al. relied on strong cryptographic assumptions to construct a code better than codes for worst-case errors.

Harsha et al. [HIKNV04] studied tradeoffs between communication complexity and time complexity and described Boolean functions with a strong communication vs. runtime tradeoff.

1.7   Technical Overview

Babai and Kimmel's Characterizing Multiset. We will use the technique of Babai and Kimmel for proving connections between the communication complexity and cryptographic primitives in both models (SM and interactive). They proved that in the SM model, Alice's behavior can be characterized by a relatively small multiset of messages. Ben-Sasson and Maor expanded it for the interactive model and proved that Alice's behavior can be characterized by a multiset of *deterministic strategies*.

We use those observations and show that the adversary can use the characterizing multisets to find bad inputs for Alice and Bob. That is, we construct a function that for any x (Alice's input) generates a characterizing multiset of the behavior of Alice for this x. We claim that an adversary who can break the security of this function, can find bad inputs for the protocol. On the other direction, if such a protocol exists it implies the existence of a certain cryptographic primitive.

In more details: We show a construction of a function that for an Alice's input ($x \in X$) outputs a multiset that characterizes Alice's behaviour. We claim that a collision in such function induces bad inputs for the protocol as it implies two inputs that make Alice behaves similar. That is, the correctness of the protocol implies the security of the function. However, the construction is probabilistic and the function does not output a characterizing multiset for every inputs but only for at most every input. Hence, it may not be collision resistant but only one-way function. Moreover, we show it also a distributional collision resistant since it outputs a characterizing for at most every input.

2   Models and Preliminaries

2.1   Model Definition

Let f be a predicate that Alice and bob would like to compute. For a predicate f to be interesting we may assume that the f has no redundancy:

Definition 2.1 (Non-Redundant Predicate). *Predicate* $f : X \times Y \to \{0,1\}$ *is non-redundant if there are no two identical rows or two identical columns in the truth matrix. In other words,* $\forall x_1 \neq x_2 : \exists y$ *s.t.* $f(x_1, y) \neq f(x_2, y)$ *and for* $\forall y_1 \neq y_2$ *as well.*

Also, we discuss only predicates where their non-redundancy can be 'proven' or found efficiently:

Definition 2.2 (Efficiently Separable Predicate). *Let* $f : X \times Y \to \{0,1\}$ *be a non-redundant predicate, then* f *is efficiently separable if there exists PPTM* $\mathcal{M}$ *that finds the element promised by Definition 2.1. That is* $\forall x_1 \neq x_2 \in X$:

$$\Pr_{y \leftarrow \mathcal{M}(x_1, x_2)} [f(x_1, y) \neq f(x_2, y)] = 1 - \mathrm{negl}(n)$$

and similarly for $\forall y_1 \neq y_2 \in Y$ *as well.*

Note 2.3. It is not clear that a Non-Redundant Predicate that is *not* Efficiently Separable implies the existence of one-way functions. In fact, it seems that hard problems in NP ("Pessiland") already implies the existence of such predicates, and hence as far as we know it is not a sufficient assumption for mounting meaningful cryptography.

The only specific predicate we discuss is the equality predicate, $EQ(x, y) = \mathbb{1}_{\{x=y\}}$. For the equality predicate it is easy to see that both Definitions 2.1 and 2.2 hold.

Now, we define the communication layouts:

Definition 2.4 (Interactive Communication Model). *Alice and Bob are given x and y respectively and should compute some function f. They may send each other messages without any limit (but the total number of bits sent is the complexity).*

Definition 2.5 (Simultaneous Messages (SM) Model). *In the simultaneous messages model, Alice and Bob are given x and y respectively and should compute some function f without communicating with each other. Instead, each one sends a message to a third party (a referee) who calculates $f(x, y)$ given the messages from Alice and Bob.*

Following Babai and Kimmel we assume without loss of generality that the referee is deterministic.

Fact 2.6. *In the SM model there exist protocols for the equality predicate of complexity $O(\sqrt{n})$. The protocols found independently by Ambainis, Babai and Kimmel, Naor and Newman; see [BK97] for references.*

Fact 2.6 is an example of the possible gap between probabilistic and deterministic protocols in the SM model because the equality predicate is non-redundant and because of the following well known fact:

Fact. In the SM model, the deterministic communication complexity of any non-redundant predicate is $\Omega(n)$.

Now, we are ready to define our model formally, in the above described communication layouts. Recall that our model is *computational*. That is, the participants' running time is bounded by some poly(λ) for some security parameter $\lambda = $ poly(n), it's important especially for the adversarial participant. That is, any PPTM run time is bounded by poly(λ).

Definition 2.7 (Preset Public Coins). *A protocol for a function f in the preset public coins is defined by the following game: Let Alice and Bob be PPTMs with running time* poly(λ).

1. *A public uniform random string r_{pub} is sampled[6].*
2. *The adversary sees r_{pub} and chooses $(x, y) \in X \times Y$.*
3. *Alice and Bob get (x, r_{pub}) and (y, r_{pub}) respectively.*
4. *Alice and Bob send message(s) (optionally using private coins) in order to compute some target function.*
5. *Optionally: More steps that depend on the communication settings. For instance, in the SM model the referee steps in here.*

We say that a protocol is ε-secure in this model if for every PPTM adversary $\mathcal{A}dv$ with running time poly(λ) the probability that the computation of Alice and Bob will be correct is at least $1 - \varepsilon$:

$$\Pr_{\substack{r_{pub} \\ (x,y) \leftarrow \mathcal{A}dv(r_{pub}) \\ \text{Alice and Bob private coins}}} [Protocol\ Fails] \leq \varepsilon$$

Amplification. The usual requirements in communication complexity is for $\varepsilon = 1/3$ and then to argue for amplification by repetition. Here we have to be a bit more careful, since the correctness requirement is computational. However, we know that for games of a certain structure we get parallel amplification: Bellare et al. [BIN97] showed that parallel repetition of computationally sound protocols doesn't always lower the error as one may expect. However, they proved that for three-round protocols the error does go down exponentially fast[7] as in the information-theoretic case.

A protocol in our model can be evaluated in the following 3 rounds:

---

[6] Can be generalized to a sample from any known efficient distribution.

[7] See Canetti et al. [CHS05] for better parameters.

1. The prover chooses the public random string.
2. The adversary chooses the inputs of Alice and Bob.
3. The prover chooses Alice's and Bob's private random string.

Note 2.8. Alice's and Bob's algorithms are public and since they don't have any secret state or secret input they can be simulated (also by the adversarial participant). It is a core fact when we are using the technique of Babai and Kimmel in computational settings in the proofs of Theorems 3.2 and 3.14 and Theorem 4.1.

2.2   Free Talk Model

We consider a variation to the SM model where Alice and Bob are allowed to communicate freely in a preprocessing phase, before the inputs are chosen:

Free talk. Free talk is a 'free' communication that Alice and Bob can have before the inputs are chosen by the adversary. Alice and Bob can generate states (possibly secret) in the free talk phase. Those states can be used afterward to reduce the communication complexity.

However, the adversary is also stronger, in two ways:

Free Talk Eavesdropping. The transcript of the free talk phase is known to the adversary and it may choose the inputs depending also on it.

Rushing. Rushing adversary decides Bob's input at the 'last moment': Rushing adversary chooses the input of Bob *after* Alice produces its message. That is, first Alice's input is chosen and Alice sends its message, and afterwards, Bob's input is chosen depending on Alice's message and Bob sends its message.

Definition 2.9 (SM Preset Public Coins With Stateful Free Talk and Rushing Adversary). *A protocol for a function f in the SM Preset Public Coins With stateful free talk and rushing adversary is defined by the following game: Let Alice and Bob be PPTMs with running time* $\mathrm{poly}(\lambda)$.

1. *Alice and Bob toss coins and communicate in order to generate their (possibly secret) states τ_A and τ_B respectively.*
2. *The adversary sees their full communication (but not their internal states τ_A and τ_B) and sets Alice's input $x \in X$.*
3. *Alice (that has τ_A as her internal state) gets x and sends a message m_A to the referee.*
4. *The adversary sees m_A and chooses Bob's input $y \in Y$, optionally depending on m_A and the free talk's transcript.*
5. *Bob (that has τ_B as his internal state) gets y and sends a message m_B to the referee.*
6. *The referee, as a function of m_A and m_B, computes the target predicate.*

To simplify the description we assume, without loss of generality, that Alice and Bob are probabilistic only in the first step. (This is wlog since they can toss coins in the first step and save them in their private states for later use.)

In the stateful model we consider a scenario with a 'patient' adversary: there are multiple sessions between Alice and Bob and the (rushing) adversary can choose one session to attack among them, after seeing the message Alice choose.

Definition 2.10 (Stateful Free Talk ε-Secure Protocol). *We say that a protocol is ε-secure in the stateful model if for every PPTM adversary $\mathcal{A}dv$ with running time $\mathrm{poly}(\lambda)$ who involved in $\mathrm{poly}(\lambda)$ sessions and chooses among them one session as the defining one (after seeing Alice's message) the probability that the computation of Alice and Bob will be correct for the chosen session is at least $1 - \varepsilon$.*

2.3 Notation

Messages Space. Denote by M_A and M_B Alice's and Bob's messages spaces. In the interactive model we consider Alice's and Bob's deterministic strategies, every strategy is represented by a rooted binary tree of depth c (the total communication): The protocol begins in the root, each vertex is owned by one party who chooses one of the children and informs the other party by sending a bit. Finally, the leaves represent the protocol's result. We denote the set of deterministic strategies of Alice and Bob by S_A and S_B respectively.

Private random string. Denote by $r_A \in R_A$ the private random string of Alice.

Public random string. Denote by $r_{\mathrm{pub}} \in R_{\mathrm{pub}}$ the public random string in the protocol (it is given also to the adversary).

Secret State. When Alice and Bob have secret states we denote them by τ_A and τ_B respectively.

Participant. In the SM model, for a public random string r_{pub} denote the strategy of Alice by $A_{r_{\mathrm{pub}}} : X \times R_A \to M_A$ and Bob by $B_{r_{\mathrm{pub}}} : X \times R_B \to M_B$. When the public random string r_{pub} is clear from the context we may omit the subscript. (When Alice and Bob have a secret state we denote Alice and Bob as a function that gets a secret state τ instead of private random string).

Referee. In the SM model denote the referee by a function $\rho_{r_{\mathrm{pub}}} : M_A \times M_B \to \{0,1\}$ for a public random string r_{pub} or ρ when r_{pub} is clear from the context.

Communication Complexity. Denote the length of the total communication by $c = c(n, \lambda)$.

Protocol. We denote the protocol by π, and $\pi(x, y)$ denotes running the protocol on inputs x and y.

2.4 Probability

To measure distance between two distributions we use the *total variation distance*:

Definition 2.11 (Statistical Distance). *Let D_1 and D_2 be two distributions and $D(E)$ be the probability of event E under the distribution D.*

$$\Delta(D_1, D_2) = \max_{Event\ E} |D_1(E) - D_2(E)|$$

We use in our proofs the following concentration lemma:

Lemma 2.12. *Let $X_1, X_2, \ldots, X_t$ be mutually independent random variables where $\mathbf{E}[X_i] = 0$ and $|X_i| \leq 1$. Let $S = \frac{1}{t} \sum_{i=1}^{t} X_i$ then*

$$\mathbf{Pr}[S > \delta] < e^{-\delta^2 t/2}$$

which is a rephrasing of the following Chernoff bound:

Theorem 2.13 (Chernoff Bound [AS08, Theorem A.1.16]). *Let $X_1, \ldots,$ X_t be mutually independent random variables where $\mathbf{E}[X_i] = 0$ and $|X_i| \leq 1$ and let $S = \sum_{i=1}^{t} X_i$. Then*

$$\mathbf{Pr}[S > a] < e^{-a^2/2t}$$

2.5 Collision Resistant Hash Functions

A collision resistant hash function (CRH) is a function that any efficient algorithm has at most a negligible probability of a collision:

Definition 2.14 (CRH). *Let a functions family $\mathcal{H}$ be a family of functions that (1) compress (2) are computable in polynomial time. $\mathcal{H}$ is a family of CRHs if for every polynomial $p(\cdot)$ for every PPTM $\mathcal{A}dv$ and large enough λ,*

$$\Pr_{\substack{h \in \mathcal{H} \\ (x,y) \leftarrow \mathcal{A}dv(h)}} [x \neq y \wedge h(x) = h(y)] < \frac{1}{p(\lambda)}$$

Note that, the output of the function cannot be too small with respect to the security parameter. Otherwise, collisions can be found easily by trying sufficient inputs.

Simon [Sim98] showed that a CRH cannot be built from black-box one-way functions. Since one-way functions are existential equivalent to a lot of basic cryptographic primitives, we know that also they cannot be black-box used to construct CRHs. For an example, see Wee [Wee07] who ruled out constructions for statistically hiding commitments with low round complexity that are based only on black-box one-way functions.

Distributional Collision Resistant Hash Functions Distributional collision resistant hash functions (dCRH) are functions where it is hard for any adversary to generate collisions that *are close to random collisions*. We first have to define an ideal collision finder:

Definition 2.15 (Ideal Collision Finder COL). *The random function COL gets a description of a hash function h and outputs (x, x') s.t. x is uniformly random and x' is uniformly random from $h^{-1}(x)$. Note that:*

1. *The marginal distribution of x and x' is the same: x and x' are uniformly random (but not independent).*
2. *It is possible that $x = x'$.*

That notion of distributional collision resistance hash functions is due to Dubrov and Ishai [DI06]. However, Bitansky et al. [BHKY19] deviated from this definition and used a stronger definition[8]. Since our results hold also for the stronger definition we will use it:

Definition 2.16 (dCRH). *Let a functions family $\mathcal{H}$ be a family of functions that (1) compress (2) are computable in polynomial time. $\mathcal{H}$ is a family of distributional CRHs if there exists some polynomial $p(\cdot)$ s.t. for every PPTM $\mathcal{A}dv$, and large enough λ,*

$$\Delta(COL(h), \mathcal{A}dv(h)) \geq \frac{1}{p(\lambda)}$$

where $h \leftarrow \mathcal{H}$.

This definition is a generalization of distributional one-way functions[9] and hence implies it. Furthermore, Bitansky et al. showed that dCRHs can be used for applications that one-way functions aren't known to achieve (and are black-box separated) [BHKY19].

Although the notion of dCRH is much weaker than CRH, as noted by Dubrov and Ishai [DI06], the black-box separation result of Simon [Sim98] applied also for dCRH: Its collision finder is the same as COL in our definition (Definition 2.15). Simon proved that relative to COL one-way functions exist (although (d)CRHs do not).

2.6 Adversarially Robust Property-Preserving Hash Functions

Here we define the notion of adversarially robust property-preserving hash functions. We follow Boyle et al.'s notion of direct-access robust property-preserving hash functions:

Definition 2.17 (Direct-Access Robust PPHs). *Let a functions family $\mathcal{H}$ be a family of functions that (1) compress (2) are computable in polynomial time and let Eval be a deterministic polynomial time algorithm. $\mathcal{H}$ (with Eval) is a*

---

[8] By switching the order of quantifiers, they require one polynomial for any adversary and not that for any adversary there exists a polynomial. See the comparison in [BHKY19].

[9] Functions where it is hard to sample uniformly from $h^{-1}(h(x))$ for random x. Such functions are known to exist if and only if one-way functions exist [IL89]. (in contrast to dCRH).

family of Direct-Access Robust PPHs for a predicate $P : X \times X \to \{0, 1, *\}^{10}$ if for every polynomial $p(\cdot)$ for every PPTM Adv and large enough λ,

$$\Pr_{\substack{h \in \mathcal{H} \\ (x,y) \leftarrow \mathcal{A}dv(h)}} [P(x,y) \neq * \wedge P(x,y) \neq Eval(h, h(x), h(y)) \neq P(x,y)] < \frac{1}{p(\lambda)}$$

2.7   Secret Key Agreement and Its Amplification

In a secret key agreement protocol two participants who do not have a common secret, but each one has its own source of randomness, both output a value (the secret). The participants' output has to satisfy two properties: it should be the same value for the two participants (agreement), and it has to be unknown to any efficient observer (secrecy). We follow the definition of Holenstein [Hol05]:

Definition 2.18 ((α, β)-Secret Bit Agreement (SBA)). *An efficient two party protocol without input (aside from the security parameter λ), with one bit output for each participant b and b' respectively where $b, b' \in \{0, 1\}$ is an (α, β)-secret bit agreement if*

$$\Pr[b = b'] \geq \frac{1 + \alpha}{2}$$

and for every PPTM Adv with running time bounded by $\mathrm{poly}(\lambda)$

$$\Pr[\mathcal{A}dv(\tau) = b \mid b = b'] \leq 1 - \frac{\beta}{2}$$

where τ is the complete transcript of the protocol.

The previous definition is a weaker notion of the usually desirable stronger notion:

Definition 2.19 (Secret Key Agreement). *(α, β)-secret bit agreement is a secret key agreement protocol if $\alpha = 1 - \mathrm{negl}(\lambda)$ and $\beta = 1 - \mathrm{negl}(\lambda)$.*

Holenstein [Hol06] proved when an (α, β)-secret bit agreement can be amplified efficiently to a secret key agreement:

Theorem 2.20 ([Hol06, Corollary 7.5]). *Let efficiently computable functions $\alpha(\lambda), \beta(\lambda)$, be given such that*

$$\frac{1 - \alpha}{1 + \alpha} < \beta$$

Let $\varphi = \max(2, \frac{8}{\log(\frac{\beta(1+\alpha)}{1-\alpha})})$ and $\gamma = \frac{1}{\log(1 + ((1-\alpha)/(1+\alpha))^\varphi)}$, and assume that $\frac{\varphi \cdot 2^{4\gamma}}{\alpha} \in \mathrm{poly}(\lambda)$. If there exists an (α, β)-secret bit agreement protocol for all but finitely many k, then there exists a computationally secure key agreement.

Note that a secret key agreement is unlikely to be based (only) on one-way permutations and collision resistant hash functions in a black-box manner: It is known that any secret key agreement protocol in the random oracle model[11] can be broken using an $O(n^2)$ queries attack [IR89, BM09] and this is tight.

---

[10] $*$ is a don't care symbol, see [BLV18] for a comparison of "total vs. partial predicates".
[11] CRHs exist in this model.

3   Collision Resistance and the Preset Public Coins Model

3.1   CRHs Imply Succinct Protocols

We start by noting that the lower bounds shown in Sect. 3.2 (about the necessity of dCRHs) are almost tight, since using a CRH one can break those bounds ($\Omega(\sqrt{n})$ in the SM model (Theorem 3.2) and $\Omega(\log n)$ in the interactive model (Theorem 3.14)). See the full version for details.

Theorem 3.1. *If CRHs exist, then given a family of CRHs $\{h : \{0,1\}^n \to \{0,1\}^\lambda\}$,*

In the preset public coins SM model: *There exist protocols of communication complexity $O(\sqrt{\lambda})$ for the Equality predicate.*

In the preset public coins interactive model: *There exist protocols of communication complexity $O(\log \lambda)$ for the Equality predicate.*

3.2   Succinct Protocols Imply dCRHs

Theorem 3.2. *Let $c(n) \leq o(\sqrt{n})$. Given a protocol for an efficiently separable predicate (Definition 2.2) of complexity $c(n)$ in the preset public coins SM model, then distributional CRH functions exist and it is possible to construct them from the protocol.*

Proof. Our intuition is that after fixing the public random string r_{pub}, the model is similar to the private coins SM model where the adversary is faced with a problem defined by the random string. We therefore appeal to Babai and Kimmel's definitions and techniques. Furthermore, in Lemma 3.5 we will also repeat the proof of [BK97, Lemma 2.3] with a different constant and make it constructive.

For each multiset of Alice's messages and one message from Bob we consider the probability of acceptance by the referee:

Definition 3.3 (Referee's Expected Value for a Multiset). *For any r_{pub}, for a multiset T of members from M_A and $m_B \in M_B$, let*

$$Q(T, m_B) = \underset{i \in [t]}{\mathbf{E}} [\rho_{r_{pub}}(T[i], m_B)] = \frac{1}{t} \sum_{i \in [t]} \rho_{r_{pub}}(T[i], m_B)$$

where $t = |T|$.

Now, we show that for every input of Alice $x \in X$, there exists a multiset *characterizing* the behavior of Alice on x. In other words, instead of running Alice, we can approximate the protocol's result (referee's output) by a uniform sample from the multiset. Furthermore, we prove that such a multiset can be found (w.h.p.) by some (relatively few) independent samples from the distribution defined by Alice (given x and r_{pub}).

Definition 3.4 (Characterizing Multiset). *For any r_{pub}, a multiset T of elements from M_A characterizes Alice for $x \in X$ if $\forall m_B \in M_B$,*

$$\left| Q(T, m_B) - \Pr_{r_A}[\rho_{r_{pub}}(A_{r_{pub}}(x, r_A), m_B) = 1] \right| \leq 0.1$$

where $Q(T_x, m_B)$ is the referee's expected value for the multiset T_x and Bob's possible message $m_B \in M_B$ (Definition 3.3).

Lemma 3.5 (Sample a Characterizing Multiset). *For any r_{pub}, for $x \in X$, let $r' = (r_A^1, ..., r_A^t)$ be t independent uniform samples from R_A where $t = 2 \cdot 200 \cdot \ln(2|M_B|)$. Then, for the multiset $T_x = \{A_{r_{pub}}(x, r_A^i) : i \in [t]\}$ it holds that $\forall m_B \in M_B$,*

$$\Pr_{r'} \left[\left| Q(T_x, m_B) - \Pr_{r_A}[\rho_{r_{pub}}(A_{r_{pub}}(x, r_A), m_B) = 1] \right| \leq 0.1 \right] \geq 1 - \frac{1}{2|M_B|}$$

(i.e., T_x characterizes Alice for x)

Proof. Let T_x be as defined. $\forall i \in [t], m_B \in M_B$,

$$\mathbf{E}[\rho_{r_{pub}}(T_x[i], m_B)] = \Pr_{r_A}[\rho_{r_{pub}}(A_{r_{pub}}(x, r_A), m_B) = 1]$$

$$\implies \mathbf{E}\left[\rho_{r_{pub}}(T_x[i], m_B) - \Pr_{r_A}[\rho_{r_{pub}}(A_{r_{pub}}(x, r_A), m_B) = 1] \right] = 0$$

where the probability is over the random choice $T_x[i] \leftarrow A_{r_{pub}}(x)$.

Now, for $i \in [i]$, define random variables

$$\eta(i) = \rho_{r_{pub}}(T_x[i], m_B) - \Pr_{r_A}[\rho_{r_{pub}}(A_{r_{pub}}(x, r_A), m_B) = 1].$$

Since the members of T_x are independent random variables, we have that all $\{\eta(i) : i \in [t]\}$ are independent random variables with expectation 0. Hence, we can use a Chernoff bound to bound the probability that, for a fixed $m_B \in M_B$,

$$\left| \sum_{i \in [t]} \eta(T_x[i]) \right| > 0.1 \cdot t.$$

In other words, the probability that

$$\left| Q(T_x, m_B) - \Pr_{r_A}[\rho_{r_{pub}}(A_{r_{pub}}(x, r_A), m_B) = 1] \right| > 0.1$$

is bounded by

$$\Pr_{r'}[|\sum_{i \in [t]} \rho_{r_{pub}}(T_x[i], m_B) - \mathbf{E}[\sum_{i \in [t]} \rho_{r_{pub}}(T_x[i], m_B)]| > 0.1] < 2e^{-\frac{(0.1)^2 \cdot t}{2}} \quad \text{(Lemma 2.12)}$$

$$= 2e^{-\frac{t}{200}}$$

$$= 2e^{-2\ln(2|M_B|)}$$

$$= \frac{1}{2|M_B|^2}.$$

By the union bound (over all $m_B \in M_B$),

$$\Pr_{r'}\left[\exists m_B \text{ s.t. } \left|Q(T, m_B) - \Pr_{r_A}[\rho_{r_{\text{pub}}}(A_{r_{\text{pub}}}(x, r_A), m_B) = 1]\right| > 0.1\right] < \frac{|M_B|}{2\,|M_B|^2}$$

$$= \frac{1}{2\,|M_B|}$$

$\square$

We define a hash function by following the process of Lemma 3.5 (running Alice t times independently):

Construction 3.6. Characterizing Multiset Function

Definition: The function is defined by the public random string r_{pub} and t Alice's random tapes $r_A^1, ..., r_A^t \in R_A$.

Output: For $x \in X$, the value of the function is the multiset as in Lemma 3.5:

$$h(x) = \text{The multiset } \{A_{r_{\text{pub}}}(x, r_A^i) : i \in [t]\}$$

where the multiset is encoded as a sequence $A_{r_{\text{pub}}}(x, r_A^1), \ldots, A_{r_{\text{pub}}}(x, r_A^t)$, note that every Alice's message can be encoded using $\log |M_A| = c$ bits.

Observation 3.7. *For all $x \in X$, the function from Construction 3.6 outputs a multiset that characterizes x w.p. $1 - \frac{1}{2|M_B|}$ where the probability is over the uniform random choice of $r_A^1, ..., r_A^t \in R_A$.*

Observation 3.8. *The function from Construction 3.6 is compressing: The domain of the function is of size 2^n, but the range is of size at most*

$$(2^c)^t = 2^{400c \cdot (c+1) \cdot \ln 2} = 2^{\Theta(c^2)} = 2^{o(n)}$$

Next, we prove that any x and x' which share a characterizing multiset, induce bad inputs for the protocol (since Alice's behavior on x and x' is similar).

Proposition 3.9. *Let $x, x' \in X$ and $y \in Y$ that separates them (Definition 2.1), if there is a multiset T that is characterizing for both x and x' then, the sum of the failure probability of $\pi(x, y)$ and $\pi(x', y)$ is at least 0.8. In other words, at least one of them fails.*

Proof. Since T is a characterizing multiset (Definition 3.4) of both x and x', then $\forall m_B \in M_B$

$$\left|Q(T, m_B) - \Pr_{r_A}[\rho_{r_{\text{pub}}}(A_{r_{\text{pub}}}(x, r_A), m_B) = 1]\right| \leq 0.1$$

and the same for x'. This means

$$\Pr_{r_A}[\rho_{r_{\text{pub}}}(A_{r_{\text{pub}}}(x, r_A), m_B) = 1] \in [Q(T, m_B) \pm 0.1]$$

and

$$\Pr_{r_A}[\rho_{r_{\text{pub}}}(A_{r_{\text{pub}}}(x', r_A), m_B) = 1] \in [Q(T, m_B) \pm 0.1].$$

Putting it together we get that:

$$\left| \Pr_{r_A}[\rho_{r_{\text{pub}}}(A_{r_{\text{pub}}}(x, r_A), m_B) = 1] - \Pr_{r_A}[\rho_{r_{\text{pub}}}(A_{r_{\text{pub}}}(x', r_A), m_B) = 1] \right| \le 0.2. \tag{1}$$

Assume without loss of generality that $f(x, y) = 0$ and $f(x', y) = 1$

$$
\begin{aligned}
\Pr[\pi \text{ fails on } (x, y)] &= \Pr_{r_A, r_B}[\rho_{r_{\text{pub}}}(A_{r_{\text{pub}}}(x, r_A), B_{r_{\text{pub}}}(y, r_B)) = 1] \\
&= \mathbf{E}_{r_A, r_B}[\rho_{r_{\text{pub}}}(A_{r_{\text{pub}}}(x, r_A), B_{r_{\text{pub}}}(y, r_B))] \\
&= \mathbf{E}_{r_B}\left[\mathbf{E}_{r_A}[\rho_{r_{\text{pub}}}(A_{r_{\text{pub}}}(x, r_A), B_{r_{\text{pub}}}(y, r_B))]\right] \\
&\ge \mathbf{E}_{r_B}\left[\mathbf{E}_{r_A}[\rho_{r_{\text{pub}}}(A_{r_{\text{pub}}}(x', r_A), B_{r_{\text{pub}}}(y, r_B))] - 0.2\right] \quad \text{(Equation (1))} \\
&= \mathbf{E}_{r_B}\left[\mathbf{E}_{r_A}[\rho_{r_{\text{pub}}}(A_{r_{\text{pub}}}(x', r_A), B_{r_{\text{pub}}}(y, r_B))]\right] - 0.2 \\
&= \Pr_{r_A, r_B}[\rho_{r_{\text{pub}}}(A_{r_{\text{pub}}}(x', r_A), B_{r_{\text{pub}}}(y, r_B)) = 1] - 0.2 \\
&= \Pr[\pi \text{ succeeds on } (x', y)] - 0.2 \\
&= 1 - \Pr[\pi \text{ fails on } (x', y)] - 0.2 \\
&= 0.8 - \Pr[\pi \text{ fails on } (x', y)]
\end{aligned}
$$

Hence, the sum of the failure probability of the protocol on (x, y) and the failure probability of the protocol on (x', y) is

$$\Pr[\pi(x, y) \text{ fails}] + \Pr[\pi(x', y) \text{ fails}] \ge 0.8$$

□

However, now we deal with the fact that there exist x's s.t. the multiset $h(x)$ does not characterize x (Observation 3.7).

Lemma 3.10. *Let π be an SM protocol of complexity $c(n) = o(\sqrt{n})$ and $h(x)$ be as in Construction 3.6. If we have an efficient adversary $\mathcal{A}dv_{collision}$ that breaks the security of h as a distributional CRH for some $p \in \text{poly}(\lambda)$:*

$$\Delta\left(\mathcal{A}dv_{collision}(h), \mathcal{COL}(h)\right) \le \frac{1}{p(\lambda)}$$

Then, we can construct an adversary $\mathcal{A}dv_\pi$ *with running time of the same order as* $\mathcal{A}dv_{collision}$ *s.t.*

$$\mathbf{Pr}[\pi \text{ fails on inputs from } \mathcal{A}dv_\pi] \geq 0.4\left(1 - \frac{1}{p(\lambda)}\right) - \text{negl}(\lambda)$$

Proof. $\mathcal{A}dv_\pi$'s algorithm is:

Algorithm 3.11. Near Ideal Collision Finder for h to Bad Inputs for Protocol π

---

1. Construct $h(x)$ using the public random string of π and as in Construction 3.6.
2. $x, x' \leftarrow \mathcal{A}dv_{collision}(h)$.
3. Find $y \in Y$ which separates x and x' (promised to be efficient by Definition 2.2).
4. Pass to Alice and Bob (x, y) w.p. $1/2$ or (x', y) w.p. $1/2$.

First, we consider $\mathcal{COL}$'s distribution: A pair (x, x') that was sampled from $\mathcal{COL}$ (the ideal collisions finder, Definition 2.15) will not be usable for Algorithm 3.11 if any of the following conditions hold:

1. $x = x'$.
2. $h(x) = h(x')$ is not characterizing x or x'.

We call a pair (x, x') a *colliding* pair if neither of the above two conditions hold. In the following claims we bound the probability for those bad events.

Proposition 3.12. *The probability of sampling a pair* (x, x) *from* $\mathcal{COL}$ *(i.e., $x = x'$) is negligible. That is,*

$$\mathbf{Pr}_{(x,x')\leftarrow\mathcal{COL}}[x = x'] = \text{negl}(n)$$

Proof. First, consider the number of pairs (x, x') s.t. $x \neq x'$ but $h(x) = h(x')$. By the pigeonhole principle there exists a set of x's of size at least 2^{n-c^2} with the same image. Hence, there are at least $\binom{2^{n-c^2}}{2} = \Theta((2^{n-c^2})^2)$ many pairs (x, x') s.t. $x \neq x'$ but $h(x) = h(x')$. On the other hand, the number of pairs (x, x) is 2^n. Hence,

$$\mathbf{Pr}_{(x,x')\leftarrow\mathcal{COL}}[x = x'] = O\left(\frac{2^n}{2^n + (2^{n-o(n)})^2}\right) = \text{negl}(\lambda) \quad (c^2 = o(n))$$

□

Proposition 3.13. *For a random h, the probability of sampling from* $\mathcal{COL}$ *a pair* (x, x') *s.t. the multiset $h(x)$ does not characterize x or x' is negligible.*

Proof. Let $(x, x') \leftarrow \mathcal{COL}$, recall that the distribution of each element from $\mathcal{COL}$ (x and x') is uniform (Definition 2.15). For each element in the pair, the probability that the multiset $h(x)$ does not characterize it is at most 2^{-c} (Observation 3.7) and by the union bound the claim follows.   □

By Propositions 3.12 and 3.13, a sample from $\mathcal{COL}$ is colliding w.p. $1 - \mathrm{negl}(\lambda)$. However, the distribution of $\mathrm{Adv}_{\mathrm{collision}}$ is not exactly the same as $\mathcal{COL}$, but

$$\frac{1}{p(\lambda)} \geq \Delta(\mathcal{COL}, \mathrm{Adv}_{\mathrm{collision}})$$

$$\geq \left| \Pr_{(x,x')\leftarrow \mathrm{Adv}_{\mathrm{collision}}} [(x, x') \text{ not colliding}] - \Pr_{(x,x')\leftarrow \mathcal{COL}} [(x, x') \text{ not colliding}] \right|$$

and we can conclude that the probability that Algorithm 3.11 does not get a colliding pair (x, x') in step 2 is bounded by,

$$\Pr_{(x,x')\leftarrow \mathrm{Adv}_{\mathrm{collision}}} [(x, x') \text{ isn't colliding}] \leq \frac{1}{p(\lambda)} + \mathrm{negl}(\lambda)$$

To conclude: In cases that a colliding pair (x, x') was found by the adversary. The adversary chooses at random a pair from (x, y) and (x', y) (where y separates x and x', and can be found efficiently by Definition 2.2). By Proposition 3.9,

$$\Pr[\pi(x, y) \text{ fails}] + \Pr[\pi(x', y) \text{ fails}] \geq 0.8$$

and hence the failure probability over the random choice of the pair is at least

$$\Pr_{(z,y)\leftarrow \mathrm{Adv}_{\pi}} [\pi(z, y) \text{ fails}] \geq 0.4$$

Now, put it together with the probability of finding a colliding pair (for h) and we get the probability that the protocol π fails on inputs from the adversary:

$$\Pr[\mathrm{Adv}_{\pi} \text{ finds a colliding } (x, x')] \cdot \Pr_{(z,y)\leftarrow \mathrm{Adv}_{\pi}} [\pi(z, y) \text{ fails}]$$

$$\geq \left(1 - \frac{1}{p(\lambda)} - \mathrm{negl}(\lambda) \right) \cdot \frac{4}{10}$$

□

We get that given an adversary for the distributional CRH we can find bad inputs for the protocol as required for the proof.   □

Interactive Protocols

For general (interactive) protocols we can also prove a similar implication as in Theorem 3.2 for a logarithmic bound by the technique adaptation of Ben-Sasson and Maor [BM15]:

Theorem 3.14. *Let $c(n) < \delta_\varepsilon \log n$, where $\delta_\varepsilon < 1/2$ is a constant that depends only on ε. For an efficiently separable predicate (satisfying Definition 2.2), given a protocol of complexity $c(n)$ in the preset public coins interactive model, a distributional CRH can be constructed.*

Ben-Sasson and Maor studied protocols in the general communication settings and instead of using a characterizing multiset of *messages* they used a characterizing multiset of *deterministic strategies*. They have a variation of [BK97, Lemma 2.3] that says that there exists a strategies multiset of size $2^{O(c)}$ that characterizes the behavior of Alice for $x \in X$.

For a detailed proof see the full version.

A Corollary for PPHs

Corollary 3.15. *Without assuming the existence of distributional CRHs one cannot get better than $\sqrt{\cdot}$ compression for a direct-access robust equality PPH, even when extending the definitions for randomized hash functions.*

Proof. Observe that any PPH can be used to solve the same problem in the preset public coins SM model. Hence, this corollary is simply rephrasing Theorem 3.2 in the terms of adversarially robust property-preserving hash functions.   □

Note that the other direction is true as well: Every protocol in the preset public coins SM model for $f(x, y)$ of $c(n)$ bits 'induces' a PPH for f of $c(n) \cdot n^\varepsilon$ bits for some $\varepsilon > 0$. That is, we start with any preset public coins SM protocol and repeat it n^ε times to make the error probability negligible. This protocol defines a family of PPHs and its random coins are fixed when sampling a function from the family.

4   No Ultra Short Interactive Communication

The power of the preset public coins model power lies between the public and the private coins models. As noted, the public random coins model is strictly more powerful than the private one: there are protocols of $O(1)$ bits only in this model. We show (unconditionally) that in our model there are *no* functions with $o(\log \log n)$ communication complexity:

Theorem 4.1. *Let $c(n) : \mathcal{N} \mapsto \mathcal{N}$ be s.t. $2^{3c(n)} = O(\log n)$ and let $f : X \times Y \to \{0, 1\}$ be an efficiently separable predicate (satisfying Definition 2.2, i.e., non redundant s.t. can be proven efficiently). In the preset public coins interactive communication model, if the adversary has a running time of $\mathrm{poly}(\lambda)$ (where λ is the security parameter) then, there are no protocols of complexity $O(c(n))$.*

Proof. Assume there is such a protocol in the preset public coins interactive model for some non-redundant function f of complexity $c(n)$.

In the proof of Theorem 3.14 we adapted Construction 3.6 for interactive protocols. The constructed hash function has the following properties:

- Random collisions in the function induce (w.h.p.) bad inputs in the protocol (Lemma 3.10).
- The range of the function is of size

$$|S_A|^t = |S_A|^{2^{2 \cdot 200 \ln(2|S_B|)}}$$

Those properties are the key points of the adversary described by Algorithm 4.2 that searches for random collisions in a brute force manner.

Algorithm 4.2. Finding Bad Inputs in Ulta-Succinct Protocols

---

1. Construct a characterizing function $h(\cdot)$ (Construction 3.6).
2. Repeat at most $3 \cdot 2^{2^{3c}} = \text{poly}(\lambda)$ times:
   (a) Choose a pair $x \neq x' \in X$ uniformly at random.
   (b) If $h(x) = h(x')$:
       i. Find $y \in Y$ that separates x and x' (can be done efficiently, as promised by Definition 2.2).
       ii. Output (x, y) w.p. $1/2$ or (x', y) w.p. $1/2$
       iii. Halt

Let h be a characterizing function of the protocol (Construction 3.6). The proof relies on the following two claims.   □

Proposition 4.3. *There must be a collision in h.*

Proof. The range of the characterizing function $h(x)$ is of size (number of possible characterizing sets):

$$|S_A|^{2^{2 \cdot 200 \ln(2|S_B|)}} = 2^{2^c \cdot 2 \cdot 200 \ln\left(2^{2^c}+1\right)} < 2^{2^{3c}}$$

Hence, since $2^{3c} = O(\log n) = o(n)$ there must be a collision in the function.   □

Proposition 4.4. *The adversary described in Algorithm 4.2 finds a collision w.h.p.*

Proof. Since the range is small (same order as the running time of the adversary $2^{2^{3c}} = \text{poly}(\lambda)$), the adversary can find random collisions easily. The probability for a random pair to collide is at least $\frac{1}{2^{2^{3c}}}$ and hence, after $3 \cdot 2^{2^{3c}}$ trials, the probability that a collision was not found is at most:

$$\Pr_{x,x'}[h(x) \neq h(x')]^{3 \cdot 2^{2^{3c}}} \leq \left(\left(1 - \frac{1}{2^{2^{3c}}}\right)^{2^{2^{3c}}}\right)^3 \to e^{-3}$$

$$\implies \Pr_{x,x'}[h(x) \neq h(x')]^{3 \cdot 2^{2^{3c}}} < 0.05$$

    □

We get that w.h.p. the adversary finds a collision in the function h. However, not every collision implies bad inputs for the protocol: the construction of the characterizing function implies that there exist also bad collisions: x and x' s.t. $h(x) = h(x')$ but $h(x)$ doesn't characterizes x or x' (recall Observation 3.7). However, in almost all collisions it is not the case and $h(x)$ characterizes x and x' (recall Proposition 3.13). Now, since the collision that Algorithm 4.2 finds is completely random we can conclude,

$$\mathbf{Pr}[\text{the adversary finds a colliding pair}] \geq 1 - 0.05 - \frac{1}{|S_B|}$$

and by Proposition 3.9

$$\mathbf{Pr}[\text{the protocol will fail}] \geq \frac{1}{2} \cdot \frac{8}{10}\left(1 - 0.05 - \frac{1}{|S_B|}\right) > \frac{1}{3}.$$

$\square$

5   Secret Key Agreement from Efficient SM Protocols

5.1   Optimal Protocols from SKA

Our first observation is that it is possible to obtain an optimal protocol (in terms of the error as a function of the communication) for the equality predicate once given a secret key agreement protocol, following relatively simple principles. The error is 2^{-c} (where c is the communication complexity after the free talk) plus a negligible factor reflecting the probability of breaking the secret-key exchange. For details see the full version.

Theorem 5.1. *In the stateful preset public coins SM with free talk model: Given a secret key agreement protocol there is, for any $c(n)$, a protocol for the equality predicate of complexity $c(n)$, where any adversary can cause an incorrect answer with probability at most $2^{-c} + \mathrm{negl}(n)$, satisfying Definition 2.10.*

5.2   SKA from Near Optimal Protocols

Theorem 5.2. *An SM protocol with stateful free talk for the equality predicate of complexity $c(n) = O(\log \log n)$ for $c(n)$ larger from some constant, that is ε-secure (Definition 2.10) with $\varepsilon \leq 2^{-0.7c(n)}$, implies the existence of secret key-agreement protocols.*

Proof. Assume we have such a protocol π for the equality predicate $EQ : \{0,1\}^n \times \{0,1\}^n \rightarrow \{0,1\}$. We will use π for constructing a secret key-agreement protocol. The idea is to construct a weak secret bit agreement (Definition 2.18) that can be amplified into a full secret key agreement (α and β according to Theorem 2.20). The construction is based on the following: (α, β)-SBA protocol:

Algorithm 5.3. Weak Bit Agreement

1. Alice and Bob communicate and toss coins according to the free talk of protocol π to generate their secret states τ_A and τ_B respectively.
2. Alice selects at random a bit $b \in \{0,1\}$ and uniformly random inputs $x_0, x_1 \in \{0,1\}^n$.
3. Alice evaluates $m_A = A(x_b, \tau_A)$ (that is, a message of the protocol π for $EQ(\cdot, \cdot)$).
4. Alice sends to Bob (m_A, x_1).
5. Bob evaluates $m_B = B(x_1, \tau_B)$.
6. Alice outputs b and Bob outputs $b' = \rho(m_A, m_B)$.

Lemma 5.4. *Algorithm 5.3 is a $\left(\alpha = 1 - 2^{-c/2-3}, \beta = 2^{-c/2+1}\right)$-SBA protocol.*

Proof. Let $c = c(n)$. We have to show its agreement and secrecy properties:

Agreement. By the properties of protocol π, specifically that the error $\varepsilon \leq 2^{-0.7c(n)}$:

$$\mathbf{Pr}[b = b'] \geq 1 - \left(\frac{1}{2}\right)^{0.7c} \geq 1 - \left(\frac{1}{2}\right)^{0.5c-2} = \frac{1 + (1 - 2^{-c/2-3})}{2} = \frac{1 + \alpha}{2}.$$

Secrecy. We should show that for every PPTM adversary $\mathcal{Adv}_{\text{sba}}$

$$\mathbf{Pr}[\mathcal{Adv}_{\text{sba}}(m_A, x_1) = b \mid b = b'] \leq \frac{2 - \beta}{2} = \frac{2 - 2^{-c/2+1}}{2} = \frac{2^{c/2} - 1}{2^{c/2}}.$$

Assume towards contradiction that $\mathbf{Pr}[\mathcal{Adv}_{\text{sba}}(m_A, x_1) = b \mid b = b'] > \frac{2^{c/2}-1}{2^{c/2}}$. We show that given $\mathcal{Adv}_{\text{sba}}$, we can construct $\mathcal{Adv}_{\text{eq}}$ that finds bad inputs for the protocol π (with probability higher than ε):

Lemma 5.5. *Given an adversary $\mathcal{Adv}_{sba}$ with success probability (guessing b when it is equal to b') at least $\frac{2^{c/2}-1}{2^{c/2}}$, we can construct an adversary $\mathcal{Adv}_{eq}$ with running time $O(6 \cdot 2^{c+1})$ s.t.*

$$\mathbf{Pr}[\pi \text{ fails on inputs from } \mathcal{Adv}_{eq}] > 2^{-0.7c} \geq \varepsilon.$$

Proof. The strategy of the adversary $\mathcal{Adv}_{\text{eq}}$ to find bad inputs is:

Algorithm 5.6. $\mathcal{Adv}_{\text{eq}}$ – Find Bad Inputs Using $\mathcal{Adv}_{\text{sba}}$

1. Repeat at most $6 \cdot 2^{c+1}$ times:
   (a) Select uniformly at random $x \in \{0,1\}^n$ and set it as Alice's input.
   (b) Let Alice's message (output) be $m_A \in M_A$.
   (c) Select uniformly at random $x' \in \{0,1\}^n$.
   (d) If $\mathcal{Adv}_{\text{sba}}(x, m_A) = 1$ and $\mathcal{Adv}_{\text{sba}}(x', m_A) = 1$:
      i. Pass the message m_A to the referee and set Bob's input to be either $y = x$ w.p. $1/2$ or $y = x'$ w.p. $1/2$.
      ii. Halt.
   (e) Otherwise, continue to the next session.

Recall that the private states of Alice and Bob are τ_A and τ_B (unknown to the adversary). The success of the adversary $\mathcal{A}dv_{eq}$ relies on choosing a *colliding* x' (i.e., x' s.t. $A(x, \tau_B) = A(x', \tau_B)$).

For $x \in \{0,1\}^n$ denote by p_x^0 and p_x^1 the probability of a random $x' \in \{0,1\}^n$ to be bad in the following sense:

1. Let p_x^0 be the probability that for a random x': x and x' collide yet are not identified by $\mathcal{A}dv_{sba}$ as such. I.e.,

$$p_x^0 = \Pr_{x', \mathcal{A}dv}[A(x) = A(x') \wedge \mathcal{A}dv_{sba}(x', A(x, \tau_A)) = 0].$$

2. Let p_x^1 be the probability that for a random x': x and x' do not collide yet are identified by $\mathcal{A}dv_{sba}$ as such. I.e.,

$$p_x^1 = \Pr_{x', \mathcal{A}dv}[A(x) \neq A(x') \wedge \mathcal{A}dv_{sba}(x', A(x, \tau_A)) = 1].$$

Let $p_x = \max(p_x^0, p_x^1)$. For a random free talk session and over the random choice of $x \in \{0,1\}^n$, we know that $\mathbf{E}_x[p_x] = \sum_{p_x} p_x \mathbf{Pr}[p_x] \leq 2^{-c/2+1}$.

We will analyze the probability of success of each session and then argue that at least one session succeeds in outputting a value w.h.p. We need to show the probability of outputting a pair of strings that agree on the message Alice sends ("Correct") is not much smaller than outputting a pair that does not agree ("Wrong"). To compare the probability of outputting a wrong value to the probability of outputting the correct value, note that the probability of outputting a wrong value is at most $\sum_{\text{all } p_x} \Pr[p_x] \cdot p_x \leq 2^{-c/2}$. On the other hand we will argue that the probability of outputting a correct value (with identification) is roughly (at least) 2^{-c}. The ratio between them is roughly $2^{-0.5c}$ and we get an attack of the equality protocol that is better than its purported security.

For the rest of the proof see the full version. □

Lemma 5.5 implies the secrecy of Algorithm 5.3 (otherwise, we get a contradiction for the security of protocol π).

This means that Algorithm 5.3 is an $(1 - 2^{-c/2-3}, 2^{-c/2+1})$-SBA and the proof of Lemma 5.4. □

Finally, we have to show that Theorem 2.20 can be used to amplify the secret bit agreement:

Proposition 5.7. *For the functions $\alpha(c) = 1 - 2^{-c/2-3}$ and $\beta(c) = 2^{-c/2+1}$ the conditions in Lemma 2.20 hold.*

For proof see the full version.

We conclude, by Proposition 5.7 that the SBA of Algorithm 5.3 (Lemma 5.4) can be amplified efficiently into a full-fledged secret key agreement protocol. □

6   Conclusions

Role of Private Randomness. In this paper we introduced a computational model for communication complexity. However, it can also be seen as a generalization of (deterministic) property preserving hash functions to probabilistic algorithms. We studied some relations between the power of private randomness and cryptographic primitives such as collision resistance. The main open problem left from this point is whether CRHs are equivalent to preset public coins SM protocols of complexity $o(\sqrt{n})$ and whether we can break that bound using a primitive weaker than CRHs. Another direction could be to show how to use $o(\sqrt{n})$ equality protocols in order to get low communication string commitment.

Boyle et al.'s Lower Bounds. Boyle et al. [BLV18] proved two general lower bounds for property preserving hash functions using communication complexity[12]:

1. A lower bound for *reconstructing* predicates: Boyle et al. proved that for predicates that can be used for reconstructing the original string there cannot exist (compressing) property preserving hash functions. This lower bound is also true for our preset public coins SM model. However, we didn't necessarily consider reconstructing predicates (for instance, the equality predicate is not a reconstructing predicate).
2. General lower bound from one-way communication: Boyle et al. proved that any property preserving hash function cannot compress better than the one-way communication complexity[13]. This lower bound is also true in our model, but it is too loose in our context since in our model the inputs and the public random string may be dependent (e.g., the equality predicate complexity is $O(1)$ in the one-way communication complexity model).

Multi CRHs (MCRH). For $k \geq 3$, A familty of hash function is k-multi-collision resistant if finding a collision of size k is hard: no PPTM can succeed in finding $x_1, \ldots, x_k$ s.t. $h(x_1) = \ldots = h(x_k)$ with non-negligible probability (for $k = 2$ it is the regular notion of collision resistance); see [KNY18,KY18,RV22] for the relationship between MCRHs, dCRHS and CRHs. One question is whether MCRHs can be constructed from succinct protocols in a black-box manner.

Secret Key Agreement. We showed a tight relationship between secret key agreement protocols and succinct protocols for the equality predicate in the SM preset public coins stateful free talk model. On the one hand, SKA can be used for constructing an equality protocol in this model, and on the other hand, equality protocols with good error in this model can be used for constructing SKA protocols. The open questions are (i) whether the existence of protocols with much worse error probability (e.g., constant error probability for c which $O(\log \log \lambda)$)

---

[12] See also Hardt and Woodruff [HW13] who proved robustness limitations for *linear* functions.
[13] See Fleischhacker and Simkin [FS21] and Fleischhacker et al. [FLS22] for more such lower bounds.

also imply SKA and (ii) whether the fact that we allowed the adversary $\mathcal{A}dv_{eq}$ to be *rushing* was essential.

Acknowledgments. We thank Shahar Dobzinski, Ilan Komargodski, Guy Rothlbum and Eylon Yogev for useful discussions and suggestions and the Crypto 2022 referees for the helpful comments and questions.

References

[AS08] Alon, N., Spencer, J.H.: The Probabilistic Method, 3rd edn. Wiley, Hoboken (2008)

[BGK15] Bottesch, R., Gavinsky, D., Klauck, H.: Equality, revisited. In: Italiano, G.F., Pighizzini, G., Sannella, D.T. (eds.) MFCS 2015. LNCS, vol. 9235, pp. 127–138. Springer, Heidelberg (2015). https://doi.org/10.1007/978-3-662-48054-0_11

[BHKY19] Bitansky, N., Haitner, I., Komargodski, I., Yogev, E.: Distributional collision resistance beyond one-way functions. In: Ishai, Y., Rijmen, V. (eds.) EUROCRYPT 2019. LNCS, vol. 11478, pp. 667–695. Springer, Cham (2019). https://doi.org/10.1007/978-3-030-17659-4_23

[BIN97] Bellare, M., Impagliazzo, R., Naor, M.: Does parallel repetition lower the error in computationally sound protocols? In: Proceedings 38th Symposium on Foundations of Computer Science, pp. 374–383. IEEE (1997)

[BK97] Babai, L., Kimmel, P.G.: Randomized simultaneous messages: solution of a problem of YAO in communication complexity. In: Proceedings of Computational Complexity. Twelfth IEEE Conference, pp. 239–246. IEEE (1997)

[BLV18] Boyle, E., LaVigne, R., Vaikuntanathan, V.: Adversarially robust property-preserving hash functions. In: ITCS 2019 (2018)

[BM15] Ben-Sasson, E., Maor, G.: Lower bound for communication complexity with no public randomness. Electron. Colloquium Comput. Complex. **22**, 139 (2015)

[BM09] Barak, B., Mahmoody-Ghidary, M.: Merkle puzzles are optimal — an $O(n^2)$-query attack on any key exchange from a random oracle. In: Halevi, S. (ed.) CRYPTO 2009. LNCS, vol. 5677, pp. 374–390. Springer, Heidelberg (2009). https://doi.org/10.1007/978-3-642-03356-8_22

[CHS05] Canetti, R., Halevi, S., Steiner, M.: Hardness amplification of weakly verifiable puzzles. In: Kilian, J. (ed.) TCC 2005. LNCS, vol. 3378, pp. 17–33. Springer, Heidelberg (2005). https://doi.org/10.1007/978-3-540-30576-7_2

[DI06] Dubrov, B., Ishai, Y.: On the randomness complexity of efficient sampling. In: Proceedings of the Thirty-eighth ACM Symposium on Theory of Computing, pp. 711–720 (2006)

[FLS22] Fleischhacker, N., Larsen, K.G., Simkin, M.: Property-preserving hash functions for hamming distance from standard assumptions. In: Dunkelman, O., Dziembowski, S. (eds.) EUROCRYPT 2022, Part II. LNCS, vol. 13276, pp. 764–781. Springer, Cham (2022). https://doi.org/10.1007/978-3-031-07085-3_26

[FS21] Fleischhacker, N., Simkin, M.: Robust property-preserving hash functions for hamming distance and more. In: Canteaut, A., Standaert, F.-X. (eds.) EUROCRYPT 2021. LNCS, vol. 12698, pp. 311–337. Springer, Cham (2021). https://doi.org/10.1007/978-3-030-77883-5_11

[GHY20] Grossman, O., Holmgren, J., Yogev, E.: Transparent error correcting in a computationally bounded world. In: Pass, R., Pietrzak, K. (eds.) TCC 2020. LNCS, vol. 12552, pp. 530–549. Springer, Cham (2020). https://doi.org/10.1007/978-3-030-64381-2_19

[HIKNV04] Harsha, P., Ishai, Y., Kilian, J., Nissim, K., Venkatesh, S.: Communication versus computation. In: Díaz, J., Karhumäki, J., Lepistö, A., Sannella, D. (eds.) ICALP 2004. LNCS, vol. 3142, pp. 745–756. Springer, Heidelberg (2004). https://doi.org/10.1007/978-3-540-27836-8_63

[Hol05] Holenstein, T.: Key agreement from weak bit agreement. In: Proceedings of the 37th ACM Symposium on Theory of Computing, pp. 664–673 (2005)

[Hol06] Holenstein, T.: Strengthening key agreement using hard-core sets. Ph.D thesis, ETH Zurich (2006)

[HW13] Hardt, M., Woodruff, D.: How robust are linear sketches to adaptive inputs? In: Proceedings of the Forty-Fifth ACM Symposium on Theory of Computing, pp. 121–130 (2013)

[IL89] Impagliazzo, R., Luby, M.: One-way functions are essential for complexity based cryptography. In: 30th IEEE Symposium on Foundations of Computer Science, pp. 230–235. IEEE Computer Society (1989)

[IR89] Impagliazzo, R., Rudich, S.: Limits on the provable consequences of one-way permutations. In: Proceedings of the 21st ACM symposium on Theory of Computing, pp. 44–61 (1989)

[KN96] Kushilevitz, E., Nisan, N.: Communication Complexity. Cambridge University Press, Cambridge (1996)

[KNY18] Komargodski, I., Naor, M., Yogev, E.: Collision resistant hashing for paranoids: dealing with multiple collisions. In: Nielsen, J.B., Rijmen, V. (eds.) EUROCRYPT 2018. LNCS, vol. 10821, pp. 162–194. Springer, Cham (2018). https://doi.org/10.1007/978-3-319-78375-8_6

[KY18] Komargodski, I., Yogev, E.: On distributional collision resistant hashing. In: Shacham, H., Boldyreva, A. (eds.) CRYPTO 2018. LNCS, vol. 10992, pp. 303–327. Springer, Cham (2018). https://doi.org/10.1007/978-3-319-96881-0_11

[Lip94] Lipton, R.J.: A new approach to information theory. In: Enjalbert, P., Mayr, E.W., Wagner, K.W. (eds.) STACS 1994. LNCS, vol. 775, pp. 699–708. Springer, Heidelberg (1994). https://doi.org/10.1007/3-540-57785-8_183

[MNS11] Mironov, I., Naor, M., Segev, G.: Sketching in adversarial environments. SIAM J. Comput. 40(6), 1845–1870 (2011)

[MPSW10] Micali, S., Peikert, C., Sudan, M., Wilson, D.A.: Optimal error correction for computationally bounded noise. IEEE Trans. Inf. Theory 56(11), 5673–5680 (2010)

[New91] Newman, I.: Private vs common random bits in communication complexity. Inf. Process. Lett. 39(2), 67–71 (1991)

[NR09] Naor, M., Rothblum, G.N.: The complexity of online memory checking. J. ACM 56(1), 1–46 (2009)

[NS96] Newman, I., Szegedy, M.: Public vs. private coin flips in one round communication games. In: Proceedings of the Twenty-Eighth ACM Symposium on Theory of Computing, pp. 561–570 (1996)

[RV22] Rothblum, R.D., Vasudevan, P.N.: Collision-resistance from multi-collision-resistance. Electron. Colloquium Comput. Complex. 17 (2022)

[RY20] Rao, A., Yehudayoff, A.: Communication Complexity: and Applications. Cambridge University Press, Cambridge (2020)

[Sim98] Simon, D.R.: Finding collisions on a one-way street: can secure hash func-
         tions be based on general assumptions? In: Nyberg, K. (ed.) EUROCRYPT
         1998. LNCS, vol. 1403, pp. 334–345. Springer, Heidelberg (1998). https://
         doi.org/10.1007/BFb0054137
[Wee07] Wee, H.: One-way permutations, interactive hashing and statistically hid-
         ing commitments. In: Vadhan, S.P. (ed.) TCC 2007. LNCS, vol. 4392, pp.
         419–433. Springer, Heidelberg (2007). https://doi.org/10.1007/978-3-540-
         70936-7_23
[Yao79] Yao, A.C.-C.: Some complexity questions related to distributive comput-
         ing. In: Proceedings of the 11th ACM Symposium on Theory of Computing,
         STOC 1979, pp. 209–213 (1979)

Cryptanalysis II

Cryptanalysis II

Accelerating the Delfs–Galbraith Algorithm with Fast Subfield Root Detection

Maria Corte-Real Santos[1(✉)], Craig Costello[2], and Jia Shi[3]

[1] University College London, London, UK
maria.santos.20@ucl.ac.uk
[2] Microsoft Research, Redmond, USA
craigco@microsoft.com
[3] University of Waterloo, Waterloo, Canada
j96shi@uwaterloo.ca

Abstract. We give a new algorithm for finding an isogeny from a given supersingular elliptic curve $E/\mathbb{F}_{p^2}$ to a subfield elliptic curve $E'/\mathbb{F}_p$, which is the bottleneck step of the Delfs–Galbraith algorithm for the general supersingular isogeny problem. Our core ingredient is a novel method of rapidly determining whether a polynomial $f \in L[X]$ has any roots in a subfield $K \subset L$, while avoiding expensive root-finding algorithms. In the special case when $f = \Phi_{\ell,p}(X, j) \in \mathbb{F}_{p^2}[X]$, i.e., when f is the ℓ-th modular polynomial evaluated at a supersingular j-invariant, this provides a means of efficiently determining whether there is an ℓ-isogeny connecting the corresponding elliptic curve to a subfield curve. Together with the traditional Delfs–Galbraith walk, inspecting many ℓ-isogenous neighbours in this way allows us to search through a larger proportion of the supersingular set per unit of time. Though the asymptotic $\tilde{O}(p^{1/2})$ complexity of our improved algorithm remains unchanged from that of the original Delfs–Galbraith algorithm, our theoretical analysis and practical implementation both show a significant reduction in the runtime of the subfield search. This sheds new light on the concrete hardness of the general supersingular isogeny problem (i.e. the foundational problem underlying isogeny-based cryptography), and has immediate implications on the bit-security of schemes like B-SIDH and SQISign for which Delfs–Galbraith is the best known classical attack.

Keywords: Isogeny-based cryptography · supersingular isogeny problem · Delfs–Galbraith algorithm

1 Introduction

In its most general form, the *supersingular isogeny problem* asks to find an isogeny

$$\phi \colon E_1 \to E_2$$

M. Corte-Real Santos—Supported by EPSRC grant EP/S022503/1.
J. Shi—Part of this work was done while Jia was an intern at Microsoft Research.

Y. Dodis and T. Shrimpton (Eds.): CRYPTO 2022, LNCS 13509, pp. 285–314, 2022.
https://doi.org/10.1007/978-3-031-15982-4_10

between two given supersingular curves, $E_1/\bar{\mathbb{F}}_p$ and $E_2/\bar{\mathbb{F}}_p$. We emphasize that this is the general problem, where we do not assume knowledge of the degree of the isogeny, or any torsion point information. The best known classical attack against the supersingular isogeny problem is the Delfs–Galbraith algorithm [13], which, for two curves E_1 and E_2 defined over $\mathbb{F}_{p^2}$, has two steps. The first step computes random walks in the ℓ-isogeny graph (for some choice of ℓ) to find isogenies $\phi_1 \colon E_1 \to E_1'$ and $\phi_2 \colon E_2 \to E_2'$, such that $E_1'/\mathbb{F}_p$ and $E_2'/\mathbb{F}_p$ are *subfield curves*. There are around $\lfloor p/12 \rfloor$ supersingular curves up to isomorphism and $O(p^{1/2})$ of them are subfield curves, therefore this step runs in $\tilde{O}(p^{1/2})$ bit operations. The second step searches for a *subfield* isogeny $\phi' \colon E_1' \to E_2'$ that connects ϕ_1 and ϕ_2, and it requires $\tilde{O}(p^{1/4})$ bit operations [13]. It follows that the entire algorithm runs in $\tilde{O}(p^{1/2})$ operations on average, with the cost dominated by the first step, i.e., the search for paths to subfield curves.

Solver. To our knowledge, a precise complexity analysis of the Delfs–Galbraith algorithm has not been conducted. We fill this gap by presenting an optimised implementation of the Delfs–Galbraith algorithm, called Solver, and conducting experiments over many thousands of instances of the subfield search problem to determine its concrete complexity. Though Solver finds the full path, we focus on the optimisation and complexity of the bottleneck step: finding subfield curves. These optimisations include:

- *Choice of ℓ.* In their high-level description of the algorithm, Delfs and Galbraith do not specify which ℓ-isogeny graph to walk in. Framing the problem of taking a step in the ℓ-isogeny graph as computing the roots of a polynomial of degree ℓ, in Solver we chose the simplest and most efficient choice: $\ell = 2$.
- *Fast square root finding in $\mathbb{F}_{p^2}$.* We use the techniques presented in [25, §5.3] to construct an optimised algorithm for finding square roots in $\mathbb{F}_{p^2}$, which only requires two $\mathbb{F}_p$ exponentiations and a few $\mathbb{F}_p$ multiplications and additions.
- *Random walks in the 2-isogeny graph.* We implement a depth-first search to find subfield nodes in the 2-isogeny graph and give a precise complexity analysis on the number of $\mathbb{F}_p$ operations required.

SuperSolver. The main contribution of this paper is a new state-of-the-art algorithm for solving the general supersingular isogeny problem, called SuperSolver. This is a variant of the Delfs–Galbraith algorithm that exploits a combination of our new *subfield root detection* algorithm and the use of modular polynomials. We show that we can efficiently determine whether a polynomial $f \in L[X]$ has a root in a subfield $K \subset L$, without finding any roots explicitly. Though this algorithm works for general fields and polynomials (and may be of use in other contexts), we apply it to the case where $f = \Phi_{\ell,p}(X, j) \in \mathbb{F}_{p^2}[X]$, i.e., where f is the ℓ-th modular polynomial evaluated at a supersingular j-invariant. This provides a means of quickly determining whether there is an ℓ-isogeny connecting the corresponding elliptic curve to a subfield curve: we develop this Neighbour-InFp subroutine in Sect. 4, and use it as the core of our SuperSolver algorithm in Sect. 5.

In Sect. 7, we conduct extensive experiments using both our Solver and Super-Solver libraries, all of which show that SuperSolver performs much faster than Solver. In Table 1, we give a taste of the types of improvements we see in searching for subfield nodes over supersingular sets of various sizes, taking a number of primes from the isogeny-based literature. These primes were specifically chosen because the Delfs–Galbraith algorithm for the general supersingular isogeny problem is the best known classical attack against the cryptosystems they target.

Our Solver and SuperSolver algorithms are written in Sage [30] and Python and can be found at

$$\text{https://github.com/microsoft/SuperSolver.}$$

Table 1. The number of nodes inspected per 10^8 field multiplications for primes targeting schemes where Delfs–Galbraith is the best known classical attack. The Solver column corresponds to optimised Delfs–Galbraith walks in $\mathcal{X}(\mathbb{F}_p, 2)$ – see Sect. 3. The SuperSolver columns correspond to enabling our fast subfield root detection algorithm with the three fastest sets of ℓ's (left to right) – see Sect. 5. Numbers in round brackets are the approximate number of $\mathbb{F}_p$ multiplications per node inspected at each step, as computed during the precomputation phase that predicts which sets of ℓ's will perform fastest.

prime p	Solver		SuperSolver		
B-SIDH-p247 [11]	**246,461**	(406)	{3,5,7,11,13}	{3,5,7,11,13,9}	{3,5,7,11}
			1,726,427 (58.0)	1,723,345 (58.1)	1,711,713 (58.5)
TwinSmooth-p250 [12]	**233,511**	(430)	{3,5,7,11,13,9}	{3,5,7,11,13}	{3,5,7,11,9}
			1,699,825 (59.1)	1,697,769 (59.1)	1,680,379 (59.8)
SQISign-p256 [15]	**246,459**	(407)	{3,7,5,11,13}	{3,7,5,11,13,9}	{3,7,5,11}
			1,726,427 (58.0)	1,723,345 (58.1)	1,711,713 (58.5)
TwinSmooth-p384 [12]	**163,331**	(610)	{3,5,7,11,13,9}	{3,5,7,11,13}	{3,5,7,11,13,9,17}
			1,529,025 (65.2)	1,494,725 (66.6)	1,487,919 (67.0)
TwinSmooth-p512 [12]	**127,511**	(786)	{3,5,7,11,13,9,8}	{3,5,7,11,13,9}	{3,5,7,11,13,9,8,17}
			1,397,761 (71.7)	1,391,645 (72.0)	1,355,575 (73.9)

Cryptographic Implications. This paper has implications on the classical bit-security of any supersingular isogeny-based scheme for which the Delfs–Galbraith algorithm is the best known attack; this includes the key exchange scheme B-SIDH [11], the signature scheme in [16, §4], and the signature scheme SQISign [15]. For any proposed instantiation of such schemes, our SuperSolver suite allows the analysis in Sect. 7 to be conducted on input of any prime p, and determines a precise estimate on the number of operations required (on average) to solve the corresponding supersingular isogeny problem. This is especially accurate when the cardinality of the class group is known, which has recently been shown to be feasible for primes up to 512 bits [5]. On the other hand, we point out that the improvements in this paper have no direct impact on the classical security of SIDH [14] and SIKE [19]. Though the Delfs–Galbraith algorithm can be used to attack any supersingular isogeny-based cryptosystem, there are much faster *claw-finding* algorithms (see [1,14]) for solving the special instances of isogeny problems that arise in those schemes.

Roadmap. We give the preliminaries in Sect. 2. In Sect. 3, we present our optimised instantiation of the traditional Delfs–Galbraith algorithm, called Solver. In Sect. 4, we construct an efficient algorithm to detect whether a polynomial has a root in a subfield. We use this algorithm to build SuperSolver in Sect. 5. In Sect. 6, we present a worked example to highlight the differences between both algorithms, and in Sect. 7 we present a number of implementation results that illustrate the concrete improvements offered by SuperSolver.

2   Preliminaries

In this section we briefly set notation and give the requisite background for this paper. Readers familiar with the paragraph headings below are welcome to skip to the final two paragraphs.

Modular Polynomials. We will use $\Phi_\ell(X,Y) \in \mathbb{Z}[X,Y]$ to denote the classical modular polynomial (see [29]) that parameterises pairs of elliptic curves with cyclic ℓ-isogeny in terms of their j-invariants: $\Phi_\ell(j_1, j_2) = 0$ if and only if j_1 and j_2 are the j-invariants of ℓ-isogenous elliptic curves. Readers unfamiliar with modular polynomials are encouraged to look at Sutherland's database[1], which contains $\Phi_\ell(X,Y)$ for all $\ell \leq 300$ and for all primes $\ell \leq 1000$. The polynomial Φ_ℓ is symmetric in X and Y, i.e., $\Phi_\ell(X,Y) = \Phi_\ell(Y,X)$, and if $\ell = \prod_{i=1}^{n} \ell_i^{e_i}$ is ℓ's prime decomposition, the degree of $\Phi_\ell(X,Y)$ in both X and Y is

$$N_\ell := \deg\left(\Phi_\ell(X,Y)\right) = \prod_{i=1}^{n}(\ell_i + 1)\ell_i^{e_i-1}. \tag{1}$$

The difficulty in computing $\Phi_\ell(X,Y)$ is in the size, rather than the number, of its coefficients. As discussed in [29], storing $\Phi_\ell(X,Y)$ requires $O(\ell^3 \log \ell)$ bits, which corresponds to several gigabytes for $\ell \approx 1000$ and many terabytes for $\ell \approx 10^4$. Fortunately, for our purposes, the modular polynomials already contained in Sutherland's database are more than sufficient. Moreover, we will be using them in the context of cryptanalysing instances of the supersingular isogeny problem over a fixed finite field $\mathbb{F}_{p^2}$, meaning we can reduce all of the large coefficients

---

[1] See [28], a database computed using techniques from various joint works of his [6,29].

modulo p as a precomputation. Indeed, even before the target j-invariants are known, $\Phi_\ell(X, Y) \in \mathbb{Z}[X, Y]$ will be preprocessed into

$$\Phi_{\ell,p}(X, Y) \in \mathbb{F}_p[X, Y],$$

where we note the additional subscript, defined by reducing all coefficients of $\Phi_\ell(X, Y)$ modulo p. By the symmetry of $\Phi_\ell(X, Y)$, this means we must store around $N_\ell^2/2$ coefficients in $\mathbb{F}_p$, requiring only $O(\ell^2 \log p)$ bits.

Supersingular Isogeny Graphs. Following [13, §1], let $p > 3$ be a prime and let S_{p^2} denote the set of all supersingular j-invariants in $\mathbb{F}_{p^2}$. The number of such j-invariants is $\#S_{p^2} = \lfloor p/12 \rfloor + b$, where $b \in \{0, 1, 2\}$ is determined by the value of $p \bmod 12$ [27, Theorem V.4.1(c)]. For any positive integer ℓ with $p \nmid \ell$, we use $\mathcal{X}(\bar{\mathbb{F}}_p, \ell)$ to denote the *supersingular isogeny graph* whose nodes correspond to the j-invariants in S_{p^2} and whose edges are ℓ-isogenies defined over $\bar{\mathbb{F}}_p$. When ℓ is prime, these graphs are fully connected [23], and (with the possible exception of a few nodes) are $(\ell + 1)$-regular expander graphs that satisfy the Ramanujan property [24]. Crucial to both the Delfs–Galbraith algorithm and this paper is the subset S_p of supersingular j-invariants defined over $\mathbb{F}_p$. The size of this set is $\#S_p = \tilde{O}(p^{1/2})$ [13, Equation 1], and since $\#S_{p^2} = O(p)$, the expected number of randomly chosen elements in S_{p^2} we would have to take before finding one in S_p is in $\tilde{O}(p^{1/2})$.

The Delfs–Galbraith Algorithm. The Delfs–Galbraith paper largely focusses on the problem of finding an isogeny $\phi' \colon E_1' \to E_2'$ between two supersingular curves, $E_1'/\mathbb{F}_p$ and $E_2'/\mathbb{F}_p$, whose j-invariants are in S_p. One of their main results is an algorithm [13, Algorithm 1] that computes such a ϕ' in $\tilde{O}(p^{1/4})$ bit operations. At the end of their paper [13, Section 4], they show how this can be used as a subroutine to give an algorithm for the general supersingular isogeny problem, which asks to find an isogeny

$$\phi \colon E_1 \to E_2$$

between two supersingular curves, $E_1/\mathbb{F}_{p^2}$ and $E_2/\mathbb{F}_{p^2}$, whose j-invariants are in S_{p^2}. The idea is to perform simple non-backtracking random walks in $\mathcal{X}(\bar{\mathbb{F}}_p, \ell)$ until hitting an elliptic curve with a j-invariant defined over $\mathbb{F}_p$. Finding a walk from $E_1/\mathbb{F}_{p^2}$ to $E_1'/\mathbb{F}_p$ yields an isogeny $\psi_1 \colon E_1 \to E_1'$, and finding a walk from $E_2/\mathbb{F}_{p^2}$ to $E_2'/\mathbb{F}_p$ yields an isogeny $\psi_2 \colon E_2 \to E_2'$. A full isogeny $\phi \colon E_1 \to E_2$ is then found as the composition $\phi = (\hat{\psi}_2 \circ \phi' \circ \psi_1)$, where $\hat{\psi}_2 \colon E_2' \to E_2$ is the dual of ψ_2, and $\phi' \colon E_1' \to E_2'$ is the subfield isogeny above that can be computed in $\tilde{O}(p^{1/4})$ bit operations. The bottleneck in the Delfs–Galbraith algorithm is finding the paths from the curves with $j \in S_{p^2} \setminus S_p$ to the curves with $j \in S_p$. From the above discussion, the number of j-invariants in S_{p^2} we expect to search over before finding one in S_p is $\tilde{O}(p^{1/2})$. Following [13, Section 4], the steps taken in $\mathcal{X}(\bar{\mathbb{F}}_p, \ell)$ are non-backtracking, meaning that one stores the current j-invariant, j_c, and the previous j-invariant j_p. To take the next step, one then chooses one of the $N_\ell - 1$ roots (see Eq. 1) of

$$\Phi_\ell(X, j_c)/(X - j_p)$$

at random. Since ℓ and N_ℓ are fixed and small, it follows that the asymptotic complexity of the search for subfield j-invariants is $\tilde{O}(p^{1/2})$. Before presenting our improved search for subfield j-invariants, in Sect. 3 we present an optimised version of this algorithm, and subsequently replace the $\tilde{O}$ above with a precise, concrete complexity.

Factoring Polynomials in Finite Fields. Let $f(X) \in \mathbb{F}_q[X]$ be a monic polynomial of degree ℓ with $q = p^k$ for a prime p, and for the purposes of this paper, assume that p is very large (i.e., cryptographically sized) and ℓ is relatively small (i.e., $\ell < 100$). The literature contains a number of methods for finding the irreducible factors of f in $\mathbb{F}_q[x]$, and we briefly mention the most applicable and well-known algorithms for our scenario. Berlekamp's algorithm [4] factors f using an expected number of $O(\ell^3 + \ell^2 \log \ell \log q)$ operations in $\mathbb{F}_q$ [26, Theorem 20.12]. This appears to be superior to the Cantor-Zassenhaus algorithm [8], which uses an expected number of $O(\ell^3 \log q)$ operations in $\mathbb{F}_q$ [26, Theorem 20.9], however one can take advantage of certain time-memory trade-offs to implement Cantor-Zassenhaus so that it requires $O(\ell^3 + \ell^2 \log q)$ operations in $\mathbb{F}_q$ [26, Exercise 20.13]. Note that both of these big-O complexities hide a number of subtleties, that $\mathbb{F}_q$-inversions are included as $\mathbb{F}_q$ operations, and moreover that both of these algorithms are probabilistic. Their deterministic variants have worse complexities [26, §20.6].

Polynomial GCD. Euclid's integer GCD algorithm is easily adapted to compute polynomial GCD's [26, §17.3]. Computing the GCD of two polynomials $g, h \in \mathbb{F}_q[x]$ requires $O(\deg(g) \cdot \deg(h))$ operations in $\mathbb{F}_q$. Again, here each $\mathbb{F}_q$ inversion is counted as an $\mathbb{F}_q$ operation. In order to make our algorithms run as fast as possible, one of the necessary subroutines we derive in Sect. 4 is an inversion-free polynomial GCD algorithm, for which we state a tight upper bound on the concrete complexity.

Measuring Complexity. Throughout this paper we will avoid stating asymptotic (i.e., big-O-style) complexities in favour of stating concrete ones. One of our goals in Sect. 3 is to replace the $\tilde{O}(p^{1/2})$ complexity of the original Delfs–Galbraith algorithm with a closed formula that can be used to give precise estimates on the classical security of the relevant cryptographic instantiations. We will use the metric of $\mathbb{F}_p$ multiplications as convention, noting that it is relatively straightforward to convert this into a more fine-grained metric (e.g. bit operations, machine operations, cycle counts, gate counts, circuit depth, etc.) depending on the context and on the implementation of the $\mathbb{F}_p$ arithmetic. For simplicity, we will count $\mathbb{F}_p$ squarings as multiplications and ignore additions. We justify this by noting that, roughly speaking, the ratio of multiplications to additions in all of the algorithms in this work are similar, and the complexity of $\mathbb{F}_p$ additions have a minimal impact on any of the aforementioned metrics.

Subfield Search Complexity Determines Concrete Bit Security. Both the Solver implementation detailed in Sect. 3 and the SuperSolver implementation detailed in Sect. 5 solve *all* instances of the general supersingular isogeny problem. On input of any prime p and any two supersingular j-invariants in S_{p^2}, both implementations will always terminate with an isogeny that solves the corresponding problem. We emphasise that henceforth our sole focus is on the $\tilde{O}(p^{1/2})$ subfield search phase of the Delfs–Galbraith algorithm. Finding a path between subfield nodes requires $\tilde{O}(p^{1/4})$ operations, which is negligible in both the asymptotic sense and in the sense of obtaining cryptographic security estimates. To see this, suppose the asymptotic $\tilde{O}(p^{1/2})$ complexity of the first phase is replaced by a concrete complexity of $c_p \cdot p^{1/2}$, and the asymptotic $\tilde{O}(p^{1/4})$ complexity of the second phase is replaced by a concrete complexity of $d_p \cdot p^{1/4}$, where c_p and d_p are polynomials in $\log p$. The total complexity of the Delfs–Galbraith algorithm is then

$$c_p \cdot p^{1/2} + d_p \cdot p^{1/4}.$$

For primes of cryptographic size, small changes in c_p have an immediate influence on the total runtime of the algorithm, while much larger changes in d_p will not play a part in the bit security of the problem. For $p > 2^{200}$, a factor 2 change in c_p changes the bit security of the problem by 1, while d_p would have to change by a factor of at least 2^{50} to have the same impact on the bit security.

3   Solver: Optimised Delfs–Galbraith Subfield Searching in $\mathcal{X}(\bar{\mathbb{F}}_p, 2)$

Recall from the previous section that the non-backtracking walks in $\mathcal{X}(\bar{\mathbb{F}}_p, \ell)$ store the current j-invariant, j_c, and the previous j-invariant j_p, and then take a step in $\mathcal{X}(\bar{\mathbb{F}}_p, \ell)$ by choosing one of the $N_\ell - 1$ roots of $\Phi_\ell(X, j_c)/(X - j_p)$. In determining the asymptotic $\tilde{O}(p^{1/2})$ complexity of these walks, Delfs and Galbraith did not need to analyse the cost of a single step. However, to set the stage for our improved search in Sect. 5, we must optimise this process and determine its concrete cost. The first parameter that must be specified is ℓ, i.e., the isogeny graph to walk around in. Considering both Equation (1) and the complexity of the factorisation algorithms in Sect. 2, we chose $\ell = 2$ to obtain most efficient and simplest choice where we are able to take advantage of fast explicit methods for computing square roots in $\mathbb{F}_{p^2}$.

Scott's Fast Square Roots in $\mathbb{F}_{p^2}$. Optimal computation of square roots in extension fields of large characteristic requires careful attention to detail. A 2013 paper by Adj and Rodríguez-Henríquez [2] cost the process of computing square roots in $\mathbb{F}_{p^2}$ at two $\mathbb{F}_p$ residuosity tests, two $\mathbb{F}_p$ square roots, and one $\mathbb{F}_p$ inversion, for a total of five exponentiations in $\mathbb{F}_p$. In [25, §5.3], Scott shows that these operations can be combined in a clever way to significantly reduce this cost. The inputs into the Tonelli-Shanks $\mathbb{F}_p$ square root algorithm [22, Algorithm 3.34] can be tweaked in such a way that the two residuosity tests are absorbed into the two square roots. Moreover, he shows that most of the inversion cost can also be absorbed by application of Hamburg's combined 'square-root-and-inversion' trick [17]. This reduces the bulk of cost of an $\mathbb{F}_{p^2}$ square root from five $\mathbb{F}_p$ exponentiations to just two. In addition, there are a handful of $\mathbb{F}_p$ multiplications and additions that either update the Tonelli-Shanks outputs depending on the residuosity outcomes or collect and combine the results according to the "complex" formula in [25, §5.3]. We use this to construct a general square root algorithm in our implementation that is highly optimised with respect to the number of $\mathbb{F}_p$ operations it incurs[2].

Taking a Step in $\mathcal{X}(\bar{\mathbb{F}}_p, 2)$. After stepping from $j_p \in \mathbb{F}_{p^2}$ to $j_c \in \mathbb{F}_{p^2}$, a non-backtracking walk in $\mathcal{X}(\bar{\mathbb{F}}_p, 2)$ will step to one of two new nodes: j_0 and j_1. These are computed by solving the quadratic equation that arises from the modular polynomial $\Phi_\ell(X, Y)$ with $\ell = 2$:

$$\Phi_2(X, Y) = -X^2 Y^2 + X^3 + Y^3 + 1488 \cdot (X^2 Y + Y^2 X) - 162000 \cdot (X^2 + Y^2)$$
$$+ 40773375 \cdot XY + 8748000000 \cdot (X + Y) - 157464000000000.$$

The three neighbours of j_c in $\mathcal{X}(\bar{\mathbb{F}}_p, 2)$ are j_p, j_0, and j_1, meaning that $\Phi_2(X, j_c)$ factorises as

$$\Phi_2(X, j_c) = (X - j_p)(X - j_0)(X - j_1).$$

This yields a quadratic equation, whose solutions are j_0, j_1, defined by $X^2 + \alpha X + \beta = 0$, where

$$\alpha = -j_c^2 + 1488 \cdot j_c + j_p - 162000,$$
$$\beta = j_p^2 - j_c^2 j_p + 1488 \cdot (j_c^2 + j_c j_p) + 40773375 \cdot j_c - 162000 \cdot j_p + 8748000000.$$

Computing these coefficients costs a small, constant number of $\mathbb{F}_p$ operations, so the process of computing both j_0 and j_1 from j_p and j_c boils down to solving the quadratic equation, which essentially requires one $\mathbb{F}_{p^2}$ square root. Since this square root incurs two $\mathbb{F}_p$ exponentiations and a few additional $\mathbb{F}_p$ operations, it follows that the cost of computing each new $j \in S_{p^2}$ during the walks in $\mathcal{X}(\bar{\mathbb{F}}_p, 2)$ is (on average) approximately one $\mathbb{F}_p$ exponentiation.

---

[2] Note that the fixed exponentiations that take place in the calls to Tonelli-Shanks could be further optimised for a specific p by tailoring a larger window or a different addition chain, but the impact (for our purposes and comparisons) of this improvement would be minor.

The Depth First Search in $\mathcal{X}(\mathbb{F}_p, 2)$. Repeating the process described above allows us to perform the search for subfield nodes using a depth first search in a binary tree with d levels as follows. We write $j_{m,n}$ for the n-th node at level m, where $0 \leq m \leq d$ and $0 \leq n \leq 2^m - 1$. The first three levels are depicted in Fig. 1. We initialise the root node $j_{0,0}$ as the target $j \in S_{p^2}$, and set $j_{1,0}$ and

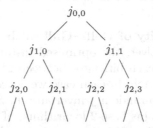

Fig. 1. Levels 0, 1, and 2 of the binary tree in the depth first search of $\mathcal{X}(\mathbb{F}_p, 2)$.

$j_{1,1}$ as two of its three neighbours[3] in $\mathcal{X}(\mathbb{F}_p, 2)$. The depth first search starts by setting $j_c = j_{1,0}$ and $j_p = j_{0,0}$. We then solve the quadratic equation above to obtain $j_{2,0}$ and $j_{2,1}$, and repeat this procedure with $j_c = j_{i+1,0}$ and $j_p = j_{i,0}$ for $1 \leq i \leq d-1$ until the leftmost leaf $j_{d,0}$ is computed and the path stack is fully initialised as

$$\mathtt{path} = [j_{0,0}, \ j_{1,0}, \ldots, j_{d-1,0}, \ j_{d,0}].$$

To avoid any waste, we also maintain a stack of the other solution to the quadratic equations that were computed along the way, which we call sibling nodes

$$\mathtt{siblings} = [j_{1,1}, \ldots, j_{d-1,1}, \ j_{d,1}].$$

The algorithm then proceeds back up the levels by popping path until its last element is the root of a subtree that has not been checked in its entirety. At this point siblings is popped and pushed into path. When the last element of path is the root of a subtree that has not been exhausted, we initialise the process of solving quadratic equations, pushing one of the two solutions into path and the other into siblings until path contains $d + 1$ elements. Each time the quadratic equation solver is called, the two roots (i.e., j-invariants) are immediately checked; if either of them lie in $\mathbb{F}_p$, it is added to path and the process is terminated. Otherwise, the process is repeated recursively until path $= [j_{0,0}]$, in which case the $2^{d+1} - 1$ nodes in the tree have been exhausted without finding a solution. To guarantee that a solution is found, one could increase d and start again, but our code proceeds by simply storing the first (leftmost) leaf and its parent in separate memory so that the process can restart

---

[3] Initially we do not have a j_p, so all three neighbours can be computed using generic root finding; our code does this during the setup phase.

here and avoid recomputing any prior j's. As Delfs and Galbraith point out, setting the depth $d = \frac{1}{2} \log_2 p$ should be enough. Since the number of nodes in the tree is 2^d, increasing d by ϵ makes the failure probability diminish by $1/2^\epsilon$. Setting $\epsilon = 10$ was sufficient in all of our experiments. Finally, as pointed out by Delfs and Galbraith in [13, §4], this process parallelises perfectly. For P processors, one can simply compute a binary tree of depth $\lceil \log_2 P \rceil$ during setup and distribute P of the leaf nodes as individual starting points.

The Concrete Complexity of Delfs–Galbraith. Table 2 reports on experiments conducted using Solver, the optimised instantiation of the traditional Delfs–Galbraith walk. For each bitlength between 21 and 40, we solved 10,000 instances of the subfield search. In each case we chose 100 random primes and, for each prime, 100 pseudo-random j-invariants in S_{p^2}. The numbers in each column report the averages (as base-2 logarithms) of these search complexities. In all cases the number of $\mathbb{F}_p$ multiplications is found to be

$$\#(\mathbb{F}_p \text{ muls.}) = c \cdot \sqrt{p} \cdot \log_2 p,$$

with $0.75 \leq c \leq 1.05$. In Sect. 7, we shed more light on the concrete complexity of both Solver and SuperSolver.

Table 2. The concrete cost of the subfield search phase of the Delfs–Galbraith over small fields of various bitlengths. Further explanation in text.

bitlengths of primes p	21	22	23	24	25	26	27	28	29	30
av. number of nodes visited	8.8	9.4	10.0	10.3	10.9	11.4	11.9	12.3	13.1	13.5
av. number of $\mathbb{F}_p$ multiplications	14.5	15.0	15.7	16.0	16.7	17.2	17.8	18.2	19.0	19.5

bitlengths of primes p	31	32	33	34	35	36	37	38	39	40
av. number of nodes visited	13.5	14.2	14.7	15.3	15.8	16.3	17.1	17.3	17.6	18.1
av. number of $\mathbb{F}_p$ multiplications	19.5	20.5	20.8	21.3	21.9	22.4	23.2	23.6	24.1	24.6

Remark 1 (Vélu's formulas). There is no traditional elliptic curve arithmetic found in either Solver or SuperSolver. All of the steps taken within $\mathcal{X}(\bar{\mathbb{F}}_p, 2)$ and the rapid inspections conducted in $\mathcal{X}(\bar{\mathbb{F}}_p, \ell)$ use the modular polynomials. We point out there *may* be specific instances of p where one could perform walks faster than repeatedly solving the $\Phi_{2,p}(X, j)$ quadratic by, say, employing Vélu's formulas [31] with the optimal strategies of De Feo–Jao–Plût [14]. For example, with a prime $p = 2^e 3^f - 1$, the price of computing a 2e-isogeny (i.e., walking through e nodes in $\mathcal{X}(\bar{\mathbb{F}}_p, 2)$) in this way may be cheaper than the price of computing e square roots in $\mathbb{F}_{p^2}$ (note that the latter reveals 2 nodes each time). However, we argue that these scenarios are likely to only exist for special instances of the supersingular isogeny problem that are geared towards cryptosystems like SIDH [14] and SIKE [19]. As discussed in Sect. 1, here

there are claw-finding algorithms that are much faster than the Delfs–Galbraith algorithm (though the number of $\mathbb{F}_p$ operations required to compute an ℓ^e-isogeny still grows with p, and therefore our fast subfield root detection would also be useful in that context). In the case of both general primes and the types of primes in Table 1, it is highly unlikely that using Vélu's formulas [31] will be competitive with the binary tree depth-first search in $\mathcal{X}(\bar{\mathbb{F}}_p, 2)$; computing general $(\prod \ell_i^{e_i})$-isogenies from kernel elements is much more expensive than ℓ^e-isogenies when $\ell \in \{2, 3\}$, and one travels through fewer nodes in S_{p^2} per $(\prod \ell_i^{e_i})$-isogeny when the ℓ_i grow larger.

Remark 2 (Radical isogenies). Another alternative to solving the quadratic equation that arises from $\Phi_2(X, j_c)/(X - j_p)$ is to instead take steps in $\mathcal{X}(\bar{\mathbb{F}}_p, 2)$ using formulas for radical isogenies [10]. For example, given a supersingular Montgomery curve parameterised as $E_A : y^2 = x^3 + Ax^2 + x$ or as $E_\alpha = x(x - \alpha)(x - 1/\alpha)$, one can compute non-backtracking chains of 2-isogenies as either $A \to A' \to A'' \ldots$, or as $\alpha \to \alpha' \to \alpha'' \ldots$, rather than computing the chain of j-invariants $j \to j' \to j'' \ldots$, as we do. Computing the next value in all of these chains requires one square root (which dominates the cost for primes of cryptographic size) and a small handful of additional field operations, the number of which depends on the choice of chain. In the case of computing the chains $A \to A' \to A'' \ldots$ or $\alpha \to \alpha' \to \alpha'' \ldots$, the number of additional operations are fewer (see [7,9]) than those which we incur using the modular polynomial, however we have not opted to exploit this minor speedup for the following reasons. Indeed, it is not true in general that $j(E_A) \in \mathbb{F}_p$ implies $A \in \mathbb{F}_p$ or that $j(E_\alpha) \in \mathbb{F}_p$ implies $\alpha \in \mathbb{F}_p$. Since $j(E_A) = 256(A^2 - 3)^3/(A^2 - 4)$, in general there are six values of A corresponding to a given j. Similarly, since $j(E_\alpha) = 256(\alpha^4 - \alpha^2 + 1)^3/(\alpha^4(\alpha^2 - 1)^2)$, in general there are twelve values of α corresponding to a given j. For large primes it is typically the case that most (or all) of the A's and α's corresponding to a given $j \in S_p$ are not defined over $\mathbb{F}_p$. Thus, if radical isogenies were used to compute chains of α's or A's in the context of Delfs–Galbraith, we would need to compute a value that determines whether the corresponding j lies in $\mathbb{F}_p$. We note that this can be achieved without inverting the denominators in the expressions for $j(E_\alpha)$ or $j(E_A)$, i.e., $(a + b \cdot \beta)/(c + d \cdot \beta)$ is in $\mathbb{F}_p$ if and only if $ad = bc$ for $a, b, c, d \in \mathbb{F}_p$ and $\mathbb{F}_{p^2} = \mathbb{F}_p(\beta)$. Thus, the original Delfs–Galbraith walk in $\mathcal{X}(\bar{\mathbb{F}}_p, 2)$ is likely to save a small, fixed number of multiplications per 2-isogeny by computing chains of A's or α's instead of j's. However, when invoking our fast subfield root detection in the sections that follow, it is critical (for Algorithm 2) that the j-invariants of each node are computed explicitly, so that the higher ℓ-degree modular polynomials can be used to probe for ℓ-isogenous subfield neighbours. This subsequent computation of the j-invariant seems to require an additional field exponentiation (we could not see a way to merge the square roots and inversions into one exponentiation in these instances), which would kill the potential advantage of radical isogenies in the optimised SuperSolver algorithm.

Remark 3 (Alternative modular functions). There are several well-known modular functions other than the j-function — see [29]. A natural question in the context of this paper is whether any such functions can be used to make the search for subfield nodes in supersingular isogeny graphs more efficient. For example, the modular polynomials for Weber's f-function [28] are the same degree as those of the j-function, but have *much* smaller coefficients, many of which are zero. If these more compact modular polynomials could be used in the same way as those for the j-function, the practical gains would be significant. However, their applicability in the context of SuperSolver appears to be hampered by reasons similar to those discussed in Remark 2. Weber's f is related to j via $j = (f^{24} - 16)^3/f^{24}$, meaning there can be as many as 72 f's corresponding to a single j-invariant, and it is not true in general that given $j \in \mathbb{F}_p$, the corresponding $f \in \mathbb{F}_p$. Although this makes the Weber polynomials unreliable replacements in the context of the SuperSolver algorithm, our search for alternative modular functions that would be compatible with SuperSolver was far from exhaustive, and it is likely that the j-function is not optimal across all of them. We leave any further investigations in this direction as future work.

4   Fast Subfield Root Detection

In this section we derive a method for determining whether a polynomial $f(X) = a_n X^n + ... + a_1 X + a_0 \in \mathbb{F}_{q^d}[X]$ with $d \geq 2$ has a root lying in the subfield $\mathbb{F}_q$, where q is a power of prime p. Though this can be achieved by factoring the polynomial, the methods described in Sect. 2 become too costly for our purposes; the number of $\mathbb{F}_q$ operations required depends on the size of q, which hampers their relative efficiency as q grows large. Our aim in this section is to detail a much faster algorithm that detects whether a root lies in a subfield and show that the number of $\mathbb{F}_q$ operations required by our algorithm only depends on the degree of f and the degree of the extension d.

As the algorithms in this section may be of independent interest, we leave them as general as possible before specialising back to the application at hand in Sect. 5. The results up to Proposition 1 are presented for general finite field extensions of the form $\mathbb{F}_{q^d}/\mathbb{F}_q$, but we will later specialise to the quadratic extensions of prime fields, i.e., where $q = p$ and $d = 2$. The inversion-free GCD in Algorithm 1 is derived for an arbitrary polynomial ring $K[x]$, but we will only need to use it in $\mathbb{F}_p[x]$.

In this section, for a polynomial in $\mathbb{F}_{q^d}[X]$, we will reduce the the problem of detecting a root in $\mathbb{F}_q$ to computing the greatest common divisor of d related polynomials $g_1, ..., g_d$. In the case where $d > 2$, we will need to compute the GCD of more than two polynomials. This can be done by recursively computing the GCD of two polynomials and using the following identity:

$$\gcd(g_1, g_2, ..., g_d) = \gcd(g_1, \gcd(g_2, ..., g_d)). \tag{2}$$

We aim to minimise the number of $\mathbb{F}_q$ multiplications needed to compute the GCD and so we construct these polyomials so that they are defined over $\mathbb{F}_q$. To achieve this, we will will need two results. The first is a theorem by Lidl and Niederreiter [21, Theorem 2.24].

Theorem 1. *Let F be a finite extension of a finite field K, both considered as vector spaces over K. Then the linear transformations from F into K are exactly the mappings $L_\beta(\alpha)$, for $\beta \in F$, where $L_\beta(\alpha) = Tr_{F/K}(\beta\alpha)$ for all $\alpha \in F$. Furthermore, we have $L_\beta \neq L_\gamma$ whenever β, γ are distinct elements of F.*

The second result we will need is the following lemma.

Lemma 1. *For $n \in \mathbb{N}$, let $f_1, ..., f_n \in \mathbb{F}_{q^d}[X]$ be polynomials and $A \in \mathrm{GL}_n(\mathbb{F}_{q^d})$. Defining $(g_1, ..., g_n) := A \cdot (f_1, ..., f_n)$, we have*

$$\gcd(f_1, ..., f_n) = \gcd(g_1, ..., g_n).$$

Proof. If a polynomial $h \in \mathbb{F}_{q^d}[X]$ divides $f_1, ..., f_n$, then h divides any linear combination of the $f_1, ..., f_n$. Therefore, h divides $g_1, ..., g_n$. Since A is invertible, by swapping the roles of g_i and f_i we see that the converse holds.   □

We are now ready to present the main result of this section.

Proposition 1. *For some $d \geq 2$, let π be the q-power Frobenius endomorphism in $\mathrm{Gal}(\mathbb{F}_{q^d}/\mathbb{F}_q)$ and consider a polynomial $f(X) = a_n X^n + ... + a_1 X + a_0 \in \mathbb{F}_{q^d}[X]$. Let β be a primitive element of the extension $\mathbb{F}_{q^d}/\mathbb{F}_q$, in the sense that the field extension is generated by a single element β, i.e., $\mathbb{F}_q(\beta) = \mathbb{F}_{q^d}$. For $i = 1, .., d$, define the following polynomials over $\mathbb{F}_{q^d}$:*

$$g_i := \sum_{j=0}^{d-1} \pi^j(\beta^{i-1}f).$$

Then $g_i(X) \in \mathbb{F}_q[X]$, and $\gcd(g_1, ..., g_d)$ divides f. In particular, if $\gcd(g_1, ..., g_d)$ is of degree 1, then f has a root in $\mathbb{F}_q$. Furthermore, if $\gcd(g_1, ..., g_d) = 1$, then $f(X)$ does not have any roots in $\mathbb{F}_q$.

Proof. Using the notation in Theorem 1, we have

$$g_i(X) = [(\beta^{i-1}a_n + \pi(\beta^{i-1}a_n) + ... + \pi^{d-1}(\beta^{i-1}a_n))X^n + ... + (\beta^{i-1}a_0 + ... + \pi^{d-1}(\beta^{i-1}a_0))]$$

$$= \sum_{m=0}^{n} L_{\beta^{i-1}}(a_m)X^m.$$

By Theorem 1, for all $i = 1, ..., d$ and $m = 0, ... n$, we have $L_{\beta^{i-1}}(a_m) \in \mathbb{F}_q$, implying that $g_i(X) \in \mathbb{F}_q[X]$. Setting $(d \times d)$ matrix A to be

$$A = \begin{bmatrix} 1 & 1 & \cdots & 1 \\ \beta & \pi(\beta) & \cdots & \pi^{d-1}(\beta) \\ \vdots & \vdots & \ddots & \vdots \\ \beta^{d-1} & \pi(\beta^{d-1}) & \cdots & \pi^{d-1}(\beta^{d-1}) \end{bmatrix} = \begin{bmatrix} 1 & 1 & \cdots & 1 \\ \beta & \beta^q & \cdots & \beta^{q^{d-1}} \\ \vdots & \vdots & \ddots & \vdots \\ \beta^{d-1} & (\beta^{d-1})^q & \cdots & (\beta^{d-1})^{q^{d-1}} \end{bmatrix},$$

we have $(g_1, ..., g_d) := A \cdot (f, \pi(f)..., \pi^{d-1}(f))$. As for Vandermonde matrices [18, §6.2], we find $\det(A) = \prod_{0 \leq i < j \leq d-1}(\beta^{q^j} - \beta^{q^i})$, which is non-zero for β a primitive element of the extension $\mathbb{F}_{q^d}/\mathbb{F}_q$ and so $A \in \mathrm{GL}_d(\mathbb{F}_{q^d})$. By Lemma 1, we have

$$\gcd(f, \pi(f), ..., \pi^{d-1}(f)) = \gcd(g_1, ..., g_d),$$

therefore $\gcd(g_1, ..., g_d) \mid f$. If $\gcd(g_1, ..., g_d)$ is of degree 1, then $(X - r) \mid f$ for some $r \in \mathbb{F}_q$, and so f has a root in $\mathbb{F}_q$.

We further note that $\gcd(f, \pi(f), ..., \pi^{d-1}(f))$, and therefore $\gcd(g_1, ..., g_d)$, is precisely the largest divisor of f that is defined over $\mathbb{F}_q$. As a result, if $\gcd(g_1, ..., g_d) = 1$, then $f(X)$ does not have any roots in $\mathbb{F}_q$.   □

Applying Proposition 1 to Detect Subfield Nodes. The proof of Proposition 1 tells us that $\gcd(g_1, ..., g_d)$ is precisely the largest divisor of $f \in \mathbb{F}_{q^d}[X]$ that is defined over $\mathbb{F}_q[X]$. In our target application of searching for subfield nodes in large supersingular isogeny graphs, i.e., when $d = 2$ and $q = p$, we will most commonly encounter $\gcd(g_1, g_2) = 1$, which immediately rules out subfield neighbours in the ℓ-isogeny graph. Non-trivial GCD's will, with overwhelmingly high probability, be of degree 1 and reveal a single subfield node; this is why our implementation of Algorithm 1 below terminates and returns **true** when the degree of the GCD is 1.

For large supersingular isogeny graphs, the only way for the degree of $\gcd(g_1, g_2)$ to be larger than 1 is when a given j-invariant is ℓ-isogenous to multiple subfield nodes, or when a given j-invariant is ℓ-isogenous to conjugate j-invariants in $\mathbb{F}_{p^2}$.[4]

In our scenario where $d = 2$, we see that $\pi(\beta) + \beta = 0$, meaning that $\pi^k(\beta) = (-1)^k \beta$. As a result, to detect a subfield root, we compute $\gcd(g_1, \beta g_2)$ where $g_1 = f + \pi(f)$ and $g_2 = f - \pi(f)$. In this case we do not need to calculate any more powers of β and we only need to do one GCD computation.

Inversion-Free Polynomial GCD. To complete the detection of roots in a subfield, we must compute the GCD of polynomials in polynomial ring $K[X]$, where K is a field. In Algorithm 1, we modify Euclid's polynomial-adapted algorithm [26, §17.3] to compute the GCD of two polynomials $g, h \in K[X]$ while avoiding inversions in K. We use $\mathrm{LC}(f)$ to denote the leading coefficient of the polynomial f. Note that, for the purposes of incorporating it into our target application of subfield searching in the next section, the algorithm outputs the boolean **true** when the GCD has degree 1 in $K[X]$.

---

[4] A real-world attack should check any non-trivial GCD, since either of these scenarios are a win for the cryptanalyst; the latter case reveals information about the secret endomorphism ring of the target isomorphism class (see [20, §5.3]), and the former case gives multiple solutions to the subfield search problem.

Algorithm 1. InvFreeGCD(): Inversion-free GCD

Input: Polynomials $g, h \in K[X]$, such that $\deg g \geq \deg h$
1: Initialise $r, s \leftarrow \mathrm{LC}(h) \cdot g, \mathrm{LC}(g) \cdot h$
2: **while** $\deg r \geq 1$ and $r \neq s$ **do**
3:    $r \leftarrow r - X^{\deg r - \deg s} \cdot s$
4:    $r, s \leftarrow \mathrm{LC}(s) \cdot r, \mathrm{LC}(r) \cdot s$
5:    **if** $\deg r \leq \deg s$ **then**
6:       $r, s \leftarrow s, r$
7: **return** $\neg(\deg r = 1$ and $r \neq s)$

Proposition 2. *Given input $g, h \in K[X]$ such that $\deg g \geq \deg h$, Algorithm 1 terminates using at most*

$$\frac{1}{2}(\deg g + \deg h + 2)(\deg g + \deg h + 3) - 6$$

multiplications in K.

Proof. Line 1 incurs at most $\deg g + \deg h + 2$ multiplications in K. Setting $r_0 := r, s_0 := s$, we define this to be loop 0. For $i \geq 1$, we denote by r_i, s_i (where $\deg s_i \geq \deg r_i$) the polynomials in loop i of Lines 2-6. Using this notation, we move to Line 7 when $\deg r_i \leq 1$ or $r_i = s_i$. Now, in loop $i \geq 1$ we replace r_i by $r_i - X^{\deg r_i - \deg s_i} s_i$, meaning $\deg r_{i-1} - \deg r_i \geq 1$, and compute $r_i \cdot \mathrm{LC}(s_i)$ and $s_i \cdot \mathrm{LC}(r_i)$. This requires $\deg r_i + \deg s_i + 2$ multiplications in K. In the worst case, we have $\deg r_{i-1} - \deg r_i = 1$ for $i \geq 1$, where the number of multiplications will decrease by exactly 1 after each loop. In the final loop we have $\deg r_i, \deg s_i = 1$, so we compute 4 multiplications in K. In summary, in the worst case we begin with $\deg g + \deg h + 2$ multiplications, decreasing by 1 until we get to 4. Therefore, the total number of multiplications is at most $\sum_{n=4}^{\deg g + \deg h + 2} n$, which is the bound above.   □

In summary, Proposition 1 shows that detecting subfield roots of $f \in \mathbb{F}_{q^d}[X]$ amounts to computing the GCD of d related polynomials in $\mathbb{F}_q[X]$. We showed that computing this GCD is simpler when $d = 2$. Proposition 2 gives an upper bound on the number of $\mathbb{F}_q$ multiplications required to compute such a GCD in $\mathbb{F}_q[X]$. In the next section we use these tools to build a faster algorithm for finding subfield nodes in supersingular isogeny graphs.

5 SuperSolver: Optimised Subfield Searching With Fast Subfield Root Detection in $\mathcal{X}(\overline{\mathbb{F}}_p, \ell)$

SuperSolver is an algorithm which, given two j-invariants in S_{p^2} corresponding to two supersingular curves $E_1/\mathbb{F}_{p^2}$ and $E_2/\mathbb{F}_{p^2}$, will, on average, solve the supersingular isogeny problem with lower concrete complexity than the traditional Delfs–Galbraith Solver algorithm described in Sect. 3. As in the Delfs–Galbraith algorithm, SuperSolver takes non-backtracking walks in $\mathcal{X}(\bar{\mathbb{F}}_p, 2)$ until they hit a j-invariant in $\mathbb{F}_p$. However, at each step of the random walk, SuperSolver also inspects $\mathcal{X}(\bar{\mathbb{F}}_p, \ell)$, for carefully chosen $\ell > 2$, to efficiently detect whether j has any ℓ-isogenous neighbours in $\mathbb{F}_p$. Traditionally, inspecting $\mathcal{X}(\bar{\mathbb{F}}_p, \ell)$ for a subfield neighbour requires fully factoring a degree-N_ℓ polynomial and determining whether any of the roots lie in $\mathbb{F}_p$. Performing this for each ℓ would require $O(\ell^3 + 2\ell^2 \log p)$ operations in $\mathbb{F}_{p^2}$ using the modified Cantor-Zassenhaus algorithm (see Sect. 2), which is prohibitively costly. Following the results from Sect. 4, however, SuperSolver conducts the inspection of $\mathcal{X}(\bar{\mathbb{F}}_p, \ell)$ with $O(\ell^2)$ multiplications in $\mathbb{F}_p$. We make this count precise later in this section. Crucially, the number of $\mathbb{F}_p$ operations is no longer dependent on the size of p, and this means that as p grows large, the set of ℓ's that are optimal to use also grows, and the more profitable (relatively speaking) SuperSolver becomes. We reiterate that, although both Solver and SuperSolver return the full isogeny between $E_1/\mathbb{F}_{p^2}$ and $E_2/\mathbb{F}_{p^2}$, our discussion focusses on the bottleneck problem of finding an isogeny from $E_1/\mathbb{F}_{p^2}$ (resp. $E_2/\mathbb{F}_{p^2}$) to $E_1'/\mathbb{F}_p$ (resp. $E_2/\mathbb{F}_p$). If, at some node j, we detect an ℓ-isogenous neighbour in $\mathbb{F}_p$, SuperSolver will then factorise the degree-N_ℓ polynomial $\Phi_{\ell,p}(X, j)$ to determine the subfield j-invariant. We view this as a post-computation step, since we are only interested in the concrete complexity of the average step taken in the walk (which we assume does not find a subfield node). Note that the paths between $E_1/\mathbb{F}_{p^2}$ and $E_2/\mathbb{F}_{p^2}$ returned by both Solver and SuperSolver both look the same: in general, both start and finish with a chain of 2-isogenies that is connected in the middle by a chain of different prime-degree isogenies. The main difference, as the results in Sect. 7 illustrate, is that 2-isogeny chains at each end are *much* shorter. Recall that in the original Delfs–Galbraith algorithm, each step consists of finding the roots of a quadratic equation in $\mathbb{F}_{p^2}[X]$, which reveals two neighbouring nodes in $\mathcal{X}(\bar{\mathbb{F}}_p, 2)$. In Super-Solver, after forming a list of carefully chosen $\ell > 2$, each step will also include the rapid inspection of $\mathcal{X}(\bar{\mathbb{F}}_p, \ell)$ for every ℓ in this list. Though the inspection of the neighbours in $\mathcal{X}(\bar{\mathbb{F}}_p, \ell)$ increases the total number of $\mathbb{F}_p$ multiplications at each step, more nodes are checked. We first describe the process of taking a step in SuperSolver, and then move to describing how to choose the list of $\ell > 2$ in order to minimise the number of $\mathbb{F}_p$ multiplications per node inspected.

Remark 4 (Odd ℓ only). With the exception of the leaf nodes in the last level of the binary tree, it is redundant to perform rapid node inspections in $\mathcal{X}(\bar{\mathbb{F}}_p, 2\ell)$ if rapid inspections in $\mathcal{X}(\bar{\mathbb{F}}_p, \ell)$ are also part of the routine, since the latter inspections will detect (or exclude) subfield nodes at the next level of the walk down the tree. We therefore find it optimal to only include odd ℓ_i in the lists constructed at the end of this section. Note that there is no redundancy in including odd composite ℓ_i's in our lists, even if they have proper divisors that are also in the list.

Rapid Inspection of the ℓ-Isogenous Neighbours. Here we describe Algorithm 2: NeighbourInFp. On input of ℓ, $j \in \mathbb{F}_{p^2}$ and p, it outputs true if j is ℓ-isogenous to a $j' \in \mathbb{F}_p$, and false otherwise. Recall from Equation (1) that the degree of $\Phi_{\ell,p}$ in X and Y is N_ℓ. The first subroutine of NeighbourInFp is EvalModPolyj(ℓ, j, p): it evaluates $\Phi_{\ell,p}(X, Y)$ at $Y = j$ by computing $j^2, ..., j^{N_\ell}$, and then multiplying these by the corresponding coefficients of $\Phi_{\ell,p}$, returning the coefficients $a_{N_\ell}, ..., a_0$ of X in $\Phi_{\ell,p}(X, j)$. Note that, since we typically have a list of multiple ℓ, i.e., $\ell_1 < \cdots < \ell_t$, the powers of j (up to N_{ℓ_t}) are computed once-and-for-all at every j, and recycled among the $\ell_i < \ell_t$. We follow Sect. 4 to detect whether $\Phi_{\ell,p}(X, j) \in \mathbb{F}_{p^2}[X]$ has a root in $\mathbb{F}_p$. Letting $\beta \in \mathbb{F}_{p^2}$ be such that $\mathbb{F}_{p^2} = \mathbb{F}_p(\beta)$, we first compute the related polynomials

$$g_1 := (1/2) \cdot [\Phi_{\ell,p}(X, j) + \pi(\Phi_{\ell,p}(X, j))] \quad \text{and}$$
$$g_2 := (-\beta/2) \cdot [\Phi_{\ell,p}(X, j) - \pi(\Phi_{\ell,p}(X, j))],$$

where $\pi \in \text{Gal}(\mathbb{F}_{p^2}/\mathbb{F}_p)$ is the Frobenius endomorphism. By Proposition 1, we have $g_1, g_2 \in \mathbb{F}_p[X]$ and

$$\deg(\gcd(g_1, g_2)) = 1 \implies \Phi_{\ell,p}(X, j) \text{ has a root in } \mathbb{F}_p.$$

We then complete the inspection of $\mathcal{X}(\bar{\mathbb{F}}_p, \ell)$ by using Algorithm 1 to calculate $\gcd(g_1, g_2)$. If $\gcd(g_1, g_2) \neq 1$, then (for large enough p) it is overwhelmingly likely that $\deg(\gcd(g_1, g_2)) = 1$, which is why our implementation uses the degree of the GCD as the criterion for terminating the subfield search. Another possibility is to terminate whenever $\gcd(g_1, g_2)$ is non-constant, and then to inspect the higher degree GCD according to the two possible scenarios discussed in Sect. 4.

Note that if we have a polynomial $f(X) = a_n X^n + a_{n-1} X^{n-1} + ... + a_1 X + a_0 \in \mathbb{F}_{p^2}[X]$ then

$$\frac{1}{2}[f + \pi(f)] = \text{Re}(a_n)X^n + \text{Re}(a_{n-1})X^{n-1} + ... + \text{Re}(a_1)X + \text{Re}(a_0) \in \mathbb{F}_p[X],$$
$$\frac{-\beta}{2}[f - \pi(f)] = \text{Im}(a_n)X^n + \text{Im}(a_{n-1})X^{n-1} + ... + \text{Im}(a_1)X + \text{Im}(a_0) \in \mathbb{F}_p[X],$$

where, for $a + b\beta \in \mathbb{F}_{p^2}$, $\text{Re}(a + b\beta) = a$ and $\text{Im}(a + b\beta) = b$, in analogy with the notation used for complex numbers. As a result, we can obtain g and h directly from $f = \Phi_{\ell,p}$ by computing

$$g_1 = X^{N_\ell} + ... + \text{Re}(a_0), \quad \text{and} \quad g_2 = \text{Im}(a_{N_\ell-1})X^{N_\ell-1} + ... + \text{Im}(a_0).$$

This avoids having to compute any $\mathbb{F}_{p^2}$ multiplications to calculate the related polynomials g_1, g_2.

Cost of Inspecting the ℓ-isogeny Graph. Evaluating $\Phi_{\ell,p}(X, Y)$ at $Y = j$ with EvalModPolyj requires at most $9N_\ell(N_\ell-1)$ multiplications in $\mathbb{F}_p$, noting that one $\mathbb{F}_{p^2}$ multiplication is equivalent to 3 $\mathbb{F}_p$ multiplications. By Proposition 2, we compute InvFreeGCD(g_1, g_2) with at most $(2N_\ell+1)(N_\ell+1) - 6 \mathbb{F}_p$ multiplications.

Algorithm 2. NeighbourInFp(): Detect whether $j \in \mathbb{F}_{p^2}$ is ℓ-isogenous to a $j' \in \mathbb{F}_p$

Input: ℓ, j, p

1: $a_{N_\ell}, ..., a_0 \leftarrow$ EvalModPolyj(ℓ, j, p)
2: $g_1 \leftarrow X^{N_\ell} + ... + \mathrm{Re}(a_0)$
3: $g_2 \leftarrow \mathrm{Im}(a_{N_\ell - 1})X^{N_\ell - 1} + ... + \mathrm{Im}(a_0)$
4: **return** InvFreeGCD(g_1, g_2)

Therefore, for a fixed ℓ, the cost of inspecting $\mathcal{X}(\bar{\mathbb{F}}_p, \ell)$ is

$$\mathrm{cost}_\ell = \frac{1}{N_\ell}[\#\mathbb{F}_p \text{ multiplications needed to inspect } \ell\text{-isogenous neighbours}]$$
$$\leq \frac{1}{N_\ell}[11N_\ell^2 - 6N_\ell - 5],$$

which depends only on ℓ. This means that, for each ℓ, cost_ℓ can be computed once for all primes. In Table 3 we present the ℓ with the lowest cost, ordering them by increasing cost_ℓ from left to right.

Table 3. The cost of inspecting ℓ-isogenous neighbours, cost_ℓ, for ℓ ordered by increasing cost from left to right.

ℓ	3	5	7	11	13	9	17	19	23	29
N_ℓ	4	6	8	12	14	12	18	21	24	30
$\mathbb{F}_p$ muls per node	16.3	24.5	32.6	48.8	56.8	58.5	72.8	80.9	96.9	120.9
ℓ	31	25	15	37	41	43	27	21	47	53
N_ℓ	32	30	24	38	42	44	36	32	48	54
$\mathbb{F}_p$ muls per node	128.9	139.5	145.3	152.9	168.9	176.9	186.3	187.5	192.4	216.9

The important takeaway from Table 3 is that the number of $\mathbb{F}_p$ multiplications incurred by our algorithm does not grow with p. This count is fixed and depends only on ℓ. Looking back at the root solving algorithms in Sect. 2, we see a stark difference in expected performance. Those algorithms have many constants hidden by the big-O, have a leading ℓ^3 term (compared to our ℓ^2 term), and, importantly, the number of field operations they incur grows as the field grows due to their implicit dependency on $\log p$. Moreover, as mentioned in Sect. 2, the complexities cited are for *probabilistic* root finding algorithms. Their deterministic variants have even worse complexities [26, §20.6].

Choosing the ℓ_i to Minimise the Cost of a Step. We consider the cost of each step in SuperSolver, which we denote by the ratio

$$\mathrm{cost} = \frac{\text{total \# of } \mathbb{F}_p \text{ multiplications}}{\text{total \# of nodes revealed}}. \tag{3}$$

The aim of this section is to describe how to construct a list of ℓ_i that minimises the cost. Recall from in Table 3 that the ℓ's that give the cheapest cost per node inspected are (from left to right)

$$[3, 5, 7, 11, 13, 9, 17, 19 \ldots]. \tag{4}$$

We will use L_b to denote each list of ℓ_i and cost_{L_b} to denote the corresponding cost, where the bit representation of b specifies the set of ℓ's from Equation (4); the least significant bit of b determines if 3 is included, the second least significant bit of b determines if 5 is included, and so on. For example, $L_0 = \{\}$, $L_2 = \{5\}$, and and $L_{11} = \{3, 5, 7\}$. Each step will always include revealing 2 neighbours in $\mathcal{X}(\mathbb{F}_p, 2)$, therefore for a node j we have for each step:

total # of $\mathbb{F}_p$ muls. $\geq$ #$\mathbb{F}_p$ muls. needed to find roots of $\Phi_{2,p}(X, j)$;

total # of nodes revealed ≥ 2.

Here, equality holds only when we take the list to be L_0, which corresponds to the original Delfs–Galbraith algorithm. Minimising the cost in Equation (3) is a nontrivial task. We first restrict the L_b to only contain ℓ such that $\text{cost}_\ell < \text{cost}_{L_0}$, otherwise it would be more advantageous to take another step by moving to a neighbouring node in $\mathcal{X}(\mathbb{F}_p, 2)$. We emphasise that cost_{L_0} grows with p, whereas cost_ℓ stays fixed. This signifies that the condition on ℓ becomes less restrictive as p increases. Suppose that, imposing this condition we get $L_b \subseteq [\ell_1, ..., \ell_n]$. We then exhaust all $b < 2^n$, corresponding to subsets of $[\ell_1, ..., \ell_n]$, to determine the L_b that minimise Equation (3). It is important to note that, as this optimisation depends only on the prime p, L_b can be determined in the precomputation.

6   A Worked Example

We now use a worked example to illustrate how the Solver and SuperSolver programs solve the supersingular isogeny problem, and to highlight the differences between them. Our SuperSolver suite is written in Sage/Python and a boolean variable supersolver specifies whether Solver or SuperSolver is used. For a prime p, and two supersingular j-invariants j_1 and j_2 defined over $\mathbb{F}_{p^2} = \mathbb{F}_p(\beta)$, Solver runs by entering

$$\text{Solver}(p, j10, j11, j20, j21, \text{false})$$

and SuperSolver runs by calling

$$\text{Solver}(p, j10, j11, j20, j21, \text{true}),$$

where $j10 = \text{Re}(j_1)$, $j11 = \text{Im}(j_1)$ and similary for $j20$, $j21$.
    We picked

$$p = 2^{20} - 3,$$

the smallest of the primes from Table 4 (of Sect. 7), and generated two pseudo-random[5] j-invariants in $S_{p^2} \setminus S_p$:

$$j_1 = 129007\beta + 818380 \qquad \text{and} \qquad j_2 = 97589\beta + 660383.$$

---

[5] We do this by taking long walks in $\mathcal{X}(\mathbb{F}_p, 3)$ away from a known subfield curve.

Preprocessing. The preprocessing phase of both programs starts by constructing the extension field $\mathbb{F}_{p^2} = \mathbb{F}_p(\beta)$, where β^2 is the first non-square in the sequence $-1, -2, 2, -3, 3, \ldots$. It then computes a list of constants for the Tonelli-Shanks subroutine, most notably the exponent $(p - 2^e - 1)/2^{e+1}$, where e is the maximum integer such that $2^e \mid (p-1)$. This exponent is Scott's 'progenitor' [25, p. 3], which essentially determines the complexity of $\mathbb{F}_p$ square roots, and therefore of $\mathbb{F}_{p^2}$ square roots. As a result, it determines the cost of taking a step in $\mathcal{X}(\bar{\mathbb{F}}_p, 2)$ – see Sect. 3. The preprocessing phase then computes a set of integers $\ell \geq 3$ (according to the optimisations in Sect. 5 and the relevant heuristics in [13]), fetches the associated files (originally from Sutherland's database [28]) containing $\Phi_\ell(X, Y) \in \mathbb{Z}[X, Y]$ and reduces all of the coefficients to store a set of new, more compact files containing elements of $\mathbb{F}_p$ that define each of the $\Phi_{\ell,p}(X, Y) \in \mathbb{F}_p[X, Y]$. Note that this is done for both Solver and SuperSolver, since both of these programs use the original Delfs–Galbraith subfield path algorithm [13, Algorithm 1] after the searches for subfield nodes is complete. It is important to note, especially in the cryptanalytic context, that all of these preprocessing steps only depend on p and can therefore be done without knowledge of j_1 and j_2.

Solver. The optimised walk in $\mathcal{X}(\bar{\mathbb{F}}_p, 2)$ proceeds exactly as described in Sect. 3, i.e., using the depth first search through the binary trees rooted at j_1 and j_2, until both searches find the subfield nodes $j_1' \in \mathbb{F}_p$ and $j_2' \in \mathbb{F}_p$. In the case of our example, paths were found to $j_1' = 760776$ and $j_2' = 35387$, depicted in Fig. 2 and Fig. 3. They correspond to $\phi_1 \colon E_1 \to E_1'$ and $\phi_2 \colon E_2 \to E_2'$, where $j(E_1) = j_1$, $j(E_1') = j_1'$, $j(E_2) = j_2$, and $j(E_2') = j_2'$.

Solver then computes a connecting path between the subfield nodes following Delfs–Galbraith [13, Algorithm 1]. This is depicted in Fig. 4. Solver simply reverses the steps in ϕ_2 to obtain its dual, $\hat{\phi}_2$, and outputs the full path as $\phi \colon E_1 \to E_2$ as $\phi = \hat{\phi}_2 \circ \phi' \circ \phi_1$.

SuperSolver. With $p = 2^{20} - 3$, the preprocessing phase determined that Super-Solver is optimal with $L_3 = \{3, 5\}$ (see also Table 4 in the next section). Before departing the starting node $j_1 = 129007\beta + 818380$, SuperSolver performs the rapid inspection of its 3- and 5-isogenous neighbours as described in Sect. 5. It then takes steps in $\mathcal{X}(\bar{\mathbb{F}}_p, 2)$ as in Sect. 3, but at each new node it performs the rapid inspection of the 3- and 5-isogenous neighbours. In our example, both walks found a subfield node after 2 steps in $\mathcal{X}(\bar{\mathbb{F}}_p, 2)$. The walk from j_1 found a 3-isogenous neighbour and the walk from j_2 found a 5-isogenous neighbour. The final step that finds ϕ' is implemented in SuperSolver exactly as it was for Solver. The three isogenies ϕ_1, ϕ_2, and ϕ', comprising the full isogeny $\phi = \hat{\phi}_2 \circ \phi' \circ \phi_1$, are depicted in Fig. 5.

To illustrate the core idea in this paper, we focus on the isogeny ϕ_1 depicted at the top of Fig. 5 and walk through the steps of the NeighbourInFp algorithm. Evaluating the third modular polynomial at the intermediate j-invariants (Step 1

$$\phi_1 : j_1 \xrightarrow{\quad 2 \quad} 219247\beta + 863507 \xrightarrow{\quad 2 \quad} 489342\beta + 132142$$

$$\downarrow 2$$

$$174188\beta + 794346 \xleftarrow{\quad 2 \quad} 291380\beta + 146098 \xleftarrow{\quad 2 \quad} 148602\beta + 24450$$

$$\downarrow 2$$

$$263095\beta + 184707 \xrightarrow{\quad 2 \quad} 37438\beta + 90559 \xrightarrow{\quad 2 \quad} 1027930\beta + 498080$$

$$\downarrow 2$$

$$612554\beta + 208821 \xleftarrow{\quad 2 \quad} 994015\beta + 681197 \xleftarrow{\quad 2 \quad} 206051\beta + 982009$$

$$\downarrow 2$$

$$649416\beta + 751358 \xrightarrow{\quad 2 \quad} 203489\beta + 43055 \xrightarrow{\quad 2 \quad} 393773\beta + 1028490$$

$$\downarrow 2$$

$$318158\beta + 140927 \xleftarrow{\quad 2 \quad} 175225\beta + 937858 \xleftarrow{\quad 2 \quad} 971263\beta + 725197$$

$$\downarrow 2$$

$$348684\beta + 935077 \xrightarrow{\quad 2 \quad} 341898\beta + 405481 \xrightarrow{\quad 2 \quad} 274229\beta + 367729$$

$$\downarrow 2$$

$$j_1' = 760776$$

Fig. 2. A walk through $\mathcal{X}(\overline{\mathbb{F}}_p, 2)$ for $p = 2^{20} - 3$ during Solver. The walk starts at $j_1 = 129007\beta + 818380 \in S_{p^2}$ and finds the subfield node $j_1' = 760776 \in S_p$ after 21 steps.

$$\phi_2 : j_2 \xrightarrow{\quad 2 \quad} 867493\beta + 220256 \xrightarrow{\quad 2 \quad} 252807\beta + 1011175$$

$$\downarrow 2$$

$$657423\beta + 286117 \xleftarrow{\quad 2 \quad} 440840\beta + 706619 \xleftarrow{\quad 2 \quad} 953362\beta + 11601$$

$$\downarrow 2$$

$$734841\beta + 660440 \xrightarrow{\quad 2 \quad} 919529\beta + 442520 \xrightarrow{\quad 2 \quad} 219960\beta + 646080$$

$$\downarrow 2$$

$$638727\beta + 940073 \xleftarrow{\quad 2 \quad} 219719\beta + 594710 \xleftarrow{\quad 2 \quad} 619876\beta + 961666$$

$$\downarrow 2$$

$$407014\beta + 868179 \xrightarrow{\quad 2 \quad} 535787\beta + 1046047 \xrightarrow{\quad 2 \quad} 138865\beta + 8726$$

$$\downarrow 2$$

$$1016378\beta + 696447 \xleftarrow{\quad 2 \quad} 289439\beta + 170877 \xleftarrow{\quad 2 \quad} 665078\beta + 700037$$

$$\downarrow 2$$

$$895198\beta + 793471 \xrightarrow{\quad 2 \quad} 562302\beta + 547814 \xrightarrow{\quad 2 \quad} 68076\beta + 946405$$

$$\downarrow 2$$

$$j_2' = 35387$$

Fig. 3. A walk through $\mathcal{X}(\overline{\mathbb{F}}_p, 2)$ for $p = 2^{20} - 3$ during Solver. The walk starts at $j_2 = 97589\beta + 660383 \in S_{p^2}$ and finds the subfield node $j_2' = 35387 \in S_p$ after 21 steps.

$$\phi' : j_1' \xrightarrow{31} 815910 \xrightarrow{17} 848568 \xrightarrow{31} 157399 \xrightarrow{29} 451011 \xrightarrow{31} 820763$$

$$\Big\downarrow 31$$

$$j_2' \xleftarrow[17]{} 286978 \xleftarrow[37]{} 76159$$

Fig. 4. A path connecting two subfield j-invariants by taking steps in $\mathcal{X}(\overline{\mathbb{F}}_p, \ell)$ with $\ell \in \{17, 29, 31, 37\}$. The walk starts at $j_1' = 760776 \in S_p$ and connects to $j_2' = 35387 \in S_p$ after 8 steps.

$$\phi_1 : j_1 \xrightarrow{2} 219247\beta + 863507 \xrightarrow{2} 489342\beta + 132142 \xrightarrow{3} j_1' = 35387$$

$$\phi_2 : j_2 \xrightarrow{2} 867493\beta + 220256 \xrightarrow{2} 252807\beta + 1011175 \xrightarrow{5} j_2' = 292917$$

$$\phi' : j_1' \xrightarrow{17} 658300 \xrightarrow{29} 343840 \xrightarrow{31} 560315$$

$$\Big\downarrow 17$$

$$j_2' \xleftarrow[37]{} 439276$$

Fig. 5. The three paths found comprising an isogeny from E_1 to E_2 as found by Super-Solver.

of Algorithm 2) yields

$$\Phi_{3,p}(X, 219247\beta + 863507) = X^4 + (212814\beta + 479338)X^3 + (408250\beta + 920025)X^2$$
$$+ (811739\beta + 93038)X + 942336\beta + 847782;$$
$$\Phi_{3,p}(X, 489342\beta + 132142) = X^4 + (872004\beta + 13960)X^3 + (1031755\beta + 822066)X^2$$
$$+ (969683\beta + 747785)X + 813010\beta + 255391.$$

Though the theory tells us that these two polynomials split over $\mathbb{F}_{p^2}[X]$, to the naked eye there is no way to distinguish which (if any) of these polynomials has a root in $\mathbb{F}_p$. In both cases, setting $g_1 = 1/2 \cdot (\Phi_{3,p} + \pi(\Phi_{3,p}))$ (Step 2 of Algorithm 2) and $g_2 = -\beta/2 \cdot (\Phi_{3,p} - \pi(\Phi_{3,p}))$ (Step 3 of Algorithm 2) respectively yields

$$g_1 = X^4 + 479338X^3 + 920025X^2 + 93038X + 847782;$$
$$g_2 = 425628X^3 + 816500X^2 + 574905X + 836099,$$

and

$$g_1 = X^4 + 13960X^3 + 822066X^2 + 747785X + 255391;$$

$$g_2 = 695435X^3 + 1014937X^2 + 890793X + 577447.$$

In the first case, Step 4 of Algorithm 2 outputs $\gcd(g_1, g_2) = 1$, meaning that $\Phi_{3,p}(X, 219247\beta + 863507)$ has no subfield roots. In the second case, we see $\gcd(g_1, g_2) = X + 1013186$, meaning that $-1013186 = 35387$ is a subfield root. In our example, we note that the total number of steps between j_1 and j_2 returned by SuperSolver is 10, which is much shorter than the 50 steps taken by Solver. Since the middle subfield path finding algorithm is the same in both routines, there is no guarantee that the total path will always be smaller for SuperSolver. It is worth pointing out, however, that the two *outer* paths from elements in $S_{p^2} \setminus S_p$ to S_p (i.e., ϕ_1 and ϕ_2) returned by SuperSolver will never be longer than those returned by Solver. Indeed, Solver can be viewed as a special case of SuperSolver where the list of ℓ's is chosen to be L_0. Finally, we note that both Solver and SuperSolver always conclude by checking the correctness of the full path from j_1 to j_2.

7   Implementation Results

In this section we present some experimental results highlighting the efficacy of SuperSolver. The experiments focus solely on the search for subfield nodes (i.e., the bottleneck step of Delfs–Galbraith) and come in two flavours: many j-invariants over small primes, and one j-invariant over a large, cryptographic prime.

Small Primes and Many Walks. Tables 4 and 5 report experiments that were run on the largest primes of the 30 bitlengths from 20 to 49. We started at 5000 pseudo-random[6] supersingular j-invariants in $S_{p^2} \setminus S_p$ for the primes of bitlengths 20–24, at 1000 j's for the primes of bitlengths 25–29, at 500 j's for the primes of bitlengths 30–34, at 100 j's for the primes of bitlengths 35–39, at 50 j's for the primes of bitlengths 40–44, and at 10 j's for the primes of bitlengths 45–49. For every j, we ran both Solver and SuperSolver (with the five sets of ℓ's that were predicted to perform best during preprocessing) until all walks hit a subfield j-invariant. Throughout, we will denote these fast sets of ℓ's by L_b, as in Sect. 5. In all cases we counted the exact number of $\mathbb{F}_p$ multiplications, squarings and additions required to find the subfield node. Following our metric in Sect. 2, Table 5 reports the average number of $\mathbb{F}_p$ multiplications by counting squarings as multiplications, and highlights in red which of the five predicted sets of ℓ's performed best on average.

Table 4 reports the average number of nodes visited in each of the walks, along with $\lceil \#S_{p^2}/\#S_p \rceil$, the expected number of random elements in S_{p^2} that would

---

[6] Just as in Sect. 6, we used long walks in $\mathcal{X}(\overline{\mathbb{F}}_p, 3)$ away from a known starting curve to achieve uniformity in S_{p^2}.

need to be sampled to find a subfield element in S_p. Here, the primes are small enough that S_p can be computed precisely (see Sect. 2). For each prime, Table 4 highlights in red the column that matches up with the least multiplications reported in Table 5. Note that, for SuperSolver, the number of nodes visited is the number of nodes that are actually walked onto in $\mathcal{X}(\overline{\mathbb{F}}_p, 2)$, not the number of nodes inspected using our fast subfield detection algorithm. Thus, in general, the lowest average number of nodes visited does not correspond to the lowest average number of multiplications. Indeed, the walks with fewer ℓ's spend less compute time inspecting ℓ-isogenous neighbours and therefore move onto new nodes faster, but do not cover as much of the supersingular set during the fast inspection.

The key trend to highlight is that, relatively speaking, SuperSolver gains more advantage over Solver as the primes get larger. This is not as evident for the small primes in Tables 4 and 5 as it is for the larger primes below.

Table 4. The average number of nodes visited in the search for subfield j-invariants in Solver and SuperSolver. Further explanation in text.

prime p	p mod 8	$\left\lceil \frac{\#S_p^2}{\#S_p} \right\rceil$	muls per step	fastest L_j's $[L_{(i)} \cdots, L_{(v)}]$	Average number of nodes visited					
					Solver DG	SuperSolver $L_{(i)}$	$L_{(ii)}$	$L_{(iii)}$	$L_{(iv)}$	$L_{(v)}$
$2^{20} - 3$	5	530	54	$[L_3, L_7, L_{11}, L_1, L_{15}]$	812	127	257	76	107	193
$2^{21} - 9$	7	156	53	$[L_3, L_7, L_1, L_5, L_{11}]$	459	86	218	53	87	111
$2^{22} - 3$	5	584	60	$[L_3, L_7, L_{15}, L_{11}, L_5]$	885	170	108	288	146	145
$2^{23} - 15$	1	583	71	$[L_7, L_3, L_{15}, L_{11}, L_5]$	838	172	106	169	121	430
$2^{24} - 3$	5	1277	64	$[L_3, L_7, L_{15}, L_{11}, L_5]$	1897	318	209	311	618	273
$2^{25} - 39$	1	1231	71	$[L_7, L_3, L_{15}, L_{11}, L_5]$	1873	360	223	359	933	259
$2^{26} - 5$	3	732	62	$[L_3, L_7, L_{15}, L_{11}, L_5]$	1362	352	194	691	271	233
$2^{27} - 39$	1	2348	73	$[L_7, L_3, L_{15}, L_{11}, L_5]$	3455	917	438	579	497	1766
$2^{28} - 57$	7	2965	64	$[L_3, L_7, L_{15}, L_{11}, L_5]$	9748	1788	1022	3065	1314	1306
$2^{29} - 3$	5	2953	74	$[L_7, L_3, L_{15}, L_{11}, L_{13}]$	4384	1053	526	712	603	2161
$2^{30} - 35$	5	3965	75	$[L_7, L_3, L_{15}, L_{11}, L_{13}]$	5555	1443	749	961	849	2825
$2^{31} - 1$	7	9009	75	$[L_7, L_3, L_{15}, L_{11}, L_{13}]$	27103	4501	2602	3755	3136	8794
$2^{32} - 5$	3	5142	75	$[L_7, L_3, L_{15}, L_{11}, L_{13}]$	10149	2520	1445	2108	1702	5335
$2^{33} - 9$	7	6638	77	$[L_7, L_3, L_{15}, L_{11}, L_{13}]$	20387	3832	2342	3756	2676	10562
$2^{34} - 41$	7	10526	78	$[L_7, L_3, L_{15}, L_{11}, L_{13}]$	32640	6443	3790	6094	4531	16320
$2^{35} - 31$	1	117571	99	$[L_{15}, L_7, L_{11}, L_3, L_{13}]$	150101	14893	27873	23076	20921	9850
$2^{36} - 5$	3	29040	83	$[L_7, L_{15}, L_3, L_{11}, L_{13}]$	63384	15929	9127	11974	10807	5249
$2^{37} - 25$	7	70328	84	$[L_7, L_{15}, L_3, L_{11}, L_{13}]$	218775	26241	16098	29226	24153	10405
$2^{38} - 45$	3	100268	86	$[L_7, L_{15}, L_{11}, L_3, L_{13}]$	217145	43595	21343	27187	26982	14897
$2^{39} - 7$	1	174817	96	$[L_7, L_{15}, L_{11}, L_3, L_{13}]$	230235	28802	48488	36770	38318	19677
$2^{40} - 87$	1	266662	95	$[L_7, L_3, L_5, L_6, L_{23}]$	394908	49855	80764	66646	56901	28016
$2^{41} - 21$	3	205227	92	$[L_7, L_3, L_5, L_6, L_{23}]$	448883	52656	105639	69940	62212	27395
$2^{42} - 11$	5	557046	99	$[L_7, L_3, L_5, L_6, L_{23}]$	720206	93920	189498	147651	102116	64309
$2^{43} - 57$	7	198777	95	$[L_7, L_3, L_5, L_6, L_{23}]$	705224	69021	153095	95778	81922	44112
$2^{44} - 17$	7	307870	98	$[L_7, L_3, L_5, L_6, L_{23}]$	808057	131220	285136	145263	142750	72964
$2^{45} - 55$	1	3120225	108	$[L_7, L_3, L_5, L_6, L_{23}]$	2298828	301730	410169	579449	404520	226542
$2^{46} - 21$	3	2759728	102	$[L_7, L_3, L_5, L_6, L_{23}]$	9075335	516826	788898	957832	730020	382101
$2^{47} - 115$	5	4234340	108	$[L_7, L_3, L_5, L_6, L_{23}]$	5182631	650377	866413	650377	801837	781907
$2^{48} - 59$	5	2706129	111	$[L_7, L_3, L_5, L_6, L_{23}]$	6739857	546014	899553	756358	651990	491312
$2^{49} - 81$	7	1239417	107	$[L_7, L_3, L_5, L_6, L_{23}]$	3582205	288124	660449	326050	319641	252270

Remark 5 ($\mathcal{X}(\mathbb{F}_p, 2)$ clusters in $\mathcal{X}(\overline{\mathbb{F}}_p, 2)$). An interesting trend to highlight in Table 4 is that the average number of nodes visited in the optimised Delfs–Galbraith walk through $\mathcal{X}(\overline{\mathbb{F}}_p, 2)$ is significantly more than the expected number of elements one would need to select randomly from S_{p^2} in order to find an element of S_p. The reason for this is that components of $\mathcal{X}(\mathbb{F}_p, 2)$ *cluster together* in $\mathcal{X}(\bar{\mathbb{F}}_p, 2)$. Thus, with respect to finding subfield nodes, walks in $\mathcal{X}(\bar{\mathbb{F}}_p, 2)$ are significantly different from selecting nodes at random from S_{p^2}. The types of clusterings in $\mathcal{X}(\bar{\mathbb{F}}_p, 2)$ depend on the value of $p \bmod 8$ [13, Theorem 2.7], which is why this value is given alongside p in each row. Write N for the ratio between the number of nodes we visited on average (i.e., the bold column) and the number of elements we would expect to draw at random from S_{p^2} before finding one in S_p (i.e., $\#S_{p^2}/\#S_p$). Table 4 shows that (i) when $p \equiv 1 \bmod 4$, we typically see $1 \le N \le 2$; (ii) when $p \equiv 3 \bmod 8$, we typically see $2 \le N \le 3$; and (iii) when $p \equiv 7 \bmod 8$, we often see $N > 3$. For more experimental data illustrating this phenomenon, see [3, §4.3]. In practice, we do not see the $N > 1$ as enough of a reason to incur the significant overhead of walking in $\mathcal{X}(\bar{\mathbb{F}}_p, \ell)$ for $\ell > 2$ instead. In any case, the method of fast subfield root detection proposed in this paper will work regardless of the ℓ-isogenies that are used to take steps in a given walk. In fact, if walking in $\mathcal{X}(\bar{\mathbb{F}}_p, \ell)$ for $\ell > 2$ results in better concrete performance than for $\ell = 2$, the greater cost of taking a step in $\mathcal{X}(\bar{\mathbb{F}}_p, \ell)$ is likely to increase the size of the set of "fast ℓ's" and the relative efficacy of invoking subfield root detection.

Table 5. The average number of $\mathbb{F}_p$ multiplications used to search for subfield j-invariants in Solver and SuperSolver. Further explanation in text.

prime	muls per step	fastest L_j's	Average number of $\mathbb{F}_p$ multiplications					
			Solver	SuperSolver				
p	step	$[L_{(i)} \cdots L_{(v)}]$	DG	$L_{(i)}$	$L_{(ii)}$	$L_{(iii)}$	$L_{(iv)}$	$L_{(v)}$
$2^{20}-3$	54	$[L_3, L_7, L_{11}, L_1, L_{15}]$	**44848**	20601	22585	22235	23459	24951
$2^{21}-9$	53	$[L_3, L_7, L_1, L_5, L_{11}]$	**24187**	13648	18578	15453	18770	14064
$2^{22}-3$	60	$[L_3, L_7, L_{15}, L_{11}, L_5]$	**52385**	28062	31962	26410	32555	38348
$2^{23}-15$	71	$[L_7, L_3, L_{15}, L_{11}, L_5]$	**59691**	30508	32883	39703	33370	44556
$2^{24}-3$	64	$[L_3, L_7, L_{15}, L_{11}, L_5]$	**112878**	53900	62725	70482	59206	73117
$2^{25}-39$	71	$[L_3, L_7, L_{15}, L_{11}, L_5]$	**128703**	63021	68210	83333	94434	70878
$2^{26}-5$	62	$[L_7, L_3, L_{15}, L_{11}, L_5]$	**85437**	59484	58286	65813	61261	62216
$2^{27}-39$	73	$[L_7, L_3, L_{15}, L_{11}, L_5]$	**251304**	164036	135672	136633	137780	185819
$2^{28}-57$	64	$[L_3, L_7, L_{15}, L_{11}, L_5]$	**631157**	305345	308003	298049	299314	351102
$2^{29}-3$	74	$[L_7, L_3, L_{15}, L_{11}, L_{13}]$	**326888**	199985	171489	173335	177986	235902
$2^{30}-35$	75	$[L_7, L_3, L_{15}, L_{11}, L_{13}]$	**412457**	260188	232753	228089	236360	301541
$2^{31}-1$	75	$[L_7, L_3, L_{15}, L_{11}, L_{13}]$	**1998840**	809040	807306	889210	871068	934319
$2^{32}-5$	75	$[L_3, L_7, L_{15}, L_{11}, L_{13}]$	**758637**	455571	449889	501335	474549	572203
$2^{33}-9$	77	$[L_7, L_3, L_{15}, L_{11}, L_{13}]$	**1564701**	700390	733705	900515	751310	1153911
$2^{34}-41$	78	$[L_7, L_3, L_{15}, L_{11}, L_{13}]$	**2537688**	1184024	1191084	1467113	1276654	1799292
$2^{35}-31$	99	$[L_{15}, L_7, L_{11}, L_3, L_{13}]$	**15272705**	5037679	5790782	6109529	6396752	6213090
$2^{36}-5$	83	$[L_7, L_{15}, L_3, L_{11}, L_{13}]$	**5244914**	3006618	2913909	2942626	3099020	3211580
$2^{37}-25$	84	$[L_7, L_{15}, L_3, L_{11}, L_{13}]$	**18322417**	4979176	5155517	7211517	6950196	6375918
$2^{38}-45$	86	$[L_7, L_{15}, L_3, L_{11}, L_{13}]$	**18402937**	8315681	6856578	6735588	7791309	9143526
$2^{39}-7$	96	$[L_7, L_{15}, L_{11}, L_3, L_{13}]$	**22505327**	9627241	9879376	9587856	11562406	12332858
$2^{40}-87$	95	$[L_7, L_3, L_5, L_6, L_{23}]$	**38602102**	16664021	16455546	17377853	17169885	17559520
$2^{41}-21$	92	$[L_7, L_3, L_5, L_6, L_{23}]$	**41185437**	17284297	20890068	17817383	18399209	17006068
$2^{42}-11$	99	$[L_7, L_3, L_5, L_6, L_{23}]$	**70760036**	31439715	38704889	99170000	00004014	40337712
$2^{43}-57$	95	$[L_7, L_3, L_5, L_6, L_{23}]$	**66820000**	22863425	30733754	24686759	24474388	27514948
$2^{44}-17$	98	$[L_7, L_3, L_5, L_6, L_{23}]$	**79795521**	43991657	58381667	38022655	43217829	45803624
$2^{45}-55$	108	$[L_7, L_3, L_5, L_6, L_{23}]$	**247697962**	103871110	87674099	156886333	126109617	144250917
$2^{46}-21$	102	$[L_7, L_3, L_5, L_6, L_{23}]$	**923415913**	174816651	163893709	198006728	205399202	220786555
$2^{47}-115$	108	$[L_7, L_3, L_5, L_6, L_{23}]$	**550653552**	222915969	183895536	175113230	248769348	272706341
$2^{48}-59$	111	$[L_7, L_3, L_5, L_6, L_{23}]$	**729589278**	188237971	192728454	205161765	251091015	310387211
$2^{49}-81$	107	$[L_7, L_3, L_5, L_6, L_{23}]$	**385982057**	99186957	141171527	88278361	99648273	160633132

Large Primes and Optimal Node Coverage. Table 6 illustrates the increased efficacy of SuperSolver over Solver as the supersingular isogeny graphs get larger. Recall that we reported some of the results from this table up front in Sect. 1, namely from the experiments using primes from the isogeny literature. We chose the largest prime below 2^k for $k \in \{50, 100, \ldots 800\}$, and started from a pseudorandom j-invariant in $S_{p^2} \setminus S_p$ as usual. Since these instances are too large to actually run the full subfield search until it terminates, in each case we ran both Solver and SuperSolver (for the three sets of ℓ's that were predicted to perform best during preprocessing) until the number of $\mathbb{F}_p$ multiplications used exceeded 10^8, and then immediately stopped. The numbers reported in bold in Table 6 are the total number of nodes covered (i.e., both walked onto *and* inspected) during these walks. For the smallest prime $p = 2^{50} - 27$, SuperSolver covers between 3 and 4 times the number of nodes that Solver does; for the largest prime $p = 2^{800} - 105$, SuperSolver covers between 18 and 19 times the number of nodes. Though primes beyond this size are unlikely to be of cryptographic interest, it is worth pointing out that this trend continues: the larger p grows, the more profitable it becomes to keep adding ℓ's in the fast subfield inspection algorithm.

Table 6. The number of nodes inspected per 10^8 field multiplications for the largest primes of various bitlengths. The Solver column corresponds to optimised Delfs–Galbraith walks in $\mathcal{X}(\overline{\mathbb{F}}_p, 2)$ – see Sect. 3. The SuperSolver columns correspond to enabling our fast subfield root detection algorithm with the three fastest sets of ℓ's (left to right) – see Sect. 5. Numbers in round brackets are the approximate number of $\mathbb{F}_p$ multiplications per node inspected, as computed during the precomputation phase that determines which sets of ℓ's will perform fastest.

prime p	Solver		SuperSolver		
$2^{50} - 27$	**882,999**	(113)	{3,5,7} 2,859,201 (35.0)	{3,5} 2,736,613 (36.5)	{3,7} 2,533,945 (39.4)
$2^{100} - 15$	**443,951**	(223)	{3,5,7} 2,165,681 (46.0)	{3,5,7,11} 2,121,313 (47.8)	{3,5,7,11,9} 2,006,215 (49.7)
$2^{150} - 3$	**317,209**	(315)	{3,5,7,11} 1,895,169 (52.8)	{3,5,7,11,13} 1,852,237 (54.0)	{3,5,7,11,9} 1,847,371 (54.1)
$2^{200} - 75$	**241,989**	(415)	{3,5,7,11,13} 1,716,767 (58.3)	{3,5,7,11,13,9} 1,715,449 (58.4)	{3,5,7,11,9} 1,700,791 (58.9)
$2^{250} - 207$	**191,115**	(526)	{3,5,7,11,13,9} 1,607,145 (62.3)	{3,5,7,11,13} 1,586,495 (63.2)	{3,5,7,11,9} 1,561,645 (64.2)
$2^{300} - 153$	**164,275**	(609)	{3,5,7,11,13,9} 1,531,993 (65.3)	{3,5,7,11,13} 1,498,175 (66.8)	{3,5,7,11,13,9,17} 1,489,991 (67.1)
$2^{350} - 113$	**141,097**	(708)	{3,5,7,11,13,9} 1,452,529 (68.8)	{3,5,7,11,13,9,17} 1,432,345 (69.8)	{3,5,7,11,13} 1,406,543 (71.1)
$2^{400} - 593$	**123,649**	(809)	{3,5,7,11,13,9} 1,380,849 (72.4)	{3,5,7,11,13,9,17} 1,378,991 (72.5)	{3,5,7,11,13,9,17,19 } 1,346,081 (74.3)
$2^{450} - 501$	**110,407**	(907)	{3,5,7,11,13,9,17} 1,332,176 (75.2)	{3,5,7,11,13,9} 1,321,701 (75.9)	{3,5,7,11,13,9,17,19} 1,316,198 (76.4)
$2^{500} - 863$	**97,510**	(1032)	{3,5,7,11,13,9,17} 1,280,243 (78.6)	{3,5,7,11,13,9,17,19} 1,274,001 (79.0)	{3,5,7,11,13,9} 1,251,602 (80.4)
$2^{550} - 5$	**90,321**	(1111)	{[3,5,7,11,13,9,17 } 1,243,309 (80.6)	{[3,5,7,11,13,9,17,19 } 1,240,916 (80.7)	{3,5,7,11,13,9,19} 1,216,189 (82.6)
$2^{600} - 95$	**81,544**	(1232)	{3,5,7,11,13,9,17,19} 1,203,358 (83.3)	{3,5,7,11,13,9,17} 1,198,900 (84.0)	{3,5,7,11,13,9,19} 1,170,561 (85.8)
$2^{650} - 611$	**76,569**	(1311)	{3,5,7,11,13,9,17,19} 1,184,513 (85.0)	{3,5,7,11,13,9,17} 1,161,998 (86.1)	{3,5,7,11,13,9,17,19,23} 1,144,708 (87.4)
$2^{700} - 1113$	**71,037**	(1409)	{3,5,7,11,13,9,17,19} 1,148,963 (82.5)	{3,5,7,11,13,9,17} 1,127,317 (82.6)	{3,5,7,11,13,9,17,19,23} 1,123,125 (82.9)
$2^{750} - 161$	**66,239**	(1510)	{3,5,4,7,11,13,9,8,17,19,6} 1,121,045 (84.4)	{3,5,4,7,11,13,9,8,17,19} 1,101,767 (84.4)	{3,5,4,7,11,13,9,8,17,6} 1,093,351 (85.1)
$2^{800} - 105$	**62,191**	(1609)	{3,5,4,7,11,13,9,8,17,19,6} 1,096,056 (86.1)	{3,5,4,7,11,13,9,8,17,19} 1,082,072 (86.3)	{3,5,4,7,11,13,9,8,17,6} 1,062,658 (87.2)

Storing and Accessing the Reduced Modular Polynomials. The unreduced modular polynomials $\Phi_\ell(X, Y) \in \mathbb{Z}[X, Y]$ require a significant amount of storage, but recall that the preprocessing phase immediately reduces all of the coefficients into $\mathbb{F}_p$ to produce $\Phi_{\ell,p}(X, Y) \in \mathbb{F}_p[X, Y]$. This can be done once-and-for-all for a specific prime, and this makes the storage and access of the $\Phi_{\ell,p}(X, Y)$ a non-issue. Storing $\Phi_{\ell,p}(X, Y)$ requires at most $(N_\ell^2/2) \cdot \log_2(p)$ bits. For example, the largest $\Phi_{\ell,p}(X, Y)$ for the 250-bit prime above is $\Phi_{13,p}(X, Y)$, which requires the storage of at most $N_{13}^2/2 = 14^2/2 = 98$ elements of $\mathbb{F}_p$, around 3KB. The largest $\Phi_{\ell,p}(X, Y)$ for the 800-bit prime above requires the storage of at most $N_{19}^2/2 = 20^2/2 = 200$ elements of $\mathbb{F}_p$, around 20KB. Any of these would comfortably fit into the L1 cache on a modern CPU.

Concrete Security of the Supersingular Isogeny Problem. Our Super-Solver suite makes it straightforward to obtain precise estimates on the concrete classical security offered by the general supersingular isogeny problem in S_{p^2}, for any prime p. Combining a small experiment (like those reported in Table 6) with the expected number of nodes one must cover before reaching a subfield node allows us to obtain accurate counts on the expected number of $\mathbb{F}_p$ multiplications, squarings and additions that must be carried out during a full cryptanalytic attack. It is then a matter of costing these $\mathbb{F}_p$ operations with respect to the appropriate metric, whether that be bit operations, cycle counts, gate counts, or circuit depth.

Take, for example, the 256-bit prime

$$p = 73743043621499797449074820543863456997944695372324032511999999999999999999999$$

underlying SQISign [15] to illustrate how our software can be used to obtain precise security estimates. The precomputation phase of SuperSolver (which takes a few seconds on input of p) reveals that taking an optimised step in $\mathcal{X}(\bar{\mathbb{F}}_p, 2)$ costs 407 multiplications in $\mathbb{F}_p$. Based on this cost, the precomputation further determines that the fastest set of ℓ's to proceed with are

$$\ell \in \{3, 5, 7, 11, 13\}.$$

On average, the combination of this set of ℓ's and Algorithm 2 reduces the cost of the subfield search from 407 multiplications in $\mathbb{F}_p$ per node to 58.0 multiplications in $\mathbb{F}_p$ per node (see Table 1). Thus, on average, solving the supersingular isogeny problem costs

$$58.0 \times \left(\frac{\#S_{p^2}}{\#S_p}\right) \mathbb{F}_p \text{ multiplications.}$$

Since $p \equiv 7 \bmod 12$, we have $\#S_{p^2} = \lfloor p/12 \rfloor + 1$ [27, Theorem V.4.1(c)], and since $p \equiv 7 \bmod 8$, $\#S_p$ is exactly the class number of the imaginary quadratic field $\mathbb{Q}(\sqrt{-p})$ [13, Equation 1]. We suppose this class number is N, i.e., $\#S_p = N$. Writing $N - 2^k$, where k is correct to 3 decimal places, we would obtain that the average cost of breaking this instance of SQISign is $2^{257.622-k}$ multiplications in $\mathbb{F}_p$.[7]

---

[7] For large, cryptographic sized primes p, computing class numbers is very computationally expensive. Indeed, a recent class group computation for a 512-bit prime terminated in ≈ 52 core years.

In Table 7 we give average counts for the cost of breaking the supersingular isogeny problem using SuperSolver for a number of primes underlying either B-SIDH or SQISign.

Table 7. The average number of $\mathbb{F}_p$ multiplications required to solve the supersingular isogeny problem using SuperSolver. When $p \equiv 1 \bmod 4$, we assume that $N = 2^k$ is the class number of $\mathbb{Q}(\sqrt{-4p})$, where k correct to 3 decimal places. Otherwise, it is the class number of $\mathbb{Q}(\sqrt{-p})$. As N varies for each prime, we will index N and k by the row in the table, i.e., $N_i = 2^{k_i}$ will be the class number of the i-th prime in the table. The number of $\mathbb{F}_p$ multiplications per node using SuperSolver is taken from Table 1.

prime p	$p \bmod 8$	Average number of $\mathbb{F}_p$ mults. per node	$\#S_{p^2}$	$\#S_p$	Average cost of SuperSolver
B-SIDH-p247 [11]	7	58.0	$2^{242.559}$	2^{k_1}	$2^{248.417-k_1}$
TwinSmooth-p250 [12]	1	59.1	$2^{246.220}$	2^{k_2-1}	$2^{251.105-k_2}$
SQISign-p256 [15]	7	58.0	$2^{251.764}$	2^{k_3}	$2^{257.622-k_3}$
TwinSmooth-p384 [12]	1	65.2	$2^{379.735}$	2^{k_4-1}	$2^{384.762-k_4}$
TwinSmooth-p512 [12]	5	71.7	$2^{507.896}$	2^{k_5-1}	$2^{513.060-k_5}$

Acknowledgements. Thanks to Sam Frengley, Michael Naehrig, Krijn Reijnders, Benjamin Smith, Greg Zaverucha, and the CRYPTO2022 reviewers for their valuable comments on an earlier version of this paper. We also thank Drew Sutherland for answering our questions about alternative modular functions.

References

1. Adj, G., Cervantes-Vázquez, D., Chi-Domínguez, J., Menezes, A., Rodríguez-Henríquez, F.: On the cost of computing isogenies between supersingular elliptic curves. In: Cid, C., Jacobson, M., Jr. (eds.) SAC 2018. LNCS, vol. 11349, pp. 322–343. Springer, Cham (2018). https://doi.org/10.1007/978-3-030-10970-7_15
2. Adj, G., Rodríguez-Henríquez, F.: Square root computation over even extension fields. IEEE Trans. Comput. **63**(11), 2829–2841 (2013)
3. Arpin, S., et al.: Adventures in supersingularland. Exp. Math. 1–28 (2021)
4. Berlekamp, E.R.: Factoring polynomials over large finite fields. Math. Comput. **24**(111), 713–735 (1970)
5. Beullens, W., Kleinjung, T., Vercauteren, F.: CSI-FiSh: efficient isogeny based signatures through class group computations. In: Galbraith, S.D., Moriai, S. (eds.) ASIACRYPT 2019. LNCS, vol. 11921, pp. 227–247. Springer, Cham (2019). https://doi.org/10.1007/978-3-030-34578-5_9
6. Bruinier, J.H., Ono, K., Sutherland, A.V.: Class polynomials for nonholomorphic modular functions. J. Number Theory **161**, 204–229 (2016)
7. Burdges, J., De Feo, L.: Delay encryption. In: Canteaut, A., Standaert, F. (eds.) EUROCRYPT 2021, Part I. LNCS, vol. 12696, pp. 302–326. Springer, Cham (2021). https://doi.org/10.1007/978-3-030-77870-5_11
8. Cantor, D.G., Zassenhaus, H.: A new algorithm for factoring polynomials over finite fields. Math. Comput. **36**, 587–592 (1981)

9. Castryck, W., Decru, T.: CSIDH on the surface. In: Ding, J., Tillich, J.-P. (eds.) PQCrypto 2020. LNCS, vol. 12100, pp. 111–129. Springer, Cham (2020). https:// doi.org/10.1007/978-3-030-44223-1_7

10. Castryck, W., Decru, T., Vercauteren, F.: Radical isogenies. In: Moriai, S., Wang, H. (eds.) ASIACRYPT 2020, Part II. LNCS, vol. 12492, pp. 493–519. Springer, Cham (2020). https://doi.org/10.1007/978-3-030-64834-3_17

11. Costello, C.: B-SIDH: supersingular isogeny Diffie-Hellman using twisted torsion. In: Moriai, S., Wang, H. (eds.) ASIACRYPT 2020. LNCS, vol. 12492, pp. 440–463. Springer, Cham (2020). https://doi.org/10.1007/978-3-030-64834-3_15

12. Costello, C., Meyer, M., Naehrig, M.: Sieving for twin smooth integers with solutions to the Prouhet-Tarry-Escott problem. In: Canteaut, A., Standaert, F.-X. (eds.) EUROCRYPT 2021. LNCS, vol. 12696, pp. 272–301. Springer, Cham (2021). https://doi.org/10.1007/978-3-030-77870-5_10

13. Delfs, C., Galbraith, S.D.: Computing isogenies between supersingular elliptic curves over $\mathbb{F}_p$. Des. Codes Cryptogr. **78**(2), 425–440 (2016)

14. De Feo, L., Jao, D., Plût, J.: Towards quantum-resistant cryptosystems from supersingular elliptic curve isogenies. J. Math. Cryptol. **8**(3), 209–247 (2014)

15. De Feo, L., Kohel, D., Leroux, A., Petit, C., Wesolowski, B.: SQISign: compact post-quantum signatures from quaternions and isogenies. In: Moriai, S., Wang, H. (eds.) ASIACRYPT 2020. LNCS, vol. 12491, pp. 64–93. Springer, Cham (2020). https://doi.org/10.1007/978-3-030-64837-4_3

16. Galbraith, S.D., Petit, C., Silva, J.: Identification protocols and signature schemes based on supersingular isogeny problems. J. Cryptol. **33**(1), 130–175 (2020)

17. Hamburg, M.: Fast and compact elliptic-curve cryptography. Cryptol. ePrint Arch. Report 2012/309 (2012). https://ia.cr/2012/309

18. Horn, R.A., Johnson, C.R.: Topics in Matrix Analysis. Cambridge University Press, Cambridge (1994)

19. Jao, D., et al.: SIKE: supersingular isogeny key encapsulation. Manuscript available at sike.org/ (2017)

20. Leonardi, C.: Security analysis of isogeny-based cryptosystems. Ph.D. thesis, University of Waterloo, Ontario, Canada (2020)

21. Lidl, R., Niederreiter, H.: Introduction to Finite Fields and their Applications. Cambridge University Press, Cambridge (1994)

22. Menezes, A.J., van Oorschot, P.C., Vanstone, S.A.: Handbook of Applied Cryptography. CRC Press, Boca Raton (2018)

23. Mestre, J.-F.: La méthode des graphes. Examples et applications. In: Proceedings of the International Conference on Class Numbers and Fundamental Units of Algebraic Number Fields (Katata), pp. 217–242. Citeseer (1986)

24. Pizer, A.K.: Ramanujan graphs and Hecke operators. Bull. Am. Math. Soc. **23**(1), 127–137 (1990)

25. Scott, M.: A note on the calculation of some functions in finite fields: tricks of the trade. IACR Cryptol. ePrint Arch. 1497 (2020)

26. Shoup, V.: A Computational Introduction to Number Theory and Algebra. Cambridge University Press, Cambridge (2009)

27. Silverman, J.H.: The Arithmetic of Elliptic Curves, vol. 106. Springer, New York (2009). https://doi.org/10.1007/978-0-387-09494-6

28. Sutherland, A.V.: Modular polynomials. https://math.mit.edu/~drew/ClassicalMo dPolys.html. Accessed 30 Sept 2021
29. Sutherland, A.V.: On the evaluation of modular polynomials. Open Book Ser. **1**(1), 531–555 (2013)
30. The Sage Developers. SageMath, the Sage Mathematics Software System (Version 9.2) (2021). https://www.sagemath.org
31. Vélu, J.: Isogénies entre courbes elliptiques. CR Acad. Sci. Paris Sér. AB **273**(A238–A241), 5 (1971)

Secret Can Be Public: Low-Memory AEAD Mode for High-Order Masking

Yusuke Naito[1($\boxtimes$)], Yu Sasaki[2], and Takeshi Sugawara[3]

[1] Mitsubishi Electric Corporation, Kanagawa, Japan
Naito.Yusuke@ce.MitsubishiElectric.co.jp
[2] NTT Social Informatics Laboratories, Tokyo, Japan
yu.sasaki.sk@hco.ntt.co.jp
[3] The University of Electro-Communications, Tokyo, Japan
sugawara@uec.ac.jp

Abstract. We propose a new AEAD mode of operation for an efficient countermeasure against side-channel attacks. Our mode achieves the smallest memory with high-order masking, by minimizing the states that are duplicated in masking. An s-bit key-dependent state is necessary for achieving s-bit security, and the conventional schemes always protect the entire s bits with masking. We reduce the protected state size by introducing an *unprotected* state in the key-dependent state: we protect only a half and give another half to a side-channel adversary. Ensuring independence between the unprotected and protected states is the key technical challenge since mixing these states reveals the protected state to the adversary. We propose a new mode HOMA that achieves s-bit security using a tweakable block cipher with the $s/2$-bit block size. We also propose a new primitive for instantiating HOMA with $s = 128$ by extending the SKINNY tweakable block cipher to a 64-bit plaintext block, a 128-bit key, and a $(256 + 3)$-bit tweak. We make hardware performance evaluation by implementing HOMA with high-order masking for $d \leq 5$. For any $d > 0$, HOMA outperforms the current state-of-the-art PFB_Plus by reducing the circuit area larger than that of the entire S-box.

Keywords: Authenticated Encryption · High-Order Masking · Side-Channel Attack · Mode of Operation · Lightweight Cryptography

1 Introduction

There is a growing demand for extending information systems to the physical world by using network-enabled embedded devices, and lightweight cryptography (LWC) is the key technology enabling secure network communication in such resource-constrained devices. Designing lightweight symmetric-key cryptography is arguably the central topic in LWC research because extremely resource-constrained devices cannot afford the cost of implementing public-key cryptography. The National Institute of Standards and Technology (NIST) is currently conducting the LWC competition to determine the next standard of authenticated encryption with associated data (AEAD) schemes [33].

© International Association for Cryptologic Research 2022
Y. Dodis and T. Shrimpton (Eds.): CRYPTO 2022, LNCS 13509, pp. 315–345, 2022.
https://doi.org/10.1007/978-3-031-15982-4_11

Such embedded devices that need LWC can be used in a hostile environment wherein a local attacker mounts power and/or electromagnetic side-channel attacks (SCAs) [24]. Thus, LWC designers face an even more challenging task of realizing an SCA-resistant implementation with limited resources. In fact, countermeasures against SCAs are explicitly mentioned as design requirements in NIST's competition, and ISAP [13], which was designed with a focus on robustness against SCA, has recently been chosen as a finalist in the competition [34].

Masking, which splits the target value into a number of shares, is arguably the most common countermeasure against SCA [20,32]. The security of masking is based on the $\tilde{d}$-probing model, which considers an attacker who can probe d wires [20]. A masking scheme with the protection order d resists attacks with up to d probes. A common strategy is to design a *gadget*, typically a secure Boolean AND operation, that securely maps the input shares into the corresponding output shares and to construct a target symmetric-key algorithm using them while ensuring the compositional security.

Large performance overhead is the major drawback of masking. In particular, the number of shares significantly impacts computational complexity. The early schemes used $(td + 1)$ shares with $t > 1$ for achieving the protection order d and thus called $(td + 1)$-masking [20]. Later, the researchers invented a new scheme that achieves the same protection order by using $(d + 1)$ shares only [39]. In this paper, we focus on the $(d + 1)$-masking schemes because they have a significant performance advantage over the $(td + 1)$-masking schemes.

Such a masking scheme is also effective against statistical SCA with several assumptions regarding the noise level and leakage function; the number of side-channel traces to mount an attack, which is the key difficulty indicator, increases exponentially with the protection order d [37]. A sufficient protection order heavily depends on the target, and the recent experimental evaluations suggests that $d \approx 5$ is practical. For example, Cassiers et al. verified their masking scheme up to $d = 3$ using 9 million traces which is close to the practical limit [9,10].

1.1 Low-Memory AEAD for Masking

As we reduce the circuit area for combinatorial logic gates by exploiting the area-latency trade-off with sophisticated serial architectures [26,27], memory (register) becomes more and more dominant. The overhead of masking is also critical because it duplicates the target state for shared representation. Since reducing the memory size within a block cipher is difficult, researchers have been tackling the problem at the higher layer, and have proposed several masking-friendly AEAD modes achieving small memory sizes after masking [21,26,29].

We summarize the memory costs for achieving s-bit security in the state-of-the-art AEAD schemes in Table 1. All conventional schemes, including the conventional block cipher (BC) based and permutation (P) based schemes [12, 25], use the total memory size of $3s$ bits without SCA protection (see the column with $d = 0$). That is because we need (i) $2s$-bit information carried between blocks to achieve s-bit security against internal-state collisions, and (ii) an s-bit key indispensable for the security against exhaustive search.

Table 1. Memory size for masking implementations with s-bit security. The security of the existing schemes are evaluated in the conventional AE-security [30] or its related notions. HOMA is evaluated in a new security notion, which ensures the same security properties as the conventional one while leaking unprotected values to adversaries.

Scheme	Public	Key-Dependent		Key[†]	(d+1) Masking				Ref.
		Protected[†]	Unprotected		$d=0$[‡]	$d=1$	$d=2$	$d=\hat{d}$	
P-based	—	$2s$	—	s	$3s$	$6s$	$9s$	$3s(\hat{d}+1)$	[12]
BC-based	—	$2s$	—	s	$3s$	$6s$	$9s$	$3s(\hat{d}+1)$	[25]
TBC-based[§]	s	s	—	s	$3s$	$5s$	$7s$	$2s(\hat{d}+1)+s$	[21,26,29]
HOMA	$1.5s$	$0.5s$	$0.5s$	s	$3.5s$	$5s$	$6.5s$	$1.5s(\hat{d}+1)+2s$	Ours

[†] The key and the key-dependent protected state are encoded into $(d+1)$ shares in $(d+1)$-masking.
[‡] $d=0$ corresponds to an implementation without any SCA countermeasure.
[§] This category includes PFB, Romulus, and PFB_Plus.

In contrast, the schemes have different memory sizes after masking. As summarized in Table 1, the memory is categorized into three types:

- *Public:* a state that can be computed only with input values to the encryption or decryption algorithm (without a key),
- *Key-dependent:* a state that requires knowledge of the key,
- *Key:* a secret key.

The public state needs no SCA protection, and the scheme with a larger public state has a smaller memory size after masking (see the column with $d > 0$). In particular, the recent beyond-the-birthday-bound schemes using Tweakable BC (TBC), namely PFB [29], Romulus [21], and PFB_Plus [26], use a public tweak for reducing the size of the key-dependent state within the internal state. These schemes achieve $2s(d+1) + s$ bits of memory with $(d+1)$-masking, which is better than the conventional BC-based or P-based schemes with $3s(d+1)$ bits.

In this paper, we pursue this direction and study a new mode of operation that minimizes the state size after $(d+1)$-masking. The key technical challenge is to reduce the key-dependent state beyond the conventional schemes. The existing masking-friendly AEADs (PFB, Romulus, and PFB_Plus) use masking to both the key-dependent state and the key. The s-bit memory for the secret key has no room for improvement. Besides, protecting the remaining key-dependent s-bit state has also been believed to be necessary for achieving s-bit security. We refer to this as "the s-bit secret barrier" hereafter. The existing masking-friendly AEADs are optimal under this belief.

1.2   Summary of Contributions

This paper makes three main contributions: (i) a new mode HOMA, (ii) an instantiation for HOMA, including a new TBC as an underlying primitive, and (iii) concrete implementations and performance benchmarking of HOMA.

(i) New Mode (Sect. 3) and Its Proof (Sect. 4). First, we propose a new TBC-based AEAD mode-of-operation HOMA that achieves the smallest memory of all existing schemes for $(d + 1)$ masking (see Fig. 1-(center) and -(right) for its core procedure). For further reducing memory, we consider dropping SCA protection from a part of the s-bit key-dependent states. Hence, we decompose the key-dependent state into "unprotected" and "protected" states.

- *Unprotected:* a key-dependent state without SCA protection in a raw form
- *Protected:* a key-dependent state with SCA protection in a shared form

The protected state is protected with high-order masking using $(d+1)$ shares, and has the protection order d. The unprotected state is represented without shares and an SCA adversary potentially has unlimited access. To capture this worst-case scenario, we define a security notion that all the unprotected values are revealed whereas the protected values are secret. With the leakage of the unprotected state, the secret state becomes smaller than s bits, which allows a birthday attack with $s/2$-bit complexity, as we discuss in Sect. 3. HOMA addresses this attack by introducing random IV without increasing memory size.

A TBC's internal state, directly updated with a key, must be protected. Hence, we design a mode such that a TBC's internal state is the only state that requires SCA protection. Moreover, the TBC's block size should be as small as possible. PFB_Plus's idea of using a small block size is beneficial to our mode. PFB_Plus divides the s-bit key-dependent state and updates a half by a TBC and another half by XORing the TBC output, as shown in Fig. 1-(left). However, simply unprotecting the latter $s/2$ bits in PFB_Plus ends up with a trivial attack. We consider $v_3 = v_1 \oplus v_2$ in Fig. 1-(left). Unprotecting the latter half of the state means that both v_3 and v_1 are revealed. This immediately reveals supposedly protected v_2 because $v_2 = v_1 \oplus v_3$. Then, a collision on the whole state can be generated only by a collision on v_3 because the difference in v_2 can be canceled by injecting the difference from A_{i+1}. Hence, security decreases to $s/2$ bits.

Addressing the issue, HOMA uses the structure in Fig. 1-(center) and -(right). Considering that each TBC call produces an $s/2$-bit random value, HOMA calls a TBC twice to sufficiently mix the s-bit internal state (and additionally calls a TBC to encrypt a plaintext block in the encryption), which enables us to prove the s-bit security of HOMA. In Fig. 1-(center) and -(right), the red lines are protected and represented with $(d+1)$ shares and the TBC and fix0 implementations are protected with $(d + 1)$-masking, and the black lines remain unprotected.

With the above security notion, we prove that by fixing the TBC size to n bits, HOMA achieves $2n$-bit security. As a result, HOMA ensures s-bit security only with a protected state of size $s/2$ bits (smaller than s bits) and an s-bit key. As a drawback, HOMA needs three (resp. two) TBC calls for each data block for encryption (resp. AD processing). This yields some overhead in latency, but its impact on memory size is negligible. Another drawback is that HOMA requires a random IV of s bits, which is crucial to ensure the s-bit security when the unprotected state is $s/2$ bits, in addition to a nonce that is an additional overhead of traffic data. Note that we can comfortably assume the availability of a random generator because it is necessary for masking[1].

---

[1] Some masking implementations use non-cryptographic PRNGs, e.g., a simple LFSR, insufficient for the random IV. A hardware TRNG for seeding should be used instead.

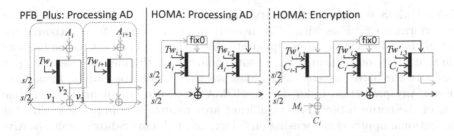

Fig. 1. PFB_Plus's structure (left) and HOMA's structure (center and right). A_j is an AD block and M_i/C_i is a plaintext/ciphertext block. The red (resp. black) lines are protected (resp. unprotected). Tw_j is a tweak. fix0 is a function fixing a LSB to 0. Each dotted circle of PFB_Plus represents a component of processing one data block. (Color figure online)

As summarized in Table 1, HOMA uses a $1.5s$-bit public state, a $0.5s$-bit protected state, a $0.5s$-bit unprotected state, and an s-bit key. Hence, without masking implementation, the state size is $3.5s$ bits, which is worse than those of existing modes. However, with $(d+1)$ masking, HOMA achieves $1.5(d+1)+2s$, which is the smallest for $d > 0$ and asymptotically reduces memory by 25%.

(ii) Instantiation of HOMA with a New TBC (Sect. 5). HOMA for $s = 128$ requires a TBC that supports a 64-bit block, a 128-bit key, and a $(256+3)$-bit tweak, where the 3 bits are for domain separation of the mode. No existing TBC efficiently supports those configurations. Moreover, tweak- and key-schedules must be designed so that the tweak (public) is not mixed with the key (key-dependent) to avoid $(d+1)$ masking of the tweak state. We found that the tweak- and key-schedules of SKINNY [3] satisfy this requirement, thus we design a new TBC "SKINNYee" by basing its structure on SKINNY. The tweaky (a combination of a tweak and a key) size of SKINNY is 64, 128, or 192 bits, and SKINNYe [26] extended it to 256 bits, while our TBC needs $(128+256+3) = 387$ bits of key and tweak. This is challenging because the tweakey size extension done by SKINNY and SKINNYe cannot exceed 256 bits due to the limited design space. We resolve it by processing a key and a tweak as independent objects. Moreover, we absorb the 3-bit tweak by initializing a linear feedback shift register (LFSR) to a tweak-dependent value, which is more efficient than existing methods to extend the tweak size by a few bits [11,27]. Besides, we modify the LFSR clocking method of SKINNY so that the implementation is optimized for small memory.

(iii) Implementation (Sect. 6). We propose a hardware architecture for HOMA instantiated with SKINNYee and make a concrete performance comparison with the conventional state-of-the-art PFB_Plus. For the high-order masking, we use Cassiers et al.'s HPC2 [9,10] for its glitch resistance, composability, and availability of an open-source implementation [8]. This is also the first HPC2 implementation of the SKINNY-based primitives and its S-box. We make an ASIC performance evaluation for the protection order $d \in \{0, \cdots, 5\}$ using a

45-nm CMOS standard cell library (see Table 3). As a result, HOMA always outperformed PFB_Plus with SCA protection, i.e., for any $d > 0$. Although the cost of the S-box circuit grows quadratically with d, in contrast to the memory size that grows only linearly, the results confirm that the memory elements still dominate the hardware cost with those practical protection orders. In particular, for any protection order $d > 0$, HOMA saved the circuit area larger than that of the entire S-box. This significant area reduction is impossible with the conventional approaches focusing on S-box, i.e., reducing S-box's multiplicative complexity [1,16,17] and improving each AND gadget [9,10].

1.3   Related Work

Optimization for $(td + 1)$ Masking. PFB_Plus is optimized for $(td+1)$ masking with $t > 1$, for Nikova et al.'s threshold implementation (TI) [32] in particular. $(td + 1)$-masking use the different number of shares between the linear and non-linear states: those states require $(d+1)$ and $(td+1)$ shares, respectively. To exploit this property, PFB_Plus increases the ratio of a linearly updated state, within the s-bit secret barrier, and achieves a smaller memory after $(td + 1)$-masking. Unfortunately, PFB_Plus's benefit disappears with a $(d + 1)$-masking, which uses the same number of shares for non-linearly and linearly updated states. TI's extension to $d \geq 2$ turned out to be non-trivial [7,38], and researchers are studying $(d + 1)$-masking as a viable option for high-order masking [39]. HOMA takes another approach of breaking the s-bit secret barrier and achieves a smaller memory with $(d+1)$ masking as shown in Table 1. Moreover, even with the 3-share TI, HOMA achieves the same memory size as PFB_Plus.

Leakage-Resilient (LR) Cryptography. LR cryptography studies symmetric-key schemes, including AEAD, with provable security against SCA [2, 5,6,13–15,36]. The early LR schemes relied on the bounded leakage model that limits the amount of leakage for each measurement [15]. However, limiting the number of measurements turned out to be impractical with a stateless primitive [4]. Addressing the issue, some recent LR schemes, including TEDT [6] and Spook [5], use a leak-free primitive supposedly realized with masking [14]. These modes can be faster than HOMA because they efficiently use unprotected primitives. Meanwhile, TEDT/Spook is not optimized for memory usage; protecting its s-bit TBC with masking requires the similar memory size as the other TBC-based schemes in Table 1. The additional components, including an independent unprotected TBC/Permutation implementation, can further increase the memory size.

Other LR schemes, including ISAP [13], pursue exclusive use of leaky primitives by limiting the target to non-adaptive attackers. ISAP can go beyond Table 1 because it does not rely on masking, and the memory size is independent of the protection order d. Meanwhile, the security of these schemes relies entirely on the restricted input space to the leaky primitives, which has several limitations compared with masking. In particular, they provide no guarantee against template attacks [14] and single-trace attacks [23].

Masking-Friendly Primitives. Those primitives use the S-box with a small multiplicative complexity to be easy to mask [1,16,17]. HOMA has a high affinity for masking-friendly primitives. Most of designs as stand-alone primtives are for block ciphers, while there are several TBCs designed along with a mode. Clyde-128 [5], Scream, and iScream [18] are such examples. Here we design a SKINNY variant for making the performance comparison clearer.

2 Preliminaries

Notation. Let ε denote the empty string. For a positive integer i, let $\{0,1\}^i$ denote the set of all i-bit strings. Let $\{0,1\}^*$ denote the set of all bit strings. For integers $i \leq j$, let $[i,j] := \{s \mid i \leq s \leq j\}$ be the set of integers from i to j. For a positive integer i, let $[i] := [1,i]$ and $(i) := [0,i]$. For a finite set T, $T \xleftarrow{\$} T$ denotes an element is chosen uniformly at random from T and is assigned to T. The concatenation of two bit strings X and Y is written as $X\|Y$ or XY when no confusion is possible. For integers $0 \leq i \leq j$ and $X \in \{0,1\}^j$, let $\mathsf{msb}_i(X)$ resp. $\mathsf{lsb}_i(X)$ be the most resp. least significant i bits of X, and $|X|$ be the number of bits of X, i.e., $|X| = j$. For an integer $n > 0$ and a bit string X, we denote the parsing into fixed-length n-bit strings as $(X_1, X_2, \ldots, X_\ell) \xleftarrow{n} X$, where if $X \neq \varepsilon$ then $X = X_1\|X_2\|\cdots\|X_\ell$, $|X_i| = n$ for $i \in [\ell-1]$, and $0 < |X_\ell| \leq n$; if $X = \varepsilon$ then $\ell = 1$ and $X_1 = \varepsilon$.

TBC. Let n be a block size. A TBC is a set of n-bit permutations indexed by a key and a public input called tweak, that is, fixing a key and a tweak, it becomes an n-bit permutation. Let $\mathcal{K}$ be the set of keys, $\mathcal{TW}$ be the set of tweaks, and n be the input/output-block size. An encryption is denoted by $\widetilde{E} : \mathcal{K} \times \mathcal{TW} \times \{0,1\}^n \to \{0,1\}^n$, $\widetilde{E}$ having a key $K \in \mathcal{K}$ is denoted by $\widetilde{E}_K$. For an input $(K,Y,X) \in \mathcal{K} \times \mathcal{TW} \times \{0,1\}^n$, the output is denoted by $\widetilde{E}_K(Y,X)$.

In this paper, a TBC is assumed to be a secure tweakable-pseudo-random permutation (TPRP), i.e., indistinguishable from a tweakable random permutation (TRP). A tweakable permutation (TP) $\widetilde{P} : \mathcal{TW} \times \{0,1\}^n \to \{0,1\}^n$ is a set of n-bit permutations indexed by a tweak in $\mathcal{TW}$. A TP $\widetilde{P}$ having a tweak $TW \in \mathcal{TW}$ is denoted by $\widetilde{P}^{TW}$. Let $\widetilde{\mathsf{Perm}}(\mathcal{TW}, \{0,1\}^n)$ be the set of all TPs: $\mathcal{TW} \times \{0,1\}^n \to \{0,1\}^n$. A TRP is defined as $\widetilde{P} \xleftarrow{\$} \widetilde{\mathsf{Perm}}(\mathcal{TW}, \{0,1\}^n)$. In the TPRP-security game, an adversary $\mathbf{A}$ has access to either $\widetilde{E}_K$ or $\widetilde{P}$, where $K \xleftarrow{\$} \mathcal{K}$ and $\widetilde{P} \xleftarrow{\$} \widetilde{\mathsf{Perm}}(\mathcal{TW}, \{0,1\}^n)$, and after the interaction, $\mathbf{A}$ returns a decision bit $\in \{0,1\}$. The output of $\mathbf{A}$ with access to $\mathcal{O}$ is denoted by $\mathbf{A}^{\mathcal{O}} \in \{0,1\}$. Then, the TPRP-security advantage function of $\mathbf{A}$ is defined as $\mathbf{Adv}_{\widetilde{E}_K}^{\mathsf{tprp}}(\mathbf{A}) := \Pr[\mathbf{A}^{\widetilde{E}_K} = 1] - \Pr[\mathbf{A}^{\widetilde{P}} = 1]$, where the probabilities are taken over K, $\widetilde{P}$, and $\mathbf{A}$. The maximum advantage over all adversaries, running in time at most t and making at most q queries, is denoted by $\mathbf{Adv}_{\widetilde{E}_K}^{\mathsf{tprp}}(q,t) := \max_{\mathbf{A}} \left(\mathbf{Adv}_{\widetilde{E}_K}^{\mathsf{tprp}}(\mathbf{A}) \right)$.

AEAD. An AEAD scheme based on a TBC $\widetilde{E}_K$, denoted by $\Pi[\widetilde{E}_K]$, is a pair of encryption and decryption algorithms $(\Pi.\mathsf{Enc}[\widetilde{E}_K], \Pi.\mathsf{Dec}[\widetilde{E}_K])$. $\mathcal{K}$, $\mathcal{IV}$, $\mathcal{M}$, $\mathcal{C}$, $\mathcal{A}$, and $\mathcal{T}$ are the sets of keys, initialization vectors, plaintexts, ciphertexts, associated data (AD), and tags of $\Pi[\widetilde{E}_K]$, respectively. For our scheme, the set of keys of $\Pi[\widetilde{E}_K]$ is equal to that of the underlying TBC. The encryption algorithm takes an initial vector $IV \in \mathcal{IV}$, an AD $A \in \mathcal{A}$, and a plaintext $M \in \mathcal{M}$, and returns, deterministically, a pair of a ciphertext $C \in \mathcal{C}$ and a tag $T \in \mathcal{T}$. The decryption algorithm takes a tuple $(IV, A, C, T) \in \mathcal{IV} \times \mathcal{A} \times \mathcal{C} \times \mathcal{T}$ and returns, deterministically, either the distinguished invalid symbol **reject** $\notin \mathcal{M}$ or a plaintext $M \in \mathcal{M}$. We require that for any $(IV, A, M), (IV', A', M') \in \mathcal{IV} \times \mathcal{A} \times \mathcal{M}$, $|\Pi.\mathsf{Enc}[\widetilde{E}_K](IV, A, M)| = |\Pi.\mathsf{Enc}[\widetilde{E}_K](IV, A, M')|$ is satisfied if $|M| = |M'|$. We also require that $\Pi.\mathsf{Dec}(IV, A, \Pi.\mathsf{Enc}[\widetilde{E}_K](IV, A, M)) = M$ for $IV \in \mathcal{IV}$, $A \in \mathcal{A}$, and $M \in \mathcal{M}$.

In this paper, $\mathcal{IV}$ consists of a set of nonces denoted by $\mathcal{N}$ and a set of random IVs denoted by $\mathcal{R}$ thus $\mathcal{IV} = \mathcal{N} \times \mathcal{R}$. For nonces of $\Pi.\mathsf{Enc}[\widetilde{E}_K]$, repeating the same nonce is forbidden within the same key.[2] For an input tuple $(N, R, A, M) \in \mathcal{N} \times \mathcal{R} \times \mathcal{A} \times \mathcal{M}$ of $\Pi.\mathsf{Enc}[\widetilde{E}_K]$, a random IV R is chosen independently of other elements (N, A, M) and uniformly at random from $\mathcal{R}$. Then, (N, R, A, M) is passed to $\Pi.\mathsf{Enc}[\widetilde{E}_K]$.

AE Security. We explain the AE-security notion [30], on which our security goal is based.[3]

The AE-security is the indistinguishability between the real and ideal worlds. The real-world oracles are $(\Pi.\mathsf{Enc}[\widetilde{E}_K], \Pi.\mathsf{Dec}[\widetilde{E}_K])$ wherein the key K is defined as $K \xleftarrow{\$} \mathcal{K}$. The ideal-world oracles are $(\$, \perp)$ wherein $\$$ is a random-bits oracle that returns a random bit string of length $|\Pi.\mathsf{Enc}_K[\widetilde{E}](N, R, A, M)|$ for an encryption query (N, A, M), and $\perp$ is a reject oracle that returns **reject** for any decryption query. Note that for each encryption query (N, A, M), the random IV is defined as $R \xleftarrow{\$} \mathcal{R}$. The AE-advantage function of an adversary $\mathbf{A}$ that returns a decision bit after interacting with $\Pi[\widetilde{E}_K]$ in the real world or with $(\$, \perp)$ in the ideal world is defined as $\mathbf{Adv}^{\mathsf{ae}}_{\Pi[\widetilde{E}_K]}(\mathbf{A}) = \Pr[\mathbf{A}^{\Pi.\mathsf{Enc}[\widetilde{E}_K], \Pi.\mathsf{Dec}[\widetilde{E}_K]} = 1] - \Pr[\mathbf{A}^{\$, \perp} = 1]$, where the probabilities are taken over $K, \$, \mathbf{A}$, and random IVs. $\mathbf{A}$ is nonce-respecting, that is, all nonces in queries to $\Pi.\mathsf{Enc}[\widetilde{E}_K]/\$$ are distinct. In this game, making a trivial query $(N, R, A, C, \hat{T})$ to $\Pi.\mathsf{Dec}[\widetilde{E}_K]/\perp$ is forbidden, which is defined by some previous query to $\Pi.\mathsf{Enc}[\widetilde{E}_K]/\$$.

3   Design of AEAD Mode for High-Order Masking

3.1   Intuition and Design of HOMA

High-Level Structure. To design an s-bit secure mode, the size of the key-dependent state must be at least s bits, whereas to design a masking-friendly mode, the size of the protected state must be less than s bits to be smaller than the existing designs. The minimum size of the protected state is the block size of the underlying TBC, since a state in a TBC includes information of the

---

[2] For $\Pi.\mathsf{Dec}[\widetilde{E}_K]$, nonces and random IVs can be repeated.

[3] The AE-security notion does not take into account SCA.

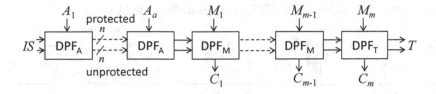

Fig. 2. The high-level structure of HOMA.

key. Thus, the security of a masking-friendly mode must be beyond the block size. HOMA is designed so that, with a TBC of n-bit block, the security level is $2n$ bits, the key-dependent state size is $2n$ bits, and the unprotected state size is n bits. In other words, for the target security level s, HOMA has the s-bit key-dependent state with $s/2$-bit protected and $s/2$-bit unprotected ones.

Figure 2 shows the high-level structure of HOMA. It starts from the $2n$-bit initial state IS and updates the state by iterating a data processing function (DPF). In this iteration, we first process AD blocks $A_1, \ldots, A_a$ and then process plaintext blocks $M_1, \ldots, M_m$ while generating ciphertext blocks $C_1, \ldots, C_m$. Each DPF takes as input a public state, including a nonce and a counter, but we omit them from the figure for simplicity. In the process of the last plaintext block M_m, we define a tag T as well as the last ciphertext block C_m.

We then specify DPFs. DPFs for processing AD, plaintext blocks before the last block, and the last plaintext block (with tag generation) are similar but slightly different. We denote them by $\mathsf{DPF_A}$, $\mathsf{DPF_M}$, and $\mathsf{DPF_T}$, respectively. To design DPFs, we need to carefully define protected and unprotected states. This is because once a protected value v_p is mixed with an unprotected value v_{up} and the resulting value v is unprotected, the protected value can be leaked (e.g., if $v = v_p \oplus v_{up}$, then one can obtain v_p ($= v \oplus v_{up}$)). With this important point in mind, we designed $\mathsf{DPF_A}$, $\mathsf{DPF_M}$, and $\mathsf{DPF_T}$, which are depicted in Fig. 3.

$\underline{\mathsf{DPF_A}}$. Each $\mathsf{DPF_A}$ must randomize the entire $2n$-bit state to avoid a state collision so that the protected state must not be mixed with the unprotected one. We thus call a TBC twice to provide $2n$-bit randomness as Fig. 3(top,left). For each TBC call, the tweak is a concatenation of a domain separation d_i, a nonce N, a counter, the AD block A_i, and the current unprotected state value. fix0 is a function that fixes the LSB to 0.[4]

$\underline{\mathsf{DPF_M}}$. To process each plaintext block, we first call a TBC to generate an n-bit key stream, then the same procedure as $\mathsf{DPF_A}$ is performed to update the whole state. $\mathsf{DPF_M}$ is shown in Fig. 3(top,right).

$\underline{\mathsf{DPF_T}}$. The DPF encrypts the last plaintext block and generates a tag simultaneously. As shown in Fig. 3(bottom), we first call a TBC to generate an n-bit key stream to encrypt the plaintext block, then a TBC is iteratively applied twice to

---

[4] The function is introduced for the security proof that ensures that the TBC output provides a randomness to the unprotected state. It ensures that the output is chosen uniformly at random from at least 2^{n-1} elements. Note that fix0 can be removed by reserving a bit in a tweak space that takes the LSB of the TBC input.

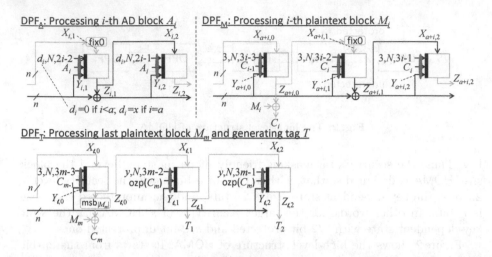

Fig. 3. DPFs of HOMA. The red lines are protected and the others are unprotected. (Color figure online)

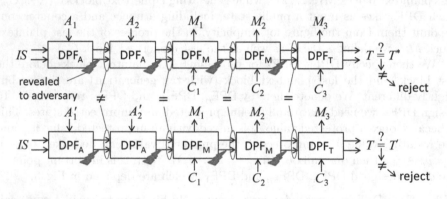

Fig. 4. A collision in decryption procedures.

generate the $2n$-bit tag. For the encryption, a tag is a conventional output, thus no protection is required, while for the decryption, the tag must be protected, since no information should be output for an invalid tag.

Random IV. For the encryption, we use a random IV of $2n - 1$ bits as the initial state IS. This is because, without a random IV, the AEAD in Fig. 2 is vulnerable against a state-collision attack. The details are as follows.

Assume that IS is not random. Then an adversary can fix IS to some constant in both the encryption and decryption procedures. The SCA adversary first interacts with the decryption oracle to cause a collision of DPF, which is shown in Fig. 4. In decryption queries, the adversary can make IS values the same even in the nonce-respect setting. In this attack, distinct ADs, an identical ciphertext, and any tag are used to cause a collision of the state after processing AD (after the second AD block in Fig. 4). The key point here is that the SCA adversary can access to the unprotected state, which enables to detect the oc-

---

Algorithm 1. HOMA

Encryption HOMA.Enc$[\widetilde{E}_K](N, R, A, M)$

1: $(H_1, H_2, C_0) \leftarrow$ HOMA.Hash$[\widetilde{E}_K](N, R, A)$
2: $(C, T) \leftarrow$ HOMA.Main$[\widetilde{E}_K](N, H_1, H_2, C_0, M)$; **return** (R, C, T)

Decryption HOMA.Dec$[\widetilde{E}_K](N, R, A, C, \hat{T})$

1: $(H_1, H_2, C_0) \leftarrow$ HOMA.Hash$[\widetilde{E}_K](N, R, A)$
2: $(M, T) \leftarrow$ HOMA.Main$[\widetilde{E}_K](N, H_1, H_2, C_0, C)$
3: **if** $\hat{T} = T$ **then return** M; **else return reject**

Processing AD HOMA.Hash$[\widetilde{E}_K](N, R, A)$

1: St $\leftarrow$ msb$_{n-1}(R)\|0$; Sb $\leftarrow$ lsb$_n(R)$; $(A_1, \ldots, A_a) \xleftarrow{n} A$
2: **for** $i = 1, \ldots, a - 1$ **do** (St, Sb) $\leftarrow$ SUF$[\widetilde{E}_K](0, N, 2(i - 1), A_i, \text{St}, \text{Sb})$
3: **if** $|A| \bmod n = 0$ **then** $x = 1$; **else** $x = 2$
4: (St, Sb) $\leftarrow$ SUF$[\widetilde{E}_K](x, N, 2(a - 1), \text{ozp}(A_a), \text{St}, \text{Sb})$; **return** (St, Sb, ozp(A_a))

Main HOMA.Main$[\widetilde{E}_K](N, H_1, H_2, C_0, D)$ ▷ If D is a plaintext M (resp. ciphertext C), then D' is the ciphertext C (resp. plaintext M).

1: $D' \leftarrow \varepsilon$; St $\leftarrow H_1$; Sb $\leftarrow H_2$; $(D_1, \ldots, D_m) \xleftarrow{n} D$
2: **for** $i = 1, \ldots, m - 1$ **do**
3:     St $\leftarrow \widetilde{E}_K((3, N, 3(i - 1), C_{i-1}, \text{Sb}), \text{St})$; $D'_i \leftarrow$ St $\oplus D_i$
4:     (St, Sb) $\leftarrow$ SUF$[\widetilde{E}_K](3, N, 3(i - 1) + 1, C_i, \text{St}, \text{Sb})$
5: **end for**
6: St $\leftarrow \widetilde{E}_K((3, N, 3(m - 1), C_{m-1}, \text{Sb}), \text{St})$; $D'_m \leftarrow$ msb$_{|D_m|}(\text{St}) \oplus D_m$
7: **if** $|D| \bmod n = 0$ **then** $y = 4$; **else** $y = 5$
8: $T_1 \leftarrow \widetilde{E}_K((y, N, 3(m - 1) + 1, \text{ozp}(C_m), \text{Sb}), \text{St})$
9: $T_2 \leftarrow \widetilde{E}_K((y, N, 3(m - 1) + 2, \text{ozp}(C_m), \text{Sb}), T_1)$; **return** $(D'_1\| \cdots \|D'_m, T_1\|T_2)$

State Update SUF$[\widetilde{E}_K](d, N, u, D, \text{St}, \text{Sb})$

1: St $\leftarrow$ fix0(St); St $\leftarrow \widetilde{E}_K((d, N, u, D, \text{Sb}), \text{St})$ ▷ The TBC output is unprotected
2: Sb $\leftarrow$ St $\oplus$ Sb; St $\leftarrow \widetilde{E}_K((d, N, u + 1, D, \text{Sb}), \text{St})$; **return** (St, Sb)

---

currence of the collision of the entire state without knowing the protected state by observing if collisions on the unprotected state occur in all subsequent blocks. After finding a collision, an adversary makes an encryption query with the same (A_1, A_2), and the modified plaintext (M_1^*, M_2^*, M_3^*) under the same IS to obtain the tag T^*. Since T^* is also valid for (A_1', A_2') and (M_1^*, M_2^*, M_3^*), the integrity is broken by $O(2^n)$ queries (from the birthday analysis).

By introducing a random IV, the adversary cannot perform the attack unless a random IV of $2n$ bits is predicted by spending $O(2^{2n})$ complexity.

3.2   Specification of HOMA

The specification of HOMA is given in Algorithm 1. Let ν and c be nonce and counter sizes. Thus, $\mathcal{N} := \{0, 1\}^\nu$. Let $\mathcal{R} := \{0, 1\}^{2n-1}$, $\mathcal{A} := \{0, 1\}^*$, $\mathcal{M} :=$

$\{0,1\}^*$, $\mathcal{C} := \mathcal{M}$, and $\mathcal{T} := \{0,1\}^{2n}$. Let $\mathsf{ozp} : \{0,1\}^{\leq n} \rightarrow \{0,1\}^n$ be the one-zero padding function: for $X \in \{0,1\}^{\leq n}$, $\mathsf{ozp}(X) = X$ if $|X| = n$; $\mathsf{ozp}(X) = X \| 10^{n-1-|X|}$ if $|X| < n$. The set of tweaks is defined as $\mathcal{TW} := (5) \times \mathcal{N} \times \{0,1\}^c \times \{0,1\}^n \times \{0,1\}^{2n}$. HOMA.Enc (resp. HOMA.Dec) is the encryption (resp. decryption) of HOMA. HOMA.Enc takes a nonce $N \in \mathcal{N}$, a random IV $R \in \mathcal{R}$, an AD $A \in \mathcal{A}$, and a plaintext $M \in \mathcal{M}$, and returns the ciphertext $C \in \{0,1\}^{|M|}$ and the tag $T \in \mathcal{T}$, where it is required that R is chosen uniformly at random from $\mathcal{R}$ and N is a non-repeated value within the same key. HOMA.Dec takes a nonce $N \in \mathcal{N}$, an IV $R \in \mathcal{R}$, an AD $A \in \mathcal{A}$, a ciphertext $C \in \mathcal{C}$ and a tag $\hat{T} \in \mathcal{T}$, and returns the plaintext $M \in \{0,1\}^{|C|}$ if the tag is valid and **reject** if the tag is invalid. HOMA.Hash is a function that processes a nonce $N \in \mathcal{N}$, an IV $R \in \mathcal{R}$, and an AD $A \in \mathcal{A}$. HOMA.Main is a function that processes a nonce $N \in \mathcal{N}$, a plaintext/ciphertext and generates a tag. $\mathsf{SUF}[\widetilde{E}_K]$ is a function that updates the $2n$-bit state,[5] where d is a domain separation value, u is a counter value, D is a data block, St is the protected state, and Sb is the unprotected state. In HOMA, domain separation values are 0 when processing AD blocks except for the last AD block, $x \in \{1,2\}$ when processing the last AD block,[6] 3 when processing the plaintext/ciphertext blocks except for the last block, and $y \in \{4,5\}$ when processing the last plaintext/ciphertext block and generating a tag.[7] The counter value at the i-th TBC call in HOMA.Hash/HOMA.Main is $i - 1$. In Algorithm 1, counter values are denoted by integers for simplicity, but the values are handled as the c-bit strings.

3.3   Protected and Unprotected Values of HOMA

We define unprotected TBC outputs in each DPF: $\mathsf{DPF_A}$: the first TBC output; $\mathsf{DPF_M}$: the second TBC output; $\mathsf{DPF_T}$: none. These outputs are the colored TBC one in SUF of Algorithm 1. Other TBC outputs are protected. In HOMA, all tweaks and a state updated with an unprotected TBC output are unprotected except for TBC computations. In Fig. 3, the colored lines are protected and other lines are unprotected.[8]

4   Security Claim and Proof of HOMA

4.1   AE Security for Masking

We define AEL-security, the security for masking, by extending the conventional AE-security [30] so that SCA adversaries for AEAD schemes with masking implementations can be considered. AEL-security is defined so that for a query to the

---

[5] The function SUF is the same for $\mathsf{DPF_A}$. In $\mathsf{DPF_M}$, a TBC is performed to encrypt/decrypt a plaintext/ciphertext block, then SUF is performed.

[6] If the length of the last block equals n, then $x = 1$, and otherwise $x = 2$.

[7] If the length of the last block equals n, then $y = 4$, and otherwise $y = 5$.

[8] For the encryption, T_0 and T_1 can be unprotected but plaintext blocks must be protected. The latter is necessary to ensure the privacy of plaintexts in real-world implementations but not in the security proof as an adversary chooses a plaintext.

target AEAD scheme $\Pi[\widetilde{E}_K]$, the adversary can obtain the unprotected values as well as the conventional output. Unlike the existing extension of the conventional AE-security in [2], our extension covers a larger class of leakage functions. Below, we define real-world and ideal-world oracles with leakage functions to access unprotected values.

First, the real-world oracles are defined. Let $\mathsf{EncUPV}[\widetilde{E}_K](N, R, A, M)$ resp. $\mathsf{DecUPV}[\widetilde{E}_K](N, R, A, C, \hat{T})$ be a leakage function for the encryption resp. the decryption, which returns unprotected values in the process of $\Pi.\mathsf{Enc}[\widetilde{E}_K](N, R, A, M)$ resp. $\Pi.\mathsf{Dec}[\widetilde{E}_K](N, R, A, C, \hat{T})$.

- Enc. oracle $\mathsf{EncL_R}[\widetilde{E}_K]$: For a query $(N, A, M) \in \mathcal{N} \times \mathcal{A} \times \mathcal{M}$, $R \xleftarrow{\$} \mathcal{R}$, and returns the outputs of $\Pi.\mathsf{Enc}[\widetilde{E}_K](N, R, A, M)$ and of $\mathsf{EncUPV}[\widetilde{E}_K](N, R, A, M)$.
- Dec. oracle $\mathsf{DecL_R}[\widetilde{E}_K]$: For a query $(N, R, A, C, \hat{T}) \in \mathcal{N} \times \mathcal{R} \times \mathcal{A} \times \mathcal{C} \times \mathcal{T}$, returns the outputs of $\Pi.\mathsf{Dec}[\widetilde{E}_K]$ $(N, R, A, C, \hat{T})$ and of $\mathsf{DecUPV}[\widetilde{E}_K](N, R, A, C, \hat{T})$.

Next, the ideal-world oracles are defined. The leakage of unprotected values is supported by introducing a simulator $\mathcal{S} = (\mathcal{S}_{\mathsf{encL}}, \mathcal{S}_{\mathsf{decL}})$ that simulates $(\mathsf{EncUPV}[\widetilde{E}_K], \mathsf{DecUPV}[\widetilde{E}_K])$.

- Enc. oracle $\mathsf{EncL_I}$: For a query $(N, A, M) \in \mathcal{N} \times \mathcal{A} \times \mathcal{M}$, $\mathsf{EncL_I}$ returns the outputs of $\$(N, A, M)$ and of $\mathcal{S}_{\mathsf{encL}}(N, R, A, C, T)$ where $(R, C, T) = \$(N, A, M)$.
- Dec. oracle $\mathsf{DecL_I}$: For a query $(N, R, A, C, \hat{T}) \in \mathcal{N} \times \mathcal{R} \times \mathcal{A} \times \mathcal{C} \times \mathcal{T}$, returns the outputs of $\perp$ and of $\mathcal{S}_{\mathsf{decL}}(N, R, A, C, \hat{T})$.

The simulator's task is to simulate unprotected values of the real world by using only public values.[9] If such simulator exists, i.e., the real and ideal worlds are indistinguishable, then one can ensure that the unprotected values provide nothing to differentiate the AEAD scheme from an ideal AEAD $(\$, \perp)$. Note that the simulator must be a polynomial-time algorithm, since the simulator represents a procedure of some polynomial-time adversary in the ideal world.

The AEL-security advantage function of an adversary $\mathbf{A}$, that returns a decision bit, after making all queries, is defined as

$$\mathbf{Adv}^{\mathsf{ael}}_{\Pi[\widetilde{E}_K], \mathcal{S}}(\mathbf{A}) = \Pr[\mathbf{A}^{\mathsf{EncL_R}[\widetilde{E}_K], \mathsf{DecL_R}[\widetilde{E}_K]} = 1] - \Pr[\mathbf{A}^{\mathsf{EncL_I}, \mathsf{DecL_I}} = 1],$$

where the probabilities are taken over $K, R, \$, \mathcal{S}, \mathbf{A}$. Hereafter, we refer a query to $\mathsf{EncL_R}[\widetilde{E}_K]/\mathsf{EncL_I}$ (resp. $\mathsf{DecL_R}[\widetilde{E}_K]/\mathsf{DecL_I}$) an encryption (resp. decryption) query. This game forbids $\mathbf{A}$ making a trivial query: some encryption query-responses are forwarded to the decryption oracle.

A scheme $\Pi[\widetilde{E}_K]$ is AEL-secure if there exists a simulator such that the advantage function is bounded by a negligible probability. The goal of HOMA is to obtain a bound of $2n$-bit security (negligible up to $O(2^{2n})$ query complexity).

---

[9] To ensure the privacy, a plaintext M must be kept private to an adversary. Thus, the plaintext must not be included in a tuple of simulator's inputs.

Comparisons with Existing Notions. Barwell et al. [2] extended the conventional AE-security notion, where two oracles $\ell(\Pi.\mathsf{Enc}[\widetilde{E}_K]), \ell(\Pi.\mathsf{Dec}[\widetilde{E}_K])$ are introduced in addition to the standard oracles $\Pi.\mathsf{Enc}[\widetilde{E}_K]$, $\Pi.\mathsf{Dec}[\widetilde{E}_K]$, \$, and $\perp$. $\ell(\Pi.\mathsf{Enc}[\widetilde{E}_K])$ (resp. $\ell(\Pi.\mathsf{Dec}[\widetilde{E}_K])$) returns leak values of $\Pi.\mathsf{Enc}[\widetilde{E}_K]$ (resp. $\Pi.\mathsf{Dec}[\widetilde{E}_K]$) as well as the output of $\Pi.\mathsf{Enc}[\widetilde{E}_K]$ (resp. $\Pi.\mathsf{Dec}[\widetilde{E}_K]$). The real-world oracles are $(\Pi.\mathsf{Enc}[\widetilde{E}_K], \Pi.\mathsf{Dec}[\widetilde{E}_K], \ell(\Pi.\mathsf{Enc}[\widetilde{E}_K]), \ell(\Pi.\mathsf{Dec}[\widetilde{E}_K]))$ and the ideal-world ones are $(\$, \perp, \ell(\Pi.\mathsf{Enc}[\widetilde{E}_K]), \ell(\Pi.\mathsf{Dec}[\widetilde{E}_K]))$. Hence, this notion does not permit adversaries to obtain leak values of the first or second oracle. AEL-security is defined so that there is no such restriction.

Berti et al. [6] defined two notions for privacy and integrity. The notion for integrity, called CIML2, is the integrity part of the AE-security one with encryption and decryption leakages. The notion for privacy, called muCIML2, is different from the privacy part of the AE-security one. The adversary's goal of muCIML2 is to guess a bit b of a challenge ciphertext C_b while having access to leakage functions as well as the encryption and decryption oracles, where two plaintext M_1 and M_2 are chosen by an adversary, b is a random bit, and C_b is the encrypted value of M_b. Since \$ and $\perp$ leak no information of plaintexts, any scheme indistinguisbale from $(\$, \perp)$ is secure in the sense of the goal of muCIML2. Hence, the AEL-security notion covers the security goals of CIML2 and of muCIML2. Berti et al. designed an AEAD mode secure regarding CIML2 and muCIML2 in the multi-user setting and the misuse setting. On the other hand, our security proof of HOMA don't consider these settings. Note that the AEL-security notion can be extended to the one covering these settings by adding multiple users and permitting adversaries to make misuse queries.

4.2   AEL-Security of HOMA

The following theorem shows that $\mathsf{HOMA}[\widetilde{E}_K]$ is AEL-secure up to $O(2^{2n})$ decryption query complexity.

Theorem 1. *(Security of* HOMA*) There exists a simulator $\mathcal{S}$ such that for any adversary $\mathbf{A}$ running in time t, $\mathbf{Adv}^{\mathsf{ael}}_{\mathsf{HOMA}[\widetilde{E}_K],\mathcal{S}}(\mathbf{A}) \leq \mathbf{Adv}^{\mathsf{tprp}}_{\widetilde{E}}(\sigma, t + O(\sigma)) + \frac{19\sigma_{\mathcal{D}}}{2^{2n}}$, and $\mathcal{S}$ runs in time $t + O(\sigma)$ and requires an $O(\sigma)$-bit memory, where $\sigma_{\mathcal{D}}$ (resp. σ) is the number of TBC calls in all* HOMA.Dec *(resp.* HOMA*) procedures.*

Intuition of the Security of HOMA. Assume that the TBC is a TRP. Then, there are the following differences between the real and ideal worlds.

1. Enc.: (real) ciphertexts and tags are defined by a TRP; (ideal) those are defined by \$.
2. Dec.: (real) a plaintext might be returned; (ideal) all responses are **reject**.
3. Unprotected values: (real) the values are defined by HOMA; (ideal) the values are defined by a simulator.

For the difference (1), in the real world, since each tweak includes a nonce and a counter, each output of $\widetilde{P}$ in the encrypt is random. Thus, the difference yields no attack.

For the difference (2), we consider two-types of decryption query in the real world: In a decryption query, (2)-1: the nonce is not in the previous encryption queries; (2)-2: the nonce is in some previous encryption query. In the type (2)-1, the tag is chosen independently from all tags in encryption queries, and thus the probability of forging the tag is $O(1/2^{2n})$. In the case (2)-2, forging the tag implies that an internal state collision occurs between the encryption and decryption queries (the nonces are the same).[10] As mentioned in Sect. 3, a collision in previous decryption queries with the same nonce cannot be used without detecting the random IV in the encryption query. The probability of detecting the random IV is $O(1/2^{2n})$. Then, to obtain the internal state collision, some $2n$-bit internal state, which is freshly defined in the decryption query, must collide with some internal state in the encryption query. The collision probability is at most $O(\ell/2^{2n})$ for the data length ℓ. Summing the bound $O(\ell/2^{2n})$ for each decryption query, the probability of forging a tag in some decryption query, i.e. the distinguishing probability from the difference is at most $O(\sigma_D/2^{2n})$.

For the difference (3), we define a simulator so that unprotected values include no information differentiating the real and ideal worlds. The detail is given in Sect. 4.

Hence, we obtain the AEL-Security bound $O(\sigma_D/2^{2n})$.

4.3 Proof of Theorem 1

First, the TBC $\widetilde{E}_K$ is replaced with a TRP $\widetilde{P}$. Then, for any adversary $\mathbf{A}$, there exists an adversary $\mathbf{A}'$ such that $\mathbf{Adv}^{\mathsf{ael}}_{\mathsf{HOMA}[\widetilde{E}_K],\mathcal{S}}(\mathbf{A}) \leq \mathbf{Adv}^{\mathsf{tprp}}_{\widetilde{E}}(\sigma, t + O(\sigma)) + \mathbf{Adv}^{\mathsf{ael}}_{\mathsf{HOMA}[\widetilde{P}],\mathcal{S}}(\mathbf{A}')$. Hereafter, we bound $\mathbf{Adv}^{\mathsf{ael}}_{\mathsf{HOMA}[\widetilde{P}],\mathcal{S}}(\mathbf{A}')$, the AEL-security advantage of HOMA using $\widetilde{P}$.

Simulator $\mathcal{S}$. Our simulator is defined below. Both of $\mathcal{S}_{\mathsf{encL}}$ and $\mathcal{S}_{\mathsf{decL}}$ run the decryption procedure HOMA.Dec and return unprotected values defined in this procedure. The underlying TBC is instantiated with a TRP $\widetilde{P}' \in \widetilde{\mathsf{Perm}}(\mathcal{TW}, \{0,1\}^n)$, which the simulators realize by lazy sampling.[11]

---

[10] A TRP offers independent permutations if the tweaks are distinct. In HOMA, a nonce is a tweak element, thus HOMA procedures with distinct nonces are independently performed (even if the R values are the same). Thus, encryption queries whose nonces are different from the nonce of the decryption query do not affect the internal state collision probability.

[11] A TRP $\widetilde{P}$ keeps a table $\mathcal{L}$ that is initially empty. For an input $(X,Y) \in \{0,1\}^n \times \mathcal{TW}$ to $\widetilde{P}$, the output Z is defined as follows: if $\mathcal{L}(X,Y) = \varepsilon$ then $Z \xleftarrow{\$} \{0,1\}^n \setminus \mathcal{L}(*,Y)$ and $\mathcal{L}(X,Y) \leftarrow Z$, where $\mathcal{L}(*,Y)$ is the set of all outputs whose tweaks are Y, and otherwise $Z \leftarrow \mathcal{L}(X,Y)$.

- $\mathcal{S}_{\mathsf{encL}}(N, R, A, C, T)$: runs $\mathsf{HOMA.Dec}[\widetilde{P}'](N, R, A, C, T)$; returns the unprotected values defined in $\mathsf{HOMA.Dec}[\widetilde{P}'](N, R, A, C, T)$.
- $\mathcal{S}_{\mathsf{decL}}(N, R, A, C, \hat{T})$: runs $\mathsf{HOMA.Dec}[\widetilde{P}'](N, R, A, C, \hat{T})$; returns the unprotected values defined in $\mathsf{HOMA.Dec}[\widetilde{P}'](N, R, A, C, \hat{T})$.

$\mathcal{S}$ runs in time $t + O(\sigma)$ and requires an $O(\sigma)$-bit memory. Note again that the TRP $\widetilde{P}'$ is realized by the simulators as well as the decryption procedure $\mathsf{HOMA.Dec}[\widetilde{P}']$, which is given in Algorithm 1 where $\widetilde{E}_K$ is replaced with $\widetilde{P}'$.

Notations. Let $q_{\mathcal{E}}$ (resp. $q_{\mathcal{D}}$) be the number of encryption (resp. decryption) queries, and $q := q_{\mathcal{E}} + q_{\mathcal{D}}$. Let $\sigma_{\mathcal{D},A}$ (resp. $\sigma_{\mathcal{D},C}$) be the total number of TRP calls in $\mathsf{HOMA.Hash}$ (resp. $\mathsf{HOMA.Main}$) by decryption queries, thus $\sigma_{\mathcal{D}} = \sigma_{\mathcal{D},A} + \sigma_{\mathcal{D},C}$. For convenience, we express the α-th encryption (resp. β-th decryption) query as the α-th (resp. $(\beta+q_{\mathcal{E}})$-th) query. For $\alpha, \beta \in [q]$ such that the β-th query is made after the α-th query, the relation is denoted by $\alpha \lhd \beta$. Let $\ell := a + m$ denote the total length of data blocks by a query. For the j-th TRP call at the i-th DPF call in HOMA, the input block, the output block, and the tweak in $\mathsf{HOMA.Hash}$ (resp. $\mathsf{HOMA.Main}$) are denoted by $X_{i,j}$, $Z_{i,j}$, and $Y_{i,j}$, (resp., $X_{i,j-1}$, $Z_{i,j-1}$, and $Y_{i,j-1}$). See also Fig. 3. Let $XY_{i,j} := X_{i,j}\|Y_{i,j}$. Note that in the ideal world, these values are defined by $\mathcal{S}$. For $\alpha \in [q]$, a value V defined at the α-th query is denoted by $V^{(\alpha)}$. The lengths a, m and ℓ of the α-th query are denoted by a_α, m_α and ℓ_α. For $\alpha \in [q]$, let $\mathcal{C}_i^{(\alpha)} := (XY_{a_\alpha,1}^{(\alpha)}, C_1^{(\alpha)}, \ldots, C_i^{(\alpha)})$ be an array of an input to the second last TRP call in $\mathsf{HOMA.Hash}$ and the ciphertext blocks up to the i-th block defined at the α-th query, $\mathcal{C}_0^{(\alpha)} := (XY_{a_\alpha,1}^{(\alpha)})$.

Transcript. In the following proof, for each encryption query, if $|C| \bmod n \neq 0$, i.e., $|C_m| < n$, then a $(n-|C_m|)$-bit string C_L is appended to the ciphertext C and the modified ciphertext $\check{C} = C\|C_L$ is returned instead of C. In the real world, $C_L := \mathsf{lsb}_{n-|C_m|}(Z_{\ell,0})$ (thus, $Z_{\ell,0} = (M_m\|0^{n-|C_m|}) \oplus (C_m\|C_L)$), and in the ideal world $C_L \xleftarrow{\$} \{0,1\}^{n-|C_m|}$. For $i \in [m-1]$, let $\tilde{C}_i := C_i$ and $\tilde{C}_m := C_m\|C_L$, thus $\tilde{C} = \tilde{C}_1\|\cdots\|\tilde{C}_m$. Let $\tilde{M}_i := M_i$ and $\tilde{M}_m := M_m\|0^{n-|M_m|}$.

The following proof, in addition to the standard outputs, permits $\mathbf{A}'$ to obtain the following protected values after making all queries but before returning a decision bit.

- $\mathcal{Z}_2 := \{Z_{i,2}^{(\alpha)} \mid \alpha \in [q], i \in [\ell_\alpha - 1]\}$.
- $\mathcal{Z}_{0,1} := \{Z_{a_\beta+i,0}^{(\beta)} \mid \beta \in [q_{\mathcal{E}}+1, q], i \in [m_\beta - 1] \text{ s.t. } \forall \alpha \in [q_{\mathcal{E}}] \text{ s.t. } \alpha \lhd \beta : N^{(\alpha)} \neq N^{(\beta)}\}$.
- $\mathcal{Z}_{0,2} := \{Z_{a_\beta+i,0}^{(\beta)} \mid \beta \in [q_{\mathcal{E}}+1, q], i \in [m_\beta - 1] \text{ s.t. } \exists \alpha \in [q_{\mathcal{E}}] \text{ s.t. } \alpha \lhd \beta \wedge N^{(\alpha)} = N^{(\beta)} \wedge \mathcal{C}_{i-1}^{(\alpha)} \neq \mathcal{C}_{i-1}^{(\beta)}\}$.
- $\mathcal{Z}_t := \{T_1^{(\beta)}, T_2^{(\beta)} \mid \beta \in [q_{\mathcal{E}}+1, q]\}$.

Note that the TBC outputs $Z_{a_\alpha+i,0}^{(\alpha)}, Z_{\ell_\alpha,1}^{(\alpha)}, Z_{\ell_\alpha,2}^{(\alpha)}$ for $\alpha \in [q_{\mathcal{E}}], i \in [m_\alpha]$ (defined by encryption queries) remain secret (in the ideal world). Then, a transcript τ that $\mathbf{A}'$ obtains in the game consists of

- $((N^{(\alpha)}, A^{(\alpha)}, M^{(\alpha)}), (R^{(\alpha)}, \tilde{C}^{(\alpha)}, T^{(\alpha)}))$ for $\alpha \in [q_\mathcal{E}]$,
- $((N^{(\beta)}, R^{(\beta)}, A^{(\beta)}, C^{(\beta)}, \hat{T}^{(\beta)}), RV^{(\beta)})$ for $\beta \in [q_\mathcal{E} + 1, q]$, where $RV^{(\beta)}$ is an output of the β-th query: plaintext $M^{(\beta)}$ or **reject**,
- $Z_{i,1}^{(\alpha)}$ for $\alpha \in [q]$ and $i \in [\ell_\alpha - 1]$,
- $\mathcal{Z}_2, \mathcal{Z}_{0,1}, \mathcal{Z}_{0,2}$, and $\mathcal{Z}_t$.

Bound of the Advantage. Let τ be a transcript that $\mathbf{A}'$ obtains by queries in the game. Let T_R be a transcript in the real world obtained by sampling $\widetilde{P}$ and R. Let T_I be a transcript in the ideal world obtained by sampling \$, $\widetilde{P}'$, and R. We call a transcript τ *valid* if $\Pr[\mathsf{T}_I = \tau] > 0$. Let $\mathcal{T}$ be all valid transcripts such that $\forall \tau \in \mathcal{T} : \Pr[\mathsf{T}_R = \tau] \leq \Pr[\mathsf{T}_I = \tau]$. Then, we have $\mathbf{Adv}_{\mathsf{HOMA}[\widetilde{P}], \mathcal{S}}^{\mathsf{ael}}(\mathbf{A}') = \mathsf{SD}(\mathsf{T}_R, \mathsf{T}_I) = \sum_{\tau \in \mathcal{T}}(\Pr[\mathsf{T}_I = \tau] - \Pr[\mathsf{T}_R = \tau])$. We bound the statistical distance $\mathsf{SD}(\mathsf{T}_R, \mathsf{T}_I)$ using the following collision event: coll_m:

- coll_m: $\exists \alpha \in [q_\mathcal{E}], \beta \in [q_\mathcal{E} + 1, q], i \in [m_\alpha]$ s.t.
$$XY_{a_\alpha+i-1,1}^{(\alpha)} \neq XY_{a_\beta+i-1,1}^{(\beta)} \wedge XY_{a_\alpha+i,1}^{(\alpha)} = XY_{a_\beta+i,1}^{(\beta)}.$$

Let coll_m^r (resp. coll_m^i) be the real (resp. ideal) world event. Using the event, we have $\mathsf{SD}(\mathsf{T}_R, \mathsf{T}_I) \leq \Pr[\mathsf{coll}_m^r] + \Pr[\mathsf{coll}_m^i] + \mathsf{SD}(\mathsf{T}_R^*, \mathsf{T}_I^*)$, where T_R^* (resp. T_I^*) is the transcript T_R (resp. T_I) conditioned on $\neg\mathsf{coll}_m^r$ (resp. $\neg\mathsf{coll}_m^i$). The bounds of $\Pr[\mathsf{coll}_m^r]$, $\Pr[\mathsf{coll}_m^i]$, and $\mathsf{SD}(\mathsf{T}_R^*, \mathsf{T}_I^*)$ are given in the following analyses, ensuring $\mathbf{Adv}_{\mathsf{HOMA}[\widetilde{P}], \mathcal{S}}^{\mathsf{ael}}(\mathbf{A}') \leq \frac{8\sigma_{\mathcal{D},C}}{2^{2n}} + \frac{11\sigma_\mathcal{D}}{2^{2n}} \leq \frac{19\sigma_\mathcal{D}}{2^{2n}}$.

Bounds of $\Pr[\mathsf{coll}_m^r], \Pr[\mathsf{coll}_m^i]$. The following analysis holds for both worlds. Fix $\alpha \in [q_\mathcal{E}], \beta \in [q_\mathcal{D} + 1, q]$, and $i \in [m_\alpha]$ such that $XY_{a_\alpha+i-1,1}^{(\alpha)} \neq XY_{a_\beta+i-1,1}^{(\beta)}$ and $N^{(\alpha)} = N^{(\beta)}$. For $\gamma \in \{\alpha, \beta\}$, $X_{a_\gamma+i,1}^{(\gamma)} = \mathsf{fix0}(Z_{a_\gamma+i,0}^{(\gamma)})$ is satisfied, and $Z_{a_\alpha+i,0}^{(\alpha)}$ and $Z_{a_\beta+i,0}^{(\beta)}$ are sampled separately and uniformly at random from at least $2^n - 1$ elements. We thus have $\Pr[X_{a_\alpha+i,1}^{(\alpha)} = X_{a_\beta+i,1}^{(\beta)}] \leq 2/2^n$. $Z_{a_\alpha+i-1,1}^{(\alpha)}$ and $Z_{a_\beta+i-1,1}^{(\beta)}$, which are used to define $Y_{a_\alpha+i,1}^{(\alpha)}$ and $Y_{a_\beta+i,1}^{(\beta)}$, respectively, are sampled separately and uniformly at random from at least 2^{n-1} elements due to fix0. We thus have $\Pr[Y_{a_\alpha+i,1}^{(\alpha)} = Y_{a_\beta+i,1}^{(\beta)}] \leq 2/2^n$. Summing the bound $4/2^{2n}$ for each β, i, we have $\Pr[\mathsf{coll}_m^r] \leq 4\sigma_{\mathcal{D},C}/2^{2n}$ and $\Pr[\mathsf{coll}_m^i] \leq 4\sigma_{\mathcal{D},C}/2^{2n}$.

Bound of $\mathsf{SD}(\mathsf{T}_R^*, \mathsf{T}_I^*)$. We bound $\mathsf{SD}(\mathsf{T}_R^*, \mathsf{T}_I^*)$ by using the coefficent H technique [35]. Here, $\mathcal{T}$ is partitioned into two transcripts: good transcripts $\mathcal{T}_{\mathsf{good}}$ and bad transcripts $\mathcal{T}_{\mathsf{bad}}$.

Lemma 1. (Coefficent H technique [35]) *If $\forall \tau \in \mathcal{T}_{\mathsf{good}} : \frac{\Pr[\mathsf{T}_R^* = \tau]}{\Pr[\mathsf{T}_I^* = \tau]} \geq 1 - \mu$ s.t. $0 \leq \mu \leq 1$, then $\mathsf{SD}(\mathsf{T}_R^*, \mathsf{T}_I^*) \leq \Pr[\mathsf{T}_I^* \in \mathcal{T}_{\mathsf{bad}}] + \mu$.*

In the following proof, good and bad transcripts are defined. Then $\Pr[\mathsf{T}_I^* \in \mathcal{T}_{\mathsf{bad}}]$ is upper-bounded, and $\frac{\Pr[\mathsf{T}_R^* = \tau]}{\Pr[\mathsf{T}_I^* = \tau]}$ is lower-bounded. Finally, an upper-bound of $\mathsf{SD}(\mathsf{T}_R^*, \mathsf{T}_I^*)$ is obtained, putting the bounds into the above lemma.

Good and Bad Transcripts. We define bad events below.

- forge: $\exists \alpha \in [q_\mathcal{D} + 1, q]$ s.t. $T^{(\alpha)} = \hat{T}^{(\alpha)}$.
- coll_{iv}: $\exists \alpha \in [q_\mathcal{E}], \beta \in [q_\mathcal{E} + 1, q]$ s.t. $\beta \lhd \alpha \wedge (N^{(\alpha)}, R^{(\alpha)}) = (N^{(\beta)}, R^{(\beta)})$.
- coll_h: $\exists \alpha \in [q_\mathcal{E}], \beta \in [q_\mathcal{E} + 1, q]$ s.t.
$$(R^{(\alpha)}, A^{(\alpha)}) \neq (R^{(\beta)}, A^{(\beta)}) \wedge XY_{a_\alpha,1}^{(\alpha)} = XY_{a_\beta,1}^{(\beta)}.$$
- coll_c: $\exists \alpha \in [q_\mathcal{E}], \beta \in [q_\mathcal{E} + 1, q], i \in [m_\alpha]$ s.t.
$$\mathcal{C}_{i-1}^{(\alpha)} \neq \mathcal{C}_{i-1}^{(\beta)} \wedge (\mathsf{fix0}(\tilde{M}_i^{(\alpha)} \oplus \tilde{C}_i^{(\alpha)}), Y_{a_\alpha+i,1}^{(\alpha)}) = (X_{a_\beta+i,1}^{(\beta)}, Y_{a_\beta+i,1}^{(\beta)}).$$

Note that if $i > m_\beta$, then $X_{a_\beta+i,1}^{(\beta)} := \varepsilon$ and $Y_{a_\beta+i,1}^{(\beta)} := \varepsilon$.

We define bad transcripts $\mathcal{T}_\mathsf{bad}$ that satisfy one of the bad events. Good transcripts are defined as $\mathcal{T}_\mathsf{good} := \mathcal{T} \setminus \mathcal{T}_\mathsf{bad}$.

Lower-Bound of $\Pr[\mathsf{T}_R^* = \tau] / \Pr[\mathsf{T}_I^* = \tau]$. We give an overview of this evaluation. The detail is given in the full version of this paper [28].

There are the following differences between the real and ideal worlds.

1. Dec.: (real) a plaintext might be returned; (ideal) all responses are **reject**.
2. Enc.: (real) ciphertexts and tags are defined by a TRP; (ideal) those are defined by $\$$.
3. Protected and unprotected values: (real) the values are defined by HOMA; (ideal) the values are defined by the simulator.

We thus show that as long as no bad event occurs, the differences yield no distinguishing attack.

For the difference (1), by $\neg\mathsf{forge}$, the difference yields no attack.

For the difference (2), in the real world, since each tweak includes a nonce and a counter, each output of $\widetilde{P}$, which is used to encrypt a plaintext, is random. Thus, the difference yields no attack.

For the difference (3), in the real world, protected values and unprotected values are defined by a TRP as well as ciphertext blocks, whereas in the ideal world, these values are defined by a TRP but independently of ciphertext blocks that are defined by $\$$. The detail of the difference is shown below, where $\alpha \in [q_\mathcal{E}], \beta \in [q_\mathcal{E} + 1, q]$ and $i \in [m_\alpha]$ such that $N^{(\alpha)} = N^{(\beta)}$ and $(R^{(\alpha)}, A^{(\alpha)}, C_1^{(\alpha)}, \ldots, C_{i-1}^{(\alpha)}) \neq (R^{(\beta)}, A^{(\beta)}, C_1^{(\beta)}, \ldots, C_{i-1}^{(\beta)})$.

- **Real**: If $(\mathsf{fix0}(\tilde{M}_i^{(\alpha)} \oplus \tilde{C}_i^{(\alpha)}), Y_{i,1}^{(\alpha)}) = (X_{i,1}^{(\beta)}, Y_{i,1}^{(\beta)})$ then $Z_{i,1}^{(\alpha)} = Z_{i,1}^{(\beta)}$, since $X_{i,1}^{(\alpha)} = \mathsf{fix0}(Z_{i,0}^{(\alpha)}) \wedge Z_{i,0}^{(\alpha)} = \tilde{M}_i^{(\alpha)} \oplus \tilde{C}_i^{(\alpha)}$.
- **Ideal**: It occurs that $(\mathsf{fix0}(\tilde{M}_i^{(\alpha)} \oplus \tilde{C}_i^{(\alpha)}), Y_{i,1}^{(\alpha)}) = (X_{i,1}^{(\beta)}, Y_{i,1}^{(\beta)}) \wedge Z_{i,1}^{(\alpha)} \neq Z_{i,1}^{(\beta)}$, since $X_{i,1}^{(\alpha)} = \mathsf{fix0}(Z_{i,0}^{(\alpha)})$ but $\tilde{C}_i^{(\alpha)}$ is defined independently of $Z_{i,0}^{(\alpha)}$.

In both worlds, by $\neg\mathsf{coll}_h \wedge \neg\mathsf{coll}_{iv}$, $\mathcal{C}_{i-1}^{(\alpha)} \neq \mathcal{C}_{i-1}^{(\beta)}$ is satisfied. Then, in the real world, by $\neg\mathsf{coll}_m$, $(\mathsf{fix0}(\tilde{M}_i^{(\alpha)} \oplus \tilde{C}_i^{(\alpha)}), Y_{i,1}^{(\alpha)}) \neq (X_{i,1}^{(\beta)}, Y_{i,1}^{(\beta)})$ is satisfied, thus the real-word event does not occur. By $\neg\mathsf{coll}_c$, the ideal-world event does not occurs. Hence, no attack using the difference (3) exists.

Hence, the real and ideal worlds are indistinguishable, that is, $\forall \tau \in \mathcal{T}_\mathsf{good}$: $\Pr[\mathsf{T}_R^* = \tau] / \Pr[\mathsf{T}_I^* = \tau] \geq 1$.

Upper-Bound of $\Pr[\mathsf{T}_I \in \mathcal{T}_{\mathsf{bad}}]$. $\Pr[\mathsf{T}_I \in \mathcal{T}_{\mathsf{bad}}]$ is bounded by $\Pr[\mathsf{forge}] + \Pr[\mathsf{coll}_{iv}] + \Pr[\mathsf{coll}_h] + \Pr[\mathsf{coll}_c] \leq \frac{q_\mathcal{D}}{2^{2n}} + \frac{2q_\mathcal{D}}{2^{2n}} + \frac{2\sigma_{\mathcal{D},A}}{2^{2n}} + \frac{8\sigma_{\mathcal{D},C}}{2^{2n}} \leq \frac{11\sigma_\mathcal{D}}{2^{2n}}$, where for each event ev of the four events, $\Pr[\mathsf{ev}]$ is the probability that ev occurs as long as other events have not occurred. The bounds are given in the following analyses.

$\Pr[\mathsf{forge}]$. For each $\alpha \in [q_\mathcal{E} + 1, q]$, each of $T_1^{(\alpha)}$ and $T_2^{(\alpha)}$ is chosen uniformly at random from $\{0,1\}^n$, thus $\Pr[\mathsf{forge}] \leq q_\mathcal{D}/2^{2n}$.

$\Pr[\mathsf{coll}_{iv}]$. For each $\alpha \in [q_\mathcal{E}], \beta \in [q_\mathcal{E} + 1, q]$ such that $\beta \lhd \alpha$ and $N^{(\alpha)} = N^{(\alpha)}$, $R^{(\alpha)}$ is chosen uniformly at random from $\{0,1\}^{2n-1}$, thus $\Pr[\mathsf{coll}_{iv}] \leq 2q_\mathcal{D}/2^{2n}$.

$\Pr[\mathsf{coll}_h]$. We first fix $\alpha \in [q_\mathcal{E}], \beta \in [q_\mathcal{D} + 1, q]$ such that $N^{(\alpha)} = N^{(\beta)} \wedge (R^{(\alpha)}, A^{(\alpha)}) \neq (R^{(\beta)}, A^{(\beta)})$, and consider an event $\mathsf{coll}_h[\alpha, \beta]$: coll_h occurs due to the α-th and β-th queries. By $(R^{(\alpha)}, A^{(\alpha)}) \neq (R^{(\beta)}, A^{(\beta)})$, $\mathsf{coll}_h[\alpha, \beta]$ implies that an internal-state collision occurs in $\mathsf{HOMA}.\mathsf{Hash}[\widetilde{P}]$: $\exists i \in [a_\beta]$ s.t. $XY_{i-1,1}^{(\alpha)} \neq XY_{i-1,1}^{(\beta)} \wedge XY_{i,1}^{(\alpha)} = XY_{i,1}^{(\beta)}$. If $XY_{i-1,1}^{(\alpha)} \neq XY_{i-1,1}^{(\beta)}$, then the outputs $Z_{i-1,1}^{(\alpha)}$ and $Z_{i-1,1}^{(\beta)}$ are sampled separately, and the next outputs $Z_{i-1,2}^{(\alpha)}$ and $Z_{i-1,2}^{(\beta)}$ are sampled separately. We thus have $\Pr[XY_{i,1}^{(\alpha)} = XY_{i,1}^{(\beta)}] \leq (2/2^n) \cdot (1/2^n) = 2/2^{2n}$.

Using the bound $2/2^{2n}$, we have $\Pr[\mathsf{coll}_h] \leq \sum_{\beta=1}^{q_\mathcal{D}} 2a_\beta/2^{2n} \leq 2\sigma_{\mathcal{D},A}/2^{2n}$.

$\Pr[\mathsf{coll}_c]$. Fix $\alpha \in [q_\mathcal{E}], \beta \in [q_\mathcal{D} + 1, q], i \in [m_\alpha]$ s.t. $N^{(\alpha)} = N^{(\beta)} \wedge C_{i-1}^{(\alpha)} \neq C_{i-1}^{(\beta)}$. For the condition $Y_{a_\alpha+i,1}^{(\alpha)} = Y_{a_\beta+i,1}^{(\beta)}$, by $\neg\mathsf{coll}_m$, $XY_{a_\alpha+i-1,1}^{(\alpha)} \neq XY_{a_\beta+i-1,1}^{(\beta)}$ is satisfied, thus the outputs $Z_{a_\alpha+i-1,1}^{(\alpha)}$ and $Z_{a_\beta+i-1,1}^{(\beta)}$ are separately sampled from at least 2^{n-1} elements due to fix0. Thus, we have $\Pr[Y_{a_\alpha+i,1}^{(\alpha)} = Y_{a_\beta+i,1}^{(\beta)}] \leq 2/2^n$. For the condition $\mathsf{fix0}(\tilde{M}_i^{(\alpha)} \oplus \tilde{C}_i^{(\alpha)}) = X_{a_\beta+i,1}^{(\beta)}$, since $\tilde{C}_i^{(\alpha)}$ is chosen from $\{0,1\}^n$, $Z_{a_\beta+i,0}^{(\beta)}$ is chosen from at least $2^n - 1$ elements, and $X_{a_\beta+i,1}^{(\beta)} = \mathsf{fix0}(Z_{a_\beta+i,0}^{(\beta)})$ is satisfied, we have $\Pr[\mathsf{fix0}(\tilde{M}_i^{(\alpha)} \oplus \tilde{C}_i^{(\alpha)}) = X_{a_\beta+i,1}^{(\beta)}] \leq 2/(2^n - 1) \leq 4/2^n$.

Summing the bound $(2/2^n) \cdot (4/2^n)$ for each β, i, we have $\Pr[\mathsf{coll}_c] \leq 8\sigma_{\mathcal{D},C}/2^{2n}$.

5 A TBC Optimized for HOMA

HOMA requires a TBC that accepts a $0.5s$-bit plaintext, an s-bit key, and a $2s + 3$-bit tweak, where $s = 128$ for 128-bit security. We design a new TBC, SKINNYee, which is optimized to be used in HOMA by basing the scheme on SKINNY64 [3]. We conjecture that SKINNYee is a TPRP and satisfies the requirement of HOMA.

5.1 SKINNY64 and SKINNYe with TK4

SKINNY64 is a TBC that supports a block size of 64 bits. SKINNY64 adopts the tweakey framework [22], which enables the designers to avoid making a distinction between a tweak and a key, and those two are treated as a single object "tweakey." The design is called TKn when the tweakey size is n times as big as the block size. SKINNY64 supports the tweakey size of 64 bits (TK1), 128 bits (TK2), and 192 bits (TK3). Later, Naito et al. [26] proposed SKINNYe (version 2) to extend the tweakey size of SKINNY64 to 256 bits (TK4). Here we describe the specifications of SKINNYe, which is a base of our work.

SKINNYe operates on the data structure (state) of 16 sequences of 4-bit data (nibble) $d_0, \ldots, d_{15}$ that are formatted into a 4×4 two-dimensional array; The first row is $d_0 \ldots, d_3$, the second row is $d_4 \ldots, d_7$, and so on. A 64-bit plaintext is divided into 16 nibbles, and those form a data state. A 256-bit tweakey forms 4 tweakey states. Then, the following round transformation is iterated 44 times.

SubCells(SC). A 4-bit S-box is applied to each nibble.

AddConstants(AC). A 7-bit constant specified for each round is XORed to particular 7 bits of the state.

AddRoundTweakey(ART). A 32-bit value called sub-tweakey is generated from the 256-bit tweakey state, and those are XORed to the top two rows of the data state. Then 3 tweakey states are updated as explained later.

ShiftRows(SR). The position of each nibble in row $i, i \in \{0, 1, 2, 3\}$ is cyclically shifted to right by i positions.

MixColumns(MC). Let (x, y, z, w) be 4 nibbles in a column. The value is updated to $(x \oplus z \oplus w, x, y \oplus z, x \oplus z)$. This transformation is applied to each column.

Regarding AC, a 6-bit affine LFSR denoted by $(rc_5, rc_4, rc_3, rc_2, rc_1, rc_0)$ is used to generate round constants. In each round, this LFSR is updated by $(rc_5 \| rc_4 \| \cdots \| rc_0) \rightarrow (rc_4 \| rc_3 \| rc_2 \| rc_1 \| rc_0 \| rc_5 \oplus rc_4 \oplus 1)$. Then, 3 nibble values $rc_3 \| rc_2 \| rc_1 \| rc_0$, $0 \| 0 \| rc_5 \| rc_4$, and $\texttt{0x2}$ are XORed to the first, the second, and the third rows of the left-most column of the state, respectively.

Regarding ART, first, the 32-bit sub-tweakey value is computed by extracting the top 2 rows from each of 4 tweakey states and XORing them. Second, nibble positions are permuted by the permutation P_T: $(0, \ldots, 15) \rightarrow (9, 15, 8, 13, 10, 14, 12, 11, 0, 1, 2, 3, 4, 5, 6, 7)$. All tweakey states are updated with the same P_T. Third, all nibbles in the second, the third, and the fourth tweakey states are updated by applying the following $LFSR_2$, $LFSR_3$, and $LFSR_4$, respectively.

$$LFSR_2 : (x_3 \| x_2 \| x_1 \| x_0) \rightarrow (x_2 \| x_1 \| x_0 \| x_3 \oplus x_2),$$
$$LFSR_3 : (x_3 \| x_2 \| x_1 \| x_0) \rightarrow (x_0 \oplus x_3 \| x_3 \| x_2 \| x_1),$$
$$LFSR_4 : (x_3 \| x_2 \| x_1 \| x_0) \rightarrow (x_1 \| x_0 \| x_3 \oplus x_2 \| x_2 \oplus x_1).$$

5.2   Elastic-Tweak Framework for Small Tweaks

Elastic-tweak is a design to convert BCs or TBCs to accept a few (more) bits of tweak [11]. The input tweak is first expanded to a relatively large size for security reasons and then XORed to the data state in every few rounds. The framework was later improved to be more lightweight by realizing the expanded tweak state with LFSR [27], but it still preserves the principle of expanding the tweak, which is disadvantageous for small implementations.

5.3 Design Approach of SKINNYee

We first give an overview of our approach to design our TBC. Recall that HOMA requires a 64-bit block TBC that supports a 128-bit key and a 259-bit tweak. By adopting the same approach as SKINNYe, such TBCs are realized if the tweakey size of SKINNY64 can be extended to 448 bits (TK7). However, we found that this approach is not reasonable for two reasons.

– The idea behind the tweakey of SKINNY is to not make any distinction between a key and a tweak. For example, a 192-bit tweakey can be an x-bit key and a $(192 - x)$-bit tweak for some x, $1 \leq x \leq 192$. This functionality is not necessary for HOMA because the key size and the tweak size are fixed.
– We actually investigated the possibility of designing TK7 by searching for $LFSR_5$, $LFSR_6$, and $LFSR_7$ for the extra tweakey states. Because the search space is limited, all 4-bit LFSRs can be tested exhaustively. Our experiments showed that no LFSR exists to ensure security for TK7. TK7 can still be achieved by replacing LFSRs with more complex computations, but this requires to compromise implementation efficiency.

Our aim is not a general-purpose TBC. From the above considerations, we determined to treat a key and a tweak as independent objects instead of a tweakey.

Among 259 bits of the tweak, 3 bits are for the domain separation. The elastic-tweak gives us a hint that those can be processed efficiently by introducing different computations from the other tweak value. However, we found that the elastic-tweak is not suitable for HOMA because an additional computation to process a small tweak increases the memory size. Instead, we enlarge the size of an LFSR to compute the round constant by a few bits and initialize the LFSR to be different values depending on the 3-bit tweak.

Lastly, we design SKINNYee by reusing as many components of SKINNY as possible for two reasons. First, the benchmark becomes fair when we later compare the benchmark of our scheme with other SKINNY-based schemes. Second, SKINNY has received a lot of third-party security analysis, and the fact that SKINNY still stands against any cryptanalytic attempts enhances the reliability of the design. To take over those cryptanalytic attempts, the amount of modification from SKINNY should be minimized. In the end, we decided not to modify SC, SR, and MC from the original. So, modifications from SKINNY are made on AC, ART, and a new operation to process a 128-bit key.

5.4 Specifications of SKINNYee

SKINNYee accepts a 128-bit key, a 256-bit tweak, and a 3-bit tweak for the domain separation. The design is based on SKINNYe (TK4). The round transformation of SKINNYee is given in Fig. 5. Modifications we made are listed below.

– The 256-bit tweak is assigned to the 256-bit tweakey of SKINNYe.
– A new operation AddRoundKey is added between SB and SR. The 128-bit key is divided into four 32-bit data K_0, K_1, K_2, K_3. In round i, a 32-bit subkey is $K_{i \bmod 4}$. The subkey is XORed to the bottom two rows of the data state.

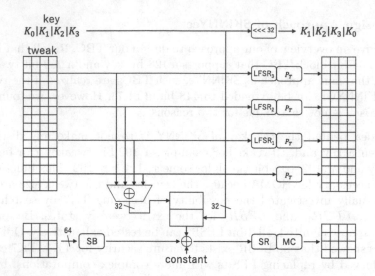

Fig. 5. Round Transformation of SKINNYee.

- **AC** is drastically modified. We define a 10-bit LFSR $rc_9, \ldots, rc_0$, which clocks $(rc_9 \| \cdots \| rc_0)$ to $(rc_8 \| rc_7 \| rc_6 \| rc_5 \| rc_4 \| rc_3 \| rc_2 \| rc_1 \| rc_0 \| rc_9 \oplus rc_3 \oplus rc_2 \oplus rc_0)$. At the beginning, $rc_9 \| rc_8 \| rc_7$ is initialized to the 3-bit tweak for the domain separation, and the other 7 bits are initialized to $rc_8 = \ldots = rc_1 = 0$ and $rc_0 = 1$. In each round, for $i = 0, 1, \ldots, 15$, we first XOR the 4-bit value $(rc_3 \| rc_2 \| rc_1 \| rc_0)$ to the i-th nibble of the data state and then clock the LFSR.
- The number of rounds increases to 56.

5.5   Design Rationale

Rationale for the AddRoundKey is as follows. First, the tweak value is not mixed with the secret value derived by the key, which enables us not need to protect tweak states, otherwise the mixed state needs to be duplicated into several shares. Second, if both the subtweak and the subkey are XORed in the top two rows, some unknown interaction between the tweak and the key may occur. Specifically, when all nibbles in the first tweak state (never updated with LFSR) and all nibbles of the key have the same value, the XOR of the subtweak and the subkey can be a constant value. To avoid such cases, we decided to XOR subkeys to the bottom two rows. Note that the TPRP security required by the mode is a security notion for a single key, thus we exclude the use case that the adversary injects some difference in the key. Hence, we do not have to worry about related-key attacks. Moreover, the tweak value is computed by the HOMA mode, and the adversary cannot control it to be suitable for the attack. For the key schedule, we chose to use 4 parts of 32 bits of the 128-bit key in turn. This avoids using extra memory for the key schedule, thus it is very suitable for our goal. Also note that the key schedule forms a cycle in every 4 rounds, and the key state is back to the original after the whole encryption process (56 rounds). This saves us the cost to implement the key schedule inverse.

We drastically modified AC. The first modification is the small-tweak dependent initialization of the LFSR. A single-bit difference in the initial value of the LFSR significantly changes the generated constant sequences, which is sufficient to separate the TBC invocations for different small-tweak values. Besides, we XOR the 4-bit constant to all nibbles by repeating exactly the same procedure 16 times in each round. This modification increases the total computational cost, thus may speed-down the round-based implementation, which was the original goal of SKINNY. Meanwhile, our goal is a small memory, thus iterating the same procedure 16 times is more suitable. The size of the LFSR was determined from the number of clocks for the whole encryption procedure. Our constant generation requires 16 clocks per round, thus it requires $16 \times 56 = 896$ clocks. We chose the LFSR size to be 10 bits to avoid having the same LFSR state. The feedback function of the 10-bit LFSR was chosen so that the cycle period is 1,023.

The number of rounds increased from that of SKINNY64 with TK3 (40 rounds) and SKINNYe with TK4 (44 rounds). This is because, in SKINNYee, each key nibble is XORed to the data state only in every 4 rounds, while in the previous designs, each key nibble is XORed in every 2 rounds. This does not immediately imply that the number of rounds of SKINNYee must be doubled. Many cryptanalyses, e.g. differential cryptanalysis, are divided into a 'distinguisher' and a 'key-recovery part.' The distinguisher is usually irrelevant to the key schedule, and the less-frequent use of each key nibble only affects the key-recovery part. We expect that the number of key-recovery rounds should be doubled in the worst-case scenario for SKINNY64 and SKINNYe. The maximum number of key-recovery rounds in literature was 11 [40],[12] thus we increased the number of rounds of SKINNYee by 12 from SKINNYe.

5.6 Security Analysis Against Various Cryptanalyses

The security goal of SKINNYee is the TPRP security, which is a notion for a single-key. Hence, we focus on the evaluation in the single-key setting. When an adversary can inject any difference in the plaintext and the tweak, the number of active S-boxes for SKINNYee (in the single-key) is the same as one for SKINNYe in the related-tweakey (TK4) setting. The minimum number of active S-boxes can be evaluated by using mixed integer linear programming (MILP). The results are shown in Table 2, which show that 29 rounds ensure at least 64 S-boxes [26], and the maximum differential characteristic probability is upper-bounded by $2^{-2 \times 64} = 2^{-128}$. Hence 56 rounds of SKINNYee is sufficiently secure.

Another popular approach is linear cryptanalysis. It has some advantage with respect to working in the known-plaintext setting, which allows an attacker to ignore the effects of random IV implemented in HOMA. The evaluation with

---

[12] The longest attack in literature with respect to the number of distinguisher rounds plus key-recovery rounds reaches $22 + 8 = 30$ rounds with TK3 [19].

Table 2. Tight bounds of the number of active Sboxes of SKINNYee.

	1	2	3	4	5	6	7	8	9	10	11	12	13	14	15
Diff	0	0	0	0	0	0	0	0	1	2	3	6	9	12	16
Lin	1	2	5	8	13	19	25	32	38	43	48	52	55	58	64

	16	17	18	19	20	21	22	23	24	25	26	27	28	29	30
Diff	19	21	24	30	35	39	41	43	46	50	54	58	62	66	72
Lin	70	76	80	85	90	96	102	107	110	115	121	127	130	135	141

MILP ensures at least 64 linearly active S-boxes only after 15 rounds [26]. Hence we conclude that HOMA is secure against linear cryptanalysis.

There are several cryptanalytic approaches that focus on features defined over 4 plaintext-ciphertext pairs. Boomerang-type attacks and differential-linear attacks are such examples. Roughly speaking, boomerang-type attacks combine 2 independent relatively short differential characteristics instead of a single long differentials characteristic, meanwhile the probability of each active S-box is squared. Table 2 shows that two 15-round characteristic with 16 active S-boxes may be able to be combined to construct 30-round distinguisher with probability $(2^{(-2) \times 16})^2 \times (2^{(-2) \times 16})^2 = 2^{-128}$. Dependency between two characteristics may increase or decrease the number of rounds a bit, but we conclude that 56 rounds of SKINNYee is sufficiently secure. In differential-linear attacks two differential characteristics and one linear characteristic is combined. For example, two 15-round differential characteristic with 16 active S-boxes may be able to be combined with a 8-round linear characteristic with 32 S-boxes. Again, dependency between two characteristics may increase or decrease the number of rounds a bit, but we conclude that 56 rounds of SKINNYee is sufficiently secure.

Meet-in-the-middle attacks divide the computation structure to two independently computed sub-parts. The designers of SKINNY [3] evaluated the maximum number of attacked rounds based on the number of rounds required for the full diffusion, which showed that the meet-in-the-middle attack would not reach 23 rounds. The use of large tweak in SKINNYee may extend the number of rounds for the full diffusion by 3, which may increase the number of rounds of independently computed parts and two techniques (partial-matching and initial structure) by 3. Hence, the number of attacked rounds is at most $23 + 5 \times 3 = 38$ even with an optimistic evaluation for the attacker.

Some attacks, such as invariant subspace and non-linear invariant, work regardless of the number of rounds (often with a weak key restriction), but no such attacks have been reported for SKINNY or its variants.

6   Implementation

6.1   Targets and Design Policy

We evaluate the hardware performance of HOMA instantiated with SKINNYee. Hereafter, we refer to the SKINNYee's 256-bit tweak as $TK_1 \| TK_2 \| TK_3 \| TK_4$ wherein each TK_i is a 64-bit chunk scheduled independently. We use them for the following purposes:

- TK_1: Upper 64 bits of the nonce,
- TK_2: Upper 36 bits: a lower part of the nonce, lower 28 bits: a counter,
- TK_3: Unprotected data,
- TK_4: Either an associated data block A_i or a ciphertext block C_i (see Fig. 1).

For a fair comparison, we also implement the current state-of-the-art PFB_Plus instantiated with SKINNYe [26] (see Table 1) with the same design policy. The circuit components needed for SKINNYe and SKINNYee are mostly common, which help us to evaluate the difference from the modes of operation. We respect PFB_Plus's original tweak configuration: $TK_1 \| TK_2$ stores the secret key, while $TK_3 \| TK_4$ stores the nonce and counter concatenated.[13]

We follow the design policy of the conventional PFB_Plus implementation [26], which works as a coprocessor that provides a set of commands for block-wise processing. We can realize all AEAD operations by combining those commands. The implementation keeps the key, nonce, and a counter during their lifetime to avoid the hidden cost of an external storage.

6.2   Masked S-box Implementation

We choose Cassiers et al.'s HPC2 [9,10] as a target masking scheme for its glitch resistance, composability, and the availability of an open-source implementation [8]. In particular, composability ensures the security of a circuit composed of the gadgets, which greatly simplifies the security analysis of the entire implementation [9]. Although HPC2 is a great option, we stress that HOMA's low-memory advantage (see Table 1) is independent of a particular masking scheme. An efficient masking scheme in the future will make the HOMA's advantage even higher because an efficient masking makes memory elements even more dominant in hardware cost.

Figure 6-(left) shows our 3-stage pipelined implementation of the SKINNY 4-bit S-box using the HPC2 AND gadgets. The gadget has built-in registers, and its two input ports have different latency. We arrange the gadgets in the pipeline in a way that minimizes the number of pipeline stages on the basis of Cassiers et al.'s S-box representation optimized for HPC2 [10]. The circuit uses four HPC2 AND gadgets, and each pipeline stage calculates (a part of) the S-box independently. Each AND gadget uses $(7d^2 + 11d + 4)/2$ bits of internal

---

[13] For both implementations, we use 28 bits as a counter and the remaining bits as a nonce, by following the conventional PFB_Plus implementation [26].

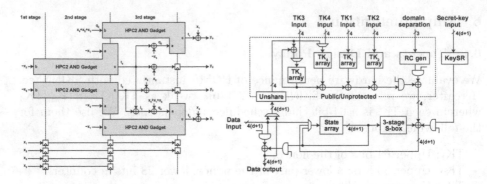

Fig. 6. (Left) three-stage pipelined implementation of the SKINNY 4-bit S-box. The shaded boxes are the HPC2 AND gadgets. We follow the original expression for the symbol names [10]. (Right) hardware architecture of HOMA.

registers. We also need $10d$ bits of the pipeline registers, as shown in the bottom of Fig. 6-(left), for carrying the inputs to later stages. As a result, the S-box circuit uses $(14d^2 + 18d + 8)$ bits of registers in total. Each HPC2 AND gadget uses $d(d+1)/2$ bits of a random number, and the S-box circuit consumes $2d(d+1)$ random bits/cycle at maximum. The total number of random bits for running a TBC is $2d(d+1) \times 16 \times N_{round}$ wherein N_{round} is the round number.

6.3 Hardware Design

Architecture. Figure 6-(right) shows the proposed nibble-serial hardware architecture, which uses the 2-dimensional arrays of registers as a basic building block, by following the conventional PFB_Plus and SKINNY implementations [3,26].

The state array is a 64-bit register arranged in a 4×4 matrix, which efficiently realizes the nibble-wise data scan, as well as the MixColumns and ShiftRows operations. We use a scan flip-flop, a special register with a built-in 2-way selector, for efficiently implementing the array. Each round function takes 24 cycles, and the entire SKINNYee operation finishes in 1344 ($=24 \times 56$) cycles.[14] The TK_1–TK_4 arrays are the similar 4×4 matrices that efficiently realize the nibble-wise data scan and the tweakey schedule [26]. We implement the newly-introduced 128-bit key $K_0 \| K_1 \| K_2 \| K_3$ using a simple (4×32)-bit shift register shown as KeySR in Fig. 6-(right).

HOMA needs to update TK_3 and TK_4 using the TBC output namely Y_{TBC}, such as $TK_3 \leftarrow TK_3 \oplus Y_{TBC}$ and $TK_4 \leftarrow M_i \oplus Y_{TBC}$, in addition to SKINNYee encryption. Our architecture implements those operations in a nibble-oriented manner. The TK_2 array also integrates a 28-bit adder for updating the counter in place, meanwhile the state array integrates the fix0 operation.

---

[14] 19 cycles for S-box calculation with pipeline latency, 4 cycles for MixColumns, and 1 cycle for ShiftRows.

Table 3. Hardware performances in gate equivalent (GE) for $d \in \{0, \cdots, 5\}$.

Component	HOMA						PFB_Plus					
	$d=0$	$d=1$	$d=2$	$d=3$	$d=4$	$d=5$	$d=0$	$d=1$	$d=2$	$d=3$	$d=4$	$d=5$
Total	4,981	6,283	8,226	10,392	12,782	15,487	4,569	6,884	9,667	12,675	15,941	19,724
S-box	161	501	1,087	1,897	2,931	4,189	161	501	1,087	1,897	2,931	4,189
State array	542	1,046	1,573	2,097	2,621	3,240	540	1,049	1,571	2,094	2,619	3,238
TK_1 array	636	549	549	549	549	549	637	1,231	1,845	2,459	3,083	3,818
TK_2 array	844	749	744	748	744	748	674	1,296	1,938	2,578	3,239	3,989
TK_3 array	675	585	586	585	585	586	746	656	657	656	656	656
TK_4 array	675	577	576	577	577	576	865	782	782	780	780	781
KeySR	735	1,468	2,201	2,935	3,668	4,402	—	—	—	—	—	—
Shift reg.	—	—	—	—	—	—	377	754	1,131	1,508	1,885	2,262

Implementation of Shares. The state array and KeySR are simply duplicated for masking, which ensures the component-wise independence. The components in the unprotected region (see Fig. 6-(right)) have no SCA protection. The Unshare module interfaces the protected and unprotected regions by converting the data in shared representation into its bare form. Besides the S-box circuit, this Unshare module is the only place wherein shares can interact. To avoid an exploitable leakage by unsharing the unwanted intermediate data, the Unshare module has a dedicated input register, which strictly controls the incoming data from flowing into the XOR gates that make actual unsharing.

PFB_Plus Implementation. Our PFB_Plus design follows the conventional one [26] and is adjusted for the pipelined S-box circuit in Fig. 6. As a result, the state array and the S-box circuit are mostly the same between our HOMA and PFB_Plus implementations. Meanwhile, there are important differences in the tweakey arrays. In particular, the TK_1 and TK_2 arrays for PFB_Plus store the secret key, which stays in the protected region and is duplicated for masking. PFB_Plus needs an additional state outside the TBC, and we implemented it using a simple shift register similar to KeySR.

6.4 Performance Evaluation and Comparison

We describe the HOMA and PFB_Plus implementations at the register-transfer level except for the direct instantiation of the scan flip-flops [26]. We evaluate the performances by synthesizing the circuits using Synopsys Design Compiler with the NanGate 45-nm standard cell library [31]. To make component-wise comparison, we preserve the hierarchy of the components shown in Fig. 6-(right). Tables 3 show the post-synthesis performances of HOMA and PFB_Plus. We examine the protection orders $d \in \{0, \cdots, 5\}$ by considering the experimental security evaluation in the original paper [9,10].

The results are consistent with the memory advantage in Table 1, and HOMA outperforms PFB_Plus in all the cases with SCA protection, i.e., $d > 0$. In those cases, HOMA's area reduction is larger than that of the entire S-box. For example, at $d = 5$, HOMA saves 4,237 GE wherein the S-box circuit uses 4,189 GE. In other words, HOMA achieves the area reduction that is impossible with the conventional approaches focusing on S-box, i.e., reducing S-box's multiplicative complexity [1,16,17] and improving each AND gadget [9,10].

The results confirm that the memory elements still dominate the overall circuit area with the practical protection orders, and HOMA saves a considerable amount of hardware resources. As discussed in Sect. 6.2, the cost of the AND gadgets and the entire S-box circuit grows quadratically with the protection order d, which will eventually overwhelm the memory elements that grow only linearly. Although we can confirm the S-box circuit's quadratic growth in Tables 3, the memory elements still dominate the total cost with $d \in \{0, \cdots, 5\}$. Besides, the simple key schedule of SKINNYee greatly contributes to the small area: the shift-register based KeySR achieves lower per-bit cost than that of the TK_1 and TK_2 arrays that PFB_Plus uses for storing the key.

HOMA essentially trades the area with latency; HOMA (resp. PFB_Plus) calls the TBC twice (resp. once) for each 64-bit message block. Also, the number of clock cycles for each TBC is extended by roughly 56/44 because SKINNYee has 56 rounds compared with 44 rounds of SKINNYe. However, we believe the area has priority in embedded-system applications, and that would be why serialized architectures having only a single S-box circuit is popular in previous literature.

7 Conclusions

We proposed an AEAD scheme that has the smaller memory usage with $(d+1)$ high-order masking. Achieving this goal, we proposed the strategy that a key-dependent state is separated into public and secret states. We then proposed the new mode HOMA that the half of the state is public, and the new TBC needed for its instantiation. We proved that for $(d+1)$ high-order masking, our scheme outperforms the previous state-of-the-art with respect to circuit area.

Designing an AEAD scheme with a smaller memory usage with $(d+1)$ high-order masking is an interesting future research. One promising approach is to extend the ratio of unprotected state in our design strategy. While SKINNYee was designed based on SKINNY for the purpose of clarifying performance comparisons, designing a new TBC with a new structure for the extended mode that requires a higher number of TK states is another interesting challenge.

References

1. Albrecht, M.R., Rechberger, C., Schneider, T., Tiessen, T., Zohner, M.: Ciphers for MPC and FHE. In: Oswald, E., Fischlin, M. (eds.) EUROCRYPT 2015. LNCS, vol. 9056, pp. 430–454. Springer, Heidelberg (2015). https://doi.org/10.1007/978-3-662-46800-5_17
2. Barwell, G., Martin, D.P., Oswald, E., Stam, M.: Authenticated encryption in the face of protocol and side channel leakage. In: Takagi, T., Peyrin, T. (eds.) ASIACRYPT 2017. LNCS, vol. 10624, pp. 693–723. Springer, Cham (2017). https://doi.org/10.1007/978-3-319-70694-8_24

3. Beierle, C., et al.: The SKINNY family of block ciphers and its low-latency variant MANTIS. In: Robshaw, M., Katz, J. (eds.) CRYPTO 2016. LNCS, vol. 9815, pp. 123–153. Springer, Heidelberg (2016). https://doi.org/10.1007/978-3-662-53008-5_5

4. Belaïd, S., Grosso, V., Standaert, F.-X.: Masking and leakage-resilient primitives: one, the other(s) or both? Cryptogr. Commun. **7**(1), 163–184 (2014). https://doi.org/10.1007/s12095-014-0113-6

5. Bellizia, D., et al.: Spook: sponge-based leakage-resistant authenticated encryption with a masked tweakable block cipher. IACR Trans. Symmetric Cryptol. **2020**(S1), 295–349 (2020)

6. Berti, F., Guo, C., Pereira, O., Peters, T., Standaert, F.: TEDT, a leakage-resist AEAD mode for high physical security applications. IACR Trans. Cryptogr. Hardw. Embed. Syst. **2020**(1), 256–320 (2020)

7. Bilgin, B., Gierlichs, B., Nikova, S., Nikov, V., Rijmen, V.: Higher-order threshold implementations. In: Sarkar, P., Iwata, T. (eds.) ASIACRYPT 2014. LNCS, vol. 8874, pp. 326–343. Springer, Heidelberg (2014). https://doi.org/10.1007/978-3-662-45608-8_18

8. Cassiers, G.: FullVerif (2021). https://github.com/cassiersg/fullverif

9. Cassiers, G., Gregoire, B., Levi, I., Standaert, F.X.: Hardware private circuits: from trivial composition to full verification. IEEE Trans. Comput. 1 (2020)

10. Cassiers, G., Levi, I.: AND depth 2, 4 ANDs, 4-bit (optimized) S-boxes. IACR Cryptol. ePrint Arch. **2020**, 185 (2020). https://eprint.iacr.org/2020/185

11. Chakraborti, A., Datta, N., Jha, A., Mancillas-López, C., Nandi, M., Sasaki, Y.: Elastic-tweak: a framework for short tweak tweakable block cipher. IACR Cryptol. ePrint Arch. **2019**, 440 (2019). https://eprint.iacr.org/2019/440

12. Chakraborti, A., Datta, N., Nandi, M., Yasuda, K.: Beetle family of lightweight and secure authenticated encryption ciphers. IACR Trans. Cryptogr. Hardw. Embed. Syst. **2018**(2), 218–241 (2018)

13. Dobraunig, C., et al.: ISAP v2.0. IACR Trans. Symmetric Cryptol. **2020**(S1), 390–416 (2020)

14. Dobraunig, C., Mennink, B.: Leakage resilient value comparison with application to message authentication. In: Canteaut, A., Standaert, F.-X. (eds.) EUROCRYPT 2021. LNCS, vol. 12697, pp. 377–407. Springer, Cham (2021). https://doi.org/10.1007/978-3-030-77886-6_13

15. Dziembowski, S., Pietrzak, K.: Leakage-resilient cryptography. In: IEEE Symposium on Foundations of Computer Science, FOCS 2008. pp. 293–302 (2008)

16. Gérard, B., Grosso, V., Naya-Plasencia, M., Standaert, F.-X.: Block ciphers that are easier to mask: how far can we go? In: Bertoni, G., Coron, J.-S. (eds.) CHES 2013. LNCS, vol. 8086, pp. 383–399. Springer, Heidelberg (2013). https://doi.org/10.1007/978-3-642-40349-1_22

17. Goudarzi, D., et al.: Pyjamask: block cipher and authenticated encryption with highly efficient masked implementation. IACR Trans. Symmetric Cryptol. **2020**, 31–59 (2020)

18. Grosso, V., et al.: SCREAM & iSCREAM side-channel resistant authenticated encryption with masking. Submitted to CAESAR (2014)

19. Hadipour, H., Bagheri, N., Song, L.: Improved rectangle attacks on SKINNY and CRAFT. IACR Cryptol. ePrint Arch. 1317 (2020)

20. Ishai, Y., Sahai, A., Wagner, D.: Private circuits: securing hardware against probing attacks. In: Boneh, D. (ed.) CRYPTO 2003. LNCS, vol. 2729, pp. 463–481. Springer, Heidelberg (2003). https://doi.org/10.1007/978-3-540-45146-4_27

21. Iwata, T., Khairallah, M., Minematsu, K., Peyrin, T.: Duel of the titans: the romulus and remus families of lightweight AEAD algorithms. IACR Trans. Symmetric Cryptol. **2020**(1), 43–120 (2020)

22. Jean, J., Nikolić, I., Peyrin, T.: Tweaks and keys for block ciphers: the TWEAKEY framework. In: Sarkar, P., Iwata, T. (eds.) ASIACRYPT 2014. LNCS, vol. 8874, pp. 274–288. Springer, Heidelberg (2014). https://doi.org/10.1007/978-3-662-45608-8_15

23. Kannwischer, M.J., Pessl, P., Primas, R.: Single-trace attacks on Keccak. IACR Trans. Cryptogr. Hardw. Embed. Syst. **2020**(3), 243–268 (2020)

24. Kocher, P.C., Jaffe, J., Jun, B.: Differential power analysis. In: Wiener, M. (ed.) CRYPTO 1999. LNCS, vol. 1666, pp. 388–397. Springer, Heidelberg (1999). https://doi.org/10.1007/3-540-48405-1_25

25. Naito, Y., Matsui, M., Sugawara, T., Suzuki, D.: SAEB: a lightweight blockcipher-based AEAD mode of operation. IACR Trans. Cryptogr. Hardw. Embed. Syst. **2018**(2), 192–217 (2018)

26. Naito, Y., Sasaki, Y., Sugawara, T.: Lightweight authenticated encryption mode suitable for threshold implementation. In: Canteaut, A., Ishai, Y. (eds.) EUROCRYPT 2020. LNCS, vol. 12106, pp. 705–735. Springer, Cham (2020). https://doi.org/10.1007/978-3-030-45724-2_24

27. Naito, Y., Sasaki, Y., Sugawara, T.: LM-DAE: low-memory deterministic authenticated encryption for 128-bit security. IACR Trans. Symmetric Cryptol. **2020**(4), 1–38 (2020)

28. Naito, Y., Sasaki, Y., Sugawara, T.: Secret can be public: low-memory AEAD mode for high-order masking. IACR Cryptol. ePrint Arch. 2022, **812** (2022). https://eprint.iacr.org/2022/812

29. Naito, Y., Sugawara, T.: Lightweight authenticated encryption mode of operation for tweakable block ciphers. IACR Trans. Cryptogr. Hardw. Embed. Syst. **2020**(1), 66–94 (2020)

30. Namprempre, C., Rogaway, P., Shrimpton, T.: Reconsidering generic composition. In: Nguyen, P.Q., Oswald, E. (eds.) EUROCRYPT 2014. LNCS, vol. 8441, pp. 257–274. Springer, Heidelberg (2014). https://doi.org/10.1007/978-3-642-55220-5_15

31. NanGate: NanGate FreePDK45 Open Cell Library (2021). https://si2.org/open-cell-library/. Accessed 06 May 2021

32. Nikova, S., Rechberger, C., Rijmen, V.: Threshold implementations against side-channel attacks and glitches. In: Ning, P., Qing, S., Li, N. (eds.) ICICS 2006. LNCS, vol. 4307, pp. 529–545. Springer, Heidelberg (2006). https://doi.org/10.1007/11935308_38

33. NIST: National Institute of Standards and Technology: Submission Requirements and Evaluation Criteria for the Lightweight Cryptography Standardization Process (2018). https://csrc.nist.gov/Projects/lightweight-cryptography

34. NIST: National Institute of Standards and Technology: Lightweight Cryptography Standardization: Finalists Announced (2021). https://csrc.nist.gov/News/2021/lightweight-crypto-finalists-announced

35. Patarin, J.: The "coefficients H" technique. In: Avanzi, R.M., Keliher, L., Sica, F. (eds.) SAC 2008. LNCS, vol. 5381, pp. 328–345. Springer, Heidelberg (2009). https://doi.org/10.1007/978-3-642-04159-4_21

36. Pereira, O., Standaert, F., Vivek, S.: Leakage-resilient authentication and encryption from symmetric cryptographic primitives. In: CCS 2015, pp. 96–108 (2015)

37. Prouff, E., Rivain, M.: Masking against side-channel attacks: a formal security proof. In: Johansson, T., Nguyen, P.Q. (eds.) EUROCRYPT 2013. LNCS, vol. 7881, pp. 142–159. Springer, Heidelberg (2013). https://doi.org/10.1007/978-3-642-38348-9_9

38. Reparaz, O.: A note on the security of higher-order threshold implementations. IACR Cryptol. ePrint Arch. 1 (2015). http://eprint.iacr.org/2015/001

39. Reparaz, O., Bilgin, B., Nikova, S., Gierlichs, B., Verbauwhede, I.: Consolidating masking schemes. In: Gennaro, R., Robshaw, M. (eds.) CRYPTO 2015. LNCS, vol. 9215, pp. 764–783. Springer, Heidelberg (2015). https://doi.org/10.1007/978-3-662-47989-6_37

40. Tolba, M., Abdelkhalek, A., Youssef, A.M.: Impossible differential cryptanalysis of reduced-round SKINNY. In: Joye, M., Nitaj, A. (eds.) AFRICACRYPT 2017. LNCS, vol. 10239, pp. 117–134. Springer, Cham (2017). https://doi.org/10.1007/978-3-319-57339-7_7

Partial Key Exposure Attacks
on BIKE, Rainbow and NTRU

Andre Esser[1]($\boxtimes$)(iD), Alexander May[2](iD), Javier Verbel[1](iD), and Weiqiang Wen[3]

[1] Technology Innovation Institute, Abu Dhabi, UAE
{andre.esser,javier.verbel}@tii.ae
[2] Ruhr University Bochum, Bochum, Germany
alex.may@rub.de
[3] LTCI, Telecom Paris, Institut Polytechnique de Paris, Palaiseau, France
weiqiang.wen@telecom-paris.fr

Abstract. In a so-called partial key exposure attack one obtains some information about the secret key, e.g. via some side-channel leakage. This information might be a certain fraction of the secret key bits (erasure model) or some erroneous version of the secret key (error model). The goal is to recover the secret key from the leaked information.

There is a common belief that, as opposed to e.g. the RSA cryptosystem, most post-quantum cryptosystems are usually resistant against partial key exposure attacks. We strongly question this belief by constructing partial key exposure attacks on code-based, multivariate, and lattice-based schemes (BIKE, Rainbow and NTRU). Our attacks exploit the redundancy that modern PQ cryptosystems inherently use for efficiency reasons. The application and development of techniques from information set decoding plays a crucial role for achieving our results.

On the theoretical side, we show non-trivial information leakage bounds that allow for a polynomial time key recovery attack. As an example, for all schemes the knowledge of a constant fraction of the secret key bits suffices to reconstruct the full key in polynomial time.

Even if we no longer insist on polynomial time attacks, most of our attacks extend well and remain feasible up to large erasure and error rates. In the case of BIKE for example we obtain attack complexities around 60 bits when half of the secret key bits are erased, or a quarter of the secret key bits are faulty.

Our results show that even highly error-prone key leakage of modern PQ cryptosystems may lead to full secret key recoveries.

Keywords: Erasure/Error Model, Asymptotics, Cold Boot Key Recovery

1 Introduction

Ideally, cryptographic schemes should enjoy robustness against key leakage in the following informal sense. If a scheme uses n-bit keys and $k < n$ bits of information

A. May—Funded by DFG under Germany's Excellence Strategy - EXC 2092 CASA - 390781972.

are leaked, then the scheme should offer the security of $(n-k)$-bit keys. The LWE problem is known to provide this *leakage robustness* property [15]. Therefore, it is widely believed that modern post-quantum schemes provide a good level of resistance against computing the secret key from partial information, i.e., against so-called *partial key exposure attacks*.

Notice that leakage robustness of a cryptographic problem does not imply any resistance against side-channel attacks, see e.g. [12]. It just tells us that the leakage of a certain amount of information does not completely destroy the problem's hardness. Moreover, a cryptographic scheme that relies on a leakage robust problem might not automatically inherit its leakage robustness, since the scheme may introduce weaknesses, e.g. via additional secret key redundancy.

As a main result, our work shows that a certain amount of side-channel information (wherever it may come from) suffices to fully recover the secret key in polynomial time - or from a more practical perspective in reasonable time, say 2^{60} operations - for the post-quantum cryptosystems BIKE, Rainbow, NTRU. We chose these schemes as representative candidates for code-, multivariate- and lattice-based cryptography. NTRU, respectively BIKE, is a NIST 3rd round finalist, respectively alternate, encryption scheme, and Rainbow is a finalist signature scheme.

Partial Key Exposure Attacks on RSA in the Erasure and Error Model. It is well-known that RSA does not enjoy leakage robustness. For instance, by a famous result of Coppersmith [9] an RSA modulus $N = pq$ can be factored in polynomial time given only half of the bits of p. Similar results have been shown for fully recovering the secret key d [7], the RSA plaintext m [9], and also RSA CRT-exponents [6] from partial knowledge in polynomial time.

All of these attacks are in what we call the *erasure model*, i.e., we obtain a certain fraction of the bits, and have to recover the remaining bits. Moreover, the above mentioned attacks usually require that the known as well as the unknown bits are in *consecutive positions*. An erasure model with *known bits in random positions* was first addressed by Heninger and Shacham [18].

The erasure model is from a theoretical perspective convenient, because it usually provides a good starting point for reasoning about algorithms that recover complete secret keys from incomplete information. In practice however, side-channel analysis often gives us full keys with some faults that stem from the side-channel's noisiness. This is what we call the *error model*, which might be further refined by its error type.

In the error model Henecka, May, Meurer [17] showed that an RSA secret key in which bits are randomly flipped with a certain error rate $r \ll \frac{1}{2}$ can be recovered in polynomial time. This was further refined by Paterson, Polychroniadou, Sibborn [23] introducing asymmetric bit-flip rates, where bits may flip from 1 to ground state 0 with large error rate p_1, whereas the inverse direction has only small probability p_0. Such an *asymmetric error* accurately models e.g. the side-channel obtained by *Cold Boot Attacks* from Halderman et al. [16].

Previous Work on PQC Partial Key Exposure Attacks. For post-quantum cryptography, in 2017 a first partial key exposure on NTRU was proposed by Paterson and Villanueva-Polanco [24], followed by two more attacks from Villanueva-Polanco on BLISS [27] and LUOV [28]. The PhD thesis of Villanueva-Polanco [25] contains a more systematic study of partial key exposure attacks also for Rainbow and McEliece.

However, the results achieved by Paterson and Villanueva-Polanco seem to support the strong belief in *leakage robustness* of post-quantum cryptosystems. For example considering NTRU, even in the asymmetric error setting their attacks experimentally cannot reach with good success probability rather small error probabilities $p_1 = 0.1$ and $p_0 = 0.001$. Similar for Rainbow, the attack in [25] only reaches error probabilities of $p_1 = 0.001$ and $p_0 = 0.001$ even for toy Rainbow parameters.

These results stand in quite sharp contrast to our attacks, that handle relatively large erasure/error rates, sometimes even in polynomial time. We see two main reasons for our substantial improvement over previous work.

First, we heavily use the key redundancy provided by many modern post-quantum systems to recover secret keys much more efficiently. Key redundancy has already been exploited by Albrecht, Deo, Paterson [1] by using the NTT representation of Kyber keys. However, [1] still only tolerates comparatively small error probabilities around 1%.

Second, we use and further develop more advanced techniques from information set decoding and lattices, thereby building on the work of Horlemann, Puchinger, Renner, Schamberger, Wachter-Zeh [19] for decoding with hints and the work of Dachman-Soled, Ducas, Gong, Rossi [10] for lattices with hints. Especially, our new decoding techniques might be of independent interest.

Our Results with Polynomial Time Key Recovery. To the best of our knowledge, our work is the first that achieves polynomial time partial key exposure attacks on post-quantum cryptosystems for non-trivial erasure/error rates. Our results are summarized in Table 1.

Table 1. Summary of (asymptotic) bounds on erasure/error probability for polynomial-time key recovery.

Polynomial Attacks	key format	erasure	error
BIKE	standard	0.500	$\frac{\log n}{\sqrt{n}}$
	compact	0.092	$\frac{1}{\log^2 n}$
Rainbow	first layer	$\frac{n}{n+1}$	$\frac{\log n}{n}$
	full key	$\frac{1}{\sqrt{n}}$	$\frac{\log n}{n}$
NTRU	(un)packed	$n^{-\frac{2}{3}}$	$\frac{\sqrt{\log n}}{n}$
	"consecutive"	0.250	

Let us briefly discuss our results, what we mean by the different key formats, and how we exploit key redundancies.

BIKE. For BIKE keys we achieve erasure rates of $p = \frac{1}{2}$ (standard) and $p = 0.092$ (compact). Let $(\mathbf{s}, \mathbf{e}) \in \mathbb{F}_2^{n/2} \times \mathbb{F}_2^{n/2}$ be a BIKE secret key in standard format, i.e., $(\mathbf{s}, \mathbf{e})$ is given as a bit-vector. Then half of the secret key bits suffice to recover the full secret key in polynomial time.

This might be surprising at first glance, but a BIKE secret key fulfills an LWE/LPN-relation $A\mathbf{s} = \mathbf{e}$. From this alone one can see that $\mathbf{s}$ suffices to efficiently recover $\mathbf{e}$. Our attack now simply shows that any $n/2$ bits suffice. Thus, in comparison to LWE/LPN, BIKE secret keys are redundant, since they store the secret $\mathbf{s}$ and the error $\mathbf{e}$. Both parts are required in BIKE for proper decryption (as opposed to LWE-type schemes).

If $(\mathbf{s}, \mathbf{e})$ is stored compactly, i.e., only the few non-zero positions of both vectors are encoded, then one can only recover the key efficiently given all but a 0.092-fraction of its bits.

In the error setting, our BIKE results tolerate roughly an $\frac{1}{\sqrt{n}}$-error in the standard case, i.e. roughly $\sqrt{n}$ error positions. However, notice that somewhat surprisingly the compact case allows for a huge number of $n/\log^2 n$ error positions.

We would like to point out that all of our BIKE results also hold identically for HQC [22] secret keys.

Rainbow. For Rainbow keys, our partial key exposure attacks are even stronger. This stems from our main observation that a single row of Rainbow's secret key matrix suffices to fully recover the first half of the key (labeled as "first layer" in Table 1). Here, in the erasure setting, we can tolerate rates that converge to 1. In other words, a linear fraction of the secret key matrix is already enough to recover this part of the key.

In order to recover the full key in polynomial time, slightly more information is needed, which leads to only $\sqrt{n}$ manageable errors. However, a Rainbow secret key, inherently contains a (quadratic) redundancy factor, which is heavily exploited by our attacks.

For error recovery our results are significantly worse. Here, we can only tolerate $\log n$ error positions per key.

NTRU. Eventually, for the NTRU cryptosystem we achieve for errors/erasures in random positions only small tolerable rates. The NTRU encryption scheme can be considered as a Ring-LWE instance. As explained for BIKE, the consequence is that NTRU secret keys provide less redundancy than BIKE secret keys, since NTRU does not store the LWE error. Thus, it is not surprising that we obtain weaker bounds for NTRU.

Yet, if we look into the setting of erasures in consecutive positions of an NTRU secret key, then we can recover the full secret key from only a 3/4-

fraction of all positions. This consecutive partial key exposure attack heavily exploits NTRU's ring structure. We are not aware of any cryptanalytic results in the literature that exploit the ring structure with such a significant gain.

Concrete Parameters: The Erasure Case. While from a theoretical perspective it is desirable to understand for which erasure/error rates we can achieve polynomial time attacks, it might be even more interesting to see how our attacks perform on concrete parameter sets. Table 2 shows the results of our attacks on Category-1 parameter sets (equivalent to AES-128 security), when we allow for attack bit complexities of 45, 60 and 80 bit.[1]

Table 2. Tolerable erasure rates for different key formats that allow for a key recovery with bit complexity less than 45, 60 and 80 on the Category-1 parameter sets.

Erasures	key format	bit complexity bound		
		45	60	80
BIKE	standard	0.570	0.650	0.730
	compact	0.410	0.425	0.445
Rainbow	full key	0.710	0.810	0.890
NTRU	unpacked	0.219	0.300	0.422
	packed	0.065	0.092	0.138

Recall from Table 1 that polynomial time attacks on BIKE are feasible for erasure rates of 0.5 (standard key format), respectively roughly 0.1 (compact key format). We observe from Table 1 that the allowed errors in the standard format are significantly larger, namely in the interval [0.57, 0.73], whereas in compact format we even improve to rates beyond 0.4. Hence, BIKE's redundancy leads to efficient key recoveries in practice given roughly half of the secret key bits.

Rainbow with its large key redundancy tolerates even larger rates than BIKE for Category-1 parameters.[2] Here, erasure rates in the interval [0.71, 0.89] still allow for key recovery as shown in Table 2.

Asymptotically, NTRU has least key redundancy and therefore tolerates only small erasure rates. This is reflected by the results of Table 2, where we can recover erasure rates in the interval [0.22, 0.42]. However, compared to previous results from Paterson and Villanueva-Polanco [24], our results still improve by orders of magnitude. The reason for this improvement comes from using more involved lattice techniques than the simple key enumeration from [24]. Even

---

[1] The code to rerun our experiments and bitcomplexity calculations is available at https://github.com/Crypto-TII/partial-key-exposure-attacks.

[2] For Rainbow Category-3 and -5 parameters tolerable rates are lower, as we discuss in Sect. 4.

for the least redundant *packed* key format, we still obtain erasure rates in the interval $[0.06, 0.14]$.

Table 3. Tolerable error rates for key recovery of Category-1 parameter sets with bit complexities bounded by 45, 60 and 80. In the asymmetric setting we fix $p_0 = 0.001$.

Errors			bit complexity				
	key format	45		60		80	
		asym.	sym.	asym.	sym.	asym.	sym.
BIKE	standard	0.050	0.050	0.150	0.120	0.300	0.200
	compact	0.175	0.030	0.240	0.060	0.275	0.080
Rainbow	full key	0.240	0.120	0.375	0.190	0.540	0.270
NTRU	unpacked	0.033	0.002	0.099	0.009	0.273	0.019
	packed	0.009	0.003	0.020	0.008	0.040	0.015

Concrete Parameters: The Error Case. Analogous to Table 2, we denote in Table 3 the error rates that we can recover for Category-1 parameter sets when using bit-complexities of 45, 60, and 80 bits.

Noteworthy, we achieve high error rates in the *asymmetric* error setting. For Rainbow, this again stems from the larger key redundancy. However, for BIKE and NTRU we exploit the partial key information to significantly lower the dimension of the underlying problems. This in turn speeds up our decoding/lattice reduction algorithms. Most impressive is maybe the error correction of unpacked NTRU keys with error rate $p_1 = 0.27$ within a complexity of 80 bit. Observe that our attack is not yet very effective for 45 bits (with error $p_1 = 0.03$), since it requires a large polynomial overhead.

Conclusion. As opposed to the common belief, current post-quantum schemes allow for effective partial key exposure attacks, both in the erasure and the error setting. We demonstrate this for representative post-quantum candidates from codes, multivariate and lattices. As a rule of thumb, the higher the key redundancy, the more effective are our attacks. But even the least redundant NTRU scheme still allows for quite impressive erasure/error rates.

Organization of the Paper. We elaborate on our erasure/error model in Sect. 2, where we also recap the basics of information set decoding attacks. All our BIKE results, asymptotically and for concrete parameters, are given in Sect. 3. Our Rainbow results can be found in Sect. 4, and we conclude with the NTRU results in Sect. 5.

2   Preliminaries

We denote vectors and matrices as bold lower case and bold capital letters. For a matrix $\mathbf{M} \in \mathbb{F}_q^{k \times n}$ and a set $I \subseteq \{1, \ldots, n\}$ we let $\mathbf{M}_I$ be the matrix obtained by projecting $\mathbf{M}$ onto the columns defined by I. We use the same notation for vectors. We refer by $\mathbf{O}$ to the all-zero matrix. All logarithms are base 2 if not stated otherwise. We use standard Landau notation for complexity statements and call a probability p high if $p = 1 - o(1)$.

2.1   Key Exposure Models

Throughout this work we consider two different key exposure models - the *error* and the *erasure* model. In the error model one obtains knowledge of a faulty version of the full secret key, whereas in the erasure setting only certain parts of the secret key are known but guaranteed to be correct.

In our theoretical treatment we work with errors and erasures on the field level, while for practical considerations we work with errors and erasures on the bit level. This distinction allows us to keep the theoretical consideration (mostly) independent of the chosen key-representation. In our practical analysis we then analyze the performance of our attacks using specific key formats. Let us more formally define both models, starting with the field level.

Errors and Erasures in Fields. For all schemes that we consider the private keys are either vectors (or matrices) over $\mathbb{F}_q$ or polynomials with coefficients over $\mathbb{F}_q$, which are represented via their coefficient vector. Field erasures then correspond to a set of indices for which the corresponding coordinates or coefficients are unknown, while the rest is known.

Definition 1 (Erasures). *Let* $n \in \mathbb{N}$, $\mathbf{f} = (f_1, \ldots, f_n) \in \mathbb{F}_q^n$ *and* $I \subseteq \{1, \ldots, n\}$ *denote the erasure positions. For* $\mathbf{u}_i$ *denoting the* i-*th unit vector we let*

$$\tilde{\mathbf{f}} := \sum_{i \notin I} f_i \mathbf{u}_i + \sum_{i \in I} y_i \mathbf{u}_i,$$

with $y_i \in \mathbb{F}_q$. *In the erasure model* I *and* $\tilde{\mathbf{f}}$ *are known, while the* y_i *are unknown. Each coordinate of* $\mathbf{f}$ *gets erased with probability* $p := \Pr[i \in I]$, *which we denote as* $\mathbb{F}_q$-*erasure probability. We call* $\tilde{\mathbf{f}}$ *a* partially erased *version of* $\mathbf{f}$.

In a concrete attack scenario of Definition 1 $\mathbf{f}$ would be the secret key, and the goal is to recover $\mathbf{f}$ from the partially erased version $\tilde{\mathbf{f}}$. We call such an attack a *(key recovery) attack in the erasure model*.

Let us analogously define the error model.

Definition 2 (Errors). *Let* $n \in \mathbb{N}$ *and* $\mathbf{f} = (f_1, \ldots, f_n) \in \mathbb{F}_q^n$. *Further let* $\mathbf{e} = (e_1, \ldots, e_n) \in \mathbb{F}_q^n$ *be an error vector. In the error model one is given*

$$\tilde{\mathbf{f}} := (\tilde{f}_1, \ldots, \tilde{f}_n) = \mathbf{f} + \mathbf{e} = (f_1 + e_1, \ldots, f_n + e_n),$$

while the f_i and e_i are unknown. Every coordinate of the error is different from zero with probability $p := \Pr[e_i \neq 0]$, which we refer to as $\mathbb{F}_q$- error probability. If $e_i \neq 0$, then e_i is uniformly distributed in $\mathbb{F}_q \setminus \{0\}$, i.e., $\Pr[e_i = 0] = (1 - p)$ and $\Pr[e_i = k] = \frac{p}{q-1}$ for all $k \in \mathbb{F}_q \setminus \{0\}$. We call $\tilde{\mathbf{f}}$ an erroneous version of $\mathbf{f}$.

Again, in a partial key exposure scenario $\mathbf{f}$ would be the secret key and $\tilde{\mathbf{f}}$ the known erroneous version of it. The goal is to recover $\mathbf{f}$ from $\tilde{\mathbf{f}}$. We call such an attack a *(key recovery) attack in the error model.*

Errors and Erasures of Bits. For our practical analysis we switch from field to bit errors, i.e., every bit in the binary representation of the secret key is flipped (error model) or erased (erasure model) with a certain probability. One obtains a definition for the erasure and error model considering bit-errors/-erasure by letting $\mathbf{f}$ of Definition 1 and 2 be the binary representation of the secret key and correspondingly setting $q = 2$. In these cases we might use the term *bit-error* and *bit-erasure* rather than $\mathbb{F}_2$-error and $\mathbb{F}_2$-erasure. Once it is known how the secret key is represented on the bit-level, one can relate the field- and bit-error/-erasure.

Speaking of the error model, in a practical scenario, which is often motivated via cold-boot attacks, we usually find asymmetric error probabilities, i.e., the probability p_0 of a zero flipping to one is different from the probability p_1 of a one becoming a zero. Let the binary representation of the secret key be $\mathbf{f} \in \mathbb{F}_2^n$ and the error be $\mathbf{e} \in \mathbb{F}_2^n$. An attack in the error model then asks to recover $\mathbf{f}$ from $\tilde{\mathbf{f}} := \mathbf{f} + \mathbf{e}$. Therefore

$$p_0 := \Pr[e_i = 1 \mid f_i = 0] \text{ and } p_1 := \Pr[e_i = 1 \mid f_i = 1].$$

Usually one of the probabilities is rather small, since bits are more likely to flip to the ground state of the respective memory region to which all bits decay over time. Following the initial work of Halderman et al. [16] we assume in our analysis that all bits decay to the same ground state for simplification. Moreover we consider the ground state to be zero and adopt the choice of $p_0 = 10^{-3}$, experimentally observed in [16].

2.2   Decoding

Some of our attacks make use of information set decoding (ISD) algorithms to decode linear codes. A linear code $\mathcal{C}$ is a k dimensional subspace of $\mathbb{F}_q^n$. We call n the *code length* and k the *code dimension*. Such a code can be represented via the kernel of a matrix $\mathbf{H} \in \mathbb{F}^{(n-k)\times n}$ of rank $n - k$, i.e., $\mathcal{C} := \{\mathbf{c} \in \mathbb{F}_q^n \mid \mathbf{H}\mathbf{c}^\top = \mathbf{0}\}$. Hence, recovering a codeword $\mathbf{c} \in \mathcal{C}$ from a given faulty string $\mathbf{y} = \mathbf{c} + \mathbf{f}$ is equivalent to recover $\mathbf{f}$ from the *syndrome* $\mathbf{s} := \mathbf{H}\mathbf{y} - \mathbf{H}(\mathbf{c} + \mathbf{f}) = \mathbf{H}\mathbf{f}$.

Definition 3 (Syndrome Decoding Problem). *Let $n, k \in \mathbb{N}$. Given the parity check matrix $\mathbf{H} \in \mathbb{F}_q^{(n-k)\times n}$ of a linear code over $\mathbb{F}_q$, a syndrome $\mathbf{s} \in \mathbb{F}_q^{n-k}$ and an error-weight $\delta \in \mathbb{N}$, the syndrome decoding problem asks to find a vector*

$\mathbf{f} \in \mathbb{F}_q^n$ *of weight* $\mathrm{wt}(\mathbf{f}) = \delta$ *satisfying* $\mathbf{Hf} = \mathbf{s}$. *We call* $(\mathbf{H}, \mathbf{s}, \delta)$ *an* instance *of the* syndrome decoding problem *and* $\mathbf{f}$ *the* solution.

The class of ISD algorithms, initiated by Prange in 1962 [26], allows to solve the syndrome decoding problem.

Prange's Information Set Decoding (ISD). For a permutation matrix $\mathbf{P} \in \mathbb{F}_2^{n \times n}$, $\mathbf{P}^{-1}\mathbf{f}$ forms a solution to the permuted syndrome decoding instance $(\mathbf{HP}, \mathbf{s}, \delta)$. We let the permuted error be $\mathbf{P}^{-1}\mathbf{f} =: (\mathbf{f}_1, \mathbf{f}_2) \in \mathbb{F}_q^{n-k} \times \mathbb{F}_q^k$ and the permuted parity check matrix $\mathbf{HP} := (\mathbf{H}_1 \mid \mathbf{H}_2)$ with $\mathbf{H}_1 \in \mathbb{F}_q^{(n-k) \times (n-k)}$. From $\mathbf{Hf} = \mathbf{s}$ it follows that

$$(\mathbf{H}_1)^{-1}(\mathbf{HP})(\mathbf{P}^{-1}\mathbf{f}) = (\mathbf{I}_{n-k} \mid \mathbf{H}_2')(\mathbf{f}_1, \mathbf{f}_2) = \mathbf{f}_1 + \mathbf{H}_2'\mathbf{f}_2 = (\mathbf{H}_1)^{-1}\mathbf{s} =: \mathbf{s}',$$

where $\mathbf{H}_2' = (\mathbf{H}_1)^{-1}\mathbf{H}_2$. Let us further assume that the permutation distributes the weight on $(\mathbf{f}_1, \mathbf{f}_2)$ such that $\mathrm{wt}(\mathbf{f}_2) = \gamma$ and, hence, $\mathrm{wt}(\mathbf{f}_1) = \delta - \gamma$. Then finding a solution corresponds to finding an $\mathbf{f}_2$ of weight γ for which the corresponding $\mathbf{f}_1 = \mathbf{s}' - \mathbf{H}_2'\mathbf{f}_2$ has weight $\delta - \gamma$. In the following we call any selection of $n - k$ columns (defined by the permutation) that leads to an $\mathbf{f}_1$ of weight $\delta - \gamma$ an *information set*. Further for $\gamma = 0$ an information set contains the whole error. Prange's algorithm now chooses a random permutation matrix, computes $\mathbf{H}_2'$ and $\mathbf{s}'$ and then enumerates all possible $\mathbf{f}_2$ of weight γ until it finds an $\mathbf{f}_1$ of weight $\delta - \gamma$. This process is repeated with fresh initial permutations until success. The expected complexity of Prange's algorithm (up to polynomial factors) is

$$T_{\text{Prange}} = \underbrace{\frac{\binom{n}{\delta}}{\binom{n-k}{\delta-\gamma}\binom{k}{\gamma}}}_{\text{Permutations}} \underbrace{\binom{k}{\gamma}(q-1)^\gamma}_{\text{Enumeration}} = \frac{(q-1)^\gamma \cdot \binom{n}{\delta}}{\binom{n-k}{\delta-\gamma}}. \tag{1}$$

Obviously, $\gamma = 0$ minimizes the running time. However, for large δ, namely for $\delta > n - k$, choosing γ equal to zero is not possible.

To derive our asymptotic bounds we show the following theorem, specifying a small error regime for which Prange's algorithm has polynomial complexity.

Theorem 1. *Let* $\mathbf{H}$ *be the parity-check matrix of a code with length* n *and co-dimension* $n - k = c \cdot n$, *for constant* c. *Then a syndrome decoding instance* $(\mathbf{H}, \mathbf{s}, \delta)$ *with* $\delta = \mathcal{O}(\log n)$ *can be solved in polynomial time.*

Proof. The complexity of Prange's algorithm to solve such an instance is (up to polynomial factors) given by Eq. 1 as

$$\frac{\binom{n}{\delta}}{\binom{n-k}{\delta}} = \frac{\binom{n}{\delta}}{\binom{cn}{\delta}} = \prod_{i=0}^{\delta-1} \frac{n-i}{cn-i} = \prod_{i=0}^{\delta-1} \frac{1}{c - \frac{(c-1)i}{n-i}} = \left(\frac{1}{c - o(1)}\right)^\delta = n^{\mathcal{O}(1)}. \quad \square$$

3   BIKE

For BIKE the private key is the solution to a syndrome decoding instance $(\mathbf{H}, \mathbf{s}, \delta)$ over $\mathbb{F}_2$, of code length n and dimension k, defined via the public key $\mathbf{H}$. Hence, the secret key is a vector $\mathbf{f} \in \mathbb{F}_2^n$. The scheme uses a code rate of $R = \frac{1}{2}$, i.e., $n = 2k$ and $\delta := \mathrm{wt}(\mathbf{f}) = \Theta(\sqrt{n}) = \Theta(\sqrt{k})$.

We consider two different key formats in our analysis. The *standard key format* stores the secret key as bitstring of length n, while the *compact key format* stores only the δ one entries of $\mathbf{f}$.[3] In a nutshell our attacks on both formats follow a similar strategy: Initially, we generate likely candidates for the one positions in the secret key based on the given key material. Then to obtain polynomial attacks we upper-bound the total number of candidates dependent on the error/erasure probability. In our practical attacks we consider constant error/erasure probabilities, which lead to a large set of candidates. Our attacks then speed up Prange's ISD procedure by prioritizing the set of candidates.

3.1   Standard Format Keys

We say the secret key is stored in *standard* format or using *standard* representation when it stores the secret value $\mathbf{f} \in \mathbb{F}_2^n$ as a sequence of n bits.

The Erasure Model. First let us investigate the erasure model. Since the parity-check matrix $H \in \mathbb{F}_2^{n/2 \times n}$ defines $n/2$ linear equations in $\mathbf{f}$, we can directly recover $\mathbf{f}$ whenever the number of unknowns is at most $n/2$.

Theorem 2 (Polynomial Erasure Attack on Standard Format). *Let $\tilde{\mathbf{f}}$ be a given partially erased BIKE secret key in the standard format with $\mathbb{F}_2$-erasure probability $p \leq \frac{1}{2}$. Then, the secret key $\mathbf{f} \in \mathbb{F}_2^n$ can be recovered in polynomial time with success probability at least $\frac{1}{2}$.*

Proof. Let X by a random variable for the number of erased coordinates of $\mathbf{f}$. Since X is binomially distributed with parameters n and $p \leq \frac{1}{2}$, we have

$$\Pr[X \leq n/2] = \sum_{i=0}^{n/2} \binom{n}{i} p^i (1-p)^{n-i} \geq 2^{-n} \sum_{i=0}^{n/2} \binom{n}{i} \geq \frac{1}{2}.$$

Thus, with probability at least $\frac{1}{2}$ we have at most $n/2$ unknowns. In this case, matrix H with rank $n/2$ provides $n/2$ linearly independent equations in at most $X \leq n/2$ unknowns. Therefore, we recover $\mathbf{f}$ via Gaussian elimination in time $\mathcal{O}(n^3)$. □

---

[3] Both formats can be found in the NIST submission [4] or the implementation accompanying it.

356   A. Esser et al.

The Error Model. Next let us consider the error model for the standard key format. According to Sect. 2.1 this corresponds to a given syndrome decoding instance $(\mathbf{H}, \mathbf{s}, \delta)$ together with a faulty solution vector $\tilde{\mathbf{f}} = \mathbf{f} + \mathbf{e}$, where $\Pr[e_i = 1] = p$. Note that we can again easily transform such an instance into a different syndrome decoding instance with weight $\delta' = \mathrm{wt}(\mathbf{e})$. Therefore we just let the new syndrome be $\mathbf{s}' := \mathbf{s} + \mathbf{H}\tilde{\mathbf{f}}$, since

$$\mathbf{s}' := \mathbf{s} + \mathbf{H}\tilde{\mathbf{f}} = \mathbf{H}\mathbf{f} + \mathbf{H}(\mathbf{f} + \mathbf{e}) = \mathbf{H}\mathbf{e}.$$

This gives a first improvement, whenever $\delta' < \delta$. However, intuitively as long as $p \neq \frac{1}{2}$ (which corresponds to a uniform error) the problem should become easier.

To obtain a speedup whenever $p < \frac{1}{2}$, we exploit that the distribution of the weight on the candidate $\tilde{\mathbf{f}}$ in this case carries information about the weight distribution of $\mathbf{f}$. Observe that the expected weight of $\tilde{\mathbf{f}}$ is

$$\delta_{\tilde{\mathbf{f}}} := \mathbb{E}[\mathrm{wt}(\tilde{\mathbf{f}})] = (1 - p)\delta + p(n - \delta),$$

where the first addend counts the ones of $\mathbf{f}$ contributing to $\delta_{\tilde{\mathbf{f}}}$, while the second counts the contribution from $\mathbf{e}$. Let γ_1 be the random variable counting the weight of $\mathbf{f}$ restricted to the coordinates where $\tilde{f}_i = 1$, then it follows that $\mathbb{E}[\gamma_1] = \delta(1 - p)$. Analogously, the rest of the weight, namely $\gamma_0 := \delta - \gamma_1$, must then distribute over the coordinates where $\tilde{f}_i = 0$.

In the following we adapt the choice of columns selected by Prange's algorithm for finding an information set based on the given key material. Put simple, if a higher fraction of the error-weight is located on the coordinates of $\tilde{\mathbf{f}}$ with $\tilde{f}_i = 1$ than on those with $\tilde{f}_i = 0$, overall more coordinates are taken from the one-associated coordinates and vice versa. More precisely, we introduce a parameter $\rho_1 \leq \delta_{\tilde{\mathbf{f}}}$ determining how many of the $n - k$ columns, belonging to the information set, are chosen from the block defined by the one-coordinates of $\tilde{\mathbf{f}}$. Consequently, the remaining $\rho_0 := n - k - \rho_1$ are taken from the block defined by the zeros of $\tilde{\mathbf{f}}$. The probability that $n - k$ columns selected this way form an information set that contains the whole error becomes

$$q := \frac{\binom{\delta_{\tilde{\mathbf{f}}} - \gamma_1}{\rho_1 - \gamma_1}}{\binom{\delta_{\tilde{\mathbf{f}}}}{\rho_1}} \cdot \frac{\binom{n - \delta_{\tilde{\mathbf{f}}} - \gamma_0}{\rho_0 - \gamma_0}}{\binom{n - \delta_{\tilde{\mathbf{f}}}}{\rho_0}} = \frac{\binom{\rho_1}{\gamma_1}\binom{\rho_0}{\gamma_0}}{\binom{\delta_{\tilde{\mathbf{f}}}}{\gamma_1}\binom{n - \delta_{\tilde{\mathbf{f}}}}{\gamma_0}}. \tag{2}$$

Let us assume that the binomially distributed random variable γ_1 stays below its expectation, which happens with constant probability. Then, we can bound the expected amount of sets to be selected until we find such an information set as

$$\mathbb{E}\left[q^{-1} \mid \gamma_1 \leq \mathbb{E}[\gamma_1]\right] \leq \frac{\binom{\rho_1}{(1-p)\delta}\binom{n-k-\rho_1}{p\delta}}{\binom{\delta_{\tilde{\mathbf{f}}}}{(1-p)\delta}\binom{n-\delta_{\tilde{\mathbf{f}}}}{p\delta}}. \tag{3}$$

The following theorem states up to which error probability the expected attack complexity, i.e., Eq. 3, stays in the polynomial time regime, using Theorem 1.

Theorem 3 (Polynomial Error Attack on Standard Format). *Let $\tilde{\mathbf{f}}$ be a given erroneous BIKE secret key in the standard format with $\mathbb{F}_2$-error probability $p = \mathcal{O}\left(\frac{\log n}{\sqrt{n}}\right)$. Then the secret key $\mathbf{f} \in \mathbb{F}_2^n$ can be recovered in polynomial time with constant probability.*

Proof. Given in the full version [14].

Note that the above attack can easily be adapted to asymmetric error probabilities. In this case the expected weight of $\tilde{\mathbf{f}}$ changes to $\delta_{\tilde{\mathbf{f}}} = \delta(1-p_1)+p_0(n-\delta)$. Again the first addend counts the number of ones contributed from $\mathbf{f}$, which lets the fraction of ones in $\tilde{\mathbf{f}}$ also present in $\mathbf{f}$ become $\gamma_1 := \delta(1-p_1)$. Now the adaptation of the ISD algorithm works as before, where Eq. 2 yields the probability of success in each iteration.

3.2   Compact Format Keys

If the secret key is stored via δ integers encoding its one positions, we say the key is stored in *compact* format or representation. Since BIKE's secret key is balanced, i.e., it has weight $\frac{\delta}{2}$ on each half of the coordinates, every integer encoding a position requires $\log k$ bits. We find that the compact compared to standard format allows for improved asymptotic bounds in the error model, while giving a slight disadvantage in the erasure model.

To allow for a direct comparison between the error- and erasure-probabilities for both key formats we stay with bit-errors and -erasures, i.e., we treat the secret key in compact format as a sequence of $\delta \log k$ bits, where any bit might be erroneous or get erased, rather than as δ integers.

The Erasure Model. Our strategy for key recovery in the erasure model is again to generate candidates for the one coordinates of the key, based on the given information, and include those candidates in the information set. As long as the amount of candidates stays smaller than the co-dimension, which is $n - k = k$ in the case of BIKE, we can recover the secret key in polynomial time via Gaussian elimination. We get a slightly worse bound than for the standard format because ε bit-erasures in any integer lead to 2^ε candidates, i.e., we have an exponential amplification in the amount of candidates.

Theorem 4 (Polynomial Erasure Attack on Compact Format). *Let $\tilde{\mathbf{f}}$ be a given partially erased BIKE secret key in the* compact *format with $\mathbb{F}_2$-erasure probability $p \leq 0.092$. Then the secret key $\mathbf{f} \in \mathbb{F}_2^{\delta \log k}$ can be recovered in polynomial time with constant success probability.*

Proof. Given in the full version [14].

Overall this corresponds to a constant factor disadvantage to the standard key format.

The Error Model. Interestingly, if we turn our focus to the error-model, the compact key representation allows for an asymptotic increase in the error probability while staying in the polynomial time regime. This is because the compact representation allows to derive more candidates than the standard format and, hence, exploit the full size of the information set.[4] Therefore, we again generate candidates for each index of the secret key based on the given erroneous indices.

Theorem 5 (Polynomial Error Attack on Compact Format). *Let* $\tilde{\mathbf{f}}$ *be a given erroneous BIKE secret key with* $\mathbb{F}_2$*-error probability* $p = \mathcal{O}\left(\frac{1}{\log^{2+\kappa} k}\right)$ *for a small constant* $\kappa > 0$. *Then the secret key* $\mathbf{f} \in \mathbb{F}_2^{\delta \log k}$ *can be recovered in polynomial time with high success probability.*

Proof. Given in the full version [14]. □

Summarizing, the compact key representation of BIKE allows for a polynomial time key recovery in the error setting up to an error rate of $p = \frac{1}{\log^{2+\kappa} k}$ for a small $\kappa > 0$ in comparison to the less compact variant which only allows for an error-rate of $\frac{\log k}{\sqrt{k}}$.

3.3 Practical Attacks on BIKE

The Erasure Model. Our practical approach for key recovery in the standard format extends the idea from Sect. 3.1 in the following way. Let I be the set of erased coordinates and $\bar{I} := \{1, \ldots, n\} \setminus I$, i.e., all coordinates of $\mathbf{f}_I$ are unknown, while those of $\mathbf{f}_{\bar{I}}$ are known. Now from $\mathbf{H}\mathbf{f} = \mathbf{s}$ it follows that

$$\mathbf{H}_I \mathbf{f}_I = \mathbf{s} + \mathbf{H}_{\bar{I}} \mathbf{f}_{\bar{I}},$$

where only $\mathbf{f}_I$ is unknown. Recovering $\mathbf{f}_I$ now corresponds to solving a syndrome decoding instance with code length $n' := |I|$, unchanged co-dimension $n - k$ and error weight $\delta' := |\{i \in I \mid f_i = 1\}|$, which is the number of missing one coordinates of the secret key. Note that for $n' \leq n - k$ we can solve for $\mathbf{f}_I$ via Gaussian Elimination again.

For the compact format we also slightly extend our previous approach from Sect. 3.2. Recall, that the secret key is represented as a vector of integers. We first check if there are erasure-free indices. Any of those decreases the searched error weight and the code length by one. Next, we generate a set of candidates for the remaining one positions of the secret key, i.e., whenever we find ε erasures in an index it contributes with 2^ε candidates. Any coordinate not identified as one in the first step and not appearing among the candidates must be zero, which shortens the code further. Finally this gives a syndrome decoding instance with code length $\tilde{n}$, which is the amount of distinct candidates, unchanged co-dimension $n - k$ and error weight $\tilde{\delta} := \delta - \beta$, where β denotes the number of erasure-free indices identified in the first step.

---

[4] Recall, that for the standard format the most likely candidates are given by the one coordinates of the erroneous secret key, which are only $\delta_{\tilde{\mathbf{f}}} = o(n)$.

For our simulation we generate a BIKE secret key in the respective format and simulate the bit-erasures. Next we derive the parameters of the reduced syndrome decoding instances and use the *Syndrome Decoding Estimator* tool by Esser and Bellini [13] to obtain the bit complexity of Stern's algorithm to solve the resulting instance.

In Fig. 1 we illustrate the averaged complexity (solid marks) of several experiments (transparent marks) as a function of the bit-erasure rate. Coherent to our theoretical analysis we find that attacks on the standard format are more efficient in the erasure model than attacks on the compact format. However, we also observe that for practical parameters in the compact format the point where the reduced code length $\tilde{n}$ exceeds the co-dimension (which marks the transition to the non-polynomial regime) is $p \approx 0.38$, rather than the theoretically proven $p = 0.092$. The difference stems from the fact that in our theoretical analysis we neglected the possibility of collisions between candidates from different blocks.

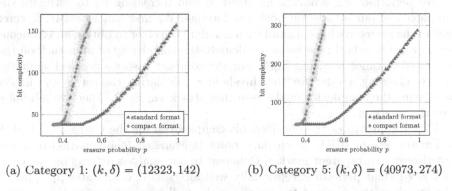

(a) Category 1: $(k, \delta) = (12323, 142)$ (b) Category 5: $(k, \delta) = (40973, 274)$

Fig. 1. Bit complexity of partial key exposure attack in the *erasure* model on the compact and standard key representations based on experiments.

The Error Model. In our practical consideration we consider asymmetric error probabilities, again let those be p_0 and p_1 as defined in Sect. 2.1.

For the compact format, contrary to what the proof of Theorem 5 suggests, we do not take the error-weight as criterion to derive a list of candidate positions, rather we use a maximum-likelihood approach. Therefore let $\tilde{I}$ with $|\tilde{I}| = \delta$ be the given set of erroneous (integer) indices. Then for every $i \in \tilde{I}$ we compute a set S_i containing those $x \in \{1, \ldots, n\}$ for which the probability $p_x := \Pr\left[x \in I \mid i \in \tilde{I}\right]$ is maximized, where I is the set of coordinates representing the true secret key. More precisely, we define a threshold τ and only include those x with $p_x > \tau$. We then compute the union of the S_i as $S = \bigcup_i S_i$. Intuitively, S contains the most likely candidates for true secret key indices. Now, we are in a similar setting to the attack on the standard format, where the set S corresponds to a set of coordinates containing more weight than $\{1, \ldots, n\} \backslash S$.

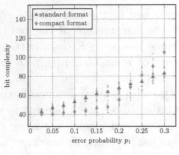
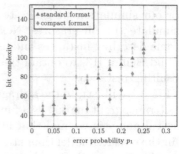

(a) Category 1: $(k, \delta) = (12323, 142)$ (b) Category 5: $(k, \delta) = (40973, 274)$

Fig. 2. Bit complexity of partial key exposure attacks on the compact and standard key representations based on experiments for $p_0 = 10^{-3}$.

We performed experiments for fixed p_0 and increasing p_1 to estimate the complexity of our attacks on both key formats. We first generate BIKE secret keys in the respective formats and then simulate the error to obtain an erroneous key. For the standard case we now calculate the complexity of an attack on the generated instance by using Eq. 2. For the compact case we proceed similarly, by first choosing a value for the threshold τ calculating the set S and finally calculating the complexity of the resulting attack via Eq. 2. Then we minimize over the choice of τ.

Figure 2 illustrates the obtained bit complexities for the Category-1 and -5 parameter sets of BIKE. Each data point is averaged (solid marks) over ten experiments (transparent marks). Coherent to our analysis attacks on the compact key format perform exceptionally well for "small" error rates $p_1 \le 0.225$. The attack on the compact format also scales well when increasing the parameters of the scheme, as shown in Fig. 2, where the break-even point is shifted to $p_1 \approx 0.3$.

We also applied the experiment for symmetric error probabilities. In this case the amount of candidates in the compact format increases drastically, which leads to an overall inferior attack on the compact format, as also reflected in Table 3.

4   Rainbow

We consider two *layers* Rainbow with parameters (q, v, o_1, o_2). Let $n := v + o_1 + o_2$, $\mathbf{x} := (x_1, \dots, x_n)$ be a vector of unknowns, and $\mathbb{F}_q[\mathbf{x}]$ be the ring of polynomials with coefficients in $\mathbb{F}_q$.

A *Rainbow central map* is a quadratic map $\mathcal{F} = (f_1, \dots, f_{o_1+o_2}) \in (\mathbb{F}_q[\mathbf{x}])^{o_1+o_2}$, where the polynomials in $(f_1, \dots, f_{o_1})$ (resp. $(f_{o_1+1}, \dots, f_{o_1+o_2})$) are of the form $\sum_{i=1}^{v} \sum_{j=1}^{v+o_1} a_{i,j} x_i x_j$ (resp. $\sum_{i=1}^{v+o_1} \sum_{j=1}^{n} a_{i,j} x_i x_j$). The sequence $(f_1, \dots, f_{o_1})$ (resp. $(f_{o_1+1}, \dots, f_{o_1+o_2})$) is called the *first layer* (resp. *second layer*) of $\mathcal{F}$.

Public and Secret Keys: The public key is a sequence of quadratic polynomials over $\mathbb{F}_q[\mathbf{x}]$ given by $(p_1, \ldots, p_{o_1+o_2}) = \mathcal{S} \circ \mathcal{F} \circ \mathcal{T}$, where $\mathcal{S} : \mathbb{F}_q^{o_1+o_2} \to \mathbb{F}_q^{o_1+o_2}$, $\mathcal{T} : \mathbb{F}_q^n \to \mathbb{F}_q^n$ are linear maps. The secret key is given by $\mathcal{S}^{-1}, \mathcal{T}^{-1}$, and $\mathcal{F}$.

In order to reduce the size of the private key, Ding et al. [11] proposed to use $\mathcal{S}$ and $\mathcal{T}$ such that for all $\mathbf{y} \in \mathbb{F}_q^{o_1+o_2}$ and all $\mathbf{x} \in \mathbb{F}_q^n$ we have

$$\mathcal{S}^{-1}(\mathbf{y}) = \underbrace{\begin{bmatrix} \mathbf{I}_{o_1} & \mathbf{S}' \\ \mathbf{O} & \mathbf{I}_{o_2} \end{bmatrix}}_{:=\mathbf{S}^{-1}} \mathbf{y} \text{ and } \mathcal{T}^{-1}(\mathbf{x}) = \underbrace{\begin{bmatrix} \mathbf{I}_v & \mathbf{T}^{(1)} & \mathbf{T}^{(4)} \\ \mathbf{O} & \mathbf{I}_{o_1} & \mathbf{T}^{(3)} \\ \mathbf{O} & \mathbf{O} & \mathbf{I}_{o_2} \end{bmatrix}}_{:=\mathbf{T}^{-1}} \mathbf{x}, \qquad (4)$$

where $\mathbf{S}, \mathbf{T}^{(3)} \in \mathbb{F}_q^{o_1 \times o_2}$, $\mathbf{T}^{(4)} \in \mathbb{F}_q^{v \times o_2}$, and $\mathbf{T}^{(1)} \in \mathbb{F}_q^{v \times o_1}$. So far none of the known attacks on Rainbow can benefit from secret matrices $\mathbf{S}$ and $\mathbf{T}$ chosen as in Eq. 4.

Remark 1. Suppose that the secret maps $\mathcal{S}$ and $\mathcal{T}$ are homogeneous, and they are represented by the matrices $\mathbf{S}$ and $\mathbf{T}$, respectively. Then, the polynomials of the public key and the central map $\mathcal{F}$ are related by the equation $\sum_{j=1}^{o_1+o_2} s_{i,j} p_j(\mathbf{x}) = f_i(\mathbf{Tx})$, for $i = 1, \ldots, o_1 + o_2$, where $\mathbf{S}^{-1} := [s_{i,j}]$.

We conclude the overview on Rainbow by stating the three suggested parameter sets, which are Rainbow-I ($q = 16, v = 36, o_1 = 32, o_2 = 32$), Rainbow-III ($q = 256, v = 68, o_1 = 32, o_2 = 48$) and Rainbow-V ($q = 256, v = 96, o_1 = 36, o_2 = 64$).

4.1 Attack Strategy

Our partial key exposure attacks exploit the structure of the maps $\mathcal{S}^{-1}$ and $\mathcal{T}^{-1}$ given in Eq. (4) and work in two steps. The first step consists in recovering the outer layer, corresponding to $\mathbf{S}', \mathbf{T}^{(3)}$ and $\mathbf{T}^{(4)}$ and the second step recovers the inner rainbow layer, i.e., the matrix $\mathbf{T}^{(1)}$.

For the first step, we derive in Proposition 1 linear relations between some coefficients of polynomials in $\mathcal{F}$ and coordinates of the matrix $\mathbf{S}'$. We then use the erroneous/ partially erased private key to find one complete row of $\mathbf{S}'$ by either solving an instance of the syndrome decoding problem (in the error model) or enumerating the minimum amount of information so that we obtain one row by solving a linear system (in the erasure model). We finally observe that this single row of $\mathbf{S}'$ is already sufficient to recover the full outer layer in polynomial time. In a second step, we recover a few columns of $\mathbf{T}^{(1)}$ from the faulty/erased key material by enumeration. Eventually, we observe that these columns together with the outer layer suffice to recover the full matrix $\mathbf{T}^{(1)}$.

Let us introduce the *vinegar part* of a homogeneous quadratic polynomial.

Definition 4 (Vinegar Part). *Let p be a homogeneous quadratic polynomial in $\mathbb{F}_q[x_1, \ldots, x_n]$. The* vinegar part *of p is the homogeneous quadratic polynomial $p^{\mathbf{v}} \in \mathbb{F}_q[x_1, \ldots, x_v]$ such that $p(x_1, \ldots, x_n) - p^{\mathbf{v}}(x_1, \ldots, x_v)$ contains no monomials of the form $x_i x_j$ where $1 \leq i, j \leq v$.*

We observe the following relation between the vinegar parts of the public polynomials and the polynomials in the hidden central map, which forms the basis of our attacks.

Proposition 1. *Let f_i be the i-th polynomial in the first layer of a Rainbow central map, that is, $i \leq o_1$. Let $(p_1, \ldots, p_{o_1+o_2})$ be a Rainbow public key, where the corresponding secret maps S and T are homogeneous, and their matrix representations are as shown in Eq. (4). Then, we have*

$$p_i^{\mathbf{v}}(x_1, \ldots, x_v) + \sum_{j=o_1+1}^{o_1+o_2} s_{i,j} \cdot p_j^{\mathbf{v}}(x_1, \ldots, x_v) = f_i^{\mathbf{v}}(x_1, \ldots, x_v),$$

where $(s_{i,1}, \ldots, s_{i,o_1+o_2})$ is the i-th row of $\mathbf{S}^{-1}$.

Proof. Given in the full version [14].

As a second key ingredient for our attacks, we show the following theorem, which allows us to recover the full Rainbow secret key in polynomial time from a single known row of $\mathbf{S}'$ and a constant number of columns from $\mathbf{T}^{(1)}$.

Theorem 6 (Rainbow Full Key Recovery). *Let (q, v, o_1, o_2) be a Rainbow parameter set, and $\mathbf{S}'$ and $\mathbf{T}$ as defined in Eq. 4. Then, (1) knowledge of any single row of $\mathbf{S}'$ is sufficient to recover the secret matrices $\mathbf{S}', \mathbf{T}^{(3)}$, and $\mathbf{T}^{(4)}$ in polynomial time in the input parameters. (2) The additional knowledge of any set of $\lceil v/o_1 \rceil$ columns of $\mathbf{T}^{(1)}$ allows to recover the full matrix $\mathbf{T}^{(1)}$ in time polynomial in the input parameters q, v, o_1, o_2.*

Proof. Given in the full version [14].

4.2 $\mathbb{F}_q$-Errors and -Erasures

All over this section we treat o_2 as the major security parameter by assuming that $o_1 = c_{o_1} o_2, v = c_v o_2, q = c_q o_2$, where c_{o_1}, c_v and c_q are considered constant. This allows us to state our results only as a function of o_2.

The Erasure Model. In the erasure model we use Proposition 1 together with the given partially erased information to derive linear equations in the unkown coordinates of a single row of $\mathbf{S}'$. We then proceed similar for $\mathbf{T}^{(1)}$ by deriving quadratic equations in the unknown coordinates of its columns.

Theorem 7 (Polynomial Erasure Attack). *Given a partially erased Rainbow secret key with $\mathbb{F}_q$-erasure probability $p = \mathcal{O}\left(\frac{1}{\sqrt{o_2}}\right)$. Then the secret key can be recovered in polynomial time with constant success probability.*

Proof. Let $\mathbf{s}_i$ denote the i-th row of $\mathbf{S}'$ from Eq. 4 and f_i^{v} be the vinegar part of polynomial f_i in the first layer. Denote by $I_{\mathbf{s}_i}$ the indices of erased coordinates of $\mathbf{s}_i$ and by $I_{f_i^{\mathrm{v}}}$ the indices of unknown coefficients in f_i^{v}. Note that there exists one i with $|I_{\mathbf{s}_i}| \le po_2$ and $|I_{f_i^{\mathrm{v}}}| \le p\frac{v(v-1)}{2}$ with constant probability. Now, by Proposition 1, every coefficient of f_i^{v} is equal to a linear combination of the entries of the $\mathbf{s}_i$. Hence, every known coefficient of f_i^{v} leads to a linear equation in the $|I_{\mathbf{s}_i}| \le p \cdot o_2$ unknown variables of $\mathbf{s}_i$. Thus, we expect to find the remaining unknown entries of $\mathbf{s}_i$ whenever

$$p \cdot o_2 \le (1-p)\frac{v(v-1)}{2} \Leftrightarrow p \le \frac{1}{1+\frac{2}{c_v v}} = \frac{1}{1+o(1)}.$$

From the found row of $\mathbf{S}'$, we recover the full matrix $\mathbf{S}'$ (Theorem 6) and can compute the polynomials $(f_1(\mathbf{Tx}), \ldots, f_{o_1}(\mathbf{Tx}))$, where the f_i's are the secret polynomials of the first layer.

We now recover the secret matrix $\mathbf{T}^{(1)}$. Let $\mathbf{t} \in \mathbb{F}_q^v$ be any column of $\mathbf{T}^{(1)}$. Then with constant probability there are less than $p \cdot v = \mathcal{O}(\sqrt{o_2})$ erasures in $\mathbf{t}$. Since $\mathbf{t}$ satisfies the quadratic equations $f_1(\mathbf{Tt}) = \cdots = f_{o_1}(\mathbf{Tt}) = 0$, where $o_1 = \mathcal{O}(o_2)$, we can solve for the $\mathcal{O}(\sqrt{o_2})$ erased coordinates in polynomial time. We repeat this process $\lceil v/o_2 \rceil = \mathcal{O}(1)$ many times and then use the obtained columns to recover $\mathbf{T}^{(1)}$ using Theorem 6. □

Note that the proof of Theorem 7 shows that we can recover $\mathbf{S}', \mathbf{T}^{(3)}$ and $\mathbf{T}^{(4)}$, corresponding to the first layer of Rainbow, even up to an erasure probability of $\frac{1}{1+o(1)}$ in polynomial time. In order to also recover $\mathbf{T}^{(1)}$ the probability bound then drops to $p = \mathcal{O}\left(\frac{1}{\sqrt{o_2}}\right)$. Note that the remaining inner layer of Rainbow forms a small instance of the unbalanced oil and vinegar (UOV) scheme [20]. This indicates that UOV is strictly less vulnerable against this kind of partial key exposure attack than Rainbow.

The Error Model. For our attack in the error model, we first show a reduction from the recovery of the secret matrices $\mathbf{S}', \mathbf{T}^{(3)}$, and $\mathbf{T}^{(4)}$ to the syndrome decoding problem. Then we study the complexity of solving the corresponding syndrome decoding instance. We give the reduction in the following lemma.

Lemma 1 (Reduction to Syndrome Decoding). *Recovering the Rainbow secret matrices $\mathbf{S}', \mathbf{T}^{(3)}$, and $\mathbf{T}^{(4)}$ from a given erroneous candidate with $\mathbb{F}_q$-error probability p can polynomially be reduced to solving an instance of the syndrome decoding problem $(\mathbf{H}, \mathbf{b}, \delta_p)$, where $\mathbf{H} \in \mathbb{F}_q^{r \times (r+o_2)}$ and $\delta_p := p(r + o_2)$ and $1 \le r \le \frac{v(v-1)}{2}$.*

Proof. Given in the full version [14].

Next in Theorem 8, we describe a polynomial-time partial key exposure attack in the error model, that uses the previous reduction.

Theorem 8. *Given an erroneous Rainbow secret key with $\mathbb{F}_q$-error probability*
$p = \mathcal{O}\left(\frac{\log o_2}{o_2}\right)$. *Then the secret key can be recovered in polynomial time with constant probability.*

Proof. Lemma 1 states that recovering any row of $\mathbf{S}'$ from the given erroneous secret matrices $\mathbf{S}'$, $\mathbf{T}^{(3)}$, and $\mathbf{T}^{(4)}$ is equivalent to solving an instance of the syndrome decoding problem $(\mathbf{H}, \mathbf{b}, \delta_p)$, where $\mathbf{H} \in \mathbb{F}_q^{r \times (r+o_2)}$, $\mathbf{b} \in \mathbb{F}_q^r$ and $\delta_p = p(r+o_2)$. In the following we set $r = o_2$, which is a valid choice since according to Lemma 1 $r \leq \frac{v(v-1)}{2} = \mathcal{O}(o_2^2)$. For this choice we find $\delta_p \leq \log(o_2)$ with constant probability.

Note that the resulting syndrome decoding instance possesses a unique solution with high probability, since the expected amount of random solutions is

$$\frac{\binom{r+o_2}{\delta_p}(q-1)^{\delta_p}}{q^{o_2}} = \frac{\binom{2o_2}{\log o_2}(q-1)^{\log o_2}}{q^{o_2}} < \frac{(2o_2)^{\log o_2}}{q^{o_2 - \log o_2}} = o(1).$$

However, the searched row of $\mathbf{S}'$ is a solution by construction. Now, by Theorem 1 we can find this unique solution in polynomial time.

Let us turn our focus to $\mathbf{T}^{(1)}$. Any column of $\mathbf{T}^{(1)}$ is error-free with probability

$$q := (1-p)^v = \left(1 - \frac{c_p \log o_2}{o_2}\right)^{c_v o_2} \xrightarrow{o_2 \to \infty} e^{-c_v c_p \log o_2} = o_2^{-c_v c_p \log e},$$

where $p = \frac{c_p \log o_2}{o_2}$. Note that the number of error-free columns is distributed binomially with parameter $o_1 = c_{o_1} o_2$ and probability q. It follows that the expected number of error-free columns is $v \cdot q = o_2^{1 - c_v c_p \log e}$, where we can ensure $v \cdot q \geq \lceil v/o_1 \rceil$ by an appropriate choice of constant c_p. Now with constant probability we have at least $v \cdot q \geq \lceil v/o_1 \rceil$ error-free columns. Finally, we iterate over any combination of $\lceil v/o_1 \rceil = \mathcal{O}(1)$ columns until the recovery via Theorem 6 yields the correct $\mathbf{T}^{(1)}$. $\qquad\square$

4.3 Practical Attacks on Rainbow

In our Rainbow bit complexity estimations we assume a field multiplication to cost $\log^2 q$ bit operations.

The Erasure Model. Our attack again splits in the two parts of recovering both layers of rainbow separately, starting with the first. Let again $\mathbf{s}_i$ denote the i-th row of $\mathbf{S}'$, and let f_i denote the i-th polynomial in the first layer of the Rainbow central map. Recall, that our strategy to recover any row $\mathbf{s}_i$ used in Theorem 7 requires to know $o_2 - k$ coordinates of the $\mathbb{F}_q$-vector representation of f_i^v, where k is the number of known coordinates of the $\mathbb{F}_q$-vector representation of $\mathbf{s}_i$.

Our (S, F)-Strategy to Recover a Row of $\mathbf{S}'$. For a fixed integer k, which is later optimized, let n_{b_i} for $i = 0, \ldots, o_1$ be the minimum amount of bits we have to enumerate of $(\mathbf{s}_i, f_i^{\mathsf{v}})$ to obtain k coordinates from $\mathbf{s}_i$ and $o_2 - k$ coefficients from f_i^{v}. For each guess, we need to solve a linear system in the $o_2 - k$ unknowns over $\mathbb{F}_q$. Finally, we need to check if the derived solution leads to the correct Rainbow private key, which requires $(v + o_1 + o_2)^3$ field multiplications (for details we refer to the full version [14]). Therefore, the amount of field multiplications to recover one row of the secret matrix $\mathbf{S}'$ is $2^{n_b} \cdot \left(o_2^3 + (v + o_1 + o_2)^3 \right)$, where $n_b = \min_i \{ n_{b_i} \}$.

Recovering $\mathbf{T}^{(1)}$ *via Partial Enumeration.* Note that after recovering the first layer Rainbow polynomials, we can recover $\mathbf{T}^{(1)}$ without any extra information in time

$$\mathcal{O}\left((v + o_1)^4 \cdot q^{v - o_1} \right),$$

using the Kipnis-Shamir attack [20]. In the case of the Rainbow-I parameter set this is already less than the complexity for the recovery of $\mathbf{S}'$. However, in the case of the Rainbow-V parameter set the Kipnis-Shamir attack becomes inefficient. Here, we make use of the given partial information to recover $\lceil v/o_1 \rceil$ columns of $\mathbf{T}^{(1)}$.

Recall that, once $\mathbf{S}'$ is recovered, we can compute the first layer Rainbow polynomials, i.e., the polynomials $g_i := (f_i \circ \mathcal{T})$ for $i = 1, \ldots, o_1$. Further, for any column $\mathbf{t}$ of $\mathbf{T}^{(1)}$ we have $g_i(\mathbf{t}) = 0$. Our attack now proceeds as follows: For an integer $k \leq o_1$, which has to be optimized, we enumerate the minimum amount of bits, namely n_b, so that we obtain all but k coordinates of one column $\mathbf{t}$ of $\mathbf{T}^{(1)}$. Then, we solve the system $g_i(\mathbf{t}) = 0$ for $i = 1, \ldots, o_1$. Overall this yields a time complexity of $q^{n_b} \cdot S$, where S corresponds to the time complexity for solving a quadratic system with k unknowns and o_1 equations over $\mathbb{F}_q$. In our estimations, we use the *MQ-Estimator* of Bellini et al. [5] to estimate S.

The resulting bit complexities of our key recovery attacks are shown in Fig. 3. For each p, we computed for ten randomly generated erased private keys the complexity of the key recovery (transparent marks), and the corresponding averaged complexity (solid marks). The attack on Category-1 parameters is dominated by our (S, F) strategy to recover the first layer, while the attack on Rainbow-V is dominated by the recovery of $\mathbf{T}^{(1)}$. We compare against naive enumeration strategies, which enumerate the least amount of erased bits to obtain one row of $\mathbf{S}'$ (Rainbow-I) or $\lceil v/o_1 \rceil$ columns of $\mathbf{T}^{(1)}$ (Rainbow-V).

Note that our strategies outperforms naive enumeration for both parameter sets and all values of p.

The Error Model. We again start with the recovery of $\mathbf{S}'$ to obtain the first layer Rainbow polynomials, after which we recover $\mathbf{T}^{(1)}$.

Recovery of $\mathbf{S}'$. Our attack in the error model uses the reduction to the syndrome decoding problem given in Lemma 1. Here we assume that every field element is represented as a sequence of $\log q$ bits, relating the bit-error probability p and

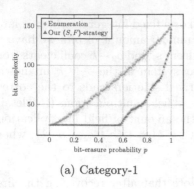
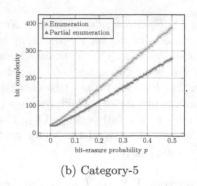

(a) Category-1   (b) Category-5

Fig. 3. Bit complexities of our partial key exposure attack in the erasure model on Rainbow.

the field error probability p_q via $p_q = 1 - (1-p)^{\log q}$. More precisely, from a given faulty Rainbow secret key with bit-error rate p we derive a syndrome decoding instance $(\mathbf{H}, \mathbf{s}, \delta)$ where $\mathbf{H} \in \mathbb{F}_q^{r \times (r+o_2)}$, $\mathbf{s} \in \mathbb{F}_q^r$, and $\delta := \left(1 - (1-p)^{\log q}\right)(r + o_2)$ with $1 \le r \le \frac{v(v-1)}{2}$ for the respective value of v of the corresponding parameter set.

To solve the resulting syndrome decoding instance we then use an ISD algorithm. For deriving the concrete bit complexity we adapted the *Syndrome Decoding Estimator* by Esser and Bellini [13] to the $\mathbb{F}_q$ case. In this adaptation we assume $\log^2 q$ bit operations per field multiplication. We finally minimize over the choice of r. In contrast to our theoretical analysis the choice of r might result in an instance with multiple solutions. As only a single of these solutions leads to the Rainbow secret key we need to reapply the ISD algorithm for each solution and finally check if it leads to the correct Rainbow private key. This check requires $(o_1 + o_2 + v)^3$ field multiplications. Now if there exist E solutions and the cost for finding all of them is T_{ISD}, then the total cost of our partial key exposure attack becomes $T = T_{\text{ISD}} + (o_1 + o_2 + v)^3 \cdot E$.

Recovering $\mathbf{T}^{(1)}$ by Partial Enumeration. Again, for the Rainbow-I parameter set we use the efficient Kipnis-Shamir modeling to recover $\mathbf{T}^{(1)}$ without using any extra information.

In the case of Rainbow-V, we use a similar strategy as in the erasure setting. Therefore, let $\mathbf{t}$ be a given erroneous column of $\mathbf{T}^{(1)}$ with ω erroneous $\mathbb{F}_q$ coordinates. We treat a random choice of $k \le o_1$ of the coordinates of $\mathbf{t}$ as unknowns, and assume that among these k coordinates are δ faulty entries. Then, among the remaining $v - k$ coordinates we enumerate all possible choices for $\omega - \delta$ errors. For each choice of k unknowns and every guess for the remaining $\omega - \delta$ errors, we then solve the system $g_i(\mathbf{t}) = 0$ for $i = 1, \ldots, o_1$, where g_i are the already recovered first layer Rainbow polynomials. The time complexity then amounts to

$$\frac{\binom{v}{\omega}}{\binom{k}{\delta}\binom{v-k}{\omega-\delta}}\left(\frac{(v-k)\log q}{c}\right)\cdot\mathcal{S},$$

where c is the maximum number of occurred bit errors over any choice of $\omega - \delta$ of the ω faulty $\mathbb{F}_q$ coordinates of $\mathbf{t}$. Further, $\mathcal{S}$ is the complexity to solve the quadratic system over $\mathbb{F}_q$. We repeat this strategy for each column for increasing values of c, to exploit the variance of the error.

In Fig. 4 we plot the computed bit complexity of our attacks for Rainbow-I and Rainbow-V parameters. Note that in the case of Rainbow-V the complexity of computing $\mathbf{T}^{(1)}$ dominates, while for Rainbow-I the recovery of $\mathbf{S}'$ is more costly. For comparison we also give the complexity of a naive enumeration of the error on the initial row of $\mathbf{S}'$ (Rainbow-I) and the complexity of a naive enumeration of the error on $\lceil v/o_1 \rceil$ columns of $\mathbf{T}^{(1)}$ (Rainbow-V). For Rainbow-V we sampled for each p twenty randomly generated erroneous private keys and computed the complexity of the key recovery (transparent marks), and the corresponding averaged complexity (solid marks). In the case of Rainbow-I we used the expected error weight to compute the bit complexity.

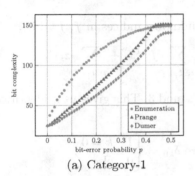

(a) Category-1

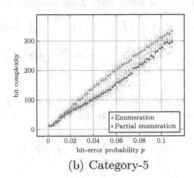

(b) Category-5

Fig. 4. Bit complexity of our key recovery attacks on Rainbow in the error model.

5   NTRU

Let n be an integer, $q > 3$ a prime number, and let the ternary field $\mathbb{F}_3$ be represented by the elements $\{-1, 0, 1\}$. We define the ring $R_q := \mathbb{F}_q[x]/\langle x^n - 1\rangle$. During this section, we identify polynomials $v = \sum_{i=0}^{n-1} v_i x^i \in R_q$ with their coefficient vector $\mathbf{v} = (v_{n-1}, v_{n-2}, \ldots, v_0)^{\mathrm{T}}$.

In NTRU, the secret key is given by a polynomial $f \in R_q \cap R_3$ that is invertible in R_q and in R_3. A public $h \in R_q$ associated with f is given by $h = f^{-1} \cdot g \bmod q$, where $g \in R_q \cap R_3$. For efficiency reasons the current NTRU NIST submission [8] stores both f and f_3^{-1} as the private key. Therefore, we refer to (f, f^{-1}) as the

NTRU private key, where we drop for convenience the subscript 3 of f_3^{-1}. Note that an NTRU private key fulfills the two equations

$$f \cdot h = g \bmod q \text{ and } f \cdot f^{-1} = 1 \bmod 3.$$

5.1 $\mathbb{F}_q$-Errors and -Erasures

The results of this section heavily exploit the key redundancy from the second equation $f \cdot f^{-1} = 1 \bmod 3$. We first show how to recover in polynomial time $\mathcal{O}(\sqrt{n})$ erasures in *random* positions, and second that in the case of *consecutive* positions we can even recover $n/4$ erasures.

For the error setting, an application of Theorem 1 shows how to correct $\mathcal{O}(\sqrt{\log n})$ errors.

The Erasure Model. Let us start with a polynomial-time attack in the erasure model that exploits the second key equation, i.e., $f \cdot f^{-1} = 1 \bmod 3$.

Theorem 9. *Given a partially erased NTRU secret key* $(\tilde{f}, \tilde{f}^{-1})$ *with* $\mathbb{F}_q$-*erasure probability* $p = \frac{1}{\sqrt{2n}}$. *Then the secret key* $(f, f^{-1}) \in R_q \times R_3$ *can be recovered in polynomial time with high success probability.*

Proof. Let $I_f, I_{f^{-1}} \subset \{1, \ldots, n\}$ denote the unknown indices in f, f^{-1}, i.e.,

$$f = \sum_{i \notin I_f} f_i x^i + \sum_{i \in I_f} y_i x^i \text{ and } f^{-1} = \sum_{i \notin I_{f^{-1}}} f_i^{-1} x^i + \sum_{i \in I_{f^{-1}}} z_i x^i.$$

Let us use the secret key equation $f \cdot f^{-1} = 1 \bmod 3$. This gives us n identities, where the k-th identity is

$$\sum_{i+j=k \bmod n} f_i \cdot f_j^{-1} = \delta_{k0}, \text{ where } \delta_{k0} = \begin{cases} 1 & k = 0 \\ 0 & \text{else} \end{cases}.$$

Let X_k be an indicator variable that takes value 1 iff the k-th identity is linear in the variables y, z. Notice that for any (i, j) with $i + j = k \bmod n$ we obtain a quadratic term $y_i z_j$ with probability $p^2 = \frac{1}{2n}$. A union bound shows that we obtain for any (i, j) a quadratic term with probability at most $np^2 = \frac{1}{2}$. Thus, $\mathbf{E}[X_k] \geq \frac{1}{2}$. Let $X = X_0 + \ldots + X_{n-1}$ denote the number of linear equations. Then by linearity of expectation $\mathbf{E}[X] \geq \frac{n}{2}$.

Any secret key coefficient is unknown with probability p. Thus, we have an expected number of $2np = \sqrt{2n}$ unknowns. An application of Markov's equality shows that the number of linear equations exceeds the number of unknowns with high probability. Therefore, we can solve the resulting system of linear equations in time polynomial in n, thereby recovering all secret key coefficients. $\square$

Remark 2. Note that the expected number of linear equations $\mathbf{E}[X] \geq n(1-np^2)$ drops to 0 when $p = \frac{1}{\sqrt{n}}$. This shows that our partial key exposure attack from Theorem 9 does not extend to larger error rates, even when we do not restrict to polynomial time.

Consecutive Erasure Attack. In the following, instead of having coefficients of f and f^{-1} erased in random positions, we assume that the erasures appear in consecutive positions. Surprisingly, in this case the erasure rate for a polynomial-time attack increases significantly. While Theorem 9 allows on expectation $2np = \sqrt{2n}$ erasures, the following theorem can handle $n/4$ erasures.

Theorem 10. *Let $(\tilde{f}, \tilde{f}^{-1})$ be a partially erased NTRU secret key having $n/4$ $\mathbb{F}_q$-erasures in (cyclically) consecutive positions of both $\tilde{f}$ and $\tilde{f}^{-1}$. Then the secret key $(f, f^{-1}) \in R_q \times R_3$ can be recovered in polynomial time.*

Proof. We assume without loss of generality that the erasures are in position $0, \ldots, \frac{n}{4} - 1$, i.e., we obtain the coefficients of f and f^{-1} in positions $\frac{n}{4}, \ldots, n-1$. By cyclicity, the following argument extends to all other (cyclically) consecutive positions. We have

$$f = \sum_{i=0}^{n/4-1} y_i x^i + \sum_{i=n/4}^{n-1} f_i x^i \text{ and } f^{-1} = \sum_{j=0}^{n/4-1} z_j x^j + \sum_{j=n/4}^{n-1} f_j^{-1} x^j.$$

The key identity $f \cdot f^{-1} = 1 \bmod 3$ gives n equations, where the k-th equation is

$$\sum_{i+j=k \bmod n} f_i f_j^{-1} = \delta_{k0} \text{ with } \delta_{k0} = \begin{cases} 1 & k = 0 \\ 0 & \text{else} \end{cases}.$$

Notice that we obtain quadratic terms $y_i z_j$ only if $0 \leq i + j \leq 2(\frac{n}{4} - 1)$. Thus, all equations with $2(\frac{n}{4} - 1) < k < n$ are linear. These are $n - (\frac{n}{2} - 2) > n/2$ linear equations. Thus, the number of linear equations exceeds the amount $\frac{n}{2}$ of unknowns y_i, z_j. Solving for the unknowns recovers the secret key in time polynomial in n. $\qquad\square$

Theorem 10 shows that we can recover $1/4$ of the secret key bits, whenever the unknowns are in consecutive positions. The following remark shows that we can recover even up to a $1/3$-fraction if certain (unrealistic) conditions are met.

Remark 3. Assume that $3|n$, and we obtain erasures y_i, z_j in positions $i, j \in \{0, 3, 6, \ldots, n-3\}$. Then for all $k = i + j$ we have $3|k$. Thus, we obtain quadratic terms only in the k-th equation with $k = 0 \bmod 3$. This in turn gives us $n - \frac{n}{3} = \frac{2}{3}n$ linear equations and also $\frac{2}{3}n$ unknowns.

The Error Model. Next we give a polynomial-time attack in the error model, again exploiting the second key equation $f \cdot f^{-1} = 1 \bmod 3$.

Theorem 11. *Let $(\tilde{f}, \tilde{f}^{-1})$ be an erroneous NTRU secret key with $\mathbb{F}_q$-error probability $p = \mathcal{O}\left(\frac{\sqrt{\log n}}{n}\right)$. Then the secret key (f, f^{-1}) can be recovered in polynomial time with high success probability.*

Proof. Given in the full version [14].

5.2   Practical Attacks on NTRU

In Sect. 5.1, we exploited the key equation $f \cdot f^{-1} = 1 \bmod 3$ to recover the secret key in polynomial time. However, Remark 2 already indicates limitations for scaling our strategy to larger error rates. Hence, in our practical attacks we devise a new strategy based on the key equation $h \cdot f = g$ instead. First we derive an LWE instance from the given partially erased or erroneous key material, whose complexity is then estimated using the LWE estimator [3] in combination with the asymptotic lattice reduction exponent of 0.3496 obtained in [2]. Second, we give a combinatorial attack that achieves the best complexities for a compact key representation.

Key Formats. The NTRU documentation specifies two key formats, a *packed* and an *unpacked* format. The unpacked format stores each coefficient of a ternary polynomial via two bits. Therefore the values 0, 1 and −1 are represented in binary as 00, 01 and 10. This key format is used whenever the secret key is accessed, e.g., during decryption. The packed format is used to store the secret key in the meantime, by packing five ternary coefficients, with total information $5 \log 3 \approx 7.92$ bits, into 8 bits. Let us detail how we translate bit to field errors/erasures for the different key formats.

Unpacked Format. For the unpacked format we observe that a single bit-erasure of the form ?1 and 1?, where "?" denotes an erased bit can directly be recovered to 01 and 10 coefficients. For every coefficient the probability of a single bit-erasure is $2p(1 - p)$, while the probability for two bit-erasures is p^2. Since the secret key is drawn randomly from all ternary polynomials, the probability that we can directly recover a single-bit affected coefficient is $1/3$.[5] Thus, we can reduce the total amount of expected erasure-affected $\mathbb{F}_3$-coefficients from $(2p - p^2)n$ to

$$(2p - p^2)n - \frac{2p(1 - p)n}{3} = \frac{np}{3}(4 - p),$$

or put differently obtain a field-erasure probability of $\frac{p}{3}(4 - p)$.

For the translation of bit-*errors* to field-*errors* we proceed similar, treating a coefficient as erroneous as long as any bit in its binary representation is error-prone. Hence, a bit-error probability of p results in a field error probability of $1 - (1 - p)^2 = 2p - p^2$.

Packed Format. For the packed format an erased or erroneous bit in its binary representation might affect multiple coefficients of the polynomial in unpacked form. We determine the field-error and -erasure rates caused by a certain bit-error/-erasure by an exhaustive enumeration of all possibilities. We start with the erasure translation. We enumerate all possible 3^5 values for an 8-bit block in packed representation and all possible positions for i bit-erasures for $i =$

---

[5] The secret key coefficient can take the values 01, 10 and 00 while only the two (out of 6) possible single-bit erasures ?1 and 1? can be recovered directly.

$1, \ldots, 8$, to derive the proportion of i bit-erasures leading to j field-erasures. Essentially, for every combination of value and i erasure positions, we enumerate all possibilities for these i bits and transform for each guess to unpacked form. This results in five ternary coefficients. Now, those coefficients which are equal among all guesses are known, while those differing among at least two guesses are treated as erased. For a table with the derived proportions we refer to the full version of this work [14].

For the bit- to field- *error* translation we proceed similar by enumerating all possible value-error pairs and counting the errors caused in the unpacked representation. We give a table with the obtained frequencies in the full version of this work [14].

Practical Attack in the Erasure Model. For our attack in the erasure model we derive a dimension-reduced small-secret LWE instance from the partially erased key material. Let $\tilde{f}$ be a partially erased version of f, where I_f denotes the set of erased coefficients. The key equation gives $h \cdot f = g$ or equivalently $\mathbf{Hf} = \mathbf{g}$, where $\mathbf{H}$ is the multiplication matrix of h and $\mathbf{f}, \mathbf{g}$ are the coefficient vectors of f and g. By denoting the columns of $\mathbf{H}$ as $\mathbf{h}_i$, we obtain

$$\mathbf{Hf} = \mathbf{g} \Leftrightarrow \sum_{i=1}^{n} \mathbf{h}_i f_i = \mathbf{g} \Leftrightarrow \sum_{i \in I_f} \mathbf{h}_i f_i - \mathbf{g} = - \sum_{i \notin I_f} \mathbf{h}_i f_i.$$

By letting $\widehat{\mathbf{H}}$ denote the matrix containing the columns $\mathbf{H}$ indexed by I_f, and analogously $\widehat{\mathbf{f}}$ denote the vector containing the coordinates of $\mathbf{f}$ indexed by I_f, we obtain $\widehat{\mathbf{H}}\widehat{\mathbf{f}} - \mathbf{g} = - \sum_{i \notin I_f} \mathbf{h}_i f_i$. Note that since the right hand side of the equation is known and $\mathbf{g}$ is small by definition this yields an LWE instance with secret $\widehat{\mathbf{f}}$ of dimension $|I_f|$, which is the number of erased $\mathbb{F}_q$ coefficients.

To determine the bit complexity of the outlined attack for various erasure probabilities p, we proceed as follows. First, we relate the bit-erasure probability p to a field-erasure probability. For the unpacked format, as outlined in Sect. 5.2, we simply use the field-erasure probability $\frac{p}{3}(4 - p)$. For the packed format we computed by exhaustive enumeration how to translate a certain number of bit-erasures in an 8-bit block to a certain number of field-erasures. For a table with the computed frequencies see the full version of this work [14].

We now first calculate the expected number N_i of blocks out of the total $n/5$ affected by i bit-erasures, $i = 1, \ldots, 8$. Then we compute the number of expected field-erasures as $\sum_i N_i E_i$, where E_i is the expected number of field erasures observed in a block with i bit erasures.

From there we use the LWE estimator to determine the bit complexity for solving the derived LWE instances. Our results for both formats are depicted in Fig. 5. The vertical dashed line represents the erasure probability up to which our polynomial time attacks from Sect. 5.1 can be applied.

Practical Attack in the Error Model. Our practical attack in the error model is quite similar to the attack in erasure model. Let us first outline the

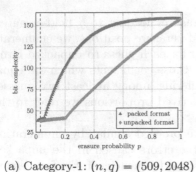
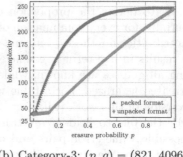

(a) Category-1: $(n, q) = (509, 2048)$ (b) Category-3: $(n, q) = (821, 4096)$

Fig. 5. Bit complexity of our partial key exposure attack in the erasure model on NTRU.

attack for a symmetric error, which does not exploit any dimension reduction. In the error setting, we obtain a noisy version $\tilde{f} = f + e$ of f. Similar to before we have

$$\mathbf{H}\tilde{\mathbf{f}} = \mathbf{He} + \mathbf{Hf} = \mathbf{He} + \mathbf{g}, \tag{5}$$

which defines an LWE instance of dimension n and secret $\mathbf{e}$, where $\mathbf{e}$ has expected $p_q \cdot n$ entries different from zero, where p_q is the field-error probability.

To derive the bit complexity of recovering the secret key for a given bit-error probability p we again first relate p to the field-error probability p_q. Then we use the LWE estimator to estimate the hardness of the above LWE instance.

For the unpacked format we have $p_q = 2p - p^2$ (compare to Sect. 5.2). For the packed format we again compute the number N_i of expected 8-bit blocks affected by $i = 1, \ldots, 8$ errors. Then we derive the number of field-errors as $\sum_i N_i E_i$, where E_i is the expected number of field-errors caused by i bit-errors.

In Fig. 6 we plot the derived bit-complexity as a function of the error-probability p. Since already a few errors in packed representation often lead to multiple errors in the unpacked form, we see a steep incline for our attack in packed form. Therefore we give a second, combinatorial approach based on a meet-in-the-middle technique.

Combinatorial Approach. Imagine we guess the first $\ell < n$ coordinates of $\mathbf{g}$ in Eq. 5. This gives an equation of the form $\mathbf{H}_\ell(\tilde{\mathbf{f}} - \mathbf{e}) = \mathbf{g}_\ell$, where $\mathbf{H}_\ell$ is the matrix formed by the first ℓ rows of $\mathbf{H}$ and analogously $\mathbf{g}_\ell$ contains the first ℓ coordinates of $\mathbf{g}$.

From here we perform a meet-in-the-middle attack on $\mathbf{e}$. Therefore let $\mathbf{e} = (\mathbf{e}_1, \mathbf{e}_2) \in \mathbb{F}_3^{n/2} \times \mathbb{F}_3^{n/2}$, $\tilde{\mathbf{f}} = (\tilde{\mathbf{f}}_1, \tilde{\mathbf{f}}_2) \in \mathbb{F}_3^{n/2} \times \mathbb{F}_3^{n/2}$ and $\mathbf{H}_\ell = (\mathbf{H}_1 \mid \mathbf{H}_2)$, which gives

$$\mathbf{H}_1(\tilde{\mathbf{f}}_1 - \mathbf{e}_1) = \mathbf{g}_\ell - \mathbf{H}_2(\tilde{\mathbf{f}}_2 - \mathbf{e}_2).$$

Now we enumerate all possible values for $\mathbf{e}_1$ (*resp.* $\mathbf{e}_2$) and store the corresponding value of the right-hand side (*resp.* left-hand side) of the above equation in a

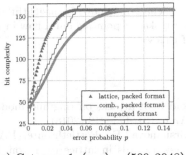
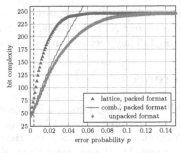

(a) Category-1: $(n, q) = (509, 2048)$ (b) Category-3: $(n, q) = (821, 4096)$

Fig. 6. Bit complexity of key recovery on NTRU in the symmetric error model.

list L_1 (*resp.* L_2). Then we search between those lists for equal elements, where by construction one matching pair reveals $\mathbf{e} = (\mathbf{e}_1, \mathbf{e}_2)$.

Note that the expected amount of matching pairs is $L := \frac{|L_1| \cdot |L_2|}{q^\ell}$ and that the matching can be performed in time $\mathcal{O}(\max\{|L|, |L_1|, |L_2|\})$. The list construction requires per element (after the first) roughly 2ℓ field multiplications, if a gray-code style enumeration for $\mathbf{e}_1$ and $\mathbf{e}_2$ is chosen. Moreover to check if an element of $\mathbf{x} \in L$ reveals the searched error we need to compute $\mathbf{H}_\ell \mathbf{x}$, which costs ℓn field multiplications. Thus by accounting for a single field multiplication $\log^2 q$ bit operations, and observing that $|L_1| = |L_2|$, we find a bit complexity of

$$\mathcal{O}\big(\max\{\ell n \cdot |L|, \ell \cdot |L_1|\} \cdot 3^\ell \log^2 q\big).$$

In the packed form, we enumerate the error first[6], subtract it from the respective part of the key material and then convert it to unpacked form. Thus, more precisely, the lists contain $\mathbf{H}_1 \cdot \mathrm{unpack}(\tilde{\mathbf{f}}_1 - \mathbf{e}_1)$ and $\mathbf{g}_\ell - \mathbf{H}_2 \cdot \mathrm{unpack}(\tilde{\mathbf{f}}_2 - \mathbf{e}_2)$ respectively. This is possible since every 8-bit block of the packed form can be converted to unpacked form independently.

In the packed form the bit length of $\tilde{\mathbf{f}}$ is roughly $\frac{8n}{5}$, hence the expected Hamming weight of the binary representation of $\mathbf{e}$ is $\frac{8np}{5}$. Thus, in expectation we have $|L_1| = |L_2| = \mathcal{O}\big(\binom{4n/5}{4np/5}\big)$.

This combinatorial attack yields an improved key recovery attack on the packed format (see Fig. 6), because it benefits from the small bit length of $\tilde{\mathbf{f}}$ in packed representation.

In [21] May gives further advanced combinatorial attacks extending the here presented meet-in-the-middle by a search-tree approach and the representation technique. We leave it as an open research task to determine the gain of those advancements in our settings.

An improved practical attack when facing asymmetric error probabilities is given in the full version of this work [14].

---

[6] The factor 3^ℓ can be slightly improved by guessing zero coordinates of $\mathbf{g}$ instead of enumerating the first ℓ coordinates.

Acknowledgments. The authors want to thank Elena Kirshanova for insightful discussions on our NTRU attacks, and Simona Samardjiska for pointing out a flaw in the Rainbow full key recovery in an earlier version of this work.

References

1. Albrecht, M.R., Deo, A., Paterson, K.G.: Cold boot attacks on ring and module LWE keys under the NTT. Cryptol. ePrint Arch. (3), 173–213 (2018)
2. Albrecht, M.R., Ducas, L., Herold, G., Kirshanova, E., Postlethwaite, E.W., Stevens, M.: The general Sieve Kernel and new records in lattice reduction. In: Ishai, Y., Rijmen, V. (eds.) EUROCRYPT 2019. LNCS, vol. 11477, pp. 717–746. Springer, Cham (2019). https://doi.org/10.1007/978-3-030-17656-3_25
3. Albrecht, M.R., Player, R., Scott, S.: On the concrete hardness of learning with errors. J. Math. Cryptol. **9**(3), 169–203 (2015)
4. Aragon, N., et al.: BIKE: bit flipping key encapsulation (2020)
5. Bellini, E., Makarim, R.H., Sanna, C., Verbel, J.: An estimator for the hardness of the MQ problem. Cryptology ePrint Archive, Paper 2022/708 (2022). https://eprint.iacr.org/2022/708
6. Blömer, J., May, A.: New partial key exposure attacks on RSA. In: Boneh, D. (ed.) CRYPTO 2003. LNCS, vol. 2729, pp. 27–43. Springer, Heidelberg (2003). https://doi.org/10.1007/978-3-540-45146-4_2
7. Boneh, D., Durfee, G., Frankel, Y.: An attack on RSA given a small fraction of the private key bits. In: Ohta, K., Pei, D. (eds.) ASIACRYPT 1998. LNCS, vol. 1514, pp. 25–34. Springer, Heidelberg (1998). https://doi.org/10.1007/3-540-49649-1_3
8. Chen, C., et al.: NTRU algorithm specifications and supporting documentation (2019). https://ntru.org/f/ntru-20190330.pdf
9. Coppersmith, D.: Small solutions to polynomial equations, and low exponent RSA vulnerabilities. J. Cryptol. **10**(4), 233–260 (1997)
10. Dachman-Soled, D., Ducas, L., Gong, H., Rossi, M.: LWE with side information: attacks and concrete security estimation. In: Micciancio, D., Ristenpart, T. (eds.) CRYPTO 2020. LNCS, vol. 12171, pp. 329–358. Springer, Cham (2020). https://doi.org/10.1007/978-3-030-56880-1_12
11. Ding, J., Chen, M.S., Petzoldt, A., Schmidt, D., Yang, B.Y.: Rainbow. NIST CSRC (2020). https://csrc.nist.gov/Projects/post-quantum-cryptography/round-3-submissions
12. Espitau, T., Fouque, P.A., Gérard, B., Tibouchi, M.: Side-channel attacks on BLISS lattice-based signatures: exploiting branch tracing against strongswan and electromagnetic emanations in microcontrollers. In: Proceedings of the 2017 ACM SIGSAC Conference on Computer and Communications Security, pp. 1857–1874 (2017)
13. Esser, A., Bellini, E.: Syndrome decoding estimator. In: Hanaoka, G., Shikata, J., Watanabe, Y. (eds.) PKC 2022. LNCS, vol. 13177, pp. 112–141. Springer, Heidelberg (2022). https://doi.org/10.1007/978-3-030-97121-2_5
14. Esser, A., May, A., Verbel, J., Wen, W.: Partial key exposure attacks on BIKE, Rainbow and NTRU. Cryptology ePrint Archive (2022)
15. Goldwasser, S., Kalai, Y.T., Peikert, C., Vaikuntanathan, V.: Robustness of the learning with errors assumption. In: ICS, pp. 230–240. Tsinghua University Press, Beijing (2010)
16. Halderman, J.A., et al.: Lest we remember: cold-boot attacks on encryption keys. Commun. ACM **52**(5), 91–98 (2009)

17. Henecka, W., May, A., Meurer, A.: Correcting errors in RSA private keys. In: Rabin, T. (ed.) CRYPTO 2010. LNCS, vol. 6223, pp. 351–369. Springer, Heidelberg (2010). https://doi.org/10.1007/978-3-642-14623-7_19
18. Heninger, N., Shacham, H.: Reconstructing RSA private keys from random key bits. In: Halevi, S. (ed.) CRYPTO 2009. LNCS, vol. 5677, pp. 1–17. Springer, Heidelberg (2009). https://doi.org/10.1007/978-3-642-03356-8_1
19. Horlemann, A., Puchinger, S., Renner, J., Schamberger, T., Wachter-Zeh, A.: Information-set decoding with hints. In: Wachter-Zeh, A., Bartz, H., Liva, G. (eds.) CBCrypto 2021. LNCS, vol. 13150, pp. 60–83. Springer, Heidelberg (2021). https://doi.org/10.1007/978-3-030-98365-9_4
20. Kipnis, A., Patarin, J., Goubin, L.: Unbalanced oil and vinegar signature schemes. In: Stern, J. (ed.) EUROCRYPT 1999. LNCS, vol. 1592, pp. 206–222. Springer, Heidelberg (1999). https://doi.org/10.1007/3-540-48910-X_15
21. May, A.: How to meet ternary LWE keys. In: Malkin, T., Peikert, C. (eds.) CRYPTO 2021. LNCS, vol. 12826, pp. 701–731. Springer, Cham (2021). https://doi.org/10.1007/978-3-030-84245-1_24
22. Melchor, C.A., et al.: Hamming quasi-cyclic (HQC) (2020)
23. Paterson, K.G., Polychroniadou, A., Sibborn, D.L.: A coding-theoretic approach to recovering noisy RSA keys. In: Wang, X., Sako, K. (eds.) ASIACRYPT 2012. LNCS, vol. 7658, pp. 386–403. Springer, Heidelberg (2012). https://doi.org/10.1007/978-3-642-34961-4_24
24. Paterson, K.G., Villanueva-Polanco, R.: Cold boot attacks on NTRU. In: Patra, A., Smart, N.P. (eds.) INDOCRYPT 2017. LNCS, vol. 10698, pp. 107–125. Springer, Cham (2017). https://doi.org/10.1007/978-3-319-71667-1_6
25. Polanco, R.V.: Cold boot attacks on post-quantum schemes. Ph.D. thesis, Royal Holloway. University of London (2019)
26. Prange, E.: The use of information sets in decoding cyclic codes. IRE Trans. Inf. Theory 8(5), 5–9 (1962)
27. Villanueva-Polanco, R.: Cold boot attacks on bliss. In: Schwabe, P., Thériault, N. (eds.) LATINCRYPT 2019. LNCS, vol. 11774, pp. 40–61. Springer, Cham (2019). https://doi.org/10.1007/978-3-030-30530-7_3
28. Villanueva-Polanco, R.: Cold boot attacks on LUOV. Appl. Sci. 10(12), 4106 (2020). http://orcid.org/10.3390/app10124106

Improving Support-Minors Rank Attacks: Applications to GeMSS and Rainbow

John Baena[1], Pierre Briaud[2,3](✉), Daniel Cabarcas[1], Ray Perlner[4], Daniel Smith-Tone[4,5], and Javier Verbel[6]

[1] Universidad Nacional de Colombia, Bogotá, Colombia
[2] Sorbonne Universités, UPMC Univ Paris 06, Paris, France
[3] Inria, Team COSMIQ, Paris, France
`pierre.briaud@inria.fr`
[4] National Institute of Standards and Technology, Gaithersburg, USA
[5] University of Louisville, Louisville, USA
[6] Technology Innovation Institute, Abu Dhabi, UAE

Abstract. The Support-Minors (SM) method has opened new routes to attack multivariate schemes with rank properties that were previously impossible to exploit, as shown by the recent attacks of [9,40] on the Round 3 NIST candidates GeMSS and Rainbow respectively. In this paper, we study this SM approach more in depth and we propose a greatly improved attack on GeMSS based on this Support-Minors method. Even though GeMSS was already affected by [40], our attack affects it even more and makes it completely unfeasible to repair the scheme by simply increasing the size of its parameters or even applying the recent projection technique from [36] whose purpose was to make GeMSS immune to [40]. For instance, our attack on the GeMSS128 parameter set has estimated time complexity 2^{72}, and repairing the scheme by applying [36] would result in a signature with slower signing time by an impractical factor of 2^{14}. Another contribution is to suggest optimizations that can reduce memory access costs for an XL strategy on a large SM system using the Block-Wiedemann algorithm as subroutine when these costs are a concern. In a memory cost model based on [7], we show that the rectangular MinRank attack from [9] may indeed reduce the security for all Round 3 Rainbow parameter sets below their targeted security strengths, contradicting the lower bound claimed by [41] using the same memory cost model.

Keywords: Support-Minors · GeMSS · Rainbow · multivariate cryptography

1 Introduction

The MinRank problem 1 introduced in [12] has shown to be essential in establishing the security of several post-quantum cryptosystems, in particular multivariate schemes (MPKCs). Many MPKCs are indeed either directly based on the hardness of MinRank [20] or strongly related to it, such as [23,37,39].

© International Association for Cryptologic Research 2022
Y. Dodis and T. Shrimpton (Eds.): CRYPTO 2022, LNCS 13509, pp. 376–405, 2022.
https://doi.org/10.1007/978-3-031-15982-4_13

Problem 1. (MinRank problem) *Given $d \in \mathbb{N}$, N matrices $\boldsymbol{M}_1, \ldots, \boldsymbol{M}_N \in$ $\mathbb{F}_q^{n_r \times n_c}$, find field elements $x_1, x_2, \ldots, x_N \in \mathbb{F}_q$, not all zero, such that*

$$rank\left(\sum_{i=1}^{N} x_i \boldsymbol{M}_i\right) \leq d.$$

The currently most high profile application of MinRank is the cryptanalysis of Rainbow [22], which was selected as a finalist to the NIST post-quantum standardization process. Rainbow is a multilayer variant of the well-known UOV signature scheme, and a key-recovery attack on the scheme can be performed by solving one of several particular MinRank instances [9,10,28]. This problem also shows up in the analysis of other types of MPKCs, namely those relying on the so-called *big-field* construction by using a field extension $\mathbb{F}_{q^n}$ over $\mathbb{F}_q$. This is the case of the historical proposals C* [33] and HFE [37], but also more recently of the HFEv- schemes [38] GeMSS [13] and Gui [21]. In this context, a difference with the original formulation from Problem 1 is that the coefficients x_i's or the entries of the $\boldsymbol{M}_i$'s may belong to the extension field $\mathbb{F}_{q^n}$.

Support-Minors is a method proposed by Bardet *et al.* [5] to reduce the Min-Rank problem to the problem of solving a system of bilinear equations. This algebraic modeling is in particular the crux of the recent attacks on MPKCs and rank-based cryptosystems [4,5,9,40]. When the corresponding MinRank instance has a unique solution, which was the case in rank-based cryptography or Rainbow [5,9], this system can be solved using a variant of the XL algorithm [19]. In particular, this approach benefits from the extreme sparsity of the resulting linear system as one can use the Block-Wiedemann algorithm [17]. However, the situation is quite different for big-field schemes, since there are naturally n solutions coming from the big-field structure. In particular, using the XL algorithm proposed in [5] neither directly yields a solution nor reduces the problem to a simpler one. Of course, it is still possible to use a general purpose Gröbner basis algorithm, but this approach can be inefficient and one faces the challenging task of establishing the solving degree to precisely estimate its complexity. In particular, the authors of [40] conjectured from experiments that the *first degree fall* d_{ff} of their Support-Minors attack on GeMSS was equal to 3. Then, based on the common heuristic that the solving degree is close to d_{ff}, they derive the complexity given in Column "support minors modeling" from [40, Table 1]. However, one may wonder if such a small value for d_{ff} is not only due to the small scale of their experiments. Moreover, the assumption that d_{ff} coincides with the solving degree remains a conjecture. It is known this is not true in general, see for example [6], and if this solving degree were higher than 3 in the case of GeMSS, the complexity of the attack in [40] would dramatically change.

Also, even when there is justification for the time complexity of an attack, there remains the question of how to measure the complexity of memory intensive cryptanalytic attacks, an issue which has been a major point of discussion throughout the NIST PQC competition. In an effort to obtain more efficient parameters while still claiming high security, a number of submitters [1,7,15,32] have introduced cost models which treat memory intensive attacks as being more expensive than indicated by time complexity estimates using the more common Random Access Machine model. The question of the effect of memory access on the cost of MinRank attacks in particular, has been brought to the fore recently. In response to the rectangular MinRank attack [9], the Rainbow team put forward a statement [41] arguing that even though this attack reduces the security of Rainbow relative to prior cryptanalysis, it does not bring any of the third round Rainbow parameters below their targeted security levels if memory costs are properly accounted for. This argument in particular states that, although the rectangular MinRank attack can use the Wiedemann algorithm and therefore does not require as much memory as attacks requiring Gröbner basis algorithms like F4 [26] and F5 [27], its complexity is dominated by a large number of random access queries to a memory, which is nonetheless fairly large.

Table 1. Time complexity of our attack (Improved SM, $\log_2(\#\text{gates})$) in comparison to [40].

Scheme	Minors [40]	SM (conjectural) [40]	Improved SM
GeMSS128	139	118	72
BlueGeMSS128	119	99	65
RedGeMSS128	86	72	49
GeMSS192	154	120	75
BlueGeMSS192	132	101	67
RedGeMSS192	95	75	51
GeMSS256	166	121	75
BlueGeMSS256	141	103	68
RedGeMSS256	101	76	52

Contributions. As a first contribution, we provide solid ground to understand the Gröbner basis computation on the Support-Minors system for HFEv- and we significantly speed up the attack in [40] which used minors modeling [25]. We provide a necessary and sufficient condition for solving the SM system at degree 2, under mild assumptions. In the case of GeMSS, we show that it can always be solved at degree 2. This material allows us to give a precise complexity formula for the Support-Minors attack on GeMSS, which is also considerably smaller than the conjectured one in [40], which relied on the aforementioned degree fall assumption (see Column "SM (conjectural) [40]" in Table 1). In particular, with our attack we can also clearly break the proposed parameters for pHFEv-, which were an attempt by [36] to repair GeMSS in the aftermath of the attacks from [40]. Also, it makes it completely unfeasible to repair GeMSS by simply increasing the size of its parameters or even applying the projection technique without becoming impractical. These improvements come from some technical observations which are described more thoroughly throughout the paper. We show that by direct linearization on the Support-Minors equations, one can already obtain linear equations. Then, one can derive a quadratic system in only $n - 1$ variables by substitution of these linear polynomials in the original system, and our attack proceeds by solving this second system. For the sake of completeness, we also provide an estimate for the memory complexity. All in all, since the time complexity of our attack on GeMSS is much reduced, the memory access cost also remains limited and it is not an obstacle to perform the attack. In particular, we have been able to perform experiments in the Magma Computer Algebra System [11] for the main step of our attack—linearization on the SM equations—on parameters which are not too far from those of the smallest GeMSS instances. Apart from GeMSS which is the focus of this work in light of the current situation, the efficiency of our approach also suggests that it might be feasible to use rank attacks in order to solve the 24 year old HFE Challenge 2 [37]. Until now, note that previous unsuccessful attempts [18,34] are direct attacks and not MinRank attacks. More generally, we demonstrate that the Support-Minors method may be used to tackle any MinRank instance with multiple solutions belonging to an extension field as long as one can benefit from this extension field structure and from a quite specific parameter range.

As a second major contribution, we propose and analyze a strategy to obviate much of the memory access cost in implementing the Wiedemann algorithm as a subroutine for XL. We exemplify the strategy on the rectangular MinRank attack on Rainbow [9] and we determine the cost on average of memory accesses in this case. While the memory access cost of the Wiedemann algorithm when applied to a Macaulay matrix of size V and row weight w over $\mathbb{F}_q$ was estimated by [41] to require remotely accessing $3wV^2 \log_2 V$ bits within a memory of size V, we conjecture that by organizing memory locally, this figure can be reduced to the equivalent of $3V^2 \log_2 q$ bits worth of remote access to memory, saving a factor of $w \log_2 V / \log_2 q$. Our strategy precisely aims at coming close to this figure, still under the assumption that the cost of memory access scales with either the square root or the cube root of the size of memory. Our concrete analysis shows that, even assuming the same cost for remote memory access as [41], the rectangular MinRank attack does indeed reduce the security of all round 3 Rainbow parameter sets below their targeted security strengths. To evaluate this memory access cost, we provide a theoretical analysis of both the memory savings and the extra costs which are associated to our strategy. We also examined various costs which were suggested to be possibly significant by [41] such as parallelization costs, and the cost of generating Macaulay matrix coefficients "on the fly", finding that incorporating these costs in our cost model does not affect our conclusion at least in the case of Rainbow. Finally, we want to insist on the fact that our methodology is limited to theoretical arguments. Of course real benchmarks would be greatly appreciated to support our claims, but it is probable that software implementations would not be a good indicator for these memory costs. Indeed, the estimates from [7,41] aim to give relative costs in an ASIC implementation which may be used by an adversary with significant resources. In particular, we believe that providing such an involved implementation is far beyond the scope of this paper.

Along with this paper, we also provide a SageMath notebook [2], where the reader may verify our results for the GeMSS attack.

2 Preliminaries

2.1 Notation

Row vectors and matrices will be written in **bold**. We denote by v_i the i-th component of a vector $\boldsymbol{v}$, and the entries of a matrix $\boldsymbol{M}$ of size $n_r \times n_c$ will be denoted by $\boldsymbol{M}_{i,j}$, where i (resp. j) is an integer in $\{1..n_r\}$ (resp. $\{1..n_c\}$). The support $\mathrm{Supp}(\boldsymbol{v}) := \{i \mid v_i \neq 0\}$ of a vector $\boldsymbol{v}$ is the set of indices of its non-zero coordinates. For $I \subset \{1..n_r\}$ and $J \subset \{1..n_c\}$, we use the notation $\boldsymbol{M}_{I,J}$ for the submatrix of $\boldsymbol{M}$ formed by its rows (resp. columns) with indexes in I (resp. J), and we adopt the shorthand notation $\boldsymbol{M}_{*,J} = \boldsymbol{M}_{\{1..n_r\},J}$ and $\boldsymbol{M}_{I,*} = \boldsymbol{M}_{I,\{1..n_c\}}$. We also denote by $|\boldsymbol{M}|$ (resp. $|\boldsymbol{M}|_{*,J}$) the determinant of $\boldsymbol{M}$ (resp. $\boldsymbol{M}_{*,J}$). Finally, we use $\#I$ to denote the number of elements of a set I.

A field with q elements is denoted by $\mathbb{F}_q$. The big field schemes take their name from a field extension $\mathbb{F}_{q^n}$ of degree n over $\mathbb{F}_q$, and in the following we consider ϕ an isomorphism $\mathbb{F}_{q^n} \to \mathbb{F}_q^n$ between vector spaces. For $j \in \mathbb{Z}_{\geq 0}$ and $\boldsymbol{v} = (v_1, \ldots, v_k) \in \mathbb{F}_{q^n}^k$, we define

$$\boldsymbol{v}^{[j]} := (v_1^{q^j}, \ldots, v_k^{q^j}).$$

This corresponds to applying the Frobenius automorphism $x \mapsto x^q$ j times on each coordinate of $\boldsymbol{v}$. Note that this field automorphism is the identity on $\mathbb{F}_q$. We will adopt the same notation for matrices, namely the matrix $\boldsymbol{M}^{[j]}$ is the matrix obtained from $\boldsymbol{M}$ by raising all its entries to the power q^j.

Polynomial Systems and Coding Theory. We use $\boldsymbol{x} = (x_1, \ldots, x_N)$ to denote a vector of variables, and $\mathbb{F}_q[\boldsymbol{x}]$ denotes the ring of polynomials in the variables $\boldsymbol{x}$ and coefficients in $\mathbb{F}_q$. When q is an odd prime power, and g a quadratic form in $\mathbb{F}_q[\boldsymbol{x}]$, we denote by $\boldsymbol{G}$ the symmetric matrix defined by $g(\boldsymbol{x}) = \boldsymbol{x}\boldsymbol{G}\boldsymbol{x}^{\mathsf{T}}$ and $g'(\boldsymbol{x}, \boldsymbol{y}) = g(\boldsymbol{x} + \boldsymbol{y}) - g(\boldsymbol{x}) - g(\boldsymbol{y}) + g(0)$ the polar form associated to g. The evaluation of a polynomial system $\mathcal{P} = (p_1, \ldots, p_m)$ at $\boldsymbol{s} \in \mathbb{F}_q^n$ is the vector $\mathcal{P}(\boldsymbol{s}) := (p_1(\boldsymbol{s}), \ldots, p_m(\boldsymbol{s}))$, and we denote by $\mathcal{P}^h = (p_1^h, \ldots, p_m^h)$ the homogeneous sequence such that p_i^h is the homogeneous part of highest degree in p_i for $1 \leq i \leq m$. We also consider the Macaulay matrix $\boldsymbol{M}(\mathcal{P}) \in \mathbb{F}_q^{m \times n_{\mathcal{M}}}$ whose columns are indexed by the monomials in $\mathcal{P}$ and such that the entries in the i-th row correspond to the coefficients of p_i for $1 \leq i \leq m$. If this matrix is full rank, then the rowspace is an m-dimensional $\mathbb{F}_q$-subspace of $\mathbb{F}_q^{n_{\mathcal{M}}}$ which can be viewed as a linear code $\mathcal{M}$ of parameters $[n_{\mathcal{M}}, m]_q$. A *generating matrix* is precisely given by $\boldsymbol{M}(\mathcal{P})$, and the *dual* is the $[n_{\mathcal{M}}, n_{\mathcal{M}} - m]_q$-linear code $\mathcal{M}^{\perp}$ defined by

$$\mathcal{M}^{\perp} := \left\{ \boldsymbol{h} \in \mathbb{F}_q^{n_{\mathcal{M}}} \mid \forall \boldsymbol{c} \in \mathcal{M}, \ \boldsymbol{c}\boldsymbol{h}^{\mathsf{T}} = 0 \right\},$$

which coincides with the right kernel of this matrix. Finally, the *puncturing* and *shortening* operations are classical ways to construct new linear codes from existing ones, and we use them in Sect. 5.1.

Definition 1. (Punctured code). *Let* $\mathcal{C} \subset \mathbb{F}_q^n$ *be a code of parameters* $[n, K]_q$ *and let* $I \subset \{1..n\}$. *The puncturing* $\mathcal{P}_I(\mathcal{C}) \subset \mathbb{F}_q^{n-\#I}$ *of* $\mathcal{C}$ *at* I *is the* $[n - \#I, K' \leq K]_q$-*code defined by:*

$$\mathcal{P}_I(\mathcal{C}) := \{ \boldsymbol{c}_{\{1..n\} \setminus I} \mid \boldsymbol{c} \in \mathcal{C} \}.$$

Definition 2. (Shortened code). *Let* $\mathcal{C} \subset \mathbb{F}_q^n$ *be a code of parameters* $[n, K]_q$ *and let* $I \subset \{1..n\}$. *The shortening* $\mathcal{S}_I(\mathcal{C}) \subset \mathbb{F}_q^{n-\#I}$ *of* $\mathcal{C}$ *at* I *is the* $[n - \#I, K' \geq K - \#I]_q$-*code defined by:*

$$\mathcal{S}_I(\mathcal{C}) := \{ \boldsymbol{c}_{\{1..n\} \setminus I} \mid \boldsymbol{c} \in \mathcal{C}, \ \boldsymbol{c}_I = 0_I \}.$$

The shortening operation is in some sense dual to puncturing, namely one has $\mathcal{S}_I(\mathcal{C}^\perp) = \mathcal{P}_I(\mathcal{C})^\perp$ and $\mathcal{S}_I(\mathcal{C})^\perp = \mathcal{P}_I(\mathcal{C}^\perp)$.

2.2 Relevant Material for the Attack on GeMSS

GeMSS [13] is a specific instance of HFEv-which was selected as an alternative candidate in the third round of the NIST PQC standardization process.

HFEv-. The HFEv- signature scheme is a variant of HFE [37] that includes both the Minus and the Vinegar modifiers. In this description we consider that q is an odd prime power. The secret polynomial $f : \mathbb{F}_{q^n} \times \mathbb{F}_q^v \rightarrow \mathbb{F}_{q^n}$ is of the form

$$f(X, \boldsymbol{y}_v) = \sum_{\substack{i,j \in \mathbb{N} \\ q^i + q^j \leq D}} \alpha_{i,j} X^{q^i + q^j} + \sum_{\substack{i \in \mathbb{N} \\ q^i \leq D}} \beta_i(\boldsymbol{y}_v) X^{q^i} + \gamma(\boldsymbol{y}_v),$$

where $\boldsymbol{y}_v = (y_1, \ldots, y_v)$ are the vinegar variables, $\alpha_{i,j} \in \mathbb{F}_{q^n}$, the β_i's are linear maps $\mathbb{F}_q^v \rightarrow \mathbb{F}_{q^n}$ and γ is a quadratic map $\mathbb{F}_q^v \rightarrow \mathbb{F}_{q^n}$. The special shape of such an f gives rise to a quadratic central map over the base field $\mathcal{F} = \phi \circ f \circ \psi : \mathbb{F}_q^{n+v} \rightarrow \mathbb{F}_q^n$, where

$$\psi : \mathbb{F}_q^n \times \mathbb{F}_q^v \longrightarrow \mathbb{F}_{q^n} \times \mathbb{F}_q^v$$
$$(x, y) \longmapsto (\phi^{-1}(x), y).$$

The public key is then given by a quadratic map $\mathcal{P} = \mathcal{T} \circ \mathcal{F} \circ \mathcal{S}$, where $\mathcal{S} : \mathbb{F}_q^{n+v} \rightarrow \mathbb{F}_q^{n+v}$ and $\mathcal{T} : \mathbb{F}_q^n \rightarrow \mathbb{F}_q^{n-a}$ are secret affine maps of maximal rank. For simplification, we assume in the rest of the paper that $\mathcal{S}$ (resp. $\mathcal{T}$) is a linear map described by a matrix $\boldsymbol{S} \in \mathbb{F}_q^{(n+v) \times (n+v)}$ (resp. $\boldsymbol{T} \in \mathbb{F}_q^{n \times (n-a)}$), so that the components of $\mathcal{P} = (p_1, \ldots, p_{n-a})$ are homogeneous polynomials in $N = n + v$ variables $\boldsymbol{x} = (x_1, \ldots, x_{n+v})$. When q is an odd prime power, we recall that $\boldsymbol{P}_i$ is the symmetric matrix associated to p_i by $p_i(\boldsymbol{x}) = \boldsymbol{x} \boldsymbol{P}_i \boldsymbol{x}^\mathsf{T}$ for $1 \leq i \leq n - a$.

MinRank Attack on HFEv- from [40]. Tao et al. recently proposed in [40] the most efficient key recovery attack on HFEv- so far. To describe this attack, we assume that q is an odd prime power, but the results can be extended to the even characteristic. Let $(\theta_1, \ldots, \theta_n)$ be a basis of the vector space $\mathbb{F}_{q^n}$ over $\mathbb{F}_q$, let $\boldsymbol{H} \in \mathbb{F}_{q^n}^{n \times n}$ be the associated Moore matrix defined by $\boldsymbol{H} := [\theta_{i+1}^{q^j}]_{i,j=0}^{n-1}$ and let $\widetilde{\boldsymbol{H}} := \begin{pmatrix} \boldsymbol{H} & 0 \\ 0 & \boldsymbol{I}_v \end{pmatrix}$. The main step of the attack is by solving the following MinRank problem to recover the first n rows of the invertible matrix U defined by

$$U := \widetilde{\boldsymbol{H}}^{-1} \boldsymbol{S}^{-1} \in \mathbb{F}_{q^n}^{(n+v) \times (n+v)}, \tag{1}$$

Problem 2. (Underlying MinRank problem) *Let* $d := \lceil \log_q (D) \rceil$ *and let* $\boldsymbol{u} \in \mathbb{F}_{q^n}^{n+v}$ *be the first row of* U. *Let* $\boldsymbol{P}_1, \ldots, \boldsymbol{P}_{n-a} \in \mathbb{F}_q^{(n+v) \times (n+v)}$ *denote the symmetric matrices associated with the HFEv- public key and let* $(\boldsymbol{e}_1, \ldots, \boldsymbol{e}_{n+v})$ *be the canonical basis for* $\mathbb{F}_q^{n+v}$. *For* $1 \leq i \leq n + v$, *we define the matrix* $\boldsymbol{M}_i \in \mathbb{F}_q^{(n-a) \times (n+v)}$ *by*

$$\boldsymbol{M}_i := \boldsymbol{e}_i \boldsymbol{P}_* := \begin{pmatrix} \boldsymbol{e}_i \boldsymbol{P}_1 \\ \vdots \\ \boldsymbol{e}_i \boldsymbol{P}_{n-a} \end{pmatrix}.$$

Then, the vector $\boldsymbol{u} := (u_1, \ldots, u_{n+v})$ *is a solution to the MinRank instance described by the* $\boldsymbol{M}_i$'s *with target rank* d.

We refer to [40, Theorem 2] for extra details. Also, note that the first n rows of U are the Frobenius iterates of $\boldsymbol{u}$, more precisely we have

$$U = \begin{pmatrix} \boldsymbol{u} \\ \vdots \\ \boldsymbol{u}^{[n-1]} \\ \boldsymbol{R} \end{pmatrix},$$

where the block $\boldsymbol{R} \in \mathbb{F}_q^{v \times (n+v)}$ is full rank, see [40, Alg. 1, 4.]. Then, it is shown in [40, 4.3] how one can efficiently derive an equivalent key and finish the attack. Finally, to keep the same notation as in [40, Thm. 2], we set

$$Z := \sum_{i=1}^{n+v} u_i \boldsymbol{M}_i \in \mathbb{F}_q[\boldsymbol{u}]^{(n-a) \times (n+v)}. \tag{2}$$

Fact 1. (On the number of solutions) *Let* $\boldsymbol{u} \in \mathbb{F}_{q^n}^{n+v}$ *be a solution to the MinRank problem 2. Then, for any* $\lambda \in \mathbb{F}_{q^n}^*$, *the vector* $\lambda \boldsymbol{u} := (\lambda u_1, \ldots, \lambda u_{n+v})$ *is another solution. Moreover, for any* $0 \leq j \leq n - 1$, *the same goes for the vector* $\boldsymbol{u}^{[j]} := (u_1^{q^j}, \ldots, u_{n+v}^{q^j})$ *with corresponding rank* d *matrix* $\boldsymbol{Z}^{[j]}$.

This fact is inherent to the big-field structure used in HFEv- and was already observed in the previous rank attacks on big-field MPKC [8,29,31,42].

Projection Modifier. The projection modification was introduced in [14] in order to repair the previously broken SFLASH signature scheme [24] and devise the new PFLASH signature scheme. In reaction to the attack on GeMSS from [40], the authors of [36] also applied this modifier to HFEv-, leading to pHFEv-. The proposed parameters for the scheme are secure against this former attack, and the point of projecting is that it appears to be more efficient than simply increasing the degree D of f to obtain the same security. The projection modifier consists in replacing the map $S : \mathbb{F}_q^{n+v} \to \mathbb{F}_q^{n+v}$ by $S = \overline{L} \circ S' : \mathbb{F}_q^{n+v-p} \to \mathbb{F}_q^{n+v}$, where $S' : \mathbb{F}_q^{n+v-p} \to \mathbb{F}_q^{n+v-p}$ is full rank and $\overline{L} : \mathbb{F}_q^{n+v-p} \to \mathbb{F}_q^{n+v}$ is full rank represented by a matrix $\begin{pmatrix} \Lambda & 0 \\ 0 & I_v \end{pmatrix} \in \mathbb{F}_q^{(n+v-p)\times(n+v)}$. The authors of [36] have studied the effect of projection on the rank of the HFEv- central map. When $p > 0$, the rank of Z from Eq. (2) is bounded by $d' := d + p$ instead of d (cf. [36, Prop. 2]), and this bound is believed to be tight from practical experiments. Moreover, the number of solutions to the corresponding MinRank problem is expected to be unchanged compared to plain HFEv-. In Table 2, we give the current GeMSS parameter sets as well as those of pHFEv- . In [36], a secure pHFEv- parameter set is constructed from a given GeMSS parameter set by choosing the least value of p such that the minors attack from [40] is just above the security level.

Table 2. GeMSS and pHFEv- parameter sets.

Scheme	q	n	v	D	a	p from [36]
GeMSS128	2	174	12	513	12	0
BlueGeMSS128	2	175	14	129	13	1
RedGeMSS128	2	177	15	17	15	4
GeMSS192	2	265	20	513	22	5
BlueGeMSS192	2	265	23	129	22	7
RedGeMSS192	2	266	25	17	23	10
GeMSS256	2	354	33	513	30	10
BlueGeMSS256	2	358	32	129	34	11
RedGeMSS256	2	358	35	17	34	14

2.3   Relevant Material on Rainbow for Section 8.3

Rainbow is a third round finalist of the NIST PQC standardization process for digital signatures. In this paper, we are mainly interested in the recent rectangular MinRank attack from [9, §7] on this scheme.

Rainbow. For clarity, we adopt the simplified description from [9]. The version of Rainbow submitted to the NIST PQC project is a 2-layered variant of the well-know UOV signature scheme: the trapdoor consists of 3 $\mathbb{F}_q$-subspaces $O_2 \subset O_1 \subset \mathbb{F}_q^n$ and $W \subset \mathbb{F}_q^m$ of dimension o_2, m and o_2 respectively, and the public system $\mathcal{P}$ contains m quadratic equations in n variables such that $\mathcal{P}(z) \in W$ for all $z \in O_1$ and $\mathcal{P}'(x, y) \in W$ for all $x \in \mathbb{F}_q^n$ and $y \in O_2$, where $\mathcal{P}'$ is the system of *polar forms* associated to $\mathcal{P}$. To perform a key-recovery on Rainbow, it had already been noted that the hardest part is to recover the space O_2: once O_2 is found, it is then easy to recover both W and O_1. Thus, the rectangular MinRank attack from [9] targets secret vectors $y \in O_2$.

Rectangular MinRank attack. The rectangular MinRank attack by [9] is currently the best key-recovery attack on Rainbow so far. For $y \in \mathbb{F}_q^n$, let

$$L_y := \begin{pmatrix} \mathcal{P}'(e_1, y) \\ \vdots \\ \mathcal{P}'(e_n, y) \end{pmatrix},$$

where $(e_1, \ldots, e_n)$ is the canonical basis of $\mathbb{F}_q^n$. The attack heavily exploits the fact that $\mathcal{P}'(x, y) \in W$ for any $x \in \mathbb{F}_q^n$ and $y \in O_2$. Indeed, when $y \in O_2$, the rows of L_y lie in W, so that the rank of this matrix is at most $\dim W := o_2$. Also $L_y = \sum_{i=1}^n y_i L_{e_i}$ by linearity, and therefore a solution to the MinRank instance described by the L_{e_i}'s with target rank o_2 is very likely to reveal a vector y in O_2. Finally, as noted in [9], it is possible to fix $o_2 - 1$ entries in y at random in order to obtain a 1-dimensional solution space. The resulting MinRank instance is then solved by relying on the recent Support-Minors modeling [5], see Sect. 3. Moreover, [9] suggests to also use the fact that $\mathcal{P}(y) = 0$, which allows to consider a system with more equations while keeping the same variables as in the Support-Minors system. The concrete improvement of this trick compared to the plain MinRank attack remains modest, see [9, Table 6].

3   Support-Minors Modeling (SM)

Support-Minors is an efficient method to model and solve the MinRank problem [5]. It has been used to cryptanalyze MPKC and rank-based cryptosystems [4, 5, 9]. The idea is to factor the secret matrix $M \in \mathbb{K}^{n_r \times n_c}$ of rank $\leq d$ as

$$M := \sum_{i=1}^N u_i M_i := DC, \tag{3}$$

where $D \in \mathbb{K}^{n_r \times d}$ and the support matrix $C \in \mathbb{K}^{d \times n_c}$ are unknown matrices. For $1 \leq j \leq n_r$, one then considers the matrix

$$C_j := \begin{pmatrix} r_j \\ C \end{pmatrix},$$

where $r_j := M_{\{j\},*}$ is the j-th row of M whose components are linear forms in the so-called *linear* variables u_i's. The rank of C_j is at most d, and equations are obtained by setting all $(d+1) \times (d+1)$ minors of this matrix to zero, namely $Q_{j,J} := |C_j|_{*,J}$ for $J \subset \{1..n_c\}$, $\#J = d+1$. The Support-Minors system then contains a total of $n_r \binom{n_c}{d+1}$ polynomials by considering $1 \leq j \leq n_r$. Moreover, by using Laplace expansion along the first row of C_j, one notices that these equations are bilinear in the u_i variables and in the so-called *minor* variables $c_T := |C|_{*,T}$, where $T \subset \{1..n_c\}$, $\#T = d$. The following fact will be used several times in the paper.

Fact 2. (Structure of the SM system) *Each SM equation contains at most $N(d+1)$ bilinear monomials. More precisely, given $J \subset \{1..n_c\}$, $\#J = d+1$ and $1 \leq j \leq n_r$, the monomials of $Q_{j,J}$ belong to a set of $N(d+1)$ elements which only depends on J.*

Proof. Let $J := \{j_1 < \cdots < j_{d+1}\}$ and $1 \leq j \leq n_r$. By Laplace expansion along the first row of $(C_j)_{*,J}$, one has that the monomials in $Q_{j,J}$ are in the set

$$A_J := \{u_i c_{J \setminus j_u} : 1 \leq u \leq d+1, \ 1 \leq i \leq N\}.$$

This set contains $N(d+1)$ elements which are independent from j. $\square$

Solving the SM System. When the corresponding MinRank problem has a unique solution, [5] proposes a dedicated XL approach by multiplying the SM equations by monomials in the linear variables. This is typically the case for Rainbow [9] or rank-based cryptography [4,5]. The attack constructs the Macaulay matrix $M(\mathcal{Q}_b)$, where $\mathcal{Q}_b$ is the system of all degree $b+1$ polynomials of the form $\mu_u f$, where μ_u is a monomial of degree $b-1$ in the linear variables and f is a SM equation. Note that direct linearization corresponds to $b=1$ with $\mathcal{Q}_1 = \mathcal{Q}$. The value of b is chosen such that the rank of $M(\mathcal{Q}_b)$ is equal to the number of columns minus one. In this case, the linear system $M(\mathcal{Q}_b)x^\mathsf{T} = 0$ has a non-trivial solution, and this solution easily yields a solution to the initial MinRank problem. The situation is quite different when there are $N' > 1$ solutions to this original MinRank instance, *e.g.* HFE, see Fact 1, but the approach can be adapted. There still exists a value of b for which the kernel of $M(\mathcal{Q}_b)$ is non-trivial and can be computed, but the dimension N'' of this kernel is expected to be > 1. In particular, the second step to solve the initial MinRank problem from arbitrary kernel vectors is no longer straightforward. By finding a basis of that kernel one can at least reduce the initial MinRank problem to a new one with N'' matrices with the same dimensions and the same target rank d, but this secondary MinRank instance has no reason to be much easier to solve.

The linear system $M(\mathcal{Q}_b)x^\mathsf{T} = 0$ is usually sparse, especially when $b > 1$, and in this case it is often advantageous to use the Wiedemann algorithm. Another idea to reduce the cost of linear algebra is to start from a Macaulay matrix of smaller size by selecting only $n' \leq n_c$ columns in M (for example the first n' ones), which yields a SM system with $n_r \binom{n'}{d+1}$ equations and $N \binom{n'}{d}$ monomials $u_i c_T$, where this time $T \subset \{1..n'\}$.

4   Improved Attack on GeMSS Using Support-Minors

In this section, we describe our approach to solve the MinRank instance 2 arising from HFEv- using Support-Minors. As noted in Fact 1, this problem is expected to have several solutions which are triggered by the big-field structure, hence we cannot directly apply the XL techniques from [5]. Two remarks are in order before we describe the attack. From the definition of Z in Equation (2) and the fact that the M_i's are over the small field, it is important to notice that the coefficients of the SM system are in $\mathbb{F}_q$, whereas the solutions may belong to the extension field $\mathbb{F}_{q^n}$. Also, as discussed in [5], we will consider a subset of the SM equations coming from a submatrix of $Z^{\mathsf{T}} \in \mathbb{F}_q[u]^{(n+v) \times (n-a)}$ obtained by selecting a subset J of $n' \in [d+1, n-a]$ columns.

4.1   Fixing Variables in the Support-Minors System

Up to relabelling of the linear variables, one can fix $u_{n+v} = 1$ as in [40]. In this case, one expects to obtain n solutions which correspond to the first n rows of U, namely $u, u^{[1]}, \ldots, u^{[n-1]}$. Also, since we can choose an arbitrary submatrix $Z^{\mathsf{T}}_{*,J}$ of Z^{T} with $\#J = n'$, we can make sure that this submatrix is full rank on its first d columns. Therefore, we will fix the minor variable $c_{\{1\ldots d\}}$ to 1.

Modeling 1. (Support-Minors modeling on Z^{T}) *Let Z be as defined in Equation (2). We consider the SM equations obtained by choosing $n' \leq n - a$ columns in Z^{T}, with coefficients in $\mathbb{F}_q$ and solutions in $\mathbb{F}_{q^n}$. Moreover, we fix $u_{n+v} = 1$ and $c_{\{1\ldots d\}} = 1$.*

The system from Modeling 1 contains $(n+v)\binom{n'}{d+1}$ affine bilinear equations in $(n+v)\binom{n'}{d}$ monomials, and $(n+v-1)(\binom{n'}{d}-1)$ of them are bilinear monomials. Also, one can choose a number of columns $n' \leq n - a$ that yields a sub-system with more equations than monomials. Indeed, this will be the case when $(n+v)\binom{n'}{d+1} \geq (n+v)\binom{n'}{d}$, and this condition is equivalent to $n' \geq 2d+1$. Finally, in GeMSS the value of $n-a$ is much higher than $2d+1$, which allows to choose $n' \in [2d+1, n-a]$.

4.2   Solving via Gröbner Bases when $n' \geq 2d + 1$

In the case when $n' \geq 2d + 1$, there are more equations than monomials in the SM system, but once again it is not possible to solve by direct linearization because the resulting linear system has a large kernel. More precisely, since we expect the system to have n solutions and since these solutions correspond to n linearly independent vectors $\{v, v^{[1]}, \ldots, v^{[n-1]}\}$ such that the first $n + v - 1$ components of v are $u_1, \ldots, u_{n+v-1}$, its dimension should be at least n. For large enough n, in every single instance we have tested, the linearization process triggers no spurious solutions, thus the dimension of the solution space is equal to n. Therefore, we adopt the following Assumption 1 in the rest of the analysis.

Assumption 1. *Let $n' \geq 2d + 1$. Then, the number of linearly independent equations in Modeling 1 is equal to*

$$\mathcal{N}_1 := (n + v)\binom{n'}{d} - n.$$

Our attack works in two steps. First, by forming linear combinations between the equations from Modeling 1, we are able to produce a system $\mathcal{L}$ of degree 1 polynomials (Step 1). Then, using $\mathcal{L}$ to substitute some of the variables, we get a quadratic system in $n_u = n - 1$ of the linear variables. Finally (Step 2) we solve this second system.

Step 1: Linear Polynomials Produced at $b = 1$. Here we explain how the system $\mathcal{L}$ is obtained at Step 1. We start by proving

Fact 3. *Under Assumption 1, by linear algebra on the affine SM equations, one can generate $\mathcal{N}_L$ linearly independent degree 1 polynomials, where*

$$\mathcal{N}_L \geq \binom{n'}{d} + v - 1. \tag{4}$$

Proof. By Assumption 1, the system given in Modeling 1 contains $\mathcal{N}_1 := (n + v)\binom{n'}{d} - n$ linearly independent equations. Moreover, one has

$$\mathcal{N}_1 \geq (n + v - 1)\left(\binom{n'}{d} - 1\right),$$

so that the number of linearly independent *affine bilinear* equations is greater than the number of *bilinear* monomials. In particular, there are non-trivial linear combinations between the bilinear parts of the equations that are zero. This means that by performing linear algebra operations on the equations in Modeling 1, one can generate at least

$$\underbrace{\left((n + v)\binom{n'}{d} - n\right)}_{\mathcal{N}_1} - \underbrace{(n + v - 1)\left(\binom{n'}{d} - 1\right)}_{\#\text{bilinear monomials}} = \binom{n'}{d} + v - 1$$

linearly independent affine degree 1 polynomials in the u_i's and in the c_T variables. □

The linear equations from Fact 3 are often referred to in the literature as *degree falls* from degree 2 to degree 1, and we denote by $M(\mathcal{L})$ the Macaulay matrix of this linear system $\mathcal{L}$. By considering an ordering on the columns such that $c_T > u_{n+v-1} > \cdots > u_1 > u_{n+v} = 1$, we choose to eliminate first and foremost all the $n_{c_T} := \binom{n'}{d} - 1$ minor variables.

Lemma 1. *Under Assumption 1, the reduced row echelon form of $M(\mathcal{L})$ is of the form*

$$L = \begin{pmatrix} I_{n_{c_T}} & * \\ 0 & K \end{pmatrix} \in \mathbb{F}_q^{\mathcal{N}_L \times (n_{c_T} + n + v)}, \tag{5}$$

where $K \in \mathbb{F}_q^{(\mathcal{N}_L - n_{c_T}) \times (n+v)}$ is row reduced. Moreover, we have that $\mathcal{N}_L = \binom{n'}{d} + v - 1$.

Proof. Let L denote the echelon form of $M(\mathcal{L})$, namely

$$L := \begin{pmatrix} N & * \\ 0 & K \end{pmatrix}, \text{where } N \in \mathbb{F}_q^{n_{c_T} \times n_{c_T}} \text{ and } K \in \mathbb{F}_q^{(\mathcal{N}_L - n_{c_T}) \times (n+v)}.$$

Assume that this matrix is not systematic on its first n_{c_T} rows. On that hypothesis, there is a set of $v_0 \geq \mathcal{N}_L - n_{c_T} + 1 \geq v + 1$ linearly independent vectors in the row space of L which have zero in their leftmost n_{c_T} entries. This yields v_0 linearly independent vectors $\boldsymbol{h}_1, \ldots, \boldsymbol{h}_{v_0} \in \mathbb{F}_q^{n+v}$ such that for all i, $\boldsymbol{u}\boldsymbol{h}_i^\mathsf{T} = 0$, where $\boldsymbol{u} \in \mathbb{F}_{q^n}^{n+v}$ denotes the first row of the matrix U defined in Equation (1). Then, by applying the Frobenius isomorphism and using the fact that it is the identity on $\mathbb{F}_q$, it follows that $\boldsymbol{u}^{[j]}\boldsymbol{h}_i^\mathsf{T} = 0$ for all i and $0 \leq j \leq n-1$. Therefore, the matrix

$$U_{\{1..n\},*} = \begin{pmatrix} \boldsymbol{u} \\ \vdots \\ \boldsymbol{u}^{[n-1]} \end{pmatrix} \in \mathbb{F}_{q^n}^{n \times (n+v)},$$

is not full-rank, which is a contradiction since U is invertible. This gives $N = I_{n_{c_T}}$.

For the second part of the proof, the number of rows $\mathcal{N}_L - n_{c_T}$ in K is at least v by Fact 3. Since $\boldsymbol{u}$ is a solution to the MinRank problem, there exists a vector $\boldsymbol{v} \in \mathbb{F}_{q^n}^{n_{c_T}}$ corresponding to the minor variables such that

$$M(\mathcal{L}) \cdot (\boldsymbol{v}, u_{n+v-1}, \ldots, u_1, u_{n+v})^\mathsf{T} = \boldsymbol{0}.$$

Since the matrix $M(\mathcal{L})$ has its entries in $\mathbb{F}_q$ we obtain n linearly independent vectors in the right kernel, namely

$$\forall\, 0 \leq j \leq n-1, \ M(\mathcal{L}) \cdot (\boldsymbol{v}^{[j]}, u_{n+v-1}^{[j]}, \ldots, u_1^{[j]}, u_{n+v}^{[j]})^\mathsf{T} = \boldsymbol{0}.$$

This shows that the rank of K is at most $(n+v-n) = v$, so that $\mathcal{N}_L - n_{c_T} = v$. □

By Lemma 1, it is possible to express all the minor variables as well as v linear variables in terms of the remaining $n-1$ linear variables. Moreover, by reordering the linear variables if necessary, we may further assume that the remaining ones are $u_1, \ldots, u_{n-1}$. In this case, the matrix corresponding to the homogeneous degree 1 parts (by dropping the last column of L) is of the form

$$L^{(h)} := \begin{pmatrix} I_{n_{c_T}} & 0 & Y \\ 0 & I_v & W \end{pmatrix} \in \mathbb{F}_q^{\mathcal{N}_L \times (n_{c_T}+n+v-1)}, \tag{6}$$

where $Y \in \mathbb{F}_q^{n_{c_T} \times n_u}$, $W \in \mathbb{F}_q^{v \times n_u}$ and $n_u := n-1$.

Step 2: Solving the Resulting Quadratic System. By using the linear equations from $\mathcal{L}$ to substitute variables in Modeling 1, we obtain the following

Modeling 2. (Quadratic system). *We consider the quadratic system in* $n_u = n - 1$ *linear variables* $u_1, \ldots, u_{n-1}$ *obtained by plugging the linear polynomials of* $\mathcal{L}$ *into the equations from Modeling 1.*

We now focus on the task of solving this quadratic system using Gröbner bases, and in Proposition 1 we prove at which degree the computation terminates as long as $n_{c_T} \geq n_u$. The proof relies on Assumption 1 and the following Assumption 2 on the echelon form $\boldsymbol{L}$ from Equation (6).

Assumption 2. *The matrix* $\boldsymbol{Y} \in \mathbb{F}_q^{n_{c_T} \times n_u}$ *in Equation* (6) *is full rank.*

Note that this assumption should hold with high probability if $\boldsymbol{Y}$ behaves as a random matrix. Also, we have performed different simulations to experimentally verify Assumptions 1 and 2. According to the results obtained for different sets of parameters (q, n, v, D, a), it seems that if n' is chosen such that $n' \geq 2d + 1$ and $n_{c_T} \geq n_u$, then the 2 assumptions are satisfied almost 100% of the times. The reader might find helpful to experimentally explore these assumptions using the SageMath notebook [2].

Proposition 1. *Under Assumptions 1 and 2, if* $n_{c_T} \geq n_u$, *a Gröbner basis of the system from Modeling 2 can be obtained by Gaussian elimination on the initial equations, i.e. it is found at degree 2.*

Proof. By Assumption 1 and the first part of Lemma 1, the number of degree 2 affine equations which remain after the linear algebra step in Modeling 1 is equal to $\mathcal{N}_1 - \mathcal{N}_L = (n + v - 1)\left(\binom{n'}{d} - 1\right)$. As we cannot construct extra degree falls between them, this implies that the linear span of these equations contains an equation with leading monomial $u_i c_T$ for any T, $\#T = d$, $T \neq \{1..d\}$ and any $1 \leq i \leq n_u + v$. Let

$$\boldsymbol{L}^{(h)} := \begin{pmatrix} \boldsymbol{I}_{n_{c_T}} & 0 & \boldsymbol{Y} \\ 0 & \boldsymbol{I}_v & \boldsymbol{W} \end{pmatrix} \in \mathbb{F}_q^{\mathcal{N}_L \times (n_{c_T} + n + v - 1)},$$

where $\boldsymbol{Y} \in \mathbb{F}_q^{n_{c_T} \times n_u}$, $\boldsymbol{W} \in \mathbb{F}_q^{v \times n_u}$ and $n_u := n - 1$ as defined in Equation (6). We also denote by $\boldsymbol{c}$ the row vector of length n_{c_T} whose components are the minor variables and $(u_1, \ldots, u_{n+v-1}) := (\boldsymbol{u}_+, \boldsymbol{u}_-)$, where $\boldsymbol{u}_+$ is of length n_u (remaining linear variables) and $\boldsymbol{u}_-$ is of length v (removed linear variables). Then, there is a vector of constants $\alpha \in \mathbb{F}_q^{n_{c_T}}$ such that

$$\boldsymbol{c}^\mathsf{T} = -\boldsymbol{Y}\boldsymbol{u}_+^\mathsf{T} - \alpha^\mathsf{T} \tag{7}$$

Since $\boldsymbol{Y}$ is full rank by Assumption 2, the linear system given by Equation (7) can be inverted when $n_{c_T} \geq n_u$, and therefore all the $\binom{n_u+1}{2}$ quadratic leading monomials will be found in the span of Modeling 2. $\qquad\square$

When $n_{c_T} < n_u$, we conjecture that the Gröbner basis algorithm terminates in degree 3. Finally, note that the content of the current Sect. 4 also applies to pHFEv- with rank equal to $d' = d + p$, since what really matters in the analysis is the number of solutions to the MinRank problem. We simply have to replace the condition $n' \geq 2d + 1$ by $n' \geq 2d' + 1$.

5   Complexity of the Attack

This section analyses the cost of our attack on GeMSS. In Sects. 5.1 and 5.2, we estimate the time complexity. This complexity comes down to two major steps, first generating Modeling 2 from Modeling 1 (Step 1) and then solving Modeling 2 via Gröbner bases (Step 2). Then, in Sect. 5.3, we evaluate the corresponding memory complexity. First, note that choosing $n' = 2d + 1$ already ensures $n_{c_T} \geq n_u$ for all the GeMSS and pHFEv- parameters, see Table 2. In particular, Proposition 1 implies that the system in Modeling 2 will be solved at degree 2. In the following, we then adopt $n' = 2d + 1$ and we will also consider that $v = o(n)$.

5.1   Time Complexity of Step 1

This first step can be performed by echelonizing the equations from Modeling 1 using Strassen's algorithm. The complexity in this case is

$$\mathcal{O}\left((n+v)\binom{2d+1}{d} \left((n+v)\binom{2d+1}{d} \right)^{\omega-1} \right) = \mathcal{O}\left(n_{c_T}^{\omega} n_u^{\omega} \right) \qquad (8)$$

$\mathbb{F}_q$-operations, where $n_u = n - 1$, $n_{c_T} = \binom{2d+1}{d} - 1$ and $\omega \approx 2.81$ is the linear algebra constant.

An alternative path is to use Coppersmith's Block-Wiedemann algorithm (BW). Let $\mathcal{M}$ be the rowspace of the Macaulay matrix $M(\mathcal{Q})$ of the SM system. By Assumption 1, it can be seen as a linear code of length $(n+v)\binom{2d+1}{d}$ and dimension $\mathcal{N}_1 = (n+v)\binom{2d+1}{d} - n$, so that we expect the right kernel of $M(\mathcal{Q})$ to be of dimension n. In particular, by running BW roughly n times, we hope to obtain a basis for this kernel which corresponds to the dual code $\mathcal{C} := \mathcal{M}^{\perp}$. Let I be the subset of positions of $\mathcal{M}$ corresponding to the bilinear monomials. We then puncture $\mathcal{C}$ at I to obtain $\mathcal{P}_I(\mathcal{C})$. Since the dual of the punctured code is the shortening of the dual, we have that $\mathcal{P}_I(\mathcal{C})^{\perp} = \mathcal{S}_I(\mathcal{M})$, and the dimension of this code corresponds to the number of independent linear equations $\mathcal{N}_L$ given by Fact 3. By Lemma 1, we have that $\mathcal{N}_L = \binom{2d+1}{d} + v - 1$. Also, the cost of obtaining the shortened code $\mathcal{S}_I(\mathcal{M})$ from $\mathcal{P}_I(\mathcal{C})$ is negligible compared to the BW step to obtain $\mathcal{P}_I(\mathcal{C})$. Finally, by Fact 2, there are at most $(d+1)(n+v)$ monomials in one SM equation, so that the overall complexity using the Wiedemann algorithm n times to find a basis of $\mathcal{C}$ is

$$\mathcal{O}\left(n \times (n+v)(d+1) \left((n+v)\binom{2d+1}{d} \right)^2 \right) = \mathcal{O}\left(d n_{c_T}^2 n_u^4 \right). \qquad (9)$$

5.2 Time Complexity of Step 2

As the choice $n' = 2d + 1$ ensures $n_u \leq n_{c_T}$ for all the parameters of GeMSS and pHFEv-, the system given by Modeling 2 can be solved at degree 2 by Proposition 1. Thus, the cost of this second step is simply the cost of row reducing the Macaulay matrix of this quadratic system. The number of columns is the number of initial monomials which is equal to $1 + n_u + \binom{n_u+1}{2}$ and there are more equations than monomials, so that the complexity of the second step is

$$\mathcal{O}\left(n_{c_T}(n + v - 1) \times \left(1 + n_u + \binom{n_u + 1}{2}\right)^{\omega-1}\right) = \mathcal{O}\left(n_{c_T} n_u^{2\omega-1}\right) \qquad (10)$$

$\mathbb{F}_q$-operations. Note that Step 1 is expected to be more costly since $n_u \leq n_{c_T}$.

5.3 Memory Cost

In this section, we estimate the space complexity of the attack on GeMSS, which is dominated by the space complexity of Step 1 as the system from Modeling 2 is much smaller. We choose $q = 2$ to be in accordance with the GeMSS parameters, so that one element in $\mathbb{F}_q$ occupies one bit in memory. We start by describing two approaches to store the Macaulay matrix $M(\mathcal{Q})$ associated with the system $\mathcal{Q}$ from Modeling 1 when used within the Block-Wiedemann algorithm.

Standard Approach. This approach uses the sparsity of the matrix $M(\mathcal{Q})$ in a naive way. Recall from Fact 2 that every SM equation contains at most $(n+v)(d+1)$ nonzero monomials. Thus, one way to store a single row of $M(\mathcal{Q})$ is by storing the indexes corresponding to nonzero positions. Hence we must store at most $(n+v)(d+1)$ column indexes per row. Since the Macaulay matrix has $(n + v)\binom{2d+1}{d}$ columns and assuming that several rows can be dropped to get a square matrix, the space complexity is given by

$$\binom{2d+1}{d}(d+1)(n+v)^2 \log_2\left(\binom{2d+1}{d}(n+v)\right) = \mathcal{O}\left(dn_u^2 n_{c_T} \log_2(n_{c_T})\right). \qquad (11)$$

Optimized Approach. Here we adapt to the SM equations the strategy used by Niederhagen for a generic Macaulay matrix [35, 4.5.3]. By Fact 2, recall that for a given subset $J \subset \{1..n_c\}$, $\#J = d + 1$, all SM equations of the form $Q_{i,J}$ for $1 \leq i \leq n_r$ have the same set of potential nonzero monomials. Hence, the set of columns in $M(\mathcal{Q})$ potentially allocating nonzero entries are the same for each row which correspond to one of these equations.

To store the system $\mathcal{Q}$ we use four arrays, namely V_1, V_2, V_3, and V_4. The array V_1 is implemented as a 2-dimensional array of size $n_r \times (Nn_o)$ in which we store the coordinates of the MinRank input matrices M_i's. The array V_2, instead, stores the monomials of all SM equations. More precisely, for each subset $J \subset \{1..n_c\}$, $\#J = d + 1$, we store in V_2 the coordinates corresponding to potential nonzero monomials in SM equations associated to J. Finally, it remains to store the information about how to read from V_1 the coefficients of a given $Q_{i,J}$ equation. This information is given a list of $N(d+1)$ coordinates in V_1 that belong to the same row. The set of column indexes is stored in V_3, while the row index is stored in V_4. A more detailed description of this storage can be found in the long version, see [3, Appendix A.3], and overall we obtain a space complexity of

$$\binom{2d+1}{d}(n+v)(d+1)\log_2\left(\binom{2d+1}{d}(n+v)\right) = \mathcal{O}\left(dn_u n_{c_T}\log_2(n_{c_T})\right), \quad (12)$$

which saves a factor of order $n+v$ compared to the Standard approach. This Optimized approach also has better memory access than the Standard approach. Indeed, both approaches require to retrieve the same amount of information, but in the Standard approach the size of the memory is larger. For instance, if one uses the 2-dimensional model of [7,41] stating that retrieving b consecutive bits from a memory of M bits costs

$$2^{-5}(b+\log N)\sqrt{M},$$

where N is the length of the array we are reading from. In the Standard approach, one can check that both $(b+\log N)$ and $\sqrt{M}$ factors are larger in each vector-vector multiplication of the Block-Wiedemann algorithm.

Table 3. Memory ($\log_2(\#\text{bytes})$) needed to store the Macaulay matrix $M(\mathcal{Q})$ from Step 1 to be used in BW or Strassen's algorithm.

Scheme	BW Standard	BW Optimized	Strassen
GeMSS128	38.665	34.553	48.935
BlueGeMSS128	34.332	30.258	41.263
RedGeMSS128	27.645	23.729	29.873
GeMSS192	39.930	35.213	50.166
BlueGeMSS192	35.586	30.917	42.478
RedGeMSS192	28.897	24.410	31.073
GeMSS256	40.836	35.686	51.049
BlueGeMSS256	36.488	31.389	43.353
RedGeMSS256	29.800	24.905	31.940

Table 3 shows the space complexity of the first step of our attack. Keep in mind that the memory demand for the BW algorithm will not be much more than the one to fully store the Macaulay matrix. It can even be significantly lower, if rows are generated on-demand, but this would increase the time complexity. In contrast, the space complexity of Strassen's algorithm is dominated by the memory demand to store a square dense matrix of size $\binom{2d+1}{d}(n+v)$, see Column "Strassen". As we can see in Table 3, the Optimized storage requires only a few

GigaBytes of shared memory to execute Step 1 with BW on any of the proposed parameters for GeMSS, whereas for the Standard approach requires up to a few TeraBytes. To perform this step with Strassen's algorithm, one would need up to more than two Petabytes. To sum up, the amount of memory required by BW is small enough to be allocated even in a shared memory device, especially if one uses the Optimized storage.

6 Application to GeMSS and pHFEv- Parameter Sets

In this section, we use the results developed in Sect. 5 to determine the effect of our attack on the security of the GeMSS and pHFEv- signature schemes. In Table 4, we give the time complexity of our attack on the current GeMSS parameters. We use Equation (8) or Equation (9) for Step 1 (Strassen or BW) and Equation (10) for Step 2. We use $\omega = 2.81$ and a conservative constant of 7 for the concrete complexity of Strassen's algorithm [43], while a constant of 3 for the concrete complexity of BW [30, Theorem 7]. One can check that for the specific parameters proposed by the GeMSS team, the value $n' = 2d + 1$ is high enough to ensure to solve at degree 2 in Step 2, i.e. $n_u \leq n_{c_T}$. Similarly, the behavior of our attack on pHFEv- is given in Table 5. We adopt the parameters from [36, Table 2] using $\omega = 2.81$. In this paper, the value of p was chosen such that the minors attack from [40] is just above the security level. On these parameters, one notices that our attack always succeeds in solving at degree 2 with $n' = 2d' + 1 = 2(d + p) + 1$. As before, for those parameters the values of d' are indeed high enough to guarantee $n_u \leq n_{c_T}$.

Table 4. Complexity of our attack ($\log_2(\#\text{gates})$) versus known attacks from [40] for the GeMSS parameters.

Scheme	Minors [40]	SM [40]	SM Step 1 (Strassen/BW)	SM Step 2 (Strassen)	n'
GeMSS128	139	118	76/72	54	21
BlueGeMSS128	119	99	65/65	51	17
RedGeMSS128	86	72	49/53	45	11
GeMSS192	154	120	78/75	57	21
BlueGeMSS192	132	101	67/67	53	17
RedGeMSS192	95	75	51/55	48	11
GeMSS256	166	121	79/77	59	21
BlueGeMSS256	141	103	68/69	55	17
RedGeMSS256	101	76	52/57	50	11

The nature of our approach, although in theory similar to the one used in [40], allows us to reduce significantly the complexity of the Support-Minors attack performed by Tao et al. against GeMSS. This is important since this improvement makes it completely infeasible to repair GeMSS by simply increasing the size of its parameters without turning it into an impractical scheme. The dominant cost of our attack is the initial linear algebra step (dense or sparse) on the Support-Minors equations, whereas in [40] an attacker needs to multiply these equations by linear and/or minor variables to solve the system. This explains why we obtain a much smaller cost than the one presented in column "SM [40]". Another noticeable difference between our work and the one in [40] is that their complexity estimate is conjectural, whereas ours is proven under mild assumptions in comparison.

The results from Table 5 also suggest that the projection modifier on HFEv- will not be sufficient to repair the scheme as we have significantly broken the parameters given in [36]. To meet the new security levels, the value of p should be increased by a consequential amount, making the scheme inefficient. For example, to achieve security level 128 with the former GeMSS128 parameters, one should take $p = 14$, increasing the signing time by a factor q^{14}, which is considerable.

Table 5. Complexity of our attack ($\log_2(\#\text{gates})$) versus known attacks from [40] for pHFEv-. The pHFEv- parameter set for level x consists of (q, n, v, D, a, p), where (q, n, v, D, a) is taken from GeMSSx and $p \geq 0$ is the smallest value such that the cost of the minors attack [40] is just above x.

Scheme	p	Minors [36,40]	SM Step 1 (Strassen/BW)	SM Step 2 (Strassen)	n'
GeMSS128	0	139	76/72	54	21
BlueGeMSS128	1	128	71/69	53	19
RedGeMSS128	4	128	71/69	53	19
GeMSS192	5	201	105/95	67	31
BlueGeMSS192	7	201	105/95	67	31
RedGeMSS192	10	205	105/95	67	31
GeMSS256	10	256	134/117	79	41
BlueGeMSS256	11	256	129/113	77	39
RedGeMSS256	14	263	129/113	77	39

7   Experiments for Step 1

We have performed experiments in Magma-2.23-8 in order to explore the feasibility of the attack on GeMSS. We focus on Step 1, because its cost dominates the total cost as discussed in Sect. 5. We measure the running time of this step for larger parameters so that a trend can be observed. For these experiments, we selected $a = v \approx n/10$, a small prime $q > 2$ and $d = \lceil \log_q(D) \rceil \geq 3$. We chose the number of columns n' to be the smallest integer such that $n_{c_T} \geq n_u$, i.e. $\binom{n'}{d} \geq n$, so the system from Step 2 is solved at degree 2.

Figure 1 summarizes the results of these experiments. In the graph, the theoretical value is the logarithm in base two of the time complexity given in Equation (8) with $n_u = n - 1$, $n_{c_T} = \binom{n'}{d} - 1$, $\omega = 2.81$ and a hidden constant from the Strassen's algorithm taken equal to 7. The experimental complexity is measured in terms of clock cycles of the CPU given by the Magma command ClockCycles(). The matrix reduction was done via the Magma command GroebnerBasis($\mathcal{Q}$, 2), which is equivalent to Reduce($\mathcal{Q}$) in this context[1], yet more efficient.

Our goal here is to discuss how feasible an attack on GeMSS is. For example, the level I parameter set RedGeMSS128 is $(q, n, v, D, a) = (2, 177, 15, 17, 15)$, so that $d = 5$. According to our estimates its complexity is upper bounded by 2^{49}, as shown in Table 4. For this value of d, we have been able to run experiments up to $n = 160$, which is quite close to the goal of 177. Figure 1 also shows that the estimated complexity is a good upper bound for the computation's complexity. Note that the jump in the $d = 4$ curves corresponds to a change in the value of n'. Indeed, one can solve the system from Step 2 at degree 2 with $n' = 2d + 1 = 9$ as long as $n \leq 126$, and otherwise one has to consider $n' > 2d + 1$, for instance $n' = 2d + 2$ for the rest of the data points in these curves.

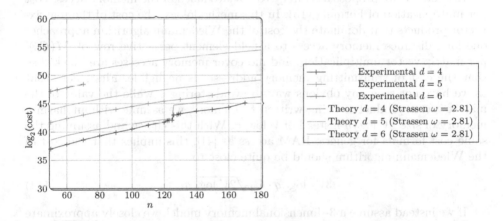

Fig. 1. Experimental vs Theoretical value of the complexity of Step 1.

8   Memory Management Strategy for the Support-Minors Equations Within Block Wiedemann

This section is dedicated to the study of the memory complexity associated to the XL strategy on a very large Support-Minors system $\mathcal{Q}_b$ with possibly $b > 1$

---

[1] The two procedures are equivalent because the system is bilinear, hence quadratic, and Gröbner bases are automatically reduced in Magma.

such as in attacks on rank metric code-based cryptosystems [5] or in the recent rectangular MinRank attack on Rainbow [9]. The core operation here is the use of Block-Wiedemann, whose cost is dominated by the combined cost of a large number of matrix-vector multiplications, where the matrix is a fixed, full-rank, square submatrix $M(\mathcal{Q}_b)'$ of the initial Macaulay matrix $M(\mathcal{Q}_b)$. Note that this matrix-vector product occurs approximately $3V$ times, where V is the dimension of the vector $\boldsymbol{v}$ being multiplied. While the cost of these multiplications is often expressed in terms of the number of field operations involved, it is likely that for cryptographically-interesting instances, this cost is dominated instead by queries to a large memory. In [41], the cost of a random access memory query is estimated by the formula

$$C_2 \log_2 V \sqrt{V \log_2 q}, \tag{13}$$

where $C_2 > 0$ is a constant, and it is asserted that such a random access must occur every time a field multiplication is performed in the Wiedemann algorithm. Here, [41] follows [7] in estimating the cost of moving a bit in a memory of size $V \log_2 q$—the size of $\boldsymbol{v}$—as $C_2 \sqrt{V \log_2 q}$. The constant $C_2 = 2^{-5}$ is used in [7], [41] and, where we provide concrete numbers, in our paper.

In Sect. 8.1, we propose a strategy to obviate much of the memory access cost per multiplication of Formula (13). In this methodology, the cost of the matrix-vector products that dominate the cost of the Wiedemann algorithm approaches one long distance memory access to a field element per active row of $M(\mathcal{Q}_b)'$ per matrix-vector multiplication, and moreover memory accesses are blocked so that the cost of transmitting memory addresses is negligible. First, note that as we have not seen any obvious way to avoid storing $\boldsymbol{v}$ while the value of the matrix-vector product is being written to memory, we assume without harm a memory of size $2V \log_2 q$ instead of $V \log_2 q$. With this choice and assuming the same cost formula for generic RAM access as [41], this implies that the cost of the Wiedemann algorithm should be quite close to

$$3V^2 \log_2 q \cdot C_2 \sqrt{2V \log_2 q}. \tag{14}$$

If we instead assume a 3-dimensional memory model, we closely approximate a similar formula for the cost with $(2V \log_2 q)^{1/3}$ substituted for $\sqrt{2V \log_2 q}$ and a different constant. In Sect. 8.2, we analyze the memory costs associated to our strategy with this 2-dimensional memory model in mind with the understanding that it is a trivial matter to adjust them to the 3-dimensional model. Finally, we apply our formulae in Sect. 8.3 to the rectangular MinRank attack [9] to show that at least in this case our results are indeed close to Formula (14).

8.1   Hashing Strategy on the Main Memory

Each coordinate of a matrix-vector product performed within the Wiedemann algorithm is obtained from a vector-vector product of the form

$$\boldsymbol{r}\boldsymbol{v}^{\mathsf{T}} = \sum_{i \in \mathrm{Supp}(\boldsymbol{r})} r_i v_i,$$

where r is a row of the Macaulay matrix with support $\mathrm{Supp}(r)$ of size w, whose elements can be cheaply computed on the fly. The cost estimates in [41] effectively assign a cost of w random access queries in a memory of size V to perform this vector-vector product. This would be accurate if the corresponding sum is computed by a central processor which first computes the nonzero elements r_i, then fetches v_i for $i \in \mathrm{Supp}(r)$ from memory, and finally multiplies each r_i by the corresponding v_i and sums the products.

The strategy we propose, however, will partition the main memory in which the v_i's are stored, so that for each row r, the v_i's with $i \in \mathrm{Supp}(r)$ will be clustered into a small number of groups such that the v_i's in each group are all in the same memory partition. This allows a distributed approach where a processor assigned to each memory partition Π computes the nonzero r_i's for $v_i \in \Pi$ and then computes the partial sum $\sum_{v_i \in \Pi} r_i v_i$. This partial sum is then transmitted by each such processing cluster to that cluster among them located in the section of memory where the total sum is to be written. Thus, most of the arithmetic is performed locally, within each partition, with "remote" communication only between the small number of relevant processing clusters.

To establish this partition, we observe that each pair of memory addresses— a read address for a coordinate of the vector v and a write address for the same coordinate of the product $M(\mathcal{Q}_b)'v^{\mathsf{T}}$— corresponds to a fixed bi-degree $(b, 1)$ monomial. Also, any row r is associated to an equation of $\mathcal{Q}_b$ of the form $\mu Q_{i,J}$, where J is a collection of $d + 1$ columns of the matrix M. The thing each monomial in such an equation has in common is that the minor variable present corresponds to a subset of J of size d; that is, it belongs to the set $\{c_{J\setminus\{j\}}, j \in J\}$. We may thus define an h-bit hash H for each monomial, where bit $i \in \{1, \dots, h\}$ of $H(\mu c_{J\setminus\{j\}})$ is 1 exactly when $i \in J \setminus \{j\}$. Since there is significant overlap in which columns are present in a minor corresponding to a minor variable within each equation, we expect each row r to involve relatively few possible hash values, thereby minimizing "remote" communication.

We may assume, as in [16,41], that the cost of distributing the MinRank instance and a seed for a PRNG to generate the same square submatrix of the Macaulay matrix to the 2^h processing clusters arising from our hashing strategy is insignificant in comparison to the cost of running the Wiedemann algorithm. Thus, the hashing strategy has the potential to produce a significant savings in memory access cost by making the vast majority of the multiplications in the Wiedemann algorithm local.

8.2   Memory Savings from Our Approach

In this section, we analyze the memory savings of our approach compared to a naive XL implementation which does not take advantage of structure within the SM system, see Fact 2. First, note that rows of the full Macaulay matrix $M(\mathcal{Q}_b)$ can be grouped in blocks of size n_r of the form $\{\mu Q_{i,J}, 1 \le i \le n_r\}$, where $J \subset \{1..n_c\}$, $\#J = d + 1$ and where μ is a fixed monomial of degree $b - 1$ in the linear variables. While not all of these n_r rows of $M(\mathcal{Q}_b)$ are present in the square submatrix $M(\mathcal{Q}_b)'$ input into the Wiedemann algorithm, on average

$$n_r' = \frac{\mathrm{rank}(M(\mathcal{Q}_b))}{\#\mathrm{blocks}} \approx \frac{\#\mathrm{cols}(M(\mathcal{Q}_b))}{\#\mathrm{blocks}} = \frac{\binom{N+b-1}{b}\binom{n_c}{d}}{\binom{N+b-2}{b-1}\binom{n_c}{d+1}}$$

such equations are included from each block. Fact 2 states that these equations have potential nonzero coefficients for $N(d+1)$ monomials all involving the same set of minor variables, and thus memory access patterns arising from vector-vector products involving these rows will be the same.

In our approach, each of these equations is considered by a given processing cluster in function of the presence or absence of the first h columns of M in the calculation of that equation. Note that the total number of choices of $d+1$ of the $n_c \geq h$ columns can be written

$$\underbrace{\binom{n_c}{d+1}}_{\#\mathrm{All\ patterns}} = \sum_{i=d+h+1-n_c}^{h} \binom{h}{i}\binom{n_c-h}{d+1-i},$$

where we have partitioned the choices by the hash value, and where binomial coefficients with a negative second argument, if they occur, are interpreted as zero. Therefore, for each hash value of Hamming weight i, there are $\binom{n_c-h}{d+1-i}$ choices of $d+1$ among the n_c columns of M including exactly that hash specified choice of i of these first h columns.

Memory Access Cost of One Field Element Within a Partition. The portion of memory required by the processing cluster corresponding to a hash H of Hamming weight i is of size $2V_i := 2\binom{n_c-h}{d+1-i}\binom{N+b-1}{b}$. This quantity includes all V_i memory locations associated with bidegree $(b, 1)$ monomials $\mu u_k c_T$, where $u_k c_T$ is a bilinear monomial from the initial SM system and such that $H_j = 1$ if and only if $j \in \{1..h\} \cap T$, as well as an equal amount of memory for writing output values. The total cost of reading every value of v within such a partition, that is, exactly half of the partition's values, is the product of the number of such values, the square root of memory size in bits and the communication cost for transmitting a field element and an address. This product is $(2\log_2 q)^{1/2}(\log_2 q + \log_2(2V_i \log_2 q))V_i^{3/2}$. Thus, summing this quantity across all $\binom{h}{i}$ hashes H of Hamming weight i for all values of i and dividing by the total size, $V = \binom{N+b-1}{b}\binom{n_c}{d}$, of read memory, we find that the average memory access cost of a field element within some memory partition is given by

$$\psi_1 = \frac{C_2(2\log_2 q)^{1/2}}{V} \sum_{i=d+h+1-n_c}^{h} \binom{h}{i}(\log_2 q + \log_2(2V_i \log_2 q))V_i^{3/2}. \quad (15)$$

Additional Costs Due to the Hashing Strategy. Still, our hash-based management scheme creates overhead that must be taken into account in the final cost. For any given row of the Macaulay matrix, there is a $(d+1)/n_c$ probability that the i-th column of M is used. Therefore, we expect the average vector-vector product to require $h(d+1)/n_c$ processing clusters to locally add products and then transmit to the designated accumulator. We further note that all of the processing clusters can transmit all of their partial sums of size $\log_2 q$ for every equation to the designated accumulator in a canonical order, removing the need for the transmission of an address of size $\log_2(2V)$ between the processing cluster and the accumulator for every equation. Therefore, dividing by $N(d+1)$, which is the number of monomials in any equation, we compute the average overhead incurred by using the hash strategy per multiplication to be

$$\psi_2 = C_2 \frac{h \log_2 q}{n_c N} \sqrt{2V \log_2 q}. \qquad (16)$$

Total Cost Per $\mathbb{F}_q$ -Multiplication. Putting these pieces together, we compute the memory access cost per multiplication for solving a generic SM system with the Wiedemann algorithm as follows. Since each equation belongs to a set of, on average, n'_r equations having the exact same $N(d+1)$ monomials, and noting that even for very large SM systems the quantity $N(d+1) \log_2 q$ is small, each processing cluster may retrieve these values only once and store them in its local cache while computing each of the n'_r partial sums. Thus, each field element is accessed $\rho := 1/n'_r$ times on average per multiplication by a processing cluster. Multiplying this average number of accesses by the average access cost ψ_1 within that partition and adding the above computed overhead ψ_2, we obtain

$$\text{Total Memory Cost Per Multiplication} = \rho\psi_1 + \psi_2. \qquad (17)$$

Recall that the validity of Eqs. (15) and (16) depends on the acceptance of a two-dimensional nearest-neighbor topology being optimal for large scale memory. If we prefer a three-dimensional nearest-neighbor topology of a similar nature, the above formulae still work when each exponent of $1/2$ is replaced by $1/3$, $3/2$ is replaced by $4/3$ and C_2 is replaced by a new constant C_3.

Neglected Costs. There are many costs to consider that arise from the hashing strategy that are either slight or negligible, hence they are not included in Equation (17). We provide a detailed analysis of some of these costs in [3, Appendix B].

8.3   Application to the Rainbow Rectangular MinRank Attack [9]

In this section, we estimate the memory access cost of our hashing scheme applied to the rectangular MinRank attack [9]. In comparison to our GeMSS attack, the sizes of the SM systems encountered there can be significant. In particular, [41] pointed out that it may be vital to consider memory access costs in this context. Recall from Sect. 2.3 that the "MinRank $+ \mathcal{P} = 0$" version of this attack considers the hybrid system $\mathcal{H}$ combining the SM equations $\mathcal{Q}$ with the m public equations $\mathcal{P}(\boldsymbol{y}) = 0$ which are quadratic in the linear variables present in $\mathcal{Q}$. In this case, the Macaulay matrix $\boldsymbol{M}(\mathcal{H}_b)$ in bi-degree $(b, 1)$ is obtained by taking the rows of $\boldsymbol{M}(\mathcal{Q}_b)$ together with these bi-degree $(2, 0)$ public equations p_i for $1 \le i \le m$ multiplied by all degree $(b - 2, 1)$ monomials ν. The effect of adding $\mathcal{P} = 0$ to SM is that for a fixed number of columns n_c of $\boldsymbol{M}$, the resulting hybrid system may be solved at a smaller degree b than the initial Support-Minors one. In general, the system $\mathcal{H}$ can be solved in degree $(b, 1)$ with any subset of the SM and $\mathcal{P} = 0$ equations of rank $V = \binom{N+b-1}{b}\binom{n_c}{d} - 1$. As derived in [9], under standard genericity assumptions such a subset exists at degree $(b, 1)$ when the coefficient of t^b in $(1 - t^2)^N G'(t)$ is non-positive, where $G'(t)$ is the generating function for the quotient of the polynomial ring by $\mathcal{Q}$. In particular, since both b and n_c are parameters of the SM equations, it is possible to construct an augmented SM system s.t. $\operatorname{rank}(\boldsymbol{M}(\mathcal{Q}_b)) < V$ while $\operatorname{rank}(\boldsymbol{M}(\mathcal{H}_b)) = V$. Note that the rank $R_{SM,b}$ of $\boldsymbol{M}(\mathcal{Q}_b)$ is given by [5, Heuristic 2] when this quantity is smaller than V, and therefore $\boldsymbol{M}(\mathcal{H}_b)$ will be of full rank if there exist at least $V - R_{SM,b}$ linearly independent equations in bi-degree $(b, 1)$ derived from $\mathcal{P} = 0$. In practice, as is found in [9, Table 6], optimization of this attack often occurs at a lower value of n_c and a higher value of b than when considering the SM system alone.

Adapting the Approach to the $\mathcal{P} = 0$ Equations. To take these augmented $\mathcal{P} = 0$ equations into account in our hashing methodology, a first remark is that they trivially come in groups of size m of the form $\{\nu p_i, \ 1 \le i \le m\}$ with the same monomial content, a set of $\binom{N+1}{2}$ monomials all involving the unique minor variable which divides ν, where we set $N := n - o_2 + 1$ and $d := o_2$ to stick to the notation from Sect. 3. This structure implies that any vector-vector product $\boldsymbol{r}\boldsymbol{v}^{\mathsf{T}}$ where $\boldsymbol{r}$ corresponds to a $\mathcal{P} = 0$ equation can be computed by a single processing cluster under the strategy we outlined in Sect. 8.1. Having at most one processing cluster required to compute the vector-vector product and having at most one long distance transmission of the sum to the designated processor that writes the value in memory, the $\mathcal{P} = 0$ equations are much more efficient than the SM equations, even if they contain many more monomials per equation, as $\binom{N+1}{2} > N(d + 1)$ for most parameters.

Another important remark is that any basis of the rowspace of $\boldsymbol{M}(\mathcal{H}_b)$ can be made to contain as many of the $\mathcal{P} = 0$ equations as are linearly independent. First, note that the first fall degree of the polynomial system $\mathcal{P}$—which was extensively tested in direct attacks on UOV/Rainbow—is significantly higher than the solving degree of the SM system using the $(b, 1)$ XL strategy. Also, the assumptions which were proposed and empirically verified on pages 22–23 of [9] for the hybrid system are actually stronger than assuming that merely the $\mathcal{P} = 0$ quadratic system is generic. Thus, there seems to be no harm in assuming that with high probability, the number $R_{P,b}$ of linearly independent $\mathcal{P} = 0$ equations can be calculated as $R_{P,b} = \binom{n_c}{d}[t^b]H(t)$, where $H(t) = \frac{1-(1-t^2)^m}{(1-t)^N}$ and where $[t^b]H(t)$ represents the coefficient of t^b in the power series expansion of H. Finally, recall that we have to add as many SM equations as possible to these

$\mathcal{P} = 0$ equations in order to reach the final rank V. Since SM equations occur in the span of the augmented $\mathcal{P} = 0$ polynomials, the rank of the Macaulay will not always increase by 1 each time we add a random SM equation. Under the standard heuristic that these equations behave as random vectors in a space of the appropriate dimension, any random subset of $R_{P,b}$ of these $\mathcal{P} = 0$ equations should be linearly independent with probability around $1 - q^{-1}$, and a similar argument under the same heuristic can be used again to verify that this system can be extended to a full rank system with randomly chosen SM equations with a similarly high probability. For clarity, we do not add the factor corresponding to this probability in our estimations as we can treat it as a constant.

Overall Costs. Naturally, using fewer of the SM equations requires a recalculation of the average number n'_r of equations included in the system from among each block of equations with the exact same monomial content. With the above strategy, we have

$$n'_r = \frac{V - R_{P,b}}{\#\text{blocks}},$$

and the value of $\rho := 1/n'_r$ is adjusted accordingly. Thus we may compute the total cost of the hybrid attack against Rainbow. Let σ_{SM} denote the ratio $(V - R_{P,b})/V$ of SM equations to total equations in the hybrid system corresponding to $M(\mathcal{H}_b)'$ and let $\sigma_P = R_{P,b}/V$ represent the ratio of $\mathcal{P} = 0$ equations. Then, the total cost under the same assumptions on memory cost of [41] and using the method described in Sect. 8.1 is given by

$$3(\rho\psi_1 + \psi_2)V^2\sigma_{\text{SM}}N(d+1)$$
$$+ 3\left(\frac{\psi_1}{m} + C_2 \log_2 q(2V \log_2 q)^{1/2}\right)V^2\sigma_P\binom{N+1}{2},$$

where we recall that $N = n - o_2 + 1$ and where ψ_1 is defined in Equation (15). Since $R_{P,b}$ is significantly smaller than $V - R_{P,b}$ and the $\mathcal{P} = 0$ equations are much more memory efficient than the SM equations, we find that the contribution of the $\mathcal{P} = 0$ equations in complexity ends up being a negligible fraction of the total cost for all the parameters we consider. Finally, we present the total estimated cost of applying XL using the hash method to the rectangular Min-Rank attack on Rainbow in the 2-dimensional case in Table 6, and we compare it to the conjectured formula given by (14).

9   Conclusion

The Support-Minors modeling of the MinRank problem [5] has changed our perspective of the applicability of rank methods in cryptanalysis. This new technique has changed the complexity of many MinRank instances by a significant amount *in the exponent*. In addition, this advance has opened up new avenues for cryptanalysis by making newly discovered attacks that exploit rank viable,

Table 6. Optimal hash size (h) and total attack cost including idle costs for the MinRank (SM) and "MinRank + $\mathcal{P} = 0$" (SM+$\mathcal{P}$) attacks in the 2D nearest-neighbor topology model for Rainbow variants compared with the conjectured bound (2D Conj.) of Formula (14) and the required security level using the constant $C_2 = 2^{-5}$.

Scheme (q, n, m, d)		2D SM	2D SM+$\mathcal{P}$	2D Conj.	Security Level
Rainbow-I $(16, 100, 64, 32)$	cost (hash)	$2^{146.9}$ ($h = 12$)	$2^{139.5}$ ($h = 14$)	$2^{135.8}$	2^{143}
Rainbow-III $(256, 148, 80, 48)$	cost (hash)	$2^{205.9}$ ($h = 16$)	$2^{201.2}$ ($h = 16$)	$2^{197.4}$	2^{207}
Rainbow-V $(256, 196, 100, 64)$	cost (hash)	$2^{272.4}$ ($h = 18$)	$2^{260.9}$ ($h = 19$)	$2^{256.9}$	2^{272}

e.g. [9,40]. This new MinRank algorithm has inspired recent efforts to repair broken schemes, see [36], and work to estimate the real-world complexity of implementing Support-Minors via XL, see [41]. In particular, [36] claims to offer protection from the Support-Minors method by way of a modification of GeMSS called pHFEv- while [41] offers a first approximation of a memory cost analysis for solving Support-Minors.

In this work, we provide a technique for solving a Support-Minors MinRank instance with solutions in an extension field, verifying that both GeMSS and pHFEv- remain insecure for all practical parameters. Indeed, it turns out that the advantage of using Support-Minors in this scenario is significant and the complexity of the attack is much smaller than that of [40]. The attack is efficient enough so that with more effort it may finally be feasible to practically solve HFE Challenge 2 [18].

Also, with our hashing strategy, we give theoretical arguments of the same level as in [41] to show that much of the memory access cost described there may be obviated when solving large Support-Minors systems using XL. Moreover, while this hash strategy depends intimately on the structure of the Support-Minors system, it does not seem to depend strongly on the solving degree in the XL algorithm. This fact suggests that it may even be possible to fully parallelize XL generically. This task remains an important direction for future work.

Acknowledgments. The Magma experiments of Sect. 7 were carried out using the Grid'5000 testbed, supported by a scientific interest group hosted by Inria and including CNRS, RENATER and several Universities as well as other organizations (see https://www.grid5000.fr). This work was supported by a grant from the Simons Foundation (712530, DCST).

References

1. Albrecht, M.R., et al.: Classic McEliece: round 3 (2020). www.classic.mceliece.org/nist/mceliece-20201010.pdf. Accessed 10 Sep. 2021
2. Baena, J., Verbel, J.: Sage tool for the GeMSS attack (2021). www.github.com/jbbaena/Attack_on_GeMSS/blob/main/Attack_on_GeMSS.ipynb
3. Baena, J., Briaud, P., Cabarcas, D., Perlner, R., Smith-Tone, D., Verbel, J.: Improving support-minors rank attacks: applications to GeMSS and Rainbow. Cryptology ePrint Archive, Paper 2021/1677 (2021). www.eprint.iacr.org/2021/1677
4. Bardet, M., Briaud, P.: An algebraic approach to the rank support learning problem. In: Cheon, J.H., Tillich, J.-P. (eds.) PQCrypto 2021 2021. LNCS, vol. 12841, pp. 442–462. Springer, Cham (2021). https://doi.org/10.1007/978-3-030-81293-5_23
5. Bardet, M., et al.: Improvements of algebraic attacks for solving the rank decoding and MinRank problems. In: Moriai, S., Wang, H. (eds.) ASIACRYPT 2020. LNCS, vol. 12491, pp. 507–536. Springer, Cham (2020). https://doi.org/10.1007/978-3-030-64837-4_17
6. Bardet, M., Mora, R., Tillich, J.P.: Decoding Reed-Solomon codes by solving a bilinear system with a Gröbner basis approach. In: 2021 IEEE International Symposium on Information Theory (ISIT), pp. 872–877 (2021)
7. Bernstein, D.J., et al.: NTRU prime: round 3 (2020). www.ntruprime.cr.yp.to/nist/ntruprime-20201007.pdf. Accessed 26 Sep. 2021
8. Bettale, L., Faugère, J.C., Perret, L.: Cryptanalysis of HFE, multi-HFE and variants for odd and even characteristic. Des. Codes Cryptogr. **69**(1), 1–52 (2013)
9. Beullens, W.: Improved cryptanalysis of UOV and rainbow. In: Canteaut, A., Standaert, F.-X. (eds.) EUROCRYPT 2021. LNCS, vol. 12696, pp. 348–373. Springer, Cham (2021). https://doi.org/10.1007/978-3-030-77870-5_13
10. Billet, O., Gilbert, H.: Cryptanalysis of rainbow. In: De Prisco, R., Yung, M. (eds.) SCN 2006. LNCS, vol. 4116, pp. 336–347. Springer, Heidelberg (2006). https://doi.org/10.1007/11832072_23
11. Bosma, W., Cannon, J., Playoust, C.: The Magma algebra system. I. The user language. J. Symb. Comput. **24**(3–4), 235 265 (1997). https://doi.org/10.1006/jsco.1996.0125
12. Buss, J.F., Frandsen, G.S., Shallit, J.O.: The computational complexity of some problems of linear algebra. J. Comput. Syst. Sci. **58**(3), 572–596 (1999)
13. Casanova, A., Faugère, J.C., Macario-Rat, G., Patarin, J., Perret, L., Ryckeghem, J.: GeMSS: a great multivariate short signature. NIST CSRC (2020). www.polsys.lip6.fr/Links/NIST/GeMSS_specification_round2.pdf
14. Chen, M.S., Yang, B.Y., Smith-Tone, D.: PFLASH—Secure asymmetric signatures on smart cards. In: Lightweight Cryptography Workshop 2015 (2015). www.csrc.nist.gov/groups/ST/lwc-workshop2015/papers/session3-smith-tone-paper.pdf
15. Chen, C., et al.: NTRU: round 3 (2019). www.ntru.org/f/ntru-20190330.pdf
16. Cheng, C.-M., Chou, T., Niederhagen, R., Yang, B.-Y.: Solving quadratic equations with XL on parallel architectures. In: Prouff, E., Schaumont, P. (eds.) CHES 2012. LNCS, vol. 7428, pp. 356–373. Springer, Heidelberg (2012). https://doi.org/10.1007/978-3-642-33027-8_21
17. Coppersmith, D.: Solving homogeneous linear equations over GF(2) via block Wiedemann algorithm. Math. Comput. **62**(205), 333–350 (1994)
18. Courtois, N.: Algebraic attacks over GF(2k), application to HFE challenge 2 and Sflash-v2, pp. 201–217 (2004)

19. Courtois, N., Klimov, A., Patarin, J., Shamir, A.: Efficient algorithms for solving overdefined systems of multivariate polynomial equations. In: Preneel, B. (ed.) EUROCRYPT 2000. LNCS, vol. 1807, pp. 392–407. Springer, Heidelberg (2000). https://doi.org/10.1007/3-540-45539-6_27

20. Courtois, N.T.: Efficient zero-knowledge authentication based on a linear algebra problem MinRank. In: Boyd, C. (ed.) ASIACRYPT 2001. LNCS, vol. 2248, pp. 402–421. Springer, Heidelberg (2001). https://doi.org/10.1007/3-540-45682-1_24

21. Ding, J., Chen, M.S., Petzoldt, A., Schmidt, D.: Gui. NIST CSRC (2017). http://www.csrc.nist.gov/Projects/post-quantum-cryptography/Round-1-Submissions

22. Ding, J., Chen, M.S., Petzoldt, A., Schmidt, D., Yang, B.Y.: Rainbow. NIST CSRC (2020). http://www.csrc.nist.gov/Projects/post-quantum-cryptography/round-3-submissions

23. Ding, J., Petzoldt, A., Wang, L.: The cubic simple matrix encryption scheme. In: Mosca, M. (ed.) PQCrypto 2014. LNCS, vol. 8772, pp. 76–87. Springer, Cham (2014). https://doi.org/10.1007/978-3-319-11659-4_5

24. Dubois, V., Fouque, P.-A., Shamir, A., Stern, J.: Practical cryptanalysis of SFLASH. In: Menezes, A. (ed.) CRYPTO 2007. LNCS, vol. 4622, pp. 1–12. Springer, Heidelberg (2007). https://doi.org/10.1007/978-3-540-74143-5_1

25. Faugère, J.C., Safey El Din, M., Spaenlehauer, P.J.: Computing loci of rank defects of linear matrices using Göbner bases and applications to cryptology. In: ISSAC 2010–35th International Symposium on Symbolic and Algebraic Computation, pp. 257–264. ACM, Munich (2010). http://www.hal.archives-ouvertes.fr/hal-01057840

26. Faugére, J.C.: A new efficient algorithm for computing Gröbner bases (F4). J. Pure Appl. Algebra **139**, 61–88 (1999)

27. Fauqére, J.C.: A new efficient algorithm for computing Gröbner bases without reduction to zero (F5). In: ISSAC 2002, pp. 75–83. ACM Press (2002)

28. Goubin, L., Courtois, N.T.: Cryptanalysis of the TTM cryptosystem. In: Okamoto, T. (ed.) ASIACRYPT 2000. LNCS, vol. 1976, pp. 44–57. Springer, Heidelberg (2000). https://doi.org/10.1007/3-540-44448-3_4

29. Jiang, X., Ding, J., Hu, L.: Kipnis-Shamir attack on HFE revisited. In: Pei, D., Yung, M., Lin, D., Wu, C. (eds.) Inscrypt 2007. LNCS, vol. 4990, pp. 399–411. Springer, Heidelberg (2008). https://doi.org/10.1007/978-3-540-79499-8_31

30. Kaltofen, E.: Analysis of Coppersmith's block Wiedemann algorithm for the parallel solution of sparse linear systems. Math. Comput. **64**(210), 777–806 (1995). https://www.jstor.org/stable/2153451

31. Kipnis, A., Shamir, A.: Cryptanalysis of the HFE public key cryptosystem by relinearization. In: Wiener, M. (ed.) CRYPTO 1999. LNCS, vol. 1666, pp. 19–30. Springer, Heidelberg (1999). https://doi.org/10.1007/3-540-48405-1_2

32. Longa, P., Wang, W., Szefer, J.: The cost to break SIKE: a comparative hardware-based analysis with AES and SHA-3. In: Malkin, T., Peikert, C. (eds.) CRYPTO 2021. LNCS, vol. 12827, pp. 402–431. Springer, Cham (2021). https://doi.org/10.1007/978-3-030-84252-9_14

33. Matsumoto, T., Imai, H.: Public quadratic polynomial-tuples for efficient signature-verification and message-encryption. In: Barstow, D., et al. (eds.) EUROCRYPT 1988. LNCS, vol. 330, pp. 419–453. Springer, Heidelberg (1988). https://doi.org/10.1007/3-540-45961-8_39

34. Mohamed, M.S.E., Ding, J., Buchmann, J.: Towards algebraic cryptanalysis of HFE challenge 2. In: Kim, T., Adeli, H., Robles, R.J., Balitanas, M. (eds.) ISA 2011. CCIS, vol. 200, pp. 123–131. Springer, Heidelberg (2011). https://doi.org/10.1007/978-3-642-23141-4_12

35. Niederhagen, R.: Parallel cryptanalysis. Ph.D. thesis. Eindhoven University of Technology (2012). http://www.polycephaly.org/thesis/index.shtml
36. Øygarden, M., Smith-Tone, D., Verbel, J.: On the effect of projection on rank attacks in multivariate cryptography. In: Cheon, J.H., Tillich, J.-P. (eds.) PQCrypto 2021 2021. LNCS, vol. 12841, pp. 98–113. Springer, Cham (2021). https://doi.org/10.1007/978-3-030-81293-5_6
37. Patarin, J.: Hidden fields equations (HFE) and isomorphisms of polynomials (IP): two new families of asymmetric algorithms. In: Maurer, U. (ed.) EUROCRYPT 1996. LNCS, vol. 1070, pp. 33–48. Springer, Heidelberg (1996). https://doi.org/10.1007/3-540-68339-9_4
38. Petzoldt, A., Chen, M.-S., Yang, B.-Y., Tao, C., Ding, J.: Design principles for HFEv- based multivariate signature schemes. In: Iwata, T., Cheon, J.H. (eds.) ASIACRYPT 2015. LNCS, vol. 9452, pp. 311–334. Springer, Heidelberg (2015). https://doi.org/10.1007/978-3-662-48797-6_14
39. Porras, J., Baena, J., Ding, J.: ZHFE, a new multivariate public key encryption scheme. In: Mosca, M. (ed.) PQCrypto 2014. LNCS, vol. 8772, pp. 229–245. Springer, Cham (2014). https://doi.org/10.1007/978-3-319-11659-4_14
40. Tao, C., Petzoldt, A., Ding, J.: Efficient key recovery for all HFE signature variants. In: Malkin, T., Peikert, C. (eds.) CRYPTO 2021. LNCS, vol. 12825, pp. 70–93. Springer, Cham (2021). https://doi.org/10.1007/978-3-030-84242-0_4
41. The Rainbow Team: Response to recent paper by Ward Beullens (2020). http://www.troll.iis.sinica.edu.tw/by-publ/recent/response-ward.pdf
42. Vates, J., Smith-Tone, D.: Key recovery attack for all parameters of HFE-. In: Lange, T., Takagi, T. (eds.) PQCrypto 2017. LNCS, vol. 10346, pp. 272–288. Springer, Cham (2017). https://doi.org/10.1007/978-3-319-59879-6_16
43. Volker, S.: Gaussian elimination is not optimal. Numerische Mathematik **13**, 354–356 (1969)

Distributed Algorithms

log*-Round Game-Theoretically-Fair Leader Election

Ilan Komargodski[1,2]($\boxtimes$) (iD), Shin'ichiro Matsuo[2,3] (iD), Elaine Shi[4], and Ke Wu[4] (iD)

[1] School of Computer Science and Engineering, Hebrew University of Jerusalem,
91904 Jerusalem, Israel
ilank@cs.huji.ac.il
[2] NTT Research, Sunnyvale 94085, USA
shinichiro.matsuo@ntt-research.com
[3] Department of Computer Science, Georgetown University,
Washington D.C. 20057, USA
[4] Computer Science Department, Carnegie Mellon University, Pittsburgh 15213, USA
kew2@andrew.cmu.edu

Abstract. It is well-known that in the presence of majority coalitions, *strongly fair* coin toss is impossible. A line of recent works have shown that by relaxing the fairness notion to game theoretic, we can overcome this classical lower bound. In particular, Chung et al. (CRYPTO'21) showed how to achieve approximately (game-theoretically) fair leader election in the presence of majority coalitions, with round complexity as small as $O(\log \log n)$ rounds.

In this paper, we revisit the round complexity of game-theoretically fair leader election. We construct $O(\log^* n)$ rounds leader election protocols that achieve $(1 - o(1))$-approximate fairness in the presence of $(1 - o(1))n$-sized coalitions. Our protocols achieve the same round-fairness trade-offs as Chung et al.'s and have the advantage of being conceptually simpler. Finally, we also obtain game-theoretically fair protocols for committee election which might be of independent interest.

The full version of this paper is available at [KMSW22].

Y. Dodis and T. Shrimpton (Eds.): CRYPTO 2022, LNCS 13509, pp. 409–438, 2022.
https://doi.org/10.1007/978-3-031-15982-4_14

1   Introduction

Suppose that Murphy, Murky, and Moody co-authored a paper that proved a ground-breaking theorem and the paper got accepted at the prestigious CRYPTO'22 conference. Murphy, Murky, and Moody want to run a coin toss protocol over the Internet to elect a winner who will present the paper at the conference. Since everyone wants to go to the beautiful beaches of Santa Barbara, all of them want to be the winner. They each are worried that the other coauthors might deviate from the honest protocol to gain an unfair advantage. There is both good and bad news. The bad news is that due to a famous lower bound by Cleve [Cle86], there is no *strongly fair* coin toss protocol when half of the parties may be corrupt and misbehaving—roughly speaking, strong fairness requires that the coalition cannot bias the outcome of the coin toss whatsoever. The good news is that a more recent line of work [CCWS21, GGS, CGL+18, WAS22] has shown that a relaxed fairness notion called *game-theoretic* fairness is indeed possible for the leader election problem, even when an arbitrary number of parties may be corrupt. To see why, first observe that the original Blum's coin toss protocol [Blu83] actually gives a game-theoretically fair leader election scheme for $n = 2$ parties. Imagine that each party first commits to a random coin, they then open their coin, and the XOR of the two bits is used to elect a random winner. If one party fails to commit or correctly open, it is eliminated and the remaining party is declared the winner. Blum's coin toss satisfies *game-theoretic* fairness in the following sense. As long as the commitment scheme is not broken, a corrupt layer cannot bias the coin *to its own favor* no matter how it deviates from the protocol. Note that Blum's protocol is not strongly fair since a corrupt party can indeed bias the coin, but only to the other player's advantage.

For the more general case of the n parties, we can use a folklore tournament-tree protocol to accomplish the same purpose. Suppose that n is a power of 2 for simplicity. We first divide the n parties into $n/2$ pairs, and each pair elects a winner using Blum's coin toss. The winner survives to the next round, where we again divide the surviving $n/2$ parties into $n/4$ pairs. The protocol continues after a final winner is elected after $\log_2 n$ rounds. At any point in the protocol, if a party fails to commit or correctly open its commitment, it is eliminated and its opponent survives to the next round.

The recent work of Chung et al. [CCWS21] argued that this simple tournament tree protocol satisfies a strong notion of game-theoretic fairness as explained below. Suppose that the winner obtains a utility of 1 and everyone else obtains a utility of 0. As long as the commitment scheme is not broken, the tournament tree protocol guarantees that 1) no coalition of any size can *increase its own expected utility* no matter what (polynomially-bounded) strategy it adopts; and 2) no coalition of any size can *harm any individual honest player's expected utility*, no matter what (polynomially-bounded) strategy it adopts. Recent work in this space [CCWS21, GGS, CGL+18, WAS22] calls the former notion cooperative-strategy-proofness (or *CSP-fairness* for short), and calls the latter notion *maximin fairness*. Philosophically, CSP-fairness guarantees that any rational, profit-seeking individual or coalition has no incentive to deviate from the honest protocol; and maximin fairness ensures that any paranoid individual who wants to maximally protect itself in the worst-case scenario has no incentive to deviate either. In summary, the honest protocol is an equilibrium and also the best response for every player and coalition. Therefore, prior works [CGL+18, CCWS21, WAS22, GGS] have argued that game-theoretic notions of fairness are compelling and worth investigating because 1) they are arguably more natural (albeit strictly weaker) than the classical strong fairness notion in practical applications; and 2) the game-theoretic relaxation allows us to circumvent classical impossibility results pertaining to strong fairness in the presence of majority coalitions [Cle86].

Having established the general feasibility of game-theoretically fair leader election in the presence of majority-sized coalitions, Chung et al. [CCWS21] asked the following natural question: *what is the round complexity of game-theoretically fair leader election in the presence of majority coalitions?* Specifically, can we asymptotically outperform the logarithmic round complexity of the folklore tournament tree protocol? They then gave a partial answer to this question, showing that for any desired round complexity parameter $\Theta(\log \log n) \leq R \leq \log n$, there is an $O(R)$-round n-party leader election protocol that achieves $\left(1 - \frac{1}{2^{\Theta(R)}}\right)$-fairness against coalitions of size up to $\left(1 - \frac{1}{2^{\Theta(R)}}\right) n$. In particular, their result statement adopts an approximate notion of game-theoretic fairness. Roughly speaking, a protocol is $(1 - \epsilon)$-fair if it satisfies the aforementioned game theoretic fairness (including CSP-fairness and maximin fairness) up to an ϵ slack. More specifically, we want that the coalition's expected utility cannot exceed $1/(1-\epsilon)$ times its normal utility had everyone behaved honestly, and we require that any honest individual's expected utility cannot drop below $(1 - \epsilon)$ times its normal utility had everyone behaved honestly. Chung et al.'s result [CCWS21] enables a smooth and mathematically quantifiable trade-off between the efficiency of the protocol and its resilience to strategic behavior. However, their result requires the protocol to have at least $\Theta(\log \log n)$ rounds to give any meaningful fairness guarantee. Indeed, a more careful examination suggests that their framework has a *sharp* cutoff at $\Theta(\log \log n)$ rounds, i.e., the approach fundamentally fails when we want round complexity to be less than $\log \log n$. Therefore, an obvious gap in our understanding is the following:

In the presence of majority-sized coalitions, can we achieve any meaningful fairness guarantee for small-round protocols whose round complexity is less than $\log \log n$?

1.1 Our Results and Contributions

In this paper, we revisit the round complexity of game-theoretically fair leader election. We make the following contributions. First, we show positive results in the style of Chung et al. [CCWS21], but now for a broader range of parameters as explained in the following Theorem 1.1. In particular, our result shows that under standard cryptographic assumptions, there is a $O(\log^* n)$-round leader election protocol that achieves $(1 - o(1))$-game-theoretic-fairness, in the presence of $(1 - o(1)) \cdot n$-sized coalitions.

Second, we give conceptually simpler constructions than those of Chung et al. [CCWS21], which also result in simpler analyses. More specifically, Chung et al.'s construction relies on combinatorial objects called extractors, which we get rid of in our construction. We believe that our conceptually simpler constructions can lend to better understanding and make it easier for future work to extend our framework. Interestingly, our constructions are inspired and have structural resemblance to Feige's famous lightest bin leader election protocol [Fei99]. We stress, however, that Feige's protocol itself does not satisfy game-theoretic fairness, but rather, achieves only a much weaker notion of resilience, i.e., an honest party is elected leader with constant probability. At a very high level, our approach augments Feige's protocol lightest-bin protocol with a "commit and open" and a "virtual identity" mechanism, and we prove that the resulting protocol satisfies the desired game-theoretic properties.

Third, we also present results for the more generalized problem of fair committee election, where the goal is to elect a committee of size c. The leader election problem can be viewed as a special case of committee election where $c = 1$. Our main results are summarized in the following theorems.

Theorem 1.1 (Game-theoretically fair leader election). *Assume the existence of enhanced trapdoor permutations, and collision-resistant hash functions. Fix n and let $\log^* n \leq R \leq C \log n$ be the round complexity we want to achieve for some constant C. Then there exists an $O(R)$-round leader election that achieves $(1 - \frac{1}{2^{\Theta(R)}})$-game-theoretic fairness against a non-uniform p.p.t. coalition of size at most $(1 - \frac{L}{\Theta(R)})n$, where L is the smallest integer such that $\log^{(L)} n \leq 2^R$.*

For readers who are familiar with the line of work on approximate *strong* fairness [Cle86, MNS09, AO16, BOO10, HT14], an interesting observation is that for game-theoretic fairness, the efficiency-fairness tradeoff is exponentially better than that of strong fairness. Specifically, it is known that any R-round protocol cannot achieve $\Omega(1/R)$ *strong* fairness[1] against an $n/2$-sized coalition, whereas we show that R-round protocols can achieve $(1 - 1/2^{\Theta(R)})$-fairness.

Theorem 1.2 (Game-theoretically fair committee election). *Assume the existence of enhanced trapdoor permutations and collision-resistant hash functions. Fix n and c. Let L^* be the smallest integer such that $\log^{(L^*)} n \leq c$. Then for any $L^* \leq R \leq C_0 \log n$ for some constant C_0, we have that*

- *If $c \geq 2^R$, there exists an $O(R)$-round committee election that achieves $(1 - \frac{1}{c^{\Theta(1)}})$-game-theoretic fairness against a non-uniform p.p.t. coalition of size at most $(1 - \frac{L^*}{\Theta(R)})n$.*
- *If $c < 2^R$, there exists an $O(R)$-round committee election that achieves $(1 - \frac{1}{2^{\Theta(R)}})$-game-theoretic fairness against a non-uniform p.p.t. coalition of size at most $(1 - \frac{L}{\Theta(R)})n$, where L is the smallest integer such that $\log^{(L)} n \leq 2^R$.*

---

[1] The approximate strong fairness line of work defines what we call $(1 - \epsilon)$-fairness as ϵ-fairness (but for the notion of strong fairness instead). Following the notations of Chung et al. [CCWS21], we flipped this notation to make it more intuitive: with our notation, 1-fair is more fair than 0-fair which agrees with our intuition.

Below are some interesting examples with respect to different committee size c and the round complexity R.

- For committee size $c = 1$, i.e., leader election, and round complexity $R = O(\log^* n)$, our protocol achieves $\Theta(1)$-game-theoretic fairness against a coalition of size $\Theta(n)$ assuming $\log * n$ is a constant;
- For committee size $c = 1$, i.e., leader election, and round complexity $R = \log \log \log n$, out protocol achieves $(1 - \frac{1}{\text{poly} \log \log n})$-fairness against a coalition of size $n - \frac{n}{\Theta(\log \log \log n)}$.
- For committee size $c = \text{poly} \log \log n$ and for constant round complexity $R = \Theta(1)$, our protocol achieves $(1 - \frac{1}{\text{poly} \log \log n})$-fairness against $\Theta(n)$-sized coalition.

In this paper, we consider the standard notions of approximate CSP-fairness and maximin-fairness. The standard notion of approximate CSP-fairness is also sometimes referred to as *approximate coalition-resistant Nash equilibrium* in some earlier works such as Fruitchain [PS17]. It is also known [CCWS21] that the standard notion of approximate CSP-fairness (or maximin-fairness) is equivalent in some sense to approximate notions of fairness formulated by the more classical Rational Protocol Design (RPD) paradigm [GKM+13, GTZ15, GKTZ15].

Although the standard notion of approximate fairness seems the most natural one, Chung et al. [CCWS21] pointed out that when defining approximate fairness, one can in fact adopt a strengthened notion which they call sequential fairness. Their game-theoretically fair leader election result is in fact stated for the sequential notion. In this sense, our result is incomparable to theirs: they consider a stronger solution concept but their approach inherently cannot give any meaningful result for protocols of $o(\log \log n)$ rounds. By contrast, we consider the more standard non-sequential notion and we are able to generalize the smooth tradeoff between efficiency and fairness shown by Chung et al. [CCWS21] to a broader range of parameters.

1.2 Additional Related Work

Game Theory Meets Cryptography. Some recent efforts have instigated the intersection of the game theory [Nas51, Aum74] and multi-party computation [GMW19, Yao82]. See [Kat08, DR+07] for a survey. There have been two classes of questions that have attracted a lot of interests.

Some work [HT04, KN08, ADGH06, OPRV09, AL11, ACH11] explore how to define game-theoretic notions of security, as opposed to cryptography security notions for distributed computing tasks such as secure function evaluation. Existing works in this line considered a different notion of utility than our work. Their utility functions are often defined assuming that players prefer to compute the function correctly, or prefer to learn others' secret data and prefers that other players do not gain knowledge about their own secrets. Garay et al. propose a paradigm called Rational Protocol Design [GKM+13] and develop this paradigm in subsequent works [GTZ15, GKTZ15]. As mentioned in Sect. 1, the standard notion of approximate CSP-fairness (or maximin fairness) is in some sense equivalent to the approximate notion of fairness formulated in RPD paradigm.

Another line of work explores how cryptography can help traditional game theory. Many works in game theory assumed the existence of a trusted mediator, which can be realized under cryptography [DHR00,IML05,GK12,BGKO11].

Recently, there has been renewed interest in the connection between game theory and cryptography. Besides the work of Chung et al. [CCWS21] that inspires our work, and [GGS] that generalized the lower bound of the round complexity of game-theoretically fair leader election, the recent work [CGL+18, WAS22] have also suggested game-theoretically fair multi-party binary-coin toss. Binary-coin toss considers tossing a binary coin among n players, while in leader election, we consider tossing an n-way coin among n players. These two formulations are different and they exhibit starkly different theoretical landscape.

Leader Election in Other Models. Leader election has been studied extensively. A line of work [BK14,ADMM14] considered how to achieve "financially-fair" n-party lottery over cryptocurrencies. Their game-theoretic notion of fairness is similar to ours, yet they rely on collateral and penalty mechanisms to achieve fairness. As a comparison, our fairness can be achieved without relying on additional assumptions such as collateral and penalty. Moreover, [ADGH06] studied an incomparable game-theoretic notion for leader election. In their notions, all users prefer to have a leader, and users may have different preferences of who the leader is.

Besides, leader election was considered in the full information model [RZ01, RSZ02,Fei99,Dod06]. Their notion of security concentrates on electing an honest leader with some *small constant* probability, assuming honest majority [Fei99]. This notion is much weaker than the game-theoretic notion considered in our work, which are more suitable in some decentralized applications, where honest majority assumption is not applicable. Moreover, in the full-information model, leader election is impossible against a majority coalition even under this weak notion of security. Interestingly, our committee election protocol actually builds on Feige's lightest bin protocol [Fei99].

Approximate Strong Fairness. As mentioned in Sect. 1, the *de facto* notion of fairness considered in the multi-party computation literature is strong fairness or unbiasability. The celebrated result of Cleve [Cle86] showed that it is not possible to achieve $\Omega(\frac{1}{R})$-unbiasable coin toss against a coalition consisting of half or more players. Moran et al. [MNS09] showed how to obtain an R-round protocol that achieves $\Omega(\frac{1}{R})$-unbiasability in the two-party setting, that matches Cleve's lower bound. Recent work [AO16,BOO10,HT14] have been making encouraging progress on building fair multi-party coin toss. However, they rely on constant number of players to ensure polynomial round complexity. We cannot directly rely on multi-party unbiasable coin toss to build game-theoretically fair leader election because our trade-off curve between round complexity and the fairness slack ϵ is exponentially better than that of the unbiasability.

2 Technical Roadmap

2.1 Electing Poly-logarithmically Sized Committees: Achieving CSP-Fairness

We start by observing that a single iteration of Feige's lightest-bin proto-col [Fei99] can elect a committee of size $c \geq \text{poly} \log n$ while satisfying *CSP-fairness against relatively large coalitions*. Feige's ingenious protocol works as follows (we describe a single iteration of the protocol): each player $i \in [n]$ chooses a random bin b_i among a total of $B = n/c$ bins, and broadcasts its choice b_i. At this moment, we identify the lightest bin, and everyone who has placed itself in the lightest bin is elected as a committee member. A simple analysis shows that this protocol satisfies CSP-fairness against relatively large coalitions. Specifi-cally, the lightest bin cannot exceed a capacity of $c = n/B$. Moreover, applying the standard Chernoff bound and the union bound, we know that with proba-bility at least $1 - n \cdot \exp(-\Omega(\epsilon^4 \cdot c))$, a good event that every bin has at least $(1 - \epsilon^2) \cdot (1 - \beta) \cdot c$ honest players must happen, where $\beta \cdot n$ is the maximum coalition size for $\beta \in (0, 1)$. Now we show that if the coalition has size larger than $\epsilon \cdot n$, then Feige's lightest bin is $(1 - \Theta(\epsilon))$-CSP-fair. Given that the good event happens, the expected fraction of corrupted players in the committee is at most $1 - (1 - \epsilon^2) \cdot (1 - \beta) \leq \frac{\beta}{1-2\epsilon}$. For large n, it is easy to see that the good event happens with $1 - \text{negl}(n)$ probability and the expected fraction of coali-tion in the committee is at most $\frac{\beta}{1-\Theta(\epsilon)}$. For small n, however, the calculation is more involved, as we will describe below. The overall expected fraction of the coalition in the committee is at most $\frac{\beta}{1-2\epsilon} + \delta$, where $\delta = n \cdot \exp(-\Omega(\epsilon^4 \cdot c))$ is the probability that the good event does not happen. To guarantee that the expected fraction of the coalition in the committee is at most $\frac{\beta}{1-\Theta(\epsilon)}$, we need the failure probability $\delta \leq \beta \cdot \Theta(\epsilon)$. The expected fraction of the coalition in the committee is thus $\frac{\beta}{1-2\epsilon} + \delta \leq \beta(\frac{1}{1-2\epsilon} + \Theta(\epsilon)) \leq \frac{\beta}{1-\Theta(\epsilon)}$. For example, if we pick $\epsilon = \frac{1}{\log n}$ and $c = (\log n)^{10}$, then the probability that the good event does not happen is at most $n \exp\{-\Omega((\log n)^6)\} \leq \epsilon^2 \leq \beta \cdot \epsilon$ for any $n \geq 3$. Henceforth the protocol satisfies $(1 - \Theta(\epsilon))$ -CSP-fairness as long as the coalition contains at least ϵn players.

Unfortunately, the protocol does not satisfy CSP-fairness for small coalitions. For example, a single individual $i \in [n]$ (i.e., a coalition of size 1) can examine all others' bin choices and then decide to place itself in the lightest bin. In this case, if the lightest bin (not counting player i) is at least 2 lighter than the second lightest bin, player i is elected into the committee. This happens with a probability at least $\frac{6}{5} \cdot \frac{c}{n}$ for large n, which is significantly higher than the normal probability c/n that player i ought to be elected in an all-honest execution.

Commit-and-Reveal Lightest Bin. We introduce commit-and-reveal version of Feige's lightest bin protocol which achieves CSP-fairness not just against large coalitions, but also against small coalitions as well. The idea is quite simple— below we describe the scheme assuming ideal commitments, although in our formal technical sections we will instantiate the commitments using standard non-malleable commitments. Everyone first commits to a random bin number among $B = n/c$ bins. They then open their commitments. Those who land in the lightest bin are declared the committee, and like before, anyone who fails to commit or correctly open is kicked out. Using the same argument as before, we can show that the commit-and-reveal lightest bin protocol also achieves $(1 - \Theta(\epsilon))$-CSP-fairness against coalitions of size at least ϵn.

We now argue why it also satisfies CSP-fairness against small coalitions of size $\beta n < \epsilon n$. Intuitively, the coalition's best strategy is to pick a bin with the fewest number of honest players (henceforth called the *honest-lightest* bin), and place as many coalition members in it as possible while still maintaining that it is the lightest. However, the coalition does not know which one is the honest-lightest bin when committing to its own bin choices. In fact, even when conditioned on the coalition's view during the commitment phase, each bin is the honest-lightest bin with equal probability. No matter how the coalition spreads its members across the bins, the expected number of coalition members in a *randomly chosen* bin is at most $\beta \cdot n/B = \beta \cdot c$. Further, with $1 - n \cdot \exp(-\Omega(\epsilon^4 \cdot c))$ probability, the good event that honest-lightest bin should have at least $(1 - \epsilon^2)(1 - \beta)c$ honest players happens. Therefore, the coalition's expected representation on the committee cannot exceed $\frac{\beta}{(1-\epsilon^2)(1-\beta)} \leq \frac{\beta}{1-2\epsilon}$ given that the good event happens. Overall, the expected fraction of the coalition in the committee is at most $\frac{\beta}{1-2\epsilon} + \delta$, where $\delta = n \cdot \exp(-\Omega(\epsilon^4 \cdot c))$ is the probability that the good event does not happen. Still, as long as $\delta \leq \beta\epsilon$, by the same analysis as before, the expected fraction of the coalition in the committee is at most $\frac{\beta}{1-\Theta(\epsilon)}$.

2.2 Electing Poly-logarithmically Sized Committees: Achieving Maximin Fairness

Although simple and cute, the commit-and-reveal lightest bin protocol does not satisfy maximin fairness. For example, a $\Theta(n)$-sized coalition can target a victim player $i \in [n]$ and prevent it from being elected with high probability using the following strategy. During the commitment phase, spread the coalition members evenly across all bins. During opening, first observe which bin (denoted b^*) player i lands in. Then, all coalition members fail to open except those whose choice was b^*.

To achieve maximin fairness, we are inspired by a virtual identity technique originally proposed by Chung et al. [CCWS21], but unfortunately, directly applying this idea to the lightest bin does not work. At a high level, a strawman idea is as follows:

1. Every player $i \in [n]$ selects a random virtual identity v_i from a sufficiently large space, and commits to the pair (i, v_i).
2. Every player $i \in [n]$ selects a random bin b_i among $B = n/c$ bins, and commits to the pair (v_i, b_i) where v_i is its secret virtual identity.
3. Everyone $i \in [n]$ opens their commitment of (v_i, b_i). The virtual identities contained in the lightest bin will be elected committee.

4. Everyone opens their real-virtual identity mapping (i, v_i). This will allow everyone to compute the real identities of those elected to the committee.

Now, as long as the coalition does not know an honest player i's virtual ID, it does not know who to target during the commit-and-reveal lightest bin steps (Steps 2 and 3). Therefore, as long as the good event that each bin contains at least $(1 - \epsilon)(1 - \beta)c$ honest players happens, an honest player i will be elected into the committee with probability at least $\frac{(1-\epsilon)(1-\beta)c}{(1-\beta)n} = \frac{(1-\epsilon)c}{n}$. By law of total probability, the probability that an honest player i gets elected into the committee with probability at least $\frac{(1-\epsilon)(1-\delta)c}{n}$, where $1 - \delta$ is the probability that the good event happens. Henceforth, as long as $\delta \leq \epsilon$, an honest player i gets elected into the committee with probability at least $\frac{(1-\Theta(\epsilon))c}{n}$.

Unfortunately, this idea does not work if the coalition can eavesdrop on the network channel and observe who sent which (bin, virtual ID) pair in the commit-and-reveal lightest bin protocol. This would allow the coalition to immediately learn the correspondance between virtual and real identities.

To salvage this idea, our high-level idea is simple but realizing it turns out to be somewhat subtle as we explain later. First, if we are willing to assume the existence of an idealized anonymous communication network where players can post messages anonymously, then we can overcome the aforementioned problem by running Steps 2 and 3 over an anonymous communication network. Therefore, it suffices to find a suitable anonymous communication protocol to realize anonymous communication. Although anonymous communication has been extensively studied in the literature [Cha81, Cha88, Abe99, CGF10, DMS04, SGR99, ZZZR05], in our setting, it is tricky to adopt existing schemes directly. The main technicality is that in the presence of a majority coalition, we cannot guarantee the liveness of the anonymous communication protocol.

To overcome this problem, one naïve idea is to rely on an anonymous communication protocol with identifiable abort, and if the protocol fails, we kick out an offending player and retry. Unfortunately, the vanilla notion of identifiable abort does not work for us because we cannot afford to kick out offending players one by one since we are aiming for small round complexity. Our idea is to devise an anonymous communication protocol not just with identifiable abort, but with *plentiful identifiable aborts*. In other words, if the protocol fails, we want to kick out sufficiently many players, such that we can eventually succeed without too many retries.

Therefore, we adapt an anonymous communication protocol inspired by DC-nets [Cha88] to achieve such a plentiful identifiable abort notion. Assuming an upper bound of βn on the coalition size, our protocol kicks out at least $(1 - \beta)n$ players in the event of failure. Thus the round complexity is at most $\frac{1}{1-\beta}$. For example, if $\beta = 99\%$, we can still succeed in $O(1)$ rounds.

We give a formal description of our poly-logarithmically-sized committee election protocol and prove its security in Sect. 4. We present a formal description of our anonymous communication protocol in Sect. 6.2.

2.3   Leader Election

Although the lightest bin protocol via anonymous broadcast (denoted as LBin-V below) achieves CSP-fairness and maximin-fairness simultaneously, it cannot be directly used to select a leader, i.e., $c = 1$. Indeed, the fairness of LBin-V depends on the occurrence of the good event that each bin has at least $(1 - \epsilon^2)(1 - \beta)c$ number of honest players, where $\beta \cdot n$ is the maximum coalition size for $\beta \in (0, 1)$. If we are to choose a leader directly using LBin-V, then the probability that this good event happens is 0, which makes our protocol unfair.

To construct a leader election protocol, we compose the committee election LBin-V for multiple iterations. In each iteration: we choose a log-sized committee. In the first iteration we choose a poly log-sized committee C_1, and then in the second iteration we choose a poly log log sized committee C_2 from C_1, and so on. As analyzed earlier, each iteration of LBin-V is $(1 - \Theta(\epsilon))$-game-theoretically fair given that the failure probability δ that the good event does not happen in this iteration is small compare to $\beta \cdot \epsilon$.

However, as the committee size becomes smaller in each iteration, the probability that the good event does not happen becomes larger. In the last few rounds, when the committee becomes constant size, the probability that the good event does not happen becomes a constant. Therefore, we need to cut off at some point and instead run the "almost perfect" tournament tree protocol. As shown in Chung et al. [CCWS21], the tournament tree protocol among c players chooses a leader in $O(\log c)$ rounds and is $(1 - \mathsf{negl})$-game-theoretically fair. If we want to achieve a round complexity of R, then we can stop running LBin-V when the committee size becomes smaller than $2^{\Theta(R)}$ and run the tournament tree protocol among the committee to elect a leader.

Now suppose that we run L iterations of committee election LBin-V and get a committee of size $2^{\Theta(R)}$. Then we need to guarantee that the round complexity of these L iterations of LBin-V is at most $O(R)$. By the analysis above, if we kick out $(1 - \beta)n$ players in each anonymous communication protocol, the round complexity of each LBin-V is at most $\frac{1}{1-\beta}$. This requires that the fraction of coalition $\beta \leq 1 - \frac{L}{\Theta(R)}$.

Now since the probability that the good event does not happen increases in each iteration, the probability that there is an iteration in which the good event does not happen is dominated by $L \cdot \delta_L$, where $\delta_L = \exp\{-\epsilon^4 \cdot 2^{-\Theta(R)}\}$ is the probability that good event does not happen in the last iteration. As long as this probability is smaller than $\beta \cdot \epsilon$, the protocol is $(1 - \Theta(\epsilon))$-fair. Picking $\epsilon = \frac{1}{2^R}$ suffices. Therefore, if we run LBin-V multiple iterations to elect a committee C of size is $2^{\Theta(R)}$, and then run the tournament tree protocol among C to elect a leader, our leader election protocol achieves $(1 - \frac{1}{2^{\Theta(R)}})$-game-theoretic fairness.

In Sect. 5, we give a generalized protocol that combines multiple iterations of LBin-V and the tournament tree protocol to elect an arbitrary-sized committee, including the special case of committee size 1, i.e., leader election.

3   Preliminaries

Notation. Throughout, we use λ to denote the security parameter. The notation $\log^{(\ell)} n$ means taking logarithm ℓ times over n. For example, $\log^{(3)} n \equiv \log\log\log n$. Moreover, we use $\log^* n$ to denote the smallest integer ℓ such that $\log^{(\ell)} n \leq 1$. For an event E, we denote $\overline{E}$ as the event that E does not happen. For a vector X of length M, we use $X[j]$ for $j \in [M]$ to denote the j-th element of X. By *t-out-of-n SS*, we refer to a Shamir secret sharing protocol in which any $t + 1$ players can reconstruct the secret, while any t players know nothing about the secret [Sha79]. We use the acronym p.p.t. for non-uniform probabilistic polynomial time. We use $\{X_\lambda\}_\lambda \equiv_c \{Y_\lambda\}_\lambda$ to denote that two distribution ensembles $\{X_\lambda\}_\lambda$ and $\{Y_\lambda\}_\lambda$ are computationally indistinguishable, i.e., for all non-uniform p.p.t. $\mathcal{A}$, there exists a negligible function $\mathsf{negl}(\cdot)$, such that for any $\lambda \in \mathbb{N}$, $|\Pr[x \xleftarrow{\$} X_n, \mathcal{A}(x) = 1] - \Pr[y \xleftarrow{\$} Y_n, \mathcal{A}(y) = 1]| < \mathsf{negl}(\lambda)$.

3.1   Probability Tools

Lemma 3.1 (Chernoff bound, Corollary A.1.14 [AS16]). *Let* $X_1, \ldots, X_n$ *be independent Bernoulli random variables. Let* $\mu = \mathbb{E}\left[\sum_{i=1}^{n} X_i\right]$. *Then, for any* $\epsilon \in (0, 1)$, *it holds that*

$$\Pr\left[\sum_{i=1}^{n} X_i \leq (1 - \epsilon)\mu\right] \leq e^{-\epsilon^2 \mu / 2}.$$

3.2   Fairness Notions for Committee Election

Since a leader is a special case of a 1-sized committee, we will define correctness and fairness with respect to committee election protocol.

In a (c, n)-committee election protocol, n players interact through pairwise private channels and a public broadcast channel. We assume that each player has identity $1, 2, \ldots, n$, respectively. We assume that all communication channels are authenticated, i.e., messages carry the sender's identity. Moreover, the network is synchronous, and the protocol proceeds in rounds.

The protocol execution is parametrized with the security parameter λ. We assume that the coalition (adversary) A performs a *rushing* attack. In every round r, it waits for all honest players (those not in A) to send messages in round r and decide what messages the players in the coalition send in round r. At the end of the committee election, the protocol outputs a set of at most c players called the *committee*. The output is defined as a deterministic, polynomial-time function over all *public messages posted to the broadcast channel*. Since we assume that all players wish to be selected into the committee, the utility function we consider is as follows: each player elected into the committee gains a utility of 1, while everyone else gains a utility of 0. If all players behave honestly, the committee is chosen uniformly at random.

Correctness. We say that a (c, n)-committee election protocol is correct, if in an all honest execution, every subset $C \subset [n]$ of size c has an equal probability of being elected as the committee, where the probability is taken over the randomness of (an honest execution) the protocol.

For the fairness notion, we recall the definitions proposed by Chung et al. [CCWS21]. The first notion of fairness (CSP-fairness) protects against a malicious coalition from increasing its utility. The second notion (maximin-fairness) protects against a malicious coalition from decreasing the utility of any honest party. Each of these notions is natural and useful on its own, and in some sense, they complement each other. A protocol that satisfies both simultaneously is called *game-theoretically fair*.

Approximate CSP-Fairness. The CSP-fairness requires that no coalition can increase its own expected utility by more than a $(1 - \epsilon)$ multiplicative factor, no matter how it deviates from the honest protocol.

Definition 3.2 $((1 - \epsilon)$-CSP-fair committee election). *A (c, n)-committee election is $(1 - \epsilon)$-CSP-fair against a non-uniform probabilistic polynomial time (p.p.t.) coalition A of size βn, iff no matter what strategy A adopts,*

$$\mathbb{E}[\widetilde{\beta}] \leq \frac{\beta}{1 - \epsilon},$$

where $\widetilde{\beta}$ is the fraction of players in the coalition among the committee, where the expectation is taken over the randomness of the protocol.

In our proof, we will also make use of another fairness notion:

Definition 3.3 $((1 - \epsilon, \delta)$-CSP-fair committee election). *A (c, n)-committee election is $(1 - \epsilon, \delta)$-CSP-fair against a non-uniform probabilistic polynomial time (p.p.t.) coalition A of size βn, if there exists an event GOOD, where $\Pr[\mathsf{GOOD}] \geq 1 - \delta$, such that no matter what strategy A adopts,*

$$\mathbb{E}[\widetilde{\beta} \mid \mathsf{GOOD}] \leq \frac{\beta}{1 - \epsilon},$$

where $\widetilde{\beta}$ is the fraction of the coalition's representation in the committee, and the expectation is taken over the randomness of the protocol.

Analogously, we define $(1 - \epsilon)$-maximin-fair and $(1 - \epsilon, \delta)$-maximin-fair committee election, which requires that the probability that an honest individual gets into the committee is large enough given that the good event happens.

Approximate Maximin-Fairness. Maximin-fairness requires that no coalition can harm any honest individual by more than a $(1-\epsilon)$ multiplicative factor, no matter how it deviates from the honest protocol.

Definition 3.4 $((1 - \epsilon)$-maximin-fair committee election). *A (c, n)-committee election is $(1 - \epsilon)$-maximin-fair against a non-uniform probabilistic polynomial time (p.p.t.) coalition A of size βn, iff for any honest individual i, the probability that i gets into the committee is*

$$\Pr[i \text{ is in the committee}] \geq \frac{(1 - \epsilon)c}{n},$$

no matter what strategy A adopts. The probability is taken over the randomness of the protocol.

Definition 3.5 $((1-\epsilon, \delta)$-maximin-fairness). *A (c, n)-committee election is $(1 - \epsilon, \delta)$-maximin-fair against a non-uniform probabilistic polynomial time (p.p.t.) coalition A of size βn, if there exists an event GOOD, where $\Pr[\text{GOOD}] \geq 1 - \delta$, such that no matter what strategy A adopts,*

$$\Pr[i \text{ is in the committee} \mid \text{GOOD}] \geq \frac{(1 - \epsilon)c}{n},$$

for any honest individual i. The probability is taken over the randomness of the protocol.

Although committee election is a constant-sum game, these two notions of fairness are non-equivalent. See Sect. 4 for more explanation.

Finally, we define *game-theoretical fairness*. This notion of fairness requires CSP and maximin-fairness simultaneously.

Definition 3.6 $((1 - \epsilon)$-game-theoretical fairness). *A (c, n)-committee election is $(1 - \epsilon)$ game-theoretically fair committee election against a non-uniform probabilistic polynomial time (p.p.t.) coalition A, iff it is $(1-\epsilon)$-CSP-fair and $(1-\epsilon)$-maximin-fair against A.*

Definition 3.7 $((1 - \epsilon, \delta)$-game-theoretical fairness). *A (c, n)-committee election is $(1 - \epsilon)$ game-theoretically fair committee election against a non-uniform probabilistic polynomial time (p.p.t.) coalition A, iff it is $(1 - \epsilon, \delta)$-CSP-fair and $(1 - \epsilon, \delta)$-maximin-fair against A.*

By definition, a $(1 - \epsilon)$-game-theoretically fair committee election is also $(1 - \epsilon, 0)$-game-theoretically fair. Next we give the translation from $(1 - \epsilon, \delta)$-CSP/maximin-fair to $(1 - \epsilon)$-CSP/maixin-fair.

Lemma 3.8. *Let n be the number of parties and fix a parameter c. Let CElect be an R-round $(1 - \epsilon, \delta)$-CSP-fair (c, n)-committee election protocol against a coalition of size βn. Then the above leader election protocol is $(1 - \epsilon_1)$-CSP-fair against a coalition of size βn, with a round complexity $R + O(\log c)$, where*

$$\epsilon_1 = \frac{\beta \epsilon + \delta(1 - \epsilon)}{\beta + \delta(1 - \epsilon)} + \mathsf{negl}(\lambda).$$

Lemma 3.9. *Let n be the number of parties and fix a parameter c. Let CElect be an R-round $(1 - \epsilon, \delta)$-maximin-fair (c, n)-committee election protocol against a coalition of size βn. Then the above leader election protocol is $(1 - \epsilon_2)$-maximin-fair, with a round complexity $R + O(\log c)$, where*

$$\epsilon_2 = \epsilon + \delta + \mathsf{negl}(\lambda).$$

The proofs of these two lemmas are available in the full version.

Hybrid vs. Real Worlds. For ease of presentation and modularity purposes, we shall sometimes consider protocols in a hybrid setting where we assume some "generic" functionality is given for free. This is called a "hybrid world". That is, we say that a protocol is in the $\mathcal{F}$-hybrid world if players interacting in this protocol have access to an ideal functionality $\mathcal{F}$. A protocol in the (plain) real world is a protocol without any ideal functionalities or setup assumptions. Specifically for us, we say that a (c, n)-committee election protocol achieves $(1 - \epsilon)$-game-theoretic fairness against a coalition A in the $\mathcal{F}$-hybrid world, if the protocol achieves $(1 - \epsilon)$-game-theoretic fairness against this coalition A, assuming the ideal functionality $\mathcal{F}$.

3.3 Publicly Verifiable Concurrent Non-Malleable Commitment

A publicly verifiable commitment scheme $(\mathsf{C}, \mathsf{R}, \mathsf{V})$ consists of a pair of interacting Turing machines, the committer C, the receiver R, and a deterministic, polynomial-time public verifier V. We assume that the protocol has two phases, a commitment phase and an opening phase. The public verifier, upon receiving a transcript Γ of the commitment protocol, outputs either a bit $b \in \{0, 1\}$ to accept or $\perp$ to reject. We use $\langle \mathsf{C}^*(z), \mathsf{R}^*(z') \rangle$ to denote an execution between C^* on input $z, 1^\lambda$, and R^* on input $z', 1^\lambda$, where λ is the security parameter.

Correctness. Correctness guarantees that an honest committer always completes the protocol and correctly opens its input bit; and will not be stuck by a malicious, non-aborting receiver. Formally, for $b \in \{0, 1\}$, for any $\lambda \in \mathbb{N}$, if C is honest and receives input bit b, then $\langle \mathsf{C}(z), \mathsf{R}^*(z') \rangle$ will complete with the accepting bit b with probability 1, for any non-aborting R^*. If the messages sent by R^* are outside the valid range, it is treated as aborting.

Perfect Binding. Perfect binding guarantees that the commitment phase will determine only one bit that can be successfully opened. Formally, let $(\Gamma_c, \Gamma_o) \in \{0, 1\}^{\ell(\lambda)}$ be the transcripts of the commitment phase and the opening phase, respectively, where $\ell(\lambda)$ is a fixed polynomial function denoting the maximum length of the transcripts. Then for any $\lambda \in \mathbb{N}$, any transcripts $\Gamma_c, \Gamma_o, \Gamma_o'$, if $\mathsf{V}(1^\lambda, \Gamma_c, \Gamma_o) = b$ and $\mathsf{V}(1^\lambda, \Gamma_c, \Gamma_o') = b'$, where $b, b' \in \{0, 1\}$, it must be that $b = b'$.

Computationally Hiding. Computationally hiding guarantees that at the end of the commitment phase, the receiver learns only a negligible amount of information about the input that the committer commits to. Formally, let $p_\lambda(v)$ denote the probability that R^* outputs 1 at the end of the commitment phase in an execution $\langle \mathsf{C}^*(1^\lambda, v), \mathsf{R}^*(1^\lambda) \rangle$, then for any non-uniform p.p.t. R^*, there exists a negligible function $\mathsf{negl}(\cdot)$ such that for every $\lambda \in \mathbb{N}$ and every $v_1, v_2 \in \{0,1\}^\lambda$, it holds that $|p_\lambda(v_1) - p_\lambda(v_2)| \leq \mathsf{negl}(\lambda)$.

Concurrent Non-malleability. We follow the definition of Lin et al. [LPV08]. Consider a man-in-the-middle adversary A that participate on the left m interactions with an honest committer who runs commitment phase committing to values $v_1, \ldots, v_m$ with identity $\mathsf{id}_1, \ldots, \mathsf{id}_m$, and on the right m interactions with an honest receiver trying to commit to values $v_1', \ldots, v_m'$ with identity $\mathsf{id}_1', \ldots, \mathsf{id}_m'$. If any of the right commitments are invalid its value is set to $\perp$. For every $i \in [m]$, if $\mathsf{id}_j' = \mathsf{id}_i$ for some $j \in [m]$, then v_j' is set to be $\perp$. Let $\mathsf{mitm}^A(1^\lambda, v_1, v_2, \ldots, v_m, z)$ denote the view of A and the values $v_1', \ldots, v_m'$.

Definition 3.10. *A commitment scheme is concurrent non-malleable if for every polynomial $p(\cdot)$, for every non-uniform p.p.t. adversary A that participates in at most $m = p(\lambda)$ concurrent executions, there exists a polynomial time simulator S such that*

$$\{\mathsf{mitm}^A(1^\lambda, v_1, v_2, \ldots, v_m, z)\}_{v_1, \ldots, v_m \in \{0,1\}, z \in \{0,1\}^*, \lambda \in \mathbb{N}} \equiv_c$$
$$\{S(1^\lambda, z)\}_{v_1, \ldots, v_m \in \{0,1\}, z \in \{0,1\}^*, \lambda \in \mathbb{N}}.$$

Theorem 3.11 ([LPV08]). *Assume that one-way permutations exist. Then there exists a constant-round, publicly verifiable commitment scheme that is perfectly correct, perfectly binding, and concurrent non-malleable.*

In this paper, we will only consider bounded concurrency. Without loss of generality, the number of concurrent calls to public verifiable concurrent non-malleable commitment in our protocol is upper bounded by n^2, where n is the number of players.

4 Game-Theoretically Fair Committee Election

In this section, we present our game-theoretically fair committee election that extends Feige's lightest bin protocol. Later, in Sect. 5, we will use it as a building block to get our committee election protocol that achieves game-theoretic fairness for arbitrary committee size.

4.1 Electing Poly-logarithmically Sized Committees: Achieving CSP-Fairness

In this section, we give a CSP-fair committee election protocol. This is the first step towards our game-theoretically fair committee election (that needs to be CSP-fair and maximin fair, simultaneously).

Our CSP-fair protocol is a commit-and-reveal variant of Feige's well-known lightest bin protocol [Fei99]. Specifically, we require all parties to (cryptographically) commit to their bin choices and only afterward to reveal their choices. The parties whose choices correspond to the lightest bin are the committee. The commitments that we use are *interactive*. To commit to a string, a player invokes n instances of NMC, one for each of the n receivers. To open the commitments, the committer posts the openings for all n instances in the broadcast channel, and the opening is correct iff all of the n instances are correctly opened to the same string. Without loss of generality, we assume that the committer only needs to send one message in the opening phase. Moreover, we assume that messages are posted to the broadcast channel, and it can be checked publicly if a commitment is correctly opened. This is why we also require public verifiability of the commitment scheme. We say that a player fails to commit if the player fails to commit in an instance, where the receiver is non-aborting.

LBin-C: **Commit-and-Reveal Lightest Bin**

Parameters: Let c be an upper bound of the size of the required committee and n is the number of players. Fix $B = \lceil \frac{n}{c} \rceil$ as the number of bins. For simplicity, we assume c divides n.

Building Blocks: A publicly verifiable concurrent non-malleable commitment as in Sect. 3.3, NMC.

Protocol:

1. <u>Round 1</u>: Every player i randomly chooses a bin $b_i \in [B]$, invokes n NMC instances and run the commit phase with n receivers to commit to b_i. The messages are sent in a broadcast channel. Exclude those players who fail to commit.
2. <u>Round 2</u>: Every player i runs the opening phase with n receivers to open its bin choice b_i. Exclude those players who fail to open all n instances correctly.
3. Let $\hat{b}$ be the lightest bin after exclusion (break ties with lexicographically the smallest bin). The players who choose bin $\hat{b}$ constitute the committee.

Theorem 4.1. *Assume that* NMC *is publicly verifiable concurrent non-malleable commitment as in Sect. 3.3. For $n, c \in \mathbb{N}$, $\epsilon \in (0, 1/2)$, and $\beta \in (0, 1)$, the protocol* LBin-C *is a constant round $(1 - 2\epsilon, \delta)$-CSP-fair (c, n)-committee election protocol against a coalition $\mathcal{K}$ of size βn, where*

$$\delta = \frac{n}{c} \exp \left\{ -\frac{\epsilon^4}{2}(1 - \beta)c \right\}. \tag{1}$$

Proof. Fix n, c, ϵ, and β as in the statement. Define GOOD to be the event that each bin has at least $(1 - \epsilon^2)(1 - \beta)c$ honest players. Let $\tilde{\beta}$ denote the fraction of players in $\mathcal{K}$ among the committee. Then, we have the following lemma.

Lemma 4.2. $\mathbb{E}\left[\widetilde{\beta} \mid \mathsf{GOOD}\right] \leq \frac{\beta}{1-2\epsilon}$.

For now assume that Lemma 4.2 holds and we explain why Theorem 4.1 follows from it. The proof of Lemma 4.2 appears right afterwards. By Chernoff bound (Lemma 3.1) and the union bound,

$$\Pr\left[\mathsf{GOOD}\right] \geq 1 - \frac{n}{c}\exp\left\{-\frac{\epsilon^4}{2}(1-\beta)c\right\}. \tag{2}$$

Combing Lemma 4.2 and (2), LBin-C is a $(1 - 2\epsilon, \delta)$-CSP-fair committee election protocol by Definition 3.5. □

Proof sketch of Lemma 4.2. We split into two cases. First, assume that $\beta \geq \epsilon$. In this case, the claim follows directly from the assumption that GOOD holds: The fraction of players in $\mathcal{K}$ among the committee must satisfy $\widetilde{\beta} \leq 1 - (1 - \epsilon^2)(1-\beta) = \beta\left(1 + \frac{\epsilon^2}{\beta} - \epsilon^2\right) \leq \frac{\beta}{1-2\epsilon}$ as required.

Now, we focus on the case where $\beta < \epsilon$. By the perfect binding property, at the end of commit phase, player i's bin choice are fixed. Let $\{b_i\}_{i=1}^n$ denote the bin choices of n players at the end of the commit phase. To compute $\mathbb{E}[\widetilde{\beta} \mid \mathsf{GOOD}]$, we define a random variable γ, which depends only on $\{b_i\}_{i=1}^n$, that upper bounds $\widetilde{\beta}$ in an execution of LBin-C. Let $\widetilde{b} \in [B]$ be the index of the bin that contains least number of honest players; and $b^* \in [B]$ be index of the lightest bin at the end of the commit phase. Note that by the way the protocol works, $\widetilde{b}$ and b^* depends only on $\{b_i\}_{i=1}^n$. Below, for $l \in [B]$, we use h_l to denote the number of honest players in bin l, and f_l to denote the number of players in $\mathcal{K}$ in bin l.

Given the bin choices $\{b_i\}_{i=1}^n$ at the end of the commit phase, the fraction of players in $\mathcal{K}$ among the committee is at most $\gamma := \frac{f_{\widetilde{b}}}{h_{b^*}+f_{b^*}}$. This is because by the perfect binding property and public verifiability of the commitment scheme, the only way the coalition can deviate is essentially to refuse to open some of their bin choices in the opening phase and get excluded at the end of Round 2, in order to change the lightest bin. To maximize the fraction of the coalition in the committee, the best strategy for the coalition is to choose bin $l = \widetilde{b}$, which contains the least number of honest players. Since the number of honest players in bin l is h_l, the fraction of players in $\mathcal{K}$ in bin $l = \widetilde{b}$, after excluding the misbehaved players, is at most $1 - \frac{h_{\widetilde{b}}}{f_{b^*}+h_{b^*}} \leq \frac{f_{\widetilde{b}}}{h_{b^*}+f_{b^*}}$.

Therefore, to upper bound $\mathbb{E}[\widetilde{\beta} \mid \mathsf{GOOD}]$, it suffices to bound $\mathbb{E}[\gamma \mid \mathsf{GOOD}]$. Since when GOOD happens, the number of honest players in every bin is at least $(1 - \epsilon^2)(1-\beta)c$, we have that

$$\mathbb{E}[\gamma \mid \mathsf{GOOD}] \leq \frac{1}{(1-\epsilon^2)(1-\beta)n}\sum_{l=1}^{B}\mathbb{E}\left[f_l \mid \widetilde{h} = l, \mathsf{GOOD}\right].$$

By the non-malleability of the commitment scheme, $\mathbb{E}[\gamma \mid \mathsf{GOOD}]$ in the protocol should be negligibly close to the conditional expectation of γ in an idealized world where the bin choices of the players in $\mathcal{K}$ are independent from the honest players' bin choices, i.e., $\tilde{b}$ is independent from f_ℓ. Therefore,

$$\mathbb{E}[\gamma \mid \mathsf{GOOD}] = \frac{1}{(1-\epsilon^2)(1-\beta)n} \sum_{l=1}^{B} \mathbb{E}\left[f_l\right] + \mathsf{negl}(\lambda) \leq \frac{\beta}{(1-\epsilon^2)(1-\epsilon)} + \mathsf{negl}(\lambda),$$

where the last inequality comes from the assumption that $\beta < \epsilon$. Putting together, the expectation $\mathbb{E}\left[\tilde{\beta} \mid \mathsf{GOOD}\right]$ in the committee election LBin-C is at most $\frac{\beta}{(1-\epsilon^2)(1-\epsilon)} + \mathsf{negl}(\lambda) \leq \frac{\beta}{1-2\epsilon}$.

4.2   Electing Poly-logarithmically Sized Committees: Achieving Maximin-Fairness

In Sect. 4.1 we gave a commit-and-reveal variant of Feige's lightest bin protocol for committee election and showed that it is CSP-fair. The protocol is, however, not maximin-fair. While the adversary cannot gain too much utility by deviating from the protocol, it can still harm the utility of an honest individual. Specifically, consider the following adversarial strategy. The coalition generates commitments so that the coalition's representations in each bin are equal. Then, when it wants to target at a specific player i to not participate in the committee, it waits to see which bin l was chosen by that honest party and then it refuses to reveal commitments from some other bin l' which will then be lighter than the bin l chosen by honest player i. This attack prevents an honest individual i from being elected into the committee.

By the properties of the commitment scheme and how our protocol works, this is the only useful attack for the adversary. Thus, we modify our protocol to withstand this attack by masking the identity of parties. Namely, we hide which bin choice belongs to which party. We achieve this by requiring players to choose a random virtual ID and use it throughout the execution. Players will only reveal their virtual IDs at the end of the protocol, after the lightest bin has been fixed. A-priori, it seems hard to implement such a system because once a party sends its message, everybody knows who sent it (recall that we are in the broadcast model). We overcome this by implementing an "anonymous" broadcast channel on top of our existing broadcast channel.

Thus, we first describe our anonymous broadcast functionality $\mathcal{F}_{\mathsf{anon}}^{t,\mathcal{O}}$. Then, we show that in a $\mathcal{F}_{\mathsf{anon}}^{t,\mathcal{O}}$-hybrid model, we can build a committee election protocol that ensures CSP-fairness and maximin-fairness simultaneously.

Anonymous Broadcast Functionality. Let $\mathcal{O}$ be the set of all players involving in the protocol. Our anonymous broadcast functionality $\mathcal{F}_{\mathsf{anon}}^{t,\mathcal{O}}$ works as follows.

$\mathcal{F}_{\mathsf{anon}}^{t,\mathcal{O}}$: **Anonymous broadcast with t-identifiable abort**

Parameters: $\mathcal{O}$ is the set of players involving in the protocol and t is a bound on the number of misbehaved players to exclude.

Functionality:

1. **Input:** Every player i sends a single message m_i or $\perp$ to $\mathcal{F}_{\text{anon}}^{t,\mathcal{O}}$.
2. **Output:** $\mathcal{F}_{\text{anon}}^{t,\mathcal{O}}$ computes a multiset $\text{Out} = \{m_i : i \in \mathcal{O} \text{ and } m_i \neq \perp\}$.
   If the number of corrupted players is smaller than t, send (ok, Out) to everyone in $\mathcal{O}$. Otherwise, send Out to the adversary $\mathcal{A}$.
   - If receives ok from $\mathcal{A}$, $\mathcal{F}_{\text{anon}}^{t,\mathcal{O}}$ sends (ok, Out) to every honest player in $\mathcal{O}$.
   - Otherwise, it receives a set $\mathcal{D}$ of corrupted IDs of size at least t from the adversary $\mathcal{A}$, and then send $(\text{fail}, \mathcal{D})$ to every honest player in $\mathcal{O}$.

We say that an adversary A is *admissible* if 1) it sends only one message for each corrupt player, and 2) it either sends ok, or a set of corrupted players of size at least t in Step 2.

The functionality exhibits several appealing properties that are important for us. Specifically, in the ideal functionality $\mathcal{F}_{\text{anon}}^{t,\mathcal{O}}$, it holds that:

1. Each player can only send one message.
2. The coalition has to choose their messages independently from honest players' messages.
3. The coalition cannot tell which honest player sends which message.
4. The output is either (ok, Out), or $(\text{fail}, \mathcal{D})$ with a set $\mathcal{D}$ of size at least t.

Formal Description of the Protocol. Here we present the formal description of our lightest bin via anonymous broadcast protocol in the $\mathcal{F}_{\text{anon}}^{t,\mathcal{O}}$-hybrid model.

LBin-V(c, n, β): **Lightest Bin via Anonymous Broadcast**

Parameters: Let c be an upper bound of the required committee and n is the number of players. Fix $B = \lceil \frac{n}{c} \rceil$ as the number of bins. For simplicity, we assume c divides n. Let $\mathcal{O}$ be initialized as $[n]$ that denotes the set of active players. $\beta \cdot n$ is the maximum size of the coalition for $\beta \in (0, 1)$.

Building Blocks: A publicly verifiable concurrent non-malleable commitment as in Sect. 3.3, NMC.

Protocol:

1. Every player i randomly chooses a string $v_i \leftarrow \{0,1\}^\lambda$ as its virtual ID, invokes n instances of NMC, and runs the commit phase with n receivers to commit to (i, v_i). Exclude those players who fail to commit.
2. Each player randomly chooses a bin $b_i \leftarrow [B]$ with fresh randomness, and sets $m_i = (b_i, v_i)$. Broadcast m_i using $\mathcal{F}_{\text{anon}}^{t,\mathcal{O}}$ with $t = \lfloor (1 - \beta)n \rfloor$.

> - If the output is (fail, $\mathcal{D}$), exclude the players in $\mathcal{D}$ from $\mathcal{O}$ (namely, set $\mathcal{O} = \mathcal{O} \setminus \mathcal{D}$). Then, the remaining players (i.e., those in the updated $\mathcal{O}$) re-run step 2.
> - If the output is (ok, Out), go to the next step.
> 3. Let b^* be the lightest bin. Every player opens its virtual ID (i, v_i). Let U_{b^*} be the set of virtual IDs that are *unique* and choose the lightest bin b^*. Those who open the (i, v_i) successfully with $v_i \in U_{b^*}$ are chosen to be the committee.

Note that in LBin-V, players do not need to commit to their bin choices and then open, since the functionality $\mathcal{F}_{\text{anon}}^{t,\mathcal{O}}$ guarantees that the malicious coalition has to choose their messages, i.e., bin choices, independently from honest players' messages. In the following theorem we show that the protocol LBin-V described above is both maximin-fair and CSP-fair in the $\mathcal{F}_{\text{anon}}^{t,\mathcal{O}}$-hybrid model.

Theorem 4.3. *Assume that* NMC *is a publicly verifiable concurrent non-malleable commitment as in Sect. 3.3. For any $n, c \in \mathbb{N}$ and $\epsilon \in (0, 1/2), \beta \in (0, 1)$, the committee election protocol* LBin-V(c, n, β) *is a $(1 - \epsilon, \delta)$-maximin-fair and a $(1 - 2\epsilon, \delta)$-CSP-fair (c, n)-committee election[2] in the $\mathcal{F}_{\text{anon}}^{t,\mathcal{O}}$-hybrid model, against a coalition $\mathcal{K}$ of size βn, where*

$$\delta = \frac{2n}{(1-\beta)c} \exp\left\{ -\frac{\epsilon^4}{2}(1-\beta)c \right\} + \mathsf{negl}(\lambda).$$

Moreover, the round complexity of LBin-V *is at most $\frac{2}{1-\beta} + 2$.*

Proof. Fix n, c, ϵ, and β as in the statement. Let Unique be the event that honest players choose unique virtual IDs, and their virtual IDs do not collide with any players in the coalition. Let GOOD be the event that in every execution of $\mathcal{F}_{\text{anon}}^{t,\mathcal{O}}$ in Step 2, each bin has at least $(1 - \epsilon^2)(1 - \beta)c$ honest players.

We use the following lemma to prove maximin-fairness and CSP-fairness. The proof to the lemma appears afterward.

Lemma 4.4. $\Pr[\text{Unique}, \text{GOOD}] \geq 1 - \delta$.

Maximin-fairness. Let H_i denote the event that an honest player i is chosen into the committee. The claimed maximin-fairness follows from the following lemma. The proof of the lemma appears below.

Lemma 4.5. $\Pr[\mathsf{H}_i \mid \text{Unique}, \text{GOOD}] \geq (1 - \epsilon)c/n$.

Combining Lemmas 4.4 and 4.5, we have that LBin-V is a $(1 - \epsilon, \delta)$-maximin-fair committee election protocol against a coalition of size βn by Definition 3.7.

CSP-fairness. Let $\widetilde{\beta}$ denote the fraction of the coalition in the committee. Now, the claimed CSP-fairness follows from the following lemma. The proof of the lemma appears below.

---

[2] Theorem 4.3 implies that the protocol LBin-V is a $(1 - 2\epsilon, \delta)$-game-theoretic fairness by Definition 3.7.

Lemma 4.6. $\mathbb{E}\left[\tilde{\beta} \mid \mathsf{GOOD}, \mathsf{Unique}\right] \leq \frac{\beta}{1-2\epsilon}$.

Combining Lemmas 4.4 and 4.6, we have that LBin-V is a $(1-2\epsilon, \delta)$-CSP-fair committee election protocol against a coalition of size βn by Definition 3.5. □

Proof sketch of Lemma 4.4. By the non-malleability property of the commitment scheme, $\Pr[\mathsf{Unique}]$ in an real execution of the protocol should be negligibly close to this probability in an idealized world where the virtual IDs of players in $\mathcal{K}$ are chosen independently from honest players' virtual IDs. Therefore, $\Pr[\mathsf{Unique}] = 1 - \mathsf{negl}(\lambda)$. By Chernoff's bound (Lemma 3.1) and the union bound over B bins, in a single execution of $\mathcal{F}_{\mathsf{anon}}^{t,\mathcal{O}}$, each bin contains at least $(1-\epsilon^2)(1-\beta)c$ honest players with probability $p = 1 - \frac{n}{c}\exp\left\{-\frac{\epsilon^4}{2}(1-\beta)c\right\}$.

Each time $\mathcal{F}_{\mathsf{anon}}^{t,\mathcal{O}}$ is invoked, it either outputs ok or wipes out a set of players in the coalition of size at least t. Since $t = \lfloor(1-\beta)n\rfloor$, we will run at most $\frac{\beta n}{\lfloor(1-\beta)n\rfloor} < \frac{2}{1-\beta}$ rounds of $\mathcal{F}_{\mathsf{anon}}^{t,\mathcal{O}}$. Hence, $\Pr[\mathsf{GOOD}, \mathsf{Unique}] \geq p^{\frac{2}{1-\beta}}(1 - \mathsf{negl}(\lambda))$. Lemma 4.4 thus follows.

Proof sketch of Lemma 4.5. In LBin-V, the players choose their bins in Step 2 with their virtual IDs and broadcast the bin choices using $\mathcal{F}_{\mathsf{anon}}^{t,\mathcal{O}}$. By the property of the functionality, in each execution of $\mathcal{F}_{\mathsf{anon}}^{t,\mathcal{O}}$, the coalition has to choose their bins independently from honest players' bin choices. If the coalition chooses to fail a call to $\mathcal{F}_{\mathsf{anon}}^{t,\mathcal{O}}$, honest players will choose bins with *fresh* randomness in the next call to $\mathcal{F}_{\mathsf{anon}}^{t,\mathcal{O}}$. Therefore, the coalition's strategy S_l of whether to fail the l-th call to $\mathcal{F}_{\mathsf{anon}}^{t,\mathcal{O}}$ in Step 2 depends only on the output of the first l calls $\mathsf{Out}_1, \ldots, \mathsf{Out}_l$ to $\mathcal{F}_{\mathsf{anon}}^{t,\mathcal{O}}$, and the view $\mathsf{view}_K^{\mathsf{comm}}$ of the coalition $\mathcal{K}$ in Step 1. Still, we use $\mathcal{H}$ to denote the set of honest players, where $|\mathcal{H}| = n - \beta n$.

Let L denote the total number of $\mathcal{F}_{\mathsf{anon}}^{t,\mathcal{O}}$ calls. Now consider the l-th call to $\mathcal{F}_{\mathsf{anon}}^{t,\mathcal{O}}$. Let $\mathsf{H}_{i,j}$ denote the event that honest player i chooses bin j in that $\mathcal{F}_{\mathsf{anon}}^{t,\mathcal{O}}$ call. Since honest players choose their bins independently in different calls to $\mathcal{F}_{\mathsf{anon}}^{t,\mathcal{O}}$, it follows that

$$\Pr\left[\mathsf{H}_{i,j} \mid \mathsf{Out}_1, \ldots, \mathsf{Out}_L, \mathsf{view}_K^{\mathsf{comm}}, S_1, \ldots, S_L\right] = \Pr\left[\mathsf{H}_{i,j} \mid \mathsf{Out}_l, \mathsf{view}_K^{\mathsf{comm}}\right].$$

By the non-malleability and the anonymity of $\mathcal{F}_{\mathsf{anon}}^{t,\mathcal{O}}$, the map between the honest virtual ID and the honest players' identity remains hidden from the coalition $\mathcal{K}$. For $j \in [B]$, we use V_j to denote the set $V_j = \{v_i : (v_i, j) \in \mathsf{Out}_l\}$, i.e., the set of virtual IDs choosing bin j. Then we have

$$\Pr[\mathsf{H}_{i,j} \mid \mathsf{Out}_l = \{(v_i, b_i)\}_{i\in[n]}, \mathsf{view}_K^{\mathsf{comm}} = v] \geq \frac{h_j}{|\mathcal{H}|} - \mathsf{negl}(\lambda),$$

where h_j is the number of honest players in bin j. Given the assumption that GOOD happens, $h_j \geq (1-\epsilon^2)(1-\beta)c$ for every $j \in [B]$. Let view_K denote the view of the adversary at the end of Step 2, which includes $\mathsf{view}_K^{\mathsf{comm}}$, all the outputs $\mathsf{Out}_1, \ldots, \mathsf{Out}_L$, as well as $\mathcal{A}$'s strategy $S_1, \ldots, S_L$. Then, the lightest bin b^* is deterministic given view_K. For any $i \in \mathcal{H}$ we have

$$\Pr[\mathsf{H}_i \mid \mathsf{GOOD}] = \sum_{j \in [B]} \Pr[\mathsf{H}_{i,j}, b^* = j \mid \mathsf{GOOD}] \geq \frac{(1 - \epsilon^2)c}{n} - \mathsf{negl}(\lambda).$$

Therefore, at the end of Step 2, the probability that an honest player i's virtual ID is in the lightest bin b^* is at least $(1 - \epsilon^2)c/n - \mathsf{negl}(\lambda)$. This implies that the honest player i will be elected into the committee with a probability at least $(1 - \epsilon^2)c/n - \mathsf{negl}(\lambda) \geq (1 - \epsilon)c/n$, given that GOOD and Unique happens.

Proof sketch of Lemma 4.6. The proof to this Lemma is similar to the proof of Lemma 4.2, except that honest players' bin choices are now hidden from the coalition by the anonymous broadcast functionality $\mathcal{F}_{\mathsf{anon}}^{t,\mathcal{O}}$.

5 Fairness Amplification Though Iteration

This section gives our final game-theoretically fair committee election and leader election protocols to select arbitrary committee size with good fairness parameters. The committee election protocol LBin-V introduced in Sect. 4.2 does not achieve fairness with good parameter for arbitrary committee size. For example, if we want to choose a $\log \log n$-sized committee from n players using LBin-V, the probability that the GOOD event does not happen is upper bounded by $\frac{n}{\log \log n} \exp\{-\frac{\epsilon^4}{2} \log \log n\}$, which is even larger than 1. This makes LBin-V not fair enough for electing a small sized-committee.

Therefore, to build a fair committee election protocol that works for arbitrary committee size, we compose LBin-V for multiple iterations, and combine it with the tournament tree protocol if necessary.

We first give the formal description of the tournament tree protocol and its "almost perfect" fairness. Then we give our final committee election protocol that achieves game-theoretic fairness for arbitrary committee size.

5.1 Preliminary: Fairness of Tournament Tree Protocol

This section gives a formal description of the tournament tree protocol.

Tournament tree protocol $\mathsf{Tourn}(\mathcal{O})$

Let n be the size of $\mathcal{O}$.

- If $n = 1$, return the single player in $\mathcal{O}$.
- Otherwise, let $n_1 = \lfloor \frac{n}{2} \rfloor$ and $n_2 = \lceil \frac{n}{2} \rceil$. Let $\mathcal{O}_1$ be the first n_1 players in $\mathcal{O}$ and $\mathcal{O}_2$ be the remaining players.
- In parallel, run $\mathsf{Tourn}(\mathcal{O}_1)$ and $\mathsf{Tourn}(\mathcal{O}_2)$, and denote the output as O_1 and O_2, respectively.

– The final winner is determined by the duel protocol between O_1 and O_2 such that O_i wins with probability n_i/n. This is described below.

Duel Protocol between O_1 and O_2

Let $\frac{k_1}{k_1+k_2}$ and $\frac{k_2}{k_1+k_2}$ be the probability that player O_1 and O_2 wins, respectively.

– Let $k = k_1 + k_2$, and $\ell = \lceil \log k \rceil$. Each player O_i commits to an ℓ-bit random string that represents some $s_i \in \mathbb{Z}_{k-1}$ for $i = 1, 2$.
– Each player O_i opens its commitment and reveals s_i. If $s_1 + s_2 \mod k \in \{0, \dots, k_1 - 1\}$, player O_1 wins. Otherwise, O_2 wins.
– If a player aborts or fails to open the commitment correctly, it is treated as forfeiting and the other player wins.

Lemma 5.1 (Theorem 3.5 of Chung et al. [CCWS21]). *Let n be the number of players and λ be the security parameter. Then, the tournament-tree protocol, when instantiated with a suitable publicly verifiable, non-malleable commitment scheme as defined in Sect. 3.3, satisfies $(1 - \mathsf{negl}(\lambda))$-CSP-fairness and $(1 - \mathsf{negl}(\lambda))$-maximin-fairness against coalition of arbitrarily sizes. Moreover, the round complexity is $O(\log n)$.*

5.2   Our Final Game-Theoretically Fair Committee Election

In this section, we give our fair committee election protocol that works for arbitrary committee size. Our final protocol runs multiple iterations of LBin-V and combines it with the tournament tree protocol if necessary. The $\mathcal{F}_{\mathsf{anon}}^{t,\mathcal{O}}$ ideal functionality in LBin-V can be instantiated in real-world cryptography, with only a constant round blowup. The instantiation will be given in Sect. 6.

Let c be the upper bound of the committee size we want to achieve. The final committee election is given below.

Committee election protocol CElect(n, c)

Parameter: Let c be the upper bound of the committee size and R be the round complexity we want to achieve. The initial committee is $\mathcal{C}_0 = [n]$, $c_0 = n$. The fraction of the coalition is $\beta_0 = \beta$. If $c \geq 2^R$, let $L \leq R$ be the smallest integer such that $\log^{(L)} n \leq c^{0.1}$ and $\epsilon = \frac{1}{c^{0.1}}$; otherwise, set $L \leq R$ be the smallest integer such that $\log^{(L)} n \leq 2^R$ and $\epsilon = \frac{1}{2^R}$.

Protocol

1. For $\ell = 1, \dots, L - 1$:
   – Let $c_\ell = (\log^{(\ell)} n)^{10}$, $\mathcal{O} = \mathcal{C}_{\ell-1}$, $\beta_\ell = \beta_{\ell-1}(1 - \epsilon^2) + \epsilon^2$.
   – Run LBin-V($c_\ell, \mathcal{C}_{\ell-1}, \beta_{\ell-1}$). That is, we choose a committee $\mathcal{C}_\ell$ of size $c_\ell = (\log^{(\ell)} n)^{10}$ from $\mathcal{C}_{\ell-1}$.
   – $\ell = \ell + 1$.

2. If $c \geq 2^R$, set $c_L = c$; otherwise, set $c_L = 2^{11R}$. Run the committee election protocol LBin-V$(c_L, \mathcal{C}_{L-1}, \beta_{L-1})$ to elect a committee $\mathcal{C}_L$ of size at most c_L.
3. If $c_L \geq c$, run c number of parallel instances of Tourn$^{sid}(\mathcal{C}_L)$ for $sid \in [c]$. Let the final committee be the set of elected leaders in these c instances of tournament tree protocol.

Note that in the protocol, β_ℓ is just a parameter that passes to LBin-V, together with c and $\mathcal{O}$. It is *not* the real fraction of the coalition in committee $\mathcal{C}_\ell$. Instead, it is the upper bound of the real fraction of the coalition in $\mathcal{C}_\ell$ if *good* event happens in each round up to ℓ. The parameter β_ℓ is only used to set the parameter t of $\mathcal{F}_{\text{anon}}^{t,\mathcal{O}}$ in the ℓ-th LBin-V call.

Theorem 5.2. *Assume the existence of enhanced trapdoor permutations and collision-resistant hash functions. Fix n and c. Let L^* be the smallest integer such that $\log^{(L^*)} n \leq c$. Then for any $L^* \leq R \leq C_0 \log n$ for some constant C_0, we have that*

- *If $c \geq 2^R$, there exists an $O(R)$-round committee election that achieves $(1 - \frac{1}{c^{\Theta(1)}})$-game-theoretic fairness against a non-uniform p.p.t. coalition of size at most $(1 - \frac{L^*}{\Theta(R)})n$.*
- *If $c < 2^R$, there exists an $O(R)$-round committee election that achieves $(1 - \frac{1}{2^{\Theta(R)}})$-game-theoretic fairness against a non-uniform p.p.t. coalition of size at most $(1 - \frac{L}{\Theta(R)})n$, where L is the smallest integer such that $\log^{(L)} n \leq 2^R$.*

Our final leader election protocol can be gained directly by picking $c = 1$ in Theorem 5.2.

Theorem 5.3. *Assume the existence of enhanced trapdoor permutations, and collision-resistant hash functions. Fix n and let $\log^* n \leq R \leq C \log n$ be the round complexity we want to achieve for some constant C. Then there exists an $O(R)$-round leader election that achieves $(1 - \frac{1}{2^{\Theta(R)}})$-game-theoretic fairness against a non-uniform p.p.t. coalition of size at most $(1 - \frac{L}{\Theta(R)})n$, where L is the smallest integer such that $\log^{(L)} n \leq 2^R$.*

The full proof of Theorem 5.2 and Theorem 5.3 are available in the full version.

6   Instantiation of the Ideal Functionalities

In this section, we show how to instantiate the ideal functionalities $\mathcal{F}_{\text{anon}}^{t,\mathcal{O}}$ used in committee election LBin-V. Recall that the ideal functionality $\mathcal{F}_{\text{anon}}^{t,\mathcal{O}}$ receives one message from each player and either sends the set of all messages it receives to everyone or a set of corrupt players of size at least t to everyone. We will first give our protocol in a IdealZK*-hybrid model in which players have access to an ideal zero-knowledge proof functionality. Then we use the elegant techniques of Pass [Pas04] to instantiate the protocol with real-world cryptography. Next. we will first describe the IdealZK* functionality in Sect. 6.1, and then we will give our protocol in the IdealZK*-hybrid world in Sect. 6.2.

6.1   Ideal Zero-Knowledge Functionality IdealZK*

Basically, IdealZK* either sends success to everyone indicating that the proof is correct, or the identity of the prover/verifier who leads to the failure of the proof. Formally,

---

Ideal Zero-knowledge Functionality IdealZK*[x, L, i, j]

The functionality involves n parties $1, \ldots, n$, and is parametrized with a statement x, the language L, the prover's identity i and the verifier's identity j.

1. If both the prover i and the verifier j are corrupted, receive a bit b from the prover i. If $b = 1$, send (success, i, j) to everyone.
2. Receive ok or $\perp$ from the verifier j.
3. If received $\perp$ from the verifier, send (fail, j) to everyone.
4. Receive w or $\perp$ from the prover.
5. If $\mathcal{R}(x, w) = 1$, send (success, i, j) to everyone. Otherwise send (fail, i) to everyone.

In an n-party IdealZK*-hybrid protocol, the players can invoke the ideal zero-knowledge functionality IdealZK*[x, L, i, j] between any prover $i \in [n]$ and any verifier $j \in [n]$, and for arbitrary NP language L. Without loss of generality, in every round, there can be at most n^2 concurrent invocations of IdealZK*. Given an n-party IdealZK*-hybrid protocol, we can instantiate IdealZK* with actual cryptography using the elegant techniques suggested by Pass [Pas04].

Theorem 6.1. *(Constant-round, bounded concurrent secure computation [Pas04]). Assume the existence of enhanced trapdoor permutations and collision-resistant hash functions. Then, given an n-party IdealZK*-hybrid protocol Π^*, in which the number of concurrent calls of IdealZK* is upper bounded by a priori known bound $m = \mathsf{poly}(\lambda)$, there exists a real-world protocol Π such that the following hold:*

- **Simulatability**: *For every real-world non-uniform p.p.t. adversary $\mathcal{A}$ controlling an arbitrary subset of up to $n - 1$ players in Π, there exists a non-uniform p.p.t. adversary $\mathcal{A}^*$ in the protocol Π^*, such that for any input $(x_1, \ldots, x_n)$, every auxiliary string $z \in \{0, 1\}^*$,*

$$\mathsf{Exec}^{\Pi, \mathcal{A}}(1^\lambda, x_1, \ldots, x_n, z) \equiv_c \mathsf{Exec}^{\Pi^*, \mathcal{A}^*}(1^\lambda, x_1, \ldots, x_n, z).$$

In the above, the notation $\mathsf{Exec}^{\Pi, \mathcal{A}}$ (or $\mathsf{Exec}^{\Pi^*, \mathcal{A}^*}$) outputs each honest players' outputs as well as the corrupt players' (arbitrary) outputs.
- **Round efficiency**: *The round complexity of Π is at most a constant factor worse than that of Π^*.*

This real-world protocol is fulfilled by replacing the IdealZK* instance with the bounded concurrent zero-knowledge proofs. All the zero-knowledge proof messages are posted to the broadcast channel. The full proof of Theorem 6.1 is available in the full version.

Now it suffices to show how to replace $\mathcal{F}_{\text{anon}}^{t,\mathcal{O}}$ with a protocol $\text{Anon}^{t,\mathcal{O}}$ in the IdealZK*-hybrid world. In the protocol, we will omit the language L when it is clear from the context.

6.2 Implementing Anonymous Broadcast Functionality

In this section, we describe how to implement $\mathcal{F}_{\text{anon}}^{t,\mathcal{O}}$ in the IdealZK*-hybrid model. The protocol makes use of a perfect binding, statistically hiding commitment scheme comm. Also, every player keeps track of two sets, $\mathcal{D}_s$ and $\mathcal{D}_r$, the set of players who fail to share and the set of players who fail to reconstruct, respectively, to guarantee the identifiable abort property. Still, we use $\mathcal{K}$ to represent the set of corrupted players, $\mathcal{H}$ to represent the set of honest players. The number of parallel sessions is set to be λ. The protocol $\text{Anon}^{t,\mathcal{O}}$ is given below.

$\text{Anon}^{t,\mathcal{O}}$: instantiating $\mathcal{F}_{\text{anon}}^{t,\mathcal{O}}$ in the IdealZK* -hybrid world

Parameters: Let $M = 2n$ be the number of slots. Let $\mathcal{D}_s$, $\mathcal{D}_r$ and Out be initially empty sets. Without loss of generality we assume that $\mathcal{O} = [n]$.

Building blocks: A perfectly binding, computationally hiding commitment scheme comm.

Input: Each player has an input $m_i \in \mathbb{F}$ for a finite field $\mathbb{F}$ with size larger than 2^λ. The sum of tuples is computed entry-wise, i.e., $(a_1, b_1, c_1) + (a_2, b_2, c_2) = (a_1 + a_2, b_1 + b_2, c_1 + c_2)$.

Preparation Phase. Run the following for λ independent, parallel sessions:

1. Player i uniformly randomly choose a nonce $\text{mid}_i \in \mathbb{F}$. It then uniformly randomly chooses a slot $l_i \leftarrow [M]$ and computes a vector $\mathbf{S}_i \in (\mathbb{F}^3)^M$ such that $\mathbf{S}_i[l] = (0,0,0)$ if $l \neq l_i$, and $\mathbf{S}_i[l] = (m_i, \text{mid}_i, 1)$ if $l = l_i$.
2. Player i then splits $\mathbf{S}_i$ into $(n-t)$-out-of-n Shamir secret shares. Let $\mathbf{X}_{i,j}$ be the j-th share of $\mathbf{S}_i$. Let $\widehat{\mathbf{X}}_{i,j} = \text{comm}(\mathbf{X}_{i,j}, r_{i,j})$ where $r_{i,j}$ are fresh randomness. Broadcast the commitments $\{\widehat{\mathbf{X}}_{i,j}\}_{j \in [n]}$.
3. If a player i fails to broadcast the commitments, add i to the set $\mathcal{D}_s$.

Validation Phase. For $sid \in [\lambda]$, let $*^{sid}$ denote the variable $*$ in session sid. Player i invoke IdealZK*$[\text{stmt}_i, i, j]$ for each $j \in [n]$, with the statement $\text{stmt}_i = \{\widehat{\mathbf{X}}_{i,j}^{sid}\}_{j \in [n], sid \in [\lambda]}$, and send the witness $w = (m_i, \text{mid}_i, \{\mathbf{S}_i^{sid}\}_{sid \in [\lambda]}, \{\mathbf{X}_{i,j}^{sid}, r_{i,j}^{sid}\}_{j \in [n], sid \in [\lambda]})$ to prove that

- For each $sid \in [\lambda]$, for each $j \in [n]$, $(\mathbf{X}_{i,j}^{sid}, r_{i,j}^{sid})$ is the correct opening of $\widehat{\mathbf{X}}_{i,j}^{sid}$;

- For each $sid \in [\lambda]$, $\{\mathbf{X}_{i,j}^{sid}\}_{j\in[n]}$ forms a valid $(n-t)$-out-of-n secret sharing of $\mathbf{S}_i^{sid}$;
- For each $sid \in [\lambda]$, the vector $\mathbf{S}_i^{sid}$ contains only one non-zero slot $(m_i, \mathsf{mid}_i, 1)$.

For each $i \in [n]$, if there exists a j that $\mathsf{IdealZK}^*[\mathsf{stmt}_i, i, j]$ outputs (fail, i), i.e., the prover fails to prove the statement to receiver j, add i to the set $\mathcal{D}_s^{sid}$ for all $sid \in [\lambda]$.

Sharing Phase. Continue the following for λ independent, parallel sessions:

1. For $j \in [n]$, player i sends $(\mathbf{X}_{i,j}, r_{i,j})$ to player j.
2. Player i does the following: for every $j \in [n] \setminus \mathcal{D}_s$, if it receives a message $(\mathbf{X}_{j,i}, r_{j,i})$ that is a correct opening with respect to $\widehat{\mathbf{X}}_{j,i}$, record $(\mathbf{X}_{j,i}, r_{j,i})$ and broadcast (ok, i, j). Otherwise, broadcast $(\mathsf{complain}, i, j)$ to complain about j.
3. Player i does the following: for all j such that there is a complain $(\mathsf{complain}, j, i)$ in Step 2, player i broadcasts the corresponding opening $(i, j, \mathbf{X}_{i,j}, r_{i,j})$.
4. Unless player i broadcasts all correct openings for those players who has sent $(\mathsf{complain}, j, i)$ to complain about i, add i to the set $\mathcal{D}_s$.
5. Player i does the following: for $j \in [n] \setminus \mathcal{D}_s$, if player i sent $(\mathsf{complain}, i, j)$ in Step 2, and j broadcast a correct opening $(\mathbf{X}_{j,i}, r_{j,i})$ in Step 3. Then record the correct opening $(\mathbf{X}_{j,i}, r_{j,i})$.

Reconstruction Phase. Run the following for λ independent, parallel sessions:

1. Player i computes $\mathbf{Y}_i = \sum_{j \in [n] \setminus \mathcal{D}_s} \mathbf{X}_{j,i}$ and broadcast $\mathbf{Y}_i$. If a player j fails to broadcast, add j to the set $\mathcal{D}_r$.
2. Player i does the following for each $j \in [n]$: invoke $\mathsf{IdealZK}^*[\mathsf{stmt}'_i, i, j]$ with the statement $\mathsf{stmt}'_i = (\mathcal{D}_s, \mathbf{Y}_i, \{\widehat{\mathbf{X}}_{j,i}\}_{j\in[n]\setminus\mathcal{D}_s})$. It sends the witness $w' = (\{\mathbf{X}_{j,i}, r_{j,i}\}_{j\in[n]\setminus\mathcal{D}_s})$ to the ideal functionality $\mathsf{IdealZK}^*$ to prove that
   - For any $j \in [n] \setminus \mathcal{D}_s$, $(\mathbf{X}_{j,i}, r_{j,i})$ is a correct opening of $\widehat{\mathbf{X}}_{j,i}$;
   - $\mathbf{Y}_i = \sum_{j\in[n]\setminus\mathcal{D}_s} \mathbf{X}_{j,i}$.
3. If there exists a j such that $\mathsf{IdealZK}^*[\mathsf{stmt}'_i, i, j]$ outputs (fail, i), i.e., the prover fails to prove the statement to receiver j, add i to the set $\mathcal{D}_r$.
4. If $|\mathcal{D}_r| \geq t$, everyone stores $(\mathsf{fail}, \mathcal{D}_r \cup \mathcal{D}_s)$ for the reconstruction phase of this session.
5. Otherwise, every player uses all broadcast shares $\{\mathbf{Y}_i\}_{i\in[n]\setminus\mathcal{D}_r}$ to reconstruct the sum $\mathbf{S} = \sum_{i \notin \mathcal{D}_s} \mathbf{Y}_i$. Store $(\mathsf{ok}, \mathbf{S})$ for the reconstruction phase of this session.

Output Phase. For each $sid \in [\lambda]$, we use $(\mathsf{fail}, \mathcal{D}^{sid})$ or $(\mathsf{ok}, \mathbf{S}^{sid})$ to denote the value each player stores in the reconstruction phase of session sid. Each player i does the following:

1. If there is a $sid \in [\lambda]$ such that player i stores $(\mathsf{fail}, \mathcal{D}^{sid})$ for that session, outputs $(\mathsf{fail}, \cup_{sid \in [\lambda]} \mathcal{D}^{sid})$, where $\mathcal{D}^{sid} = \emptyset$ for those successfully reconstructed sessions.
2. Otherwise, each player does the following: We say that (m, mid) *appears* in session sid if there exists a slot $l \in [M]$ such that $\mathbf{S}^{sid}[l] = (m, \mathsf{mid}, 1)$. For each pair (m, mid) that appears in a majority number of sessions, add a copy of m to Out.
3. Output $(\mathsf{ok}, \mathsf{Out})$.

Theorem 6.2. *If the commitment scheme* comm *is perfectly binding and computationally hiding, then* $\mathsf{Anon}^{t,\mathcal{O}}$ *securely realizes* $\mathcal{F}_{\mathsf{anon}}^{t,\mathcal{O}}$ *in the* $\mathsf{IdealZK}^*$*-hybrid model as long as* $|\mathcal{O}| - t \geq |\mathcal{K}|$. *Moreover,* $\mathsf{Anon}^{t,\mathcal{O}}$ *runs in constant number of rounds.*

The full proof of the above theorem is available in the full version.

Acknowledgement. This work is in part supported by NSF awards under the grant numbers 2044679 and 1704788, a Packard Fellowship, and a generous gift from Nikolai Mushegian.

References

[Abe99]   Abe, M.: Mix-networks on permutation networks. In: Lam, K.-Y., Okamoto, E., Xing, C. (eds.) ASIACRYPT 1999. LNCS, vol. 1716, pp. 258–273. Springer, Heidelberg (1999). https://doi.org/10.1007/978-3-540-48000-6_21

[ACH11]   Asharov, G., Canetti, R., Hazay, C.: Towards a game theoretic view of secure computation. In: Paterson, K.G. (ed.) EUROCRYPT 2011. LNCS, vol. 6632, pp. 426–445. Springer, Heidelberg (2011). https://doi.org/10.1007/978-3-642-20465-4_24

[ADGH06] Abraham, I., Dolev, D., Gonen, R., Halpern, J.: Distributed computing meets game theory: robust mechanisms for rational secret sharing and multiparty computation. In: PODC (2006)

[ADMM14] Andrychowicz, M., Dziembowski, S., Malinowski, D., Mazurek, L.: Secure multiparty computations on bitcoin. In: S&P (2014)

[AL11]   Asharov, G., Lindell, Y.: Utility dependence in correct and fair rational secret sharing. J. Cryptol. **24**(1), 157–202 (2011)

[AO16]   Alon, B., Omri, E.: Almost-optimally fair multiparty coin-tossing with nearly three-quarters malicious. In: Hirt, M., Smith, A. (eds.) TCC 2016. LNCS, vol. 9985, pp. 307–335. Springer, Heidelberg (2016). https://doi.org/10.1007/978-3-662-53641-4_13

[AS16]   Alon, N., Spencer, J.H.: The Probabilistic Method. Wiley, Hoboken (2016)

[Aum74]   Aumann, R.J.: Subjectivity and correlation in randomized strategies. J. Math. Econ. **1**(1), 67–96 (1974)

[BGKO11] Beimel, A., Groce, A., Katz, J., Orlov, I.: Fair computation with rational players. Cryptology ePrint Archive (2011)

[BK14]   Bentov, I., Kumaresan, R.: How to use bitcoin to design fair protocols. In: Garay, J.A., Gennaro, R. (eds.) CRYPTO 2014. LNCS, vol. 8617, pp. 421–439. Springer, Heidelberg (2014). https://doi.org/10.1007/978-3-662-44381-1_24

[Blu83]   Blum, M.: Coin flipping by telephone a protocol for solving impossible problems. SIGACT News (1983)

[BOO10]   Beimel, A., Omri, E., Orlov, I.: Protocols for multiparty coin toss with dishonest majority. In: Rabin, T. (ed.) CRYPTO 2010. LNCS, vol. 6223, pp. 538–557. Springer, Heidelberg (2010). https://doi.org/10.1007/978-3-642-14623-7_29

[CCWS21] Chung, K.-M., Chan, T.-H.H., Wen, T., Shi, E.: Game-theoretic fairness meets multi-party protocols: the case of leader election. In: Malkin, T., Peikert, C. (eds.) CRYPTO 2021. LNCS, vol. 12826, pp. 3–32. Springer, Cham (2021). https://doi.org/10.1007/978-3-030-84245-1_1

[CGF10]   Corrigan-Gibbs, H., Fordm, B.: Dissent: accountable anonymous group messaging. In: CCS (2010)

[CGL+18] Chung, K.-M., Guo, Y., Lin, W.-K., Pass, R., Shi, E.: Game theoretic notions of fairness in multi-party coin toss. In: Beimel, A., Dziembowski, S. (eds.) TCC 2018. LNCS, vol. 11239, pp. 563–596. Springer, Cham (2018). https://doi.org/10.1007/978-3-030-03807-6_21

[Cha81]   Chaum, D.L.: Untraceable electronic mail, return addresses, and digital pseudonyms. Commun. ACM **24**(2), 84–90 (1981)

[Cha88]   Chaum, D.: The dining cryptographers problem: unconditional sender and recipient untraceability. J. Cryptol. **1**(1), 65–75 (1988)

[Cle86]   Cleve, R.: Limits on the security of coin flips when half the processors are faulty. In: STOC (1986)

[DHR00]   Dodis, Y., Halevi, S., Rabin, T.: A cryptographic solution to a game theoretic problem. In: Bellare, M. (ed.) CRYPTO 2000. LNCS, vol. 1880, pp. 112–130. Springer, Heidelberg (2000). https://doi.org/10.1007/3-540-44598-6_7

[DMS04]   Dingledine, R., Mathewson, N., Syverson, P.: Tor: the second-generation onion router. Technical report (2004)

[Dod06]   Dodis, Y.: Fault-tolerant leader election and collective coin-flipping in the full information model (2006)

[DR+07]   Dodis, Y., Rabin, T., et al.: Cryptography and game theory. Algorithmic Game Theory 181–207 (2007)

[Fei99]   Feige, U.: Noncryptographic selection protocols. In: FOCS (1999)

[GGS]   Gelashvili, R., Goren, G., Spiegelman, A.: Short paper: on game-theoretically-fair leader election

[GK12]   Groce, A., Katz, J.: Fair computation with rational players. In: Pointcheval, D., Johansson, T. (eds.) EUROCRYPT 2012. LNCS, vol. 7237, pp. 81–98. Springer, Heidelberg (2012). https://doi.org/10.1007/978-3-642-29011-4_7

[GKM+13] Garay, J., Katz, J., Maurer, U., Tackmann, B., Zikas, V.: Rational protocol design: cryptography against incentive-driven adversaries. In: FOCS (2013)

[GKTZ15] Garay, J., Katz, J., Tackmann, B., Zikas, V.: How fair is your protocol? A utility-based approach to protocol optimality. In: PODC (2015)

[GMW19]   Goldreich, O., Micali, S., Wigderson, A.: How to play any mental game, or a completeness theorem for protocols with honest majority. In: STOC (2019)

[GTZ15] Garay, J., Tackmann, B., Zikas, V.: Fair distributed computation of reactive functions. In: Moses, Y. (ed.) DISC 2015. LNCS, vol. 9363, pp. 497–512. Springer, Heidelberg (2015). https://doi.org/10.1007/978-3-662-48653-5_33

[HT04] Halpern, J., Teague, V.: Rational secret sharing and multiparty computation. In: STOC (2004)

[HT14] Haitner, I., Tsfadia, E.: An almost-optimally fair three-party coin-flipping protocol. In: STOC (2014)

[IML05] Izmalkov, S., Micali, S., Lepinski, M.: Rational secure computation and ideal mechanism design. In: FOCS (2005)

[Kat08] Katz, J.: Bridging game theory and cryptography: recent results and future directions. In: Canetti, R. (ed.) TCC 2008. LNCS, vol. 4948, pp. 251–272. Springer, Heidelberg (2008). https://doi.org/10.1007/978-3-540-78524-8_15

[KMSW22] Komargodski, I., Matsuo, S., Shi, E., Wu, K.: log*-round game-theoretically-fair leader election. Cryptology ePrint Archive, Paper 2022/791 (2022). https://eprint.iacr.org/2022/791

[KN08] Kol, G., Naor, M.: Cryptography and game theory: designing protocols for exchanging information. In: Canetti, R. (ed.) TCC 2008. LNCS, vol. 4948, pp. 320–339. Springer, Heidelberg (2008). https://doi.org/10.1007/978-3-540-78524-8_18

[LPV08] Lin, H., Pass, R., Venkitasubramaniam, M.: Concurrent non-malleable commitments from any one-way function. In: Canetti, R. (ed.) TCC 2008. LNCS, vol. 4948, pp. 571–588. Springer, Heidelberg (2008). https://doi.org/10.1007/978-3-540-78524-8_31

[MNS09] Moran, T., Naor, M., Segev, G.: An optimally fair coin toss. In: Reingold, O. (ed.) TCC 2009. LNCS, vol. 5444, pp. 1–18. Springer, Heidelberg (2009). https://doi.org/10.1007/978-3-642-00457-5_1

[Nas51] Nash, J.: Non-cooperative games. Ann. Math. 286–295 (1951)

[OPRV09] Ong, S.J., Parkes, D.C., Rosen, A., Vadhan, S.: Fairness with an honest minority and a rational majority. In: Reingold, O. (ed.) TCC 2009. LNCS, vol. 5444, pp. 36–53. Springer, Heidelberg (2009). https://doi.org/10.1007/978-3-642-00457-5_3

[Pas04] Pass, R.: Bounded-concurrent secure multi-party computation with a dishonest majority. In: STOC (2004)

[PS17] Pass, R., Shi, E.: FruitChains: a fair blockchain. In: PODC (2017)

[RSZ02] Russell, A., Saks, M., Zuckerman, D.: Lower bounds for leader election and collective coin-flipping in the perfect information model. SIAM J. Comput. 31(6), 1645–1662 (2002)

[RZ01] Russell, A., Zuckerman, D.: Perfect information leader election in log* n+ o (1) rounds. J. Comput. Syst. Sci. 63(4), 612–626 (2001)

[SGR99] Syverson, P., Goldschlag, D., Reed, M.: Onion routing for anonymous and private internet connections. Commun. ACM 42(2), 5 (1999)

[Sha79] Shamir, A.: How to share a secret. Commun. ACM 22(11), 612–613 (1979)

[WAS22] Wu, K., Asharov, G., Shi, E.: A complete characterization of game-theoretically fair, multi-party coin toss. In: Dunkelman, O., Dziembowski, S. (eds.) EUROCRYPT 2022. LNCS, vol. 13275, pp. 120–149. Springer, Cham (2022). https://doi.org/10.1007/978-3-031-06944-4_5

[Yao82] Yao, A.C.: Protocols for secure computations. In: FOCS (1982)

[ZZZR05] Zhuang, L., Zhou, F., Zhao, B.Y., Rowstron, A.: Cashmere: resilient anonymous routing. In: NSDI (2005)

Gossiping for Communication-Efficient Broadcast

Georgios Tsimos[1](✉), Julian Loss[2], and Charalampos Papamanthou[3]

[1] University of Maryland, College Park, USA
tsimos@umd.edu
[2] CISPA Helmholtz Center for Information Security, Saarbrücken, Germany
[3] Yale University, New Haven, USA

Abstract. Byzantine Broadcast is crucial for many cryptographic protocols such as secret sharing, multiparty computation and blockchain consensus. In this paper we apply *gossiping* (propagating a message by sending to a few random parties who in turn do the same, until the message is delivered) and propose new communication-efficient protocols, under dishonest majority, for Single-Sender Broadcast (BC) and Parallel Broadcast (PBC), improving the state-of-the-art in several ways.

As our warm-up result, we present a randomized protocol for BC which achieves $O(n^2\kappa^2)$ communication complexity from plain public key setup assumptions. This is the first protocol with subcubic communication in this setting, but operates only against static adversaries.

Using ideas from our BC protocol, we move to our central contribution and present two protocols for PBC that are secure against adaptive adversaries. To the best of our knowledge we are the first to study PBC *specifically*: All previous approaches for Parallel Broadcast naively run n instances of single-sender Broadcast, increasing the communication complexity by an undesirable factor of n. Our insight of avoiding black-box invocations of BC is particularly crucial for achieving our asymptotic improvements. In particular:

1. Our first PBC protocol achieves $\tilde{O}(n^3\kappa^2)$ communication complexity and relies only on plain public key setup assumptions.
2. Our second PBC protocol uses trusted setup and achieves nearly optimal communication complexity $\tilde{O}(n^2\kappa^4)$.

Both PBC protocols yield an almost linear improvement over the best known solutions involving n parallel invocations of the respective BC protocols such as those of Dolev and Strong (SIAM Journal on Computing, 1983) and Chan et al. (Public Key Cryptography, 2020). Central to our PBC protocols is a new problem that we define and solve, which we name "Converge". In Converge, parties must run an adaptively-secure and *efficient* protocol such that by the end of the protocol, all honest parties that remain possess a superset of the union of the initial honest parties' inputs.

© International Association for Cryptologic Research 2022
Y. Dodis and T. Shrimpton (Eds.): CRYPTO 2022, LNCS 13509, pp. 439–469, 2022.
https://doi.org/10.1007/978-3-031-15982-4_15

1   Introduction

Since its formalization by Lamport et al. [19], the broadcast problem has been studied in many works and lies at the core of many cryptographic protocols such as secret sharing, multiparty computation, and blockchain consensus protocols (e.g., [23]). In its *single-sender* version, BC involves a designated sender s that distributes a value v such that (1) all parties output the same value v' (consistency); (2) all parties output v in case s is honest (validity). *Parallel* BC (PBC) (also known as interactive consistency [26]) is a generalization of the single-sender setting where all parties act as designated senders, and in the end each party outputs values, satisfying the above conditions, from every sender. PBC comprises a central component of protocols like verifiable secret sharing and multiparty computation (e.g., [2,20]), where whenever broadcast is used in these protocols, it is always a *parallel broadcast*. Any improvement in PBC therefore yields an improvement in these protocols as well.

A crucial distinction among broadcast protocols is which *implementation model* they use: In the *bulletin PKI* model, no trusted setup is required, all parties register their public keys to a public bulletin board before the start of the protocol and no assumption is made on how parties generate their keys. In the stronger *trusted PKI* model, trusted setup is required: A trusted party generates all keys honestly and distributes them to the parties prior to protocol execution. An important efficiency metric for broadcast protocols, which is the focus of this paper, is their *communication complexity*, i.e., how many bits are exchanged during the protocol. Often, it depends on the implementation model and directly affects the efficiency of the underlying protocols using BC or PBC.

Contributions. In this work, we revisit the communication complexity of both BC and PBC (See Table 1.) We focus on the dishonest majority setting with both a static and an adaptive adversary. Our first (warm-up) result provides the first statically-secure BC protocol with subcubic communication in the bulletin PKI model. We then continue with our central contributions comprising two new PBC protocols. Our main observation is that no results exist on the communication complexity of PBC *specifically*. In particular, all protocols for PBC, to the best of our knowledge, are implemented via simultaneous calls to n BC instances, leading to increased communication complexity. Leveraging this insight, we use ideas of our first warmup BC protocol to build the first adaptively-secure PBC protocol with cubic communication complexity in the bulletin PKI model (Again, one defining feature of our PBC protocol is that it is non-black-box, in that it does not use n simultaneous calls to BC.) Our final PBC result shows how to improve the PBC complexity to quadratic, by switching to the trusted PKI model. To the best of our knowledge, all three results comprise significant improvements (i.e., by a linear factor) in the communication complexity of the state-of-the-art.

Message Propagation. We achieve our improvements by optimizing one of the fundamental aspects of BC protocols: their *message propagation*. When an honest party sends out a message at some round, propagation ensures that all honest parties receive this message soon. In most protocols, this is implemented via an expensive SEND-ALL instruction delivering the message in a single round [8,10]. Such instructions might not always be needed. For example, it might not be crucial to deliver the message strictly in the next round. Our proposed protocols minimize the use of SEND-ALL instructions via *gossiping*, eventually yielding much better communication. In particular, in message propagation via gossiping, a party first sends the message M only to a small random set of parties, who in turn do the same, until M is delivered. Somewhat surprisingly, the effect of this technique on the complexity of broadcast has not been explored before. Our current protocols are for the binary case only and might become inefficient when messages become longer.

Table 1. Comparison of BULLETINBC, BULLETINPBC and TRUSTEDPBC, in terms of communication complexity in bits (CC) and round complexity (RC), to existing work. Number of parties is n. Also $\epsilon < 1$.

protocol	model	CC	RC	adversary	dishonest	type
Abraham et al. [1]	trusted PKI	$\tilde{O}(n \cdot \kappa)$	$O(1)$	adaptive	$< n/2$	BC
Momose and Ren [25]	bulletin PKI	$\tilde{O}(n^2 \cdot \kappa)$	$O(n)$	adaptive	$< n/2$	BC
Chan et al. [8]	trusted PKI	$O(n^2 \cdot \kappa^2)$	$O(\kappa)$	adaptive	$< (1-\epsilon) \cdot n$	BC
Dolev and Strong [10]	bulletin PKI	$O(n^3 \cdot \kappa)$	$O(n)$	adaptive	$< n$	BC
BULLETINBC §3	bulletin PKI	$O(n^2 \cdot \kappa^2)$	$O(n)$	static	$< (1-\epsilon)n$	BC
BULLETINPBC §5	bulletin PKI	$\tilde{O}(n^3 \cdot \kappa^2)$	$O(n \log n)$	adaptive	$< (1-\epsilon)n$	PBC
TRUSTEDPBC §6	trusted PKI	$\tilde{O}(n^2 \cdot \kappa^4)$	$O(\kappa \log n)$	adaptive	$< (1-\epsilon)n$	PBC

1.1   Communication-Efficient BC in the Bulletin PKI Model

In our first contribution (Sect. 3) we use gossiping to achieve communication-efficient BC protocols *in the bulletin PKI model*. When using bulletin PKI, it is known that BC can be solved for arbitrary $t < n$ malicious parties with $O(n^3 \cdot \kappa)$ bits of communication using the seminal result of Dolev and Strong [10] (Here κ is the security parameter and represents the size of a digital signature.) However, to the best of our knowledge no protocol with better communication complexity exists. We resolve this question by introducing BULLETINBC (see Fig. 2), the first BC protocol that achieves communication complexity of $\tilde{O}(n^2 \cdot \kappa^2)$ bits in the bulletin PKI model. Our protocol is randomized and works for $t < (1 - \epsilon) \cdot n$ corrupted parties where $\epsilon \in (0, 1)$ is a constant. On the downside, we assume a static model of corruption where the adversary must decide which t parties to corrupt before the execution—but the corrupted parties are byzantine.

Technical Highlights. Our protocol follows a similar framework with the Dolev-Strong protocol [10]. Recall that in Dolev-Strong, for all rounds $r < n$, whenever an honest party p has observed r signatures on a bit b for the first time, p adds her signature and sends a message x of $r + 1$ signatures *to all parties*, using a SEND-ALL(x) instruction. Our proposed protocol *just replaces* the

SEND-ALL(x) instruction with a SEND-RANDOM(m, x) instruction and runs for an additional $O(\log n)$ rounds. Our SEND-RANDOM(m, x) instruction is implemented by sending message x to party i (for all $i \in [n]$) with probability m/n for some fixed $m = \Theta(\kappa)$. It is important to note, however, that our protocol does not merely implement SEND-ALL(x) via a sequence of SEND-RANDOM(m, x) instructions as this would still lead to cubic communication complexity—again, it just replaces the instructions directly. We remark that while the resulting changes in the protocol are minimal and only cause the protocol to run for roughly an additional $\log n$ many steps, the security proof is affected substantially. In particular, our gossiping technique does not protect against adaptive adversaries who can simply wait and corrupt all recipients of particular SEND-RANDOM(m, x) commands during the protocol. Still, this is not fundamental: We show next that gossiping, when used in PBC can (quite surprisingly) overcome this issue.

1.2 Communication-Efficient PBC for Bulletin and Trusted PKI

Recall that in PBC all n parties simultaneously act as a sender and wish to consistently distribute their message. As we mentioned before, all PBC protocols in the literature are derived trivially by calling BC multiple times in a black-box fashion, which leads to a multiplicative n-factor in the communication complexity. For example, deriving PBC for $t < (1 - \epsilon) \cdot n$ via n parallel executions of the Dolev-Strong protocol [10], would yield $\tilde{O}(n^4)$ communication complexity. Instead, we do not use a BC protocol as a black-box but we instantiate protocols specifically for PBC. This leads to our next contributions (Sects. 5, 6).

The $\mathcal{M}$-Converge Problem. Central to our PBC protocols is the $\mathcal{M}$-Converge problem (Sect. 4) that we define for the first time and could be of independent interest. In the $\mathcal{M}$-Converge problem, there is a fixed message set $\mathcal{M}$ and all initial honest parties $p \in \mathcal{H}$ begin with a set of messages $M_p \subseteq \mathcal{M}$ and a constraint set of messages $\mathcal{C}_p \subseteq \mathcal{M}$. In the end, all remaining honest parties q (we consider an adaptive adversary) should output a set S_q that is a *superset* of $\bigcup_p M_p - \bigcup_p \mathcal{C}_p$. (We consider superset since the adversary can inject messages as well.) Clearly, there is a simple protocol that solves the $\mathcal{M}$-Converge problem in the presence of an adaptive adversary and in a single round: Have all honest parties send their sets M_p and $\mathcal{C}_p$ to all other n parties—however this protocol leads to $O(n^2|\mathcal{M}|)$ communication since both M_p and $\mathcal{C}_p$ are subsets of $\mathcal{M}$. Instead, in our $\mathcal{M}$-CONVERGERANDOM protocol (see Fig. 6), every honest party runs in a few more rounds (around $O(\log n)$) and in every round sends every message in her local set to a randomly-chosen subset of parties and *not to all of them*. This reduces the communication to $\tilde{O}(n|\mathcal{M}| + n^2)$, which, for the case of $|\mathcal{M}| = \Omega(n)$ (as in our applications), leads to a much improved worst-case communication complexity! The main idea of our protocol is as follows.

1. In round 1, honest party p, for every message $x \in M_p - \mathcal{C}_p$, picks $i \in [n]$ as a recipient with probability m/n (Again, m is $\Theta(\kappa)$.) Then p constructs lists $\mathcal{L}_j$ (for $j = 1, \ldots, n$) containing messages $x \in M_p - \mathcal{C}_p$ that were assigned to recipient j. Each list $\mathcal{L}_j$ is first padded to at most $2m\lceil |\mathcal{M}|/n \rceil$ elements

(which is enough to ensure no overflows by Chernoff) and then encrypted to ensure an adaptive adversary does not gain any advantage. Then $\mathcal{L}_j$ is sent out to party j for $j = 1, \ldots, n$.

2. In rounds $i = 2, \ldots, \lceil \log \epsilon \cdot n \rceil$, every honest party p adds to her constraint set $\mathcal{C}_p$ all messages sent in the previous round $i-1$, collects all lists $\mathcal{L}_p$ from round $i-1$ into a new set M_p and performs the same task as in round 1 (random assigning of elements in $M_p - \mathcal{C}_p$, compilation into lists and sending).

We prove that with overwhelming probability, the above gossiping protocol delivers every element contained in the sets of the initially-honest parties (except the ones in the initial constraint sets) to all remaining honest parties, see Lemma 9. The communication complexity is indeed $\tilde{O}(n|\mathcal{M}| + n^2)$ since in every round all n parties send to all n parties a message of size $2m\lceil |\mathcal{M}|/n \rceil \le 2|\mathcal{M}| \cdot m/n + 2$.

We emphasize that constraint sets used in $\mathcal{M}$-CONVERGERANDOM are crucial in reducing the communication complexity of our $\mathcal{M}$-CONVERGERANDOM protocol, in particular when $\mathcal{M}$-CONVERGERANDOM has to be called a large number of times by another protocol. This is because any message m that is sent by party p in round 1 of $\mathcal{M}$-CONVERGERANDOM enters p's constraint set and is therefore never sent again by p. A protocol can thus avoid resending messages during future calls of $\mathcal{M}$-CONVERGERANDOM, by initializing future constraint sets to contain already sent messages. We finally note that one of our protocols presented in this paper (TRUSTEDPBC) invokes $\mathcal{M}$-CONVERGERANDOM a small number of times, so for simplicity we do not use constraint sets.

While the above protocol achieves the desired communication complexity bounds, the crucial question is whether it achieves *adaptive security* (It does.) Recall that the danger with picking a few random parties to send the message in an adaptive setting (as in our statically secure broadcast protocol) was that the adversary can corrupt the specific set of recipients for the sent message. This cuts off the propagation and leaves the sender as the only honest party who has the message! Our protocol avoids that because it never reveals which are the true recipients of the message by padding each list $\mathcal{L}_j$ to the same size and then encrypting it (Secure state erasures are required as well for adaptive security.) More intuitively, this can be understood as having the (different) messages that are sent by a sender in a particular round of this process pose as "cover traffic" for one another. This cover traffic hides to whom a particular message is being sent (since all the recipients of a single sender obtain the same amount of encrypted information), and hence makes it impossible to trace the path of that message.

Technical Highlights for BULLETINPBC (Sect. 5). This protocol follows a similar framework as the Dolev-Strong protocol [10]. Recall that in Dolev-Strong, for all rounds $r < n$, whenever an honest party p has observed r signatures on a bit b for the first time, p adds bit b to the a local set (which we call Extracted), adds her signature and sends a message x of $r+1$ signatures *to all parties*, using a SEND-ALL(x) instruction. As r goes to n, this instruction incurs $O(n^3 \cdot \kappa)$ communication complexity, since all parties potentially send $O(n)$ sized lists of signatures to all. Combining n of these protocols naively would yield a PBC protocol with prohibitive communication complexity of $O(n^4 \cdot \kappa)$.

To overcome this issue, we observe that the main communication overhead in this naive protocol comes from steps where all parties send lists of $O(n)$ signatures *for the same designated sender*. For example, it could be possible that all parties hold the same list of r signatures in some round r that made them accept a message s for some slot i in that round. Clearly, it is extremely wasteful for *all* honest parties to send *all* of these signatures to *all* parties via SEND-ALL(x) (after appending their own respective signatures), since there is a large amount of redundancy among these lists.

Our proposed protocol deals with this situation by viewing it as an instance of the $\mathcal{M}$-Converge problem, where input sets consist of the signatures in the parties' lists and the constraint sets ensure that signatures which were already sent will not be repeated. Hence, we use our $\mathcal{M}$-CONVERGERANDOM protocol to propagate lists in that case much more efficiently, namely with $O(n^2 \cdot \kappa^2)$ complexity (rather than naively within $O(n^3 \cdot \kappa)$). However, in the above discussion we focused on only a single slot i. Yet, there is an issue when applying this strategy to a single instance of Dolev-Strong BC: since there are $O(n)$ rounds where parties might call $\mathcal{M}$-CONVERGERANDOM, the total communication complexity is $O(n^3 \cdot \kappa^2)$, even worse than the original DS protocol! It is here that we once again leverage the inherent parallel structure of PBC. Namely, in our protocol, we use $\mathcal{M}$-CONVERGERANDOM to propagate messages for all slots *simultaneously*, regardless of what slot they belong to. Moreover, we run one instance of $\mathcal{M}$-CONVERGERANDOM per step of the protocol, for a total of $O(n)$ many instances. While it is possible that for some of these instances, the complexity increases to $O(n^3 \cdot \kappa^2)$, thanks to the constraint sets we bound the number of such instances by $O(1)$. This results in a total of $O(n^3 \cdot \kappa^2)$ complexity, or an amortized $O(n^2 \cdot \kappa^2)$ complexity per slot.

Technical Highlights for TRUSTEDPBC (Sect. 6). Our starting point for this protocol is the recent protocol by Chan et al. [8] that solves BC in the trusted PKI model with $O(n^2 \cdot \kappa^2)$ communication complexity. We call this protocol ChBC from now on. ChBC is essentially a Dolev-Strong protocol run among a random committee of κ parties—for the rest of honest parties to agree with the committee, a distribution phase takes place. More concretely, ChBC at round $r < \kappa$ instructs parties to perform the following.

1. (Voting) Whenever an honest committee party p has observed r signatures on a bit b for the first time, p adds her signature and sends a message of $r+1$ signatures *to all parties*, using a SEND-ALL instruction. This step is executed only by the committee and the message's size is at most κ signatures of κ bits each; hence the induced communication complexity is $O(n \cdot \kappa^3)$;
2. (Distribution) When an honest party p observes r signatures on a bit b for the first time, p just forwards the r signatures *to all parties*, using a SEND-ALL instruction. Note that this step is executed by all parties and therefore induces $O(n^2 \cdot \kappa^2)$ communication complexity (It is $n^2 \cdot \kappa^2$ since every party sends once to all n parties a list of at most κ signatures of κ bits each.)

We then observe that if we naively use the ChBC protocol for the parallel case, the communication complexity of the distribution phase grows to $O(n^3 \cdot \kappa^2)$, since the SEND-ALL instruction would have to be used at most $2 \cdot n$ times (instead of twice), for each bit b and for each sender slot p. To overcome this issue we once again observe that we can abstract each step (there are κ many) of the protocol as an instance of the $\mathcal{M}$-Converge problem to improve communication complexity. This leads to the final version of our TRUSTEDPBC protocol, with amortized linear complexity $O(n \cdot \kappa^4)$ per sender slot.

1.3   Related Work

The problem of BC was originally introduced in the celebrated work of Lamport, Shostak, and Pease [19]. Their work also gave the first (setup-free) protocol for $t < n/3$ and showed optimality of their parameters. However, their solution required an exponential amount of communication and was soon improved upon by protocols requiring only polynomial amounts of communication [11,14]. More recently, a line of work initiated by King et al. [5,17,18] gave setup-free protocols for the case of $t < n/3$ that require $\tilde{O}(n^{3/2})$ communication and Momose and Ren [25] provide a protocol in the bulletin PKI model with $\tilde{O}(n^2 \cdot \kappa)$ communication complexity but in the honest majority setting. For the setting of $t < n$ corruptions, Dolev and Strong [10] gave the first protocol with polynomial efficiency. Their protocol uses a bulletin board PKI, requires $O(n^3 \cdot \kappa)$ bits of communication, and solves BC for any $t < n$. Much more recently, the work of Chan et al. [8] gives a protocol that requires $\tilde{O}(n^2 \cdot \kappa)$ bits of communication and requires trusted setup. What can be seen as a statically secure version of Chan et al.'s protocol was suggested by Buterin [6] and gives a protocol with $O(n \cdot \kappa)$ communication complexity and also requires trusted setup (to elect a random committee at the onset of the protocol). In the range of $t < n/3$ and $t < n/2$, the works of Micali [23], Micali and Vaikuntnathan [24], and Abraham et al. [1] present solution with subquadratic communication complexity using trusted setup. Somewhat surprisingly, in the setting with setup (for $t < n$), any efficiency improvement to the early work of Dolev and Strong has been aimed exclusively at improving the *round complexity* rather than the communication complexity. This has been the subject of several works [8,12,13,27]. Finally, the problem of interactive consistency or parallel broadcast was originally introduced by Pease et al. [26]. Another line of works studies the *round complexity* of BC, e.g., [8,13,27]. See Table 1 for overview of communication-efficient protocols.

Gossip protocols (also known as flooding protocols) are a simple, efficient type of information propagation and are used as a background layer in many infrastructures (e.g., blockchain protocols). Loosely speaking, they are based on the principle of exponential graph expansion: a party sends its message to a small random sample of its neighbours who in turn do the same. It is well-known [9] and easy to see that within $O(\log(n))$ rounds, all n parties learn the message. Some works [16] consider more refined versions of data dissemination, where parties keep sending until they hear from a certain number of their neighbours. These protocols work well in the presence of random, benign (i.e., crash) faults, but fail completely in the presence of malicious (byzantine) faults. This was addressed in a line of works such as [4,21]. However, as recently noticed by [22], none of these protocols work in the presence of a fully adaptive adversary that can corrupt parties based on the propagation of a specific message. It is easy to see why: an adaptive adversary can simply corrupt all the (randomly elected) neighbours an honest party sent to and inhibit further propagation of a message in this manner. Such attacks are sometimes referred to as "eclipsing attacks" in the cryptocurrency space. Hence, in [22] they considered flooding protocols in the presence of an adaptive adversary who dynamically chooses who to corrupt, but whose corruptions take a while to become active. This gives the nodes time to propagate the messages as necessary. An example of gossip used in a byzantine consensus protocol is [15]: this work shows how to obtain, using gossip, a reliable broadcast protocol with quasi-linear (in n) communication for an asynchronous network. Being asynchronous, their protocol heavily relies on the fact that fewer than $n/3$ parties are corrupted.

2   Preliminaries and Notation

We denote as $X \leftarrow \Pi$ the random variable X output by probability experiment Π. Our protocols are run among a set of n parties out of which $t = (1 - \epsilon) \cdot n$ can be malicious, for constant $\epsilon < 1$. We use κ to indicate the security parameter.

Bulletin PKI vs. Trusted PKI. We briefly recall the difference between Bulletin PKI and Trusted PKI here. For the first part of our work, we assume that parties share a *public key infrastructure* (Bulletin PKI). That is, each party i has a secret key sk_i and a public key pk_i, where pk_i is known to all parties. The secret key sk_i and the public key pk_i are not assumed to be computed in a trusted manner. Instead, we assume only that each party i generates its keys (sk_i, pk_i) locally and then makes pk_i known by using a public bulletin board. For the final result of this work, we use the Trusted PKI setting, where a trusted party computes and distributes secret/public key pairs to the protocol participants, enabling the use use of more powerful cryptographic primitives in our constructions, such as verifiable random functions.

Signatures. Party i computes a *signature* σ on a message m via $\sigma \leftarrow sig(sk_i, m)$. Later σ can be verified via $ver(pk_i, \sigma, m)$. As is standard for this line of work, we assume signatures are *idealized* in the sense that it is impossible, without sk_i, to create a signature σ on a message m such that $ver(pk_i, \sigma, m) = 1$. We also assume *perfect correctness*, i.e., for any m, $ver(pk_i, sig(sk_i, m), m) = 1$. We write $sig_i(m)$ to indicate $sig(sk_i, m)$ and $ver_i(\sigma, m)$ to indicate $ver(pk_i, \sigma, m)$.

Communication Model. We consider the standard synchronous model of communication. In this model, parties are assumed to share a global clock that progresses at the same rate for all parties. Furthermore, they are connected via pairwise, authenticated channels. Any message that is sent by an honest party at time T is guaranteed to arrive at every honest party at time $T + \Delta$, where Δ is the maximum network delay. In particular, this means that messages of honest parties can not be dropped from the network and are always delivered. It is assumed that all parties know the parameter Δ. As such we consider protocols that execute in a round based fashion, where every round in the protocol is of length Δ and parties start executing the r-th round of a protocol at time $(r - 1) \cdot \Delta$. Let $\mathcal{M}$ be a set of messages and $\mathcal{P}$ be a set of parties. When a party i calls SEND($\mathcal{M}, \mathcal{P}$) at round r, then the set of messages $\mathcal{M}$ is delivered to parties in $\mathcal{P}$ by round $r + 1$. When a party i calls RECEIVE() in round r, then all messages that were sent to i in round $r - 1$ via SEND commands are stored in i's local storage. Finally, we assume secure erasures, namely a party p can safely erase her state so that the adversary cannot access it whenever the adversary corrupts p (after the state has been erased), e.g. [3,17].

t-Secure Broadcast and t-Secure Parallel Broadcast. We now provide the definitions of t-Secure Broadcast and t-Secure Parallel Broadcast which are the focus of the paper's main body.

Definition 1 (t-Secure Broadcast). *A protocol Π executed by n parties, where a designated party $s \in [n]$ (the sender) holds an input v and all parties terminate upon output, is a t-secure broadcast protocol if the following properties hold with probability $1 - \mathsf{negl}(\kappa)$ whenever at most t parties are corrupted:*

    t-validity: if the sender is honest, all honest parties output v.

    t-consistency: all honest parties output the same value v'.

Definition 2 (t-Secure Parallel Broadcast). *A protocol Π executed by n parties, where each party i holds an input v_i and terminates upon outputting an n-value vector $\mathbf{V}_i$, is a t-secure parallel broadcast protocol if the following properties hold with probability $1 - \mathsf{negl}(\kappa)$ whenever at most l parties are corrupted:*

    t-validity: If party s is honest, then all honest parties i have $\mathbf{V}_i(s) = v_s$.

    t-consistency: all honest parties output the same vector $\mathbf{V}'$.

We define a "*slot*" s to denote in PBC the equivalent of the execution of a single sender BC, if party p_s was the designated sender. Thus, the output bit of a party p_i for a slot s is $\mathbf{V}_i(s)$. A slot s is honest, if p_s is honest.

Adversary Model. In general for all our protocols we consider a polynomial-time adversary that can corrupt up to t parties in a malicious fashion. The adversary can make them deviate from the protocol description arbitrarily. Our adversary is also rushing, being able to observe the honest parties' messages in any synchronous round r of a protocol, and delay them until the end of that round. In this way, it can choose its own messages for that round before delivering any of the honest messages. For Sect. 3, we consider a *static adversary*, who chooses all the parties to corrupt before the execution of the protocol. For Sects. 4 to 6, we consider an *adaptive adversary*, able to corrupt up to t parties, each at any point during the execution of the protocol, learning its internal state which consists of any longterm secret keys and ephemeral values that have not been deleted at that point. However, we do not consider *strongly* adaptive adversaries that could, after corrupting a party, observe what message that party attempted to send during that round and then replace its message with another one (or simply delete it). Moreover, we assume *atomic sends* [3]: an honest party p can send to multiple parties simultaneously, without the adversary being able to corrupt p in between sending to two parties.

MPC Model. One part of our parallel broadcast protocol is modeled using the ideal functionality $\mathcal{F}_{\mathsf{prop}}$ (See Fig. 4.) To show that a specific implementation realizes $\mathcal{F}_{\mathsf{prop}}$, we are using the definition of synchronous MPC in the standalone model by Canetti [7] which we briefly recall here. Let f be a (possibly randomized) function that takes n inputs. In the real world execution of a protocol Π for computing f, party P_i initially holds 1^κ and an input x_i. The adversary holds 1^κ and an auxiliary input z. The goal of running Π is for all honest parties P_i to learn output y_i, where $[y_1, \ldots, y_n] \leftarrow f(x_1, \ldots, x_n)$. During the execution, the adversary $\mathcal{A}$ can corrupt any party adaptively, upon which it learns the internal state of this party. At the end of the execution, each honest party outputs its local output (as instructed by Π) and the adversary $\mathcal{A}$ outputs its entire view. We write $\mathbf{Real}_{\Pi,\mathcal{A}}(1^\kappa, \mathbf{x}, z)$ to denote the distribution over the vector of outputs of honest parties and the set of corrupted parties in the above (real-world) experiment. We define security of Π relative to an ideal world where a trusted party securely computes f and outputs the result to all parties. Parties hold inputs as above; the adversary in the ideal world is denoted as $\mathcal{S}$. The ideal-world execution now works as follows.

> **Initial corruptions.** $\mathcal{S}$ adaptively corrupts parties and learns their inputs.
> **Evaluation by trusted party.** The inputs $\mathbf{x}$ of honest parties are sent to the trusted party. The ideal-world adversary $\mathcal{S}$ can specify the inputs on behalf of any of the parties it has corrupted. The trusted party evaluates the function f and returns the computed outputs y_i to the respective party i.
> **Additional corruptions.** At any point in time (after output has been provided by the trusted party), $\mathcal{S}$ may adaptively corrupt additional parties i.[1]
> **Output.** The honest parties output their view.
> **Post-execution corruptions.** $\mathcal{S}$ may corrupt additional parties and output (any function of) its view.

$\mathbf{Ideal}_{f,\mathcal{S}}(1^\kappa, \mathbf{x}, z)$ denotes the distribution over the vector of outputs of honest parties and the set of corrupted parties in the above (ideal-world) experiment.

Definition 3 (Secure Computation). *Π t-securely computes f if for all PPT adversaries $\mathcal{A}$ corrupting at most t parties, there exists a PPT simulator $\mathcal{S}$ such that* $\{\mathbf{Real}_{\Pi,\mathcal{A}}(1^\kappa, \mathbf{x}, z)\}_{\kappa \in \mathbb{N}, \mathbf{x}, z \in \{0,1\}^*} \approx \{\mathbf{Ideal}_{f,\mathcal{S}}(1^\kappa, \mathbf{x}, z)\}_{\kappa \in \mathbb{N}, \mathbf{x}, z \in \{0,1\}^*}.$

3   Single-Sender Broadcast

We are now ready to describe our proposed communication-efficient BC protocol in detail. As we mentioned in the introduction, our protocol replaces Dolev-Strong's SEND-ALL instruction with a SEND-RANDOM instruction. We model SEND-RANDOM with a randomized procedure that we call ADDRANDOMEDGES (see Fig. 1) that simulates the propagation of messages from honest nodes to the rest of the network in our protocol, between two consecutive rounds. Aanalyzing it seperately, allows us to argue about the consistency and validity of our protocol BULLETINBC in a structured manner.

---

[1] Since we assume erasure, the adversary learns nothing new from such corruptions.

```
1: procedure G ← ADDRANDOMEDGES(V, S₂, S₃, S, m)
   Input. Set of n nodes V; disjoint subsets of V: S₂, S₃;
   S ⊆ V − (S₂ ∪ S₃); Integer m ≤ n.
   Output. A graph G.

2:     Let G be an empty graph with node set V;
3:     for every node v ∈ S do
4:         for every node u ∈ V do
5:             Add an edge (v, u) to G with probability m/n;
6:     return G;
```

Fig. 1. The ADDRANDOMEDGES procedure.

3.1   The Procedure AddRandomEdges

ADDRANDOMEDGES works over a graph G whose n vertices V are partitioned into three disjoint sets and which is initially empty, i.e., has no edges. Given an arbitrary partition of V into three disjoint sets S_1, S_2, S_3, and a set $S \subseteq S_1$, ADDRANDOMEDGES adds the edge (v, u) to the graph G with probability m/n for every pair of nodes $v \in S$ and $u \in V$. Note that S_1 is fully defined by S_2, S_3 and V as $S_1 = V - (S_2 \cup S_3)$, therefore S_1 is not an input to ADDRANDOMEDGES. The procedure outputs the resulting graph G (i.e., with all the added edges). Looking ahead, S represents the set of parties that send a message q at a specific round r and S_2 represents the set of parties that have not received q in a previous round. An edge from $v \in S$ to $u \in V$ represents that party v sends q to party u in round r. We want to compute how many parties in S_2 receive q (for the first time) during round r, so we study the degree of nodes in S_2. We define the following indicator random variables.

Definition 4. *Let* $G \leftarrow$ ADDRANDOMEDGES(V, S_2, S_3, S, m). *For all* $u \in S_2$ *let* $Z_u \in \{0, 1\}$ *such that* $Z_u = 1$ *if and only if* u *has nonzero degree in* G.

In Lemma 1 we show that the number of nodes in S_2 that acquire an edge in G is at least twice the number of nodes in S. Intuitively, this allows us to show that messages propagate very quickly in our broadcast protocol.

Lemma 1. *Let* (S_1, S_2, S_3) *be a partition of n nodes into disjoint sets with* $\tau = |S_1| \leq \epsilon \cdot n/3$, $|S_2| = \epsilon \cdot n - |S_1|$, $|S_3| = n - \epsilon \cdot n$, *where* $\epsilon \in (0, 1)$ *is a constant. Let also* $S \subseteq S_1$ *with* $|S| \geq 2 \cdot \tau/3$ *and let* $\{Z_u\}_{u \in S_2}$ *be the random variables defined by* ADDRANDOMEDGES(V, S_2, S_3, S, m) *per Definition 4. Then for* $m \geq 15/\epsilon$,

$$\Pr\left[\sum_{u \subset S_2} Z_u \geq 2 \cdot \tau\right] \geq 1 - p, \text{ where } p = \max\left\{\epsilon \cdot n \cdot e^{-\epsilon \cdot m/9}, \left(\frac{e}{2}\right)^{-\epsilon \cdot m/4}\right\}.$$

3.2   The Protocol BULLETINBC

We now describe our protocol BULLETINBC. For simplicity, we describe our protocol for the case where values agreed upon are from the binary domain.

Intuition: From SEND-ALL to Gossiping. As we mentioned in the introduction, our protocol is inspired by the protocol of Dolev and Strong [10] that achieves $O(n^3 \cdot \kappa)$ communication complexity in the bulletin board PKI model. We give a detailed description of the Dolev-Strong protocol here. Each party $i \in [n]$ maintains a set $\mathsf{Extracted}_i$ that is initialized as empty. The protocol proceeds in $t+1$ rounds as follows (Again, $t < n$ is the number of corrupted parties.) In the first round, the designated sender s signs her input bit and sends the signature to all $n - 1$ parties. In rounds $2 \leq r \leq t$, for each bit $b \in \{0,1\}$, if an honest party i has seen at least r signatures on b (including a signature from the designated sender) and b is not in her extracted set, then party i adds b to her local extracted set, signs b and sends the $r + 1$ signatures to all $n - 1$ parties. In the final round $t + 1$, i accepts a bit b iff b is the only bit in $\mathsf{Extracted}_i$.

What makes the above protocol work is the fact that when party i sends the $r + 1$ signatures, *all* honest parties see these signatures in the next round, since these signatures are sent to *all* other $n - 1$ parties. In the final round, it is not necessary to send again, since holding $t + 1$ signatures on b means that at least one honest party has sent $r + 1$ signatures upon receiving r signatures on b in round $r < t + 1$. Hence, all parties must have received these $r + 1$ signatures in round $r + 1$ and added b to their extracted sets in that round. In terms of communication complexity, note that all honest parties send an $O(t \cdot \kappa)$-sized message to $n - 1$ parties (κ is due to the size of the signature), which results in $O(n^2 \cdot t \cdot \kappa)$ communication. Given that $t = O(n)$, this is $O(n^3 \cdot \kappa)$.

Our protocol does away with the SEND-ALL instructions, and introduces a form of gossiping: it does not require an honest party to send the $r+1$ signatures to all $n - 1$ parties. Instead, an honest party sends the $r + 1$ signatures to each other party with probability $\frac{m}{n}$. The hope is that after a certain number of rounds, enough honest parties see these messages. As expected, the total number of rounds must now increase. Fortunately, our protocol requires just an additional $R = O(\log n)$ rounds, yielding a communication complexity of $O(n^2 \cdot m \cdot \kappa) = O(n^2 \cdot \kappa^2)$ and a round complexity of $O(n)$.

Formal Description and Proof of BulletinBC. Figure 2 contains the pseudocode of our protocol from the view of an honest party p (i.e., this is the algorithm that runs at each distributed (honest) node p). It takes as input an initial bit b in the case of the designated sender (no input else) and returns the final bit b'. Note three major differences from the Dolev-Strong protocol [10]: (1) we increase the number of rounds from t to $t + R$ (Line 5); (2) instead of sending to all parties we send to each party randomly with probability m/n (Line 12); (3) for all rounds $r \geq t+1$ we do not require $r + 1$ signatures to add to the extracted set but just $t + 1$—that is why we use the expression $\min\{r, t+1\}$ in Line 9. We now continue with the proof of consistency and validity of BulletinBC. We first define, using notation consistent with AddRandomEdges, the following sets of parties (w.r.t. a bit b and a round r):

1. $S(b, r)$: honest parties i that added b to their $\mathsf{Extracted}_i$ set *at* round r;
2. $S_1(b, r)$: honest parties i that added b to their $\mathsf{Extracted}_i$ set *by* round r;
3. $S_2(b, r)$: honest parties i that have *not* added b to their $\mathsf{Extracted}_i$ set by r.

```
1:  procedure b' ← BULLETINBC_p()
        Input. A bit b if p = s, no input otherwise.
        Output. Decision bit b'.

2:      Extracted_p = Local_p = ∅;
3:      if p is the designated sender s then
4:          SEND(sig_s(b), [n]);
5:      for round r = 1 to t + R do
6:          Local_p ← Local_p ∪ RECEIVE();
7:          for bit x ∈ {0, 1} do
8:              S ← DISTINCTSIGS(x, Local_p, s);
9:              if |S| ≥ min{r, t + 1} ∧ x ∉ Extracted_p then
10:                 Extracted_p = Extracted_p ∪ x;
11:                 for party i = 1 to n do
12:                     SEND(sig_p(x) ∪ S, i) with probability m/n;
13:     return b' ∈ Extracted_p if |Extracted_p| = 1, otherwise return canonical bit 0;
```

Fig. 2. Our BULLETINBC$_p$ protocol for party p. DISTINCTSIGS(x, Local$_p$, s) returns the set of valid signatures from distinct signers on x contained in Local$_p$ if this set includes a signature from s, otherwise it returns $\emptyset$. Note that only the designated sender receives an input bit in the protocol.

Define S_3 be the set of malicious parties ($|S_3| = n - \epsilon n$). We show (roughly) that the number of parties that receive a message at round r' that was sent at round $r < r'$ increases exponentially with $r' - r$ with overwhelming probability.

Lemma 2 (Gossiping bounds). *For a specific bit b, let r be the first round of* BULLETINBC *where an honest party i adds b to* Extracted$_i$. *Let $R = \lceil \log_3(\epsilon \cdot n) \rceil$. Let p be the probability defined in Lemma 1. Then:*

1. *For all rounds ρ such that $r \leq \rho \leq r + R$ and $|S_1(b, \rho - 1)| \leq \epsilon \cdot n/3$, we have that with probability at least $(1 - p)^{\rho - r}$:*

$$|S(b, \rho)| \geq (2/3) \cdot |S_1(b, \rho)| \text{ and } |S_1(b, \rho)| \geq 3^{\rho - r}.$$

2. *Let $r^* > r$ be a round such that $|S_1(b, r^* - 1)| > \epsilon \cdot n/3$. Then, $|S_1(b, r^*)| = \epsilon \cdot n$ with probability at least $(1 - p^*) \cdot (1 - p)^{r^* - r - 1}$, where $p^* = \epsilon \cdot n \cdot e^{-2\epsilon \cdot m/9}$.*

Lemma 3 (t-consistency: BULLETINBC). *Let $R = \lceil \log_3(\epsilon n) \rceil$, $m = \Theta(\kappa)$.* BULLETINBC *satisfies t-consistency (Definition 7), with probability $1 - \mathsf{negl}(\kappa)$.*

Proof. Suppose an honest party i adds bit b to Extracted$_i$ at some round r. We prove that by the end of the protocol all honest parties j add b to their Extracted$_j$ sets with probability $1 - \mathsf{negl}(\kappa)$—this means that all honest parties have identical Extracted sets by the end of the protocol, which is equivalent to consistency. We distinguish the two cases:

Case $r < t + 1$: We distinguish two cases. If $S_1(b, r) > \epsilon \cdot n/3$, then by Item (2) of Lemma 2, all $\epsilon \cdot n$ honest parties add bit b in their extracted set by the next round with probability at least $1 - \epsilon \cdot n \cdot e^{-2\epsilon \cdot m/9} = 1 - \mathsf{negl}(\kappa)$, since $n = poly(\kappa)$. Now, if $S_1(b, r) \leq \epsilon \cdot n/3$, let $\mathbf{r}$ be the round $r + R - 1$. If $S_1(b, \mathbf{r}) > \epsilon \cdot n/3$, the previous case applies. Otherwise, Item (1) of Lemma 2 applies, meaning that at round $\mathbf{r} + 1 = r + R$ we have $S_1(b, r + R) \geq 3^R = 3^{\lceil \log_3(\epsilon \cdot n) \rceil} \geq 3^{\log_3(\epsilon \cdot n)} = \epsilon \cdot n$, with probability at least $(1 - p)^R \geq 1 - R \cdot p$, by Bernoulli's inequality[2] and since $-p \geq -1, R \geq 1$. Note that for $m = \Theta(\kappa)$, $R \cdot p$ is $\mathsf{negl}(k)$, since $n = poly(\kappa)$.

Case $r \geq t + 1$: Suppose an honest party i adds bit b to $\mathsf{Extracted}_i$ at some round $r \geq t + 1$. Then, i has received valid signatures on b from $t + 1$ distinct parties. Thus, an honest party j added bit b to $\mathsf{Extracted}_j$ at some round $r'' < t + 1$. So, case $\underline{r'' < t + 1}$ applies to honest party j. Thus all honest parties add b to their $\mathsf{Extracted}$ sets by the end of the protocol, with probability $1 - \mathsf{negl}(\kappa)$.   □

Lemma 4 (t-validity: BULLETINBC). *Let* $R = \lceil \log_3(\epsilon \cdot n) \rceil$, $m = \Theta(\kappa)$. *BULLETINBC satisfies t-validity, per Definition 7, with probability $1 - \mathsf{negl}(\kappa)$.*

Proof. Follows from the proof of consistency in Lemma 3. After $R = \lceil \log_3(\epsilon \cdot n) \rceil$ rounds, all honest parties have received the bit of the honest sender, with probability $1 - \mathsf{negl}(\kappa)$.   □

Theorem 1 (Communication complexity: BULLETINBC). *Let* $m = \Theta(\kappa)$ *and* $R = \lceil \log_3(\epsilon n) \rceil$. *The total number of bits exchanged by all parties in BULLETINBC is $O(n^2 \cdot \kappa^2)$, with probability $1 - \mathsf{negl}(\kappa)$.*

Proof. Every honest party sends at most one time for each bit to a number of $O(m) = O(\kappa)$ parties with overwhelming probability in κ, a message of at most t signatures. Since there are $O(n)$ honest parties, $t = O(n)$ and the size of each signature is κ, the total number of bits exchanged is $O(n^2 \cdot m \cdot \kappa) = O(n^2 \cdot \kappa^2)$.   □

4   The $\mathcal{M}$-Converge Problem

In this section we introduce the $\mathcal{M}$-Converge problem, an efficient solution of which is used as a black box in our parallel broadcast protocols. Informally, in the $\mathcal{M}$-Converge problem, honest parties begin with individual subsets (of a fixed set $\mathcal{M}$) as inputs and in the end of the protocol all honest parties must have a superset of the union of all the initial honest-owned subsets. We want to design $\mathcal{M}$-Converge protocols in the presence of an adversary that can corrupt at most t parties, adaptively. We now define the $\mathcal{M}$-Converge problem formally.

Definition 5. *(t-secure $\mathcal{M}$-Converge problem).* *Let $\mathcal{M} \subseteq \{0, 1\}^*$ be an efficiently recognizable set (This is a set for which membership can be efficiently decided.) A protocol Π executed by n parties where every honest party p initially holds input set $M_p \subseteq \mathcal{M}$ and constraint set $\mathcal{C}_p \subseteq \mathcal{M}$ is a t-secure $\mathcal{M}$-Converge protocol if all remaining honest parties upon termination, with probability $1 - \mathsf{negl}(\kappa)$, output a set S_p s.t.*

$$S_p \supseteq \bigcup_{p \in \mathcal{H}} M_p - \bigcup_{p \in \mathcal{H}} \mathcal{C}_p,$$

---

[2] For every $x, r \in \Re, x \geq -1, r \geq 1$ it holds that $(1 + x)^r \geq 1 + rx$.

whenever at most t parties are corrupted and where $\mathcal{H}$ is the set of honest parties in the beginning of the protocol.

We note that the trivial solution of outputting $\mathcal{M}$ does not work: We cannot necessarily enumerate the elements of $\mathcal{M}$ since we only assume that membership can be efficiently decided. An example of such a setting is where $\mathcal{M}$ consists of signatures of n parties on a bit b, computed with the parties' secret keys. In such a setting, PPT parties can easily verify membership in $\mathcal{M}$ but cannot enumerate $\mathcal{M}$, even if $\mathcal{M}$ is polynomial-sized (Note that the latter could be true depending on the signature scheme.) As we already noted in the introduction, there is a very simple t-secure $\mathcal{M}$-Converge protocol: All honest parties just send their local sets M_p to all other parties, in one round. Unfortunately, the communication complexity of this protocol is $\Omega(n^2 \cdot \min_{p \in \mathcal{H}}\{|M_p - \mathcal{C}_p|\})$, which would be prohibitively expensive. In this section we propose a protocol, $\mathcal{M}$-CONVERGERANDOM (see Fig. 6) that uses gossiping to reduce communication to $\tilde{O}(n \cdot |\mathcal{M}| + n^2)$. First, we introduce some tools necessary for the analysis and clear exposition of our protocol, the functionality $\mathcal{F}_{\text{prop}}$ and the procedure ADDRANDOMEDGESADAPTIVE, required for analyzing $\mathcal{F}_{\text{prop}}$.

4.1   The Procedure ADDRANDOMEDGESADAPTIVE

Here we face an adaptive adversary and introduce the respective standalone randomized procedure which we call ADDRANDOMEDGESADAPTIVE (Fig. 3). Analyzing this process helps with proving the security of $\mathcal{M}$-CONVERGERANDOM.

In ADDRANDOMEDGESADAPTIVE, a set of honest senders $S \subseteq H$ (H is the set of initial honest nodes) are sending a message x to the rest of the parties, by picking each party independently to be a recipient of the message with probability m/n. The set of malicious nodes are not fixed a priori and the adversary $\mathcal{A}$ decides who to corrupt *after* the edges have been placed. We define a specific set of honest parties $S_2 \subseteq H$ as the *target set* which does not contain any of the senders in S (The meaning of target set will depend on our application.) Our goal is to prove that after the adversary has finished with the adaptive corruptions, still a good amount (in particular $2 \cdot |H - S_2|$) among the remaining honest nodes of S_2 is receiving message x with overwhelming probability. Clearly if we do not confine the view of the adversary, we cannot prove anything meaningful since the adversary can go ahead and corrupt exactly the nodes that received x. For this reason, in ADDRANDOMEDGESADAPTIVE we strategically allow the adversary to access just the list RevealedEdges (see Line 8) before making the next corruption—these are the edges that correspond to nodes that *have already been corrupted* (Note that this restriction of the adversary is enforced by the implementation of our protocol later.) We formalize this intuition in Lemma 5.

Definition 6. *Let $(G, H') \leftarrow$ ADDRANDOMEDGESADAPTIVE$_{\mathcal{A}}(V, S, H, m)$. Let $S_2 \subseteq H$. Then for all $u \in S_2$ define random variables $Z_u \in \{0, 1\}$ such that $Z_u = 1$ if and only if u has nonzero degree in G and $u \in H'$.*

---

procedure $(G, H') \leftarrow$ ADDRANDOMEDGESADAPTIVE$_{\mathcal{A}}(V, S, H, m)$
Input. Set of n nodes V; sets S and H with $S \subseteq H \subseteq V$; Integer $m \leq n$.
Output. A graph G a set of nodes $H' \subseteq H$.

  Let G be an empty graph with node set V;
  for every node $v \in S$ **do**
      for every node $u \in V$ **do**
          Add a directed edge (v, u) to G with probability m/n;
  Initialize RevealedEdges to be all edges incident to nodes in $v \in V - H$;
  while $|H| \geq \epsilon \cdot n$ **do**
      $v_i \leftarrow \mathcal{A}(V, H, \text{RevealedEdges})$ such that $v_i \in H$;
      if $v_i \neq null$ **then**
          Add $\{(u, v_i) : u \in \text{in\_neighbor}(v_i)\}$ to RevealedEdges;
          $H = H - v_i$;
      else break;
  Set $H' = H$;
  return (G, H');

Fig. 3. The experiment with an adaptive adversary, ADDRANDOMEDGESADAPTIVE.

Lemma 5. *Let $\epsilon \in (0, 1)$, $S_2 \subseteq H$ with $|H - S_2| \leq \epsilon \cdot n/3$ and $S \subseteq H - S_2$ with $|S| \geq 2|H - S_2|/3$. Let $(G, H') \leftarrow$ ADDRANDOMEDGESADAPTIVE$_{\mathcal{A}}(V, S, H, m)$. Then for $m \geq 19/\epsilon$,*

$$\Pr\left[\sum_{u \in S_2} Z_u \geq 2|H - S_2|\right] \geq 1 - p,$$

where $p = \max\{n \cdot e^{-4\epsilon \cdot m/45}, (\frac{\epsilon}{2})^{-\epsilon \cdot m/2}\}$.

Proof. For any set H^*, define E_{H^*} to be the event that ADDRANDOMEDGE-SADAPTIVE$_{\mathcal{A}}(V, S, H, m)$ outputs $(\cdot, H^*)$. Also, $\mathrm{supp}(\mathsf{E}) = \{H' : \Pr[\mathsf{E}_{H'}] > 0\}$. Fix $H^* \in \mathrm{supp}(\mathsf{E})$ such that

$$\Pr\left[\sum_{u \in S_2} Z_u \geq 2|H - S_2| \ \Big|\ \mathsf{E}_{H'}\right] \geq \Pr\left[\sum_{u \in S_2} Z_u \geq 2|H - S_2| \ \Big|\ \mathsf{E}_{H^*}\right],$$

for all $H' \in \mathrm{supp}(\mathsf{E})$. Therefore

$$\Pr\left[\sum_{u \in S_2} Z_u \geq 2|H - S_2|\right] = \sum_{H' \in \mathrm{supp}(\mathsf{E})} \Pr\left[\sum_{u \in S_2} Z_u \geq 2|H - S_2| \ \Big|\ \mathsf{E}_{H'}\right] \Pr[\mathsf{E}_{H'}]$$

$$\geq \sum_{H' \in \mathrm{supp}(\mathsf{E})} \Pr\left[\sum_{u \in S_2} Z_u \geq 2|H - S_2| \ \Big|\ \mathsf{E}_{H^*}\right] \Pr[\mathsf{E}_{H'}] \geq \Pr\left[\sum_{u \in S_2 \cap H^*} Z_u \geq 2|H - S_2| \ \Big|\ \mathsf{E}_{H^*}\right],$$

since $S_2 \cap H^* \subseteq S_2$. The remaining proof lower-bounds the probability $\Pr[\sum_{u \in S_2 \cap H^*} Z_u \geq 2|H - S_2| \mid \mathsf{E}_{H^*}]$. This is done in three steps.

Step 1 : Computing the probabilities $\Pr[Z_u = 1 \mid \mathsf{E}_{H^*}]$ *for all $u \in S_2 \cap H^*$.*

For $u \in S_2 \cap H^*$ let Y_u be a random variable such that $Y_u = 1$ iff u has nonzero degree in G. By definition of Z_u ($Z_u = (Y_u = 1) \cap (u \in H')$, for $u \in S_2$) we have that, for all $u \in S_2 \cap H^*$: $Pr[Z_u = 1 \mid \mathsf{E}_{H^*}] = Pr[Y_u = 1 \mid \mathsf{E}_{H^*}]$.

Suppose now $H^* = H - \{v_1, \ldots, v_\ell\}$, where $v_1, \ldots, v_\ell$ are nodes chosen by the adversary in Line 8 of the experiment. Because the adversary, in his picking $v_1, \ldots, v_\ell$, never accesses information related to nodes in H^* (his access is confined to information in $V - H^*$ through the RevealedEdges list), it follows that E_{H^*} (the event of the adversary picking $v_1, \ldots, v_\ell$) and Y_u (for every $u \in S_2 \cap H^*$) are independent events. Therefore for all $u \in S_2 \cap H^*$ it is

$$Pr[Z_u = 1 \mid \mathsf{E}_{H^*}] = Pr[Y_u = 1 \mid \mathsf{E}_{H^*}] = Pr[Y_u = 1] = 1 - (1 - m/n)^{|S|}.$$

Step 2 : Showing $\{Z_u\}_{u \in S_2 \cap H^*}$, conditioned on E_{H^*}, are independent. By using the above findings and by the independence of Y_u we have that for all $b_u \in \{0, 1\}$

$$Pr\left[\left(\bigcap_{u \in S_2 \cap H^*} Z_u = b_u\right) \mid \mathsf{E}_{H^*}\right] = Pr\left[\left(\bigcap_{u \in S_2 \cap H^*} Y_u = b_u\right) \mid \mathsf{E}_{H^*}\right]$$

$$= Pr\left[\bigcap_{u \in S_2 \cap H^*} Y_u = b_u\right] = \prod_{u \in S_2 \cap H^*} Pr[Y_u = b_u] = \prod_{u \in S_2 \cap H^*} Pr[Z_u = b_u \mid \mathsf{E}_{H^*}]$$

and therefore $\{Z_u\}_{u \in S_2 \cap H^*}$ are independent conditioned on E_{H^*}.

Step 3 : Applying a Chernoff bound. We consider two cases, one for $|S| > 4\epsilon \cdot n/45$ and one for $|S| \leq 4\epsilon \cdot n/45$. For $|S| > 4\epsilon \cdot n/45$, we have that for $u \in S_2 \cap H^*$

$$Pr[Z_u = 0 \mid \mathsf{E}_{H^*}] = (1 - m/n)^{|S|} < (1 - m/n)^{4\epsilon \cdot n/45} \leq e^{-4\epsilon \cdot m/45},$$

where the last step is derived from the inequality $(1 - x) \leq e^{-x}, \forall x \in \mathbb{R}$ and the fact that $(1 - m/n) > 0$ and $4\epsilon \cdot n/45 > 0$. Note that we have $|H^* - S_2| \leq |H - S_2| \leq \epsilon n/3$ and $|H^*| \geq \epsilon n$. So, by using the set equality $A = (A - B) \cup (A \cap B)$, for $A = H^*$ and $B = S_2$, we get that $|S_2 \cap H^*| \geq 2\epsilon n/3$. Also, $|H - S_2| \leq \epsilon \cdot n/3$, so it is $|S_2 \cap H^*| \geq 2|H - S_2|$. Therefore

$$Pr\left[\sum_{u \in S_2 \cap H^*} Z_u \geq 2 \cdot |H - S_2| \mid \mathsf{E}_{H^*}\right] \geq Pr\left[\sum_{u \in S_2 \cap H^*} Z_u = |S_2 \cap H^*| \mid \mathsf{E}_{H^*}\right]$$

$$= Pr\left[\bigcap_{u \in S_2 \cap H^*} Z_u = 1 \mid \mathsf{E}_{H^*}\right] = 1 - Pr\left[\bigcup_{u \in S_2 \cap H^*} Z_u = 0 \mid \mathsf{E}_{H^*}\right]$$

$$\geq 1 - \sum_{u \in S_2 \cap H^*} Pr[Z_u = 0 \mid \mathsf{E}_{H^*}] > 1 - |S_2 \cap H^*| \cdot e^{-4\epsilon \cdot m/45}$$

$$> 1 - n \cdot e^{-4\epsilon \cdot m/45}, \text{ since } |S_2 \cap H^*| < n.$$

For the case $|S| \leq 4\epsilon \cdot n/45$, since Z_u ($u \in S_2 \cap H^*$) are independent random variables conditioned on E_{H^*} we can use the lower tail Chernoff bound for $Z = \sum_{u \in S_2 \cap H^*} Z_u$, i.e.,

$$Pr[Z < (1 - \delta)\mu \mid \mathsf{E}_{H^*}] < \left(\frac{e^{-\delta}}{(1 - \delta)^{1-\delta}}\right)^\mu.$$

Now $\mu = \mathbb{E}\left[Z \mid \mathsf{E}_{H^*}\right] = \sum_{u \in S_2 \cap H^*} \Pr[Z_u = 1 \mid \mathsf{E}_{H^*}] \geq 2\epsilon \cdot n \cdot (1 - (1 - m/n)^{|S|})/3$, since $|S_2 \cap H^*| \geq 2\epsilon \cdot n/3$. Also, since $|S| \geq 1$ we have

$$\mu \geq 2\epsilon \cdot n \cdot (1 - (1 - m/n)^{|S|})/3 \geq 2\epsilon \cdot n \cdot (1 - (1 - m/n))/3 = 2\epsilon \cdot m/3.$$

For $\delta = 1/2$ this yields $\Pr[Z < \mu/2 \mid \mathsf{E}_{H^*}] < \left(\frac{e^{-0.5}}{(0.5)^{0.5}}\right)^{2\epsilon \cdot m/3} = \left(\frac{e}{2}\right)^{-\epsilon \cdot m/3}$.

Recall however that we must bound the probability $\Pr[Z < 2|H - S_2| \mid \mathsf{E}_{H^*}]$. Therefore it is enough to also show that $\mu \geq 4 \cdot |H - S_2|$. Recall that $|S| \geq 2|H - S_2|/3$ and since $|S| \leq 4\epsilon n/45$, then $|H - S_2| \leq 2\epsilon n/15$. From $\mu \geq 2\epsilon \cdot n \cdot (1 - (1 - m/n)^{|S|})/3$ and by $1 + x \leq e^x$ and $m \leq n$ we have that

$$\mu \geq \frac{2}{3}\epsilon \cdot n \cdot (1 - e^{-\frac{m}{n}|S|}) \geq 5 \cdot |H - S_2| \cdot \left(1 - e^{\frac{-2m \cdot \epsilon |S|}{15|H - S_2|}}\right),$$

$$\text{since } (n \geq 15|H - S_2|/2\epsilon \text{ and for } \alpha > 0, \; f(n) = n\left(1 - e^{-\frac{\alpha}{n}}\right) \nearrow \text{ in } n)$$

$$\geq 5 \cdot |H - S_2| \cdot \left(1 - e^{\frac{-4m \cdot \epsilon}{45}}\right), (\text{since } |S|/|H - S_2| \geq 2/3)$$

$$> 4 \cdot |H - S_2|, (\text{since } m \geq 19/\epsilon > \frac{45\ln 5}{4\epsilon}). \quad \square$$

4.2   The Ideal Functionality $\mathcal{F}_{\mathsf{prop}}$

To facilitate the exposition of our $\mathcal{M}$-CONVERGERANDOM protocol, we use an ideal functionality $\mathcal{F}_{\mathsf{prop}}$—see Fig. 4. In summary, $\mathcal{F}_{\mathsf{prop}}$ enables a party i to send a set of messages M to, on average, m out of n randomly selected parties without leaking *which those parties are* to the adversary. (We stress that each message in M is sent to different parties.) In our protocol $\mathcal{F}_{\mathsf{prop}}$ is called, via (SendRandom, M), by all honest parties i in the beginning of every round β and returns a set O_i, in the end of round β, which contains messages sent from other parties to i in the beginning of round β. The adversary in $\mathcal{F}_{\mathsf{prop}}$ gets a special interface to the functionality via the instruction (SendDirect, $\mathbf{x}$, J) by which it can send messages in $\mathbf{x}$ to parties specified in the vector J directly rather than randomly. We also assume that the adversary learns the input set of an honest party to $\mathcal{F}_{\mathsf{prop}}$. Finally the adversary gets access to all the sets O_i for the parties i that have been corrupted. We note here that $\mathcal{F}_{\mathsf{prop}}$ does not maintain state across calls and therefore all $O_i = \emptyset$, in the beginning of every round.

Implementing the Ideal Functionality $\mathcal{F}_{\mathsf{prop}}$ with PROPAGATE(). In Fig. 5 we define the process that instantiates $\mathcal{F}_{\mathsf{prop}}$ and give it the fitting name PROPAGATE(). As usual, we describe the protocol PROPAGATE() from the view of a party p. Consistent with the interface of $\mathcal{F}_{\mathsf{prop}}$, PROPAGATE() takes as input a set of messages M_p (that are to be sent out to other parties) and returns a set of messages O_p that were sent to p. In the first step of PROPAGATE(), every party creates a fresh pair of secret and public keys.

Next, note that PROPAGATE() does not send a message $x \in M_p$ directly to party j (with probability m/n) since this would reveal the recipient of x to the adversary. Instead, before sending, it locally computes a list $\mathcal{L}_j$, for every party

---

Functionality: $\mathcal{F}_{\mathsf{prop}}$

Let n be the number of parties and $m = 10/\epsilon + \kappa$. For every party $i \in [n]$, $\mathcal{F}_{\mathsf{prop}}$ keeps a set O_i which is initialized to $\emptyset$. Let M_i be party i's input messages' set.
On input (SendRandom, M_i) by honest party i:
  - For all $x \in M_i$ and for all $j \in [n]$ add (i,x) to O_j with probability m/n;
  - **return** M_i to adversary $\mathcal{A}$;
  - **return** O_i to party i.
On input (SendDirect, $\mathbf{x}$, J) by adversary $\mathcal{A}$ (for a corrupted party i):
  - Add $(i, x[j])$ to O_j for all $j \in J$;
  - **return** O_i to adversary $\mathcal{A}$.

Fig. 4. Functionality $\mathcal{F}_{\mathsf{prop}}$.

$j \in [n]$, and adds x to $\mathcal{L}_j$ with probability m/n. All lists $\mathcal{L}_j$ are padded to the size of the maximum sized list for the current call of PROPAGATE by the party (say party p), which we call Λ_p and are encrypted using the fresh public keys (Recall that $\mathcal{M}$ is the fixed set of the $\mathcal{M}$-Converge problem.) Then *the plaintext lists are erased from memory* and only after erasure the encrypted lists are sent out. In the end, the fresh secret key is also erased from memory. Intuitively, security is guaranteed because (i) the communication pattern of each sender does not reveal anything (irrespectively of who the recipient of x is, the adversary just sees equally-sized encrypted lists sent to all parties from each sender); and (ii) even if the adversary adaptively corrupts a party, no information about who that party sent to is revealed (because of erasure of plaintext lists and secret key)—the only information that is revealed is from whom that party received, which is harmless. We show that the lists $\mathcal{L}_j$ constructed by PROPAGATE$_p$() is of the same order as the message list M_p of party p with overwhelming probability.

Lemma 6. *If M_p is the input set of party p, the number of elements added to list $\mathcal{L}_j$ at Line 7 of PROPAGATE() is $\leq |M_p| \cdot 2m/n \leq \Lambda_p$ with probability $1 - \mathsf{negl}(\kappa)$.*

Lemma 7. *Let s be the length in bits of a message in $\mathcal{M}$. The communication complexity of PROPAGATE() for party p with input M_p, is $O(\max\{n, |M_p|\} \cdot m \cdot s)$.*

Security of PROPAGATE(). The lemma below proves that PROPAGATE() securely instantiates $\mathcal{F}_{\mathsf{prop}}$. The key property that we leverage is that each sender sends the same amount of information to every other party, regardless of their inputs. This trivializes the simulation of honest parties' communication in the protocol, since it is independent of the actual values they input to PROPAGATE().

Lemma 8. *Assuming a CPA-secure PKE scheme (KeyGen, Enc, Dec) and secure erasure, PROPAGATE() t-securely computes $\mathcal{F}_{\mathsf{prop}}$ according to Definition 3.*

```
1:  procedure PROPAGATE_p(SendRandom, M_p)
    Input. A set of of messages M_p.
    Output. A set of messages O_p.

2:      Set (sk_p, pk_p) ← KeyGen(1^κ);           ▷ at time 0
3:      SEND(pk_p, [n]);
4:      RECEIVE();                                ▷ at time Δ
5:      for all x ∈ M_p do
6:          for j = 1 to n do
7:              Add x to list L_j with probability m/n;
8:      Let Λ_p = 2m ⌈ |M_p|/n ⌉;
9:      for j = 1 to n do
10:         Pad list L_j to maximum size Λ_p;
11:         ct_j ← Enc(pk_j, L_j);
12:         Erase L_j from memory;
13:     for j = 1 to n do
14:         SEND(ct_j, j);
15:     C ← RECEIVE();                            ▷ at time 2Δ
16:     for all ct ∈ C do
17:         Decrypt ct using sk_p and output a list L;
18:         Add L to O_p;
19:     Erase sk_p from memory;
20:     return O_p;
```

Fig. 5. PROPAGATE(), a secure instantiation of $\mathcal{F}_{\text{prop}}$. We note that the secret and public keys that are generated in Line 2 are one-time and are never used again.

4.3 Our $\mathcal{M}$-CONVERGERANDOM Protocol

We now analyze the $\mathcal{M}$-CONVERGERANDOM protocol, depicted in Fig. 6, solving the $\mathcal{M}$-Converge problem with improved communication. Our protocol proceeds in $\lceil \log(\epsilon \cdot n) \rceil$ rounds. In each round, every honest party p uses $\mathcal{F}_{\text{prop}}$ to send messages in their local set that are not in their constraint set, to a few randomly selected parties (Line 3). To decide what to send in the next round, p takes the union of the received messages (Line 4), and from the resulting set of messages, keeps only the ones that belong in set $\mathcal{M}$ (Line 6) and are not in p's constraint set. For example, messages $m \notin \mathcal{M}$, sent by the adversary can be safely discarded and so can any message $m \in \mathcal{C}_p$.

The proof of Lemma 9 requires defining and proving some properties of the standalone probabilistic experiment ADDRANDOMEDGESADAPTIVE (Fig. 3), which encapsulates how $\mathcal{M}$-CONVERGERANDOM works.

Lemma 9 (Propagation in presence of an adaptive adversary). *Fix an initially-honest party p and a message $\mathsf{m}^* \in M_p - \bigcup_{h \in \mathcal{H}} \mathcal{C}_h$. Then, with probability $1 - \mathsf{negl}(\kappa)$, all remaining honest parties after $\mathcal{M}$-CONVERGERANDOM terminates have received m^*.*

1: **procedure** $S_p \leftarrow \mathcal{M}\text{-CONVERGERANDOM}_p(M_p, \mathcal{C}_p)$
    Input. Sets $M_p \subseteq \mathcal{M}, \mathcal{C}_p \subseteq \mathcal{M}$
    Output. A set S_p.

2:     **for** round $\beta = 1$ to $\lceil \log(\epsilon \cdot n) \rceil$ **do**
3:         $\text{RECEIVE}^{\mathcal{F}_{\text{prop}}} \leftarrow \mathcal{F}_{\text{prop}}(\text{SendRandom}, M_p - \mathcal{C}_p)$;
4:         $\text{Local}_p \leftarrow \text{Local}_p \cup \text{RECEIVE}^{\mathcal{F}_{\text{prop}}}$;
5:         $\mathcal{C}_p = \mathcal{C}_p \cup M_p$;
6:         $M_p = \text{Local}_p \cap \mathcal{M}$;
7:     **return** M_p;

Fig. 6. Our $\mathcal{M}$-CONVERGERANDOM$_p$ protocol.

Proof. Let $h_\beta \geq \epsilon \cdot n$ be the set of parties that remain honest after the adversary has performed corruptions for round β of $\mathcal{M}$-CONVERGERANDOM. Thus, for all $\beta \geq 0$, $h_{\beta+1} \subseteq h_\beta$. Also, let R_β denote the set of parties that *i.* remain honest after the adversary has performed corruptions for round β; and *ii.* receive m* for the first time during round β. Let

$$\omega_\beta = \left(\bigcup_{i=1}^{\beta} R_i \right) \cap h_\beta = (R_\beta \cap h_\beta) \cup \left(\left(\bigcup_{i=1}^{\beta-1} R_i \right) \cap h_\beta \right)$$

$$= R_\beta \cup \left(\left(\bigcup_{i=1}^{\beta-1} R_i \right) \cap h_{\beta-1} \cap h_\beta \right) = R_\beta \cup (\omega_{\beta-1} \cap h_\beta)$$

We shall use the above notation for sets interchangeably with the notation for their cardinality, which will be clear depending on the context of the operations. We first prove that with probability $1 - \text{negl}(\kappa)$, for all rounds $\beta \leq \lceil \log(\epsilon \cdot n) \rceil$:

1. If $\omega_{\beta-1} \leq \epsilon \cdot n/3$, then $R_\beta \geq (2/3) \cdot \omega_\beta$ and $\omega_\beta \geq 2^\beta$
2. If $\omega_{\beta-1} > \epsilon \cdot n/3$, then $\omega_\beta = h_\beta \geq \epsilon \cdot n$

(1.) In $\mathcal{M}$-CONVERGERANDOM, a message m* at round β is propagated in a randomized fashion using $\mathcal{F}_{\text{prop}}$. So, the adversary does not see which party receives the message unless this party is already corrupted—this is exactly what is modeled by ADDRANDOMEDGESADAPTIVE with the use of RevealedEdges. Thus, since $h_\beta \geq \epsilon \cdot n$, we can compute the number of "new" honest receivers R_β of message m in the end of round β by (almost) directly applying Lemma 5, with S_2 being $h_\beta - \omega_{\beta-1}$ (the set of honest parties that have never received m* by that round of the protocol) and $R_{\beta-1}$ being S, i.e. the set of honest senders of m* for round β. Also $R_0 = \omega_0 \geq 1$, since there is at least one honest sender for m* (namely p) for round 1. We use induction. For $\beta = 1$, if $R_0 \leq \epsilon n/3$, by applying Lemma 5:

$$\Pr[R_1 \geq 2\omega_0] = \Pr[R_1 \geq 2R_0] \geq 1 - p = 1 - \text{negl}(\kappa),$$

where $p = \max\{n \cdot e^{-4\epsilon \cdot m/45}, (\frac{\epsilon}{2})^{-\epsilon \cdot m/2}\}$ and since $m = \Theta(\kappa)$ and $\kappa = \text{poly}(n)$. Then, we have that $\omega_1 = R_1 + \omega_0 \geq 3\omega_0 \geq 2$, with probability $1 - \text{negl}(\kappa)$. Also,

$$\frac{\omega_1}{R_1} = \frac{R_1 + \omega_0 \cap h_0}{R_1} = \frac{R_1 + \omega_0}{R_1} \leq \frac{R_1 + R_1/2}{R_1} = 3/2,$$

thus $R_1 \geq (2/3)\omega_1$ with probability $1 - \mathsf{negl}(\kappa)$. Therefore, the base case holds. Let us assume the claim holds for round $\beta - 1 \leq \lceil \log(\epsilon \cdot n) \rceil - 1$. Then, if $\omega_{\beta-1} \leq \epsilon n/3$, we prove that $R_\beta \geq (2/3) \cdot \omega_\beta$ and $\omega_\beta \geq 2^\beta$. By $\mathcal{M}$-CONVERGERANDOM, all honest receivers in round $\beta - 1$ become senders in round β. So, for applying Lemma 5, we match the sets as follows: $h_{\beta-1} - \omega_{\beta-1} := S_2, h_{\beta-1} := H, h_\beta := H', R_{\beta-1} := S$. Notice that the $u \in S_2$ s.t. $Z_u^{(\beta)} = 1$ are exactly the $u \in R_\beta$ and thus $\sum_{u \in S_2} Z_u^{(\beta)} = R_\beta$. Also, notice that

$$H - S_2 = h_{\beta-1} - (h_{\beta-1} - \omega_{\beta-1}) = h_{\beta-1} \cap \omega_{\beta-1} = \omega_{\beta-1},$$

meaning: $|H - S_2| = \omega_{\beta-1} \leq \epsilon n/3$ and $S = R_{\beta-1} \geq 2\omega_{\beta-1}/3 \geq 2|H - S_2|/3$.

Finally, we have $m = \Theta(\kappa) \geq 19/\epsilon = \Theta(1)$. Therefore, we can use Lemma 5 for round β: Thus, $\Pr[R_\beta \geq 2|H - S_2|] = \Pr[R_\beta \geq 2\omega_{\beta-1}] \geq 1 - p = 1 - \mathsf{negl}(\kappa)$. Therefore, $\omega_\beta \geq R_\beta \geq 2\omega_{\beta-1} \geq 2 \cdot 2^{\beta-1} = 2^\beta$, with probability $1 - \mathsf{negl}(\kappa)$. Also,

$$\frac{\omega_\beta}{R_\beta} = \frac{R_\beta + \omega_{\beta-1} \cap h_\beta}{R_\beta} \leq \frac{R_\beta + \omega_{\beta-1}}{R_\beta} \leq \frac{R_\beta + R_\beta/2}{R_\beta} = 3/2,$$

thus $R_\beta \geq (2/3)\omega_\beta$, with probability $1 - \mathsf{negl}(\kappa)$, which completes the proof.

(2.) For every party $p_i : i = 1, \ldots, n$ we define Bernoulli R.V.s $Z_i^{(\beta)} = 1$ if and only if party p_i received m^* at round β. If $\beta = 1$ and $\omega_0 > \epsilon n/3$, then from the first round there are $\geq \epsilon n/3$ honest senders for m^*. We bound the probability

$$\Pr\left[\bigcup_{i=1}^{n} \{Z_i^{(1)} = 0\}\right] \leq \sum_{i=1}^{n} \Pr\left[Z_i^{(1)} = 0\right] = n \cdot \left(1 - \frac{m}{n}\right)^{R_0} \leq n \cdot \left(1 - \frac{m}{n}\right)^{\epsilon n/3}$$

$$= n \cdot \left[\left(1 - \frac{m}{n}\right)^{n/m}\right]^{\epsilon m/3} \leq n \cdot e^{-\epsilon m/3} = \mathsf{negl}(\kappa).$$

Now, if $\beta > 1$, then there was some round $\beta^* \leq \beta$ s.t. $\beta^* \stackrel{\text{def}}{=} \arg\min_{i \geq 0}\{\omega_i > \epsilon n/3\}$. If $\beta^* = 0$, we already showed that all parties receive m^* in the first round. Thus, for all subsequent rounds i, $\omega_i = h_i$. Else, if $\beta^* > 0$, by definition $\omega_{\beta^*-1} \leq \epsilon n/3$. So, we can apply (1.), meaning that $R_{\beta^*} \geq 2\omega_{\beta^*}/3 \geq 2\epsilon n/9$. Accordingly, for round β^*, we can again bound the probability

$$\Pr\left[\bigcup_{i=1}^{n} \{Z_i^{(\beta^*)} = 0\}\right] \leq n \cdot \left[\left(1 - \frac{m}{n}\right)^{n/m}\right]^{2\epsilon m/9} \leq n \cdot e^{-2\epsilon m/9} = \mathsf{negl}(\kappa),$$

So, for all subsequent rounds $i \geq \beta^*$, $\omega_i = h_i$.

The results from (1.),(2.) combined mean that, if the protocol runs for more than $\lceil \log \epsilon n/3 \rceil$ rounds without reaching case (2.), it is definite that, after applying (1.) for round $\beta = \lceil \log(\epsilon n/3) \rceil$, case (2.) will hold for the next round. Therefore, with probability $1 - \mathsf{negl}(\kappa)$, all remaining honest parties after $\mathcal{M}$-CONVERGERANDOM terminates have received the message m^*. $\square$

Theorem 2. *Protocol $\mathcal{M}$-CONVERGERANDOM from Fig. 6 is an adaptively t-secure $\mathcal{M}$-Converge protocol for all $t < (1 - \epsilon) \cdot n$ and fixed $\epsilon \in (0, 1)$. The number of bits sent by one party is*

$$O\left(n \log n \cdot m \cdot s + \sum_{i=1}^{\lceil \log \epsilon n \rceil} |M_p^{(i)} - C_p^{(i)}| \cdot m \cdot s\right),$$

where s is the length in bits of a message in $\mathcal{M}$ and $M_p^{(i)} - \mathcal{C}_p^{(i)}$ denotes the set given as input to the i-th call of PROPAGATE.

Proof. Security follows by applying Lemma 9 for all initially-honest parties and for all of their initial messages. Every message m^* is delivered to all honest parties that remain after the termination of the protocol, as required by Definition 5. The communication complexity (CC) is dominated by the calls to $\mathcal{F}_{\text{prop}}$. Each call to $\mathcal{F}_{\text{prop}}$ is securely instantiated by executing PROPAGATE with the same input set (Lemma 8). By Lemma 7, the i-th such call to PROPAGATE invokes a total of $O(\max\{n, |M_p^i - \mathcal{C}_p^i|\} \cdot m \cdot s) = O(n \cdot m \cdot s + |M_p^{(i)} - \mathcal{C}_p^{(i)}| \cdot m \cdot s)$ communication, where $M_p^i - \mathcal{C}_p^i$ is the corresponding set of messages input to PROPAGATE at that call. Thus, the number of bits sent by one party is

$$\sum_{i=1}^{\lceil \log \epsilon n \rceil} O(n \cdot m \cdot s + |M_p^{(i)} - \mathcal{C}_p^{(i)}| \cdot m \cdot s) = O\left(n \log n \cdot m \cdot s + \sum_{i=1}^{\lceil \log \epsilon n \rceil} |M_p^{(i)} - \mathcal{C}_p^{(i)}| \cdot m \cdot s\right)$$

with probability $1 - \mathsf{negl}(\kappa)$. □

4.4   An Extension: The $\mathcal{M}$-DistinctConverge Protocol

Recall that the $\mathcal{M}$-Converge problem was defined with respect to a message set $\mathcal{M}$. For achieving PBC with low communication complexity in the trusted PKI setting (see Sect. 6), we need a slightly different version of the $\mathcal{M}$-Converge problem, namely the $\mathcal{M}$-DistinctConverge problem, defined with respect to a parameter k. Now, some elements of the set $\mathcal{M}$, while different, are considered the "same" because their k-bit prefixes are the same. Looking ahead, our set $\mathcal{M}$ is the set of all possible valid r-batches (a valid r-batch is a set of at least r signatures) on bit-slot pairs (b, s), denoted (b, s, r). In this set, two valid r-batches with different set of signatures but on the same (b, s) are considered the same. Our prior analysis applies as is to $\mathcal{M}$-DistinctConverge.

Definition 7 (distinct$_k$ function). *For any set M, $\mathsf{distinct}_k(M)$ is a subset of M that contains all messages in M with distinct k-bit prefixes.*

E.g., for $M = \{01001, 01111, 11000, 10000\}$ we have that $\mathsf{distinct}_2(M) = \{01001, 11000, 10000\}$. Note that $\mathsf{distinct}_k$ is an one-to-many function. For example, $\mathsf{distinct}_2(M)$ is also $\{01111, 11000, 10000\}$. We are now ready to present the $\mathcal{M}$-DistinctConverge problem.

Definition 8 (t-secure $\mathcal{M}$-DistinctConverge protocol). *Let $\mathcal{M} \subseteq \{0,1\}^*$ be an efficiently recognizable set. A protocol Π executed by n parties, where every honest party p initially holds input set $M_p \subseteq \mathcal{M}$ and constraint set $\mathcal{C}_p \subseteq \mathcal{M}$, is a t-secure $\mathcal{M}$-DistinctConverge protocol if all remaining honest parties upon termination, with probability $1 - \mathsf{negl}(\kappa)$, output a set*

$$S_p \supseteq \mathsf{distinct}_k \left(\bigcup_{p \in \mathcal{H}} M_p - \bigcup_{p \in \mathcal{H}} \mathcal{C}_p \right),$$

```
1: procedure S_p ← M-DISTINCTCV_p(M_p, C_p, k)
       Input. Sets M_p ⊆ M, C_p ⊆ M and parameter k.
       Output. A set S_p.

2:     for round β = 1 to ⌈log(ε · n)⌉ do
3:         RECEIVE^{F_prop} ← F_prop(SendRandom, distinct_k(M_p − C_p));
4:         Local_p ← Local_p ∪ RECEIVE^{F_prop};
5:         C_p = C_p ∪ M_p;
6:         M_p = Local_p ∩ M;
7:     return M_p;
```

$$\text{Fig. 7. Our } \mathcal{M}\text{-DISTINCTCV}_p \text{ protocol.}$$

when at most t parties are corrupted and where $\mathcal{H}$ is the set of honest parties in the beginning of the protocol.

Figure 7 shows $\mathcal{M}$-DISTINCTCV, a modification of $\mathcal{M}$-CONVERGERANDOM.

Theorem 3. *Let $k > 0$. Protocol $\mathcal{M}$-DISTINCTCV from Fig. 7 is an adaptively t-secure $\mathcal{M}$-DistinctConverge protocol for all $t < (1 − \epsilon) \cdot n$ and fixed $\epsilon \in (0, 1)$. The total number of bits sent by all parties is*

$$\tilde{O}(n \cdot \max\{n, |\text{distinct}_k(\mathcal{M})|\} \cdot m \cdot s).$$

5   Parallel Broadcast in the Bulletin PKI Model

We present a protocol to achieve PBC in the Bulletin PKI model. This lack of trusted setup induces additional difficulty to the problem. Still, the proposed protocol uses communication cubic in n. We describe the high-level idea of the protocol. Each party internally maintains state for every signature. Each triplet (b, s, j) (for $b \in \{0, 1\}, s, j \in [n]$) defines a specific signature, so there could be $2 \cdot n^2$ signatures overall, each of size κ (where κ denotes the security parameter). The propagation of a specific signature $\sigma_j := \text{sig}_j(b, s)$ is independent of whether b was added to Extracted$_i^s$ at that given round. Instead, whenever a party i observes a new signature, i.e. $\text{sig}_j(b, s)$ for some (b, s, j) that i never observed before, they proceed to propagate the signature exactly twice. If the signature was observed during the subround of some $\mathcal{M}$-CONVERGERANDOM, then they continue propagating it only during the next subround (due to how $\mathcal{M}$-CONVERGERANDOM updates C_p). They also initiate the next round's $\mathcal{M}$-CONVERGERANDOM with the signature being on their input set but not on their constraint set. Notice that $\mathcal{M}$-CONVERGERANDOM is defined with respect to the set $\mathcal{M}$. Here, we fix $\mathcal{M}$ to consist of all of the parties' valid signatures for messages $[b, s]$, where b is a bit and s a slot in $[n]$. Next, we prove the security of our protocol.

Lemma 10 (t-consistency: BULLETINPBC). BULLETINPBC *satisfies consistency (Definition 2) in the ($\mathcal{F}_{\text{prop}}$)-hybrid world, with probability $1 − \text{negl}(\kappa)$.*

1: **procedure** $\{b_1, \ldots, b_n\} \leftarrow$ BULLETINPBC$_p(b_p)$
    Input. Local bit b_p.
    Output. Decision bits $b_1, \ldots, b_n$.
    ▷ Fix set $\mathcal{M} = \{\mathsf{sig}_v([b, s])$ such that $b \in \{0, 1\}, s, v \in [n]\}$

2:    Extracted$_p^i = \emptyset$, for $i = 1, \ldots, n$;   ▷ global variable
3:    Local$_p = \emptyset$;   ▷ global variable
4:    SEND($\mathsf{sig}_p([b_p, p]), [n]$);
5:    **for** round $r = 1$ to $t + 1$ **do**   ▷ t: bound on dishonest parties
6:        ADDMYSIGNATURE$_p(r)$;
7:        FORWARDSIGNATURES$_p(r)$;

8:    **for** slot $i = 1, \ldots, n$ **do**
9:        **return** $b_i \in$ Extracted$_p^i$ **if** $|$Extracted$_p^i| = 1$, **else return** canonical bit **0**;

1: **procedure** ADDMYSIGNATURE$_p(r)$

2:    Local$_p \leftarrow$ Local$_p \cup$ RECEIVE();
3:    **for all** $[b, s]$ such that $b \notin$ Extracted$_p^s$ **do**
4:        **if** Local$_p$ contains $\geq r$ valid signatures on $[b, s]$ (including $\mathsf{sig}_s([b, s])$) **then**
5:            Add b to Extracted$_p^s$;
6:            Add $\mathsf{sig}_p([b, s])$ to Local$_p$;

1: **procedure** FORWARDSIGNATURES$_p(r)$

2:    **if** $r \leq t$ **then**
3:        Let C_p contain all signatures that p has propagated exactly twice via CONVERGERANDOM;
4:        Local$_p \leftarrow \mathcal{M}$-CONVERGERANDOM(Local$_p, C_p$);

Fig. 8. The protocols for PBC in the Bulletin-PKI. The main PBC protocol BULLET-INPBC invokes the procedures ADDMYSIGNATURE and FORWARDSIGNATURES. The later calls a $\mathcal{M}$-Converge protocol, i.e. $\mathcal{M}$-CONVERGERANDOM, in order for each honest party to convey its internal view to all other parties.

Proof. Suppose for some slot s, an honest party p adds bit b to Extracted$_p^s$ at some round r. We prove that by the end of the protocol, all honest parties j add b to their Extracted$_j^s$ sets with probability at least $1 - \mathsf{negl}(\kappa)$. We distinguish the following cases according to the round when p adds bit b to Extracted$_p^s$ (We sometimes omit "with probability $1 - \mathsf{negl}(\kappa)$" when it is clear from the context.)

If $r \leq t$, then p has at least r distinct, valid signatures for (b, s) and also p creates its own signature. So, p observed each of these $\geq r + 1$ signatures for the first time at some round $r - k$ where $k \in \{0, \ldots, r - 1\}$. For every signature σ with $k \geq 1$, p called a $\mathcal{M}$-CONVERGERANDOM with σ in its initial input set M_p and not in its constraint set C_p. (Suppose not. Then σ is observed during some $\mathcal{M}$-CONVERGERANDOM by p, sent once with PROPAGATE and never sent again by p, a contradiction, since only signatures sent twice go in C_p.) For the signatures with $k = 0$, p initiates a $\mathcal{M}$-CONVERGERANDOM during round r. From Theorem 2, by round $r + 1$ every honest party j has $\geq r + 1$ valid signatures for (b, s) and adds b to their $\mathsf{Extracted}_j^s$ set during $\textsc{AddMySignature}_j(r+1)$.

Else, if $r > t$ then, p observes $t + 1$ valid signatures for (b, s). At least one of the signatures comes from an honest party h. So, h has added b to $\mathsf{Extracted}_h^s$ by some round $r' \leq t$. Thus, for honest party h the case $r' \leq t$ can be applied, and so all honest parties j add b to their $\mathsf{Extracted}_j^s$ sets by round $r' + 1$. □

Lemma 11 (t-validity: $\textsc{BulletinPBC}$). $\textsc{BulletinPBC}$ *satisfies validity (Definition 2), in the $(\mathcal{F}_{\mathsf{prop}})$-hybrid world with probability $1 - \mathsf{negl}(\kappa)$.*

Proof. Follows directly from the proof of consistency (Lemma 10) and the idealized signature scheme. Every honest sender s with input bit b_s, executes Line 4 and thus sends to all parties their signature for (b_s, s) at the start of the protocol. So, all honest parties h add b_s to their $\mathsf{Extracted}_h^s$ sets. By the idealized signature scheme, no other bit b' could bare a valid signature from honest sender s, thus no other bit b' could be in an h's $\mathsf{Extracted}_h^s$ set. □

Theorem 4 (Communication Complexity of $\textsc{BulletinPBC}$). *The total number of bits exchanged by all parties in $\textsc{BulletinPBC}$ is $\tilde{O}(n^3 \cdot \kappa^2)$.*

Proof. The communication complexity (CC) of $\textsc{BulletinPBC}$ is dominated by the CC of $\mathcal{M}\text{-}\textsc{ConvergeRandom}$. By Theorem 2 each such call invokes $O(n \log n \cdot ms + \sum_{i=1}^{\lceil \log \epsilon n \rceil} |M_p^{(i)} - C_p^{(i)}| \cdot ms)$ communication for each party, where $M_p^{(i)} - C_p^{(i)}$ is the corresponding set of messages input to $\textsc{Propagate}$. The sets input to $\textsc{Propagate}$ by the protocol are sets containing signatures of size κ each. During each super-round j of the protocol, $\mathcal{M}\text{-}\textsc{ConvergeRandom}$ is called once, with input set $M_p^{(j)} - C_p^{(j)}$. Due to $\mathcal{M}\text{-}\textsc{ConvergeRandom}$, when a message is input by party p to $\textsc{Propagate}$ at some subround, it is subsequently added to C_p and thus won't be input to $\textsc{Propagate}$ again during that super-round. Let for a fixed party p, $I_p^{(j,i)}$ denote the input set $M_p - C_p$ for its call of $\mathcal{M}\text{-}\textsc{ConvergeRandom}$ at subround i of round j. In $\textsc{BulletinPBC}$, parties only propagate signatures they have propagated less than twice. Thus, each message can be propagated by the same party at most twice meaning that, for each party p, during all sub-rounds of all super-rounds of the protocol, it holds that $\sum_{j=1}^{(t+1)} \sum_{i=1}^{\lceil \log \epsilon n \rceil} |I_p^{(j,i)}| \leq 2|\mathcal{M}| = O(n^2)$.

We can count the overall CC of each party during the protocol, so we have

$$\mathsf{CC}(p) = \sum_{j=1}^{(t+1)} O(n \log n \cdot m\kappa + \sum_{i=1}^{\lceil \log \epsilon n \rceil} |I_p^{(j,i)}| \cdot m\kappa) = O(\sum_{j=1}^{(t+1)} \sum_{i=1}^{\lceil \log \epsilon n \rceil} |I_p^{(j,i)}| \cdot m \cdot \kappa)$$

$$+ O(n^2 \log n \cdot m \cdot \kappa) = \tilde{O}(n^2 \cdot \kappa^2),$$

where, we used the fact that $\sum_{j=1}^{(t+1)} \sum_{i=1}^{\lceil \log \epsilon n \rceil} |I_p^{(j,i)}| = O(n^2)$. Thus, the CC of $\mathcal{M}\text{-}\textsc{ConvergeRandom}$ for all parties is $\tilde{O}(n^3 \cdot \kappa^2)$. □

6 Parallel Broadcast in the Trusted PKI Model

In this section we use trusted setup to reduce the communication complexity of PBC from cubic to quadratic. Our new protocol $\textsc{TrustedPBC}$ uses protocol

---

Functionality: $\mathcal{F}_{\text{mine}}$

$\mathcal{F}_{\text{mine}}$ is parameterized by parties $1, \ldots, n$ and "mining" probability p_{mine}. Let $s \in [n]$ and $b \in \{0, 1\}$. Let *call* be vector of n entries initialized with -1.
   On input (Mine, b, s) from party i:
      – If $call_i = -1$ output $b = 1$ with probability p_{mine} or $b = 0$ with probability $1 - p_{\text{mine}}$ and set $call_i = b$;
      – Else output $call_i$.
   On input (Verify, b, s, j) from party i output 1 if $call_j = 1$ and 0 otherwise.

Fig. 9. Functionality $\mathcal{F}_{\text{mine}}$.

$\mathcal{M}$-DISTINCTCV from Sect. 4.4. To facilitate the exposition and our proof, TRUSTEDPBC in Fig. 10 is given in a hybrid world where two functionalities exist. The first one is $\mathcal{F}_{\text{prop}}$ which was presented and instantiated in Sect. 4.2.

The second functionality is $\mathcal{F}_{\text{mine}}$ (Fig. 9), which was also presented in Chan et al. [8] and was shown to be instantiable from standard assumptions (with setup) by [1]. We assume that when a party calls $\mathcal{F}_{\text{mine}}$ then it returns instantaneously. A party p in our protocol queries $\mathcal{F}_{\text{mine}}$ on input (Mine, b, s) in some round i, where $s \in [n]$ refers to one of the slots and $b \in \{0, 1\}$. If it receives response 1, it considers itself a member of a randomly selected subset of all the parties, which we refer to as the "(b, s)-*committee*". More concretely, when $\mathcal{F}_{\text{mine}}$ receives such a query, it flips a random coin to decide whether the party p is in that committee. $\mathcal{F}_{\text{mine}}$ keeps the information and returns the same answer to all future identical queries by any party. Next, we provide some definitions and necessary results.

Definition 9 ((b, s)-committee). *For each pair of bit b and slot s, the (b, s)-committee is a subset of parties such that for each party c in the (b, s)-committee, whenever the $\mathcal{F}_{\text{mine}}$ is queried on input (Verify, b, s, c), $\mathcal{F}_{\text{mine}}$ outputs 1.*

Lemma 12 (Honest Committees). *Let $R = 2\kappa/\epsilon$ and let the probability of success for $\mathcal{F}_{\text{mine}}$ be $p_{\text{mine}} = \min\{1, \kappa/(\epsilon \cdot n)\}$. Then, with probability $1 - \text{negl}(\kappa)$, for each bit $b \in \{0, 1\}$ and slot $s \in [n]$, the (b, s)-committee contains (i) at least one honest party and (ii) at most R dishonest parties.*

Definition 10 (Valid r-batch). *A valid r-batch on pair (b, s) is the element*
$$b||s||\text{SIG}_r,$$
where SIG_r is a set of at least r signatures on $[b, s]$ consisting of one signature from party s and at least $r - 1$ signatures from parties in the (b, s)-committee.

Definition 11. *We define $\mathcal{M}_r$ to be a set that contains all possible valid r-batches for all $b \in \{0, 1\}$ and for all $s \in [n]$.*

Lemma 13. *It is $|\text{distinct}_{k^*}(\mathcal{M}_r)| = 2 \cdot n$, where k^* is the number of bits needed to represent $b||s$ and where distinct_{k^*} is defined in Definition 7.*

```
1: procedure {b₁,...,bₙ} ← TRUSTEDPBCₚ(bₚ)
      Input. Local bit bₚ.
      Output. Decision bits b₁,...,bₙ.

2:    Extractedₚⁱ = ∅, for i = 1,...,n;                    ▷ global variable
3:    Votedₚⁱ = ∅, for i = 1,...,n;                        ▷ global variable
4:    Localₚ = ∅;                                           ▷ global variable
5:    SEND(sigₚ([bₚ,p]),[n]);
6:    for round r = 1 to R + 1 do              ▷ R is also a global variable
7:        DISTRIBUTEₚ(r);
8:        VOTEₚ(r);
9:    for slot i = 1,...,n do
10:       return bᵢ ∈ Extractedₚⁱ if |Extractedₚⁱ| = 1 else return canonical bit 0;

1: procedure DISTRIBUTEₚ(r)

2:    Localₚ ← Localₚ ∪ RECEIVE();
3:    Let 𝒱 = {vᵢ} be valid r-batches (in Localₚ) on {[bᵢ,sᵢ]} s.t. bᵢ ∉ Extractedₚˢⁱ;
4:    for all vᵢ ∈ 𝒱 do Add bᵢ to Extractedₚˢⁱ;
5:    if r ≤ R then Localₚ ← 𝓜ᵣ-DISTINCTCVₚ(𝒱,∅,k*);

1: procedure VOTEₚ(r)

2:    if r ≤ R then
3:        Let 𝒱 = {vᵢ} be valid r-batches (in Localₚ) on {[bᵢ,sᵢ]} s.t. bᵢ ∉ Votedₚˢⁱ;
4:        for all vᵢ ∈ 𝒱 s.t. ℱmine(Mine,bᵢ,sᵢ) = 1 do
5:            Add bᵢ to Votedₚˢⁱ;
6:            Add bᵢ in Extractedₚˢⁱ if bᵢ ∉ Extractedₚˢⁱ;
7:            Extend vᵢ to a valid (r+1)-batch vᵢ′ by adding p's signature on [bᵢ,sᵢ];
8:            SEND(vᵢ′,[n]);
```

Fig. 10. TRUSTEDPBC calls two procedures, i.e. DISTRIBUTE and VOTE. During each execution, DISTRIBUTE calls the $\mathcal{M}_r$-DISTINCTCV protocol, for each honest party to convey its internal view to all other parties. $\mathcal{M}_r$ follows Definition 11.

Proof. Follows from the fact that $\mathcal{M}_r$ contains exactly $2 \cdot n$ elements with unique $b\|s$ prefixes, since $b \in \{0, 1\}$ and $s \in [n]$. □

Our protocol (see Fig. 10) is inspired by the single-sender protocol of Chan et al. [8] (ChBC protocol), of which we gave a detailed overview in the introduction. In particular, our protocol works in $R + 1$ rounds as follows (Round $R + 1$ is only used for updating the local sets and no sending takes place.) Every party p maintains n Extracted$_s^p$ and Voted$_s^p$ sets, $s \in [n]$, that are initialized as $\emptyset$. Roughly speaking, a bit $b \in$ Extracted$_s^p$ if p has observed a valid r-batch on $[b, s]$; a bit $b \in$ Voted$_s^p$ if it has already been revealed that p is part of the (b, s)-committee (i.e., p has "voted"). In round 0, party i (for all $i \in [n]$) signs her input bit b_i, adds it to her Extracted$_i^i$ set and sends b_i to all $n - 1$ parties along with its signature on b_i, sig$_i([b_i, i])$. Afterwards, the distribution and voting phases follow, for every round $r = 1, \ldots, R$. These are non-trivial modifications (for many slots and using parallel gossiping) of the distribution and voting phases of ChBC. Our new distribution/voting phases, for round $r \leq R$, work as follows.

1. (Distribution) An honest party p first collects the set $\mathcal{V}$ of valid r-batches $v_1, \ldots, v_w$ on messages $[b_1, s_1], \ldots, [b_w, s_w]$ that are not in the respective p's Extracted sets. Instead of every node using a SEND-ALL to send each v_i (as ChBC would do), all nodes run $\mathcal{M}_r$-DISTINCTCV from Fig. 7 ($\mathcal{M}_r$ defined per Definition 11), with their initial constraint sets $\mathcal{C}_p$ empty. $\mathcal{M}_r$-DISTINCTCV assures that all parties eventually see the other parties' inputs but since there is overlap between input messages, it uses less communication.

2. (Voting) An honest party p checks which valid r-batches in their local set correspond to pairs $(b, s) : b \notin \mathsf{Voted}_p^s$. For each such pair, they check whether they are members of the respective committee via $\mathcal{F}_{\mathsf{mine}}$. If they are, they add their own signature to extend the valid r-batch to a valid $(r + 1)$-batch.

Lemma 14 (t-consistency). *Let $R = 2\kappa/\epsilon$. TRUSTEDPBC satisfies t-consistency, per Definition 2, in the $(\mathcal{F}_{\mathsf{mine}}, \mathcal{F}_{\mathsf{prop}})$-hybrid world with probability $1 - \mathsf{negl}(\kappa)$.*

Lemma 15 (t-validity). *Let $R = 2\kappa/\epsilon$. TRUSTEDPBC satisfies t-validity, per Definition 2, in the $(\mathcal{F}_{\mathsf{mine}}, \mathcal{F}_{\mathsf{prop}})$-hybrid world with probability $1 - \mathsf{negl}(\kappa)$.*

Theorem 5 (Communication). *Let $R = 2\kappa/\epsilon$. The total number of bits exchanged by all parties in TRUSTEDPBC is $\tilde{O}(n^2 \cdot \kappa^4)$ with probability $1 - \mathsf{negl}(\kappa)$.*

Acknowledgments. This research was supported in part by the National Science Foundation, VMware, the Ethereum Foundation and Protocol Labs.

References

1. Abraham, I., Hubert Chan, T.-H., Dolev, K.N.D., Pass, R., Ren, L., Shi, E.: Communication complexity of byzantine agreement, revisited. In: Proceedings of ACM Symposium on Principles of Distributed Computing (PODC), pp. 317–326 (2019)
2. Baum, C., Orsini, E., Scholl, P., Soria-Vazquez, E.: Efficient constant-round MPC with identifiable abort and public verifiability. In: Micciancio, D., Ristenpart, T. (eds.) CRYPTO 2020. LNCS, vol. 12171, pp. 562–592. Springer, Cham (2020). https://doi.org/10.1007/978-3-030-56880-1_20
3. Blum, E., Katz, J., Liu-Zhang, C.-D., Loss, J.: Asynchronous byzantine agreement with subquadratic communication. In: Pass, R., Pietrzak, K. (eds.) TCC 2020. LNCS, vol. 12550, pp. 353–380. Springer, Cham (2020). https://doi.org/10.1007/978-3-030-64375-1_13
4. Bortnikov, E., Gurevich, M., Keidar, I., Kliot, G., Shraer, A.: Brahms: byzantine resilient random membership sampling. In: Proceedings of ACM PODC, pp. 145–154 (2008)
5. Boyle, E., Ran, Goel, A.: Breaking the $o(\sqrt{n})$-bit barrier: Byzantine agreement with polylog bits per party. In: Proceedings of ACM PODC, pp. 319–330 (2021)

6. Buterin, V.: A guide to 99% fault tolerant consensus. Blog Post (2018)
7. Canetti, R.: Security and composition of multiparty cryptographic protocols. J. Cryptology **13**, 143–202 (2000)
8. Chan, T.-H.H., Pass, R., Shi, E.: Sublinear-round byzantine agreement under corrupt majority. In: Kiayias, A., Kohlweiss, M., Wallden, P., Zikas, V. (eds.) PKC 2020. LNCS, vol. 12111, pp. 246–265. Springer, Cham (2020). https://doi.org/10.1007/978-3-030-45388-6_9
9. Demers, A.J.: Epidemic algorithms for replicated database maintenance. In: Proceedings of ACM PODC, pp. 1–12 (1987)
10. Dolev, D., Strong, H.R.: Authenticated algorithms for byzantine agreement. SIAM J. Comput. **12**(4), 656–666 (1983)
11. Feldman, P., Micali, S.: Optimal algorithms for byzantine agreement. In: Proceedings of ACM STOC, pp. 148–161 (1988)
12. Fitzi, M., Nielsen, J.B.: On the number of synchronous rounds sufficient for authenticated byzantine agreement. In: Keidar, I. (ed.) DISC 2009. LNCS, vol. 5805, pp. 449–463. Springer, Heidelberg (2009). https://doi.org/10.1007/978-3-642-04355-0_46
13. Garay, J.A., Katz, J., Koo, C.-Y., Ostrovsky, R.: Round complexity of authenticated broadcast with a dishonest majority. In: Proceedings of IEEE FOCS, pp. 658–668 (2007)
14. Garay, J.A., Moses, Y.: Fully polynomial byzantine agreement in $t+1$ rounds. In: Proceedings of ACM STOC, pp. 31–41 (1993)
15. Guerraoui, R., Kuznetsov, P., Monti, M., Pavlovic, M., Seredinschi, D.A.: Scalable Byzantine reliable broadcast. In: Proceedings of DISC, vol. 146, pp. 22:1–22:16 (2019)
16. Haas, Z.J., Halpern, J.Y., Li, L.: Gossip-based ad hoc routing. IEEE/ACM Trans. Netw. **14**, 479–491 (2006)
17. King, V., Saia, J.: Breaking the $O(n^2)$ bit barrier: scalable byzantine agreement with an adaptive adversary. In: Proceedings of ACM PODC, pp. 420–429 (2010)
18. King, V., Saia, J., Sanwalani, V., Vee, E.: Scalable leader election. In: Proceedings of ACM-SIAM SODA, pp. 990–999 (2006)
19. Lamport, L., Shostak, R., Pease, M.: The byzantine generals problem. Trans. Programm. Lang. Syst. **4**, 382–401 (1982)
20. Libert, B., Joye, M., Yung, M.: Born and raised distributively: fully distributed non-interactive adaptively-secure threshold signatures with short shares. In: Proceedings of ACM PODC, pp. 303–312 (2014)
21. Malkhi, D., Mansour, Y., Reiter, M.K.: On diffusing updates in a byzantine environment. In: Proceedings of the IEEE Symposium on Reliable Distributed Systems, pp. 134–143 (1999)
22. Matt, C.: Jesper Buus Nielsen, and Søren Eller Thomsen. Formalizing delayed adaptive corruptions and the security of flooding networks, Cryptology ePrint Archive (2022)
23. Micali, S.: Very simple and efficient byzantine agreement. In: Proceedings of ITCS, vol. 67, pp. 6:1–6:1 (2017)
24. Micali, S., Vaikuntanathan, V.: Optimal and player-replaceable consensus with an honest majority. Technical report, MIT (2017)
25. Momose, A., Ren, L.: Optimal communication complexity of authenticated byzantine agreement. In: Proceedings of DISC, pp. 32:1–32:16 (2021)

26. Pease, M.C., Shostak, R.E., Lamport, L.: Reaching agreement in the presence of faults. J. ACM **27**, 228–234 (1980)
27. Wan, J., Xiao, H., Shi, E., Devadas, S.: Expected constant round byzantine broadcast under dishonest majority. In: Pass, R., Pietrzak, K. (eds.) TCC 2020. LNCS, vol. 12550, pp. 381–411. Springer, Cham (2020). https://doi.org/10.1007/978-3-030-64375-1_14

Secure Hash Functions

Nearly Optimal Property Preserving Hashing

Justin Holmgren[1], Minghao Liu[2], LaKyah Tyner[2], and Daniel Wichs[1,2](✉)

[1] NTT Research, Sunnyvale, CA 94085, USA
[2] Northeastern University, Boston, MA 02115, USA
wichs@ccs.neu.edu

Abstract. *Property-preserving hashing (PPH)* consists of a family of compressing hash functions h such that, for any two inputs x, y, we can correctly identify whether some property $P(x, y)$ holds given only the digests $h(x), h(y)$. In a basic PPH, correctness should hold with overwhelming probability over the choice of h when x, y are worst-case values chosen a-priori and independently of h. In an adversarially *robust* PPH (RPPH), correctness must hold even when x, y are chosen adversarially and adaptively depending on h. Here, we study (R)PPH for the property that the *Hamming distance* between x and y is at most t.

The notion of (R)PPH was introduced by Boyle, LaVigne and Vaikuntanathan (ITCS '19), and further studied by Fleischhacker, Simkin (Eurocrypt '21) and Fleischhacker, Larsen, Simkin (Eurocrypt '22). In this work, we obtain improved constructions that are conceptually simpler, have nearly optimal parameters, and rely on more general assumptions than prior works. Our results are:

- We construct information-theoretic non-robust PPH for Hamming distance via syndrome list-decoding of linear error-correcting codes. We provide a lower bound showing that this construction is essentially optimal.
- We make the above construction robust with little additional overhead, by relying on homomorphic collision-resistant hash functions, which can be constructed from either the discrete-logarithm or the short-integer-solution assumptions. The resulting RPPH achieves improved compression compared to prior constructions, and is nearly optimal.
- We also show an alternate construction of RPPH for Hamming distance under the minimal assumption that standard collision-resistant hash functions exist. The compression is slightly worse than our optimized construction using homomorphic collision-resistance, but essentially matches the prior state of the art constructions from specific algebraic assumptions.
- Lastly, we study a new notion of randomized robust PPH (R2P2H) for Hamming distance, which relaxes RPPH by allowing the hashing algorithm itself to be randomized. We give an information-theoretic construction with optimal parameters.

Research supported by NSF grant CNS-1750795, CNS-2055510 and the Alfred P. Sloan Research Fellowship.

Y. Dodis and T. Shrimpton (Eds.): CRYPTO 2022, LNCS 13509, pp. 473–502, 2022.
https://doi.org/10.1007/978-3-031-15982-4_16

1   Introduction

This work studies the problem of how to compress a large input into a small digest that nevertheless preserves some class of properties of the input. This high level goal is of central importance and lies behind many prominent topics in computer science, such as sketching algorithms, locality sensitive hash functions, streaming algorithms, and compressed sensing.

We focus on an important variant of this problem, called *(robust) property-preserving hashing (R)PPH*, which was recently introduced by Boyle, LaVigne and Vaikuntanthan [BLV19] and further studied by Fleischhacker, Simkin [FS21] and Fleischhacker, Larsen, Simkin [FLS22]. An (R)PPH for a property P (a binary predicate) consists of a compressing family of deterministic hash function h such that, for any x, y, we can determine whether the property $P(x, y)$ holds given only the digests $h(x), h(y)$. In more detail, there is an Eval procedure that operates on the digests and whose goal is to ensure correctness: $\mathsf{Eval}(h(x), h(y)) = P(x, y)$.[1] The basic notion of PPH requires that correctness holds with overwhelming probability over the choice of h, when the inputs x, y are worst-case values chosen *ahead of time and independently of the choice of* h. A robust PPH (RPPH), on the other hand, requires that correctness holds with overwhelming probability over the choice of h, even when the inputs x, y are chosen by an adversary *adaptively depending on the hash function h*. The difference between non-robust and robust PPH is exemplified by the difference between universal hashing and collision-resistant hashing. Concretely, if we consider the *equality property* "$P(x, y) = 1$ iff $x = y$", then universal hashing gives an information-theoretic (non-robust) PPH for equality, while collision-resistant hashing gives an RPPH for equality.

The interesting problem is to construct (R)PPH for more complex properties beyond equality. Most naturally, we'd like to do so for properties $P(x, y)$ that hold if x, y are "similar" in some metric. For example, Apple recently suggested a method for privately detecting users who store known Child Sexual Abuse Material (CSAM) [App, NYT, Scha]. A key component of their system was a hash function called NeuralHash, which was essentially intended to be an RPPH for the property that two images are similar. However, it became clear that NeuralHash is not robust, and it is possible to adversarially find images that are completely different, yet their hashes identify them as being similar [Schb, Cru]. This leads to privacy violations in the overall system, which is one of the reasons that Apple ended up abandoning the CSAM detection system for the time being. The above highlights the need for a better understanding of RPPH, what it can achieve, and what are its limitations.

(R)PPH for Hamming Distance. In this work, following prior works [BLV19, FS21, FLS22], we study (R)PPH for Hamming distance over the binary alphabet. In particular, for some distance bound t, we consider the property $P(x, y)$,

---

[1] Technically, the Eval procedure also takes as input the description of the hash function h, but for simplicity we omit this throughout the introduction.

which holds iff the Hamming distance between x, y is $||x - y||_0 \leq t$. There are several reasons for focusing on Hamming distance. Firstly, Hamming distance is arguably the most basic metric to study and understanding it is likely to be a prerequisite for understanding more complex metrics. Secondly, a common approach to defining "similarity" between complex objects is to first translate these objects into binary "feature vectors" that represent a list of potential features and indicates whether or not the object has them, and then looking at the Hamming distance between the feature vectors. In this case, a good (R)PPH for Hamming distance gives a good (R)PPH for testing similarity of more complex objects. Lastly, by focusing on Hamming distance, we can make use of an extensive set of tools from coding theory to help us along.

The main measure of efficiency that we seek to optimize is the output length m of the (R)PPH, as a parameter that depends on the input length n, the distance parameter t and the security parameter λ. In particular, we would like the RPPH to be as compressing as possible by minimizing m for any choice of n, t, λ.

Prior Work. The work of Boyle, LaVigne and Vaikuntanthan [BLV19] initiated the general study of (R)PPH. They provided definitions for both the non-robust and robust variants of PPH.[2] Although [BLV19] does not directly offer any constructions of RPPH for the exact Hamming distance property studied here, their main positive results consider a relaxation called RPPH for *gap-Hamming distance*, where the goal is only to distinguish between the case where the Hamming distance between x and y is $\leq t$ versus $> (1 + \delta)t$, for some distance t and gap parameter $\delta > 0$. In other words, this relaxation only requires $\mathsf{Eval}(h(x), h(y))$ to output 1 in the former case and 0 in the latter case, but any output is permissible in the gap between them. The work of [BLV19] gave two constructions of RPPH for gap-Hamming distance with any constant gap $\delta > 0$. The first construction is based on only the existence of collisions-resistant hash functions (CRHFs). Assuming CRHFs with output length $\ell = \ell(\lambda)$, they showed that for any constant *compression factor* $\eta > 0$, there exists some constant $\rho > 0$ such that for any distance $t \leq \rho \cdot n/(\ell \cdot \log \ell)$, there is an RPPH for gap Hamming distance with output length $m \leq \eta \cdot n$.[3] Their second construction is based on a new but plausible computational assumption that they introduce and call the

---

[2] They also considered two additional intermediate variants of PPH, where the adversary does not get the full description of the hash function but gets some partial oracle access before choosing x, y. Our notion of robust PPH is the strongest notion they considered and is also referred to as a "direct access robust" PPH in their work.

[3] Asymptotically, the existence of CRHFs with output length $\ell(\lambda) = \lambda$ is equivalent to those with output length $\ell(\lambda) = \lambda^\varepsilon$ for $\varepsilon > 0$. Moreover, it may be plausible to even conjecture the existence of CRHFs with (e.g.,) output length $\ell(\lambda) = \log \lambda \log \log \lambda$. However, these choices will have vastly different exact security. All the constructions/reductions referred to in this work preserve exact security. Therefore, we find it more informative to phrase all results in terms of the exact output length $\ell(\lambda)$ of the underlying primitive and the construction with inherit the exact security of that primitive with the given output length.

Sparse Short Vector (SSV) assumption. Under that assumption, they got somewhat better parameters, showing that for any constant $\eta > 0$, there exists some constant $\rho > 0$ such that for any $t \leq \rho \cdot n / \log n$ there is an RPPH for gap Hamming distance with output size $m \leq \eta \cdot n$.

The work of Fleischhacker, Simkin [FS21] gave the first construction of RPPH for exact Hamming distance. They did so under a new assumption in bilinear groups, which they called the *q-Strong Bilinear Discrete Logarithm (q-SBDL) Assumption*. They showed that, assuming q-SBDL holds in a group whose elements can be represented using $\ell = \ell(\lambda)$ bits, for any distance t there is an RPPH for exact Hamming distance with output length $m = O(t\ell)$. In particular, the RPPH is non-trivially compressing for $t = O(n/\ell)$.

The work of Fleischhacker, Larsen, Simkin [FLS22], gave a similar result as above but under the *Short-Integer Solution (SIS)* assumption, which is a well-studied assumption (it is implied by learning-with-errors (LWE)) and can be based on the hardness of worst-case lattice problems [Ajt96]. In particular, under the SIS assumption, they showed that for any distance t there is an RPPH for exact Hamming distance with output size $m = O(t\ell \cdot \log n)$, where $\ell = \ell(\lambda)$ is the output length of Ajtai's hash function based on SIS. In particular, the output size is non-trivially compressing for $t = O(n/(\ell \cdot \log n))$.

To summarize, the best prior RPPH constructions for exact Hamming distance at the very least required output size $m \geq t\ell(\lambda)$, where ℓ is some polynomial. They also required specific algebraic assumptions, namely SIS or the q-SBDL assumption in bilinear maps. For gap Hamming distance, we knew how to get slightly better output length $m \geq t \log n + \ell(\lambda)$, but only under a new non-standard variant of SIS, or we knew how to get $m \geq t\ell(\lambda) \log n$ under just collision-resistance.

1.1 Our Results

In this work, we give new constructions of (R)PPH for exact Hamming distance. Our constructions are conceptually simpler, are based on more general assumptions, and achieve improved compression compared to prior work. Our results are as follows.

Non-Robust PPH. Our first result is to construct a *non-robust PPH for Hamming distance* via a simple connection to syndrome list-decoding of linear error-correcting codes. In terms of parameters, the output size of our hash function is $m = \eta \cdot n + \lambda$, where $1 - \eta$ is the optimal rate of a linear list-decodable error-correcting code that can correct t errors. Inefficiently, we can go up to the Hamming bound with $\eta = H(t/n)$, where H is the Shannon binary entropy function. Efficiently we can go up to the slightly weaker *Blokh-Zyablov* bound. In either case, this implies $m = O(t \log n) + \lambda$. However, it also implies non-trivial compression for larger distances up to $t = O(n)$. In particular, for any constant compression factor $\eta > 0$ there exists some $\rho > 0$ such that there is a (non-robust) PPH with output length $m = \eta n + \lambda$ for all distances $t \leq \rho \cdot n$.

We give a matching lower bound, showing that the output size has to satisfy $m > (H(t/n) - o(1)) \cdot n$.

RPPH from Homomorphic Collision-Resistance. Our next result extends the above idea to add robustness and achieve *RPPH for Hamming distance* by leveraging *homomorphic collision-resistant hash functions*, which we in turn construct under either the standard *discrete logarithm (DLOG)* assumption or the *short-integer-solution (SIS)* assumption. The construction adds a constant factor overhead of at most $(\log_2 3)$ compared to our non-robust PPH, giving $m = (\log_2 3)\eta \cdot n + \ell$, where $1 - \eta$ is the optimal rate of a linear list-decodable error-correcting code that can correct t errors, and $\ell = \ell(\lambda)$ is the output length of the homomorphic CRHF (e.g., the bit-length of a group element). In particular, our output length is bounded by $m = O(t \cdot \log n + \ell)$, while previous constructions [FS21,FLS22] achieved $m = O(t \cdot \ell)$. Since we always assume $n = \text{poly}(\lambda)$, we can conclude that $\log n = O(\log \lambda)$ is asymptotically smaller than $\ell = \text{poly}(\lambda)$. Moreover, for any constant compression factor $\eta > 0$ there exists some constant $\rho > 0$ such that we get an RPPH for Hamming distances $t \leq \rho \cdot n$ with output size $m \leq \eta \cdot n$. Previous constructions of RPPH for Hamming distance [FS21,FLS22] only achieved non-trivial compression $\eta < 1$ for sub-linear distances $t = O(n/\ell)$, while we do so for up to linear distances $t = O(n)$.

RPPH from Standard Collision-Resistance. We also construct the first RPPH for Hamming distance based on the minimal assumption that (standard) collision-resistant hash functions (CRHFs) exist. Previously, we only knew how to do this for gap-Hamming distance [BLV19], while we show how to do for exact Hamming distance. In fact, we show how to using syndrome decoding to generically upgrade an RPPH for gap-Hamming distance into one for exact Hamming distance. The achieved parameters are slightly worse than those of our optimized construction based on homomorphic CRHFs above, but are comparable to those achieved by prior constructions for exact Hamming distance [FS21,FLS22] based on specific algebraic assumptions. In particular, assuming CRHFs with output length $\ell = \ell(\lambda)$, we get an RPPH for distance t with output length $m = O(t \cdot \ell \cdot \log(n/t))$.

Randomized RPPH (R2P2H). We also consider a *randomized* notion of RPPH (R2P2H), where the computations of the hash function $h(x)$ can itself be a randomized. The adversary can choose worst-case values x, y after seeing the description of h, but before knowing the internal randomness that will be employed in the computation of $h(x), h(y)$. The adversary wins if $\text{Eval}(h(x), h(y)) \neq P(x, y)$, and we require that the can only happen with negligible probability over the choice of the hash function h and the internal randomness used to compute $h(x), h(y)$. We emphasize that, aside for allowing the hash function to be randomized, the security guarantee provided by R2P2H is also qualitatively weaker than that of deterministic RPPH. For deterministic RPPH, the security definition implicitly allows the adversary to choose y after seeing $h(x)$, since the adversary can compute $h(x)$ himself. This is not the case for R2P2H, where seeing $h(x)$ can reveal something about the internal randomness employed in the computation that would allow the adversary to find a bad y that breaks security. Surprisingly, this relaxation to R2P2H allows us to get non-trivial information-theoretic constructions. It was previously known that one can achieve information-theoretic R2P2H for the equality predicate, where the output length is $m = O(\sqrt{n})$ and that this is optimal [NS96,BK97,MNS08,CN22]. We extend this to showing a construction of information-theoretic R2P2H for Hamming distance t, where the output length is $O(\sqrt{\lambda n} \log n) + \eta n)$, where $1 - \eta$ is the optimal rate of a linear list-decodable error-correcting code that can correct t errors; in particular $\eta n \le O(t \log n)$.

1.2 Our Techniques

On a technical level, our constructions are quite different than those of [FS21,FLS22]. The common theme of all our results is the reliance on syndrome decoding.

PPH from Syndrome Decoding. We start with a simple construction of a non-robust PPH based on *syndrome (list) decoding* of linear error-correcting codes. Assume there exists some linear error-correcting code over a field $\mathbb{F}$, having codeword length n, message length k, and the ability to (efficiently) correct up to t errors. This is equivalent to the existence of a *parity check* matrix $P \in \mathbb{F}^{(n-k) \times n}$ such that for any *error-vector* $e \in \mathbb{F}^n$ with Hamming weight $\|e\|_0 \le t$ we can (efficiently) recover e from the *syndrome* $P \cdot e$. More generally, a code that allows (efficient) list-decoding of up to t errors implies that given a syndrome $P \cdot e$ as above we can (efficiently) recover a polynomial-sized list $\mathcal{L}$ of potential error vectors with the guarantee that $e \in \mathcal{L}$. Without loss of generality, we can assume that each $e_i \in \mathcal{L}$ has Hamming-weight $\|e_i\|_0 \le t$.

For our construction of PPH, assume we have a list-decodable code as above over the binary field $\mathbb{F}_2$ and let P be the parity check matrix. We will also make use of the universal hash function $h_{univ}(x) = A \cdot x$ where $A \leftarrow \mathbb{F}_2^{\lambda \times n}$ is a random matrix. This ensures that for any $x_1 \ne x_2 \in \mathbb{F}_2^n$ chosen a-priori, we have $\Pr_A[Ax_1 = Ax_2] = 2^{-\lambda}$. We will rely on the fact that this universal hash function is linearly homomorphic with $h_{univ}(x_1) - h_{univ}(x_2) = x_1 - x_2$.[4]

The description of the PPH h consists of the random matrix A of the universal hash function. Given an input x, the PPH output $y = h(x)$ is defined as $y = (P \cdot x, A \cdot x)$, consisting of the syndrome and the universal-hash of x. Given $y_1 = h(x_1), y_2 = h(x_2)$ with $y_1 = (v_1, w_1), y_2 = (v_2, w_2)$ the procedure $\mathsf{Eval}(y_1, y_2)$ does the following. It runs the syndrome list-decoding algorithm on $v_1 - v_2 = P \cdot (x_1 - x_2)$ to recover a list of potential error-vectors $\mathcal{L}$. If there exists some $e_i \in \mathcal{L}$ such that $A \cdot e_i = w_1 - w_2$ than the Eval algorithm accepts else it rejects.

To see that the above construction satisfies the definition of a PPH, we consider two cases. First, suppose x_1 and x_2 are "close": i.e., $\|x_1 - x_2\|_0 \le t$.

---

[4] Since we're working over $\mathbb{F}_2$, addition and subtraction are equivalent, but we use subtraction to make it easier to compare to later constructions that work in larger fields.

Then, during the computation of $\mathsf{Eval}\big(h(x_1), h(x_2)\big)$, the correctness of syndrome list-decoding for the syndrome $v_1 - v_2 = P \cdot (x_1 - x_2)$ ensures that $x_1 - x_2$ appears in the list $\mathcal{L}$. Moreover $A \cdot (x_1 - x_2) = w_1 - w_2$ and therefore the Eval algorithm will accept with probability 1. Next, suppose that x_1 and x_2 are instead "far": i.e., $\|x_1 - x_2\|_0 > t$. Then, during the computation of $\mathsf{Eval}\big(h(x_1), h(x_2)\big)$, no matter what list $\mathcal{L}$ is generated, we know that $x_1 - x_2 \notin \mathcal{L}$ since the list only contains vectors with Hamming weight at most t. Furthermore, the list $\mathcal{L}$ is independent of A and is polynomial in size. This ensures that the probability over A that there exists some $e_i \in \mathcal{L}$ such that $A \cdot e_i = w_1 - w_2 = A \cdot (x_1 - x_2)$ is at most $|\mathcal{L}| \cdot 2^{-\lambda} = \mathrm{negl}(\lambda)$.

The output size of the above PPH is $m = (n - k) + \lambda$ bits, where k is determined by the optimal rate of the code that can list-decode up to t errors. It is known that, inefficiently, such linear list-decodable codes exist with rates k/n arbitrarily close to $1 - H(t/n)$ where H is the binary entropy function [GHK10]. The well-known *Hamming bound* states that it is impossible to do better. This gives an inefficient PPH with output length $m \approx H(t/n) \cdot n + O(\lambda)$. For efficiently list-decodable codes, it is a well known open problem to match the Hamming bound. Instead, the best known constructions [GR09] achieve a slightly worse bound called the *Blokh-Zyablov* bound [BZ82] (see Fact 3 for the exact expression). While this bound is somewhat difficult to interpret, we can always bound the output length by at most $m = O(t \log n + \lambda)$. Moreover, for any constant compression factor $\eta > 0$, there is some constant $\rho > 0$ such that we get a PPH for all distances $t \leq \rho \cdot n$ with output length $m \leq \eta \cdot n + \lambda$.

Remark: Weak Robustness and Heuristic RPPH. As a remark, we mention that we can leverage the result of [BLV19], who showed that one can generically upgrade a non-robust PPH into a weak form of "double-oracle access robust" PPH, where security holds even if the adversary is given oracle access to the hash function h and the evaluation procedure Eval but does not get the code of h itself. This transformation only relies on one-way functions and only adds a small $O(\lambda)$ additive overhead. The idea is to encrypt the output of the non-robust PPH using symmetric-key authenticated encryption whose key is stored as part of the hash function (and which can even be made deterministic), and the Eval procedure first decrypts the non-robust PPH digests and then does what the non-robust Eval procedure would do.

Moreover, we can heuristically convert any such "double-oracle access robust" PPH into a fully robust RPPH by obfuscating the code of the hash function h and the Eval procedure, without increasing the output size of the hash at all. Therefore, this gives heuristic evidence that we can robustly match the above parameters of our non-robust PPH without any additional overhead. Our main results show how to almost match the above parameters robustly under standard assumptions.

Lower Bound. We also prove a lower bound on the output length m of any (not necessarily robust or efficiently computable) PPH for Hamming distance, showing that we require $m > \log \binom{n}{t}$ which implies $m \geq (H(t/n) - o(1)) \cdot n$ and

$m \geq t\log(n/t)$. Our lower bound is simpler than the previous lower bound of [FLS22] and, more importantly, for constant error-rate $\rho = t/n$, it gives a tight bound on compression factor $\eta = m/n$, showing $\eta = H(\rho) - o(1)$. Our upper bound shows how to match the lower bound of $\eta \approx H(\rho)$ inefficiently. Efficiently, our upper bound gives a slightly worse η matching the Blokh-Zyablov bound. Closing this gap between our inefficient and efficient constructions boils down to the fundamental coding theoretic problem of improving the rate of efficiently list-decodable linear codes from the Blokh-Zyablov bound to the better Hamming bound.

The idea behind the lower bound is as follows. For a random x, we show that if we can correctly guess the PPH output $y = h(x)$ as well as some value x' that's exactly at distance t from x, then we can recover x. If we select y, x' uniformly at random then our guess is good with probability $\frac{1}{2^m} \cdot \frac{\binom{n}{t}}{2^n}$, but this can then be at most the probability of guessing x, which is $\frac{1}{2^n}$.

RPPH from Homomorphic Collision-Resistance. We take our construction of PPH for Hamming distance and show how to make it robust. At a high level, the idea is exactly the same as before, and we simply replace the homomorphic universal hash function h_{univ} with a homomorphic collision-resistant hash function h_{CR}. We have such hash functions under the discrete-logarithm (DLOG) assumption—namely, the Pedersen hash function $h_{CR}(x_1, \ldots, x_n) = \prod g_i^{x_i}$, where g_i are random group elements in some prime-order cyclic group. We also have such hash functions under the *short-integer-solution (SIS)* problem— namely, Ajtai's hash function $h_{CR}(x) = A \cdot x$, where A is a random compressing matrix over $\mathbb{Z}_q$ and $||x||_\infty$ is small. In both cases, the output size can be bounded by some polynomial $\ell = \ell(\lambda)$.

There is only one catch: the above hash functions are homomorphic over $\mathbb{Z}_q$ for some $q > 2$ rather than over $\mathbb{Z}_2$. In particular, given $w_1 = h_{CR}(x_1), w_2 = h_{CR}(x_2)$ we can compute $h_{CR}(x_1 - x_2)$ where the subtraction is now over $\mathbb{Z}_q$. Since our PPH construction applies the hash function to values $x_1, x_2 \in \{0,1\}^n$ we have $x_1 - x_2 \in \{-1, 0, 1\}^n$ is the same when computed mod q or over the integers. Therefore, to make the overall PPH construction work, we will also need to use a linear (list decodable) code over some field $\mathbb{F}$ of characteristic $p > 2$ so that, given the syndrome $P \cdot (x_1 - x_2)$ computed over $\mathbb{F}$, we can recover a list containing $x_1 - x_2 \in \{-1, 0, 1\}^n$ computed over the integers. For simplicity, we can just use codes over $\mathbb{F}_3$ instead of $\mathbb{F}_2$. With these changes, the construction and proof of security are essentially the same as in the non-robust case, but now we rely on collision-resistance instead of universality to achieve security even when x_1, x_2 are chosen adaptive depending on the description of the hash function h.

The parameters of the resulting RPPH are essentially the same as those of the non-robust PPH, with the only difference that the hash output now contains $n - k$ elements of $\mathbb{F}_3$ rather than bits. This increases the bit-length of the output by a multiplicative factor of at most $\log_2(3) \approx 1.58$.[5] It is an interesting open problem to get rid of this constant-factor increase by constructing CRHFs that are homomorphic over $\mathbb{Z}_2^n$.[6]

RPPH from Standard Collision-Resistance. Next, we show how to construct RPPH for Hamming distance using just standard collision-resistant hash functions (CRHFs). The output size is larger than that of our optimized construction using homomorphic collision-resistance, but essentially matches the prior state of the art constructions [FS21, FLS22] from specific assumptions.

Our construction relies on two ingredients. The first is an RPPH for *gap Hamming distance*, which was previously constructed from CRHFs by [BLV19]. Namely, assuming a CRHF with output length $\ell = \ell(\lambda)$, they gave a construction of an RPPH for gap Hamming distance with any constant gap $\delta > 0$ and any constant-factor compression, for distances up to $t = O(n/\ell \log \ell)$. We generalize their analysis to showing that for smaller distances t we can get even smaller compression, and in general, for any t, we can make the output as small as $O(t\ell \log(n/t))$. Our second ingredient is a linear error-correcting code over $\mathbb{F}_2$ with a parity check matrix $P \in \mathbb{F}_2^{(n-k) \times n}$ that enables efficient (unique) syndrome decoding from $(1 + \delta)t$ errors.

We use syndrome decoding to upgrade an RPPH for gap Hamming distance h_{gap} with some constant gap $\delta > 0$, into an RPPH for exact Hamming distance h_{exact}. We define $h_{exact}(x) = (P \cdot x, h_{gap}(x))$. Given two hashes $h_{exact}(x_1) = (P \cdot x_1, h_{gap}(x_1))$, $h_{exact}(x_2) = (P \cdot x_2, h_{gap}(x_2))$, we can define the Eval_{exact} procedure that tests whether $\|x_1 - x_2\|_0 \leq t$ as follows. First, it runs $\mathsf{Eval}_{gap}(h_{gap}(x_1), h_{gap}(x_2))$ and if that outputs 0 then we know that $\|x_1 - x_2\|_0 > t$ and hence output 0. Otherwise, if Eval_{gap} outputs 1 then we know that $\|x_1 - x_2\|_0 \leq (1 + \delta)t$. In this case we apply syndrome decoding on $P \cdot (x_1 - x_2)$ to uniquely recover $(x_1 - x_2)$ and if the Hamming weight is $\leq t$ we outputs 1 else 0.

The end result is an RPPH for exact Hamming distance, where the output length is the sum of $n - k$ and the output length of the RPPH for gap Hamming distance from CRHFs. Using Reed-Solomon codes, the former can be bounded by $O(t \log n)$. Therefore the second term dominates, and we get the same parameters for exact Hamming distance as the previous construction for gap Hamming distance by [BLV19].

---

[5] On the other hand, it allows us to use codes over $\mathbb{F}_3$ which may have slightly improved rate compared to ones over $\mathbb{F}_2$.

[6] A heuristic construction would be to define the hash function h_{CR} whose description consists of an obfuscated program that has a hard-coded random matrix $A \leftarrow \mathbb{Z}_2^{\lambda \times n}$ and a key k for a pseudorandom permutation $\pi_k : \{0,1\}^\lambda \rightarrow \{0,1\}^\lambda$. On input ("hash", x) the program would output $\pi_k(Ax)$, which we would also define as the output of the hash function $h_{CR}(x)$. On input ("homomorphism", y_1, y_2) the program would output $\pi_k(\pi_k^{-1}(y_1) - \pi_k^{-1}(y_2))$, which would allow us to implement the homomorphic operation on the hash outputs.

R2P2H. Finally, we turn to the construction of randomized RPPH (R2P2H). We go back to our initial construction of a (non-robust) PPH for Hamming distance, where $h(x)$ outputs a syndrome of x and a homomorphic universal hash of x. We can think of the universal hash function as a (deterministic, non-rboust) PPH for equality. By taking that construction and replacing the universal hash function with a R2P2H for quality we get our R2P2H for Hamming distance. We just need the R2P2H for equality to satisfy an appropriate homomorphic property, and we show how to adapt known constructions to do so.

Open Question. While our work gives nearly optimal constructions of (R)PPH for exact Hamming distance, it leaves open the question whether one can get significantly better parameters for gap Hamming distance. Recall that, in the non-robust case, we had a lower bound of $m \geq \log \binom{n}{t} \geq t \log(n/t)$ on the output length of a (even non-robust) PPH for exact Hamming distance. As pointed out in [BLV19], using the result of [KOR00], it turns out that one can do much better for gap Hamming distance: for any constant gap $\delta > 0$ there is a non-robust PPH for gap Hamming distance with output length just $O(\lambda)$ independent of n, t. A very interesting open question is whether it is possible to match this with robustness or not. Currently, we don't even have heuristic constructions that would beat the $m \geq t \log(n/t)$ lower bound in the gap setting with robustness. On the other hand, we also currently don't have any techniques for proving any lower bounds on the cost of robustness – all current lower bounds for RPPH also hold for non-robust PPH.

1.3 Other Related Work

Locality sensitive hash functions [IM98] can be thought of as a strengthening of PPH, where we want $h(x_1) = h(x_2)$ to collide iff $P(x_1, x_2)$ holds. In other words, we can think of this as a special case of PPH where Eval just outputs 1 iff the digests are equal. While there is a simple construction of locality sensitive hash functions for gap Hamming distance [IM98], there are strong lower bounds showing that they cannot achieve a negligible correctness error, even in the non-robust setting [MNP07, OWZ11]. In particular, they cannot be robust.

Secure sketches [DORS08] ensure that, given a hash (called a "sketch") $h(x_1)$ and some x_2 within distance t of x_1, we can recover x_1. While the original notion of secure sketches did not require the digest to be compressing, one of the constructions of [DORS08] for Hamming distance is based on syndrome decoding and is compressing. Secure sketches easily yield a relaxation of PPH (resp. RPPH), where we can determine whether $P(x_1, x_2)$ holds given one digest $h(x_1)$ and the other input x_2 in the clear. In particular, we simply append a universal (resp. collision resistant) hash function of x_1 to the output of the sketch; then, given x_2, we first use the sketch to attempt to recover a candidate x_1' for x_1, then check that it matches the universal (resp. collision resistant) hash, and finally check that it is within distance t of x_2. This type of relaxed notion of (R)PPH was also defined by [BLV19], and referred to as a "single-input property" (R)PPH. Given the above, the main novelty of our work and previous works on

RPPH for Hamming distance, is that we need to decide whether $P(x_1, x_2)$ holds given only the two digests $h(x_1), h(x_2)$, without having either of the inputs in the clear.

2 Preliminaries

Notation. When X is a distribution, or a random variable following this distribution, we let $x \leftarrow X$ denote the process of sampling x according to the distribution X. If X is a set, we let $x \leftarrow X$ denote sampling x uniformly at random from X. We use the notation $[k] = \{1, \ldots, k\}$. If $x \in \{0,1\}^k$ and $i \in [k]$ then we let $x[i]$ denote the i'th bit of x. If $s \subseteq [k]$, we let $x[s]$ denote the list of values $x[i]$ for $i \in s$.

Predictability and Entropy. The *predictability* of a random variable X is $\mathbf{Pred}(X) \overset{\text{def}}{=} \max_x \Pr[X = x]$. The *min-entropy* of a random variable X is $\mathbf{H}_\infty(X) = -\log(\mathbf{Pred}(X))$. Following Dodis et al. [DORS08], we define the conditional predictability of X given Y as $\mathbf{Pred}(X|Y) \overset{\text{def}}{=} \mathbb{E}_{y \leftarrow Y}[\mathbf{Pred}(X|Y = y)]$ and the (average) conditional min-entropy of X given Y as: $\mathbf{H}_\infty(X|Y) = -\log(\mathbf{Pred}(X|Y))$. Note that $\mathbf{Pred}(X|Y)$ is the success probability of the optimal strategy for guessing X given Y.

Lemma 1 ([DORS08]). *For any random variables X, Y, Z where Y is supported over a set of size T we have $\mathbf{H}_\infty(X|Y, Z) \leq \mathbf{H}_\infty(X|Z) - \log T$.*

Universal Hashing. We recall the definition of universal hash function and a simple well-known construction via matrix multiplication.

Definition 1. *A family of hash functions $\mathcal{H} = \{h : \{0,1\}^n \rightarrow \{0,1\}^m\}$ is a universal hash family if for all $x_1, x_2 \in \{0,1\}^n$ such that $x_1 \neq x_2$, we have:*

$$\Pr[h(x_1) = h(x_2) : h \leftarrow \mathcal{H}] \leq 2^{-m}$$

We will rely on the following simple universal hash function family, which also has the additional feature of being homomorphic over $\mathbb{Z}_2^n$ with $h(x_1) + h(x_2) = h(x_1 + x_2)$.

Lemma 2. *For any n, m, the hash function family $\mathcal{H}$ consisting of hash functions $h_A(x) = A \cdot x$ with $A \in \mathbb{Z}_2^{m \times n}$, is a universal hash family.*

Proof. Let $x_1, x_2 \in \{0,1\}^n$ such that $x_1 \neq x_2$ and let $v = (x_1 - x_2) \neq 0^n$. Denote the bits of $v = (v_1, \ldots, n_n)$. Then there exists some $i \in [n]$ such that $v_i = 1$. Denote the columns of A by $A = [a_1, \ldots, a_n]$ with $a_i \in \mathbb{Z}_2^m$. Then $\Pr_A[Ax_1 = Ax_2] = \Pr_A[Av = 0] = \Pr_A\left[a_i = -\sum_{j \neq i} a_j \cdot v_j\right] = \frac{1}{2^m}$.

2.1   Coding Theory

Definition 2. *An $[n,k]_q$ code for $n, k, q \in \mathbb{Z}^+$ is an injective linear function $C : \mathbb{F}_q^k \to \mathbb{F}_q^n$. We call k the* message length *and n the* block length *of C.*
A codeword *of C is any element of the image of C.*

Definition 3 (Parity Checks/Syndromes). *A* parity check matrix[7] *for an $\mathbb{F}$-linear code $C : \mathbb{F}^k \to \mathbb{F}^n$ is a matrix $P \in \mathbb{F}^{(n-k) \times n}$ such that $c \in \mathbb{F}^n$ is a codeword of C if and only if $P \cdot c = 0$.*
When C and P are fixed, we call $P \cdot y$ the syndrome *of y.*

Definition 4 (Distance). *The* distance *of a code C is the minimum Hamming distance between two different codewords of C.*

Definition 5 (List-Decoding). *An $[n,k]_q$ code $C : \mathbb{F}_q^k \to \mathbb{F}_q^n$ is said to be* combinatorially list decodable *against t errors if for any $y \in \Sigma_k^n$, there are at most[8] $\mathrm{poly}(n)$ codewords of C within Hamming distance t of any $y \in \mathbb{F}_q^n$. If there is a $\mathrm{poly}(n)$-time algorithm that outputs all such codewords, then C is said to be* efficiently *list decodable against t errors.*

Syndrome decoding is another standard but less common way of characterizing list decodability.

Definition 6 (Syndrome Decoding). *Let $C : \mathbb{F}_q^k \to \mathbb{F}_q^n$ be an $[n,k]_q$ code with parity check matrix P.*
C is said to be combinatorially syndrome list decodable *against t errors if for every $s \in \mathbb{F}_q^{n-k}$, there are at most $\mathrm{poly}(n)$ vectors $e \in \mathbb{F}_q^n$ with Hamming weight at most t such that $P \cdot e = s$.*
C is said to be efficiently syndrome list decodable *against t errors if there is a $\mathrm{poly}(n)$-time algorithm that on input $s \in \mathbb{F}_q^{n-k}$ enumerates all $e \in \mathbb{F}_q^n$ with Hamming weight at most t for which $P \cdot e = s$.*

Fact 1. *An $[n,k]_q$ code C with parity check matrix P is combinatorially list decodable against t errors if and only if it is combinatorially syndrome list decodable against t errors. Moreover C is efficiently list decodable against t errors if and only if it is efficiently syndrome list decodable against t errors.*

Proof. For any $[n,k]_q$ code $C : \mathbb{F}_q^k \to \mathbb{F}_q^n$ with parity check matrix $P \in \mathbb{F}_q^{(n-k) \times n}$, any $t \in \mathbb{Z}^+$, and any $y \in \mathbb{F}_q^n$ with syndrome $s = P \cdot y \in \mathbb{F}_q^{n-k}$, there is a bijective correspondence between:

- $e \in \mathbb{F}_q^n$ such that $P \cdot e = s$ and $\|e\|_0 \leq t$; and
- $m \in \mathbb{F}_q^k$ such that $\|y - C(m)\|_0 \leq t$.

---

[7] There are multiple possible parity check matrices for any code, but the specific choice will be unimportant for us.

[8] The asymptotic bound of $\mathrm{poly}(n)$ in fact assumes that we have a family of codes for an infinite and dense set of n.

Specifically, any such e can be mapped to $m = C^{-1}(y - e)$. This is well-defined because $P \cdot (y - e) = P \cdot y - P \cdot e = s - s = 0$, so $y - e$ is in the image of C. In the other direction, any such m can be mapped to $e = y - C(m)$, which satisfies $P \cdot e = P \cdot y - P \cdot C(m) = s - 0 = s$. It is easy to check that these maps are inverses of each other.

Known Results

Definition 7 (q-ary Entropy Function). *The q-ary entropy function H_q is defined as*

$$H_q(\rho) \overset{\text{def}}{=} \rho \log_q(q - 1) - \rho \log_q \rho - (1 - \rho) \log_q(1 - \rho).$$

We use H without a subscript to refer to the binary entropy function H_2.

We first state the fact that inefficiently (combinatorially) list-decodable codes exist matching the Hamming bound.

Fact 2 (Combinatorially List-Decodable Codes [GHK10]). *For all $q \in \mathbb{Z}^+$, all $0 < \rho < 1 - \frac{1}{q}$, all $0 < R < 1 - H_q(\rho)$, and for all sufficiently large n, there exists an $[n, Rn]_q$ code that is combinatorially list decodable against $\rho \cdot n$ errors. Moreover the list size is inversely proportional to $1 - H_q(\rho) - R$.*[9]

When it comes to efficiently list-decodable codes, we only have construction matching the slightly weaker Blokh-Zyablov bound as stated below.

Fact 3 (Blokh-Zyablov bound [BZ82, GR09]). *For any $q \in \mathbb{Z}^+$, any $\rho \in (0, \frac{1}{2})$, any*

$$0 < R < 1 - \underbrace{\left(H_q(\rho) + \rho \cdot \int_0^{1 - H_q(\rho)} \frac{dx}{H_q^{-1}(1 - x)} \right)}_{H_q^{\mathsf{BZ}}(\rho)}, \tag{1}$$

and any sufficiently large n, there is an explicit $[n, \lceil Rn \rceil]_q$ code that is efficiently list decodable against ρn errors.

We define the quantity $H_q^{\mathsf{BZ}}(\rho)$ as in Eq. (1). Note that $\lim_{\rho \to 0} H_q^{\mathsf{BZ}}(\rho) = 0$. In particular, for every $\eta > 0$ there exists some $\rho > 0$ such that $\eta > H_q^{\mathsf{BZ}}(\rho)$.

Lastly, when the distance d is small (say $d \approx n^\varepsilon$ for constant $\varepsilon > 0$) then we can get nearly optimal high-rate codes via Reed-Solomon. While Reed-Solomon codes are usually expressed over a large field, if the field is an extension-field of some small field $\mathbb{F}_q$ (e.g., $q = 2$) then we can always re-interpret the codes as just being linear codes over $\mathbb{F}_q$. Therefore Reed-Solomon yields essentially optimal high-rate codes over $\mathbb{F}_2$ when the distance is small.

---

[9] In fact, a random linear code is known to have the stated list decodability with high probability.

Fact 4 (Efficiently Decodable High-Rate Codes). *For all n, all q, and all d and for $k = n - d \log_q n$ there exists an $\mathbb{F}_q$-linear code $C : \mathbb{F}_q^k \to \mathbb{F}_q^n$ that is efficiently uniquely decodable against $\lfloor \frac{d}{2} \rfloor$ errors.*

Proof. We start with a Reed-Solomon code $C' : (\mathbb{F}')^{k'} \to (\mathbb{F}')^{n'}$, where $n' = n/\log_q n$ and $k' = k/\log_q n$ and $\mathbb{F}' = \mathbb{F}_{q^{\log_q n}}$ is an extension field of $\mathbb{F}_q$ satisfying $|\mathbb{F}'| \geq n \geq n'$. By standard properties of Reed-Solomon codes, C' is $\mathbb{F}'$-linear, has distance $d = n' - k' + 1$, and is efficiently uniquely decodable against $\lfloor d/2 \rfloor$ errors [Pet60].

Using the fact that $\mathbb{F}' \cong \mathbb{F}_q^{\log_q n}$, we can view C' as a code $C : \mathbb{F}_q^k \to \mathbb{F}_q^n$. The code C inherits its distance and efficient unique decodability from C', because if two strings differ in at most d symbols when interpreted as string over $\mathbb{F}_q$, then they also differ in at most d symbols when interpreted as string over $\mathbb{F}'$.

Finally, it is easy to see (e.g., see [RRR21, Proposition 6.6]) that C is $\mathbb{F}_q$-linear.

3   Definition of (R)PPH

We recall the definition of (R)PPH from [BLV19]. We first define a general notion for arbitrary properties P and then discuss the specific Hamming distance property considered in this work. For the general notion, we also potentially consider partial predicates $P(x_1, x_2)$ that can sometimes output $\bot$, in which case we do not care what output the (R)PPH gives.

Definition 8. *Let $n = n(\lambda), m = m(\lambda)$ be some polynomials in the security parameter λ. A (n, m)-Property Preserving Hash (PPH) family $\mathcal{H} = \{h : \{0,1\}^n \to \{0,1\}^m\}$ for a two-input (partial) predicate $P : \{0,1\}^n \times \{0,1\}^n \to \{0, 1, \bot\}$ is a family of efficiently computable functions with the following algorithms:*

- *$\mathsf{Samp}(1^\lambda) \to h$ is a PPT algorithm that samples a random $h \in \mathcal{H}$.*
- *$\mathsf{Eval}(h, y_1, y_2)$ is a deterministic polynomial-time algorithm that on input $h \in \mathcal{H}$ and $y_1, y_2 \in \{0,1\}^m$, outputs a single bit.*

Additionally, $h \in \mathcal{H}$ must satisfy the following correctness property:

- *Correctness: $\forall x_1, x_2 \in \{0,1\}^n$*

$$\Pr_{h \leftarrow \mathsf{Samp}(1^\lambda)} [P(x_1, x_2) \neq \bot \land \mathsf{Eval}(h, h(x_1), h(x_2)) \neq P(x_1, x_2)] = \mathrm{negl}(\lambda)$$

Definition 9. *A (n, m)-PPH is a robust PPH (RPPH) if it satisfies the following additional robustness property.*

- *Robustness: For any PPT adversary $\mathcal{A}$,*

$$\Pr_{\substack{h \leftarrow \mathsf{Samp}(1^\lambda) \\ (x_1, x_2) \leftarrow \mathcal{A}(h)}} [P(x_1, x_2) \neq \bot \land \mathsf{Eval}(h, h(x_1), h(x_2)) \neq P(x_1, x_2)] = \mathrm{negl}(\lambda)$$

The main focus of this work is (R)PPH for the (exact) Hamming distance property, which is defined by the following (total) predicate.

Definition 10. *For $n \in \mathbb{N}$, $0 < t < n$, the (two-input)* HAMMING$_{n,t}$ *predicate is a predicate defined as*

$$\mathrm{HAMMING}_{n,t}(x_1, x_2) = \begin{cases} 1 & \text{if } \|x_1 \oplus x_2\|_0 \leq t \\ 0 & \text{if } \|x_1 \oplus x_2\|_0 > t \end{cases}$$

As a tool in one of our constructions, we will also consider a relaxation of (R)PPH to *gap-Hamming distance*, which is defined by the following (partial) predicate.

Definition 11. *For $n \in \mathbb{N}$, $0 < t < n$, $\delta > 0$, the (two-input)* GAPHAMMING$_{n,t,\delta}$ *predicate is a partial predicate defined as*

$$\mathrm{GAPHAMMING}_{n,t,\delta}(x_1, x_2) = \begin{cases} 1 & \text{if } \|x_1 \oplus x_2\|_0 \leq t \\ 0 & \text{if } \|x_1 \oplus x_2\|_0 \geq (1 + \delta)t \\ \bot & \text{otherwise.} \end{cases}$$

4 Non-robust PPH

In this section, we present the construction of an information-theoretically secure non-robust property preserving hash (PPH) for Hamming distance. The construction relies on syndrome list-decoding and universal hashing.

(n, m)-PPH for Hamming$_{n,t}$.

Let $P \in \mathbb{F}_2^{(n-k) \times n}$ be a parity check matrix of an $[n, k]_2$-linear code which is efficiently list decodable against t errors.

- Samp(1^λ): Sample $A \leftarrow \mathbb{F}_2^{\lambda \times n}$ uniformly at random. Output the function h defined below, whose description contains A.
- $h(x) := (P \cdot x, A \cdot x)$.
- Eval(h, y_1, y_2) : Let $y_1 = (v_1, w_1)$ and $y_2 = (v_2, w_2)$. Use syndrome list-decoding for the syndrome $v_1 - v_2$ to recover a list $\mathcal{L} = \{e_1, \ldots, e_L\}$ of possible error vectors $e_i \in \mathbb{F}_2^n$ such that $Pe_i = v_1 - v_2$ and $\|e_i\|_0 \leq t$. Then
    - output 1, if there exists $e_i \in \mathcal{L}$ such that $A \cdot e_i = w_1 - w_2$,
    - otherwise output 0.

Fig. 1. Construction of (n, m)-PPH for HAMMING$_{n,t}$

Theorem 5. *Let λ be a security parameter. For any polynomial n, t, k such that there exists an $[n, k]_2$-linear code which is efficiently list decodable against* *t errors, the construction above is a (n, m)-PPH for* $\text{HAMMING}_{n,t}$ *with output length* $m = (n - k) + \lambda$. *If the code is only combinatorially (inefficiently) list decodable, then the resulting PPH is inefficient.*

Proof. Let $x_1, x_2 \in \mathbb{F}_2^n$ be arbitrary values chosen a priori. Let $h \leftarrow \mathsf{Samp}(1^\lambda)$ and let $y_1 = h(x_1), y_2 = h(x_2)$ with $y_1 = (v_1, w_1)$ and $y_2 = (v_2, w_2)$. Let $\mathcal{L}$ be the list recovered during the computation of $\mathsf{Eval}(h, y_1, y_2)$. We consider two cases:

- If $\|x_1 - x_2\|_0 \leq t$, then $e := x_1 - x_2 \in \mathcal{L}$ by the correctness of syndrome list-decoding for the syndrome $v_1 - v_2 = P \cdot (x_1 - x_2)$. Therefore $A \cdot e = A \cdot (x_1 - x_2) = A \cdot x_1 - A \cdot x_2 = w_1 - w_2$ and hence Eval will output 1.
- If $\|x_1 - x_2\|_0 > t$, then for all $e_i \in \mathcal{L}$, we have $\|e_i\|_0 \leq t$ and therefore $e_i \neq x_1 - x_2$. Note that the list $\mathcal{L}$ is independent of A. Hence for each $e_i \in \mathcal{L}$, we have $\Pr_A[A \cdot e_i = w_1 - w_2] = \Pr_A[A \cdot e_i = A \cdot (x_1 - x_2)] = 2^{-\lambda}$, by Lemma 2. By a union bound, the probability $\Pr_A[\exists e_i \in \mathcal{L} : A \cdot e_i = w_1 - w_2] \leq |\mathcal{L}| \cdot 2^{-\lambda} = \mathrm{negl}(\lambda)$. Therefore, with all but negligible probability, Eval will output 0.

Plugging in Facts 3 and 4, we obtain the following corollaries for PPH.

Corollary 1. *For all constant* $0 < \rho < 1/2$ *and* $\eta > H_2^{\mathsf{BZ}}(\rho)$ *(see Fact 3), for all polynomial* n, *there exists an efficient* (n, m)-PPH *for* $\text{HAMMING}_{n,t}$ *with* $t = \rho \cdot n$, *having output length* $m = \eta \cdot n + \lambda$. *In particular, for every constant* $\eta > 0$, *there exists some constant* $\rho > 0$ *such that the above holds.*

Corollary 2. *For all polynomial* n *and* t, *there exists an* (n, m)-PPH *for* $\text{HAMMING}_{n,t}$ *where* $m = 2t \cdot \log_2 n + \lambda$.

Lastly, plugging in Fact 2, we obtain the following bound for *inefficient* PPH.

Corollary 3. *For all constant* $0 < \rho < 1/2$ *and* $\eta > H_2(\rho)$ *there exists an inefficient* (n, m)-PPH *for* $\text{HAMMING}_{n,t}$ *with* $t = \rho \cdot n$, *having output length* $m = \eta \cdot n + \lambda$.

5   Lower Bounds on PPH Output

In this section we provide a lower bound on the output size of any (not necessarily robust) PPH for the Hamming distance predicate. Previous lower bounds on PPH [BLV19,FLS22] mainly come from communication complexity lower bounds, and are usually presented as asymptotic bounds. In particular, in [FLS22] the authors presented an output size bound of $\Omega(t \log(\min n/t, 1/\delta))$ for RPPHs for $\text{HAMMING}_{n,t}$ with error probability δ. We obtain an exact lower bound, without asymptotic. In particular, this lets us argue that we cannot beat the Hamming bound.

As with all previous lower bounds on RPPH ([BLV19,FLS22]), our lower bound works for non-robust PPH as well. It remains unclear how robustness is factored into RPPH lower bounds.

Theorem 6. *For any (n, m)-PPH for* HAMMING$_{n,t}$ *with correctness error $\delta <$ $\frac{1}{2n}$, the output size m must satisfy $m \geq \log\binom{n}{t}$. In particular, this implies $m \geq$ $t \log \frac{n}{t}$ and $m \geq \left(H\left(\frac{t}{n}\right) - o(1)\right) \cdot n$, where H is the binary entropy function.*

Proof. Let (Samp, Eval) be an (n, m)-PPH for HAMMING$_{n,t}$. We first show that there is some function Rec such that, for all x, y with $||x - y||_0 = t$, we have

$$\Pr_{h \leftarrow \mathsf{Samp}()}[\mathsf{Rec}(h, h(x), y) = x] > \frac{1}{2}.$$

In particular, we define $\mathsf{Rec}(h, h(x), y)$ as follows:

- For each $i \in [n]$, define the string $y^{(i)}$ to be the same as y except that we flip the i'th bit. Then compute $b_i = \mathsf{Eval}(h, h(x), h(y^{(i)}))$. Let $\tilde{x}_i = b_i \oplus y_i$, where y_i denotes the i'th bit of y.
- Output $\tilde{x} = (\tilde{x}_1, \ldots, \tilde{x}_n)$.

Observe that for each $i \in [n]$, if $x_i = y_i$, we have $||x - y^{(i)}||_0 = t + 1$ and if $x_i \neq x_i'$, we have $||x \oplus y^{(i)}||_0 = t - 1$. Therefore, as long as for each $i \in [n]$, we get $b_i = 0$ in the former case and $b_i = 1$ in the latter case, we get $\tilde{x} = x$. By the correctness of the PPH, this occurs with overwhelming probability, since the probability of Eval giving the wrong answer in any position i is $< \frac{1}{2n}$, and by the union bound, the probability of there being any error overall is then $< \frac{1}{2}$.

Now let us define a (randomized) function $P(h, h(x))$ whose goal is to predict x given $h, h(x)$:

- Sample a uniformly random $y \leftarrow \{0, 1\}^n$ and output $\mathsf{Rec}(h, h(x), y)$,

We have for all $x \in \{0, 1\}^n$:

$$\Pr_{h \leftarrow \mathsf{Samp}()}[P(h, h(x)) = x]$$

$$\geq \Pr_{y \leftarrow \{0,1\}^n}[\ ||x - y||_0 = t\ ]\Pr_{h,y}[\ \mathsf{Rec}(h, h(x), y) = x\ |\ ||x - y||_0 = t\ ]$$

$$> \frac{\binom{n}{t}}{2^n} \cdot \frac{1}{2}.$$

Now consider X to be a random variable uniformly distributed over $\{0, 1\}^n$ and h to be a random variable distributed according to $\mathsf{Samp}()$. Then

$$\mathbf{H}_\infty(X \mid h, h(X)) \leq -\log(\mathbf{Pred}(X \mid h, h(X))) \leq -\log(\Pr_{h,x}[P(h, h(x)) = x]) < n - \log\binom{n}{t} + 1.$$

On the other hand

$$\mathbf{H}_\infty(X \mid h, h(X)) \geq \mathbf{H}_\infty(X \mid h) - m \geq \mathbf{H}_\infty(X) - m \geq n - m.$$

The first inequality follows from Lemma 1, the second inequality follows since h, X are independent, and the third since X is uniformly random over $\{0, 1\}^n$.

Combining the above two inequalities, we get $m > \log\binom{n}{t} - 1$, but since m is an integer, this implies $m \geq \log\binom{n}{t}$.

Optimality of Our Construction. Our lower bound in Theorem 6 shows that our PPH construction from the previous section achieves essentially tight parameters. We look at two concrete settings.

When $t = \rho \cdot n$ for some constant $\rho > 0$ then the lower bound shows $m \geq (H(\rho) - o(1)) \cdot n$. This essentially matches our upper bound from Corollary 3 which shows that inefficiently we can achieve $m \approx H(\rho) \cdot n + \lambda$. Therefore, our inefficient construction is tight, including constant factors! Efficiently, Corollary 1 allows us to achieve a slightly worse compression $m \approx H_2^{\mathsf{BZ}}(\rho) \cdot n + \lambda$, where $H_2^{\mathsf{BZ}}(\rho)$ is a slightly larger constant than $H(\rho)$. The small gap between our efficient upper bounds and the lower bound is due to the fact that current constructions of efficiently list-decodable linear codes are slightly sub-optimal compared to combinatorially (inefficiently) list-decodable counterparts – future advances in coding theory will hopefully allows us to close this gap.

For smaller distances $t = n^\varepsilon$ for some constant $\varepsilon > 0$, then the lower bound shows that $m \geq t \log(n/t) = \Omega(t \log n)$. This essentially matches our upper bound of $m = O(t \log n)$ from Corollary 2, up to constant factors.

6   RPPH from Homomorphic Collision Resistance

In this section, we present the construction of a robust property preserving hash (RPPH) from homomorphic collision resistant hash functions. The construction is analogous to that of non-robust PPH, with the main difference being that we replace the homomorphic universal hash function $h_{univ}(x) = A \cdot x$ with a cryptographic homomorphic collision-resistant hash function. We begin by defining this notion and showing how to construct it.

6.1   Homomorphic CRHFs

We rely on the following definition of a homomorphic collision-resistant hash function.

Definition 12 (Homomorphic CRHF). *Let* $n = n(\lambda), \ell = \ell(\lambda)$ *be some polynomials with* $\ell < n$. *A family of* Homomorphic Collision Resistant Hash Functions (Samp, $\mathcal{H}$) *consists of a sampling algorithm* $h \leftarrow \mathsf{Samp}(1^\lambda)$ *that generates a hash function* $h \in \mathcal{H}$ *with* $h : \mathbb{Z}_q^n \to \{0,1\}^\ell$ *for some integer* q *specified by* h. *We require require the following properties:*

- Efficiency: *For any* $h \leftarrow \mathsf{Samp}(1^\lambda)$ *the function* $h(x)$ *can be computed in* poly(λ) *time.*
- Collision-Resistance: *For any ppt adversary* $\mathcal{A}$:

$$\Pr \left[\begin{array}{c} h(x_1) = h(x_2) \\ \wedge \ (x_1 \neq x_2) \\ \wedge \ x_1, x_2 \in \{-1, 0, 1\}^n \end{array} \quad : \quad \begin{array}{c} h \leftarrow \mathsf{Samp}(1^\lambda), \\ (x_1, x_2) \leftarrow \mathcal{A}(h) \end{array} \right] \leq \mathsf{negl}(\lambda).$$

- Homomorphism: *The description of* h *determines some operation* $\div$ *computable in* poly(λ) *time such that for all* $x_1, x_2 \in \mathbb{Z}_q^n$ *we have*

$$h(x_1) \div h(x_2) = h(x_1 - x_2).$$

Note that, while for homomorphism we consider the domain of the hash function to be $\mathbb{Z}_q^n$ and the subtraction $x_1 - x_2$ is computed in $\mathbb{Z}_q^n$, for collisions we only need to consider inputs in a restricted sub-domain $\{-1, 0, 1\}^n \subseteq \mathbb{Z}_q^n$. This will be important for our construction from the SIS assumption.

Construction from Discrete Log. We observer that the Pedersen hash function [Ped92] (a deterministic version of Pedersen commitment) is a good homomorphic collision-resistant hash function under the discrete logarithm assumption.

Let $\mathcal{G} = (\mathbb{G}, g, q) \leftarrow \mathsf{GroupGen}(1^\lambda)$ be a group generation algorithm that generates the description of a cyclic group $\mathbb{G} = \langle g \rangle$ of prime order $|\mathbb{G}| = q$, with a generator g, such that the group operation (written as multiplication) can be computed in $\mathrm{poly}(\lambda)$ time and group elements can be efficiently represented using $\ell = \ell(\lambda)$ bits.

The discrete logarithm (DLOG) assumption relative to the above $\mathsf{GroupGen}$ algorithm says the following.

Definition 13 (Discrete Log Assumption). *For any ppt adversary $\mathcal{A}$ we have:*
$$\Pr[\mathcal{A}(\mathcal{G}, g^x) = x \; : \; \mathcal{G} \leftarrow \mathsf{GroupGen}(1^\lambda), x \leftarrow \mathbb{Z}_q] \leq \mathrm{negl}(\lambda).$$

For any polynomial input length $n = n(\lambda)$, the Pederson hash functions $(\mathsf{Samp}, \mathcal{H})$ is defined as follows:

- $h \leftarrow \mathsf{Samp}(1^\lambda)$: Sample $\mathcal{G} = (\mathbb{G}, g, q) \leftarrow \mathsf{GroupGen}(1^\lambda)$, and let $g_1, \ldots, g_n \leftarrow \mathbb{G}$ be random group elements. The description of the hash function h consists of $(\mathcal{G}, g_1, \ldots, g_n)$.
- $y = h(x)$: Given an input $x = (x_1, \ldots, x_n) \in \mathbb{Z}_q^n$ define $h(x) = \prod_{i \in [n]} g_i^{x_i}$.
- The $\div$ operation is defined as $h(x) \div h(x') = h(x)/h(x') = h(x - x')$.

Theorem 7 ([Ped92]). *The above hash function family is a homomorphic collision-resistant hash function under the discrete logarithm assumption.*

Construction from SIS. We observe that Ajtai's hash function [Ajt96] based on the short-integer solution (SIS) problem is is a good homomorphic collision-resistant hash function.

Definition 14. *The short integer solution $SIS_{m,q,B}$ assumption with some parameters $m = m(\lambda), q = q(\lambda)$ and $B = B(\lambda)$ says that for all polynomial $n = n(\lambda)$ and all ppt $\mathcal{A}$ we have:*
$$\Pr[A \cdot x = 0 \wedge x \neq 0 \wedge x \in [-B, B]^n \; : \; A \leftarrow \mathbb{Z}_q^{m \times n}, x \leftarrow \mathcal{A}(A)] \leq \mathrm{negl}(\lambda).$$

For any polynomial input length $n = n(\lambda)$, Ajtai's hash functions $(\mathsf{Samp}, \mathcal{H})$ is defined as follows:

- $h \leftarrow \mathsf{Samp}(1^\lambda)$: Sample $A \leftarrow \mathbb{Z}_q^{m \times n}$ and let the description of the hash function $h : \mathbb{Z}_q^n \to \mathbb{Z}_q^m$ consist of the matrix A.
- $y = h(x)$: Given an input $x \in \{0, 1\}^n$ define $h(x) = A \cdot x$.

- The $\div$ operation is defined as $h(x_1) \div h(x_2) = h(x_1) - h(x_2)$.

Theorem 8 ([Ajt96]). *The above hash function family is a homomorphic collision-resistant hash function under the $SIS_{m,q,B}$ assumption with $B = 2$.*

Proof. Assume otherwise, that there is some ppt $\mathcal{A}$ such that

$$\Pr[A \cdot x_1 = A \cdot x_2 \wedge x_1 \neq x_2 \wedge x_1, x_2 \in \{-1,0,1\}^n : A \leftarrow \mathbb{Z}_q^{m \times n}, (x_1, x_2) \leftarrow \mathcal{A}(A)] = \mu(\lambda)$$

for some non-negligible μ. Whenever $A \cdot x_1 = A \cdot x_2 \wedge x_1 \neq x_2 \wedge x_1, x_2 \in \{-1,0,1\}^n$ occurs, we can define $x^* = (x_1 - x_2) \in [-2,2]^n$ such that $x^* \neq 0$ and $Ax^* = 0$. Therefore if we define a ppt $\mathcal{A}'$ that runs $(x_1, x_2) \leftarrow \mathcal{A}(A)$ and outputs $x^* = (x_1 - x_2)$ then

$$\Pr[A \cdot x^* = 0 \wedge x^* \neq 0 \wedge x^* \in [-2,2]^n \ : \ A \leftarrow \mathbb{Z}_q^{m \times n}, x^* \leftarrow \mathcal{A}'(A)] = \mu(\lambda).$$

and therefore $\mathcal{A}'$ breaks the $SIS_{m,q,B}$.

6.2 RPPH from Homomorphic CRHFs

We now give our construction of RPPH from homomorphic CRHFs. The construction is essentially identical to the non-robust PPH construction in Fig. 1. The main difference is that we now use a homomorphic CRHF in place of a homomorphic universal hash function. Another difference arises from the fact that the homomorphic CRHF is over $\mathbb{Z}_q^n$ for some arbitrary q rather than just over $\mathbb{Z}_2$. Although we will still apply the CRHF on inputs $x_1, x_2 \in \{0,1\}^n$, when we subtract over $\mathbb{Z}_q^n$ we get $x_1 - x_2 \in \{-1,0,1\}^n$. If $q \neq 2$ then $-1 \neq 1$. This means that we need to use a linear error-correcting code over some field $\mathbb{F}$ of characteristic $p > 2$ so that when we apply syndrome decoding over $\mathbb{F}$ we correctly recover the same value $x_1 - x_2 \in \{-1,0,1\}^n$.

Theorem 9. *Assume the existence of a homomorphic CRHF with output length $\ell(\lambda)$. For any polynomial t, k and odd prime power Q such that there exists an $[n, k]_Q$ code that is efficiently list decodable against t errors, the construction above is an (n, m)-RPPH for $\mathrm{HAMMING}_{n,t}$ with output length $(n - k) \cdot \log_2 Q + \ell(\lambda)$.*

Proof. Let $h \leftarrow \mathsf{Samp}(1^\lambda)$, let $x_1, x_2 \in \{0,1\}^n$ be arbitrary values chosen by an adversary adaptively after seeing h. Let $y_1 = h(x_1), y_2 = h(x_2)$ with $y_1 = (v_1, w_1)$ and $y_2 = (v_2, w_2)$. Let $\mathcal{L}$ be the list recovered during the computation of $\mathsf{Eval}(h, y_1, y_2)$. We consider two cases:

- If $\|x_1 - x_2\|_0 \leq t$, then $e := x_1 - x_2 \in \mathcal{L}$ by the correctness of syndrome list-decoding for the syndrome $v_1 - v_2 = P \cdot (x_1 - x_2)$. Therefore $g(e) = g(x_1 - x_2) = g(x_1) \div g(x_2) = w_1 \div w_2$ and hence Eval will output 1. Note that, since $x_1, x_2 \in \{0,1\}^n$, the difference $x_1 - x_2 \in \{-1,0,1\}^n$ is the same when computed over the field $\mathbb{F}$ of characteristic $p \geq 3$ as when just computed over the integers.

(n, m)-RPPH for Hamming$_{n,t}$.

Let $n = n(\lambda)$ and $\ell = \ell(\lambda)$. Let $P \in \mathbb{F}^{(n-k) \times n}$ be a parity check matrix of an $[n, k]_Q$ code that is efficiently list decodable against t errors, where Q is an odd prime power. Let $(\mathsf{Samp}_{CR}, \mathcal{H}_{CR})$ be a family of collision Resistant Homomorphic Hash Functions with input length n and output length ℓ. The RPPH family $(\mathsf{Samp}, \mathsf{Eval})$ is defined as follows:

- $\mathsf{Samp}(1^\lambda)$: Sample $g \leftarrow \mathsf{Samp}_{CR}(1^\lambda)$ to generate a homomorphic collision-resistant hash function $g : \mathbb{Z}_q^n \to \{0,1\}^\ell$ for some q. Output the function h defined below, whose description contains g.
- $h(x) := (P \cdot x, g(x))$.
- $\mathsf{Eval}(h, y_1, y_2)$: Let $y_1 = (v_1, w_1)$ and $y_2 = (v_2, w_2)$. Use syndrome list-decoding for the syndrome $v_1 - v_2 \in \mathbb{F}^{n-k}$ to recover a list $\mathcal{L} = \{e_1, \ldots, e_L\}$ of possible error vectors $e_i \in \mathbb{F}^n$ such that $Pe_i = v_1 - v_2$ and $\|e_i\|_0 \leq t$. Then
  - output 1, if there exists $e_i \in \mathcal{L}$ such that $g(e_i) = w_1 \div w_2$ and $e_i \in \{-1, 0, 1\}^n$,
  - otherwise output 0.

Fig. 2. Construction of (n, m)-RPPH for Hamming$_{n,t}$

– If $\|x_1 - x_2\|_0 > t$, then for all $e_i \in \mathcal{L}$, we have $\|e_i\|_0 \leq t$ and therefore $e_i \neq x_1 - x_2 \pmod{q}$. If there exists some i such that $e_i \in \{-1, 0, 1\}^n$ and $g(e_i) = g(x_1 - x_2)$ it means that we found a valid collision $e_i \neq (x_1 - x_2)$ in the hash function g. But, by collision resistance, the probability of this is negligible. Therefore, with overwhelming probability, no such index i exists and Eval will output 0.

Plugging in Facts 3 and 4, and using $Q = 3$, we obtain the following corollaries for PPH.

Corollary 4. *Assume the existence of a homomorphic CRHF with output length $\ell = \ell(\lambda)$. For all constants $0 < \rho < 1/2$ and $\eta > H_3^{\mathsf{BZ}}(\rho) \cdot (\log_2 3)$ (see Fact 3), for all polynomial n, there exists an efficient (n, m)-PPH for Hamming$_{n,t}$ with $t = \rho \cdot n$, having output length $m = \eta \cdot n + \ell$. In particular, for every constant $\eta > 0$, there exists some constant $\rho > 0$ such that the above holds.*

Corollary 5. *Assume the existence of a homomorphic CRHF with output length $\ell = \ell(\lambda)$. For all polynomial n and t, there exists an (n, m)-RPPH for Hamming$_{n,t}$ where $m = O(t \cdot \log n + \ell)$.*

In the case where $l = \rho \cdot n$ for a constant $\rho > 0$, the first corollary gives constant compression factor $\eta \approx H_3^{\mathsf{BZ}}(\rho) \cdot (\log_2 3)$. We know from our lower bound (Theorem 6) that we cannot do better than $\eta > H(\rho)$. The small gap between the constant in our upper bounds and lower bounds comes from: (1) the fact that current constructions of efficiently list-decodable linear codes are slightly sub-optimal compared to combinatorially (inefficiently) list-decodable counterparts, which reuslts in our upper bound having H^{BZ} instead of H, (2) the fact that our constructions of homomorphic hash functions work over $\mathbb{Z}_q$ for $q > 2$ rather than over $\mathbb{Z}_2$, which necessitates the $\log_2 3$ factor. It is plausible that future advances in list-decodable codes and homomorphic hashing could remove either/both of these gaps.

In the case of smaller distances t in the range $\ell < t < n^\varepsilon$ for some constant $\varepsilon > 0$, the lower bound (Theorem 6) shows that $m \geq t\log(n/t) = \Omega(t\log n)$, which essentially matches our upper bound of $m = O(t\log n)$, up to constant factors.

7 RPPH from Standard Collision Resistance

In this section, we present our construction of RPPH for exact Hamming distance from standard collision-resistant hash functions. We do so by starting with the construction of RPPH for gap Hamming distance due to Boyle, LaVigne, and Vaikuntanathan in [BLV19], and then showing how to generically upgrade an RPPH for gap Hamming to an RPPH for exact Hamming using syndrome decoding.

7.1 RPPH for Gap-Hamming

We start with a RPPH construction for $\mathrm{GAPHAMMING}_{n,t,\delta}$ described by Boyle, LaVigne, and Vaikuntanathan in [BLV19]. We give a generalized (and somewhat simplified) analysis of the construction that explicitly shows how the output length m scales as a function of the input length n, the distance t and the security parameter λ for general setting of parameters.

Theorem 10 (Generalizing [BLV19] Theorem 16). *Let λ be a security parameter and let $\delta > 0$ be a constant. Assuming CRHFs with output size $\ell = \mathrm{poly}(\lambda)$, for any $n = \mathrm{poly}(\lambda)$, any $0 < t < n$, there exists a (n,m)-RPPH for $\mathrm{GAPHAMMING}_{n,t,\delta}$ with output length $m = O((t\log\frac{n}{t} + \lambda)\ell)$.*

The main idea of the construction is to use a bipartite "expander graph" to map the n locations of the input into k subsets for some $k \ll n$. Then, we apply a standard CRHF on the bits of x in each of the k sets of locations and set the k CRHF outputs as the output of the RPPH. The expander ensures that there is some threshold μ such that:

- If x_1, x_2 differ in $\leq t$ locations then they will differ $< \mu \cdot k$ of the k subsets and therefore at most that many of the CRHF output will differ.
- If x_1, x_2 differ in $> (1 + \delta)t$ locations then they will differ $> \mu \cdot k$ of the k subsets and therefore at least that many of the CRHF output will differ.

This allows us to distinguish the two cases.

In [BLV19], they rely on standard expander graphs to achieve the above properties. We observe that the expansion is somewhat stronger than what we need: it guarantees that for *every* small set $S \subseteq [n]$, must have a large number of neighbors, whereas we only need this to hold when $|S| \geq (1+\delta)t$. As a result, we obtain a more straightforward analysis for the same construction and a more general range of parameters.

Definition 15. *Let $G = (L \cup R, E)$ be a bipartite graph with $E \subseteq L \times R$. For a set $S \subseteq L$ let $N(S) \subseteq R$ denote the neighbors of S. We say that G is (n, k, t, δ)-nice if it has $|L| = n, |R| = k$, and there exists some threshold $\mu > 0$ such that:*

1. *For every "small" $S \subseteq L$ such that $|S| \leq t$, we have $|N(S)| < \mu k$.*
2. *For every "large" $S \subseteq L$ such that $|S| \geq (1+\delta)t$ we have have $|N(S)| > \mu k$.*

We show that such nice graphs exist and can be sampled efficiently via a probabilistic argument. Indeed, a random graph is nice with overwhelming probability. We can rely on randomized constructions since we can include the description of the graph G as part of the description of the RPPH.

Lemma 3. *For any n, $0 < t < n$, and any constant $\delta > 0$, a (n, k, t, δ)-nice bipartite graph is efficiently constructible (with all but $e^{-\Omega(\lambda)}$ probability) with $k = O(t \log(n/t) + \lambda)$.*

Proof. We show that a random graph satisfies the requirement with all but negligible probability. Define the following constants that depend on δ:

$$\mu_0 = \frac{\delta}{2(1+\delta)^2}, \quad \mu_1 = (1 + \delta/2)\mu_0, \quad \rho = \frac{\delta}{4+\delta}, \quad \mu = (1+\rho)\mu_0 = (1-\rho)\mu_1.$$

Sample a bipartite graph $G = (L \cup R, E)$ with $|L| = n$, $|R| = k$, where for any $(v, w) \in L \times R$, the edge (v, w) is included in E independently with probability $p = \frac{\mu_0}{t}$. We show that this graph is (n, k, t, δ)-nice with overwhelming probability. We do so by showing that each of the two properties holds separately.

First, we show property 1 holds. Fix any set $S \subseteq L$ of size $|S| = t$. For any $w \in R$, we can rely on the union bound to show:

$$\Pr[w \in N(S)] = \Pr\left[\bigcup_{v \in S}(v, w) \in E\right] \leq \sum_{v \in S}\Pr[(v, w) \in E] \leq t \cdot p \leq \mu_0.$$

Define the indicator random variables X_w which are 1 iff $w \in N(S)$. Then these random variables are independent and $\mathbb{E}[\sum_{w \in R} X_w] = \mu_0 \cdot k$. By the Chernoff bound, we therefore have:

$$\Pr[\,|N(S)| \geq \mu \cdot k\,] = \Pr\left[\sum_{w \in R} X_w \geq (1+\rho)\mu_0 k\right] \leq \exp\left(-\rho^2 \mu_0 k/3\right).$$

Finally, by the union bound over all such sets S, we can bound the probability that property 1 does *not* hold by:

$$\Pr[\exists S \subseteq L, |S| = t \;:\; |N(S)| \geq \mu \cdot k] \leq \binom{n}{t} \cdot \exp\left(-\rho^2 \mu_0 k/3\right).$$

By choosing a sufficiently large $k = O(t \log \frac{n}{t} + \lambda)$, we can bound the above by $2^{-\Omega(\lambda)}$.

Second, we show property 2 holds. Fix any set $S \subseteq L$ of size $|S| \geq (1 + \delta)t$. For any $w \in R$, we can rely on the inclusion-exclusion principle to show:

$$
\begin{aligned}
\Pr[w \in N(S)] = \Pr\left[\bigcup_{v \in S} (v, w) \in E\right] \\
\geq \sum_{v \in S} \Pr[(v, w) \in E] - \sum_{v_1 \neq v_2 \in S} \Pr[(v_1, w) \in E \wedge (v_2, w) \in E] \\
\geq (1 + \delta)tp - [(1 + \delta)t]^2 p^2 \\
= (1 + \delta)tp - (\delta/2)tp \\
= (1 + \delta/2)tp = \mu_1.
\end{aligned}
$$

Define the indicator random variables X_w which are 1 iff $w \in N(S)$. Then these random variables are independent and $\mathbb{E}[\sum_{w \in R} X_w] = \mu_1 \cdot k$. By the Chernoff bound, we therefore have:

$$
\Pr[\, |N(S)| \leq \mu \cdot k \,] = \Pr\left[\sum_{w \in R} X_w \leq (1 - \rho)\mu_1 k\right] \leq \exp\left(-\rho^2 \mu_0 k/2\right).
$$

Finally, by the union bound over all such sets S, we can bound the probability that property 2 does *not* hold by:

$$
\Pr\left[\exists S \subseteq L, |S| = (1 + \delta)t \, : \, |N(S)| \geq \mu \cdot k\right] \leq \binom{n}{(1 + \delta)t} \exp\left(-\rho^2 \mu_0 k/2\right).
$$

By choosing a sufficiently large $k = O(t \log \frac{n}{t} + \lambda)$, we can bound the above by $e^{-\Omega(\lambda)}$.

Therefore, for each property, the probability that it fails to hold is negligible, and by the union bound, the probability that either property fails to hold is then also negligible. This shows that the samples graph G is (n, k, t, δ)-nice with all but $e^{-\Omega(\lambda)}$ probability.

The proof of Theorem 10 is similar to the proof of Theorem 16 in [BLV19], modulo parameter settings and the graph G defined above. We present the proof for completeness.

Proof (Proof of theorem 10). We show that the construction in Fig. 3 yields an RPPH construction. We split the proof of robustness into two cases:

- Suppose $x_1, x_2 \in \{0, 1\}^n$ satisfy $\|x_1 \oplus x_2\|_0 \leq t$. Let $S \subseteq L$ be the set of indices where x_1, x_2 differ, and $T = N(S)$. We have $|S| \leq t$. Since G is nice with overwhelming probability, by the first property we have $|T| < \mu k$ with overwhelming probability.

(n, m)-RPPH for GapHamming$_{n,t,\delta}$

Given parameters $n, 0 < t < n, \delta > 0$ and a CRHF family $(\mathsf{Samp}_{CR}, \mathcal{G})$:

- $\mathsf{Samp}(1^\lambda)$: Set $k = O(t \log \frac{n}{t} + \lambda)$ appropriately and sample a (n, k, t, δ)-nice bipartite graph $G = (L \cup R, E)$ per Lemma 3. Sample a CRHF $g \leftarrow \mathsf{Samp}_{CR}(1^\lambda)$ with output size $\ell = \ell(\lambda)$. Output $h = (G, g)$.
- $h(x)$: For every $j \in [k]$, compute the (ordered) set of neighbors of the j-th right vertex in G, denoted $N(j)$. Let $\hat{x}^{(j)} := x|_{N(j)}$ be x restricted to the set $N(j)$. Output $h(x) := g(\hat{x}^{(1)}), ..., g(\hat{x}^{(k)})$.
- $\mathsf{Eval}(h = (G, g), y_1, y_2)$. Parse $y_1 = (\hat{y}_1^{(1)}, ..., \hat{y}_1^{(k)})$ and $y_2 = (\hat{y}_2^{(1)}, ..., \hat{y}_2^{(k)})$. Compute

$$\Delta = \sum_{j=1}^{k} \mathbb{1}(\hat{y}_1^{(j)} \neq \hat{y}_2^{(j)})$$

Let μ be the threshold parameter for the (n, k, t, δ)-nice bipartite graph G per definition 15. If $\Delta \leq \mu k$, output 1. Otherwise, output 0.

Fig. 3. Construction of (n, m)-RPPH family for GapHamming$_{n,t,\delta}$ from CRHFs

Now for every $j \in R$ such that $j \notin T$, the subsampled values satisfy $\hat{x}_1^{(j)} = \hat{x}_2^{(j)}$ and in turn $\hat{y}_1^{(j)} = \hat{y}_2^{(j)}$. Therefore

$$\Delta = \sum_{j=1}^{k} \mathbb{1}(\hat{y}_1^{(i)} \neq \hat{y}_2^{(i)}) \leq |T| < \mu k$$

so Eval will output 1 with overwhelming probability.
- Now suppose $x_1, x_2 \in \{0, 1\}^n$ satisfy $\|x_1 \oplus x_2\|_0 \geq (1 + \delta)t$. Define S, T as above, then $|S| \geq (1 + \delta)t$. Since G is nice, by the second property we have $|T| > \mu k$, with overwhelming probability.
Now for every $j \in T$, $\hat{x}_1^{(j)} \neq \hat{x}_2^{(j)}$. We show that $\hat{y}_1^{(j)} \neq \hat{y}_2^{(j)}$ with all but negligible probability for (x_1, x_2) chosen by a PPT adversary. Suppose not, then the $\hat{x}_1^{(j)}, \hat{x}_2^{(j)}$ are a collision on the CHRF, which contradicts collision resistance.
Therefore with all but negligible probability for each $j \in T$ we have $\hat{y}_1^{(j)} \neq \hat{y}_2^{(j)}$. Using a union bound this holds for all $j \in T$ still with all but negligible probability, in which case $\Delta > \mu \cdot k$ and Eval will output 0.

7.2 From Gap-Hamming to Hamming

Now we are ready to use syndrome decoding to generically amplify any RPPH for gap Hamming distance to a RPPH for exact Hamming distance. In this section, we rely on unique decoding rather than list decoding.

(n, m)-RPPH for Hamming$_t$

Given n, $0 < t < n$: Let $\delta > 0$ be any constant. Fix a (n, m_{gap})-RPPH
($\mathsf{Samp}_{\mathsf{gap}}, \mathsf{Eval}_{\mathsf{gap}}$) for GapHamming$_{n,t,\delta}$ with output size m_{gap} and a
parity-check matrix $P \in \mathbb{F}_2^{(n-k) \times n}$ of a (n, k)-linear code that allows
efficient (unique) decoding up to $(1 + \delta)t$ errors.

- $\mathsf{Samp}(1^\lambda)$: Sample $g \leftarrow \mathsf{Samp}_{\mathsf{gap}}(1^\lambda)$. Output the hash function h
  defied below, whose description consists of the description of g.
- $h(x) := (Px, g(x))$.
- $\mathsf{Eval}(h, y_1, y_2)$: Parse $y_1 = (Px_1, g(x_1))$ and $y_2 = (Px_2, g(x_2))$.
  Let $s := Px_1 \oplus Px_2 = P(x_1 \oplus x_2)$. Apply syndrome decoding to
  obtain e such that $P \cdot e = s$ and $\|e\|_0 \leq (1 + \delta)t$, or output 0 if no
  such e exists. Set $b = \mathsf{Eval}_{\mathsf{gap}}(g, g(x_1), g(x_2))$. Then
  - output 1 if $\|e\|_0 \leq t$ and $b = 1$.
  - output 0 otherwise.

Fig. 4. Construction of RPPH for Hamming$_{n,t}$ from RPPH for GapHamming$_{n,t,\delta}$

Theorem 11. *Let λ be a security parameter and $\delta > 0$ be any constant. Assume
there exist a (n, m_{gap})-RPPH for GapHamming$_{n,t,\delta}$ with output size m_{gap} and
an efficiently decodable (n, k)-linear code that corrects up to $(1+\delta)t$ errors. Then
the construction in Fig. 4 is a (n, m)-RPPH for Hamming$_{n,t}$ with output length
$m = n - k + m_{gap}$.*

Proof. We analyze robustness. Suppose a PPT adversary $\mathcal{A}$ outputs $x_1, x_2 \in \{0, 1\}^n$:

- If x_1, x_2 satisfy $\|x_1 - x_2\|_0 \leq t$, then syndrome decoding of $s = P \cdot (x_1 - x_2)$
  always recovers $e = x_1 - x_2$, since $\|e\|_0 \leq t$. Now since g is a RPPH for
  GapHamming$_{n,t,\delta}$, by its robustness we have $\mathsf{Eval}_{\mathsf{gap}}(g, g(x_1), g(x_2)) = 1$
  with probability $1 - \mathsf{negl}(\lambda)$. Therefore $\mathsf{Eval}(h, h(x_1), h(x_2))$ will output 1
  with probability $1 - \mathsf{negl}(\lambda)$.
- If x_1, x_2 satisfy $\|x_1 - x_2\|_0 \geq t + 1$, we further distinguish between two cases:
  (1) If $t + 1 \leq \|x_1 - x_2\|_0 \leq (1 + \delta)t$, syndrome decoding always recovers
  $e = (x_1 - x_2)$ and $\|e\|_0 > t$ so Eval will output 0 with probability 1. (2) If
  $\|x_1 \oplus x_2\|_0 > (1 + \delta)t$, by the robustness of g, $\mathsf{Eval}_{\mathsf{gap}}(g, g(x_1), g(x_2)) = 0$
  with probability $1 - \mathsf{negl}(\lambda)$, so Eval will output 0 with probability at least
  $1 - \mathsf{negl}(\lambda)$.

Plugging in Theorem 10 along with Fact 4 to the above, and setting (e.g.,)
$\delta = 1$, gives the following corollary.

Corollary 6. *Assume there exists a CRHF with output length $\ell = \ell(\lambda)$. For any
polynomial n and t, there exists an (n, m)-RPPH for Hamming$_{n,t}$ with output
length $m = O(\ell \cdot t \cdot \log(n/t) + \ell \cdot \lambda)$.*

The above essentially matches the parameters of prior works [FS21, FLS22] that
relied on specific algebraic asssumptions: the q-Strong Bilinear Discrete Logarithm (q-SBDL) Assumption in the former case, and the Short-Integer Solution

(SIS) in the latter case. It also essentially matches (a generalized form of) the parameters achieved by the prior work of [BLV19] for gap Hamming distance, but does so for exact Hamming distance.

7.3 The Necessity of Collision-Resistance

We also show that collision-resistant hash functions are necessary for RPPH for Hamming distance, and therefore our construction above is based on a minimal assumption. This result follow implicitly as a special case of a result of [BLV19] (Corollary 30), but we include a simple stand-alone proof for completeness.

Theorem 12. *Let $n = n(\lambda)$ and $t = t(\lambda)$ be polynomials with $t < n/2$. Any (n, m)-RPPH for* HAMMING$_{n,t}$ *is also necessarily a collision-resistant hash function.*

Proof. First observe that for any $x_1, x_2 \in \{0, 1\}^n$ with $x_1 \neq x_2$ we can efficiently find y such that $||x_1 - y||_0 \leq t$ and $||x_2 - y||_0 > t$. In particular, if $||x_1 - x_2||_0 > t$ then $y = x_1$ satisfies this, and otherwise define y by flipping some arbitrary t positions of x_1 in which x_1, x_2 agree.

Now assume we have an RPPH construction which is not collision-resistant, meaning that there is some PPT $\mathcal{A}$ such that, given $h \leftarrow \mathsf{Samp}(1^\lambda)$, the output $(x_1, x_2) \leftarrow \mathcal{A}(h)$ is a valid collision with non-negligible probability, meaning: $x_1 \neq x_2$ and $h(x_1) = h(x_1)$. Whenever $\mathcal{A}(h)$ finds a valid collision (x_1, x_2), we can use it to find inputs on which the RPPH give the wrong answer. Namely, we can find y as above with $||x_1 - y||_0 \leq t$ and $||x_2 - y||_0 > t$. Then HAMMING$_{n,t}(x_1, y) \neq$ HAMMING$_{n,t}(x_2, y)$, but $\mathsf{Eval}(h, h(x_1), h(y)) = \mathsf{Eval}(h, h(x_2), h(y))$, since $h(x_1) = h(x_2)$. Therefore it must hold that for one of the input pairs (x_b, y) we have $\mathsf{Eval}(h, h(x_b), h(y)) \neq$ HAMMING$_{n,t}(x_b, y)$, meaning that we get a valid attack contradicting RPPH security.

8 Randomized Robust PPH (R2P2H)

In this section, we consider a randomized notion of RPPH, denoted R2P2H, where the hash function h itself can be a randomized function. For robustness, we assume that the adversary can choose the inputs x_1, x_2 adaptively depending on the description of h, but before knowing the internal randomness that will be used in the computations of $h(x_1), h(x_2)$. The adversary wins if $\mathsf{Eval}(h, h(x_1), h(x_2)) \neq P(x_1, x_2)$. Formally, the definition is identical to that in Sect. 3, with two modifications:

- We now allow the hash functions $h : \{0, 1\}^n \rightarrow \{0, 1\}^m$ to be randomized functions.
- The definition of robustness (Definition 9) is modified accordingly so that the probability is taken also over the internal randomness used in the computation of $h(x_1), h(x_2)$.

R2P2H is a relaxation of RPPH. At first sight, it may seem that allowing randomness does not alter the problem significantly, and that RPPH and R2P2H are "morally equivalent". This is not the case. On the positive side, for interesting regimes, RPPH is known to require collision-resistant hash functions, while R2P2H can be constructed information-theoretically. On the negative side, we caution that R2P2H provides qualitatively weaker security than RPPH. For deterministic RPPH, the security definition implicitly allows the adversary to choose x_2 after seeing $h(x_1)$, since the adversary can compute $h(x_1)$ himself. This is not the case for R2P2H, where seeing $h(x_1)$ can reveal something about the internal randomness used to compute it and could allow the adversary to find a bad x_2 that breaks security. Indeed, this will be the case for our construction.

The notion of R2P2H for the equality predicate was studied implicitly in [NS96,BK97,MNS08] and the connection was recently made explicit in [CN22].

Lemma 4. *Let* $T \subseteq [\ell]$ *be an arbitrary set of size* $|T| \geq \delta \cdot \ell$ *for some constant* $\delta > 0$. *Let* $S_A, S_B \subseteq [n]$ *be chosen as uniformly random and independent sets of size* $|S_A| = |S_B| = \sqrt{\lambda\ell}$ *where* $\ell > \lambda$. *Then* $\Pr[|S_A \cap S_B \cap T| = \emptyset] \leq 2^{-\Omega(\lambda)}$.

For lack of space, we defer the proof of the above lemma to the full version.

(n, m)-**R2P2H for Hamming**$_{n,t}$.

Notation: For a string $y \in \{0,1\}^\ell$ and a subset $S \subseteq [\ell]$, let $y_S \in \{0,1\}^{|S|}$ denote the bits of y in the positions indexed by S.
Scheme: Set $\ell = 2n$. Let $G \in \mathbb{F}_2^{\ell \times n}$ be the generator matrix of an $[\ell, n]_2$-code which with distance $\delta\ell$ for some constant $\delta > 0$. Let $P \in \mathbb{F}_2^{(n-k) \times n}$ be a parity check matrix of an $[n, k]_2$-linear code which is efficiently list decodable against t errors.

- $h(x)$: Choose a set $S \subseteq [\ell]$ of size $|S| = \sqrt{\lambda\ell}$ uniformly at random. Let $C(x) = G \cdot x$. Output $h(x) := (P \cdot x, S, C(x)_S)$
- $\mathsf{Eval}(y_1, y_2)$: Let $y_1 = (v_1, S_1, C(x_1)_{S_1})$ and $y_2 = (v_2, S_2, C(x_2)_{S_2})$. Let $S^* = S_1 \cap S_2$. Use syndrome list-decoding for the syndrome $v_1 - v_2$ to recover a list $\mathcal{L} = \{e_1, \ldots, e_L\}$ of possible error vectors $e_i \in \mathbb{F}_2^n$ such that $Pe_i = v_1 - v_2$ and $\|e_i\|_0 \leq t$.
  - output 1, if there exists some $e_i \in \mathcal{L}$ such that $C(e_i)_{S^*} = C(x_1)_{S^*} - C(x_2)_{S^*}$.
  - otherwise output 0.

Fig. 5. Construction of (n, m)-R2P2H for HAMMING$_{n,t}$

Theorem 13. *Let* λ *be a security parameter. For any polynomial* n, t, k *such that there exists an* $[n, k]_2$-*linear code which is efficiently list decodable against* t *errors, the construction above is a* (n, m)-*R2P2H for* HAMMING$_{n,t}$ *with output length* $m = O(\sqrt{\lambda n} \log n) + (n - k)$. *In particular: (1) there exist* (n, m)-*RPPH* for $\text{HAMMING}_{n,t}$ with output length $m = O(\sqrt{\lambda n} \log n) + 2t \log n$, and (2) for any constant $\eta > 0$, there exists some constant $\rho > 0$ such that there exist (n, m)-RPPH for $\text{HAMMING}_{n,t}$ with $t = \rho n$ and $m = O(\sqrt{\lambda n} \log n) + \eta \cdot n$.

Proof. Let $x_1, x_2 \in \mathbb{F}_2^n$ be arbitrary values. Let $y_1 = h(x_1)$ and $y_2 = h(x_2)$ with $y_1 = (v_1, S_1, C(x_1)_{S_1})$ and $y_2 = (v_2, S_2, C(x_2)_{S_2})$. Define T to be the set of locations where $C(e) \neq C(x_1 - x_2)$ We consider two cases:

- If $\|x_1 - x_2\|_0 \leq t$, then $e = x_1 - x_2 \in \mathcal{L}$ and $C(e)_{S^*} = C(x_1 - x_2)_{S^*} = C(x_1)_{S^*} - C(x_2)_{S^*}$. Therefore $\mathsf{Eval}(y_1, y_2)$ will output 1 with probability 1.
- If $\|x_1 - x_2\|_0 > t$, for any $e_i \in \mathcal{L}$, we have $\|e_i\|_0 \leq t$ and therefore $e_i \neq x_1 - x_2$. Define the set $T_i = \{j : C(x_1 - x_2)_j \neq C(e_i)_j\}$ of locations on which $C(x_1 - x_2)$ and $C(e_i)$ disagree. Since the minimum distance of the code is $\delta \ell$, we have $|T_i| > \delta \ell$. By Lemma 4, we have

$$\Pr[\exists i \in [L] S_1 \cap S_2 \cap T_i = \emptyset] \leq \sum_{i \in [L]} \Pr[S_1 \cap S_2 \cap T_i = \emptyset] \leq L 2^{-\Omega(\lambda)} = \mathsf{negl}(\lambda).$$

As long as the above event does not occur, $\mathsf{Eval}(y_1, y_2)$ will output 0, since for every $i \in [L]$ we have $S_1 \cap S_2 \cap T_i \neq \emptyset$ and therefore there exists some $j \in S^*$ such that $C(x_1)_j - C(x_2)_j \neq C(e_i)_j$. Overall, this shows that $\mathsf{Eval}(y_1, y_2) = 0$ with all but negligible probability.

References

[Ajt96] Ajtai, M.: Generating hard instances of lattice problems (extended abstract). In: 28th ACM STOC, pp. 99–108. ACM Press (1996)

[App] Apple csam detection. https://www.apple.com/child-safety/pdf/CSAM_Detection_Technical_Summary.pdf. Accessed 13 Feb 2022

[BK97] Babai, L., Kimmel, P.G.: Randomized simultaneous messages: solution of a problem of yao in communication complexity. In: Twelfth Annual IEEE Conference on Proceedings of Computational Complexity, pp. 239–246 (1997)

[BLV19] Boyle, E., LaVigne, R., Vaikuntanathan, V.: Adversarially robust property-preserving hash functions. In: Blum, A., (ed.) ITCS 2019, vol. 124, pp. 16:1–16:20. LIPIcs (2019)

[BZ82] Blokh, E.L., Zyablov, V.: Linear concatenated codes. Nauka (1982)

[CN22] Cohen, S.P., Naor, M.: Low communication complexity protocols, collision resistant hash functions and secret key-agreement protocols. Cryptol. ePrint Arch. Paper 2022/312, 2022. https://eprint.iacr.org/2022/312

[Cru] Apple's csam detection tech is under fire - again. https://techcrunch.com/2021/08/18/apples-csam-detection-tech-is-under-fire-again/. Accessed 13 Feb 2022

[DORS08] Dodis, Y., Ostrovsky, R., Reyzin, L., Smith, A.D.: Fuzzy extractors: how to generate strong keys from biometrics and other noisy data. SIAM J. Comput. **38**(1), 97–139 (2008)

[FLS22] Fleischhacker, N., Larsen, K.G., Simkin, M.: Property-preserving hash functions from standard assumptions. EUROCRYPT (2022)

[FS21]   Fleischhacker, N., Simkin, M.: Robust property-preserving hash functions for hamming distance and more. In: Canteaut, A., Standaert, F.-X. (eds.) EUROCRYPT 2021. LNCS, vol. 12698, pp. 311–337. Springer, Cham (2021). https://doi.org/10.1007/978-3-030-77883-5_11

[GHK10] Guruswami, V., Hastad, J., Kopparty, S.: On the list-decodability of random linear codes. In: Schulman, L.J. (ed.) Proceedings of the 42nd ACM Symposium on Theory of Computing, STOC 2010, Cambridge, Massachusetts, USA, 5–8 June 2010, pp. 409–416. ACM (2010)

[GR09]   Guruswami, V., Rudra, A.: Better binary list decodable codes via multilevel concatenation. IEEE Trans. Inf. Theory **55**(1), 19–26 (2009)

[IM98]   Indyk, P., Motwani, R.: Approximate nearest neighbors: towards removing the curse of dimensionality. In: Vitter, J.S., (ed.) Proceedings of the Thirtieth Annual ACM Symposium on the Theory of Computing, Dallas, Texas, USA, May 23–26, 1998, pp. 604–613. ACM (1998)

[KOR00] Kushilevitz, E., Ostrovsky, R., Rabani, Y.: Efficient search for approximate nearest neighbor in high dimensional spaces. SIAM J. Comput. **30**(2), 457–474 (2000)

[MNP07] Motwani, R., Naor, A., Panigrahy, R.: Lower bounds on locality sensitive hashing. SIAM J. Discret. Math. **21**(4), 930–935 (2007)

[MNS08] Mironov, I., Naor, M., Segev, G.: Sketching in adversarial environments. In: Ladner, R.E., Dwork, C., (eds.) 40th ACM STOC, pp. 651–660. ACM Press, May 2008

[NS96]   Newman, I., Szegedym M.: Public versus private coin flips in one round communication games (extended abstract). In: 28th ACM STOC, pp. 561–570. ACM Press, May 1996

[NYT]   Apple wants to protect children. but it's creating serious privacy risks. https://www.nytimes.com/2021/08/11/opinion/apple-iphones-privacy.html. Accessed 13 Feb 2022

[OWZ11] O'Donnell, R., Wu, Y., Zhou, Y.: Optimal lower bounds for locality sensitive hashing (except when q is tiny). In: Chazelle, B. (ed.) Innovations in Computer Science - ICS 2011. Tsinghua University, Beijing, China, January 7–9, 2011. Proceedings, pp. 275–283. Tsinghua University Press (2011)

[Ped92] Pedersen, T.P.: Non-interactive and information-theoretic secure verifiable secret sharing. In: Feigenbaum, J. (ed.) CRYPTO 1991. LNCS, vol. 576, pp. 129–140. Springer, Heidelberg (1992). https://doi.org/10.1007/3-540-46766-1_9

[Pet60] Peterson, W.: Encoding and error-correction procedures for the Bose-Chaudhuri codes. IRE Trans. Inf. Theory **6**(4), 459–470 (1960)

[RRR21] Reingold, O., Rothblum, G.N., Rothblum, R.D.: Constant-round interactive proofs for delegating computation. SIAM J. Comput. **50**(3) (2021)

[Scha]   Apple adds a backdoor to imessage and icloud storage. https://www.schneier.com/blog/archives/2021/08/apple-adds-a-backdoor-to-imesssage-and-icloud-storage.html. Accessed 13 Feb 2022

[Schb]   Apple's neuralhash algorithm has been reverse-engineered. https://www.schneier.com/blog/archives/2021/08/apples-neuralhash-algorithm-has-been-reverse-engineered.html. Accessed 13 Feb 2022

Collision-Resistance from Multi-Collision-Resistance

Ron D. Rothblum[1] and Prashant Nalini Vasudevan[2]($\boxtimes$)

[1] Technion, Haifa, Israel
rothblum@cs.technion.ac.il
[2] National University of Singapore, Singapore, Singapore
prashant@comp.nus.edu.sg

Abstract. Collision-resistant hash functions (CRH) are a fundamental and ubiquitous cryptographic primitive. Several recent works have studied a relaxation of CRH called *t-way multi-collision-resistant hash functions* (*t*-MCRH). These are families of functions for which it is computationally hard to find a *t*-way collision, even though such collisions are abundant (and even $(t-1)$-way collisions may be easy to find). The case of $t = 2$ corresponds to standard CRH, but it is natural to study *t*-MCRH for larger values of *t*.

Multi-collision-resistance seems to be a qualitatively weaker property than standard collision-resistance. Nevertheless, in this work we show a *non-blackbox* transformation of any moderately shrinking *t*-MCRH, for $t \in \{3, 4\}$, into an (infinitely often secure) CRH. This transformation is non-constructive – we can prove the existence of a CRH but cannot explicitly point out a construction.

Our result partially extends to larger values of *t*. In particular, we show that for suitable values of $t > t'$, we can transform a *t*-MCRH into a t'-MCRH, at the cost of reducing the shrinkage of the resulting hash function family and settling for infinitely often security. This result utilizes the list-decodability properties of Reed-Solomon codes.

1 Introduction

Collision-Resistant Hashing (CRH) is a fundamental primitive that is important throughout cryptography. These are functions that shrink their input but for which it is computationally infeasible to find two inputs (called "colliding" inputs) that map to the same output, even though many such pairs exist.

Recently, natural relaxations of such hash functions, called Multi-Collision-Resistant Hash Functions (*t*-MCRH for some integer *t*) have been studied [KNY17, BDRV18, BKP18, KNY18, KY18]. These are functions where it is computationally infeasible to find a set of *t* distinct inputs that are all mapped to the same output, even though many such collisions exist and moreover, it might even be possible to find sets of $(t-1)$ colliding inputs efficiently. Clearly, a CRH is a *t*-MCRH for any value of $t \geq 2$. In this paper, we address the question of whether the existence of a *t*-MCRH for some $t > 2$ implies the existence of a CRH.

© International Association for Cryptologic Research 2022
Y. Dodis and T. Shrimpton (Eds.): CRYPTO 2022, LNCS 13509, pp. 503–529, 2022.
https://doi.org/10.1007/978-3-031-15982-4_17

The existing evidence in this regard is ambiguous. In some important applications like constant-round statistically hiding commitments, CRH may be replaced by MCRH [BDRV18,KNY18]. Further, MCRH imply a different relaxation of CRH called distributional CRH [KY18]. Similar to CRH, there is also a blackbox separation between MCRH and one-way permutations [BDRV18,KNY18]. These suggest that MCRH might be as powerful as CRH.

On the other hand, CRH have properties that MCRH are not known to possess. For instance, it is well-known that for CRH, shrinkage of even a single bit suffices to construct a CRH of essentially any desired shrinkage (see [Gol04, Section 6.2.3] for details). Such a transformation for t-MCRH that preserves the number t of collisions resisted is not known. A non-trivial transformation that somewhat increases the t is known, however, if starting with a t-MCRH that already has substantial shrinkage [BKP18].

1.1 Our Results

Loosely speaking, we show that the existence of t-MCRH for $t = 3$ or 4 that are sufficiently shrinking implies the existence of CRH. Our proof of this is non-constructive and non-blackbox. It is non-constructive because, even when given an explicit t-MCRH, we can only prove that a CRH exists but cannot explicitly point out a specific construction. It is non-blackbox because we make non-blackbox use of a potential CRH adversary.

Before stating our results formally, we define these primitives. Throughout this work, for a function $h : \{0,1\}^n \to \{0,1\}^*$, integer $t \in \mathbb{N}$ and set $X \subseteq \{0,1\}^n$, we denote by t-coll$_h(X)$ the event that (1) $|X| = t$ and (2) $h(x) = h(x')$ for every $x, x' \in X$.

Definition 1. *For functions $t = t(n)$ and $\ell = \ell(n)$, a (t, ℓ)-multi-collision-resistant hash function ((t, ℓ)-MCRH) consists of a probabilistic polynomial-time algorithm* Gen *that on input 1^n outputs a circuit $h : \{0,1\}^n \to \{0,1\}^{n-\ell(n)}$ such that the following holds. For every family of polynomial-size circuits $A = (A_n)_{n \in \mathbb{N}}$, every polynomial p and all sufficiently large $n \in \mathbb{N}$, it holds that:*

$$\Pr_{\substack{h \leftarrow \mathsf{Gen}(1^n) \\ X \leftarrow A_n(h)}} [t\text{-coll}_h(X)] < 1/p(n). \tag{1}$$

Observe that for a (t, ℓ)-MCRH to be non-trivial, we need $\ell(n) \geq \log t(n)$. The standard definition of CRH is equivalent to $(2, 1)$-MCRH. As noted earlier, while a $(2, 1)$-MCRH can be used to construct a $(2, cn)$-MCRH for any $c < 1$, this is not known to be true for a $(t, \log t)$-MCRH for $t > 2$. This potentially qualitative difference between t-MCRH with different levels of shrinkage also shows up in the theorems we are able to prove in this paper. Thus, it is important to be explicit about the shrinkage ℓ of an MCRH in our terminology. (Nevertheless, in some informal discussions we may use the terminology t-MCRH without explicitly stating the shrinkage.)

Variants of MCRH. We also consider certain variants of the definition of MCRH. In an *infinitely-often* MCRH we require every adversary to fail on infinitely many

n's (rather than *all* sufficiently large n's). More precisely, we say that Gen is a (t, ℓ)-ioMCRH if Eq. (1) only holds for infinitely many n's (rather than all sufficiently large n's). Every MCRH is also an ioMCRH but the converse is not necessarily true.

We say that a hash function family is *non-uniform* if the sampling algorithm is non-uniform. That is, instead of an algorithm Gen that samples the hash functions h when run as Gen(1^n), there is a family of probabilistic circuits $(\mathsf{Gen}_n)_{n \in \mathbb{N}}$ such that Gen_n has size poly(n) and outputs h. In this work, we follow the standard practice of modeling adversaries as non-uniform circuits. Jumping ahead, as some of our constructions make use of a potential non-uniform adversary, the hash functions we construct will also be non-uniform.

Remark 1. Hsiao and Reyzin [HR04] consider a variant of CRH in which the adversary is given also the coins used by the generator to sample the hash function h. An analogous variant may be considered for MCRH (with or without the infinitely-often and non-uniform qualifiers). We remark that all of our results can be easily adapted to the [HR04] setting as well.

Main Results. With the above definitions in hand, we are ready to state our main results. The first result, which is easiest to state, is the construction of an (infinitely-often and non-uniform) CRH from a sufficiently shrinking 3-MCRH. Similar to standard CRH, the shrinkage of non-uniform infinitely often secure CRH can also be generically increased from a single bit to cn for any $c < 1$, so we often do not specify it. The parameters stated in the theorems below result in CRH with shrinkage $\Omega(\log n)$.

Theorem 1. *Suppose there exists a* $(3, n/2 + \omega(\log n))$*-MCRH. Then there exists a non-uniform ioCRH.*

The same conclusion also holds under the weaker assumption that the 3-MCRH in the hypothesis above is non-uniform and/or only infinitely-often secure (this is true for the remaining theorems as well). Given Theorem 1, it is natural to wonder for what values of t we can construct ioCRH from t-MCRH. Curiously, while we are able to show such an implication from a sufficiently shrinking 4-MCRH, our techniques stop working when $t \geq 5$.

Theorem 2. *Suppose there exists a* $(4, \frac{5}{6}n + \omega(\log n))$*-MCRH. Then there exists a non-uniform ioCRH.*

We discuss the limitation of our techniques to $t \leq 4$ in Sect. 4. Getting around this and constructing ioCRH from t-MCRH for larger constants t (let alone all constants or even super constant values of t) is an interesting open problem. Despite this restriction, for large enough constants t, we are able to show that t-MCRH generically implies t'-ioMCRH for many values of $t' < t$.

Theorem 3. *Consider any constants* t, k, $t_f \geq \max\left[(2t\sqrt{k-1})^{2/3}, 24\right]$, *and function* $\ell = \ell(n)$. *If there exists a* (t, ℓ)*-MCRH then there exists a* (t_f, ℓ_f)*-ioMCRH, for* $\ell_f(n) = \min\left[(\ell(n) - n/k), (\ell(kn) - n(k-1) - O(\log n))\right]$.

Theorem 3 is only meaningful if t is larger than t_f (and thus larger than 24). These bounds are not optimized, and our construction works for some smaller values of t and t_f as well. Starting with any (t, ℓ), the parameter k controls a tradeoff between the best values of t_f and ℓ_f we can obtain from the above theorem. It may be verified that, for the $\ell_f(n)$ above to be positive for some value of k, we need to start with an ℓ such that $\ell(n) > n/2$. With appropriate choices of the parameters, the theorem can be applied multiple times in sequence to get a (t'_f, ℓ'_f)-ioMCRH from the (t_f, ℓ_f)-ioMCRH for some $t'_f < t_f$, etc. For $t > 4$, however, there is no sequence of parameters that can be used to get all the way down to a $(2, 1)$-ioMCRH.

For an example of an instantiation, consider a 100-MCRH that has output of length $n/10$ – that is, a $(100, 9n/10)$-MCRH. With $k = 2$, noting that $(2 \cdot 100 \cdot 1)^{2/3} \approx 34$, the above theorem gives us a $(35, 4n/10)$-ioMCRH (ignoring additive $O(\log n)$ terms). Similarly, with $k = 4$ and $k = 9$, we can get a $(50, 6n/10)$-ioMCRH and a $(69, n/10)$-ioMCRH, respectively. Values of k outside the range $[2, 9]$ lead to negative values for $\ell_f(n)$ and thus do not result in shrinking hash functions.

1.2 Our Techniques

In this overview we focus on Theorem 1, that is, our approach for constructing an (infinitely-often and non-uniform) CRH from a 3-MCRH. Suppose we have a $(3, \ell)$-MCRH, for a shrinkage parameter $\ell = \ell(n)$ to be determined below. At a high-level, we will construct two families of functions such that if neither of them is a CRH, then 3-way collisions can be found in the original hash function family.

Our approach is inspired by a recent construction of Komargodski and Yogev [KY18] of *distributional* CRH from MCRH. Distributional CRH (or DCRH), introduced by Dubrov and Ishai [DI06], are a different relaxation of CRH in which it should be hard to find *random* collisions (although it may be easy to find some specific collisions). In contrast to [KY18] who construct (infinitely-often) DCRH from MCRH, we show that MCRH imply *worst-case* collision-resistance. We defer a thorough comparison of our techniques and results with those of [KY18] to Sect. 1.3.

The Candidate CRHs. Fix some input length n. Let $\mathcal{H} = \{h : \{0, 1\}^n \to \{0, 1\}^{n-\ell}\}$ be a $(3, \ell)$-MCRH (for simplicity we assume that the hash functions are sampled uniformly at random from this family). Since it may be possible to find 2-way collisions for functions in $\mathcal{H}$, we will have to modify $\mathcal{H}$. Toward this end we introduce an additional *non-cryptographic* function family $\mathcal{G} = \{g : \{0, 1\}^n \to \{0, 1\}^m\}$, with $m = m(n) < \ell(n)$. The exact properties that we need from $\mathcal{G}$, as well as setting of the parameter $m = m(n)$, will be specified below.

Thus, our first family of hash functions is $\mathcal{F} = \{f_{h,g} : \{0, 1\}^n \to \{0, 1\}^{n-\ell+m}\}$, where $h \in \mathcal{H}$, $g \in \mathcal{G}$. The evaluation $f_{h,g}(x)$ is simply the concatenation $f_{h,g}(x) = (h(x), g(x))$. There are two possibilities: either $\mathcal{F}$ is a CRH or it is not. If the former is true then we are done and so we might as well assume the latter. Namely, assume that there exists an efficient (non-uniform) adversary A that, given $f_{h,g} \in \mathcal{F}$ as input, outputs (x_0, x_1) such that $x_0 \neq x_1$ but $f_{h,g}(x_0) = f_{h,g}(x_1)$. For simplicity, let us assume that A is *perfect* – that is, that A finds a valid collision for *any* $f_{h,g} \in \mathcal{F}$.

We will use A – an adversary for $\mathcal{F}$ – to construct a second family of hash functions. We denote the family by $\mathcal{F}_A = \{f_{h,A} : \mathcal{G} \to \{0,1\}^{n-\ell}\}$. Each function $f_{h,A}$ takes as its input the description of a function g from $\mathcal{G}$, runs $A(f_{h,g})$ to get (x_0, x_1) – a collision for $f_{h,g}$ – and outputs $h(x_0)$. The fact that $\mathcal{F}_A$ depends on an adversary A is what makes our construction non-blackbox, non-uniform, and non-constructive. In particular, as the description of the family $\mathcal{F}_A$ involves the description of a purported adversary A for $\mathcal{F}$, unless this adversary were explicitly given, we would be unable to point out an explicit construction of $\mathcal{F}_A$ (even given $\mathcal{H}$).

What makes $\mathcal{F}_A$ interesting for our purposes is that, intuitively, a pairwise collision $g_0, g_1 \in \mathcal{G}$ for $\mathcal{F}_A$ actually specifies four inputs (namely, $(x_{00}, x_{01}) \leftarrow A(f_{h,g_0})$ and $(x_{10}, x_{11}) \leftarrow A(f_{h,g_1})$) that all collide under h. We will attempt to leverage this fact to argue that $\mathcal{F}_A$ must be collision-resistant.

Thus, assume toward a contradiction that $\mathcal{F}_A$ is not a CRH. That is, that there exists an efficient adversary A' that finds collisions for $\mathcal{F}_A$. We assume again that A' is also perfect in the same manner as A, and show how to use A' to find a 3-way collision for $\mathcal{H}$.

Finding 3-way Collisions. For any $h \in \mathcal{H}$, given A and A' as above, we can find a collision for h as follows:

1. Run $A'(f_{h,A})$ to get (g_0, g_1).
2. Run $A(f_{h,g_0})$ to get (x_{00}, x_{01}).
3. Run $A(f_{h,g_1})$ to get (x_{10}, x_{11}).
4. Identify three distinct elements among $\{x_{00}, x_{01}, x_{10}, x_{11}\}$ and output them if they exist.

We make the following observations about this procedure:

1. The fact that A finds valid collisions implies that $x_{00} \neq x_{01}$ and $x_{10} \neq x_{11}$.
2. The fact that g_0 and g_1 are a collision for $f_{h,A}$ implies that, whether given f_{h,g_0} or f_{h,g_1} as input, A will find collisions that have the same output under h – that is, $h(x_{00}) = h(x_{01}) = h(x_{10}) = h(x_{11})$.
3. The definition of f_{h,g_0} and f_{h,g_1} implies that $g_0(x_{00}) = g_0(x_{01})$ and $g_1(x_{10}) = g_1(x_{11})$. Further, the fact that A' finds valid collisions implies that $g_0 \neq g_1$.

Property 2 above implies that the set $X = \{x_{00}, x_{01}, x_{10}, x_{11}\}$ forms a collision under h, while Property 1 implies that X contains at least 2 distinct elements. Unfortunately though, nothing so far guarantees that this set contains *more* than 2 elements. A particularly alarming, but so far possible, scenario is that $x_{00} = x_{10}$ and $x_{01} = x_{11}$. Thus, it is not at all immediate that the set X contains a 3-way collision. This is the point where we will need to use special properties of the family of functions $\mathcal{G}$. In particular, we will choose $\mathcal{G}$ in such a way that Property 3 above will ensure that X does indeed contain a 3-way collision for h.

The Family $\mathcal{G}$. Let $\mathbb{F}$ denote the finite field of size $2^{n/2}$. Functions in $\mathcal{G}$ correspond to elements of $\mathbb{F}$. Thus, for each $\alpha \in \mathbb{F}$, there is a function $g_\alpha \in \mathcal{G}$, which is computed as follows. Given input $x \in \{0,1\}^n$, divide x into two halves $x_L, x_R \in \{0,1\}^{n/2}$ and interpret them as elements of $\mathbb{F}$ in the natural way. The evaluation of $g_\alpha(x)$ is simply the value of the line specified by (x_L, x_R) at the point α – that is, $g_\alpha(x) = x_L + \alpha \cdot x_R$ (computations performed over $\mathbb{F}$).

If for some $x_0, x_1 \in \{0,1\}^n$ and some $g_\alpha \in \mathcal{G}$ we have $g_\alpha(x_0) = g_\alpha(x_1)$, this implies that the lines specified by x_0 and x_1 intersect at $(\alpha, g_\alpha(x_0))$. Since any two distinct lines can intersect at at most one point, $\mathcal{G}$ has the following property: for any two distinct $x_0, x_1 \in \{0,1\}^n$, there is at most one function $g \in \mathcal{G}$ such that $g(x_0) = g(x_1)$.

Consider now the two pairwise collisions that we have: both $\{x_{00}, x_{01}\}$ and $\{x_{10}, x_{11}\}$ are pairs of distinct inputs such that $g_0(x_{00}) = g_0(x_{01})$ and $g_1(x_{10}) = g_1(x_{11})$. Suppose that these two sets are identical to one another: for example that $x_{00} = x_{10}$ and $x_{01} = x_{11}$. Since $g_0 \neq g_1$, this implies that there are two distinct functions in G such that x_{00} and x_{01} collide on them, a contradiction of the above property of G.

Thus, these two sets cannot be identical, implying that the set of collisions X above contains at least 3 distinct elements. This gives us a 3-way collision for h. We conclude that if $\mathcal{H}$ is a 3-MCRH, then either A or A' cannot exist. That is, either $\mathcal{F}$ is collision-resistant, or $\mathcal{F}_A$, constructed using the corresponding adversary A, is collision-resistant.

Shrinkage. It remains to argue that both $\mathcal{F}$ and $\mathcal{F}_A$ are in fact shrinking. As noted earlier, a CRH with one bit of shrinkage is sufficient to construct a CRH with essentially any desired shrinkage (and the same holds for non-uniform ioCRH). So it would be sufficient for $\mathcal{F}$ and $\mathcal{F}_A$ to shrink by even one bit.

By construction, functions in $\mathcal{G}$ map n-bit inputs to $n/2$-bit outputs. This means that $\mathcal{F}$ maps n bits to $(\frac{3}{2}n - \ell)$ bits and is shrinking as long as $\ell > n/2$. As noted above, each member of $\mathcal{G}$ is described by an element of $\mathbb{F}$, in other words a string of length $n/2$. Thus, functions in $\mathcal{F}_A$ map $n/2$ bits to $(n - \ell)$ bits. So again, if $\ell > n/2$, this is shrinking.

Coping with Imperfect Adversaries. Above, we assumed that the adversaries A and A' work perfectly – given a hash function, they always find a collision for it. This was done for simplicity of presentation here. In the actual construction, there are several difficulties that arise from dealing with imperfect adversaries. First, if A and A' are standard CRH adversaries, this would only imply that they find collisions for an infinite set of input lengths n, rather than all large enough n. We can only make the above arguments for the set of n's for which both of them work, and this set could well be empty. This is the reason that we can only argue that $\mathcal{F}$ or $\mathcal{F}_A$ is an *infinitely often* CRH rather than a standard CRH.

In addition, in the actual construction we only know that A succeeds with non-negligible probability, rather than with probability 1 as assumed above. This means that $\mathcal{F}_A$ might only be defined for a relatively small (but non-negligible) fraction of its domain. We resolve this second difficulty by showing how, in general, to transform collision-resistant hash functions that only work on a small subset of their domain, to full-fledged CRH. This transformation, which we find to be of independent interest, is based on the so-called "reverse randomization" technique, introduced by Lautemann [Lau83] and used in several works in cryptography since [Nao89, DNR04, DN07, BV17]. We defer the details to Sect. 2. We remark that this transformation introduces a small overhead and in particular leads to our hypothesis being that ℓ is larger than $n/2 + \omega(\log n)$ rather than just $n/2$ as above.

Improving Collision Resistance in General t-MCRH. A simple generalization of the above approach to getting a t_f-MCRH from a t-MCRH for some $t_f < t$ is to keep the construction as is and just change the arguments in the proof. Let $t_f = \lceil (t+1)/2 \rceil$, and let the families $\mathcal{F}$, $\mathcal{G}$, and $\mathcal{F}_A$ be just as defined above. If $\mathcal{F}$ were not a t_f-MCRH and $\mathcal{F}_A$ were not a CRH, then we can find a t-wise collision for functions in $\mathcal{H}$ in the same manner we found 3-wise collisions above – given $h \in \mathcal{H}$, find a pairwise collision (g_0, g_1) for $f_{h,A} \in \mathcal{F}_A$, and then for each g_b, find a t_f-wise collision $(x_{b1}, \ldots, x_{bt_f})$ for f_{h,g_b}. By the same argument as above, the sets $\{x_{0i}\}$ and $\{x_{1i}\}$ can have at most one element in common, and they all have the same value of $h(x_{bi})$. This gives a $(2t_f - 1)$-wise collision for h, which is a contradiction. Thus, either $\mathcal{F}$ is a t_f-MCRH or $\mathcal{F}_A$ is a CRH. The only guarantee we have, however, is that the weaker of these statements holds, meaning that a t_f-MCRH exists.

The price of this transformation is that the shrinkage of the resulting hash functions decreases by at least $n/2$ from that of $\mathcal{H}$, as this is the size of the output of functions in $\mathcal{G}$. For one, this precludes the transformation from being applied twice in order to get a t'_f-MCRH for some $t'_f < t_f$. In order to obtain better shrinkage and also to improve how much smaller t_f can be than t, we generalize our construction. For any $k \geq 2$, denote by $\mathbb{F}_k$ the finite field of size $2^{n/k}$ (assume that k divides n). Now, instead of $\mathcal{G}$ being the set of functions representing evaluations of lines in $\mathbb{F}_2$, we set it to be the functions representing evaluations of polynomials of degree $(k-1)$ over $\mathbb{F}_k$. That is, each function $g \in \mathcal{G}$ corresponds to an element $\lambda \in \mathbb{F}_k$, and given input $x \in \{0,1\}^n$, interprets it as a list of elements $x_0, \ldots, x_{k-1} \in \mathbb{F}_k$, and outputs $\sum_{i=0}^{k-1} x_i \lambda^i$.

Notice that the shrinkage of $\mathcal{F}$ is now $(\ell(n) - n/k)$, as opposed to the $(\ell(n) - n/2)$ earlier. The shrinkage of $\mathcal{F}_A$ can be computed to be $(\ell(kn) - n(k-1))$, which can be made better than $(\ell(n) - n/2)$ by an appropriate choice of k. We claim now that, for certain values of t_f, either $\mathcal{F}$ is a t_f-MCRH, or the $\mathcal{F}_A$ constructed using the corresponding adversary A is a t_f-MCRH. If they were not, given an $h \in \mathcal{H}$, we can proceed along the same lines as earlier to first get a set of functions $g_1, \ldots, g_{t_f} \in \mathcal{G}$ that collide under $\mathcal{F}_A$. Then, we can use A on each f_{h,g_i} to get t_f sets $X_i = \{x_{i1}, \ldots, x_{it_f}\}$, each of size t_f, such that all the x_{ij}'s have the same value under h and all the elements of each X_i have the same value under g_i.

If we can also prove that there are at least t distinct x_{ij}'s in the union of these sets, we would have a t-wise collision for h and thus a contradiction. Notice that each set X_i corresponds to a set of t_f polynomials (given by $x_{i1}, \ldots, x_{it_f}$) that all have the same evaluation at the field element, say λ_i, corresponding to g_i.

Thus we end up with the following question: given t_f sets X_i of t_f polynomials each and t_f pairs (λ_i, y_i) with the guarantee that for each $x \in X_i$ we have $x(\lambda_i) = y_i$, what is the smallest possible number of distinct polynomials in the union $\cup_{i=1}^{t_f} X_i$?

This is closely related to bounds on the list-decodability of Reed-Solomon codes, which we use to show that as long as t_f is at least roughly $(2t\sqrt{k-1})^{2/3}$, there have to be at least t distinct elements among the above sets. This gives us a transformation from t-MCRH to t_f-MCRH for such values of t, which is again much better than the transformation to $\lceil (t+1)/2 \rceil$-MCRH that followed from our original construction. We elaborate on this in Sect. 3.3. By paying attention to details, we show that this transformation can be used to go from a 4-MCRH to a 3-MCRH with a loss of $n/3$ in shrinkage, and then on to a CRH with an additional loss of $n/2$. This approach, however, cannot be used to get a CRH starting from a 5-MCRH. We discuss this barrier in Sect. 4.

1.3   Related Work

Multi-Collision-Resistance was first studied by Joux [Jou04], who showed that for a certain class of hash functions called iterated hash functions, certain collision-finding attacks can be augmented to find multi-collisions without much overhead. Subsequent work has studied similar attacks on some other specific classes of hash functions [NS07, YW07, ...]. The formal theoretical study of MCRH began with the work of Komargodski et al. [KNY17], who defined MCRH and showed connections to problems arising from Ramsey theory.

A more detailed study of MCRH was done later in three concurrent and independent works [BKP18, KNY18, BDRV18]. Berman *et al.* [BDRV18] showed that $(n^2, \sqrt{n})$-MCRH can be constructed from the hardness of a variant of the Entropy Approximation problem [DGRV11]. Both Berman *et al.* and Komargodski *et al.* [BDRV18, KNY18] showed that constant-round statistically hiding commitment schemes can be constructed from MCRH with various parameters, which implies a blackbox separation between such MCRH and one-way permutations [HHRS15]. This separation extends the well-known separation between CRH and one-way permutations [Sim98]. The latter separation was also extended in other directions by Bitansky and Degwekar [BD19].

Komargodski *et al.* also showed how to use MCRH to construct succinct argument-systems. Additionally, they claimed to show a blackbox separation between CRH and $(3, n/2)$-MCRH, but there is a gap in the proof [BD19, Per], and for the time being such a separation is not known.

Bitansky *et al.* [BKP18] studied MCRH and also considered a keyless version of MCRH. They used both variants to construct round-efficient succinct zero-knowledge arguments. Notably, they use the keyless version of MCRH to construct 3-message zero-knowledge arguments. Holmgren and Lombardi [HL18] showed how to construct MCRH (and even CRH) from exponentially secure one-way functions with certain direct product properties.

The paper closest to ours is that of Komargodski and Yogev [KY18] on distributional CRH (DCRH). DCRH, first defined by Dubrov and Ishai [DI06], is a relaxation of CRH where the adversary's task is to sample a *random* collision – given a function h, to sample (x, x') where x is a uniformly random input and x' is uniformly random conditioned on $h(x) = h(x')$. Whereas with some primitives like one-way functions the distributional version implies the full-fledged one [IL89], this is not known to be the case with CRH. See also Bitansky *et al.* [BHKY19] for more recent work on DCRH.

Detailed Comparison with [KY18]. Komargodski and Yogev show that the existence of a $(t, \Omega(n))$-MCRH for any constant t implies the existence of an infinitely often DCRH.[1] Their construction is also non-explicit and non-blackbox, and their approach is quite similar to ours. Our results are technically incomparable – they obtain a weaker primitive (DCRH as opposed to our CRH), but they can work with any t-MCRH, whereas we are limited to 4-MCRH. We describe their approach at a high level here and discuss the salient differences.

Let $\mathcal{H} = \{h : \{0,1\}^n \rightarrow \{0,1\}^{n/2}\}$ be a $(3, n/2)$-MCRH. They also construct two families of hash functions such that at least one of them has to be a DCRH. The first family is $\mathcal{H}$ itself. Suppose $\mathcal{H}$ is not a DCRH and there is an adversary A that samples uniformly random collisions for $h \in \mathcal{H}$. Note that A is necessarily randomized. Without loss of generality (by padding), we can assume that the number ρ of random bits that A uses is larger than n. The second family of hash functions is then defined as $\mathcal{H}_A = \{f_{h,A} : \{0,1\}^\rho \rightarrow \{0,1\}^{n/2}\}$, where $h \in \mathcal{H}$. The function $f_{h,A}(r)$ is computed by first running $A(h;r)$ to get a collision (x_0, x_1), and then outputting $h(x_0)$.

If $\mathcal{H}_A$ is also not a DCRH, then there is another adversary A' that finds random collisions for $f_{h,A} \in \mathcal{H}_A$. This A' can be used to find a pair of uniformly random (r_0, r_1) such that $A(h; r_0)$ and $A(h; r_1)$ both find collisions that have the same output under h. That is, if $(x_{00}, x_{01}) \leftarrow A(h; r_0)$ and $(x_{10}, x_{11}) \leftarrow A(h; r_1)$, then $h(x_{00}) = h(x_{01}) = h(x_{10}) = h(x_{11})$. Further, as r_0 and r_1 are uniformly random upto this condition, and A also samples uniformly random collisions, this set of x's is also random conditioned on colliding under h. Thus, with very high probability, they will all be distinct, giving a 3-way collision for h.

Essentially, the work of our family of functions $\mathcal{G}$ is here performed by the randomness of the distributional collision-finding adversary A. Such a distributional adversary is much more powerful than the normal collision-finding adversary that we have access to. The distinctness of the collisions found comes for free with a distributional adversary, whereas we have to use $\mathcal{G}$ to get it. It also enables the constructed DCRH above to not lose any shrinkage compared to the original 3-MCRH. This allows them to start from $(t, \Omega(n))$-MCRH for any

---

[1] Their paper states this theorem for $(t, n/2)$-MCRH, but their proof immediately extends to any $(t, \Omega(n))$-MCRH. They define MCRH security as holding only against uniform adversaries and thus obtain a uniform i.o. DCRH secure against uniform adversaries. Under our definition of MCRH with security against non-uniform adversaries, their approach would also result in a non-uniform construction secure against non-uniform adversaries. They also construct DCRH from the average-case hardness of problems in SZK, but this result is not relevant here.

constant t and iteratively perform the above process to eventually get a DCRH, while the best we can do is start from a $(4, 5n/6)$-MCRH.

1.4   Open Questions

We show using non-blackbox techniques that CRH exist assuming the existence of sufficiently shrinking 3-MCRH (or 4-MCRH). This indicates that blackbox separations are not necessarily the last word in classifying the power of cryptographic primitives. Still, our proof is non-constructive. The question that follows immediately from this observation is whether an explicit construction of CRH from MCRH is possible.

Question 1. Can *explicit* CRH (or even ioCRH) be constructed from 3-MCRH?

The answer to this question is unclear to us. If it were positive, such a construction, apart from being useful in obtaining explicit and usable CRH, would likely require novel and interesting techniques.

The other direction in which our results can be improved is constructing primitives that are secure in the standard cryptographic sense rather than only infinitely often secure. Infinitely often security (or hardness) comes up regularly in cryptography and complexity theory, and we are not aware of any techniques to convert such security to standard security without additional assumptions. Being able to construct such primitives is also likely to require new and interesting techniques.

Question 2. Can a standard (as opposed to i.o.) CRH be constructed from a 3-MCRH?

The third obvious question arising from our work is to construct a CRH from t-MCRH for $t > 4$, even assuming the best possible shrinkage. As discussed in Sect. 4, our approach itself is not sufficient for this purpose and new techniques, or at least non-trivial modifications to ours, will be needed here.

Question 3. Can CRH be constructed from $(t, n - \mathsf{polylog}(n))$-MCRH for all constant t?

Apart from these, there are several adjacent questions about the primitives we deal with here. As noted above, Berman et al. [BDRV18] construct n^2-MCRH from assumptions about problems related to the complexity class SZK. Their construction does not extend to t-MCRH for constant t, and it would be interesting to see whether something like this is possible.

Question 4. Can t-MCRH for some constant t be constructed based on the average-case hardness of the Entropy Approximation problem (or the variant used by [BDRV18])?

Perhaps the most intriguing question is whether the classic separation of CRH from one-way permutations [Sim98] can be side-stepped using non-blackbox techniques such as those in this paper. Even a non-constructive answer to this question would be pivotal to our understanding of the relative power of these key cryptographic primitives.

Question 5. Can non-blackbox techniques be used to construct CRH (or even MCRH) from One-Way Permutations?

Unfortunately, while our techniques are non-blackbox, they still relativize – they work in the presence of any oracle that the construction and adversaries may have access to. The existing separation [Sim98] essentially demonstrates an oracle relative to which one-way permutations exists but CRH's do not. Thus, our approach cannot be used as is to get around it.[2]

An interesting approach towards answering this question was formulated by Holmgren and Lombardi [HL18], who showed that exponentially secure one-way functions with strong enough direct product properties can be used to construct CRH (or MCRH if starting from a weaker security property). They point out that proving that one-way permutations have such properties would then answer the above question.

1.5   Organization

In Sect. 2 we define *partial domain* MCRH (resp., CRH) and show how to transform such hash functions to standard, full domain MCRH (resp., CRH). This notion, and the transformation, are important for our main results – the transformations from t-MCRH to t_f-MCRH for suitable $t_f < t$, which are presented in Sect. 3. Finally, in Sect. 4 we show some inherent barriers to our approach.

2   Partial Domain MCRH

In this section we introduce and study *partial-domain* MCRH. Loosely speaking, these are MCRH defined over only a (potentially small) part of their domain. The main result shown in this section is a transformation from such partial-domain MCRH to full-fledged MCRH – a transformation that will be used to establish our main theorems in Sect. 3. We remark that an impatient reader can skip directly to Sect. 3 after reviewing only the definition of partial-domain MCRH.

A *partial domain* MCRH $\mathcal{H} = (\mathcal{H}_n)_{n \in \mathbb{N}}$ is defined similarly to an MCRH except that for every $h \leftarrow \mathsf{Gen}(1^n)$, some of the inputs in the domain of h may be defined as "invalid". On such invalid inputs the hash function outputs $h(x) = \bot$. A collision finding adversary for such a partial domain MCRH needs to find a tuple of *valid* colliding inputs. We require that the number of valid inputs is a noticeable fraction of the domain. We proceed to the formal definition.

---

[2] Thanks to Iftach Haitner for pointing this out to us.

Definition 2. *A partial-domain (t, ℓ)-MCRH consists of a probabilistic polynomial-time algorithm* Gen *that on input 1^n outputs a circuit $h : \{0,1\}^n \to (\{0,1\}^{n-\ell} \cup \{\bot\})$ such that the following holds.*

1. *For every family of polynomial-size circuits $A = (A_n)_{n\in\mathbb{N}}$, every polynomial p and all sufficiently large $n \in \mathbb{N}$ it holds that:*

$$\Pr_{\substack{h \leftarrow \mathsf{Gen}(1^n) \\ X \leftarrow A_n(h)}} \left[\left(t\text{-coll}_h(X)\right) \text{ and } \left(\forall i \in [t], \ h(x_i) \neq \bot\right) \right] < 1/p(n). \qquad (2)$$

2. *There exists a polynomial q such that with all but negligible probability over $h \leftarrow \mathsf{Gen}(1^n)$ it holds that $\left|\{x \in \{0,1\}^n : h(x) \neq \bot\}\right| \geq \frac{1}{q(n)} \cdot 2^n$.*

To highlight the distinction from partial domain MCRH, we will sometimes refer to a standard MCRH as a *full domain* MCRH. We also generalize the definition of partial domain to the case of infinitely often MCRH and non-uniform MCRH in the natural way. We emphasize that the extension of Definition 2 to the infinitely often case requires Condition 1 to hold infinitely often, whereas Condition 2 remains unchanged – that is, it should hold for all sufficiently large n.

The following lemma shows how to transform a partial domain MCRH to a full domain MCRH. The proof technique is based on Lautemann's [Lau83] proof that BPP is contained in the polynomial hierarchy (this technique has been used in several works in cryptography since then [Nao89, DNR04, DN07, BV17]).

Lemma 1. *If there exists a partial domain (t, ℓ)-MCRH, then there exists a full domain $(t, \ell - O(\log(n)))$-MCRH. The same is true if both the initial and resulting MCRH are non-uniform and/or merely ioMCRH.*

Proof (Proof of Lemma 1). We prove the lemma with respect to standard MCRH. The proof extends readily also to non-uniform and/or ioMCRH.

Let Gen be the sampling algorithm for a partial domain (t, ℓ)-MCRH and let $q = q(n)$ be the polynomial guaranteed in the definition (i.e., for all but a negligible fraction of hash functions at least $2^n/q(n)$ of the inputs are valid). We construct a new *full domain* hash function family using a sampling algorithm Gen′ as follows.

On input 1^n, the algorithm Gen′ first invokes $\mathsf{Gen}(1^n)$ to obtain a hash function $h : \{0,1\}^n \to \{0,1\}^{n-\ell}$. The algorithm further samples $z_1, \ldots, z_k \in \{0,1\}^n$, where $k = 2n \cdot q(n)$. The algorithm constructs a hash function h' that on input x, outputs $h'(x) = \left(h(x \oplus z_i), i\right) \in \{0,1\}^{n-\ell} \times \{0, \ldots, k\}$, were i is the minimal index such that $h(x \oplus z_i) \neq \bot$ and in case no such i exists it outputs a default value $(0,0)$. We will sometimes denote the hash function by $h' = (h, z_1, \ldots, z_k)$ and note that $h' : \{0,1\}^n \to \{0,1\}^{n-\ell+O(\log n)}$.

Denote the subset of hash functions in the support of $\mathsf{Gen}(1^n)$ for which at least $1/q(n)$ fraction of the inputs are valid by H. By definition of partial domain MCRH we have that:

Claim 1. $\Pr_{h \leftarrow \mathsf{Gen}(1^n)}[h \notin H] = \mathrm{negl}(n)$.

Next we argue that for $h \in H$, with overwhelming probability over the z_i's, no input for the hash function $h' = (h, z_1, \ldots, z_k)$ is mapped to the default value.

Claim 2. *For every $h \in H$, with all but 2^{-n} probability over $z_1, \ldots, z_k$, no input for the hash function $h' = (h, z_1, \ldots, z_k)$ is mapped to the default value.*

Proof. For every fixed $x \in \{0,1\}^n$ and every $i \in [k]$, the probability over z_i that $h(x \oplus z_i) = \bot$ is at most $1 - 1/q(n)$. Therefore, the probability that $h(x \oplus z_i) = \bot$ for *all* $i \in [k]$ is at most $(1 - 1/q(n))^{2n \cdot q(n)} \leq 2^{-2n}$. The claim follows by taking a union bound over all $x \in \{0,1\}^n$.

Consider $h' = (h, z_1, \ldots, z_k) \in H$ such that no input is mapped to the default value. In such a case, every t-way collision $\{x_1, \ldots, x_t\}$ for h' must satisfy that $h(x_1 \oplus z_i) = h(x_2 \oplus z_i) = \cdots = h(x_t \oplus z_i)$ for some $i \in [k]$. Thus, we have a t-way collision $\{x_1 \oplus z_i, \ldots, x_t \oplus z_i\}$ of size t also for h.

Applying Claims 1 and 2, we conclude that a collision finding algorithm wrt Gen', which succeeds with probability $\epsilon = \epsilon(n)$, yields a collision finding algorithm for Gen that succeeds with probability $\epsilon(n) - \mathrm{negl}(n) - 2^{-n}$ and the lemma follows.

3   Improving Collision-Resistance in MCRH

In this section, we prove Theorems 1 to 3 (which were stated in Sect. 1.1). We start by setting up a common framework for the proofs of all of the theorems. The proofs of Theorems 1 to 3 will be completed in Sects. 3.1 to 3.3, respectively.

Setup. Consider a constant t and a (shrinkage) function $\ell : \mathbb{N} \to \mathbb{N}$. Let t_f and k parameters that will be determined later such that $k < t_f < t$. Define the function $\ell_f(n) = \min [\ell(n) - n/k, \ell(kn) - n(k-1)]$. Let Gen be (a sampler for) a (t, ℓ)-ioMCRH. We will use Gen to construct a (t_f, ℓ_f)-ioMCRH.[3] Below, when it is clear from the context, we sometimes use ℓ as a shorthand for $\ell(n)$. For simplicity, we will assume that k, whatever it is set to, divides n; our proof can be easily extended to work when this is not the case.

Let $\mathbb{F}$ be the finite field of size $2^{n/k}$.[4] We view an input $x \in \{0,1\}^n$ for a hash function $h \leftarrow \mathsf{Gen}(1^n)$ as representing a degree $(k-1)$ univariate polynomial over $\mathbb{F}$ as follows: x is interpreted as a vector $(x_0, \ldots, x_{k-1}) \in \mathbb{F}^k$, and the polynomial is defined as $P_x(\xi) = \sum_{i=0}^{k-1} x_i \cdot \xi^i$ (where the arithmetic is over the field). For ease of notation, for $\lambda \in \mathbb{F}$, we use $x(\lambda)$ to denote the evaluation of the polynomial P_x at the point λ.

---

[3] Actually, it may be the case that the shrinkage of the hash function we construct is *larger* than this ℓ_f. In such a case, we can simply pad the output of the hash function with 0's to ensure that the shrinkage is exactly ℓ' (without any effect on its collision-resistance properties).

[4] We assume the field elements can be represented using $\log_2(|\mathbb{F}|)$ bits (in the natural way) and that field operations (i.e., arithmetic operations as well as sampling of random field elements) can be performed in $\mathsf{polylog}(|\mathbb{F}|)$ time. See, e.g., [Sho88] for details.

The First Hash Family. We construct a new hash function family defined by the sampler Gen′ that, on input 1^n, works as follows:

1. Invoke Gen(1^n) to obtain a hash function $h : \{0,1\}^n \to \{0,1\}^{n-\ell}$.
2. Sample a random $\lambda \in \mathbb{F}$.
3. Output the hash function[5] $h' : \{0,1\}^n \to \{0,1\}^{n-\ell+n/k}$ defined as $h'(x) = \big(h(x), x(\lambda)\big)$.

If Gen′ is a (t_f, ℓ')-ioMCRH, where $\ell'(n) = (\ell(n) - n/k)$, then we are done. Thus, we may assume that it is not – namely, that there exists a polynomial-size circuit family $A' = (A'_n)_{n \in \mathbb{N}}$ and a polynomial p' such that for all sufficiently large $n \in \mathbb{N}$ it holds that:

$$\Pr_{\substack{h' \leftarrow \mathsf{Gen}'(1^n) \\ X \leftarrow A'_n(h')}} \left[t_f\text{-coll}_{h'}(X) \right] \geq \frac{1}{p'(n)}. \tag{3}$$

Using the definition of h', Eq. (3) can be rewritten as:

$$\Pr_{\substack{h \leftarrow \mathsf{Gen}(1^n) \\ \lambda \leftarrow \mathbb{F} \\ X \leftarrow A'_n(h,\lambda)}} \left[\big(t_f\text{-coll}_h(X)\big) \text{ and } \big(\forall x_1, x_2 \in X, \; x_1(\lambda) = x_2(\lambda)\big) \right] \geq \frac{1}{p'(n)}. \tag{4}$$

For every h in the support of Gen(1^n), define:

$$\delta_h = \Pr_{\substack{\lambda \leftarrow \mathbb{F} \\ X \leftarrow A'_n(h,\lambda)}} \left[\big(t_f\text{-coll}_h(X)\big) \text{ and } \big(\forall x_1, x_2 \in X, \; x_1(\lambda) = x_2(\lambda)\big) \right].$$

Thus, Eq. (4) implies that $\mathbb{E}_{h \leftarrow \mathsf{Gen}(1^n)}[\delta_h] \geq \frac{1}{p'(n)}$. We shall aim to restrict our attention to hash functions h for which δ_h is relatively large (i.e., close to the expectation). The following lemma describes a sampling algorithm for such hash functions.

Lemma 2. *There exists a probabilistic polynomial time algorithm $\widetilde{\mathsf{Gen}}$ that on input 1^n outputs a hash function $h : \{0,1\}^n \to \{0,1\}^{n-\ell}$ in the support of Gen(1^n) such that the following holds for all sufficiently large n:*

– $\Pr_{h \leftarrow \widetilde{\mathsf{Gen}}(1^n)}\left[\delta_h > \frac{1}{4p'(n)} \right] = 1 - 2^{-\Omega(n)}.$
– *For every event E:*

$$\Pr_{h \leftarrow \mathsf{Gen}(1^n)} \left[h \in E \right] \geq \frac{1}{3p'(n)} \cdot \Pr_{h \leftarrow \widetilde{\mathsf{Gen}}(1^n)} \left[h \in E \right] - 2^{-\Omega(n)}.$$

The first item in Lemma 2 states that with very high probability, a hash function h sampled by $\widetilde{\mathsf{Gen}}$ has relatively large δ_h. The second item relates the distributions Gen and $\widetilde{\mathsf{Gen}}$ and in particular implies that events that happen with non-negligible probability over the latter also happen with non-negligible probability

---

[5] Note that for Gen′ to be non-trivial we must have $\ell(n) > n/k$.

over the former. The proof of Lemma 2 is deferred to Sect. 3.4 but on first reading, the reader may find it convenient to think of the simpler case in which all h have $\delta_h \geq \frac{1}{4p'(n)}$ in which case we can simply take $\widetilde{\mathsf{Gen}} = \mathsf{Gen}$.

The Second Hash Family. We now use the adversary A' to construct a new *partial domain non-uniform hash function family* defined by a sampler $\mathsf{Gen}'' = (\mathsf{Gen}''_n)_{n \in \mathbb{N}}$ as follows. The sampler[6] $\mathsf{Gen}''_{n/k}$ works as follows:

1. Invoke $\widetilde{\mathsf{Gen}}(1^n)$ to obtain a hash function $h : \{0,1\}^n \to \{0,1\}^{n-\ell}$.
2. Output a hash function[7] $h'' : \{0,1\}^{n/k} \to (\{0,1\}^{n-\ell}) \cup \{\perp\}$ that is computed as follows:
   - The input to h'', which is a vector in $\{0,1\}^{n/k}$, is interpreted as a field element $\lambda \in \mathbb{F}$ in the natural way (recall that $|\mathbb{F}| = 2^{n-k}$).
   - To hash λ, first invoke[8] $A'_n(h, \lambda)$ and then consider two cases:
     (a) Case 1: If $A'_n(h, \lambda)$ outputs $X \subseteq \{0,1\}^n$ such that $t_f\text{-coll}_h(X)$ and $\forall x_1, x_2 \in X$, $x_1(\lambda) = x_2(\lambda)$. In such a case $h''(\lambda)$ outputs $h(x)$ for an arbitrary $x \in X$ (the specific choice does not matter since all elements in X collide under h).
     (b) Case 2: If $A'_n(h, \lambda)$ does not generate an output as above (which can be easily tested in polynomial-time) $h''(\lambda)$ outputs $\perp$.

Recall that we currently have two assumptions in place – Gen is a (t, ℓ)-ioMCRH and Gen' is *not* a (t_f, ℓ')-ioMCRH, with the above A' being the corresponding adversary. Under these assumptions we will prove the following lemma.

Lemma 3. Gen'' *is a partial-domain non-uniform* (t_f, ℓ'')-ioMCRH, *where* $\ell''(n) = \ell(kn) - n(k-1)$.

Lemma 3, for various values of t and t_f, together with with transformation of partial-domain MCRH into full-domain MCRH (Lemma 1), implies Theorems 1 to 3. To prove it, we will need to show that Gen'' satisfies the two conditions from Definition 2, and that it has shrinkage ℓ''. The latter follows by construction. We will show in Proposition 1 that Gen'' satisfies Condition 2 of Definition 2 irrespective of the choice of t_f and k. The proof that Gen'' satisfies Condition 1 is where the proofs of the three theorems diverge. For different values of t_f and k, the fact that it does is proven in Sects. 3.1 to 3.3, leading to Theorems 1 to 3.

Proposition 1. *There exists a polynomial q such that, for all sufficiently large n, with all but negligible probability over $h'' \leftarrow \mathsf{Gen}''_n$, it holds that $\left| \{x \in \{0,1\}^n : h''(x) \neq \perp\} \right| \geq \frac{1}{q(n)} \cdot 2^n$.*

---

[6] For sake of consistency we define the hash function w.r.t. "security parameter" n/k, since its domain is $\{0,1\}^{n/k}$.

[7] As in Footnote 5, this is only interesting if $\ell(n) > (n - n/k)$.

[8] This is the point where we use the adversary in a non-blackbox manner. Since the adversary is non-uniform, this also makes the construction non-uniform.

Proof. By the first item in Lemma 2, with all but $2^{-\Omega(n)}$ probability over $h \leftarrow \widetilde{\text{Gen}}(1^n)$ it holds that $\delta_h \geq 1/(4p'(n))$. If $\delta_h \geq 1/(4p'(n))$ then the corresponding h'' (that is output by $\text{Gen}''_{n/k}$ when it samples h from $\widetilde{\text{Gen}}(1^n)$) does not output $\perp$ on an inverse polynomial fraction of its domain. Thus, Gen'' satisfies the requirements of the proposition.

3.1   From 3-MCRH to CRH $(t = 3, t_f = 2)$

In this subsection, we prove that Gen'' satisfies Condition 1 of Definition 2 under the parameter setting $t = 3$, $t_f = 2$, and $k = 2$. This is stated in the following proposition. This proves Lemma 3 under this setting, which, together with Lemma 1, completes the proof of Theorem 1.

Proposition 2. *Let $t = 3$ and $k = 2$. For every family of polynomial-size circuits $A'' = (A''_n)_{n \in \mathbb{N}}$, every polynomial p'' and infinitely many $n \in \mathbb{N}$ it holds that:*

$$\Pr_{\substack{h'' \leftarrow \text{Gen}''_n \\ (\lambda_1, \lambda_2) \leftarrow A''_n(h'')}} \left[(\lambda_1 \neq \lambda_2) \text{ and } (h''(\lambda_1) = h''(\lambda_2) \neq \perp) \right] < 1/p''(n).$$

Proof. Fix a hash function $h'' \leftarrow \text{Gen}''_{n/k}(1^{n/k})$ and consider a pair $\lambda_1, \lambda_2 \in \mathbb{F}$ such that $\lambda_1 \neq \lambda_2$ and $h''(\lambda_1) = h''(\lambda_2) \neq \perp$. Let $\{x_{1,1}, x_{1,2}\} = A'_n(h, \lambda_1)$ and $\{x_{2,1}, x_{2,2}\} = A'_n(h, \lambda_2)$. Recall that h'' can be recast as a function $h \leftarrow \widetilde{\text{Gen}}(1^n)$.

Claim 3. *The set $\{x_{i,j}\}_{i,j \in \{1,2\}}$ contains a 3-way collision for h.*

Proof. Since $h''(\lambda_1) \neq \perp$ we have that $x_{1,1} \neq x_{1,2}$ but $h(x_{1,1}) = h(x_{1,2})$ and $x_{1,1}(\lambda_1) = x_{1,2}(\lambda_2)$. Similarly, since $h''(\lambda_2) \neq \perp$, we have that $x_{2,1} \neq x_{2,2}$ but $h(x_{2,1}) = h(x_{2,2})$ and $x_{2,1}(\lambda_1) = x_{2,2}(\lambda_2)$. In addition, since $h''(\lambda_1) = h''(\lambda_2)$ we have that $h(x_{1,1}) = h(x_{2,1})$. Overall, this means that $h(x_{1,1}) = h(x_{1,2}) = h(x_{2,1}) = h(x_{2,2})$ so all of the elements do indeed collide.

Thus we only need to show that the set $\{x_{1,1}, x_{1,2}, x_{2,1}, x_{2,2}\}$ contains at least 3 distinct elements. Suppose that $x_{1,1} = x_{2,1}$ and $x_{1,2} = x_{2,2}$ (the other case is handled similarly). In such a case we have that the line $x_{1,1}$ and the line $x_{1,2}$, which are distinct lines, agree on the distinct points λ_1 and λ_2. But this is a contradiction since two distinct lines (i.e., degree 1 polynomials) can agree on at most one point.

Thus, the existence of an adversary A'' contradicting the proposition's hypothesis immediately yields a method for finding a 3-way collision for a random $h \leftarrow \widetilde{\text{Gen}}(1^n)$, with probability at least $1/p''(n)$, for all sufficiently large n. By the second item of Lemma 2, this method also works for $h \leftarrow \text{Gen}(1^n)$ with probability at least $\frac{1}{3p'(n) \cdot p''(n)} - 2^{-\Omega(n)}$ (again, for all sufficiently large n) – a contradiction.

3.2   From 4-MCRH to 3-MCRH $(t = 4, t_f = 3)$

Having handled the case of $t = 3$, we proceed to the special case of $t = 4$. We show how to transform a sufficiently shrinking 4-MCRH into a 3-ioMCRH. If the latter is sufficiently shrinking, we can then apply Theorem 1 to obtain an ioCRH.

Thus, we need to show that Gen'' satisfies Condition 1 of Definition 2 under the parameter setting $t = 4$, $t_f = 3$, and $k = 3$. This is stated in the following proposition. This proves Lemma 3 under this setting, which, together with Lemma 1, completes the proof of Theorem 1.

Proposition 3. *Let $t = 4$ and $k = 3$. For every family of polynomial-size circuits $A'' = (A_n'')_{n \in \mathbb{N}}$, every polynomial p'' and infinitely many $n \in \mathbb{N}$ it holds that:*

$$\Pr_{\substack{h'' \leftarrow \text{Gen}_n'' \\ (\lambda_1, \lambda_2, \lambda_3) \leftarrow A_n''(h'')}} \left[(\lambda_1, \lambda_2, \lambda_3 \text{ are distinct}) \text{ and } (h''(\lambda_1) = h''(\lambda_2) = h''(\lambda_3) \neq \bot) \right] < 1/p''(n).$$

As the proof mirrors that of Proposition 2, we provide only a sketch.

Proof (Proof Sketch). Similarly to Proposition 2, each λ_i yields a 3-way collision $x_{i,1}, x_{i,2}, x_{i,3}$ and the set $\{x_{i,j}\}_{i, \in \{1,2,3\}}$ all collide on h. What remains to be shown is that this set contains 4 distinct elements.

Suppose not. Then, wlog, it must be the case that $x_{1,1} = x_{2,1} = x_{3,1}$, $x_{2,1} = x_{2,2} = x_{2,3}$ and $x_{1,3}, = x_{2,3} = x_{3,3}$. Each one of $x_{1,1}, x_{1,2}, x_{1,3}$ specifies a degree $k - 1$ polynomial, that is, a quadratic polynomial. Thus, we have 3 distinct quadratic polynomials that agree on the 3 points $\lambda_1, \lambda_2, \lambda_3$ – a contradiction.

Overall, we get that a 3-way collision finder for Gen'' yields a 4-way collision finder for $\widetilde{\text{Gen}}$, and therefore, as in the proof of Proposition 2, also for Gen.

Overall, this yields a $(3, \ell_f - O(\log n))$-ioMCRH from a $(4, \ell)$-MCRH, where $\ell_f = \min[\ell(n) - n/3, \ell(3n) - 2n]$. In particular, if $\ell(n) > \frac{5}{6} \cdot n + \omega(\log n)$, we get that $\ell_f > \frac{1}{2}n + \omega(\log n)$. At this point we can apply Theorem 1 to derive a (non-uniform) ioMCRH, thereby establishing Theorem 2.

3.3   From General t-MCRH to t_f-MCRH

In this subsection, we consider a generic constant t and show that Gen'' satisfies Condition 1 of Definition 2 under the certain settings of t_f and k. This is captured by the following lemma.

Lemma 4. *Consider any t, k, and $t_f \geq \max\left[(2t\sqrt{k-1})^{2/3}, 24\right]$. For every family of polynomial-size circuits $A'' = (A_n'')_{n \in \mathbb{N}}$, every polynomial p, and infinitely many $n \in \mathbb{N}$, it holds that.*

$$\Pr_{\substack{h'' \leftarrow \text{Gen}''(1^n) \\ X \leftarrow A_n''(h'')}} \left[(t_f\text{-coll}_{h''}(X)) \text{ and } (\forall i \in [t], \, h''(x_i) \neq \bot) \right] < 1/p(n). \quad (5)$$

Under the above setting of parameters, Lemma 3 follows from Lemma 4. Combined with Lemma 1 (the partial to full domain transformation), this completes the proof of Theorem 3. The proof of Lemma 4 makes use of list-decoding bounds for Reed-Solomon codes.

Proof. Assume toward a contradiction that there exists a polynomial-size circuit family $A'' = (A_n'')_{n \in \mathbb{N}}$ and a polynomial p'' such that for all sufficiently large $n \in \mathbb{N}$ it holds that:

$$\Pr_{\substack{h'' \leftarrow \mathsf{Gen}_{n/k}'' \\ \Lambda \leftarrow A_{n/k}''(h'')}} \left[(t_f\text{-coll}_{h''}(\Lambda)) \text{ and } (\forall \lambda \in \Lambda : h''(\lambda) \neq \bot) \right] \geq 1/p''(n).$$

Fix a large enough n such that both $A_{n/k}''$ and A_n' have such non-negligible success probability. Fix also an h in the support of $\widetilde{\mathsf{Gen}}(1^n)$ and the corresponding h'' (that is output by $\mathsf{Gen}_{n/k}''$ when it samples h from $\widetilde{\mathsf{Gen}}(1^n)$) such that for the $\Lambda = \{\lambda_1, \ldots, \lambda_{t_f}\}$ output by $A_{n/k}''(h'')$, the conditions in the above probability statement hold. Denote $X_i = A_n'(h, \lambda_i)$.

Claim 4. *It holds that:*

1. *For every $i \in [t_f]$, the set X_i contains t_f distinct elements and for every $x_1, x_2 \in X_i$ it holds that $x_1(\lambda_i) = x_2(\lambda_i)$.*
2. *For every $i, j \in [t_f]$ and $x_1 \in X_i$, $x_2 \in X_j$ it holds that $h(x_1) = h(x_2)$.*

Proof. The fact that the event $t_f\text{-coll}_{h''}(\Lambda)$ holds implies that all of the λ_i's are distinct but $h''(\lambda_1) = \cdots = h''(\lambda_{t_f}) \neq \bot$. By the definition of Gen'', this means that for every $i \in [t_f]$, it holds that $A'(h, \lambda_i)$ outputs a set $X_i = \{x_{i,1}, \ldots, x_{i,t_f}\}$ such that $t_f\text{-coll}_{(h,\lambda_i)}(X_i)$. This implies Item 1 in the claim as well as the fact that $h(x_{i,j}) = h(x_{i,j'})$ for every $i, j, j' \in [t_f]$.

On the other hand, the fact that $h''(\lambda_1) = \cdots = h''(\lambda_t) \neq \bot$ means that $h(x_{1,1}) = \cdots = h(x_{t_f,1})$. Overall, we conclude that *all* of the $x_{i,j}$'s collide under h. This establishes Item 2.

Let $X \subseteq \{0,1\}^n$ be the multi-set $X = \cup_{i \in [t_f]} X_i$. We emphasize that X is a multi-set, where the *multiplicity* of an element $x \in X$ is equal to the number of $i \in [t_f]$ such that $x \in X_i$. The following proposition shows that X contains a t-way collision for h.

Proposition 4. $t\text{-coll}_h(X)$ *holds.*

Proof. By Item 2 in Claim 4, all elements in the set X indeed collide under h and so we only need to show that the set contains at least t *distinct* elements. Define a function $f : \Lambda \to \mathbb{F}$ as $f(\lambda_i) = x_i(\lambda_i)$, where x_i is an arbitrary element in X_i (by Item 1 in Claim 4, the specific choice does not matter). Let $d = k - 1$. Let $X_{close} \subseteq X$ denote the set of points $x \in X$ such that x, viewed as a degree d polynomial over $\mathbb{F}$, agrees with f on at least $\sqrt{2t_f d}$ points in Λ. By construction, all $x \in X \backslash X_{close}$ have multiplicity at most $\sqrt{2t_f d}$.

Claim 5. *The number of* distinct *elements in X_{close} is at most $\sqrt{2t_f/d}$.*

This claim follows immediately from the following lemma of Sudan [Sud97], which is a special case of an earlier lemma of Goldreich *et al.* [GRS00].[9]

Lemma 5 ([Sud97, GRS00]). *Let $\mathbb{F}$ be a finite field and let $\{(x_i, y_i)\}_{i=1}^n \in (\mathbb{F} \times \mathbb{F})^n$ be a sequence of N pairs. The number of degree d polynomials f such that $|\{i : f(x_i) = y_i\}| \geq \sqrt{2dN}$ is at most $\sqrt{2N/d}$.*

Thus, the multi-set X, which contains $(t_f)^2$ elements overall (counting multiplicities), has at most $\sqrt{2t_f/d}$ elements with multiplicity at least $\sqrt{2t_f d}$. This means that the number of distinct elements in X is at least:

$$\frac{(t_f)^2 - \sqrt{2t_f/d} \cdot t_f}{\sqrt{2t_f d}} \geq \frac{(t_f)^{3/2}}{2\sqrt{d}} \geq t$$

where the first inequality holds for any $t_f \geq 24$ and $d \geq 1$, and the second inequality follows from the condition in the hypothesis that $t_f \geq (2t\sqrt{k-1})^{2/3}$.

Thus, under the assumption that such an A'' exists, we are able to find a t-way collision for a random $h \leftarrow \widetilde{\mathsf{Gen}}(1^n)$ with probability at least $1/p''(n)$ for all large enough n. By the second item of Lemma 2, this method also works for $h \leftarrow \mathsf{Gen}(1^n)$ with probability at least $\left(\frac{1}{3p'(n)\cdot p''(n)} - 2^{-\Omega(n)}\right)$ for all large enough n – a contradiction to our assumption that Gen is a (t, ℓ)-ioMCRH. So such an A'' cannot exist, which proves Lemma 4.

3.4   Proof of Lemma 2

Consider the following basic process $\mathsf{Gen}_0(1^n)$ (this is not yet the eventual process $\widetilde{\mathsf{Gen}}$ which we need to show in order to prove Lemma 2).

$\mathsf{Gen}_0(1^n)$:

1. Sample $h \leftarrow \mathsf{Gen}(1^n)$.
2. Sample $\lambda_1, \ldots, \lambda_\ell \leftarrow \mathbb{F}$, where $\ell = \Theta((p'(n))^2 \cdot n \cdot r(n))$ where r is a polynomial bounding the number of random coins that $\mathsf{Gen}(1^n)$ uses. Use $\lambda_1, \ldots, \lambda_\ell$ to compute an approximation $\hat{\delta}_h$ for δ_h by setting

$$\hat{\delta}_h = \frac{1}{\ell} \cdot \left|\left\{i \in [\ell] : (t_f\text{-coll}_h(X)) \text{ and } (\forall x_1, x_2 \in X, \ x_1(\lambda_i) = x_2(\lambda_i)), \text{ where } X \leftarrow A'_n(h, \lambda_i)\right\}\right|.$$

3. If $\hat{\delta}_h > 1/(3p'(n))$ output h otherwise output $\perp$.

---

[9] Sudan additionally established bounds on the *algorithmic* list-decoding properties of Reed-Solomon codes, whereas for our purposes a combinatorial bound (such as that established in [GRS00]) suffices.

Denote by $p_\perp = \Pr[\mathsf{Gen}_0(1^n) = \perp]$. Let μ denote the distribution obtained by sampling from $\mathsf{Gen}_0(1^n)$ conditioned on *not* getting $\perp$.

Proposition 5. $p_\perp \leq 1 - 1/(3p'(n))$.

Proof. Since $E_{h \leftarrow \mathsf{Gen}(1^n)}[\delta_h] \geq 1/p'(n)$ (see Eq. (4)), by Markov's inequality, with probability $1/2p'(n)$ over $h \leftarrow \mathsf{Gen}(1^n)$ it holds that $\delta_h \geq 1/(2p'(n))$.

Assume that such an h is sampled in Step 1 of $\mathsf{Gen}_0(1^n)$. By the Chernoff bound, the probability that it passes the check in Step 2 is at least 0.99. In case these two events occur the process outputs $h \neq \perp$ and so we have that $p_\perp \leq 1 - 1/(3p'(n))$. $\qquad\blacksquare$

Proposition 6. *For every event E it holds that:*

$$\Pr_{h \leftarrow \mathsf{Gen}(1^n)}[h \in E] \geq (1 - p_\perp) \cdot \Pr_{h \leftarrow \mu}[h \in E].$$

Proof. By linearity, it suffices to prove the claim for the case that $E = \{h\}$ is a singleton. Furthermore, we can view the distribution μ as sampling from $\mathsf{Gen}_0(1^n)$ repeatedly until a function $h \neq \perp$ is obtained. With that in mind we have that

$$\Pr[\mu = h] = \sum_{i=0}^{\infty} \Pr[\mu \text{ outputs } h \text{ in iteration } i+1 \text{ and } \perp \text{ in all previous iterations}]$$

$$= \sum_{i=0}^{\infty} \Pr[\mathsf{Gen}_0(1^n) = h] \cdot (p_\perp)^i$$

$$\leq \Pr[\mathsf{Gen}(1^n) = h] \cdot \frac{1}{1 - p_\perp},$$

where the final inequality follows from the fact that $\Pr[\mathsf{Gen}_0(1^n) = h] \leq \Pr[\mathsf{Gen}(1^n) = h]$ and a standard bound on the sum of a geometric series. $\qquad\blacksquare$

Consider the "rejection sampling with cutoff" sampler $\widetilde{\mathsf{Gen}}(1^n)$ defined as follows:

1. Repeat $\Theta(p'(n) \cdot n)$ times:
   (a) Sample $h \leftarrow \mathsf{Gen}_0(1^n)$.
   (b) If $h \neq \perp$ output h and abort. Otherwise continue to the next iteration.
2. If this step has been reached, then output some default hash function in the support of $\mathsf{Gen}(1^n)$.

Note that $\widetilde{\mathsf{Gen}}$ can indeed be implemented in probabilistic polynomial-time.

Proposition 7. *The statistical distance between μ and $\widetilde{\mathsf{Gen}}(1^n)$ is at most $2^{-\Omega(n)}$.*

Proof. The statistical distance between the two distributions is equal to the probability that $\widetilde{\mathsf{Gen}}$ gets to Step 2. It follows from Proposition 5 that the latter probability is bounded by $(1 - 1/(3p'(n)))^{\Omega(p'(n) \cdot n)} \leq 2^{-\Omega(n)}$.

Combining Propositions 5 to 7 we have that for every event E,

$$\Pr_{h \leftarrow \mathsf{Gen}(1^n)} [h \in E] \geq (1 - p_\perp) \cdot \Pr_{h \leftarrow \mu} [h \in E]$$

$$\geq \frac{1}{3p'(n)} \cdot \Pr_{h \leftarrow \mu} [h \in E]$$

$$\geq \frac{1}{3p'(n)} \cdot \Pr_{h \leftarrow \widetilde{\mathsf{Gen}}(1^n)} [h \in E] - 2^{-\Omega(n)}. \tag{6}$$

This establishes the second part of Lemma 2. The following proposition establishes also the first part.

Proposition 8. $\Pr_{h \leftarrow \widetilde{\mathsf{Gen}}(1^n)} \left[\delta_h < \frac{1}{4p'(n)} \right] = 2^{-\Omega(n)}.$

Proof. Fix h with $\delta_h < \frac{1}{4p'(n)}$. For $\mathsf{Gen}_0(1^n)$ to output h, the approximation must deviate by at least an $\frac{1}{12p'(n)}$ factor which, by the Chernoff bound, happens with probability at most $2^{-(2n+p'(n)+r(n))}$.

By taking a union bound over the $O(p'(n) \cdot n)$ iterations in $\widetilde{\mathsf{Gen}}(1^n)$, the probability that an h as above is sampled by the rejection sampling process is at most $\frac{O(p'(n) \cdot n)}{2^{2n+p'(n)+r(n)}} \leq 2^{-(n+r(n))}$. By another application of the union bound we have that:

$$\Pr_{h \leftarrow \widetilde{\mathsf{Gen}}(1^n)} \left[\delta_h < \frac{1}{4p'(n)} \right] = \sum_{h \,:\, \delta_h < \frac{1}{4p'(n)}} \Pr[\widetilde{\mathsf{Gen}}(1^n) = h] \leq 2^{r(n)} \cdot 2^{-(n+r(n))} = 2^{-n}.$$

Lemma 2 follows from Eq. (6) and Proposition 8.

4 Limitations of Our Approach

In this section, we discuss why our approach to constructing a CRH (more precisely a non-uniform ioCRH) cannot work when starting from a t-MCRH for $t > 4$. Our discussion will not be completely formal, but should convince the reader of this claim. We will consider, in fact, a generalization of the construction presented in previous sections that uses an unspecified (list-decodable) code rather than the Reed-Solomon code. For simplicity, we go back some of the assumptions made in the presentation in Sect. 1.2 – that we start with a (t, ℓ)-MCRH that simply samples uniformly random functions from a set $\mathcal{H} = \{ h : \{0,1\}^n \to \{0,1\}^{n-\ell} \}$, and that all collision-finding adversaries below are perfect. Say we wish to construct from this a (t_f, ℓ_f)-ioMCRH for some $t_f \leq t$.

Formalizing Our Approach. The generalized version of our construction may be described as follows. Let C be a code with message length of n bits and codewords of length N over an alphabet Σ. In particular, C is a subset of Σ^N of size 2^n. (The constructions in Sect. 3 correspond to taking C to be the Reed-Solomon code of various degrees over fields of characteristic 2.) We will also write $C(x)$ for an $x \in \{0,1\}^n$ to denote the codeword that x is mapped to by the code. Our construction defines the following families of functions:

- $\mathcal{G} = \{g_\lambda : \{0,1\}^n \to \Sigma\}_{\lambda \in [N]}$: for any $x \in \{0,1\}^n$ and $\lambda \in [N]$, $g_\lambda(x)$ is the λth symbol of $C(x)$.
- $\mathcal{F} = \{f_{h,g} : \{0,1\}^n \to \{0,1\}^{n-\ell} \times \Sigma\}_{h \in \mathcal{H}, g \in \mathcal{G}}$: $f_{h,g}(x)$ is simply the concatenation $(h(x), g(x))$. Suppose $\mathcal{F}$ is not a t_f-ioMCRH, and the corresponding adversary is A.
- $\mathcal{F}_A = \{f_{h,A} : [N] \to \{0,1\}^{n-\ell}\}_{h \in \mathcal{H}}$: given input $\lambda \in [N]$, the function $f_{h,A}$ first runs $A(h, g_\lambda)$ to get $x_1, \ldots, x_{t_f} \in \{0,1\}^n$, and outputs $h(x_1)$. (Here g_λ is the function corresponding to λ in $\mathcal{G}$.)

We would like to show then that if $\mathcal{F}$ is not a t_f-ioMCRH and $\mathcal{F}_A$ constructed using the adversary A is also not a t_f-ioMCRH, then we can find t-wise collisions for functions in $\mathcal{H}$, which is a contradiction. In order to do this, we make use of the collision-finding adversary A' for $\mathcal{F}_A$. The process then proceeds as follows:

1. Given an $h \in \mathcal{H}$, first run $A'(f_{h,A})$ to get functions $g_1, \ldots, g_{t_f} \in \mathcal{G}$ that collide under $f_{h,A}$.
2. Then, for each g_i, run $A(f_{h,g_i})$ to get a set $X_i = \{x_{i1}, \ldots, x_{it_f}\}$ whose elements collide under f_{h,g_i}.
3. If there are t distinct elements in the union $\cup_{i=1}^{t_f} X_i$, output them.

Arguments outlined in Sect. 1.2 and Sect. 3 explain why all the x_{ij}'s have the same output under h, and only the following question remains: can we ensure that there are indeed t distinct elements among the X_i's while $\mathcal{F}$ and $\mathcal{F}_A$ are both shrinking? Note that the shrinkage of $\mathcal{F}$ is $(\ell - \log|\Sigma|)$, and that of $\mathcal{F}_A$ is $(\log N - (n - \ell))$.

The question of the existence of t distinct x_{ij}'s may be recast as follows. We are given t_f sets of codewords $C_i = \{c_{i1}, \ldots, c_{it_f}\}$, where each of the t_f codewords in C_i are distinct. Each C_i corresponds to a statement that, for some $\lambda_i \in [N]$ (where the λ_i's are distinct), all the codewords in C_i agree on the λ_i^{th} coordinate. In other words, there are t_f tuples $(\lambda_i, y_i) \in [N] \times \Sigma$ such that for all $c_{ij} \in C_i$, we have $c_{ij}[\lambda_i] = y_i$. We would then like to claim that there is no set of codewords $T \subseteq C$ such that $|T| < t$, for each i we have $C_i \subseteq T$, and still $c_{ij}[\lambda_i] = y_i$ for all $i, j \in [t_f]$. At the very least, this requires that no set of $(t-1)$ codewords agree on t_f coordinates.

Optimality of Current Choices. It turns out, however, that (an extension of) the Singleton bound implies that in order for this to happen for $t_f < t$, the alphabet Σ has to be quite large, thus implying an upper bound on the shrinkage of the resulting family $\mathcal{F}$. Let us start with the simple case of $t = 3$ and $t_f = 2$. Here, the condition stated above becomes the following: any 2 codewords agree on at most 1 coordinate. In other words, the distance of the code has to be at least $(N-1)$.

Proposition 9. *In any code $C \subseteq \Sigma^N$ where $|C| = 2^n$ and any 2 codewords agree on at most 1 coordinate, it has to be that $|\Sigma| \geq 2^{n/2}$.*

Proof. This is simply the Singleton bound. Consider truncating all the codewords in C to the first two coordinates. As no two codewords agree on more than one coordinate, this set of truncated codewords still has no repetitions and so has size at least 2^n. This implies that $|\Sigma|^2 \geq 2^n$, which implies that $|\Sigma| \geq 2^{n/2}$.

Proposition 9 implies that the shrinkage of $\mathcal{F}$ is $(\ell - \log|\Sigma|) \leq (\ell - n/2)$. In particular, this says that using a different code in place of the Reed-Solomon code (of degree 1 in this case) in our transformation from $(3, \ell)$-MCRH to CRH cannot improve the shrinkage ℓ that we can start with.

We can similarly show that our choices in our transformation from 4-MCRH to CRH were also close to optimal. To start with, note that we cannot use our approach to go directly from 4-MCRH to CRH. This would require showing that 2 sets C_i of size 2 each have *no* intersection, which implies that for any codeword $c \in C$, there exists at most one λ for which there is some c' such that $c[\lambda] = c'[\lambda]$. A simple counting argument shows that this cannot happen unless $|\Sigma| \geq 2^n$, at which point all shrinkage is lost.

So to get a CRH from a 4-MCRH, we have to construct a 3-MCRH first. The following proposition implies that the loss in shrinkage in going from a 4-MCRH to a 3-MCRH is at least $n/3$ irrespective of the choice of the code C. So, in order to go from a $(4, \ell)$-MCRH to a CRH, ℓ would have to be at least $(n/3 + n/2) = 5n/6$, which is what we obtained.

Proposition 10. *In any code $C \subseteq \Sigma^N$ where $|C| = 2^n$ and any 3 codewords all agree on at most 2 coordinates, it has to be that $|\Sigma| \geq \Omega(2^{n/3})$.*

Proof. Again, truncate the codewords in C to the first 3 coordinates. This set of truncated codewords has to have at least $2^n/2$ distinct elements. Otherwise, this would mean that some 3 codewords in C agreed on the first 3 coordinates, which is precluded by the hypothesis. Thus, $\Sigma^3 \geq 2^n/2$, which implies that $\Sigma \geq (2^n/2)^{1/3}$.

Obstructions to Improvement. More generally, the above techniques can be used to prove the following general bound.

Proposition 11. *In any code $C \subseteq \Sigma^N$ where $|C| = 2^n$ and any p codewords all agree on at most q coordinates, it has to be that $|\Sigma| \geq (2^n/(p-1))^{1/(q+1)}$.*

Proposition 11 implies, for instance, that going from a 5-MCRH to a 4-MCRH (resp. 3-MCRH) using our approach would incur a loss of at least $n/4$ (resp. $n/3$) in shrinkage. Further, we can show that going from a 5-MCRH to a 3-MCRH in fact incurs a loss of at least $n/2$. In order to do this, we show that if the alphabet Σ is of size somewhat less than $2^{n/2}$, then there actually does exist a $T \subseteq C$ of size 4 such that the sets C_1, C_2, C_3 with their requisite properties are subsets of T. This is implied immediately by the following proposition.

Proposition 12. *For any code $C \subseteq \Sigma^N$ such that $|C| = 2^n$ and $|\Sigma| \leq 2^{n/2}/2$, there exist codewords $c, c_1, c_2, c_3 \in C$ such that on each of the first three coordinates, at least two of the c_i's agree with c.*

Proof. Consider just the first three coordinates of codewords in C. Let S_1 be the set of all codewords c such that there exists another codeword c' such that $c[1] = c'[1]$ and $c[2] = c'[2]$. Let S_2 and S_3 denote similar sets of codewords that instead look at the first and third, and second and third coordinates, respectively. If we can prove that there exists a codeword c that is contained in all of the S_i's then we would be done.

We do this by showing that each S_i has to be large. Take S_1, for instance. By definition, S_1 is the set of all codewords that have some "collision" in the first two coordinates. Since the first two coordinates are supported on Σ^2, the number of codewords that do not have any collisions in these coordinates can be at most $|\Sigma|^2$. Thus, S_1 (and similarly S_2 and S_3) is of size at least $(2^n - |\Sigma|^2) \geq (3/4) \cdot 2^n$. So there has to exist at least one codeword in the intersection of all three S_i's. Take this codeword to be c, and its colliding codeword in each S_i to be the respective c_i. This proves the proposition.

To go from a 5-MCRH to a CRH, we would first have to go to a 4-MCRH or a 3-MCRH, and then to a CRH from there. As noted above, going from a 4-MCRH (resp. 3-MCRH) to a CRH already incurs a loss of at least $5n/6$ (resp. $n/2$) in shrinkage. Following the above bounds on constructions of 4- or 3-MCRH from 5-MCRH, neither of these routes is viable, and our approach as is cannot be used to construct a CRH from a 5-MCRH (and thus also from t-MCRH for $t > 5$).

Potential Workarounds. One possibility to getting a CRH from even a 5-MCRH is to use the hash function h itself to split up codewords that may otherwise appear together in the sets C_i. The codewords in any given c_i correspond to a set of inputs that collide under both h and g, but so far we have only used the fact that they collide under g. Could their collision under h be used meaningfully somehow to improve this approach? Of course, there might also be approaches significantly different from ours that construct CRH from such MCRH.

Acknowledgments. We thank Itay Berman and Akshay Degwekar for being part of much of our exploration of multicollision resistance, for helpful discussions, and for their collaboration in general. We also thank Iftach Haitner for helpful discussions.

Rothblum was supported in part by the Israeli Science Foundation (Grants No. 1262/18 and 2137/19), by grants from the Technion Hiroshi Fujiwara cyber security research center and Israel cyber directorate, and by the European Union. Views and opinions expressed are however those of the author(s) only and do not necessarily reflect those of the European Union or the European Research Council. Neither the European Union nor the granting authority can be held responsible for them.

Vasudevan was supported by funds from an NUS Presidential Young Professorship.

References

[BD19]   Bitansky, N., Degwekar, A.: On the complexity of collision resistant hash
           functions: new and old black-box separations. In: Hofheinz, D., Rosen, A.
           (eds.) TCC 2019, Part I. LNCS, vol. 11891, pp. 422–450. Springer, Cham
           (2019). https://doi.org/10.1007/978-3-030-36030-6_17

[BDRV18]   Berman, I., Degwekar, A., Rothblum, R.D., Vasudevan, P.N.: Multi-
           collision resistant hash functions and their applications. In: Nielsen and
           Rijmen [NR18], pp. 133–161

[BHKY19]   Bitansky, N., Haitner, I., Komargodski, I., Yogev, E.: Distributional colli-
           sion resistance beyond one-way functions. In: Ishai, Y., Rijmen, V. (eds.)
           EUROCRYPT 2019, Part III. LNCS, vol. 11478, pp. 667–695. Springer,
           Cham (2019). https://doi.org/10.1007/978-3-030-17659-4_23

[BKP18]   Bitansky, N., Kalai, Y.T., Paneth, O.: Multi-collision resistance: a paradigm
           for keyless hash functions. In: Diakonikolas, I., Kempe, D., Henzinger, M.
           (eds.) Proceedings of the 50th Annual ACM SIGACT Symposium on The-
           ory of Computing, STOC 2018, Los Angeles, CA, USA, 25–29 June 2018,
           pp. 671–684. ACM (2018)

[BV17]   Bitansky, N., Vaikuntanathan, V.: A note on perfect correctness by deran-
           domization. In: Coron, J.-S., Nielsen, J.B. (eds.) EUROCRYPT 2017, Part
           II. LNCS, vol. 10211, pp. 592–606. Springer, Cham (2017). https://doi.org/
           10.1007/978-3-319-56614-6_20

[DGRV11]   Dvir, Z., Gutfreund, D., Rothblum, G.N., Vadhan, S.P.: On approximating
           the entropy of polynomial mappings. In: Chazelle, B. (ed.) Innovations in
           Computer Science - ICS 2011, Tsinghua University, Beijing, China, 7–9
           January 2011, Proceedings, pp. 460–475. Tsinghua University Press (2011)

[DI06]   Dubrov, B., Ishai, Y.: On the randomness complexity of efficient sampling.
           In: Kleinberg, J.M. (ed.) Proceedings of the 38th Annual ACM Symposium
           on Theory of Computing, Seattle, WA, USA, 21–23 May 2006, pp. 711–720.
           ACM (2006)

[DN07]   Dwork, C., Naor, M.: Zaps and their applications. SIAM J. Comput. 36(6),
           1513–1543 (2007)

[DNR04]   Dwork, C., Naor, M., Reingold, O.: Immunizing encryption schemes from
           decryption errors. In: Cachin, C., Camenisch, J.L. (eds.) EUROCRYPT
           2004. LNCS, vol. 3027, pp. 342–360. Springer, Heidelberg (2004). https://
           doi.org/10.1007/978-3-540-24676-3_21

[Gol04]   Goldreich, O.: The Foundations of Cryptography - Volume 2: Basic Appli-
           cations. Cambridge University Press, Cambridge (2004)

[GRS00]   Goldreich, O., Rubinfeld, R., Sudan, M.: Learning polynomials with queries:
           the highly noisy case. SIAM J. Discret. Math. 13(4), 535–570 (2000)

[HHRS15]   Haitner, I., Hoch, J.J., Reingold, O., Segev, G.: Finding collisions in inter-
           active protocols - tight lower bounds on the round and communication
           complexities of statistically hiding commitments. SIAM J. Comput. 44(1),
           193–242 (2015)

[HL18] Holmgren, J., Lombardi, A.: Cryptographic hashing from strong one-way functions (or: one-way product functions and their applications). In: Thorup, M. (ed.) 59th IEEE Annual Symposium on Foundations of Computer Science, FOCS 2018, Paris, France, 7–9 October 2018, pp. 850–858. IEEE Computer Society (2018)

[HR04] Hsiao, C.-Y., Reyzin, L.: Finding collisions on a public road, or do secure hash functions need secret coins? In: Franklin, M. (ed.) CRYPTO 2004. LNCS, vol. 3152, pp. 92–105. Springer, Heidelberg (2004). https://doi.org/10.1007/978-3-540-28628-8_6

[IL89] Impagliazzo, R., Luby, M.: One-way functions are essential for complexity based cryptography (extended abstract). In: 30th Annual Symposium on Foundations of Computer Science, Research Triangle Park, North Carolina, USA, 30 October–1 November 1989, pp. 230–235. IEEE Computer Society (1989)

[Jou04] Joux, A.: Multicollisions in iterated hash functions. Application to cascaded constructions. In: Franklin, M. (ed.) CRYPTO 2004. LNCS, vol. 3152, pp. 306–316. Springer, Heidelberg (2004). https://doi.org/10.1007/978-3-540-28628-8_19

[KNY17] Komargodski, I., Naor, M., Yogev, E.: White-box vs. black-box complexity of search problems: ramsey and graph property testing. In: Umans, C. (ed.) 58th IEEE Annual Symposium on Foundations of Computer Science, FOCS 2017, Berkeley, CA, USA, 15–17 October 2017, pp. 622–632. IEEE Computer Society (2017)

[KNY18] Komargodski, I., Naor, M., Yogev, E.: Collision resistant hashing for paranoids: dealing with multiple collisions. In: Nielsen and Rijmen [NR18], pp. 162–194

[KY18] Komargodski, I., Yogev, E.: On distributional collision resistant hashing. In: Shacham, H., Boldyreva, A. (eds.) CRYPTO 2018, Part II. LNCS, vol. 10992, pp. 303–327. Springer, Cham (2018). https://doi.org/10.1007/978-3-319-96881-0_11

[Lau83] Lautemann, C.: BPP and the polynomial hierarchy. Inf. Process. Lett. **17**(4), 215–217 (1983)

[Nao89] Naor, M.: Bit commitment using pseudo-randomness. In: Brassard, G. (ed.) CRYPTO 1989. LNCS, vol. 435, pp. 128–136. Springer, New York (1990). https://doi.org/10.1007/0-387-34805-0_13

[NR18] Nielsen, J.B., Rijmen, V. (eds.): Advances in Cryptology - EUROCRYPT 2018, Part II. LNCS, vol. 10821. Springer, Cham (2018)

[NS07] Nandi, M., Stinson, D.R.: Multicollision attacks on some generalized sequential hash functions. IEEE Trans. Inf. Theory **53**(2), 759–767 (2007)

[Per] Personal communication with the authors of [KNY18]

[Sho88] Shoup, V.: New algorithms for finding irreducible polynomials over finite fields. In: 29th Annual Symposium on Foundations of Computer Science, White Plains, New York, USA, 24–26 October 1988, pp. 283–290 (1988)

[Sim98] Simon, D.R.: Finding collisions on a one-way street: can secure hash functions be based on general assumptions? In: Nyberg, K. (ed.) EUROCRYPT 1998. LNCS, vol. 1403, pp. 334–345. Springer, Heidelberg (1998). https://doi.org/10.1007/BFb0054137

[Sud97] Sudan, M.: Decoding of Reed Solomon codes beyond the error-correction bound. J. Complex. **13**(1), 180–193 (1997)

[YW07] Yu, H., Wang, X.: Multi-collision attack on the compression functions of MD4 and 3-Pass HAVAL. In: Nam, K.-H., Rhee, G. (eds.) ICISC 2007. LNCS, vol. 4817, pp. 206–226. Springer, Heidelberg (2007). https://doi.org/10.1007/978-3-540-76788-6_17

Post-quantum Cryptography

Post-quantum Simulatable Extraction with Minimal Assumptions: Black-Box and Constant-Round

Nai-Hui Chia[1], Kai-Min Chung[2], Xiao Liang[3(✉)] [iD], and Takashi Yamakawa[4]

[1] Rice University, Houston, USA
nc67@rice.edu
[2] Academia Sinica, Taipei, Taiwan
kmchung@iis.sinica.edu.tw
[3] Stony Brook University, Stony Brook, USA
xiao.crypto@gmail.com
[4] NTT Social Informatics Laboratories, Tokyo, Japan
takashi.yamakawa.ga@hco.ntt.co.jp

Abstract. From the minimal assumption of post-quantum semi-honest oblivious transfers, we build the first ε-*simulatable* two-party computation (2PC) against quantum polynomial-time (QPT) adversaries that is both constant-round and black-box (for both the construction and security reduction). A recent work by Chia, Chung, Liu, and Yamakawa (FOCS'21) shows that post-quantum 2PC with standard simulation-based security is impossible in constant rounds, unless either **NP** $\subseteq$ **BQP** or relying on non-black-box simulation. The ε-simulatability we target is a relaxation of the standard simulation-based security that allows for an arbitrarily small noticeable simulation error ε. Moreover, when quantum communication is allowed, we can further weaken the assumption to post-quantum secure one-way functions (PQ-OWFs), while maintaining the constant-round and black-box property.

Our techniques also yield the following set of *constant-round and black-box* two-party protocols secure against QPT adversaries, only assuming black-box access to PQ-OWFs:

- extractable commitments for which the extractor is also an ε-simulator;
- ε-zero-knowledge commit-and-prove whose commit stage is extractable with ε-simulation;
- ε-simulatable coin-flipping;
- ε-zero-knowledge arguments of knowledge for **NP** for which the knowledge extractor is also an ε-simulator;
- ε-zero-knowledge arguments for **QMA**.

At the heart of the above results is a black-box extraction lemma showing how to efficiently extract secrets from QPT adversaries while disturbing their quantum states in a controllable manner, i.e., achieving ε-simulatability of the after-extraction state of the adversary.

© International Association for Cryptologic Research 2022
Y. Dodis and T. Shrimpton (Eds.): CRYPTO 2022, LNCS 13509, pp. 533–563, 2022.
https://doi.org/10.1007/978-3-031-15982-4_18

1 Introduction

Extractability is an important concept in cryptography. A typical example is extractable commitments, which enable an extractor to extract a committed message from a malicious committer. Extractable commitments have played a central role in several major cryptographic tasks, including (but not limited to) secure two-party and multi-party computation (e.g., [19,36,38,61]), zero-knowledge (ZK) protocols (e.g., [56,63]), concurrent zero-knowledge protocols (e.g., [59,62]), non-malleable commitments (e.g., [37,52]) etc. Recently, two concurrent works by Grilo, Lin, Song, and Vaikuntanathan [40] and Bartusek, Coladangelo, Khurana, and Ma [5] (based on earlier works [7,11,22,23]) demonstrate new applications of extractable commitments in quantum cryptography. They show that quantumly secure extractable commitments are sufficient for constructing maliciously secure quantum oblivious transfers (OTs), which can be compiled into general-purpose quantum MPC [26,49].[1]

As noted in [40], it is surprisingly non-trivial to construct quantumly secure extractable commitments. The reason is that quantum extractability requires an extractor to extract the committed message *while simulating the committer's post-execution state*. However, known rewinding-based classical extraction techniques are not directly applicable as it is unclear if they could provide any simulation guarantee when used against quantum adversaries. To address this issue, recent works [5,40] propose new polynomial-round *quantum* constructions of quantumly secure extractable commitments from post-quantum one-way functions (PQ-OWFs), which are functions efficiently computable in the classical sense but one-way against quantum polynomial-time (QPT) adversaries. Relying on assumptions stronger than PQ-OWFs, *classical* constructions of quantumly secure extractable commitments (which we call *post-quantum* extractable commitments) are known [4,9,10,43,58]. However, those constructions require (at least) the existence of OTs.

Moreover, all existing post-quantum extractable commitments make *non-black-box* use of their building-block primitives. This is not ideal as *black-box* constructions are often preferred over non-black-box ones. A black-box construction only depends on the input/output behavior of its building-block cryptographic primitive(s). In particular, such a construction is independent of the specific implementation or code of the building-block primitive. Black-box constructions enjoy certain advantages. For example, they remain valid even if the building-block primitive/oracle is based on a *physical* object such as a noisy channel or tamper-proof hardware [21,34,66]. Also, since the efficiency of black-box constructions does not depend on the implementation details of the primitive, their efficiency can be theoretically independent of the code of lower-level primitives. Indeed, it has been an important theme to obtain black-box constructions for

---

[1] They actually rely on extractable and *equivocal* commitments. However, since equivocality can be added easily, extractable commitments are the essential building block.

major cryptographic objects, e.g., [15,18,24,29,31–33,36,37,39,41,44,46,47,49–52,54,55,61].

In the classical setting, it is well-known that constant-round extractable commitments can be obtained assuming only black-box access to OWFs [25,61–63].[2] Therefore, it is natural to ask the following analog question in the quantum setting: Is it possible to construct constant-round post-quantum extractable commitments assuming only black-box access to PQ-OWFs? We remark that this question is open even if we do not require the scheme to be constant-round or black-box.

The Black-Box Extraction Barrier. We observe that the recent lower bound on black-box post-quantum ZK [17] suggests a negative answer to the above question. Namely, if we have constant-round post-quantum extractable commitment with black-box extraction, then we can construct constant-round post-quantum ZK arguments for **NP** with black-box simulation based on standard techniques (see [16, Appendix A] for details). However, [17] showed that such a ZK argument cannot exist unless **NP** ⊆ **BQP**, which seems unlikely.[3]

ε-**Simulation Security.** On the other hand, another recent work [18] showed that we can bypass the impossibility result by relaxing the requirement of ZK to the so-called ε-ZK [8,27,28]. The standard ZK property requires a simulator to simulate the verifier's view in a way that no distinguisher can distinguish it from the real one with non-negligible advantage. In contrast, the ε-ZK property only requires the existence of a simulator such that for any noticeable $\varepsilon(\lambda)$, the simulated view can be distinguished from the real one with advantage at most ε. As explained in [18], ε-ZK is still useful in several applications of ZK. The results in [18] suggest the possibility of post-quantum extractable commitments if we relax the simulation requirement on the extractor to a similar ε-close[4] version. We will refer to this weakened notion as *extractability with ε-simulation*.[5] It seems natural to hope that the techniques in [18] could be used in the context of extractable commitments. Indeed, by plugging the ZK argument from [18] into the OT-based construction [9,10,43,58], we can obtain a non-black-box construction of constant-round post-quantum extractable commitments with ε-simulation, assuming constant-round post-quantum OTs. However, if we focus on *black-box constructions* from the *minimal assumption* of PQ-OWFs, it is unclear if the techniques in [18] would help. Therefore, we ask the following question:

---

[2] The term "black-box" here refers to both black-box constructions and black-box extraction.

[3] A concurrent work by Lombardi, Ma, and Spooner [57] showed that the impossibility of [17] can be avoided if we consider a stronger computational model for simulators. We provide more discussion in [16, Sect. 1.3].

[4] Throughout this paper, "ε-close" means that the adversary's distinguishing advantage is at most ε.

[5] In the main body, we call it *strong* extractability with ε-simulation since we also define a weaker variant of that.

Table 1. Comparison of Quantumly Secure Extractable Commitment.

Reference	#Round	Cla. Const.	BB Const.	BB Ext.	Siml. Err.	Assumption
[40]	$\text{poly}(\lambda)$			✓	negl	OWF
[5]	$\text{poly}(\lambda)$		✓	✓	negl	OWF
[10]	$O(1)$	✓			negl	QFHE+QLWE
folklore[a]	$\text{poly}(\lambda)$	✓		✓	negl	OT
folklore+[18]	$O(1)$	✓		✓	ε	$O(1)$-round OT
Ours	$O(1)$	✓	✓	✓	ε	OWF

The "Cla. Const.", "BB Const.", and "BB Ext." columns indicate if the scheme relies on classical constructions, black-box constructions, and extraction, respectively. In the "Siml. Err." column, negl and ε mean that the construction achieves the standard quantum extractability and quantum extractability with ε-simulation, respectively. In "Assumption" column, QFHE and QLWE means quantum fully homomorphic encryption and the quantum hardness of learning with errors, respectively.
[a] As noted in [9], the construction is implicit in [10, 43, 58].

Question 1: *Is it possible to have constant-round post-quantum extractable commitments with ε-simulation, assuming only black-box access to PQ-OWFs?*

In the more general context of 2PC and MPC, the implication of [17] is that to obtain constant-round constructions with post-quantum security, we have to

1. rely on non-black-box simulation, *or*
2. aim for a relaxed security notion (e.g., ε-close simulation security).

The first approach was taken in [2] (based on [10]), leading to a constant-round post-quantum MPC protocol with non-black-box simulation. On the other hand, the second approach has not been explored in the existing literature of post-qauntum 2PC or MPC (except for the special case of ZK as in [18]). It is possible to construct constant-round post-quantum 2PC with ε-close simulation by combining constant-round post-quantum semi-honest OTs and the constant-round post-quantum ε-ZK in [18]. However, the naive approach will lead to a non-black-box construction. In contrast, in the classical setting, constant-round *black-box constructions* of 2PC [61] and MPC [19, 36] are known from the minimal assumption of constant-round semi-honest OT. The above discussion suggests that one has to relax the security requirement when considering the post-quantum counterparts of these tasks. We will refer to 2PC and MPC with ε-close simulation as ε-2PC and ε-MPC respectively. Then, an interesting question is:

Question 2: *Do there exist constant-round black-box post-quantum ε-2PC and ε-MPC, assuming only constant-round semi-honest OTs secure against QPT adversaries?*

1.1 Our Results

We answer **Question 1** affirmatively and address **Question 2** partially, showing a positive answer only for the two-party case. We first construct constant-round black-box post-quantum extractable commitments with ε-simulation from PQ-OWFs. See Table 1 for comparisons among quantumly secure extractable commitments. Such commitments imply new constant-round and black-box protocols for general-purpose 2PC secure against QPT adversaries. In particular, we get

- post-quantum ε-2PC from semi-honest OTs, and
- post-quantum ε-2PC from PQ-OWFs, assuming that quantum communication is possible. (Henceforth, we will use OWFs to denote PQ-OWFs.)

As an intermediate tool to achieve the above results, we construct a constant-round post-quantum ε-ZK commit-and-prove, assuming only black-box access to OWFs. Black-box zero-knowledge commit-and-prove [37,39,45,47,50,53] is a well-studied primitive in classical cryptography; it enables a prover to commit to some message and later to prove in zero-knowledge that the committed message satisfies a given predicate in a *black-box* manner. In addition to being secure in the post-quantum setting, our construction enjoys the extra property that the commit stage is extractable (albeit with only ε-simulation of the adversary's post-extraction state). Such a constant-round ε-simulatable ExtCom-and-Prove protocol implies the following set of two-party protocols:

- constant-round black-box post-quantum coin-flipping with ε-simulation,
- constant-round black-box post-quantum ε-ZK arguments of knowledge for **NP** with ε-simulating knowledge extractor, and
- constant-round black-box ε-ZK arguments for **QMA**.

In the following, we provide more discussion about them.

Coin-Flipping. Coin-flipping is a two-party protocol to generate a uniformly random string that cannot be biased by either of parties (w.r.t. the standard simulation-based security). In the classical setting, constant-round black-box constructions from OWFs are known [61]. On the other hand, known post-quantum constructions are based on stronger assumptions (like QLWE) than OWFs, and require either polynomial rounds [58] or non-black-box simulation [2]. Our construction can be understood as the post-quantum counterpart of the classical construction by Pass and Wee [61], albeit with ε-simulation.

Arguments of Knowledge with Simulating Extractor. Arguments of knowledge intuitively require an extractor to extract a witness from any efficient malicious prover whenever it passes the verification. In the classical setting, constant-round black-box constructions from OWFs are known [61]. In the post-quantum setting, there are two existing notions of arguments of knowledge depending on whether we require the extractor to simulate the prover's post-execution state or not. For the "without-simulation" version, Unruh [64] gave a polynomial-round black-box construction from OWFs.[6] For the "with-simulation" version, all existing constructions require both polynomial rounds *and* assumptions stronger

---

[6] Though Unruh originally assumes *injective* OWFs, [18] pointed out that any OWF suffices.

than OWFs (like QLWE) [3,43,58].[7] Our construction improves both the round complexity and the required assumption, at the cost of weakening ZK and extractability to their ε-simulation variants. On the other hand, we note that the construction in [3] achieves *proofs of knowledge*, while ours only achieves *arguments of knowledge*. We also note that even without knowledge extractability, our construction improves the construction in [18, Sect. 6], which is a *non-black-box construction* of constant-round ε-ZK arguments for **NP** from OWFs.

ZK Arguments for QMA. **QMA** is a quantum analog of **NP**. Known constructions of ZK proofs or arguments for **QMA** rely on either polynomial-round communication [12–14] or non-black-box simulation [10]. If we relax the ZK requirement to ε-ZK, constant-round black-box ε-ZK *proofs* were already constructed in [18]; but that construction needs to assume collapsing hash functions, which are stronger than OWFs. Our construction improves the assumption to the existence of OWFs at the cost of weakening the soundness to the computational one (i.e., an argument system).

Discussion. Due to space constraints, we provide additional discussion on minimality of assumptions, other potential applications, and a comparison with the concurrent work by Lombardi, Ma, and Spooner [57] in the full version [16, Sects. 1.2 and 1.3].

2   Technical Overview

2.1   Extractable Commitment with ε-Simulation

Our main technical tool for constructing ε-simulatable extractable commitments is a generalization of the extract-and-simulate technique from [18].

Extract-and-Simulation Lemma in [18]. We briefly recall the extract-and-simulate lemma shown in [18, Lemma 4.2].[8] At a high level, that lemma can be interpreted as follows.[9] Let $\mathcal{A}$ be a quantum algorithm with an initial state ρ. Suppose that $\mathcal{A}$ outputs some *unique* classical string s^* or otherwise outputs a failure symbol Fail. Then, there exists a simulation-extractor $\mathcal{SE}$ such that for any noticeable function ε (on the security parameter), the following two experiments are ε-close:

---

[7] Though not claimed explicitly, it seems also possible to obtain constant-round construction with non-black-box simulation from QLWE and QFHE based on [10].

[8] In [18], the lemma was called "extraction lemma". Here, we add "simulation" to emphasize that the extractor not only extracts but also simulates the adversary's state.

[9] There are two versions of their lemma: the statistically-binding case and the strong collapse-binding case. The abstraction given here is a generalization of the statistically-binding case.

$\mathsf{Exp}_{\mathsf{real}}$	$\mathsf{Exp}_{\mathsf{ext}}$
	$(s_{\mathsf{Ext}}, \rho_{\mathsf{Ext}}) \leftarrow \mathcal{SE}^{\mathcal{A}(\rho)}(1^{\varepsilon^{-1}})$
Run $\mathcal{A}(\rho)$,	Run $\mathcal{A}(\rho_{\mathsf{Ext}})$,
If $\mathcal{A}$ outputs Fail,	*If* $\mathcal{A}$ outputs Fail $\lor\ s_{\mathsf{Ext}} \neq s^*$,
Output Fail	*Output* Fail
Else output $\mathcal{A}$'s final state.	*Else output* $\mathcal{A}$'s final state.

Generalizing the Lemma. Note that their lemma will enable us to extract s^* from $\mathcal{A}$ *only if* $\mathcal{A}$ *reveals the value* s^* *at the end*. As shown in [18], this already suffices for the constant-round ZK proof by Goldreich and Kahan [35], where the verifier first commits to the challenge and opens it (i.e., "reveals it at the end") later. However, this does not seem to help obtain extractable commitments, because the committed message is not revealed *at the end the commit stage* (i.e., before decommitment happens); but the definition of extractable commitments does require extraction before decommitment happens.

To deal with this issue, we generalize the [18] lemma as follows. Let $\mathcal{A}$ be a quantum algorithm that on an initial state ρ, outputs a classical symbol Succ or Fail. Moreover, suppose that there are a unique classical string s^* and a "simulation-less extractor" $\mathsf{Ext}_{\mathsf{Sim\text{-}less}}$ that outputs s^* or otherwise Fail. Also, suppose that

$$\Pr[\mathsf{Ext}_{\mathsf{Sim\text{-}less}}^{\mathcal{A}(\rho)} = s^*] \geq (\Pr[\mathcal{A}(\rho) = \mathsf{Succ}])^c - \mathsf{negl}(\lambda) \qquad (1)$$

for some constant c. Our generalized lemma says that the ε-closeness between $\mathsf{Exp}_{\mathsf{real}}$ and $\mathsf{Exp}_{\mathsf{ext}}$ holds in this setting as well.

One can think of $\mathcal{A}$ as a joint execution of a malicious committer and honest receiver where it outputs Succ if and only if the receiver accepts. In this setting, one can understand the above lemma as a lifting lemma from "simulation-less extractor" to "ε-simulation extractor" in the setting where the extracted string is unique. In the main body, we present the lemma in a more specific form (Lemma 1), where it is integrated with Watrous' rewinding lemma [65] and Unruh's rewinding lemma [64], because that is more convenient for our purpose. We will overview the intuition behind the above generalized lemma toward the end of this subsection.

Weakly Extractable Commitment. Next, we explain how to construct post-quantum extractable commitments using our extract-and-simulate lemma. We go through the following two steps:

1. Construct a commitment scheme wExtCom that satisfies a weak version of post-quantum extractability with ε-simulation.
2. Upgrade wExtCom into a scheme ExtCom with full-fledged post-quantum extractability with ε-simulation (which we call *strong* extractability with ε-simulation to distinguish it from the weak one).

We first explain Step 1, the construction of wExtCom. Actually, our construction of wExtCom is exactly the same as the classical extractable commitments from OWFs given in [61], which are in turn based on earlier works [25,62,63]. Let

Com be a computationally-hiding and statistically-binding commitment scheme (say, Naor's commitment [60]). Then, the commitment scheme wExtCom works as follows.

Commit Stage:

1. To commit to a message m, the committer C generates $k = \omega(\log \lambda)$ pairs of 2-out-of-2 additive secret shares $\{(v_i^0, v_i^1)\}_{i=1}^k$, i.e., they are uniformly chosen conditioned on that $v_i^0 \oplus v_i^1 = m$ for each $i \in [k]$. Then, C commits independently to each v_i^b $(b \in \{0,1\})$ in parallel by using Com. We denote these commitments by $\{(\mathsf{com}_i^0, \mathsf{com}_i^1)\}_{i=1}^k$.
2. R randomly chooses $\mathbf{c} = (c_1, ..., c_k) \leftarrow \{0,1\}^k$ and sends it to C.
3. C decommits $\{\mathsf{com}_i^{c_i}\}_{i=1}^k$ to $\{v_i^{c_i}\}_{i=1}^k$, and R checks that the openings are valid.

Decommit Stage:

1. C sends m and opens all the remaining commitments; R checks that all openings are valid *and* $v_i^0 \oplus v_i^1 = m$ for all $i \in [k]$.

Suppose that a malicious committer C^* generates commitments $\{(\mathsf{com}_i^0, \mathsf{com}_i^1)\}_{i=1}^k$ in Step 1, and let ρ be its internal state at this point. Then, we consider $\mathcal{A}(\rho)$ that works as follows:

- Choose $\mathbf{c} = (c_1, ..., c_k) \leftarrow \{0,1\}^k$ at random.
- Send $\mathbf{c}$ to C^* and simulate Step 3 of C^* in the commit stage to get $\{v_i^{c_i}\}_{i=1}^k$ and the corresponding decommitment information.
- If all the openings are valid, output Succ; otherwise output Fail.

To use our extract-and-simulate lemma, we need to construct a simulation-less extractor $\mathsf{Ext}_{\mathsf{Sim-less}}$ satisfying Inequality (1). A natural idea is to use Unruh's rewinding lemma [64]. His lemma directly implies that if $\mathcal{A}$ returns Succ with probability δ, then we can obtain valid $\{v_i^{c_i}\}_{i=1}^k$ and $\{v_i^{c_i'}\}_{i=1}^k$ for two uniformly random challenges, $\mathbf{c} = (c_1, \ldots, c_k)$ and $\mathbf{c}' = (c_1', \ldots, c_k')$, with probability at least δ^3. In that case, unless $\mathbf{c} = \mathbf{c}'$ (which happens with negligible probability), we can "extract" $m = v_i^0 \oplus v_i^1$ from position $i \in [k]$ that satisfies $c_i \neq c_i'$. However, such an "extractor" does not satisfy the assumption for our generalized extract-and-simulate lemma in general, because $v_i^0 \oplus v_i^1$ may be different for each $i \in [k]$.

Therefore, to satisfy this requirement, we have to introduce an additional assumption that $\{(\mathsf{com}_i^0, \mathsf{com}_i^1)\}_{i=1}^k$ is *consistent*, i.e., if we denote the corresponding committed messages as $\{(v_i^0, v_i^1)\}_{i=1}^k$, then there exists a unique m such that $v_i^0 \oplus v_i^1 = m$ for all $i \in [k]$.[10] With this assumption, we can apply our generalized extract-and-simulate lemma. It enables us to extract the committed message *and* simultaneously ε-simulate C^*'s state, conditioned on that the receiver accepts in the commit stage. The case where the receiver rejects can be easily handled using Watrous' rewinding lemma [65] as we will explain later. As a result, we get an ε-simulating extractor that works well conditioned on that

---

[10] The corresponding message is well-defined (except for negligible probability) since we assume that Com is statistically binding.

the commitments generated in Step 1 are consistent. We will refer to such a weak notion of simulation-extractability as *weak extractability with ε-simulation* (see Definition 7 for the formal definition).

Moreover, since Unruh's rewinding lemma naturally gives a simulation-less extractor in the parallel setting (where C^* interacts with many copies of R in parallel), we can prove the parallel version of the weak extractability with ε-simulation similarly. More generally, we prove that wExtCom satisfies a further generalized notion of extractability which we call the *special parallel weak extractability with ε-simulation* (see Definition 10 for the formal definition). Roughly speaking, it requires an ε-simulating extractor to work in n-parallel execution as long as the commitments in some subset of $[n]$ are consistent and the committed messages in those sessions determine a unique value. We remark that this parallel extractability will play an important role in the weak-to-strong compiler which we discuss next.

Weak-to-Strong Compiler. The reason why we cannot directly prove that wExtCom satisfies the strong extractability with ε-simulation is related to an issue that is often referred to as *over-extraction* in the classical literature (e.g., [30,37,52]). Over-extraction means that an extractor may extract some non-⊥ message from an invalid commitment, instead of detecting the invalidness of the commitment. In particular, there does not exist a unique "committed message" when the commitment is ill-formed in wExtCom, and extraction of such a non-unique message may collapse the committer's state. To deal with this issue, we have to add some mechanism which could help the receiver (and thus the extractor) detect (in)validness of the commitment.

One possible approach is to revisit the techniques developed in the classical setting, performing necessary surgery to make the proof work against QPT adversaries. However, as demonstrated by the above cited works, existing techniques in the classical setting are already delicate. Even if it would work eventually, such a non-black-box treatment would further complicate the proof undesirably. Therefore, we present an alternative approach that deviates from existing ones in the classical setting. As we will show later, this new approach turns out to be quantum-friendly.

Roughly speaking, our construction ExtCom works as follows:

Commit Stage:

1. The committer C generates shares $\{v_i\}_{i=1}^n$ of a *verifiable secret sharing* (VSS) scheme of the message to be committed to, and then commits to each v_i using wExtCom separately in parallel.
2. C and the receiver R execute a "one-side simulatable" coin-flipping protocol based on wExtCom to generate a random subset T of $[n]$ of a certain size.[11] Specifically, they do the following:
   (a) R commits to a random string r_1 by wExtCom.

---

[11] We remark that it is a non-trivial task to construct constant-round two-party coin-flipping from OWFs in the quantum setting, achieving the (even ε-)simulation-based security *against both parties*. Indeed, that will be one application of the strongly extractable commitment with ε-simulation, which we are now constructing. How-

    (b) C sends a random string r_2 in the clear.

    (c) R opens r_1. Then, both parties derive the subset T from $r_1 \oplus r_2$.

3. C opens the commitments corresponding to the subset T, and R checks their validness and consistency.

Decommit Stage:

1. C opens all the commitments. R checks those openings are valid. If they are valid, R runs the reconstruction algorithm of VSS to recover the committed message.

Using a similar argument as that for the soundness of the *MPC-in-the-head paradigm* [36,48], we can show that if a malicious committer passes the verification in the commit stage, then:

1. Most of the commitments of wExtCom generated in Step 1 are valid *as a commitment*; **and**

2. The committed shares in those valid commitments determines a *unique* message that can be recovered by the reconstruction algorithm of VSS.

Then, we can apply the special parallel weak extractability with ε-simulation of wExtCom to show the strong extractability with ε-simulation of ExtCom. We remark that essentially the same proof can be used to show that the *parallel* execution of ExtCom is still *strongly* extractable (with ε-simulation). We refer to this as the parallel-strong extractability with ε-simulation. It will play a critical role in our construction of ExtCom-and-Prove (see Sect. 2.2).

Dealing with Rejection in Commit Stage. So far, we have only focused on the case where the receiver accepts in the commit stage. However, the definition of (both weak and strong) extractability requires that the final state should be simulated even in the case where the receiver rejects in the commit stage. In this case, of course, the extractor does not need to extract anything, and thus the simulation is straightforward. A non-trivial issue, however, is that the extractor does not know if the receiver rejects in advance. This issue can be solved by a technique introduced in [10]. The idea is to just guess if the receiver accepts, and runs the corresponding extractor assuming that the guess is correct. This gives an intermediate extractor that succeeds with probability almost $1/2$ and its output correctly simulates the desired distribution conditioned on that it does not abort. Such an extractor can be compiled into a full-fledged extractor that does not abort by Watrous' rewinding lemma [65].

Proof Idea for the Generalized Extract-and-Simulate Lemma. Finally, we briefly explain the idea for the proof of our generalized extract-and-simulate lemma. The basic idea is similar to the original extract-and-simulate lemma in [18]—Use Jordan's lemma to decompose the adversary's internal state into "good" and "bad" subspaces, and amplify the extraction probability in the good subspace while effectively ignoring the bad-subspace components. However, the

---

ever, this is not a circular reasoning. Here, we need simulation-based security only against a malicious receiver. For such a one-side simulatable coin-flipping, the weakly extractable commitment wExtCom (with ε-simulation) suffices.

crucial difference is that in [18], they define those subspaces with respect to the success probability of $\mathcal{A}$ whereas we define them with respect to the success probability of $\mathsf{Ext}_{\mathsf{Sim\text{-}less}}$. That is, for a noticeable δ, we apply Jordan's lemma to define a subspaces $S_{<\delta}$ and $S_{\geq\delta}$ such that

1. When $\mathsf{Ext}_{\mathsf{Sim\text{-}less}}$'s input is in $S_{<\delta}$ (resp. $S_{\geq\delta}$), it succeeds in extracting s^* with probability $<\delta$ (resp. $\geq\delta$).
2. Given a state in $S_{\geq\delta}$, we can extract s^* with overwhelming probability within $O(\delta^{-1})$ steps.
3. The above procedure does not cause any interference between $S_{<\delta}$ and $S_{\geq\delta}$.

We define $\mathcal{SE}$ to be an algorithm that runs the procedure in Item 2 and outputs s (which is supposed to be s^* in the case of success) and the post-execution state of $\mathcal{A}$. First, we consider simpler cases where the initial state of the experiments is a pure state $|\psi\rangle$ that is in either $S_{\geq\delta}$ or $S_{<\delta}$.

Case of $|\psi\rangle \in S_{\geq\delta}$: In this case, Item 2 implies that $\mathcal{SE}$ outputs s^* with overwhelming probability. In general, such an almost-deterministic quantum procedure can be done (almost) without affecting the state (e.g., see the *Almost-as-Good-as-New Lemma* in [1, Lemma 2.2]). Therefore, $\mathsf{Exp}_{\mathsf{real}}$ and $\mathsf{Exp}_{\mathsf{ext}}$ are negligibly indistinguishable in this case.

Case of $|\psi\rangle \in S_{<\delta}$: For any state $|\psi_{<\delta}\rangle \in S_{<\delta}$, Item 1 implies

$$\Pr[\mathsf{Ext}_{\mathsf{Sim\text{-}less}}^{\mathcal{A}(|\psi_{<\delta}\rangle)} = s^*] \leq \delta.$$

On the other hand, our assumption (i.e., Inequality (1)) implies

$$\Pr[\mathsf{Ext}_{\mathsf{Sim\text{-}less}}^{\mathcal{A}(|\psi_{<\delta}\rangle)} = s^*] \geq (\Pr[\mathcal{A}(|\psi_{<\delta}\rangle) = \mathsf{Succ}])^c - \mathsf{negl}(\lambda)$$

for some constant c. By combining them, we have

$$\Pr[\mathcal{A}(|\psi_{<\delta}\rangle) = \mathsf{Succ}] \leq (\delta + \mathsf{negl}(\lambda))^{1/c}.$$

We note that the second output of $\mathcal{SE}$ in $\mathsf{Exp}_{\mathsf{ext}}$ is in $S_{<\delta}$ if the initial state is in $S_{<\delta}$ by Item 3. Therefore, if we run $\mathsf{Exp}_{\mathsf{real}}$ or $\mathsf{Exp}_{\mathsf{ext}}$ with an initial state in $S_{<\delta}$, it outputs Fail with probability $> 1 - (\delta + \mathsf{negl}(\lambda))^{1/c}$. Recall that when an experiment outputs Fail, no information about the internal state of $\mathcal{A}$ is revealed. Thus, the distinguishing advantage between those experiments can be bounded by $O(\delta^{1/c})$.

In general, the initial state is a superposition of $S_{<\delta}$ component and $S_{\geq\delta}$ component. Thanks to Item 3, we can reduce the general case to the above two cases. When doing that, there occurs an additional loss of the 4-th power of δ due to a technical reason. Still, we can bound the distinguishing advantage between the two experiments by $O(\delta^{1/(4c)})$. This can be made to be an arbitrarily small noticeable function because δ is an arbitrarily small noticeable function. This suffices for establishing the ε-closeness of those experiments.

2.2   Black-Box ε-Simulatable ExtCom-and-Prove

Black-box zero-knowledge commit-and-prove allows a committer to commit to some message m (the Commit Stage), and later prove in zero-knowledge that the committed m satisfies some predicate ϕ (the Prove Stage). What makes this primitive non-trivial is the requirement of black-box use of cryptographic building blocks; otherwise, it can be fulfilled easily by giving a standard commitment to m first, and then running any zero-knowledge system over the commitment in a non-black-box manner.

Our construction follows the classical "MPC-in-the-head" paradigm [37,47] with the following modifications. To make the commitment stage extractable, we ask the committer to use the ε-simulatable parallel-strongly extractable commitment. We remark that the parallel-strong extractability is essential for obtaining a constant round construction since the committer has to parallelly commit to many secret shares of its message in the construction. Another caveat is that the protocol relies on coin-flipping to conduct a "cut-and-choose" type of argument. As explained in Sect. 2.1, we can implement a "one-sided simulatable" coin flipping from (weakly) extractable commitments. Based on this observation, we upgrade the classical security proof to the quantum setting.

Due to space constraints, we provide a more detailed overview of this construction in [16, Sect. 2.2].

2.3   Black-Box ε-Simulatable 2PC

It is well-known that there exist black-box constant-round constructions of general-purpose 2PC from semi-honest OTs and (simulation-secure) commitments in the universally-composable (UC) model [19,42,49]. In the stand-alone setting, it had been a folklore that a similar conversion works if we assume suitable parallel-simulation-secure commitments, but we are not aware of any work that *formally* proved it until the recent work of [40]. [40] addressed this issue by defining a functionality called $\mathcal{F}_{\text{SO-COM}}^t$, and showed that the above conversion works in the $\mathcal{F}_{\text{SO-COM}}^t$-hybrid model *in the stand-alone setting*. $\mathcal{F}_{\text{SO-COM}}^t$ is a two-party ideal functionality that allows a committer to commit to an a-priori fixed polynomial number $t(\lambda)$ of messages in parallel, and later decommit to a subset of these commitments named by the receiver (thus, "SO" stands for "selectively opening").

Thus, for obtaining a black-box constant-round construction of general-purpose ε-simulatable 2PC, all we need to do is to construct a constant-round black-box commitment scheme that implements $\mathcal{F}_{\text{SO-COM}}^t$ with ε-close simulation. It is straightforward to construct such a commitment scheme based on our ExtCom-and-Prove protocol, since it enables the committer to prove any predicate on committed values, which of course supports revealing a subset of them.

Moreover, if we are allowed to use quantum communication, [40] showed that we can construct black-box constant-round (maliciously-secure) OTs in the $\mathcal{F}_{\text{SO-COM}}^t$-hybrid model. Thus, we can drop the additional assumption of semi-honest OTs in this case.

We provide a more detailed technical overview in [16, Sect. 2.3].

3 Preliminaries

We postpone basic notations, definitions, and known lemmas to [16, Sect. 3].

3.1 Post-quantum Extractable Commitment

We give a definition of post-quantum (strongly) extractable commitments with ε-simulation. We will omit the security parameter from the input to parties when it is clear from the context.

Definition 1 (Post-quantum Commitment). *A post-quantum commitment scheme* Π *is a classical interactive protocol between interactive* PPT *machines* C *and* R. *Let* $m \in \{0,1\}^{\ell(\lambda)}$ *(where* $\ell(\cdot)$ *is some polynomial) is a message that* C *wants to commit to. The protocol consists of the following stages:*

- **Commit Stage:** $C(m)$ *and* R *interact with each other to generate a transcript (which is also called a commitment) denoted by* com,[12] C*'s state* ST_C, *and* R*'s output* $b_{\mathrm{com}} \in \{0,1\}$ *indicating acceptance (i.e.,* $b_{\mathrm{com}} = 1$*) or rejection (i.e.,* $b_{\mathrm{com}} = 0$*). We denote this execution by* $(\mathsf{com}, \mathsf{ST}_C, b_{\mathrm{com}}) \leftarrow \langle C(m), R \rangle(1^\lambda)$. *When* C *is honest,* ST_C *is classical, but when we consider a malicious quantum committer* $C^*(\rho)$, *we allow it to generate any quantum state* ST_{C^*}. *Similarly, a malicious quantum receiver* $R^*(\rho)$ *can output any quantum state, which we denote by* OUT_{R^*} *instead of* b_{com}.
- **Decommit Stage:** C *generates a decommitment* decom *from* ST_C. *We denote this procedure by* decom $\leftarrow C(\mathsf{ST}_C)$.[13] *Then it sends a message* m *and decommitment* decom *to* R, *and* R *outputs a bit* $b_{\mathrm{dec}} \in \{0,1\}$ *indicating acceptance (i.e.,* $b_{\mathrm{dec}} = 1$*) or rejection (i.e.,* $b_{\mathrm{dec}} = 0$*). We assume that* R*'s verification procedure is deterministic and denote it by* $\mathsf{Verify}(\mathsf{com}, m, \mathsf{decom})$.[14] *W.l.o.g., we assume that* R *always rejects (i.e.,* $\mathsf{Verify}(\mathsf{com}, \cdot, \cdot) = 0$*) whenever* $b_{\mathrm{com}} = 0$. *(Note that w.l.o.g.,* com *can include* b_{com} *because we can always modify the protocol to ask* R *to send* b_{com} *as the last round message.)*

The scheme satisfies the following correctness requirement:

1. **Correctness.** *For any* $m \in \{0,1\}^{\ell(\lambda)}$, *it holds that*

$$\Pr\left[b_{\mathrm{com}} = b_{\mathrm{dec}} = 1 : \begin{array}{l} (\mathsf{com}, \mathsf{ST}_C, b_{\mathrm{com}}) \leftarrow \langle C(m), R \rangle(1^\lambda) \\ \mathsf{decom} \leftarrow C(\mathsf{ST}_C) \\ b_{\mathrm{dec}} \leftarrow \mathsf{Verify}(\mathsf{com}, m, \mathsf{decom}) \end{array}\right] = 1.$$

---

[12] That is, we regard the whole transcript as a commitment.

[13] We could define ST_C to be decom itself w.l.o.g. However, we define them separately because this is more convenient when we define ExtCom-and-Prove, which is an extension of post-quantum extractable commitments.

[14] Note that Verify is well-defined since our syntax does not allow R to keep a state from the commit stage.

Definition 2 (Computationally Hiding). *A post-quantum commitment* Π *is computationally hiding if for any* $m_0, m_1 \in \{0,1\}^{\ell(\lambda)}$ *and any non-uniform QPT receiver* $R^*(\rho)$, *the following holds:*

$$\{\mathsf{OUT}_{R^*} : (\mathsf{com}, \mathsf{ST}_C, \mathsf{OUT}_{R^*}) \leftarrow \langle C(m_0), R^*(\rho) \rangle (1^\lambda)\}_\lambda$$
$$\overset{c}{\approx} \{\mathsf{OUT}_{R^*} : (\mathsf{com}, \mathsf{ST}_C, \mathsf{OUT}_{R^*}) \langle C(m_1), R^*(\rho) \rangle (1^\lambda)\}_\lambda.$$

Definition 3 (Statistically Binding). *A post-quantum commitment* Π *is statistically binding if for any unbounded-time comitter* C^*, *the following holds:*

$$\Pr\left[\begin{array}{l} \exists \{m_b, \mathsf{decom}_b\}_{b \in \{0,1\}}, m_0 \neq m_1 \\ \wedge \ \mathsf{Verify}(\mathsf{com}, m_b, \mathsf{decom}_b) = 1 \quad : (\mathsf{com}, \mathsf{ST}_{C^*}, b_{\mathsf{com}}) \leftarrow \langle C^*, R \rangle (1^\lambda) \\ \text{for } b \in \{0,1\} \end{array} \right] = \mathsf{negl}(\lambda).$$

Definition 4 (Committed Values). *For a post-quantum commitment* Π, *we define the value function as follows:*

$$\mathsf{val}_\Pi(\mathsf{com}) := \begin{cases} m & \text{if } \exists \text{ unique } m \text{ s.t. } \exists \text{ decom}, \mathsf{Verify}(\mathsf{com}, m, \mathsf{decom}) = 1 \\ \bot & \text{otherwise} \end{cases}.$$

We say that com *is valid if* $\mathsf{val}_\Pi(\mathsf{com}) \neq \bot$ *and invalid if* $\mathsf{val}_\Pi(\mathsf{com}) = \bot$.

Then we give the definition of the strong extractability with ε-simulation. The definition is similar to that of post-quantum extractable commitments in [9,10] except that we allow an (arbitrarily small) noticeable approximation error similarly to post-quantum ε-zero-knowledge [18]. We note that we call it the *strong* extractability since we also define a weaker version of extractability in Definition 7 in Sect. 5.1.

Definition 5 (Strong Extractability with ε-Simulation). *A commitment scheme* Π *is strongly extractable with ε-simulation if there exists a QPT algorithm* $\mathcal{SE}$ *(called the ε-simulation strong-extractor) such that for any noticeable* $\varepsilon(\lambda)$ *and any non-uniform QPT* $C^*(\rho)$,

$$\left\{ \mathcal{SE}^{C^*(\rho)}(1^\lambda, 1^{\varepsilon^{-1}}) \right\}_\lambda \overset{c}{\approx}_\varepsilon \left\{ (\mathsf{val}_\Pi(\mathsf{com}), \mathsf{ST}_{C^*}) : (\mathsf{com}, \mathsf{ST}_{C^*}, b_{\mathsf{com}}) \leftarrow \langle C^*(\rho), R \rangle (1^\lambda) \right\}_\lambda.$$

We also define the parallel version.

Definition 6 (Parallel-Strong Extractability with ε-Simulation). *A commitment scheme* Π *is parallelly strongly extractable with ε-simulation if for any integer* $n = \mathsf{poly}(\lambda)$, *there exists a QPT algorithm* $\mathcal{SE}_{\mathsf{par}}$ *(called the ε-simulation parallel-strong-extractor) such that for any noticeable* $\varepsilon(\lambda)$ *and any non-uniform QPT* $C^*(\rho)$,

$$\left\{ \mathcal{SE}_{\mathsf{par}}^{C^*(\rho)}(1^\lambda, 1^{\varepsilon^{-1}}) \right\}_\lambda$$
$$\overset{c}{\approx}_\varepsilon \left\{ (\Lambda_{\{b_{\mathsf{com},j}\}_{j=1}^n}(\{\mathsf{val}(\mathsf{com}_j)\}_{j=1}^n), \mathsf{ST}_{C^*}) : \begin{array}{l} (\{\mathsf{com}_j\}_{j=1}^n, \mathsf{ST}_{C^*}, \{b_{\mathsf{com},j}\}_{j=1}^n) \\ \leftarrow \langle C^*(\rho), R^n \rangle (1^\lambda) \end{array} \right\}_\lambda$$

where $(\{\mathsf{com}_j\}_{j=1}^n, \mathsf{ST}_{C^*}, \{b_{\mathsf{com},j}\}_{j=1}^n) \leftarrow \langle C^*(\rho), R^n \rangle(1^\lambda)$ *means that* $C^*(\rho)$
interacts with n *copies of the honest receiver* R *in parallel and the execution
results in transcripts* $\{\mathsf{com}_j\}_{j=1}^n$, *the final state* ST_{C^*}, *and outputs* $\{b_{\mathsf{com},j}\}_{j=1}^n$
of each copy of R *and*

$$\Lambda_{\{b_{\mathsf{com},j}\}_{j=1}^n}(\{\mathsf{val}(\mathsf{com}_j)\}_{j=1}^n) := \begin{cases} \{\mathsf{val}_\Pi(\mathsf{com}_j)\}_{j=1}^n & \text{if } \forall\, j \in [n]\ b_{\mathsf{com},j} = 1 \\ \perp & \text{otherwise} \end{cases}.$$

Remark 1. We remark that the above definition only requires the extractor to
extract the committed values when R accepts in all the parallel sessions. In
particular, when R accepts in some sessions but not in others, the extractor
does not need to extract the committed values at all. An alternative stronger
(and probably more natural) definition would require the extractor to extract
$\mathsf{val}_\Pi(\mathsf{com}_j)$ for all $j \in [n]$ such that R accepts in the j-th session. But we define
it in the above way since it suffices for our purpose and we do not know if our
construction satisfies the stronger one.

4   Extract-and-Simulate Lemma

We prove a lemma that can be seen as an ε-simulation variant of Unruh's rewinding lemma ([64, Lemma 7]) in typical applications. This lemma is the technical
core of all the results in this paper.

4.1   Statement of Extract-and-Simulate Lemma

Our lemma is stated as follows.

Lemma 1 (Extract-and-Simulate Lemma). *Let* C *be a finite set. Let*
$\{\Pi_i\}_{i \in C}$ *be orthogonal projectors on a Hilbert space* $\mathcal{H}$ *such that the measurement*
$\{\Pi_i, I - \Pi_i\}$ *can be efficiently implemented. Let* $|\psi_{\mathsf{init}}\rangle \in \mathcal{H}$ *be a unit vector.*

Suppose that there are a subset $S \in C^2$ *and a QPT algorithm* $\mathcal{A} = (\mathcal{A}_0, \mathcal{A}_1)$
that satisfies the following:

1. S *consists of an overwhelming fraction of* C^2, *i.e.,* $\frac{|S|}{|C|^2} = 1 - \mathsf{negl}(\lambda)$.
2. *For all* $i \in C$, *there exists a classical string* s_i *such that*

$$\Pr\left[\mathcal{A}_0\left(i, \frac{\Pi_i|\psi_{\mathsf{init}}\rangle}{\|\Pi_i|\psi_{\mathsf{init}}\rangle\|}\right) = s_i\right] = 1.$$

3. *There exists a classical string* s^* *such that for any* $(i, j) \in S$,

$$\Pr[\mathcal{A}_1(i, j, s_i, s_j) = s^*] = 1.$$

Let $\mathsf{Exp}(\lambda, \{\Pi_i\}_{i \in C}, |\psi_{\mathsf{init}}\rangle)$ *be an experiment that works as follows:*

- *Choose* $i \leftarrow C$.
- *Apply the measurement* $\{\Pi_i, I - \Pi_i\}$ *on* $|\psi_{\mathsf{init}}\rangle$.

- If the state is projected onto Π_i, the experiment outputs i, the classical string s^*, and the resulting state $\frac{\Pi_i|\psi_{\text{init}}\rangle}{\|\Pi_i|\psi_{\text{init}}\rangle\|}$. [15]
- If the state is projected onto $I - \Pi_i$, the experiment outputs i, $\perp$, and the resulting state $\frac{(I-\Pi_i)|\psi_{\text{init}}\rangle}{\|(I-\Pi_i)|\psi_{\text{init}}\rangle\|}$.

Then, there is a QPT algorithm $\mathcal{SE}$ such that for any noticeable ε,

$$\{\mathcal{SE}(1^\lambda, 1^{\varepsilon^{-1}}, \{\Pi_i\}_{i\in C}, \mathcal{A}, |\psi_{\text{init}}\rangle)\}_\lambda \overset{s}{\approx}_\varepsilon \{\mathsf{Exp}(\lambda, \{\Pi_i\}_{i\in C}, |\psi_{\text{init}}\rangle)\}_\lambda.$$

Due to space constraints, we postpone the proof to the full version [16, Sect. 4.2]. But note that the key ideas of this proof are already described in Sect. 2.1.

5 Black-Box ε-Simulation-Extractable Commitments in Constant Rounds

In this section, we present our construction of post-quantum commitment that satisfies the (parallel) strong extractability with ε-simulation. Namely, we prove the following lemma.

Lemma 2. *Assume the existence of post-quantum secure OWFs. Then, there exists a constant-round construction of post-quantum commitment that satisfies computational hiding (Definition 2), statistical binding (Definition 3), and (parallel) strongly extractable commitment with ε-simulation. Moreover, this construction makes only black-box use of the assumed OWF.*

Toward proving that, we first construct a scheme that satisfies a weaker notion of ε-simulatable extractability in Sect. 5.1. In Sect. 5.2, we present a compiler that converts the weak scheme in Sect. 5.1 into one that satisfies the (parallel) strong extractability with ε-simulation.

5.1 Weakly Extractable Commitment

We construct a commitment scheme that satisfies weak notions of extractability defined in Definitions 7 and 10 based on OWFs. The description of the scheme is given in Protocol 1, where Com is a statistically-binding and computationally-hiding commitment scheme (e.g., Naor's commnitment). We remark that the scheme is identical to the *classical* extractable commitment in [61], which in turn is based on earlier works [25,62,63].

Protocol 1: Extractable Commitment Scheme wExtCom
The extractable commitment scheme, based on any commitment scheme Com, works in the following way.   **Input:**

---

[15] We stress that we do not assume that the experiment is efficient. Especially, it may be computationally hard to find s^* from $\frac{\Pi_i|\psi_{\text{init}}\rangle}{\|\Pi_i|\psi_{\text{init}}\rangle\|}$.

- both the committer C and the receiver R get security parameter 1^λ as the common input.
- C gets a string $m \in \{0,1\}^{\ell(\lambda)}$ as his private input, where $\ell(\cdot)$ is a polynomial

Commitmment Phase:

1. The committer C commits using Com to $k = \lambda$ pairs of strings $\{(v_i^0, v_i^1)\}_{i=1}^k$ where $(v_i^0, v_i^1) = (\eta_i, m \oplus \eta_i)$ and η_i are random strings in $\{0,1\}^\ell$ for $1 \le i \le k$.[16] We denote those commitments by $\overline{\text{com}} = \{{}_i^0, {}_i^1\}_{i=1}^k$.
2. Upon receiving a challenge $\mathbf{c} = (c_1, \ldots, c_k)$ from the receiver R, S opens the commitments to $\mathbf{v} := (v_1^{c_1}, \ldots, v_k^{c_k})$ with the corresponding decommitment $\overline{\text{decom}} := (\text{decom}_1^{c_1}, \ldots, \text{decom}_k^{c_k})$.
3. R checks that the openings are valid.

Decommitment Phase:

- C sends σ and opens the commitments to all k pairs of strings. R checks that all the openings are valid, and also that $m = v_1^0 \oplus v_1^1 = \cdots = v_k^0 \oplus v_k^1$.

Proof of Security. The correctness and the statistically-binding property of wExtCom follows straightforwardly from that of Com. The computationally-hiding property of wExtCom can be reduced to that of Com by standard arguments.

Lemma 3 (Computational Hiding). wExtCom *is computationally hiding.*

The proof is similar to the classical counterpart in [61]. We postpone it to the full version [16, Sect. 5.1].

We prove that wExtCom satisfies a weak version of the extractability which we call the *weak extractability with ε-simulation.* Intuitively, it requires the simulation-extractor to perform extraction *and* ε-simulation properly, *as long as the commitment is valid.* A formal definition is given below.

Definition 7 (Weak Extractability with ε-Simulation). *A commitment scheme Π is weakly extractable with ε-simulation if there exists a QPT algorithm $\mathcal{SE}_{\text{weak}}$ (called the ε-simulation weak-extractor) such that for any noticeable $\varepsilon(\lambda)$ and any non-uniform QPT $C^*(\rho)$,*

$$\left\{ \Gamma_{\text{com}}(m_{\text{Ext}}, \widetilde{\text{ST}}_{C^*}) : (\text{com}, m_{\text{Ext}}, \widetilde{\text{ST}}_{C^*}) \leftarrow \mathcal{SE}^{C^*(\rho)}(1^\lambda, 1^{\varepsilon^{-1}}) \right\}_\lambda$$

$$\overset{c}{\approx}_\varepsilon \left\{ \Gamma_{\text{com}}(\text{val}_\Pi(\text{com}), \text{ST}_{C^*}) : (\text{com}, \text{ST}_{C^*}, b_{\text{com}}) \leftarrow \langle C^*(\rho), R \rangle(1^\lambda) \right\}_\lambda$$

where $\Gamma_{\text{com}}(m, \text{ST}_{C^*}) := \begin{cases} (m, \text{ST}_{C^*}) & \text{if } \text{val}_\Pi(\text{com}) \neq \bot \\ \bot & \text{otherwise} \end{cases}$.

Lemma 4 (Weak Extractability with ε-Simulation). wExtCom *is weakly extractable with ε-simulation (as per Definition 7).*

Before proving Lemma 4, we prepare several definitions.

---

[16] Actually, the scheme will be secure as long as we use Com to commit $k = \omega(\log \lambda)$ pairs of strings.

Definition 8 (Validness of $\overline{\text{com}}$). *For a sequence $\overline{\text{com}} = \{\text{com}_i^0, \text{com}_i^1\}_{i=1}^k$ of commitments of the scheme* Com, *we say that $\overline{\text{com}}$ is valid if there exis $m \in \{0,1\}^\ell$ such tat $\text{val}_{\text{Com}}(\text{com}_i^b) \neq \bot$ for all $i \in [k]$ and $b \in \{0,1\}$ and $\text{val}_{\text{Com}}(\text{com}_i^0) \oplus \text{val}_{\text{Com}}(\text{com}_i^1) = m$ for all $i \in [k]$ where $\text{val}_{\text{Com}}(\text{com}_i^b)$ is the value function as defined in Definition 4. We denote by $\text{val}_{\text{Com}}(\overline{\text{com}})$ to mean such m if $\overline{\text{com}}$ is valid and otherwise $\bot$.*

Definition 9 (Accepting Opening of $\overline{\text{com}}$). *For a sequence $\overline{\text{com}} = \{\text{com}_i^0, \text{com}_i^1\}_{i=1}^k$ of commitments of the commitment scheme* Com *and $\mathbf{c} = (c_1, ..., c_k) \in \{0,1\}^k$, we say that $(\mathbf{v} = (v_1, ..., v_k), \overline{\text{decom}} = (\text{decom}_1, ..., \text{decom}_k))$ is an accepting opening of $\overline{\text{com}}$ w.r.t. $\mathbf{c}$ if $\text{Verify}_{\text{Com}}(\text{com}_i^{c_i}, v_i, \text{decom}_i) = 1$ for all $i \in [k]$.*

Then we prove Lemmma 4.

Proof of Lemma 4. For simplicity, we assume that Com satisfies perfect binding. It is straightforward to extend the proof to the statistically binding case by excluding the bad case where any commitment of Com is not bounded to a unique message, which happens with a negligible probability.

Remark that the weak extractability with ε-simulation only requires the extractor to correctly extract and simulate if the commitment generated in the commit stage is valid in the sense of Definition 4. When the commitment is valid, $\overline{\text{com}}$ generated in Step 1 is also valid in the sense of Definition 8 (because otherwise a committer cannot pass the verification in the decommitment stage). Therefore, it suffices to prove that the extractor works for any fixed valid $\overline{\text{com}}$.

Let $C^*(\rho)$ be a non-uniform QPT malicious committer. For $\mathbf{c} \in \{0,1\}^k$, let $U_\mathbf{c}$ be the unitary corresponding to the action of C^* in Step 2. That is, for the state ρ' before Step 2, it applies $U_\mathbf{c}$ to get $U_\mathbf{c} \rho' U_\mathbf{c}^\dagger$ and measures designated registers $\mathbf{V}$ and $\mathbf{D}$ to get the message $\mathbf{v}$ and opening information $\overline{\text{decom}}$ in Step 2. Let $\Pi_\mathbf{c}^{\text{test}}$ be the projection that maps onto states that contain an accepting opening $\mathbf{v}$ and $\overline{\text{decom}}$ of $\overline{\text{com}}$ w.r.t. $\mathbf{c}$ (as defined in Definition 9) in $\mathbf{V} \otimes \mathbf{D}$. For $\mathbf{c} \in \{0,1\}^k$, we define $\Pi_\mathbf{c} := U_\mathbf{c}^\dagger \Pi_\mathbf{c}^{\text{test}} U_\mathbf{c}$.

We apply Lemma 1 for $\{\Pi_\mathbf{c}\}_{\mathbf{c} \in \{0,1\}^k}$ with the following correspondence.

- $\mathcal{H}$ is the internal space of C^*.
- The initial state is ρ'.[17]
- $C = \{0,1\}^k$.
- $S = \{((c_1, ..., c_k), (c_1', ..., c_k')) : \exists i \in [k] \text{ s.t. } c_i \neq c_i'\}$
- $\mathcal{A}_0$ applies $U_\mathbf{c}$ on its input, measures $\mathbf{V}$ to get $\mathbf{v}$, applies $U_\mathbf{c}^\dagger$, and outputs $\mathbf{v}$.
- $\mathcal{A}_1$ is given as input $(\mathbf{c}, \mathbf{c}') \in S$, $\mathbf{v}_\mathbf{c} = (v_1^{c_1}, ..., v_k^{c_k})$, and $\mathbf{v}_{\mathbf{c}'} = (v_1^{c_1'}, ..., v_k^{c_k'})$. $\mathcal{A}_1$ outputs $v_i^{c_i} \oplus v_i^{c_i'}$ for the smallest $i \in [k]$ such that $c_i \neq c_i'$. Note that such i exists since we assume $(\mathbf{c}, \mathbf{c}') \in S$.

If $\overline{\text{com}}$ is valid, we can see that the assumptions for Lemma 1 are satisfied as follows:

---

[17] Though we assume that the initial state $|\psi_{\text{init}}\rangle$ is a pure state in Lemma 1, the lemma holds for any mixed state since a mixed state can be seen as a probability distribution over pure states.

1. By the definition of S, it is easy to see that $\frac{|S|}{|C|^2} = 1 - 2^{-k} = 1 - \mathsf{negl}(\lambda)$.
2. For any $\mathbf{c}$, if $\mathcal{A}_0$ takes a state in the span of $\Pi_{\mathbf{c}}$ as input, it outputs $s_{\mathbf{c}} := (\mathsf{val}_{\mathsf{Com}}(\mathsf{com}_1^{c_1}), ..., \mathsf{val}_{\mathsf{Com}}(\mathsf{com}_k^{c_k}))$ with probability 1 by the definition of $\Pi_{\mathbf{c}}$ and the perfect binding property of Com.
3. For any $(\mathbf{c}, \mathbf{c}') \in S$, if $\mathcal{A}_1$ takes as input the $s_{\mathbf{c}}$ and $s_{\mathbf{c}'}$ defined as follows:

$$\begin{cases} s_{\mathbf{c}} = (\mathsf{val}_{\mathsf{Com}}(\mathsf{com}_1^{c_1}), \ldots, \mathsf{val}_{\mathsf{Com}}(\mathsf{com}_k^{c_k})) \\ s_{\mathbf{c}'} = (\mathsf{val}_{\mathsf{Com}}(\mathsf{com}_1^{c_1'}), \ldots, \mathsf{val}_{\mathsf{Com}}(\mathsf{com}_k^{c_k'})) \end{cases} ;$$

then, it outputs $s^* := \mathsf{val}_{\mathsf{Com}}(\overline{\mathsf{com}})$ as defined in Definition 8 since we assume that $\overline{\mathsf{com}}$ is valid.

Let $\widetilde{\mathcal{SE}}$ be the ε-simulation extractor of Lemma 1 in the above setting. Then Lemma 1 gives us the following:

$$\{\widetilde{\mathcal{SE}}(1^\lambda, 1^{\varepsilon^{-1}}, \{\Pi_{\mathbf{c}}\}_{\mathbf{c}\in\{0,1\}^k}, \mathcal{A}, \rho')\}_\lambda \overset{s}{\approx}_\varepsilon \{\mathsf{Exp}(\lambda, \{\Pi_{\mathbf{c}}\}_{\mathbf{c}\in\{0,1\}^k}, \rho')\}_\lambda$$

where $\mathsf{Exp}(\lambda, \{\Pi_{\mathbf{c}}\}_{\mathbf{c}\in\{0,1\}^k}, \rho')$ is as defined in Lemma 1. That is, $\mathsf{Exp}(\lambda, \{\Pi_{\mathbf{c}}\}_{\mathbf{c}\in\{0,1\}^k}, \rho')$ works as follows:

- Choose $\mathbf{c} \leftarrow \{0,1\}^k$.
- Apply the measurement $\{\Pi_{\mathbf{c}}, I - \Pi_{\mathbf{c}}\}$ on ρ'.
  - If the state is projected onto $\Pi_{\mathbf{c}}$, the experiment outputs $\mathbf{c}$, the classical string $\mathsf{val}_{\mathsf{Com}}(\overline{\mathsf{com}})$, and the resulting state.
  - If the state is projected onto $I - \Pi_{\mathbf{c}}$, the experiment outputs $\mathbf{c}$, $\perp$, and the resulting state.

One can see that the state in the third output of $\mathsf{Exp}(\lambda, \rho')$ is similar to the final state of C^* in the real execution except that C^* applies the unitary $U_{\mathbf{c}}$ instead of the measurement $\{\Pi_{\mathbf{c}}, I - \Pi_{\mathbf{c}}\}$ and measures $\mathbf{V}$ and $\mathbf{D}$. By noting that $\Pi_{\mathbf{c}}^{\mathsf{test}} U_{\mathbf{c}} = U_{\mathbf{c}} \Pi_{\mathbf{c}}$ and that measuring $\mathbf{V}$ and $\mathbf{D}$ is the same as first applying the measurement $\{\Pi_{\mathbf{c}}^{\mathsf{test}}, I - \Pi_{\mathbf{c}}^{\mathsf{test}}\}$ and then measuring $\mathbf{V}$ and $\mathbf{D}$, if we apply $U_{\mathbf{c}}$ on the third output of $\mathsf{Exp}(\lambda, \{\Pi_{\mathbf{c}}\}_{\mathbf{c}\in\{0,1\}^k}, \rho')$ and then measure $\mathbf{V}$ and $\mathbf{D}$, the state is exactly the same as the final state of C^*.

Therefore, the following extractor $\mathcal{SE}_{\mathsf{weak}}$ works for the weak ε-simulation extractability:

$$\mathcal{SE}_{\mathsf{weak}}^{C^*(\rho)}(1^\lambda, 1^{\varepsilon^{-1}}):$$

1. Run the commit stage of wExtCom between $C^*(\rho)$ and the honest receiver R until C^* sends $\overline{\mathsf{com}}$ in Step 1. Let ρ' be the internal state of C^* at this point.
2. Run $(\mathbf{c}, m_{\mathsf{Ext}}, \rho_{\mathsf{Ext}}) \leftarrow \widetilde{\mathcal{SE}}(1^\lambda, 1^{\varepsilon^{-1}}, \{\Pi_{\mathbf{c}}\}_{\mathbf{c}\in\{0,1\}^k}, \mathcal{A}, \rho')$ where $\mathcal{A} = (\mathcal{A}_0, \mathcal{A}_1)$ is as defined above. Remark that the definition of $\Pi_{\mathbf{c}}$ depends on $\overline{\mathsf{com}}$, and it uses $\overline{\mathsf{com}}$ generated in the previous step.
3. Apply $U_{\mathbf{c}}$ on ρ_{Ext} to generate $U_{\mathbf{c}} \rho_{\mathsf{Ext}} U_{\mathbf{c}}^\dagger$ and measures registers $\mathbf{V}$ and $\mathbf{D}$ to get $\mathbf{v}$ and $\overline{\mathsf{decom}}$. Let ρ_{final} be the state after the measurement.
4. Output $(m_{\mathsf{Ext}}, \rho_{\mathsf{final}})$. □

On the Parallel Execution of wExtCom. We can prove that wExtCom satisfies a parallel version of the weak extractability with ε-simulation in a similar way. In the following, we prove that wExtCom satisfies even a generalized version of that, which we call *special parallel weak extractability with ε-simulation*. Looking ahead, this will be used in the proof of the (parallel) ε-simulation strong extractability of Protocol 2 in Sect. 5.2.

Intuitively, it requires the following: Suppose that a malicious committer C^* interacts with n copies of the honest receiver R in parallel, and let com_j be the commitment generated in the j-th execution. Suppose that com_j is valid for all $j \in V$ for some subset $V \subseteq [n]$. Let $F : \{0,1\}^\ell \cup \{\bot\} \to \{0,1\}^*$ be a function that is determined by $\{\mathsf{val}(\mathsf{com}_j)\}_{j \in V}$, i.e., $F(m_1, ..., m_n)$ takes a unique value m^* as long as $m_j = \mathsf{val}(\mathsf{com}_j)$ for all $j \in V$. Then, the extractor can extract m^* while simulating the post-execution state of C^*. A formal definition is given below.

Definition 10 (Special Parallel Weak Extractability with ε-Simulation). *We say that a commitment scheme Π satisfies the* special parallel weak extractability with ε-simulation *if the following is satisfied. For any integer $n = \mathrm{poly}(\lambda)$ and an efficiently computable function $F : \{\{0,1\}^\ell \cup \{\bot\}\}^n \to \{0,1\}^*$, there exists $\mathcal{SE}_F$ that satisfies the following: For commitments $\{\mathsf{com}_j\}_{j=1}^n$, we say that $\{\mathsf{com}_j\}_{j=1}^n$ is F-good if it satisfies the following:*

1. *there exists $V \subseteq [n]$ such that com_j is valid (i.e., $\mathsf{val}_\Pi(\mathsf{com}_j) \neq \bot$) for all $j \in V$; and*
2. *there exists a unique m^* such that $F(m_1', ..., m_n') = m^*$ for all $(m_1', ..., m_n')$ such that $m_j' = \mathsf{val}_\Pi(\mathsf{com}_j)$ for all $j \in V$.*

Then it holds that

$$\left\{ \Gamma_{F,\{\mathsf{com}_j\}_{j=1}^n}(m_{\mathsf{Ext}}, \mathsf{ST}_{C^*}) : (\{\mathsf{com}_j\}_{j=1}^n, m_{\mathsf{Ext}}, \mathsf{ST}_{C^*}) \leftarrow \mathcal{SE}_F^{C^*(\rho)}(1^\lambda, 1^{\varepsilon^{-1}}) \right\}_\lambda$$

$$\stackrel{c}{\approx}_\varepsilon \left\{ \begin{array}{l} \Gamma_{F,\{\mathsf{com}_j\}_{j=1}^n}(F(\mathsf{val}_\Pi(\mathsf{com}_1), ..., \mathsf{val}_\Pi(\mathsf{com}_n)), \mathsf{ST}_{C^*}) \\ : (\{\mathsf{com}_j\}_{j=1}^n, \mathsf{ST}_{C^*}, \{b_{\mathsf{com},j}\}_{j=1}^n) \leftarrow \langle C^*(\rho), R^n \rangle (1^\lambda) \end{array} \right\}_\lambda,$$

where $(\{\mathsf{com}_j\}_{j=1}^n, \mathsf{ST}_{C^*}, \{b_{\mathsf{com},j}\}_{j=1}^n) \leftarrow \langle C^*(\rho), R^n \rangle (1^\lambda)$ means that $C^*(\rho)$ interacts with n copies of the honest receiver R in parallel and the execution results in transcripts $\{\mathsf{com}_j\}_{j=1}^n$, the final state ST_{C^*}, and outputs $\{b_{\mathsf{com},j}\}_{j=1}^n$ of each copy of R and

$$\Gamma_{F,\{\mathsf{com}_j\}_{j=1}^n}(m, \mathsf{ST}_{C^*}) := \begin{cases} (m, \mathsf{ST}_{C^*}) & \text{if } \{\mathsf{com}_j\}_{j=1}^n \text{ is } F\text{-good} \\ \bot & \text{otherwise} \end{cases}.$$

Lemma 5 (Special Parallel Weak Extractability with ε-Simulation). wExtCom *satisfies the special parallel weak extractability with ε-simulation (as per Definition 10).*

The proof of Lemma 5 is similar to that of Lemma 4. Due to space constraints, we postpone it to the full version [16, Sect. 5.1].

5.2 Strongly Extractable Commitment

In this section, we present the *strongly* extractable commitment with ε-simulation. The scheme is shown in Protocol 2. It relies on the following building blocks:

1. the ε-simulatable *weakly* extractable commitment wExtCom given in Protocol 1. We remark that the security of Protocol 2 relies on the particular wExtCom presented in Protocol 1 because we also need the special parallel weak extractability with ε-simulation (Definition 10); we do not know if Protocol 2 can be based on any wExtCom satisfying the weak extractability with ε-simulation as in Definition 7.
2. a $(n+1,t)$-perfectly verifiable secret sharing scheme VSS = (VSS$_{\text{Share}}$, VSS$_{\text{Recon}}$). We require that t is a constant fraction of n such that $t \leq n/3$. There are known constructions (without any computational assumptions) satisfying these properties [6,20].

Protocol 2: ε(-Simulatable Strongly Extractable Commitment ExtCom

---

Let $n(\lambda)$ be a polynomial on λ. Let t be a constant fraction of n such that $t \leq n/3$.

Input: both the (committer) C and the receiver R get security parameter 1^λ as the common input; C gets a string $m \in \{0,1\}^{\ell(\lambda)}$ as his private input, where $\ell(\cdot)$ is a polynomial.

Commit Stage:

1. C emulates $n+1$ (virtual) players $\{P_i\}_{i\in[n+1]}$ to execute the VSS$_{\text{Share}}$ protocol "in his head", where the input to P_{n+1} (i.e., the Dealer) is m. Let $\{v_i\}_{i\in[n+1]}$ be the views of the $n+1$ players describing the execution.
2. C and R involve in n executions of wExtCom in parallel, where in the i-th instance $(i \in [n])$, C commits to v_i.
3. R picks a random string r_1 and commits to it using wExtCom.
4. C picks a random string r_2 and sends it to R.
5. R sends to C the value r_1 together with the corresponding decommitment information w.r.t. the wExtCom in Step 3. Now, both parties learn a coin-tossing result $r = r_1 \oplus r_2$, which specifies a size-t random subset $T \subseteq [n]$.
6. C sends to R in *one round* the following messages: $\{v_i\}_{i\in T}$ together with the corresponding decommitment information w.r.t. the wExtCom in Step 2.
7. R checks the following conditions:
   (a) All the decommitments in Step 6 are valid; **and**
   (b) for any $i,j \in T$, views (v_i, v_j) are consistent w.r.t. the VSS$_{\text{Share}}$ execution as described in Step 1.
   If all the checks pass, R accepts; otherwise, R rejects.

Decommit Stage:

1. C sends $\{v_i\}_{i\in[n]}$ together with all the corresponding information w.r.t. the wExtCom in Step 1 of the Commit Stage.
2. R constructs $\{v_i'\}_{i\in[n]}$ as follows: in Step 1 of the Decommit Stage, if the i-th decommitment is valid, R sets $v_i' := v_i$; otherwise, R sets $v_i' := \perp$.
3. R outputs $m' := \text{VSS}_{\text{Recon}}(v_1', \ldots, v_n')$.

Security. Correctness and statistical binding property of ExtCom follows straightforwardly from that of wExtCom. We show that ExtCom is computationally-hiding and (parallel) strong extractable with ε-simulation.

Lemma 6 (Computational Hiding). ExtCom *is computationally hiding.*

Computational hinding property can be shown based on the weak extractability of wExtCom used in Step 3, computational hiding property of wExtCom used in Step 2, and the secrecy property of VSS by a standard hybrid argument. The proof is postponed to the full version [16, Sect. 5.2].

In the following, we prove the (parallel-)strong extractability with ε-simulation. Though we finally prove the parallel version, we first give a proof for the stand-alone version since that is simpler and the proof is readily extended to that of the parallel version.

Lemma 7 (Strong Extractability with ε-Simulation). ExtCom *is strongly extractable with ε-simulation (as per Definition 5).*

Proof. Suppose that a non-uniform QPT committer C^* interacts with the honest receiver R in the commit stage of ExtCom. We consider two cases where R accepts or rejects, respectively. By using Watrous' rewinding lemma [65] in a similar way to the proof of Lemma 1, it suffices to construct a simulator that correctly extracts and simulates for each case separately. Moreover, when R rejects, the commitment is invalid and thus the extractor does not need to extract anything. Thus, there is a trivial perfect simulation extractor for this case: it can simply run the interaction between $C^*(\rho)$ and R by playing the role of R and outputs the final state of C^*. What is left is to construct an extractor that correctly extracts and simulates assuming that R accepts in the committing stage. That is, it suffices to prove the following claim.

Claim 1 (Extraction and Simulation for Accepting Case). *There exists a QPT algorithm $\mathcal{SE}_{\mathsf{Acc}}$ such that for any noticeable $\varepsilon(\lambda)$ and any non-uniform QPT $C^*(\rho)$, it holds that*

$$\left\{ \Gamma_{b_{\mathsf{com}}}(m_{\mathsf{Ext}}, \mathsf{ST}_{C^*}) : (m_{\mathsf{Ext}}, \mathsf{ST}_{C^*}, b_{\mathsf{com}}) \leftarrow \mathcal{SE}_{\mathsf{Acc}}^{C^*(\rho)}(1^\lambda, 1^{\varepsilon^{-1}}) \right\}_\lambda$$

$$\overset{c}{\approx}_\varepsilon \left\{ \Gamma_{b_{\mathsf{com}}}(\mathsf{val}_{\mathsf{ExtCom}}(\mathsf{com}), \mathsf{ST}_{C^*}) : (\mathsf{com}, \mathsf{ST}_{C^*}, b_{\mathsf{com}}) \leftarrow \langle C^*(\rho), R \rangle(1^\lambda) \right\}_\lambda,$$

where $\Gamma_{b_{\mathsf{com}}}(m, \mathsf{ST}_{C^*}) := \begin{cases} (m, \mathsf{ST}_{C^*}) & \text{if } b_{\mathsf{com}} = 1 \\ \perp & \text{otherwise} \end{cases}$.

Remark 2. One may think that the above claim is similar to the weak extractability with ε-simulation (Definition 7). However, the crucial difference is that the extractor $\mathcal{SE}_{\mathsf{Acc}}$ should declare if the simulation has succeeded by outputting b_{com} in the clear. On the other hand, in Definition 7, $\mathcal{SE}_{\mathsf{weak}}$ is only required to indirectly declare that depending on if com is valid, which may not be known by $\mathcal{SE}_{\mathsf{weak}}$.

Proof of Claim 1. Let wExtCom.com$_i$ be the i-th commitment of wExtCom in Step 2 in the commit stage. In the execution of $(\mathsf{com}, \mathsf{ST}_{C^*}, b_{\mathsf{com}}) \leftarrow \langle C^*(\rho), R \rangle (1^\lambda)$, let Good be the event that $\{\mathsf{wExtCom.com}_i\}_{i=1}^n$ is VSS$_{\mathsf{Recon}}$-good in the sense of Definition 10, i.e.,

- there exists $V \subseteq [n]$ such that wExtCom.com$_i$ is valid (i.e., val$_{\mathsf{wExtCom}}$ (wExtCom.com$_i$) $\neq \bot$) for all $i \in V$, and
- there exists m^* such that $\mathsf{VSS}_{\mathsf{Recon}}(v_1', \ldots, v_n') = m^*$ for all $(v_1', \ldots, v_n')$ such that

$$\forall i \in V, \ v_i' = \mathsf{val}_{\mathsf{wExtCom}}(\mathsf{wExtCom.com}_i).$$

Let Bad be the complementary event of Good. We prove the following claim.

Claim 2. *It holds that*

$$\Pr[\mathsf{Bad} \wedge b_{\mathsf{com}} = 1 : (\mathsf{com}, \mathsf{ST}_{C^*}, b_{\mathsf{com}}) \leftarrow \langle C^*(\rho), R \rangle (1^\lambda)] = \mathsf{neglnegl}(\lambda). \quad (2)$$

Claim 2 can be proven based on a similar argument to those used in previous black-box commit-and-prove literature [37,39,47,54]. We postpone the proof to [16, Section 5.2].

Given Claim 2, it is straightforward to finish the proof of Lemma 1 by using Lemma 5. Claim 2 means that the Good occurs whenever $b_{\mathsf{com}} = 1$ except for negligible probability. Since $\mathcal{SE}_{\mathsf{Acc}}$ is only required to correctly extract and simulate when $b_{\mathsf{com}} = 1$, it suffices to give an extractor that correctly extracts and simulates when $\{\mathsf{wExtCom.com}_i\}_{i=1}^n$ satisfies the condition for Good. Since wExtCom satisfies the special parallel weak extractability with ε-simulation as shown in Lemma 5, $\mathcal{SE}_{\mathsf{VSS}_{\mathsf{Recon}}}$ given in Definition 10 (where we set $F := \mathsf{VSS}_{\mathsf{Recon}}$) directly gives $\mathcal{SE}_{\mathsf{Acc}}$. Specifically, $\mathcal{SE}_{\mathsf{Acc}}$ as described below suffices for Lemma 1. $\mathcal{SE}_{\mathsf{Acc}}^{C^*(\rho)}(1^\lambda, 1^{\varepsilon^{-1}})$:

1. Run $(\{\mathsf{wExtCom.com}_i\}_{i=1}^n, m_{\mathsf{Ext}}, \mathsf{ST}_{C_2^*}) \leftarrow \mathcal{SE}_{\mathsf{VSS}_{\mathsf{Recon}}}^{C_2^*(\rho)}(1^\lambda, 1^{\varepsilon^{-1}})$ where C_2^* denotes the action of C^* until Step 2 in the commit stage where it outputs $\{\mathsf{wExtCom.com}_i\}_{i=1}^n$.
2. Simulate the interaction between C^* and R from Step 3 where the state of C^* is initialized to be $\mathsf{ST}_{C_2^*}$. Let b_{com} be R's decision (i.e., $b_{\mathsf{com}} = 1$ if and only if R accepts) and ST_{C^*} be the post-execution state of S
3. Output $(m_{\mathsf{Ext}}, \mathsf{ST}_{C^*}, b_{\mathsf{com}})$.

This finishes the proof of Lemma 1.   □

This eventually concludes the proof of Claim 7.   □

The above proof can be extended to prove the parallel-strong extractability (i.e. Lemma 8). We postpone it to the full version [16, Sect. 5.2].

Lemma 8 (Parallel-Strong Extractability with ε-Simulation). ExtCom *is parallel-strongly extractable with ε-simulation.*

6 Black-Box ε-Simulatable ExtCom-and-Prove in Constant Rounds

Roughly speaking, ε-simulatable ExtCom-and-Prove is a strongly extractable commitment scheme with ε-simulation with the additional functionality that the committer can later prove any statement of the committed message. Besides the security requirements as strongly extractable commitments with ε-simulation, we additionally require soundness, which states that the committer cannot prove a false statement on the committed message, and ε-zero-knowledge property, which is defined similarly to in [18]. See [16, Definition 17] for the formal definition.

We show the following lemma.

Lemma 9. *Assume the existence of post-quantum secure OWFs. Then, there exists a constant-round ε-simulatable ExtCom-and-Prove scheme. Moreover, this construction makes only black-box use of the assumed OWF.*

Construction. The construction is shown in Protocol 3. It makes black-box use of the following building blocks:

1. The ε-simulatable, *parallel-strong* extractable commitment ExtCom constructed in Sect. 5.2, which in turn makes black-box use of any post-quantum secure OWFs.
2. A statistically-binding, computationally-hiding (against QPT adversaries) commitment Com. This is also known assuming only black-box access to post-quantum secure OWFs.
3. A $(n + 1, t)$-perfectly secure verifiable secret sharing scheme VSS = (VSS$_{\mathsf{Share}}$, VSS$_{\mathsf{Recon}}$) (see [16, Section 3.3]);
4. A (n, t)-perfectly secure MPC protocol Π_{MPC} (see [16, Sect. 3.4]).

For the VSS and MPC protocols, we require that t is a constant fraction of n such that $t \leq n/3$. There are information-theoretical constructions satisfying these properties [6,20].

Protocol 3: ε-Simulatable ExtCom-and-Prove

Parameter Setting: Let $n(\lambda)$ be a polynomial on λ. Let t be a constant fraction of n such that $t \leq n/3$.

Input: Both P and the receiver V get 1^λ as the common input; P gets a string $m \in \{0,1\}^{\ell(\lambda)}$ as his private input, where $\ell(\cdot)$ is a polynomial.

Commit Stage:
1. P emulates $n + 1$ (virtual) players $\{P_i\}_{i \in [n+1]}$ to execute the VSS$_{\mathsf{Share}}$ protocol "in his head", where the input to P_{n+1} (i.e., the Dealer) is m. Let $\{\mathsf{v}_i\}_{i \in [n+1]}$ be the views of the $n + 1$ players describing the execution.
2. P and V involve in n executions of ExtCom in parallel, where in the i-th instance $(i \in [n])$, P commits to v_i.

Decommit Stage:
1. P sends $\{\mathsf{v}_i\}_{i \in [n]}$ together with the corresponding decommitment information w.r.t. the ExtCom in Step 2 of the Commit Stage.

2. V checks that all the decommitments in Step 1 of the Decommit Stage are valid. If so, V outputs $\mathsf{VSS_{Recon}}(\mathsf{v}_1, \ldots, \mathsf{v}_n)$ and then halts; otherwise, V outputs $\bot$ and then halts.

Prove Stage: both parties learn a polynomial-time computable predicate ϕ.

1. P emulates "in his head" n (virtual) players $\{P_i\}_{i \in [n]}$, where P_i's input is v_i (from Step 1 of the Commit Stage). These n parties execute Π_{MPC} for the following functionality: the functionality reconstructs $m' := \mathsf{VSS_{Recon}}(\mathsf{v}_1, \ldots, \mathsf{v}_n)$ and sends the value $\phi(m')$ to all the parties as their output. For $i \in [n]$, let v_i' be the view of party P_i during Π_{MPC}.

2. P and V involve in n executions of Com in parallel, where in the i-th instance ($i \in [n]$), P commits to v_i'.

3. V picks a random string r_1 and commits to it using ExtCom.

4. P picks a random string r_2 and sends it to V.

5. V sends to P the value r_1 together with the corresponding decommitment information w.r.t. the ExtCom in Step 3. Now, both parties learn a coin-tossing result $r = r_1 \oplus r_2$, which specifies a size-t random subset $T \subseteq [n]$.

6. P sends to V in *one round* the following messages:
   (a) $\{\mathsf{v}_i\}_{i \in T}$ together with the corresponding decommitment information w.r.t. the ExtCom in Step 2 of the Commit Stage; **and**
   (b) $\{\mathsf{v}_i'\}_{i \in T}$ together with the corresponding decommitment information w.r.t. the Com in Step 2 of the Prove Stage.

7. V checks the following conditions:
   (a) All the decommitments in Step 6a and 6b are valid; **and**
   (b) for any $i \in T$, v_i is the prefix of v_i' ; **and**
   (c) for any $i, j \in T$, views $(\mathsf{v}_i', \mathsf{v}_j')$ are consistent w.r.t. the $\mathsf{VSS_{Share}}$ execution in Step 1 of the Commit Stage and the Π_{MPC} execution as described in Step 1 of the Prove Stage.

If all the checks pass, V accepts; otherwise, V rejects.

Security. It is straightforward to see that Protocol 3 is constant-round and makes only black-box access to OWFs. Completeness follows from that of VSS, ExtCom, Com, and Π_{MPC}. In the following, we show ε-simulatable extractability (in Lemma 10), soundness (in Lemma 11), and ε-zero-knowledge (in Lemma 12). Due to space constraints, we postpone their proofs to [16, Sect. 6.5].

Lemma 10 (ε-Simulation Extractability). *Assume* ExtCom *is parallel-strongly extractable with ε-simulation. Then, Protocol 3 satisfies security as ε-simulation extractable commitment.*

Lemma 11 (Soundness). *Assume* ExtCom *and* Com *are statistically binding,* ExtCom *is computationally-hiding,* VSS *is $(n+1, t)$-perfectly verifiable-committing and* Π_{MPC} *is (n, t)-perfectly robust. Then, Protocol 3 satisfies the soundness requirement (see [16, Definition 17]).*

Lemma 12 (ε-Zero-Knowledge). *Assume* ExtCom *and* Com *are computationally-hiding,* ExtCom *is weakly extractable with ε-simulation,* VSS *is $(n+1, t)$-secret (see [16, Definition 1]), and* Π_{MPC} *is (n, t)-semi-honest computationally private* *(see* [16, Definition 4]*). Then, Prot. 3 satisfies the ε-zero-knowledge property defined in* [16, Definition 17].

Applications. Applications of our ε-simulatable ExtCom-and-Prove protocol are postponed to the full version, where we will show to to obtain ε-simulatable coin-flipping [16, Sect. 6.2], zero-knowledge argument of knowledge with an ε-simulatable knowledge extractor [16, Sect. 6.3], and black-box ε-zero-knowledge for **QMA** [16, Sect. 6.4].

7   Black-Box ε-Simulatable PQ-2PC in Constant Rounds

The ε-simulatable ExtCom-and-Prove protocol constructed in Sect. 6 yields the following theorems. Due to space constraints, their proofs are postponed to the full version [16, Sects. 7 and 8].

Theorem 3. *Assuming the existence of a constant-round semi-honest bit-OT secure against QPT adversaries, there exists a black-box, constant-round construction of ε-simulatable 2PC protocol secure against QPT adversaries.*

Theorem 4. *Assuming the existence of OWFs secure against QPT adversaries, there exists a black-box, constant-round construction of ε-simulatable 2PC protocol secure against QPT adversaries. This protocol makes use of quantum communication.*

Acknowledgments. Kai-Min Chung is supported in part by Ministry of Science and Technology, Taiwan, under Grant no. MOST 109-2223-E-001-001-MY3, the 2021 Academia Sinica Investigator Award (AS-IA-110-M02), and the Air Force Office of Scientific Research under award number FA2386-20-1-4066.

Xiao Liang is supported in part by Omkant Pandey's DARPA SIEVE Award HR00112020026 and NSF grants 1907908 and 2028920. Any opinions, findings and conclusions or recommendations expressed in this material are those of the author(s) and do not necessarily reflect the views of the United States Government, DARPA, or NSF.

References

1. Aaronson, S.: Limitations of quantum advice and one-way communication. Theory Comput. **1**(1), 1–28 (2005)
2. Agarwal, A., Bartusek, J., Goyal, V., Khurana, D., Malavolta, G.: Post-quantum multi-party computation. In: Canteaut, A., Standaert, F.-X. (eds.) EUROCRYPT 2021, Part I. LNCS, vol. 12696, pp. 435–464. Springer, Cham (2021). https://doi.org/10.1007/978-3-030-77870-5_16
3. Ananth, P., Chung, K.-M., Placa, R.L.L.: On the concurrent composition of quantum zero-knowledge. In: Malkin, T., Peikert, C. (eds.) CRYPTO 2021. LNCS, vol. 12825, pp. 346–374. Springer, Cham (2021). https://doi.org/10.1007/978-3-030-84242-0_13

4. Ananth, P., La Placa, R.L.: Secure quantum extraction protocols. In: Pass, R., Pietrzak, K. (eds.) TCC 2020, Part III. LNCS, vol. 12552, pp. 123–152. Springer, Cham (2020). https://doi.org/10.1007/978-3-030-64381-2_5

5. Bartusek, J., Coladangelo, A., Khurana, D., Ma, F.: One-way functions imply secure computation in a quantum world. In: Malkin, T., Peikert, C. (eds.) CRYPTO 2021, Part I. LNCS, vol. 12825, pp. 467–496. Springer, Cham (2021). https://doi.org/10.1007/978-3-030-84242-0_17

6. Ben-Or, M., Goldwasser, S., Wigderson, A.: Completeness theorems for non-cryptographic fault-tolerant distributed computation (extended abstract). In: 20th ACM STOC, pp. 1–10. ACM Press (1988). https://doi.org/10.1145/62212.62213

7. Bennett, C.H., Brassard, G., Crépeau, C., Skubiszewska, M.H.: Practical quantum oblivious transfer. In: Feigenbaum, J. (ed.) CRYPTO 1991. LNCS, vol. 576, pp. 351–366. Springer, Heidelberg (1992). https://doi.org/10.1007/3-540-46766-1_29

8. Bitansky, N., Kalai, Y.T., Paneth, O.: Multi-collision resistance: a paradigm for keyless hash functions. In: Diakonikolas, I., Kempe, D., Henzinger, M. (eds.) 50th ACM STOC, pp. 671–684. ACM Press (2018). https://doi.org/10.1145/3188745.3188870

9. Bitansky, N., Lin, H., Shmueli, O.: Non-malleable commitments against quantum attacks. Cryptology ePrint Archive, Report 2021/920 (2021). https://ia.cr/2021/920

10. Bitansky, N., Shmueli, O.: Post-quantum zero knowledge in constant rounds. In: Makarychev, K., Makarychev, Y., Tulsiani, M., Kamath, G., Chuzhoy, J. (eds.) 52nd ACM STOC, pp. 269–279. ACM Press (2020). https://doi.org/10.1145/3357713.3384324

11. Bouman, N.J., Fehr, S.: Sampling in a quantum population, and applications. In: Rabin, T. (ed.) CRYPTO 2010. LNCS, vol. 6223, pp. 724–741. Springer, Heidelberg (2010). https://doi.org/10.1007/978-3-642-14623-7_39

12. Brakerski, Z., Yuen, H.: Quantum garbled circuits (2020)

13. Broadbent, A., Grilo, A.B.: QMA-hardness of consistency of local density matrices with applications to quantum zero-knowledge. In: 61st FOCS, pp. 196–205. IEEE Computer Society Press (2020). https://doi.org/10.1109/FOCS46700.2020.00027

14. Broadbent, A., Ji, Z., Song, F., Watrous, J.: Zero-knowledge proof systems for QMA. SIAM J. Comput. 49(2), 245–283 (2020)

15. Chatterjee, R., Liang, X., Pandey, O.: Improved black-box constructions of composable secure computation. In: Czumaj, A., Dawar, A., Merelli, E. (eds.) ICALP 2020. LIPIcs, vol. 168, pp. 28:1–28:20. Schloss Dagstuhl (2020). https://doi.org/10.4230/LIPIcs.ICALP.2020.28

16. Chia, N.H., Chung, K.M., Liang, X., Yamakawa, T.: Post-quantum simulatable extraction with minimal assumptions: Black-box and constant-round. Cryptology ePrint Archive, Paper 2021/1516 (2021). https://eprint.iacr.org/2021/1516

17. Chia, N.H., Chung, K.M., Liu, Q., Yamakawa, T.: On the impossibility of post-quantum black-box zero-knowledge in constant rounds. In: 62nd FOCS (2021)

18. Chia, N.H., Chung, K.M., Yamakawa, T.: A black-box approach to post-quantum zero-knowledge in constant rounds. In: Malkin, T., Peikert, C. (eds.) CRYPTO 2021, Part I. LNCS, vol. 12825, pp. 315–345. Springer, Cham (2021). https://doi.org/10.1007/978-3-030-84242-0_12

19. Choi, S.G., Dachman-Soled, D., Malkin, T., Wee, H.: Simple, black-box constructions of adaptively secure protocols. In: Reingold, O. (ed.) TCC 2009. LNCS, vol. 5444, pp. 387–402. Springer, Heidelberg (2009). https://doi.org/10.1007/978-3-642-00457-5_23

20. Cramer, R., Damgård, I., Dziembowski, S., Hirt, M., Rabin, T.: Efficient multi-party computations secure against an adaptive adversary. In: Stern, J. (ed.) EURO-CRYPT 1999. LNCS, vol. 1592, pp. 311–326. Springer, Heidelberg (1999). https://doi.org/10.1007/3-540-48910-X_22

21. Crépeau, C., Kilian, J.: Achieving oblivious transfer using weakened security assumptions (extended abstract). In: 29th FOCS, pp. 42–52. IEEE Computer Society Press (1988). https://doi.org/10.1109/SFCS.1988.21920

22. Crépeau, C., Kilian, J.: Weakening security assumptions and oblivious transfer. In: Goldwasser, S. (ed.) CRYPTO 1988. LNCS, vol. 403, pp. 2–7. Springer, New York (1990). https://doi.org/10.1007/0-387-34799-2_1

23. Damgård, I., Fehr, S., Lunemann, C., Salvail, L., Schaffner, C.: Improving the security of quantum protocols via commit-and-open. In: Halevi, S. (ed.) CRYPTO 2009. LNCS, vol. 5677, pp. 408–427. Springer, Heidelberg (2009). https://doi.org/10.1007/978-3-642-03356-8_24

24. Damgård, I., Ishai, Y.: Constant-round multiparty computation using a black-box pseudorandom generator. In: Shoup, V. (ed.) CRYPTO 2005. LNCS, vol. 3621, pp. 378–394. Springer, Heidelberg (2005). https://doi.org/10.1007/11535218_23

25. Dolev, D., Dwork, C., Naor, M.: Nonmalleable cryptography. SIAM J. Comput. **30**(2), 391–437 (2000)

26. Dulek, Y., Grilo, A.B., Jeffery, S., Majenz, C., Schaffner, C.: Secure multi-party quantum computation with a dishonest majority. In: Canteaut, A., Ishai, Y. (eds.) EUROCRYPT 2020, Part III. LNCS, vol. 12107, pp. 729–758. Springer, Cham (2020). https://doi.org/10.1007/978-3-030-45727-3_25

27. Dwork, C., Naor, M., Sahai, A.: Concurrent zero-knowledge. J. ACM **51**(6), 851–898 (2004)

28. Fleischhacker, N., Goyal, V., Jain, A.: On the existence of three round zero-knowledge proofs. In: Nielsen, J.B., Rijmen, V. (eds.) EUROCRYPT 2018. LNCS, vol. 10822, pp. 3–33. Springer, Cham (2018). https://doi.org/10.1007/978-3-319-78372-7_1

29. Garg, R., Khurana, D., Lu, G., Waters, B.: Black-box non-interactive non-malleable commitments. In: Canteaut, A., Standaert, F.-X. (eds.) EUROCRYPT 2021, Part III. LNCS, vol. 12698, pp. 159–185. Springer, Cham (2021). https://doi.org/10.1007/978-3-030-77883-5_6

30. Garg, S., Goyal, V., Jain, A., Sahai, A.: Concurrently secure computation in constant rounds. In: Pointcheval, D., Johansson, T. (eds.) EUROCRYPT 2012. LNCS, vol. 7237, pp. 99–116. Springer, Heidelberg (2012). https://doi.org/10.1007/978-3-642-29011-4_8

31. Garg, S., Gupta, D., Miao, P., Pandey, O.: Secure multiparty RAM computation in constant rounds. In: Hirt, M., Smith, A. (eds.) TCC 2016, Part I. LNCS, vol. 9985, pp. 491–520. Springer, Heidelberg (2016). https://doi.org/10.1007/978-3-662-53641-4_19

32. Garg, S., Kiyoshima, S., Pandey, O.: A new approach to black-box concurrent secure computation. In: Nielsen, J.B., Rijmen, V. (eds.) EUROCRYPT 2018, Part II. LNCS, vol. 10821, pp. 566–599. Springer, Cham (2018). https://doi.org/10.1007/978-3-319-78375-8_19

33. Garg, S., Liang, X., Pandey, O., Visconti, I.: Black-box constructions of bounded-concurrent secure computation. In: Galdi, C., Kolesnikov, V. (eds.) SCN 2020. LNCS, vol. 12238, pp. 87–107. Springer, Cham (2020). https://doi.org/10.1007/978-3-030-57990-6_5

34. Gennaro, R., Lysyanskaya, A., Malkin, T., Micali, S., Rabin, T.: Algorithmic tamper-proof (ATP) security: theoretical foundations for security against hardware tampering. In: Naor, M. (ed.) TCC 2004. LNCS, vol. 2951, pp. 258–277. Springer, Heidelberg (2004). https://doi.org/10.1007/978-3-540-24638-1_15

35. Goldreich, O., Kahan, A.: How to construct constant-round zero-knowledge proof systems for NP. J. Cryptol. **9**(3), 167–189 (1996). https://doi.org/10.1007/BF00208001

36. Goyal, V.: Constant round non-malleable protocols using one way functions. In: Fortnow, L., Vadhan, S.P. (eds.) 43rd ACM STOC, pp. 695–704. ACM Press (2011). https://doi.org/10.1145/1993636.1993729

37. Goyal, V., Lee, C.K., Ostrovsky, R., Visconti, I.: Constructing non-malleable commitments: A black-box approach. In: 53rd FOCS, pp. 51–60. IEEE Computer Society Press (2012). https://doi.org/10.1109/FOCS.2012.47

38. Goyal, V., Lin, H., Pandey, O., Pass, R., Sahai, A.: Round-efficient concurrently composable secure computation via a robust extraction lemma. In: Dodis, Y., Nielsen, J.B. (eds.) TCC 2015, Part I. LNCS, vol. 9014, pp. 260–289. Springer, Heidelberg (2015). https://doi.org/10.1007/978-3-662-46494-6_12

39. Goyal, V., Ostrovsky, R., Scafuro, A., Visconti, I.: Black-box non-black-box zero knowledge. In: Shmoys, D.B. (ed.) 46th ACM STOC, pp. 515–524. ACM Press (2014). https://doi.org/10.1145/2591796.2591879

40. Grilo, A.B., Lin, H., Song, F., Vaikuntanathan, V.: Oblivious transfer is in MiniQCrypt. In: Canteaut, A., Standaert, F.-X. (eds.) EUROCRYPT 2021. LNCS, vol. 12697, pp. 531–561. Springer, Cham (2021). https://doi.org/10.1007/978-3-030-77886-6_18

41. Haitner, I.: Semi-honest to malicious oblivious transfer– the black-box way. In: Canetti, R. (ed.) TCC 2008. LNCS, vol. 4948, pp. 412–426. Springer, Heidelberg (2008). https://doi.org/10.1007/978-3-540-78524-8_23

42. Haitner, I., Ishai, Y., Kushilevitz, E., Lindell, Y., Petrank, E.: Black-box constructions of protocols for secure computation. SIAM J. Comput. **40**(2), 225–266 (2011). https://doi.org/10.1137/100790537

43. Hallgren, S., Smith, A., Song, F.: Classical cryptographic protocols in a quantum world. In: Rogaway, P. (ed.) CRYPTO 2011. LNCS, vol. 6841, pp. 411–428. Springer, Heidelberg (2011). https://doi.org/10.1007/978-3-642-22792-9_23

44. Hazay, C., Venkitasubramaniam, M.: On the power of secure two-party computation. In: Robshaw, M., Katz, J. (eds.) CRYPTO 2016, Part II. LNCS, vol. 9815, pp. 397–429. Springer, Heidelberg (2016). https://doi.org/10.1007/978-3-662-53008-5_14

45. Hazay, C., Venkitasubramaniam, M.: Round-optimal fully black-box zero-knowledge arguments from one-way permutations. In: Beimel, A., Dziembowski, S. (eds.) TCC 2018, Part I. LNCS, vol. 11239, pp. 263–285. Springer, Cham (2018). https://doi.org/10.1007/978-3-030-03807-6_10

46. Ishai, Y., Kushilevitz, E., Lindell, Y., Petrank, E.: Black-box constructions for secure computation. In: Kleinberg, J.M. (ed.) 38th ACM STOC, pp. 99–108. ACM Press (2006). https://doi.org/10.1145/1132516.1132531

47. Ishai, Y., Kushilevitz, E., Ostrovsky, R., Sahai, A.: Zero-knowledge from secure multiparty computation. In: Johnson, D.S., Feige, U. (eds.) 39th ACM STOC, pp. 21–30. ACM Press (2007). https://doi.org/10.1145/1250790.1250794

48. Ishai, Y., Kushilevitz, E., Ostrovsky, R., Sahai, A.: Cryptography with constant computational overhead. In: Ladner, R.E., Dwork, C. (eds.) 40th ACM STOC, pp. 433–442. ACM Press (2008). https://doi.org/10.1145/1374376.1374438

49. Ishai, Y., Prabhakaran, M., Sahai, A.: Founding cryptography on oblivious transfer – efficiently. In: Wagner, D. (ed.) CRYPTO 2008. LNCS, vol. 5157, pp. 572–591. Springer, Heidelberg (2008). https://doi.org/10.1007/978-3-540-85174-5_32
50. Khurana, D., Ostrovsky, R., Srinivasan, A.: Round optimal black-box "commit-and-prove". In: Beimel, A., Dziembowski, S. (eds.) TCC 2018, Part I. LNCS, vol. 11239, pp. 286–313. Springer, Cham (2018). https://doi.org/10.1007/978-3-030-03807-6_11
51. Kilian, J.: Founding cryptography on oblivious transfer. In: 20th ACM STOC, pp. 20–31. ACM Press (1988). https://doi.org/10.1145/62212.62215
52. Kiyoshima, S.: Round-efficient black-box construction of composable multi-party computation. In: Garay, J.A., Gennaro, R. (eds.) CRYPTO 2014, Part II. LNCS, vol. 8617, pp. 351–368. Springer, Heidelberg (2014). https://doi.org/10.1007/978-3-662-44381-1_20
53. Kiyoshima, S.: Round-optimal black-box commit-and-prove with succinct communication. In: Micciancio, D., Ristenpart, T. (eds.) CRYPTO 2020, Part II. LNCS, vol. 12171, pp. 533–561. Springer, Cham (2020). https://doi.org/10.1007/978-3-030-56880-1_19
54. Liang, X., Pandey, O.: Towards a unified approach to black-box constructions of zero-knowledge proofs. In: Malkin, T., Peikert, C. (eds.) CRYPTO 2021, Part IV. LNCS, vol. 12828, pp. 34–64. Springer, Cham (2021). https://doi.org/10.1007/978-3-030-84259-8_2
55. Lin, H., Pass, R.: Black-box constructions of composable protocols without set-up. In: Safavi-Naini, R., Canetti, R. (eds.) CRYPTO 2012. LNCS, vol. 7417, pp. 461–478. Springer, Heidelberg (2012). https://doi.org/10.1007/978-3-642-32009-5_27
56. Lindell, Y.: A note on constant-round zero-knowledge proofs of knowledge. J. Cryptol. **26**(4), 638–654 (2013). https://doi.org/10.1007/s00145-012-9132-7
57. Lombardi, A., Ma, F., Spooner, N.: Post-quantum zero knowledge, revisited (or: how to do quantum rewinding undetectably). Cryptology ePrint Archive, Report 2021/1543 (2021). https://ia.cr/2021/1543
58. Lunemann, C., Nielsen, J.B.: Fully simulatable quantum-secure coin-flipping and applications. In: Nitaj, A., Pointcheval, D. (eds.) AFRICACRYPT 2011. LNCS, vol. 6737, pp. 21–40. Springer, Heidelberg (2011). https://doi.org/10.1007/978-3-642-21969-6_2
59. Micciancio, D., Ong, S.J., Sahai, A., Vadhan, S.: Concurrent zero knowledge without complexity assumptions. In: Halevi, S., Rabin, T. (eds.) TCC 2006. LNCS, vol. 3876, pp. 1–20. Springer, Heidelberg (2006). https://doi.org/10.1007/11681878_1
60. Naor, M.: Bit commitment using pseudorandomness. J. Cryptol. **4**(2), 151–158 (1991). https://doi.org/10.1007/BF00196774
61. Pass, R., Wee, H.: Black-box constructions of two-party protocols from one-way functions. In: Reingold, O. (ed.) TCC 2009. LNCS, vol. 5444, pp. 403–418. Springer, Heidelberg (2009). https://doi.org/10.1007/978-3-642-00457-5_24
62. Prabhakaran, M., Rosen, A., Sahai, A.: Concurrent zero knowledge with logarithmic round-complexity. In: 43rd FOCS, pp. 366–375. IEEE Computer Society Press (Nov 2002). https://doi.org/10.1109/SFCS.2002.1181961
63. Rosen, A.: A note on constant-round zero-knowledge proofs for NP. In: Naor, M. (ed.) TCC 2004. LNCS, vol. 2951, pp. 191–202. Springer, Heidelberg (2004). https://doi.org/10.1007/978-3-540-24638-1_11

64. Unruh, D.: Quantum proofs of knowledge. In: Pointcheval, D., Johansson, T. (eds.) EUROCRYPT 2012. LNCS, vol. 7237, pp. 135–152. Springer, Heidelberg (2012). https://doi.org/10.1007/978-3-642-29011-4_10
65. Watrous, J.: Zero-knowledge against quantum attacks. SIAM J. Comput. **39**(1), 25–58 (2009)
66. Wyner, A.D.: The wire-tap channel. Bell Syst. Tech. J. **54**(8), 1355–1387 (1975)

The Gap Is Sensitive to Size of Preimages: Collapsing Property Doesn't Go Beyond Quantum Collision-Resistance for Preimages Bounded Hash Functions

Shujiao Cao[1,2] and Rui Xue[1,2(✉)]

[1] State Key Laboratory of Information Security, Institute of Information Engineering, Chinese Academy of Sciences, Beijing 100093, China
{caoshujiao,xuerui}@iie.ac.cn
[2] School of Cyber Security, University of Chinese Academy of Sciences, Beijing 100049, China

Abstract. As an enhancement of quantum collision-resistance, the collapsing property of hash functions proposed by Unruh (EUROCRYPT 2016) emphasizes the hardness for distinguishing a superposition state of a hash value from a collapsed one. The collapsing property trivially implies the quantum collision-resistance. However, it remains to be unknown whether there is a reduction from the collapsing hash functions to the quantum collision-resistant hash functions. In this paper, we further study the relations between these two properties and derive two intriguing results as follows:

- Firstly, when the size of preimages of each hash value is bounded by some polynomial, we demonstrate that the collapsing property and the collision-resistance must hold simultaneously. This result is proved via a semi-black-box manner by taking advantage of the invertibility of a unitary quantum circuit.
- Next, we further consider the relations between these two properties in the exponential-sized preimages case. By giving a construction of polynomial bounded hash functions, which preserves the quantum collision-resistance, we show the existence of collapsing hash functions is implied by the quantum collision-resistant hash functions when the size of preimages is not too large to the expected value.

Our results indicate that the gap between these two properties is sensitive to the size of preimages. As a corollary, our results also reveal the non-existence of polynomial bounded equivocal collision-resistant hash functions.

Keywords: quantum collision-resistance · collapsing property · equivocal collision-resistance · hash function

1 Introduction

As a central property of hash functions, collision-resistance plays an important role in the development of cryptography. It emphasizes the hardness of finding two distinct inputs which share the same hash value. The collision-resistant

Y. Dodis and T. Shrimpton (Eds.): CRYPTO 2022, LNCS 13509, pp. 564–595, 2022.
https://doi.org/10.1007/978-3-031-15982-4_19

hash functions can be used to construct many cryptographic objects, such as the digital signature, the Merkle tree, and succinct (zero-knowledge) arguments [6,25,29]. Indeed, the existence of collision-resistant hash function yields the existence of the primitives in MiniCrypt such as the one-way function and the pseudorandom generator. It can increase the efficiency of cryptographic schemes than simply using the one-way function in many cases. And it has been proven that the opposite direction is infeasible via the black-box reduction [36]. As a variant of collision-resistance, some other properties such as preimage resistance and second-preimage resistance have been extended and studied by Rogaway and Shrimpton [34].

When the collision-resistance is considered in the quantum case, it should also be infeasible to generate a collision for any quantum efficient adversary. Namely for a quantum secure collision-resistant hash function H_n, there doesn't exist any quantum adversary $\mathcal{A}$ that finds a distinct pair $x_0 \neq x_1$ such that $H_n(x_0) = H_n(x_1)$. However, it seems that the quantum collision-resistance is still inadequate in the quantum setting. In order to devise a quantum commitment that achieves a post-quantum secure binding property, Unruh proposed the notion of collapsing hash function, which is stronger than the quantum collision-resistant hash function [38]. Informally, a function H_n is collapsing, if given a superposition $\sum a_{x,z} |x, H(x), z\rangle$, any quantum efficient adversary can not detect wether the input register or the output register has been measured. Notice that the collapsing property implies the quantum collision-resistance trivially, since if there exists an adversary $\mathcal{A}$ that finds a distinct pair $x_0 \neq x_1$ such that $y = H_n(x_0) = H_n(x_1)$, it is easy to generate and check the state $(|x_0, y\rangle + |x_1, y\rangle)/\sqrt{2}$, which hence breaks the collapsing property of H_n. In the other direction, Unruh gave evidence showing that there exists a construction $H_n^{\mathcal{O}}$ that is quantum collision-resistant but not collapsing relative to a quantum oracle $\mathcal{O}$ [38]. Then, several quantum analogues of properties such as preimage resistance and second-preimage resistance have been formalized and discussed in [20,23]. Zhandry proved that the existence of quantum collision-resistant hash functions which is not collapsing implies the existence of quantum lightning in infinity-often sense [43]. Moreover, Amos et al. proposed another quantum security definition of hash functions called the equivocal collision-resistant hash functions and derived a construction relative to a classical oracle, which also yields a classical oracle construction of non-collapsing quantum collision-resistant hash functions [4].

However, these results don't rule out the reduction from the collapsing hash functions to the quantum collision-resistant hash functions. It remains to be unknown whether we can construct the collapsing hash functions from the quantum collision-resistant hash functions in a black-box (or non-black-box) manner. That hence raise the motivation of this work:

Does the existence of quantum collision-resistant hash functions imply the existence of collapsing hash functions?

This motivated us to further study the relations of these properties theoretically. If there is a universal construction of collapsing hash functions from quantum collision-resistant hash functions, if not, can we set up a quantum black-box barrier between these two primitives?

1.1 Our Result

In this paper, we further investigate the relations between quantum collision-resistance and collapsing property and get a surprising result. Although there is a oracle-aided construction separates these two post-quantum security definitions, these two primitives might be equivalent in many cases.

In order to exhibit our results, we firstly classify these hash functions by the upper bound of the size of preimages. Informally, we call a collection of functions $\{H_n : \mathbf{K} \times \mathbf{X} \to \mathbf{Y}\}_{n \in \mathbb{N}}$ is $\delta(n)$-bounded if any hash value of $H_n(k, \cdot)$ has at most $\delta(n)$ preimages for any $k \in \mathbf{K}$[1]. We denote it as regular bounded and polynomial bounded for simplicity if $\delta(n)$ is $O(|\mathbf{X}/\mathbf{Y}|)$ or $\texttt{poly}(n)$ for some positive polynomial $\texttt{poly}(\cdot)$ respectively. And $\{H_n\}_{n \in \mathbb{N}}$ is almost $\delta(n)$-bounded if it is $\delta(n)$-bounded with overwhelming probability over the randomness of the evaluation key (the almost regular bounded and almost polynomial bounded are defined accordingly). Hence our results can be discussed separately according to the size of preimages.

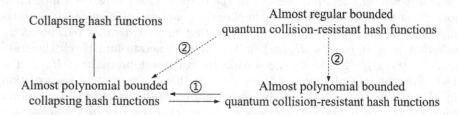

Fig. 1. The arrow "$A \to B$" means that the primitive A satisfies the property of B. The dotted arrow $A \dashrightarrow B$ indicates that if the primitive A exists, then so does B. The ①, ② are the main results proved in this paper, and other directions are implied naturally by their definitions.

Our main results can be described as the Fig. 1, where ① represents our first result. That is, for any (almost) polynomial bounded hash functions, we can prove that surprisingly, the collapsing property is equivalent to the property of quantum collision-resistance.

Theorem 1 (informal). *For any collection of (almost) polynomial bounded hash functions $\{H_n\}$, it is collapsing iff it satisfies the quantum collision-resistance.*

---

[1] In the following part, we always assume the functions as $\{H_n : \{0,1\}^{l(n)} \times \{0,1\}^n \to \{0,1\}^{m(n)}\}_{n \in \mathbb{N}}$ namely $\mathbf{X} = \{0,1\}^n$, $\mathbf{K} = \{0,1\}^{l(n)}$ and $\mathbf{Y} = \{0,1\}^{m(n)}$. Moreover, we always assume $\{H_n\}$ is compressing, namely $m(n) < n$ for all $n \in \mathbb{N}$, and $|\mathbf{X}|/|\mathbf{Y}| > C$ for general $H_n : \mathbf{X} \to \mathbf{Y}$, where $C > 1$ is a constant.

Then, as a corollary of that theorem, we can directly derive the non-existence of any polynomial bounded equivocal collision-resistant hash functions.

Corollary 1 (informal). *There doesn't exist any (almost) polynomial bounded quantum collision-resistant hash function that satisfies the equivocal property.*

The corollary above indicates that if we want to construct the equivocal collision-resistant hash functions, the input space of that function must be super-polynomially larger than the output space.

Then, as the second part of our results (which is exhibited as ② in Fig. 1) we further explore the relations when the preimages are exponentially large. Based on the equivalence in the polynomial bounded case and construction of (almost) polynomial bounded hash functions from (almost) regular bounded hash functions which preserves the quantum collision-resistance, we prove the existence of (almost) polynomial bounded collapsing hash functions is implied by the (almost) regular bounded quantum collision-resistant hash functions. That hence implies the reduction from polynomial bounded collapsing hash functions to the (almost) regular bounded quantum collision-resistant hash functions.

Theorem 2 (informal). *The existence of (almost) polynomial bounded collapsing hash functions is implied by the existence of (almost) regular bounded quantum collision-resistant hash functions.*

Our result demonstrates that the gap between these two properties is sensitive to the size of preimages. Namely, fewer preimages and more regularity the hash functions have, more "close" these properties are.

As an application of that part, we show that Ajtai's construction of hash functions based on the short integer solution (**SIS**) problem is (almost) regular bounded [2,18].

Corollary 2 (informal). *There exists a construction of collapsing hash functions based on the short integer solution (**SIS**) assumption.*

1.2 Technical Overview

In this part, we show our main technique involved in this paper. We start by a detailed description of hash functions. A collection of hash functions $\{H_n : \{0,1\}^{l(n)} \times \{0,1\}^n \to \{0,1\}^{m(n)}\}_{n \in \mathbb{N}}$ usually consists of two probabilistic polynomial-time algorithms Gen and Eval, where $\text{Gen}(1^n)$ outputs an evaluation key $k \in \{0,1\}^{l(n)}$ with the security parameter 1^n as its input, and $\text{Eval}(k, \cdot)$ calculates the function $H_n(k, \cdot)$. The properties such as collision-resistance and collapsing property of $\{H_n\}$ stress that any quantum polynomial-time adversary $\mathcal{A}$ who gets the evaluation key k generated by $\text{Gen}(1^n)$ can not break the security of $H_n(k, \cdot)$ (e.g. can not find a collision of $H_n(k, \cdot)$ for a collection of collision-resistant hash functions $\{H_n\}$).

Recall that a collection of hash functions $\{H_n : \{0,1\}^{l(n)} \times \{0,1\}^n \to \{0,1\}^{m(n)}\}_{n \in \mathbb{N}}$ is $\delta(n)$-bounded if it holds that

$$|\{x \mid H_n(k,x) = y\}| \leq \delta(n) \tag{1}$$

for any valid $k \in \{0,1\}^{l(n)}$ and $y \in \{0,1\}^{m(n)}$. In that case, we denote by regular bounded and polynomial bounded if $\delta(n) = O(2^{n-m(n)})$ and $\delta(n) = \texttt{poly}(n)$ for some positive polynomial $\texttt{poly}(\cdot)$ respectively. Similar definitions can be derived when we consider it in the keyless setting (i.e. the form $\{H_n : \times\{0,1\}^n \to \{0,1\}^{m(n)}\}_{n\in\mathbb{N}}$). And it is almost $\delta(n)$-bounded, if $H_n(k, \cdot)$ is $\delta(n)$-bounded with overwhelming probability, where the randomness is taken over the $k \leftarrow \texttt{Gen}(1^n)$.

The Equivalence in Bounded Case. Since the key generation algorithm Gen seems not involved in our first result, without loss of generality, we sometimes assume the hash functions are constructed in the keyless setting for convenience. Namely, the key generation algorithm $\texttt{Gen}(1^n)$ generates the evaluation key deterministically for each security parameter. Therefore we denote by the collection of hash functions as $\{H_n : \{0,1\}^n \to \{0,1\}^m\}_{n\in\mathbb{N}}$ for simplicity. In that case, the quantum collision-resistance stresses the quantum hardness for finding a collision of H_n, and the collapsing property indicates that there is no (computational) difference between measuring the input register or the output register of H_n.

When the preimages of H_n are limited by some polynomial, we intent to take advantage of the invertibility of a quantum circuit and show the equivalence between these two properties. The strategy is that, assuming there exists a quantum adversary $\mathcal{A}$ that breaks the collapsing property of a hash function H_n efficiently, then we can construct another quantum polynomial-time adversary $\mathcal{B}$ breaks the quantum collision-resistance of H_n as well. In order to make it clear, we divide the adversary $\mathcal{A}$ of the collapsing experiment into two phases $\mathcal{A}_1, \mathcal{A}_2$, which is formalized in Fig. 2.

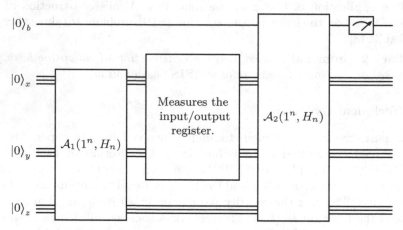

Fig. 2. The description of $\mathcal{A}$. Where the register of $|0\rangle_b$ stores the decision of $\mathcal{A}$, and $|0\rangle_x, |0\rangle_y$ store the input/ output of H_n respectively. $|0\rangle_z$ stores the auxiliary bits of $\mathcal{A}$. The second step means it would randomly toss a coin $b \leftarrow \{0,1\}$, when $b = 0$ it would measure the output register, and when $b = 1$ it would measure the input register.

At the first phase of the collapsing experiment, $\mathcal{A}_1$ gets the security parameter and the description of H_n as its input, then generates a challenge state ρ and sends it to the challenger, the challenger measures the input or the output register of ρ according to the tossed coin $b \leftarrow \{0, 1\}$. In the second phase, $\mathcal{A}_2$ receives the resulting state $\rho_{(b)}$ sent by the challenger and inherited by $\mathcal{A}_1$, and made his decision b'. $\mathcal{A}$ wins the game iff it holds that $b' = b$.

Note that, when the size of preimages is bounded by some polynomial, the trace distance between $\rho_{(0)}$ and $\rho_{(1)}$ is smaller than 1 by a non-negligible amount, which means these two states are not extremely far from each other, therefore we can deduce that the states generated by $\mathcal{A}_2$ with inputs $\rho_{(0)}$ and $\rho_{(1)}$ are similar to each other with non-negligible amount. That gives possibility to restore one from another state by the power of the inverse of $\mathcal{A}_2$.

Inspired by this observation, assuming $\mathcal{A} = (\mathcal{A}_1, \mathcal{A}_2)$ is unitary and breaks the collapsing property of H_n, if we measure the input register of the state ρ generated by the first phases $\mathcal{A}_1$ in the computational basis and get a preimage x of some hash value y, the resulting state $\rho_{(1)}$ should be non-negligibly "close" to $\rho_{(0)}$ (i.e. the state after measuring the output register of ρ). That implies the state $\mathcal{A}_2 \rho_{(1)} \mathcal{A}_2^\dagger$ is not too "far" from $\mathcal{A}_2 \rho_{(0)} \mathcal{A}_2^\dagger$. Therefore, if we apply $\mathcal{A}_2$ to $\rho_{(1)}$ and measuring the decision register, the resulting state after measuring is similar to the other case with a non-negligible amount. Therefore by applying the inverse $\mathcal{A}_2^\dagger$ to that state, we may "retrieve" the state $\rho_{(0)}$ with a non-negligible advantage. Then another preimage of the hash value y could be derived with non-negligible probability if measuring the input register again. This intuition tells us that when the preimages are bounded by some polynomial, the quantum collision-resistance and the collapsing property must hold simultaneously.

We now describe the procedure of $\mathcal{B}$ as Fig. 3. Namely, $\mathcal{B}$ firstly invokes $\mathcal{A}_1, \mathcal{A}_2$ faithfully and measures the input register between these two phases and the decision register after running $\mathcal{A}_2$. Here we denote by x the measurement of the input register in that step. Then $\mathcal{B}$ runs the inverse of $\mathcal{A}_2$ and measures the input register in the computational basis and gets x^* in result. By the discussion above, we claim it holds that $x \neq x^*$ and $H_n(x) = H_n(x^*)$ with non-negligible probability. The formal proof of that result will be exhibited in Sect. 3.

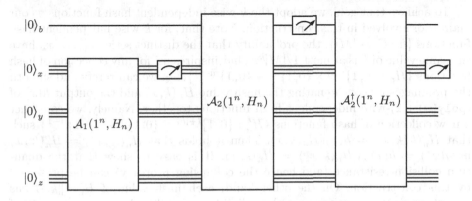

Fig. 3. The description of $\mathcal{B}$.

Note that the adversary $\mathcal{A}$ we considered can be of arbitrary form, it hence could be probably not unitary (and not invertible). That indicates the reduction above would be obstructed if it was treated in a fully black-box manner (in which case both the underlying implementation of the primitive and the adversary $\mathcal{A}$ are only treated as black-box). However, that problem can be circumvented if we consider it in a semi-black-box manner (that is, the underlying implementation of the primitive is still given as a black-box, while the description of the adversary $\mathcal{A}$ is given) [32]. In that case, the inverse of $\mathcal{A}_2$ exists because any general quantum circuit can be simulated by a unitary circuit equivalently (which is called the purification of that circuit, the existence of such simulation may refer to [1]). Therefore, we can assume the whole process of $(\mathcal{A}_1, \mathcal{A}_2)$ is unitary, then the inverse of $\mathcal{A}_2$ is its conjugate transpose $\mathcal{A}_2^\dagger$. That implies the feasibility of the quantum adversary $\mathcal{B}$ for breaking the quantum collision-resistance of H_n.

The Relation in Almost Regular Bounded Case. The second result aims to study the relation between these two properties in a general case. We believe there might be a quantum collision-resistant hash function that is not collapsing due to the existing oracle-aided constructions [4,38]. However, that doesn't obstruct the reduction from collapsing hash functions to the quantum collision-resistant hash functions.

Therefore we consider whether we can construct polynomial bounded hash functions from unbounded hash functions. Unfortunately, a universal transformation is unknown due to the sophisticated structure of preimages unbounded hash functions. However, we can prove an implication relation for some specific types of hash functions. Namely, when the collection of hash functions $\{H_n : \{0,1\}^l \times \{0,1\}^n \to \{0,1\}^m\}_{n\in\mathbb{N}}$ is almost regular bounded (i.e. almost $O(2^{n-m})$-bounded) and quantum collision-resistant, we can construct a collection of collapsing hash functions from it. The idea is simple, since the collapsing property and the quantum collision-resistance are equivalent in polynomial bounded case, it is sufficient to justify our result by constructing polynomial bounded hash functions from $O(2^{n-m})$-bounded hash functions that preserves the quantum collision-resistance.

To achieve that goal, we adopt the k-wise independent hash functions as our main tool involved in this construction. Note that, for k-wise independent hash functions $\{h : U \to [M]\}$, the probability that the distinct series $x_1, \ldots, x_k$ have the same value of h is at most $1/|M|^k$. That inspires us, for any collection of hash functions $\{H_n : \{0,1\}^{l(n)} \times \{0,1\}^n \to \{0,1\}^{m(n)}\}_{n\in\mathbb{N}}$, we can rarefy and smooth the preimages by concatenating the hash value $H_n(k,x)$ and the output $h(x)$ of $(\text{poly}(n)+1)$-wise independent hash functions together. Namely, we construct a new collection of hash functions $\{H_n' : \{0,1\}^{l+|h|} \times \{0,1\}^n \to \{0,1\}^{n-1}\}$ such that $H_n'(h\|k,x) := h(x)\|H_n(k,x)$. Then it holds that $H_n'(k',x^*) = H_n'(k',x)$ iff $h(x^*) = h(x) \wedge H_n(k,x^*) = H_n(k,x)$. It is easy to show that the quantum collision-resistance (and hence the collapsing property) can be preserved by this construction. On the other hand, each hash value of $H_n'(h\|k,\cdot)$ has more than $\text{poly}(n)$ preimages with negligible probability due to the property of the $(\text{poly}(n)+1)$-wise independent hash functions, that indicates $H_n'(h\|k,\cdot)$ is

$\texttt{poly}(n)$-bounded with overwhelming probability, which hence proves that $\{H'_n\}$ is almost polynomial bounded quantum collision-resistant hash functions, and the collapsing property can be derived according to our first result.

To show an application of that result, we give a construction of collapsing hash functions from Ajtai's construction $\{H_A(\mathbf{x}) = A\mathbf{x}, A \in \mathbb{Z}_q^{n \times m}\}$ based on the short integer solution (SIS) problem by showing $\{H_A\}$ is almost regular bounded for $\mathbf{X} = \{\mathbf{x} \in \mathbb{Z}_q^m : \|\mathbf{x}\| \leq \beta/2\}$ and $\mathbf{Y} = \mathbb{Z}_q^n$. The idea is simple, notice that any vector $\mathbf{x} \in \mathbb{Z}_q^m$ in the input space $\mathbf{X}$ belongs to the sphere $B_{\beta/2}(\mathbf{0})$, we hence give a cell $P(\Lambda_q^\perp(A), \mathbf{x})$ that contains each vector $\mathbf{x} \in \mathbf{X}$ disjointedly and show each cell is contained in a sphere $B_{\beta'/2}(\mathbf{0})$ which is slightly larger than $B_{\beta/2}(\mathbf{0})$. Then we can get an upper bounded of the size of preimages which is the volume of $B_{\beta'/2}(\mathbf{0})$ divided by the volume of the cell. Since the size of $\mathbf{X}$ is approximatively equals to the volume of $B_{\beta/2}(\mathbf{0})$, and $B_{\beta'/2}(\mathbf{0})$ is slightly larger than $B_{\beta/2}(\mathbf{0})$, we can deduce that Ajtai's construction is almost regular bounded. Hence it's feasible to transform it into a collapsing one based on our construction.

1.3 Related Works

Comparation to Concurrent Work. The concurrent work by Zhandry also discusses the relation between the two security definitions and gets the same equivalence result independently as ours but from different perspectives [44]. He gives a generalized transformation from any quantum collision-resistant hash function that satisfies a certain regularity condition called "semi-regularity" to the collapsing hash functions. Using that transformation, he derives several constructions of collapsing hash functions from different assumptions such as the learning parity with noise (LPN) problem, and some problems arising from isogenies on elliptic curves. These results greatly expand known results (since the only standard-model construction of collapsing hash functions before that was based on the learning with error (LWE) problem).

From a different perspective, our work mainly aims to figure out the implication relations between the collapsing hash functions and the quantum collision-resistant hash functions in various cases, and we consider the existence of some related primitives such as the equivocal collision-resistant hash functions. As an application, we construct collapsing hash functions from Ajtai's construction based on the quantum hardness of the short integer solution (SIS) problem.

The Collapsing Hash Functions. The concept of collapsing hash functions is proposed by Unruh to achieve the post-quantum binding property for commitment scheme [38]. He showed the random function satisfies the collapsing property, and gave an instance of a quantum collision-resistant hash function that is not collapsing relative to a quantum oracle (which is constructed by Ambainis et al. in [3]). Then he gave a concrete construction in his later work [37], which also shows the collapsing is preserved under the Merkle-Damgård construction. Czajkowski et al. proved the Sponge construction also preserves the collapsing property under some suitable assumptions [15] (which is originally in [39]). Fehr proposed a formalism and a framework which could obtain simpler proofs for the collapsing property [17]. The relations of the security notions of cryptographic hash functions against quantum attacks are further studied by Hamlin and Song in [20]. Moreover, Zhandry showed the existence of non-collapsing quantum collision-resistant hash functions implies the quantum lighting in an infinite-often sense. Then Amos et al. proposed the notion of equivocal collision-resistant hash functions, which is collision-resistant but not collapsing, and gave a classical oracle construction, which also yields a classical oracle construction separates the collapsing property and the quantum collision-resistance [4].

The Relations of Variant Hash Functions. The relations of security notions of cryptographic hash functions are studied comprehensively in both classical and quantum setting (such as [20,34]). As for the existence in the black-box manner, Hsiao and Reyzin set up a fully black-box barrier from the public-coin collision-resistant hash functions to the secret-coin collision-resistant hash functions by the two-oracle technique [22]. Simon showed the impossibility of (relativized) reduction from the collision-resistant hash functions to one-way permutation [36]. This impossibility is lifted into a quantum fully black-box setting by Hosoyamada and Yamakawa [21], which also rules out the quantum fully black-box reduction from the quantum-computable (classical-computable) collapsing hash functionsto the quantum-computable (classical-computable) one-way permutation. Asharov and Segev showed the non-existence of fully black-box construction of collision-resistant hash functions from indistinguishability obfuscator, which indicates that the collision-resistant hash function doesn't belong to the world Obfustopia [5]. As a weaker notion, the multi-collision resistant hash function was studied in [7,9], which also showed a fully black-box barrier from one-way permutation to that primitive. Inspired by Impagliazzo's five worlds [24], Komargodski et al. defined four worlds of hashing-related primitives in classical setting [26], which are Hashomania, Minihash, Unihash, Nocrypt respectively. Hashomania denotes the world that the collision-resistant hash function exists. Minihash is the world that multiple collision resistant hash exists. Unihash denotes only one-way functions exist, and Nocrypt is the world that has no one-way function. They also showed a fully black-box barrier from the multiple collision resistant hash functions to the collision-resistant hash functions. Then Komargodski et al. studied the distributional collision resistant hash functions [27], which is firstly introduced by [16], they showed the distributional collision-resistan hash functions can be guaranteed by the existence of multi-collision resistance hash in a non-black-box (and infinitely-often) case, and also implied by the the average case hardness of statistical zero-knowledge. Then Bitansky et al. showed that primitive might be stronger than one-way functions by giving a construction of constant-round statistically hiding commitment scheme [8], which seems impossible from one-way function in the fully black-box case [19].

Although there have been a lot of studies about the security notions of hash functions in the classical world. Many relations remain to be unknown in the quantum setting. Therefore, in this paper, we further study the relations of post-quantum security definitions of hash functions theoretically and take the first step to show whether collapsing hash belongs to the quantum analogue of Hashomania.

2 Preliminary

2.1 Notations

We use $\mathbb{N}$ and $\mathbb{R}$ to denote the set of positive integers and real numbers respectively, $\|\rho_1, \rho_1\|_{tr}$ is the trace distance between two mixed states ρ_1, ρ_1, and $\mathrm{Tr}(\rho)$ denotes ρ's trace. The length of a string x is denoted as $|x|$, and when refered to a set X, let $|X|$ be its Cardinality. The mathematical expectation of a random variable H is $\mathrm{E}[H]$. A function $f : \mathbb{N} \to \mathbb{R}$ is called negligible, if for any positive polynomial $p(n)$, it holds $1/p(n) > f(n)$ for all sufficiently large n. It is easy to see that for a non-negligible $f(n)$, there is some positive polynomial $p(\cdot)$ such that $1/p(n) < f(n)$ for infinite many $n \in \mathbb{N}$. For a hash function $H_n : \{0,1\}^n \to \{0,1\}^m$, we let $H_n^{-1}(y)$ denote the set of preimage for any $y \in \{0,1\}^m$, and when $y \notin H_n(\{0,1\}^n)$, let $H_n^{-1}(y) = \emptyset$.

2.2 Quantum Computation

In this part, we introduce some background information on quantum computation, we assume the familiarity with basic notions in [31]. A quantum state is a vector with norm 1 in a Hilbert space, which we usually denote it by $|\phi\rangle$. And in this work, we usually consider that state in binary form, for example

$$|\phi\rangle := \sum_x a_x |x\rangle$$

for $x \in \{0,1\}^n$ and $\sum |a_x|^2 = 1$. The family of pure states $\{|x\rangle\}_{x \subset \{0,1\}^n}$ is called the computational basis of that space. The combination of two states $|\phi_1\rangle, |\phi_2\rangle$ is the tensor product $|\phi_1\rangle \otimes |\phi_2\rangle$ and we denote by $|\phi_1, \phi_2\rangle$ for simplicity.

A quantum algorithm $\mathcal{A}$ is made up by the composition of a series of basis gates, which can be unitary (such as the Hadamard gates, Toffoli gates, and the CNOT gates), and non-unitary (such as the ancillary gates and the erasure gates). A collection of functions $\{H_n\}$ is called quantum-computable if there exists a family of polynomial-time uniform quantum circuits $\{\mathcal{C}_n\}$ to implement it, and permits the superposition calculation, namely

$$\sum_{x,y} a_{x,y} |x, y\rangle \xrightarrow{\mathcal{C}_n} \sum_{x,y} a_{x,y} |x, y \oplus H_n(x)\rangle$$

for any possible $\sum_{x,y} a_{x,y} |x, y\rangle$ (or we can define it in the bounded-error case, i.e. the distance between $\mathcal{C}_n |x, y\rangle$ and the actual $|x, y \oplus H_n(x)\rangle$ is at least $2/3$).

For a general quantum circuit $\mathcal{C}$, the output is denoted by the mixed state $\rho = \sum_i p_i |\phi_i\rangle \langle \phi_i|$ such that $\sum_i p_i = 1$. If $\mathcal{C}$ is polynomial-time quantum circuit, we can simulate it equivalently by some unitary circuits $\mathcal{C}'$ efficiently [1]. We denote by $|\phi\rangle$ the output of $\mathcal{C}'$, then we have

$$\mathrm{Tr}_z |\phi\rangle \langle \phi| = \rho,$$

where Tr_z is the partial trace respect to some auxiliary registers added in $\mathcal{C}'$. We hence say $|\phi\rangle$ is the *purification* of ρ and $\mathcal{C}'$ is the *purified circuit* of $\mathcal{C}$. And when we measure a state $|\phi\rangle$ (in some basis such as $\{|x\rangle\}_{x\in\{0,1\}^n}$), the probability that we get x in result is $|\langle x|\phi\rangle|^2$ and when measuring a mixed state ρ, the corresponding probability is $\langle x|\rho|x\rangle$.

For a quantum algorithm $\mathcal{A}$, we denote by $[\mathcal{A}(x) \to z]$ the process that it takes the classical information x as its input and output the measurement z, and the corresponding probability is denote as

$$\Pr[\mathcal{A}(x) \to z].$$

When $\mathcal{A}$ is unitary, that probability can be denoted as $\||z\rangle\langle z| \otimes I \circ \mathcal{A}|x,0\rangle\|^2$, where 0 stores the auxiliary qubits of $\mathcal{A}$, and I is the identity on the rest registers.

2.3   The Quantum Security of Hash Functions

In this part, we will introduce several security definitions of hash functions $\{H_n : \mathbf{K} \times \mathbf{X} \to \mathbf{Y}\}_{n\in\mathbb{N}}$. We usually assume the hash functions follow the binary form $\{H_n : \{0,1\}^{l(n)} \times \{0,1\}^n \to \{0,1\}^{m(n)}\}_{n\in\mathbb{N}}$, namely $\mathbf{X} = \{0,1\}^n$, $\mathbf{K} = \{0,1\}^{l(n)}$, and $\mathbf{Y} = \{0,1\}^{m(n)}$. The parameters $l(n)$ and $m(n)$ are bounded by some polynomial of n. They are denoted as l and m in brief when there is no confusion. We will always assume that $\{H_n\}$ is compressing, namely it holds that $n > m$ for all sufficiently large $n \in \mathbb{N}$, and $\{H_n\}$ is keyless if $l(n) = 0$.

The following definition of quantum collision-resistant hash functions is adapted from [21], which provides a classification due to the implementation environment[2].

Definition 1 (Quantum collision-resistant hash function [21]). *A collection of hash functions $\{H_n : \{0,1\}^l \times \{0,1\}^n \to \{0,1\}^m\}_{n\in\mathbb{N}}$ is quantum-computable (or classical-computable) quantum collision-resistant hash functions if there exists a pair of efficient quantum (classical) algorithms* Gen *and* Eval *such that:*

- Gen(1^n) *: The key generation algorithm takes the security parameter 1^n as its input, and output an evaluation key $k \in \{0,1\}^l$.*
- Eval(k,x) *The evaluation algorithm calculates the hash function $H_n(k,\cdot)$ for an evaluation key $k \in \{0,1\}^l$ and returns the hash value $y = H_n(k,x)$.*

For any quantum efficient adversary $\mathcal{A}$, we have

$$\Pr_{k\leftarrow\mathrm{Gen}(1^n)}[\mathcal{A}(1^n,k) \to (x_0,x_1), H_n(k,x_0) = H_n(k,x_0)] \leq \mathtt{negl}(n) \qquad (2)$$

for any $n \in \mathbb{N}$. The probability above is taken over the choice of $k \leftarrow$ Gen(1^n) and the randomness inside $\mathcal{A}$. Where $\mathtt{negl}(\cdot)$ is a negligible function.

---

[2] We will always follow this classification in the following definitions. It's not important to the proof in our result, but we believe it can help us clarify the underlying relations of each primitive with different perspectives.

Next, we introduce the definition of collapsing hash functions, which is originally defined by Unruh [38], here we adapt it slightly to achieve the consistency of this work.

Definition 2 (Collapsing Hash Functions [38]). *A collection of hash functions* $\{H_n : \{0,1\}^l \times \{0,1\}^n \to \{0,1\}^m\}_{n\in\mathbb{N}}$ *is quantum-computable (classical-computable) collapsing hash functions, if there exists a pair of efficient quantum (classical) algorithms* Gen *and* Eval *as Definition 1, and withstands the attack of any quantum efficient adversary* $\mathcal{A}$ *in the following experiment* $\mathrm{Exp}_{\mathcal{A}}^{coll}(n)$:

- *The adversary* $\mathcal{A}$ *is divided into two phases* $\mathcal{A}_1$, $\mathcal{A}_2$ *in that experiment.*
- *In the first phase,* $\mathcal{A}_1$ *is given the security parameter* 1^n *along with an evaluation key* $k \leftarrow \mathrm{Gen}(1^n)$ *as its input and generates the following state:*

$$|\phi\rangle := \sum_{x,y} \alpha_{x,y,z}|x,y,z\rangle \tag{3}$$

where $x \in \{0,1\}^n$ *and* $y \in \{0,1\}^{m(n)}$ *denote the input/output of* $H_n(k,\cdot)$ *respectively and* z *is the auxiliary string. Then* $\mathcal{A}_1$ *sends the registers containing the input/output of* $H_n(k,\cdot)$ *to the challenger.*
- *The challenger randomly chooses a coin* $b \leftarrow \{0,1\}$. *If* $b = 0$, *it would measure the output register of the receiving state in the computational basis; If* $b = 1$, *it would measure the input register.*
- *Then the challenger returns the resulting state to the adversary* $\mathcal{A}_2$.
- *After receiving the state from the challenger and inheriting the information from* $\mathcal{A}_1$. *The second phase* $\mathcal{A}_2$ *outputs his decision* $b' \in \{0,1\}$ *and wins iff* $b' = b$.

We let $\mathrm{Exp}_{\mathcal{A}}^{coll}(n) = 1$ *whenever the adversary* $\mathcal{A}$ *wins and* $\mathrm{Exp}_{\mathcal{A}}^{coll}(n) = 0$ *otherwise. Then* $\{H_n\}_{n\in\mathbb{N}}$ *satisfies the collapsing property if*

$$\left| \Pr[\mathrm{Exp}_{\mathcal{A}}^{coll}(n) = 1] - \frac{1}{2} \right| \leq \mathrm{negl}(n) \tag{4}$$

for any quantum efficient adversary $\mathcal{A}$, *and for all* $n \in \mathbb{N}$. *Where* $\mathrm{negl}(\cdot)$ *is a negligible function.*

Since the challenger can check the validity of $|\phi\rangle$ by invoking H_n again in the experiment, without loss of generality, we assume $\mathcal{A}_1$ always returns a valid state, which means the output register stores the correct hash value of the corresponding input.

To construct quantum lightning, one-shot chameleon hashing, and signatures schemes, Amos et al. further explored the quantum security of hash functions and proposed a new notion which is called the equivocal collision-resistant hash functions.

Definition 3 (Equivocal Collision-Resistant Hash Functions [4]). *A collection of hash functions* $\{H_n : \{0,1\}^l \times \{0,1\}^n \to \{0,1\}^m\}_{n\in\mathbb{N}}$ *is quantum-computable (classical-computable) equivocal collision-resistant hash functions, if there exists a pair of efficient quantum (classical) algorithms* Gen *and* Eval *as in Definition 1, along with the following two efficient quantum algorithms* $\mathcal{G}, \mathcal{E}$:

- $\mathcal{G}(k)$: *The generation algorithm takes the evaluation key k as its input, and outputs a hash value y of $H_n(k, \cdot)$, a description of a predicate $\mathcal{P} : \{0,1\}^n \to \{0,1\}$, and a state $\rho_{y,\mathcal{P}}$ (which probably includes the information about the evaluation key and the description of $\mathcal{P}$).*
- $\mathcal{E}(b, \rho)$: *The equivocal algorithm takes a bit $b \in \{0,1\}$ along with a state ρ as its input, and outputs a preimage x.*

The correctness stresses that if $\mathcal{P}$, y and $\rho_{y,\mathcal{P}}$ is generated by $\mathcal{G}(k)$, then the output x of $\mathcal{E}(b, \rho_{y,\mathcal{P}})$ satisfies $H_n(k, x) = y$ and $\mathcal{P}(x) = b$ with overwhelming probability for any $b \in \{0,1\}$. And the security of $\{H_n\}$ also requires quantum collision-resistance against any quantum efficient adversary $\mathcal{A}$.

Notice that here we only consider the quantum implementations of $\mathcal{G}, \mathcal{E}$ in above definition. Since if they are classical, we can apparently get a collision by repeating $\mathcal{E}(b, \rho)$ with a copied ρ (if $\mathcal{G}$ is classical, the output of $\mathcal{G}$ should be classical as well). Moreover, we can see that the quantum collision-resistance is implied by the equivocal collision-resistance, and the equivocality also rules out the collapsing property, which is shown by the following lemma.

Lemma 1. *If $\{H_n\}$ is a collection of quantum-computable (classical-computable) equivocal collision-resistant hash functions, then it is not collapsing.*

That result was claimed originally by Amos et al. in [4] (Sect. 2) without an explicit proof. We will give a detailed proof for Lemma 1 via a non-black-box manner in Appendix A for completeness.

Then we derive the following definitions of (almost) $\delta(n)$-bounded (and regular bounded) to classify the hash functions by the size of preimages.

Definition 4 ($\delta(n)$-bounded). *A collection of hash functions $\{H_n : \mathbf{K} \times \mathbf{X} \to \mathbf{Y}\}$ is $\delta(n)$-bounded if*

$$|\{x \mid H_n(k,x) = y\}| \leq \delta(n) \tag{5}$$

for all $n \in \mathbb{N}$, $k \in \mathrm{supp}(\mathtt{Gen}(1^n))$, and $y \in \{0,1\}^m$. Where $\mathrm{supp}(\mathtt{Gen}(1^n)) \subseteq \mathbf{K}$ denotes the support of the distribution of key generation algorithm $\mathtt{Gen}(1^n)$. In addition, $\{H_n\}$ is almost $\delta(n)$-bounded if

$$\Pr_{k \leftarrow \mathtt{Gen}(1^n)} [|\{x \mid H_n(k,x) = y\}| \leq \delta(n)] \geq 1 - \mathtt{negl}(n) \tag{6}$$

for all $n \in \mathbb{N}$, and $y \in \mathbf{Y}$, where $\mathtt{negl}(\cdot)$ denotes a negligible function.

Besides, $\{H_n : \mathbf{K} \times \mathbf{X} \to \mathbf{Y}\}$ is called *regular bounded* if $\delta(n) = O(|\mathbf{X}|/|\mathbf{Y}|)$, which means the preimages could not be too large to the expected value. We say a collection of hash functions $\{H_n\}$ is *polynomial bounded*, if there exists a positive polynomial $\mathtt{poly}(\cdot)$ such that $\{H_n\}$ is $\mathtt{poly}(n)$-bounded. And the notions of *almost regular bounded* and *almost polynomial bounded* are defined accordingly.

In the following part, we will classify the hash functions by this notion and start our result in a polynomial bounded setting.

A function H_n is called *regular*, if all hash values have the same size of preimages (except the empty set). Base on that notion, Ristenpart and Shrimpton further proposed the definition of regularity [33], which is also highly relative to the almost regular bounded property. Here we adapt that notion to fit our content as follows.

Definition 5 (Regularity [33]). *A collection of hash functions* $\{H_n : \mathbf{K} \times \mathbf{X} \to \mathbf{Y}\}$ *is* $\Delta(n)$-*regular if it holds that*

$$\sum_k \Pr[k = k' : \mathtt{Gen}(1^n) \to k'] \cdot \Delta(k, n) \leq \Delta(n),$$

where $\Delta(k, n)$ *is given by*

$$\Delta(k, n) := \max_y \frac{\left|\,|\{x \mid H_n(k, x) = y\}| - |\mathbf{X}|/|\mathbf{Y}|\,\right|}{|\mathbf{X}|}.$$

In addition, we say $\{H_n : \mathbf{K} \times \mathbf{X} \to \mathbf{Y}\}$ *is nearly regular if* $\Delta(n) \leq O(\frac{|\mathbf{X}|}{|\mathbf{Y}| \cdot n^{\omega(1)}})$.

Notice there are other definitions characterizing the regularity of hash functions such as [28], they also defined the *almost regularity*, we hence denote our notion by "nearly regular" instead of "almost regular" to avoid the potential confusion. It's easy to see that any regular hash function satisfies the nearly regular property, and by Markov's inequality, nearly regular hash function is almost regular bounded.

As a basic tool that will used in the second part of our result, we introduce the notion from k-wise independent hash functions, which is generalized by the universal hash functions.

Definition 6 (k-Wise Independent Hash Functions). *A family of hash functions* $\{h : U \to [M]\}$ *is called k-wise independent if for any k distinct inputs* $x_1, \ldots x_k$ *along with k outputs* $y_1, \ldots, y_k$ *(probably not distinct), it holds that*

$$\Pr_h[\wedge_{i=1}^k h(x_i) = y_i] \leq \frac{1}{M^k}. \tag{7}$$

That notion has plenty of applications in cryptography in both quantum and classical setting such as [10,11,14,35,37,41]. It can be implemented efficiently due to many concrete constructions such as [13,40].

3 The Equivalence in Polynomial Bounded Case

In this section, we will show the equivalence of the quantum collision-resistance and the collapsing property, when the preimages of each hash value are upper bounded by some polynomial of the input length. It is formalized as follows.

Theorem 3. *A collection of quantum-computable (classical-computable) polynomial bounded hash functions is collapsing if and only if it is quantum collision-resistant.*

Proof. By the definition of collapsing hash functions, it's trivial to obtain the collision-resistance from collapsing property for any quantum-computable (classical-computable) $\texttt{poly}(n)$-bounded hash functions $\{H_n : \{0,1\}^l \times \{0,1\}^n \rightarrow \{0,1\}^m\}_{n \in \mathbb{N}}$, where $\texttt{poly}(\cdot)$ is a positive polynomial. Hence it's sufficient to prove it on the other direction.

Since the evaluation key is not involved in this proof, without loss of generality, we consider this problem in the keyless setting (i.e. the collection of hash functions is denote by $\{H_n : \{0,1\}^n \rightarrow \{0,1\}^m\}_{n \in \mathbb{N}}$) for convenience, and the generalized result can be derived accordingly. We justify that result by making a contradiction. Assuming there exists a collection of quantum-computable (classical-computable) $\texttt{poly}(n)$-bounded hash functions $\{H_n : \{0,1\}^n \rightarrow \{0,1\}^m\}_{n \in \mathbb{N}}$ for some positive polynomial $\texttt{poly}(\cdot)$ which is quantum collision-resistant but not collapsing, and $\mathcal{A} = (\mathcal{A}_1, \mathcal{A}_2)$ is the corresponding quantum adversary that breaks the collapsing property of H_n. We now take advantage of $\mathcal{A}$ to construct a quantum collision-finding algorithm $\mathcal{B}$ as follows:

- $\mathcal{B}$ firstly invokes $\mathcal{A}_1(1^n)$ and produces the state ρ_1.
- $\mathcal{B}$ measures the input register of ρ_1 in the computational basis, and gets a measurement $x \in \{0,1\}^n$ with the resulting state ρ_2.
- Then $\mathcal{B}$ runs $\mathcal{A}_2$ on ρ_2 and measures the decision qubit b', and ρ_3 is the collapsed resulting state after measuring.
- $\mathcal{B}$ runs the inverse $\mathcal{A}_2^\dagger$ to ρ_3 and measures the input register in the computational basis, and gets the measurement x^*. Then outputs the pair (x, x^*) as its result.

First of all, we will justify the feasibility of $\mathcal{B}$. We consider that $\mathcal{B}$ is given the internal information of $\mathcal{A}_1, \mathcal{A}_2$ (which is stronger than only given the oracle access), in that case, we can assume both $\mathcal{A}_1, \mathcal{A}_2$ are unitary operations without loss of generality. Since if not, we can certainly replace them by their purified circuits. These processes are efficient as justified in [1]. Since $\mathcal{A}$ is an efficient quantum adversary, hence $\mathcal{B}$ is also an efficient quantum algorithm. The remaining part of this proof is to show that $\mathcal{B}$ breaks the collision-resistance of H_n with non-negligible probability, namely, the existence of some positive polynomial $\text{P}'(n)$ such that

$$\Pr[\mathcal{B}(1^n) \rightarrow (x, x^*), H_n(x) = H_n(x^*)] \geq \frac{1}{\text{P}'(n)} \qquad (8)$$

for infinitely many $n \in \mathbb{N}$. Where $\text{P}'(n)$ is some positive polynomial.

Before showing that, we give some notations which are useful in the proof. Firstly, the procedure of $\mathcal{A}_1$ is expressed as follows:

$$\mathcal{A}_1|0\rangle = \sum_{x,y,z} \alpha_{x,y,z}|x,y,z\rangle. \qquad (9)$$

where x, y are stored in the input/ output registers respectively, and z is the corresponding auxiliary string. Without loss of generality, we assume $\mathcal{A}_1$ always produces valid state, namely it holds that $y = H_n(x)$ in Eq. (9) (since if not, we can check the validity of that state by invoking $H_n(\cdot)$ and refuse the noisy part). The second phase $\mathcal{A}_2$ runs on $|0, x, y, z\rangle$ as follows

$$A_2|0, x, y, z\rangle = \sum_{b', x', y', z'} \beta^{x, y, z}_{b', x', y', z'} |b', x', y', z'\rangle. \tag{10}$$

where b' stores the decision bit of $\mathcal{A}_2$.

By our assumption, since $\mathcal{A}$ wins in $\mathrm{Exp}^{coll}_{\mathcal{A}}(n)$ with non-negligible advantage under our assumption, there exists a positive polynomial $\mathrm{P}(\cdot)$ such that

$$\left| \Pr[\mathrm{Exp}^{coll}_{\mathcal{A}}(n) = 1] - \frac{1}{2} \right| \geq \frac{1}{\mathrm{P}(n)}, \tag{11}$$

for infinitely many $n \in \mathbb{N}$.

Let $\rho_{(0)}$ denote the mixed state after measuring (tracing out) the output register of ρ_1 (i.e. $b = 0$), by the Eq. (9), it can be denoted as

$$\rho_{(0)} := \sum_y \Big(\sum_{x, z}^{x \in H_n^{-1}(y)} |\alpha_{x, y, z}|^2 \Big) \cdot |\phi_y\rangle\langle\phi_y|.$$

where $|\phi_y\rangle := \sum_{x, z}^{x \in H_n^{-1}(y)} \alpha_{x, y, z} |x, y, z\rangle / \sqrt{(\sum_{x, z} |\alpha_{x, y, z}|^2)}$, and $\rho_{(1)}$ be the state in the case $b = 1$, which is

$$\rho_{(1)} := \sum_y \sum_x^{x \in H_n^{-1}(y)} \Big(\sum_z |\alpha_{x, y, z}|^2 \Big) |\psi_{x, y}\rangle\langle\psi_{x, y}|.$$

where $|\psi_{x, y}\rangle = \sum_z \alpha_{x, y, z} |x, y, z\rangle / \sqrt{(\sum_z |\alpha_{x, y, z}|^2)}$. Recall that

$$A_2|0, x, y, z\rangle = \sum_{b', x', y', z'} \beta^{x, y, z}_{b', x', y', z'} |b', x', y', z'\rangle.$$

Let $\mathbf{E}_{b, b'}$ be the event that the measurement of decision bit is b' after invoking the $\mathcal{A}_2$ on $|0\rangle\langle 0| \otimes \rho_{(b)}$, then we can denote the probability that $\mathbf{E}_{b, b'}$ occurs as

$$\Pr[\mathbf{E}_{0, b'}] = \sum_y \sum_{x', y', z'} \Big| \sum_{x, z}^{x \in H_n^{-1}(y)} \beta^{x, y, z}_{b', x', y', z'} \alpha_{x, y, z} \Big|^2 \tag{12}$$

for $b = 0$, and

$$\Pr[\mathbf{E}_{1, b'}] = \sum_y \sum_x^{x \in H_n^{-1}(y)} \sum_{x', y', z'} \Big| \sum_z \beta^{x, y, z}_{b', x', y', z'} \alpha_{x, y, z} \Big|^2 \tag{13}$$

for $b = 1$.

Thus the success probability of $\mathcal{A}$ satisfies

$$4 \cdot \left| \Pr[\mathrm{Exp}_{\mathcal{A}}^{coll}(n) = 1] - \frac{1}{2} \right|$$

$$= \sum_{b'} \left| \Pr[\mathbf{E}_{0,b'}] - \Pr[\mathbf{E}_{1,b'}] \right|$$

$$= \sum_{b'} \left| \sum_{y,x',y',z'} \left[\left| \sum_{x,z}^{x \in H_n^{-1}(y)} \beta_{b',x',y',z'}^{x,y,z} \alpha_{x,y,z} \right|^2 - \sum_{x \in H_n^{-1}(y)} \left| \sum_z \beta_{b',x',y',z'}^{x,y,z} \alpha_{x,y,z} \right|^2 \right] \right|$$

$$= \sum_{b'} \left| \sum_{x,y,x',y',z'}^{x \in H_n^{-1}(y)} \sum_{x^* \in H_n^{-1}(y)}^{x \neq x^*} \mathrm{Re}\left(\left(\sum_z \beta_{b',x',y',z'}^{x,y,z} \alpha_{x,y,z} \right) \cdot \left(\sum_z \beta_{b',x',y',z'}^{x^*,y,z} \alpha_{x^*,y,z} \right) \right) \right|.$$

$$(14)$$

where $\mathrm{Re}(a)$ denotes the real part of a (Here the situations that $x = x_0 \wedge x^* = x_1$ and $x = x_1 \wedge x^* = x_0$ are counted as two cases, that's the reason there is no coefficient 2 in the last equation of (14)).

Since we assume that $\mathcal{A}$ breaks the collapsing property of H_n with advantage $1/\mathrm{P}(n)$, from Eq. (14), we can deduce that

$$\sum_{b'} \left| \sum_{x,y,x',y',z'}^{x \in H_n^{-1}(y)} \sum_{x^* \in H_n^{-1}(y)}^{x \neq x^*} \mathrm{Re}\left(\left(\sum_z \beta_{b',x',y',z'}^{x,y,z} \alpha_{x,y,z} \right) \right. \right.$$

$$\left. \left. \cdot \left(\sum_z \beta_{b',x',y',z'}^{x^*,y,z} \alpha_{x^*,y,z} \right) \right) \right| \geq \frac{4}{\mathrm{P}(n)} \qquad (15)$$

for infinitely many $n \in \mathbb{N}$.

We now estimate the probability that $\mathcal{B}$ successfully finds a collision. Since we denote by ρ_2 the state that $\mathcal{B}$ just measures the input register of the state produced by $\mathcal{A}_1(1^n)$, we have

$$\rho_2 = \rho_{(1)} = \sum_y \sum_x^{x \in H_n^{-1}(y)} \left(\sum_z |\alpha_{x,y,z}|^2 \right) |\psi_{x,y}\rangle\langle\psi_{x,y}|. \qquad (16)$$

Therefore $\mathcal{A}_2(|0\rangle\langle 0| \otimes \rho_2)\mathcal{A}_2^\dagger$ is denoted as

$$\sum_y \sum_x^{x \in H_n^{-1}(y)} \left(\sum_z |\alpha_{x,y,z}|^2 \right) \mathcal{A}_2 |0, \psi_{x,y}\rangle\langle 0, \psi_{x,y}| \mathcal{A}_2^\dagger$$

$$= \sum_y \sum_x^{x \in H_n^{-1}(y)} \left(\sum_{z,b',x',y',z'} \alpha_{x,y,z} \beta_{b',x',y',z'}^{x,y,z} |b', x', y', z'\rangle \right)$$

$$\cdot \left(\sum_{z,b',x',y',z'} \bar{\alpha}_{x,y,z} \bar{\beta}_{b',x',y',z'}^{x,y,z} \langle b', x', y', z'| \right).$$

Then ρ_3 can be denoted as

$$\sum_{y} \overset{x \in H_n^{-1}(y)}{\sum_{x}} \sum_{b'} (\sum_{z,x',y',z'} \alpha_{x,y,z} \beta_{b',x',y',z'}^{x,y,z} |b',x',y',z'\rangle)$$
$$\cdot (\sum_{z,x',y',z'} \bar{\alpha}_{x,y,z} \bar{\beta}_{b',x',y',z'}^{x,y,z} \langle b',x',y',z'|).$$

The finial state before measuring is $\mathcal{A}_2^{\dagger} \rho_3 \mathcal{A}_2$, which can be denoted as follows

$$\sum_{y} \overset{x \in H_n^{-1}(y)}{\sum_{x}} \sum_{b'} (\sum_{z,x',y',z'} \alpha_{x,y,z} \beta_{b',x',y',z'}^{x,y,z} \mathcal{A}_2^{\dagger} |b',x',y',z'\rangle)$$
$$\cdot (\sum_{z,x',y',z'} \bar{\alpha}_{x,y,z} \bar{\beta}_{b',x',y',z'}^{x,y,z} \langle b',x',y',z'|\mathcal{A}_2).$$

To estimate the probability that the measurement of $\mathcal{A}_2^{\dagger} \rho_3 \mathcal{A}_2$ equals $|0,x^*,y,z^*\rangle$. Note that, for any $|0,x^*,y,z^*\rangle$, we have

$$\langle 0,x^*,y,z^*| (\sum_{z,x',y',z'} \alpha_{x,y,z} \beta_{b',x',y',z'}^{x,y,z} \mathcal{A}_2^{\dagger} |b',x',y',z'\rangle)$$
$$\cdot (\sum_{z,x',y',z'} \bar{\alpha}_{x,y,z} \bar{\beta}_{b',x',y',z'}^{x,y,z} \langle b',x',y',z'|\mathcal{A}_2) |0,x^*,y,z^*\rangle$$
$$= |(\sum_{z,x',y',z'} \alpha_{x,y,z} \beta_{b',x',y',z'}^{x,y,z} \langle 0,x^*,y,z^*|\mathcal{A}_2^{\dagger} |b',x',y',z'\rangle)|^2$$
$$= |(\sum_{z,x',y',z'} \alpha_{x,y,z} \beta_{b',x',y',z'}^{x,y,z} (\sum_{b',x',y',z'} \bar{\beta}_{b',x',y',z'}^{x^*,y,z^*} \langle b',x',y',z'|) |b',x',y',z'\rangle)|^2$$
$$= | \sum_{z,x',y',z'} \alpha_{x,y,z} \beta_{b',x',y',z'}^{x,y,z} \bar{\beta}_{b',x',y',z'}^{x^*,y,z^*} |^2$$

Therefore the probability that $\mathcal{B}$ finds a collision x,x^* is at least

$$\Pr[\mathcal{B}(1^n) \to (x,x^*), H_n(x) = H_n(x^*)]$$
$$\geq \overset{x \in H_n^{-1}(y)}{\sum_{x,y,b'}} \overset{x^* \neq x}{\sum_{z^*,x^* \in H_n^{-1}(y)}} \langle 0,x^*,y,z^*| (\sum_{z,x',y',z'} \alpha_{x,y,z} \beta_{b',x',y',z'}^{x,y,z} \mathcal{A}_2^{\dagger} |b',x',y',z'\rangle)$$
$$\cdot (\sum_{z,x',y',z'} \bar{\alpha}_{x,y,z} \bar{\beta}_{b',x',y',z'}^{x,y,z} \langle b',x',y',z'|\mathcal{A}_2) |0,x^*,y,z^*\rangle$$
$$= \overset{x \in H_n^{-1}(y)}{\sum_{x,y,b'}} \overset{x^* \neq x}{\sum_{z^*,x^* \in H_n^{-1}(y)}} | \sum_{z,x',y',z'} \alpha_{x,y,z} \beta_{b',x',y',z'}^{x,y,z} \bar{\beta}_{b',x',y',z'}^{x^*,y,z^*} |^2. \tag{17}$$

Since H_n is $\texttt{poly}(n)$-bounded, and $\sum_{x,y,z} |\alpha_{x,y,z}|^2 = 1$, it holds that

$$\sum_{x,y}^{x \in H_n^{-1}(y)} \sum_{z^*,x^* \in H_n^{-1}(y)}^{x^* \neq x} \sigma(x,y) \cdot |\bar{\alpha}_{x^*,y,z^*}|^2 \leq \texttt{poly}(n), \tag{18}$$

According to the inequality (18) and

$$|\sum_{i=1}^{k} a_i b_i|^2 \leq (\sum_{i=1}^{k} |a_i|^2) \cdot (\sum_{i=1}^{k} |b_i|^2),$$

we can hence further deduce that

$$\sum_{x,y}^{x \in H_n^{-1}(y)} \sum_{z^*,x^* \in H_n^{-1}(y)}^{x^* \neq x} |(\sum_{z,x',y',z'} \alpha_{x,y,z} \beta_{b',x',y',z'}^{x,y,z} \bar{\beta}_{b',x',y',z'}^{x^*,y,z^*}|^2$$

$$\geq \Big(\sum_{x,y}^{x \in H_n^{-1}(y)} \sum_{z^*,x^* \in H_n^{-1}(y)}^{x^* \neq x} \big| \sum_{z,x',y',z'} \bar{\beta}_{b',x',y',z'}^{x^*,y,z^*} \alpha_{x,y,z} \beta_{b',x',y',z'}^{x,y,z} \big|^2 \Big)$$

$$\cdot \Big(\sum_{x,y}^{x \in H_n^{-1}(y)} \sum_{z^*,x^* \in H_n^{-1}(y)}^{x^* \neq x} |\bar{\alpha}_{x^*,y,z^*}|^2 \Big)/\texttt{poly}(n)$$

$$\geq \big| \sum_{x,y}^{x \in H_n^{-1}(y)} \sum_{z^*,x^* \in H_n^{-1}(y)}^{x^* \neq x} (\sum_{z,x',y',z'} \bar{\beta}_{b',x',y',z'}^{x^*,y,z^*} \bar{\alpha}_{x^*,y,z^*} \alpha_{x,y,z} \beta_{b',x',y',z'}^{x,y,z}) \big|^2/\texttt{poly}(n),$$

$$\tag{19}$$

for both $b' = 0, 1$.

Combining the inequalities (17), (19) with (15), we can derive the probability that $\mathcal{B}$ finds a collision satisfies

$$\Pr[\mathcal{B}(1^n) \rightarrow (x, x^*), H_n(x) = H_n(x^*)]$$

$$\geq \sum_{b'} \big| \sum_{x,y} \sum_{z^*,x^* \in H_n^{-1}(y)}^{x^* \neq x} (\sum_{z,x',y',z'} \bar{\beta}_{b',x',y',z'}^{x^*,y,z^*} \bar{\alpha}_{0,x^*,y,z^*} \alpha_{0,x,y,z} \beta_{b',x',y',z'}^{x,y,z}) \big|^2/\texttt{poly}(n)$$

$$\geq \frac{8}{\texttt{p}(n)^2 \cdot \texttt{poly}(n)}$$

for infinitely many $n \in \mathbb{N}$, which implies immediately that $\{H_n\}$ is not a collection of quantum-computable (classical-computable) collision-resistant hash functions. That hence completes the proof of Theorem 3. $\qquad\square$

Notice that Theorem 3 is proved in the semi-black-box manner [32], that is because the inverse of the second phase of adversary $\mathcal{A}_2$ is usually inaccessible via the fully black-box reduction (because $\mathcal{A}_2$ could be probably non-unitary in general case).

Since the correctness of this proof is irrelevant to the evaluation key, that method can also be adapted slightly to fit the equivalence of the general hash functions $\{H_n : \{0,1\}^l \times \{0,1\}^n \rightarrow \{0,1\}^m\}_{n\in\mathbb{N}}$. Moreover, we can further generalize the Theorem 3 into the almost bounded case, which is the following corollary.

Corollary 3. *A collection of quantum-computable (classical-computable) almost polynomial bounded hash functions is collapsing if and only if it is quantum collision-resistant.*

The proof is very similar to the proof of Theorem 3 (the only difference is that we should ignore the unbounded part of k, whose ratio is at most negligible large), which is omitted here.

Theorem 3 indicates that the quantum collision-resistance and the collapsing property must be satisfied simultaneously for any polynomial bounded hash functions, since classical-computable (quantum-computable) equivocal collision-resistance hash functions can not satisfy the collapsing property due to Lemma 1, as a corollary, we can also show the non-existence of equivocal collision-resistant polynomial bounded hash functions as follows.

Corollary 4. *There doesn't exist almost polynomial bounded equivocal collision-resistant hash functions.*

The corollary above sheds light on how to circumvent a morass for constructing the equivocal collision-resistant hash functions. That is, the preimages shouldn't be too small for each hash value. Besides, our result also partially answers the open problem raised by Amos et al. in [4], which shows that the collapsing hash functions can be implied by the unequivocal hash function in polynomial bounded case.

Besides, since any collection of polynomial bounded quantum collision-resistant hash functions must satisfies the collapsing property simultaneously, we can further deduce that, for any construction that preserves the collision-resistance and the collapsing property such as the Sponge construction and the Merkle-Damgård construction [15,37,42], it's sufficient to guarantee the collapsing property if the underlying block functions are polynomial bounded and quantum collision-resistant.

4 The Implication in Regular Bounded Case

In this section, we consider the case that the preimages are exponentially large. Firstly, we give a construction to show how to transform the almost regular bounded quantum collision-resistant hash functions to a collapsing one. Then, as an application, we show Ajtai's construction could meet the requirement of that almost regular bounded property, which hence implies a construction of collapsing hash functions based on the quantum hardness of short integer solution (**SIS**) problem.

4.1   A Construction of Collapsing Hash Functions

For a collection of (compressing) hash functions $\{H_n : \{0,1\}^l \times \{0,1\}^n \to \{0,1\}^m\}_{n \in \mathbb{N}}$ with efficient quantum (classical) algorithms Gen and Eval, we consider the following way to rarefy and smooth the preimages by extending the output size.

Firstly, we assume it holds that $n + 1 > m(n)$ for all n, since if not, we have many way to extent that gap when $n+1 = m(n)$ such as using some iterations or just omitting one random bit of the output string (and let the information of that position be the additional key of the new hash). Then we construct the new hash functions $\{H_n' : \{0,1\}^{l+|h|} \times \{0,1\}^n \to \{0,1\}^{n-1}\}_{n \in \mathbb{N}}$, with the corresponding algorithms Gen', Eval which perform as follows:

- Gen'(1^n) : The key generation algorithm takes the security parameter 1^n as its input, and generates a ($\texttt{poly}(n) + 1$)-wise independent hash function $h : \{0,1\}^n \to \{0,1\}^{n-m-1}$, where we denote by h it's description and the length is $|h|$. Then it invokes $k \leftarrow \texttt{Gen}(1^n)$ and returns $k' = h\|k$ as its output.
- Eval'(k, x) : The evaluation algorithm takes the evaluation key $k' = h\|k$ and $x \in \{0,1\}^n$ as its input, it firstly calculates $t := h(x)$, then invokes the evaluation algorithm of $H_n(k, \cdot)$ and gets $y = \texttt{Eval}(k, x)$. It would return $y' := t\|y$ as its output.

It is easy to show that $\{H_n' : \{0,1\}^{l+|h|} \times \{0,1\}^n \to \{0,1\}^{n-1}\}$ is quantum collision-resistant if $\{H_n : \{0,1\}^l \times \{0,1\}^n \to \{0,1\}^m\}_{n \in \mathbb{N}}$ is. From the following lemma by Unruh, we can further deduce the similar preservation of the collapsing property for that construction.

Lemma 2 ([15]). *If $G_k \circ H_n(k, \cdot)$ is collapsing, and G_k is quantum polynomial-time computable, then $H_n(k, \cdot)$ is collapsing.*

If $\{H_n : \{0,1\}^l \times \{0,1\}^n \to \{0,1\}^m\}_{n \in \mathbb{N}}$ is collapsing, and G_k is the operation that omits the first $n - m - 1$ bits of its input, we have $G_k \circ H_n'(k', \cdot) = H_n(k, \cdot)$. That implies H_n' is also collapsing due to the Lemma 2. Then by such construction, we further derive the implication from the almost polynomial bounded collision-resistant hash functions to the almost regular bounded collapsing hash functions which is formed as the following theorem.

Theorem 4. *The existence of the quantum-computable (classical-computable) almost polynomial bounded collapsing hash functions is implied by the existence of the quantum-computable (classical-computable) almost regular bounded collision-resistant hash functions.*

Proof. To prove that theorem, according to the result in polynomial bounded case (i.e. Theorem 3), it is sufficient to give a construction from the almost regular bounded (i.e. almost $O(2^{n-m})$-bounded in that case) quantum collision-resistant hash functions $\{H_n : \{0,1\}^l \times \{0,1\}^n \to \{0,1\}^m\}_{n \in \mathbb{N}}$ to almost $\texttt{poly}(n)$-bounded quantum collision-resistant hash functions for some positive polynomial $\texttt{poly}(\cdot)$.

We hence prove that the construction of $\{H'_n\}$ at the beginning of the Sect. 4 could meet that satisfactory.

It is easy to derive that the quantum collision-resistance is preserved in the construction above. More specifically, $\{H'_n : \{0,1\}^{l+n} \times \{0,1\}^n \to \{0,1\}^{n-1}\}_{n\in\mathbb{N}}$ is a collection of quantum-computable (classical-computable) collision-resistant hash functions if $\{H_n : \{0,1\}^l \times \{0,1\}^n \to \{0,1\}^m\}_{n\in\mathbb{N}}$ is quantum-computable (classical-computable) collision-resistant. If not, there should exist an adversary $\mathcal{A}$ finding a collision x, x^* for H'_n with non-negligible probability. Since $H'_n(k', x^*) = H'_n(k', x)$ if and only if $h(x^*) = h(x)$ and $H_n(k, x^*) = H_n(k, x)$ hold simultaneously, therefore (x, x^*) is also a collision of $H_n(k, \cdot)$. Since the collection of functions $\{H'_n\}$ is constructed from $\{H_n\}$ efficiently, that means $\{H_n\}$ is not quantum collision-resistant either, which is obviously contradictory to our assumption.

Therefore to prove the theorem, it's sufficient to estimate the number of preimages of $H'_n(k', \cdot)$. Since $h : \{0,1\}^n \to \{0,1\}^{n-m-1}$ is a $(\mathbf{poly}(n) + 1)$-wise independent hash function, we hence have

$$\Pr_h[h(x_1) = h(x_2) = \ldots = h(x_{\mathbf{poly}(n)+1})] \leq \left(\frac{1}{2^{n-m-1}}\right)^{\mathbf{poly}(n)+1} \quad (20)$$

for any distinct $x_1, \ldots x_{\mathbf{poly}(n)+1}$, where the probability is taken over the generation of the function h.

Recall that $H'_n(k', x^*) = H'_n(k', x)$ if and only if $h(x^*) = h(x)$ and $H_n(k, x^*) = H_n(k, x)$. We denote by $\mathbf{Bad}$ the event that $H'_n(k', \cdot)$ is not $\mathbf{poly}(n)$-bounded and $\mathbf{Bad}_y$ the event that y's preimages of $H'_n(k', \cdot)$ are not bounded by $\mathbf{poly}(n)$ for some specific $y \in \{0,1\}^{n-1}$, and $\mathbf{Good}_k$ denote $H_n(k, \cdot)$ is $O(2^{n-m})$-bounded for $k \in \{0,1\}^l$. For any $y \in \{0,1\}^{n-1}$, we denote by y_1 and y_2 the first $n - m - 1$ bits and the last m bits of y respectively. Then, it holds that

$$\Pr_{k,h}[\mathbf{Bad}] = \Pr_{k,h}\left[\bigvee_y \mathbf{Bad}_y\right] \leq \sum_y \Pr_{k,h}[\mathbf{Bad}_y]$$

$$\leq \sum_y \Pr_{k,h}\left[|\{x \mid H_n(k,x) = y_1 \wedge h(x) = y_2\}| > \mathbf{poly}(n)\right]$$

$$\leq \sum_y \Pr_{k,h}\left[|\{x \mid H_n(k,x) = y_1 \wedge h(x) = y_2\}| > \mathbf{poly}(n) \mid \mathbf{Good}_k\right] + \Pr_{k,h}[\neg\mathbf{Good}_k]$$

$$\overset{*}{\leq} \sum_y \left(\frac{1}{2^{n-m-1}}\right)^{\mathbf{poly}(n)+1} \cdot \frac{(C \cdot 2^{n-m}) \cdot \ldots \cdot (C \cdot 2^{n-m} - \mathbf{poly}(n))}{(\mathbf{poly}(n) + 1)!} + \mathbf{negl}(n)$$

$$\leq \frac{(2 \cdot C)^{\mathbf{poly}(n)+1} \cdot 2^{n-1}}{(\mathbf{poly}(n) + 1)!} + \mathbf{negl}(n) \quad (21)$$

which is also negligible for $n \in \mathbb{N}$, where $(*)$ follows from the definition of almost $O(2^{n-m})$-bounded hash functions and the property of $(\mathbf{poly}(n) + 1)$-wise independent hash functions, $C > 0$ is a constant.

That implies, for any $O(2^{n-m})$-bounded $H_n(k, \cdot)$, the probability that the new hash $H'_n(h\|k, \cdot)$ is $\mathbf{poly}(n)$-bounded with overwhelming probability over the generation of h. Combining with the fact that $\{H_n\}'$ preserves the quantum collision-resistance, and the efficiency of k-wise independent hash functions, we can deduce that $\{H_n'\}$ is a collection of quantum-computable (classical-computable) almost $\texttt{poly}(n)$-bounded collision-resistant hash functions if $\{H_n\}$ is quantum-computable (classical-computable) almost $O(2^{n-m})$-bounded (i.e. almost regular bounded) collision-resistant. That hence completes the proof of Theorem 4.   □

Since any collection of nearly regular hash functions is almost regular bounded, therefore based on the Theorem 4, we obtain the implication from any nearly regular quantum collision-resistant hash functions as well.

Corollary 5. *The existence of the quantum-computable (classical-computable) almost polynomial bounded collapsing hash functions is implied by the existence of the quantum-computable (classical-computable) nearly regular collision-resistant hash functions.*

These results indicate the collapsing property is not inherently "stronger" than the quantum collision-resistance in many cases, which gives evidence to show that collapsing hash functions might not be a "higher leveled" quantum cryptographic primitive than quantum collision-resistant hash functions.

Remark 1. Notice that the form of the input/output space doesn't affect the correctness of the proof of Theorem 4. Therefore, by the same method, we can generalize result of Theorem 4 to any almost $O(|\mathbf{X}|/|\mathbf{Y}|)$-bounded hash functions $\{H_n : \mathbf{K} \times \mathbf{X} \rightarrow \mathbf{Y}\}$.

4.2   Application to Ajtai's Construction

As an application, we will show how to transform Ajtai's construction into a collapsing one assuming the quantum hardness of short integer solution problem.

Firstly, we introduce the short integer solution problem $\mathbf{SIS}_{n,m,q,\beta}$ as follows:

Definition 7 (Short Integer Solution Problem). *Let $A \in \mathbb{Z}_q^{n \times m}$ be a matrix which is chosen uniformly at random, the Short Integer Solution problem $\mathbf{SIS}_{n,m,q,\beta}$ is to find a nonzero vector $\mathbf{x} \in \mathbb{Z}_q^m$ such that $A\mathbf{x} = \mathbf{0}$ and $\|\mathbf{x}\| \leq \beta$.*

Since we can trivially derive a solution of $A\mathbf{x} = \mathbf{0}$ when the parameters are chosen inappropriately (for example $\beta > q$). Therefore to guarantee it to be as hard as certain worst-case lattice problems [30], the hardness of $\mathbf{SIS}_{n,m,q,\beta}$ usually requires that $\beta \geq \sqrt{n \log q}$, $m \geq n \log q$ and $q \geq \beta \cdot \omega(\sqrt{n \log n})$. Then we introduce Ajtai's construction of a family of hash functions $\{H_A\}$ as follows [2,18]:

- $\texttt{Gen}(1^n)$: The key generation algorithm outputs a matrix $A \in \mathbb{Z}_q^{n \times m}$ uniformly at random as the evaluation key.
- $\texttt{Eval}(k, x)$: The evaluation algorithm takes a matrix $A \in \mathbb{Z}_q^{n \times m}$ and a vector $\mathbf{x} \in \mathbb{Z}_q^m$ as its input, and outputs $\mathbf{y} := H_A(\mathbf{x}) = A\mathbf{x} \bmod q$.

When the input space of $\{H_A\}$ belongs to the sphere $B_{\beta/2}(\mathbf{0}) := \{\mathbf{x} \mid \|x\| \leq \beta/2\}$, then it's not hard to see the quantum collision-resistance of Ajtai's construction assuming the quantum hardness of Short Integer Solution problem $\mathbf{SIS}_{n,m,q,\beta}$. Therefore, to adopt our construction, it's sufficient to prove that $\{H_A\}$ is almost $O(|B_{\beta/2}(\mathbf{0})|/q^n)$-bounded.

Theorem 5. *Assuming $\beta \geq m^3$, $m \geq n \log q$, and $q \geq \beta \cdot \omega(\sqrt{n \log n})$, then we have*

$$\Pr_A[\max_{\mathbf{y}} |\{\mathbf{x} \mid \|\mathbf{x}\| \leq \frac{\beta}{2} \wedge A\mathbf{x} = \mathbf{y} \bmod q\}| \leq O(\frac{\mathrm{vol}(B_{\beta/2}(\mathbf{0}))}{q^n})] \geq 1 - \frac{1}{2^m} - \frac{1}{q^{m-n}},$$

where the probability is taken over the randomness of $A \leftarrow \mathbb{Z}_q^{n \times m}$, and $\mathrm{vol}(B_{\beta/2}(\mathbf{0})$ denotes the volume of sphere $B_{\beta/2}(\mathbf{0})$.

Proof. To prove that proposition, we will firstly estimate the size of preimages of $\mathbf{0} \in \mathbb{Z}_q^n$. Notice that $\det(\Lambda_q^{\perp}(A)) = q^n$ (or $\dim(\Lambda_q^{\perp}(A)) = m-n$) with probability at least $1 - 1/q^{m-n}$ over a random chosen $A \in \mathbb{Z}_q^{n \times m}$. In the case of $\det(\Lambda_q^{\perp}(A)) = q^n$, we consider the following cell

$$P(\Lambda_q^{\perp}(A), \mathbf{x}) := \{\sum_{i=1}^{m} a_i \mathbf{v}_i + \mathbf{x} : a_i \in [-1/2, 1/2)\}. \tag{22}$$

where $\{\mathbf{v}_i \in \mathbb{Z}_q^m, i \in \{1, \ldots, m-n\}\}$ forms a basis of $\Lambda_q^{\perp}(A)$ with $\max_i\{\|v_i\|\} = \lambda_{m-n}(\Lambda_q^{\perp}(A))$ ($\lambda_{m-n}(\Lambda_q^{\perp}(A))$ is the $(m-n)$-th successive minimum). And $\{\mathbf{v}_i \in \mathbb{Z}_q^m, i \in \{m-n+1, \ldots, m\}\}$ forms a orthogonal basis with length 1 and orthogonal to the space spaned by $\{\mathbf{v}_i \in \mathbb{Z}_q^m, i \in \{1, \ldots, m-n\}\}$. Since for any $\mathbf{x}' \neq \mathbf{x} \in \mathbb{Z}_q^m$ satisfying $A\mathbf{x} = A\mathbf{x}' = \mathbf{0}$, the vector $\mathbf{x} - \mathbf{x}'$ is a linear combination of $\{\mathbf{v}_i \in \mathbb{Z}_q^m, i \in \{1, \ldots, m-n\}\}$, therefore each point $\mathbf{x} \in \Lambda_q^{\perp}(A)$ lies disjointedly in a cell $P(\Lambda_q^{\perp}(A), \mathbf{x})$.

On the other hand, for any vector $\mathbf{v} \in P(\Lambda_q^{\perp}(A), \mathbf{x})$, it holds that

$$\|\mathbf{v} - \mathbf{x}\| \leq (m \cdot \lambda_{m-n}(\Lambda_q^{\perp}(A)) + n)/2$$

Therefore the cell $P(\Lambda_q^{\perp}(A), \mathbf{x})$ of a point $\mathbf{x} \in \mathbb{Z}_q^m$ satisfying $H_A(\mathbf{x}) = A\mathbf{x} = \mathbf{0}$ and $\mathbf{x} \in B_{\beta/2}(\mathbf{0})$ should be contained in a larger sphere $B_{(\beta+m \cdot \lambda_{m-n}(\Lambda_q^{\perp}(A))+n)/2}(\mathbf{0})$. We hence have

$$|B_\beta(\mathbf{0}) \cap \Lambda_q^{\perp}(A)| \leq \frac{\mathrm{vol}(B_{(\beta+m \cdot \lambda_{m-n}(\Lambda_q^{\perp}(A))+n)/2}(\mathbf{0}))}{\mathrm{vol}(P(\Lambda_q^{\perp}(A), \mathbf{0}))}$$

$$= \frac{\mathrm{vol}(B_{(\beta+m \cdot \lambda_{m-n}(\Lambda_q^{\perp}(A))+n)/2}(\mathbf{0}))}{q^n}, \tag{23}$$

in the case that $\det(\Lambda_q^{\perp}(A)) = q^n$, where $\mathrm{vol}(\cdot)$ denotes the volume.

We notice that the covering radius μ satisfying $\mu(\Lambda_q^{\perp}(A)) > \lambda_{m-n}(\Lambda_q^{\perp}(A))/2$ and the fact that

$$\Pr_A[\frac{1}{\delta} \cdot \sqrt{m} \cdot q^{n/m} \leq 2\mu(\Lambda_q^{\perp}(A))] \leq 1/2^m, \tag{24}$$

for some constant $\delta > 0$. Therefore $\lambda_{m-n}(\Lambda_q^{\perp}(A)) < \frac{1}{\delta} \cdot \sqrt{m} \cdot q^{n/m}$ with probability at least $1 - 2^{-m}$. In that case, the inequality (23) is further estimated as follows.

$$\frac{\text{vol}(B_{(\beta + m \cdot \lambda_{m-n}(\Lambda_q^{\perp}(A)) + n)/2}(\mathbf{0}))}{q^n}$$

$$\leq \frac{\text{vol}(B_{(\beta + \frac{1}{\delta} \cdot m^{3/2} \cdot q^{n/m} + n)/2}(\mathbf{0}))}{q^n} \leq \frac{\pi^{m/2} \cdot (\beta + \frac{1}{\delta} \cdot m^{3/2} \cdot q^{n/m} + n)^m}{\Gamma(m/2 + 1) \cdot 2^m \cdot q^n}$$

$$\leq \frac{\pi^{m/2} \cdot (1 + (\frac{1}{\delta} \cdot m^{3/2} \cdot q^{n/m} + n)/\beta)^m \cdot \beta^m}{\Gamma(m/2 + 1) \cdot 2^m \cdot q^n} \leq \frac{\pi^{m/2} \cdot (1 + O(\frac{1}{m}))^m \cdot \beta^m}{\Gamma(m/2 + 1) \cdot 2^m \cdot q^n}$$

$$\leq O(\frac{\pi^{m/2} \cdot (\beta/2)^m}{\Gamma(m/2 + 1) \cdot q^n}) = O(\frac{\text{vol}(B_{\beta/2}(\mathbf{0}))}{q^n}).$$

We now turn to estimate the size of preimages for any $\mathbf{y} \neq \mathbf{0}$. Let's assume there exists a $\mathbf{t} \in \mathbb{Z}_q^m$ such that $H_A(\mathbf{t}) = A\mathbf{t} = \mathbf{y} \mod q$. It is equivalent to count the cardinality of set

$$\{\mathbf{x} : A\mathbf{x} = 0, \|\mathbf{x} + \mathbf{t}\| \leq \beta/2\}, \tag{25}$$

which is proved similarly as above, to be upper bounded by $O(\text{vol}(B_{\beta/2}(\mathbf{0}))/q^n)$ under the same conditions which are $\frac{1}{\delta} \cdot \sqrt{m} \cdot q^{n/m} > 2\mu(\Lambda_q^{\perp}(A))$ and $\det(\Lambda_q^{\perp}(A)) = q^n$.

Therefore the size of preimages of $\{H_A\}$ is bounded by $O(\text{vol}(B_{\beta/2}(\mathbf{0}))/q^n)$ with probability at least $1 - 2^{-m} - q^{n-m}$, which completes the proof of Theorem 5. □

Since the cardinality of $\{\mathbf{x} \in \mathbb{Z}_q^m : \|\mathbf{x}\| \leq \beta/2\}$ is approximately equal to the volume of sphere $B_\beta(\mathbf{0})$, therefore the size of preimages for any $\mathbf{y}$ is upper bounded by $O(|\{\mathbf{x} \in \mathbb{Z}_q^m : \|\mathbf{x}\| \leq \beta\}|/q^n)$ with overwhelming probability. That shows $\{H_A(\mathbf{x}) = A\mathbf{x}\}$ is a collection of almost regular bounded hash functions. Notice that the construction in the proof of Theorem 4 can also be applied to the cases that the input/output space are not in a binary form, which means we can transform Ajtai's construction into a collapsing one assuming the quantum hardness of $\mathbf{SIS}_{n,m,q,\beta}$.

Corollary 6. *Let $\{H_A : \mathbf{X} \to \mathbf{Y}\}$ denote Ajtai's construction of hash functions for $\mathbf{X} = \{\mathbf{x} \in \mathbb{Z}_q^m : \|\mathbf{x}\| \leq \beta/2\}$ and $\mathbf{Y} = \mathbb{Z}_q^n$. Then*

$$H_n'(h\|A, \mathbf{x}) = (h(\mathbf{x}), A\mathbf{x}) \tag{26}$$

is classical-computable almost polynomial bounded collapsing hash functions assuming the quantum hardness of $\mathbf{SIS}_{n,m,q,\beta}$ for $\beta \geq m^3$, $m \geq n \log q$, and $q \geq \beta \cdot \omega(\sqrt{n \log n})$, where $c > 1$ is a constant. $h : \mathbf{X} \to \{0,1\}^r$ is $(\text{poly}(n) + 1)$-wise independent hash function satisfying $\log |\mathbf{X}|/|\mathbf{Y}| - C \leq r < \log |\mathbf{X}|/|\mathbf{Y}|$ for any constant $C > 0$.

5 Conclusion

In this paper, we prove that the collapsing property and the quantum collision-resistance must hold simultaneously when the size of preimages of a hash function are upper bounded by some polynomial, and further deduce that these two properties are in the "same level" under the meaning of implication in "almost regular bounded" case. Our result indicates that the collapsing hash functions belong to the quantum analogue of Hashomania [26] (i.e. the world that collision-resistance hash exists) in many restrictive cases. However, the relation between these two primitives remains open in more general cases. Actually, our result doesn't obstruct the way to construct the quantum collision-resistant hash functions which are not collapsing (in the case that the size of preimages is not bounded by some polynomial). Therefore, we believe it is important to find a concrete construction for that (and even a construction of equivocal collision-resistant hash functions). Besides, since we use the inverse of an quantum circuit in our proof of Theorem 3, which means our results are proved in a semi-black-box manner. We also think it is an intriguing problem that if the relation still holds in fully black-box case, or otherwise, if we can set up a quantum black-box barrier between these two primitives with some technique like the quantum two-oracle method [12,21]?

Acknowledgment. We sincerely thank the anonymous reviewers of CRYPTO 2022 for their valuable comments on our paper, and Mark Zhandry for introducing his work to us during the preparation of this final version. This work was supported by National Natural Science Foundation of China (Grants No. 62172405).

A Proof of Lemma 1

We give a proof of Lemma 1 as follows.

Proof (of Lemma 1). Notice that if the state $\rho_{y,\mathcal{P}}$ output by $\mathcal{E}$ already contains the superposition of the preimages of y. One can obviously distinguishes the difference between measureing the input or the output register of $\rho_{y,\mathcal{P}}$ by invoking $\mathcal{E}$ which directly breaks the collapsing property. However, $\rho_{y,\mathcal{P}}$ may not contain the preimages of y directly. Therefore the main task is to construct a suitable state which contains the superposition of the preimages of y (namely, the challenging state output by the first phase of the adversary $\mathcal{A}$ that intends to break the collapsing property).

Since the evaluation key is not involved in this proof, without loss of generality, we consider this problem in the keyless setting, which is $\{H_n : \{0,1\}^n \rightarrow \{0,1\}^m\}_{n \in \mathbb{N}}$.

To proof that lemma, we firstly replace the original $\mathcal{G}$ and $\mathcal{E}$ by their purifications (i.e. assume they are unitary), then we can denote the output state of $\mathcal{G}$ as

$$|\psi\rangle = \sum_{\mathcal{P},y,z} a_{\mathcal{P},y,z}|\mathcal{P},y,z\rangle \otimes |\phi_{y,\mathcal{P},z}\rangle. \tag{27}$$

where $|\phi_{y,\mathcal{P},z}\rangle$ is the corresponding output state state when the description is $\mathcal{P}$, the hash value equals y, and the auxiliary internal information of $\mathcal{G}$ is z. Then the actual output $\rho_{y,\mathcal{P}}$ equals to the collapsed state $|\psi\rangle$ after measuring the y, $\mathcal{P}$, and tracing out the auxiliary register z which is $\sum_z |a_{\mathcal{P},y,z}|^2 |\phi_{y,\mathcal{P},z}\rangle\langle\phi_{y,\mathcal{P},z}|/(\sum_z |a_{\mathcal{P},y,z}|^2)$. Here for convenience, we denote it equivalently by the following mixed state

$$\rho = \operatorname*{Tr}_{\mathcal{P},y,z} |\psi\rangle\langle\psi| = \sum_{\mathcal{P},y,z} |a_{\mathcal{P},y,z}|^2 |\mathcal{P},y,z\rangle\langle\mathcal{P},y,z| \otimes |\phi_{y,\mathcal{P},z}\rangle\langle\phi_{y,\mathcal{P},z}|.$$

Then the final state after invoking the purified $\mathcal{E}$ on $(b, \rho_{y,\mathcal{P}})$ can be denoted as

$$\rho^{(b)} := \mathcal{E}|b,0\rangle\langle b,0| \otimes \rho\mathcal{E}^\dagger. \tag{28}$$

Equivalently, we denote by $\mathcal{E}(0, \cdot)$ (or $\mathcal{E}(1, \cdot)$) the unitary operator for the case $b = 0$ (or $b = 1$). Since the correctness of the equivocal collision-resistant hash functions indicates that $\mathcal{E}$ recovers an preimage x of y satisfying $\mathcal{P}(x) = b$ with overwhelming probability, hence $\rho^{(b)}$ must contain the preimages of y with overwhelming probability. Therefore we can rewrite the state $\rho^{(b)}$ as follows[3]

$$\rho^{(b)} = \sum_{\mathcal{P},y,z} |a_{\mathcal{P},y,z}|^2 |\mathcal{P},y,z,b\rangle\langle\mathcal{P},y,z,b| \otimes (\sum_{x,w} \beta_{\mathcal{P},y,z,b,x,w}|x,w\rangle)(\sum_{x,w} \bar{\beta}_{\mathcal{P},y,z,b,x,w}\langle x,w|),$$

where x is the output that need to be measured after running $\mathcal{E}(b, \cdot)$, and it holds that

$$\sum_{\mathcal{P},y,z} |a_{\mathcal{P},y,z}|^2 \cdot \sum_{w,x}^{\mathcal{P}(x)=b, H_n(x)=y} |\beta_{\mathcal{P},y,z,b,x,w}|^2 \geq 1 - \mathtt{negl}(n) \tag{29}$$

for some negligible function $\mathtt{negl}(\cdot)$ due to the correctness of the equivocality. Since it may not always hold that $y = H_n(x)$, we hence add an additional register to $\rho^{(b)}$ in order to store the hash value $H_n(x)$, which we denote it by

$$\tilde{\rho}^{(b)} = \sum_{\mathcal{P},y,z} |a_{\mathcal{P},y,z}|^2 |\mathcal{P},y,z,b\rangle\langle\mathcal{P},y,z,b|$$

$$\otimes (\sum_{x,w} \beta_{\mathcal{P},y,z,b,x,w}|x,H_n(x),w\rangle)(\sum_{x,w} \bar{\beta}_{\mathcal{P},y,z,b,x,w}\langle x,H_n(x),w|).$$

Hence $\tilde{\rho}^{(b)}$ contains the input and output of H_n, that inspires us to adopt that state as the challenging state in the collapsing experiment. More specifically, when we give the registers $x, H_n(x)$ of $\tilde{\rho}^{(0)}$ to the challenger of the collapsing game, then if it has been measured in the output register, the state $\rho^{(0)}$ would basically not change, which means we can retrieve some x satisfying $H_n(x) =$

---

[3] To make it clear, we denote it as a mixed state where the measurement of $\mathcal{P}, y$ is replaced by the tracing out operation, and without loss of generality, we assume the register containing the bit b is not changed by $\mathcal{E}$.

$y \wedge \mathcal{P}(x) = 1$ with overwhelming probability by invoking $\mathcal{E}(1, \cdot) \circ \mathcal{E}^\dagger(0, \cdot)$. On the other hand, if it has been measured in the input register, then the state $\rho^{(0)}$ would be probably collapsed and can not be reversible, if not, that implies we can get a collision of y with non-negligible probability.

The following is the description of the adversary $\mathcal{A}$ that breaks the collapsing property:

- $\mathcal{A}$ gets the description of the hash function $H_n(k, \cdot)$, and then invokes the purified $\mathcal{G}(1^n)$ to get the state ρ.
- $\mathcal{A}$ runs the operator $\mathcal{E}(0, \cdot)$ to the state $|0,0\rangle\langle 0,0| \otimes \rho$, and gets $\tilde{\rho}^{(0)}$ in result, then sends the input and output registers of $\tilde{\rho}^{(0)}$ to the challenger.
- After receiving the state $\tilde{\rho}^{(0)}_{(b^*)}$ from the challenger ($b^* = 0$ means the state after measuring (tracing out) the output register of $\tilde{\rho}^{(0)}$, and $b^* = 1$ denotes the state after measuring the input register), $\mathcal{A}$ invokes the $\mathcal{E}(1, \cdot) \circ \mathcal{E}^\dagger(0, \cdot)$ to that state and measures the result to get a measurement x and the corresponding y. It would output 0 if $\mathcal{P}(x) = 1 \wedge H_n(x) = y$, and output 1 if $\mathcal{P}(x) = 0 \wedge H_n(x) = y$ otherwise, it would returns a random bit $b' \leftarrow \{0,1\}$ uniformly.

We now estimate the advantage of $\mathcal{A}$. In the case that the challenger measures the output register, according to the correctness of the equivocality of H_n, we can deduce from inequality (29) that the trace distance between $\tilde{\rho}^{(0)}_{(0)}$ and $\tilde{\rho}^{(0)}$ is at most

$$\mathrm{TD}(\tilde{\rho}^{(0)}_{(0)}, \tilde{\rho}^{(0)}) \leq \mathtt{negl}_0(n)$$

for some negligible function $\mathtt{negl}_0(\cdot)$. That implies if we invoke the inverse $\mathcal{E}^\dagger(0, \cdot)$ in that case, we could recover the state $|0,0\rangle\langle 0,0| \otimes \rho$ with overwhelming probability. And hence we get the measurement x that satisfies $\mathcal{P}(x) = 1$ and $H_n(k, x) = y$ with overwhelming probability after invoking $\mathcal{E}$ again. Namely, we have

$$\Pr[\mathcal{A} \text{ outputs } 0 \mid b^* = 0] \geq 1 - \mathtt{negl}_1(n). \tag{30}$$

In the case that the challenger measures the input register (i.e. $b^* = 1$), the input register of $\tilde{\rho}^{(0)}$ would collapse to some x^* (which is the preimage of y with overwhelming probability due to the correctness of equivocality). Then we run the $\mathcal{E}(1, \cdot) \circ \mathcal{E}^\dagger(0, \cdot)$ and measure the result to get a measurement x and the corresponding $H_n(x)$. To estimate the probability that $\mathcal{A}$ wins in this case, we consider the following these events separately:

- The measurement x satisfies $\mathcal{P}(x) = 1 \wedge H_n(x) = y$, that implies we successfully find a collision x, x^*. Therefore the probability of that event occurs is bounded by some negligible function $\mathtt{negl}_2(\cdot)$ (otherwise it would induce an adversary breaks the quantum collision-resistance of $H_n(\cdot)$ with non-negligible probability).
- The measurement x satisfies $\mathcal{P}(x) = 0 \wedge H_n(x) = y$, then $\mathcal{A}$ would return 1 deterministically when that event occurs.

- The measurement x is not a preimage of y, then the probability that $\mathcal{A}$ returns 1 with probability exactly $1/2$

That implies

$$\Pr[\mathcal{A} \text{ outputs } 1 \mid b^* = 1]$$

$$= 1 - \Pr[\mathcal{P}(x) = 1 \wedge H_n(x) = y \mid b^* = 1] - \frac{1}{2}\Pr[H_n(x) \neq y \mid b^* = 1]$$

$$\geq \frac{1}{2} - \mathtt{negl}_2(n), \tag{31}$$

for some negligible function $\mathtt{negl}_2(\cdot)$.

Combining the inequality (30) with (31), we have

$$\left| \Pr[\mathsf{Exp}_{\mathcal{A}}^{coll}(n) = 1] - \frac{1}{2} \right|$$

$$\geq \left| \frac{1}{2} \cdot \Pr[\mathcal{A} \text{ outputs } 1 \mid b^* = 1] + \frac{1}{2} \cdot \Pr[\mathcal{A} \text{ outputs } 1 \mid b^* = 1] - \frac{1}{2} \right|$$

$$\geq \frac{1}{4} - \mathtt{negl}_1(n) - \mathtt{negl}_2(n), \tag{32}$$

which hence breaks the collapsing property of $H_n(\cdot)$. $\qquad\square$

Note that the inverse of the operator $\mathcal{E}(\cdot)$ is involved in our proof, which is usually infeasible in the fully black-box sense (even the semi-black-box sense), that is because the process of purification requires the internal information of the equivocal hash functions. That implies we prove the Lemma 1 via a non-black-box manner. However, we believe it is also interesting to figure out if this result still holds in the black-box manner.

References

1. Aharonov, D., Kitaev, A.Y., Nisan, N.: Quantum circuits with mixed states. In: Vitter, J.S. (ed.) Proceedings of the Thirtieth Annual ACM Symposium on the Theory of Computing, pp. 20–30. ACM, Dallas, Texas, USA (1998)
2. Ajtai, M.: Generating hard instances of lattice problems (extended abstract). In: Miller, G.L. (ed.) Proceedings of the Twenty-Eighth Annual ACM Symposium on the Theory of Computing, pp. 99–108. ACM, Philadelphia, Pennsylvania, USA (1996)
3. Ambainis, A., Rosmanis, A., Unruh, D.: Quantum attacks on classical proof systems: the hardness of quantum rewinding. In: 55th IEEE Annual Symposium on Foundations of Computer Science, FOCS 2014, pp. 474–483. IEEE Computer Society, Philadelphia, PA, USA (2014)
4. Amos, R., Georgiou, M., Kiayias, A., Zhandry, M.: One-shot signatures and applications to hybrid quantum/classical authentication. In: Makarychev, K., Makarychev, Y., Tulsiani, M., Kamath, G., Chuzhoy, J. (eds.) Proccedings of the 52nd Annual ACM SIGACT Symposium on Theory of Computing, STOC 2020, pp. 255–268. ACM, Chicago, IL, USA (2020)

5. Asharov, G., Segev, G.: Limits on the power of indistinguishability obfuscation and functional encryption. In: Guruswami, V. (ed.) IEEE 56th Annual Symposium on Foundations of Computer Science, FOCS 2015, pp. 191–209. IEEE Computer Society, Berkeley, CA, USA (2015)

6. Barak, B., Goldreich, O.: Universal arguments and their applications. SIAM J. Comput. **38**(5), 1661–1694 (2008)

7. Berman, I., Degwekar, A., Rothblum, R.D., Vasudevan, P.N.: Multi-collision resistant hash functions and their applications. In: Nielsen, J.B., Rijmen, V. (eds.) EUROCRYPT 2018. LNCS, vol. 10821, pp. 133–161. Springer, Cham (2018). https://doi.org/10.1007/978-3-319-78375-8_5

8. Bitansky, N., Haitner, I., Komargodski, I., Yogev, E.: Distributional collision resistance beyond one-way functions. In: Ishai, Y., Rijmen, V. (eds.) EUROCRYPT 2019. LNCS, vol. 11478, pp. 667–695. Springer, Cham (2019). https://doi.org/10.1007/978-3-030-17659-4_23

9. Bitansky, N., Kalai, Y.T., Paneth, O.: Multi-collision resistance: a paradigm for keyless hash functions. In: Diakonikolas, I., Kempe, D., Henzinger, M. (eds.) Proceedings of the 50th Annual ACM SIGACT Symposium on Theory of Computing, STOC 2018, pp. 671–684. ACM, Los Angeles, CA, USA (2018)

10. Bitansky, N., Paneth, O., Wichs, D.: Perfect structure on the edge of Chaos. In: Kushilevitz, E., Malkin, T. (eds.) TCC 2016. LNCS, vol. 9562, pp. 474–502. Springer, Heidelberg (2016). https://doi.org/10.1007/978-3-662-49096-9_20

11. Canetti, R., Lin, H., Tessaro, S., Vaikuntanathan, V.: Obfuscation of probabilistic circuits and applications. In: Dodis, Y., Nielsen, J.B. (eds.) TCC 2015. LNCS, vol. 9015, pp. 468–497. Springer, Heidelberg (2015). https://doi.org/10.1007/978-3-662-46497-7_19

12. Cao, S., Xue, R.: Being a permutation is also orthogonal to one-wayness in quantum world: Impossibilities of quantum one-way permutations from one-wayness primitives. Theor. Comput. Sci. **855**, 16–42 (2021)

13. Carter, L., Wegman, M.N.: Universal classes of hash functions (extended abstract). In: Hopcroft, J.E., Friedman, E.P., Harrison, M.A. (eds.) Proceedings of the 9th Annual ACM Symposium on Theory of Computing, pp. 106–112. ACM, Boulder, Colorado, USA (1977)

14. Cramer, R., Shoup, V.: Universal hash proofs and a paradigm for adaptive chosen Ciphertext secure public-key encryption. In: Knudsen, L.R. (ed.) EUROCRYPT 2002. LNCS, vol. 2332, pp. 45–64. Springer, Heidelberg (2002). https://doi.org/10.1007/3-540-46035-7_4

15. Czajkowski, J., Groot Bruinderink, L., Hülsing, A., Schaffner, C., Unruh, D.: Post-quantum security of the sponge construction. In: Lange, T., Steinwandt, R. (eds.) PQCrypto 2018. LNCS, vol. 10786, pp. 185–204. Springer, Cham (2018). https://doi.org/10.1007/978-3-319-79063-3_9

16. Dubrov, B., Ishai, Y.: On the randomness complexity of efficient sampling. In: Kleinberg, J.M. (ed.) Proceedings of the 38th Annual ACM Symposium on Theory of Computing, pp. 711–720. ACM, Seattle, WA, USA (2006)

17. Fehr, S.: Classical proofs for the quantum collapsing property of classical hash functions. In: Beimel, A., Dziembowski, S. (eds.) TCC 2018. LNCS, vol. 11240, pp. 315–338. Springer, Cham (2018). https://doi.org/10.1007/978-3-030-03810-6_12

18. Goldreich, O., Goldwasser, S., Halevi, S.: Collision-free hashing from lattice problems. Electron. Colloquium Comput. Complex. (42) (1996)

19. Haitner, I., Hoch, J.J., Reingold, O., Segev, G.: Finding collisions in interactive protocols - tight lower bounds on the round and communication complexities of statistically hiding commitments. SIAM J. Comput. **44**(1), 193–242 (2015)

20. Hamlin, B., Song, F.: Quantum security of hash functions and property-preservation of iterated hashing. In: Ding, J., Steinwandt, R. (eds.) PQCrypto 2019. LNCS, vol. 11505, pp. 329–349. Springer, Cham (2019). https://doi.org/10.1007/978-3-030-25510-7_18

21. Hosoyamada, A., Yamakawa, T.: Finding collisions in a quantum world: quantum black-box separation of collision-resistance and one-wayness. In: Moriai, S., Wang, H. (eds.) ASIACRYPT 2020. LNCS, vol. 12491, pp. 3–32. Springer, Cham (2020). https://doi.org/10.1007/978-3-030-64837-4_1

22. Hsiao, C.-Y., Reyzin, L.: Finding collisions on a public road, or do secure hash functions need secret coins? In: Franklin, M. (ed.) CRYPTO 2004. LNCS, vol. 3152, pp. 92–105. Springer, Heidelberg (2004). https://doi.org/10.1007/978-3-540-28628-8_6

23. Hülsing, A., Rijneveld, J., Song, F.: Mitigating multi-target attacks in hash-based signatures. In: Cheng, C.-M., Chung, K.-M., Persiano, G., Yang, B.-Y. (eds.) PKC 2016. LNCS, vol. 9614, pp. 387–416. Springer, Heidelberg (2016). https://doi.org/10.1007/978-3-662-49384-7_15

24. Impagliazzo, R.: A personal view of average-case complexity. In: Proceedings of the Tenth Annual Structure in Complexity Theory Conference, pp. 134–147. IEEE Computer Society, Minneapolis, Minnesota, USA (1995)

25. Katz, J., Lindell, Y.: Introduction to Modern Cryptography. CRC Press (2020)

26. Komargodski, I., Naor, M., Yogev, E.: Collision resistant hashing for paranoids: dealing with multiple collisions. In: Nielsen, J.B., Rijmen, V. (eds.) EUROCRYPT 2018. LNCS, vol. 10821, pp. 162–194. Springer, Cham (2018). https://doi.org/10.1007/978-3-319-78375-8_6

27. Komargodski, I., Yogev, E.: On distributional collision resistant hashing. In: Shacham, H., Boldyreva, A. (eds.) CRYPTO 2018. LNCS, vol. 10992, pp. 303–327. Springer, Cham (2018). https://doi.org/10.1007/978-3-319-96881-0_11

28. Mazor, N., Zhang, J.: Simple constructions from (Almost) regular one-way functions. In: Nissim, K., Waters, B. (eds.) TCC 2021. LNCS, vol. 13043, pp. 457–485. Springer, Cham (2021). https://doi.org/10.1007/978-3-030-90453-1_16

29. Merkle, R.C.: A certified digital signature. In: Brassard, G. (ed.) CRYPTO 1989. LNCS, vol. 435, pp. 218–238. Springer, New York (1990). https://doi.org/10.1007/0-387-34805-0_21

30. Micciancio, D., Regev, O.: Worst-case to average-case reductions based on gaussian measures. SIAM J. Comput. **37**(1), 267–302 (2007)

31. Nielsen, M.A., Chuang, I.: Quantum Computation and Quantum Information (2002)

32. Reingold, O., Trevisan, L., Vadhan, S.: Notions of reducibility between cryptographic primitives. In: Naor, M. (ed.) TCC 2004. LNCS, vol. 2951, pp. 1–20. Springer, Heidelberg (2004). https://doi.org/10.1007/978-3-540-24638-1_1

33. Ristenpart, T., Shrimpton, T.: How to build a hash function from any collision-resistant function. In: Kurosawa, K. (ed.) ASIACRYPT 2007. LNCS, vol. 4833, pp. 147–163. Springer, Heidelberg (2007). https://doi.org/10.1007/978-3-540-76900-2_9

34. Rogaway, P., Shrimpton, T.: Cryptographic hash-function basics: definitions, implications, and separations for preimage resistance, second-preimage resistance, and collision resistance. In: Roy, B., Meier, W. (eds.) FSE 2004. LNCS, vol. 3017, pp. 371–388. Springer, Heidelberg (2004). https://doi.org/10.1007/978-3-540-25937-4_24

35. Rompel, J.: One-way functions are necessary and sufficient for secure signatures. In: Ortiz, H. (ed.) Proceedings of the 22nd Annual ACM Symposium on Theory of Computing, pp. 387–394. ACM, Baltimore, Maryland, USA (1990)
36. Simon, D.R.: Finding collisions on a one-way street: can secure hash functions be based on general assumptions? In: Nyberg, K. (ed.) EUROCRYPT 1998. LNCS, vol. 1403, pp. 334–345. Springer, Heidelberg (1998). https://doi.org/10.1007/BFb0054137
37. Unruh, D.: Collapse-binding quantum commitments without random oracles. In: Cheon, J.H., Takagi, T. (eds.) ASIACRYPT 2016. LNCS, vol. 10032, pp. 166–195. Springer, Heidelberg (2016). https://doi.org/10.1007/978-3-662-53890-6_6
38. Unruh, D.: Computationally binding quantum commitments. In: Fischlin, M., Coron, J.-S. (eds.) EUROCRYPT 2016. LNCS, vol. 9666, pp. 497–527. Springer, Heidelberg (2016). https://doi.org/10.1007/978-3-662-49896-5_18
39. Unruh, D.: Collapsing sponges: Post-quantum security of the sponge construction. IACR Cryptol. ePrint Arch. 282 (2017)
40. Wegman, M.N., Carter, L.: New hash functions and their use in authentication and set equality. J. Comput. Syst. Sci. **22**(3), 265–279 (1981)
41. Zhandry, M.: Secure identity-based encryption in the quantum random oracle model. In: Safavi-Naini, R., Canetti, R. (eds.) CRYPTO 2012. LNCS, vol. 7417, pp. 758–775. Springer, Heidelberg (2012). https://doi.org/10.1007/978-3-642-32009-5_44
42. Zhandry, M.: How to record quantum queries, and applications to quantum indifferentiability. In: Boldyreva, A., Micciancio, D. (eds.) CRYPTO 2019. LNCS, vol. 11693, pp. 239–268. Springer, Cham (2019). https://doi.org/10.1007/978-3-030-26951-7_9
43. Zhandry, M.: Quantum lightning never strikes the same state twice. In: Ishai, Y., Rijmen, V. (eds.) EUROCRYPT 2019. LNCS, vol. 11478, pp. 408–438. Springer, Cham (2019). https://doi.org/10.1007/978-3-030-17659-4_14
44. Zhandry, M.: New constructions of collapsing hashes. In: Dodis, Y., Shrimpton, T. (eds.) CRYPTO 2022. LNCS, vol. 13509, pp. 596–624. Springer, Cham (2022)

New Constructions of Collapsing Hashes

Mark Zhandry[1,2]([✉])

[1] NTT Research, Sunnyvale, USA
mzhandry@gmail.com
[2] Princeton University, Princeton, USA

Abstract. Collapsing is a post-quantum strengthening of collision resistance, needed to lift many classical results to the quantum setting. Unfortunately, the only existing standard-model proofs of collapsing hashes require LWE. We construct the first collapsing hashes from the quantum hardness of any one of the following problems:

- LPN in a variety of low noise or high-hardness regimes, essentially matching what is known for collision resistance from LPN.
- Finding cycles on exponentially-large expander graphs, such as those arising from isogenies on elliptic curves.
- The "optimal" hardness of finding collisions in *any* hash function.
- The *polynomial* hardness of finding collisions, assuming a certain plausible regularity condition on the hash.

As an immediate corollary, we obtain the first statistically hiding post-quantum commitments and post-quantum succinct arguments (of knowledge) under the same assumptions. Our results are obtained by a general theorem which shows how to construct a collapsing hash H' from a post-quantum collision-resistant hash function H, regardless of whether or not H itself is collapsing, assuming H satisfies a certain regularity condition we call "semi-regularity".

1 Introduction

Collision resistance is one of the most important cryptographic concepts, with numerous applications throughout cryptography. A collision resistant hash function $H : \{0,1\}^m \to \{0,1\}^n$ is one where $n < m$, thus guaranteeing that collisions exist in abundance, but where actually finding such collisions is computationally intractable. Collision resistance provably follows from most number-theoretic problems used in cryptography, and is one of the main design goals in constructions built from symmetric key tools, such as SHA2 or SHA3.

What happens when quantum computers enter the picture? For any application that required collision resistance classically, certainly a *minimal* condition is that it remains intractable for quantum algorithms to find a collision. We will call this notion a "post-quantum" collision resistant hash function (PQ-CRHF). Post-quantum security rules out constructions based on discrete logarithms or factoring due to Shor's algorithm [Sho94]. Surprisingly, however, even PQ-CRHFs are often *insufficient* for applications, as first demonstrated by Ambainis, Rosmanis, and Unruh [ARU14, Unr16b] with a counterexample. The issue usually stems

© International Association for Cryptologic Research 2022
Y. Dodis and T. Shrimpton (Eds.): CRYPTO 2022, LNCS 13509, pp. 596–624, 2022.
https://doi.org/10.1007/978-3-031-15982-4_20

from rewinding, which is known to be problematic quantumly [VDG98,Wat06]. Examples include commitments and more generally interactive protocols.

To remedy the situation, Unruh [Unr16b] proposes a strengthening of collision resistance called *collapsing*. Very roughly, collapsing means that measuring the hash of a quantum superposition of messages is quantum computationally indistinguishable from measuring the message superposition itself, even though both operations are information-theoretically very different. Since its introduction, collapsing hashes have become recognized as the preferred notion of post-quantum security, being the appropriate post-quantum replacement for classical collision resistance whenever there is rewinding [CCY21,CMSZ21,LMS21], and sometimes even when rewinding is not present [AMRS20]. Unsurprisingly, collapsing is also a natural property beyond hash functions, being the right notion of post-quantum commitments [Unr16b] (whereas PQ computational binding is useless), identification protocols underlying post-quantum signatures [DFMS19,LZ19], and general argument systems [LMS21].

Given their importance to post-quantum security, it is crucial to understand how to construct collapsing hash functions. Unfortunately, there are essentially only two classes of constructions. The first are idealized model proofs [Unr16b,Unr17], where one proves collapsing relative to, say, a random oracle. The second are standard-model proofs [Unr16a,LZ19], where the only existing paradigm leverages lossy functions or closely related concepts, whose only known post-quantum instantiations require LWE (or equivalently, SIS by Regev's reduction [Reg05]).

On the other hand, the only hash functions which are provably PQ-CRHFs but *not* collapsing are contrived and require either complex oracles [Unr16b,AGKZ20] or un-tested conjectures [Zha19b][1]. Zhandry [Zha19b] even shows that such a separation between the notions could be used to build public key quantum money and stronger objects, which have been notoriously hard to build. In summary, neither of the following scenarios would contradict any long-standing conjectures:

- Collapsing is ubiquitous, and *every* non-relativized PQ-CRHF is collapsing.
- Collapsing is rare, and the *only* standard-model collapsing hash functions are those requiring LWE.

On Random Oracle-based Hashes. One may argue that we can simply conjecture that some hash function is collapsing, and then trivially "build" collapsing hashes from that function. In particular, random oracles are collapsing [Unr16b] and symmetric key hash functions such as SHA2 or SHA3 are often modeled as random oracles.

However, collapsing is an inherently quantum notion, which is potentially much harder to reason about than typical classically-defined notions such as collision resistance, pseudorandomness, etc. Indeed, the random oracle heuristic is based on extensive cryptanalytic studies of the hash functions with respect

---

[1] [Zha19b] gives a proof relative to a novel computational assumption, but it has been cryptanalyzed [Rob21].

to classically-defined tasks. This is true even for works considering quantum attacks [HS21, AMG+16], where the cryptanalysis goal is still classically-defined, such as finding collisions. Some works have proved the post-quantum *indifferentiability* of these functions [Zha19a, CHS19, Cza21]; while these are important for understanding security, they punt the cryptanalysis effort to the underlying round function, which again have largely been studied for their classical security.

Aside from idealized model justifications, we are not aware of *any* cryptanalysis effort on hash functions like SHA2 or SHA3 with regards to collapsing. Therefore, it seems plausible that the random oracle heuristic could hold on symmetric hash functions relative to classically-defined security properties, but fails for collapsing. For this reason, the current evidence for SHA2 or SHA3 being collapsing appears much weaker than evidence for their (post-quantum) collision resistance.

Our Results. In this work, we build a collapsing hash function H' from any PQ-CRHF H that satisfies a mild structural condition we call *semi-regularity*. Semi-regularity essentially means that no output has too many more pre-images than the "average" output. Note that H itself may be equivocal, and indeed the counter-example of [ARU14] is semi-regular. Yet when plugged into our construction, the resulting H' is collapsing. We then show the following:

- Hash functions based on expanders [TZ94, CLG09, FLLT21], or a variety of LPN settings [BLVW19, YZW+19] satisfy our regularity condition. In these cases, we thus achieve collapsing hashes under the same assumptions used to achieve post-quantum collision resistance.
- We do not know how to prove semi-regularity for symmetric hash function such as SHA2 or SHA3, but it is a natural property and it is reasonable to conjecture it holds for these functions. In particular, random oracles are semi-regular. Under this conjecture together with post-quantum collision resistance for SHA2 or SHA3, we obtain collapsing hashes. This is the first standard-model collapsing hash function from *classically defined* assumptions in Minicrypt; that is, they do not imply public key encryption.
- As an alternative approach, we show that H can be compiled into a collapsing hash function if it is *optimally* collision resistant, even if it is not semi-regular. Optimal collision resistance means that every polynomial-time algorithm can only find collisions with probability poly/|Range|. Note that the optimal generic classical and quantum [BHT97] collision-finding algorithms make T queries and succeed with probability $O(T^2)/|\text{Range}|$ and $O(T^3)/|\text{Range}|$, respectively. Symmetric hashes such as SHA2 or SHA3 are often designed with the goal of achieving optimal collision resistance, and so we obtain collapsing hashes under the assumed optimal collision resistance of either of these functions.

As immediate corollaries of our results, we obtain post-quantum statistically hiding commitments [Unr16b] and succinct arguments [CMSZ21] under any of the above assumptions. Our results show that semi-regularity is an important design consideration for constructing post-quantum hash functions.

1.1 Why PQ-CRHFs Are Not Enough

For completeness, we give a brief explanation of why rewinding is problematic with PQ-CRHFs. Consider the following game. An adversary sends a hash y to the challenger. The challenger then flips a random bit b. The adversary then wins if it can produce a pre-image x of y such that the first bit of x is b. Clearly, an adversary could always set y to be the hash of an arbitrary x, in which case the first bit of x is b with probability $1/2$. But can the adversary do better?

Classically, the answer is no, assuming the hash is collision resistant. Suppose for a given y that the adversary could win with probability $1/2 + \epsilon$. Then it must win with probability at least ϵ conditioned on $b = 0$, and also with probability at least ϵ conditioned on $b = 1$. By running the adversary on $b = 0$, rewinding until just after the adversary sends y, and running again on $b = 1$, one obtains (with probability at least ϵ^2) pre-images x_0 and x_1 whose first bits are 0,1 respectively. Since $x_0 \neq x_1$ and they are both pre-images of y, we have thus found a collision.

Quantumly, however, the above breaks down. Measuring x_0 on the first execution potentially destroys the quantum state of the adversary, meaning the adversary is no longer guaranteed to produce x_1. Ambainis et al.'s counter-example gives a hash function (relative to an oracle) where the probability to produce x_1 indeed becomes negligible. This creates problems for computationally binding commitments, where Ambainis et al.'s construction yields commitments that are equivocal, despite being binding in the usual sense. Likewise, this equivocation is problematic for many proof systems that demonstrate soundness by extracting two colliding transcripts from an adversary through rewinding.

Unruh's notion of collapsing hashes resolves this problem. Basically, the adversary's first message y results in the output of the hash being measured. Collapsing implies that this is indistinguishable from measuring the input. Measuring the input corresponds exactly to extracting x_0. While such extraction could potentially alter the quantum state, it cannot alter it in any detectable way. In particular this means the second run to recover x_1 must still succeed. This completes the reduction from collision resistance. Note that collision resistance is implied by collapsing as explained by Unruh, and hence collapsing implies the adversary can only win with probability $1/2 + \mathsf{negl}$, as desired.

1.2 Techniques

We call a function $\leq\!\ell\text{-to-1}$ if no image has more than ℓ pre-images. We start with the following observation (Sect. 3):

Theorem 1 (Informal). *For poly ℓ, any $\leq\!\ell\text{-to-1}$ PQ-CRHF is also collapsing.*
To see why this might be true, consider some $\leq\!\ell\text{-to-1}$ function H. Let

$$|\phi\rangle = \sum_x \alpha_x |x\rangle$$

be a superposition of inputs. Now consider measuring the output of H applied to $|\phi\rangle$ in superposition. If the measurement results in outcome y, then the state

$|\phi\rangle$ collapses to the partially-measured state

$$|\phi_y\rangle \propto \sum_{x:H(x)=y} \alpha_x |x\rangle \ .$$

Since H is $\leq\ell$-to-1, the support of $|\phi_y\rangle$ contains at most ℓ different x.

Non-collapsing means that there is some operation M which distinguishes $|\phi_y\rangle$ from the result of measuring $|\phi_y\rangle$, the latter yielding a distribution over singletons $|x\rangle$ such that $H(x) = y$. Suppose that M actually simply accepted $|\phi_y\rangle$ and rejected all orthogonal states. In this case, if we measure $|\phi_y\rangle$—thus obtaining one pre-image x—and then apply M, there is a non-negligible chance we get back to $|\phi_y\rangle$. This is because $|\phi_y\rangle$ must have a significant overlap with $|x\rangle$, as $|\phi_y\rangle$ is the sum of only ℓ of the $|x\rangle$ vectors. But then if we were to measure again, we will get some x' that is *also* a pre-image. Moreover, $|\phi_y\rangle$ is itself not a singleton, since otherwise measuring it would have no effect and the distinguishing M would be impossible. Therefore there is a non-negligible chance that $x \neq x'$. We thus obtain a collision.

We show that the above actually holds, no matter what $|\phi_y\rangle$ is, and no matter what M does, thus proving Theorem 1.

Generalization. Unfortunately, Theorem 1 appears somewhat limited. One may hope that symmetric hash functions such as SHA2 or SHA3, when restricted to a domain that is only slightly larger than the range, might be $\leq\ell$-to-1 for a polynomial ℓ. After all, if we model them as random oracles, it is straightforward to show this. However, for other hash functions based on post-quantum assumptions, such as LPN [BLVW19, YZW+19] or expanders [CLG09], we cannot reasonably apply the random oracle heuristic due to significant structure. There are two potential problems:

1. The image might be a sparse subset of the co-domain. In this case, even if the hash function only compressed by a single bit, it may be exponentially-many-to-1 and Theorem 1 will not apply. It is not hard to modify Unruh's counterexample [Unr16b] to give such a non-collapsing hash (relative to an oracle). We will give an example of where this is relevant below.
2. Looking ahead, we will see that LPN- and expander-based hash functions will eventually achieve some level of regularity, but this is only guaranteed once the input size is somewhat larger than the output. In such a case, the function is inherently exponentially-many-to-1.

We therefore propose a generalization of Theorem 1 which overcomes these two specific issues above. First, observe that any $\leq\ell$-to-1 hash on its own is not very useful, as it offers only minimal compression. However, by domain extension techniques, we can compile it into a hash function with arbitrary compression.

Imagine using Merkle-Damgård (MD) for domain extension, compiling a "small" hash H into a "big" hash H'. MD is already guaranteed to preserve collapsing [Unr16b]. Imagine at each iteration, we only incorporate a single bit of the input at a time. Since the input to each iteration of H is just an output of H concatenated with a single bit, the number of possible inputs to H is never more than twice the number of possible outputs. In other words, H is 2-to-1 *on average*, over the set of possible inputs it will be evaluated on. If H were "sufficiently random looking", we would therefore expect that most outputs to H would only have relatively few pre-images, so that H could be $\leq \ell$-to-1 for a polynomial ℓ.

We formalize this intuition: assuming H is "sufficiently regular", we show that we can make H "sufficiently random looking" by pre-pending it with a (almost) ℓ-wise independent permutation for a polynomially-large ℓ. Here, "sufficiently regular" essentially means that the most common output of H is only polynomially-more likely than the average output. This is formalized by a notion we call *semi-regularity* (Definition 4), which says roughly that the most common output is only a polynomial factor more likely than the "average" output. The result is the following:

Theorem 2. *If H is a semi-regular PQ-CRHF, then it can be compiled into a collapsing hash function H'.*

Applications. We show that several candidate post-quantum hash functions satisfy the necessary semi-regularity conditions, thus allowing us to construct novel collapsing hash functions:

- Section 5: Hash functions based on LPN [BLVW19, YZW+19] for a variety of low noise or high-hardness settings, matching the LPN assumptions under which plain post-quantum collision resistance exists.
- Section 6: Hash functions based on walks on exponentially-large expander graphs, as proposed by Charles, Goren, and Lauter [CLG09], abstracting earlier ideas of [TZ94]. A particular instantiation suggested by [CLG09] allows for obtaining a collapsing hash function from the hardness of certain problems on isogenies over elliptic curves. Another candidate was recently proposed by Fuchs et al. [FLLT21] based on Markov Triples.

Remark 1. The output of an expander-based hash is the label of the final node in the walk. In general, the set of labels may be sparse, in which case we would run into Problem 1. An example of such an expander is that of Fuchs et al., where the range is $\mathbb{Z}_p^3$, but the size of the graph is only $O(p^2)$. Likewise, the Charles et al. expander from isogenies has labels in $\mathbb{Z}_p^2$ but the graph size is only $O(p)$. For this reason, in the case of expander hashes, we need the full power of Theorem 2.

Remark 2. We emphasize that we do not prove the constructions of [BLVW19, YZW+19, CLG09, FLLT21] are collapsing. Instead, we only prove semi-regularity, which allows us to compile (through a Merkle-Damgård-like construction) into a collapsing hash. We leave as an interesting open question whether the base constructions could be proven collapsing.

Remark 3. Other instantiations of [CLG09] have been proposed, such as the use of LPS graphs [CLG09], the original proposal of [TZ94], and Morgenstern graphs [PLQ12]. Some weaknesses have been shown in these graphs [PLQ08], though there are still versions that remain secure. See [PLQ08] for discussion. For any version that is post-quantum collision resistant, our result immediately lifts it to a hash that is collapsing.

Symmetric Key Hash Functions. We do not know how to prove that symmetric hash functions such as SHA2 or SHA3 are semi-regular, and leave this as an interesting open question. However, we observe that random oracles are readily shown to be semi-regular. Thus, either of two things happen:

- The hash function is not semi-regular, therefore violating the random oracle heuristic for a classically defined statistical property. This case could be considered as demonstrating a significant weakness of the hash function.
- The hash function is semi-regular, in which we can compile it into a collapsing hash function based on the assumed (post-quantum) collision resistance of the function, which is a widely studied security property.

Thus we establish semi-regularity as an important design principle in the design of symmetric-key based hash functions.

We also provide additional evidence that SHA2 or SHA3 can be compiled into a collapsing hash. Concretely, SHA2 and SHA3 are widely believed to have *optimal* collision resistance, meaning that any polynomial-time algorithm only has a polynomial advantage over the trivial algorithm of guessing two random inputs and hoping they collide. The assumed optimal collision resistance is the basis for the current parameter settings of these functions. If SHA2 or SHA3 did not have optimal collision resistance, it would show that the parameter settings are too aggressive, and this would be considered a serious weakness.

In Sect. 7, we show that any optimally (post-quantum) collision resistant hash function that compresses by only a few bits is in fact collapsing, even if it is not semi-regular. Thus under the highly likely optimal collision resistance of SHA2 or SHA3, we obtain a collapsing hash function.

1.3   Collapsing from Group Actions?

A group action is a relaxation of a standard cryptographic group, roughly allowing exponentiation but not multiplication. The advantage of such a restricted structure is that it prevents Shor's algorithm [Sho94], and therefore maintains plausible post-quantum security. This was observed concurrently by Couveignes [Cou06] and Rostovtsev and Stolbunov [RS06], both works also proposing an instantiation of plausible post-quantum group actions using isogenies over elliptic curves.

The restricted structure of group actions preserves plausible post-quantum security, but it also restricts applications. In particular, the usual way of obtaining collision resistance from discrete logarithms, namely

$$(x, y) \mapsto g^x h^y \ ,$$

no longer can be computed without the ability to multiply elements. One could consider another natural construction, namely:

$$(x, b) \mapsto \begin{cases} g^x & \text{if } b = 0 \\ h^x & \text{if } b = 1 \end{cases},$$

where b is a single bit. This is a 2-to-1 function where finding collisions is intractable by the hardness of discrete logarithms on the group action. For group actions based on isogenies, the discrete logarithm problem is exactly the problem of computing isogenies. However, with currently known group actions from isogenies, the bit-length of g^x is roughly *twice* the bit-length of x, meaning the images are sparse and the function is not compressing despite being 2-to-1. Such functions are not useful for hashing. It remains a major open question whether collision resistant compressing hashing can be based on the discrete log problem for group actions of this form, and in particular if such collision resistance can be based on the hardness of computing isogenies.

Call a group action *compact* if g^x has the same bit length as x. For compact group actions, the above hash function would be compressing, and collision resistance would follow from the hardness of computing discrete logarithms. Then applying Theorem 1, we immediately conclude that compact group actions also yield collapsing hash functions.. We leave finding a plausible post-quantum compact group action as an intriguing open question.

Remark 4. The isogeny-based hash of [CLG09] relies on a different problem, namely finding a non-trivial cycle on the isogeny graph. The hardness of finding cycles is a *stronger* assumption that the hardness of computing isogenies.

1.4   Collapsing from Arbitrary Collision Resistance?

While it seems most natural hash functions are semi-regular (at least in some parameter settings), it is not hard to construct contrived hash functions that are not semi-regular. Therefore, our restriction to semi-regular functions potentially limits the applicability of our approach. An interesting conjecture is the following:

Conjecture 1. From *any* PQ-CRHF, one can build a collapsing hash function.

Removing the semi-regularity restriction seems challenging. Consider a construction of H' from H where the output of H' is just the concatenation of t outputs of H on different inputs. More generally, perhaps the output of H' is an injective function applied to t outputs of H. This structure would allow for immediately translating an H' collision into an H collision. It seems difficult to devise an H' that is not of this form while still proving the collision resistance of H' (let alone collapsing) just on the collision resistance of H.

For an H' of this form, if H has n-bit outputs, H' has tn-bit outputs, and therefore H' must have at least $(tn + 1)$-bit inputs in order to be compressing. Suppose H was not semi-regular, and had some outputs that represented an

f-fraction of the domain, where f is much larger than the fraction for "average" outputs, which we will denote g. Then H' will have (information-theoretically) outputs that represent an approximately f^t-fraction of the domain, where the average output would be approximately g^t. Thus H' is not semi-regular, and in fact has even worse regularity if $t > 1$.

Therefore, it seems challenging, if not impossible, to generically remove semi-regularity from a collision resistant hash function. One may hope to prove H' is collapsing despite not being semi-regular. But there would be little hope of using our techniques alone to prove collapsing, since the calls to H could be on inputs mapping to the highly-likely outputs, in which case H is super-poly-to-1.

On the other hand, our situation can be seen as roughly analogous to the case of constructing pseudorandom generators (PRGs) from one-way functions (OWFs). Specifically, Goldreich, Krawczyk, and Luby [GKL88] initially show that PRGs can be constructed from any regular one-way function. This was then improved to PRGs from arbitrary one-way functions by Håstad et al. [HILL99]. Likewise, our hope is that future ideas will allow for proving Conjecture 1.

1.5 Concurrent and Independent Work

In a current and independent work, Cao and Xue [CX22] also study collapsing hash functions. Their core result is identical to Theorem 1, namely that collision resistance when the number of pre-images is polynomially bounded implies collapsing. Somewhat analogous to Theorem 2, they also identify a relaxation they call *almost-regularity*, and show that almost-regular PQ-CRHFs can be used to build collapsing hashes. Almost-regularity is a somewhat stronger requirement than semi-regularity, resulting in fewer applications. [CX22] show that the SIS hash function is almost-regular, thus giving a collapsing hash function from SIS, arriving at the same feasibility result as [Unr16a] though through entirely different means. Our work gives several applications not covered in [CX22], namely collapsing hashes from LPN, expanders, and optimal collision resistance. The former two applications rely on our more general Theorem 2.

2   Preliminaries

Quantum Computation. We give a very brief overview of quantum computation. A pure state is a unit column vector, usually denoted in ket notation as $|\psi\rangle$, in a complex Hilbert space $\mathcal{H}$. The conjugate transpose of $|\psi\rangle$, a row vector, is denoted in bra notation as $\langle\psi|$. We usually think of $\mathcal{H}$ as a product of n 2-dimensional spaces, which are called qubits. For each qubit, we will fix some preferred basis $\{|0\rangle, |1\rangle\}$, which we call the computational basis. An n qubit space is therefore associated with the set of n-bit strings, and we say that $|\psi\rangle$ is a superposition over n-bit strings.

A mixed state is a probability distribution over pure states. If state $|\psi_i\rangle$ occurs with probability p_i, the mixed state is characterized by a density matrix, given by $\sum_i p_i |\psi_i\rangle\langle\psi_i|$. Mixed states are usually denoted as ρ.

A quantum algorithm contains two types of operations: unitary transformations and projective measurements. A unitary is a linear operator U such that $UU^\dagger = \mathbf{I}$, where $U^\dagger$ is the Hermitian transpose. The action of U on $|\psi\rangle$ is given by $U|\psi\rangle$. A projective measurement is specified by a set of projections $\mathcal{P} = (P_1, \ldots, P_t)$ such that $\sum_i P_i = \mathbf{I}$. When applying measurement $\mathcal{P}$ to state $|\psi\rangle$, the result is to output i with probability p_i and the quantum system "collapses" to the state $|\psi_i\rangle$, where:

$$|\psi_i\rangle := \frac{P_i|\psi\rangle}{\sqrt{\langle\psi|P_i|\psi\rangle}} \quad , \quad p_i := \langle\psi|P_i|\psi\rangle \ .$$

When the measurement is applied to a mixed state ρ, the result is to output i with probability p_i and the system collapses to ρ_i, where

$$\rho_i := \frac{1}{p_i} P_i \rho P_i \quad , \quad p_i := \mathsf{Tr}(P_i\rho) \ .$$

For a qubit, measurement in the computational basis is the measurement $(|0\rangle\langle 0|, |1\rangle\langle 1|)$. For a projective measurement $\mathcal{P}$ acting on pure state $|\psi\rangle$ or mixed state ρ, we will write $(i, \rho') \leftarrow \mathcal{P}(|\psi\rangle)$ or $(i, \rho') \leftarrow \mathcal{P}(\rho)$ to denote the output i of applying the measurement $\mathcal{P}$ to ρ, together with the resulting state ρ'. Sometimes we will ignore the actual result of measurement i, focusing just on the resulting state, in which case we write $\rho' \leftarrow \mathcal{P}(|\psi\rangle)$ or $\rho' \leftarrow \mathcal{P}(\rho)$. Other times, we will ignore the resulting state and just focus on the measurement outcome, in which case we write $i \leftarrow \mathcal{P}(|\psi\rangle)$ or $i \leftarrow \mathcal{P}(\rho)$.

Consider a joint system $\mathcal{H} = \mathcal{H}_0 \otimes \mathcal{H}_1$, and applying two measurements $\mathcal{P}_0, \mathcal{P}_1$ to the sub-systems $\mathcal{H}_0, \mathcal{H}_1$. We write the resulting measurement as $\mathcal{P}_0 \otimes \mathcal{P}_1$.

Efficient quantum algorithms are given by a polynomial number of unitaries from some constant-sized universal set and a polynomial number of computational basis measurements. We say such algorithms are *quantum polynomial time* (QPT).

Throughout this work, we will make use of the following fact:

Fact 1. *Any efficient quantum computation over a space $\mathcal{H}$ can be turned into an efficient computation that is also a projective measurement $\mathcal{P}$ over a space $\mathcal{H} \otimes \mathcal{H}'$ for some $\mathcal{H}'$.*

Hash Functions. A hash function will be specified by a family of distributions $\mathcal{H} = (\mathcal{H}_\lambda)_\lambda$ over classically efficiently computable functions $h : \mathcal{X}_\lambda \to \mathcal{Y}_\lambda$ between some domain $\mathcal{X}_\lambda$ and co-domain $\mathcal{Y}_\lambda$. We require non-trivial compression, namely that $|\mathcal{X}_\lambda| \geq 2 \times |\mathcal{Y}_\lambda|$. We will consider two security properties. The first is plain collision resistance but again quantum attackers:

Definition 1 (PQ-CRHF). $\mathcal{H}$ *is a post-quantum collision resistant hash function if, for every QPT algorithm $\mathcal{A}$, there exists a negligible function* negl *such that*

$$\Pr\left[{x_0 \neq x_1, \text{ and} \atop h(x_0) = h(x_1)} : {h \leftarrow \mathcal{H}_\lambda \atop (x_0, x_1) \leftarrow \mathcal{A}(h)}\right] < \mathsf{negl}(\lambda) \ .$$

The second definition is collapsing, due to Unruh [Unr16b]. Consider a superposition $|\psi\rangle$ over $\mathcal{X}_\lambda$. Consider two measurements:

- $\mathcal{M}_{\mathcal{X}} = (|x\rangle\langle x|)_{x \in \mathcal{X}_\lambda}$, which is just the computational basis measurement of $|\psi\rangle$.
- $\mathcal{M}_{\mathcal{Y}}^h = (\sum_{x:h(x)=y} |x\rangle\langle x|)_{y \in \mathcal{Y}_\lambda}$. This is the measurement corresponding to the following process:
  - First map $|\psi\rangle = \sum_x \alpha_x |x\rangle$ to $|\psi_1\rangle = \sum_x \alpha_x |x\rangle|h(x)\rangle$, a superposition over $\mathcal{X}_\lambda \times \mathcal{Y}_\lambda$.
  - Measure the $\mathcal{Y}_\lambda$ registers to obtain y. The $|\psi_1\rangle$ collapses to a state proportional to $\sum_{x:h(x)=y} \alpha_x |x\rangle|y\rangle$.
  - Discard the $\mathcal{Y}_\lambda$ registers.

The collapsing definition essentially says that, for any superposition of inputs the adversary can produce, if either $\mathcal{M}_{\mathcal{X}}$ or $\mathcal{M}_{\mathcal{Y}}^h$ is applied to the state, it is computationally infeasible to tell which. This holds even if the adversary maintained an arbitrary internal state that could be entangled with the superposition of inputs.

Definition 2 (Collapsing Hash [Unr16b]). $\mathcal{H}$ *is a* collapsing *hash function if, for every QPT algorithm* $\mathcal{A} = (\mathcal{A}_0, \mathcal{A}_1)$, *there exists a negligible function* negl *such that*

$$|\Pr[1 \leftarrow \mathcal{A}_1 \circ (\mathbf{I} \otimes \mathcal{M}_{\mathcal{X}}) \circ \mathcal{A}_0(h)] - \Pr[1 \leftarrow \mathcal{A}_1 \circ (\mathbf{I} \otimes \mathcal{M}_{\mathcal{Y}}^h) \circ \mathcal{A}_0(h)]| < \mathsf{negl}(\lambda) \ ,$$

where both probabilities are over the choice of $h \leftarrow \mathcal{H}_\lambda$. *We call the quantity on the left above the* advantage *of* $\mathcal{A}$. *Note that* $\mathcal{A}_0$ *outputs both a (quantum) internal state and a superposition over* $\mathcal{X}_\lambda$. *The internal state is passed unaffected to* $\mathcal{A}_1$, *as is the result of applying* $\mathcal{M}_{\mathcal{X}}$ *or* $\mathcal{M}_{\mathcal{Y}}^h$ *to the superposition over* $\mathcal{X}_\lambda$.

Definition 3 (t-wise independence). *A family* Π *of injections from* $\mathcal{X}$ *to* $\mathcal{Y}$ *(*$|\mathcal{Y}| \geq |\mathcal{X}|$*) is a* t-wise δ-dependent injection *if, for any distinct* $x_1, \ldots, x_t \in \mathcal{X}$, *the distribution* $(\pi(x_1), \ldots, \pi(x_t))$ *for* $\pi \leftarrow \Pi$ *is* δ-close *to* t *uniformly random distinct* elements of $\mathcal{Y}$.

Distributions and Rényi Entropy. For a distribution D over a finite set I, and $\alpha > 1$, define the *Rényi Entropy* as

$$H_\alpha(D) := -\frac{1}{\alpha - 1} \log\left(\sum_{i \in I} \Pr[i \leftarrow D]^\alpha\right)$$

$$H_\infty(D) := -\log \max_{i \in I} \Pr[i \leftarrow D]$$

The choice of base in the logarithm is irrelevant for our purposes, as long as the same base is used for all α. For our purposes, it will be convenient to map Rényi entropy to the norm of the probability vector. Write

$$\|D\|_\alpha := \left(\sum_{i \in I} \Pr[i \leftarrow D]^\alpha\right)^{1/\alpha} = 2^{-\left(1 - \frac{1}{\alpha}\right)H_\alpha(D)}$$

$$\|D\|_\infty := \max_{i \in I} \Pr[i \leftarrow D] = 2^{-H_\infty(D)}$$

For $\beta > \alpha \geq 1$, we have the following inequalities, where the left and right inequalities are identical just phrased in terms of entropies vs vector norms:

$$H_\alpha(D) \geq H_\beta(D) \qquad\qquad (\|D\|_\alpha)^{\frac{\alpha}{\alpha-1}} \leq (\|D\|_\beta)^{\frac{\beta}{\beta-1}} \quad (1)$$

$$\left(1 - \frac{1}{\alpha}\right) H_\alpha(D) \leq \left(1 - \frac{1}{\beta}\right) H_\beta(D) \qquad\qquad \|D\|_\alpha \geq \|D\|_\beta \qquad (2)$$

$$H_\alpha(D) \leq \log|I| \qquad\qquad \|D\|_\alpha \geq |I|^{-1} \qquad (3)$$

Let $\Delta_\alpha(D) := H_\alpha(D) - H_\infty(D)$ to be the *Entropy Gap* of D. When α is not specified, we will mean $\alpha = 2$.

For a finite set $\mathcal{X}$, we abuse notation and use $\mathcal{X}$ to denote the uniform distribution over $\mathcal{X}$. For a function $h : \mathcal{X} \to \mathcal{Y}$ and a distribution D on $\mathcal{X}$, we let $h(D)$ be the distribution obtained by sampling $x \leftarrow D$ and then outputting $h(x)$. We also define $H_\alpha(h) := H_\alpha(h(\mathcal{X}))$, $\|h\|_\alpha := \|h(\mathcal{X})\|_\alpha$, and $\Delta_\alpha(h) := \Delta_\alpha(h(\mathcal{X}))$.

3   From Non-collapsing to Equivocation

Here, we prove that a failure to be collapsing leads to equivocation. We consider the following setup:

- A secret set S of size ℓ, which is a subset of some set $\mathcal{U}$.
- Another set $\mathcal{V}$.
- A state ρ that is a superposition over pairs $(v, s) \in \mathcal{V} \times S$.
- A binary-outcome projective measurement $\mathcal{P} = (\mathbf{P}, \mathbf{I} - \mathbf{P})$.

Our goal is to, starting in the state ρ, obtain two distinct values $i, j \in S$. The only operations we can perform are the measurement $\mathcal{P}$ and the measurement in the computational basis for $\mathcal{U}$. Without any further promises, this goal is impossible. By applying $\mathcal{U}$ to ρ, one obtains a single element of S. If $\mathcal{P}$, say, commutes with $\mathcal{U}$, then no sequence of operations will ever change the state, and we will never obtain a second element.

Therefore, we are given the promise that $\mathcal{P}$ is sufficiently non-commuting with $\mathcal{U}$. Concretely, we are promised that:

$$|\Pr[1 \leftarrow \mathcal{P}(\rho)] - \Pr[1 \leftarrow (\mathcal{P} \circ (\mathbf{I} \otimes \mathcal{U}))(\rho)]| \geq \epsilon$$

for some non-negligible quantity ϵ. In other words, $\mathcal{P}$ distinguishes between ρ and the result of measuring ρ in the computational basis for $\mathcal{U}$.

The Algorithm. Since we are now only allowed to use $\mathcal{U}$ and $\mathcal{P}$, there is nothing that can be done except alternate them. Concretely, we apply $\mathcal{U}$, $\mathcal{P}$, and then $\mathcal{U}$ again. We will show that, with non-negligible probability, the two applications of $\mathcal{U}$ output distinct elements of S.

Lemma 1. *For $\ell, S, \rho, \mathcal{P}, \mathcal{U}, \mathcal{V}$ as defined above,*

$$\Pr\left[\begin{matrix} i,j \in S \\ i \neq j \end{matrix} : \begin{matrix} (i,\rho') \leftarrow (\mathbf{I} \otimes \mathcal{U})(\rho) \\ \rho'' \leftarrow \mathcal{P}(\rho') \\ j \leftarrow (\mathbf{I} \otimes \mathcal{U})(\rho'') \end{matrix}\right] \geq \frac{2}{\ell-1}\left|\begin{matrix} \Pr[1 \leftarrow \mathcal{P}(\rho)] \\ -\Pr[1 \leftarrow (\mathcal{P} \circ (\mathbf{I} \otimes \mathcal{U}))(\rho)] \end{matrix}\right|^2.$$

Before proving Lemma 1, we observe that it is tight. Let q be the quantity on the left, and r the quantity inside $|\cdot|$ on the right. Consider the case where $\mathcal{V}$ is empty, ρ is the pure state $|\psi\rangle := \ell^{-1/2}\sum_{i \in S}|i\rangle$, and $\mathbf{P}$ is the projection onto $|\psi\rangle$. In this case, Applying $\mathcal{P}$ to $|\psi\rangle$ outputs 0 with certainty. Meanwhile, measuring $|\psi\rangle$ gives a random $|i\rangle$, and applying $\mathcal{P}$ to any $|i\rangle$ will give 0 with probability $1/\ell$. Therefore, $r = 1 - 1/\ell$, and the right-hand side becomes $2(\ell-1)/\ell^2$.

On the other hand, for computing q, there are two cases: (1) if applying $\mathcal{P}$ to $|i\rangle$ outputs 0, or (2) it outputs 1. If it outputs 0 (which occurs with probability $1/\ell$), then the state is back to $|\psi\rangle$, and measuring again will give an $j \neq i$ with probability $1 - 1/\ell$. If it outputs 0 (which occurs with probability $1 - 1/\ell$), then the state becomes $|i\rangle - \ell^{-1/2}|\psi\rangle$. In this case, a simple calculation shows that measurement will give $j \neq i$ with probability $1/\ell$. Taken together, the overall probability q of obtaining a $j \neq i$ is exactly $2(\ell-1)/\ell^2$, exactly matching the right-hand side.

We now give the proof of Lemma 1.

Proof. We focus on the case of pure states, the mixed state setting then following from convexity. Therefore we assume $\rho = |\psi\rangle\langle\psi|$ for some pure state $|\psi\rangle = \sum_{v,i}\alpha_{v,i}|v,i\rangle$.

We first analyze q. The probability of obtaining i in the first measurement is $p_i = \mathsf{Tr}\left[(\mathbf{I} \otimes |i\rangle\langle i|)\rho\right]$, in which case ρ' becomes $\rho_i := \frac{1}{p_i}(\mathbf{I} \otimes |i\rangle\langle i|)\rho(\mathbf{I} \otimes |i\rangle\langle i|)$.

Now we apply $\mathcal{P}$, and disregard the output of the measurement. The resulting mixed state is $\rho'_i := \mathbf{P}\rho_i\mathbf{P} + (\mathbf{I} - \mathbf{P})\rho_i(\mathbf{I} - \mathbf{P})$. Now we apply $(\mathbf{I} \otimes \mathcal{U})$ again. The probability of obtaining j is $\mathsf{Tr}\left[(\mathbf{I} \otimes |j\rangle\langle j|)\rho'_i\right]$. Summing over all $i \in S$ and $j \in S \setminus \{i\}$, we have that the probability of obtaining distinct $i, j \in S$ is q where

$$q = \mathsf{Tr}\left[\sum_{i,j \in S, i \neq j} \begin{matrix} (\mathbf{I} \otimes |j\rangle\langle j|)\mathbf{P}(\mathbf{I} \otimes |i\rangle\langle i|)\rho(\mathbf{I} \otimes |i\rangle\langle i|)\mathbf{P} \\ +(\mathbf{I} \otimes |j\rangle\langle j|)(\mathbf{I} - \mathbf{P})(\mathbf{I} \otimes |i\rangle\langle i|)\rho(\mathbf{I} \otimes |i\rangle\langle i|)(\mathbf{I} - \mathbf{P}) \end{matrix}\right]$$

$$= 2\mathsf{Tr}\left[\sum_{i,j \in S, i \neq j} (\mathbf{I} \otimes |j\rangle\langle j|)\mathbf{P}(\mathbf{I} \otimes |i\rangle\langle i|)\rho(\mathbf{I} \otimes |i\rangle\langle i|)\mathbf{P}\right]$$

$$= 2\mathsf{Tr}\left[\sum_{\substack{i,j \in S, i \neq j \\ v,v' \in \mathcal{V}}} \alpha_{v,i}\alpha_{v',i}^\dagger(\mathbf{I} \otimes |j\rangle\langle j|)\mathbf{P}(|v\rangle\langle v'| \otimes |i\rangle\langle i|)\mathbf{P}\right]$$

$$= 2\left[\sum_{\substack{i,j \in S, i \neq j \\ v,v' \in \mathcal{V}}} \alpha_{v,i}\alpha_{v',i}^\dagger(\langle v'|\langle i|)\mathbf{P}(\mathbf{I} \otimes |j\rangle\langle j|)\mathbf{P}(|v\rangle|i\rangle)\right]$$

$$= 2 \left[\sum_{\substack{i,j \in S, i \neq j \\ v,v',v'' \in \mathcal{V}}} \alpha_{v,i} \alpha_{v',i}^\dagger \langle v', i | \mathbf{P} | v'', j \rangle \, \langle v'', j | \mathbf{P} | v, i \rangle \right] .$$

Then if we define $\mathbf{w}$ as the vector indexed by tuples $(i, j, v''), i \neq j$ such that $\mathbf{w}_{(i,j,v'')} := \sum_v \alpha_{v,i} \langle v'', j | \mathbf{P} | v, i \rangle$, we have that $q = 2|\mathbf{w}|^2$.

Next we analyze the right hand side, r, of Lemma 1. We have

$$r = \mathsf{Tr}\,[\mathbf{P}\rho] - \mathsf{Tr}\left[\mathbf{P} \sum_{i \in S} (\mathbf{I} \otimes |i\rangle\langle i|) \rho (\mathbf{I} \otimes |i\rangle\langle i|)\right]$$

$$= \left[\sum_{\substack{i,j \in S \\ v,v' \in \mathcal{V}}} \alpha_{v,i} \alpha_{v',j}^\dagger \langle v' | \langle i | \mathbf{P} | v \rangle | j \rangle - \sum_{\substack{i \in S \\ v,v' \in \mathcal{V}}} \alpha_{v,i} \alpha_{v',i}^\dagger \langle v' | \langle i | \mathbf{P} | v \rangle | i \rangle \right]$$

$$= \left[\sum_{\substack{i,j \in S, i \neq j \\ v,v' \in \mathcal{V}}} \alpha_{v,i} \alpha_{v',j}^\dagger \langle v' | \langle i | \mathbf{P} | v \rangle | j \rangle \right] .$$

Then if we define $\mathbf{x}$ as the vector $\mathbf{x}_{(i,j,v'')} := \alpha_{v'',j}$, we have that $r = \mathbf{x} \cdot \mathbf{w}$. Note that

$$|\mathbf{x}|^2 = \sum_{\substack{i,j \in S, i \neq j \\ v'' \in \mathcal{V}}} |\alpha_{v'',j}|^2 = \sum_{j \in S, v'' \in \mathcal{V}} (\ell - 1) |\alpha_{v'',j}|^2 = \ell - 1 .$$

Therefore, by the Cauchy-Schwartz inequality, we have that $|\mathbf{w}|^2 |\mathbf{x}|^2 \geq |\mathbf{w} \cdot \mathbf{x}|^2$. The lemma follows. $\qquad\square$

3.1   Application: Hashing with Small Compression

We now use Lemma 1 to show that any hash function which is $\leq \ell$-to-1 for a polynomial ℓ is collapsing.

Theorem 1. *Let $\mathcal{H}$ be a post-quantum collision-resistant hash function with domain $\mathcal{X}$, and ℓ a polynomial. Suppose that, with overwhelming probability over the choice of $h \leftarrow \mathcal{H}$, that h is $\leq \ell$-to-1. Then $\mathcal{H}$ is collapsing.*

Proof. Assume toward contradiction that $\mathcal{H}$ is not collapsing. Let $\mathcal{A} = (\mathcal{A}_0, \mathcal{A}_1)$ be the adversary for the collapsing game, with non-negligible advantage ϵ. We will think of $\mathcal{A}_1$ as being a projective measurement on the joint system $\mathcal{V} \times \mathcal{X}_\lambda$, where $\mathcal{V}$ is the adversary's internal state.

Observe that $\mathcal{M}_\mathcal{X}$ is equivalent to the composition of $\mathcal{M}_\mathcal{Y}$ followed by $\mathcal{M}_\mathcal{X}$, since the domain element uniquely determines the range element. Therefore, we can think of both sides of the collapsing experiment as applying $\mathcal{M}_\mathcal{Y}$, and then the only difference is whether an additional $\mathcal{M}_{\mathcal{X}}$ is applied. We will therefore always think of the output of $\mathcal{A}_0$ as having $\mathcal{M}_{\mathcal{Y}}$ applied.

For a fixed h and result y from $\mathcal{M}_{\mathcal{Y}}$, suppose $\mathcal{A}_1$ has a distinguishing advantage ϵ_h. Then we can apply Lemma 1 to extract two pre-images of y (and hence a collision) with probability at least $2\epsilon_h^2/(\ell-1)$. By averaging over all h and y and invoking convexity, we see that the overall probability of finding a collision is at least $2\epsilon^2/(\ell-1)$, which is non-negligible. $\square$

By combining with the fact that standard domain extension works for collapsing hash functions, we have the following corollary:

Corollary 1. *Assuming the existence of $\leq\ell$-to-1 PQ-CRHFs for a polynomial ℓ, there exist collapsing hash functions for arbitrary domains.*

4 The Main Theorem

We now generalize the $\leq\ell$-to-1 case to a somewhat more general class of hash functions. The main challenge, of course, is that general hash functions may not be $\leq\ell$-to-1 for any polynomial ℓ. This can be a problem *even if* the domain is only slightly larger than the co-domain. Here, we show how to somewhat relax the conditions on the hash function.

Definition 4. *Let $\mathcal{H} = (\mathcal{H}_\lambda)_\lambda$ be a family of hash functions with domain $\mathcal{X}_\lambda$ and co-domain $\mathcal{Y}_\lambda$. We say that $\mathcal{H}$ is* semi-regular *if there exists a polynomial r and negligible* negl *such that*

$$\Pr_{h \leftarrow \mathcal{H}_\lambda}[\Delta_2(h) > \log r(\lambda)] < \mathsf{negl}(\lambda) \ .$$

Equivalently, $\|h\|_\infty \leq r(\lambda) \times \|h\|_2^2$, except with negligible probability.

For a function h, we will call $\|h\|_\infty/\|h\|_2^2$ the *regularity* of h. A semi-regular hash function is therefore one where the regularity is a polynomial except with negligible probability.

Main Theorem. We now give our main theorem.

Theorem 2. *If there exists a semi-regular PQ-CRHF, then there exists a collapsing hash function.*

The remainder of this section is devoted to proving Theorem 2. We start by considering the following hash function:

Construction 1. *Let $\mathcal{H}$ be a family of post-quantum collision resistant hash functions with domain $\mathcal{X}_\lambda$ and co-domain $\mathcal{Y}_\lambda$. For parameters $\ell \in \mathbb{Z}, \delta \in [0,1]$, let $\mathcal{F}$ be a ℓ-wise δ-dependent injection with domain $\mathcal{Y}_\lambda \times \{0,1\}$ and co-domain $\mathcal{X}_\lambda$. Then for any polynomial $m = m(\lambda)$, we construct the following function family $\mathcal{H}'$ with domain $\{0,1\}^m$ and co-domain $\mathcal{Y}_\lambda$, where $h' \leftarrow \mathcal{H}'$ is sampled as follows: sample $h \leftarrow \mathcal{H}$ and for $i = 1,\ldots, m \times t$, sample $f_i \leftarrow \mathcal{F}$, where t is a parameter to be specified later. Also fix an arbitrary $y_0 \in \mathcal{Y}_\lambda$. Then output $h' : \{0,1\}^m \to \mathcal{Y}_\lambda$ defined as:*

- *For $i = 1, \ldots, u = (m-1) \times t + 1$:*
    - *Let $z_i = y_{i-1} \| x_j$ if $i = t(j-1) + 1$, otherwise let $z_i = y_{i-1} \| 0$.*
    - *Let $y_i = h(f_i(z_i))$.*
- *Output y_u*

The operation of h' is also given in Fig. 1.

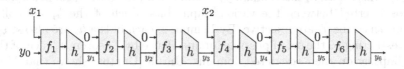

Fig. 1. The first few iterations of Construction 1 for $t = 3$.

Remark 5. Note that Construction 1 is only defined for a bounded domain, since it needs independent f_i for each application of h. However, we can set m to be large enough so that $2^m \gg \mathcal{Y}_\lambda$, obtaining a compressing collapsing function. Then we can plug the result into a plain Merkle-Damgård or other domain extender, which are known to preserve collapsing [Unr16a]. The result is an arbitrary-domain hash function that is collapsing.

Remark 6. Observe that some iterations of Construction 1 incorporate bits of the input into the z_i, while others just incorporate 0's. This is mostly an artifact of our proof of collapsing, and it is unclear if it is strictly needed. Looking ahead, in each iteration that incorporates an input bit, the number of possible z_i values potentially doubles, while in other iterations, we show that the number of possible z_i values decreases with noticeable probability. By inserting sufficiently many 0 iterations, we can make sure the number of possible z_i values never gets too large, which we can then use to apply Lemma 1.

For the remainder of the proof, we omit λ subscripts and write $\mathcal{X} = \mathcal{X}_\lambda$ and $\mathcal{Y} = \mathcal{Y}_\lambda$ to keep notation simple. Let $\mathcal{Y}_i$ be the set of possible values for z_i as x ranges over all possible inputs, and $N_i = |\mathcal{Y}_i|$. Let M_i be the number of possible values for y_i. Observe that $N_i = 2M_i$ for $i = t(j-1) + 1$ and $N_i = M_i$ otherwise. Define the following quantities:

$$r = \|h\|_\infty / \|h\|_2^2 \tag{4}$$

$$\ell = \max(2re, 3\log|\mathcal{Y}|) \tag{5}$$

$$\delta = |\mathcal{Y}|^{-2} \binom{|\mathcal{Y}|}{\ell}^{-1} \tag{6}$$

$$t = 200\ell \tag{7}$$

Lemma 2. *Except with negligible probability over the choice of h, f_i, the following hold:*

- $N_i \leq \|h\|_2^{-2}$ for all i
- For all i, the function $h_i(y) = h(f_i(y))$, when restricted to $\mathcal{Y}_{i-1}$, is $< \ell$-to-1.

Before proving Lemma 2, we first demonstrate that it allows for proving Construction 1 is collapsing. Note that only the second bullet is needed to prove collapsing; the first bullet is facilitates our proof of Lemma 2 by induction.

Construction 1 is just Merkle-Damgård, composed of u functions $h_i(y) = h(f_i(y))$, where each h_i has domain $\mathcal{Y}_{i-1}$ and the input to the hash has a number of zeros inserted between the various input bits. Each of the h_i are collision resistant since the f_i are injective. By Lemma 2, each of the h_i are also $< \ell$-to-1 when restricting to the set of possible inputs. Hence by Theorem 1, each of the h_i are collapsing on their restricted domains. Unruh [Unr16a] shows that Merkle-Damgård is collapsing if the component h_i are collapsing, hence Construction 1 is collapsing. The exact same proof works here, the only difference is that the h_i are only collapsing on the outputs of h_{i-1}, but are potentially not collapsing on the entire domain $\mathcal{Y}_\lambda \times \{0,1\}$. Nevertheless the same proof works here: imagine y_u is measured. Now measure z_u, then z_{u-1}, then z_{u-2}, etc., until we measure z_1. The application of each measurement is undetectable by the collapsingness of the h_i on their restricted domains. By the time we have measured all of the z_i's, we have measured the entire input. Hence measuring y_u (the output of h') is indistinguishable from measuring the input x.

For completeness, we work out the proof here. We need to show that measuring the final output y_u vs measuring the input x is computationally indistinguishable. We will do this through a hybrid argument. Let $\mathcal{A} = (\mathcal{A}_0, \mathcal{A}_1)$ be a a collapsing adversary for $\mathcal{H}_0'$, where the probability of distinguishing the measurement $\mathcal{M}_{\mathcal{Y}}^{h'}$ from $\mathcal{M}_{\mathcal{X}}$ is a non-negligible ϵ.

Consider evaluating h' on a quantum superposition, writing the output y_u to a new register Y_u. During iteration j, a number of intermediate values will be stored in a register, including z_j which will be stored in a register Z_j. After the final output y_u of h' is produced and written to a register Y_u, all the intermediate registers including the Z_j will be uncomputed.

In Hybrid i, register Y_u is measured to give y_u, and also registers Z_j for $j = i, \ldots, u$ are all measured before uncomputation, giving z_j. Let p_i be the probability $\mathcal{A}$ outputs 1 in Hybrid i.

Hybrid $u+1$ means none of the Z_j registers are measured, whereas in Hybrid 1, all of the Z_j are measured, which is equivalent to measuring the input registers. Thus $|p_1 - p_{u+1}| = \epsilon$, by our assumption that $\mathcal{A}$ is a collapsing adversary. For each i, we obtain a collapsing adversary $\mathcal{B}^{(i)} = (\mathcal{B}_0^{(i)}, \mathcal{B}_1^{(i)})$ for h_i with advantage $\epsilon_i = |p_i - p_{i+1}|$. $\mathcal{B}_0^{(i)}(h_i)$ works as follows:

- It first chooses f_j for $j \neq i$, and constructs h' as above. Then it simulates $\mathcal{A}_0(h')$.
- $\mathcal{A}_0$ produces $\rho_{\mathsf{state}, X}$, where state is a register containing the adversary's state that gets forwarded to the next stage, and X is a register containing a superposition of inputs to h'.

$\mathcal{B}_0^{(i)}$ evaluates h' on register X, and measures the registers $Z_{i+1}, \ldots, Z_u$. During the uncomputation step, it uncomputes Y_u and all the registers containing all the intermediate values, *except* for the register Z_i.

- $\mathcal{B}_0^{(i)}$ then outputs the joint system $\rho_{\mathsf{state}', Z_i}$, where $\mathsf{state}' = (\mathsf{state}, X)$.

$\mathcal{B}_1^{(i)}$, upon receiving $\rho_{\mathsf{state}', Z_i}$, uncomputes the Z_i registers, obtaining the system $\rho_{\mathsf{state}'} = \rho_{\mathsf{state}, X}$, which it feeds into $\mathcal{A}_1$. It outputs whatever $\mathcal{A}_1$ outputs.

Since $\mathcal{B}^{(i)}$ measures register Z_{i+1} to obtain z_{i+1} which includes $y_i = h_i(z_i)$, if the challenger for $\mathcal{B}^{(i)}$ measures the output of h_i, the measurement is redundant and has no effect on the state. Therefore, $\mathcal{B}^{(i)}$ perfectly simulates Hybrid $i + 1$. On the other hand, if the challenger measures the input, this is exactly the same as measuring Z_i to obtain z_i. Hence $\mathcal{B}^{(i)}$ perfectly simulates Hybrid i in this case. Therefore, $\mathcal{B}^{(i)}$ has advantage exactly $\epsilon_i = |p_i - p_{i+1}|$.

We then turn each $\mathcal{B}^{(i)}$ into a collision-finder for h, which we call $\mathcal{C}^{(i)}$, following Theorem 1. Conditioned on Lemma 2 holding, the functions h_i are $<\ell$-to-1, meaning $\mathcal{C}^{(i)}$ finds a collision with probability at least $2\epsilon_i^2/(\ell - 1)$. Notice that $\sum_i \epsilon_i \geq \epsilon$. Therefore, we can obtain an overall collision-finder $\mathcal{C}$, which runs $\mathcal{C}^{(i)}$ for a random choice of i. By Cauchy-Schwartz, the probability $\mathcal{C}$ obtains a collision is at least

$$\frac{2}{u(\ell - 1)} \sum_i \epsilon_i^2 \geq \frac{2\epsilon^2}{u^2(\ell - 1)} \ ,$$

which is non-negligible. This contradicts the assumed collision resistance of h. We now turn to proving Lemma 2.

Proof. We prove by induction on i. Clearly $N_0 = 2$ and h_1 is at most 2-to-1. We now fix h and $f_1, \ldots, f_{i-1}$, which determines $\mathcal{Y}_{i-1}$ and N_{i-1}. We inductively assume $N_{i-1} \leq \|h\|_2^{-2}$. We first prove, with overwhelming probability over the choice of f_i, that h_i is $\leq \ell$-to-1 when restricted to $\mathcal{Y}_{i-1}$.

Toward that end, for any $y \in \mathcal{Y}$, let p_y be the probability a random input to h maps to y. For any set of ℓ inputs $x_1, \ldots, x_\ell$, the probability they all map to the same output of h is:

$$
\begin{aligned}
\Pr[h_i(x_1) = \cdots = h_i(x_\ell)] &\leq \Pr_{\substack{w_j \leftarrow \mathcal{X} \\ w_{j_1} \neq w_{j_2} \forall j_1 \neq j_2}} [h(w_1) = \cdots = h(w_\ell)] + \delta \\
&\leq \Pr_{w_j \leftarrow \mathcal{X}} [h(w_1) = \cdots = h(w_\ell)] + \delta \\
&= \sum_{y \in \mathcal{Y}} p_y^\ell + \delta = \|h\|_\ell^\ell + \delta
\end{aligned}
$$

Let V be the event that h_i is *not* $<\ell$-to-1. Union-bounding over all sets of ℓ inputs in $\mathcal{Y}_{i-1}$, we have that

$$
\begin{aligned}
\Pr[V] &\leq \binom{N_{i-1}}{\ell} (\|h\|_\ell^\ell + \delta) \\
&\leq \frac{N_{i-1}^\ell \|h\|_\ell^\ell}{\ell!} + \delta \binom{N_{i-1}}{\ell}
\end{aligned}
$$

$$\leq \frac{N_{i-1}^{\ell}\|h\|_{\infty}^{\ell-1}}{\ell!} + |\mathcal{Y}|^{-2} \qquad \text{Equations (1) and (6)}$$

$$\leq \frac{(N_{i-1}\|h\|_{\infty})^{\ell}\|h\|_{\infty}^{-1}}{\ell!} + |\mathcal{Y}|^{-2}$$

$$\leq \frac{(N_{i-1}r\|h\|_2^2)^{\ell}|\mathcal{Y}|}{\ell!} + |\mathcal{Y}|^{-2} \qquad \text{Equation (4)}$$

$$\leq \frac{r^{\ell}|\mathcal{Y}|}{\ell!} + |\mathcal{Y}|^{-2} \qquad \text{Inductive assumption}$$

$$\leq \left(\frac{re}{\ell}\right)^{\ell}|\mathcal{Y}| + |\mathcal{Y}|^{-2} \qquad \text{Stirling's Approximation}$$

$$\leq 2^{-\ell}|\mathcal{Y}| + |\mathcal{Y}|^{-2} = 2 \times |\mathcal{Y}|^{-2} \qquad \text{Equation (5)}$$

$|\mathcal{Y}|$ must be superpolynomial by the assumed collision resistance of h, and so the above quantity is negligible. Now it remains to prove the desired size bounds. First recall that $N_{t(j-1)+1} \leq 2N_{t(j-1)}$ and $N_i \leq N_{i-1}$ for all i not of the form $t(j-1)+1$. The following suffices to prove the size bound in Lemma 2:

Claim. $N_{t(j-1)} \leq \|h\|_2^{-2}/2$ for all j.

This claim implies that $N_{t(j-1)+1} \leq \|h\|_2^{-2}$, and therefore all $N_{t(j-1)+k} \leq \|h\|_2^{-2}$ for all $k = 2,\ldots,t$, thus proving Lemma 2. We now prove the claim by induction. Clearly for $j = 1$ we have that $N_{t(j-1)} = N_0 = 1$, which is $\leq \|h\|_2^{-2}/2$ since $\|h\|_2^2$, the collision probability of two random inputs to h, must be negligible. This establishes the base case.

We now inductively assume that $N_{t(j-1)+1} \leq \|h\|_2^{-2}$. Our goal is to prove that $N_{t(j-1)+t} \leq \|h\|_2^{-2}/2$. Note that if *any* i in the interval $t(j-1)+2,\ldots,tj$ satisfy $N_i \leq \|h\|_2^{-2}/2$, then we are done since all subsequent i in the interval have $N_i \leq N_{i-1}$. From now on, we will therefore assume towards contradiction that $N_i > \|h\|_2^{-2}/2$ for all i in the interval.

Let C_i be the number of distinct pairs of colliding inputs to h_i. We observe the following:

Claim. If h_i is $<\ell$-to-1, then $M_i < N_{i-1} - \frac{2}{\ell}C_i$.

The claim is proved as follows: by linearity, it suffices to consider the case where h_i has a single output, meaning $M_i = 1$ and $N_i < \ell$. In this case, we have that

$$N_{i-1} - \frac{2}{\ell}C_i = N_{i-1} - \frac{2}{\ell}\binom{N_{i-1}}{2} = N_{i-1} - \frac{N_{i-1}}{\ell}(N_{i-1} - 1)$$
$$> N_{i-1} - (N_{i-1} - 1) = 1 = M_i \ .$$

Therefore, to bound $N_i = M_i$ for $i = t(j-1)+2,\ldots,tj$, we need to bound C_i. To do so, let P_2 be the probability that two random distinct inputs to h map to the same image. Then

$$P_2 = \sum_y p_y\left(\frac{p_y|\mathcal{X}| - 1}{|\mathcal{X}| - 1}\right) = \frac{|\mathcal{X}|\|h\|_2^2 - 1}{|\mathcal{X}| - 1} \geq \|h\|_2^2 - |\mathcal{X}|^{-1} \ .$$

For a set $L \subseteq \mathcal{Y}_{i-1}$, let E_L be the indicator function for the event that all L map to the same value under h_i. Then $C_i = \sum_{L \subseteq \mathcal{Y}_{i-1}:|L|=2} E_L$. We now calculate the mean of C_i:

$$\mathbb{E}[C_i] = \sum_{L \subseteq \mathcal{Y}_{i-1}:|L|=2} \mathbb{E}[E_L] \geq \sum_{L \subseteq \mathcal{Y}_{i-1}:|L|=2} (P_2 - \delta) \geq \binom{N_{i-1}}{2} P_2 - 1$$

$$\geq \binom{N_{i-1}}{2}(\|h\|_2^2 - |\mathcal{X}|^{-1}) - 1 = \frac{N_{i-1}^2 - N_{i-1}}{2}(\|h\|_2^2 - |\mathcal{X}|^{-1}) - 1$$

$$\geq \frac{N_{i-1}^2}{2}(\|h\|_2^2 - |\mathcal{X}|^{-1}) - 2 \ .$$

Recall that $\|h\|_2^2 \geq |\mathcal{Y}|^{-1} \geq 2|\mathcal{X}|^{-1}$ and that $N_{i-1}\|h\|_2^2 \in (1/2, 1]$ by assumption. Therefore, $\mathbb{E}[C_i] \geq N_{i-1}/8 - 2$.

From above we know that $\Pr[V] \leq 2|\mathcal{Y}|^{-2}$. Now we have, for $i = t(j-1) + 2, \dots, tj$ and assuming each such $N_{i-1} > \|h\|_2^{-2}$,

$$\mathbb{E}[N_i] = \mathbb{E}[N_i | \neg V](1 - \Pr[V]) + \mathbb{E}[N_i | V] \Pr[V]$$

$$\leq \mathbb{E}[N_{i-1} - (2/\ell)C_i | \neg V](1 - \Pr[V]) + N_{i-1} \Pr[V]$$

$$\leq (N_{i-1} - (2/\ell) \mathbb{E}[C_i | \neg V])(1 - \Pr[V]) + N_{i-1} \Pr[V]$$

$$\leq N_{i-1} - (2/\ell)(\mathbb{E}[C_i] - \mathbb{E}[C_i | V] \Pr[V]) + N_{i-1} \Pr[V]$$

$$\leq N_{i-1} - (2/\ell)(N_{i-1}/8 - 2) + (2/\ell \, \mathbb{E}[C_i | V] + N_{i-1}) \Pr[V]$$

$$\leq N_{i-1} - (2/\ell)(N_{i-1}/8 - 2) + N_{i-1}^2 \Pr[V]$$

$$\leq N_{i-1} - (2/\ell)(N_{i-1}/8 - 2) + 2$$

$$\leq N_{i-1} - N_{i-1}/5\ell$$

Since N_i is between 1 and N_{i-1}, we must have that

$$\Pr[N_i < N_{i-1}(1 - 1/10\ell)] \geq 1/10\ell \ .$$

Call an i "good" $N_i < N_{i-1}(1 - 1/10\ell)$. Let T be the number of good i. Suppose there are $\geq T$ good i in the interval $t(j-1) + 2, \dots, tj$. Then $N_{tj} < (1 - 1/10\ell)^{10\ell} N_{t(j-1)+1} \leq (e^{-1} - o(1))\|h\|_2^{-2} \leq \|h\|_2^{-2}/2$. Since we assumed this was not the case, it must be that $T < 10\ell$. But $\mathbb{E}[T] \geq t/10\ell = 20\ell$, so by Hoeffding's inequality,

$$\Pr[T < 10\ell] \leq \Pr[T - \mathbb{E}[T] < -10\ell] < e^{-2(10\ell)^2/t} = e^{-\ell} \ .$$

Thus, except with negligible probability, N_{tj} must in fact be $\leq \|h\|_2^{-2}/2$. This completes the proof of Lemma 2 and hence Theorem 2. $\qquad\square$

5   Collapsing Hashes from LPN

In this section, we construct collapsing hash functions from the hardness of learning parities with noise (LPN) in certain extreme parameter regimes.

5.1   LPN-Based Hashing

For positive integers $n, m > n$ and error rate $\epsilon \in [0, 0.5]$, define $LPN_\epsilon^{n \times m}$ to be the following distribution: choose a random $s \leftarrow \mathbb{Z}_2^n$ and random $A \leftarrow \mathbb{Z}_2^{n \times m}$. Choose a random $e \in B_\epsilon^m$, B_ϵ is the Bernoulli distribution: output 1 with probability ϵ and 0 otherwise. The output of $LPN_\epsilon^{n \times m}$ is then $(A, s^T \cdot A + e^T \bmod 2)$. The LPN assumption states that it is computationally infeasible to distinguish $LPN_\epsilon^{n \times m}$ from the uniform distribution $\mathbb{Z}_2^{(n+1) \times m}$. Specifically:

Assumption 1. *For parameters* $\epsilon = \epsilon(n), m = m(n), T = T(n)$, *The* (ϵ, m, T)-*LPN assumption is that, for any adversary $\mathcal{A}$ running in time at most T, there exists a negligible* negl(n) *such that*

$$| \Pr[1 \leftarrow \mathcal{A}(LPN_\epsilon^{n \times m})] - \Pr[1 \leftarrow \mathcal{A}(\mathbb{Z}_2^{(n+1) \times m})]| < \mathsf{negl}(n).$$

Brakerski et al. [BLVW19] and Yu et al. [YZW+19] show how to construct a hash function from the LPN problem as follows:

Construction 2. *Let $S_w^m \subseteq \{0, 1\}^m$ be the set of length-m vectors, where the domain is divided into w blocks of size m/w, and each block contains exactly a single 1. Let* LPNHash$_w^{n \times m}$ *be the hash function family defined as follows:* $h : S_w^m \to \{0, 1\}^n$ *is specified by a random matrix $A \in \mathbb{Z}_2^{n \times m}$. Then $h(x) = A \cdot x \bmod 2$.*

Remark 7. Brakerski et al. allow for a slightly more general domain where the inputs can have w 1's in any position. For our analysis of semi-regularity, however, it will be convenient to use the domain S_w^m as defined.

Theorem 3 ([BLVW19]). *Under the $(O(\log^2 n/n), \mathsf{poly}, \mathsf{poly})$-LPN assumption,* LPNHash$_w^{n \times m}$ *is a PQ-CRHF for $m = \mathsf{poly}(n)$ and $w = O(n/\log n)$.*

Theorem 4 ([YZW+19]). *The following are true:*

- *Under the $(O(1), 2^{O(n^{0.5})}, 2^{O(n^{0.5+\epsilon})})$-LPN assumption,* LPNHash$_w^{n \times m}$ *is a PQ-CRHF for $n = O(\log^2 \lambda)$, $m = \lambda$, and $w = O(\log^{1+2\epsilon} \lambda)$.*
- *Under the $(O(1), 2^{O(n/\log n)}, \mathsf{poly})$-LPN assumption,* LPNHash$_w^{n \times m}$ *is a PQ-CRHF for $m = \mathsf{poly}(n)$ and $w = O(n/\log n)$.*
- *Under the $(O(n^{-0.5}), 2^{O(n^{0.5}/\log n)}, \mathsf{poly})$-LPN assumption,* LPNHash$_w^{n \times m}$ *is a PQ-CRHF for $m = \mathsf{poly}(n)$ and $w = O(n/\log n)$.*

5.2   Semi-regularity of LPN-Based Hashing

We now prove that LPNHash is semi-regular, for appropriate parameter choices.

Theorem 5. *For any m, n, w, let $\alpha := \sqrt{n(w/m) \ln 2}$. If $\alpha \leq 1/2$ and $\alpha^w \leq 2^{-n}$, then* LPNHash$_w^{n \times m}$ *is semi-regular.*

Before proving Theorem 5, we observe an immediate corollary:

Corollary 2. *If LPN is hard in any of the parameter regimes in Theorems 3 or 4, then collapsing hash functions exist:*

Proof. By Theorem 2, it suffices to show that the settings of parameters in Theorems 3 and 4 satisfy the conditions of Theorem 5. For the settings where $m = \mathsf{poly}(n)$ and $w = O(n/\log n)$, we just need to set $m = n^c$ and $w = dn \log n$ where $cd \geq 2$. Then $\alpha = o(1)$ and

$$\alpha^w = \left(\frac{dn^2 \ln 2}{n^{1+c} \log n} \right)^{dn/2 \log n} \leq \left(\frac{1}{n^{c-1}} \right)^{dn/2 \log n} \leq 2^{-n} .$$

For the setting where $n = O(\log^2 \lambda), m = \lambda = 2^{n^{0.5}}, w = O(\log^{1+2\epsilon} \lambda)) = O(n^{0.5+\epsilon})$, we have $\alpha = \mathsf{poly}(n) 2^{-O(n^{0.5})} \leq 2^{-O(n^{0.5-\epsilon/2})} = o(1)$ and $\alpha^w \leq 2^{-O(n^{1+\epsilon/2})} < 2^{-n}$. $\qquad\square$

We now prove Theorem 5.

Proof. Our goal is to show that $\|h(S_w^m)\|_\infty = \mathsf{poly}/2^n$, which implies $H_\infty(h) \geq n - O(\log n)$. Since $H_2(h) \leq n$, this would establish semi-regularity.

We will write $A = (v_1, \ldots, v_m)$ for vectors $v_i \in \mathbb{Z}_2^n$. Let D_i be the distribution $v_{j_1} + v_{m/w+j_2} + \cdots v_{(m/w)(i-1)+j_i}$, where each j_i is uniform in $[m/w]$. Then $h(S_w^m) = D_w$.

Lemma 3. *Fix $v_1, \ldots, v_{(m/w)i}$. Suppose $\|D_i\|_\infty = f/2^n$. Then except with probability 2^{-n} over the choice of $v_{(m/w)i+1}, \ldots, v_{(m/w)(i+1)}$, $\|D_{i+1}\|_\infty \leq (1+g)/2^n$, where $g = f\sqrt{n(w/m)\ln 2}$*

Proof. For each x in $\{0,1\}^n$, define $p_x^{(i)} := \Pr[x \leftarrow D_i]$. Then

$$p_x^{(i+1)} = \frac{w}{m} \sum_{j=1}^{w/m} p_{x \oplus v_{(m/w)i+j}}^{(i)} .$$

The $v_{(m/w)i+j}$ are just independent random vectors, so we can think of $p_x^{(i+1)}$ as a random variable which is the mean of w/m random samples of $p_{x'}^{(i)}$ for random x'. Each of the $p_{x'}^{(i)}$ are non-negative random variables with mean 2^{-n} (since they must sum to 1) and maximum $f \times 2^{-n}$. By Hoeffding's inequality,

$$\Pr[p_x^{(i+1)} > (1+g)/2^n] = \Pr[p_x^{(i+1)} - 2^{-n} > g/2^n] < e^{-2(m/w)\frac{g^2}{f^2}} .$$

Union-bounding over all 2^n different x, we have that

$$\Pr[\|D_{i+1}\|_\infty > (1+g)/2^n] < 2^n \times e^{-2(m/w)\frac{g^2}{f^2}} .$$

By setting $g = f\sqrt{n(w/m)\ln 2}$, the right-hand side becomes 2^{-n}, as desired. $\quad\square$

Notice that $\|D_0\|_\infty = 1$. Let $\alpha = \sqrt{n(w/m)\ln 2}$. Union-bounding over all $i = 1, \ldots, w$, we therefore have that

$$\|D_{i+1}\|_\infty \leq \alpha\|D_i\|_\infty + 2^{-n} .$$

for all i. Then

$$\|D_w\|_\infty \leq \alpha^w\|D_0\|_\infty + \left(\sum_{i=0}^{w-1} \alpha^i\right) \times 2^{-n} \leq \alpha^w + \frac{1}{1-\alpha} \times 2^{-n} .$$

If we set α so that $\alpha^w \leq 2^{-n}$ and $\alpha \leq 1/2$, we have that $\|D_w\|_\infty \leq 3 \times 2^{-n}$, showing that LPNHash is semi-regular. $\qquad\square$

6   Collapsing Hashes from Expanders

Charles, Goren, and Lauter [CLG09], abstracting earlier ideas of Tillich and Zémor [TZ94], propose an elegant way to construct collision resistant hash functions from exponentially-large expander graphs, whose collision-resistance follows from the assumed difficulty of finding cycles in the graphs. A number of graphs have been proposed for use in hash functions, such as:

- Charles et al. [CLG09] propose using isogeny graph on certain elliptic curves.
- Fuchs et al. [FLLT21] propose using the graph of Markov Triples.

We show that expander-based hashes satisfy our regularity condition, and hence we can obtain collapsing hash functions under the same computational assumptions on expanders as for collision resistance.

6.1   Expander Graphs

Let $G = (V, E)$ be an undirected graph. G is d-regular if every $v \in V$ has exactly d neighbors. Throughout, we will always assume our graphs are regular. Let $A = A(G)$ denote the adjacency matrix of G: the $|V| \times |V|$ matrix such that $A_{i,j}$ if $(i, j) \in E$ and 0 otherwise. Since A is symmetric, it has $|V|$ real eigenvalues $\lambda_1 \geq \lambda_2 \geq \cdots \geq \lambda_n$. For a d-regular graph, $\lambda_1 = d$.

There are several equivalent definitions of expander graphs; the following linear-algebraic definition captures the only property we will need.

Definition 5. *A connected d-regular graph G is a $(|V|, d, \delta)$-expander graph if $\lambda_2 \leq \delta d$.*

Walks on Expanders. Let G be a d-regular graph, and let $v_0 \in V$ be a node. A walk on G starting from v_0 is simply a sequence $(v_0, v_1, v_2, \ldots)$ such that $(v_{i-1}, v_i) \in E$ for all $i > 0$. A *random walk* is one where v_{i+1} is chosen uniformly from the set of neighbors of v_i. A *non-backtracking* walk is one where $v_{i-1} \neq v_{i+1}$ for all $i > 0$, and a *random non-backtracking* walk is a walk where v_{i+1} is chosen uniformly from the neighbors of v_i other than v_{i-1}.

For a d regular graph, the nodes v_i for a random walk and random non-backtracking walk will converge to the uniform distribution over V as $i \to \infty$. We will use the notion of *mixing* time to characterize how fast this occurs.

Definition 6. *The* mixing time *of a random walk starting at v_0 is defined as*

$$\tau(G) = \min_t \left\{ \left| \Pr[v_t = u] - \frac{1}{|V|} \right| \leq \frac{1}{2V} \forall u \in V \right\} ,$$

where $\Pr[v_t = u]$ is the probability that $v_t = u$ in the walk. The mixing time for a random non-backtracking walk is defined as $\tilde{\tau}(G)$, and is defined analogously.

For both backtracking and non-backtracking walks, the mixing time is at most $O(\log(|V|)/(1 - \delta))$. The backtracking case has long been known, and the non-backtracking case follows from the fact that non-backtracking walks mix at least as fast, as shown by [ABLS07].

6.2   Hash Functions Based on Expanders

Let $\mathcal{G} = (\mathcal{G}_\lambda)_\lambda$ where each $\mathcal{G}_\lambda$ is a family of d-regular connected graphs where each $G = (V, E) \in \mathcal{G}_\lambda$ is exponentially large and *implicitly represented*. That is, $V \subseteq \{0, 1\}^{n(\lambda)}$, and each G is represented by a polynomial-size string $\mathsf{Desc}(G)$. There is an efficient procedure which computes the neighbors of any $v \in V$, given $\mathsf{Desc}(G)$. We assume that $\mathsf{Desc}(G)$ includes a distinguished node v_0, and that it is possible to efficiently sample $\mathsf{Desc}(G)$ for a random $G \leftarrow \mathcal{G}_\lambda$.

Definition 7. *The* Cycle Finding *problem is hard in $\mathcal{G}$ if, for any QPT $\mathcal{A}$, $\mathcal{A}(\mathsf{Desc}(G)), G \leftarrow \mathcal{G}_\lambda$ outputs a simple cycle in G with negligible probability.*

Based on cycle finding hardness, [CLG09] constructs the following hash:

Construction 3 ([CLG09]). *Let $\mathsf{ExHash}_\mathcal{G}$ be the distribution over functions $h_{\mathsf{Desc}(G)} : [d-1]^t \to \{0,1\}^{n(\lambda)}$ for a random $G \leftarrow \mathcal{G}_\lambda$ defined as follows: interpret each element x of $[d-1]^n$ as a length-n non-backtracking walk in G starting from v_0. That is, on the ith step, if the walk is currently at node v_i and was previously at v_{i-1}, then x_i selects amongst the $d - 1$ neighbors of v_i other than v_{i-1}. That neighbor will be v_{i+1}. Let v_t be the end of the walk. Then $h_{\mathsf{Desc}(G)}(x) = v_t$.*

Theorem 6 ([CLG09]). *$\mathsf{ExHash}_\mathcal{G}$ is a PQ-CRHF if cycle finding is hard in $\mathcal{G}$.*

Proof. We give the proof for completeness. Any collision in $h_{\mathsf{Desc}(G)}$ gives two non-backtracking walks $W_0 \neq W_1$ that start at v_0 and end at the same node v. Assume without loss of generality that the nodes immediately before v in W_1, W_1 are different. Let v_1 be the last node before v where the walks coincide. Then by concatenating the two paths from v_1 to v under W_0, W_1 gives a simple cycle. $\square$

[CLG09] propose using expander graphs as a minimal criteria for selecting $\mathcal{G}$ where the cycle finding problem is hard. A uniformly random input to $\mathsf{ExHash}_\mathcal{G}$ corresponds to a random non-backtracking walk on $\mathcal{G}$. Since the mixing time of an expander is logarithmic in $|V|$, it is polynomial for implicitly represented graphs. Once the walk mixes, no node in the graph is more likely than $2/|V|$, implying $\|h\|_\infty \leq 2/|V|$. Meanwhile, $\|h\|_2^2 \geq 1/|V|$. Therefore, for a polynomial-length input, $\mathsf{ExHash}_\mathcal{G}$ is semi-regular with $r \leq 2$. Therefore, we have the following:

Corollary 3. *Suppose $\mathcal{G}$ is a family of $(|V_\lambda|, d, \delta)$-expander graph for a constant δ. Then if cycle finding is hard for $\mathcal{G}$, there exists collapsing hash functions.*

When V is an appropriate set of elliptic curves and E are isogenies as proposed by [CLG09], cycle-finding is a well-known challenging problem. The graph of Markov triples has been explored by [FLLT21]. Other instantiations have been proposed [CLG09, TZ94, PLQ12], but they have weaknesses [PLQ08].

7   Toward Collapsing Hashes from General Collision Resistance

Here, we discuss the possibility of obtaining collapsing hashes from more general PQ-CRHFs. In particular, we are interested in the case of symmetric hash functions such as SHA2 or SHA3. It seems plausible that SHA2 or SHA3 would be semi-regular: after all, if a hash function had certain images that were far more likely than others, this would be considered a significant design weakness. Unfortunately, we do not know how to prove unconditionally that, say, SHA2 or SHA3 are semi-regular. Instead, we simply conjecture it. The following shows that this assumption is justified in the random oracle mode:

Lemma 4. *Random oracles are semi-regular. In particular, for λ bit outputs, a compressing random oracle has regularity at most λ.*

Proof. By a standard balls-and-bins argument, for a random function $F : \{0,1\}^m \to \{0,1\}^\lambda$, the most likely output has probability $H_\infty(F) \leq O(\lambda 2^{-\lambda})$, with all but negligible probability. On the other hand, $\|F\|_2^2 \geq 2^{-\lambda}$. Thus F has regularity at most $O(\lambda)$. □

Since SHA2 or SHA3 are often modeled as random oracles, it therefore seems reasonable to conjecture that they are semi-regular. Note that this is potentially very different than assuming SHA2 or SHA3 are collapsing, even though random oracles are collapsing. Indeed, the analysis of SHA2 and SHA3 has usually focused on classical security properties. Semi-regularity is a simple classical property, whereas collapsing is a more complicated *inherently quantum* property. Under the assumed quantum collision resistance and assumed regularity of either SHA2 or SHA3, we therefore obtain a standard-model collapsing hash function from classically-defined properties, which are much better understood.

7.1   Collapsing from Optimal Collision Resistance

Here, we give another, simpler, approach for justifying building collapsing hashes from SHA2 or SHA3. Namely, we observe that symmetric hash functions are usually treated as having optimal collision resistance, defined as follows:

Definition 8 (Optimal Collision Resistance). *$\mathcal{H}$ is a post-quantum optimally collision resistant if, for every QPT algorithm $\mathcal{A}$, there exists a a polynomial $q(\lambda)$ such that*

$$\Pr\left[\begin{smallmatrix} x_0 \neq x_1, \text{ and} \\ h(x_0) = h(x_1) \end{smallmatrix} : \begin{smallmatrix} h \leftarrow \mathcal{H}_\lambda \\ (x_0, x_1) \leftarrow \mathcal{A}(h) \end{smallmatrix}\right] < \frac{q(\lambda)}{|\mathcal{Y}_\lambda|} \ ,$$

where $\mathcal{Y}_\lambda$ is the co-domain of h.

If SHA2 or SHA3 turned out to not be optimally collision resistant, this would be considered a major weakness of the functions. It is therefore plausible to conjecture such hardness.

Theorem 7. *Suppose $\mathcal{H}$ is a hash function with domain $\mathcal{X}_\lambda$ and co-domain $\mathcal{Y}_\lambda$ such that $|\mathcal{X}_\lambda|/|\mathcal{Y}|_\lambda$ is polynomial. Equivalently, suppose $\mathcal{H}$ compressed by at most logarithmically many bits. Then if $\mathcal{H}$ is post-quantum optimally collision resistant, it is also collapsing.*

Note that the function $\mathcal{H}$ may be optimally collision resistant, but fail to be semi-regular: for example there may be a single input that is very likely, but infeasible to find a pre-image of in polynomial time. Such an $\mathcal{H}$ is not semi-regular, but could plausibly be optimally collision resistant. Thus, Theorem 7 offers a distinct alternative to assuming semi-regularity, trading off a structural assumption for a stronger hardness assumptions. Depending on the analysis performed, either approach may be preferred.

Proof. Let $\mathcal{A}$ be a collapsing adversary with non-negligible advantage ϵ. Let $|\psi\rangle$ be the superposition of inputs to h produced by $\mathcal{A}$, and y be the measured image of $|\psi\rangle$. We give a simple adversary $\mathcal{B}$ for optimal collision resistance. $\mathcal{B}$ first runs $\mathcal{A}(h)$ to get $|\psi\rangle$, and then applies the measurement $\mathcal{M}_{\mathcal{Y}}^h$ to get y. Then it simply measures $|\psi\rangle$ to get a pre-image x_0 such that $h(x_0) = y$. It finally chooses a uniformly random input $x_1 \in \mathcal{X}_\lambda$ and outputs (x_0, x_1).

By the optimal collision resistance of $\mathcal{H}$, we know that $\mathcal{B}$ finds a collision with probability at most $p/|\mathcal{Y}_\lambda|$ for a polynomial p. But the probability $\mathcal{B}$ finds a collision is just the expected fraction of $\mathcal{X}_\lambda$ that are pre-images of y but not equal to x_0. Since $\mathcal{X}_\lambda$ is only polynomially larger than $\mathcal{Y}_\lambda$, we therefore have that the expected number of pre-images of y is polynomial ℓ. In particular, with probability at least $1/2$, the number of pre-images is at most 2ℓ.

But now we can use Lemma 1 to construct a different collision finding adversary $\mathcal{C}$. This is basically identical to the proof of Theorem 1: if y has ℓ pre-images, then $\mathcal{C}$ finds a collision with probability at least $2\epsilon^2/(\ell-1)$. Therefore, $\mathcal{C}$ finds a collision with probability at least $\epsilon^2/2\ell$, which is non-negligible and in particular violates the optimal security of $\mathcal{H}$.   □

References

[ABLS07] Alon, N., Benjamini, I., Lubetzky, E., Sodin, S.: Non-backtracking random walks mix faster. Commun. Contemp. Math. **9**, 585–603 (2007)

[AGKZ20] Amos, R., Georgiou, M., Kiayias, A., Zhandry, M.: One-shot signatures and applications to hybrid quantum/classical authentication. In: Makarychev, K., Makarychev, Y., Tulsiani, M., Kamath, G., Chuzhoy, J. (eds.) 52nd ACM STOC, pp. 255–268. ACM Press (2020)

[AMG+16] Amy, M., Di Matteo, O., Gheorghiu, V., Mosca, M., Parent, A., Schanck, J.: Estimating the cost of generic quantum pre-image attacks on SHA-2 and SHA-3. In: Avanzi, R., Heys, H. (eds.) SAC 2016. LNCS, vol. 10532, pp. 317–337. Springer, Cham (2017). https://doi.org/10.1007/978-3-319-69453-5_18

[AMRS20] Alagic, G., Majenz, C., Russell, A., Song, F.: Quantum-access-secure message authentication via blind-unforgeability. In: Canteaut, A., Ishai, Y. (eds.) EUROCRYPT 2020, Part III. LNCS, vol. 12107, pp. 788–817. Springer, Cham (2020). https://doi.org/10.1007/978-3-030-45727-3_27

[ARU14] Ambainis, A., Rosmanis, A., Unruh, D.: Quantum attacks on classical proof systems: the hardness of quantum rewinding. In: 55th FOCS, pp. 474–483. IEEE Computer Society Press (2014)

[BHT97] Brassard, G., Høyer, P., Tapp, A.: Quantum algorithm for the collision problem. ACM SIGACT News (Cryptol. Column) **28**, 14–19 (1997)

[BLVW19] Brakerski, Z., Lyubashevsky, V., Vaikuntanathan, V., Wichs, D.: Worst-case hardness for LPN and cryptographic hashing via code smoothing. In: Ishai, Y., Rijmen, V. (eds.) EUROCRYPT 2019, Part III. LNCS, vol. 11478, pp. 619–635. Springer, Cham (2019). https://doi.org/10.1007/978-3-030-17659-4_21

[CCY21] Chia, N.-H., Chung, K.-M., Yamakawa, T.: A black-box approach to post-quantum zero-knowledge in constant rounds. In: Malkin, T., Peikert, C. (eds.) CRYPTO 2021, Part I. LNCS, vol. 12825, pp. 315–345. Springer, Cham (2021). https://doi.org/10.1007/978-3-030-84242-0_12

[CHS19] Czajkowski, J., Hülsing, A., Schaffner, C.: Quantum indistinguishability of random sponges. In: Boldyreva, A., Micciancio, D. (eds.) CRYPTO 2019, Part II. LNCS, vol. 11693, pp. 296–325. Springer, Cham (2019). https://doi.org/10.1007/978-3-030-26951-7_11

[CLG09] Charles, D.X., Lauter, K.E., Goren, E.Z.: Cryptographic hash functions from expander graphs. J. Cryptol. **22**(1), 93–113 (2009)

[CMSZ21] Chiesa, A., Ma, F., Spooner, N., Zhandry, M.: Post-quantum succinct arguments. In: Proceedings of FOCS (2021)

[Cou06] Couveignes, J.-M.: Hard homogeneous spaces. Cryptology ePrint Archive, Report 2006/291 (2006). https://eprint.iacr.org/2006/291

[CX22] Cao, S., Xue, R.: The gap is sensitive to size of preimages: collapsing property doesn't go beyond quantum collision-resistance for preimages bounded hash functions. In: Dodis, Y., Shrimpton, T. (eds.) CRYPTO 2022, LNCS 13509, pp. 564–595 (2022)

[Cza21] Czajkowski, J.: Quantum indifferentiability of SHA-3. Cryptology ePrint Archive, Report 2021/192 (2021). https://eprint.iacr.org/2021/192

[DFMS19] Don, J., Fehr, S., Majenz, C., Schaffner, C.: Security of the Fiat-Shamir transformation in the quantum random-oracle model. In: Boldyreva, A., Micciancio, D. (eds.) CRYPTO 2019, Part II. LNCS, vol. 11693, pp. 356–383. Springer, Cham (2019). https://doi.org/10.1007/978-3-030-26951-7_13

[FLLT21] Fuchs, E., Lauter, K., Litman, M., Tran, A.: A cryptographic hash function from Markoff triples. Cryptology ePrint Archive, Report 2021/983 (2021). https://eprint.iacr.org/2021/983

[GKL88] Goldreich, O., Krawczyk, H., Luby, M.: On the existence of pseudorandom generators (extended abstract). In: 29th FOCS, pp. 12–24. IEEE Computer Society Press (1988)

[HILL99] Håstad, J., Impagliazzo, R., Levin, L.A., Luby, M.: A pseudorandom generator from any one-way function. SIAM J. Comput. **28**(4), 1364–1396 (1999)

[HS21]   Hosoyamada, A., Sasaki, Yu.: Quantum collision attacks on reduced SHA-256 and SHA-512. In: Malkin, T., Peikert, C. (eds.) CRYPTO 2021, Part I. LNCS, vol. 12825, pp. 616–646. Springer, Cham (2021). https://doi.org/10.1007/978-3-030-84242-0_22

[LMS21] Lombardi, A., Ma, F., Spooner, N.: Post-quantum zero knowledge, revisited (or: how to do quantum rewinding undetectably). Cryptology ePrint Archive, Report 2021/1543 (2021). https://eprint.iacr.org/2021/1543

[LZ19]   Liu, Q., Zhandry, M.: Revisiting post-quantum Fiat-Shamir. In: Boldyreva, A., Micciancio, D. (eds.) CRYPTO 2019, Part II. LNCS, vol. 11693, pp. 326–355. Springer, Cham (2019). https://doi.org/10.1007/978-3-030-26951-7_12

[PLQ08] Petit, C., Lauter, K., Quisquater, J.-J.: Full cryptanalysis of LPS and Morgenstern hash functions. In: Ostrovsky, R., De Prisco, R., Visconti, I. (eds.) SCN 2008. LNCS, vol. 5229, pp. 263–277. Springer, Heidelberg (2008). https://doi.org/10.1007/978-3-540-85855-3_18

[PLQ12] Petit, C., Lauter, K.E., Quisquater, J.-J.: Cayley hashes: a class of efficient graph-based hash functions (2012)

[Reg05] Regev, O.: On lattices, learning with errors, random linear codes, and cryptography. In: Gabow, H.N., Fagin,R. (eds.) 37th ACM STOC, pp. 84–93. ACM Press (2005)

[Rob21] Roberts, B.: Security analysis of quantum lightning. In: Canteaut, A., Standaert, F.-X. (eds.) EUROCRYPT 2021, Part II. LNCS, vol. 12697, pp. 562–567. Springer, Cham (2021). https://doi.org/10.1007/978-3-030-77886-6_19

[RS06]   Rostovtsev, A., Stolbunov, A.: Public-key cryptosystem based on isogenies. Cryptology ePrint Archive, Report 2006/145 (2006). https://eprint.iacr.org/2006/145

[Sho94] Shor, P.W.: Algorithms for quantum computation: discrete logarithms and factoring. In: 35th FOCS, pp. 124–134. IEEE Computer Society Press (1994)

[TZ94]   Tillich, J.-P., Zémor, G.: Hashing with SL_2. In: Desmedt, Y.G. (ed.) CRYPTO 1994. LNCS, vol. 839, pp. 40–49. Springer, Heidelberg (1994). https://doi.org/10.1007/3-540-48658-5_5

[Unr16a] Unruh, D.: Collapse-binding quantum commitments without random oracles. In: Cheon, J.H., Takagi, T. (eds.) ASIACRYPT 2016, Part II. LNCS, vol. 10032, pp. 166–195. Springer, Heidelberg (2016). https://doi.org/10.1007/978-3-662-53890-6_6

[Unr16b] Unruh, D.: Computationally binding quantum commitments. In: Fischlin, M., Coron, J.-S. (eds.) EUROCRYPT 2016, Part II. LNCS, vol. 9666, pp. 497–527. Springer, Heidelberg (2016). https://doi.org/10.1007/978-3-662-49896-5_18

[Unr17] Unruh, D.: Collapsing sponges: post-quantum security of the sponge construction. Cryptology ePrint Archive, Report 2017/282 (2017). https://eprint.iacr.org/2017/282

[VDG98] Van De Graaf, J.: Towards a formal definition of security for quantum protocols. Ph.D. thesis, CAN (1998). AAINQ35648

[Wat06] Watrous, J.: Zero-knowledge against quantum attacks. In: Kleinberg, J.M. (ed.) 38th ACM STOC, pp. 296–305. ACM Press (2006)

[YZW+19] Yu, Y., Zhang, J., Weng, J., Guo, C., Li, X.: Collision resistant hashing from L-exponential learning parity with noise. In: Galbraith, S.D., Moriai, S. (eds.) ASIACRYPT 2019, Part II. LNCS, vol. 11922, pp. 3–24. Springer, Cham (2019). https://doi.org/10.1007/978-3-030-34621-8_1

[Zha19a] Zhandry, M.: How to record quantum queries, and applications to quantum indifferentiability. In: Boldyreva, A., Micciancio, D. (eds.) CRYPTO 2019, Part II. LNCS, vol. 11693, pp. 239–268. Springer, Cham (2019). https://doi.org/10.1007/978-3-030-26951-7_9

[Zha19b] Zhandry, M.: Quantum lightning never strikes the same state twice. In: Ishai, Y., Rijmen, V. (eds.) EUROCRYPT 2019, Part III. LNCS, vol. 11478, pp. 408–438. Springer, Cham (2019). https://doi.org/10.1007/978-3-030-17659-4_14

Statistically Sender-Private OT from LPN and Derandomization

Nir Bitansky and Sapir Freizeit[(✉)]

Tel Aviv University, Tel Aviv, Israel
nirbitan@tau.ac.il, sapirfreizeit@gmail.com

Abstract. We construct a two-message oblivious transfer protocol with statistical sender privacy (SSP OT) based on the Learning Parity with Noise (LPN) Assumption and a standard Nisan-Wigderson style derandomization assumption. Beyond being of interest on their own, SSP OT protocols have proven to be a powerful tool toward minimizing the round complexity in a wide array of cryptographic applications from proofs systems, through secure computation protocols, to hard problems in statistical zero knowledge (SZK).

The protocol is plausibly post-quantum secure. The only other constructions with plausible post quantum security are based on the Learning with Errors (LWE) Assumption. Lacking the geometric structure of LWE, our construction and analysis rely on a different set of techniques.

Technically, we first construct an SSP OT protocol in the common random string model from LPN alone, and then derandomize the common random string. Most of the technical difficulty lies in the first step. Here we prove a robustness property of the inner product randomness extractor to a certain type of linear splitting attacks. A caveat of our construction is that it relies on the so called *low noise regime* of LPN. This aligns with our current complexity-theoretic understanding of LPN, which only in the low noise regime is known to imply hardness in SZK.

1 Introduction

Learning Parity with Noise [16,17] is a prominent hardness assumption in cryptography. The search version of the problem LPN_ε postulates that given access to polynomially many samples $(\mathbf{a}_i, \mathbf{a}_i^t \mathbf{s} + e_i)$ where $\mathbf{s} \leftarrow \mathbb{F}_2^n$ is a uniformly random secret, each $\mathbf{a}_i \leftarrow \mathbb{F}_2^n$ is a uniformly random vector, and each $e_i \leftarrow \text{Bern}(\varepsilon)$ is a random Bernouli noise bit, it is hard to find the secret $\mathbf{s}$. In the decision version, which is equivalently hard [34], the samples are indistinguishable from completely random samples, where $e_i \leftarrow \mathbb{F}_2$ is uniformly random.

Much of the appeal of the LPN assumption stems from its direct relation to the long-studied problem of decoding random linear codes, as well as its plausible resilience to quantum attacks. Furthermore, in terms of applications, LPN has led to simple and efficient constructions, for a both symmetric-key and asymmetric-key primitives (c.f. [3,24,37,44]). Yet, our understanding of LPN,

---

A full version of this work is available [12].

Y. Dodis and T. Shrimpton (Eds.): CRYPTO 2022, LNCS 13509, pp. 625–653, 2022.
https://doi.org/10.1007/978-3-031-15982-4_21

both in terms of hardness and in terms of applications, still seems to be lacking, and in particular to be far behind our understanding of its cousin, the Learning with Errors (LWE) assumption [46]. In LWE, instead of $\mathbb{F}_2$, we consider $\mathbb{F}_q$ for a large (at least polynomial) modulus q, and instead of Bernouli noise e_i, we consider (discrete) Gaussian noise e_i of norm $\ll q$.

Although the two have a similar flavour, the geometric structure endowed by the two mentioned differences has made LWE substantially more versatile than LPN. While LWE has led to a wide array of applications, including ground-breaking ones such as fully-homomorphic encryption [23, 28], the set of applications known from LPN is far more restricted (see also Sect. 1.3). At the same time, there is no formal indication that LPN is less powerful than LWE, and the effort to expand its reach continues.

Statistically Sender-Private OT. One powerful primitive that has been constructed from LWE [18, 25] and has yet to be achieved under LPN is *two-message statistically sender-private oblivious transfer* (SSP OT in short) [2, 41]. Recall that in an OT protocol [27, 45], the sender S holds two messages $(m_0\, m_1)$ and the receiver R holds a choice bit $c \in \{0, 1\}$. The goal is for R to learn the message m_c of its choice, without learning anything on the other message m_{1-c}, and without having S learn anything about the choice c. SSP OT requires that this is done in minimal round complexity with a single message from the receiver R and a single message returned from the sender S. Security is also taken to the extreme, requiring that sender privacy, namely the hiding of m_{1-c}, is statistical (statistical receiver-privacy is impossible in this setting, as it would enable a non-uniform malicious receiver to learn both sender messages).

As for the formal security notion, the gold-standard simulation guarantee against malicious parties is known to be unobtainable (even with computational sender privacy), without reliance on some form of setup. In contrast, in the common random string model, Döttling, Garg, Hajiabadi, and Wichs [24] construct a simulatable protocol with computational security (for both the receiver and sender) from LPN$_{n^{\frac{1}{2}-\varepsilon}}$. The standard security notion in this setting, introduced in [2, 41], relaxes the simulation requirement in a meaningful manner. On the receiver side, receiver messages corresponding to different choice bits should be computationally indistinguishable. On the sender side, any receiver message information-theoretically fixes a choice $c^* \in \{0, 1\}$, so that sender messages corresponding to different m_{1-c^*} are statistically indistinguishable.

Such SSP OT protocols have turned out to be highly useful, in particular toward obtaining protocols with low round complexity. They have been used to achieve two-message (statistically) witness indistinguishable protocols [5, 33] and weak zero-knowledge protocols [13, 32], multi-party computation protocols with minimal round complexity [4, 6, 7], improved round complexity for non-malleable commitments [35, 36], malicious circuit privacy for fully-homomorphic encryption [42], and correctness amplification for indistinguishability obfuscators [14].

Up until recently, SSP OT protocols were only known based on number-theoretic assumptions such as DDH [2, 41] and QR and DCR [30], which are not resilient to quantum attacks. Brakerski and Dötling [18] gave the first construction that is plausibly post-quantum secure, based on LWE. Dötling et al. [25] and Aggarwal et al. [1] provided additional constructions from LWE that also achieve constant rate. The construction of [18] strongly relies on the tight connection between LWE and lattices and in particular, the transference principle [9]. The construction by [25] relies on trapdoor hash functions and the one by Aggarwal et al. [1] is based on Algebraic Restriction Codes and a special form of linear homomorphic encryption. Aiming to construct SSP OT from LPN, we are once again faced with the fact that LPN lacks the geometrical structure and expressiveness of LWE; in particular, in the context of LPN, there is no analogous transference principle, and neither trapdoor hash functions nor linear homomorphic encryption are known.

1.1   Our Results

We construct SSP OT assuming $\text{LPN}_{\frac{\log^2 n}{n}}$ and a standard Nisan-Wigderson style derandomization assumption, namely that there exists functions with (uniform) time complexity $2^{O(n)}$ and non-deterministic circuit complexity $2^{\Omega(n)}$. Toward this, we first construct SSP OT in the common random string model, which is already meaningful on its own, and where most of the technical difficulty lies. We then show how to derandomize the common random string.

In more detail, we prove the following three results:

1. Assuming $\text{LPN}_{\frac{\log^2 n}{n}}$, there exists SSP OT in the *common random string model*.
2. Any SSP OT in the common random string model, can be converted to one in a relaxed model, where the receiver need not trust the common string. We refer to this as the *sender random string model*, as the sender can generate the common string.
3. Under the aforementioned derandomization assumption, any SSP OT in the sender random string model can be transformed into one in the plain model, provided that it has a certain *bad-crs certification* property. We prove that the construction from the first result (in the common random string model) satisfies this property, and that it is preserved by the transformation given by the second result.

On Low-Noise LPN. Our construction relies on LPN in the so called low-noise regime, where we could expect at most quasi-polynomial hardness [17]. This indeed makes it mostly of theoretical interest. Improving the noise rate is an intriguing problem that may very well require a significant leap in our understanding of the complexity of LPN. Indeed, a folklore fact is that SSP OT (even in the common random string model) implies lossy public-key encryption, and thus a construction of SSP OT from LPN_ε would imply that $\text{LPN}_\varepsilon \in \text{BPP}^{\text{SZK}}$. However, so far it is only known that $\text{LPN}_\varepsilon \in \text{BPP}^{\text{SZK}}$ for $\varepsilon = O(\log^2 n/n)$ [22], and there is no indication that this is also true for larger ε. We also note that there are in fact much more basic primitives than SSP OT, such as collision resistant hashing (which is not even broken in SZK), that to date are only known in the low noise regime.

On the Derandomization Assumption. Starting from the work of Barak, Ong, and Vadhan [10], the use of Nisan-Wigderson syle derandomization has become quite commonly used in cryptographic applications (c.f. [8,15,31]). The corresponding assumption is a worst-case assumption that is considered to be a natural generalization of the assumption that **EXP** $\not\subset$ **NP**. We also note that there is a universal candidate for the assumption, by instantiating the hard function with any **E**-complete language under linear reductions. In the body, we actually use an even weaker uniform variant of the derandomization assumption. (See further discussion in [10].)

1.2   Technical Overview

We now provide a technical overview of our constructions and proofs. Most of the overview is dedicated to our protocol in the common random string model (CRS), where most of the technical challenge lies. We then explain the second step in which the CRS is derandomized.

A Basic Protocol. We start by describing the basic protocol in the CRS model.

- The CRS $(\mathbf{A}, \mathbf{v})$ will consist of a random matrix $\mathbf{A} \leftarrow \mathbb{F}_2^{\ell \times n}$ and a random vector $\mathbf{v} \leftarrow \mathbb{F}_2^{\ell}$, for a parameter $\ell = \text{poly}(n)$.
- The receiver, with choice $c \in \{0,1\}$, samples a secret $\mathbf{s} \leftarrow \mathbb{F}_2^n$ and a noise vector $\mathbf{e} \leftarrow \text{Bern}(\varepsilon)^{\ell}$, and sends $\mathbf{v}_0 := \mathbf{As} + \mathbf{e} + c\mathbf{v}$.
- The sender, with messages $m_0, m_1 \in \{0,1\}$, samples a vector $\mathbf{x} \leftarrow \mathcal{X}$ from some low hamming-weight distribution $\mathcal{X}$ on $\mathbb{F}_2^{\ell}$, and sends back $(\mathbf{x}^t\mathbf{A}, \mathbf{x}^t\mathbf{v}_0 + m_0, \mathbf{x}^t\mathbf{v}_1 + m_1)$, where $\mathbf{v}_1 = \mathbf{v}_0 + \mathbf{v}$.
- The receiver, now uses $\mathbf{s}$ to compute $\mathbf{x}^t\mathbf{v}_c + m_c - \mathbf{x}^t\mathbf{As} = m_c + \mathbf{x}^t\mathbf{e}$.

Correctness and SSP Against Semi-honest Receivers. In the above basic protocol, the computational privacy of the receiver's choice follows directly from LPN_ε. The essential tradeoff is between correctness and statistical sender privacy (SSP). On one hand, to ensure correctness we aim that $\mathbf{x}^t\mathbf{e} = 0$ with high enough probability, and thus want $\mathbf{x}$ to be as sparse as possible. On the other hand, given that $\mathbf{x}^t\mathbf{A}$ already leaks n bits of information about $\mathbf{x}$, it should have min-entropy greater than n, and thus cannot be too sparse.

To understand how to balance this tradeoff, let us first restrict attention to a simple case of semi-honest receivers that follow the protocol as prescribed (here in fact the receiver may also send the CRS). A simple intuition for SSP in this setting is the fact that for the negative choice bit $1 - c$, the receiver obtains

$$\mathbf{x}^t\mathbf{v}_{1-c} + m_{1-c} = \mathbf{x}^t(\mathbf{As} + \mathbf{e}) + \mathbf{x}^t\mathbf{v} + m_{1-c} \ .$$

Here the inner product $\mathbf{x}^t\mathbf{v}$ acts as a strong randomness extractor, so as long as the min-entropy remaining in $\mathbf{x}$ is large enough $\mathbf{H}_\infty\left(\mathbf{x} \mid \mathbf{x}^t\mathbf{A}\right) \gg n$, the message m_{1-c} will remain statistically hidden. A back of the envelop calculation shows that this already restricts our possible choice of parameters. It requires that we choose $\varepsilon = O(\log^2 n/n)$, which lets us choose $\mathcal{X}$ so to guarantee that $\mathbf{x}^t\mathbf{e} = 0$ with probability at least $\frac{1}{2} + \frac{1}{\text{poly}(n)}$ (the exact choice of $\mathcal{X}$ does not matter at this point, e.g. it can be $\text{Bern}(\delta)^\ell$ for an appropriate δ). Once we have this correctness guarantee, we can amplify it, using standard parallel repetition.

Malicious Receivers. The main technical challenge and the bulk of our work is proving that the above protocol is in fact also SSP against malicious receivers (for an appropriate choice of distribution $\mathcal{X}$). The challenge lies in the fact that a malicious receiver may now choose $\mathbf{v}_0$ arbitrarily and adaptively depending on the seed $\mathbf{v}$ and the matrix $\mathbf{A}$. Still, we need to ensure that any $\mathbf{v}_0 \in \mathbb{F}_2^\ell$, now chosen as a function of $\mathbf{v}, \mathbf{A}$, fixes some $c^* \in \{0,1\}$ such that $\mathbf{x}^t\mathbf{v}_{1-c^*}$ is statistically close to uniform for $\mathbf{x} \leftarrow \mathcal{X}$, even given $\mathbf{x}^t\mathbf{A}$. (To be more precise, as described so far, the sender's message includes an extra bit of leakage on $\mathbf{x}$, since it includes both $\mathbf{x}^t\mathbf{v}_0 + m_0$ and $\mathbf{x}^t\mathbf{v}_1 + m_1$. In the actual scheme, we use two independent samples $\mathbf{x}_0$ and $\mathbf{x}_1$ for these two parts, so this is not an issue.)

One could hope that the inner product extractor is generally resilient to such *linear splitting attacks.* That is, given the seed $\mathbf{v}$ the attacker may split it adaptively to $\mathbf{v}_0, \mathbf{v}_1$ that sum to $\mathbf{v}$, we can still hope that one of the seeds still functions as a good extractor. However, it turns out that this is generally not true. As an example, consider the distribution $\mathcal{X}'$, where $\mathbf{x}$ is sampled by first choosing a uniformly random $\mathbf{x} \leftarrow \mathbb{F}_2^\ell$, then flipping a random bit $b \leftarrow \{0,1\}$, and then zeroing out the first or second half of $\mathbf{x}$ according to b. Then an attacker, given a seed $\mathbf{v} = (v_1, \ldots, v_\ell)$ could split $\mathbf{v}$ into its two halves $\mathbf{v}_0 = (v_1, \ldots, v_{\frac{\ell}{2}}, 0, \ldots, 0)$ and $\mathbf{v}_1 = (0, \ldots, 0, v_{\frac{\ell}{2}+1}, \ldots, v_\ell)$. Then neither $\mathbf{v}_0$ nor $\mathbf{v}_1$ is a good extractor: if we leak b, then although $\mathbf{x}|b$ has high entropy, either bit will be predictable with probability $3/4$. Indeed, this counter example strongly relies on the fact that $\mathbf{v}_0$ is chosen adaptively depending on $\mathbf{v}$.

Back to Our Case. While we cannot simply rely on the inner product being a strong extractor, in our case the leakage on $\mathbf{x}$ has a specific form $\mathbf{x}^t\mathbf{A}$, and we also have the liberty of choosing the distribution $\mathcal{X}$ (provided that the previous correctness guarantees still hold). Indeed, we manage to prove that for an appropriate choice of $\mathcal{X}$ SSP does hold. We now proceed to describe our choice of distribution $\mathcal{X}$, and the main steps in the proof, which is quite intricate.

Inspired by the LPN smoothing reduction of Brakerski et al. [22], we choose a distribution $\mathcal{X}$ that behaves somewhat nicely in terms of Fourier analysis. Specifically, we use the *sampling with replacement* distribution

$$\mathcal{X}_{\ell,k} := \sum_{i=1}^k U\{\mathbf{e}_1, \ldots, \mathbf{e}_l\} \ ,$$

which is the sum of k independent random unit vectors over $\mathbb{F}_2^\ell$. By choosing the hamming weight $k \approx n/\log n$, we guarantee that $\mathbf{x}^t \mathbf{e} = 0$ with probability noticeably greater than half as required. Considering the attacker's choice of $\mathbf{v}_0$ and the corresponding $\mathbf{v}_1 = \mathbf{v}_0 + \mathbf{v}$, we aim to show that for some $\mathbf{w} \in \{\mathbf{v}_0, \mathbf{v}_1\}$ we are guaranteed that $\mathbf{x}^t \mathbf{w}$ is close to uniform, even given $\mathbf{x}^t \mathbf{A}$.

Relating Statistical Unpredictability to Coset Balance. We first observe that if $\mathbf{w}$ is *too close* to the code generated by $\mathbf{A}$, namely $\mathbf{w} = \mathbf{A}\mathbf{s}^* + \mathbf{e}^*$ for some low hamming weight $\mathbf{e}^*$, then $\mathbf{x}^t \mathbf{w} = \mathbf{x}^t \mathbf{A}\mathbf{s}^* + \mathbf{x}^t \mathbf{e}^*$ becomes predictable. Indeed, $\mathbf{x}^t \mathbf{A}\mathbf{s}^*$ is determined by $\mathbf{x}^t \mathbf{A}$ and $\mathbf{x}^t \mathbf{e}^*$ is likely to be zero (this is exactly what enables correctness). This is in fact also the case if $\mathbf{w}$ is *too far* from some codeword, namely $\mathbf{w} = \mathbf{A}\mathbf{s}^* + \mathbf{1} + \mathbf{e}^*$, where $\mathbf{1}$ is the all one vector. Predicting $\mathbf{x}^t \mathbf{w}$ is similar to the previous case, except that we need to also predict $\mathbf{x}^t \mathbf{1}$, but this will be exactly $k \mod 2$.

In conclusion, to guarantee statistical unpredictability, it is necessary that all the vectors $\mathbf{w} + \mathbf{A}\mathbf{s}$ in the coset $\mathbf{w} + \mathbf{A} = \{\mathbf{w} + \mathbf{A}\mathbf{s} : \mathbf{s} \in \mathbb{F}_2^n\}$ will be rather *balanced*, namely they should have hamming weight $\|\mathbf{w} + \mathbf{A}\mathbf{s}\|_0 \approx \ell/2$. Using Fourier analysis, we show that to some extent this is also sufficient. That is, we characterize the unpredictability of $\mathbf{x}^t \mathbf{w}$ in terms of the *balance parameter* $\beta_{\mathbf{t}} := 1 - (2/\ell) \|\mathbf{t}\|_0$ of any coset member $\mathbf{t} \in \mathbf{w} + \mathbf{A}$. Specifically, we prove:

$$ SD\left(\left(\mathbf{x}^t \mathbf{A}, \mathbf{x}^t \mathbf{w} \right), \left(\mathbf{x}^t \mathbf{A}, u \right) \right) \le \frac{1}{2} \sum_{\mathbf{s} \in \mathbb{F}_2^n} \left| \beta_{\mathbf{A}\mathbf{s}+\mathbf{w}} \right|^k , $$

for any matrix $\mathbf{A} \in \mathbb{F}_2^{\ell \times n}$, vector $\mathbf{w} \in \mathbb{F}_2^\ell$, $\mathbf{x} \leftarrow \mathcal{X}_{\ell,k}$, and $u \leftarrow \mathrm{Bern}(1/2)$. The proof can be found in Sect. 3.2.

Our goal is thus to show that for at least one $\mathbf{w} \in \{\mathbf{v}_0, \mathbf{v}_1 = \mathbf{v}_0 + \mathbf{v}\}$, the total balance $\sum_{\mathbf{s} \in \mathbb{F}_2^n} \left| \beta_{\mathbf{A}\mathbf{s}+\mathbf{w}} \right|^k$ is negligible. To show this, we prove that the following two coset balance properties hold with overwhelming probability over the choice of the CRS $(\mathbf{v}, \mathbf{A})$:

1. **Property 1: v is A-balanced for sums.** This property means that for any decomposition $\mathbf{v}_0 + \mathbf{v}_1 = \mathbf{v}$, for at least one $\mathbf{w} \in \{\mathbf{v}_0, \mathbf{v}_1\}$, the coset $\mathbf{w} + \mathbf{A}$ is *somewhat balanced*. Specifically, for every $\mathbf{s}$, $|\beta_{\mathbf{A}\mathbf{s}+\mathbf{w}}| \le 3/5$.
2. **Property 2: A is affinely balanced.** This property means that in any coset $\mathbf{w} + \mathbf{A}$ most members are *well balanced*. Specifically, except for a set E of at most $2^{o(k)}$ vectors $\mathbf{s}$, it holds that $|\beta_{\mathbf{A}\mathbf{s}+\mathbf{w}}| \le 2^{-\omega(n/k)}$.

Combining these two properties, we can guarantee that for the $\mathbf{w} \in \{\mathbf{v}_0, \mathbf{v}_1\}$ such that Property 1 holds:

$$ \sum_{\mathbf{s}} \left| \beta_{\mathbf{A}\mathbf{s}+\mathbf{w}} \right|^k \le \sum_{\mathbf{s} \in E} (3/5)^k + \sum_{\mathbf{s} \notin E} 2^{-\omega(n)} , $$

which is negligible for our choice of $k \approx n/\log n$. We refer the reader to Sect. 3 for more details regarding the proof, and in particular the proof that the above two properties hold.

From the CRS Model to the Sender Random String Model. We now explain how to compile an SSP OT protocol (S, R) in the CRS model to a protocol (S', R') in the sender random string model (SRS), where receiver privacy is guaranteed even if the common string is chosen by a malicious sender. The transformation is based on the idea of reverse randomization from Dwork and Naor's *NIZK to ZAP transformation* [26].

In the new protocol, the sender random string consists of many random strings $scrs_1, \ldots, scrs_k$. The receiver R', given the sender random string, will sample a single random string $rcrs$ of its own, and will generate k corresponding common strings $crs_i = scrs_i \oplus rcrs$ for the underlying protocol (S, R). It will then run the underlying S in k parallel copies using crs_i and his choice bit c. The sender S' will secret share each of its two messages m_0 and m_1 into $m_0^1, \ldots, m_0^k$ and $m_1^1, \ldots, m_1^k$, and respond in each copy i by running the underlying S with messages m_0^i, m_1^i.

The computational receiver privacy is shown via a standard hybrid argument. For SSP, k is chosen to be large enough to guarantee that for any receiver choice of $rcrs$, at least one crs_i will ensure SSP, this is sufficient due to the use of secret sharing.

From the SRS Model to the Plain Model Using Derandomization. We now explain how to derandomize the SRS to get a protocol in the plain model. Here we again draw inspiration from the case of ZAPs. Barak, Ong, and Vadhan [10] observe that in ZAPs a *bad CRS*, namely one relative to which there exist false proofs, can be identified non-deterministically in *fixed* polynomial time (for a given false statement, the certificate for badness is an accepting ZAP). This allows them to derandomize the CRS using *hitting set generators* (HSG) against co-nondeterministic circuits, which in turn can be constructed from the aforementioned worst-case assumption [29]. Such a generator G deterministically computes in polynomial time a set $S = \{crs_i\}$ of strings. G guarantees that if a random string crs is *not* bad with high probability, then the set S will include *at least one* string crs_i that is not bad. This is sufficient for derandomizing ZAPs, by running parallel ZAP instances with each crs_i.

In our setting a bad SRS is one for which SSP does not hold. If such badness is certifiable then we can rely on a similar transformation. As in ZAPs, we can run the SSP OT protocol with each crs_i in the generated set S, and like the transformation from the previous paragraph, use secret sharing on the sender's end to guarantee SSP. However, unlike the case of ZAPs, for a general SSP OT the badness of a given crs might not be certifiable. Hence we need to require this explicitly from the underlying SSP OT. This means that we have to guarantee that our SSP OT has this additional *bad CRS certification* property.

Guaranteeing Bad CRS Certification. Guaranteeing bad CRS certification boils down to showing that our protocol in the CRS model has the property; indeed, it is not hard to show that the transformation to the SRS model would preserve bad CRS certification. Recall that in our construction, we proved that if a CRS $(\mathbf{A}, \mathbf{v})$ possesses Properties 1 and 2, then it is not bad. It is not hard to see that if Property 1—$\mathbf{v}$ is $\mathbf{A}$-balanced for sums—is not satisfied then this can be certified. The witness is a decomposition $\mathbf{v}_0, \mathbf{v}_1$ such that $\mathbf{v} = \mathbf{v}_0 + \mathbf{v}_1$ along with $\mathbf{s}_0, \mathbf{s}_1$, such that both $\mathbf{As}_i + \mathbf{v}_i$ are not somewhat balanced.

In contrast, it is not clear how to certify Property 2—$\mathbf{A}$ is affinely balanced. For this purpose we identify an alternative algebraic property that is both certifiable and implies affine balance; surprisingly we call it *strong affine balance*. The property states that for any $\mathbf{w}$, in any set of $d \approx n/\log^2 n$ linearly independent vectors $\mathbf{s}_1, \ldots, \mathbf{s}_d \in \mathbb{F}_2^n$ at least one coset member $\mathbf{As}_i + \mathbf{w}$ is well balanced. If this property does not hold, then this can be certified; the witness is $\mathbf{w}, \mathbf{s}_1, \ldots, \mathbf{s}_d$ that do not satisfy the property. Furthermore, we show that strong affine balance implies affine balance. We refer the reader to Sect. 3 for more details.

1.3 More Related Work

Other Applications of LPN. The works of Brakerski et al. and Yu et al. build collision-resistant hash function based on $LPN_{\log^2 n/n}$ [22,48] (the latter also shows certain tradeoffs between hardness and shrinkage) . [21] construct anonymous identity-based encryption assuming the hardness of $LPN_{\log^2 n/n}$. Brakerski, Mour, and Koppula [19] construct non-interactive zero-knowledge arguments based on $LPN_{n-(1/2+\epsilon)}$ and the existence of trapdoor-hash-functions (which can be constructed from DDH). Bartusek et al. construct maliciously-secure, two-round reusable multiparty computation in the CRS model based on $LPN_{1/n^{1-\epsilon}}$ [11].

The Hardness of LPN. The gap between LWE and LPN is also expressed in hardness results. While the hardness of LWE can be based on the worst-case hardness of long-studied lattice problems (c.f. [20,43,46]), worst-case to average case reductions for LPN have only been recently discovered and are still very limited (they essentially show that solving the relatively "easy case" of $LPN_{\frac{\log^2 n}{n}}$ in the worst case can be reduced to solving a very "hard case" of $LPN_{\frac{1}{2}-\frac{1}{\mathrm{poly}(n)}}$ in the average case) [22,47].

2 Preliminaries

We rely on the following standard notation.

- Throughout, we identify $\{0,1\}^\ell$ with $\mathbb{F}_2^\ell$ in the natural way, addition and multiplication of elements in $\mathbb{F}_2$ refers to the corresponding field operations.
- We denote vectors and matrices in bold, whereas scalars are not bold.
- For a binary vector $\mathbf{x}$, we denote by $\|\mathbf{x}\|_0$ the hamming weight of $\mathbf{x}$.
- We denote by $\mathbb{E}[X]$ the expected value of random variable X.
- For a distribution D, $x \leftarrow D$ denotes sampling x from D. For a set S, $x \leftarrow S$ denotes uniformly sampling from S.

We rely on the standard notions of Turing machines and Boolean circuits.

- We say that a Turing machine is PPT if it is probabilistic and runs in polynomial time.
- For a PPTalgorithm M, we denote by $M(x; r)$ the output of M on input x and random coins r. For such an algorithm, and any input x, we may write $m \in M(x)$ to denote the fact that m is in the support of $M(x; \cdot)$.
- A polynomial-size circuit family $\mathcal{C}$ is a sequence of circuits $\mathcal{C} = \{C_n\}_{n \in \mathbb{N}}$, such that each circuit C_n is of polynomial size $n^{O(1)}$ and has $n^{O(1)}$ input and output bits. We also consider probabilistic circuits that may toss random coins.
- We follow the standard convention of modeling any efficient adversary as a family of polynomial-size circuits. For an adversary A corresponding to a family of polynomial-size circuits $\{\mathsf{A}_n\}_{n \in \mathbb{N}}$, we sometimes omit the subscript n, when it is clear from the context.
- A function $f : \mathbb{N} \to [0, 1]$ is negligible if $f(n) = n^{-\omega(1)}$ and is noticeable if $f(n) = n^{-O(1)}$.
- Two ensembles of random variables $\mathcal{X} = \{X_i\}_{n \in \mathbb{N}, i \in I_n}$, $\mathcal{Y} = \{Y_i\}_{n \in \mathbb{N}, i \in I_n}$ over the same set of indices $I = \cup_{n \in \mathbb{N}} I_n$ are said to be *computationally indistinguishable* (respectively, *statistically indistinguishable*), denoted by $\mathcal{X} \approx_c \mathcal{Y}$, if for every polynomial-size (respectively, unbounded) distinguisher $\mathsf{A} = \{\mathsf{A}_n\}_{n \in \mathbb{N}}$ there exists a negligible function μ such that for all $n \in \mathbb{N}, i \in I_n$,

$$\left| \Pr\left[\mathsf{A}(X_i) = 1\right] - \Pr\left[\mathsf{A}(Y_i) = 1\right] \right| \le \mu(n) \ .$$

Definition 2.1 (Distribution $\mathcal{X}_{\ell,k}$: sampling with replacement). *Let $\ell, k \in \mathbb{N}$. We denote by $\mathcal{X}_{\ell,k}$ the distribution over $\mathbb{F}_2^\ell$, where $\mathbf{x} \leftarrow \mathcal{X}_{\ell,k}$ is the sum of k uniformly random standard basis vectors, sampled independently with repetitions:*

$$\mathbf{x} := \sum_{i=1}^{k} \mathbf{x}_i, \ where \ \forall i \in [k], \ \mathbf{x}_i \leftarrow \{\mathbf{e}_1, \ldots, \mathbf{e}_\ell\} \ ,$$

where $\mathbf{e}_j$ is the j-th standard basis vector.

We rely on the following basic lemmas.

Lemma 2.2 (Piling-Up Lemma [39]). *Let $v_1, .., v_k \in \mathbb{F}_2$ i.i.d random variables such that $\mathbb{E}[v_i] = \varepsilon$, then:*

$$\Pr\left[\sum_{i=1}^{k} v_i = 1\right] = \frac{1}{2} - \frac{1}{2}(1 - 2\varepsilon)^k \ .$$

Lemma 2.3 (Random Vectors Are Balanced). *Let $\ell \subset \mathbb{N}$ and $\beta \ge \sqrt{1/\ell}$, then:*

$$\Pr_{\mathbf{w} \leftarrow \mathbb{F}_2^\ell}\left[\left| \|\mathbf{w}\|_0 - \frac{\ell}{2} \right| \ge \beta\ell\right] \le 2^{-\beta^2 \ell} \ .$$

The latter lemma follows directly from a Chernoff-Hoeffding bound.

2.1   Learning Parity with Noise

We recall the Learning Parity with Noise (LPN) assumption.

Definition 2.4 (*LPN* **Assumption**). *For noise rate $\varepsilon(n) \in [0, 1/2]$, the LPN_ε assumption is that for any $m(n) = n^{O(1)}$,*

$$\{\mathbf{A}, \mathbf{As} + \mathbf{e}\}_{n \in \mathbb{N}} \approx_c \{\mathbf{A}, \mathbf{u}\}_{n \in \mathbb{N}} \ ,$$

where $\mathbf{A} \leftarrow \mathbb{F}_2^{m \times n}, \mathbf{s} \leftarrow \mathbb{F}_2^n, \mathbf{e} \leftarrow \mathrm{Bern}(\varepsilon)^m$, and $\mathbf{u} \leftarrow \mathbb{F}_2^m$.

2.2   Derandomization: Hitting Set Generators

We next define hitting set generators (HSGs) and state relevant results from the literature. We address both HSGs against non-uniform circuits as well against uniform algorithms. The non-uniform version is somewhat more common in the literature and simpler to state. However, the (weaker) uniform version will suffice for our purpose.

Definition 2.5 (**Co-nondeterministic Circuits and Algorithms**). *A co-nondeterministic boolean circuit $C(x, w)$ (respectively, uniform algorithm $A(x, w)$) takes x as a primary input and w as a witness. We define $C(x) := 0$ (respectively, $A(x) := 0$) if and only if there exists w such that $C(x, w) = 0$ (respectively, $A(x, w) = 0$).*

Definition 2.6 (**Hitting Set Generators**). *A deterministic polynomial-time algorithm $H(1^m, 1^s)$ that outputs a set of strings of length m, is a hitting set generator against co-nondeterministic circuits, if for every $m, s \in \mathbb{N}$, and every co-non-deterministic circuit $C : \{0, 1\}^m \to \{0, 1\}$ of size at most s:*

$$\Pr_{x \leftarrow \{0,1\}^m} [C(x) = 1] > 1/2 \Longrightarrow \exists y \in H(1^m, 1^s) : C(y) = 1 \ .$$

Definition 2.7 (**Uniform Hitting Set Generators**). *A deterministic polynomial-time algorithm $H(1^m, 1^{s(m)})$ that outputs a set of strings of length m, is a hitting set generator against co-non-deterministic **uniform algorithms**, if for every co-nondeterministic uniform algorithm $A : \{0, 1\}^* \to \{0, 1\}$ of running time at most $s(m)$, and for sufficiently large m:*

$$\Pr_{x \leftarrow \{0,1\}^m} [A(x) = 1] > 1/2 \Longrightarrow \exists y \in H(1^m, 1^{s(m)}) : A(y) = 1 \ .$$

In the literature, a more general notion of ε-HSGs is often defined, where the bound $1/2$ is replaced by ε. In terms of computational assumptions, this difference is inconsequential due to general amplification results for HSGs [29].

Theorem 2.8 ([40]). *Assume there exists a function f in $\mathbf{E} = \mathbf{Dtime}(2^{O(n)})$ with non-deterministic circuit complexity $2^{\Omega(n)}$. Then, there exists an efficient HSG against co-nondeterministic circuits.*

Gutfreund, Shaltiel and Ta-Shma [29] show that HSGs against co-nondeterministic *uniform* algorithm can be obtained from a relaxed (uniform) hardness assumption.

Definition 2.9 (AM). *A probabilistic nondeterministic algorithm $A(x, r, y)$ takes in addition to its regular input x a randomness input r as well a nondeterministic input y. We say that A computes a function $f : \{0,1\}^* \to \{0,1\}$ if for any x:*

- *$f(x) = 1 \implies \Pr_r [\exists y : A(x, r, y) = 1] = 1$,*
- *$f(x) = 0 \implies \Pr_r [\exists y : A(x, r, y) = 1] \leq \frac{1}{2}$.*

AM *is the class of all languages decidable by probabilistic nondeterministic algorithms running in time $\mathrm{poly}(n)$ where $n = |x|$. Similarly,* **AMTIME**$(t(n))$ *is the class of all languages decidable by probabilistic nondeterministic algorithms running in time at most $t(n)$. Finally,* $[i.o. - \textbf{AMTIME}](t(n))$ *denotes the class of all languages which have a probabilistic nondeterministic $t(n)$-running-time algorithm deciding them for infinitely-many input lengths.*

Theorem 2.10 ([29]). *Assume $E \nsubseteq [i.o. - \textbf{AMTIME}](2^{\delta n})$ for some $\delta > 0$. Then, there exists an efficient HSG against co-nondeterministic uniform algorithms.*

Note that the uniform assumption (as in Theorem 2.10) is indeed a relaxation of the non-uniform one (as in Theorem 2.8), since non-uniformity can simulate randomness. We also note that both assumptions are worst-case assumptions, and that similar (or stronger) assumptions have by now become quite common in cryptographic applications (c.f. [10,15,31]).

2.3 Statistical Sender-Private Oblivious Transfer

Oblivious Transfer (OT) is a protocol between two parties: a sender S and a receiver R. The sender input consists of two secret messages m_0, m_1, and the receiver input is a secret choice bit c. The protocol allows the receiver to learn m_c, and guarantees that the receiver gains no information regarding m_{1-c}, whereas the sender gains no information regarding the receiver choice bit c. We focus on statistical sender privacy (SSP); namely, sender privacy holds even against unbounded malicious receivers. Receiver privacy is computational. Furthermore, we restrict attention to protocols with two messages (one from each party).

We consider three models of trusted setup:

- **The common random string model:** Here a common random string crs is generated once and for all. The string is trusted by both the receiver and sender.
- **The sender random string model:** This model is similar to the common random string model, except that the receiver need not trust the string crs; namely, receiver privacy holds for any choice of crs (even if adversarially made by the sender).

- **The plain model:** Here there is no trusted setup at all. Equivalently, the setup procedure generating crs is deterministic.

We next define the notion in the common random string model, and then extend it to the sender random string model and the plain model. In all definitions, n indicates the security parameter.

Definition 2.11 (Two-message Statistically Sender-Private OT in CRS model). *A two-message Statistically sender-private OT in the common-random-string model consists of PPT algorithms* $R = (R.Enc, R.Dec)$ *and* S, *and an associated polynomial* ρ, *with the following syntax:*

1. $R.Enc(crs, c)$: *Gets* $crs \in \{0,1\}^{\rho(n)}$ *and choice bit* $c \in \mathbb{F}_2$ *and outputs a message* rm *and secret key* sk.
2. $S(crs, m_0, m_1, rm)$: *Gets* $crs \in \{0,1\}^{\rho(n)}$, *two bits* $m_0, m_1 \in \mathbb{F}_2$, *and* rm, *and outputs a message* sm.
3. $R.Dec(crs, sk, sm)$: *Gets* $crs \in \{0,1\}^{\rho(n)}$, *secret key* sk, *and message* sm, *and outputs a message bit.*

We require the following:

- **Correctness:** *For every* c, m_0, m_1,

$$\Pr\left[R.Dec(crs, sk, sm) = m_c \;\middle|\; \begin{array}{l} crs \leftarrow \{0,1\}^{\rho(n)} \\ (rm, sk) \leftarrow R.Enc(crs, c) \\ sm \leftarrow S(crs, m_0, m_1, rm) \end{array}\right] \geq 1 - n^{-\omega(1)} \;.$$

- **Receiver Privacy:**

$$\left\{ crs, rm \;\middle|\; \begin{array}{l} crs \leftarrow \{0,1\}^{\rho(n)} \\ (rm, sk) \leftarrow R.Enc(crs, 0) \end{array}\right\}_{n \in \mathbb{N}} \approx_c$$

$$\left\{ crs, rm \;\middle|\; \begin{array}{l} crs \leftarrow \{0,1\}^{\rho(n)} \\ (rm, sk) \leftarrow R.Enc(crs, 1) \end{array}\right\}_{n \in \mathbb{N}} \;.$$

- **Statistical Sender Privacy:** *There exists an (unbounded)* OTExt, *such that for any (unbounded)* R^*:

$$\left\{ crs, sm \;\middle|\; \begin{array}{l} crs \leftarrow \{0,1\}^{\rho(n)} \\ rm \leftarrow R^*(crs) \\ sm \leftarrow S(crs, m_0, m_1, rm) \end{array}\right\}_{n, m_0, m_1} \approx_s$$

$$\left\{ crs, sm \;\middle|\; \begin{array}{l} crs \leftarrow \{0,1\}^{\rho(n)} \\ rm \leftarrow R^*(crs) \\ b \leftarrow OTExt(crs, rm) \\ sm \leftarrow S(crs, m_b, m_b, rm) \end{array}\right\}_{n, m_0, m_1} \;,$$

where $n \in \mathbb{N}, m_0, m_1 \in \{0,1\}$.

We now derive the definitions in the sender-random-string model and in the plain model.

Definition 2.12 (Two-message Statistically Sender-Private OT in SRS model). *A two-message Statistically sender-private OT in the sender-random-string model is defined similarly to Definition 2.11, except that receiver privacy holds for any choice of* crs:

$$\left\{ \mathsf{rm} \mid (\mathsf{rm}, \mathsf{sk}) \leftarrow \mathsf{R}.\mathsf{Enc}(\mathsf{crs}, 0) \right\}_{n,\mathsf{crs}} \approx_c \left\{ \mathsf{rm} \mid (\mathsf{rm}, \mathsf{sk}) \leftarrow \mathsf{R}.\mathsf{Enc}(\mathsf{crs}, 1) \right\}_{n,\mathsf{crs}} \ ,$$

where $n \in \mathbb{N}, \mathsf{crs} \in \{0, 1\}^{\rho(n)}$.

Definition 2.13 (Two-message Statistically Sender-Private OT in plain model). *A two-message Statistically sender-private OT in the plain model is defined similarly to Definition 2.11, except that* crs *is ignored by all algorithms.*

Enhancements. We define two natural enhancements to the definition of SSP-OT protocols in the CRS/SRS model. Relying on these enhancements, we will show transformations between the three models (CRS, SRS, and plain). Furthermore, our core protocol (presented in Sect. 3) will satisfy these enhancements.

Bad CRS Certification. The first enhancement is for sender privacy, roughly saying that there is an NP witness for a CRS being "bad for sender privacy". The exact definition follows.

Definition 2.14 (Bad CRS Certification). *A two-message SSP OT protocol in the CRS/SRS model has* bad CRS certification *if there exists a set* B *such that:*

- *Statistical Sender Privacy Outside* B: *There exists an (unbounded)* OTExt, *such that for any (unbounded)* R*:*

$$\left\{ \mathsf{sm} \ \middle| \ \begin{matrix} \mathsf{rm} \leftarrow \mathsf{R}^*(\mathsf{crs}) \\ \mathsf{sm} \leftarrow \mathsf{S}(\mathsf{crs}, m_0, m_1, \mathsf{rm}) \end{matrix} \right\}_{n,\mathsf{crs},m_0,m_1} \approx_s$$

$$\left\{ \mathsf{sm} \ \middle| \ \begin{matrix} \mathsf{rm} \leftarrow \mathsf{R}^*(\mathsf{crs}) \\ b \leftarrow \mathsf{OTExt}(\mathsf{crs}, \mathsf{rm}) \\ \mathsf{sm} \leftarrow \mathsf{S}(\mathsf{crs}, m_b, m_b, \mathsf{rm}) \end{matrix} \right\}_{n,\mathsf{crs},m_0,m_1} ,$$

  where $n \in \mathbb{N}, \mathsf{crs} \in \{0, 1\}^{\rho(n)} \setminus \mathsf{B}, m_0, m_1 \in \{0, 1\}$.
- *Negligible Density:* $\Pr\left[\mathsf{crs} \in \mathsf{B} \mid \mathsf{crs} \leftarrow \{0, 1\}^{\rho(n)}\right] \leq n^{-\omega(1)}$.
- *Certification:* $\mathsf{B} \in \mathbf{NP}$.

Remark 2.15 (Relation to the SSP in Definition 2.11). We note that SSP as given by Definition 2.11 is in fact equivalent to the first two above conditions. That is, if SSP holds, then there exists a set B satisfying the first two conditions, and vice versa. The fact that the first two conditions imply SSP follows directly from the definition. The other direction follows by an averaging argument.

Specifically, given that SSP holds, consider the malicious receiver R* that given crs, chooses the message rm that maximizes the statistical distance between

$S(\mathsf{crs}, m_0, m_1, \mathsf{rm})$ and $S(\mathsf{crs}, m_b, m_b, \mathsf{rm})$ where b is the extracted bit. Letting ν be the statistical distance for a random crs, it holds that for all but a $\sqrt{\nu}$ fraction of crs, the maximal statistical distance between $S(\mathsf{crs}, m_0, m_1, \mathsf{rm})$ and $S(\mathsf{crs}, m_b, m_b, \mathsf{rm})$, over any choice of rm, is at most $\sqrt{\nu}$. The corresponding set B consists of this $\sqrt{\nu}$ fraction.

CRS-Free Correctness. The second enhancement is for the correctness property, saying that correctness holds for *any* choice of CRS.

Definition 2.16. *A two-message SSP OT protocol in the CRS/SRS model has CRS-free correctness if:*

$$\min_{\substack{\mathsf{crs}\in\{0,1\}^{\rho(n)} \\ m_0, m_1, c \in \{0,1\}}} \Pr\left[\mathsf{R.Dec}(\mathsf{crs}, \mathsf{sk}, \mathsf{sm}) = m_c \;\middle|\; \begin{array}{l} (\mathsf{rm}, \mathsf{sk}) \leftarrow \mathsf{R.Enc}(\mathsf{crs}, c) \\ \mathsf{sm} \leftarrow \mathsf{S}(\mathsf{crs}, m_0, m_1, \mathsf{rm}) \end{array}\right]$$

$$\geq 1 - n^{-\omega(1)},$$

where the probability is over the coins of the sender S and receiver R.

In Sect. 4.1, we show that this property can always be obtained for free with no additional assumptions.

3   Two-Message SSP OT in the CRS Model

In this section, we present our two-message, statistically sender-private oblivious transfer in the common random string model. We prove the following theorem.

Theorem 3.1. *Under the $LPN_{\frac{\log^2(n)}{n}}$ assumption, there exists a two-message statistically-sender-private OT protocol in the CRS model. Moreover, the protocol has CRS-free correctness and bad-CRS certification.*

We describe the protocol in Fig. 1 and then proceed to analyze it. We describe the protocol in its interactive form. The receiver algorithms R.Enc and R.Dec correspond to the generation of the receiver message, and the decryption of the sender message, respectively.

Parameters: $n \in \mathbb{N}$ is the security parameter, $\delta > 1$ is a constant, $\ell = n^{1+\frac{1}{\delta}}$, $\varepsilon = \frac{\log^2(n)}{n}$, $k = 4\delta \cdot \frac{n}{\log(n)}$, and $r = n^{64\delta+1}$.

3.1   Correctness and Receiver Privacy

We first prove correctness.

Proposition 3.2. *The protocol is correct.*

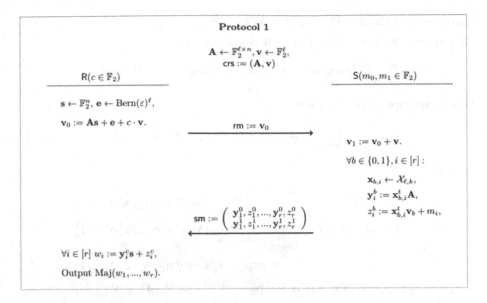

Fig. 1. Two-message statistically-sender-private OT in the CRS model

Proof. In fact, we show CRS-free correctness. Fix any $\mathbf{A} \in \mathbb{F}_2^{\ell \times n}$, $\mathbf{v} \in \mathbb{F}_2^{\ell}$, $c, m_0, m_1 \in \mathbb{F}_2$. Recall that, R samples $\mathbf{s} \leftarrow \mathbb{F}_2^{n}$, $\mathbf{e} \leftarrow \mathrm{Bern}(\varepsilon)^{\ell}$, sends $\mathbf{v}_0 := \mathbf{As} + \mathbf{e} + c \cdot \mathbf{v}$, and then S sets $\mathbf{v}_1 := \mathbf{v}_0 + \mathbf{v}$. It follows that $\mathbf{v}_c = \mathbf{As} + \mathbf{e}$ and for every $i \in [r]$,

$$z_i^c = \mathbf{x}_{c,i}^t \mathbf{As} + \mathbf{x}_{c,i}^t \mathbf{e} + m_c$$
$$w_i = \mathbf{x}_{c,i}^t \mathbf{e} + m_c \qquad \text{where } \mathbf{x}_{c,i} \leftarrow \mathcal{X}_{\ell,k}.$$

Thus, it suffices to show that the majority of $(\mathbf{x}_{c,1}^t \mathbf{e}, ..., \mathbf{x}_{c,r}^t \mathbf{e})$ equals 1 with negligible probability.

Claim. Let ε, ℓ, k, r be functions of n as in our setting of parameters. Let $\mathbf{e} \leftarrow \mathrm{Bern}(\varepsilon)^{\ell}$, and $\mathbf{x}_1, ..., \mathbf{x}_r \leftarrow \mathcal{X}_{\ell,k}$ be independent random variables. Then for large enough n:

$$\Pr_{\mathbf{e}, \mathbf{x}_1, ..., \mathbf{x}_r}\left[\mathrm{Maj}(\mathbf{x}_1^t \mathbf{e}, ..., \mathbf{x}_r^t \mathbf{e}) = 1\right] \leq \exp\left(-\varepsilon\ell/3\right) + \exp\left(-r \cdot 2^{-16k\varepsilon}/4\right) \leq n^{-\omega(1)}.$$

Proof. First, by Lemma 2.2, for any $\mathbf{w} \in \mathbb{F}_2^{\ell}$ with $\|\mathbf{w}\|_0 = \eta \leq 2\varepsilon\ell$,

$$\Pr_{\mathbf{x} \leftarrow \mathcal{X}_{\ell,k}}\left[\mathbf{x}^t \mathbf{w} = 1\right] = \Pr\left[\sum_{i=1}^{k} \mathrm{Bern}\left(\frac{\eta}{\ell}\right) = 1\right] = \frac{1}{2} - \frac{1}{2}\left(1 - 2\frac{\eta}{\ell}\right)^k$$
$$\leq \frac{1}{2} - \frac{1}{2}\left(1 - 4\varepsilon\right)^k \leq \frac{1}{2} - \frac{1}{2} \cdot 2^{-8\varepsilon k},$$

where we used the fact that $\forall y \in [0, 1/2]$, $2^{-2y} \leq 1 - y$.

For any such $\mathbf{w}$, it holds by Chernoff-Hoeffding that

$$\Pr_{\mathbf{x}_1,\ldots,\mathbf{x}_r} \left[\mathrm{Maj}(\mathbf{x}_1^t \mathbf{w}, \ldots, \mathbf{x}_r^t \mathbf{w}) = 1 \right] \leq \exp(-r \cdot 2^{-16\varepsilon k}/4) \ .$$

Also by multiplicative Chernoff,

$$\Pr_{\mathbf{e} \leftarrow \mathrm{Bern}(\varepsilon)^\ell} [\|\mathbf{e}\|_0 > 2\varepsilon\ell] \leq \exp(-\varepsilon\ell/3) \ .$$

Overall,

$$\Pr_{\mathbf{e}, \mathbf{x}_1, \ldots, \mathbf{x}_r} \left[\mathrm{Maj}(\mathbf{x}_1^t \mathbf{e}, \ldots, \mathbf{x}_r^t \mathbf{e}) = 1 \right]$$

$$\leq \Pr_{\mathbf{e}} \left[\|\mathbf{e}\|_0 > 2\varepsilon\ell \right] + \max_{\substack{\mathbf{e}: \\ \|\mathbf{e}\|_0 \leq 2\varepsilon\ell}} \Pr_{\mathbf{x}_1, \ldots, \mathbf{x}_r} \left[\mathrm{Maj}(\mathbf{x}_1^t \mathbf{e}, \ldots, \mathbf{x}_r^t \mathbf{e}) = 1 \right]$$

$$\leq \exp(-\varepsilon\ell/3) + \exp(-r \cdot 2^{-16\varepsilon k}/4)$$

$$\leq \exp(-n^{\frac{1}{\delta}}(\log^2 n)/3) + \exp(-n^{64\delta+1} \cdot n^{-64\delta}/4) \leq n^{-\omega(1)} \ ,$$

where the first to last inequality is by our setting of the parameters.

This concludes the proof of CRS-free correctness.

Receiver privacy follows directly from the LPN_ε assumption:

Proposition 3.3. *Under the LPN_ε assumption, the protocol satisfies receiver privacy.*

Proof. Under LPN_ε, the receiver message $\mathbf{v}_0$ is pseudorandom, regardless of its choice bit c.

3.2   Statistical Sender Privacy Analysis

In this section we analyze the statistical sender privacy of the protocol. First, in Sect. 3.2, we relate the statistical sender privacy to a certain measure of balance on code cosets. Then in Sect. 3.2, we analyze the required balance conditions, and deduce sufficient conditions for them to hold. Finally, in Sect. 3.2, we tie the two together to deduce statistical sender privacy with bad-CRS certification.

Statistical Distance and Balanced Cosets. To prove statistical sender privacy, we aim to characterize which matrices $\mathbf{A} \in \mathbb{F}_2^{\ell \times n}$ and vectors $\mathbf{w} \in \mathbb{F}_2^\ell$ are such that $\mathbf{x}^t \mathbf{w}$ is statistically close to uniform even given the leakage $\mathbf{x}^t \mathbf{A}$, when $\mathbf{x} \leftarrow \mathcal{X}_{\ell,k}$. We prove the following proposition, which relates the relevant statistical distance to how balanced are vectors in the coset $\mathbf{w} + \mathbf{A}$ of the linear code given by $\mathbf{A}$.

Lemma 3.4. *Let* $\mathbf{A} \in \mathbb{F}_2^{\ell \times n}$, $\mathbf{w} \in \mathbb{F}_2^{\ell}$. *Also, for* $\mathbf{t} \in \mathbb{F}_2^{\ell}$, *let* $\beta_{\mathbf{t}} := 1 - \frac{2}{\ell} \|\mathbf{t}\|_0$. *Then,*

$$SD\left((\mathbf{x}^t \mathbf{A}, \mathbf{x}^t \mathbf{w}), (\mathbf{x}^t \mathbf{A}, u)\right) \leq \frac{1}{2} \sum_{\mathbf{s} \in \mathbb{F}_2^n} |\beta_{\mathbf{As}+\mathbf{w}}|^k \ ,$$

where $\mathbf{x} \leftarrow \mathcal{X}_{\ell,k}$, *and* $u \leftarrow \mathrm{Bern}\left(\frac{1}{2}\right)$.

We prove the lemma using Fourier analysis on the Boolean cube. We start by recalling the definition of the Hadamard matrix (corresponding to the Boolean Fourier transform), and then state and prove two lemmas needed to prove Lemma 3.4.

Definition 3.5 (Hadamard matrix). *The Hadamard matrices* $\{\mathbf{H}^{\otimes n} \in \{\pm 1\}^{2^n \times 2^n}\}_{n \in \mathbb{N}}$ *are defined inductively:*

$$\mathbf{H}^{\otimes 0} = \begin{pmatrix} 1 \end{pmatrix} \ ,$$

$$\mathbf{H}^{\otimes n} = \begin{pmatrix} \mathbf{H}^{\otimes(n-1)} & \mathbf{H}^{\otimes(n-1)} \\ \mathbf{H}^{\otimes(n-1)} & -\mathbf{H}^{\otimes(n-1)} \end{pmatrix} \ .$$

Note that for every $\mathbf{x}, \mathbf{y} \in \mathbb{F}_2^n$: $\mathbf{H}_{\mathbf{x},\mathbf{y}}^{\otimes n} = (-1)^{\langle \mathbf{x},\mathbf{y} \rangle}$, where we identify strings in $\mathbb{F}_2^n$ with indices in $[2^n]$ in the natural way.

Lemma 3.6. *Let* $\ell \in \mathbb{N}$, $n \in \mathbb{N}$, $\mathbf{A} \in \mathbb{F}_2^{\ell \times n}$, $\mathbf{w} \in \mathbb{F}_2^{\ell}$, *and let* D *be a distribution over* $\mathbb{F}_2^{\ell}$, *then:*

$$\begin{pmatrix} \Pr_{\mathbf{x} \leftarrow D}\left[\mathbf{x}^t \mathbf{A} = \vec{\mathbf{0}}, \mathbf{x}^t \mathbf{w} = 0\right] - \Pr_{\mathbf{x} \leftarrow D}\left[\mathbf{x}^t \mathbf{A} = \vec{\mathbf{0}}, \mathbf{x}^t \mathbf{w} = 1\right] \\ \vdots \\ \Pr_{\mathbf{x} \leftarrow D}\left[\mathbf{x}^t \mathbf{A} = \vec{\mathbf{1}}, \mathbf{x}^t \mathbf{w} = 0\right] - \Pr_{\mathbf{x} \leftarrow D}\left[\mathbf{x}^t \mathbf{A} = \vec{\mathbf{1}}, \mathbf{x}^t \mathbf{w} = 1\right] \end{pmatrix}$$

$$= \frac{1}{2^n} \mathbf{H}^{\otimes n} \begin{pmatrix} \mathbb{E}_{\mathbf{x} \leftarrow D}\left[(-1)^{\mathbf{x}^t(\mathbf{A}\vec{\mathbf{0}}+\mathbf{w})}\right] \\ \vdots \\ \mathbb{E}_{\mathbf{x} \leftarrow D}\left[(-1)^{\mathbf{x}^t(\mathbf{A}\vec{\mathbf{1}}+\mathbf{w})}\right] \end{pmatrix} \ ,$$

where above we consider all 2^n *strings* $\vec{\mathbf{0}}, \dots, \vec{\mathbf{1}} \in \{0,1\}^n$ *according to lexicographic order.*

Proof. For any $k \in \mathbb{N}$ and $\mathbf{B} \in \mathbb{F}_2^{\ell \times k}$, consider the distribution $(\mathbf{x}^t \mathbf{B}, \mathbf{x}^t \mathbf{w})_{\mathbf{x} \leftarrow D}$. Note that for any $\mathbf{b} \in \mathbb{F}_2^k$:

$$\Pr_{\mathbf{x} \leftarrow D}\left[\mathbf{x}^t \mathbf{B} = \mathbf{b}\right] = \mathbb{E}_{\mathbf{x} \leftarrow D}\left[\mathbb{1}_{\mathbf{x}^t \mathbf{B} = \mathbf{b}}\right] = \mathbb{E}_{\mathbf{x} \leftarrow D}\left[\frac{1}{2^k} \sum_{\mathbf{s} \in \mathbb{F}_2^k} (-1)^{\langle \mathbf{x}^t \mathbf{B} + \mathbf{b}, \mathbf{s} \rangle}\right]$$

$$= \frac{1}{2^k} \sum_{\mathbf{s} \in \mathbb{F}_2^k} (-1)^{\langle \mathbf{b}, \mathbf{s} \rangle} \cdot \mathbb{E}_{\mathbf{x} \leftarrow D}\left[(-1)^{\mathbf{x}^t \mathbf{Bs}}\right] \ ,$$

which means

$$\begin{pmatrix} \Pr_{\mathbf{x} \leftarrow D} \left[\mathbf{x}^t \mathbf{B} = \vec{\mathbf{0}} \right] \\ \vdots \\ \Pr_{\mathbf{x} \leftarrow D} \left[\mathbf{x}^t \mathbf{B} = \vec{\mathbf{1}} \right] \end{pmatrix} = \frac{1}{2^k} \mathbf{H}^{\otimes k} \begin{pmatrix} \mathbb{E}_{\mathbf{x} \leftarrow D} \left[(-1)^{\mathbf{x}^t \mathbf{B} \vec{\mathbf{0}}} \right] \\ \vdots \\ \mathbb{E}_{\mathbf{x} \leftarrow D} \left[(-1)^{\mathbf{x}^t \mathbf{B} \vec{\mathbf{1}}} \right] \end{pmatrix}.$$

Now, Because $\mathbf{H}^{\otimes (n+1)} = \begin{pmatrix} \mathbf{H}^{\otimes n} & \mathbf{H}^{\otimes n} \\ \mathbf{H}^{\otimes n} & -\mathbf{H}^{\otimes n} \end{pmatrix}$, the lemma follows when taking $\mathbf{B} = (\mathbf{w} | \mathbf{A}) \in \mathbb{F}_2^{\ell \times (n+1)}$.

Lemma 3.7. *Let* $\mathbf{A} \in \mathbb{F}_2^{\ell \times n}$, $\mathbf{w} \in \mathbb{F}_2^{\ell}$. *Also, for* $\mathbf{t} \in \mathbb{F}_2^{\ell}$ *let* $\beta_{\mathbf{t}} := 1 - \frac{2}{\ell} \|\mathbf{t}\|_0$. *Then for* $\mathbf{x} \leftarrow \mathcal{X}_{\ell,k}$,

$$\begin{pmatrix} \Pr_{\mathbf{x}} \left[\mathbf{x}^t \mathbf{A} = \vec{\mathbf{0}}, \mathbf{x}^t \mathbf{w} = 0 \right] - \Pr_{\mathbf{x}} \left[\mathbf{x}^t \mathbf{A} = \vec{\mathbf{0}}, \mathbf{x}^t \mathbf{w} = 1 \right] \\ \vdots \\ \Pr_{\mathbf{x}} \left[\mathbf{x}^t \mathbf{A} = \vec{\mathbf{1}}, \mathbf{x}^t \mathbf{w} = 0 \right] - \Pr_{\mathbf{x}} \left[\mathbf{x}^t \mathbf{A} = \vec{\mathbf{1}}, \mathbf{x}^t \mathbf{w} = 1 \right] \end{pmatrix} = \frac{1}{2^n} \mathbf{H}^{\otimes n} \begin{pmatrix} \beta_{\mathbf{A}\vec{\mathbf{0}} + \mathbf{w}}^k \\ \vdots \\ \beta_{\mathbf{A}\vec{\mathbf{1}} + \mathbf{w}}^k \end{pmatrix},$$

where above we consider all 2^n *strings* $\vec{\mathbf{0}}, \ldots, \vec{\mathbf{1}} \in \{0,1\}^n$ *according to lexicographic order.*

Proof. The lemma follows directly from Lemma 3.6, and the observation that for any $\mathbf{t} \in \mathbb{F}_2^{\ell}$,

$$\mathbb{E}_{\mathbf{x} \leftarrow \mathcal{X}_{\ell,k}} \left[(-1)^{\langle \mathbf{x}, \mathbf{t} \rangle} \right] = \mathbb{E}_{\mathbf{x}_1, \ldots, \mathbf{x}_k \leftarrow \{\mathbf{e}_1, \ldots, \mathbf{e}_\ell\}} \left[\prod_{i=1}^{k} (-1)^{\langle \mathbf{x}_i, \mathbf{t} \rangle} \right]$$

$$= \prod_{i=1}^{k} \mathbb{E}_{\mathbf{x}_1 \leftarrow \{\mathbf{e}_1, \ldots, \mathbf{e}_\ell\}} \left[(-1)^{\langle \mathbf{x}_1, \mathbf{t} \rangle} \right] = \left(1 - \frac{2}{\ell} \|\mathbf{t}\|_0 \right)^k.$$

We are now ready to prove Lemma 3.4.

Proof (Proof of Lemma 3.4).

$$SD_{\mathbf{x} \leftarrow \mathcal{X}_{\ell,k}, u \leftarrow \mathrm{Bern}(\frac{1}{2})} \left((\mathbf{x}^t \mathbf{A}, \mathbf{x}^t \mathbf{w}), (\mathbf{x}^t \mathbf{A}, u) \right)$$

$$= \frac{1}{2} \sum_{\mathbf{a} \in \mathbb{F}_2^n} \left(\left| \Pr_{\mathbf{x}} \left[\mathbf{x}^t \mathbf{A} = \mathbf{a}, \mathbf{x}^t \mathbf{w} = 0 \right] - \frac{1}{2} \Pr_{\mathbf{x}} \left[\mathbf{x}^t \mathbf{A} = \mathbf{a} \right] \right| \right.$$

$$\left. + \left| \Pr_{\mathbf{x}} \left[\mathbf{x}^t \mathbf{A} = \mathbf{a}, \mathbf{x}^t \mathbf{w} = 1 \right] - \frac{1}{2} \Pr_{\mathbf{x}} \left[\mathbf{x}^t \mathbf{A} = \mathbf{a} \right] \right| \right)$$

$$= \frac{1}{2} \sum_{\mathbf{a} \in \mathbb{F}_2^n} \left(\frac{1}{2} \left| \Pr_{\mathbf{x}} \left[\mathbf{x}^t \mathbf{A} = \mathbf{a}, \mathbf{x}^t \mathbf{w} = 0 \right] - \Pr_{\mathbf{x}} \left[\mathbf{x}^t \mathbf{A} = \mathbf{a}, \mathbf{x}^t \mathbf{w} = 1 \right] \right| \right.$$

$$\left. + \frac{1}{2} \left| \Pr_{\mathbf{x}} \left[\mathbf{x}^t \mathbf{A} = \mathbf{a}, \mathbf{x}^t \mathbf{w} = 1 \right] - \Pr_{\mathbf{x}} \left[\mathbf{x}^t \mathbf{A} = \mathbf{a}, \mathbf{x}^t \mathbf{w} = 0 \right] \right| \right)$$

$$= \frac{1}{2} \sum_{\mathbf{a} \in \mathbb{F}_2^n} \left| \Pr_{\mathbf{x}} \left[\mathbf{x}^t \mathbf{A} = \mathbf{a}, \mathbf{x}^t \mathbf{w} = 0 \right] - \Pr_{\mathbf{x}} \left[\mathbf{x}^t \mathbf{A} = \mathbf{a}, \mathbf{x}^t \mathbf{w} = 1 \right] \right|$$

$$= \frac{1}{2} \left\| \begin{pmatrix} \Pr_{\mathbf{x} \leftarrow \mathcal{X}_{\ell,k}} \left[\mathbf{x}^t \mathbf{A} = \vec{\mathbf{0}}, \mathbf{x}^t \mathbf{w} = 0 \right] - \Pr_{\mathbf{x} \leftarrow \mathcal{X}_{\ell,k}} \left[\mathbf{x}^t \mathbf{A} = \vec{\mathbf{0}}, \mathbf{x}^t \mathbf{w} = 1 \right] \\ \vdots \\ \Pr_{\mathbf{x} \leftarrow \mathcal{X}_{\ell,k}} \left[\mathbf{x}^t \mathbf{A} = \vec{\mathbf{1}}, \mathbf{x}^t \mathbf{w} = 0 \right] - \Pr_{\mathbf{x} \leftarrow \mathcal{X}_{\ell,k}} \left[\mathbf{x}^t \mathbf{A} = \vec{\mathbf{1}}, \mathbf{x}^t \mathbf{w} = 1 \right] \end{pmatrix} \right\|_1$$

$$= \frac{1}{2} \left\| \frac{1}{2^n} \mathbf{H}^{\otimes n} \begin{pmatrix} \beta_{\mathbf{A}\vec{\mathbf{0}}+\mathbf{w}}^k \\ \vdots \\ \beta_{\mathbf{A}\vec{\mathbf{1}}+\mathbf{w}}^k \end{pmatrix} \right\|_1 \qquad \text{(by Lemma 3.7)}$$

$$\leq \frac{1}{2} \left\| \frac{1}{2^{n/2}} \mathbf{H}^{\otimes n} \begin{pmatrix} \beta_{\mathbf{A}\vec{\mathbf{0}}+\mathbf{w}}^k \\ \vdots \\ \beta_{\mathbf{A}\vec{\mathbf{1}}+\mathbf{w}}^k \end{pmatrix} \right\|_2 \qquad \text{(Cauchy-Schwartz)}$$

$$= \frac{1}{2} \left\| \begin{pmatrix} \beta_{\mathbf{A}\vec{\mathbf{0}}+\mathbf{w}}^k \\ \vdots \\ \beta_{\mathbf{A}\vec{\mathbf{1}}+\mathbf{w}}^k \end{pmatrix} \right\|_2 \qquad (2^{-n/2}\mathbf{H}^{\otimes n} \text{ is orthonormal})$$

$$\leq \frac{1}{2} \left\| \begin{pmatrix} \beta_{\mathbf{A}\vec{\mathbf{0}}+\mathbf{w}}^k \\ \vdots \\ \beta_{\mathbf{A}\vec{\mathbf{1}}+\mathbf{w}}^k \end{pmatrix} \right\|_1.$$

This concludes the proof.

Balance of Code Cosets. Following Lemma 3.4 from the previous section, in this section we analyze the balance properties of code cosets. Concretely, our goal is to find sufficient conditions to guarantee that no matter how an adversarial receiver decomposes $\mathbf{v}$ into $\mathbf{v}_0 + \mathbf{v}_1 = \mathbf{v}$, it must be that one of the cosets $\mathbf{v}_i + \mathbf{A}$ will be balanced (in which case we can invoke Lemma 3.4).

Step I: In Any Decomposition, One Coset is Somewhat Balanced. Our first step is to show that when $\mathbf{v}$ as chosen at random (as in the CRS), then any sum decomposition $\mathbf{v} = \mathbf{v}_0 + \mathbf{v}_1$ will induce at least one coset $\mathbf{v}_i + \mathbf{A}$ in which all members are *somewhat balanced*. Jumping ahead, this balance alone will not suffice, and our second step will deal with the additional balance properties required.

Definition 3.8. *For all* $\mathbf{A} \in \mathbb{F}_2^{\ell \times n}, \mathbf{v} \in \mathbb{F}_2^\ell$, *we use the (abuse of) notion* $\|\mathbf{A} + \mathbf{v}\|_0$ *to denote the minimal distance between* $\mathbf{v}$ *and the image of* $\mathbf{s} \mapsto \mathbf{As}$, *formally:* $\|\mathbf{A} + \mathbf{v}\|_0 := \min_{\mathbf{s} \in \mathbb{F}_2^n} \|\mathbf{As} + \mathbf{v}\|_0$.

Note that $\|\mathbf{A} + \mathbf{v}\|_0$ satisfies the triangle inequality:

$$\|\mathbf{A} + (\mathbf{v}_0 + \mathbf{v}_1)\|_0 \leq \|\mathbf{A} + \mathbf{v}_0\|_0 + \|\mathbf{A} + \mathbf{v}_1\|_0 .$$

Definition 3.9. *Let* $\mathbf{A} \in \mathbb{F}_2^{\ell \times n}$, $\mathbf{v} \in \mathbb{F}_2^{\ell}$. *We say that* $\mathbf{v}$ *is* $\mathbf{A}$-*balanced for sums if for all* $\mathbf{v}_0, \mathbf{v}_1$ *such that* $\mathbf{v}_0 + \mathbf{v}_1 = \mathbf{v}$, *there exists* $i \in \{0, 1\}$ *such that for all* $\mathbf{s} \in \mathbb{F}_2^n$:

$$\frac{\ell}{5} \leq \|\mathbf{As} + \mathbf{v}_i\|_0 \leq \frac{4\ell}{5} .$$

Proposition 3.10 (A random $\mathbf{v}$ **is** $\mathbf{A}$-**balanced for sums).** *For any* $\mathbf{A} \in \mathbb{F}_2^{\ell \times n}$:

$$\Pr_{\mathbf{v} \leftarrow \mathbb{F}_2^{\ell}} [\mathbf{v} \text{ is } \mathbf{A}\text{-balanced for sums}] \geq 1 - \frac{2^{n+1}}{2^{\Omega(\ell)}} .$$

Proof. Define $\mathbf{A}' := (\mathbf{A}|\vec{\mathbf{1}}) \in \mathbb{F}_2^{\ell \times (n+1)}$. Observe that:

$$\Pr_{\mathbf{v} \leftarrow \mathbb{F}_2^{\ell}} \left[\|\mathbf{A}' + \mathbf{v}\|_0 \geq \frac{2}{5}\ell \right] \geq \Pr_{\mathbf{v} \leftarrow \mathbb{F}_2^{\ell}} \left[\forall \mathbf{s} \in \mathbb{F}_2^{n+1} : \left| \|\mathbf{A}'\mathbf{s} + \mathbf{v}\|_0 - \frac{\ell}{2} \right| \leq \frac{1}{10}\ell \right]$$

$$\geq 1 - \frac{2^{n+1}}{2^{\Omega(\ell)}} ,$$

where the above follows from Lemma 2.3 and the fact that for any $\mathbf{s}$, $\mathbf{A}'\mathbf{s} + \mathbf{v}$ is uniformly random over $\mathbb{F}_2^{\ell}$, as well as a union bound.

Now, for any $\mathbf{v}_0, \mathbf{v}_1 \in \mathbb{F}_2^{\ell}$ such that $\mathbf{v}_0 + \mathbf{v}_1 = \mathbf{v}$, by the triangle inequality,

$$\|\mathbf{A}' + \mathbf{v}\|_0 \geq \frac{2}{5}\ell \implies \exists i \in \{0, 1\} : \|\mathbf{A}' + \mathbf{v}_i\|_0 \geq \frac{1}{5}\ell .$$

Finally, observe that for every $\mathbf{w} \in \mathbb{F}_2^{\ell}$ and $\gamma \leq 1/2$, if $\|\mathbf{A}' + \mathbf{w}\|_0 \geq \gamma\ell$ then $\forall \mathbf{s} \in \mathbb{F}_2^n : \left| \|\mathbf{As} + \mathbf{w}\|_0 - \frac{1}{2}\ell \right| \leq (\frac{1}{2} - \gamma)\ell$. Indeed, for all $\mathbf{s} \in \mathbb{F}_2^{\ell}$:

$$\|\mathbf{As} + \mathbf{w}\|_0 \geq \gamma\ell \implies \gamma\ell - \frac{1}{2}\ell \leq \|\mathbf{As} + \mathbf{w}\|_0 - \frac{1}{2}\ell ,$$

$$\left\|\mathbf{As} + \mathbf{w} + \vec{\mathbf{1}}\right\|_0 \geq \gamma\ell \implies \ell - \|\mathbf{As} + \mathbf{w}\|_0 \geq \gamma\ell \implies \|\mathbf{As} + \mathbf{w}\|_0 - \frac{1}{2}\ell \leq \frac{1}{2}\ell - \gamma\ell .$$

The lemma now follows when setting $\gamma = \frac{1}{5}$.

Step II: Almost All Coset Members Are Well Balanced. The balance property defined above is still not sufficient for meaningfully invoking the statistical distance bound given by Lemma 3.4. Indeed, directly using the bound $\sum_{\mathbf{s} \in \mathbb{F}_2^n} |\beta_{\mathbf{As} + \mathbf{w}}|^k$ given by the lemma would require that the maximum bias β is such that $\beta \ll 2^{-n/k}$. However, in our case, to guarantee correctness $k \approx n/\log n$ and bounding β by a constant is insufficient. Using a more careful analysis, we will prove that in fact, for a random matrix $\mathbf{A}$, it is the case that in all cosets $\mathbf{w} + \mathbf{A}$, almost all members are well (rather than somewhat) balanced, and in particular have maximal bias $\beta \ll 2^{-n/k}$. This will allow using the relatively weak balance property from Step I on a sufficiently small set. We proceed with the relevant definitions and analysis.

Definition 3.11 $((\beta, D)$-**Affine-Balance**$)$. *Let* $\beta \in [0,1]$, $D \in \mathbb{N}$ *and* $\mathbf{A} \in \mathbb{F}_2^{\ell \times n}$. *We say that* $\mathbf{A}$ *is* (β, D)-*affinely-balanced if for all* $\mathbf{w} \in \mathbb{F}_2^{\ell}$ *there exists a set* $E_{\mathbf{w}} \subseteq \mathbb{F}_2^n$ *such that* $|E_{\mathbf{w}}| < D$, *and:*

$$\forall \mathbf{s} \in \mathbb{F}_2^n \setminus E_{\mathbf{w}} : (1 - \beta)\frac{\ell}{2} \le \|\mathbf{A}\mathbf{s} + \mathbf{w}\|_0 \le (1 + \beta)\frac{\ell}{2}$$

We also define (and achieve) a stronger balance property that will be useful for showing bad-CRS certification.

Definition 3.12 $((\beta, d)$-**Strong-Balance**$)$. *Let* $\beta \in [0,1]$, $d \in \mathbb{N}$ *and* $\mathbf{A} \in \mathbb{F}_2^{\ell \times n}$. *We say that* $\mathbf{A}$ *is* (β, d)-*strongly-balanced if for all* $\mathbf{w} \in \mathbb{F}_2^{\ell}$, *and any set of* d **linearly independent** *vectors* $\mathbf{s}_1, ..., \mathbf{s}_d \in \mathbb{F}_2^n$, *there exists some* $i \in [d]$ *such that:*

$$(1 - \beta)\frac{\ell}{2} \le \|\mathbf{A}\mathbf{s}_i + \mathbf{w}\|_0 \le (1 + \beta)\frac{\ell}{2} .$$

Proposition 3.13 (From strong to affine balance). *Any* $\mathbf{A} \in \mathbb{F}_2^{\ell \times n}$ *which is* (β, d)-*strongly-balanced, is also* $(\beta, 2^d)$-*affinely balanced.*

Proof. The proposition follows from the fact that any set of 2^d vectors over $\mathbb{F}_2^n$ contains a set of d linearly independent vectors.

Proposition 3.14. *For* $\beta \ge \ell^{-1/2}$, *a random* $\mathbf{A} \xleftarrow{\$} \mathbb{F}_2^{\ell \times n}$ *is* (β, d)-*strongly-balanced with probability at least:*

$$\Pr_{\mathbf{A} \leftarrow \mathbb{F}_2^{\ell \times n}} [\mathbf{A} \text{ is } (\beta, d) - \text{strongly-balanced}] \ge 1 - 2^{\ell + n \cdot d + 2d - \frac{1}{4} d \beta^2 \ell} .$$

Proof. Assume $\mathbf{A} \xleftarrow{\$} \mathbb{F}_2^{\ell \times n}$. We will bound the probability that $\mathbf{A}$ is not (β, d)-strongly-balanced. This happens when there exists $\mathbf{w} \in \{0,1\}^{\ell}$ and d linearly independent vectors $\mathbf{s}_1, ..., \mathbf{s}_d$ such that $\forall i \in [d] : \left| \|\mathbf{A}\mathbf{s}_i + \mathbf{w}\|_0 - \frac{\ell}{2} \right| > \frac{1}{2}\beta\ell$. We bound the probability that such $\mathbf{w}, \mathbf{s}_1, ..., \mathbf{s}_d$ exist.
First, for any fixed $\mathbf{w} \in \mathbb{F}_2^{\ell}$ and $0 \ne \mathbf{s} \in \mathbb{F}_2^n$ it holds that $\mathbf{A}\mathbf{s} + \mathbf{w}$ is uniformly distributed over $\{0,1\}^{\ell}$, and therefore from Lemma 2.3 we get:

$$\Pr_{\mathbf{A}} \left[\left| \|\mathbf{A}\mathbf{s} + \mathbf{w}\|_0 - \frac{\ell}{2} \right| > \frac{1}{2}\beta\ell \right] \le 2^{-\frac{1}{4}\beta^2\ell} .$$

Similarly, for any fixed $\mathbf{w} \in \mathbb{F}_2^{\ell}$, and any set of d linearly independent vectors $\{\mathbf{s}_1, ..., \mathbf{s}_d\} \subseteq \mathbb{F}_2^n$ it holds that $(\mathbf{A}\mathbf{s}_1 + \mathbf{w}, ..., \mathbf{A}\mathbf{s}_d + \mathbf{w})$ is uniformly distributed over $\{0,1\}^{\ell \times d}$, and independence implies:

$$\Pr_{\mathbf{A}} \left[\forall i \in [d] : \left| \|\mathbf{A}\mathbf{s}_i + \mathbf{w}\|_0 - \frac{\ell}{2} \right| > \frac{1}{2}\beta\ell \right] \le \left(2^{-\frac{1}{4}\beta^2\ell} \right)^d$$

Finally, by the union bound, and the fact that $\binom{m}{k} \le \left(\frac{m \cdot e}{k} \right)^k$,

$$\Pr_{\mathbf{A}} \left[\exists \mathbf{w} \in \{0,1\}^{\ell}, \text{linearly independent } \mathbf{s}_1, ..., \mathbf{s}_d : \forall i \in [d], \left| \|\mathbf{A}\mathbf{s}_i + \mathbf{w}\|_0 - \frac{\ell}{2} \right| > \frac{1}{2}\beta\ell \right]$$

$$\le 2^{\ell} \binom{2^n}{d} \left(2^{-\frac{1}{4}\beta^2\ell} \right)^d \le 2^{\ell + n \cdot d + 2d - \frac{1}{4} d \beta^2 \ell} .$$

Putting Things Together: Statistical Sender Privacy. We are now ready to prove that the protocol is statistically-sender-private. In fact we will prove the stronger property of bad-CRS certifiability.

Proposition 3.15. *The protocol is statistically-sender-private. Moreover, it is bad-CRS certifiable.*

Proof. In what follows, $\delta = 1 + \Theta(1)$, $\ell = n^{1+\frac{1}{\delta}}$ and $k = 4\delta n/\log(n)$ are as previously set in our construction, and $d(n) = n/\log^2(n)$, $\beta(n) = 4\sqrt{n/\ell} = 4n^{-1/(2\delta)}$.

We first define the set of bad CRSs:

$$\mathsf{B} := \bigcup_n \left\{ (\mathbf{A}, \mathbf{v}) \in \mathbb{F}_2^{\ell \times n} \times \mathbb{F}_2^{\ell} \; \middle| \; \begin{array}{l} \mathbf{A} \text{ is } \mathbf{not}(\beta, d)\text{-strongly-balanced} \\ \mathbf{OR}\, \mathbf{v} \text{ is } \mathbf{not}\,\mathbf{A}\text{-balanced for sums} \end{array} \right\} .$$

We next establish each of the three requirements of sender-statistical-privacy with bad CRS certification.

Claim. Sender statistical privacy outside of B is satisfied.

Proof. Fix $(\mathbf{A}, \mathbf{v}) \notin \mathsf{B}$ and any decomposition $\mathbf{v} = \mathbf{v}_0 + \mathbf{v}_1$. Since $\mathbf{v}$ is $\mathbf{A}$-balanced for sums, there exists $i \in \{0, 1\}$ such that for all $\mathbf{s} \in \mathbb{F}_2^n$:

$$\frac{\ell}{5} \leq \|\mathbf{As} + \mathbf{v}_i\|_0 \leq \frac{4\ell}{5} . \tag{1}$$

Let $i \in \{0, 1\}$ be (the minimal) such that the above holds.

$$\text{The extractor } \mathsf{OTExt}(\mathbf{A}, \mathbf{v}, \mathbf{v}_0) \text{ outputs } 1 - i.$$

To conclude the proof, we bound the statistical distance $SD\left((\mathbf{x}^t\mathbf{A}, \mathbf{x}^t\mathbf{v}_i), (\mathbf{x}^t\mathbf{A}, u)\right)$ for $\mathbf{x} \leftarrow \mathcal{X}_{\ell,k}$, $u \leftarrow \mathsf{Bern}\left(\frac{1}{2}\right)$. In what follows, for $\mathbf{t} \in \mathbb{F}_2^{\ell}$ let $\beta_{\mathbf{t}} := 1 - \frac{2}{\ell}\|\mathbf{t}\|_0$. Also, let $E_{\mathbf{v}_i} \subseteq \mathbb{F}_2^n$ be the set given by Definition 3.11, where its existence is guaranteed by Proposition 3.13 and the fact that $\mathbf{A}$ is (β, d)-strongly-balanced.

$$SD\left((\mathbf{x}^t\mathbf{A}, \mathbf{x}^t\mathbf{v}_i), (\mathbf{x}^t\mathbf{A}, u)\right)$$

$$\leq \sum_{\mathbf{s} \in \mathbb{F}_2^n} |\beta_{\mathbf{As}+\mathbf{v}_i}|^k \qquad\qquad\qquad\qquad \text{(By Lemma 3.4)}$$

$$= \sum_{\mathbf{s} \in E_{\mathbf{v}_i}} |\beta_{\mathbf{As}+\mathbf{v}_i}|^k + \sum_{\mathbf{s} \notin E_{\mathbf{v}_i}} |\beta_{\mathbf{As}+\mathbf{v}_i}|^k$$

$$\leq |E_{\mathbf{v}_i}| \cdot \max_{\mathbf{s} \in \mathbb{F}_2^n} |\beta_{\mathbf{As}+\mathbf{v}_i}|^k + 2^n \cdot \max_{\mathbf{s} \notin E_{\mathbf{v}_i}} |\beta_{\mathbf{As}+\mathbf{v}_i}|^k$$

$$\leq 2^d \cdot \max_{\mathbf{s} \in \mathbb{F}_2^n} |\beta_{\mathbf{As}+\mathbf{v}_i}|^k + 2^n \cdot \beta^k \qquad\qquad \text{(By Definition 3.11)}$$

$$\leq 2^d \cdot (3/5)^k + 2^n \cdot \beta^k \qquad\qquad\qquad \text{(By Equation (1))}$$

$$= 2^{\frac{n}{\log^2 n}} \cdot (3/5)^{\frac{4\delta n}{\log n}} + 2^n \cdot (4n^{-1/(2\delta)})^{\frac{4\delta n}{\log n}} \quad \text{(By our parameter setting)}$$

$$= 2^{-\Omega(n/\log n)} + 2^n \cdot 2^{\frac{8\delta n}{\log n} - 2n}$$

$$= 2^{-\Omega(n/\log n)} \ .$$

Claim. B is certifiable.

Proof. $(\mathbf{A}, \mathbf{v}) \in B$ if and only if either one of the following holds:

- **A is not (β, d)-strongly-balanced:** there exist $\mathbf{w} \in \mathbb{F}_2^\ell$ and d linearly independent vectors $\mathbf{s}_1, .., \mathbf{s}_d \in \mathbb{F}_2^n$ such that $\forall i \in [d]$:

$$\left| \|\mathbf{As}_i + \mathbf{w}\|_0 - \frac{\ell}{2} \right| > \beta \frac{\ell}{2} \ .$$

- **v is not A balanced for sums:** there exist $\mathbf{v}_0, \mathbf{v}_1 \in \mathbb{F}_2^\ell$, $\mathbf{s}_0, \mathbf{s}_1 \in \mathbb{F}_2^n$ such that $\mathbf{v} = \mathbf{v}_0 + \mathbf{v}_1$ and for both $i \in \{0, 1\}$:

$$\left| \|\mathbf{As}_i + \mathbf{v}_i\|_0 - \frac{\ell}{2} \right| > \frac{3}{5} \cdot \frac{\ell}{2} \ .$$

Given $(\mathbf{w}, \mathbf{s}_1, .., \mathbf{s}_d)$, respectively $(\mathbf{v}_0, \mathbf{v}_1, \mathbf{s}_0, \mathbf{s}_1)$, the first, respectively the second, condition can be efficiently checked. Hence $B \in \mathbf{NP}$.

Claim. B has negligible density

Proof. By Proposition 3.14,

$$\Pr_{\mathbf{A} \leftarrow \mathbb{F}_2^{\ell \times n}} [\mathbf{A} \text{ is not } (\beta, d)\text{-strongly-balanced}]$$

$$\leq 2^{\ell + n \cdot d + 2d - \frac{1}{4} d \beta^2 \ell}$$

$$= 2^{n^{1+1/\delta} + \frac{n(n+2)}{\log^2 n} - 4 \frac{n^2}{\log^2 n}}$$

$$= 2^{-\Omega(n^2/\log^2 n)} \ .$$

By Lemma 3.10, for every $\mathbf{A} \in \mathbb{F}_2^{\ell \times n}$:

$$\Pr_{\mathbf{v} \leftarrow \mathbb{F}_2^\ell} [\mathbf{v} \text{ is not } \mathbf{A}\text{-balanced for sums}] \leq \frac{2^{n+1}}{2^{\Omega(\ell)}} \leq 2^{-\Omega(n^{1+1/\delta})} \ .$$

Overall, by the union bound,

$$\Pr_{\mathbf{A}, \mathbf{v}} [(\mathbf{A}, \mathbf{v}) \in B] \leq 2^{-\Omega(n^{1+1/\delta})} \ .$$

This concludes the proof of Proposition 3.15.

4 From the CRS Model to the SRS and Plain Models

In this section, we show transformations from the CRS model to the SRS model, and then to the plain model.

4.1   From the CRS Model to the SRS Model

In this section, we show how to transform any two-message SSP OT in the common random string model into one in the sender random string model. Recall that this model is similar to the common random string model, except that receiver privacy holds even for an adversarial (rather than random) choice of the common string. The transformation is based on the idea of reverse randomization from [26] (tracing back to [38]).

In what follows, we denote the original protocol by (S, R) and its CRS length by ρ and construct a new protocol (S', R') with SRS length ρ^2. The transformation is presented in Fig. 2.

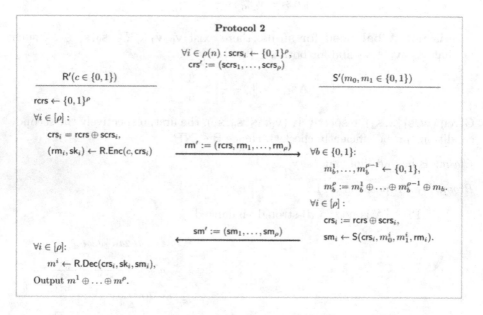

Fig. 2. Two-message statistically-sender-private OT in the SRS model

We prove:

Theorem 4.1. *Assuming (S, R) is a two-message statistically sender-private OT in CRS model, then (S', R') is a two-message statistically sender-private OT in SRS model. Moreover, (S', R') has CRS-free correctness (even if (S, R) does not), and if (S, R) has bad-CRS certification so does (S', R').*

Corollary 4.2. *Under the $LPN_{\log^2(n)}$ assumption, there exists a two-message statistically-sender-private OT protocol in the SRS model. Moreover, the protocol has CRS-free correctness and bad-CRS certification.*

We prove Theorem 4.1 in the full version of the paper [12].

4.2   From the SRS Model to the Plain Model

In this section, we show how to transform any two-message SSP OT in the sender random string model that has CRS-free correctness and bad-CRS certification into one in the plain model. We do this assuming the existence of hitting set generators (HSGs) against co-non-deterministic uniform algorithms, which are in turn known from worst-case uniform assumption commonly used for derandomizing **AM**. Similar (or even stronger) assumptions have become rather common in in the cryptographic literature. (See more details in Sect. 2.2.)

In what follows, we denote the original protocol by (S, R), its CRS length by ρ, and corresponding bad CRS set by B. Let D_B be the co-non-deterministic decider that outputs 0 on every $x \in B$ and 1 on $x \notin B$, and let $t(m) = m^{O(1)}$ be its running time. Also let H be hitting-set generator against co-non-deterministic uniform algorithms. We construct a new protocol (S', R'). The transformation is presented in Fig. 3.

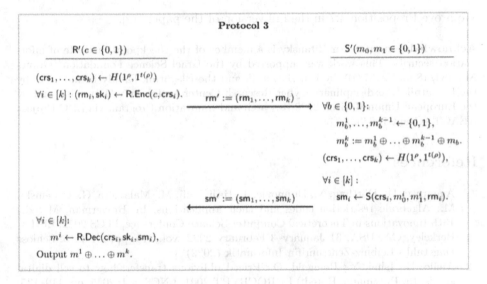

Fig. 3. Two-message statistically-sender-private OT in the plain model

We prove:

Theorem 4.3. *Assuming (S, R) is a two-message statistically sender-private OT in SRS model with CRS-free correctness and bad-CRS certification, then (S', R') is a two-message statistically sender-private OT in plain model.*

Corollary 4.4. *Under the $LPN_{\frac{\log^2(n)}{n}}$ assumption, and the existence of hitting-set generators against co-nondeterministic algorithms, there exists a two-message statistically-sender-private OT protocol in the plain model.*

To prove Theorem 4.3, we prove each of the required properties.

Proposition 4.5. *Protocol* $(\mathsf{S}', \mathsf{R}')$ *is correct.*

Proof. By the CRS-free correctness of the underlying protocol, correctness holds for each crs_i output by the hitting set generator H. It follows that except with negligible probability $n^{-\omega(1)}$ over the coins of $(\mathsf{S}', \mathsf{R}')$, the receiver learns all m_c^i and $m_c = \oplus_i m_c^i$.

Proposition 4.6. *Protocol* $(\mathsf{S}', \mathsf{R}')$ *satisfies receiver privacy.*

Proof. Recall that the underlying protocol is secure in the SRS model, implying that receiver privacy holds for any choice of CRS. In particular, it holds with respect to each crs_i output by H. Receiver privacy follows by a straightforward hybrid argument.

Proposition 4.7. *Protocol* $(\mathsf{S}', \mathsf{R}')$ *is statistically-sender-private.*

We prove Proposition 4.7 in the full version of the paper [12].

Acknowledgements. Nir Bitansky is a member of the checkpoint institute of information security. This work was supported by the Israel Science Foundation (Grants No. 484/18 and 2137/19, by Len Blavatnik and the Blavatnik Family Foundation, by the Blavatnik Interdisciplinary Cyber Research Center at Tel Aviv University, and by the European Union Horizon 2020 Research and Innovation Program via ERC Project REACT (Grant 756482).

References

1. Aggarwal, D., Döttling, N., Dujmovic, J., Hajiabadi, M., Malavolta, G., Obremski, M.: Algebraic restriction codes and their applications. In: Braverman, M (ed.) 13th Innovations in Theoretical Computer Science Conference, ITCS 2022, LIPIcs, Berkeley, CA, USA, 31 January–3 February 2022, vol. 215, pp. 2:1–2:15. Schloss Dagstuhl - Leibniz-Zentrum für Informatik (2022)
2. Aiello, B., Ishai, Y., Reingold, O.: Priced oblivious transfer: how to sell digital goods. In: Pfitzmann, B. (ed.) EUROCRYPT 2001. LNCS, vol. 2045, pp. 119–135. Springer, Heidelberg (2001). https://doi.org/10.1007/3-540-44987-6_8
3. Alekhnovich, M.: More on average case versus approximation complexity. In: Proceedings of 44th Symposium on Foundations of Computer Science (FOCS 2003), Cambridge, MA, USA, 11–14 October 2003, pp. 298–307. IEEE Computer Society (2003)
4. Ananth, P., Jain, A.: On secure two-party computation in three rounds. In: Kalai, Y., Reyzin, L. (eds.) TCC 2017, Part I. LNCS, vol. 10677, pp. 612–644. Springer, Cham (2017). https://doi.org/10.1007/978-3-319-70500-2_21
5. Badrinarayanan, S., Garg, S., Ishai, Y., Sahai, A., Wadia, A.: Two-message witness indistinguishability and secure computation in the plain model from new assumptions. In: Takagi, T., Peyrin, T. (eds.) ASIACRYPT 2017, Part III. LNCS, vol. 10626, pp. 275–303. Springer, Cham (2017). https://doi.org/10.1007/978-3-319-70700-6_10

6. Badrinarayanan, S., Goyal, V., Jain, A., Kalai, Y.T., Khurana, D., Sahai, A.: Promise zero knowledge and its applications to round optimal MPC. In: Shacham, H., Boldyreva, A. (eds.) CRYPTO 2018, Part II. LNCS, vol. 10992, pp. 459–487. Springer, Cham (2018). https://doi.org/10.1007/978-3-319-96881-0_16

7. Badrinarayanan, S., Goyal, V., Jain, A., Khurana, D., Sahai, A.: Round optimal concurrent MPC via strong simulation. In: Kalai, Y., Reyzin, L. (eds.) TCC 2017, Part I. LNCS, vol. 10677, pp. 743–775. Springer, Cham (2017). https://doi.org/10.1007/978-3-319-70500-2_25

8. Ball, M., Dachman-Soled, D., Kulkarni, M., Lin, H., Malkin, T.: Non-malleable codes against bounded polynomial time tampering. In: Ishai, Y., Rijmen, V. (eds.) EUROCRYPT 2019, Part I. LNCS, vol. 11476, pp. 501–530. Springer, Cham (2019). https://doi.org/10.1007/978-3-030-17653-2_17

9. Banaszczyk, W.: New bounds in some transference theorems in the geometry of numbers. Mathematische Annalen **296**(4), 625–636 (1993)

10. Barak, B., Ong, S.J., Vadhan, S.P.: Derandomization in cryptography. SIAM J. Comput. **37**(2), 380–400 (2007)

11. Bartusek, J., Garg, S., Srinivasan, A., Zhang, Y.: Reusable two-round MPC from LPN. IACR Cryptology ePrint Archive, p. 316 (2021)

12. Bitansky, N., Freizeit, S.: Statistically sender-private OT from LPN and derandomization. Cryptology ePrint Archive, Paper 2022/185 (2022). http://eprint.iacr.org/2022/185

13. Bitansky, N., Khurana, D., Paneth, O.: Weak zero-knowledge beyond the black-box barrier. In: Charikar, M., Cohen, E. (eds.) Proceedings of the 51st Annual ACM SIGACT Symposium on Theory of Computing, STOC 2019, Phoenix, AZ, USA, 23–26 June 2019, pp. 1091–1102. ACM (2019)

14. Bitansky, N., Vaikuntanathan, V.: Indistinguishability obfuscation: from approximate to exact. In: Kushilevitz, E., Malkin, T. (eds.) TCC 2016, Part I. LNCS, vol. 9562, pp. 67–95. Springer, Heidelberg (2016). https://doi.org/10.1007/978-3-662-49096-9_4

15. Bitansky, N., Vaikuntanathan, V.: A note on perfect correctness by derandomization. In: Coron, J.-S., Nielsen, J.B. (eds.) EUROCRYPT 2017, Part II. LNCS, vol. 10211, pp. 592–606. Springer, Cham (2017). https://doi.org/10.1007/978-3-319-56614-6_20

16. Blum, A., Furst, M., Kearns, M., Lipton, R.J.: Cryptographic primitives based on hard learning problems. In: Stinson, D.R. (ed.) CRYPTO 1993. LNCS, vol. 773, pp. 278–291. Springer, Heidelberg (1994). https://doi.org/10.1007/3-540-48329-2_24

17. Blum, A., Kalai, A., Wasserman, H.: Noise-tolerant learning, the parity problem, and the statistical query model. J. ACM **50**(4), 506–519 (2003)

18. Brakerski, Z., Döttling, N.: Two-message statistically sender-private OT from LWE. In: Beimel, A., Dziembowski, S. (eds.) TCC 2018, Part II. LNCS, vol. 11240, pp. 370–390. Springer, Cham (2018). https://doi.org/10.1007/978-3-030-03810-6_14

19. Brakerski, Z., Koppula, V., Mour, T.: NIZK from LPN and trapdoor hash via correlation intractability for approximable relations. In: Micciancio, D., Ristenpart, T. (eds.) CRYPTO 2020, Part III. LNCS, vol. 12172, pp. 738–767. Springer, Cham (2020). https://doi.org/10.1007/978-3-030-56877-1_26

20. Brakerski, Z., Langlois, A., Peikert, C., Regev, O., Stehlé, D.: Classical hardness of learning with errors. In: Boneh, D., Roughgarden, T., Feigenbaum, J. (eds.) Symposium on Theory of Computing Conference, STOC 2013, Palo Alto, CA, USA, 1–4 June 2013, pp. 575–584. ACM (2013)

21. Brakerski, Z., Lombardi, A., Segev, G., Vaikuntanathan, V.: Anonymous IBE, leakage resilience and circular security from new assumptions. In: Nielsen, J.B., Rijmen, V. (eds.) EUROCRYPT 2018, Part I. LNCS, vol. 10820, pp. 535–564. Springer, Cham (2018). https://doi.org/10.1007/978-3-319-78381-9_20

22. Brakerski, Z., Lyubashevsky, V., Vaikuntanathan, V., Wichs, D.: Worst-case hardness for LPN and cryptographic hashing via code smoothing. In: Ishai, Y., Rijmen, V. (eds.) EUROCRYPT 2019, Part III. LNCS, vol. 11478, pp. 619–635. Springer, Cham (2019). https://doi.org/10.1007/978-3-030-17659-4_21

23. Brakerski, Z., Vaikuntanathan, V.: Efficient fully homomorphic encryption from (standard) LWE. In: Ostrovsky, R. (ed.) IEEE 52nd Annual Symposium on Foundations of Computer Science, FOCS 2011, Palm Springs, CA, USA, 22–25 October 2011, pp. 97–106. IEEE Computer Society (2011)

24. Döttling, N., Garg, S., Hajiabadi, M., Masny, D., Wichs, D.: Two-round oblivious transfer from CDH or LPN. IACR Cryptology ePrint Archive, p. 414 (2019)

25. Döttling, N., Garg, S., Ishai, Y., Malavolta, G., Mour, T., Ostrovsky, R.: Trapdoor hash functions and their applications. In: Boldyreva, A., Micciancio, D. (eds.) CRYPTO 2019, Part III. LNCS, vol. 11694, pp. 3–32. Springer, Cham (2019). https://doi.org/10.1007/978-3-030-26954-8_1

26. Dwork, C., Naor, M.: Zaps and their applications. In: 41st Annual Symposium on Foundations of Computer Science, FOCS 2000, Redondo Beach, California, USA, 12–14 November 2000, pp. 283–293. IEEE Computer Society (2000)

27. Even, S., Goldreich, O., Lempel, A.: A randomized protocol for signing contracts. Commun. ACM **28**(6), 637–647 (1985)

28. Gentry, C.: Fully homomorphic encryption using ideal lattices. In: Mitzenmacher, M. (ed.) Proceedings of the 41st Annual ACM Symposium on Theory of Computing, STOC 2009, Bethesda, MD, USA, 31 May–2 June 2009, pp. 169–178. ACM (2009)

29. Gutfreund, D., Shaltiel, R., Ta-Shma, A.: Uniform hardness versus randomness tradeoffs for arthur-merlin games. In: 18th Annual IEEE Conference on Computational Complexity (Complexity 2003), Aarhus, Denmark, 7–10 July 2003, pp. 33–47. IEEE Computer Society (2003)

30. Halevi, S., Kalai, Y.T.: Smooth projective hashing and two-message oblivious transfer. J. Cryptol. **25**(1), 158–193 (2012)

31. Hubácek, P., Naor, M., Yogev, E.: The journey from NP to TFNP hardness. In: Papadimitriou, C.H. (ed.) 8th Innovations in Theoretical Computer Science Conference, ITCS 2017. LIPIcs, Berkeley, CA, USA, vol. 67, pp. 60:1–60:21. Schloss Dagstuhl - Leibniz-Zentrum für Informatik (2017)

32. Jain, A., Kalai, Y.T., Khurana, D., Rothblum, R.: Distinguisher-dependent simulation in two rounds and its applications. In: Katz, J., Shacham, H. (eds.) CRYPTO 2017, Part II. LNCS, vol. 10402, pp. 158–189. Springer, Cham (2017). https://doi.org/10.1007/978-3-319-63715-0_6

33. Kalai, Y.T., Khurana, D., Sahai, A.: Statistical witness indistinguishability (and more) in two messages. In: Nielsen, J.B., Rijmen, V. (eds.) EUROCRYPT 2018, Part III. LNCS, vol. 10822, pp. 34–65. Springer, Cham (2018). https://doi.org/10.1007/978-3-319-78372-7_2

34. Katz, J., Shin, J.S., Smith, A.D.: Parallel and concurrent security of the HB and hb^+ protocols. J. Cryptol. **23**(3), 402–421 (2010)

35. Khurana, D.: Round optimal concurrent non-malleability from polynomial hardness. In: Kalai, Y., Reyzin, L. (eds.) TCC 2017, Part II. LNCS, vol. 10678, pp. 139–171. Springer, Cham (2017). https://doi.org/10.1007/978-3-319-70503-3_5

36. Khurana, D., Sahai, A.: How to achieve non-malleability in one or two rounds. In: Umans, C. (ed.) 58th IEEE Annual Symposium on Foundations of Computer Science, FOCS 2017, Berkeley, CA, USA, 15–17 October 2017, pp. 564–575. IEEE Computer Society (2017)

37. Kiltz, E., Pietrzak, K., Cash, D., Jain, A., Venturi, D.: Efficient authentication from hard learning problems. In: Paterson, K.G. (ed.) EUROCRYPT 2011. LNCS, vol. 6632, pp. 7–26. Springer, Heidelberg (2011). https://doi.org/10.1007/978-3-642-20465-4_3

38. Lautemann, C.: BPP and the polynomial hierarchy. Inf. Process. Lett. **17**(4), 215–217 (1983)

39. Matsui, M.: Linear cryptanalysis method for DES cipher. In: Helleseth, T. (ed.) EUROCRYPT 1993. LNCS, vol. 765, pp. 386–397. Springer, Heidelberg (1994). https://doi.org/10.1007/3-540-48285-7_33

40. Miltersen, P.B., Vinodchandran, N.V.: Derandomizing Arthur-Merlin games using hitting sets. In: 40th Annual Symposium on Foundations of Computer Science, FOCS 1999, New York, NY, USA, 17–18 October 1999, pp. 71–80. IEEE Computer Society (1999)

41. Naor, M., Pinkas, B.: Efficient oblivious transfer protocols. In: Rao Kosaraju, S. (ed.) Proceedings of the Twelfth Annual Symposium on Discrete Algorithms, Washington, DC, USA, 7–9 January 2001, pp. 448–457. ACM/SIAM (2001)

42. Ostrovsky, R., Paskin-Cherniavsky, A., Paskin-Cherniavsky, B.: Maliciously circuit-private FHE. In: Garay, J.A., Gennaro, R. (eds.) CRYPTO 2014, Part I. LNCS, vol. 8616, pp. 536–553. Springer, Heidelberg (2014). https://doi.org/10.1007/978-3-662-44371-2_30

43. Peikert, C.: Public-key cryptosystems from the worst-case shortest vector problem: extended abstract. In: Mitzenmacher, M (ed.) Proceedings of the 41st Annual ACM Symposium on Theory of Computing, STOC 2009, Bethesda, MD, USA, 31 May–2 June 2009, pp. 333–342. ACM (2009)

44. Pietrzak, K.: Cryptography from learning parity with noise. In: Bieliková, M., Friedrich, G., Gottlob, G., Katzenbeisser, S., Turán, G. (eds.) SOFSEM 2012. LNCS, vol. 7147, pp. 99–114. Springer, Heidelberg (2012). https://doi.org/10.1007/978-3-642-27660-6_9

45. Rabin, M.O.: How to exchange secrets with oblivious transfer. IACR Cryptology ePrint Archive, p. 187 (2005)

46. Regev, O.: On lattices, learning with errors, random linear codes, and cryptography. In: Gabow, H.N., Fagin, R. (ed.) Proceedings of the 37th Annual ACM Symposium on Theory of Computing, Baltimore, MD, USA, 22–24 May 2005, pp. 84–93. ACM (2005)

47. Yu, Y., Zhang, J.: Smoothing out binary linear codes and worst-case sub-exponential hardness for LPN. In: Malkin, T., Peikert, C. (eds.) CRYPTO 2021, Part III. LNCS, vol. 12827, pp. 473–501. Springer, Cham (2021). https://doi.org/10.1007/978-3-030-84252-9_16

48. Yu, Y., Zhang, J., Weng, J., Guo, C., Li, X.: Collision resistant hashing from learning parity with noise. IACR Cryptology ePrint Archive, p. 1260 (2017)

Constructive Post-Quantum Reductions

Nir Bitansky[1]([✉]), Zvika Brakerski[2], and Yael Tauman Kalai[3,4]

[1] Tel Aviv University, Tel Aviv, Israel
nirbitan@tau.ac.il
[2] Weizmann Institute of Science, Rechovot, Israel
zvika.brakerski@weizmann.ac.il
[3] Microsoft Research, Cambridge, MA, USA
yael@microsoft.com
[4] Massachusetts Institute of Technology, Cambridge, MA, USA

Abstract. Is it possible to convert classical reductions into post-quantum ones? It is customary to argue that while this is problematic in the interactive setting, non-interactive reductions do carry over. However, when considering quantum auxiliary input, this conversion results in a *non-constructive* post-quantum reduction that requires duplicating the quantum auxiliary input, which is in general inefficient or even impossible. This violates the win-win premise of provable cryptography: an attack against a cryptographic primitive should lead to an algorithmic advantage.

We initiate the study of constructive quantum reductions and present positive and negative results for converting large classes of classical reductions to the post-quantum setting in a constructive manner. We show that any non-interactive non-adaptive reduction from assumptions with a polynomial solution space (such as decision assumptions) can be made post-quantum constructive. In contrast, assumptions with super-polynomial solution space (such as general search assumptions) cannot be generally converted.

Along the way, we make several additional contributions:

1. We put forth a framework for reductions (or general interaction) with *stateful* solvers for a computational problem, that may change their internal state between consecutive calls. We show that such solvers can still be utilized. This framework and our results are meaningful even in the classical setting.

2. A consequence of our negative result is that quantum auxiliary input that is useful against a problem with a super-polynomial solution space cannot be generically "restored" post-measurement. This shows that the novel rewinding technique of Chiesa et al. (FOCS 2021) is tight in the sense that it cannot be extended beyond a polynomial measurement space.

1 Introduction

The notion of provable security in cryptography has had a great impact on the field and has become a de-facto gold standard in evaluating the security of cryptographic primitives. A provably secure cryptographic primitive is stated in

A Full Version of This Work Is Available [3].

Y. Dodis and T. Shrimpton (Eds.): CRYPTO 2022, LNCS 13509, pp. 654–683, 2022.
https://doi.org/10.1007/978-3-031-15982-4_22

the form of a computational problem P, whose hardness is related by means of *reduction* to that of another problem Q which is either by itself considered intractable or in turn can be further reduced down the line. The reduction is an algorithm that solves the problem Q provided that it is given access to an algorithm that solves the problem P.

This gives rise to the "win-win principle" which stands as one of the main motivations for using provably secure cryptography. The logic is the following. Either an algorithmic solution for P cannot be found, i.e. the cryptographic primitive P is secure for all intents and purposes, or one can find an algorithmic solution for P which would imply an algorithmic solution for Q, thus contributing to the state of the art in algorithms design. Indeed, cryptographic reductions are the main working tool for the theoretical cryptographer. Numerous reductions between cryptographic primitives are known and hundreds of such reductions are published in the cryptographic literature every year.

The emergence of the quantum era in computing poses a new challenge to provable security and the win-win principle. Many existing reductions in the "pre-quantum" world implicitly or explicitly relied on the P-algorithm being classical. These reductions are thus a-priori invalid when considering quantum algorithms. A central line of investigation in the domain of post-quantum security is thus dedicated to the following question.

To what extent can pre-quantum reductions be ported to the post-quantum setting?

Such conversion may not always be possible. This is particularly a concern when considering *interactive* problems, i.e. ones where the solution to P involves multiple messages being exchanged with the solver algorithm. Indeed, one of the most prominent techniques for proving security in the interactive setting, namely the notion of *rewinding*, does not directly translate to the quantum setting and moreover one can explicitly show cases where pre-quantum reductions exist but post-quantum ones do not. In fact, this property was actually used to construct *proofs of computational quantumness* [5] in which a party proves that it is quantum by succeeding in a task for which there is a classical impossibility result (under computational assumptions). In a nutshell, the reason is that a quantum algorithm may keep a quantum state between rounds of interaction, and this quantum state is measured and thus potentially destroyed in order to produce the next message of interaction. It is therefore not possible to naively "rewind" the interaction back to a previous step as is customary in many classical proofs.

The focus of this work, therefore, is on *non-interactive cryptographic assumptions*. These are problems P whose syntax contains a (randomized) instance generator which generates some instance x, and a verifier that checks whether solutions y are valid (with respect to x or more generally the randomness that was used to generate x). The role of the solver algorithm in this case is simply to take x as input and produce a y that "verifies well" (we avoid getting into the exact formalism at this point).

Contrary to the interactive case, it is customary to postulate (often without proof) that classical reductions to non-interactive cryptographic assumptions carry over straightforwardly to the post-quantum setting since there is no rewinding. There is a simple challenge-response interface that on the face of it "does not care" whether the underlying P-solver is implemented classically or quantumly. This viewpoint, however, is overly simplistic, since the P solver may use *quantum auxiliary input*: a quantum state $|s\rangle$ that is used as a resource for solving P. The state $|s\rangle$ can be the result of some natural process upon which we have no control, or a result of some exhaustive preprocessing, or generated in the course of execution of some protocol. At any rate, the means to produce $|s\rangle$ are often not at our disposal, we just get a copy of the state.

In this case, similarly to the interactive setting, the quantum state is measured whenever the P-solver is called, and therefore, it potentially precludes us from calling the P solver more than once. This issue is often addressed in the literature by noticing that providing many copies of $|s\rangle$ would allow to call the P solver multiple times – namely there exists a quantum state $|s\rangle^{\otimes t}$ that allows to solve Q given access to the P solver. Therefore, the existence of a classical reduction still implies that if Q is intractable *even given arbitrary auxiliary input*, then the same holds for P.

We argue that the aforementioned common "solution" for post-quantum reductions in the presence of quantum auxiliary input is unsatisfactory. First and foremost, this solution violates the win-win principle. While the argument above indeed implies that (some form of) intractability for P follows from (some form of) intractability for Q, it *does not* allow to convert an auxiliary-input algorithm for P into an auxiliary-input algorithm for Q in a constructive manner, since the transformation $|s\rangle \to |s\rangle^{\otimes t}$ is not an efficient one. An additional related concern is the *durability* of such reductions. Namely, that if we wish to execute the reduction more than once (i.e. solve multiple instances of Q) then we need to duplicate the state $|s\rangle$ an a-priori unbounded number of times.

Given this state of affairs, the question we are facing is the following.

To what extent can pre-quantum reductions to non-interactive assumptions be ported to the post-quantum setting constructively and durably?

Naturally, we do not wish to redo decades of cryptographic work in re-proving each result individually. Instead, we would like to identify the broadest class of pre-quantum reductions that can be generically converted into the post-quantum regime, and at the same time characterize the limitations where such generic conversion is not possible. This is the focus of this work, and indeed we show a generic transformation for a very broad class of reductions. Along the way we develop an adversarial model for *stateful* adversaries that may be of interest in its own right, even in the *classical* setting.

1.1 Our Main Results

We prove a general positive result for converting classical reductions into post-quantum ones. In particular we consider *non-adaptive reductions*. In such reductions, the set of queries to the oracle is determined before any query is made. It turns out that an important parameter in our positive as well as our negative result is the size of the *solution space* of the computational problem P ("the cryptographic primitive"). Our positive results apply to cases where the solution space is polynomial.[1] One notable example the case where P is a "decision assumption", namely the P solver is a distinguisher that returns a single bit as output. Another notable example is the case where P is an NP search problem, with unique solutions (e.g., injective one-way functions or unique signatures). An informal result statement follows.

Theorem 1.1 (Positive result, informal). *There exists an efficient transformation for converting any classical non-adaptive black-box reduction from assumption Q to assumption P, where P is a non-interactive assumption with a polynomial solution space, into a* constructive and durable *post-quantum reduction from Q to P.*

We prove a complementary negative result, for the case where P has a large solution space. The negative result relies on the existence of classical indistinguishability obfuscation which is secure against quantum adversaries.

Theorem 1.2 (Negative result, informal). *Assume the existence of postquantum secure indistinguishability obfuscation. Then there exist non-interactive assumptions P, Q, where P has a super-polynomial solution space and the following hold. There exists a classical non-adaptive black-box reduction from assumption Q to assumption P, but there is no such constructive post-quantum reduction.*

As explained above, in order to address the question of constructiveness, we need to develop a new adversarial model and a host of tools to address this question. An account of these intermediate contributions appears in the technical overview below.

1.2 Our Techniques and Additional Contributions

Known approaches fall short of achieving constructiveness and durability since they regard quantum auxiliary input similarly to its classical counterpart, despite the inherent difference of the inability to duplicate or reuse quantum information. We assert that the process of making multiple calls to an algorithm with quantum side information is inherently *stateful*. Namely, the internal state of the "oracle" changes and evolves over time. In this work we put forth a framework for stateful solvers, namely algorithms that change their internal state and thus their behavior over time.

In the post-quantum setting, reductions start from *one-shot* solvers. That is, ones that have an initial state that allows them to provide an answer for a single

---

[1] They in fact apply even if the solution space is polynomial *per instance* (but the space is not the same for all instances), and a certain natural verifiability property is satisfied (see Definition 3.2).

instance of P successfully, but afterwards all bets are off. It seems natural (and, as we show, turns out to be useful) to consider stateful solvers that propagate their P-solving property throughout an execution, we call this property *persistence*. Persistent solvers evolve their state in an arbitrary way subject to being able, at any point in their evolution, to successfully answer a P-query (with some noticeable advantage).

A Framework for Stateful Solvers. Section 3 is dedicated to formally defining the notion of a (potentially stateful) solver and quantifying its success probability in solving a problem P. We accordingly provide definitions for a post-quantum reduction in this setting, and more specifically the notion of a post-quantum black-box reduction. The standard notion of a classical black-box reduction is recovered as a special case of our definition, when specializing to so-called *stateless* P-solvers.

Using our new formalism, the task at hand is to convert a reduction that expects to be interacting with a *stateless* solver, into one that is successful even when given a *one-shot stateful* solver.

One-Shot Solvers Imply Persistent Solvers. One-shot solvers may seem quite useless, since on the face of it they may only successfully respond to a single query. However, our first technical result, in Sect. 4, is that they can in fact be converted generically (but in a non-black-box manner) into persistent solvers. Namely, ones that can answer an *a-priori unbounded* number of queries and maintain roughly the same success probability. The persistent solver has a state of length that is polynomially related to that of the one-shot solver. The running time of the persistent solver increases with each query it is being asked. That is, the time complexity of answering the t-th query scales with $\mathrm{poly}(t)$ for a fixed polynomial. This still ensures that for any polynomial-length sequence of queries, the total time to answer all queries is bounded by a fixed polynomial. The persistent value of the resulting solver (i.e. the value that is maintained for an a-priori unbounded number of times) is itself a random variable that is determined during the conversion process. The expectation of the persistent value is equal to the one-shot value of the solver we start from. (We note that it is inherently impossible to achieve a non-probabilistic behavior, i.e. to ensure a persistent value that is always above some threshold.[2])

Our transformation is an extension of the techniques in the recent work of Chiesa, Ma, Spooner and Zhandry [7], that can be interpreted as showing such a transformation for "public-coin" cryptographic assumptions (ones where the instances are uniformly distributed and the verification requires only the in-

---

[2] To see this, consider the case where the one-shot auxiliary input $|s\rangle$ is a superposition giving weight $\sqrt{1-\varepsilon}$ to a value $|\bot\rangle$ that always makes the P-solver fail, and giving weight $\sqrt{\varepsilon}$ to a state that makes the P-solver perfectly successful. Then, by trace-distance considerations, any processing of $|s\rangle$ must be ε-statistically-indistinguishable from a case where $|s\rangle = |\bot\rangle$. Therefore, with probability at least $1-\varepsilon$ the persistent value will be trivial. Nevertheless, using a Markov argument, if we start from a one-shot solver with a non-negligible advantage, we recover, with a non-negligible probability, a many-shot solver with a non-negligible persistent advantage.

stance and the solution, and not the randomness that was used to generate the instance). It is only in this step that we have the restriction that the solution space of the problem needs to be polynomial, due to limitations of the [7] technique. Our negative result (further discussed below) proves that these limitations are inherent.

The conversion from one-shot to persistent is the only transformation that uses the solver in a non-black-box manner. In the rest of our (positive) results we take a persistent P-solver and a bound on the length of its auxiliary quantum state and only make black-box use of this solver, i.e., provide instances as input and receive solutions as output. We do not further intervene with the evolution of the state between consecutive calls to the solver.

Once we transformed our solver to being persistent, we are guaranteed that we can make multiple P queries, and each one will be answered by a "successful" solver. It may seem that our mission is complete. However, this is far from being the case. While all queries are answered by a successful solver, these solvers may be arbitrarily correlated. For example, thinking about a simple linearity test where a reduction queries $x_1, x_2, x_3 = x_1 \oplus x_2$ and checks whether a linear relation holds. It may be the case that for each query x_i we get a response y_i from an approximately-linear function, and yet the solver "remembers" that x_1, x_2 were previously made as queries, and deliberately fails on $x_1 \oplus x_2$ in the next query. Another example, that will be quite useful to illustrate our transformation is that of the Goldreich-Levin (GL) hardcore bit [12], where queries take the form $(f(x), r_i)$, always with the same $f(x)$, and with additional correlations between the r_i values across different queries. In particular, it may be the case that once a query with some value $f(x)$ has been made, the solver refuses to meaningfully answer any additional queries with the same $f(x)$.[3]

We note that attributing adversarial behavior to the solver is done for purposes of analysis. Our transformation from one-shot to persistent appears quite "innocent" and we do not know whether it can actually generate such pathological behavior that will prevent reductions from running. However, we cannot rule it out and therefore we consider a worst-case adversarial model.

When described in this way, it seems that only very specialized reductions can be carried over to the post quantum setting. For example, ones that employ a strong form of random self reduction when making solver queries. One such case is the search-to-decision reduction for the learning with errors problem [20]. However, as the GL hardcore bit example demonstrates, this doesn't even extend to all search to decision reductions. We must therefore find a new way to utilize stateful solvers. Indeed, the handle that we use is that while the solver may change its behavior adversarially, its adversarial behavior is constrained by the length of the auxiliary state $|s\rangle$ that it uses. We will indeed leverage the fact

---

[3] We note that while the *classical* GL reduction, falls under our umbrella of non-adaptive reductions, in this specific case, it is in fact known how to devise a single-query *quantum* reduction [1]. This, however, does not resolve the question of durability, and more importantly does not provide a general framework for all non-adaptive reductions.

that this state is polynomailly bounded to limit the adversarial powers of the solver and handle more general reductions.

Before moving on to describe our techniques in this context, we notice that while this adversarial model (of black-box access to a persistent solver) emerged as a by-product of our work on quantum reductions, it is nevertheless a valid model in its own right in both the quantum and classical setting. We may consider interacting with an adversary/solver that is *only* guaranteed to be noticeably successful at every point in time but, unlike the standard notion of an "oracle", may change its behavior over time. In our case, we allow the behavior to change arbitrarily, so long that the amount of information carried over between executions is bounded (in our case, by the length of the state, which is polynomially bounded).

Memoryless Persistent Solvers. Our next step, in Sect. 5, is to show that a persistent solver, even with adversarial behavior, can be effectively converted into a more predictable form of solver that we call *memoryless* (note that this is different from our final goal which is to achieve a *stateless* solver). A memoryless solver keeps track of the sequence number of the question it is asked (e.g. it knows that it is now answering query number 4) but it is not allowed to remember any information about the actual content of the previous queries that were made.

We show that a combination of a non-adaptive reduction and a persistent solver induce a memoryless (persistent) solver (more accurately a distribution over memoryless solvers). These memoryless solvers are accessible using a simulator that, given access to the reduction and the original solver, efficiently simulates the interaction of the reduction with the induced memoryless solver, up to inverse-polynomial statistical distance. Note that we require that the reduction is non-adaptive. Namely, its queries to the solver can be arbitrarily correlated (as in the GL case), but the identity of the queries must not depend on the answers to previous queries.

The transformation relies on the fact that the solver has a bounded amount of memory, say ℓ qubit of state that is propagated through the execution. Our strategy is to dazzle the solver with an abundance of i.i.d dummy queries, that are sampled from the marginal distribution of the "real" queries (for example, in the GL case, each dummy query will have the form $(f(x_i), r_i)$ where x_i, r_i are both random). In between the dummy queries, in random locations, we plant our real queries, in random order. We prove that the solver, having only ℓ qubits of state, must answer our real queries as if they were dummy queries. This requires us to develop a proper formalism and to prove a new lemma (Plug-In Lemma) using tools from quantum information theory. See Sect. 9 in Ref. [3] for the full details.

Stateless Solvers at Last. Finally, we show in Sect. 6 that memoryless solvers imply stateless solvers. This is again shown by means of simulation via a similar formalism to the previous result. Recall that a stateless solver must answer all queries according to the same distribution. This transformation again relies on the non-adaptive nature of the reduction, namely on the ability to generate all solver-queries ahead of time. To do this, we notice that we can think of a memoryless solver simply as a sequence of stateless solvers that can be queried one at a time. Therefore, we can consider the induced stateless solver that at every query picks a random solver from this collection and executes it on the query. This indeed will result in a stateless solver. The solving probability of the induced stateless solver is simply the average success probability of solvers in the collection, which is concentrated due to persistence. Moreover, this behavior can be simulated by randomly permuting the *queries*, while still calling the solvers according to their order in the sequence.[4]

This way, asking the queries in a permuted order to the memoryless solver will (almost) mimic the action of sampling a solver from the collection independently for each query. The only reason why this mimic is not perfect is that permuted queries are sampling "without repetition", i.e. none of the solvers in the sequence defined by the memoryless solver will be queried twice, whereas in the ideal strategy we described above, it is possible that the same solver from the sequence will be sampled more than once. We deal with this by making the number of solvers in the sequence so big, that the probability of hitting the same solver twice becomes very small (inversely polynomial for a polynomial of our choice). We simply add to our queries of interest a large number of dummy "0 queries", and perform a random permutation on this extended set of queries.

Putting Things Together. In Sect. 7 we put all of the components together and prove our main positive result, that any classical non-adaptive reduction which relies on a non-interactive polynomial-solution-space assumption can be made post quantum. This requires putting together the components in a careful manner.

The fact that the first step in our transformation was to produce a persistent P, allows us to continue using it even after having solved a Q instance. This means that we can solve additional instances of Q, or use it to solve additional instances of P or any other problem Q' for which a non-adaptive reduction to P exists. In particular, this property implies that our reduction is *durable*.

A Negative Result for Search Assumptions. We show in Sect. 8 that a generic conversion from classical to constructive quantum reductions is not always possible, even for the case of non-adaptive reductions to non-interactive assumptions. In particular, if P is an assumption with a large solution space (intuitively, a search assumption) this may not be possible.

We show our negative result by relying on a recently introduced primitive known as tokenized signatures [2]. These are signature schemes with the standard classical syntax, but for which it is possible to produce a quantum *signature token*. The signature token allows to generate a single classical signature for a message of the signer's choice, but only one such signature can be created. Tokenized signatures have been constructed relative to a classical oracle [2] or based on cryptographic assumptions [8].

---

[4] Remember that we have access to the memoryless solver which only allows to make queries in order.

We can define an "assumption" which is essentially the task of signing a random message using a tokenized signature scheme.[5] In the classical world, there is a trivial reduction between the task of signing one random message and the task of signing two random messages. However, if we consider a quantum solver that holds the token as auxiliary input, then by definition it should not be possible to use it to obtain two signatures for two different messages. Our negative result holds for any conversion process that is constructive, and in particular does not obtain any implicit non-uniform advice about the assumption.

1.3 Other Related Work

The question of which reductions can be translated from the classical to the post-quantum setting also received significant attention in the context of the random-oracle model (ROM), starting from the work of Boneh et al. [4]. The question asked in these works is whether it is possible to convert reductions in the classical ROM into ones the quantum ROM (QROM, where the adversary is allowed to make quantum queries to the oracle). There are several results proving that specific schemes that are secure in the ROM are also secure in the QROM [10,11,14–17,21,23,24]. Recently, a more general "lifting theorem" was given in [22], showing how to convert a proof in the ROM to one in the QROM for any "search-type game" where a challenger makes only a *constant* number of queries to the random oracle. This work also presented a negative result, showing that there are schemes that are secure in the ROM yet are insecure in the QROM. While the general motivation in these works is similar to ours, the question they ask is quite different from ours. In the ROM/QROM, the solver is allowed to make queries to the oracle (which is simulated by the reduction), which is more similar to the setting where interactive-assumptions are used.

Our memoryless transformation (Sect. 5) relies heavily on the state of the solver being bounded in length. The idea that bounded quantum memory can be used to restrict an otherwise all powerful adversary is at the core of the bounded quantum storage model. It can be shown (see, e.g., [9]) that it is possible to achieve cryptographic abilities against strong adversaries while relying only on a limit on the amount of quantum storage they can use. This setting is quite different from ours, though, since the quantum bounded storage model allows an unbounded amount of classical memory, which in our setting would make it impossible to achieve any result. Indeed, the bounded storage model requires quantum communication (whereas our reduction-solver communication is completely classical), and thus the set of tools and techniques that are used in both settings are completely different.

---

[5] The assumption is instantiated by a verification key which we can think of as non-uniformity of the assumption, see discussion in Sect. 8.

2   Preliminaries and Tools

We say that a given function $f(x_1, \ldots, x_k)$ is $\text{poly}(x_1, \ldots, x_k)$, if there exist constants c, C such that $(x_1 \cdot x_2 \cdot \ldots \cdot x_k)^c \leq f \leq (x_1 \cdot x_2 \cdot \ldots \cdot x_k)^C$.

We denote by TD the trace distance between two matrices.

Algorithms. By default, when referring to an *algorithm* we mean a classical probabilistic (resp. quantum) algorithm. Algorithms may be uniform or non-uniform, meaning that they have *classical* advice related to the input size (we specify when uniformity matters). An *efficient* algorithm is also polynomial time.

Quantum Notation. We use standard quantum information in Dirac notation. We denote quantum variables in boldface $\boldsymbol{x}$ and classical variables in lowercase x. The density matrix of $\boldsymbol{x}$ is denoted $\rho_{\boldsymbol{x}}$. Classical variables may also have (diagonal) density matrices. Quantum variables $\boldsymbol{x}, \boldsymbol{y}$ have a joint density matrix $\rho_{\boldsymbol{x},\boldsymbol{y}}$ if they can be jointly produced by an experiment. As usual, $\boldsymbol{x}, \boldsymbol{y}$ are independent if $\rho_{\boldsymbol{x},\boldsymbol{y}} = \rho_{\boldsymbol{x}} \otimes \rho_{\boldsymbol{y}}$. We never assume that quantum variables are independent unless we explicitly say so. Quantum registers are denoted in capital letters. We also sometimes use capital letters to denote distributions, where it is clear from the context. For a finite Hilbert space $\mathcal{H}$ we denote by $\mathbf{S}(\mathcal{H})$ the set of density matrices over quantum states in $\mathcal{H}$.

A quantum procedure is a general quantum algorithm that can apply unitaries, append ancilla registers in 0 state, perform measurements in the computational basis and trace out registers. The complexity of F is the number of *local* operations it performs (say, operations on up to 3 qubits are considered local). If F is a quantum procedure then we denote by $F(\boldsymbol{x})$ the application of F on $\boldsymbol{x}$. Any unitary induces a quantum procedure that implements this unitary, which does not perform measurements or trace out registers, we call this procedure "a unitary quantum circuit".

Purification of Quantum Procedures and States. A quantum procedure may introduce new ancilla qubits, perform intermediate measurement throughout its computation and discard registers or parts thereof. However, any quantum procedure can be *purified* into unitary form without much loss in complexity [19]. This is formally stated below.

Proposition 2.1. *Let C be a general quantum procedure of complexity s. Then it is possible to efficiently generate a* unitary *quantum circuit $\widehat{C}$ of size $O(s)$, such that for any quantum state $(\boldsymbol{x}, \boldsymbol{a})$, setting $(\boldsymbol{y}, \boldsymbol{z}) = \widehat{C}(\boldsymbol{x}, \boldsymbol{0})$, it holds that $(\boldsymbol{y}, \boldsymbol{a})$ has identical density matrix to $(C(\boldsymbol{x}), \boldsymbol{a})$.*

Likewise, any quantum state can be viewed as a reduced density matrix of the output of a unitary (which may be inefficient to implement).

Proposition 2.2. *Let $\boldsymbol{x}$ be a variable with density matrix $\rho_{\boldsymbol{x}}$. Then there exists a unitary U over registers XY such that applying $U(\boldsymbol{0}, \boldsymbol{0})$, the reduced density matrix of the value in the X register has density matrix $\rho_{\boldsymbol{x}}$.*

2.1   The Plug-In Lemma

The following lemma is another manifestation of information incompressibility in the quantum setting. Specifically, we are interested in an experiment in which an all powerful compressing procedure attempts to compress t samples which are arbitrarily distributed into ℓ quantum bits. We show that this is infeasible even in the weak sense in which a decoder receives the compressed value, and a $(j - 1)$-prefix of the sequence, and is required to identify the j-th element. We show that as t increases, the probability of succeeding in the experiment drops. A formal statement follows.

Lemma 2.3 (Plug-In Lemma). *Let $\vec{Y} = (Y_1, \ldots, Y_t)$ be a joint distribution over t classical random variables. Let $\vec{y}$ be distributed according to $\vec{Y}$. Let s be an ℓ-qubit random variable that has arbitrary dependence on $\vec{y}$. We let $\vec{y}_i$ denote the prefix $\vec{y}_i = (y_1, \ldots, y_i)$ for $1 \leq i \leq t$, and $\vec{y}_0$ is the empty vector (and likewise for $\vec{Y}$). Let J be the uniform distribution over $[t]$ and let $j \leftarrow J$. Define $y' \leftarrow Y_j | (\vec{Y}_{j-1} = \vec{y}_{j-1})$. Then it holds that*

$$\mathrm{TD}((j, \vec{y}_{j-1}, y_j, s), (j, \vec{y}_{j-1}, y', s)) \leq \sqrt{\ell / (2t)} . \tag{1}$$

Note that the above two distributions are *not* identical even though $(j, \vec{y}_{j-1}, y_j)$ and $(j, \vec{y}_{j-1}, y')$ are identically distributed. The reason is that in both cases, s is always generated as a function of $\vec{y}$, i.e. using y_j and not y'_j.

The lemma is proven in the full version of this paper [3].

3   Assumptions, Stateful Solvers, and Reductions

In this section, we formally define the concepts of non-interactive cryptographic assumptions, stateful solvers, and their value and advantage in breaking an assumption.

3.1   Non-Interactive Assumptions

We define the notion of a non-interactive (falsifiable) cryptographic assumption as in [13,18]. While we frame the notion as "cryptographic", it can be viewed more generally as a notion for average-case problems where the solution can be verified.

Definition 3.1 (Non-Interactive Assumption). *A non-interactive assumption is associated with polynomials $d(\lambda), n(\lambda), m(\lambda)$ and a tuple $P = (G, V, c)$ with the following syntax. The generator G takes as input 1^λ and $r \in \{0,1\}^d$, it returns $x \in \{0,1\}^n$. The verifier V takes as input 1^λ and $(r, y) \in \{0,1\}^d \times \{0,1\}^m$ and returns a single bit output. (Both G and V are deterministic.) $c(\lambda)$ is the assumption's threshold.*

We say that P is falsifiable if G, V are uniform polynomial-time algorithms (in their input size).

We also define a property called *verifiably-polynomial image* that roughly speaking requires that any instance has at most polynomial many solutions and that this can be verified in some weak sense. The property in particular captures problems where the solution space $\{0,1\}^m$ is of polynomial size such as decision problems (where $m = 1$), and problems in NP where there are a few solutions per instance (such as injective one-way functions).

Definition 3.2 (Verifiably-Polynomial Image). *A non-interactive assumption P has a* verifiably-polynomial image *if there exists an efficient verifier K and a polynomial $k = \mathrm{poly}(\lambda)$, such that for any instance $x \in \{0,1\}^n$, the set $Y_x := \{y : K(1^\lambda, x, y) = 1\}$ of K-valid solutions is of size at most k and for any valid instance $x = G(1^\lambda, r)$ and solution y such that $V(1^\lambda, r, y) = 1$, it holds that $y \in Y_x$.*

The traditional notion of the advantage in solving an assumption P is measured in terms of the distance between the solving probability (which we term the value) and the threshold c.

Definition 3.3 (Value and Advantage of Classical Functions). *Let $P = (G, V, C)$ be a non-interactive assumption and let $f = \{\, f_\lambda : \{0,1\}^n \to \{0,1\}^m \,\}_\lambda$ be a family of (possibly randomized) functions. For every $\lambda \in \mathbb{N}$, we define the corresponding value and advantage:*

$$\mathsf{val}_P[f](\lambda) := \Pr\left[V(1^\lambda, r, y) = 1 \,\middle|\, \begin{array}{l} r \leftarrow \{0,1\}^d \\ x = G(1^\lambda, r) \\ y \leftarrow f_\lambda(x) \end{array} \right], \mathsf{a}_P[f](\lambda) := |\mathsf{val}_P[f](\lambda) - c(\lambda)| \ ,$$

where the probability is also above the randomness of f_λ in case it is randomized.

3.2 Stateful Solvers

The premise of our work is that in the quantum setting, one ought to think about *stateful* solvers, which generalizes the standard treatment of a solver as a one-shot algorithm. We now define this formally.

Definition 3.4 (Stateful Solvers: Syntax). *Let P be a non-interactive assumption.*

Let $\ell = \ell(\lambda)$ be a function. A classical (resp. quantum) ℓ-stateful solver $\mathcal{B} = (B, \mathsf{state}_0 = \{\mathsf{state}_{\lambda,0}\}_\lambda)$ is defined as follows.

- *B is a classical (resp. quantum) algorithm that takes as input 1^λ, 1^t, $x \in \{0,1\}^n$ and state which is an ℓ-bit (resp. qubit) string, and outputs a value $y \in \{0,1\}^m$ and state' which is an ℓ-bit (resp. qubit) next-state. We let $B(\cdots)_\mathsf{v}$ denote the y output and $B(\cdots)_\mathsf{ot}$ denote the state' output.*
- *$\mathsf{state}_0 = \{\mathsf{state}_{\lambda,0}\}_\lambda$ is a sequence of classical (resp. quantum) states consisting of $\ell = \ell(\lambda)$ bits (resp. qubits).*

We say that $\mathcal{B}$ is efficient if B runs in time $\mathrm{poly}(\lambda, t, n)$; i.e., in polynomial time in the lengths of its inputs.

Remark 3.5 (Non-uniformity). The algorithm B may have a non-uniform classical advice. It does not have any additional quantum advice.

Remark 3.6 (Dependence on Runtime). Our definition allows the running time of efficient stateful solvers to depend polynomially on the "iteration" t. In particular, for any polynomial number of solving attempts $t = \text{poly}(\lambda)$, the overall running of the solver is polynomial. One could also consider a more stringent definition that requires that each call runs in fixed polynomial time independently of the iteration number t. Jumping forward, we will show how a solver can preserve its solving ability through time, but at the cost of running for longer in each step. Doing this according to the more stringent time-independent definition remains an open question.

It will be useful to define some properties of solvers with respect to an extension of the sovler's execution transcript. The extension corresponds to the would-be transcript of a purified version of the solver, running on a purified version of the initial state. This will allow us to get a precise well-defined handle on the evolution of quantum states throughout the lifetime of the solver. The extended transcript will only be used for purposes of definition and analysis and will never be required algorithmically.

Definition 3.7 (Stateful Solvers: Purifying Values). *Consider a solver* $\mathcal{B} = (B, \text{state}_0 = \{\text{state}_{\lambda,0}\}_\lambda)$. *Let* $B_{\lambda,t,x}$ *denote the quantum procedure that takes* s *as input and produces* $B(1^\lambda, 1^t, x, s)$ *over registers* SY. *By Proposition 2.1, we can consider its purification* $\widehat{B}_{\lambda,t,x}$ *which acts on registers* $SY\widehat{Y}$ *and takes as input* $(s, 0, 0)$. *Then define* $\widehat{B}(1^\lambda, 1^t, x, s)$ *as the algorithm that computes* $(s', y, \hat{y}) = \widehat{B}_{\lambda,t,x}(s, 0, 0)$, *measures* $(y, \hat{y})$ *in the computational basis to obtain* $(y, \hat{y})$, *and then outputs* s' *as the* state *output,* y *as the solution output, and* $\hat{y}$ *as the* purifying *output.*

In addition, by Proposition 2.2, there exists a (possibly inefficient) unitary $\widehat{B}_{0,\lambda}$ *that operates on two registers* $S\widehat{Y}$ *such that when applying* $(s_0, \hat{y}_0) \leftarrow \widehat{B}_{0,\lambda}(0, 0)$, *the reduced density matrix of* s_0 *is identical to that of* state$_0$. *Then define* $\widehat{B}_0(1^\lambda)$ *as the quantum procedure that computes* $(s_0, \hat{y}_0) \leftarrow \widehat{B}_{0,\lambda}(0, 0)$, *measures* $\hat{y}_0$ *in the computational basis, and then outputs* s_0 *as* state$_0$ *and* $\hat{y}_0$ *as the* purifying initial value.

We refer to the collection $\widehat{\mathcal{B}} = \{\widehat{B}_{i,\lambda,x}\}$ *as a* purification *of* $\mathcal{B}$ *(it is not unique).*

Remark 3.8. We note that the purifying values can be arbitrarily long. These values will only be used for analysis purposes and are never produced in an actual execution, and hence we do not require any bound whatsoever on the length of the purifying values or the complexity of producing them.

We now define the concept of a *solver interaction*, which captures the process of repeatedly invoking a stateful solver by a given algorithm.

Definition 3.9 (Solver Interaction). *Let $P = (G, V, c)$ be a non-interactive assumption. For any stateful solver $\mathcal{B} = (B, \mathsf{state}_0)$ and corresponding purification $\widehat{\mathcal{B}}$, and any algorithm A with input $z \in \{0,1\}^*$, we consider the process $A^{\mathcal{B}}(1^\lambda, z)$ of the algorithm interacting with the solver. We define this process in two different yet equivalent manners: one which is efficient given the ability to execute B, and one which may be inefficient but implies an identical output distribution. The latter will include a production of all purifying values (Definition 3.7) which will be useful for definitions and analysis.*

- *We let state_0 be as defined in $\mathcal{B}$.*
  Equivalently: We let $(\mathsf{state}_0, \hat{y}) \leftarrow \widehat{B}_0(1^\lambda)$.
- *A is invoked on input $(1^\lambda, z)$ and at every step $i \geq 1$:*
  1. *A submits a query $x_i \in \{0,1\}^n$.*
  2. *$(y_i, \mathsf{state}_i) \leftarrow B(1^\lambda, 1^i, x_i, \mathsf{state}_{i-1})$ is invoked.*
     Equivalently: $(\hat{y}_i, y_i, \mathsf{state}_i) \leftarrow \widehat{B}(1^\lambda, 1^i, x_i, \mathsf{state}_{i-1})$ is invoked.
  3. *A obtains y_i, and proceeds to the next step.*
- *At the end of the interaction A may produce an output w.*

We sometimes refer to A as a solver-aided *algorithm and use the shorthand $A_z^{\mathcal{B}}$ for the solver interaction and $A_z^{\widehat{\mathcal{B}}}$ for the purified solver interaction. We refer to the random variables $\mathsf{state}_0, \mathsf{state}_1, \mathsf{state}_2, \ldots$ as the state random variables of the interaction. We refer to the list of pairs of generated instances and solutions (x_i, y_i) as the transcript of the interaction and denote it by ts. We also define the* extended transcript $\widehat{\mathsf{ts}}$ *of the execution as consisting of the value $\hat{y}_0$ followed by a list to triples $(x_i, y_i, \hat{y}_i)$. Given an extended transcript $\widehat{\mathsf{ts}}$, we can produce the standard transcript ts by removing all purifying values. We call this action* redaction *and say that ts is the redacted transcript induced by $\widehat{\mathsf{ts}}$. Generating an extended transcript according to the purified solver interaction $A_z^{\widehat{\mathcal{B}}}$ and redacting it produces an identical distribution to the generation of the redacted transcript by direct interaction $A_z^{\mathcal{B}}$. The length of a transcript/extended-transcript is the number of pairs/triples it contains (this means that an extended transcript of length 0 is not empty since it still contains $\hat{y}_0$. The i-prefix of a transcript/extended-transcript is denoted $\mathsf{ts}_i/\widehat{\mathsf{ts}}_i$ and contains the first i pairs/triples (and also $\hat{y}_0$ in the extended case).*

We show that the purifying values indeed purify the entire solver interaction, in the sense that they determine all states state_i as pure states for any solver interaction.

Proposition 3.10. *Let $\mathcal{B} = (B, \mathsf{state}_0)$ be a solver with purification $\widehat{\mathcal{B}}$ and consider the extended transcript $\widehat{\mathsf{ts}}$ of the solver interaction $A_z^{\widehat{\mathcal{B}}}$ and let t be its length. Then for all $i \leq t$, the state state_i is pure conditioned on $\widehat{\mathsf{ts}}_i$. Specifically, it has density matrix $|s_{\widehat{\mathsf{ts}}_i}\rangle\langle s_{\widehat{\mathsf{ts}}_i}|$ that is completely determined by $\widehat{\mathsf{ts}}_i$ (and therefore by the classical string $\widehat{\mathsf{ts}}$) and does not depend on any other parameter of the execution.*

Proof. We consider the purifying description of the solver interaction $A_z^{\widehat{B}}$ and prove by induction. For $t = 0$, we recall that the pair $(\text{state}_0, \hat{y})$ is generated by applying $\widehat{B}_{0,\lambda}$ on the zero state, followed by measuring the $\hat{Y}$ register. The pre-measurement state over registers $S\hat{Y}$ is therefore pure, and can always be written as

$$\sum_{\hat{y}} \alpha_{\hat{y}} |s_{\hat{y}}\rangle_S \otimes |\hat{y}\rangle_{\hat{Y}} , \tag{2}$$

where $\alpha_{\hat{y}}$ are non-negative real values with $\sum_{\hat{y}} \alpha_{\hat{y}}^2 = 1$, and $|s_{\hat{y}}\rangle$ are fully specified unit vectors. Therefore, post-selecting on having measured the value $\hat{y}_0$ in register $\hat{Y}$, we have that the state in register S is exactly $\text{state}_0 = |s_{\hat{y}_0}\rangle\langle s_{\hat{y}_0}|$, which completes the base step of the proof.

Now assume that the above holds for all $i < t$. Consider a transcript $\widehat{\text{ts}}$ of length t s.t. $\widehat{\text{ts}} = \widehat{\text{ts}}_{t-1} \| (x, y, \hat{y})$ for some $\widehat{\text{ts}}_{t-1}, x, y, \hat{y}$.

Let us consider the state of the system right before the t-th query to the solver. At this point, $\widehat{\text{ts}}_{t-1}$ was already determined, and thus by induction we know that $\text{state}_{t-1} = |s_{\widehat{\text{ts}}_{t-1}}\rangle\langle s_{\widehat{\text{ts}}_{t-1}}|$ is a pure state. At this point x has also been determined.

By definition, state_t is produced by executing a unitary $\widehat{B}_{\lambda,t,x}$ (that acts on registers $SY\hat{Y}$) on $(\text{state}_{t-1}, \mathbf{0}, \mathbf{0})$, which is pure by the induction hypothesis, and measuring the $Y\hat{Y}$ registers. The analysis here is similar to the base case. The pre-measurement state is pure (since it is induced by applying a unitary on a pure state) and thus can always be written as

$$\sum_{y,\hat{y}} \alpha_{y,\hat{y}} |s_{y,\hat{y}}\rangle_S \otimes |y,\hat{y}\rangle_{Y\hat{Y}} , \tag{3}$$

and as above α_y are non-negative real values with $\sum_y \alpha_y^2 = 1$, and $|s_{y,\hat{y}}\rangle$ are fully specified unit vectors. Post selecting on $y, \hat{y}$ leaves us with register S containing $\text{state}_t = |s_{y,\hat{y}}\rangle\langle s_{y,\hat{y}}|$, which completes the proof.

We are now ready to define the concepts of value and advantage of stateful solvers. Traditionally, when thinking about stateless solvers, we consider their *one shot value*, namely the probability that they solve the problem on a random instance. Since they are stateless this probability does not change over time. In the case of stateful solvers, this probability may change over time. Our definition of the *many shot values* aims to capture exactly this. For any solver interaction $A_z^{\mathcal{B}}$, the value at time t, captures the probability that the solver $\mathcal{B}$ successfully solves a random instance at this time, after a given t-round interaction with A_z. This value is, in fact, a random variable that depends on the history of the interaction. To make this precise, we consider any purification $\widehat{\mathcal{B}}$, and define these values as a function of the extended transcript.

Definition 3.11 (Stateful Solvers: Value and Advantage). *Let P be a non-interactive assumption, $\mathcal{B} = (B, \text{state}_0)$ be a corresponding stateful solver, $\widehat{\mathcal{B}}$ a corresponding purification, and A a solver-aided algorithm with input z. For* *every* $\lambda, i \in \mathbb{N}$, *let* state_i *be the* i-*th pure state random variable of the solver interaction* $A_z^{\widehat{\mathcal{B}}}$ *(determined by* $\widehat{\text{ts}}_i$*). The corresponding value random variables are:*

$$\text{val}_P[i, A_z^{\widehat{\mathcal{B}}}](\lambda) := \Pr \left[V(1^\lambda, r, y) = 1 \,\middle|\, \begin{array}{c} r \leftarrow \{0,1\}^d \\ x = G(1^\lambda, r) \\ (\hat{y}_{i+1}, y, \text{state}_{i+1}) \leftarrow \widehat{B}(1^\lambda, 1^i, x, \text{state}_i) \end{array} \right],$$

where the probability is over the choice of r *and the measurement of* $\hat{y}_{i+1}, y$.

The one-shot value of $\mathcal{B}$ *is*

$$\text{val}_P[0, \mathcal{B}](\lambda) := \Pr \left[V(1^\lambda, r, y) = 1 \,\middle|\, \begin{array}{c} r \leftarrow \{0,1\}^d \\ x = G(1^\lambda, r) \\ (y, \text{state}_1) \leftarrow B(1^\lambda, x, \text{state}_0) \end{array} \right],$$

where the probability is over the choice of r, *measurements of* B, *and (the possibly mixed)* state_0. *Note that this is in fact a number, independent of any* A *or the choice of purification* $\widehat{\mathcal{B}}$.

The corresponding advantage random variables are:

$$\mathsf{a}_P[i, A_z^{\widehat{\mathcal{B}}}](\lambda) := \left| \text{val}_P[i, A_z^{\widehat{\mathcal{B}}}](\lambda) - c(\lambda) \right| \qquad \mathsf{a}_P[0, \mathcal{B}](\lambda) := \left| \text{val}_P[0, \mathcal{B}](\lambda) - c(\lambda) \right|.$$

For a distribution $\mathbb{B}$ *on solvers* $\{\mathcal{B}_\alpha\}_\alpha$, *we define the one-shot value of the distribution as:*

$$\text{val}_P[0, \mathbb{B}](\lambda) = \mathbb{E}_{\alpha \leftarrow \mathbb{B}}[\text{val}_P[0, \mathcal{B}_\alpha](\lambda)].$$

The corresponding advantage is $\mathsf{a}_P[0, \mathbb{B}](\lambda) = |c(\lambda) - \text{val}_P[0, \mathbb{B}](\lambda)|$.

As the solver's state evolves over time, its advantage in solving an assumption may reduce or disappear altogether. This is in particular relevant to the quantum setting, where when a solver is invoked its internal state is disturbed. Aiming to capture solvers that remain useful over time, we next define the notion of solvers with *persistent value*, namely, solvers whose value in solving a given assumption is preserved through time. We define it more generally for distributions over solvers; single solvers are a special case.

Definition 3.12 (Persistent Value). *Let* P *be a non-interactive assumption. A distribution* $\mathbb{B}$ *on solvers* $\{\mathcal{B}_\alpha\}_\alpha$ *is* η-*persistent if there exist purifications* $\{\widehat{\mathcal{B}}_\alpha\}_\alpha$ *such that for any algorithm* A *with input* z, *with probability* $1 - \eta$ *over the choice of solver* $\alpha \leftarrow \mathbb{B}$ *and over an extended transcript* $\widehat{\text{ts}}$ *in the solver interaction process* $A_z^{\widehat{\mathcal{B}}_\alpha}$, *there exists a value* p *such that:*

$$\max_i \left| \text{val}_P[i, A_z^{\widehat{\mathcal{B}}_\alpha}] - p \right| \leq \eta. \tag{4}$$

We call p *a persistent value. Given a random variable* $p^*(\alpha) \subseteq [0,1]$, *we say that a solver distribution is* (p^*, η)-*persistent if the condition holds for* $p^*(\alpha)$.

We next define the notion of a persistent advantage. This aims to capture the case that solvers maintain a lower bound on their advantage through time.

Definition 3.13 (Persistent Advantage). *Let P be a non-interactive assumption with threshold c. A distribution $\mathbb{B}$ on solvers $\{\mathcal{B}_\alpha\}_\alpha$ has ε-persistent advantage if there exist purifications $\{\widehat{\mathcal{B}}_\alpha\}_\alpha$ such that for any algorithm A with input z:*

$$\mathbb{E}\left[\min_i \mathsf{val}_P[i, A_z^{\widehat{\mathcal{B}}_\alpha}]\right] \geq c + \varepsilon , \tag{5}$$

where the expectation is over the choice of solver $\alpha \leftarrow \mathbb{B}$ and over an extended transcript $\widehat{\mathsf{ts}}$ in the solver interaction process $A_z^{\widehat{\mathcal{B}}_\alpha}$.

In the above, We require that the advantage has a consistent sign (for simplicity, positive). Intuitively, the reason we focus on persistence of the positive advantage $v_t - c$ at time t, rather than the absolute advantage $|v_t - c|$, is that if the sign of $v_t - c$ arbitrarily changes after each solver invocation, then the solver may not be as useful. (As a simple example, take a deterministic distinguisher and turn it into a stateful distinguisher that flips the output of the original distinguisher at random with each invocation, deeming it useless.) We note that η persistent solvers in particular preserve the sign of their advantage (up to η).

Memoryless and Stateless Solvers. A special case of the above definitions is that of *memoryless and stateless solvers*.

Definition 3.14. *A solver $\mathcal{B} = (B, \mathsf{state}_0)$ is memoryless if the size of its state is $\ell = 0$. The solver is stateless if in addition (to being memoryless), the algorithm B does not depend on 1^t (in functionality or runtime).*

Remark 3.15 (Persistent Value for Stateless and Memoryless Solvers). Note that in the case of stateless solvers, successive invocations of the solver will always result in the same output distribution. Here the one-shot (and many-shot) advantage coincide with the standard notion of advantage for functions (Definition 3.3) and values are persistent (Definition 3.12). Accordingly, stateless solvers exactly capture the traditional notion of classical solvers, given by a randomized function.

Moreover, even for memoryless solvers, when considering the definition of persistent solvers the value $\mathsf{val}_P[i, A_z^{\widehat{\mathcal{B}}}]$ does not depend on A_z at all (only on i), and therefore it is a fixed number rather than a random variable. It follows that for (p, η)-persistent memoryless solvers, Eq. (4) holds with probability 1.

3.3 Reductions

We now define the notion of a reduction. A reduction is a way to prove a claim of the form "if there exists a successful solver for assumption P then there exists a successful solver for an assumption Q". We consider *constructive reductions* in the sense that they are an explicit uniform algorithm that takes as input a successful solver for P and efficiently solves the problem Q.

The default notion of a reduction in the literature is *one shot*. In pparticular, a given quantum P-solver is only assumed to have a meaningful one-shot advantage in solving P, and there is no a priori guarantee on its advantage in any many shot solving process, in particular there may not be any value persistence. Likewise, the produced solver for the assumption Q is only required to have a meaningful one-shot advantage. Below we define both the default notion of one-shot reductions as well as the stronger notion of *durable reductions* requiring that the resulting Q-solver also has persistent advantage, meaning that with noticeable probability, the reduction can go on solving for an arbitrary polynomial number of times.

Definition 3.16 *(Reduction). A reduction from classically (resp. quantumly) solving a non-interactive assumption Q to classically (resp. quantumly) solving a non-interactive assumption P is an efficient classical (resp. quantum) uniform algorithm $\mathcal{R}$ with the following guarantee. For any solver $\mathcal{B}_P = (B_P, \mathsf{state}_0)$ for P with one-shot advantage ε and running time T, let $\mathsf{state}_0' = (\mathsf{state}_0, B_P, 1^{1/\varepsilon}, 1^T)$. Then $\mathcal{B}_Q = (\mathcal{R}, \mathsf{state}_0')$ is a solver for Q with one-shot advantage $\varepsilon' = \mathrm{poly}(\varepsilon, T^{-1}, \lambda^{-1})$ and running-time $\mathrm{poly}(T, \varepsilon^{-1}, \lambda)$. We say that the reduction is durable if $\mathcal{B}_Q$ has $\mathrm{poly}(\varepsilon, T^{-1}, \lambda^{-1})$-persistent advantage.*

We refer to a reduction from solving Q to classically (resp. quantumly) solving P as a classical-solver *(resp.* quantum-solver*) reduction.*

Remark 3.17 (Many Shot Reductions). There could be several conceivable extensions of the above definition that also account for the *many-shot advantage*. One such natural extension is requiring that the reduction works only given a solver with a persistent value (as in Definition 3.12). Jumping ahead, in Sect. 4, we show that under certain conditions, persistent solving can in fact be reduced to one-shot solving, even in the quantum setting.

Remark 3.18 (The Loss). We allow for a (fixed) polynomial loss in the advantage and running time. One could naturally extend it to more general relations.

Classical Black-Box Reductions. In this work, we prove that several general classes of *classical reductions* that a priori are only guaranteed to work for classical solvers, can be enhanced *efficiently* to also work for quantum solvers. Our focus is on black-box reductions; that is, reductions that are oblivious of the representation and inner workings of the solver that they use (in contrast to the above Definition 3.16, where the reduction obtains the full description of the solver $\mathcal{B}_P$).

We next formally define such black box reductions, using the terminology we have already developed. Specifically, we capture the notion of a classical solver for a given problem P as a stateless (classical) solver.

Definition 3.19 (Classical Black-Box Reduction). *A classical black-box reduction, from solving a non-interactive assumption Q to solving a non-interactive* *assumption P, is an efficient classical solver-aided uniform algorithm $\mathcal{R}$ with the following syntax and guarantee. $\mathcal{R}$ takes as input a security parameter 1^λ, parameter $1^{1/\varepsilon}$, and instance $x \in \{0,1\}^{n_Q}$ of Q. It interacts with a solver $\mathcal{B}$ for P (per Definition 3.9) and produces an output $y \in \{0,1\}^{m_Q}$. We require that for any distribution $\mathbb{B}$ over* **stateless classical** *solvers $\{\mathcal{B}_\alpha\}_\alpha$ such that $\mathbb{B}$ has advantage at least ε in solving P, the corresponding solver distribution $\mathbb{R}$ over solvers $\{\mathcal{R}^{\mathcal{B}_\alpha}(1^\lambda, 1^{1/\varepsilon}, \cdot)\}_\alpha$ has advantage at least $\mathrm{poly}(\varepsilon, \lambda^{-1})$ in solving Q. The advantage of $\mathcal{R}$ is positive if its value is always at least c_Q (above the assumption Q's threshold), regardless of any P-solver.*

We further say that the reduction $\mathcal{R}$ is non-adaptive *if $\mathcal{R}$ produces all of its oracle queries $x_1, \ldots, x_k \in \{0,1\}^{n_P}$ to $\mathcal{B}$ in one shot, obtains all answers $y_1, \ldots, y_k$, and then produces its output y.*

Remark 3.20. In our definition of solver interaction, a given solver $\mathcal{B}$ is only ever invoked for the instance size $n_P(\lambda)$. Accordingly, the above definition restricts attention to classical reductions that in order to solve problem Q for instance size $n_Q(\lambda)$ make queries to a P-solver on a specific related input size $n_p(\lambda)$. While this is not without loss of generality, it does capture natural reductions. (In fact, we are not aware of important reductions that do not adhere to this.)

Remark 3.21 (Deterministic Solver Reductions, Positive Advantage, and Repeated Queries). We consider classical reductions that ought to work when given a stateless solver from a distribution $\mathbb{B}$ over solvers $\{\mathcal{B}_\alpha\}$. (As a matter of fact in our model, even once a stateless solver $\mathcal{B}_\alpha$ is fixed, the process of answering any given query is randomized, but this can be modeled as sampling a deterministic stateless solver from another distribution $\mathbb{B}$ with the same advantage.) A weaker notion of classical reductions only requires that the reduction works for deterministic solvers. In the classical setting, this is typically not an issue, as long as the reduction has the power to fix the solver's randomness and repeatedly replace it as needed. Jumping forward, when considering quantum reductions, the randomness of a given solver may arise from the quantum nature of the solving process, and the reduction may not be able to control it. Accordingly, in our transformations from classical-solver reductions to quantum-solver reductions, we will naturally need the classical reduction we start from to also be able to deal with distributions over solvers.

We note that for typical assumptions Q such as search problems (with trivial threshold $c = 0$) or decision problems (with solution length $m = 1$ and trivial threshold $c = 1/2$), a classical reduction $\mathcal{R}$ from Q-solving to deterministic P-solving implies a classical reduction $\mathcal{R}'$ from Q-solving to distributional P-solving. Here two subtleties should be addressed. The first issue that could prevent $\mathcal{R}$ from working for distributional P-solvers is that the sign of the advantage of $\mathcal{R}^{\mathcal{B}}$ as a Q-solver may depend on the randomness of $\mathcal{B}$ and may cancel out in expectation. For search assumptions Q, where $c = 0$, this cannot happen as any advantage is positive. For decision problems, this can be avoided by slightly augmenting $\mathcal{R}$ to make sure that the advantage is always positive using standard black-box techniques [6]. This incurs only a polynomial overhead in solving queries, or even just a single query, at the cost of quadratically decreasing the advantage. The second issue concerns the running time of the reduction. Specifically a reduction that works for deterministic oracles, excepts to get their advantage $1^{1/\varepsilon}$ as input, where ε is the P-solver's advantage. When executing such a reduction with a solver distribution, we are given $1^{1/\varepsilon}$, where ε is the average advantage. Nevertheless, we can run the original reduction with input $1^{2/\varepsilon}$. Note that the probability that that the advantage of a sampled oracle is at least $\varepsilon/2$ is at least $\varepsilon/2$, and since the reduction has positive advantage, we are overall guaranteed to maintain a noticeable advantage.

Following the above, for typical assumptions Q, we can in particular assume w.l.o.g positive advantage. For simplicity, we also assume throughout that classical reductions We do not repeat queries. This is w.l.o.g as given a deterministic oracle, the reduction can simply store previous answers and answer consistently by itself.

4   Persistent Solvers in the Quantum Setting

In this section, invoking state restoration techniques from [7], we prove that any one-shot solver for an assumption P with a verifiably-polynomial image (in particular, decision problems) can be converted into a persistent solver for P.

Theorem 4.1 (Persistence Theorem). *Let P be a non-interactive falsifiable assumption with a verifiably-polynomial image. For any inverse polynomial function η, there exist efficient quantum algorithms S, R with the following syntax and guarantee. $S_B(\mathsf{state}_0)$ takes as input a quantum algorithm B and state state_0 and outputs a state state_0^* and a value $p^* \in [0, 1]$. $R_B(1^\lambda, 1^i, x, \mathsf{state}_{i-1}^*)$ takes as input B, a security parameter 1^λ, step 1^i, input $x \in \{0,1\}^n$, and state state_{i-1}^* and outputs a solution $y \in \{0,1\}^m$ and state state_i^*.*

For any solver $\mathcal{B} = (B, \mathsf{state}_0)$ with one-shot value $p - \mathsf{val}_P[0, \mathcal{B}]$, considering the random variable $(\mathsf{state}_0^*, p^*) \leftarrow S_B(\mathsf{state}_0)$, it holds that:

1. *$\mathbb{E}[p^*] = p$.*
2. *$\mathcal{R}^* = (R_B, \mathsf{state}_0^*)$ sampled in this process is a distribution over efficient stateful solvers that is (p^*, η)-persistent.*

Remark 4.2. The efficiency of the algorithms S, R is also polynomial in the running time of B. We avoid passing explicitly the running time bound as input to simplify notation.

The proof relies on techniques from [7] and can be found in the full version of this work [3].

5   Stateful Solvers to Memoryless Solvers

The following theorem shows that it is possible to convert stateful solvers into memoryless solvers with the same value, albeit with a few caveats. First, the distribution of queries that is to be made to the memoryless solver needs to be known ahead of time (i.e. it needs to be decided upfront in a non-adaptive manner). Second, the resulting memoryless solver might not be efficiently executable. Instead, we provide a simulator that can emulate its behavior, but only once, and only on an input that comes from the prescribed distribution. The simulator only manages to simulate the execution up to some statistical error, and its running time is polynomial in the inverse of this error. A formal theorem statement follows.

Theorem 5.1. *There exists a polynomial time oracle-aided simulator* SimMemless *with the following properties. Let $\mathcal{B}$ be a (p, η)-persistent ℓ-stateful solver for a falsifiable non-interactive assumption P and let $D = \{D_\lambda\}_\lambda$ be an efficiently samplable distribution ensemble over k-tuples of P instances. Finally, let δ be some parameter. Then there exists a (p, η)-persistent (but possibly inefficient) distribution over memoryless solvers $\mathcal{B}' = \mathcal{B}'_{\ell,D,\delta} = (B', \emptyset)$ for P such that the following holds.*

Consider sampling $\vec{x} \leftarrow D_\lambda$, and let $\mathcal{B}'(1^\lambda, \vec{x})$ be the transcript of the process that feeds the elements of $\vec{x}$ into $\mathcal{B}'$ one-by-one in order (i.e. executes $B'(1^\lambda, 1^i, x_i, \emptyset)$ in order). Then SimMemless$^{\mathcal{B},D}(1^\lambda, 1^\ell, 1^{1/\delta}, \vec{x})$ *makes non-adaptive black-box access to $\mathcal{B}$ and produces a distribution that is within at most δ statistical distance from $\mathcal{B}'(1^\lambda, \vec{x})$.*

We note that our simulator is "almost" a black-box algorithm in $\mathcal{B}$ in the sense that it takes the size of the state 1^ℓ as input, but otherwise it only makes black-box queries to $\mathcal{B}$. We also emphasize that the simulator does not depend at all on p, η or any other property of $\mathcal{B}$ (other than ℓ).

5.1   The Simulator SimMemless

We start by describing the simulator that will be used to prove Theorem 5.1. The simulator SimMemless simply "floods" the solver $\mathcal{B}$ with queries from a fixed distribution, and plants the elements of $\vec{x}$ in random positions.

Specifically, SimMemless$^{\mathcal{B},D}(1^\lambda, 1^\ell, 1^{1/\delta}, \vec{x})$ works as follows. Let t be such that $k\sqrt{\ell/2t} \leq \delta$, i.e. $t = O(\ell(k/\delta)^2)$. The simulator is also going to generate a non-adaptive sequence of queries. We start by defining our "flooding" distribution.

Definition 5.2 (Random Marginal). *Let D be a distribution over X^k, i.e. k-tuples over a domain X. Then the random marginal distribution D_U over X is a distribution obtained by sampling $(x_1, \ldots, x_k)$ according to D, sampling a random i in $[k]$, and outputting x_i as the final sample.*

The simulator starts by sampling the following values.

1. A vector $\vec{z}$ of $k \cdot t$ samples $z_{j,i} \leftarrow D_U$, where $j \in [k]$, $i \in [t]$.
2. k uniform samples $i_j \leftarrow [t]$, where $j \in [k]$.
3. A uniform permutation π over $[k]$.

It then generates a sequence of queries $\vec{z}^*$ by taking the vector $\vec{z}$ and, for all $j \in [k]$, replacing z_{j,i_j} with $x_{\pi(j)}$. Namely, thinking of $\vec{z}$ as containing k sequences of queries of length t each, we plug in a random element from $\vec{x}$ in a random location in each sequence.

The simulator then calls $\mathcal{B}$ on the queries in $\vec{z}^*$ in order, to obtain a sequence of responses $\vec{y}$. Let $y_{j,i}$ be the (j, i) element in this sequence. We define $y_j^* = y_{j,i_j}$. The simulator returns the transcript $((x_1, y^*_{\pi^{-1}(1)}), \ldots, (x_k, y^*_{\pi^{-1}(k)}))$. Namely, we output a transcript that pairs each x_i with the response that $\mathcal{B}$ produces when introduced to the query $z_{j,i_j} = x_i$, namely $\pi(j) = i$.

5.2   Proving Theorem 5.1

We now turn to prove the theorem. We start by defining a hybrid distribution which is defined with respect to purifying executions of $\mathcal{B}$. This will allow us to make claims about extended transcripts, and finally to redact to standard transcript and derive the proof of the theorem.

A Hybrid Distribution. To prove the theorem, we define the hybrid distribution $\mathcal{S}_h$, defined for every $h \in \{0, 1, \ldots, k\}$.

1. Sample a uniform permutation π over $[k]$.
2. For all $j \in [k]$, sample a random index $i_j \in [t]$.
3. Sample $\vec{x}$ from D.
4. Generate a sequence of queries $z_{j,i}$ for all $j \in [k]$, $i \in [t]$ as follows.
   (a) For all $j > h$, set $z_{j,i_j} = x_{\pi(j)}$.
   (b) Otherwise sample z_{j,i_j} from D_U.
5. Generate the extended transcript $\widehat{\mathsf{ts}}$ of executing $\mathcal{B}$ (in a purifying manner) on the entries $z_{j,i}$ in lexicographic order (i.e. starting with $(1,1), \ldots, (1,t)$ and concluding with $(k,1), \ldots, (k,t)$). We let $\widehat{\mathsf{ts}}_{j,i}$ denote the prefix of the transcript prior to making the (j, i) query. We let $|s_{j,i}\rangle$ denote the solver state respective to $\widehat{\mathsf{ts}}_{j,i}$, as guaranteed by Proposition 3.10. Notice that $|s_{1,1}\rangle$ is the initial state state_0 of $\mathcal{B}$ conditioned on $\widehat{\mathsf{ts}}_0 = \hat{y}_0$.
6. The output of the hybrid $\mathcal{S}_h$ then consists the following values, for all $j \in [k]$:
   (a) The values $i_j, \pi(j)$.
   (b) The quantum state in the beginning of the j-th run: $|s_{j,1}\rangle$.
   (c) The quantum state right before the i_j-th query in the j-th sequence is made: $|s_{j,i_j}\rangle$.
   (d) The value $x_{\pi(j)}$, which is the i_j-th query in the j-th sequence if $j > h$.
   (e) An answer $(y_{\pi(j)}, \hat{y}_{\pi(j)})$ computed as follows.
       - If $j > h$ then set $(y_{\pi(j)}, \hat{y}_{\pi(j)}) = (y_{j,i_j}, \hat{y}_{j,i_j})$ (i.e. the $(y, \hat{y})$-part of the (j, i_j)-th triplo in $\widehat{\mathsf{ts}}$).
       - Otherwise generate $(y_{\pi(j)}, \hat{y}_{\pi(j)})$ as $\widehat{\mathcal{B}}(1^\lambda, 1^{t(j-1)+i_j}, x_{\pi(j)}, |s_{j,i_j-1}\rangle)_{\mathsf{y},\hat{\mathsf{y}}}$.

In what follows, we will prove that the distributions induced by the first and last hybrids are close in trace distance, as formalized below.

Lemma 5.3. *It holds that* $\mathrm{TD}(\mathcal{S}_0, \mathcal{S}_k) \leq k\sqrt{\ell/(2t)}$.

Before proving Lemma 5.3, we argue that it implies the validity of Theorem 5.1. Indeed, we observe that the output of the simulator SimMemless can be extracted from $\mathcal{S}_0$ by simply outputting all of the pairs $((x_1, y_1), \ldots, (x_k, y_k))$. Applying the same extraction procedure on the last hybrid $\mathcal{S}_k$ will lead to a sequence $((x_1, y_1), \ldots, (x_k, y_k))$ in which $y_{\pi(j)} = B(1^\lambda, 1^{t(j-1)+i_j}, x_{\pi(j)}, |s_{j,i_j-1}\rangle)_\mathrm{y}$. However, in the hybrid $\mathcal{S}_k$, the transcript $\widehat{\mathsf{ts}}$, and therefore all states $|s_{j,i}\rangle$, are generated independently of $\vec{x}$. Therefore, for every values of $\pi, \widehat{\mathsf{ts}}$ one could define a memoryless adversary $\mathcal{B}' = (B'_{\pi, \widehat{\mathsf{ts}}}, \emptyset)$, defined by

$$B'_{\pi, \widehat{\mathsf{ts}}}(1^\lambda, 1^j, x, \emptyset) = B(1^\lambda, 1^{t(j'-1)+i_{j'}}, x, |s_{j', i_{j'}-1}\rangle)_\mathrm{y} , \tag{6}$$

with $j' = \pi^{-1}(j)$. Note that the sequence of states is hard-wired into B' and it does not require to propagate a state throughout the execution.

We therefore indeed have that the solver $\mathcal{B}'$ is a distribution over memoryless solvers indicated by sampling $\pi, \widehat{\mathsf{ts}}$ from their respective distributions and executing $B'_{\pi, \widehat{\mathsf{ts}}}$. Since $\mathcal{B}$ is (p, η)-persistent, we have that with probability $1 - \eta$ over $\widehat{\mathsf{ts}}$, all invocations of $B(1^\lambda, 1^{t(j'-1)+i_{j'}}, x, |s_{j', i_{j'}-1}\rangle)$ have value $p \pm \eta$, which would imply that $(B'_{\pi, \widehat{\mathsf{ts}}}, \emptyset)$ is (p, η)-persistent. Therefore, the distribution $\mathcal{B}'$ is also, by definition, (p, η)-persistent.

The proof of Lemma 5.3 will follow from a standard hybrid argument, given by the following lemma.

Lemma 5.4. *For all* $h \in \{0, 1, \ldots, k-1\}$ *it holds that*

$$\mathrm{TD}(\mathcal{S}_h, \mathcal{S}_{h+1}) \leq \sqrt{\ell/(2t)} . \tag{7}$$

Proof. We will show that the lemma holds true even when conditioning both $\mathcal{S}_h, \mathcal{S}_{h+1}$ on any value for $\widehat{\mathsf{ts}}_{h,1}$ (the $(h \cdot t)$-prefix of the transcript $\widehat{\mathsf{ts}}$).

We will show that the lemma follows from the following claim.

Claim 5.5. *Conditioning on any value of* $\widehat{\mathsf{ts}}_{h,1}$ *for both* $\mathcal{S}_h, \mathcal{S}_{h+1}$, *the joint distribution of:*

$$(i_h, \widehat{\mathsf{ts}}_{h,i_h}, |s_{h+1,1}\rangle), (x_{\pi(h)}, y_{\pi(h)}, \hat{y}_{\pi(h)})) \tag{8}$$

is within trace distance $\sqrt{\ell/(2t)}$ *between* $\mathcal{S}_h, \mathcal{S}_{h+1}$.

Given Claim 5.5, Lemma 5.4 follows since all other elements of the two distributions $\mathcal{S}_h, \mathcal{S}_{h+1}$ can be sampled given $\widehat{\mathsf{ts}}_{h,1}$ and $(i_h, \widehat{\mathsf{ts}}_{h,i_h}, |s_{h+1,1}\rangle), (x_{\pi(h)}, y_{\pi(h)}, \hat{y}_{\pi(h)}))$, as follows.

1. Sample the permutation π and the query vector $\vec{x}$ conditioned on the value $x_{\pi(h)}$.
2. For very $j \in [k] \setminus \{h\}$, sample i_j uniformly in $[t]$.

3. For all $j < h$, the transcript prefix $\widehat{\mathsf{ts}}_{h,1}$ determines all states $|s_{j,i}\rangle$ (for all $i \in [t]$), which in turn, together with $\vec{x}$, determines the distribution of $y_{\pi(j)}, \hat{y}_{\pi(j)}$ for all $j < h$ (since this distribution is specified by applying the solver B on $x_{\pi(j)}$ with quantum state that is determined by the h-prefix).

4. For all $j > h$ the outputs of both $\mathcal{S}_h, \mathcal{S}_{h+1}$ are determined as the outcomes of an identical quantum process applied to the state $|s_{h+1,1}\rangle$ (the initial state of the $(h+1)$-th sequence), considering that π and $\vec{x}$ have been determined.

We now proceed to prove Claim 5.5, and focus on the distribution of $(i_h, \widehat{\mathsf{ts}}_{h,i_h}, |s_{h+1,1}\rangle, (x_{\pi(h)}, y_{\pi(h)}, \hat{y}_{\pi(h)}))$ in the two hybrids, given that $\widehat{\mathsf{ts}}_{h,1}$ is fixed. The claim follows straightforwardly from our information theoretic Plug-In Lemma (Lemma 2.3), where the classical values y_i in the lemma corresponds to pairs $(z_{h,i}, y_{h,i}, \hat{y}_{h,i})$ generated in the h'th round in the hybrid experiment. Note that since we fixed $\widehat{\mathsf{ts}}_{h,1}$, the distribution over these classical values is also fixed, and indeed the value $s = |s_{h+1,1}\rangle$ depends on this sequence of t values. The triple $(x_{\pi(h)}, y_{\pi(h)}, \hat{y}_{\pi(h)})$ differs between $\mathcal{S}_h$ and $\mathcal{S}_{h+1}$ since in the former it is exactly equal to the i_{h+1} element in the h-th sequence, and in the latter it is sampled from the marginal distribution of this element. We can therefore apply the plug-in lemma directly to obtain the $\sqrt{\ell/(2t)}$ bound on the trace distance as Claim 5.5 requires. This completes the proof of the claim and thus also of the lemma.

6 Memoryless Solvers to Stateless Solvers

Theorem 6.1. *There exists a polynomial-time oracle-aided simulator* SimStateless *with the following properties. Let $\mathcal{B}$ be a (p, η)-persistent memoryless solver for a falsifiable non-interactive assumption P and let $\{D_\lambda\}_\lambda$ be an efficiently samplable distribution ensemble over k-tuples of P instances. Let δ be some parameter.*

Then there exists a (p, η)-persistent (but possibly inefficient) stateless solver $\mathcal{B}'' = \mathcal{B}''_\delta = (B'', \emptyset)$ for P such that the following holds. Consider sampling $\vec{x} \leftarrow D_\lambda$, and let $\mathcal{B}''(1^\lambda, \vec{x})$ be the transcript of the process that feeds the elements of $\vec{x}$ into $\mathcal{B}''$ (i.e. executes $B''(1^\lambda, x_i, \emptyset)$ for all x_i). Then SimStateless$^{\mathcal{B}}(1^\lambda, 1^{1/\delta}, \vec{x})$ makes non-adaptive black-box access to $\mathcal{B}$ and produces a distribution that is within at most δ statistical distance from $\mathcal{B}''(1^\lambda, \vec{x})$.

Proof. The simulator SimStateless$^{\mathcal{B}}$ runs as follows. Given $\vec{x}$ as input, it generates a query vector $\vec{x}'$ of length $t = k^2$ as follows. It samples, without repetitions, k indices $i_1, \ldots, i_k$ and sets $x'_j = x_{i_j}$. All other values of x' are set to 0 (or some other fixed value).

After making the queries in $\vec{x}$ to $\mathcal{B}$ and receiving an output vector $\vec{y}$, the simulator sets $y_j = y_{i_j}$ returns $((x_1, y_1), \ldots, (x_k, y_k))$.

Let us now define the stateless adversary $\mathcal{B}''$. On input x, $B''(1^\lambda, x)$ samples $j \leftarrow [t]$ uniformly, and outputs $y = B(1^\lambda, 1^j, x, \emptyset)_y$. The solver $\mathcal{B}''$ is also (p, η)-persistent; indeed, its value is the average of values, which are all η-close to

p. (Recall Remark 3.15 about persistent values for stateless and memoryless solvers.)

To bound the statistical distance between $\mathsf{SimStateless}^{\mathcal{B}}(1^\lambda, 1^{1/\delta}, \vec{x})$ and $\mathcal{B}''(1^\lambda, \vec{x})$, we consider the case where in the course of the execution of $\mathcal{B}''(1^\lambda, \vec{x})$, all j's that are sampled are distinct. This happens with probability at least $1 - k^2/t = 1 - \delta$. Conditioned on this event, $\mathcal{B}''(1^\lambda, \vec{x})$ is identically distributed as $\mathsf{SimStateless}^{\mathcal{B}}(1^\lambda, 1^{1/\delta}, \vec{x})$. It follows that in general the statistical distance is bounded by δ.

We conclude with a corollary that combines Theorem 5.1 and Theorem 6.1.

Corollary 6.2. *There exists a polynomial-time simulator* Sim *with the following properties. Let* $\mathcal{B}$ *be a* (p, η)*-persistent* ℓ*-stateful solver for a falsifiable non-interactive assumption* P *and let* $\{D_\lambda\}_\lambda$ *be an efficiently samplable distribution ensemble over* k*-tuples of* P *instances. Finally, let* δ *be some parameter.*

Then there exists a (p, η)*-persistent (but possibly inefficient) distribution over stateless solvers* $\mathcal{B}'' = \mathcal{B}''_{\ell, D, \delta} = (B'', \emptyset)$ *for* P*. Consider sampling* $\vec{x}^* \leftarrow D_\lambda$*, and let* $\mathcal{B}''(1^\lambda, \vec{x}^*)$ *be the transcript of the process that feeds the elements of* $\vec{x}^*$ *into* $\mathcal{B}''$ *(i.e. executes* $B''(1^\lambda, x_i^*, \emptyset)$ *for all* x_i^**). Then* $\mathsf{Sim}^{\mathcal{B}, D}(1^\lambda, 1^\ell, 1^{1/\delta}, \vec{x}^*)$ *makes non-adaptive black-box access to* $\mathcal{B}$ *and produces a distribution that is within at most* δ *statistical distance from* $\mathcal{B}''(1^\lambda, \vec{x}^*)$*.*

The proof can be found in the full version of the paper [3].

7 Classical Non-Adaptive Reductions and Quantum Solvers

In this section, we show that a wide class of classical reductions can be translated to the quantum setting. Specifically we start from any non-adaptive black-box reductions from classically solving P with a verifiably-polynomial image (Definition 3.2), to classically solving Q. We transform it into a quantum reduction from quantumly solving P to quantumly solving Q.

Theorem 7.1. *Assume there exists a classical non-adaptive black-box reduction from solving a non-interactive assumption* Q *to solving a non-interactive assumption* P *with a verifiably-polynomial image. Then there exists a quantum reduction from solving* Q *to quantumly solving* P*. This reduction is durable if the original classical reduction has positive advantage.*

Proof. Let $\mathcal{R}$ be a classical non-adaptive black-box reduction from solving a non-interactive assumption $Q = (G_Q, V_Q, c_Q)$ to solving a non-interactive assumption $P = (G_P, V_P, c_P)$. We present a quantum reduction $\mathcal{R}'$ from solving Q to quantumly solving P. We start by describing and analyzing $\mathcal{R}'$ with a one-shot advantage, and then extend it to address durability in the case that $\mathcal{R}$ has positive advantage. We assume w.l.o.g that $\mathcal{R}$ never makes the same query twice to its oracle function (see Remark 3.21).

Recalling Definition 3.16, $\mathcal{R}'$ takes as input $(1^\lambda, 1^t, x_Q, \text{state})$, where $x_Q \in \{0,1\}^{n_Q}$ is potentially an instance of Q, and its initial state is $\text{state}_0' = (\text{state}_0, B, 1^{1/\varepsilon}, 1^T)$, where we are guaranteed that $\mathcal{B} = (\text{state}_0, B)$ is a P solver with advantage at least ε that runs in time at most T.

We let ε' denote the advantage of $\mathcal{R}$ in solving Q when given access to an oracle that solves P with advantage at least $\varepsilon/2$. We are guaranteed that $\varepsilon' = \text{poly}(\varepsilon, \lambda^{-1})$. We set $\delta = \varepsilon'/2$ and $\eta = \min\{\varepsilon/4, \varepsilon'/2\}$.

We define a distribution D over $(\{0,1\}^{n_P})^k$ as the distribution over the set of oracle queries produced by first sampling a uniform r_Q' and using it to generate $x_Q' = G_Q(1^\lambda, r_Q')$, and finally executing $\mathcal{R}(1^\lambda, 1^{4/\varepsilon}, x_Q')$ to produce a k-tuple of P-instances.

Having all of these definitions in place, we can now introduce the execution of $\mathcal{R}'(1^\lambda, 1^0, x_Q, \text{state}_0')$. Namely, we start by analyzing the one-shot execution of $\mathcal{R}'$ (the case $t = 0$).

1. Let R, S be the state restoration algorithms with respect to P as guaranteed by Theorem 4.1, with parameter η as defined above. Set $(\text{state}_0^*, p^*) \leftarrow S_B(\text{state}_0)$. Define $\mathcal{B}_0 = \mathcal{R}^* = (R_B, \text{state}_0^*)$ and recall that $\mathcal{B}_0$ is (p^*, η)-persistent, and that $\mathbb{E}[p^*] = p$.
2. Execute $\mathcal{R}(1^\lambda, 1^{3/\varepsilon}, x_Q)$ to obtain the sequence of queries $\vec{x}$.
3. Recall   the simulator Sim guaranteed by Corollary 6.2. Execute $\text{Sim}^{\mathcal{B}_0, D}(1^\lambda, 1^\ell, 1^{1/\delta}, \vec{x})$ to obtain a transcript ts.
4. Extract the responses to $\vec{x}$ from ts and resume the execution $\mathcal{R}$ from step 2 with these responses. Once the execution of $\mathcal{R}$ completes and a value y_Q is output, output y_Q as the output of $\mathcal{R}'$.

To analyze the one-shot value and advantage of $\mathcal{R}'$, we start by analyzing the performance of $\mathcal{R}'$ conditioned on obtaining a fixed value p^* in step 1 of the execution. In this case $\mathcal{B}_0$ is (p^*, η)-persistent, and we can invoke Corollary 6.2 to conclude that there exists a (p^*, η)-persistent distribution over stateless adversaries $\mathcal{B}_{p^*}''$ s.t. the output of $\mathcal{R}'$ is within statistical distance δ from the execution of $\mathcal{R}^{\mathcal{B}_{p^*}''}(1^\lambda, 1^{4/\varepsilon}, x_Q)$.

In turn, the execution of $\mathcal{R}^{\mathcal{B}_{p^*}''}(1^\lambda, 1^0, x_Q, \text{state}_0')$ is equivalent to executing $\mathcal{R}^{\mathcal{B}''}(1^\lambda, 1^{4/\varepsilon}, x_Q)$, where $\mathcal{B}''$ is a distribution over stateless solvers defined as follows. First sample p^* from its designated distribution, then sample $\mathcal{B}_{p^*}''$ from the (p^*, η)-persistent distribution of stateless solvers. Recall that with probability $1 - \eta$ over the sampling of $\mathcal{B}_{p^*}''$, it holds that the outcome is a (single) (p^*, η)-persistent stateless solver and therefore that $|\text{val}_P[0, \mathcal{B}_{p^*}''] - p^*| \leq \eta$. It follows that with probability at least $1 - \eta$:

$$|\mathbb{E}[\text{val}_P[0, \mathcal{B}'']] - p| = |\mathbb{E}[\text{val}_P[0, \mathcal{B}_{p^*}''] - p^*]|$$
$$\leq \mathbb{E}[|\text{val}_P[0, \mathcal{B}_{p^*}''] - p^*|]$$
$$\leq \eta.$$

It follows that $\mathcal{B}''$ has advantage at least $\varepsilon - 2\eta \geq \varepsilon/2$ in solving P. We have therefore that $\mathcal{R}^{\mathcal{B}''}$ has advantage at least ε' in solving Q. Since the output of

$\mathcal{R}'$ is within $\delta = \varepsilon'/2$ statistical distance from $\mathcal{R}^{\mathcal{B}''}$, we conclude that $\mathcal{R}'$ has advantage at least $\varepsilon'/2$. We therefore established the one-shot value of $\mathcal{R}'$.

In the full version [3] we further show that $\mathcal{R}'$ is durable.

8   An Impossibility Result for Search Assumptions

Our result in Sect. 7 transforms a classical non-adaptive reduction $\mathcal{R}$ from solving Q to classically solving P into a reduction $\mathcal{R}$ to *quantumly* solving P. It is restricted to assumptions P with a verifiably-polynomial image. While this captures a large class of assumptions, such as all decision assumptions, it certainly does not capture all assumptions of interest. In particular, it does not capture *search assumptions* where the number of possible solutions per instance could be super polynomial, such as say the hardness of inverting a one-way function where the preimage size could be super-polynomial.

In this section we show that this is somewhat inherent. We prove that for search assumptions, such a transformation cannot exist as long as the resulting reduction $\mathcal{R}'$ is explicit in the assumptions P, Q. In particular, it may obtain as input the code of the algorithms describing P, Q, but does not get any implicit non-uniform advice regarding these assumptions. Indeed, the transformation in Sect. 7 (from classical non-adaptive reductions to quantum ones) as well as the Persistence Theorem 4.1 on which it relies, the resulting quantum reduction $\mathcal{R}'$ is in fact black-box in the assumptions P, Q, and in particular explicit.

Definition 8.1 (Assumption Pair Colletion). *An assumption pair collection $\mathcal{PQ}$ consists of pairs of assumptions (P, Q), each given by its corresponding (possibly non-uniform) algorithms (G_P, V_P, c_P) and (G_Q, V_Q, c_Q).*

Definition 8.2 (Explicit Reduction). *An explicit quantum reduction for assumption pair collection $\mathcal{PQ}$ is an efficient algorithm $\mathcal{R}$ with the following guarantee. For any $(P, Q) \in (\mathcal{P}, \mathcal{Q})$ and any quantum solver $\mathcal{B}_P = (B_P, \text{state}_0)$ for P with one-shot advantage ε and running time T, let $\text{state}'_0 = (\text{state}_0, (P, Q), B_P, 1^{1/\varepsilon}, 1^T)$. Then $\mathcal{B}_Q = (\mathcal{R}, \text{state}'_0)$ is a solver for Q with one-shot advantage $\text{poly}(\varepsilon, T^{-1}, \lambda^{-1})$ and running-time $\text{poly}(T, \varepsilon^{-1}, \lambda)$.*

We say that the reduction is strongly explicit, instead of being given the explicit description of (P, Q) as part of its input, it is given oracle access to its corresponding algorithms.

Note that in the above definition state'_0 is formally a sequence

$$\text{state}'_{0,\lambda} = (\text{state}_{0,\lambda}, (P, Q)_\lambda, B_{P,\lambda}, 1^{1/\varepsilon(\lambda)}, 1^{T(\lambda)}) ,$$

where $(P, Q)_\lambda$ consist of their corresponding algorithms (possibly along with their corresponding non-uniform advice) restricted to security parameter λ (w.l.o.g circuits).

Restating our result from Sect. 7, we proved that for any pair collection $\mathcal{PQ}$, if for any $(P, Q) \in \mathcal{P}, \mathcal{Q}$, P has verifiably-polynomial image, and there exists a classical non-adaptive black-box reduction $\mathcal{R}_{P,Q}$ from solving Q to solving P, then there also exists a strongly explicit quantum reduction $\mathcal{R}'$ for $\mathcal{P}\mathcal{Q}$. We prove that if P does not have a verifiably-polynomial image this may not be the case.

Theorem 8.3. *There exists an assumption pair collection $\mathcal{P}\mathcal{Q}$, such that for any $(P,Q) \in \mathcal{P}, \mathcal{Q}$, there exists a classical non-adaptive black-box reduction $\mathcal{R}_{P,Q}$ from solving Q to solving P, but there is no strongly explicit reduction $\mathcal{R}'$ for $\mathcal{P}\mathcal{Q}$. Assuming also post-quantum indistinguishability obfuscation, there also does not exist an explicit reduction $\mathcal{R}'$.*

The theorem is proven in the full version of the paper [3].

Acknowledgments. Nir Bitansky is a member of the checkpoint institute of information security and was supported by the Israel Science Foundation (Grants No. 484/18 and 2137/19, by Len Blavatnik and the Blavatnik Family Foundation, by the Blavatnik Interdisciplinary Cyber Research Center at Tel Aviv University, and by the European Union Horizon 2020 Research and Innovation Program via ERC Project REACT (Grant 756482). Zvika Brakerski was supported by the Israel Science Foundation (Grant No. 3426/21), and by the European Union Horizon 2020 Research and Innovation Program via ERC Project REACT (Grant 756482) and via Project PROMETHEUS (Grant 780701). Yael Tauman Kalai's work supported by DARPA under Agreement No. HR001120200. Any opinions, findings and conclusions or recommendations expressed in this material are those of the author(s) and do not necessarily reflect the views of the United States Government or DARPA.

References

1. Adcock, M., Cleve, R.: A quantum Goldreich-Levin theorem with cryptographic applications. In: Alt, H., Ferreira, A. (eds.) STACS 2002. LNCS, vol. 2285, pp. 323–334. Springer, Heidelberg (2002). https://doi.org/10.1007/3-540-45841-7_26
2. Ben-David, S., Sattath, O.: Quantum tokens for digital signatures. CoRR (2016). arxiv:abs/1609.09047
3. Bitansky, N., Brakerski, Z., Kalai, Y.T.: Constructive post-quantum reductions. CoRR, abs/2203.02314 (2022). https://arxiv.org/abs/2203.02314
4. Boneh, D., Dagdelen, Ö., Fischlin, M., Lehmann, A., Schaffner, C., Zhandry, M.: Random oracles in a quantum world. In: Lee, D.H., Wang, X. (eds.) ASIACRYPT 2011. LNCS, vol. 7073, pp. 41–69. Springer, Heidelberg (2011). https://doi.org/10.1007/978-3-642-25385-0_3
5. Brakerski, Z., Christiano, P., Mahadev, U., Vazirani, U.V., Vidick, T.: A cryptographic test of quantumness and certifiable randomness from a single quantum device. In: 59th IEEE Annual Symposium on Foundations of Computer Science, FOCS 2018, Paris, France, 7-9 October 2018, pp. 320–331 (2018)
6. Brakerski, Z., Goldreich, O.: From absolute distinguishability to positive distinguishability. In: Goldreich, O. (ed.) Studies in Complexity and Cryptography. Miscellanea on the Interplay between Randomness and Computation. LNCS, vol. 6650, pp. 141–155. Springer, Heidelberg (2011). https://doi.org/10.1007/978-3-642-22670-0_17

7. Chiesa, A., Ma, F., Spooner, N., Zhandry, M.: Post-quantum succinct arguments. CoRR, abs/2103.08140 (2021)

8. Coladangelo, A., Liu, J., Liu, Q., Zhandry, M.: Hidden cosets and applications to unclonable cryptography. In: Malkin, T., Peikert, C. (eds.) CRYPTO 2021, Part I. LNCS, vol. 12825, pp. 556–584. Springer, Cham (2021). https://doi.org/10.1007/978-3-030-84242-0_20

9. Damgård, I., Fehr, S., Salvail, L., Schaffner, C.: Cryptography in the bounded-quantum-storage model. SIAM J. Comput. **37**(6), 1865–1890 (2008)

10. Don, J., Fehr, S., Majenz, C.: The measure-and-reprogram Technique 2.0: multiround Fiat-Shamir and more. In: Micciancio, D., Ristenpart, T. (eds.) CRYPTO 2020, Part III. LNCS, vol. 12172, pp. 602–631. Springer, Cham (2020). https://doi.org/10.1007/978-3-030-56877-1_21

11. Don, J., Fehr, S., Majenz, C., Schaffner, C.: Security of the Fiat-Shamir transformation in the quantum random-oracle model. In: Boldyreva, A., Micciancio, D. (eds.) CRYPTO 2019, Part II. LNCS, vol. 11693, pp. 356–383. Springer, Cham (2019). https://doi.org/10.1007/978-3-030-26951-7_13

12. Goldreich, O., Levin, L.A.: A hard-core predicate for all one-way functions. In: Johnson D.S. (ed.) Proceedings of the 21st Annual ACM Symposium on Theory of Computing, Seattle, Washington, USA, 14–17 May 1989, pp. 25–32. ACM (1989)

13. Haitner, I., Holenstein, T.: On the (im)possibility of key dependent encryption. In: Reingold, O. (ed.) TCC 2009. LNCS, vol. 5444, pp. 202–219. Springer, Heidelberg (2009). https://doi.org/10.1007/978-3-642-00457-5_13

14. Jiang, H., Zhang, Z., Chen, L., Wang, H., Ma, Z.: IND-CCA-secure key encapsulation mechanism in the quantum random oracle model, revisited. In: Shacham, H., Boldyreva, A. (eds.) CRYPTO 2018, Part III. LNCS, vol. 10993, pp. 96–125. Springer, Cham (2018). https://doi.org/10.1007/978-3-319-96878-0_4

15. Katsumata, S., Yamada, S., Yamakawa, T.: Tighter security proofs for GPV-IBE in the quantum random oracle model. In: Peyrin, T., Galbraith, S. (eds.) ASIACRYPT 2018, Part II. LNCS, vol. 11273, pp. 253–282. Springer, Cham (2018). https://doi.org/10.1007/978-3-030-03329-3_9

16. Krämer, J., Struck, P.: Encryption schemes using random oracles: from classical to post-quantum security. In: Post-Quantum Cryptography—11th International Conference, PQCrypto 2020, Paris, France, 15–17 April 2020, Proceedings, pp. 539–558 (2020)

17. Liu, Q., Zhandry, M.: Revisiting post-quantum Fiat-Shamir. In: Boldyreva, A., Micciancio, D. (eds.) CRYPTO 2019, Part II. LNCS, vol. 11693, pp. 326–355. Springer, Cham (2019). https://doi.org/10.1007/978-3-030-26951-7_12

18. Naor, M.: On cryptographic assumptions and challenges. In: Boneh, D. (ed.) CRYPTO 2003. LNCS, vol. 2729, pp. 96–109. Springer, Heidelberg (2003). https://doi.org/10.1007/978-3-540-45146-4_6

19. Nielsen, M.A., Chuang, I.L.: Quantum Computation and Quantum Information (10th Anniversary edition). Cambridge University Press, Cambridge (2016)

20. Regev, O.: On lattices, learning with errors, random linear codes, and cryptography. In: Gabow, H.N., Fagin, R. (eds.) Proceedings of the 37th Annual ACM Symposium on Theory of Computing, 22–24 May 2005, Baltimore, MD, USA, pp. 84–93. ACM, Baltimore (2005)

21. Targhi, E.E., Unruh, D.: Post-quantum security of the Fujisaki-Okamoto and OAEP transforms. In: Hirt, M., Smith, A. (eds.) TCC 2016. LNCS, vol. 9986, pp. 192–216. Springer, Heidelberg (2016). https://doi.org/10.1007/978-3-662-53644-5_8

22. Yamakawa, T., Zhandry, M.: Classical vs quantum random oracles. In: Canteaut, A., Standaert, F.-X. (eds.) EUROCRYPT 2021, Part II. LNCS, vol. 12697, pp. 568–597. Springer, Cham (2021). https://doi.org/10.1007/978-3-030-77886-6_20

23. Zhandry, M.: Secure identity-based encryption in the quantum random oracle model. In: Safavi-Naini, R., Canetti, R. (eds.) CRYPTO 2012. LNCS, vol. 7417, pp. 758–775. Springer, Heidelberg (2012). https://doi.org/10.1007/978-3-642-32009-5_44

24. Zhandry, M.: How to record quantum queries, and applications to quantum indifferentiability. In: Boldyreva, A., Micciancio, D. (eds.) CRYPTO 2019, Part II. LNCS, vol. 11693, pp. 239–268. Springer, Cham (2019). https://doi.org/10.1007/978-3-030-26951-7_9

Symmetric Cryptanalysis

Differential Cryptanalysis
in the Fixed-Key Model

Tim Beyne[1(✉)] and Vincent Rijmen[1,2]

[1] imec-COSIC, KU Leuven, Leuven, Belgium
{tim.beyne,vincent.rijmen}@esat.kuleuven.be
[2] University of Bergen, Bergen, Norway

Abstract. A systematic approach to the fixed-key analysis of differential probabilities is proposed. It is based on the propagation of 'quasidifferential trails', which keep track of probabilistic linear relations on the values satisfying a differential characteristic in a theoretically sound way. It is shown that the fixed-key probability of a differential can be expressed as the sum of the correlations of its quasidifferential trails.

The theoretical foundations of the method are based on an extension of the difference-distribution table, which we call the quasidifferential transition matrix. The role of these matrices is analogous to that of correlation matrices in linear cryptanalysis. This puts the theory of differential and linear cryptanalysis on an equal footing.

The practical applicability of the proposed methodology is demonstrated by analyzing several differentials for RECTANGLE, KNOT, Speck and Simon. The analysis is automated and applicable to other SPN and ARX designs. Several attacks are shown to be invalid, most others turn out to work only for some keys but can be improved for weak-keys.

Keywords: Differential cryptanalysis · Hypothesis of stochastic equivalence · Correlation matrices · RECTANGLE · KNOT · Speck · Simon

1 Introduction

At CRYPTO 1990, Biham and Shamir [5] published the first reduced-round differential attacks on the block cipher DES. Differential cryptanalysis is now one of the cornerstones of the security analysis of block ciphers and hash functions. Its central problem is to count the number of inputs of a function for which a given input difference results in a particular output difference or, what amounts to the same, to compute the probability of a differential.

For functions that can be written as a composition of simple operations, the standard procedure is to analyze sequences of intermediate differences or *characteristics*. The probability of a characteristic is then heuristically estimated by multiplying the probabilities of the intermediate differentials. In the context of block ciphers, Lai, Massey and Murphy [16] showed that this procedure yields the correct value of the *key-averaged probability* for Markov ciphers.

However, since the key is fixed throughout a differential attack, even the average data-complexity cannot be computed from the average probability of

Y. Dodis and T. Shrimpton (Eds.): CRYPTO 2022, LNCS 13509, pp. 687–716, 2022.
https://doi.org/10.1007/978-3-031-15982-4_23

differentials alone. Hence, Lai *et al.* [16] introduced an additional assumption known as the *hypothesis of stochastic equivalence*. It states that the probability for each key is close to the average probability.

In practice, it turns out that the probability can vary significantly between keys. Hence, standard assumptions may lead to incorrect conclusions. Furthermore, averages may hide weak-key attacks that can considerably degrade security. Finally, the same formalism is used even when there is no key, such as for cryptographic permutations, or when the cryptanalyst has full control over the key, such as in many hash functions.

From a theoretical viewpoint, it can be argued that the standard approach to differential cryptanalysis is incomplete, since it does not offer any tools to compute probabilities beyond the average case. This is in contrast to linear cryptanalysis [20], where key-dependence is much better understood. In particular, the correlation matrix approach of Daemen *et al.* [10] shows that the correlation of a linear approximation is precisely equal to the sum of the correlations of all its linear trails.

Previous Work. Knudsen [15] already observed significant deviations from the hypothesis of stochastic equivalence for the characteristics used in the differential analysis of DES. Experiments such as those of Ankele and Kölbl [2] and Heys [14] further suggest that such deviations are the norm rather than the exception.

Daemen and Rijmen [11] showed that the fixed-key probability of two-round characteristics of AES is either zero or 2^h, with h an integer independent of the key. Such characteristics are called *plateau characteristics*, and have been used in several other contexts [9,19,21,25]. Although plateau characteristics are the only systematic method to analyze fixed-key probabilities for S-box-based ciphers, their scope remains limited. They assume that the input or output values satisfying a differential over the S-box form an affine space. In addition, their analysis becomes difficult for more than two rounds.

For constructions relying on modular additions, several techniques were developed in the context of collision attacks on hash functions. These methods keep track of additional information about the values satisfying a characteristic. For example, the breakthrough results of Wang *et al.* [26] rely on *signed differences*. De Cannière and Rechberger [12] extended these to *generalized differences*, allowing arbitrary constraints to be imposed on individual bits. Leurent [18] proposed a framework for ARX-constructions based on two-bit conditions. Xu *et al.* [27] recently introduced *signed sums*, which are single-bit conditions. Despite their merit, these techniques have significant limitations. Imposing conditions directly on values becomes difficult for keyed functions, since key-additions result in conditions that potentially depend on many unknown bits. Hence, these methods are limited to keyless functions except for local, key-independent effects in ciphers such as XTEA that use modular additions between dependent values. Furthermore, the conditions that are imposed cannot fully explain the probability of a characteristic, and the right choice of the type of conditions to use depends on the function under analysis.

Contribution. We develop a general methodology to analyze the fixed-key probabilities of differentials. It allows propagating probabilistic linear relations on the values satisfying differential characteristics in a theoretically sound way. The theoretical foundations of the proposed approach are inspired by the correlation matrix framework [10] and its recent generalization [4] that provide a natural description of linear cryptanalysis.

Section 3 builds up an extension of the difference-distribution table that we call the *quasidifferential transition matrix.* It is obtained by performing a change-of-basis on the permutation matrices describing the propagation of probability distributions of pairs through a function, analogous to the construction of correlation matrices using the Fourier transformation. Our choice of basis ensures that the difference distribution table is obtained as a submatrix, and simultaneously diagonalizes the transition matrices corresponding to round-key additions.

By construction, quasidifferential transition matrices satisfy similar properties as correlation matrices. For example, composition of functions corresponds to multiplication of quasidifferential transition matrices. This property leads to quasidifferential trails, the central notion of our methodology. In Sect. 4, we prove that the sum of the correlations of all quasidifferential trails in a characteristic is equal to its exact probability. Likewise, the probability of a differential is the sum of the correlations of all quasidifferential trails. A few quasidifferential trails often capture the essence of the key-dependence. For example, the key-dependence in the DES characteristics observed by Knudsen [15] is explained by taking into account one additional one-round quasidifferential trail.

To demonstrate the practical applicability of our methodology, we apply it to four primitives. To this end, an algorithm to compute the quasidifferential transition matrix of general functions in time proportional (up to logarithmic factors) to the size of the matrix is given in Sect. 5. In addition, the quasidifferential transition matrix of bitwise-and and modular addition are determined.

Section 6 presents an automated search tool for quasidifferential trails in RECTANGLE [28]. The implementation is provided as supplementary material[1], and can also be used for the analysis of other, similar ciphers. Our analysis shows that the best published key-recovery attack on round-reduced RECTANGLE does not work, but we show how to modify it to obtain a valid weak-key attack.

In Sect. 7 we apply the same tool to KNOT [29], a second-round candidate in the NIST lightweight cryptography competition. We show that previously proposed reduced-round forgery and collision attacks do not work, because the characteristics they rely on have probability zero. At the same time, we show that their probabilities are two orders of magnitude larger for some choices of the round constants.

Section 8 reevaluates the best published attacks on Speck. The analysis relies on an automated search tool that is provided as supplementary material. It can easily be modified for other ARX designs. We find that most of the attacks we analyzed only work for a subset of keys. However, we also show that for

---

[1] All of our source code can be found at https://github.com/TimBeyne/quasidiff erential-trails.

weak keys, attacks with lower data-complexity can be obtained. In the extended version of the paper, we provide a similar search tool for Simon.

2   Preliminaries and Related Work

Most of the notations used in this paper are standard, or will be introduced where necessary. Throughout this paper, random variables are denoted in boldface. The average of a random variable $\boldsymbol{x}$ will be denoted by $\mathsf{E}\,\boldsymbol{x}$, and its variance by $\mathrm{Var}\,\boldsymbol{x}$. All key-dependent probabilities given in this paper are with respect to a fixed key, unless it is explicity mentioned that they are averages.

2.1   Differential Cryptanalysis

Differential cryptanalysis [5,6] is a technique to analyze the propagation of differences through a function $\mathsf{F} : \mathbb{F}_2^n \rightarrow \mathbb{F}_2^m$. Typically, the cryptanalyst attempts to find a differential $(a, b) \in \mathbb{F}_2^n \times \mathbb{F}_2^m$ such that the difference equation

$$\mathsf{F}(x) + \mathsf{F}(x + a) = b, \tag{1}$$

has a large number of solutions in x. The ordered pairs $(x, x+a)$ for which Eq. (1) holds are called *right pairs* for the differential (a, b). The number of right pairs divided by 2^n is called the probability of the differential. The *difference-distribution table* $\mathsf{DDT}^{\mathsf{F}}$ is a $2^n \times 2^m$ table with rows and columns indexed by input and output differences respectively. The corresponding entries are equal to the number of right pairs for a particular differential:

$$\mathsf{DDT}^{\mathsf{F}}_{a,b} = |\{x \in \mathbb{F}_2^n \mid \mathsf{F}(x) + \mathsf{F}(x + a) = b\}| = 2^n \Pr\left[\mathsf{F}(\boldsymbol{x}) + \mathsf{F}(\boldsymbol{x} + a) = b\right],$$

with $\boldsymbol{x}$ uniform random on $\mathbb{F}_2^n$. A differential with probability $p \gg 2^{-n}$ results in a distinguisher with data-complexity $\mathcal{O}(1/p)$.

Characteristics. Computing or estimating the probability of a differential for a general function with many inputs can be computationally difficult. However, differential cryptanalysis is typically applied to functions F of the form $\mathsf{F} = \mathsf{F}_r \circ \cdots \circ \mathsf{F}_1$, where the functions F_i admit differentials with relatively high probability and are usually easier to analyze. In this case, the probability of a differential (a_1, a_{r+1}) can be estimated based on *characteristics*. A characteristic is a sequence $(a_1, a_2, \ldots, a_{r+1})$ of compatible intermediate input and output differences for each of the functions F_i. For simplicity of notation, assume that $m = n$ and the functions F_i are all n-bit functions. It holds that

$$\Pr\left[\mathsf{F}(\boldsymbol{x}) + \mathsf{F}(\boldsymbol{x} + a_1) = a_{r+1}\right] = \sum_{a_2, \ldots, a_r} \Pr\left[\textstyle\bigwedge_{i=1}^{r} \mathsf{F}_i(\boldsymbol{x}_i) + \mathsf{F}_i(\boldsymbol{x}_i + a_i) = a_{i+1}\right],$$

with $\boldsymbol{x}_1$ uniform random on $\mathbb{F}_2^n$ and $\boldsymbol{x}_i = \mathsf{F}_{i-1}(\boldsymbol{x}_{i-1})$ for $i = 2, \ldots, r$. The probability of a characteristic is often estimated using the assumption that intermediate differentials are independent:

$$\Pr\left[\textstyle\bigwedge_{i=1}^{r} \mathsf{F}_i(\boldsymbol{x}_i) + \mathsf{F}_i(\boldsymbol{x}_i + a_i) = a_{i+1}\right] = \prod_{i=1}^{r} \Pr\left[\mathsf{F}_i(\boldsymbol{z}_i) + \mathsf{F}_i(\boldsymbol{z}_i + a_i) = a_{i+1}\right].$$

Under the same independence heuristic, combining the equations above yields

$$\mathsf{DDT}^{\mathsf{F}}_{a_1,a_{r+1}}/2^n = \sum_{a_2,\ldots,a_r} \prod_{i=1}^{r} \mathsf{DDT}^{\mathsf{F}_i}_{a_i,a_{i+1}}/2^n \,. \tag{2}$$

We stress that Eq. (2) is an approximation, and it is easy to come up with examples such as $\mathsf{F} = \mathsf{F}_2 \circ \mathsf{F}_1$ with $\mathsf{F}_2 = \mathsf{F}_1^{-1}$ where it fails spectacularly.

Key-Averaged Probabilities. If the functions $\mathsf{F}_1, \ldots, \mathsf{F}_r$ depend on keys $k_1, \ldots, k_r$, then the heuristic Eq. (2) can be motivated using the *Markov cipher* assumption [16]. In particular, it can be shown that if all round keys are uniform random and independent, then the key-averaged probability of a characteristic is indeed equal to the product of the intermediate key-averaged probabilities.

Aside from the fact that most ciphers are not true Markov ciphers due to round-key dependencies introduced by the key-schedule, one is ultimately interested in fixed-key rather than key-averaged probabilities. Importantly, this is true even when computing the key-averaged data-complexity of an attack. After all, in general $\mathsf{E}\left[1/p_{\boldsymbol{k}}\right] \neq 1/\,\mathsf{E}\left[p_{\boldsymbol{k}}\right]$ with $p_{\boldsymbol{k}}$ the probability for a random key $\boldsymbol{k}$.

Hence, to bridge this gap, an additional hypothesis was introduced by Lai, Massey and Murphy [16, §2]. Informally, the *hypothesis of stochastic equivalence* states that the key-averaged probability of a characteristic is close to its fixed-key probability for any particular key. As discussed in the introduction, previous work has shown that this assumption is often unrealistic.

2.2   Linear Cryptanalysis

Although the average probability of characteristics and differentials is relatively well understood, few techniques are known to analyze fixed-key probabilities. This contrasts with linear cryptanalysis, where linear trails give a complete description of the correlation of linear approximations even in the fixed-key setting.

A natural way to describe linear cryptanalysis is by means of correlation matrices. These matrices were first introduced by Daemen *et al.* [10]. Although the scope of the present paper is limited to differential cryptanalysis only, it is useful to introduce these matrices as they provide an important motivation for the quasidifferential transition matrices that will be introduced in Sect. 3.

From the viewpoint introduced in [3,4], correlation matrices represent linear operators that act on functions $\mathbb{F}_2^n \to \mathbb{R}$ such as probability distributions. In the following, let $\mathbb{R}[\mathbb{F}_2^n]$ denote the vector space of such functions. The functions δ_x such that $\delta_x(y) = 1$ if $y = x$ and zero elsewhere form an orthonormal basis for $\mathbb{R}[\mathbb{F}_2^n]$ with respect to the inner product $\langle f, g \rangle = \sum_{x \in \mathbb{F}_2^n} f(x)\, g(x)$. Below, this basis will be referred to as the *standard basis*.

Another convenient basis for $\mathbb{R}[\mathbb{F}_2^n]$ consists of the group characters of $\mathbb{F}_2^n$. These are homomorphisms from $\mathbb{F}_2^n$ to the multiplicative group $\mathbb{C} \setminus \{0\}$. Any such homomorphism is of the form $\chi_u(x) = (-1)^{u^{\mathsf{T}}x}$ with $u \in \mathbb{F}_2^n$. The characters χ_u form an orthogonal basis for $\mathbb{R}[\mathbb{F}_2^n]$. Specifically, $\langle \chi_u, \chi_v \rangle = 2^n\, \delta_u(v)$. Hence, any function $f \in \mathbb{R}[\mathbb{F}_2^n]$ can be expressed as a linear combination of the characters

χ_u. This leads to the Fourier transformation, which is defined in Definition 2.1. The basis $\{\chi_u \mid u \in \mathbb{F}_2^n\}$ will be called the *character basis*.

Definition 2.1 (Fourier transformation). *Let* $f : \mathbb{F}_2^n \to \mathbb{R}$ *be a function. The Fourier transformation of* f *is the function* $\mathscr{F}_n f : \mathbb{F}_2^n \to \mathbb{R}$ *defined by* $(\mathscr{F}_n f)(u) = \langle \chi_u, f \rangle$. *That is,* $(\mathscr{F}_n f)(u)/2^n$ *is the coordinate corresponding to the basis function* χ_u *when* f *is expressed in the character basis.*

The motivation for using the character basis is that it simplifies the effect of translating functions by a constant. In particular, if $g(x) = f(x + t)$, then $(\mathscr{F}_n g)(u) = \chi_u(t) (\mathscr{F}_n f)(u)$ because $\chi_u(x + t) = \chi_u(t)\chi_u(x)$ by the definition of characters as group homomorphisms.

Correlation matrices describe how a function $\mathsf{F} : \mathbb{F}_2^n \to \mathbb{F}_2^m$ transforms functions in $\mathbb{R}[\mathbb{F}_2^n]$ to functions in $\mathbb{R}[\mathbb{F}_2^m]$. In the standard basis, the relation is expressed by a permutation matrix that is called the *transition matrix* in Definition 2.2. The same linear transformation can be expressed in the Fourier basis and this yields Definition 2.3.

Definition 2.2 (Transition matrix [4, Definition 3.2]). *Let* $\mathsf{F} : \mathbb{F}_2^n \to \mathbb{F}_2^m$ *be a function. Define* $T^{\mathsf{F}} : \mathbb{R}[\mathbb{F}_2^n] \to \mathbb{R}[\mathbb{F}_2^m]$ *as the unique linear operator defined by* $\delta_x \mapsto \delta_{\mathsf{F}(x)}$ *for all* $x \in \mathbb{F}_2^n$. *The transition matrix of* F *is the coordinate representation of* T^{F} *with respect to the standard bases of* $\mathbb{R}[\mathbb{F}_2^n]$ *and* $\mathbb{R}[\mathbb{F}_2^m]$.

Definition 2.3 (Correlation matrix [4, Definition 3.3]). *Let* $\mathsf{F} : \mathbb{F}_2^n \to \mathbb{F}_2^m$ *be a function. Define* $C^{\mathsf{F}} : \mathbb{R}[\mathbb{F}_2^n] \to \mathbb{R}[\mathbb{F}_2^m]$ *as the Fourier transformation of* T^{F}. *That is,* $C^{\mathsf{F}} = \mathscr{F}_m T^{\mathsf{F}} \mathscr{F}_n^{-1}$. *The correlation matrix of* F *is the coordinate representation of* C^{F} *with respect to the standard bases of* $\mathbb{R}[\mathbb{F}_2^n]$ *and* $\mathbb{R}[\mathbb{F}_2^m]$.

The coordinates of the correlation matrix C^{F} correspond to the correlations of linear approximations over F. In particular, $C_{v,u}^{\mathsf{F}} = 2 \Pr [v^{\mathsf{T}}\mathsf{F}(\boldsymbol{x}) + u^{\mathsf{T}}\boldsymbol{x} = 0] - 1$ with $\boldsymbol{x}$ uniform random. In fact, the original definition of correlation matrices due to Daemen *et al.* [10] starts from this equivalence.

Correlation matrices satisfy several natural properties, most of which are direct consequences of the properties of transition matrices and Definition 2.3. In particular, for a function $\mathsf{F} = \mathsf{F}_r \circ \cdots \circ \mathsf{F}_1$, it holds that

$$C^{\mathsf{F}} = C^{\mathsf{F}_r} C^{\mathsf{F}_{r-1}} \cdots C^{\mathsf{F}_1}.$$

Expanding the above equation in coordinates yields the following identity:

$$C_{u_{r+1},u_1}^{\mathsf{F}} = \sum_{u_2,\ldots,u_r} \prod_{i=1}^{r} C_{u_{i+1},u_i}^{\mathsf{F}_i}. \tag{3}$$

That is, the correlation of a linear approximation is equal to the sum of the correlations of all linear trails defined by the intermediate masks $u_2, \ldots, u_r$. This result should be compared with Eq. (2) for differentials. However, there is a fundamental difference: whereas Eq. (2) is heuristic and at best true on average with respect to independent uniform random round keys, Eq. (3) holds exactly without any assumptions.

As argued in the introduction, closing the gap between Eq. (2) and Eq. (3) is essential to achieve a more complete understanding of differential cryptanalysis. To this end, Sect. 3 introduces quasidifferential transition matrices as a differential analog of correlation matrices.

3   Quasidifferential Transition Matrices

The probability of differentials can be described exactly by tracking the distribution of pairs of state values. Such a distribution can be described by a function $p : \mathbb{F}_2^n \times \mathbb{F}_2^n \to [0,1] \subseteq \mathbb{R}$. There exists a transition matrix which describes the propagation of such probability distributions through a function $\mathsf{F} : \mathbb{F}_2^n \to \mathbb{F}_2^m$.

However, keeping track of pairs directly is inconvenient because it does not provide a simple description of translations – which are essential to understand key-dependence. In Sect. 3.1, we define a new basis that is nicer to work with. In Sect. 3.2, it is then shown that expressing transition matrices in this new basis leads to matrices with similar properties as correlation matrices. These *quasidifferential transition matrices* will be used in Sect. 4 to give a natural fixed-key description of differential cryptanalysis.

3.1   Quasidifferential Basis

As discussed in Sect. 2, the Fourier transformation simplifies the effect of translations on functions. However, the character basis is not suitable to describe differences between the halves of pairs in a straightforward way. The basis proposed in Defintion 3.1 below is a hybrid solution. Up to scaling, it contains the probability distributions of uniform random pairs with a fixed difference and, as shown below, it simplifies the effect of translations.

Definition 3.1 (Quasidifferential basis). *Let n be a positive integer. For any $u, a \in \mathbb{F}_2^n$, the function $\beta_{u,a} : \mathbb{F}_2^n \times \mathbb{F}_2^n \to \mathbb{R}$ is defined by*

$$\beta_{u,a}(x,y) = \chi_u(x)\, \delta_a(x+y)\,.$$

The set of all $\beta_{u,a}$ will be called the quasidifferential basis for $\mathbb{R}[\mathbb{F}_2^n \times \mathbb{F}_2^n]$.

The functions $\beta_{u,a}$ are not only linearly independent, but also orthogonal. This is shown in Theorem 3.1, which also states the important translation-invariance property.

Theorem 3.1. *The quasidifferential basis defined in Definition 3.1 is translation-invariant and orthogonal. Specifically:*

(1) For all $(u,a),(v,b) \in \mathbb{F}_2^n \times \mathbb{F}_2^n$, it holds that $\langle \beta_{v,b},\, \beta_{u,a} \rangle = 2^n\, \delta_v(u)\, \delta_b(a)$.
(2) For all $(u,a) \in \mathbb{F}_2^n \times \mathbb{F}_2^n$ and $t \in \mathbb{F}_2^n$, it holds that

$$\beta_{u,a}(x+t, y+t) = \chi_u(t)\, \beta_{u,a}(x,y)\,.$$

Proof. The first property follows from the expression

$$\langle \beta_{v,b},\, \beta_{u,a} \rangle = \sum_{(x,y) \in \mathbb{F}_2^n \times \mathbb{F}_2^n} \chi_v(x)\, \delta_b(x+y)\, \chi_u(x)\, \delta_a(x+y)\,.$$

Indeed, if $a \neq b$, then $x + y = a$ and $x + y = b$ never hold simultaneously. If $a = b$, then the result follows from the orthogonality of the characters χ_u. The translation-invariance follows from the fact that $\chi_u(x+t) = \chi_u(t)\,\chi_u(x)$. □

Similar to the Fourier transformation, we define the change-of-basis operator $\mathcal{Q}_n : \mathbb{R}[\mathbb{F}_2^n \times \mathbb{F}_2^n] \to \mathbb{R}[\mathbb{F}_2^n \times \mathbb{F}_2^n]$ by $(\mathcal{Q}_n f)(u,a) = \langle \beta_{u,a},\, f \rangle$. By Theorem 3.1 (1), $(\mathcal{Q}_n f)(u,a)/2^n$ is then indeed the coordinate corresponding to basis function $\beta_{u,a}$ when f is expressed in the quasidifferential basis.

3.2 Quasidifferential Transition Matrix

Recall from Sect. 2.2 that the correlation matrix of a function $\mathsf{F} : \mathbb{F}_2^n \to \mathbb{F}_2^m$ with transition matrix T^{F} is defined as $C^{\mathsf{F}} = \mathscr{F}_m\, T^{\mathsf{F}} \mathscr{F}_n^{-1}$. Below, we define the *quasidifferential transition matrix* similarly using the change-of-basis operator $\mathcal{Q}_n$ and the transition matrix for pairs of values. The latter matrix can be succinctly written as the Kronecker (or tensor) product $T^{\mathsf{F}} \otimes T^{\mathsf{F}}$, which is defined as a $2^{2m} \times 2^{2n}$ matrix with coordinates

$$(T^{\mathsf{F}} \otimes T^{\mathsf{F}})_{(y_1,y_2),(x_1,x_2)} = T^{\mathsf{F}}_{y_1,x_1} T^{\mathsf{F}}_{y_2,x_2} = \delta_{y_1}(\mathsf{F}(x_1))\delta_{y_2}(\mathsf{F}(x_2))\,.$$

Note that we index the coordinates of $T^{\mathsf{F}} \otimes T^{\mathsf{F}}$ directly by pairs of bitvectors. This avoids choosing an arbitrary convention for converting between integers and bitvector pairs.

Definition 3.2 (Quasidifferential transition matrix). *Let n and m be positive integers and $\mathsf{F} : \mathbb{F}_2^n \to \mathbb{F}_2^m$ a function. The quasidifferential transition matrix D^{F} is defined as the matrix-representation of $T^{\mathsf{F}} \otimes T^{\mathsf{F}}$ with respect to the quasidifferential basis defined in Defintion 3.1. That is, $D^{\mathsf{F}} = \mathcal{Q}_m (T^{\mathsf{F}} \otimes T^{\mathsf{F}}) \mathcal{Q}_n^{-1}$.*

To make Defintion 3.2 more concrete, we compute the coordinates of D^{F}. Like for $T^{\mathsf{F}} \otimes T^{\mathsf{F}}$, the coordinates of D^{F} will be indexed by pairs $(u,a) \in \mathbb{F}_2^n \times \mathbb{F}_2^n$ and $(v,b) \in \mathbb{F}_2^m \times \mathbb{F}_2^m$. By the orthogonality of the quasidifferential basis (Theorem 3.1 (1)), it holds that $\mathcal{Q}_n^{-1} = \mathcal{Q}_n^{\mathsf{T}}/2^n$ and consequently

$$D^{\mathsf{F}}_{(v,b),\,(u,a)} = \langle \delta_{(v,b)},\, \mathcal{Q}_n(T^{\mathsf{F}} \otimes T^{\mathsf{F}})\mathcal{Q}_n^{\mathsf{T}} \delta_{(u,a)} \rangle / 2^n = \langle \beta_{v,b},\, (T^{\mathsf{F}} \otimes T^{\mathsf{F}})\beta_{u,a} \rangle / 2^n\,.$$

Working this out yields the following expression:

$$
\begin{aligned}
D^{\mathsf{F}}_{(v,b),\,(u,a)} &= \frac{1}{2^n} \sum_{(x,y) \in \mathbb{F}_2^n \times \mathbb{F}_2^n} \chi_u(x)\chi_v(\mathsf{F}(x))\, \delta_a(x+y)\delta_b(\mathsf{F}(x)+\mathsf{F}(y)) \\
&= \frac{1}{2^n} \sum_{\substack{x \in \mathbb{F}_2^n \\ \mathsf{F}(x+a)=\mathsf{F}(x)+b}} (-1)^{u^{\mathsf{T}}x + v^{\mathsf{T}}\mathsf{F}(x)}\,.
\end{aligned}
\tag{4}
$$

For $u = v = 0$, Eq. (4) reduces to the probability of the differential with input difference a and output difference b. That is, $D^{\mathsf{F}}_{(0,b),(0,a)} = 2^{-n}\, \mathsf{DDT}^{\mathsf{F}}_{a,b}$. For $a = b = 0$, one obtains the coordinates of the correlation matrix of F. Specifically, $D^{\mathsf{F}}_{(v,0),(u,0)} = C^{\mathsf{F}}_{v,u}$. More generally, the right hand side of Eq. 4 can be interpreted as a kind of correlation matrix for the function F when restricted to the right pair set of the differential (a, b). That is, the coordinates of D^{F} express the correlations of probabilistic linear relations ('linear approximations') between the input and output values of the right pairs.

The following result summarizes some of the basic properties of quasidifferential transition matrices. Properties (1) to (3) are identical to those of corrrelation matrices [4, Theorem 3.1], and their proofs are nearly identical. For Theorem 3.2 (2), the Kronecker product of two quasidifferential transition matrices is defined by

$$(D^{\mathsf{F}_1} \otimes D^{\mathsf{F}_2})_{(v_1\|v_2,b_1\|b_2),(u_1\|u_2,a_1\|a_2)} = D^{\mathsf{F}_1}_{(v_1,b_1),(u_1,a_1)}\, D^{\mathsf{F}_2}_{(v_2,b_2),(u_2,a_2)}\,,$$

with $x\|y$ the concatenation of bitvectors x and y.

Theorem 3.2. *Let n and m be positive integers and $\mathsf{F} : \mathbb{F}_2^n \to \mathbb{F}_2^m$ a function. The matrix D^{F} has the following properties:*

(1) If F is a bijection, then D^{F} is an orthogonal matrix.
(2) If $\mathsf{F} = (\mathsf{F}_1, \ldots, \mathsf{F}_m)$, then $D^{\mathsf{F}} = \bigotimes_{i=1}^{m} D^{\mathsf{F}_i}$.   *(boxed maps)*
(3) If $\mathsf{F} = \mathsf{F}_2 \circ \mathsf{F}_1$, then $D^{\mathsf{F}} = D^{\mathsf{F}_2} D^{\mathsf{F}_1}$.   *(composition)*
(4) If $\mathsf{F}(x) = x + t$ for some $t \in \mathbb{F}_2^n$, then $D^{\mathsf{F}}_{(v,b),(u,a)} = \chi_v(t)\, \delta_v(u)\, \delta_b(a)$.
(5) If F is a linear function, then $D^{\mathsf{F}}_{(v,b),(u,a)} = \delta_u(\mathsf{F}^{\mathsf{T}}(v))\, \delta_b(\mathsf{F}(a))$.

Proof. Property (1) follows from the fact that $T^{\mathsf{F}} \otimes T^{\mathsf{F}}$ is a permutation matrix when F is a bijection and the fact that $\mathscr{Q}_n/\sqrt{2^n}$ is an orthogonal matrix by Theorem 3.1 (1). Property (2) follows immediately from the analogous result for $T^{\mathsf{F}} \otimes T^{\mathsf{F}}$ and the separability of the basis. Property (3) also follows from the same property for $T^{\mathsf{F}} \otimes T^{\mathsf{F}}$. The fourth property is due to the translation invariance and orthogonality of the quasidifferential basis (Theorem 3.1). Finally, Property (5) can be deduced from Eq. (4):

$$D^{\mathsf{F}}_{(v,b),\,(u,a)} = \frac{1}{2^n} \sum_{\substack{x \in \mathbb{F}_2^n \\ \mathsf{F}(x+a)=\mathsf{F}(x)+b}} (-1)^{(u+\mathsf{F}^{\mathsf{T}}(v))^{\mathsf{T}}x} = \delta_u(\mathsf{F}^{\mathsf{T}}(v))\, \delta_b(\mathsf{F}(a))\,,$$

where the second equality follows from the orthogonality of characters and the fact that $\mathsf{F}(x + a) = \mathsf{F}(x) + b$ if and only if $b = \mathsf{F}(a)$. □

Consider the S-box $\mathsf{S} : \mathbb{F}_2^4 \to \mathbb{F}_2^4$ of the lightweight block cipher RECTANGLE, given by $\mathsf{S} = (3\ \mathsf{a})(0\ 6\ 7\ 9)(1\ 5\ \mathsf{e}\ 4)(2\ \mathsf{c}\ 8\ \mathsf{b}\ \mathsf{d}\ \mathsf{f})$ in cycle notation. The 256×256 quasidifferential transition matrix of S is shown in Fig. 1, with colors representing the absolute value of the entries. The integer indices correspond to pairs (u, a) by the map $(u, a) \mapsto \mathsf{int}(u) + 16 \times \mathsf{int}(a)$, where $\mathsf{int}(u) = \sum_{i=1}^{4} u_i 2^{4-i}$.

Figure 1 immediately reveals a number of properties of quasidifferential transition matrices. The top-left square in Fig. 1 corresponds to the correlation matrix of S. Each block shows the correlations of probabilistic linear relations between the input and output values for the right pairs. Hence, Fig. 1 looks like a 'magnified' version of the difference-distribution table of S.

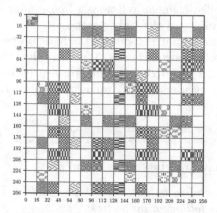

Fig. 1. The quasidifferential transition matrix D^S of the RECTANGLE S-box S. Blue cells correspond to values of absolute value 1/8, orange cells to 1/4, and green cells to 1/2. Empty cells correspond to zeros. (Color figure online)

4 Quasidifferential Trails

Motivated by the notion of *linear trails* and Eq. (3) from Sect. 2.2, the following definition defines *quasidifferential trails*. In Sect. 4.1, it will be shown that exact expressions for the probabilities of differentials can be given in terms of the correlations of quasidifferential trails.

Definition 4.1. *A quasidifferential trail for a function* $\mathsf{F} = \mathsf{F}_r \circ \cdots \circ \mathsf{F}_1$ *is a sequence* $\varpi_1, \varpi_2, \ldots, \varpi_{r+1}$ *of mask-difference pairs* $\varpi_i = (u_i, a_i)$. *The correlation of this quasidifferential trail is defined as* $\prod_{i=1}^{r} D^{\mathsf{F}_i}_{\varpi_{i+1}, \varpi_i}$.

Quasidifferential trails with $u_1 = u_2 = \ldots = u_{r+1} = 0$ correspond to characteristics. Their correlation is equal to the product of the one-round probabilities of the characteristic with differences $a_1, \ldots, a_{r+1}$:

$$\prod_{i=1}^{r} D^{\mathsf{F}}_{(0, a_{i+1}), (0, a_i)} = \prod_{i=1}^{r} \Pr\left[\mathsf{F}_i(\boldsymbol{x} + a_i) = \mathsf{F}_i(\boldsymbol{x}) + a_{i+1}\right],$$

with $\boldsymbol{x}$ uniform random on $\mathbb{F}_2^n$. This follows from Eq. (4) and Definition 4.1.

4.1   Exact Probabilities from Quasidifferential Trails

Theorem 3.2 (2) implies that the sum of the correlations of all quasidifferential trails with input and output mask-difference pairs $\varpi_1 = (0, a_1)$ and $\varpi_{r+1} = (0, a_{r+1})$ respectively, is equal to the exact probability of the differential with input difference a_1 and output difference a_{r+1}. Specifically, expanding the coordinate of $D^{\mathsf{F}} = \prod_{i=1}^{r} D^{\mathsf{F}_i}$ corresponding to this differential yields

$$D^{\mathsf{F}}_{\varpi_{r+1}, \varpi_1} = \sum_{\varpi_2, \ldots, \varpi_r} \prod_{i=1}^{r} D^{\mathsf{F}_i}_{\varpi_{i+1}, \varpi_i} . \tag{5}$$

This expression also holds when the input or output mask is nonzero. Furthermore, as shown in Theorem 4.1, quasidifferential trails also allow computing the probability of a characteristic. This result should be compared with Eq. (3).

Theorem 4.1. *Let* $\mathsf{F} : \mathbb{F}_2^n \to \mathbb{F}_2^m$ *be a function such that* $\mathsf{F} = \mathsf{F}_r \circ \ldots \circ \mathsf{F}_1$. *The probability of a characteristic with differences* $a_1, \ldots, a_{r+1}$ *is equal to the sum of the correlations of all quasidifferential trails with the same intermediate differences:*

$$\Pr\left[\bigwedge_{i=1}^{r} \mathsf{F}_i(\boldsymbol{x}_i + a_i) = \mathsf{F}_i(\boldsymbol{x}_i) + a_{i+1}\right] = \sum_{u_2, \ldots, u_r} \prod_{i=1}^{r} D^{\mathsf{F}_i}_{(u_{i+1}, a_{i+1}), (u_i, a_i)} ,$$

with $u_1 = u_{r+1} = 0$, $\boldsymbol{x}_i = \mathsf{F}_{i-1}(\boldsymbol{x}_{i-1})$ *for* $i = 2, \ldots, r$ *and* $\boldsymbol{x}_1$ *uniform random on* $\mathbb{F}_2^n$.

Proof. Substituting Eq. (4) in the right-hand side above yields

$$\prod_{i=1}^{r} D^{\mathsf{F}_i}_{(u_{i+1}, a_{i+1}), (u_i, a_i)} = \frac{1}{2^{nr}} \sum_{\substack{x_1, \ldots, x_r \\ \mathsf{F}(x_i + a_i) = \mathsf{F}(x_i) + a_{i+1}}} \prod_{i=1}^{r} (-1)^{u_i^\mathsf{T} x_i + u_{i+1}^\mathsf{T} \mathsf{F}_i(x_i)} .$$

Summing over $u_2, \ldots, u_r$ then results in the equation

$$\sum_{u_2, \ldots, u_r} \prod_{i=1}^{r} D^{\mathsf{F}_i}_{(u_{i+1}, a_{i+1}), (u_i, a_i)} = \frac{1}{2^{nr}} \sum_{\substack{x_1, \ldots, x_r \\ \mathsf{F}(x_i + a_i) = \mathsf{F}(x_i) + a_{i+1}}} \prod_{i=1}^{r} \sum_{u_i} (-1)^{u_i^\mathsf{T}(x_{i+1} + \mathsf{F}_i(x_i))}$$

$$= \frac{1}{2^n} \sum_{\substack{x_1, \ldots, x_r \\ \mathsf{F}(x_i + a_i) = \mathsf{F}(x_i) + a_{i+1}}} \prod_{i=1}^{r} \delta_{x_{i+1}}(\mathsf{F}_i(x_i)) .$$

Writing the right-hand side in terms of probabilities gives the desired result. $\square$

Theorem 4.1 can also be obtained using the following intuitive argument, illustrated in Fig. 2. Let $\mathsf{G} = (\mathsf{F}_1, \mathsf{F}_2 \circ \mathsf{F}_1, \ldots, \mathsf{F}_r \circ \cdots \circ \mathsf{F}_1)$. A differential for G with input difference a_1 and output difference $(a_2, \ldots, a_{r+1})$ is equivalent to a characteristic for $\mathsf{F} = \mathsf{F}_r \circ \cdots \circ \mathsf{F}_1$ with intermediate differences $a_2, \ldots, a_r$. For the linear function $\mathsf{L}(x) = x \| x$, Theorem 3.2 (5) yields $D^{\mathsf{L}}_{(v, b), (u, a)} = \delta_u(v_1 + v_2) \, \delta_{b_1}(a) \, \delta_{b_2}(a)$ with $v = v_1 \| v_2$ and $b = b_1 \| b_2$. Hence, all trails through G are of the form shown in Fig. 2 and the result follows from Eq. (5).

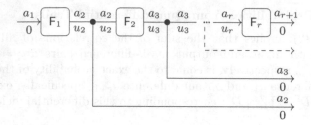

Fig. 2. Quasidifferential trail through the function G. Differences are indicated in orange (above), masks in blue (below). (Color figure online)

4.2 Example: Differential Cryptanalysis of DES

As a first example of quasidifferential trails and Theorem 4.1, we consider the effect of key-dependence on the differential cryptanalysis of DES by Biham and Shamir [5,6]. The example in this section is particularly simple, but more advanced applications will be discussed in Sects. 6 and 8.

Recall that the differential cryptanalysis of DES is based on an iterative characteristic of the form shown in Fig. 3. There exist two differences that achieve the same maximal average probability of approximately $2^{-7.87}$. For simplicity (the other case is similar), we will consider the difference $a = \mathtt{0x19600000}$. The key-dependence of this characteristic was already noted by Knudsen [15, §5], who explained it using an argument specific to DES. Below, it will be shown that the general methodology of quasidifferential trails automatically provides a simple explanation.

The round function F_k of DES consists of a linear expansion function $\mathsf{E}:\mathbb{F}_2^{32}\to\mathbb{F}_2^{48}$, which duplicates certain bits, followed by the key addition and a nonlinear layer S consisting of eight 6-bit to 4-bit S-boxes. Finally, the S-box layer is followed by a bit-permutation P. The key-averaged probability of the characteristic in Fig. 3 is easily computed from the difference-distribution tables of the first three S-boxes: $14/64 \times 8/64 \times 10/64 = 1120/64^3$.

However, the structure of the round function of DES leads to one-round quasidifferential trails, as shown on the right side of Fig. 3. In particular, since E is not surjective, there exist masks $u \neq 0$ such that $\mathsf{E}^{\mathsf{T}}(u) = 0$. For the difference a mentioned above, there exists one such quasidifferential trail with $u = \mathtt{0x001400000000}$. The correlation of this trail can be computed from the quasidifferential transition matrix for the first three S-boxes and equals $\chi_u(k_2)\,14/64 \times -8/64 \times 6/64 = -\chi_u(k_2)\,672/64^3$. It follows that a full description of the probability of the characteristic over $2r$ rounds is given by

$$p_k = \prod_{i=1}^{r}\left(\frac{1120}{64^3} - (-1)^{k_{2i,12}+k_{2i,14}}\frac{672}{64^3}\right).$$

Although for every two rounds only two trails are especially important, these trails can be combined in many ways. In particular, the expression above is

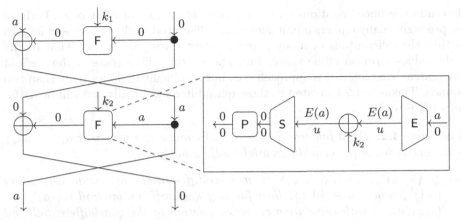

Fig. 3. Iterative characteristic for two rounds of DES.

equivalent to a sum over 2^r quasidifferential trails. This is a typical way in which a relatively small local effect can result in significant variations in the overall probability of a characteristic.

Due to the above, the probability of the thirteen round differential used in the differential attack of Biham and Shamir [6] is roughly 17 times larger for one in 64 keys and more than 244 times smaller than the average probability for an equal number of keys, as previously observed by Knudsen [15].

It is natural to wonder if there exist other quasidifferential trails with large absolute correlation. For example, a more general three-round effect can occur when $\mathsf{E}^\mathsf{T}(u) \neq 0$. However, most quasidifferential trails activating four or less additional S-boxes have correlation zero because the correlation of a linear approximation with input mask 1 or 32 and output mask 1, 2, 4 or 8 is zero for all S-boxes. This follows from the fact that the S-boxes are permutations when the first and last input bits are fixed. It can be checked that the best three-round quasidifferential trail of this type has absolute correlation at most $2^{-19.41}$.

4.3 Interpretation of Quasidifferential Trails

As discussed in Sect. 3.2, the coordinates of D^F can be interpreted as the correlations of linear approximations between the input and output values for the right pairs of a differential. Quasidifferential trails provide a way to connect such approximations through a sequence of functions.

Since $|D^\mathsf{F}_{(v,b),(u,a)}|$ never exceeds the probability of the differential (a, b), the quasidifferential trails with the highest correlation tend to have nonzero masks in only a few rounds. We refer to these quasidifferential trails as 'local'. In general, the best quasidifferential trails typically activate as few S-boxes as possible. An S-box is active if the output mask or the input difference is nonzero.

Quasidifferential trails with absolute correlation equal to the correlation of the corresponding differential trail are of particular interest. They correspond to deterministic linear relations on the intermediate values of right pairs. Perhaps surprisingly, many ciphers admit such quasidifferential trails. One reason for this is that the differentials of many popular S-boxes are *planar* [11]. That is, the right values form an affine space. Propagating this affine space is the basis of the plateau characteristics approach [11], but is difficult to do for more than two rounds. Theorem 4.2 is related to these quasidifferential trails and will be useful in Sects. 6 to 8.

Theorem 4.2. *For a function* $\mathsf{F} = \mathsf{F}_r \circ \cdots \circ \mathsf{F}_1$ *and a characteristic* $a_1, \ldots, a_{r+1}$ *with correlation* p *(as quasidifferential trail), it holds that:*

(1) If $(u_1, a_1), \ldots, (u_{r+1}, a_{r+1})$ *is a quasidifferential trail with correlation* $(-1)^b p$ *where* $b \in \{0, 1\}$, *then for any quasidifferential trail* $(v_1, a_1), \ldots,$ (v_{r+1}, a_{r+1}) *with correlation* c, *the correlation of the quasidifferential trail* $(u_1 + v_1, a_1), \ldots, (v_{r+1} + u_{r+1}, a_{r+1})$ *is* $(-1)^b c$.

(2) If the correlations of any number of quasidifferential trails with differences $a_1, \ldots, a_{r+1}$ *and correlation* $\pm p$ *sum to zero, then the probability of the characteristic* $a_1, \ldots, a_{r+1}$ *is zero.*

Proof. By Theorem 4.1 the second property follows from the first one, since it implies that the set of all quasidifferential trails can be partitioned into subsets whose correlations sum to zero. For the first property, note that the correlation of the quasidifferential trail $(u_1, a_1), \ldots, (u_{r+1}, a_{r+1})$ equals $\pm p$ if and only if $D^{\mathsf{F}_i}_{(u_{i+1}, a_{i+1}), (u_i, a_i)} = \pm D^{\mathsf{F}_i}_{(0, a_{i+1}), (0, a_i)}$ for $i = 1, \ldots, r - 1$.

By Eq. (4), this implies that $u_{i+1}^\mathsf{T} \mathsf{F}_i(x) = u_i^\mathsf{T} x + b_i$ for all x such that $\mathsf{F}_i(x + a_i) = \mathsf{F}_i(x) + a_{i+1}$. Hence, again by Eq. (4), the correlation of the ith transition of the quasidifferential trail $(u_1 + v_1, a_1), \ldots, (u_{r+1} + v_{r+1}, a_{r+1})$ is multiplied by a factor $(-1)^{b_i}$. The result then follows from $b = \sum_{i=1}^r b_i$. □

Finally, we briefly consider how strong quasidifferential trails can exist for a large number of rounds of a cipher. For every active S-box in a quasidifferential trail that is not active in the corresponding characteristic, the correlation of the trail contains a factor equal to the correlation of an ordinary linear approximation over that S-box. These approximations never have correlation ± 1, since the S-box is a nonlinear function. Hence, to avoid activating too many differentially inactive S-boxes, the masks of the quasidifferential trail should follow the differences as closely as possible. By Theorem 3.2 (5), one structural property that makes this more likely is if the linear layer L of the cipher satisfies $\mathsf{L}^{-1} = \mathsf{L}^\mathsf{T}$. Such 'self-dual' linear layers, including all bit-permutations, are in common use. Insights such as these can be used by designers to avoid strong key-dependency or, should they choose to do so, to amplify key-dependent effects on purpose.

4.4   Key-Alternating Ciphers

For key-alternating ciphers, quasidifferential trails with nonzero masks have an intuitive interpretation. Let $\mathsf{F} = \mathsf{F}_r \circ \cdots \circ \mathsf{F}_1$ with $\mathsf{F}_i(x) = \mathsf{G}_i(x) + k_i$. By Equation (5) and Theorem 3.1 (2), it holds that

$$D^{\mathsf{F}}_{\varpi_{r+1},\varpi_1} = \sum_{\varpi_2,\ldots,\varpi_r} \prod_{i=1}^{r} (-1)^{u_{i+1}^{\mathsf{T}} k_i} D^{\mathsf{G}_i}_{\varpi_{i+1},\varpi_i} , \qquad (6)$$

where $\varpi_i = (u_i, a_i)$ for $i = 1, \ldots, r+1$. It is easy to see that for $u_0 = u_r = 0$, the average of the above with respect to independent uniform random round keys $k_1, \ldots, k_r$ is equal to the sum of the average probabilities of all characteristics. More generally, one has the following result.

Theorem 4.3. *Let* $\mathsf{F} = \mathsf{F}_r \circ \cdots \circ \mathsf{F}_1$ *with* $\mathsf{F}_i(x) = \mathsf{G}_i(x) + k_i$. *If* $\boldsymbol{k} = (\boldsymbol{k}_1, \ldots, \boldsymbol{k}_r)$ *is a uniform random variable on a set* $\mathcal{K}$, *then*

$$\Pr\left[\mathsf{F}(\boldsymbol{x} + a) = \mathsf{F}(\boldsymbol{x}) + b\right] = \sum_{\substack{u_2,\ldots,u_r \\ a_2,\ldots,a_r \\ (u_2,\ldots,u_r)\perp\mathcal{K}}} \prod_{i=1}^{r} D^{\mathsf{G}_i}_{(u_{i+1},a_{i+1}),(u_i,a_i)} ,$$

where $u_1 = u_{r+1} = 0$ *and the probability is over a uniform random* $\boldsymbol{x}$ *and over the keys* $\boldsymbol{k}_1, \ldots, \boldsymbol{k}_r$. *In particular, for* $\mathcal{K} = \mathbb{F}_2^n$, *only quasidifferential trails with zero masks contribute to the key-averaged probability of the differential.*

Proof. Taking the average of both sides of Eq. (6) with respect to $\boldsymbol{k}_1, \ldots, \boldsymbol{k}_r$ yields the result, since $\sum_{i=1}^{r} u_{i+1}^{\mathsf{T}} k_i$ is zero when $(u_2, \ldots, u_r) \in \mathcal{K}^{\perp}$ and uniform random otherwise. $\qquad\square$

A result similar to Theorem 4.3 but for characteristics follows from Theorem 4.1. Furthermore, Eq. (6) allows computing the variance of the probability of a differential:

$$\mathsf{E}\left[D^{\mathsf{F}}_{\varpi_{r+1},\varpi_1}\right]^2 + \mathsf{Var}\left[D^{\mathsf{F}}_{\varpi_{r+1},\varpi_1}\right] = \sum_{\varpi_2,\ldots,\varpi_r} \prod_{i=1}^{r} \left(D^{\mathsf{G}_i}_{\varpi_{i+1},\varpi_i}\right)^2 .$$

This result is analogous to a well-known result of Nyberg [22] in the context of linear cryptanalysis, which states that the variance of the correlation of a linear approximation is equal to the sum of the squared correlations of the linear trails in the approximation.

5   Computing the Quasidifferential Transition Matrix

The differential cryptanalysis of specific primitives using quasidifferential trails requires calculating the quasidifferential transition matrix for each round transformation. For affine functions, Theorem 3.2 (4) and (5) show how to compute the quasidifferential transition matrix.

In general, calculating the quasidifferential transition matrix is nontrivial because the dimensions of the matrix D^{F} scale exponentially with the number of input and output bits of F. In the following two sections, we show that this is not an issue for most primitives: we provide efficient methods to compute the quasidifferential transition matrix for small (such as 4- or 8-bit) S-boxes, for the bitwise-and operations and for modular additions.

5.1 S-boxes

The matrix D^{F} can be computed using a number of operations roughly proportional to its number of elements. Specifically, for a function $\mathsf{F} : \mathbb{F}_2^n \to \mathbb{F}_2^m$, the matrix D^{F} can be computed in $\mathcal{O}((n+m)2^{2n+2m})$ time using a method similar to the fast Fourier transform. Specifically, the matrix $\mathscr{Q}_n$ with columns $\beta_{u,a}$ satisfies $\mathscr{Q}_n = \mathscr{Q}_1^{\otimes n}$. It follows that there exists an efficient divide-and-conquer algorithm for multiplication with $\mathscr{Q}_n$ or its transpose, analogous to the fast Fourier transform. Hence, since $D^{\mathsf{F}} = \mathscr{Q}_m (T^{\mathsf{F}} \otimes T^{\mathsf{F}}) \mathscr{Q}_n^{\mathsf{T}}/2^n$ by Definition 3.2, the matrix D^{F} can be computed by applying this divide-and-conquer multiplication algorithm to both the rows and columns of $T^{\mathsf{F}} \otimes T^{\mathsf{F}}$. A SAGE implementation of this algorithm is provided as supplementary material. It is also possible to compute the quasidifferential transition matrix from the correlation matrix of F using essentially the same approach. This is discussed in the extended version of the paper.

5.2 Bitwise-And and Modular Addition

Several ciphers use bitwise-and or modular addition as their nonlinear components. Although these functions potentially have many input and output bits, they are highly structured. This makes it possible to express the entries of their quasidifferential transition matrix in terms of relatively simple logical constraints. These constraints can be used to model the propagation of quasidifferential trails in such ciphers as an MILP, SAT or SMT problem, *cf.* Sect. 8.

In the following, the bitwise-and of $x, y \in \mathbb{F}_2^n$ will be denoted by $x \wedge y$, the bitwise or by $x \vee y$. We also define $\mathsf{and}(x\|y) = x \wedge y$. The bitwise complement of x will be written as $\bar{x}$. The addition of the integers represented by x and y modulo 2^n will be denoted by $\mathsf{add}(x\|y)$. Finally, we write $x \preccurlyeq y$ when $x_i \leq y_i$ for $i = 1, \ldots, n$.

Bitwise-And. The quasidifferential transition matrix of and is easy to compute because it acts on each bit independently. Hence, Theorem 3.2 (2) can be used. This results in the following theorem. The proof can be found in the extended version of the paper.

Theorem 5.1. *Let $a, b, c \in \mathbb{F}_2^n$ be differences and $u, v, w \in \mathbb{F}_2^n$ masks. It holds that $D^{\mathsf{and}}_{(w,c),\,(u\|v,a\|b)} \neq 0$ if and only if $c \preccurlyeq a \vee b$, $u \vee v \preccurlyeq a \vee b \vee w$ and $a \wedge u + b \wedge v = c \wedge w$. Furthermore, if these conditions hold, then*

$$D^{\mathsf{and}}_{(w,c),\,(u\|v,a\|b)} = 2^{-\,\mathrm{wt}(a\vee b)-\mathrm{wt}(w\wedge\bar{a}\wedge\bar{b})} (-1)^{u^{\mathsf{T}}(\bar{a}\wedge c)+v^{\mathsf{T}}(a\wedge c)+u^{\mathsf{T}}(a\wedge b)}.$$

Modular Addition. The quasidifferential transition matrix of add can be computed using its CCZ equivalence to a quadratic function [23] that is nearly the same as bitwise-and. This results in Theorem 5.2. The proof is given in the extended version of the paper. In Theorem 5.2, the linear map $M : \mathbb{F}_2^n \to \mathbb{F}_2^n$ is defined by $M(x)_1 = 0$ and $M(x)_i = \sum_{j=1}^{i-1} x_j$ for $i > 1$ and its 'pseudoinverse' is $M^{\dagger}(x) = [x + (x \ll 1)] \gg 1$, where $\ll$ and $\gg$ denote left and right shifts respectively.

Theorem 5.2. *Denote the map of modular addition with modulus 2^n by* add : $\mathbb{F}_2^{2n} \to \mathbb{F}_2^n$. *Furthermore, let* $a, b, c \in \mathbb{F}_2^n$ *be differences and* $u, v, w \in \mathbb{F}_2^n$ *masks. It holds that* $D^{\text{add}}_{(w,c),(u\|v,a\|b)} \neq 0$ *if and only if*

$$c_1' = 0$$
$$M^\dagger c' \preccurlyeq a' \vee b'$$
$$u' \vee v' \preccurlyeq a' \vee b' \vee M^\mathsf{T} w'$$
$$a' \wedge u' + b' \wedge v' = c' \wedge M^\mathsf{T} w'$$
$$(a_n' = b_n' = 0) \vee (a_n' u_n' + b_n' v_n' \neq w_n') \vee (a_n' v_n' = \bar{a}_n' u_n'),$$

where $(a', b', c') = (b+c, a+c, a+b+c)$ *and* $(u', v', w') = (u+w, v+w, u+v+w)$. *Furthermore, if the above conditions hold, then*

$$D^{\text{add}}_{(w,c),(u\|v,a\|b)} = 2^{z - \text{wt}(a' \vee b') - \text{wt}(M^\mathsf{T} w' \wedge \bar{a}' \wedge \bar{b}')} (-1)^{(\bar{a}' \wedge M^\dagger c' + a' \wedge b')^\mathsf{T} u' + (a' \wedge M^\dagger c')^\mathsf{T} v'},$$

where $z = (a_n' \vee b_n') \wedge (a_n' u_n' + b_n' v_n' = w_n') \wedge (a_n' v_n' \neq \bar{a}_n' u_n')$.

6 Application to **RECTANGLE**

RECTANGLE [28] is a 64-bit substitution-permutation network, with a nonlinear layer consisting of 4-bit S-boxes and a bit-permutation as the linear layer. The state is represented by a 4×16 array of bits. For the specification of RECTAN-GLE, we refer the reader to the extended version of the paper.

There are several reasons why RECTANGLE is an interesting target to illustrate the use of quasidifferential trails. The linear layer is a bit-permutation and simpler compared to similar ciphers such as PRESENT [8]. In particular, it rotates the second, third and fourth rows of the state by 1, 12 and 13 bits respectively. As discussed in Sect. 4.3, the self-duality of bit-permutations potentially results in quasidifferential trails with high absolute correlation relative to the probability of the corresponding differential trail. In addition, differential cryptanalysis is the dominant attack for RECTANGLE. The optimal differentials for RECTAN-GLE also have a limited differential effect, *i.e.* they contain few characteristics. This simplifies the analysis.

To perform the analysis in this section, we developed an SMT-based program to automate the search for quasidifferential trails in RECTANGLE. This tool is provided as supplementary material and can easily be adapted to similar ciphers such as PRESENT. Additional details can be found in the extended version of the paper.

6.1 Differentials

Table 1 lists several differentials for RECTANGLE. Differential i is a 14-round differential used in the best published key-recovery attack on RECTANGLE [28].

Although its probability is suboptimal, its input and output differences are betted suited for key-recovery. The corresponding 18-round key-recovery attack requires 2^{64} data and enough memory to hold 2^{72} counters. The time-complexity amounts to $2^{78.67}$ (80-bit key) or $2^{126.66}$ (128-bit key) 18-round encryptions. A success probability of 67% is claimed.

Differential ii has a dominant characteristic with average probability 2^{-61}. Based on the analysis of the designers (which included differential effects), this differential is believed to have a maximal average probability. Up to rotational equivalence, there are a total of 32 such differentials. However, as discussed below, these differentials all have similar behavior.

The average probability of differential iii is suboptimal, but the analysis in Sect. 6.2 shows that its probability is much larger for some keys.

Table 1. Differentials (a, b) for 14 rounds of RECTANGLE. The column p_{avg} gives an estimate of the average differential probability for independent round-keys.

a	b	p_{avg}	Comment	№
0020000600000000	0004000000000020	$2^{-63} + 2^{-66}$	18-round key-recovery	i
0100007000000000	0861008400000010	$2^{-61} + 2 \cdot 2^{-64}$	'Optimal' (1 of 32).	ii
00000000c0000600	0004000000000020	$2 \cdot 2^{-65} + 13 \cdot 2^{-68}$	'Suboptimal'.	iii

6.2 Analysis

In order to search for optimal quasidifferential trails, we model the propagation of the masks for a fixed difference as a 'Satisfiability Modulo Theories' (SMT) problem. Using Theorem 4.1, quasidifferential trails allow us to compute the probability of a characteristic. The extended version of the paper contains additional information about the SMT model and its implementation.

Differential i. For completeness, we list the two dominant characteristics for this differential in the extended version of the paper. The first two columns of Table 2 list the number of quasidifferential trails of each correlation for these two characteristics.

Any characteristic has at least one quasidifferential trail with correlation equal to its average probability p_{avg}, namely the trail with all-zero masks. The fact that the first characteristic has two quasidifferential trails with correlation $\pm p_{avg}$ and the second four, is special. Table 3 shows two of these trails (one for each characteristic) with the same masks. Only rounds 9 to 12 are shown, since the masks are zero in all other rounds. Hence, these two trails describe a local, three-round effect. This is already an interesting outcome of our approach by itself, since previous techniques such as plateau characteristics are not able to describe such three-round effects.

Table 2. Number of quasidifferential trails for 14 rounds of RECTANGLE.

$\lvert c\rvert/p_{\text{avg}}$	Differential i		Differential ii			Differential iii	
	2^{-63}	2^{-66}	2^{-61}	2^{-64}	2^{-64}	2^{-65}	2^{-65}
1	2	4	2	2	4	32	32
2^{-1}	2	4	2	2	4	32	32
2^{-2}	26	52	24	24	48	352	352
2^{-3}	26	60	24	24	56	480	480
2^{-4}	182	396	176	176	384	2656	2656

Table 3. Differences and masks for two three-round quasidifferential trails with absolute correlation 2^{-13} and 2^{-19}. The masks are the same for both trails.

Differences ($p_{\text{trail}} = 2^{-63}$)	Differences ($p_{\text{trail}} = 2^{-66}$)	Masks (both)
........2....6.	........2....6.	....
........c....2.	........c....2.	..........c.....
...........86..	...........86..	............84..
...........12..	...........92..	............12..
...........3...	...........3..8	............3...
...........8...	...........8..1	....

Note that the propagation of the masks closely follows that of the differences. As discussed in Sect. 4.3, this is beneficial to obtain quasidifferential trails with high correlation. The correlation for the quasidifferential trail corresponding to the first characteristic in rounds 9 to 12 is equal to

$$(-1)^{\kappa_1} \times D^{\mathsf S}_{(c,c),(2,0)} D^{\mathsf S}_{(2,0),(6,0)} \times D^{\mathsf S}_{(1,1),(8,8)} D^{\mathsf S}_{(2,2),(6,4)} \times D^{\mathsf S}_{(8,0),(3,3)}$$

$$= (-1)^{\kappa_1} \times \frac{-1}{8} \times \frac{1}{4} \times \frac{1}{8} \times \frac{1}{4} \times \frac{1}{8} = (-1)^{1+\kappa_1} 2^{-13},$$

where $\kappa_1 = k_{10,10} + k_{10,15} + k_{11,12} + k_{11,13}$. Similarly, for the second characteristic, the correlation of the quasidifferential trail is equal to

$$(-1)^{\kappa_1} \times D^{\mathsf S}_{(c,c),(2,0)} D^{\mathsf S}_{(2,0),(6,0)} \times D^{\mathsf S}_{(9,1),(8,8)} D^{\mathsf S}_{(2,2),(6,4)} \times D^{\mathsf S}_{(8,0),(3,3)} D^{\mathsf S}_{(1,0),(8,0)}$$

$$= (-1)^{\kappa_1} \times \frac{-1}{8} \times \frac{1}{4} \times \frac{-1}{8} \times \frac{1}{4} \times \frac{1}{8} \times \frac{1}{8} = (-1)^{\kappa_1} 2^{-19}.$$

Note the sign difference compared to the first characteristic. As shown below, it implies that the two characteristics are incompatible: for each key, one of them must have probability zero. Taking into account the first four quasidifferential trails, the probability of the first characteristic is

$$p_{i,1} \approx \left(1 - (-1)^{\kappa_1}\right)\left(1 + (-1)^{\lambda}/2\right)2^{-63} = \mathbb{1}_{\kappa_1=1}\left(1 + (-1)^{\lambda}/2\right)2^{-62},$$

where λ is a linear combination of round-key bits. Although we did not include all quasidifferential trails in the analysis, Theorem 4.2 (2) allows concluding that the characteristic has probability zero when $\kappa_1 = 0$. Furthermore, it can be argued that lower-correlation trails are typically less significant. Although it is possible that for example the 26 trails with correlation 2^{-65} contribute a term of magnitude $2^{-63.3}$, this only happens for a small fraction of keys since it requires the signs of all these trails to point in the same direction. For the second characteristic, considering the first 8 trails results in

$$p_{i,2} \approx \left(1 + (-1)^{\kappa_1} - (-1)^{\kappa_2} - (-1)^{\kappa_1 + \kappa_2}\right)\left(1 + (-1)^{\lambda}/2\right)2^{-66}$$
$$= \mathbb{1}_{\kappa_1 = 0}\mathbb{1}_{\kappa_2 = 1}\left(1 + (-1)^{\lambda}/2\right)2^{-64}.$$

Impact on the Key-Recovery Attack. The time-complexity of the 18-round key-recovery attack based on differential i is determined by the number of remaining pairs for the right key after filtering the data. For the maximal number of input structures, the number of remaining unordered pairs will be $p_i \, 2^{63}$.

If $\kappa_1 = 0$, then the number of pairs is $\mathbb{1}_{\kappa_2 = 1}(2 + (-1)^{\lambda})/4$ on average over the remaining key bits. Since this is less than one for all values of κ_2 and λ, the key-recovery advantage will be too low to improve over brute-force.

For $\kappa_1 = 1$, the average number of unordered pairs is $2 + (-1)^{\lambda}$. Using a threshold of one pair as in the original attack, this gives a time-complexity of $2^{77.65}$ (80-bit key) or $2^{125.65}$ (128-bit key) assuming that the cost of evaluating the key-schedule is negligible compared to the cost of evaluating the cipher. Assuming that the number of right pairs follows a Poisson distribution within each key class, the success probability is then approximately $(1 - e^{-1})/2 + (1 - e^{-3})/2 \approx 79\%$. Hence, for this case, the attack still marginally improves over exhaustive search. However, achieving this improvement requires filtering for weak keys using the condition $\kappa_1 = 1$ during the key-recovery phase. Otherwise, no improvement over exhaustive search is obtained. The observations above can be summarized as follows.

Result 1. *The key-recovery attack on 18-round RECTANGLE from [28] using differential i does not improve over exhaustive search. For keys with $k_{10,10} + k_{10,15} + k_{11,12} + k_{11,13} = 1$, the attack can be modified to filter out keys not satisfying this condition and then achieves a success probability of approximately 79% with a time-complexity of $2^{77.65}$ (80-bit key) or $2^{125.65}$ (128-bit key) 18-round encryptions. The attack requires 2^{64} data and enough memory to store 2^{72} counters.*

By Result 1, there is a rectified 18-round key-recovery attack on RECTANGLE with *average* success probability 39.5% and (marginally) better time-complexity than exhaustive search.

Differential ii. The analysis of differential ii is very similar to that of i. The three dominant characteristics are given in the extended version of the paper. Based on the first four trails for the first two characteristics and the first eight trails for the second, the characteristic probabilities are

$$p_{ii,1} \approx \mathbb{1}_{\kappa_1=1}\left(1 + (-1)^\lambda/2\right) 2^{-60}$$
$$p_{ii,2} \approx \mathbb{1}_{\kappa_1=1}\left(1 + (-1)^\lambda/2\right) 2^{-63}$$
$$p_{ii,3} \approx \mathbb{1}_{\kappa_1=0}\mathbb{1}_{\kappa_2=0}\left(1 + (-1)^\lambda/2\right) 2^{-62}.$$

That is, for half of the keys, the dominant characteristic actually has no right pairs. For the other keys, its probability is roughly twice as large. The second characteristic shows similar behavior. Also note that the third characteristic is not compatible with the first two.

A similar analysis was performed for all other (up to rotational equivalence) 14-round differentials with a dominant characteristic of average probability 2^{-61}. The results were essentially the same.

Differential iii. Both characteristics with probability 2^{-65} are given in the extended version of the paper. Based on the 32 quasidifferential trails with correlation 2^{-65}, we find that the first characteristic has a nonzero probability if and only if 5 linearly independent equations in the round keys hold. The average probability over these keys is 2^{-60}. For the second characteristic, we find a similar effect with slightly different conditions on the round keys. Like for the first characteristic, the average probability over these keys is 2^{-60}. Furthermore, the conditions for the two characteristics to have nonzero probability (given in the extended version) are incompatible. Hence, the sum of the probabilities of the first two characteristics is 2^{-60} for 1/16 keys and zero for all other keys.

In addition, there are 13 characteristics with an average probability of 2^{-68}. We find that each of these characteristics has nonzero probability zero for only 1/64 or 1/128 keys. The conditions for this to happen may partially overlap or be inconsistent with the conditions for the first two characteristics.

7 Application to KNOT

In order to illustrate the relevance of our techniques to the analysis of permutations, we analyze several differential attacks on the KNOT family of permutations and their authenticated-encryption and hashing modes [29]. KNOT is a large-state variant of RECTANGLE and was a second-round candidate in the NIST lightweight cryptography project. In this paper, we only consider the primary variant, which is a 256-bit permutation. The state is represented by a 4×64 rectangular array. The round function operations are similar to those of RECTANGLE, but a different S-box is used and the third and fourth row of the state are rotated by 8 and 25 positions respectively. Additional details may be found in the extended version of the paper.

7.1 Differentials

At the 2020 NIST lightweight cryptography workshop, Zhang *et al.* [30] presented several differential attacks on round-reduced KNOT authenticated encryption and hashing modes. The differentials used in these attacks are listed in

Table 4, along with their estimated probabilities (without taking into account quasidifferential trails). In this section, it will be shown that these attacks do not work because the probability of the differentials in Table 4 is much smaller than expected. Furthermore, it will be shown that there exist round constants for which their probabilities are two orders of magnitude larger. All relevant characteristics are listed in the extended version of the paper.

Table 4. Differentials for r rounds of KNOT-256. The column p_{avg} gives an estimate of the 'average' differential probability (for independent uniform random round constants). The differences are given in the extended version of the paper.

r	p_{avg}	Application	№
10	5×2^{-56}	Hash collision and AEAD forgery.	i
12	10×2^{-66}	Hash collision and AEAD forgery.	ii

7.2   Analysis

The analysis of the differentials in Table 4 is similar to the analysis for RECT-ANGLE. The SMT-model for RECTANGLE can easily be modified to efficiently search for quasidifferential trails in KNOT.

Differential i. Based on the quasidifferential trails with correlation 2^{-56} for each of the five characteristics with $p_{avg} = 2^{-56}$, we conclude that all of them have probability zero for the standard round constants of KNOT-256. Hence, the differential probability is much lower than what might be expected from the 'average'. Even if there exist other characteristics with unexpectedly large probability (a scenario considered below), this is a significant issue for the collision attack on the KNOT hash function. Indeed, the collision search consists of finding a right pair for one of the best few characteristics, since this is significantly easier than finding a right pair for the differential by random search.

Despite the observations above, it is possible that there exists a low-probability characteristic with an unexpectedly high probability for the default round constants. The differential contains four characteristics with 'average' probability 2^{-60}. However, by analyzing the corresponding quasidifferential trails, we find that they too have probability zero. Next, there are 17 characteristics with 'average' probability 2^{-62}. Again, we find that all of them have probability zero. We also considered 24 characteristics with 'average' probabilities 2^{-63} and 2^{-65} and found that they have probability zero. Although we did not analyze all characteristics with probability 2^{-66} or lower, they can only have a high nonzero probability for a very small fraction of round constants. Given the number of such characteristics, it is unlikely that a high probability characteristic exists.

On the flip side, there exist round constants for which one or more of the five characteristics have probability 2^{-50}. This is due to the existence of 64 quasidifferential characteristics with absolute correlation 2^{-56}. A careful inspection of the conditions on the round constants shows that there exist variants of KNOT with modified constants for which the probability of differential i is approximately $5 \cdot 2^{-50} = 2^{-47.7}$. Further improvements are possible by taking into account additional characteristics and quasidifferential trails.

Differential ii. The analysis of the 12-round differential is similar to the 10-round differential, and leads to similar conclusions. This is not surprising given that both characteristics follow a similar pattern up to rotational symmetry. We find that each of the 10 dominant characteristics has probability zero for the default round constants. In addition, we did not find any characteristics with 'average' probability 2^{-70} or higher with a nonzero probability. Hence, it is unlikely that the 12-round forgery and collision attacks presented by Zhang *et al.* are valid. Finally, we can identify round constants for which one or more of the 10 characteristics has a probability of 2^{-59}.

8 Application to Speck

In this section we investigate the key-dependency of several differentials for Speck from the literature. The bitvector constraints for modular addition from Theorem 5.2 are the main ingredient of our SMT-model. The same approach can be applied to any ARX block cipher or permutation. The implementation of our model is provided as supplementary material.

In Sect. 8.1 we provide a simple explanation (using a single quasidifferential trail) for an experimental observation of Ankele and Kölbl [2] on Speck-64. In Sects. 8.2 and 8.3 we analyze the differentials used in the best published attacks on all variants of Speck. In the extended version of the paper, Speck is briefly reviewed.

8.1 Explaining Observations of Ankele and Kölbl on Speck-64

Ankele and Kölbl [2] experimentally estimated the probability of a 7-round differential for Speck-64 for 10000 random keys and found that the distribution of the number of rights pairs is bimodal. Their results are reproduced in Fig. 4, but colored to indicate two key classes that follow from the analysis below.

The fact that the histogram in Fig. 4 is bimodal already suggests the presence of an important quasidifferential trail with nonzero masks. Automatic search reveals that the best such quasidifferential trail has correlation 2^{-23}. The dominant characteristic (with probability 2^{-21}) and the masks of the quasidifferential trail with correlation 2^{-23} are shown in Table 5.

The quasidifferential trail from Table 5 only involves the modular additions of the first two rounds. Figure 5 shows the propagation of the mask-difference pairs for these rounds in more detail. Following Sect. 4.3, the interpretation of this trail is that there exists a linear combination of the output of the first modular addition which is biased for the right pairs. This implies that a rotated

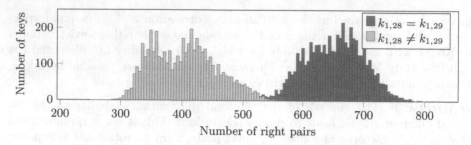

Fig. 4. Number of right pairs for the SPECK-64 differential from [2], for a total of 10000 keys. For each key, 2^{30} pairs were sampled uniformly at random.

Table 5. Differential trail with probability 2^{-21} for 7 rounds of Speck-64, and the masks of a quasidifferential trail with correlation 2^{-23}.

Differences	Masks
4...4.92 1.42..4.	....
82.2..... .12.2.. 18.....	....
..9..... ....1...	....
....8...	....
......8. ......8.	....
8.....8. 8....48.	....
..8..48.. ..8.2.84	....
8.8..a.8. 8481a4a.	....

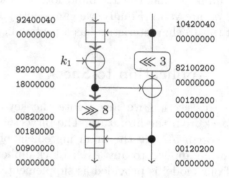

```
92400040                          10420040
00000000                          00000000

k1
82020000                          82100200
18000000                          00000000

                                  00120200
                                  00000000
00820200
00180000

00900000                          00120200
00000000                          00000000
```

Fig. 5. Quasidifferential trail with correlation $2^{-5} \times 2^{-6} = 2^{-11}$ through two rounds of Speck-64, with differences in orange and masks in blue. (Color figure online)

linear combination of the left input of the second modular addition is biased. This bias results in a smaller or larger number of right pairs, depending on the value of a linear combination of bits of k_1. Specifically, the probability can be estimated as

$$2^{-21} + (-1)^{k_{1,28}+k_{1,29}} 2^{-23}.$$

For 2^{30} random input pairs, the average number of right pairs is still $2^9 = 512$. However, the above formula predicts that the average is $512 + 2^7 = 640$ if $k_{1,28} = k_{1,29}$ and $512 - 2^7 = 384$ otherwise. This explains most of the variation in the experimental results shown in Fig. 4. Additional effects, such as the more limited bimodal behavior for $k_{1,28} \neq k_{1,29}$, can be explained by taking into account additional quasidifferential trails.

8.2 Analysis of Differential Attacks on Speck-32

The best published attacks on reduced-round Speck are differential attacks using the enumeration key-recovery strategy proposed by Dinur [13]. Given an r-round differential, an $r+3$ round attack is obtained by prepending one round (for free) and appending two rounds. For variants with longer key lengths, one performs the same attack for each guess of the last few round keys.

In this section, we analyze the best published attacks on Speck-32 reduced to 11–14 rounds. These attacks rely on the 6–9 round differentials shown in Table 6. Lee et al. [17] report on a 10-round differential with average probability $2^{-30.39}$, but it does not lead to a 15-round key-recovery attack because the time-complexity would be $2^{31.39}$ for a success probability of $1 - 1/e \approx 63\%$.

Table 6. Differentials (a, b) for r-round Speck-32.

r	a	b	p_{avg}	Reference	№
6	0211 0a04	850a 9520	2^{-13}	Abed et al. [1]	i
7	0a60 4205	850a 9520	2^{-18}	Abed et al. [1]	ii
8	1488 1008	850a 9520	$2^{-24} + 2^{-27}$	Abed et al. [1]	iii
9	8054 a900	0040 0542	$2^{-30} + 2 \cdot 2^{-33\dagger}$	Biryukov et al. [7], Song et al. [24]	iv

$\dagger$ $3060307 \cdot 2^{-47} \approx 2^{-29.45}$ with characteristics of average probability $\leq 2^{-49}$

Differentials i and ii. The six round differential i is dominated by a characteristic with average probability 2^{-13}, given in the extended version of the paper. The next-best characteristic has average probability 2^{-23} and will be ignored in our analysis. We find two quasidifferential trails with correlation $\pm 2^{-15}$ and two with correlation $\pm 2^{-17}$. There also exist trails with absolute correlation 2^{-19} and lower, but their effect on the probability is limited except for a small fraction of keys. Grouping these trails appropriately, the following estimate is obtained:

$$p_i \approx (1 + (-1)^{0003^{\mathsf{T}} k_5}/4)(1 + (-1)^{0180^{\mathsf{T}} k_5}/4)2^{-13},$$

where, for simplicity, only one trail of correlation $\pm 2^{-17}$ is included.

The analysis of the seven round differential is similar. The dominant differential trail has average probability 2^{-18} and is the same as the six round trail with one additional round at the beginning. Hence,

$$p_{ii} \approx (1 + (-1)^{0003^{\mathsf{T}} k_6}/4)(1 + (-1)^{0180^{\mathsf{T}} k_6}/4)2^{-18}.$$

Differential iii. The differential is dominated by two characteristics. The first has average probability 2^{-24}. Since the last part of these characteristics is the same as for the dominant characteristics of differentials i and ii, some of the same quasidifferential trails are obtained. However, there also exist quasidifferential trails with correlation equal to the probability of the trail. This implies that there exists keys for which these characteristics have probability zero. Specifically, for the first characteristic, we find that

$$p_{iii,1} \approx \mathbb{1}_{0600^{\mathsf{T}} k_2 = 0} \mathbb{1}_{1800^{\mathsf{T}} k_3 = 0}(1 + (-1)^{0003^{\mathsf{T}} k_7}/4)(1 + (-1)^{0180^{\mathsf{T}} k_7}/4)\, 2^{-22}.$$

That is, its probability is zero for 3/4 keys, but four times larger for the other keys. For the second characteristic, we have

$$p_{iii,2} \approx \mathbb{1}_{0600^\mathsf{T}k_2=0}\,\mathbb{1}_{1800^\mathsf{T}k_3=0}\,\mathbb{1}_{0a00^\mathsf{T}k_2=0}(1+(-1)^{0003^\mathsf{T}k_7}/4)(1+(-1)^{0180^\mathsf{T}k_7}/4)\,2^{-24}.$$

Hence, the second characteristic has nonzero probability only when the first probability is nonzero *and* $0a00^\mathsf{T}k_2 = 0$.

Differential iv. The probability is dominated by three characteristics (listed in the extended version of the paper). Additional characteristics only increase the overall probability, but more detailed analysis reveals that many additional characteristics have probability zero for most keys, and high probability for a relatively small fraction of keys.

The first characteristic has average probability 2^{-30}. Based on all quasidifferential trails with absolute correlation $\geq 2^{-32}$, we obtain

$$p_{iv,1} \approx \mathbb{1}_{000c^\mathsf{T}k_5=0}(1-(-1)^{0180^\mathsf{T}k_1}/4)\,2^{-29}.$$

For the second characteristic (with average probability 2^{-33}), the quasidifferential trails with absolute correlation $\geq 2^{-34}$ yield

$$p_{iv,2} \approx \mathbb{1}_{6000^\mathsf{T}k_2=1}(1+(-1)^{000c^\mathsf{T}k_5}/2+(-1)^{0300^\mathsf{T}k_4+000c^\mathsf{T}k_5}/2)\,2^{-32}.$$

Note that one of the two quasidifferential trails with absolute correlation 2^{-34} involves three modular additions. By Theorem 4.2, the condition $6000^\mathsf{T}k_2 = 1$ is necessary to obtain a nonzero probability. However, the conditions $0300^\mathsf{T}k_4 = 0$ and $000c^\mathsf{T}k_5 = 1$ only imply a small but possibly nonzero correlation. For the third characteristic, we consider all quasidifferential trails with absolute correlation $\geq 2^{-35}$ and obtain

$$p_{iv,3} \approx \mathbb{1}_{0c00^\mathsf{T}k_2=1}\,\mathbb{1}_{000c^\mathsf{T}k_5=0}(1-(-1)^{0180^\mathsf{T}k_1}/2)\,2^{-31}.$$

Note that the condition $000c^\mathsf{T}k_5 = 0$ is shared with the first characteristic. Since the probability of the second characteristic is too low, this implies that previous key-recovery attacks on 14 rounds of Speck-32 work for only half of the keys.

Impact on Key-Recovery Attacks. The above analysis allows us to reevaluate the best published attacks on reduced-round Speck-32. The attack on 13 rounds only works for one in four keys. Likewise, the attack on 14 rounds works only for half of the keys. Another way to formulate this is that the (key-averaged) success probability of these attacks is much lower than expected. For eleven and twelve rounds, the success probability is also slightly lower, but less so. Unfortunately, restoring the previous success-probability is not possible except by using alternative differentials.

However, if the results of our analysis are taken into account, weak-key attacks with lower data requirements are obtained. These attacks can be optimized either with respect to the number of weak keys, or with respect to the data-complexity. To minimize the data-complexity, we make assumptions on the key to maximize the probability of the differential. To maximize the number of keys for which the attack works, only conditions to ensure nonzero probabilities are imposed. Assuming that the adversary stops requesting data once the key has been found[2], these attacks require less data than what would be expected based on the average-case analysis.

Table 7. Rectified attacks on r-round Speck-32.

r	Time *encryptions*	Data *chosen plaintexts*	Weak-keys *density*	Comment
11	$2^{45.36}$	$2^{13.36}$	2^{-2}	Optimized for data
	$2^{45.88}$	$2^{13.88}$	1	Optimized for number of keys
12	$2^{50.36}$	$2^{18.36}$	2^{-2}	Optimized for data
	$2^{50.88}$	$2^{18.88}$	1	Optimized for number of keys
13	$2^{54.03}$	$2^{22.03}$	2^{-5}	Optimized for data
	$2^{56.20}$	$2^{24.20}$	2^{-2}	Optimized for number of keys
14	$2^{61.84}$	$2^{29.84}$	2^{-1}	Optimized for number of keys

The results are shown in Table 7. For example, the 6-round differential (11 round attack) has a probability at most $(1 + 1/4)^2 \, 2^{-13} \approx 2^{-12.36}$. With early stopping, the average number of pairs required is $2^{13}(1/(1 - 1/4)^2 + 2/(1 - 1/4^2) + 1/(1 + 1/4)^2)/4 \approx 2^{12.88}$. For 14 rounds, we omit the attack optimizing the data-complexity, since it requires more time than exhaustive search over a key space of size 2^{64-1} for a similar success probability.

8.3   Analysis of Differential Attacks on Larger Variants of Speck

The techniques to analyze Speck-32 in Sect. 8.2 carry over to the larger variants of Speck. In this section, we reevaluate the best published attacks on these variants. They rely on the key-recovery technique of Dinur [13] and are based on the differentials shown in Table 8 below. For 16 rounds of Speck-96, Song *et al.* [24] also propose a differential with average probability $2^{-94.94}$. However, we do not include it as its probability is too low to improve over exhaustive search.

Most of the differentials in Table 8 rely on a significant differential effect. Nevertheless, the analysis below will be limited to a few characteristics in each case. This is done only to simplify the analysis, since each characteristic has its own key-dependent behaviour that is not independent of other characteristics. Note that including additional characteristics can only increase the probability of the differential. In addition, it will be shown that key-dependence is much more significant than the differential effect for all differentials in Table 8. A detailed analysis of the differentials in Table 8 is given in the extended version.

---

[2] This is possible due to the way the key-recovery attack works.

Table 8. Differentials for r-round Speck-n (differences in the extended version). The average differential probability is p_{avg}, the average probability of the analyzed characteristics is p_{char}. The values p_{min} and p_{max} are the minimum and maximum value of the probability of the analyzed characteristics.

n	r	p_{avg}	p_{char}	p_{min}	p_{max}	Reference	№
48	11	$2^{-44.31}$	$2^{-46} + 2^{-47}$	0	2^{-43}	Song et $al.$ [24]	i
64	15	$2^{-60.56}$	2^{-62}	0	2^{-59}	Song et $al.$ [24]	ii
96	15	$2^{-81.00}$	2^{-81}	0	$2^{-73.68}$	Song et $al.$ [24]	iii
128	20	$2^{-124.35}$	$4 \cdot 2^{-128}$	0	$2^{-120.36}$	Song et $al.$ [24]	iv

Table 9. Rectified attacks on r-round Speck.

Variant	r	Time $encryptions$	Data $chosen$ $plaintexts$	Weak-keys $density$	Comment
48/72	15	2^{68}	2^{44}	2^{-3}	Optimized for data
		$2^{68.58}$	$2^{44.58}$	2^{-2}	Optimized for number of keys
48/96	16	2^{92}	2^{44}	2^{-3}	Optimized for data
		$2^{92.58}$	$2^{44.58}$	2^{-2}	Optimized for number of keys
64/96	19	2^{92}	2^{60}	2^{-3}	——
64/128	20	2^{124}	2^{60}	2^{-3}	——
96/96	18	$2^{74.68}$	$2^{74.68}$	2^{-9}	Optimized for data
		$2^{77.25}$	$2^{77.25}$	2^{-6}	Optimized for number of keys
96/144	19	$2^{122.68}$	$2^{74.68}$	2^{-9}	Optimized for data
		$2^{125.25}$	$2^{77.25}$	2^{-6}	Optimized for number of keys
128/m	20	$2^{121.36}$	$2^{121.36}$	2^{-7}	Distinguisher (data-optimized)
		$2^{125.36}$	$2^{125.36}$	2^{-3}	Distinguisher (key-optimized)

Impact on Key-Recovery Attacks. The analysis above directly impacts the key-recovery attacks based on the differentials from Table 8. Like for Speck-32, all of these attacks have lower success probability than previously expected. Nevertheless, the analysis also leads to weak-key attacks with lower data-complexity. The results are summarized in Table 9.

Note that for Speck-128, our analysis shows that the key-recovery attacks probably do not improve over exhaustive search over the reduced key-space. Improvements may be possible if checking the weak-key conditions can be made comparatively cheap, provided that checking candidate keys dominates the cost. Since a detailed analysis of the time-complexity is outside of the scope of this paper, Table 9 only lists a distinguisher for this case. Although our analysis did not include all characteristics, these would only increase the *average* differential probability by $2^{-124.9}$. Further analysis shows that the probabilities of these characteristics are strongly key-dependent. Hence, the key-recovery attacks on Speck-128 from [24] most likely do not improve over exhaustive search.

Acknowledgements. We thank Anne Canteaut and Jean-René Reinhard for responding to our questions about their attacks on PRINCE. Tim Beyne is supported by a PhD Fellowship from the Research Foundation – Flanders (FWO). This work was partially supported by the Research Council KU Leuven, grant C16/18/004 on New Block Cipher Structures.

References

1. Abed, F., List, E., Lucks, S., Wenzel, J.: Differential cryptanalysis of round-reduced SIMON and SPECK. In: Cid, C., Rechberger, C. (eds.) FSE 2014. LNCS, vol. 8540, pp. 525–545. Springer, Heidelberg (2015). https://doi.org/10.1007/978-3-662-46706-0_27
2. Ankele, R., Kölbl, S.: Mind the gap—a closer look at the security of block ciphers against differential cryptanalysis. In: SAC 2018. LNCS, vol. 11349, pp. 163–190 (2018). https://doi.org/10.1007/978-3-030-10970-7_8
3. Beyne, T.: Block cipher invariants as eigenvectors of correlation matrices. In: Peyrin, T., Galbraith, S. (eds.) ASIACRYPT 2018, Part I. LNCS, vol. 11272, pp. 3–31. Springer, Cham (2018). https://doi.org/10.1007/978-3-030-03326-2_1
4. Beyne, T.: A geometric approach to linear cryptanalysis. In: Tibouchi, M., Wang, H. (eds.) ASIACRYPT 2021, Part I. LNCS, vol. 13090, pp. 36–66. Springer, Cham (2021). https://doi.org/10.1007/978-3-030-92062-3_2
5. Biham, E., Shamir, A.: Differential cryptanalysis of DES-like cryptosystems. In: Menezes, A.J., Vanstone, S.A. (eds.) CRYPTO 1990. LNCS, vol. 537, pp. 2–21. Springer, Heidelberg (1991). https://doi.org/10.1007/3-540-38424-3_1
6. Biham, E., Shamir, A.: Differential cryptanalysis of the Full 16-round DES. In: Brickell, E.F. (ed.) CRYPTO 1992. LNCS, vol. 740, pp. 487–496. Springer, Heidelberg (1993). https://doi.org/10.1007/3-540-48071-4_34
7. Biryukov, A., Roy, A., Velichkov, V.: Differential analysis of block ciphers SIMON and SPECK. In: Cid, C., Rechberger, C. (eds.) FSE 2014. LNCS, vol. 8540, pp. 546–570. Springer, Heidelberg (2015). https://doi.org/10.1007/978-3-662-46706-0_28
8. Bogdanov, A., et al.: PRESENT: an ultra-lightweight block cipher. In: Paillier, P., Verbauwhede, I. (eds.) CHES 2007. LNCS, vol. 4727, pp. 450–466. Springer, Heidelberg (2007). https://doi.org/10.1007/978-3-540-74735-2_31
9. Canteaut, A., Lambooij, E., Neves, S., Rasoolzadeh, S., Sasaki, Y., Stevens, M.: Refined probability of differential characteristics including dependency between multiple rounds. IACR Trans. Symm. Cryptol. 2, 203–227 (2017)
10. Daemen, J., Govaerts, R., Vandewalle, J.: Correlation matrices. In: Preneel, B. (ed.) FSE 1994. LNCS, vol. 1008, pp. 275–285. Springer, Heidelberg (1995). https://doi.org/10.1007/3-540-60590-8_21
11. Daemen, J., Rijmen, V.: Plateau characteristics. IET Inf. Secur. 1(1), 11–17 (2007)
12. De Cannière, C., Rechberger, C.: Finding SHA-1 characteristics: general results and applications. In: Lai, X., Chen, K. (eds.) ASIACRYPT 2006. LNCS, vol. 4284, pp. 1–20. Springer, Heidelberg (2006). https://doi.org/10.1007/11935230_1
13. Dinur, I.: Improved differential cryptanalysis of round-reduced speck. In: Joux, A., Youssef, A. (eds.) SAC 2014. LNCS, vol. 8781, pp. 147–164. Springer, Cham (2014). https://doi.org/10.1007/978-3-319-13051-4_9

14. Heys, H.M.: Key dependency of differentials: Experiments in the differential cryptanalysis of block ciphers using small S-boxes. ePrint, Report 2020/1349 (2020)
15. Knudsen, L.R.: Iterative characteristics of DES and s^2-DES. In: Brickell, E.F. (ed.) CRYPTO 1992. LNCS, vol. 740, pp. 497–511. Springer, Heidelberg (1993). https://doi.org/10.1007/3-540-48071-4_35
16. Lai, X., Massey, J.L., Murphy, S.: Markov ciphers and differential cryptanalysis. In: Davies, D.W. (ed.) EUROCRYPT 1991. LNCS, vol. 547, pp. 17–38. Springer, Heidelberg (1991). https://doi.org/10.1007/3-540-46416-6_2
17. Lee, H., Kim, S., Kang, H., Hong, D., Sung, J., Hong, S.: Calculating the approximate probability of differentials for ARX-based cipher using SAT solver. J. Korea Inst. Inf. Secur. Cryptol. 28(1), 15–24 (2018)
18. Leurent, G.: Analysis of differential attacks in ARX constructions. In: Wang, X., Sako, K. (eds.) ASIACRYPT 2012. LNCS, vol. 7658, pp. 226–243. Springer, Heidelberg (2012). https://doi.org/10.1007/978-3-642-34961-4_15
19. Liu, Y., et al.: The phantom of differential characteristics. Des. Codes Cryptogr. 88(11), 2289–2311 (2020)
20. Matsui, M.: Linear cryptanalysis method for DES Cipher. In: Helleseth, T. (ed.) EUROCRYPT 1993. LNCS, vol. 765, pp. 386–397. Springer, Heidelberg (1994). https://doi.org/10.1007/3-540-48285-7_33
21. Mendel, F., Rijmen, V., Toz, D., Varıcı, K.: Differential analysis of the LED block cipher. In: Wang, X., Sako, K. (eds.) ASIACRYPT 2012. LNCS, vol. 7658, pp. 190–207. Springer, Heidelberg (2012). https://doi.org/10.1007/978-3-642-34961-4_13
22. Biham, E., Dunkelman, O., Keller, N.: Linear cryptanalysis of reduced round serpent. In: Matsui, M. (ed.) FSE 2001. LNCS, vol. 2355, pp. 16–27. Springer, Heidelberg (2002). https://doi.org/10.1007/3-540-45473-X_2
23. Schulte-Geers, E.: On CCZ-equivalence of addition mod 2^n. Des. Codes Cryptogr. 66(1–3), 111–127 (2013)
24. Song, L., Huang, Z., Yang, Q.: Automatic differential analysis of ARX block ciphers with application to SPECK and LEA. In: Liu, J.K., Steinfeld, R. (eds.) ACISP 2016, Part II. LNCS, vol. 9723, pp. 379–394. Springer, Cham (2016). https://doi.org/10.1007/978-3-319-40367-0_24
25. Sun, L., Wang, W., Wang(66), M.: More accurate differential properties of LED64 and Midori64. IACR Trans. Symm. Cryptol. 2018(3), 93–123 (2018)
26. Wang, X., Yu, H.: How to break MD5 and other hash functions. In: Cramer, R. (ed.) EUROCRYPT 2005. LNCS, vol. 3494, pp. 19–35. Springer, Heidelberg (2005). https://doi.org/10.1007/11426639_2
27. Xu, Z., Li, Y., Jiao, L., Wang, M., Meier, W.: Do NOT misuse the Markov cipher assumption—automatic search for differential and impossible differential characteristics in ARX ciphers. ePrint, Report 2022/135 (2022)
28. Zhang, W., Bao, Z., Lin, D., Rijmen, V., Yang, B., Verbauwhede, I.: RECTANGLE: a bit-slice lightweight block cipher suitable for multiple platforms. Sci. China Inf. Sci. 58(12), 1–15 (2015)
29. Zhang, W., Ding, T., Yang, B., Bao, Z., Xiang, Z., Ji, F., Zhao, X.: KNOT: Algorithm specifications and supporting document. Submission to NIST lightweight cryptography project (2019)
30. Zhang, W., Ding, T., Zhou, C., Ji, F.: Security analysis of KNOT-AEAD and KNOT-Hash. In: NIST Lightweight Cryptography Workshop (2020)

Simplified MITM Modeling for Permutations: New (Quantum) Attacks

André Schrottenloher[✉] and Marc Stevens

Cryptology Group, CWI, Amsterdam, The Netherlands
andre.schrottenloher@m4x.org, marc.stevens@cwi.nl

Abstract. Meet-in-the-middle (MITM) is a general paradigm where internal states are computed along two independent paths ('forwards' and 'backwards') that are then matched. Over time, MITM attacks improved using more refined techniques and exploiting additional freedoms and structure, which makes it more involved to find and optimize such attacks. This has led to the use of detailed attack models for generic solvers to automatically search for improved attacks, notably a MILP model developed by Bao et al. at EUROCRYPT 2021.

In this paper, we study a simpler MILP modeling combining a greatly reduced attack representation as input to the generic solver, together with a theoretical analysis that, for any solution, proves the existence and complexity of a detailed attack. This modeling allows to find both classical and quantum attacks on a broad class of cryptographic permutations. First, PRESENT-like constructions, with the permutations from the SPONGENT hash functions: we improve the MITM step in distinguishers by up to 3 rounds. Second, AES-like designs: despite being much simpler than Bao et al.'s, our model allows to recover the best previous results. The only limitation is that we do not use degrees of freedom from the key schedule. Third, we show that the model can be extended to target more permutations, like Feistel networks. In this context we give new Guess-and-determine attacks on reduced Simpira v2 and SPARKLE.

Finally, using our model, we find several new quantum preimage and pseudo-preimage attacks (e.g. Haraka v2, Simpira v2 ...) targeting the same number of rounds as the classical attacks.

Keywords: MITM Attacks · Permutation-based hashing · Preimage attacks · Merging algorithms · Quantum cryptanalysis

1 Introduction

Meet-in-the-middle is a general attack paradigm against cryptographic primitives where internal states are computed along two independent paths ('forwards' and 'backwards') that are then matched to produce a complete path solution. MITM attacks can be traced back to Diffie and Hellman's time-memory trade-off on Double-encryption [23]. Since then, they have been successfully applied over the years on block ciphers and hash functions [1, 14, 26, 33, 36, 37]. Moreover,

© International Association for Cryptologic Research 2022
Y. Dodis and T. Shrimpton (Eds.): CRYPTO 2022, LNCS 13509, pp. 717–747, 2022.
https://doi.org/10.1007/978-3-031-15982-4_24

MITM attacks have been improved using more refined techniques and exploiting additional freedoms and structure (e.g., using internal state guesses [26], splice-and-cut [1,33], bicliques [38], 3-subset MITM [14]), which also makes it more involved to find and optimize such attacks.

An important trend in cryptanalysis is the application of automatic tools to search for improved attacks. The search of an attack of a certain form is translated into a search or optimization problem, which is solved using an off-the-shelf SAT, constraint programming (CP), Mixed Integer Linear Programming (MILP) solver. Thus the difficulty of finding an attack by hand is replaced by that of finding a proper modeling of the attack search space into a corresponding search/optimization problem. This has naturally led to a bottom-up modeling including low-level attack details, such that any solution directly corresponds to an instantiation of the attack.

MITM Attacks on Hash Functions. Hash functions are often built from a compression function, using a simple domain extender such as Merkle-Damgård [21,41]. This compression function, in turn, can be built from a block cipher E_k using one of the twelve secure PGV modes [43], usually one of the three most common: Davies-Meyer (DM), Matyas-Meyer-Oseas (MMO) and Miyaguchi-Preneel (MP). A preimage attack on the hash function can be reduced to one on the compression function.

In [44], Sasaki introduced a MITM preimage attack on AES hashing modes targeting as much as 7 rounds. This attack already integrates advanced techniques such as the *initial structure* and *matching through MixColumns*, which is reviewed later. Bao *et al.* [3] improved the attacks of [44] by making use of degrees of freedom from the key-schedule path; that is, allowing a varying chaining value instead of considering a fixed one. In [4], an MILP framework for automatic search of MITM attacks was introduced. It applies to all *AES-based* hash functions, whose internal state is defined as an array of fixed-size cells and whose operations mimic the operations of the AES block cipher. This modeling led to many improved results; in particular, the first 8-round preimage attack on a hash function using AES-128. Later on, this modeling was improved in [5] and [25]. The former introduced the technique of *guess-and-determine* in the solver, while the latter extended the search to collision attacks and key-recovery attacks against block ciphers.

Limits of Rule-Based Modeling. In AES-based hash functions, internal states are represented as an array of cells corresponding to the S-Boxes. The MITM attack can entirely be specified by a certain coloring of these cells (backwards, forwards, unspecified). *Propagation rules* can then be defined, which specify the admissible coloring transitions at each stage of the cipher, while computing the parameters which give the time and memory complexities of the MITM attack. This is a bottom-up approach, as the validity of the path is enforced locally.

However, the definition of these rules is quite involved, and the follow-up works [5,25] added even more rules to capture new techniques. This increases, in turn, the complexity of the model, which (as reported in [5]) requires more human intervention to limit the search space.

Furthermore, the rule-based modeling in [4] is limited to AES-like ciphers. These primitives have the property that the linear layer is *strongly aligned* with the S-Box layer, and all the operations can be defined at cell-level (bytes in the case of AES), instead at bit-level. Extending the rule-based modeling to other primitives was one of the main open questions in [4], which would typically require moving to a bit-level and increasing model complexity. Our goal is to develop a powerful model that is both broadly applicable and significantly simpler than rule-based models.

Quantum Preimage Attacks. It is well-known that Grover's quantum search algorithm [30] halves the bits of preimage security that one can expect from a hash function, e.g., instead of requiring 2^{128} computations of a 128-bit hash function, Grover's search can find a preimage in about 2^{64} evaluations of a quantum circuit for the function. However, Grover search is only a generic algorithm. There might exist dedicated *quantum attacks* that, for a given design, find a preimage in less time. Such attacks determine the security margin of a hash function in a post-quantum context, especially for hash-based signature schemes [2]. But to date, while quantum collision attacks have been significantly studied [34, 35], little is known on quantum preimage attacks.

1.1 Our Contributions

Top-Down Modeling. In this work we do not follow the detailed bottom-up modeling where any solution directly corresponds to an instantiation of the attack. Ideally, the modeling should remain simple, and lead to feasible search times, while at the same time, cover a large space of potential attacks. Hence instead, we study a simpler *top-down* modeling paradigm in which we search for a greatly simplified attack representation excluding many details, for which we are able to prove the existence of an optimized attack instantiation and its corresponding complexity (see Lemma 2 and Theorem 1 in Sect. 4). This has several benefits. First, the abstract representation makes it more generically applicable to a wide set of designs. Second, it enables analysis of not only classical attacks, but quantum attacks as well with minor changes. Third, the resulting model input to the solver is significantly smaller, which typically means it can be solved faster and thus it is more practical to cover larger primitives and/or more rounds.

MITM Preimage Attacks. We apply this top-down modeling paradigm to MITM preimage attacks. Our representation is close to the dedicated solvers introduced in [16, 22], and complementary to the bottom-up modeling developed in [4, 5, 25]. Instead of defining local rules for the propagation of cell coloring between cells, we consider a global view of the MITM attack capturing only which cells belong to the forward and the backward paths, and optimize the attack time complexity as a function of the cells. This view has two advantages: first, its simplicity. Second, its genericity, as it is not limited to strongly aligned designs and allows to target a larger class than AES-based hashing. In fact, we start with applications to "PRESENT-like" permutations, and only later, rewrite AES-based primitives as "PRESENT-like", using the Super S-Box.

Our approach is so far limited to permutations: we do not use degrees of freedom of the key-schedule. This restriction makes our tool oblivious to the most advanced attacks on hashing using AES. However, many recent hash functions, especially small-range hash functions like Simpira v2 [31] or Haraka v2 [40], or more generally, Sponge designs like SHA-3, are only based on permutations.

Our modeling also admits a generic translation of classical MITM attacks into quantum attacks. We find these attacks using our automatic tool, by a mere change in the optimization goal. In fact, the valid paths for quantum attacks correspond to classical paths *under new memory constraints*. When applicable, our quantum attacks reach the same number of rounds as the classical ones.

Outline and Results. In Sect. 2, we recall previous results and elaborate on the definition and modeling of a MITM attack in [4,5,25]. The rest of the paper follows our new approach. We define our *cell-coloring representation*, and *merging-based MITM attacks*, in Sect. 3. In Sect. 4, we simplify this representation and detail our MILP modeling for classical and quantum attacks. Next, we demonstrate the versatility of our approach and obtain existing and new state-of-the-art attacks.

In Sect. 5, we study the class of PRESENT-like permutations, which have the same operations as the block cipher PRESENT: individual S-Boxes, followed by a linear layer which exchanges bits between pairs of S-Boxes. We improve the MITM step in the distinguishers on the permutations of the SPONGENT family.

In Sect. 6, we study the class of AES-like permutations. With the Super S-Box, AES itself becomes a small PRESENT-like cipher. We recover previous results on these permutations and give new quantum preimage attacks on reduced-round AES, Haraka v2 and Grøstl (these results are summarized in Table 1).

In Sect. 7, we study an extended class of permutations in which the linear layer contains XORs. In particular, we study Generalized Feistel Networks and obtain generic and *practical* guess-and-determine distinguishers on GFNs, reduced-round Simpira permutations, and reduced-step SPARKLE permutations (summarized in Tables 3 and 4). The distinguishers on Simpira are converted into preimage attacks (see Table 1).

Our code is available at: github.com/AndreSchrottenloher/mitm-milp. We used the MILP solver of the SCIP Optimization Suite [29].

2   Preliminaries

In this section, we describe the families of PRESENT-like, AES-like and Feistel-like permutations targeted in this paper. We recall MITM problems and the rule-based framework studied in [3–5,25,44]. We choose to focus only on single-target *pseudo-preimage attacks*, and refer to [3] for a clear depiction of generic techniques to convert pseudo-preimage to preimage attacks.

Table 1. Our new (pseudo)-preimage attacks, with points of comparison to previous works. QRAQM = quantum-accessible quantum memory. The generic time given can be higher than the security claims of the design. $|_n$: A partial preimage attack over n-bits. (Q): Using QRAQM.

Target	Type	Rounds	Time	Generic time	Memory	Source
AES-128	Classical	8	2^{120}	2^{128}	2^{40}	[4]
AES-128	Quantum	7	$2^{63.34}$	2^{64}	2^8 (Q)	Sect. 6.1
Haraka-256 v2	Classical	4.5/5	2^{224}	2^{256}	2^{32}	[4]
Haraka-256 v2	Quantum	4.5/5	$2^{115.55}$	2^{128}	2^{32}(Q)	Sect. 6.2
Haraka-512 v2	Classical	5.5/5	2^{240}	2^{256}	2^{128}	[4]
Haraka-512 v2	Classical	5.5/5	2^{240}	2^{256}	2^{16}	Sect. 6.2
Haraka-512 v2	Quantum	5.5/5	$2^{123.34}$	2^{128}	2^{16}(Q)	Sect. 6.2
Haraka-512 v2 $|_{32}$	Classical	5.5/5	2^{16}	2^{32}	2^{16}	Sect. 6.2
Haraka-512 v2 $|_{64}$	Classical	5/5	2^{32}	2^{64}	2^{32}	Full version [45]
SPHINCS+-Haraka	Quantum	3.5/5	$2^{64.65}$	$2^{85.33}$	negl	Sect. 6.2
Grøstl-256 OT	Classical	6/10	2^{224}	2^{256}	2^{128}	[5]
Grøstl-256 OT	Quantum	6/10	$2^{123.56}$	2^{128}	2^{112}(Q)	Sect. 6.3
Grøstl-512 OT	Classical	8/14	2^{472}	2^{512}	2^{224}	[5]
Grøstl-512 OT	Quantum	8/14	$2^{255.55}$	2^{256}	2^{56}(Q)	Sect. 6.3
Simpira-2	Classical	5/15	2^{128}	2^{256}	negl	Sect. 7.2
Simpira-2	Quantum	5/15	2^{64}	2^{128}	negl	Sect. 7.2
Simpira-4	Classical	9/15	2^{128}	2^{256}	negl	Sect. 7.2
Simpira-4	Quantum	9/15	2^{64}	2^{128}	negl	Sect. 7.2

2.1   Families of Designs

PRESENT-*like.* We name this family after the block cipher PRESENT [13]. It is a Substitution-Permutation Network (SPN) with an internal state of $b = 16$ cells of 4 bits. Its round function applies in order: (1) the round key addition, (2) the PRESENT S-Box on each cell independently, and (3) the linear layer defined by the bit-permutation:

$$P(j) = \begin{cases} 4b - 1 & \text{if } j = 4b - 1; \\ (j \cdot b) \bmod 4b - 1 & \text{otherwise.} \end{cases}$$

That is, the j-th bit of the state after an S-Box layer is moved to the $P(j)$-th bit of the state before the next key addition. In particular, each cell at a given round connects to 4 cells at the next round. Thus, PRESENT is an SPN in the strict sense that the "permutation" is a permutation of bits. In this paper, we consider the analysis of PRESENT in the known-key setting (see e.g. [10]), where the key is fixed, which turns the cipher into a permutation. The SPONGENT-π family of permutations[1], which are used in the SPONGENT hash function [11] is a generalization of the PRESENT design to larger state sizes, with b ranging from

---

[1] This denomination is from [9] . Previously the permutation did not have a name, or was named "SPONGENT" by metonymy.

22 to 192. By abstracting out the S-Box, other designs such as GIMLI [8] can be considered as PRESENT-like.

AES-like. The AES, designed by Daemen and Rijmen [20], is the standardized version of the candidate Rijndael [19] which was chosen in an open competition organized by the NIST. It is a block cipher with a state of 16 bytes (128 bits). The bytes are arranged in a 4×4 array, where the byte at position (i, j) is numbered $4j + i$. Each round contains the following operations in order: (1) AddRoundKey (ARK): the subkey is XORed to the state, (2) SubBytes (SB): the 8-bit S-Box is applied to each byte independently, (3) ShiftRows (SR): the row number i (starting from 0) is shifted by i bytes left, and (4) MixColumns (MC): the columns of the state are multiplied by an MDS matrix. Importantly, all these operations can be defined *at byte level* (strong alignment).

The class of *AES-like designs* studied in previous works [4] can then be defined as follows: the internal state is an array of cells (not necessarily bytes) and the round function combines ARK, SB, MC and operations that swap cells (SR, or MIX in Haraka). In general the mixing function must be MDS, though the extension in [25] does not require this. Since we are interested in permutations, the ARK layer is replaced by AddConstant (AC).

Feistel-like. We consider permutations based on Generalized Feistel Networks (GFNs). The state of a GFN is formed of $b \geq 2$ *branches*. We denote branches by S_i. Apart from swapping branches, the basic operation in a GFN is to apply a *round function* F on a well-chosen pair (S_i, S_j): $(S_i, S_j) \mapsto (S_i, S_j \oplus F(S_i))$. Our main example is the Simpira v2 [31] family of permutations, where the branches are AES states, and the round functions apply two rounds of AES. This is an instance of the *double-SP* structures defined in [15], and a case in which the F functions are permutations.

More generally, we can extend the class of GFN to *Feistel-like permutations* by allowing permutations to be applied in place on branches, and not only through round functions: $S_i \mapsto \Pi(S_i)$. This does not make a difference from our modeling perspective. In particular, the SPARKLE family of permutations [7] adopts such a Feistel-like structure, but with non-linear permutations on the branches, and linear mixing layers. Though it is not strictly a GFN, our modeling captures it as well.

2.2   Generic Depiction of MITM Attacks

We consider the MITM attack framework as represented in Fig. 1 using the *splice-and-cut* and *initial structure* techniques. The key schedule is ignored due to our restriction to permutations, and we reason only with the internal states.

The goal of the MITM attack is to find a sequence of internal states which satisfy a *closed computational path*: there is a relation between the value before the first round and the value after the last round. In order to do so, one starts by separating the path in two *chunks* (splice-and-cut): the **backward chunk** ◄

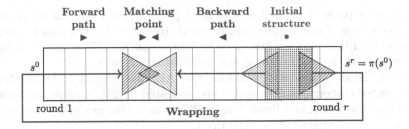

Fig. 1. MITM attack depiction with the splice-and-cut and initial structure techniques.

and the **forward chunk** ▶. Both chunks form independent computation paths. One then finds a *partial match* between them at some round.

In addition, one usually starts at some **initial structure** • which fixes some part of the internal state to constant values. The total complexity depends on (1) the amount of these global guesses, (2) the degree of freedom of both chunks, and (3) the amount of matching. All these parameters are completely determined by the definition of chunks. As an example, we detail the 7-round attack on AES of Sasaki [44] in the full version of the paper [45].

2.3 Rule-Based Modeling and Limits

A MILP model for searching MITM attacks on AES-like designs has been introduced in [4] and further improved in [5,25].

Given the byte-level structure of the design, one fixes a starting round and an ending round where the matching occurs (all possibilities are enumerated). Then, each byte is 'colored' like in Fig. 1. There are four 'colors' (backward, forwards, initial, unknown), which are encoded on two Boolean variables. Only the ARK (if the key-schedule is used) and MC operations change the colors. A series of *rules* is then enforced, as constraints, on the coloring transitions through these operations. For example, going through MC forwards, one "unknown" byte in input implies all bytes "unknown" in output; if all bytes are "initial" in input, then they are all "initial" in output, etc. Other constraints have to be enforced if we go backwards.

At the starting states, there are "initial degrees of freedom" which count the number of forward and backward bytes. The forward computation path, respectively backwards, consume these degrees of freedom under an enforcement of the propagation rules. There must remain enough degrees of freedom at the ending round, in order to ensure some matching.

This representation captures a large number of possible paths (including the key-schedule, contrary to this paper). However, there are several downsides. First of all, the rule-based modeling is complex, and the set of paths depends crucially on the implementation of the propagation rules. For example, the introduction of Guess-and-determine in [5] required to add more rules to take into account this additional technique. The approach so far is *bottom-up* in the sense that the set of possible paths is defined by the local propagation rules. (In contrast, in this paper we use a *global* approach, in which the objective function is directly computed from the coloring. Advanced techniques such as Guess-and-determine are covered by design and without the need for new rules.)

Second, the above model [4] works only for AES-like designs, and extending it to bit-oriented ciphers is far from obvious, as stated in [25]. Notably, it becomes unclear how the S-Box and linear layer will interact. Our model overcomes this problem, albeit restricted to permutations.

3   Cell-Coloring Representation of MITM Attacks

In this section, we define the classes of designs under study, and the class of *merging-based* MITM attacks which we are interested in. These attacks have been previously studied in [16,22] in a very generic setting in combination with a dedicated search tool. Although the search space is similar, our approach differs by using MILP instead. The basis of our representation is PRESENT-like designs. We extend it in two directions: AES-like designs on the one hand, more complex linear layers on the other hand. These are referred in this work as the "PRESENT-like setting", the "AES-like setting" and the "extended setting".

3.1   Cell-Based Representations

Let $\pi = \pi^{r-1} \circ \ldots \circ \pi^0$ be an r-round permutation. We consider the application of π to an initial state s^0, and write s^i the state before round i. Thus s^r is the final state and we have: $\forall i \geq 0, s^{i+1} = \pi^i(s^i)$.

For now π is assumed to be a Substitution-Permutation Network (SPN). We can cut each s^i into b *cells* of w bits, denoted as s^i_j where $0 \leq j \leq b - 1$. Each round applies individual S-Boxes S to the cells (substitution), then a linear layer between them (permutation). By abuse of notation, we also name "cell" the pair $x^i_j = (s^i_j, S(s^i_j))$. Thus cells are $2w$-bit words, which can only take 2^w values. The linear layer of round i relates the cells x^i_j to the cells x^{i+1}_j. We have now completely unfolded the equation $s^r = \pi(s^0)$, into a system of *linear equations on the cells*. So far this view is the same as in [16,22].

PRESENT-*like Setting.* The archetype of a PRESENT-like design is represented on Fig. 2. Here we have two rounds with 4 cells each, of 4 bits. The linear layer merely swaps bits. Thus, it can be entirely represented by pairwise linear relations between the cells. All the information necessary for finding attacks then holds in a simple directed, weighted graph $G = (N, E)$:

- a node $x \in N$ is a cell x with a *width* parameter w_x;
- an edge $(x, x') \in E$ is a linear relation between a cell x at a given round, and a cell x' at the next round, with a *width* $w_{x,x'}$ (we use purposefully the same term as for cells).

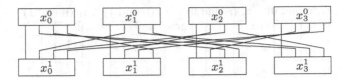

Fig. 2. Example of a 4-cell PRESENT-like design.

The width of a cell corresponds to the combined width that a set of edges needs to have to determine the cell's value. Hence, the widths of cells and edges are relative to each other. We set the width of cells to 1, and the width of edges to a fraction (0.25 in Fig. 2). It follows from the PRESENT-like structure that the combined width of incoming edges, resp., of outgoing edges, is equal to the width of the cell:

$$\forall x \in N, \quad \sum_{x'|(x,x')\in E} w_{x,x'} = \sum_{x'|(x',x)\in E} w_{x',x} = w_x \ . \tag{1}$$

To simplify, we make the following assumption on the S-Boxes similar to the "heuristic assumption" in Sect. 4.1 of [16]. It would be true on average if the S-Boxes were drawn at random, and it is not true for fixed S-Boxes. Our final complexity estimates rely in fact on a global heuristic, rather than this local one.

Assumption 1 (S-Boxes). *Given fixed edges with a combined width $u \leq 1$, a cell x of w bits can take exactly $2^{w(1-u)}$ values.*

AES-like Setting. Our cell-based representation of AES-like designs is different from the one in previous works like [4,16,22]. These works considered the S-Boxes as individual cells. Instead, we want to represent AES-like operations in a way that looks like a PRESENT-like design, with linear relations between pairs of cells. For this we use the *Super S-Box representation.*

In the analysis of AES, the Super S-Box consists in considering the MC operation, followed by SB, as a single, large S-Box of $4 \times 8 = 32$ bits. In our representation, the cells are the columns of a given AES-like state, as represented on Fig. 3 (or the rows, if MixColumns were to be replaced by MixRows). In that case, the MC operation is the one of the previous round, and the SR operation becomes an exchange of bytes between super-cells: two rounds of AES can then be represented as in Fig. 2. The relative widths of cells and edges are unchanged; each edge represents a byte, and each cell a column of 32 bits.

Extended Setting. In order to target even more designs, we show how to model any linear layer for which a bit of x^i is obtained by XORing several bits of x^{i-1}. This allows for example to model the permutation ASCON [24] (though we did not obtain interesting results on this design). This XOR operation requires the introduction of new cells:

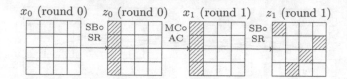

Fig. 3. 2 rounds of AES, with a single (super-)cell.

- *b-branching cells*: a cell x of width $w_x = v$, with one incoming edge and b outgoing edges of width v each;
- *b-XOR cells*: a cell x of width $w_x = bv$, with b incoming edges and one outgoing edge of width v each. The inputs are b bits, and the output is the XOR of them.

These cells allow to keep a graph structure, where the width of a cell still corresponds to a combined width of edges that allows to determine the cell's value. In b-branching cells, all edges have the same value, and in b-XOR cells, knowing b edges allows to deduce the remaining one. The difference with PRESENT-like designs is that Eq. 1 is not satisfied anymore. In order to separate successive rounds, three layers for a single round (S-Box, branching, XOR) may be needed.

3.2   Meet-in-the-Middle Problems

The goal of a MITM attack is, using the cell-based representation, to find values for all cells such that a given equation system is satisfied. The starting equation system encoding $s^r = \pi(s^0)$ is trivial, where s^r can be computed from s^0 and vice-versa. By adding new linear relations between s^0 and s^r, this becomes a *closed computational path*. The relations between s^0 and s^r can also be encoded into the undirected graph of Sect. 3.1. We mostly consider *wrapping constraints*, where we put new edges between cells s^0 and s^r, and *input-output constraints*, where we fix some bits in the s^0 and s^r to arbitrary constants.

Problem 1 (Meet-in-the-middle problem). Consider a permutation $\pi(s^0) = s^r$. Then given either u_w bits of wrapping constraints $L(s^0, s^r) = 0$; or instead u_i bits of input constraints $L(s^0) = 0$ together with u_o bits of output constraints $L(s^r) = 0$, find a pair of states (s^0, s^r) that satisfy these constraints. (Here each L is a linear function over $\mathbb{F}_2$.)

Given query access (forwards and backwards) to a random permutation, an adversary must make respectively $\mathcal{O}(2^{u_w})$ and $\mathcal{O}(2^{\min(u_i, u_o)})$ queries to solve Problem 1. These complexities are to be multiplied by the number of requested solutions. This defines the generic difficulty of the problem. Note that for solutions to exist, u_w (resp. $u_i + u_o$) cannot exceed the state size of the permutation. The number of solutions of the problem (in $\log_2$) can be computed by:

$$\left(\sum_{x \in N} w_x - \sum_{(x,x') \in E} w_{x,x'} \right) - u_i - u_o \;, \tag{2}$$

where the sum over all edges includes wrapping constraints (if applicable).

3.3 Merging-Based MITM Attacks

Now that we have defined the cell-based representation, we can move on to the definition of *merging-based attacks*. This class of attacks is borrowed from [16,22]. However, while they persue a dedicated bottom-up solver to automatically search for attacks, we follow a top-down MILP modeling approach. We focus for now on the basic PRESENT-like setting.

Reduced Lists. Let us consider a set of cells $X = (x_j^i)_{(i,j) \in IJ_X}$, i.e., nodes in the directed graph $G = (N, E)$ that represents the MITM equation system. We define the *reduced list* $\mathcal{R}[X]$ as the set of all value assignments $(v_j^i)_{(i,j) \in IJ_X}$ to X that satisfy all linear constraints between the cells of X.

E.g., we may consider in Fig. 2 a reduced list $\mathcal{R}[x_0^0, x_0^1]$, which contains all assignments $(s_0^0, S(s_0^0)), (s_0^1, S(s_0^1))$ such that $(S(s_0^0))|_1 = (s_0^1)|_0$ (the second bit of $S(s_0^0)$ is equal to the first bit of s_0^1). In particular, the list has size $|\mathcal{R}[x_0^0, x_0^1]| = 2^7$.

A reduced list is entirely determined by its defining set of cells. It forms the set of solutions to a subsystem of equations. Our goal can now be rephrased as follows: *Compute an element from the reduced list of all cells: $\mathcal{R}[\{x | x \in N\}]$.* Indeed, by definition, this is a solution to the MITM equation system.

Base Lists. We start with base lists: reduced lists $\mathcal{R}[\{x_j^i\}]$ of individual cells. These are simply the list of all input-outputs through the S-Box: $(s_j^i, S(s_j^i))$. In extended mode, base lists for branching and XOR cells are likewise trivial.

Merging Lists. Merging is the fundamental algorithmic operation to construct bigger lists. It corresponds to the "recursive combinations of solvers" considered in Sect. 4.2 of [16], where the "solvers" produce the solutions of a given equation subsystem: merging the lists corresponds to merging two subsystems.

Lemma 1. *Let $\mathcal{R}[X_1]$ and $\mathcal{R}[X_2]$ be two reduced lists. From them, the reduced list $\mathcal{R}[X_1 \cup X_2]$ can be computed in time:*

$$\max(|\mathcal{R}[X_1 \cup X_2]|, |\mathcal{R}[X_1]|, |\mathcal{R}[X_2]|) \ . \tag{3}$$

Proof. Let Y be the set of linear equations of the system whose support is included in $X_1 \cup X_2$, but not in X_1 nor X_2. Then by definition of reduced lists, we have: $|\mathcal{R}[X_1 \cup X_2]| = |\mathcal{R}[X_1]| \times |\mathcal{R}[X_2]| / (\sum_{L \in Y} \text{width}(L))$.

We separate each linear equation L of Y into its X_1-part L_1 and its X_2-part L_2: the equation becomes $L(X) = L_1(X_1) \oplus L_2(X_2) = 0$. We compute $L_1(X_1)$ for all cell assignments in $\mathcal{R}[X_1]$, likewise we compute $L_2(X_2)$ for all cell assignments in $\mathcal{R}[X_2]$. We then sort both lists with respect to these values, and we look for collisions. The collision pairs are computed efficiently by iterating over both lists, and give the matching cell assignments of $\mathcal{R}[X_1 \cup X_2]$.   □

Remark 1. The merging operation is the same in the extended setting. In the AES-like setting, there can be implicit linear relations between cells. This corresponds to *matching through MixColumns*; we explain how we model this in Sect. 4.3.

It can be shown by a trivial induction that, if Assumption 1 holds for individual cells, then the sizes of all reduced lists are exactly powers of 2. Of course this is true only on average if we consider S-Boxes drawn at random. In practice, the S-Boxes are fixed, but the deviation from this average is small.

Definition. A *merging-based MITM attack* is a *merging strategy* represented by a binary tree $\mathcal{T}$, whose nodes are identified by sets of cells X, such that: • the leaves contain individual cells; • the root contains the set of all cells; • the set of cells of a given node is the union of the set of cells of its children. Then each node represents a reduced list. The attack consists in computing the reduced lists in any order consistent with the tree. By Lemma 1, its time complexity is given by $\max_{X \in \mathcal{T}} |\mathcal{R}[X]|$.

The strategy of [16,22] is an exploration of the merging strategies, starting from individual cells and computing the complexity of reduced lists until enough cells are covered. Paths stop when the complexity exceeds the generic one. Thus, the dedicated solver that they use is also *bottom-up*, not in the definition of constraints like [4], but in the way it computes the complexity of possible attacks.

3.4 Global Edges

In all settings (PRESENT, AES, extended), an important extension of merging-based MITM attacks is the ability to guess globally the value of an edge. We use *global edges* in three cases.

Input-Output Constraints. To model input-output constraints, we create wrapping constraints and make these edges global. With this view, we remark that a MITM problem always has same or lower complexity with a given amount of wrapping constraints compared to the same amount of input-output constraints.

Reducing the Number of Solutions. In the PRESENT and AES-like setting, it can be seen that when the system admits more than 1 solution, we can set global edges of a combined width equal to the quantity of Eq. 2. As long as the width of global edges on a given cell does not exceed 1, there is on average a solution. (This is not true in the "extended" setting, where global edges can *a priori* create inconsistencies in the system and more care is required.)

Reducing the Memory. Global edges allow to reduce the size of intermediate lists in the merging strategy. We can easily prove that they do not allow to reduce the time complexity. If we consider a system with α global edges, that admits a solution with probability $2^{-\alpha}$, we can redo any merging strategy by removing these global edges: the size of lists increases by a factor 2^{α} at most. Since the time complexity is the maximum of list sizes (multiplied by the loop on global guesses), it stays the same in both cases.

Global edges correspond to the *initial structure* in previous works on MITM attacks. An interesting consequence of this remark is that the initial structure is actually not necessary to obtain the best time complexity: it suffices to share its components between the backward and forward paths.

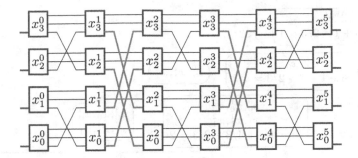

Fig. 4. 12-round MITM attack on GIMLI. The matching edges between the two final lists are highlighted in cyan.

3.5 Example: Gimli

Before we elaborate on our MILP modeling, we detail a simple example of a merging-based attack: the state-recovery on 12-round GIMLI-Cipher of [27].

GIMLI [8] is a cryptographic permutation with 384-bit state divided into 4 cells of 96 bits each. The full permutation has 24 rounds that apply an *SP-Box* to each cell individually, and then, every two round, perform a linear layer. The linear layer is either a *small swap* (32 bits are exchanged between cell 0 and 1, and between 2 and 3) or a *big swap* (32 bits are exchanged between cell 0 and 2, and between 1 and 3). In the cell-based representation, each cell has width 1, three input and three output branches of width 1/3 each, as can be seen in Fig. 4. We do not need to consider the details of the SP-Box.

The attack of [27] targets GIMLI-Cipher, where GIMLI is used in a Duplex mode. The recovery of the internal state can be reduced to the following problem. Given the cell-based representation of Fig. 4, where a single edge is fixed in the 4 input and output cells, the goal is to find the list of size $2^{4 \times 32} = 2^{128}$ (4/3 cells) of all possible values of the full state, in time less than 2^{256} (8/3 cells). The merging strategy is given in Fig. 5, where the list sizes are computed in $\log_2$ and relatively to a cell. The time and memory complexities are 2^{192} (2 cells).

4 Simplification and MILP Modeling

In Sect. 3 we have given a very generic definition of merging-based MITM attacks. We postulate that this definition contains all structural MITM attacks on permutations known to date. Unfortunately, this search space is too large for MILP solvers to be practical. Hence we consider a subset of these attacks, using only two lists, a *forward* list and a *backward* list. We motivate this definition in Sect. 4.1 and show how to obtain the list sizes from their cells. Then, we show in Sect. 4.2 how to obtain a MITM attack with a complexity determined by the list sizes. Finally in Sect. 4.3 we detail the MILP model itself.

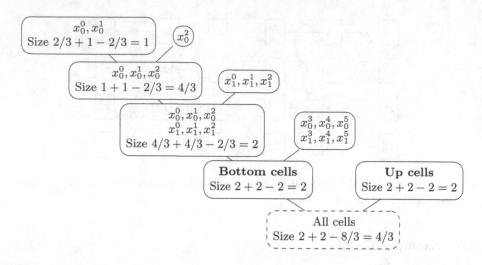

Fig. 5. Merging strategy for the 12-round attack against GIMLI-Cipher of [27]. Some lists are omitted by symmetry.

4.1 A Simpler Definition

In line with the "Meet-in-the-middle" terminology, we consider a merging strategy made of only three reduced lists: a *forward list* $\mathcal{R}[X_F]$, a *backward list* $\mathcal{R}[X_B]$ and a *merged list* $\mathcal{R}[X_F \cup X_B]$.

Forward and Backward Lists. Ultimately, the time complexity of the MITM attack is computed as a function of the list sizes, so we must define sets X_B and X_F in such a way that the list sizes $|\mathcal{R}[X_F]|$ and $-\mathcal{R}[X_B]|$ are simple functions of X_F and X_B respectively. In the generic binary trees, we used the fact that the size of leaves can be trivially computed (a list with a single cell of width w contains 2^w elements). Here we are simply making these leaves more complex, so that only two leaves are needed in the end.

Lemma 2. *Let X be a set of cells such that: (1) there is at least one round $0 \le i \le r - 1$ such that no cell x_j^i belongs to X; (2) for every global linear constraint connecting cells $x_{j_1}^i$ and $x_{j_2}^{i+1}$, then only one of these two cells can be in X, and always either the one of the lower round number (backward case) or the upper round number (forward case). Let ℓ be the quantity:*

$$\ell = \sum_{x \in X} \left(w_x - \sum_{\substack{(x,x') \in E \\ x' \in X}} w_{(x,x')} \right) - \sum_{\substack{(x,x') \in E \\ x \in X \lor x' \in X \\ (x,x') \text{ is global}}} w_{(x,x')} \ , \qquad (4)$$

then $\mathcal{R}[X]$ is of size exactly 2^ℓ. In the PRESENT-like / AES-like setting, it can be constructed in time 2^ℓ with negligible memory.

Here, *forward* and *backward* lists follow the same intuition as in standard MITM attacks, where there are two computational paths going into different directions. But this direction is only enforced because of global edges.

Proof. The size of a list is given by the sum of all widths of the cells, minus the linear constraints between them, minus the globally fixed edges. Since at least one round is cut, we can reorder the terms and associate all linear constraints (x, x') between round i and $i + 1$ to the cell x at round i: we obtain the formula for ℓ. Let us consider the backward list. We have:

$$\ell_B = \sum_{x \in X} \left(w_x - \sum_{\substack{(x,x') \in E \\ x' \in X}} w_{(x,x')} - \sum_{\substack{(x,x') \in E \\ (x,x') \text{ is global}}} w_{(x,x')} \right), \tag{5}$$

and we remark that each term is greater than zero: indeed, we cannot have $x' \in X$ and (x, x') global at the same time, by assumption, and in the PRESENT-like setting, we have $w_x \geq \sum_{(x,x') \in E} w_{(x,x')}$. This is not true in the extended setting (due to branching cells), but we can work around this in practice.

One constructs $\mathcal{R}[X]$ follows: separate X into $X_{r-1}, \ldots, X_0$, assuming that no cell is covered at round r. We start at round $r - 1$: we take values for all edges $(x, x') \in E$ with $x \in X_{r-1}$ that are not already global. Next, at round $r - 2$, we take values for all edges (x, x') with $x \in X_{r-2}$ that are neither connected to $x' \in X_{r-1}$, nor global. Each time, the number of bits to guess corresponds precisely to another term in ℓ. For the forward list, we rewrite ℓ as:

$$\ell_F = \sum_{x \in X} \left(w_x - \sum_{\substack{(x',x) \in E \\ x' \in X}} w_{(x',x)} - \sum_{\substack{(x',x) \in E \\ (x',x) \text{ is global}}} w_{(x,x')} \right), \tag{6}$$

and we change the direction of the procedure. This is a streaming procedure, which outputs the list elements without requiring any storage. In both cases, the list size corresponds exactly to the number of bits that we have to guess.   □

Simple Condition of Success. Initially, we required the merging strategy to compute the reduced list of all cells. However, we can stop as soon as *all cells can be deduced from the current list.* That is, given a valid sequence of values for the cells of $X_F \cup X_B$, we can deduce all the others without guessing new edges. Since we are studying a permutation, a sufficient condition (that we enforce) is that $X_F \cup X_B$ covers a complete round. (Intuitively, we dismiss the trivial merging steps consisting in adding the remaining cells one by one.)

Disjoint Paths. In the PRESENT- and AES-like settings (but not the "extended" setting), the sets X_F and X_B can be made disjoint at no loss. Since any intersection between X_F and X_B can either be removed from X_F, or from X_B, and in at least one case both list sizes decrease (the merged list remains unchanged).

4.2   From a Coloring to an Attack

Now we show that to any valid triple of sets X_B, X_F, $X_F \cup X_B$, there corresponds a MITM procedure whose time and memory complexities are determined solely by the size of the three lists involved. We use ℓ_B, ℓ_F, ℓ_M to denote the $\log_2$ of these list sizes, counted relatively to a cell. Our goal is to minimize this complexity. We assume for simplicity that the merging problem admits a single solution; it is easy to generalize this to multiple solutions in the classical setting.

Theorem 1. *Assume that X_B and X_F are defined as in Lemma 2, and $X_F \cup X_B$ covers at least one round completely. let g be the sum of all widths of global edges. Then there exists a classical and a quantum algorithm solving the MITM problem with the following complexities in $\log_2$, relatively to a cell size. The classical algorithm has memory complexity $m_c = \min(\ell_F, \ell_B)$ and time complexity $t_c = g + \max(\ell_F, \ell_B, \ell_M)$. The quantum algorithm has memory $m_q = m_c = \min(\ell_F, \ell_B)$ and time complexity $t_q = \frac{g}{2} + \max \left(\min(\ell_F, \ell_B), \frac{1}{2} \max(\ell_F, \ell_B, \ell_M) \right)$.*

Proof (sketch). In the classical setting, both leaf lists can be computed on the fly, we only need to store one of them (the smallest). The memory complexity is thus (in $\log_2$) $\min(\ell_F, \ell_B)$ and the time complexity $g + \max(\ell_F, \ell_B, \ell_M)$ (we must repeat the merging for every choice of global edges). One should note that by the definition of the leaf lists, there is no variance in their size. There can be a variance in the merged list size, which is usually dismissed in classical analyses.

Given a path for a two-list MITM attack, we can also write down a quantum algorithm to solve it. In short, this algorithm creates the smallest list (e.g., the forward one), then performs a Grover search in the merged list for a solution. We refer to the full version of the paper [45] for technical details. The algorithm requires quantum-accessible quantum memory (QRAQM). Assuming a single solution, the quantum time complexity can be bounded by:

$$2 \left(\frac{\pi}{4} 2^{g/2} + 1 \right) \left(2^{\ell_F} + \left(\frac{\pi}{4} \sqrt{2^{\ell_B}} + 1 \right) \left(\frac{\pi}{\sqrt{2}} \max \left(1, \sqrt{\frac{2^{\ell_M}}{2^{\ell_B}}} \right) + 6 \right) \right) \quad (7)$$

quantum evaluations of the attacked permutation, for a $1/2$ chance of success. Asymptotically, this formula can be simplified into 2^{t_q}, where:

$$t_q = \frac{g}{2} + \max \left(\min(\ell_F, \ell_B), \frac{1}{2} \max(\ell_F, \ell_B, \ell_M) \right) , \quad (8)$$

which concludes the proof.   □

Criterion for a Quantum Attack. By comparing the quantum and classical time exponents, one can see that quantum attacks require an additional constraint compared to classical attacks: One can see that a classical MITM procedure constitutes an attack if $t_c < t$ where t is the generic time exponent to solve the MITM problem; in the quantum setting, this time is reduced by a square-root factor due to Grover search, so we need $t_q < t/2$. Unsurprisingly, any quantum MITM attack turns into a classical attack: $t_q \leq t/2 \implies t_c \leq t$. In the other direction, if we have a valid classical path, and if the following additional constraint is satisfied: $\min(\ell_F, \ell_B) \leq \frac{1}{2}\max(\ell_F, \ell_B, \ell_M)$, then it also gives a valid quantum attack. This is true in particular when $\ell_M = 0$ and $\ell_F \leq \frac{1}{2}\ell_B$.

4.3   MILP Modeling

From the analysis above, we can see that we want to solve the problem:

> **Minimize** the complexity formulas of Theorem 1, under the constraints on X_F and X_B given by Lemma 2, and the constraint that $X_F \cup X_B$ covers at least one round completely.

Our MILP model essentially uses boolean variables to represent X_F and X_B, continuous variables to represent global edges, and expresses the list sizes ℓ_F, ℓ_B, and ℓ_M depending on these variables. This model can be generated from the weighted graph (N, E) defined in Sect. 3.

Present-like Setting: Variables. We start with the basic PRESENT-like constraints and explain afterwards the extensions. For each cell x, we introduce boolean *coloring* variables $\mathsf{col}_F[x]$, $\mathsf{col}_B[x]$ and $\mathsf{col}_M[x]$ to represent the sets X_F, X_B and $X_M := X_F \cup X_B$. We have the constraint $\mathsf{col}_M[x] = \max(\mathsf{col}_F[x], \mathsf{col}_B[x])$.

We constrain some round to be absent from X_F (resp. X_B), it can be chosen manually or not. For each edge (x, x'), we introduce a variable $\mathsf{global}[x, x']$ which is 1 if the edge is globally guessed, 0 otherwise. It can be relaxed to a continuous variable. We constrain $X_F \cup X_B$ to cover at least one round entirely (chosen manually or not). Finally, we impose that for each edge (x, x'):

$$\mathsf{col}_F[x] \leq 1 - \mathsf{global}[x, x'] \qquad \mathsf{col}_B[x'] \leq 1 - \mathsf{global}[x, x']$$
$$\mathsf{col}_B[x] \geq \mathsf{global}[x, x'] \qquad \mathsf{col}_F[x'] \geq \mathsf{global}[x, x']$$

Here the two constraints on the first line ensure that the conditions of Lemma 2 are satisfied. The second line is not required, but it simplifies the formula for ℓ of Lemma 2. Since each global constraints reduces the size of *both the forward and the backward lists*, we can introduce a term of *global reduction*:

$$g = \sum_{(x,x') \in E} \mathsf{global}[x, x'] w_{x,x'} \ , \tag{9}$$

which contains all of their contribution. At this point, we have defined a valid MITM strategy, and it only remains to compute the list sizes.

List Sizes. The list sizes are computed in $\log_2$ and relatively to the width of a cell (in practice cells may have different widths). For each list, there are two terms that intervene: the *contribution* of individual cells and the *global reduction*. For the forward list, following Eq. 6, we define the variables:

$$\mathsf{contrib}_F[x] \geq w_x \mathsf{col}_F(x) - \sum_{(x',x) \in E} w_{x',x} \mathsf{col}_F(x') \ , \tag{10}$$

and we have: $\ell_F = \left(\sum_{x \in N} \text{contrib}_F[x]\right) - g$. For the backward list, we define:

$$\text{contrib}_B[x] \geq w_x \text{col}_B(x) - \sum_{(x,x') \in E} w_{x,x'} \text{col}_B(x') \tag{11}$$

and we have similarly $\ell_B = \left(\sum_{x \in N} \text{contrib}_B[x]\right) - g$. For the merged list, we can go either forwards or backwards, for example:

$$\text{contrib}_M[x] \geq w_x \text{col}_M(x) - \sum_{(x,x') \in E} w_{x,x'} \text{col}_M(x'), \quad \ell_M = \sum_{x \in N} \text{contrib}_M[x] - g \ . \tag{12}$$

Since we have now expressed the list sizes, we implement the time and memory complexities using the formulas of Theorem 1, e.g., classically:

$$\text{memory} = \min(\ell_F, \ell_B), \text{time} = g + \max(\ell_F, \ell_B, \ell_M) \ .$$

The primary optimization goal is the time and the secondary goal is the memory.

Extended Setting. In the extended setting, we must allow a *negative* contribution of the cells in each list. We have lower bounds: $\text{contrib}_F[x] \geq w_x - \sum_{(y,x) \in E} w_{x,y}$ and $\text{contrib}_B[x] \geq w_x - \sum_{(x,y) \in E} w_{y,x}$ which can be negative for branching cells. This is the only required change.

AES-like Setting. So far, our model considers the AES Super S-Box as a completely unknown function. We make two modifications to allow two techniques.

First, *matching through MC*. When we know $u \geq 4$ bytes in the input and output of an AES Super S-Box, we can reduce the merged list size by $u - 4$. Indeed, these edges are individual S-Boxes, and we can write linear equations between them using MixColumns. In order to model this, we modify the definition of $\text{col}_M[x]$. We authorize a cell of the merged list to be covered even if it does not belong to $X_F \cup X_B$, as soon as enough input and output edges are covered. This should not, however, happen at two successive rounds.

Second, *optimizing the memory through MC*. This is important for reaching better memory complexities on AES-like designs, but also, better quantum times. Assume that there exists a cell that belongs to the merged list but not the forward and backward ones. Assume that there are f_i input edges from the forward list, f_o output edges from the forward list, and respectively b_i and b_o such edges for the backward list. Recall that each edge here corresponds to an individual S-Box. Then we can add some shared constraints on these cells and make these constraints global. Indeed, if we know that: $\ell_1(x_0, x_1, x_2, x_3, y_0) = 0$ and $\ell_2(x_0, x_1, x_2, x_3, y_1) = 0$, we can create a global constraint $\ell'_1(x_0, x_1, x_2) = t$ and $\ell'_2(y_0, y_1) = t$. Going through MC, we can add up to $f_i + f_o + b_i + b_o - w$ such linear constraints, where w is the cell width in number of edges (4 in the case of AES). Furthermore, we need to have less such new constraints than f_o and b_i respectively: this ensures the existence of a streaming procedure for the lists and the validity of an adapted version of Lemma 2.

Practical Improvements. Our code is more optimized than the presentation given in this section. In particular, we removed the $\mathsf{global}[x, x']$ variables attached to edges and replaced them by "global reduction" variables attached to each cell. These variables unify the PRESENT-like and AES-like settings, since they account both for the global edges and the reduction through MC.

Reducing the Search Space. There are several ways to reduce the search space without affecting the optimality. First, we can prune the graph by removing cells that do not have both input and output edges (for example in the MITM attack on PRESENT of Sect. 5, many cells from the first and last rounds can be removed). Second, when two cells in the graph have the same forward and backward connections, their colorings can always be exchanged without changing the list sizes. This reduces massively the search space size in the case of highly symmetric AES-like designs, for example Grøstl-256 (see Sect. 6.3).

5   Application to PRESENT-like Permutations

Gimli. With our tool, we can prove the optimality of the 12-round state-recovery attack recalled in Sect. 3.5. Here our 2-list MILP model is not enough, since the two lists merged at level 1 in the tree span all the rounds. So, contrary to most of our examples, we used an extension to 4 lists.

Present and Spongent. The current best distinguishers on known-key PRESENT [10] and reduced-round SPONGENT-π [47] combine a MITM layer and a truncated differential layer. By improving the MITM layer, we improve indirectly the number of rounds that can be targeted.

In a nutshell, the goal is to construct the list of 2^{56} input states that satisfy a 4-bit input constraint and a 4-bit output constraint, in time less than 2^{60}. In [10] the constraint is put at position 13; for SPONGENT-π we tried the position 0. We conjecture that due to the high amount of symmetries in the design, the number of attacked rounds should remain the same independently of this position.

The MITM layer for [10] reaches 7 rounds, in time 2^{56} and memory 2^{32}. The time is optimal, but we improve the memory to 2^{12}. Next, we find an attack with one more round. The time complexity then rises to 2^{58} (14.5 cells) and the memory complexity to 2^{43} (10.75 cells). In order to make the optimization converge, we used the following simplification: we merged pairwise the cells of the middle rounds. These pairs of cells thus have the same coloration; this simplification reduces greatly the number of variables, while still allowing interesting results.

Spongent. This strategy was extended in [47] to the SPONGENT-π permutations, which are used in the hash function SPONGENT [11] and the permutation-based AEAD Elephant [9] (in the "Dumbo" version). Following [47, Table 1], we denote the number of rounds of both phases (truncated differential and MITM) by r_0 and r_1 and report them in Table 2, where our new results appear in **bold** in the last column. The table contains all state sizes specified in [9,11,12]. Here

Table 2. Versions of SPONGENT, results from [47] and our improvements.

	State size (bits)	Rounds Attacked / full	Cells	r_0	r_1	New r_0
PRESENT	64	31 / 31	16	7	24	**8 (+ 1)**
SPONGENT-88/80/8	88	30 / 45	22	7	23	**8 (+ 1)**
SPONGENT-128/128/8	136	43 / 70	34	7	36	**8 (+ 1)**
SPONGENT-π[160]	160	80	40			**9**
SPONGENT-160/160/16	176	53 / 90	44	7	46	**9 (+ 2)**
SPONGENT-160/160/80	240	69 / 120	60	7	62	**10 (+ 3)**
SPONGENT-88/176/88	264	77 / 135	66	9	68	**10 (+ 1)**
SPONGENT-256/256/16	272	68 / 140	68	9	69	**10 (+ 1)**
SPONGENT-224/224/112	336	95 / 170	84	9	86	**10 (+ 1)**
SPONGENT-128/256/128	384	109 / 195	96	11	98	**11**
SPONGENT-160/320/160	480	132 / 240	120	9	123	**12 (+ 3)**
SPONGENT-224/448/224	672	181 / 340	168	9	172	**12 (+ 3)**
SPONGENT-256/512/256	768	192 / 385	192	11	194	**12 (+ 1)**

the notation SPONGENT-$n/c/r$ refers to [12], where n is the output hash size, c the capacity and r the rate, while SPONGENT-π refers to the permutation itself. The 160-bit version used in Elephant [9] was not studied previously, because SPONGENT-π[160] does not appear among the different parameterizations of the SPONGENT hash functions.

As in [10], the MITM layer finds all the input-output pairs such that: 4 bits of an S-Box are fixed in input, and in output, to arbitrary values. The generic complexity would be 2^{b-4} evaluations of the permutation. The lowest complexity possible is 2^{b-8} since this is the number of solutions. Since the state size becomes quite large, we do not use our tool as an optimization, but rather as a solver: we set the minimal complexity 2^{b-8} as optimization goal and kill the process if it runs for too long (say, 500 s). By our experiments, we expect solutions to be found quite quickly, if they exist.

6   Application to AES-Based Permutations

As remarked above, our model does not include degrees of freedom of the key-schedule, and some of the previous preimage attacks on AES-like hashing cannot be recovered. However, all known results on AES-based permutations [3–5,25], *except* the non-linear computation of neutral words proposed in [5] (see the example of Grøstl below), can be recovered by our simplified modeling. We only present new attacks obtained by our tool in this section. In the classical setting, we improve the attack on Haraka-512 v2 of [4]. In the quantum setting, we give attacks on reduced-round AES, Haraka and Grøstl.

Note that an AES-like state is an $n \times m$ matrix of bytes, which we represent as m cells with n input and output edges. The SR operation moves individual

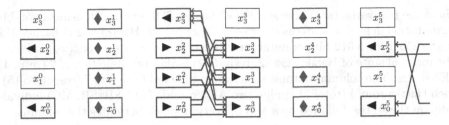

Fig. 6. AES 7-round quantum attack. ◄: **backward**, ►: **forward**, ♦: **matching** through MC (new cells in the merged list), ↔: **global edges**.

bytes between the cells. When the last MC operation is omitted, and round $r - 1$ is connected to round 0, then round 0 can actually be bypassed. Indeed, the columns at the beginning of round 1 (before SB), which correspond to the cells at round 1 in our representation, can immediately be linked to the columns at round $r - 1$ (which correspond to the cells at round $r - 1$). Though MC has been removed, we usually keep the last SR operation; this creates a special round in which bytes are exchanged between pairs of cells only.

6.1 Quantum Attack on 7-Round AES

On this example, like the following ones, our attack is a pseudo-preimage attack that, given a target t, finds x such that $x \oplus AES(x) = t$. None of the attacks known classically can be adapted in the quantum setting (they don't satisfy the condition given in Sect. 4.2), so we use our tool to find a new optimization. The path is displayed in Fig. 6.

Details of the Attack. We count the complexities in cells. The attack has 2.75 global guesses, with 0.75 global edges and 2 additional reductions through MC at round 1. For each of these 2.75 choices, we compute the three lists.

First, the **backward ◄ list** is of size 0.25. We start by x_3^2 which contributes only to 0.25. We move to x_0^0 and x_2^0 which are entirely determined by the reduction through MC of round 1. We deduce x_0^5, x_2^5. Second, the **forward ► list** is of size 1. We start by x_0^2, x_1^2, x_2^2, which have only $3 - 2 = 1$ degree of freedom by the reduction through MC of round 1. We deduce x_0^3, x_1^3, x_2^3. Third, the merged list is of size ≤ 1. We match through MC at round 4, each cell gives 0.25 degree of matching, so one would be enough.

This corresponds to an attack of classical time 2^{120} and memory 2^8, so equivalent to the attack of [44]. However, using Eq. 8, we obtain a quantum time 2^{60}, and with the precise formula of Eq. 7, we have a time of $2^{63.34}$ quantum evaluations of the primitive (Grover search would stand at $2^{64.65}$).

6.2 New Attacks on Haraka V2

Haraka v2 [40] is a short-input AES-like hash function intended for use within post-quantum signature schemes based on hash functions, such as SPHINCS+ [2].

There are two variants: (1) Haraka-256 v2 hashes 256 bits to 256 using a 256-bit permutation in feed-forward mode: $x \mapsto \pi_{256}(x) \oplus x$; (2) Haraka-512 v2 hashes 512 bits to 256 using a 512-bit permutation with a truncation: $x \mapsto \mathsf{trunc}(\pi_{512}(x) \oplus x)$. The internal state of Haraka-256 v2 (resp. -512) is the concatenation of 2 (resp. 4) AES states. The columns of these states are numbered from 0 to 7 (resp. 0 to 15). Each Haraka round (total 5) applies two AES rounds (AC, SB, SR, MC) individually on the states, followed by a MIX operation which permutes the columns:

$$\mathsf{MIX}_{512} : \quad 0, \ldots, 15 \mapsto (3, 11, 7, 15), (8, 0, 12, 4), (9, 1, 13, 5), (2, 10, 6, 14)$$
$$\mathsf{MIX}_{256} : \quad 0, \ldots, 7 \mapsto (0, 4, 1, 5), (2, 6, 3, 7)$$

The truncation trunc extracts the columns $(2, 3, 6, 7, 8, 9, 12, 13)$.

Integration in SPHINCS, SPHINCS+ and Attacks. In [39], Kölbl proposed to integrate Haraka into SPHINCS. Here both Haraka-256 v2 and Haraka-512 v2 need 256 bits of classical preimage security and 128 bits of quantum preimage security (see [39], Sect. 3). In [4], the authors found a classical 4.5-round preimage attack on Haraka-256 v2 and a 5.5-round attack (extended by 0.5 round) on Haraka-512 v2. None of the attacks of [4] apply directly to the post-quantum signature scheme SPHINCS+ [2], an "alternate" finalist of the NIST post-quantum standardization process. Here Haraka-512 is used in a Sponge with 256 bits of rate and 256 bits of capacity. The targeted security level is 128 bits due to a generic second-preimage attack. We obtain a classical MITM attack on 4.5 rounds of complexity 2^{192}, and a quantum preimage attack on 3.5 rounds of complexity 2^{64}. The details are provided in the full version of the paper [45].

New Quantum Attack on Haraka-256 v2. The attack path of [4] does not meet our criteria for quantum attacks, since both the forward and backward lists have size 1 cell, and the total time complexity is 7 cells. However, a reoptimization allows to reach an attack with 5 global guesses, a forward list of size 2, a backward list of size 1 and a merged list of size 2 (details in the full version of the paper [45]). By Eq. 7, this gives a quantum time $2^{115.55}$ against a generic 2^{128}.

Improved Attack on Haraka-512 v2. The 5.5 round attack of [4] has time complexity 2^{240} (7.5 cells) and memory complexity 2^{128} (4 cells). In order to make our optimization converge faster, we constrain the pattern in the first and last rounds to contain full active AES states, like in [4]). We obtain the path of Fig. 7, which reduces the memory down to 0.5 cell (2^{16}). The main difference with the framework of [4] is that the matching occurs in several rounds separately.

We first guess **28 bytes** •: $x_3^a[0, 1, 5, 6, 10, 11, 12, 15]$, $x_3^d[10, 11, 12, 15]$, $x_4^a[4-11]$, $x_4^b[0, 1, 2, 3, 12, 13, 14, 15]$, and we precompute two linear relations between the first and second columns of z_2^d and w_2^d, and one linear relation for each column between z_6 and w_6. The total is 46 bytes, i.e., 11.5 cells, of global guesses (including 8 for free). Then for the **forward ▶ list** (size 0.5 cells), we start from w_2^d. We have 4 bytes and two precomputed linear relations, thus 2 bytes of freedom. We continue to compute until z_6. In each column, we have one byte

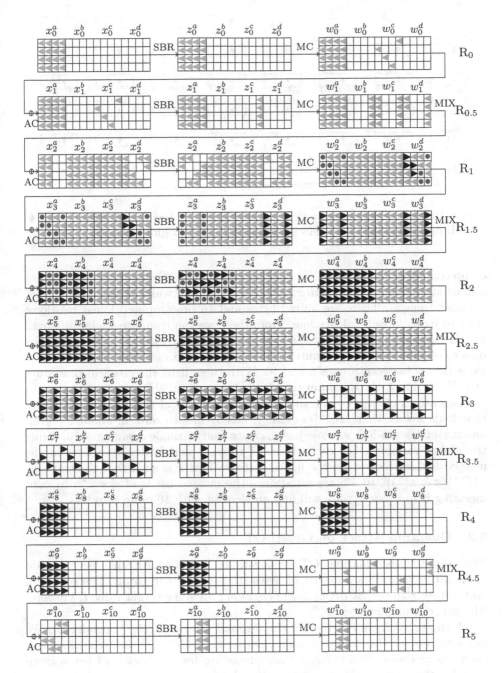

Fig. 7. Path of our improved attack on Haraka-512 v2. ◄: **backward**, ►: **forward**, •: **guessed**

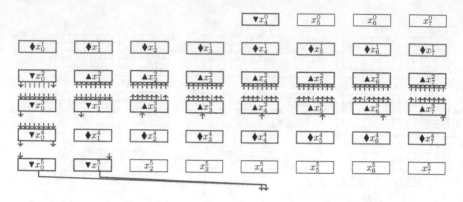

Fig. 8. Path of the quantum attack on Grøstl-256 OT. ▲: backward, ▼: forward, ♦: **matching** through MC (new cells in the merged list), ↔: **global edges**.

of precomputed linear relation, thus we can deduce all the blue bytes in w_6 immediately. We continue until x_9. Next, for the **backward** ◀ **list** (size 4 cells), we start from z_6. There are 32 red bytes and 16 precomputed linear relations, thus 16 bytes (4 cells) of freedom. From there we can compute backwards until w_2. We deduce $z_2^d[0,7]$ using the two precomputed relations, and the rest by direct computation. We compute until w_{10}^a. Finally, a matching of more than 2 bytes occurs between rounds 9 and 10. With these lists, the classical time stays at 2^{240}. By Eq. 7, the quantum time is $2^{123.34}$, against 2^{128} generically.

This attack of large complexity also yields a practical *partial preimage attack* that finds x such that $MC^{-1}(x \oplus \pi(x))$ has 32 bits to zero, in about 2^{16} evaluations of Haraka-512 v2. We just have to run a single merging step, fixing the global variables. For each choice of forward and backward values in the merged list, we recompute the initial state x. This x is such that the two cells $MC^{-1}(x \oplus \pi(x))^a[10,13]$ are zero. Since the merged list is of size 2^{16}, by enumerating it in times 2^{16}, we will find an element with 16 more zero bits.

6.3   Quantum Attack on Grøstl OT

The output transformation (OT) of Grøstl-256 [28] is an AES-like permutation P operating on an 8×8 matrix of bytes (thus 512 bits in total). The goal is to find a state x such that $\mathsf{trunc}_{256}(P(x) \oplus x) = t$ for some target value t, say zero. The generic complexity is 2^{256}.

With our tool, we can recover the 6-round attack of [25, Appendix D]. We can also recover the improved time complexity of [5] (2^{224}, 3.5 cells), but not its memory complexity, because their procedure for the backward list is more complex than a streaming procedure. We obtain only a memory 2^{224}.

New Quantum Attack. We do not know if the approach of [5] could lead to a quantum attack, as they require a memory of size 2^{128}: in the quantum setting, one cannot afford a precomputation of time 2^{128} since it already becomes larger than the limit given by Grover search. By optimizing for the quantum time complexity, our tool finds the path of Fig. 8. There are 4.25 global guesses (including 4 free guesses), with 2.5 cells of global linear constraints and 0.25 reduction through MixColumns in each of the 7 green cells at round 4. First, the **forward ▼ list** (1.75 cells): we start from x_0^2. We deduce immediately the blue cells at round 3 and 4. Then using the 1.75 cells of precomputed equations at round 4, we deduce completely x_0^5 and x_1^5. There remains 6 bytes (0.75 cells) to guess to obtain x_4^0. Second, the **backward ▲ list** (3.5 cells): we start from round 3. With the 1.75 precomputed equations and 0.75 guessed values, there remain 3.5 cells of freedom. We deduce completely the cells at round 2. Finally, matching: there is 0.75 cell of matching between round 2 and 3 and 1 cell of matching through MC between round 0 and round 2, so 1.75 in total, which gives a merged list of size 3.5 cells. By Eq. 7, the quantum time is $2^{123.56}$, against 2^{128} generically.

For 8 rounds of Grøstl-512, there are no symmetries anymore, and the model becomes quite large. We simplify it by merging the cells in groups of 4. Then, we use the results as "hints" for the detailed version. We reobtain the time complexity of [5] with a corresponding memory complexity of 2^{304} (instead of 2^{224}), and we find a quantum attack detailed in the full version of the paper [45].

7 Applications to Feistel Networks

7.1 GFNs and Simpira

The extended setting that we defined in Sect. 3 allows to model a large class of permutations, and in particular, GFNs and SPARKLE.

Simpira v2 (simply Simpira in what follows) is a family of permutations proposed in [31]. For each $b \geq 2$, Simpira-b is a b-branch GFN where each branch is a 128-bit AES state. (Though in contrast to a GFN, the branches are not swapped and the round functions are simply applied in place). Simpira-2 is a standard FN, Simpira-3 a 3-branch type-I GFN in the classification of [48], Simpira-4 a type-II 4-branch GFN, Simpira-6 and Simpira-8 have structures taken from [46]. Each round function performs 2 complete rounds of AES with a certain round constant; we use Π_i to denote them (where i indicates the current round constant). Examples for Simpira-2, -3 and -4 are depicted in the full version of the paper [45].

For $b \geq 2$, we can use any permutation in the family to define a small-range hash function G_b by feed-forwarding:

$$G_b : \begin{cases} \{0,1\}^{b \times 128} & \to \{0,1\}^{256} \\ x & \mapsto \mathsf{trunc}(\text{Simpira-}b(x) + x) \end{cases} \tag{13}$$

where trunc is the truncation to the first 256 bits. The proposal SPHINCS-Simpira [32] uses G_2 and G_4 in SPHINCS+.

The authors of Simpira claim only 128-bit preimage security for the functions G_b, although the generic classical preimage search would stand at atime 2^{256}.

Table 3. Distinguishers on Simpira: number of rounds attacked (rounds/total rounds) by our automatic MITM tool, and by a dedicated GAD approach.

b	2	3	4	6	8
MITM (automatic)	Inapplicable	8/21	7/15	9/15	9/18
GAD	5/15	11/21	9/15	9/15	9/18

SPHINCS-Simpira [32] also claims 128-bit *quantum* preimage security. The quantum security of Simpira was studied in [42], but only regarding collision attacks. Among the known results on unkeyed GFNs, e.g. a 5-round distinguisher on a 2-branch FN [18] and a 8-round distinguisher on the 4-branch, type-II GFN [17], we did not find immediate preimage attacks on the G_b.

Results of the Extended Model. By making no structural assumption on the round functions, our model represents any GFN as a directed graph of 2-XOR cells (corresponding to round functions) and 2-branching cells. We may add *dummy cells* (1-branching cells) to separate clearly the rounds. The round functions do not need to be permutations; the attacks have a complexity at least the size of one branch, which is the cost of inverting a round function by brute force.

In order to maximize the number of rounds attacked, we consider a full wrapping constraint. We remove the memory optimization: we look for attacks of time and memory complexity $2^{(b-1)w}$ against generic 2^{bw}, where w is the branch width. Then, we run our tool with a 4-list MILP model. The results are reported in Table 3.

7.2   Guess-and-Determine Attacks on GFNs

We remarked that, with the Simpira-b structures for $b \leq 8$, we could attack the same number of rounds, and more, using much simpler Guess-and-determine (GAD) attacks. These results are also given in Table 3. The increased number of rounds is due to the linearity of the XOR, which is not captured by our cell-based modeling (see Simpira-2 below).

These attacks are *partial preimage* attacks on the hash functions G_b. We find x such that $G_b(x) = 0_{128}|*$. From there, we have a full preimage of G_b in classical time 2^{128} and quantum time 2^{64}, still valid if we replace the Π_i by random functions F_i (we can invert the F_i by brute force).

Example: Simpira-2. We explain our strategy with a 5-round attack on Simpira-2 (see Fig. 16 in the full version of the paper [45]). We index the branches as follows: first, the initial state is named $S_0, \ldots, S_{b-1}$. Then, each time a new operation $S_i \leftarrow S_i \oplus F(S_j)$ is applied, the resulting state is named S_k, with the current index k (which is then incremented). So we want to solve the following equation system:

$$S_1 \oplus S_2 = \Pi_1(S_0), \quad S_2 \oplus S_4 = \Pi_3(S_3) \quad S_0 \oplus S_3 = \Pi_2(S_2)$$
$$S_0 \oplus S_3 = \Pi_4(S_4), \quad S_4 \oplus S_6 = \Pi_5(S_5), \quad S_0 = S_5 \text{ (wrapping)} \ .$$

Table 4. Distinguishers on SPARKLE. * The attacks from Table 4.9 in [6], can be extended by one step when attacking the permutation instead of the AEAD mode.

Target	Type	Steps	Time	Generic time	Memory	Source
SPARKLE-256	Classical	5/10	2^{96}	2^{128}	2^{96}	[6] *
SPARKLE-384	Classical	5/11	2^{128}	2^{192}	2^{128}	[6] *
SPARKLE-512	Classical	5/12	2^{192}	2^{256}	2^{160}	[6] *
SPARKLE-256	Practical	4/10	negl.	2^{64}	negl.	This paper
SPARKLE-384	Practical	4/11	negl.	2^{64}	negl.	This paper
SPARKLE-512	Practical	5/12	$< 2^{32}$	2^{64}	negl.	This paper

As we can see, there are 6 equations and 7 variables, since we have put a wrapping constraint on one branch. We can simplify this system by removing all variables that intervene in a single equation, i.e., S_6 and S_1. We obtain:

$$S_0 \oplus S_3 = \Pi_2(S_2), \quad S_2 \oplus S_4 = \Pi_3(S_3), \quad S_0 \oplus S_3 = \Pi_4(S_4) .$$

From this we obtain the new equation $\Pi_4(S_4) = \Pi_2(S_2)$, which is not captured by our cell-based modeling. Guessing S_4 (our only degree of freedom) we can deduce S_2, and all the other variables follow. After trying for $b = 2, 3, 4, 6, 8$, we found that this expansion of the equation system was only useful for Simpira-2 and Simpira-4. The appropriate internal guesses are found automatically using another automated tool, which would work for any GFN construction.

7.3 Application to Sparkle

SPARKLE is a family of permutations upon which the NIST LWC candidate SCHWAEMM/ESCH (respectively for AEAD and hashing) [7] is based. We refer to the submission document [6] for a complete specification of SPARKLE, since we abstract out most of its components.

There exists three variants SPARKLE-256, -384 and -512, with respectively $b = 4, 6$ and 8 branches of 64 bits. One step of SPARKLE has the following operations: (1) an ARX-box (using round constants to disrupt symmetries) is applied to all branches. (2) a linear function of the $b/2$ left branches is computed (noted ℓ' in [6], and L here). (3) each left branch $i \leq b/2$ is XORed to branch $i + b/2$; the output of L is also XORed to each branch $i + b/2$. (4) the $b/2$ right branches are swapped following a standard GFN pattern, and then, the groups of left and right branches are swapped.

SPARKLE is not a GFN since the "round function" is actually linear, and the non-linear functions (the ARX boxes) are computed alongside the branches. But this makes no difference for our extended representation. We obtain results similar to Simpira: the MILP solver finds 4-step MITM distinguishers on the 3 variants of the permutation, and these can be simplified and improved with a GAD strategy. The details are given in the full version of the paper [45].

Our results are summarized in Table 4. We found a GAD distinguisher of complexity 1 for 4-step SPARKLE-256 and -384, and a practical 5-step distinguisher for SPARKLE-512, which combines the GAD strategy with SAT solving. It highlights another limitation of our automatic approach: the ARX boxes are viewed as random permutations, although solving some ARX equations can be done practically.

As a comparison, the *birthday-differential* GAD attacks given in the NIST submission document [6], which break 4 steps in the authenticated encryption mode SCHWAEMM, can also be turned into 5-step distinguishers for the permutation. But they have large complexities, and our distinguishers are the first practical ones.

Acknowledgments. We want to thank Patrick Derbez and Léo Perrin for helpful discussions, and Xavier Bonnetain for contributing to the code used for generating some figures of this document. A.S. is supported by ERC-ADG-ALGSTRONGCRYPTO (project 740972).

References

1. Aoki, K., Sasaki, Yu.: Preimage attacks on one-block MD4, 63-step MD5 and more. In: Avanzi, R.M., Keliher, L., Sica, F. (eds.) SAC 2008. LNCS, vol. 5381, pp. 103–119. Springer, Heidelberg (2009). https://doi.org/10.1007/978-3-642-04159-4_7
2. Aumasson, J.P., et al.: SPHINCS+: submission to the NIST post-quantum project (2015)
3. Bao, Z., Ding, L., Guo, J., Wang, H., Zhang, W.: Improved meet-in-the-middle preimage attacks against AES hashing modes. IACR Trans. Symmetric Cryptol. **2019**(4), 318–347 (2019)
4. Bao, Z., et al.: Automatic search of meet-in-the-middle preimage attacks on AES-like hashing. In: Canteaut, A., Standaert, F.-X. (eds.) EUROCRYPT 2021, Part I. LNCS, vol. 12696, pp. 771–804. Springer, Cham (2021). https://doi.org/10.1007/978-3-030-77870-5_27
5. Bao, Z., Guo, J., Shi, D., Tu, Y.: MITM meets guess-and-determine: further improved preimage attacks against AES-like hashing. IACR Cryptol. ePrint Arch. **2021**, 575 (2021)
6. Beierle, C., et al.: Schwaemm and Esch: lightweight authenticated encryption and hashing using the Sparkle permutation family. Submission to the NIST lightweight standardization process (second round) (2019)
7. Beierle, C., et al.: Lightweight AEAD and hashing using the Sparkle permutation family. IACR Trans. Symmetric Cryptol. **2020**(S1), 208–261 (2020)
8. Bernstein, D.J., et al.: GIMLI: a cross-platform permutation. In: Fischer, W., Homma, N. (eds.) CHES 2017. LNCS, vol. 10529, pp. 299–320. Springer, Cham (2017). https://doi.org/10.1007/978-3-319-66787-4_15
9. Beyne, T., Chen, Y.L., Dobraunig, C., Mennink, B.: Dumbo, jumbo, and delirium: parallel authenticated encryption for the lightweight circus. IACR Trans. Symmetric Cryptol. **2020**(S1), 5–30 (2020)
10. Blondeau, C., Peyrin, T., Wang, L.: Known-key distinguisher on full PRESENT. In: Gennaro, R., Robshaw, M. (eds.) CRYPTO 2015, Part I. LNCS, vol. 9215, pp. 455–474. Springer, Heidelberg (2015). https://doi.org/10.1007/978-3-662-47989-6_22

11. Bogdanov, A., Knežević, M., Leander, G., Toz, D., Varıcı, K., Verbauwhede, I.: SPONGENT: a lightweight hash function. In: Preneel, B., Takagi, T. (eds.) CHES 2011. LNCS, vol. 6917, pp. 312–325. Springer, Heidelberg (2011). https://doi.org/10.1007/978-3-642-23951-9_21

12. Bogdanov, A., Knezevic, M., Leander, G., Toz, D., Varici, K., Verbauwhede, I.: SPONGENT: the design space of lightweight cryptographic hashing. IEEE Trans. Comput. **62**(10), 2041–2053 (2013)

13. Bogdanov, A., et al.: PRESENT: an ultra-lightweight block cipher. In: Paillier, P., Verbauwhede, I. (eds.) CHES 2007. LNCS, vol. 4727, pp. 450–466. Springer, Heidelberg (2007). https://doi.org/10.1007/978-3-540-74735-2_31

14. Bogdanov, A., Rechberger, C.: A 3-subset meet-in-the-middle attack: cryptanalysis of the lightweight block cipher KTANTAN. In: Biryukov, A., Gong, G., Stinson, D.R. (eds.) SAC 2010. LNCS, vol. 6544, pp. 229–240. Springer, Heidelberg (2011). https://doi.org/10.1007/978-3-642-19574-7_16

15. Bogdanov, A., Shibutani, K.: Double SP-functions: enhanced generalized feistel networks. In: Parampalli, U., Hawkes, P. (eds.) ACISP 2011. LNCS, vol. 6812, pp. 106–119. Springer, Heidelberg (2011). https://doi.org/10.1007/978-3-642-22497-3_8

16. Bouillaguet, C., Derbez, P., Fouque, P.-A.: Automatic search of attacks on round-reduced AES and applications. In: Rogaway, P. (ed.) CRYPTO 2011. LNCS, vol. 6841, pp. 169–187. Springer, Heidelberg (2011). https://doi.org/10.1007/978-3-642-22792-9_10

17. Chang, D., Kumar, A., Sanadhya, S.: Security analysis of GFN: 8-round distinguisher for 4-branch type-2 GFN. In: Paul, G., Vaudenay, S. (eds.) INDOCRYPT 2013. LNCS, vol. 8250, pp. 136–148. Springer, Cham (2013). https://doi.org/10.1007/978-3-319-03515-4_9

18. Coron, J.-S., Patarin, J., Seurin, Y.: The random oracle model and the ideal cipher model are equivalent. In: Wagner, D. (ed.) CRYPTO 2008. LNCS, vol. 5157, pp. 1–20. Springer, Heidelberg (2008). https://doi.org/10.1007/978-3-540-85174-5_1

19. Daemen, J., Rijmen, V.: AES proposal: Rijndael. Submission to the NIST AES competition (1999)

20. Daemen, J., Rijmen, V.: The Design of Rijndael: AES - The Advanced Encryption Standard. Information Security and Cryptography. Springer, Heidelberg (2002). https://doi.org/10.1007/978-3-662-04722-4

21. Damgård, I.B.: A design principle for hash functions. In: Brassard, G. (ed.) CRYPTO 1989. LNCS, vol. 435, pp. 416–427. Springer, New York (1990). https://doi.org/10.1007/0-387-34805-0_39

22. Derbez, P., Fouque, P.-A.: Automatic search of meet-in-the-middle and impossible differential attacks. In: Robshaw, M., Katz, J. (eds.) CRYPTO 2016, Part II. LNCS, vol. 9815, pp. 157–184. Springer, Heidelberg (2016). https://doi.org/10.1007/978-3-662-53008-5_6

23. Diffie, W., Hellman, M.E.: Special feature exhaustive cryptanalysis of the NBS data encryption standard. Computer **10**(6), 74–84 (1977)

24. Dobraunig, C., Eichlseder, M., Mendel, F., Schläffer, M.: Ascon v1.2. Submission to NIST-LWC (2nd Round) (2010)

25. Dong, X., Hua, J., Sun, S., Li, Z., Wang, X., Hu, L.: Meet-in-the-middle attacks revisited: key-recovery, collision, and preimage attacks. In: Malkin, T., Peikert, C. (eds.) CRYPTO 2021, Part III. LNCS, vol. 12827, pp. 278–308. Springer, Cham (2021). https://doi.org/10.1007/978-3-030-84252-9_10

26. Dunkelman, O., Sekar, G., Preneel, B.: Improved meet-in-the-middle attacks on reduced-round DES. In: Srinathan, K., Rangan, C.P., Yung, M. (eds.) INDOCRYPT 2007. LNCS, vol. 4859, pp. 86–100. Springer, Heidelberg (2007). https://doi.org/10.1007/978-3-540-77026-8_8

27. Flórez-Gutiérrez, A., Leurent, G., Naya-Plasencia, M., Perrin, L., Schrottenloher, A., Sibleyras, F.: Internal symmetries and linear properties: full-permutation distinguishers and improved collisions on Gimli. J. Cryptol. **34**(4), 45 (2021)

28. Gauravaram, P., Knudsen, L.R., Matusiewicz, K., Mendel, F., Rechberger, C., Schläffer, M., Thomsen, S.S.: Grøstl-a SHA-3 candidate. Submission to the SHA-3 competition (2011)

29. Gleixner, A., et al.: The SCIP Optimization Suite 6.0. Technical report, Optimization Online (2018)

30. Grover, L.K.: A fast quantum mechanical algorithm for database search. In: STOC, pp. 212–219. ACM (1996)

31. Gueron, S., Mouha, N.: Simpira v2: a family of efficient permutations using the AES round function. In: Cheon, J.H., Takagi, T. (eds.) ASIACRYPT 2016, Part I. LNCS, vol. 10031, pp. 95–125. Springer, Heidelberg (2016). https://doi.org/10.1007/978-3-662-53887-6_4

32. Gueron, S., Mouha, N.: SPHINCS-Simpira: fast stateless hash-based signatures with post-quantum security. IACR Cryptol. ePrint Arch., 645 (2017)

33. Guo, J., Ling, S., Rechberger, C., Wang, H.: Advanced meet-in-the-middle preimage attacks: first results on full tiger, and improved results on MD4 and SHA-2. In: Abe, M. (ed.) ASIACRYPT 2010. LNCS, vol. 6477, pp. 56–75. Springer, Heidelberg (2010). https://doi.org/10.1007/978-3-642-17373-8_4

34. Hosoyamada, A., Sasaki, Yu.: Finding hash collisions with quantum computers by using differential trails with smaller probability than birthday bound. In: Canteaut, A., Ishai, Y. (eds.) EUROCRYPT 2020, Part II. LNCS, vol. 12106, pp. 249–279. Springer, Cham (2020). https://doi.org/10.1007/978-3-030-45724-2_9

35. Hosoyamada, A., Sasaki, Yu.: Quantum collision attacks on reduced SHA-256 and SHA-512. In: Malkin, T., Peikert, C. (eds.) CRYPTO 2021, Part I. LNCS, vol. 12825, pp. 616–646. Springer, Cham (2021). https://doi.org/10.1007/978-3-030-84242-0_22

36. Isobe, T.: A single-key attack on the full GOST block cipher. In: Joux, A. (ed.) FSE 2011. LNCS, vol. 6733, pp. 290–305. Springer, Heidelberg (2011). https://doi.org/10.1007/978-3-642-21702-9_17

37. Isobe, T., Shibutani, K.: All subkeys recovery attack on block ciphers: extending meet-in-the-middle approach. In: Knudsen, L.R., Wu, H. (eds.) SAC 2012. LNCS, vol. 7707, pp. 202–221. Springer, Heidelberg (2013). https://doi.org/10.1007/978-3-642-35999-6_14

38. Khovratovich, D., Rechberger, C., Savelieva, A.: Bicliques for preimages: attacks on Skein-512 and the SHA-2 family. In: Canteaut, A. (ed.) FSE 2012. LNCS, vol. 7549, pp. 244–263. Springer, Heidelberg (2012). https://doi.org/10.1007/978-3-642-34047-5_15

39. Kölbl, S.: Putting wings on SPHINCS. In: Lange, T., Steinwandt, R. (eds.) PQCrypto 2018. LNCS, vol. 10786, pp. 205–226. Springer, Cham (2018). https://doi.org/10.1007/978-3-319-79063-3_10

40. Kölbl, S., Lauridsen, M.M., Mendel, F., Rechberger, C.: Haraka v2 - efficient short-input hashing for post-quantum applications. IACR Trans. Symmetric Cryptol. **2016**(2), 1–29 (2016)

41. Merkle, R.C.: One way hash functions and DES. In: Brassard, G. (ed.) CRYPTO 1989. LNCS, vol. 435, pp. 428–446. Springer, New York (1990). https://doi.org/10.1007/0-387-34805-0_40

42. Ni, B., Dong, X., Jia, K., You, Q.: (Quantum) collision attacks on reduced Simpira v2. IACR Trans. Symmetric Cryptol. **2021**(2), 222–248 (2021)

43. Preneel, B., Govaerts, R., Vandewalle, J.: Hash functions based on block ciphers: a synthetic approach. In: Stinson, D.R. (ed.) CRYPTO 1993. LNCS, vol. 773, pp. 368–378. Springer, Heidelberg (1994). https://doi.org/10.1007/3-540-48329-2_31

44. Sasaki, Yu.: Meet-in-the-middle preimage attacks on AES hashing modes and an application to whirlpool. In: Joux, A. (ed.) FSE 2011. LNCS, vol. 6733, pp. 378–396. Springer, Heidelberg (2011). https://doi.org/10.1007/978-3-642-21702-9_22

45. Schrottenloher, A., Stevens, M.: Simplified MITM modeling for permutations: New (quantum) attacks. Cryptology ePrint Archive, Report 2022/189 (2022)

46. Suzaki, T., Minematsu, K.: Improving the generalized feistel. In: Hong, S., Iwata, T. (eds.) FSE 2010. LNCS, vol. 6147, pp. 19–39. Springer, Heidelberg (2010). https://doi.org/10.1007/978-3-642-13858-4_2

47. Zhang, G., Liu, M.: Sci. China Inf. Sci. **60**(7), 1–13 (2017). https://doi.org/10.1007/s11432-016-0165-6

48. Zheng, Y., Matsumoto, T., Imai, H.: On the construction of block ciphers provably secure and not relying on any unproved hypotheses. In: Brassard, G. (ed.) CRYPTO 1989. LNCS, vol. 435, pp. 461–480. Springer, New York (1990). https://doi.org/10.1007/0-387-34805-0_42

Constructing and Deconstructing Intentional Weaknesses in Symmetric Ciphers

Christof Beierle[1]($\boxtimes$), Tim Beyne[2], Patrick Felke[3]($\boxtimes$), and Gregor Leander[1]

[1] Ruhr University Bochum, Bochum, Germany
{christof.beierle,gregor.leander}@rub.de
[2] imec-COSIC, KU Leuven, Leuven, Belgium
tim.beyne@esat.kuleuven.be
[3] University of Applied Sciences Emden/Leer, Emden, Germany
patrick.felke@hs-emden-leer.de

Abstract. Deliberately weakened ciphers are of great interest in political discussion on law enforcement, as in the constantly recurring crypto wars, and have been put in the spotlight of academics by recent progress. A paper at Eurocrypt 2021 showed a strong indication that the security of the widely-deployed stream cipher GEA-1 was deliberately and secretly weakened to 40 bits in order to fulfill European export restrictions that have been in place in the late 1990s. However, no explanation of how this could have been constructed was given. On the other hand, we have seen the MALICIOUS design framework, published at CRYPTO 2020, that allows to construct tweakable block ciphers with a backdoor, where the difficulty of recovering the backdoor relies on well-understood cryptographic assumptions. The constructed tweakable block cipher however is rather unusual and very different from, say, general-purpose ciphers like the AES.

In this paper, we pick up both topics. For GEA-1 we thoroughly explain how the weakness was constructed, solving the main open question of the work mentioned above. By generalizing MALICIOUS we – for the first time – construct backdoored tweakable block ciphers that follow modern design principles for general-purpose block ciphers, i.e., more natural-looking deliberately weakened tweakable block ciphers.

Keywords: Cryptanalysis · GPRS · GEA-1 · Stream cipher · Tweakable block cipher · LFSR · Malicious · Invariant attacks

1 Introduction

The design of deliberate and often hidden weaknesses in (symmetric) cryptographic primitives has a long history, both in practical examples as well as in academic constructions. For the former, among the most famous examples are the block cipher DES [32], for which the key size was deliberately weakened to 56 bits, and the pseudonumber generator Dual EC DRBG, which was equipped with a backdoor (see [28]) by a proper selection of its parameters. We refer to [9] for a detailed survey on the standardization and the weakness of Dual EC DRBG. We also like to mention the Russian cipher GOST (R 34.12-2015), aka Kuznyechik, where the S-box was shown to have undisclosed structures [29].

© International Association for Cryptologic Research 2022
Y. Dodis and T. Shrimpton (Eds.): CRYPTO 2022, LNCS 13509, pp. 748–778, 2022.
https://doi.org/10.1007/978-3-031-15982-4_25

In [12] a nice argument was given that this structure is indeed very unlikely to appear by chance.

For academic constructions, we have seen approaches based on hiding a highly-biased linear approximation [31,33] over a block cipher and approaches based on partitioning cryptanalysis [19], where the backdoor consists of a partition of the plaintext space that is preserved under the encryption function [5,18,27]. The latter approach is related to invariant subspace attacks [24] and nonlinear invariant attacks [36]. In the case of hash functions, the work [1] showed how to design malicious variants of SHA-1 with built-in collisions.

For all of these academic constructions, the designers either do not claim security of the backdoor in the sense that it cannot be recovered even if its general form is known, or there is an attack which recovers the backdoor from the specification of the cipher (see e.g., [39]).

The interest into deliberately weakening symmetric primitives has been increased recently, again with respect to both aspects. On the one hand, the work [8] showed that there is a strong indication that the security of the widely deployed cipher GEA-1 was deliberately and secretly weakened to 40 bits in order to fulfill European export restrictions. On the other hand, we have seen the MALICIOUS design framework [30] that allows to construct a tweakable block cipher with a backdoor. One of the interesting features within this framework is that the difficulty of recovering the backdoor relies on well-understood cryptographic principles.

The MALICIOUS Framework. The authors defined the following four notions a cryptographic backdoor can fulfill, which we directly quote from [30].

- *Undetectability:* this security notion represents the inability for an external entity to realize the existence of the hidden backdoor.
- *Undiscoverability:* it represents the inability for an attacker to find the hidden backdoor, even if the general form of the backdoor is known.
- *Untraceability:* it states that an attack based on the backdoor should not reveal any information about the backdoor itself.
- *Practicability:* this usability notion stipulates that the backdoor is practical, in the sense that it is easy to recover the secret key once the backdoor is known.

The basic idea of the MALICIOUS framework is to construct a tweakable block cipher such that for a particular malicious tweak pair (t, t'), the instance of the cipher for this tweak pair exhibits a differential property that allows for a practical cryptanalytic attack. The tweak pair (t, t') is secured by being a pair of preimages for outputs of an extendable-output function (XOF) H.

With such a construction, the backdoor fulfills the notions of practicability, undiscoverability, and undetectability, but not untraceability.

The instances given in [30] are based on the block cipher LowMC [2]. The drawback is that the round function needs to be constructed by using a rather complex (basically random) linear layer and a partial S-box layer. As suggested for future work in [30], it would be interesting to find similar constructions which are based on cryptanalytic attacks other than differential cryptanalysis, as this might lead to more natural instances.

Deliberate Weakness in GEA-1. General Packet Radio Service (GPRS) is a mobile data standard based on the GSM (2G) technology, and was widely deployed during the late 1990s s and the early 2000s. At the cryptographic level, the data processed by the GPRS protocol is protected by a stream cipher. In 1998, ETSI Security Algorithms Group of Experts (SAGE) initially designed the proprietary 64-bit encryption algorithm GEA-1 for this purpose. The cipher GEA-1 is depicted in Fig. 2 and consists of three LFSRs with different lengths and a non-linear Boolean function combining their outputs to produce the keystream.

Although classical algebraic attacks on GEA-1 (e.g., those based on linearization) are hard to conduct in practice because of the limit on the data available to an adversary, in [8] the authors showed that GEA-1 does not achieve an adequate security level. Indeed, they presented an attack on GEA-1 with complexity corresponding to a security level of 40 bits. It is based on a simple but remarkable observation: After the linear initialization procedure, the joint state of two of the LFSRs have a joint entropy of only 40 bits, whereas their joint size adds up to 64 bits. This loss of entropy directly leads to a classical meet-in-the-middle attack with time complexity 2^{40}. Recently, in [3], the authors presented an attack on GEA-1 with the same time complexity but a reduced memory complexity of only 4 MiB (instead of 44.5 GiB).

The authors of [8] further analyzed how frequently this surprising observation occurs for randomly chosen LFSRs. For this, they replaced the (two) LFSRs used in GEA-1 by primitive LFSRs in Galois mode of the corresponding size chosen uniformly at random and computed the loss of entropy. After roughly one million trials, the maximal loss that was observed was at most 9 bits,[1] demonstrating that this behavior is (i) very rare and thus (ii) most likely built in to keep the ciphers effective strength at 40 bits.

One important question was not answered in [8], namely: How was this configuration of LFSRs constructed? By extrapolating the experimental observations given in [8, Table 2], we estimate the cost of constructing this simply by randomly picking primitive LFSRs to be in the range of roughly 2^{47} trials, summing up to around 2^{65} binary operations in total.[2] Taking into account that the design is already more than 20 years old, the cost of this would have been prohibitive. This strongly indicated that there must be a more elaborated and efficient way of achieving the desired setting.

---

[1] When considering all possible combinations of two of the three registers in GEA-1, the maximal observed loss was 11 bits.

[2] We estimate the number of expected solutions to be $s \cdot 2^{-2d+1}$, where s denotes the sample space and d the desired entropy loss. For each sample, one has to solve a linear system of dimension 64 to compute the entropy loss.

1.1   Our Contribution

Deconstructing GEA-1: Choosing LFSRs with a Hidden Weakness. In the case of GEA-1 we answer the open question on how to construct a GEA-1-like cipher with such a reduced security. Our observations and analysis, relying mainly on the polynomial representation of the involved LFSRs, imply that the actual GEA-1 instance could have been obtained from our construction.

For this we describe the states, the initialization and the intersection of states by polynomials over $\mathbb{F}_2$. This description allows to formulate the conditions for a set-up that enables an attack as the one on GEA-1 in terms of divisibility of state polynomials by the characteristic polynomial of the LFSRs. In a second step, we explain a possible construction of pairs of LFSRs with the desired entropy loss. The general idea here is to turn the problem around by starting with elements in the kernel and then searching for suitable LFSRs.

We show by decomposing the kernel of GEA-1 that it can be easily constructed using our approach. As GEA-1 is then only one example of the (re?)-discovered design strategy, we elaborate about other possible parameter choices in Sect. 3.2 and discuss the limits of this approach.

As a side remark, the above mentioned use of LFSRs in Galois mode can now also be justified: A Fibonacci LFSR that is based on a random characteristic polynomial, and thus very likely has many taps, is unfavorable to implement in software and thus unusual. For an LFSR in Galois mode, the choice of a random characteristic polynomial resulting in many taps is desirable.

In contrast to the MALICIOUS framework, the weakness in GEA-1 is based on *hiding* a cryptoanalytic attack. This approach has the drawback that in principle everybody can recover this attack and can decipher messages encrypted with this system. Thus, this design fails to fulfill three of the four conditions for a backdoor proposed by [30], i.e., undiscoverability, undetectability and untraceability.

Constructing Backdoors: Trivial and Natural Variants of MALICIOUS. As described above, the original MALICIOUS framework was formulated in terms of differential cryptanalysis only. For our results, we use a naturally generalized version of the framework.

Our contribution is twofold. First, we show that *any* (tweakable) block cipher can be tweaked in a very simple way in order to comply with the MALICIOUS framework. In a nutshell, the idea of constructing such an instance is to check if the message hashes to a certain fixed value and if so, return the key instead of the encrypted message. If the hash does not match, the cipher is executed unchanged.

While this example shows that the initial goals of the MALICIOUS framework can be achieved in a trivial way, this artificial construction does not give further insights on how to construct *hidden* weaknesses. Ideally, a malicious designer would aim for constructing a rather *natural* instance which follows modern design principles in symmetric cryptography and for which a sound design rationale can be formulated. Towards achieving this goal, we propose two new instances of the MALICIOUS framework as our second contribution. While the instances presented in [30] rely on the existence of a high-probability differential, we base our construction on an invariant subspace, resp., nonlinear invariant, for the malicious tweak value. As we argue, this allows for more natural instances. In particular, in Sect. 5, we show how to use the round function of the Advanced Encryption Standard (AES) and to adapt the key schedule in order to embed a backdoor based on an *invariant subspace* over the round function. More precisely, we exploit an invariant subspace that is already known since 2004, see [23]. In Sect. 6, we construct a dedicated cipher, called Boomslang, that embeds a backdoor based on a *nonlinear invariant* over two consecutive round functions.

Compared to previous constructions not based on the MALICIOUS framework, in particular [27] and [31], our constructions also directly improve upon the usability of the backdoor as they enable significantly more practical key-recovery attacks.

Our constructions constitute the first backdoored ciphers that follow modern design principles of general-purpose block ciphers, and are expected to achieve competitive performance characteristics.

Ethical Aspect of Our Research. We (the authors) do not have the goal to support people in building intentionally weakened ciphers. A first step in order to prevent the use of intentionally weakened designs in the future is to investigate the design space of such constructions. Only when knowing what potential attackers, in this case acting as malicious developers of cryptographic primitives, are capable of doing, we are able to prevent them from doing so.

2 GEA-1 and Its Cryptoanalytic Properties

In this section we recall the description of the stream cipher GEA-1 as well as its weakness, both as presented in [8]. Before doing so, we define and recall the basic mathematics behind the cipher.

2.1 Preliminaries

As usual, a matrix $A \in \mathbb{F}_2^{m \times n}$ corresponds to a linear map from $\mathbb{F}_2^n$ to $\mathbb{F}_2^m$ by matrix-vector multiplication from the right. Thus the ith column of A is the image of $e_i := (0, 0, \ldots, 1, 0 \ldots, 0)^\top \in \mathbb{F}_2^n$, i.e., the ith canonical unit vector.

Galois Mode LFSRs. We recall some basic facts about linear feedback shift registers (LFSRs) in Galois mode, as depicted in Fig. 1. For further reading we refer to [35, p. 378 ff.] and [20, p. 227].

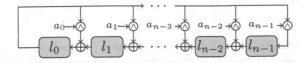

Fig. 1. An LFSR in Galois mode.

Given an LFSR L in Galois mode of degree n with entries in $\mathbb{F}_2$, clocking the state $l = (l_0, \ldots, l_{n-1})$ is equivalent to the matrix-vector multiplication

$$G_L \cdot l = \begin{bmatrix} a_0 & 1 & 0 & \cdots & 0 \\ a_1 & 0 & 1 & \cdots & 0 \\ \vdots & \vdots & \vdots & \ddots & \vdots \\ a_{n-2} & 0 & 0 & \cdots & 1 \\ a_{n-1} & 0 & 0 & \cdots & 0 \end{bmatrix} \begin{bmatrix} l_0 \\ l_1 \\ \vdots \\ l_{n-2} \\ l_{n-1} \end{bmatrix} = \begin{bmatrix} a_0 l_0 + l_1 \\ a_1 l_0 + l_2 \\ \vdots \\ a_{n-2} l_0 + l_{n-1} \\ a_{n-1} l_0 \end{bmatrix}.$$

The characteristic polynomial of G_L is

$$g := \det(X I_n + G_L) = X^n + a_0 X^{n-1} + \cdots + a_{n-2} X + a_{n-1} \in \mathbb{F}_2[X]$$

and is a multiple of the minimal polynomial of G_L. Here, I_n denotes the $n \times n$ identity matrix. Although LFSRs in Galois mode can be defined more generally, we only consider the case where g is primitive. That is, g is the minimal polynomial of an element $\alpha \in \mathbb{F}_{2^n}$ that generates the multiplicative group $\mathbb{F}_{2^n}^{\times}$. In this case, g is also the minimal polynomial of G_L. Only primitive polynomials are of cryptographic interest as they correspond to LFSRs with a maximal period of $2^n - 1$. Since primitive polynomials are necessarily irreducible, we have $a_{n-1} \neq 0$, which is equivalent to the fact that G_L is invertible. Conversely, any primitive polynomial g corresponds to an (invertible) companion matrix of an LFSR in Galois mode with minimal polynomial g.

Galois Matrices. In the sequel, the matrix G_L will be called a *Galois matrix* of degree n and the corresponding minimal polynomial the *Galois polynomial*. Moreover, given an LFSR L in Galois mode with minimal polynomial g, we also denote the Galois matrix by G_g if appropriate.

To describe our construction, we need the following properties of Galois matrices. These are well-known facts from classical ring or field theory respectively (e.g., see [25,37]). To keep the paper self-contained and to enhance readability we include a proof below.

Theorem 1. *Given a Galois matrix G_g of degree n with primitive Galois polynomial g, let $\mathbb{F}_2[G_g] := \{\sum_{i=0}^{m} t_i G_g^i \mid m \in \mathbb{N}, t \in \mathbb{F}_2^{m+1}\}$ be the subring of $\mathbb{F}_2^{n \times n}$ generated by G_g and let (g) denote the ideal generated by $g \in \mathbb{F}_2[X]$. Then the following statements are true.*

1. *The map $\psi : \mathbb{F}_2[X]/(g) \to \mathbb{F}_2[G_g]$ defined by $\psi(\sum_{i=0}^{m} t_i X^i) = \sum_{i=0}^{m} t_i G_g^i$ is a ring isomorphism.[3]*

---

[3] Note that we use $\sum_{i=0}^{m} t_i X^i$ as a shorthand for the corresponding coset of $\mathbb{F}_2[X]$.

2. *Every nonzero element $v \in \mathbb{F}_2^n$ is G_g-cyclic, i.e., $\{v, G_g v, \ldots, G_g^{n-1} v\}$ is a basis for $\mathbb{F}_2^n$.*

Proof. By the definition of minimal polynomials, the set of all polynomials p with $p(M) = 0$ for a matrix M with minimal polynomial q is equal to the ideal (q). Since (q) is a maximal ideal, $\mathbb{F}_2[X]/(q)$ is a finite field of degree n over $\mathbb{F}_2$. As remarked above, g is primitive and the minimal polynomial of G_g. Thus, the canonical map $\phi : \mathbb{F}_2[X] \longrightarrow \mathbb{F}_2[G_g] : p \mapsto p(G_g)$ has kernel (g) and hence ψ is an isomorphism by the first isomorphism theorem.

For the second claim, suppose the vectors $v, G_g v, \ldots, G_g^{n-1} v$ are linearly dependent. Then there exist $t_0, \ldots, t_{n-1} \in \mathbb{F}_2$ such that not all t_i equal zero and

$$\sum_{i=0}^{n-1} t_i G_g^i \, v = \left(\sum_{i=0}^{n-1} t_i G_g^i \right) v = 0 \ .$$

By applying the isomorphism ψ^{-1}, we get that $0 \neq \sum_{i=0}^{n-1} t_i X^i \in \mathbb{F}_2[X]/(g)$ as the degree of the polynomial $\sum_{i=0}^{n-1} t_i X^i$ is at most $n-1$ and not all t_i are equal to zero. As $\mathbb{F}_2[X]/(g)$ is a finite field, any nonzero element such as $\sum_{i=0}^{n-1} t_i X^i$ is invertible. Since any isomorphism maps invertible elements to invertible elements, it follows that $\sum_{i=0}^{n-1} t_i G_g^i$ is invertible. Hence $\left(\sum_{i=0}^{n-1} t_i G_g^i \right) v \neq 0$ as $v \neq 0$. This is a contradiction and therefore, v is G_g-cyclic. □

Remark 1. Note that $\mathbb{F}_2[X]/(g)$ is a field. The matrix G_g is the representation matrix of the linear mapping $p \mapsto Xp$ over the finite field $\mathbb{F}_2[X]/(g)$ with respect to the basis $X^{n-1}, X^{n-2}, \ldots, 1$. This connection to a central mapping in the theory of finite fields (also called Galois fields), the so-called left multiplication, leads to the name for these kind of LFSRs.

The following corollary is extensively used in the remainder of this paper. The proof is a straightforward application of Theorem 1 and therefore omitted.

Corollary 1. *Let e_0 denote the vector $e_0 := (1, 0, \ldots, 0)^\top \in \mathbb{F}_2^n$ and G_g a Galois matrix of degree n for a primitive polynomial g. Then, for $m \geq 0, t_i \in \mathbb{F}_2, i = 0, \ldots, m$, we have $\sum_{i=0}^{m} t_i G_g^i e_0 = 0$ if and only if g divides $\sum_{i=0}^{m} t_i X^i$ in $\mathbb{F}_2[X]$.*

2.2 Description of GEA-1

We now turn to the description of GEA-1, and in particular the mechanism used to initialize the LFSR registers.

Keystream Generation. The keystream is generated from three LFSRs over $\mathbb{F}_2$, called A, B and C, together with a 7-bit non-linear filter function f. The registers A, B and C have lengths $31, 32$ and 33, respectively and the LFSRs work in Galois mode. In particular, the Galois polynomials corresponding to LFSRs A,

B and C are

$$g_A = X^{31} + X^{30} + X^{28} + X^{27} + X^{23} + X^{22} + X^{21} + X^{19} + X^{18} + X^{15}$$
$$+ X^{11} + X^{10} + X^8 + X^7 + X^6 + X^4 + X^3 + X^2 + 1 ,$$
$$g_B = X^{32} + X^{31} + X^{29} + X^{25} + X^{19} + X^{18} + X^{17} + X^{16} + X^9 + X^8$$
$$+ X^7 + X^3 + X^2 + X + 1 ,$$
$$g_C = X^{33} + X^{30} + X^{27} + X^{23} + X^{21} + X^{20} + X^{19} + X^{18} + X^{17} + X^{15}$$
$$+ X^{14} + X^{11} + X^{10} + X^9 + X^4 + X^2 + 1 ,$$

respectively. The function f belongs to a class of cryptographically strong Boolean functions that can be decomposed into two bent functions on 6 bits. For the considerations below, the choice of f is irrelevant and we omit it here.

When all registers have been initialized (see below), the actual keystream generation starts. This is done by taking the bits at seven specified positions in each register to be the input to f. The outputs of the three f-functions are XORed together to produce one bit of the keystream. Figure 2 shows the particular feedback positions of each register, as well as which positions form which input to f. After calculating a single keystream bit, all registers are clocked once each before the process is repeated to generate the next bit.

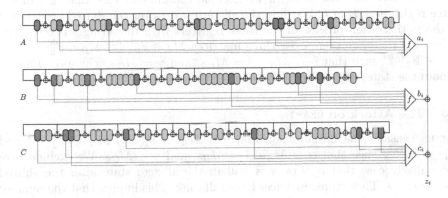

Fig. 2. Overview of the keystream generation of GEA-1 [8].

Initialization. The cipher is initialized using a non-linear feedback shift register S of length 64. This register is filled with zeros at the start of the initialization process. The input for initializing GEA-1 consists of a public 32-bit initialization vector iv, one public bit dir (indicating direction of communication/uplink or downlink in a cellular network), and a 64-bit secret key k. The initialization starts by clocking S for 97 times, feeding in one input bit with every clock. The input bits are introduced in the order $iv_0, iv_1, \ldots, iv_{31}, dir, k_0, k_1, \ldots, k_{63}$. When all input bits have been loaded, the register is clocked another 128 times with zeros as input. The feedback function consists of f, XORed with the bit that is shifted out, and XORed with the next bit from the input sequence.

After S has been clocked 225 times, the content of the register is taken as a 64-bit vector $s = (s_0, \ldots, s_{63})$. This string is taken as a seed for initializing A, B and C as follows. First, all three registers are initialized with zeros. Then, each register is clocked 64 times, with an s_i-bit XORed onto the bit that is shifted out before feedback. Register A inserts the bits from s in the natural order $s_0, s_1, \ldots, s_{63}$. The sequence s is cyclically shifted by 16 positions before being inserted to register B, so the bits are entered in the order $s_{16}, s_{17}, \ldots, s_{63}, s_0, \ldots, s_{15}$. For register C the sequence s is cyclically shifted by 32 positions before insertion starts. Figure 3 depicts the process for register B. If any of the registers A, B or C end up in the all-zero state, the bit in position zero of the register is forcibly set to one before keystream generation starts.

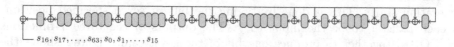

$s_{16}, s_{17}, \ldots, s_{63}, s_0, s_1, \ldots, s_{15}$

Fig. 3. Initialization of register B [8].

As already observed in [8], if we exclude the unlikely case that any of the three registers A, B or C is still in the all-zero state after the shifted insertion of s, the initialization process of the three registers with the string s is obviously linear and therefore there exist three matrices $M_A \in \mathbb{F}_2^{31 \times 64}$, $M_B \in \mathbb{F}_2^{32 \times 64}$ and $M_C \in \mathbb{F}_2^{33 \times 64}$ such that $\alpha = M_A s, \beta = M_B s$, and $\gamma = M_C s$, where α, β and γ denote the states of the three LFSRs after the initialization phase.

2.3 The Attack on GEA-1

Let us consider the initialization matrices $M_A \in \mathbb{F}_2^{31 \times 64}$, $M_B \in \mathbb{F}_2^{32 \times 64}$ and $M_C \in \mathbb{F}_2^{33 \times 64}$ such that $\alpha = M_A s, \beta = M_B s$, and $\gamma = M_C s$. We exclude here the unlikely case that α, β or γ is still in the all-zero state after the shifted insertion of s. These three matrices have full rank. This implies that the number of possible starting states after initialization is maximal when each LFSR is considered independently, i.e., there are $2^{31} - 1$ possible states for register A, $2^{32} - 1$ possible states for register B, and $2^{33} - 1$ possible states for register C, as should be expected. This corresponds to the linear mappings represented by M_A, M_B and M_C having kernels of dimension of at least 33, 32 and 31, respectively. However, when considering pairs of registers, one gets a decomposition of $\mathbb{F}_2^{64}$ as a direct sum of the kernels of the linear mappings. In [8] it was observed that if one denotes $T_{A,C} := \ker(M_A) \cap \ker(M_C)$ and $U_B := \ker(M_B)$, then

$$\dim(T_{A,C}) = 24, \quad \dim(U_B) = 32, \quad \text{and} \quad U_B \cap T_{A,C} = \{0\} .$$

From this, it directly follows that $\mathbb{F}_2^{64}$ can be decomposed into the direct sum $U_B \oplus T_{A,C} \oplus V$, where V is of dimension 8. Thus, for the key-dependent and secret string s, there exists a *unique* representation $s = u + t + v$ with $u \in U_B$, $t \in T_{A,C}$, $v \in V$ and

$$\beta = M_B(u + t + v) = M_B(t + v)$$
$$\alpha = M_A(u + t + v) = M_A(u + v)$$
$$\gamma = M_C(u + t + v) = M_C(u + v).$$

Indeed, from this decomposition, s can be computed with a meet-in-the-middle attack with a complexity[4] of 2^{37} GEA-1 evaluations to build (and sort) a table with 2^{32} entries of size 89 bit (65 keystream bits to reconstruct the key uniquely with high probability and 24 bits for t leading to this keystream) and a brute-force step of complexity 2^{40} GEA-1 evaluations for each new session key $k_0, \ldots, k_{63}$. For more details of the attack see [8]. Note that once s is recovered it is easy to recover $k_0, \ldots, k_{63}$ by clocking the S-register backwards. Hence, the attack has to be conducted only *once per GPRS session* and is done in 2^{40} operations once the table has been computed. In other words, the joint state of A and C can be described with only 40 bits and thus can take only 2^{40} possible values. This is the key observation of the attack and in [8] computer simulations are used to argue that such a decomposition of the key space is highly unlikely to occur accidentally. The main question arising in this context is how to design such a system. As demonstrated by the experiments conducted in [8], a trial and error approach is elusive. This question will be answered in the next section.

3   Deconstructing GEA-1: Shifting Matters

In this section we will give a method to build ciphers of GEA-1 type which are vulnerable to the attack described above and thereby answer the corresponding question in [8].

It will become apparent (without giving a rigorous proof) that systems of GEA-1 type with a keyspace that can be decomposed into a direct sum as above only appear for *very special choices* of the shift constants together with *very special choices* for the Galois polynomials. This is remarkable because one could intuitively expect that shifting only strengthens the system.

In general, this demonstrates that it is not recommended to modify the canonical way of feeding the key into the LFSRs. Indeed, only by modifying this initialization and by using the shifted key for the individual LFSRs, the attack becomes possible.

3.1   The Impact of Shifting

We first settle the question how to find two primitive Galois polynomials $g_1 \in \mathbb{F}_2[X]$ and $g_2 \in \mathbb{F}_2[X]$ of degree d_1 and d_2, respectively, such that for the corresponding Galois matrices G_{g_1} and G_{g_2}, the dimension of $T_{g_1,g_2,\text{cs}} := \ker(M_{g_1}) \cap$

---

[4] The complexity is measured by the amount of operations that are roughly as complex as GEA-1 evaluations (for generating a keystream of size ≤ 128 bit).

$\ker(M_{g_2,\mathsf{cs}})$ is at least ξ with $\mathsf{cs} \in \{0, 1, \ldots, \kappa - 1\}$ being the cyclic shift employed during the initialization and κ being the size of the session key (64 in case of GEA-1). Without loss of generality we focus on this case. It is a routine matter to extend the approach presented in the sequel to the case where in both initialization phases a shift is applied. First of all, note that the columns of M_{g_1} (the initialization matrix without a shift) consist of $G_{g_1}^{\kappa-i} e_0$, where $e_0 := (1, 0, \ldots, 0)^\top \in \mathbb{F}_2^{d_1}$ and $i = 0, \ldots, \kappa - 1$. Note that we have to clock the register i times before the first bit of s_i not equal to zero is plugged into the register and thus the state becomes non-zero. This explains the shape of $M_{G_{g_1}}$. Suppose $t \in \ker(G_{g_1})$, then

$$0 = M_{g_1} t = \sum_{i=0}^{\kappa-1} t_i \, G_{g_i}^{\kappa-i} \, e_0 \,.$$

By Corollary 1, the above holds if and only if g_1 divides $\sum_{i=0}^{\kappa-1} t_i X^{\kappa-i}$. In the case of g_2, a similar reasoning takes into account the effect of cs such that the columns of $M_{g_2,\mathsf{cs}}$ (the initialization matrix with a shift) consist of $G_{g_2}^{\mathsf{cs}-i} e_0$ if $i < \mathsf{cs}$ and $G_{g_2}^{\kappa-i+\mathsf{cs}} e_0$ otherwise, where $e_0 := (1, 0, \ldots, 0)^\top \in \mathbb{F}_2^{d_2}$. Note that now we have to clock the register $\kappa + i - \mathsf{cs}$ times before the first non-zero bit of s_i is plugged into the register and thus the state is non-zero. This gives the first case. The second follows in the same way. In the same vein as above we get that

$$0 = M_{g_2,\mathsf{cs}} \, t = \sum_{i=0}^{\mathsf{cs}-1} t_i \, G_{g_2}^{\mathsf{cs}-i} e_0 + \sum_{i=\mathsf{cs}}^{\kappa-1} t_i \, G_{g_2}^{\kappa-i+\mathsf{cs}} \, e_0$$

if and only if g_2 divides $\sum_{i=0}^{\mathsf{cs}-1} t_i X^{\mathsf{cs}-i} + \sum_{i=\mathsf{cs}}^{\kappa-1} t_i X^{\kappa-i+\mathsf{cs}}$. Hence, a vector $t \in \mathbb{F}_2^\kappa$ lies in $T_{g_1,g_2,\mathsf{cs}}$ if and only if g_1 divides $\sum_{i=0}^{\kappa-1} t_i X^{\kappa-i}$ and g_2 divides $\sum_{i=0}^{\mathsf{cs}-1} t_i X^{\mathsf{cs}-i} + \sum_{i=\mathsf{cs}}^{\kappa-1} t_i X^{\kappa-i+\mathsf{cs}}$. More specifically, we have the following theorem which shows how to control the dimension of $T_{g_1,g_2,\mathsf{cs}}$.

Theorem 2. *Let $g_1, g_2 \in \mathbb{F}_2[X]$ be two primitive Galois polynomials and $\mathsf{cs} \in \{0, 1, \ldots, \kappa - 1\}$ an integer. For $t \in T_{g_1,g_2,\mathsf{cs}}$ we define the associated polynomials*

$$p_1 := \sum_{i=0}^{\kappa-1} t_i \, X^{\kappa-i}, \quad p_2 := \sum_{i=0}^{\mathsf{cs}-1} t_i \, X^{\mathsf{cs}-i} + \sum_{i=\mathsf{cs}}^{\kappa-1} t_i \, X^{\kappa-i+\mathsf{cs}} \,.$$

Let

$$r_1 = \min\{k : X^k \text{ is a monomial with non-zero coefficient in } p_1\},$$
$$r_2 = \min\{k : X^k \text{ is a monomial with non-zero coefficient in } p_2\},$$
$$r_3 = \min\{r_1, r_2\}$$

Then

1. *The polynomial p_1 is divisible by g_1 and the polynomial p_2 is divisible by g_2.*
2. *For all $0 \le s \le r_3 - 1$, the shifted vectors $t^s := (0, \ldots, 0, t_0, t_1, \ldots, t_{\kappa-1-s})^\top \in \mathbb{F}_2^\kappa$ are elements of $T_{g_1,g_2,\mathsf{cs}}$.*

3. *The elements t^s are linearly independent and thus span a subspace of $T_{g_1,g_2,\mathrm{cs}}$ of dimension r_3.*

Proof. The first property was already established above. By definition, it holds that $t_{\kappa-1-(r_1-1)} = 1$, as it is the coefficient of X^{r_1} in p_1. We further have $t_{\kappa-1-(r_1-1)+1} = 0$, $t_{\kappa-1-(r_1-1)+2} = 0$, ..., $t_{\kappa-1} = 0$ from the definition of r_1. Hence, the elements t^s are linearly independent.

Since $t \in T_{g_1,g_2,\mathrm{cs}}$ we have that g_1 divides p_1 and g_2 divides p_2. By definition of r_3, the associated polynomials of t^s are of the form $X^{-s}p_1, X^{-s}p_2$ and still contained in $\mathbb{F}_2[X]$. Therefore they are also divisible by g_1 and g_2. Thus the elements t^s form a subspace of dimension r_3 of $T_{g_1,g_2,\mathrm{cs}}$. $\square$

Remark 2. Note that slightly more can be said about the structure of good choices for g_1 and g_2 and the corresponding space $T_{g_1,g_2,\mathrm{cs}}$. For example looking at the reciprocal polynomials of g_1 and g_2 results in the same dimension for the kernel.

For this let κ be even and $\mathrm{cs} = \kappa/2$. If $t \in T_{g_1,g_2,\mathrm{cs}}$ for two primitive polynomials $g_1, g_2 \in \mathbb{F}_2[X]$, we have $t^* = (t_{\kappa-1}, \ldots, t_1, t_0) \in T_{g_1^*,g_2^*,\mathrm{cs}}$, where $g_i^*(X) := X^{\deg g_i}g_i(X^{-1})$ denotes the *reciprocal polynomial* of g_i. This can be seen as follows. For the polynomials p_1 and p_2 defined in Theorem 2, we let $q_i(X) := X^\kappa p_i(X^{-1})$. Then,

$$ X q_1 = \sum_{i=0}^{\kappa-1} t_i^* X^{\kappa-i}, \quad X q_2 = \sum_{i=0}^{\mathrm{cs}-1} t_i^* X^{\mathrm{cs}-i} + \sum_{i=\mathrm{cs}}^{\kappa-1} t_i^* X^{\kappa-i+\mathrm{cs}} $$

and $t^* \in T_{g_1^*,g_2^*,\mathrm{cs}}$ if g_i^* divides $X q_i$ for $i \in \{1,2\}$. Since $q_i = X^{\kappa-\deg p_i}p_i^*$, this happens if g_i^* divides p_i^* for $i \in \{1,2\}$. By assumption, $t \in T_{g_1,g_2,\mathrm{cs}}$, so g_i divides p_i for $i \in \{1,2\}$, and therefore g_i^* also divides p_i^* for $i \in \{1,2\}$. Moreover g_i is primitive if and only if g_i^* is primitive.

3.2 Constructing the Galois Polynomials

The principle to construct systems vulnerable to the attack described in Sect. 2.3 is now fairly simple. We start with an element in the (potential) kernel, that would imply the desired dimension by the above theorem. Then, we construct the two polynomials p_1 and p_2 and check if they are divisible by primitive polynomials of the desired degree. We explain this in more detail below, first for the parameters used in GEA-1 and then for the general case.

The Case of GEA-1. We give an example for the case of $\kappa = 64$, $\mathrm{cs} = 32$, $\xi = 24$, and primitive polynomials g_1, g_2 of degree $d_1 = 31, d_2 = 33$. Those parameters correspond exactly to the case of GEA-1. Other parameter choices are discussed below.

First of all we will construct an element $t = (t_0, \ldots, t_{63})^\top$ of the form such that applying Theorem 2 yields $t \in T_{g_1,g_2,\mathrm{cs}}$, where $T_{g_1,g_2,\mathrm{cs}}$ is of dimension 24.

For this, let us fix t such that $t_i = 0$ for $i \in \{9, 10, \ldots, 31\} \cup \{41, \ldots, 63\}$ and $t_0 = t_{40} = 1$. We consider the polynomials

$$p_1 := X^{64} + \sum_{i=1}^{8} t_i X^{64-i} + \sum_{i=32}^{39} t_i X^{64-i} + X^{24} \in \mathbb{F}_2[X]$$

$$p_2 := X^{32} + \sum_{i=1}^{8} t_i X^{32-i} + \sum_{i=32}^{39} t_i X^{64-i+32} + X^{56} \in \mathbb{F}_2[X]$$

to guarantee a kernel of dimension at least 24 if there exist proper g_1, g_2 of degree 31,33 such that $t \in T_{g_1,g_2,\mathsf{cs}}$. In the positive case the lower bound for the dimension (here 24) is a direct consequence of Theorem 2. We have 2^{16} possibilities to fix such an element t, i.e., to choose the above pair of polynomials p_1, p_2. We choose such an element t uniformly at random and check if p_1 is divisible by a primitive polynomial g_1 of degree 31 and if p_2 is divisible by a primitive polynomial g_2 of degree 33.

It is well known that the number of primitive elements of a finite field of q^n elements, where q is a prime number, is $\varphi(q^n - 1)$ (see e.g., [22, p. 56]). Here, φ denotes Euler's totient function. Hence the number of primitive polynomials in our case is $\varphi(2^{31} - 1)/31$ and $\varphi(2^{33} - 1)/33$, because the 31 (resp., 33) roots of a primitive polynomial of degree 31 (resp., 33) are all primitive. By construction $p_1 = X^{24} \cdot h_1$, where $h_1 \in \mathbb{F}_2[X]$ with $\deg(h_1(X)) = 40$, independently of the choice of the t_i. Analogously, $p_2 = X^{24} \cdot h_2$, where $h_2 \in \mathbb{F}_2[X]$ with $\deg(h_2(X)) \leq 40$. The overall number of polynomials of degree 40 having a primitive divisor of degree 31 is $2^9 \cdot \varphi(2^{31} - 1)/31$ and similarly $2^8 \cdot \varphi(2^{33} - 1)/33$ for polynomials of degree at most 40 with a primitive divisor of degree 33. Therefore, under an independence assumption, we expect the probability that both h_1 has a primitive divisor of degree 31 and h_2 has a primitive divisor of degree 33 to be

$$\frac{\varphi(2^{31} - 1)}{31 \cdot 2^{31}} \frac{\varphi(2^{33} - 1)}{33 \cdot 2^{33}} \approx \frac{1}{1250}.$$

As we have 2^{16} possibilities to vary p_1 and p_2, we expect to be successful to find the sought for polynomials g_1 and g_2 with $t \in T_{g_1,g_2,\mathsf{cs}}$.

Indeed, the primitive polynomials g_A and g_C used in GEA-1 are exactly of this form. More precisely, the element t satisfying $(t_0, \ldots, t_8) = (1, 0, 1, 1, 0, 0, 1, 1, 1)$, $(t_{32}, \ldots, t_{40}) = (0, 0, 1, 1, 1, 1, 0, 0, 1)$, $t_i = 0$ for $i \in \{9, 10, \ldots, 31\} \cup \{41, \ldots, 63\}$ is contained in $T_{A,C}$. The corresponding polynomial p_1 is divided by

$$g_A = X^{31} + X^{30} + X^{28} + X^{27} + X^{23} + X^{22} + X^{21} + X^{19} + X^{18} + X^{15}$$
$$+ X^{11} + X^{10} + X^8 + X^7 + X^6 + X^4 + X^3 + X^2 + 1 \in \mathbb{F}_2[X]$$

and the corresponding polynomial p_2 is divisible by

$$g_C = X^{33} + X^{30} + X^{27} + X^{23} + X^{21} + X^{20} + X^{19} + X^{18} + X^{17} + X^{15}$$
$$+ X^{14} + X^{11} + X^{10} + X^9 + X^4 + X^2 + 1 \in \mathbb{F}_2[X] \, .$$

As expected by Theorem 2, the 24-dimensional linear space $T_{A,C}$ is spanned by the shifted elements $t^s = (0, \ldots, 0, t_0, t_1, \ldots, t_{63-s})^\top \in \mathbb{F}_2^{64}$, $0 \leq s \leq 23$.

From the 2^{16} possibilities to choose t, except from the example given above, also 47 other choices yield primitive divisors of p_1 and p_2 with degree 31 and 33, respectively. Note that once we have been successful in finding the primitive polynomials g_1 and g_2, we could choose a primitive polynomial g_3 of degree 32 and check if $U_{g_3} \cap T_{g_1,g_2,\text{cs}} = \{0\}$ in order to construct a stream cipher similar to GEA-1. In Appendix A of the full version of this paper [6], we provide a sage [34] code that allows to construct such weak GEA-1-like instances based on this construction. By the algorithm above, it is possible to find a shift cs and corresponding polynomials such that the resulting system can be broken with the attack described in Sect. 2.3.

Moreover, we conducted slightly more general experiments. Our results (given by the case of $\ell_1 = 31$ in Table 3 in Appendix B of the full version) imply that it would have been possible to design the two LFSRs A and C of GEA-1 such that they yield a kernel intersection of dimension 26, reducing the security of GEA-1 from 40 to 38 bits. Interestingly, the designers decided not to do so, which suggests that they were aiming at 40 bits security exactly.

The General Case. We now focus on the case of an arbitrary (even) key length κ and aim to construct two LFSRs of size ℓ_1 and ℓ_2 such that the kernel has a dimension of (at least) ξ. In order to simplify the discussion and the notation, we focus on the case of $\text{cs} = \kappa/2$. The case of other shift values can be handled in a similar way as long as $\text{cs} \geq \xi$.

In order to construct the two LFSRs, i.e., the corresponding primitive polynomials of degree ℓ_1 and ℓ_2, we start again by an element in the kernel that, due to Theorem 2, guarantees a kernel intersection of dimension at least ξ. That is, we consider a vector $t \in \mathbb{F}_2^\kappa$ such that

$$t_i = 0 \text{ for } i \in \left\{ \frac{\kappa}{2} - \xi + 1, \ldots, \frac{\kappa}{2} - 1 \right\} \cup \{\kappa - \xi + 1, \ldots, \kappa - 1\}$$

and $t_0 = t_{\kappa - \xi} = 1$. To this choice of t, we get the corresponding polynomials

$$p_1 := X^\kappa + \sum_{i=1}^{\frac{\kappa}{2} - \xi} t_i X^{\kappa - i} + \sum_{i=\frac{\kappa}{2}}^{\kappa - \xi - 1} t_i X^{\kappa - i} + X^\xi \in \mathbb{F}_2[X] \tag{1}$$

$$p_2 := X^{\frac{\kappa}{2}} + \sum_{i=1}^{\frac{\kappa}{2} - \xi} t_i X^{\frac{\kappa}{2} - i} + \sum_{i=\frac{\kappa}{2}}^{\kappa - \xi - 1} t_i X^{\kappa - i + \frac{\kappa}{2}} + X^{\xi + \frac{\kappa}{2}} \in \mathbb{F}_2[X] . \tag{2}$$

The number of vectors t and thus the number of pairs of polynomials (p_1, p_2) we can construct this way is $N = 2^{\kappa - 2\xi}$. To successfully construct the LFSRs with a kernel intersection of dimension at least ξ, we require that p_1 is divisible by a primitive polynomial of degree ℓ_1 and p_2 is divisible by a primitive polynomial of degree ℓ_2. To analyze the successes probability, we use as before a heuristic approach. More precisely, we assume that (p_1, p_2) behaves as a uniformly and independently chosen pair of polynomials (of degree κ and less than or equal to κ respectively) with respect to their probability of being divisible by primitive polynomials of the desired degree.

The number of polynomials of degree n with a primitive divisor of degree ℓ is, analogously as above, given by

$$P_{n,\ell} := 2^{n-\ell} \frac{\varphi(2^\ell - 1)}{\ell} .$$

In addition, the probability that a uniform random polynomial of degree n is divisible by a primitive divisor of degree ℓ is

$$\Psi_\ell := \frac{P_{n,\ell}}{2^n} = \frac{\varphi(2^\ell - 1)}{\ell 2^\ell} .$$

Note that Ψ_ℓ is also the probability of a polynomial of degree *less than or equal to* n to be divisible by a primitive divisor of degree ℓ, as both nominator and denominator are multiplied by a factor of two in this case.

While computing lower bounds on Euler's totient function is non trivial, for our purpose it is sufficient, easier, and more precise to compute $\varphi(2^\ell - 1)$ for practical relevant values of ℓ. For $\ell \leq 512$ we computed explicitly that

$$\frac{2^\ell}{\varphi(2^\ell - 1)} \leq 3.4 , \tag{3}$$

using a computer program.

Following the above heuristic on the random behavior of p_1 and p_2 we get that the probability for a successful construction for one fixed t is given by

$$\Psi_{\ell_1} \Psi_{\ell_2} = \frac{\varphi(2^{\ell_1} - 1)}{\ell_1 \cdot 2^{\ell_1}} \frac{\varphi(2^{\ell_2} - 1)}{\ell_2 \cdot 2^{\ell_2}} .$$

From Eq. (3), the expected number of trials until suitable polynomials are found can be bounded by

$$(\Psi_{\ell_1} \Psi_{\ell_2})^{-1} \leq 12 \ell_1 \ell_2$$

for $\ell_i \leq 512, i \in \{1, 2\}$. This shows that the approach is easily feasible for all practical relevant choices of ℓ_1 and ℓ_2 and can be expected to find valid solutions as long as the number of candidates N is larger than the expected number of trials. Note that for concrete parameters with a large ξ, ℓ_1, ℓ_2, it is better to check if $(\Psi_{\ell_1} \Psi_{\ell_2})^{-1} \leq N$ as N becomes relatively small and $12 \ell_1 \ell_2$ significantly larger than $(\Psi_{\ell_1} \Psi_{\ell_2})^{-1}$.

Applicability to Longer Keys. We recall that in the attack on GEA-1, the keyspace $\mathbb{F}_2^{64}$ was decomposed into the direct sum $U_B \oplus T_{A,C} \oplus V$ such that $\beta = M_B(u + t + v) = M_B(t + v)$, $\alpha = M_A(u + t + v) = M_A(u + v)$, and $\gamma = M_C(u + t + v) = M_C(u + v)$, where $\dim(U_B \oplus V) = 40$ and $\dim(T_{A,C} \oplus V) = 32$. In general, if the key size is κ, a straightforward divide-and-conquer attack could be applied by either building a table of size at least $2^{\dim(T_{A,C} \oplus V)}$ bitstrings and conducting exhaustive search of complexity $2^{\dim(U_B \oplus V)}$ cipher evaluations or vice versa.

Let us now discuss whether it is possible to build weak GEA-1-like instances operating on a larger keyspace. For this, we restrict to the case of extending the lengths of the three involved LFSRs and do not consider extending the number of LFSRs. The reason is that the attack requires two steps; (1) building a table of size exponentially in the dimension of the kernel intersection, (2) an exhaustive search of complexity exponentially in the state size of the remaining register(s). Since our construction yielding a large kernel intersection only works for two LFSRs, adding more LFSRs would increase the complexity of the second step.

For $\kappa = 96$, it is possible to choose primitive polynomials g_A and g_C of degree 47 and 49, respectively, such that for the corresponding LFSRs A and C we have $\dim T_{A,C} = 44$ (where the shift for initializing LFSR C is $\mathsf{cs} = 48$). Those parameters directly correspond to the maximal dimension that can be expected by the formulas above and are also verified experimentally (see in Table 3 in Appendix B in the full version). To find this specific polynomials we have checked if it is possible to have $\dim T_{A,C} \geq 42$, i.e., $\xi = 42$ and $\ell_1 = 47, \ell_2 = 49$. As $(\Psi_{\ell_1} \Psi_{\ell_2})^{-1} \approx 2500$ and $N = 2^{12} = 4096$ our approach should be successful with high probability. Indeed our algorithm computed the above solution with the even larger $T_{A,C}$ of dimension 44. Note that these parameters are chosen at the edge with respect to our theory. We could then choose a primitive polynomial g_B of degree 48 such that $\dim U_B = 48$ and such that the keyspace can be decomposed into $\mathbb{F}_2^{96} = U_B \oplus T_{A,C} \oplus V$ with $\dim V = 4$. Thus, we can break such a scheme with time complexity 2^{52} cipher evaluations and memory complexity $2^{48} \cdot 141$ bits.[5] The size of such a table is 4512 TiB.

For larger key sizes, this approach quickly gets infeasible. For example, if we would aim for a key length of $\kappa = 112$ bit (i.e., the minimum security required by NIST), we would choose $g_A, g_B,$ and g_C of degrees 55, 56, and 57, respectively, such that $\dim T_{A,C} = 50$, $\dim U_B = 56$ and $\dim V = 6$. Other choices would only allow for other trade-offs between memory and computation, but not for reducing both. The divide-and-conquer (or meet-in-the-middle) attack against such a GEA-1 instance would require

$$2^{\dim U_B} \cdot (\kappa + 1 + \dim T_{A,C} + \dim V) = 2^{56} \cdot (113 + 56) = 2^{56} \cdot 169$$

bits of memory, which corresponds to 1,384,448 TiB. Hence this approach is tailored to key spaces of smaller sizes.

3.3   Properties of the GEA-1 Intentional Weakness

The weakness of GEA-1 can be understood as a *hidden*, or *obfuscated*, cryptanalytic attack. It does not fulfill the property of undetectability, or even undiscov-

---

[5] The length of each entry in the table must be large enough to avoid false key candidates. Similarly as described in [8, Section 3.1], we assume that each bitstring in the table is of size $\ell + \dim(T_{A,C})$, where ℓ is the minimum integer such that $(1 - 2^{-\ell})^{2^{\kappa}} \geq 0.5$.

erability, simply because everyone who has the specification of GEA-1 and some knowledge of cryptoanalysis is in principle capable of finding the weakness and is able to exploit the attack. Of course, the fact that the GEA-1 algorithm was not made public by the designers significantly hardened the discoverability of the weakness.

In the next part, we focus on the MALICIOUS framework, which is a method for inserting a practical and undetectable backdoor within a symmetric crypto-graphic algorithm, more precisely within a tweakable block cipher.

4   Revisiting the MALICIOUS Framework

In contrast to a hidden cryptographic weakness as in the case of GEA-1, the specification of the tweakable block cipher can be published entirely.

In the following, we discuss a simple instance of the MALICIOUS frame-work [30] that inserts a practical, undetectable backdoor into a tweakable block cipher. For this, let $H: \mathbb{F}_2^\star \to \mathbb{F}_2^m$ be a cryptographic hash function and let $E: \mathbb{F}_2^\kappa \times \mathbb{F}_2^\tau \times \mathbb{F}_2^n \to \mathbb{F}_2^n$ be a (secure) tweakable block cipher with tweak length τ, key length κ, and block length n. The malicious designer chooses a tweak $t^\star \in \mathbb{F}_2^\tau$ uniformly at random and computes $s := H(t^\star)$. The chosen tweak $t^\star$ will serve as the secret backdoor. The designer then defines the tweakable block cipher $\widetilde{E}: \mathbb{F}_2^\kappa \times \mathbb{F}_2^\tau \times \mathbb{F}_2^n \to \mathbb{F}_2^n$ as

$$\widetilde{E}(k,t,x) := \begin{cases} E(k,t,x) & \text{if } H(t) \neq s \\ x + k & \text{if } H(t) = s . \end{cases} \tag{4}$$

In other words, if the backdoor $t^\star$ is used as the tweak, the tweakable block cipher $\widetilde{E}$ simply applies the permutation $x \mapsto x + k$, which allows the malicious designer to recover the key k with one known plaintext/ciphertext pair. Due to this simple key-recovery attack, the backdoor fulfills the notion of *practicability*. If we assume that the hash function H is preimage resistant up to q queries, a user having oracle access to $\widetilde{E}$ cannot recover the backdoor $t^\star$ with less than q queries. Therefore, the backdoor fulfills the notion of *undiscoverability*. More generally, under the same assumption on H, a user cannot even prove the existence of a secret backdoor with less than q queries to $\widetilde{E}$. The reason is that the user cannot distinguish between whether the tweakable block cipher defined by Eq. (4) was designed by a *malicious* designer who knows $t^\star$ and generated $s = H(t^\star)$ accordingly or by an *honest* designer who simply chose a random $s \in \mathbb{F}_2^m$ to specify $\widetilde{E}$. Therefore, the backdoor fulfills the notion of *undetectability*.

We conclude that the backdoor in the simple construction defined in Eq. (4) fulfills the same security notions as the backdoor in the original MALICIOUS framework. However, similar to the original MALICIOUS framework, the back-door in $\widetilde{E}$ does not fulfill the notion of *untraceability*; once $\widetilde{E}$ is queried with the tweak $t^\star$, the full backdoor is revealed.

5   Malicious AES

We now describe how to construct a tweakable variant of the AES with a modified key-schedule to obtain a more natural backdoored cipher based on the MALICIOUS framework. Instead of constructing a probability-one differential over the cipher for a secret pair of tweak values (as in the original MALICIOUS framework), we embed an invariant subspace that holds for a secret tweak value. For the sake of completeness, we briefly recall the definition of the AES round function. For further details, we refer to the book by Daemen and Rijmen [14].

5.1   Description of the AES

The AES is a family of block ciphers with a block length of 128 bits, supporting three different key lengths of 128, 192, and 256 bits. In this section, we concentrate on the AES variant with a 128-bit key. For each fixed key, the AES operates as a permutation on $\mathbb{F}_2^{128}$. For a simpler description of the algorithm, we represent the AES as a family of permutations on $\mathbb{F}_{2^8}^{4\times 4}$. The internal state can then be described by a 4×4 array with elements in $\mathbb{F}_{2^8}$ (also called *cells*) as

$$
\begin{bmatrix}
a_{0,0} & a_{0,1} & a_{0,2} & a_{0,3} \\
a_{1,0} & a_{1,1} & a_{1,2} & a_{1,3} \\
a_{2,0} & a_{2,1} & a_{2,2} & a_{2,3} \\
a_{3,0} & a_{3,1} & a_{3,2} & a_{3,3}
\end{bmatrix}.
$$

The unkeyed round function R: $(\mathbb{F}_{2^8})^{4\times 4} \to (\mathbb{F}_{2^8})^{4\times 4}$ of AES is defined as the composition of the operations SubBytes, ShiftRows and MixColumns such that

$$R = \mathsf{MixColumns} \circ \mathsf{ShiftRows} \circ \mathsf{SubBytes}.$$

The functions on the right-hand side are defined as follows.

SubBytes is a parallel application of the 8-bit AES S-box $S\colon \mathbb{F}_{2^8} \to \mathbb{F}_{2^8}$ to all 16 cells of the internal state. We refer to [14] for the definition of S, since its details are not important for our construction.

ShiftRows cyclically rotates the ith row of the state i positions to the left, for all $i \in \{0, 1, 2, 3\}$.

MixColumns multiplies the columns of the state with a matrix M. Again, we refer to [14] for the definition of M.

The unkeyed AES rounds are interleaved by the addition of a round key. The latter operation will be denoted by $\mathsf{Add}_{k_i}: x \mapsto x + k_i$. The ith round function of the AES is then given by

$$R_i = \mathsf{Add}_{k_i} \circ R.$$

The round keys k_i are generated from the 128-bit master key k by the AES key schedule, i.e., we have $(k_0, k_1, \ldots, k_{10}) = \mathsf{KeySchedule}(k)$. We refer to [14] for the specification of the function KeySchedule. With the above notation, the AES variant with a 128-bit key can then be described as

$$\mathsf{AES}_k = \mathsf{Add}_{k_{10}} \circ \mathsf{ShiftRows} \circ \mathsf{SubBytes} \circ \mathsf{R}_9 \circ \cdots \circ \mathsf{R}_2 \circ \mathsf{R}_1 \circ \mathsf{Add}_{k_0},$$

where $(k_0, k_1, \ldots, k_{10}) = \mathsf{KeySchedule}(k)$.

5.2 Specification of MaliciousAES

In this section, we define a tweakable variant of the AES that incorporates a backdoor based on the MALICIOUS framework. The round function of MaliciousAES is identical to that of the AES, but its key schedule is different and it supports an arbitrary-length tweak. Note that, for other reasons, changing the AES key-scheduling has been discussed previously, e.g. in [21] and [15] to increase the resistance of AES against dedicated attacks.

Key and Tweak Schedule. Let $k \in \mathbb{F}_2^\kappa$ be a κ-bit master key. The partial (64-bit) round keys $k_0, \ldots, k_{10} \in \mathbb{F}_2^{64}$ are derived from the master key using a key scheduling function. The details of this function are left open. For reasons discussed in Sect. 5.3, it will be required that there is an efficient algorithm to uniquely determine 64 bits of k given the value of k_{10}. The actual round keys are then equal to $(k_0', \ldots, k_{10}') = \mathsf{MaliciousKeySchedule}(k)$, where the ith round key k_i' is defined by

$$k_i' = \begin{bmatrix} k_{i,0} & k_{i,4} & k_{i,0} & k_{i,4} \\ k_{i,1} & k_{i,5} & k_{i,1} & k_{i,5} \\ k_{i,2} & k_{i,6} & k_{i,2} & k_{i,6} \\ k_{i,3} & k_{i,7} & k_{i,3} & k_{i,7} \end{bmatrix}, \text{ for } i = 0, \ldots, 9 \text{ and } k_{10}' = \begin{bmatrix} k_{10,0} & k_{10,4} & 0 & 0 \\ k_{10,1} & k_{10,5} & 0 & 0 \\ k_{10,2} & k_{10,6} & 0 & 0 \\ k_{10,3} & k_{10,7} & 0 & 0 \end{bmatrix},$$

with $k_{i,0}, \ldots, k_{i,7}$ being the bytes of k_i. In order to support arbitrary-length tweaks, the ith partial round tweak $t_i \in \mathbb{F}_2^{64}$ will be derived from the master tweak t using an extendable output function H, i.e., $(t_0, \ldots, t_9) = \mathsf{H}(t)$. The full round tweaks are then equal to $(t_0', \ldots, t_9') = \mathsf{MaliciousTweakSchedule}(t)$ where t_i' is defined by

$$t_i' = \begin{bmatrix} c_{i,0} & c_{i,4} & t_{i,0} & t_{i,4} \\ c_{i,1} & c_{i,5} & t_{i,1} & t_{i,5} \\ c_{i,2} & c_{i,6} & t_{i,2} & t_{i,6} \\ c_{i,3} & c_{i,7} & t_{i,3} & t_{i,7} \end{bmatrix},$$

with $t_{i,0}, \ldots, t_{i,7}$ being the bytes of t_i and $c_{i,0}, \ldots, c_{i,7}$ being the bytes of c_i. The values $c_0, \ldots, c_9$ are round constants that appear to look random but, as explained below, are not necessarily so.

Overall Structure. The ith round function is defined by $\mathsf{R}_i' = \mathsf{Add}_{k_i' + t_i'} \circ \mathsf{R}$ and the tweakable block cipher MaliciousAES can then be described as

$$\mathsf{MaliciousAES}_{k,t} = \mathsf{Add}_{k_{10}'} \circ \mathsf{ShiftRows} \circ \mathsf{SubBytes} \circ \mathsf{R}_9' \circ \cdots \circ \mathsf{R}_1' \circ \mathsf{Add}_{k_0' + t_0'},$$

where we have $(k_0', \ldots, k_{10}') = \mathsf{MaliciousKeySchedule}(k)$ and we have $(t_0', \ldots, t_9') = \mathsf{MaliciousTweakSchedule}(t)$.

Backdoor Setup. Similar to the instances of the MALICIOUS framework presented in [30], we aim to introduce a tweak input such that the cipher can easily be broken for a special secret value of the tweak. To set up a backdoored instance of MaliciousAES, the attacker chooses a secret tweak t^* and computes the values $(t_0^*, \ldots, t_9^*) = H(t^*)$. The round constants $c_0, \ldots, c_9$ are then chosen as $c_i = t_i^*$ for $i = 0, \ldots, 9$. It will be shown in Sect. 5.3 that this choice results in the desired backdoor.

5.3   Description of the Backdoor

The backdoor in MaliciousAES is based on an invariant subspace for the round function R of the AES. For the secret backdoor tweak t^*, this subspace is preserved up to the penultimate round of the cipher. Below, the invariant subspace for R, its extension to MaliciousAES and the key-recovery procedure are discussed.

Invariant Subspace for R. Consider the linear subspace $\mathcal{I} \subseteq (\mathbb{F}_{2^8})^{4 \times 4}$ in which the first column of the 4×4 state matrix is equal to the third column and the second column is equal to the fourth column, i.e.,

$$\mathcal{I} := \left\{ \begin{bmatrix} a_{0,0} & a_{0,1} & a_{0,0} & a_{0,1} \\ a_{1,0} & a_{1,1} & a_{1,0} & a_{1,1} \\ a_{2,0} & a_{2,1} & a_{2,0} & a_{2,1} \\ a_{3,0} & a_{3,1} & a_{3,0} & a_{3,1} \end{bmatrix} \;\middle|\; \forall i \in \{0,1,2,3\}, j \in \{0,1\} : a_{i,j} \in \mathbb{F}_{2^8} \right\}. \tag{5}$$

It is well known (see, e.g., [23, Prop. 5]) that $\mathcal{I}$ is an invariant subspace for the unkeyed AES round function R, i.e., $R(\mathcal{I}) = \mathcal{I}$. Indeed, $\mathcal{I}$ is invariant for all of the three operations SubBytes, ShiftRows, and MixColumns independently. However, since $\mathcal{I}$ is in general not invariant over the addition with a round key, $\mathcal{I}$ cannot be used as an invariant subspace over multiple AES rounds interleaved with round key additions.

Invariant Subspace for MaliciousAES. When the cipher is evaluated with the malicious tweak value t^*, we have that each round tweak t_i' with $i = 0, \ldots, 9$ is contained in $\mathcal{I}$ by construction. Hence, $\mathcal{I}$ is an invariant subspace for $\mathrm{Add}_{k_0' + t_0'}$ and more generally over any tweaked and keyed round function R_i', $i = 1, \ldots, 9$. The structure of the invariant subspace is depicted in Fig. 4. Iterating this property yields

$$(\mathrm{Add}_{k_{10}'} \circ \mathrm{MaliciousAES}_{k,t^*})(\mathcal{I}) = \mathcal{I}.$$

Under the assumption that for a tweak $t \neq t^*$, each value t_i of $(t_0, \ldots, t_9) = H(t)$ for $i \in \{0, \ldots, 9\}$ is randomly drawn from a uniform distribution over $\mathbb{F}_2^{64}$, the probability that, for a fixed $j \in \{0, \ldots, 9\}$, the value t_j' is contained in $\mathcal{I}$ is equal to $(2^{-8})^8 = 2^{-64}$. Therefore, we expect that for a tweak $t \neq t^*$, the invariant subspace property is already broken after the first round of MaliciousAES. For this reason, if H is a cryptographically secure function, the backdoor fulfills the notions of *undiscoverability* and *undetectability*.

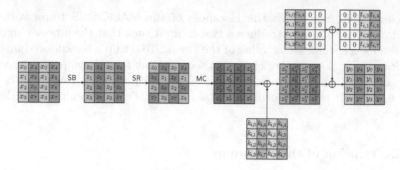

Fig. 4. An invariant subspace over one round of MaliciousAES under tweak $t^\star$. In the input state, if the first column is equal to the third column and the second column is equal to the fourth column, the same property holds for the output state after one round.

Key-Recovery Strategy. For $t^\star$, the last round key k'_{10} (which is constructed from $k_{10} \in \mathbb{F}_2^{64}$) can be recovered using a chosen plaintext attack with a single plaintext/ciphertext pair. For $x \in \mathcal{I}$ and $y = \mathsf{MaliciousAES}_{k,t^\star}(x)$, we have

$$\forall i \in \{0,1,2,3\}: \qquad k_{10,i} = y_{i,0} + y_{i,2}, \quad k_{10,4+i} = y_{i,1} + y_{i,3},$$

where $y_{i,j}$ is the byte in row i and column j of the ciphertext y. Hence, the 64-bit partial round key k_{10} can directly be recovered. From k_{10}, we can then recover k by guessing the remaining $\kappa - 64$ bits. Therefore, if κ is sufficiently small, MaliciousAES fulfills the notion of *practicability*.

Larger Keys. We only provided a very simple malicious variant of AES which uses 64-bit round keys derived from a master key of length κ bits. This approach is especially suitable when the master key is short, such as $\kappa = 64$. There are several straightforward methods to construct instances operating on larger keys. For instance, one can build a similar construction based on Rijndael-192 or Rijndael-256 [14]. For larger κ, one could also enforce other properties on the last (say the last two) round keys and use more elaborated key-guessing techniques to recover more than 64 bits of key information.

Security Arguments. We do not provide an explicit security analysis for MaliciousAES as (i) most of the security arguments for AES are equally valid for MaliciousAES and (ii) increasing the number of rounds of MaliciousAES does not invalidate the backdoor but should invalidate all potential non-backdoor based attacks.

6   A Dedicated Tweakable Block Cipher

In this section, we propose the backdoored dedicated tweakable block cipher Boomslang. Similar to MaliciousAES, the proposed cipher relies on the MALI-CIOUS framework to achieve undiscoverability. However, the backdoor is based on a nonlinear invariant rather than an invariant subspace. In fact, the back-door implies the existence of an iterative perfect linear approximation over four rounds of the cipher. Hence, it can also be compared to the recently proposed block cipher ЯооⅭ [31], which contains a backdoor based on linear cryptanalysis. However, the design rationale of ЯооⅭ is weaker and it does not offer undiscoverability, so it has only limited practicability.

6.1 Specification of Boomslang

The cipher operates on 128-bit blocks and the state will be represented by a 4×8 array of 4-bit cells. The key k is a 128-bit value, and the tweak t can be any bitstring of arbitrary (bounded) length.

Round Operations. The overall structure of the round function is shown in Fig. 5 and it closely follows that of the AES. Specifically, the unkeyed round function of Boomslang can be written as

$$R = \text{MixColumns} \circ \text{ShiftRows} \circ \text{SubBytes}.$$

Below, each of the functions on the right-hand side will be briefly discussed.

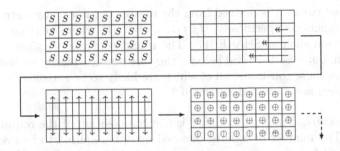

Fig. 5. Overview of the round function: SubBytes, ShiftRows, MixColumns and the addition of constants.

SubBytes consists of the parallel application of an S-box S to the 4-bit cells of the state. The S-box is the nonlinear function $S : \mathbb{F}_2^4 \to \mathbb{F}_2^4$ defined by Table 1.

ShiftRows is similar to the AES ShiftRows step. If the rows are numbered from zero to three with zero corresponding to the top row, then ShiftRows rotates the ith row of the state over $4 \cdot i$ bits to the left.

MixColumns consists of a columnwise multiplication with a lightweight matrix from the family of quasi-MDS matrices that was proposed for Qarma-64 [4]. Let us denote the cells within one column of the state by $(x_0, \ldots, x_3)$, where $x_i \in \mathbb{F}_2^4$. MixColumns maps each column $(x_0, \ldots, x_3)$ to a new column $(y_0, \ldots, y_3)$ defined by

$$y_i = x_{i+1} + (x_{i+2} \lll 1) + (x_{i+3} \lll 2),$$

for $i = 0, \ldots, 3$ and where the addition of the indices is regarded modulo 4. The inverse mapping is given by

$$x_i = y_{i+3} + (y_{i+1} \lll 2) + (y_{i+2} \lll 3),$$

for $i = 0, \ldots, 3$. In software, MixColumns can be implemented using bitslicing.

The $2i^{\text{th}}$ round function is then defined as

$$R_{2i} = \mathsf{Add}_{k_i} \circ \mathsf{Add}_{c_{2i}} \circ R,$$

Table 1. The 4-bit S-box S.

0 1 2 3 4 5 6 7 8 9 a b c d e f
8 2 4 a 5 f 7 6 0 c b 9 e d 1 3

where c_i are round constants and k_i round keys. The round keys k_i can be derived using an arbitrary key schedule. Since we do not aim for related-key security, we propose $k_i = k$ for simplicity. Similarly, the $(2i+1)^{\text{th}}$ round function is defined as

$$R_{2i+1} = \mathsf{Add}_{t_i} \circ \mathsf{Add}_{c_{2i+1}} \circ R.$$

The ith round tweak t_i is derived from the master tweak t using a strong tweak-scheduling function. Specifically, $(t_0, t_1, \ldots) = H(t)$ where H is an extendable output function such as SHAKE [17]. The round constants c_i should appear to look random, but – as discussed below – they are not necessarily so. Some specific conditions on these constants, all of which are likely to be satisfied for a uniform random choice, are discussed in Sect. 6.2.

Overall Structure. The overall cipher is the composition of the round functions $R_0, R_1, \ldots$ The number of rounds, denoted by r, is required to be even, so that the last round function always performs a round-tweak addition. Based on the analysis in Sect. 6.2, $r = 32$ is a reasonable choice. The key k is also added to the plaintext and $\sigma(k)$ is added to the state after the last round, with σ being a linear orthomorphism, i.e., we have that both $k \mapsto \sigma(k)$ and $k \mapsto \sigma(k) + k$ are permutations. Specifically, we use $\sigma(k) = (k \ggg 1) + (k \gg 63)$ as in PRINCE [13]. In summary, the overall cipher is defined by

$$\mathsf{Boomslang} = \mathsf{Add}_{\sigma(k)} \circ R_{r-1} \circ \cdots \circ R_1 \circ R_0 \circ \mathsf{Add}_k.$$

Backdoor Setup. To set up a backdoored instance of Boomslang, one must choose a secret tweak $t^\star$ and compute the corresponding round tweaks $(t_0^\star, t_1^\star, \ldots) = H(t^\star)$. The round constants c_{2i+1} should then be chosen as $c_{2i+1} = t_i^\star$ for $i = 0, \ldots, r/2 - 1$.

Given a few hundred known plaintext/ciphertext pairs encrypted under the tweak $t^\star$, it will then be possible to efficiently recover the full key. The mechanism for doing so will be explained in Sect. 6.3.

6.2   Design Rationale

In this section, we argue that the design of Boomslang follows standard modern design principles. Our security analysis focuses on differential and linear cryptanalysis, and invariants. The latter two are of particular relevance with respect to the backdoor that will be revealed in Sect. 6.3. In the following, we first motivate the overall structure of Boomslang and then discuss the choice of the individual components.

Overall Structure. The design follows the wide-trail strategy [14, Chapter 9] with some changes to obtain a more lightweight cipher. Whenever possible, the design was kept as simple as possible and close to that of the AES.

In general, the proposed cipher is geared towards hardware. This is the motivation for relying on 4-bit S-boxes rather than 8-bit S-boxes as in the AES. In software, the 4×8 state allows storing the rows as 32-bit words. The S-box and linear layer can then be implemented using bitslicing.

The key schedule is chosen as the identity function, although other key schedules could also be used. Since related-key security was not a design goal, we decided to choose the simplest option. In addition, having a linear key schedule sometimes enables more straightforward security arguments. For example, the arguments from [7] related to the choice of round constants to prevent invariants are only applicable to linear key schedules.

Finally, the choice of the tweak schedule can be motivated by the goal of supporting arbitrary-length tweaks. Since related tweak security is important, it seems necessary to use a cryptographically strong hash function or XOF to derive round tweaks from the master tweak.

Choice of the Components. We now argue that all of the basic components used in the cipher are individually acceptable choices from the current state of the art.

SubBytes. The S-box has a maximum absolute correlation of $1/2$ for nonzero masks and a maximum differential probability of $1/4$ for nonzero differences. The S-box is chosen such that it is not an involution.

ShiftRows. The cell permutation is chosen such that the cells of each column end up in different columns of the state. Shifting rows is a natural choice because it allows for an efficient software implementation, and it is the same as for the AES.

MixColumns. The MixColumns map is inspired by the linear layer of Qarma-64 [4]. Specifically, the transformation of each column is defined by a circulant matrix M of the form

$$M = \begin{bmatrix} 0 & X^a & X^b & X^c \\ X^c & 0 & X^a & X^b \\ X^b & X^c & 0 & X^a \\ X^a & X^b & X^c & 0 \end{bmatrix},$$

over the $\mathbb{F}_2$-vector space $\mathbb{F}_2[X]/(X^4+1)$. The input bitvector can be considered as an element of this space by the isomorphism $\delta_i \mapsto X^{i-1}$, where δ_i is the ith standard basis vector of $\mathbb{F}_2^4$.

The matrix M is invertible with circulant inverse of the same form if and only if $a \equiv c \pmod 4$ or $a \equiv c+2 \pmod 4$. All of these matrices have branch number four, which is the maximum possible for this type of matrix. Furthermore, we impose the following criteria:

- Unlike in Qarma-64, we require that M is not an involution. Equivalently, $2b \not\equiv 0 \pmod 4$. The motivation for this requirement is that involutions more easily lead to 2-round invariants, as demonstrated in the case of Midori-64 [10].
- M should not be orthogonal or nearly orthogonal, i.e. $M^{-1} \neq c\,M^\top$ for any $c \in \mathbb{F}_2[X]/(X^4+1)$. This requirement is motivated by the fact that any quadratic form of the type $\sum_{i=1}^m x_i^\top Q x_i$ is a nonlinear invariant for an $m \times m$ orthogonal matrix [36]. More generally, for a nearly orthogonal matrix, any such quadratic function which is also invariant under multiplication by c is a nonlinear invariant.

The second criterium leads to the requirement that $X^{a+b} \neq X^{b+c}$ or equivalently $a \not\equiv c \pmod 4$. From the viewpoint of software implementations, it makes sense to choose one of a, b or c equal to zero. Choosing $a = 0$ and $b = 1$ then gives $c = 2$.

Linear and Differential Cryptanalysis. The wide-trail strategy directly gives upper bounds on the absolute correlation of linear trails and on the probability of differential characteristics. In particular, since M has a branch number of four, the number of active S-boxes over four rounds is at least 16 [14, Theorem 9.4.1]. Hence, after 16 rounds the average probability of any differential characteristic is lower than 2^{-128} and the absolute correlation of any linear trail is at most 2^{-64}. The suggested choice of 32 rounds was obtained by taking twice as many rounds; taking into account potential improvements and key-recovery attacks.

In fact, it is to some extent possible to extend the above results to linear approximations and differentials. In particular, for independent uniform random constants, [26, Corollary 1 & 2] imply that the average probability of any 4-round differential and the average squared correlation of any 4-round linear approximation is at most $(2^{-2\times(4-1)})^4 = 2^{-24}$.

Invariants. Several lightweight ciphers have been found vulnerable to invariant subspace [24] and nonlinear invariant attacks [36]. Hence, it is natural to attempt to rule out the existence of invariants in Boomslang.

The argument from [7] can be used to rule out joint invariants over all the affine layers (i.e., linear layers together with the constant additions) for a large number of rounds using only the properties of the linear layer and the round constants. Specifically, the security argument depends on the dimension of of the smallest subspace invariant under the linear layer and containing the differences of the constants. For the linear layer L = MixColumns ∘ ShiftRows of Boomslang and constants $c_0, \ldots, c_{r-1}$, denote this space by $W_{\mathsf{L}}(c_0+c_1, c_0+c_2, \ldots, c_0+c_{r-1})$.

If $W_L(c_0 + c_1, c_0 + c_2, \ldots, c_0 + c_{r-1}) = \mathbb{F}_2^{128}$, then joint invariants over the affine layers can be ruled out with high probability. The linear map L has 16 invariant factors and its minimal polynomial is $(X + 1)^8$. Hence, by [7, Proposition 11],

$$\Pr_{c_0,\ldots,c_{23}} [\dim W_L(c_0 + c_1, c_0 + c_2, \ldots, c_0 + c_{23}) = 128] = \prod_{i=0}^{15} \left(1 - \frac{1}{2^{23-i}}\right) \geq 0.99,$$

for uniformly chosen random constants $c_0, \ldots, c_{23}$. Hence, 24 rounds are sufficient to rule out with high probability the existence of such invariants. Note that this argument does not yet rule out invariants over a small number of rounds and also does not cover generalized and closed-loop invariants [38].

Most invariants considered in previous attacks have independent cells ('rank-one', from the viewpoint of [10]), as this leads to an easier analysis of the SubBytes and ShiftRows steps. To investigate this in more detail, we used the tool from [11, §6.2] to obtain the rank-one invariants of the linear layer M. Although M has some rank-one invariants, they do not correspond to Boolean functions or sets, and there are no shared invariants between M and the S-box layer.

6.3   Description of the Backdoor

The backdoor is a two-round invariant, which is not invariant for one round. This is similar to one of the invariants of two-rounds of Midori-64 [10], but unlike in that case the property is not invariant under the linear layer. Indeed, as discussed above, that would not be possible due to the choice of the linear layer. Importantly, the invariant only exists for the secret weak tweak for which the round constants in even rounds cancel out.

Two-Round Nonlinear Invariant. Let $f : \mathbb{F}_2^4 \rightarrow \mathbb{F}_2$ and $g : \mathbb{F}_2^4 \rightarrow \mathbb{F}_2$ be the Boolean functions defined by

$$f(z_0, z_1, z_2, z_3) = (z_0 + z_2)(z_1 + z_3) + z_0 + z_2 + z_3 + 1$$
$$g(z_0, z_1, z_2, z_3) = (z_0 + z_2)(z_1 + z_3) + z_2.$$

The functions f and g can be used to form a perfect nonlinear approximation of M. This is due to the fact that the term $(z_0 + z_2)(z_1 + z_3)$ is invariant under rotations of $z_0, \ldots, z_3$. Hence, if $y = \mathsf{MixColumns}(x)$, then

$$\sum_{i=0}^{31} g(y_{4i}, y_{4i+1}, y_{4i+2}, y_{4i+3}) = \sum_{i=0}^{31} f(x_{4i}, x_{4i+1}, x_{4i+2}, x_{4i+3}).$$

Furthermore, it is easy to see that

$$\sum_{i=0}^{31} \mathsf{a}^\top (y_{4i}, y_{4i+1}, y_{4i+2}, y_{4i+3}) = \sum_{i=0}^{31} 5^\top (x_{4i}, x_{4i+1}, x_{4i+2}, x_{4i+3}).$$

The S-box S defined in Table 1 also satisfies

$$5^\top S(z_0, z_1, z_2, z_3) = g(z_0, z_1, z_2, z_3)$$
$$f(S(z_0, z_1, z_2, z_3)) = \mathsf{a}^\top(z_0, z_1, z_2, z_3).$$

Since linear functions are invariant under the addition of any constant, and because the constants are cancelled out by the tweak in even rounds, one obtains the following two-round invariant:

$$\sum_{i=0}^{31} g(y_{4i}, y_{4i+1}, y_{4i+2}, y_{4i+3}) = c + \sum_{i=0}^{31} g(x_{4i}, x_{4i+1}, x_{4i+2}, x_{4i+3}),$$

where $y = (\mathsf{R}_{2i+1} \circ \mathsf{R}_{2i})(x)$. The full nonlinear trail is illustrated in Fig. 6. Note that the last step only works for one in 2^{64} constants, but the constants are chosen such that there exists a tweak so that the constants are weak in all odd-numbered rounds.

Alternatively, the nonlinear invariant discussed above can be described from the point of view introduced in [10,11]. Let

$$w = (0, -1, 0, 0, 1, 0, 0, 0, 0, 0, 0, -1, 0, \quad 0, -1, 0)^\top/2$$
$$v = (0, \quad 0, 1, 0, 0, 0, 0, 1, 1, 0, 0, \quad 0, 0, -1, \quad 0, 0)^\top/2.$$

In the above, w and v are the Walsh-Hadamard transform of f and g respectively. It holds that $C^M w^{\otimes 4} = v^{\otimes 4}$, with C^M being the correlation matrix of the linear layer and $\otimes$ the tensor product. Furthermore, the S-box satisfies $C^S v = \delta_5$ and $C^S \delta_{\mathsf{a}} = w$. The vector v is invariant under one in four constants.

Key-Recovery Strategy. The addition of whitenening keys k and $\sigma(k)$ leads to an efficient key-recovery attack. Specifically, one can use the fact that there exist $\ell \in \mathbb{F}_2^{128}$ and $b \in \mathbb{F}_2$ such that for every plaintext/ciphertext pair (x, y) encrypted under the backdoored tweak,

$$\sum_{i=0}^{31} g(x_i + k_i) + \sum_{i=0}^{31} g(y_i + \sigma(k)_i) = \ell^\top k + b,$$

with $x_1, \ldots x_{32}, y_1, \ldots, y_{32}$ and $k_1, \ldots, k_{32}$ being the nibbles of x, y and k, respectively. Since σ is an orthomorphism, the 64 bits of k that are nonlinearly mixed with x are linearly independent from the bits of k that are nonlinearly mixed with y. Hence, given q messages, one can on average recover q bits of the key even when $q \geq 64$.

Solving the system of equations is easy because of the low number of quadratic terms. One can either use Gröbner basis methods, exploiting the low degree of regularity of the system, or one can directly rely on linearization. Since g contains only a single quadratic term, each equation contains at most 64 quadratic terms. Hence, given 192 known plaintext/ciphertext pairs, the full key can be recovered using less than $192^3 \leq 2^{23}$ bit operations.

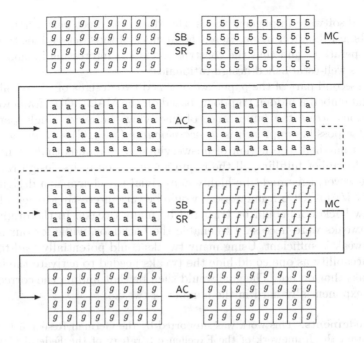

Fig. 6. Two-round invariant for Boomslang.

Construction of the Backdoor. The backdoor primarily relies on the choice of the S-box. The tool from [11, §6.2] was used to find symmetric nonlinear rank-one approximations of the linear layer M. This resulted in the choice of the vectors w and v listed above. One can then easily generate S-boxes such that the conditions $C^S v = \delta_5$ and $C^S v = \delta_{10}$ are satisfied. There are still significant degrees of freedom left in the choice of the S-box. These could be used to satisfy additional design criteria, or to argue that the S-box was generated based on certain magic constants.

7   Conclusion

Feeding a session key into LFSRs by making use of shifts is common in many designs, e.g., besides in GEA-1 and GEA-2 it is also used in A5/1. Our work demonstrates that those shifts, together with a clever choice of feedback polynomials and filtering, can be used to deliberately weaken the construction. We gave an explicit and efficient way to construct those choices for a large variety of parameters. Our construction includes the choices made for GEA-1 indicating that this (or a related) strategy was used in the actual design process. On the positive side, we again see that, in line with [8], this is unlikely to happen unintentionally. While our theory is described with a focus on LFSRs in Galois mode, it applies to LFSRs in Fibonacci mode as well. However, our construction yields random looking feedback polynomials and thus seemingly selected taps. While for Galois

LFSRs and software implementations, this does not affect performance, it does for LFSRs in Fibonacci mode. Here, the number of taps determines the number of XOR operations and thus the construction is less interesting in this case as it contradicts well-established design rationales.

In the second part of the paper, we outlined two designs of a tweakable block cipher that embed a hidden trapdoor, based on the MALICIOUS framework. Our constructions stress the importance of justifying the every single part of the design. One possible approach is *unswervingness* (see [16]) as a design requirement. In a nutshell, the notion of unswervingness demands that each instance of a (block) cipher fulfilling all the requirements given in its design rationale is secure. However, this might be highly non-trivial to achieve as a designer.

For the MALICIOUS framework, it would be very interesting to actually investigate how backdoors could be triggered by many tweaks. In the original work [30] two tweaks were necessary to enable the backdoor, while for our instances a single tweak is sufficient. Using many tweaks could potentially lead to achieving untraceability as one could hide the tweaks needed to activate the backdoor with tweaks that do not. The goal would then be that finding the correct subset becomes exponentially hard in the number of tweaks.

Acknowledgments. This work was supported by the German Research Foundation (DFG) within the framework of the Excellence Strategy of the Federal Government and the States – EXC 2092 CaSa – 39078197. Tim Beyne is supported by a PhD Fellowship from the Research Foundation – Flanders (FWO).

References

1. Albertini, A., Aumasson, J.-P., Eichlseder, M., Mendel, F., Schläffer, M.: Malicious hashing: Eve's variant of SHA-1. In: Joux, A., Youssef, A. (eds.) SAC 2014. LNCS, vol. 8781, pp. 1–19. Springer, Cham (2014). https://doi.org/10.1007/978-3-319-13051-4_1

2. Albrecht, M.R., Rechberger, C., Schneider, T., Tiessen, T., Zohner, M.: Ciphers for MPC and FHE. In: Oswald, E., Fischlin, M. (eds.) EUROCRYPT 2015. LNCS, vol. 9056, pp. 430–454. Springer, Heidelberg (2015). https://doi.org/10.1007/978-3-662-46800-5_17

3. Amzaleg, D., Dinur, I.: Refined cryptanalysis of the GPRS ciphers GEA-1 and GEA-2. In: Dunkelman, O., Dziembowski, S. (eds.) EUROCRYPT 2022. LNCS, vol. 13277, pp. 57–85. Springer, Cham (2022). https://doi.org/10.1007/978-3-031-07082-2_3

4. Avanzi, R.: The QARMA block cipher family. Almost MDS matrices over rings with zero divisors, nearly symmetric even-mansour constructions with non-involutory central rounds, and search heuristics for low-latency s-boxes. IACR Trans. Symmetric Cryptol. **2017**(1), 4–44 (2017)

5. Bannier, A., Filiol, E.: Partition-based trapdoor ciphers. IntechOpen (2017)

6. Beierle, C., Beyne, T., Felke, P., Leander, G.: Constructing and deconstructing intentional weaknesses in symmetric ciphers. Cryptology ePrint Archive, Report 2021/829 (2021). https://ia.cr/2021/829

7. Beierle, C., Canteaut, A., Leander, G., Rotella, Y.: Proving resistance against invariant attacks: how to choose the round constants. In: Katz, J., Shacham, H. (eds.) CRYPTO 2017. LNCS, vol. 10402, pp. 647–678. Springer, Cham (2017). https://doi.org/10.1007/978-3-319-63715-0_22

8. Beierle, C., et al.: Cryptanalysis of the GPRS encryption algorithms GEA-1 and GEA-2. In: Canteaut, A., Standaert, F.-X. (eds.) EUROCRYPT 2021. LNCS, vol. 12697, pp. 155–183. Springer, Cham (2021). https://doi.org/10.1007/978-3-030-77886-6_6

9. Bernstein, D.J., Lange, T., Niederhagen, R.: Dual EC: a standardized back door. In: Ryan, P.Y.A., Naccache, D., Quisquater, J.-J. (eds.) The New Codebreakers. LNCS, vol. 9100, pp. 256–281. Springer, Heidelberg (2016). https://doi.org/10.1007/978-3-662-49301-4_17

10. Beyne, T.: Block cipher invariants as eigenvectors of correlation matrices. In: Peyrin, T., Galbraith, S. (eds.) ASIACRYPT 2018. LNCS, vol. 11272, pp. 3–31. Springer, Cham (2018). https://doi.org/10.1007/978-3-030-03326-2_1

11. Beyne, T.: A geometric approach to linear cryptanalysis. In: Tibouchi, M., Wang, H. (eds.) ASIACRYPT 2021. LNCS, vol. 13090, pp. 36–66. Springer, Cham (2021). https://doi.org/10.1007/978-3-030-92062-3_2

12. Bonnetain, X., Perrin, L., Tian, S.: Anomalies and vector space search: tools for S-Box analysis. In: Galbraith, S.D., Moriai, S. (eds.) ASIACRYPT 2019. LNCS, vol. 11921, pp. 196–223. Springer, Cham (2019). https://doi.org/10.1007/978-3-030-34578-5_8

13. Borghoff, J., et al.: PRINCE – a low-latency block cipher for pervasive computing applications. In: Wang, X., Sako, K. (eds.) ASIACRYPT 2012. LNCS, vol. 7658, pp. 208–225. Springer, Heidelberg (2012). https://doi.org/10.1007/978-3-642-34961-4_14

14. Daemen, J., Rijmen, V.: The Design of Rijndael - The Advanced Encryption Standard (AES). Information Security and Cryptography, 2nd edn. Springer, Heidelberg (2020). https://doi.org/10.1007/978-3-662-04722-4

15. Derbez, P., Fouque, P., Jean, J., Lambin, B.: Variants of the AES key schedule for better truncated differential bounds. In: Cid, C., Jacobson, M., Jr. (eds.) SAC 2018. LNCS, vol. 11349, pp. 27–49. Springer, Cham (2018). https://doi.org/10.1007/978-3-030-10970-7_2

16. Dunkelman, O., Perrin, L.: Adapting rigidity to symmetric cryptography: towards "unswerving" designs. In: Mehrnezhad, M., van der Merwe, T., Hao, F. (eds.) Proceedings of the 5th ACM Workshop on Security Standardisation Research Workshop, pp. 69–80. ACM (2019)

17. Dworkin, M.: SHA-3 standard: permutation-based hash and extendable-output functions (2015)

18. Filiol, E.: BSEA-1 - a stream cipher backdooring technique. arXiv preprint arXiv:1903.11063 (2019)

19. Harpes, C., Massey, J.L.: Partitioning cryptanalysis. In: Biham, E. (ed.) FSE 1997. LNCS, vol. 1267, pp. 13–27. Springer, Heidelberg (1997). https://doi.org/10.1007/BFb0052331

20. Hoffman, K., Kunze, R.A.: Linear Algebra. PHI Learning (2004)

21. Khoo, K., Lee, E., Peyrin, T., Sim, S.M.: Human-readable proof of the related-key security of AES-128. IACR Trans. Symmetric Cryptol. **2017**(2), 59–83 (2017)

22. Koblitz, N.: Algebraic Aspects of Cryptography, Algorithms and Computation in Mathematics, vol. 3. Springer, New York (1998). https://doi.org/10.1007/978-3-662-03642-6

23. Van Le, T., Sparr, R., Wernsdorf, R., Desmedt, Y.: Complementation-like and cyclic properties of AES round functions. In: Dobbertin, H., Rijmen, V., Sowa, A. (eds.) AES 2004. LNCS, vol. 3373, pp. 128–141. Springer, Heidelberg (2005). https://doi.org/10.1007/11506447_11

24. Leander, G., Abdelraheem, M.A., AlKhzaimi, H., Zenner, E.: A cryptanalysis of PRINTCIPHER: the invariant subspace attack. In: Rogaway, P. (ed.) CRYPTO 2011. LNCS, vol. 6841, pp. 206–221. Springer, Heidelberg (2011). https://doi.org/10.1007/978-3-642-22792-9_12

25. Lidl, R., Niederreiter, H.: Finite Fields, 2nd edn. Encyclopedia of Mathematics and its Applications, Cambridge University Press (1996)

26. Park, S., Sung, S.H., Lee, S., Lim, J.: Improving the upper bound on the maximum differential and the maximum linear hull probability for SPN structures and AES. In: Johansson, T. (ed.) FSE 2003. LNCS, vol. 2887, pp. 247–260. Springer, Heidelberg (2003). https://doi.org/10.1007/978-3-540-39887-5_19

27. Paterson, K.G.: Imprimitive permutation groups and trapdoors in iterated block ciphers. In: Knudsen, L. (ed.) FSE 1999. LNCS, vol. 1636, pp. 201–214. Springer, Heidelberg (1999). https://doi.org/10.1007/3-540-48519-8_15

28. Perlroth, N., Larson, J., Shane, S.: N.S.A. able to foil basic safeguards of privacy on web. International New York Times (2013). https://www.nytimes.com/2013/09/06/us/nsa-foils-much-internet-encryption.html. Accessed 30 Sept 2021

29. Perrin, L.: Partitions in the s-box of Streebog and Kuznyechik. IACR Trans. Symmetric Cryptol. **2019**(1), 302–329 (2019)

30. Peyrin, T., Wang, H.: The MALICIOUS framework: embedding backdoors into tweakable block ciphers. In: Micciancio, D., Ristenpart, T. (eds.) CRYPTO 2020. LNCS, vol. 12172, pp. 249–278. Springer, Cham (2020). https://doi.org/10.1007/978-3-030-56877-1_9

31. Posteuca, R., Ashur, T.: How to backdoor a cipher. IACR Cryptol. ePrint Arch, p. 442 (2021)

32. Fips, P.U.B.: 46: Data Encryption Standard (DES). National Bureau of Standards, US Department of Commerce (1977)

33. Rijmen, V., Preneel, B.: A family of trapdoor ciphers. In: Biham, E. (ed.) FSE 1997. LNCS, vol. 1267, pp. 139–148. Springer, Heidelberg (1997). https://doi.org/10.1007/BFb0052342

34. Sage Developers: SageMath, the Sage Mathematics Software System (Version 9.3) (2021). https://www.sagemath.org

35. Schneier, B.: Applied Cryptography - Protocols, Algorithms, and Source Code in C, 2nd edn. Wiley (1996)

36. Todo, Y., Leander, G., Sasaki, Y.: Nonlinear invariant attack: practical attack on full SCREAM, iSCREAM, and Midori64. J. Cryptol. **32**(4), 1383–1422 (2019)

37. Wardlaw, W.P.: Matrix representation of finite fields. Math. Mag. **67**(4), 289–293 (1994)

38. Wei, Y., Ye, T., Wu, W., Pasalic, E.: Generalized nonlinear invariant attack and a new design criterion for round constants. IACR Trans. Symmetric Cryptol. **2018**(4), 62–79 (2018)

39. Wu, H., Bao, F., Deng, R.H., Ye, Q.-Z.: Cryptanalysis of Rijmen-Preneel trapdoor ciphers. In: Ohta, K., Pei, D. (eds.) ASIACRYPT 1998. LNCS, vol. 1514, pp. 126–132. Springer, Heidelberg (1998). https://doi.org/10.1007/3-540-49649-1_11

Simon's Algorithm and Symmetric Crypto: Generalizations and Automatized Applications

Federico Canale, Gregor Leander, and Lukas Stennes[✉]

Ruhr University Bochum, Bochum, Germany
{federico.canale,gregor.leander,lukas.stennes}@rub.de

Abstract. In this paper we deepen our understanding of how to apply Simon's algorithm to break symmetric cryptographic primitives.

On the one hand, we automate the search for new attacks. Using this approach we automatically find the first efficient key-recovery attacks against constructions like 5-round MISTY L-FK or 5-round Feistel-FK (with internal permutation) using Simon's algorithm.

On the other hand, we study generalizations of Simon's algorithm using non-standard Hadamard matrices, with the aim to expand the quantum symmetric cryptanalysis toolkit with properties other than the periods. Our main conclusion here is that none of these generalizations can accomplish that, and we conclude that exploiting non-standard Hadamard matrices with quantum computers to break symmetric primitives will require fundamentally new attacks.

Keywords: Symmetric Cryptanalysis · Simon's algorithm · Bernstein-Vazirani algorithm · Fourier transform · Walsh-Hadamard transform · automatic search · circuits normal form

1 Introduction

Unlike for many public-key schemes, for which the implications of the availability of quantum computers of suitable size were clear from the start, the situation is less well understood for symmetric primitives. The initial general consensus was essentially that only Grover's algorithm, which gives a quadratic speed-up for the problem of exhaustive search [12], is of interest to attack symmetric cryptosystems with quantum resources. This changed after Kuwakado and Morii published theoretical quantum attacks on two classically provable secure constructions, the 3-round Feistel [17] and Even-Mansour [18], using Simon's algorithm.

Simon's algorithm allows to efficiently compute the period of a Boolean function f, when f is accessible as a quantum oracle, and with the given premise that f is a 2 1 function having a unique period. The fact that f has to be accessible by a quantum oracle, often referred to as the Q_2 setting, makes those attacks less relevant in practice for now, but certainly an interesting research topic. Moreover, ideas like the ones presented in [2] show how this class of attacks can have implications in the Q_1 setting, where f can only be queried classically.

© International Association for Cryptologic Research 2022
Y. Dodis and T. Shrimpton (Eds.): CRYPTO 2022, LNCS 13509, pp. 779–808, 2022.
https://doi.org/10.1007/978-3-031-15982-4_26

Another closely related algorithm to efficiently compute periods uses the Bernstein-Vazirani routine [1], as was already observed in [27]. This routine, see Sect. 2.1 for details, is very similar to the one used in Simon's algorithm. It outputs a vector x that belongs to the support of the Walsh-Hadamard (or Fourier) transformation $\hat{f}$ of f, defined as

$$\hat{f}(x) := \sum_y (-1)^{f(y)+\langle x,y\rangle} = (H_0\phi)_x \tag{1}$$

where $(H_0\phi)_x$ is the x.th component of the multiplication vector between the standard Hadamard matrix H_0 and the vector

$$\phi = \left((-1)^{f(0)}, \ldots, (-1)^{f(2^n-1)}\right)^T.$$

Therefore, with enough outputs of this routine we can compute the orthogonal of the support of $\hat{f}$, which is the space of linear structures of f. Since the 0-linear structures of f are exactly the periods, the above algorithm essentially corresponds to Simon's algorithm, but highlights better its relation to the Walsh-Hadamard transformation of f.

The interest sparked by Kuwakado's and Morii's work resulted in the publication of attacks on many other constructions using quantum period finding [15,20,26], a better understanding of how the algorithm works with a relaxed premise on f [15], or without quantum oracle access to f [2,3], in the presence of noise [23], and when trying to minimize the amount of qubits required [22]. The most recent work in this context is by Bonnetain et al. who introduced Quantum Linearization attacks in [4].

The idea behind most of these attacks is to build a function f, based on the target cryptographic scheme E, that has a non-trivial period. So far, by more and more sophisticated and hand-optimized constructions, this class of attacks has made possible to come up with distinguishers on many constructions, like Feistel ciphers up to 6 rounds [8,14,17], MISTY [8,11] or forgery attacks on different kind of authenticated encryptions [13,15,25]. It should be noted that some of these attacks are highly non-trivial and can actually look fairly involved, see e.g. the attack for 6-round Feistel-FK [14]. Searching for new attacks and understanding the security of new constructions has become a cumbersome and error-prone task.

Moreover, those improvements and applications build on exploiting the periodicity of the involved construction only. However, other criteria are of interest as well. As an example, it would be of great value to be able to compute the algebraic degree and related properties of Boolean functions efficiently on a quantum computer. However, the search for efficient quantum algorithms exploiting criteria of Boolean functions other than linear structures has not yet been successful.

One large class of possible algorithms arise naturally from Simon's algorithm by replacing H_0 in Eq. (1) by any other Hadamard matrix H, which corresponds to changing the second Hadamard gate H_0 in the Bernstein-Vazirani routine with a gate that computes the unitary transformation H, as we will see in Sect. 4.

Those algorithms are therefore worth studying. In particular it is of interest to understand if they could lead to new items in the quantum toolbox of symmetric cryptanalysis.

Our Contribution

Our contribution is twofold. First, we simplify the search for new applications of Simon's algorithm and thereby overcome the increasing complexity of the attacks in the literature.

Second, we study the usefulness of the natural extensions of Simon's algorithm mentioned above in the context of symmetric cryptanalysis.

Automatizing. Towards achieving the first goal, introduced in Sect. 3, we propose to automate the search of such functions. More precisely, we present a generic algorithm that aims at finding, given a symmetric cryptographic scheme E, non-trivial periodic functions f, that can then be efficiently computed by a quantum computer.

Our approach here is to represent those functions f dependent on E by a class of circuits. Those circuits can make use of oracle gates for E and potentially further oracle gates for internal parts of the scheme E. We then automatically examine all circuits up to a certain number of gates and test each of them for periodicity, by instantiating the respective function on small dimensions. Of course, this means that many useless circuits, as well as many useless periods, are generated. The main technical contribution and work is aimed at addressing this problem, and keeping the process efficient by pruning the search tree. We discuss the details in Sect. 5.

As a proof of concept, we rediscover many of the attacks already known. Moreover, and more importantly, our algorithm automatically leads to new attacks. Indeed, it finds new periodic functions for 4-round Feistel-FK and 5-round Feistel-FK with internal permutation, as well as 4-round MISTY R-FK and 5-round MISTY L-FK. Those lead to the first known key-recovery attacks on these constructions in polynomial time. Further, we show that our approach is also applicable in the Grover-Meets-Simon case. We give new attacks for the permutation-based Encrypted Davies-Meyer and sum of key alternating ciphers constructions.

Generalizations. Regarding the generalization of Simon's algorithm we argue in Sect. 4 that none of those algorithms is likely to be helpful for speeding-up known attacks on quantum computers.

We do so by arguing that none of the new algorithms arising from this generalizaion of Simon's algorithm allow the computation of any property of Boolean functions that is invariant under linear equivalence. Since most of the properties used in cryptography, like the algebraic degree, the balancedness, the nonlinearity (order) or differential uniformity of f are indeed linear invariant, this brings us to conclude that any property related to this is unlikely to be of relevance for existing attack vectors.

While this result might not be surprising, it (i) sheds some light on the lack of alternative quantum algorithms and (ii) might be of independent interest. Indeed, it is technically based on a new characterization of the standard Hadamard matrix, proved using a general result on the structure of the automorphism group of the general linear group over $\mathbb{F}_2$ due to Dieudonné [9].

Outline

We explain preliminaries in Sect. 2, followed by the new attacks in Sect. 3. Section 4 presents our main result regarding the generalization of Simon's algorithm. Sections 5 and 6 respectively give more details about our automated search and the proof of our result on generalized Simon. We conclude our results in Sect. 7.

2   Preliminaries

Let $\mathbb{F}_2$ be the finite field with two elements and $\mathbb{F}_2^n$ a vector space of dimension n over $\mathbb{F}_2$. We will often identify the elements of $\mathbb{F}_2^n$ with the integers $\{0, \ldots, 2^n - 1\}$, without making it explicit unless required by the context. We denote by $\mathrm{GL}(n, \mathbb{F}_2)$ the general linear group of invertible matrices of order n over $\mathbb{F}_2$. We will ignore normalization factors for quantum states in order to simplify notation and concepts. We denote the rising factorial $x \cdot (x+1) \cdots (x+n-1)$ as $x^{\bar{n}}$.

2.1   Some Generalities on Boolean Functions

A Boolean function is any function $f : \mathbb{F}_2^n \to \mathbb{F}_2$. We denote the set of Boolean functions by $\mathcal{B}_n$. We may identify the set of Boolean functions over $\mathbb{F}_2^n$ with the set of polynomials $\mathbb{F}_2[X_1, \ldots, X_n]/(X_1^2, \ldots, X_n^2)$, in which case a Boolean function f can be written as

$$f(X) = \sum_{u \in \mathbb{F}_2^n} a_u X^u \tag{2}$$

for some $a_u \in \mathbb{F}_2$ and where we have denoted by X^u the monomial $X_1^{u_1} \cdots X_n^{u_n}$. Equation (2) is also known as the Algebraic Normal Form of f.

For a given Boolean function $f : \mathbb{F}_2^n \to \mathbb{F}_2$, the Walsh-Hadamard transform of f is defined as the function $\hat{f} : \mathbb{F}_2^n \to \mathbb{Z}$ such that

$$\hat{f}(\alpha) = \sum_{x \in \mathbb{F}_2^n} (-1)^{f(x) + \langle \alpha, x \rangle},$$

where we indicate with $\langle \cdot, \cdot \rangle$ the scalar product over $\mathbb{F}_2^n$ defined by $\langle x, y \rangle = x_1 y_1 + \ldots + x_n y_n$ for any $x = (x_1, \ldots, x_n)$ and $y = (y_1, \ldots, y_n)$.

Finally, let us denote the support of $\hat{f}$ by $\mathrm{supp}(\hat{f}) = \{\alpha \in \mathbb{F}_2^n : \hat{f}(\alpha) \neq 0\}$.

From the perspective of the Fourier transformation, Simon's algorithm can be interpreted as using the following relation between the Walsh-Hadamard transformation and the linear structures of a function f.

Theorem 1 (Proposition 29 in [6]). *Let $e \neq 0$ be an element of $\mathbb{F}_2^n$. We have that*

$$f(x) + f(x+e) = 0 \quad \forall x \in \mathbb{F}_2^n$$

(resp. $f(x) + f(x+e) = 1$) if and only if

$$\{0, e\} \subset supp(\widehat{f})^\perp$$

(resp. $supp(\widehat{f}) \cap \{0, e\}^\perp$ is the empty set).

We refer to [6] for more background on Boolean functions and in particular for a discussion of cryptographic criteria. We here limit ourselves to highlighting the fact that most of those criteria are invariant under linear equivalence. That is, given two Boolean functions $f, g \in \mathcal{B}_n$ such that for all $x \in \mathbb{F}_2^n$ it holds that $f(x) = g(L(x))$, where L is an isomorphism, then f and g behave identical with respect to the main criteria. Those criteria that are linear invariant include the algebraic degree, the non-linearity, the differential uniformity, and the balancedness of f and g.

2.2   Quantum Period Finding and the Hadamard Gate

We will briefly recall the Hadamard gate which will be in many ways the focus of the second part of the paper. To this end, we simply remind that the state of n qubits can be represented as a unitary vector in $\mathbb{C}^{2^n}$ and that a quantum transformation is represented as a unitary transformation. We indicate a basis for $\mathbb{C}^{2^n}$ as $|i\rangle$, where i is an integer between 0 and $2^n - 1$ written in its binary representation. No further knowledge about quantum computation is necessary for the purpose of this paper, and we refer to [24] for details.

The Hadamard gate on one qubit is such that

$$|0\rangle \mapsto (|0\rangle + |1\rangle)$$
$$|1\rangle \mapsto (|0\rangle - |1\rangle).$$

In other words, it is represented by the matrix

$$H_0 = \begin{bmatrix} 1 & 1 \\ 1 & -1 \end{bmatrix}.$$

Applied to an n-qubit vector, it is represented by the matrix $H_0^{\otimes n}$, given by

$$\left(H_0^{\otimes n} \right)_{x,y} = (-1)^{\langle x, y \rangle} \text{ for all } 0 \leq x, y \leq 2^n - 1,$$

which will act on the basis vector $|x\rangle$ as

$$|x\rangle \mapsto \sum_{y=0}^{2^n - 1} (-1)^{\langle x, y \rangle} |y\rangle.$$

For the rest of the paper, we will indicate the above transformation simply by H_0, regardless of the dimension n, unless there is possibility for ambiguity.

Let us now consider the quantum implementation of a Boolean function $f : \mathbb{F}_2^n \to \mathbb{F}_2$

$$U_f : |x\rangle |y\rangle \mapsto |x\rangle |y \oplus f(x)\rangle \text{ for any } x \in \mathbb{F}_2^n \text{ and } y \in \mathbb{F}_2.$$

The unitary transforms just presented are the building blocks for the quantum routine used in Bernstein-Vazirani algorithm (as well as Simon's), which allow to efficiently compute the support of the Walsh-Hadamard transformation, since the state before measurement is

$$\sum_{y=0}^{2^n-1} \left(\sum_{x=0}^{2^n-1} (-1)^{f(x)+\langle x,y\rangle} \right) |y\rangle |-\rangle = \sum_{y=0}^{2^n-1} \hat{f}(y) |y\rangle |-\rangle \tag{3}$$

where $|-\rangle = |0\rangle - |1\rangle$. Therefore, measuring the first n-qubit register will yield y with probability proportional to $\hat{f}(y)^2$. With a sufficient number of y, it is therefore possible to compute the space generated by the support of the Walsh-Hadamard transform of a random function f, which is exactly the orthogonal of the space of linear structures for f due to Theorem 1.

From this, it follows that this routine can be used to efficiently compute periods of a random Boolean function, as was already noted in [28]. More details about this will be given in Sect. 4.1. Note that this can be extended to find linear structures in the case where the codomain of f has dimension larger than 1 by considering each component separately, as it is discussed in [28]. A brief description of Simon's algorithm and a comparison with Bernstein-Vazirani can be found in the extended version of the paper [5].

In this work, we are mostly interested in finding new meaningful cryptographic periods (Sect. 3), and less interested in how they are computed. Therefore, we always assume that the functions we deal with are random enough to make the quantum period finding efficient. For a more thorough discussion about the precise conditions that a function has to satisfy in order for this to be possible, we refer to [2] and [28].

Furthermore, the way of efficiently computing the Walsh-Hadamard transform of f thanks to Eq. (3) leads to the question of whether it is possible to generalize the construction in order to efficiently compute other kinds of transform of f that could possibly capture different properties of f (Sect. 6.1). For this, we recall the definition of the class of Hadamard matrices.

Definition 1. *Let $H \in \mathbb{R}^{N \times N}$ be a matrix. We say that H is a Hadamard matrix of order N if*

$$(H)_{x,y} \in \{-1,1\} \text{ for all } 1 \le x, y \le N \text{ and } H^T H = N I_N,$$

where I_N is the identity matrix and $N \in \mathbb{N}$.

2.3   Description of Feistel and MISTY

In this work, we present new attacks on the Feistel and MISTY construction using quantum period finding. Therefore, we now briefly describe these families of ciphers.

Feistel. The Feistel cipher, also known as Luby-Rackoff cipher, is a simple way of turning random functions into a pseudorandom permutation. To do so, given r round functions $F_0, F_1, \ldots, F_{r-1} : \mathbb{F}_2^n \to \mathbb{F}_2^n$ and input $(L_0, R_0) \in \mathbb{F}_2^n \times \mathbb{F}_2^n$, one computes the output (L_r, R_r) by computing

$$L_{i+1} = R_i \qquad R_{i+1} = F_i(R_i) \oplus L_i$$

for $i = 0, 1, \ldots, r - 1$. If we replace the secret random permutations with one public permutation F and round keys k_i which we xor to the output of F, we obtain the so called Feistel-FK construction which we depict in Fig. 1.

MISTY. Matsui [21] proposed the MISTY structure as a way to design block ciphers with provable security against differential and linear cryptanalysis. In some ways, MISTY is similar to Feistel. That is, there is a left and a right part that are altered and swap in every round. But in contrast to Feistel, MISTY decryption requires the inverse of the round function. Furthermore, there is a left and a right version of MISTY, which we denote by MISTY L and MISTY R resp.. Let (L_i, R_i) be the input to the i-th round of MISTY L-F with round function F_i. Then the output (L_{i+1}, R_{i+1}) is defined by

$$L_{i+1} = R_i \qquad R_{i+1} = F_i(L_i) \oplus R_i.$$

For MISTY R-F we have

$$L_{i+1} = R_i \oplus F_i(L_i) \qquad R_{i+1} = F_i(L_i).$$

Analogous to Feistel, in practice we might replace the secret round functions F_i by one public permutation F in combination with round keys k_i. We can inject k_i either before we apply F or afterwards. We call the former KF and the latter FK. In this work, we study 5-round MISTY L-FK and 4-round MISTY R-FK. For both, one round is depicted in Fig. 1.

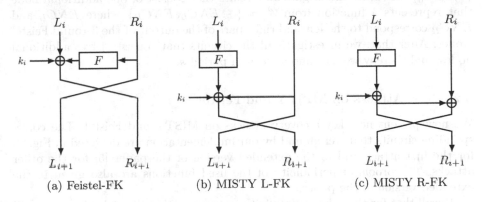

(a) Feistel-FK   (b) MISTY L-FK   (c) MISTY R-FK

Fig. 1. Feistel and MISTY constructions.

3   Finding New Applications

In this section, we first briefly describe how new applications of Simon's algorithm can be found automatically. After that, we present new attacks against MISTY and Feistel. We found these with a straightforward sage implementation of our algorithm.[1] A more detailed analysis, especially regarding the efficiency of our approach, is presented in Sect. 5.

3.1   The Idea: Finding Circuits

One goal of this work is to automate the step of searching a suitable periodic function f for some cryptographic construction E so that f leads to an attack on E based on Simon's algorithm. In a nutshell, the idea for this is to simply test all sensible functions that depend on E, which we denote informally by $\mathscr{F}^E$, for periodicity. Although this idea is simple, it raises two questions. First, what functions $\mathscr{F}^E$ do we need to test and second, how can we efficiently check whether f is periodic or not? The latter is easy to answer. We just instantiate E with a small input size s.t. we can evaluate f on all possible inputs. The former is more profound. Our approach is to represent $\mathscr{F}^E$ by a class of circuits. That is, we fix the inputs of f and the operations f consists of. We call these gate functions. Most importantly, the set of gate functions contains oracle gates for E. Then we can automatically examine all functions that consists of one gate, all functions that consists of two gates and so on. E.g., consider the quantum attack on 3-round Feistel from [17] which is based on the function

$$f(x,b) = ENC_L(x,\alpha_b) \oplus \alpha_{\bar{b}} = F_1(x \oplus F_0(\alpha_b)) \oplus \alpha_b \oplus \alpha_{\bar{b}}$$

with period $s = (F_0(\alpha_0) \oplus F_0(\alpha_1))||1$. Here, $\alpha_0, \alpha_1 \in \mathbb{F}_2^n$ are arbitrary distinct constants. Now consider Fig. 2a which shows a circuit C_f that represents f. To find this, we start with a circuit that only contains the input nodes $X = \{x, \alpha_b, \alpha_{\bar{b}}\}$. Then, we investigate all circuits that consist of one additional node that represents a function from $\mathscr{G} = \{\oplus, ENC_L, ENC_R\}$ where ENC_L and ENC_R correspond to the left and right part of the output of the 3-round Feistel cipher. After that, we investigate all the circuits that consist of two additional nodes, and thereby we encounter C_f with period s.

3.2   New Attacks on MISTY and Feistel

We now present new key-recovery attacks on MISTY and Feistel. The corresponding circuits that were found by our implementation are depicted in Fig. 2b for the first attack and in the extended version of the paper [5] for the other attacks. The proofs of periodicity of the used functions are also given in the extended version of the paper.

Recall that for the sake of simplicity, we assume that Simon's algorithm will always yield the correct period. For rigorous proofs of correctness the strategy in

---

[1] See https://www.doi.org/10.5281/zenodo.6623768.

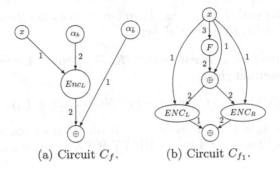

(a) Circuit C_f.   (b) Circuit C_{f_1}.

Fig. 2. Circuits for attack against 3-round Feistel cipher from [17] and against 4-round MISTY R-FK from Sect. 3.2.

[15] can be adopted to argue that either Simon's promise is sufficiently fulfilled, or differential-based attacks exist.

Because here the focus is to automatically find periodic functions, we leave this and other details such as how one can implement the functions on a quantum computer for future work.

Key-Recovery Attack on 4-Round MISTY R-FK. For 4-round MISTY R-FK, Cui et al. [8] mention a distinguishing attack but they do not give it explicitly. Our automated search yields

$$f_1(x) = ENC_L(x, x \oplus F(x)) \oplus ENC_R(x, x \oplus F(x)) \tag{4}$$

with period $s_1 = k_0$. This immediately leads to a full key-recovery attack. After we have recovered k_0 using Simon's algorithm, we can simply uncompute the first round before we make a query and extend the output of the oracle by an additional round, i.e., we use

$$L_0' = F^{-1}(R_0 \oplus k_0)$$
$$R_0' = L_0 \oplus R_0$$
$$ENC_R'(L_0, R_0) = F(ENC_L(L_0', R_0')) \oplus k_4$$
$$ENC_L'(L_0, R_0) = ENC_R(L_0', R_0') \oplus ENC_R'(L_0, R_0)$$

instead of ENC_L and ENC_R to recover k_1. Here, k_4 is of course not a secret key, but a random value chosen by us to simulate an additional round. We repeat this procedure to recover k_2 and k_3. Notice that there may be more efficient ways to recover the other round keys once k_0 is uncovered. But for sake of simplicity, we will stick to this generic argument.

Key-Recovery Attack on 5-Round MISTY L-FK. Cui et al. [8] also give a distinguisher for 5-round MISTY L-FK. Again, we improve on this and give a key-recovery attack based on the function

$$f_2(x) = ENC_L(F^{-1}(F^{-1}(x) \oplus x), F^{-1}(x)) \oplus F(x). \tag{5}$$

The corresponding period is $s_2 = k_0$. Therefore, we can use the same idea as for 4-round MISTY R-FK to recover all keys.

Key-Recovery Attack on 4-Round Feistel-FK. For 4-round Feistel-FK, our automated search algorithm yields

$$f_3(x) = ENC_R(x, \alpha) \oplus F(ENC_L(x, \alpha)) \oplus F(x) \tag{6}$$

with period $s_3 = k_0 \oplus F(\alpha)$. Here, $\alpha \in \mathbb{F}_2^n$ is an arbitrary constant. Again, we can use the same idea as for 4-round MISTY R-FK to recover all keys.

Key Recovery Attack on 5-Round Feistel-FK. This time, we use a slightly different idea for the search. That is, once we have discovered a periodic function whose period bears some information on the keys, we use this period as a constant in our next search. Thereby, we find the following functions.

$$f_4(x) = ENC_R(F(x), x) \oplus F(ENC_L(F(x), x)) \oplus F(x) \tag{7}$$
$$f_5(x) = ENC_L(F(F^{-1}(x) \oplus s_4), F^{-1}(x) \oplus s_4) \oplus F(x) \oplus F^{-1}(x) \tag{8}$$

The corresponding periods are $s_4 = F(k_0) \oplus k_1$ and $s_5 = k_0 \oplus k_2$. Notice that f_5 uses the inverse of the internal function F, and thus we have to assume that F is bijective. It is well-known that this is not necessary for Feistel networks, but we nonetheless believe that our attack is of interest.

The first step of our attack, once again, is to use Simon's algorithm to find s_4 and s_5. After that, we use a classical query to obtain an auxiliary value

$$h = ENC_R(F(s_4), s_4) \oplus F(ENC_L(F(s_4), s_4)) \oplus F(0) = k_0 \oplus k_2 \oplus k_4.$$

Now we can restore $k_4 = h \oplus s_5$. Thereby, we have learned the last round key and can continue similarly to the attacks where we learned the first round key, i.e., we add a round before we make a query and uncompute the last round afterward to find k_3. We repeat this procedure to learn k_2, k_1 and k_0.

3.3   Grover-Meets-Simon: New Attacks on pEDM and SoKAC

Our approach cannot only be used to find quantum attacks based on Simon's algorithm but leads also to attacks based on the Grover-Meets-Simon algorithm [20]. In those attacks, the attacker first makes a guess u for part of the key, say k_1, (the Grover part). Only for the correct guess, i.e., if $u = k_1$, the attacker gets a periodic function, which is then the detected with Simon's algorithm.

To find such, we add a second input node u and then check periodicity for all values of u separately.

Key Recovery Attack on pEDM. In [10], the authors introduced the permutation-based Encrypted Davies-Meyer construction. For a random permutation P and secret keys k_0 and k_1, we have

$$pEDM(x) = P(P(x \oplus k_0) \oplus (x \oplus k_0) \oplus k_1) \oplus k_0.$$

Now, it is easy to verify that

$$f(u, x) = pEDM(x) \oplus P(P(x) \oplus x \oplus u)$$

has period k_0 for $u = k_1$ and thus both keys can be recovered using the Grover-Meets-Simon attack.

Key Recovery Attack on SoKAC. Similar to the attack on pEDM, for the sum of key alternating ciphers [7] with two permutations P_1, P_2 and two keys k_0, k_1, we have

$$SoKAC(x) = P_2(P_1(x \oplus k_0) \oplus k_1) \oplus k_0 \oplus P_1(x \oplus k_0)$$

and

$$f(u, x) = SoKAC(x) \oplus P_2(P_1(x) \oplus u) \oplus P_1(x)$$

has period k_0 for $u = k_1$ and thus both keys can be recovered using the Grover-Meets-Simon attack.

3.4 Applications to Classical Cryptanalysis

Obviously, periodic functions as presented in Sect. 3.2 do not only lead to quantum attacks based on Simon's algorithm, but also to classical birthday-bound attacks. Similarly, attacks based on Grover-Meets-Simon can be converted to classical attacks too. Even more practical classical attacks, polynomial-time attacks, are special cases where one has to find a constant function, i.e. a function where all elements are periods. However, during our work we have not encountered any such function, which is not surprising at least for the constructions with classical security proofs. Nevertheless, we believe that our tool is a valuable addition to the toolbox of symmetric cryptanalysis. It can be applied to many more constructions in the future. In particularly, it might be of use already in the actual design process of a new construction as a tool to quickly rule out insecure approaches.

4   Generalizing Simon's Algorithm

There are many properties of Boolean functions that have been found to be meaningful from a cryptographic point of view, but most of them have not yet been found to be significantly more easy to compute with quantum resources.

   In this section we discuss how we attempted to address this problem by investigating whether it is possible to generalize Simon's algorithm, or rather the Bernstein-Vazirani algorithm, in order to be able to compute other potentially interesting properties of Boolean functions, focusing on linear invariant properties: we conclude that the generalization we propose does not allow to do that, by proving that the corresponding generalization of the Walsh-Hadamard transform is not linear invariant. A more formal discussion of the precise statements and proofs will be given in Sect. 6. Note that we focus on the case of Walsh-Hadamard or Fourier-transformations over $\mathbb{F}_2$ only.

4.1   The Idea: Using Non-standard Hadamard Matrices

In order to understand our idea for generalizing Simon's algorithm, we consider the following small variation of the quantum routine used in Simon's algorithm, due to Bernstein-Vazirani [1], where H_0 corresponds to the standard Hadamard transform $(H_0)_{x,y} = (-1)^{\langle x,y \rangle}$.

$$|0^n\rangle \quad \boxed{H_0} \quad \boxed{U_f} \quad \boxed{H_0} \quad \measuredangle$$
$$|-\rangle$$

This circuit outputs a vector x that belongs to the support of the Walsh-Hadamard (or Fourier) transformation $\hat{f}$ of f. This is due to the fact that the state of the n-qubit register before the final application of H_0, ignoring the constant that makes the state unitary, is represented by

$$\phi := \left((-1)^{f(0)}, \ldots, (-1)^{f(2^n-1)} \right)^T,$$

and applying H_0 to ϕ yields a vector whose components are

$$(H_0\phi)_x = \sum_y (-1)^{f(y)+\langle x,y \rangle} = \hat{f}(x). \tag{9}$$

Therefore, since a measurement of such a state results in a x such that $\hat{f}(x) \neq 0$, with enough measurements of the above circuit, we can compute the space generated by the support of $\hat{f}$ and recover the space of the linear structures of f thanks to Theorem 1. More precisely, the measurement yields x with probability $\frac{\hat{f}(x)^2}{2^{2n}}$. However, for the purpose of this work, we are simply interested in the fact that the measurement of the state at the end of the circuit is a vector x such that $\hat{f}(x) \neq 0$. For a more thorough analysis of the algorithm we refer to [27].

The idea behind our generalization is to consider Hadamard matrices other than the standard one. More precisely, in this paper we will study the class of transforms given by

$$\widehat{f}^H(x) := \sum_y (-1)^{f(y)+g(x,y)} = (H\phi)_x$$

with H being a Hadamard matrix $(H)_{x,y} = (-1)^{g(x,y)}$. This corresponds to studying the following generalization of the previous circuit, which we call $\mathtt{Simon}(H)$.

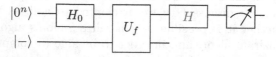

This circuit outputs x such that $\widehat{f}^H(x) \neq 0$ and could be used to compute efficiently (under the hypothesis that H can also be efficiently implemented) information about $\widehat{f}^H(x)$. In particular, echoing Simon's algorithm, the space generated by its support could be computed and could potentially correspond to a (cryptographically) relevant property of f (as is the case for $H = H_0$).

4.2 Results

There are several interesting discussions raising from this perspective. First, as the number of Hadamard matrices to consider for $\widehat{f}^H(x)$ (or equivalently $\mathtt{Simon}(H)$) is huge even for small dimensions, reducing their amount using a suitable notion of equivalence is of interest. Second, and most importantly, the question is if computing those transforms can be used to compute anything of (cryptographic) relevance.

In this paper we discuss those points. We show in Sect. 6.1 that the usual notion of equivalence for Hadamard matrices[2] nicely translates into equivalent quantum algorithms. More precisely, given two equivalent Hadamard matrices H and H', the $\mathtt{Simon}(H')$ circuit can be turned into the $\mathtt{Simon}(H)$ circuit by classical pre- and post-processing (Proposition 1).

Regarding the question of whether anything relevant can be computed with Hadamard matrices that are not equivalent to the standard Hadamard (and therefore not to the standard Fourier-transform), we argue that this is not the case for any property that is invariant under linear equivalence. This brings us to conclude that any property related to this is unlikely to be of relevance for existing attack vectors (since most of the properties used in cryptography, like the algebraic degree, the balancedness, the nonlinearity (order) of f are indeed linear invariant).

Indeed, we observe that the fact that $\mathtt{Simon}(H_0)$ allows to compute such a criterion, i.e. the existence of linear structures, can be seen as a consequence of the fact that, for any isomorphism A

$$\widehat{f \circ A} = \widehat{f} \circ B,$$

where $B^{-1} = A^T$.

Our main result, stated in the next theorem and proved in Sect. 6.2, is that this property already classifies the standard Hadamard transformation.

Theorem 2. *If for any $A \in \mathrm{GL}(n, \mathbb{F}_2)$ there exists $B \in \mathrm{GL}(n, \mathbb{F}_2)$ such that for all Boolean functions f we have*

$$\widehat{f \circ A}^H = \widehat{f}^H \circ B$$

then H is equivalent to H_0.

This result implies that, if H is not equivalent to H_0, then the transform $\widehat{f}^H$ cannot capture any linear invariant property of f, because the transform itself does not vary linearly.

Note that there is a technical caveat: indeed, we cannot strictly exclude that the circuit $\mathtt{Simon}(H)$ could be used to compute properties that are linear invariant even if H is not equivalent to H_0. For example, for the space V_f *generated by*

---

[2] A list of possible representatives of Hadamard matrices up to dimension 28 is known and can be found here: http://neilsloane.com/hadamard/.

$\mathrm{supp}(\widehat{f^H})$ Theorem 2 does not directly imply that V_f is also not linear invariant. However, such a behaviour would be very surprising.

Therefore we conclude that, unless H is equivalent to H_0, it is unlikely that the algorithm given by $\mathtt{Simon}(H)$ could compute any property of f that is linear invariant.

5   Constructing Circuits: Efficiency Considerations

We already described the basic idea of finding periodic functions in Sect. 3.1. In this section, we explain our approach in more detail. We define a notion of circuits, establish a normal form for these, and work out how many circuits there are. Furthermore, we describe how we exclude useless and enumerate good circuits, and also how we filter out trivial periods. After that, we use our algorithm to rediscover known results automatically. Thereby, we do not only demonstrate that our approach is indeed sensible, but we also gather valuable experience that we reuse when we look for novel attacks.

5.1   Circuits

Different variants of circuits are used in a variety of contexts. Our idea of a circuit is mostly inspired by Boolean circuits used in computational complexity theory and related fields. Since we are mainly interested in a practical way of automatically generating circuits, we choose to define circuits from the ground up. Thereby, we can make sure that our formalism and our implementation are well-matched.

Definition 2 (Syntax of Circuits).   *A circuit* $C = (D, X, \mathscr{G}, v_{out}, n)$ *is defined by*

- *a directed acyclic graph* $D = (V, E)$ *with labeled nodes and edges,*
- *a set of input nodes* $X \subset V$,
- *a set of gate functions* $\mathscr{G} = \{G_0, G_1, \dots, G_{g-1}\}$ *where* $G_i : \mathbb{F}_2^n \times \mathbb{F}_2^n \to \mathbb{F}_2^n$,
- *an output node* $v_{out} \in V$.

We assume $V = \{0, 1, \dots, p-1\}$ *and* $X = \{0, 1, \dots, q-1\}$ *for some* $p, q \in \mathbb{N}$. *Nodes* $v \in V \setminus X$ *are labeled with gate functions. We denote the gate function associated with* v *by* v_G. *For all* $v \in V \setminus X$ *there is a left and a right predecessor of* v *which we denote by* v_L *and* v_R *resp.. It must hold that* $v_L < v$ *and* $v_R < v$. *The edge* (v_L, v) *is labeled with* 1 *and* (v_R, v) *is labeled with* 2. *If* $v_L = v_R$, *then* (v_L, v) *is labeled with* 3. *There are no other edges. We denote* $|V \setminus X|$ *as the size of* C.

Throughout this work, we will omit parts of this formal definition if they are clear from the context. We want to stress that gate functions only take two inputs and have one output.

Definition 3 (Semantics of Circuits). *For a circuit $C = (D, X, \mathscr{G}, v_{out}, n)$ and an input assignment $A : X \to \mathbb{F}_2^n$, the output of a node v is defined as*

$$out(v) = \begin{cases} A(v) & \text{if } v \in X \\ v_G(out(v_L), out(v_R)) & \text{if } v \in V \setminus X. \end{cases}$$

The output of C is set to $out(v_{out})$. We denote the function described by C as C_f.

Of course, in our algorithm, we want to avoid checking the same function multiple times. Therefore, we want to establish a normal form for circuits next. To do so, we first define an equivalence relation in a straightforward way. Then we illustrate a non-normal circuit in Example 1 and formalize the concept of equivalent nodes, loose ends and ordered circuits. Finally, we define the circuit normal form in Definition 9.

Definition 4 (Equivalence of Circuits). *Two circuits C and C' are said to be equivalent if they correspond to the same function, i.e., if $C_f = C'_f$. We denote this as $C \sim C'$.*

Example 1. The circuit in Fig. 3a meets Definition 2 and by Definition 3 computes the function $f(x, y, z) = G_2(G_0(x, y), G_1(G_0(x, y), z))$. However, notice that there are two nodes (marked in blue) that compute the same intermediate value and another node (marked in green) that is never used. Hence, this is not a natural way of representing f. In contrast, the circuit in Fig. 3b, which also computes f, has no useless nodes and therefore, is a more sensible way to represent f.

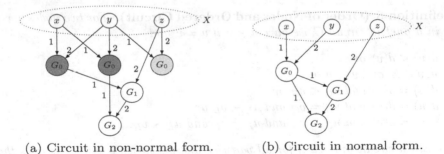

(a) Circuit in non-normal form.   (b) Circuit in normal form.

Fig. 3. A circuit in (non-)normal form.

Definition 5 (Equivalence of Nodes). *All nodes in a circuit C are equivalent to itself. For all $x \in X$ there is no other node than x that is equivalent to x. We define the equivalence of two nodes $u, v \in V \setminus X$, which we denote by $u \sim v$,* *inductively by stating that u and v are equivalent if both are assigned with the same gate function and $u_L \sim v_L$ and $u_R \sim v_R$. We call a circuit onefold if there are no two distinct nodes that are equivalent.*

Definition 6 (Loose End). *A node $v \in V \setminus X$ in a circuit C is called a loose end if $v \neq v_{out}$ and there is no edge $(v, u, l) \in E$ for some node u and a label l.*

Recall that a non-input node v in a circuit C is just a natural number that is labeled with a gate function, and that we require that v is greater than its predecessors. In other words, we assert that the order of the natural numbers $<$ is a topological order of the underlying graph of C. Thereby, starting with the empty circuit that only contains the input nodes X, $<$ describes an order in which we can add the gates to obtain the complete circuit C. But notice that this order is not always unique because C is not required to have a path that contains all nodes. Of course, we demand uniqueness so that we do not check the same circuit multiple times. Therefore, we commit to a specific topological order. As a first step, we formalize the depth of v, i.e., the length of the longest path from an input node to v.

Definition 7 (Depth of a Node). *For a node v in a circuit C we define the depth d of v as*

$$d(v) = \max\{d(v_L), d(v_R)\} + 1$$

where $d(x) = 0$ for all $x \in X$.

Now it only remains to sort nodes of the same depth. The input nodes $X = \{0, 1, \ldots, q-1\}$ are given, so we simply use $<$ for X. For non-input nodes, we use the associated gate function and the left and right predecessor. For the gate functions we assume that $\mathcal{G} = \{G_0, G_1, \ldots, G_{g-1}\}$ is ordered by $G_0 < G_1 < \cdots < G_{g-1}$. We formalize this in the following definition.

Definition 8 (Order of Nodes and Ordered Circuit). *For two nodes $u, v \in V$ in a onefold circuit C we have $u \prec v$ if $u \neq v$ and*

- *$d(u) < d(v)$ or*
- *$u, v \in X$ and $u < v$ or*
- *$d(u) = d(v)$ and $u_G < v_G$ or*
- *$d(u) = d(v)$ and $u_G = v_G$ and $u_L \prec v_L$ or*
- *$d(u) = d(v)$ and $u_G = v_G$ and $u_L = v_L$ and $u_R \prec v_R$.*

We call a circuit ordered if for all pairwise distinct nodes $u, v \in V$ it holds that $u < v \iff u \prec v$.

Definition 9 (Normal form for Circuits). *A circuit C is in normal form if C is onefold, without loose ends and ordered. We call such circuits normal.*

Lemma 1. *For every circuit C, there is an equivalent circuit C' s.t. C' is in normal form and has at most as many nodes as C.*

Proof. To bring C into normal form, we first make C onefold. To do so, for all equivalent nodes $u, v \in V$ we remove u and replace edges (u, w, l) by (v, w, l). After that, we remove all loose ends. Last, we make C ordered by permuting the underlying graph D and its labels accordingly.   □

Now that we have established our definitions for circuits, we want to study the number of possible circuits. Recall that our basic approach is to fix X and $\mathscr{G}$ based on the construction we are interested in, and also bound the number of non-input nodes by some $k \in \mathbb{N}$. The essential part here is that there are gates in $\mathscr{G}$ that correspond to oracles an attacker would have access to in the corresponding security games. For now, we only restrict the size of X and $\mathscr{G}$, i.e., we consider the circuit class

$$\mathscr{C}(q, g, k) = \{C \mid |X| = q, |\mathscr{G}| = g, |V \setminus X| = k\}.$$

Strictly speaking, we should not only consider circuits of size exactly k but circuits of size up to k. But as we will see, for our application there are by far more circuits of size k then there are circuits of size $k - 1$. So for the sake of simplicity, in our analysis, we only consider circuits of size exactly k.

Of course, we are mainly interested in the number of normal circuits, i.e., in the size of

$$\mathscr{C}_{norm}(q, g, k) = \{C \in \mathscr{C}(q, g, k) \mid C \text{ is normal}\}$$

because from Lemma 1 it immediately follows that they cover all circuits up to equivalence. Nevertheless, we will first derive the number of all circuits of size k which we will then use to estimate the number of normal circuits.

To determine the number of all circuits, we consider a tree T with root X and depth k, where every edge corresponds to adding a new gate. The leaves of this tree are the circuits in $\mathscr{C}(q, g, k)$. We call T the circuit tree of $\mathscr{C}(q, g, k)$. T is diagrammed in Fig. 4. There are $g \cdot q^2$ possible ways to add the first gate. $g \cdot (q + 1)^2$ for the next and so on. In total, the number of all leaves is

$$|\mathscr{C}(q, g, k)| = \prod_{i=0}^{k-1} g \cdot (q + i)^2 = g^k \cdot \left(\overline{q^k}\right)^2. \tag{10}$$

Therefore, the circuit size k has the highest impact on the number of all circuits and the number of input nodes q has a slightly higher impact than the number of gate functions g.

Now, to estimate the number of normal circuits, we wrote a `sage` script that essentially generates random circuits and then checks if they are normal. The results of this simulation, as well as the number of all circuits, are illustrated in Fig. 5 for the parameters $k \leq 9$ and $(q, g) \in \{(1, 3), (3, 3), (3, 5)\}$. The choice of these parameters is motivated by the idea of using $X = \{x\}$ or $X = \{x, \alpha_b, \alpha_{\overline{b}}\}$ and $\mathscr{G} = \{\oplus, ENC, DEC\}$ where ENC and DEC might be split into a left and a right half. We can draw two conclusions from Fig. 5. On the one hand, for small circuit classes, i.e., for circuit of size five or smaller, we might iterate all normal circuits with moderate computing power. On the other hand, we need

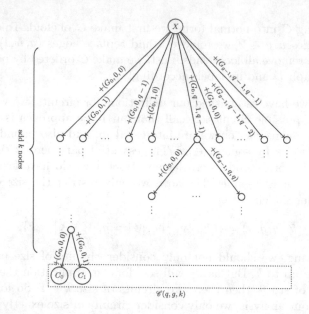

Fig. 4. Circuit tree T of $\mathscr{C}(q,g,k)$. By $+(G,l,r)$ we denote the adding of a node with gate function G, left predecessor l and right predecessor r.

to reduce the number of circuit further for larger classes. To do so, we establish a set of rules R that circuits have to comply with. These rules are basically an expansion of our already set up requirement that circuits must be normal. But they also include requirements that are based on the concrete choice of X and $\mathscr{G}$. E.g., one gate function that we always use is the XOR function, and it is natural to require that the inputs of the XOR are ordered since XOR is commutative. Thus, we consider the class of circuits

$$\mathscr{C}(X,\mathscr{G},k,R) = \{C \mid C \text{ has input nodes } X, \text{ gate functions } \mathscr{G},$$
$$|V \setminus X| = k, \forall r \in R : r(C) = 1\}.$$

Notice that here we overload the notation because we are not interested in the pure size of X and $\mathscr{G}$ anymore. In the following, we use $R(C) = \wedge_{r \in R} r(C)$ to shorten the notation.

5.2   Enumerating Circuits

The most straightforward way of enumerating $\mathscr{C}(X,\mathscr{G},k,R)$ is surely to simply enumerate all circuits of size k with input nodes X and gate functions $\mathscr{G}$. Then, for each circuit, we can check whether it complies with R. But, as we have seen in the last section, there are many more circuits than circuits in normal form. So, this approach is rather inefficient.

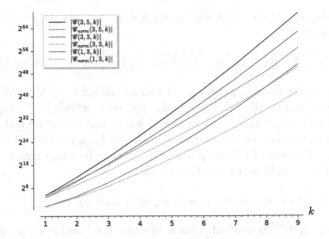

Fig. 5. Number of circuits for various parameters.

To find a better strategy, we assume that we cannot only test R on a complete circuit $C \in \mathscr{C}(X, \mathscr{G}, k, \emptyset)$ but also on every partial circuit

$$C' \in \bigcup_{1 \leq i < k} \mathscr{C}(X, \mathscr{G}, i, \emptyset)$$

in such a way that no partial circuit C' with $R(C') = 0$ can be extended to a circuit C s.t. $R(C) = 1$. E.g., again consider the XOR gate and observe that once we added a bad XOR gate, there is no way to get to a good circuit. The same applies to all other rules we use. Now recall the circuit tree T from Fig. 4. We are interested in enumerating all leaves C of T for which $R(C) = 1$ holds. Let us assume, that we have already identified the first, i.e., the leftmost, circuit C^* with this property. Then, we will first check all right siblings of C^*. After that, we test $R(C^{\dagger})$ where $C^{\dagger}$ is the first right sibling of the parent of C^*. If $R(C^{\dagger}) = 1$ we will check all children of $C^{\dagger}$. Otherwise, we continue with the next sibling of $C^{\dagger}$. At some point, there are no more siblings of $C^{\dagger}$ left. Then, we continue with the same approach on the level of the parent of $C^{\dagger}$. As soon as we hit the root of T we are finished with our search.

Notice that, since the setting is rather vague, neither can we exclude that there are more efficient ways to enumerate circuits or even find periodic circuits nor can we give a general runtime analysis of our approach. Instead, we will analyze the runtime for concrete and practical examples in Sect. 5.4.

One rule that we always want to use is

$$r_{normal}(C) = \begin{cases} 1 & \text{if } C \text{ is in normal form} \\ 0 & \text{else.} \end{cases}$$

Therefore, we now describe how r_{normal} can be checked on partial circuits. First, recall that we call a circuit normal if it is onefold, without loose ends and ordered.

For loose ends, we observe that with each new node, we can get rid of at most one loose end. So if

$$|\{v \in V \setminus X \mid \nexists u \in V : v = u_L \vee v = u_R\}| > 1 + (k - (|V| - |X|))$$

holds for a partial circuit C', there is no way of adding $k - (|V| - |X|)$ nodes to C' to obtain a circuit without loose ends. To check whether C' is ordered, we only have to test $u \prec v$ as defined in Definition 8 where v is the last added and u is the second but last added node resp. This is because we will check $R(C')$ only if the predecessor of C' complied with R. For the same reason, if v is the last added node, it suffices to check whether the set

$$\{u \in V \mid u_G = v_G \text{ and } u_L = v_L \text{ and } u_R = v_R\}$$

is empty to check if C' is onefold. This is because if C' without v is onefold then

$$u_L \sim v_L \iff u_L = v_L$$

and the same holds for the right predecessor.

5.3 Testing a Circuit for Periodicity

Testing a circuit C, i.e., the function C_f, for periodicity is fairly simple because we can evaluate C_f on all inputs and then check whether there are any periods. When we enumerate circuits, we do not evaluate each circuit from the ground up. Instead, we store the evaluation of each node s.t. after adding a node and checking that it complies with all rules, we only have to evaluate the new node.

Aside from that, we want to filter out as much trivial periods as possible. By trivial periods, we mean periods that bear no useful information. For example, consider the function

$$f(x) = E(x) \oplus E(x \oplus \alpha)$$

where E is an encryption oracle and α is an arbitrary constant. Obviously, f has a period $s = \alpha$. But this has nothing to do with the structure of E and in fact, if we replace E with a truly random function E', the period persists. Since our enumeration will encounter functions of this kind, we want to check whether a period is trivial or not. To do so, we can replace all oracles by their random version and see whether the period persists. If so, we discard the period. Notice that the period may change since the period could depend on the oracle gates, e.g., consider f as above but replace α with $E(\alpha)$. We want to remark that this essentially matches the definition of a distinguisher, i.e., a non-trivial period is a property that is present in the real but not in the random case.

Notice, since we instantiate the constructions with a small input size, we might identify or miss a period accidentally. In practice, this was never a problem and in case of uncertainty, we can always repeat the search with fresh randomness or slightly increase the input size.

5.4   Setup of Our Search

Known Attacks. Here, we rediscover known attacks with our automated search algorithm. Of course, the primary intention here is to identify sound choices for gates, inputs and rules that we can reuse when we search for novel attacks. Furthermore, we use the occasion to investigate the running time of our algorithm in a practical scenario.

Recall that the attack on the Even-Mansour cipher [18] is based on the function

$$f(x) = ENC(x) \oplus P(x) = P(x \oplus k_0) \oplus k_1 \oplus P(x) \tag{11}$$

with period $s = k_0$. Therefore, our attack requires input nodes $X = \{x\}$ and gates $\mathscr{G} = \{\oplus, ENC, P\}$. Notice that, both ENC and P are functions of one variable, but our definition requires that both are functions of two variables. Therefore, we set the rule

$$r_{SI}(C) = \begin{cases} 1 & \text{if } \forall v \in V : v_G \in \{ENC, P\} \Rightarrow v_L = v_R \\ 0 & \text{else.} \end{cases}$$

We can enforce r_{SI} simply by checking if $v_G \in \{ENC, P\} \Rightarrow v_L = v_R$ holds for each node v that we add to a circuit. Furthermore, since for Even-Mansour P is just a public permutation, only circuits that contain at least one ENC gate are of interest. Therefore, we add the rule

$$r_{1E}(C) = \begin{cases} 1 & \text{if } \exists v \in V : v_G = ENC \\ 0 & \text{else.} \end{cases}$$

This rule is of course only enforced for complete circuits, i.e., for circuits of size k. Equivalently, we can say that $r_{1E}(C') = 1$ for all partial circuits C'. Last, we add a rule that eliminates some circuits that are equivalent to another circuit because of the commutative or self inverse properties of the XOR function. That is, $r_\oplus$ excludes all circuits that contain a node v with $v_G = \oplus$ for which $v_L \prec v_R$ does not hold. Again, this can be checked each time we add a new gate. This also excludes circuits which compute the XOR of a node with itself. In addition, $r_\oplus$ shall exclude circuits for which there is a node that contributes twice to a XOR sum, and also circuits for which there are two nodes that compute the same XOR sum. To check these, for each node v we store a set Σ_v that is defined as follows

$$\Sigma_v = \begin{cases} \{v\} & \text{if } v \in X \text{ or } v_G \neq \oplus \\ \Sigma_{v_L} \cup \Sigma_{v_R} & \text{if } v_G = \oplus. \end{cases}$$

Thereby, Σ_v contains all nodes that contribute to the XOR sum if v is an XOR gate. So if we add a new node v we only have to check that the intersection $\Sigma_{v_L} \cap \Sigma_{v_R}$ is empty and that there is no other node u s.t. $\Sigma_u = \Sigma_v$.

As we saw in Sect. 3.1, the distinguishing attack by Kuwakado and Morii against 3-round Feistel cipher uses the function

$$f(x,b) = ENC_L(x, \alpha_b) \oplus \alpha_{\bar{b}} = F_1(x \oplus F_0(\alpha_b)) \oplus \alpha_b \oplus \alpha_{\bar{b}}$$

with period $s = (F_0(\alpha_0) \oplus F_0(\alpha_1))\|1$ where $\alpha_0, \alpha_1 \in \mathbb{F}_2^n$ are arbitrary distinct constants. To find this f, we use $X = \{x, \alpha_b, \alpha_{\bar{b}}\}$ and set $\mathcal{G} = \{\oplus, ENC_L, ENC_R\}$. In terms of rules, we first notice that α_b and $\alpha_{\bar{b}}$ are equivalent for the attack. Therefore, we demand that α_b appears first. Further, the output must depend on x and at least on one of α_b and $\alpha_{\bar{b}}$ because otherwise there will be trivial periods. To check this, for complete circuits, we simply check whether there is a path from x to v_{out} and from α_b or $\alpha_{\bar{b}}$ to v_{out}. All the above rules do not exclude useful periodic circuits from the search. To decrease the search space even further, we limit the number of oracle queries to one. Therefore, ENC_L and ENC_R each are allowed only once in a circuit. If they both appear in a circuit, we require them to have the same inputs. Last, we enforce that ENC_L and ENC_R depend on x. This, again, can be checked with a reachability test in the underlying digraph, and excludes circuits that, e.g., compute $ENC_L(\alpha_b, \alpha_{\bar{b}})$. Although the last two rules might exclude useful periodic circuits, based on the periodic functions from the literature and our experience, we believe that this are reasonable additions to our set of rules.

Other attacks make also use of decryption queries, e.g., in [14, Section 5] the authors present a quantum chosen-ciphertext distinguisher against 4-round Feistel. To find such, we add decryption oracles to the set of gate functions. So, for Feistel, we have $\mathcal{G} = \{\oplus, ENC_L, ENC_R, DEC_L, DEC_R\}$. Naturally, we add a rule to exclude circuits that, e.g., decrypt an unaltered ciphertext. Further, we demand that DEC gates depend on ENC gates.

We now briefly discuss the complexity of the searches on Even-Mansour and Feistel. Consider Fig. 5 for k up to 6 and compare it with Fig. 6 which shows the complexity, i.e., the number of tests our algorithm needs. The solid lines are essentially the same in both plots. A trivial search algorithm would test all circuits (solid lines) for normality and then test all normal circuits (dotted lines from Fig. 5) for periodicity. Our algorithm does not only test for normality, but also for other rules defined by R. But these tests are done in a sophisticated way on (partial) circuits. Therefore, for our choices of R, a single test is not more complex than a test for normality. But the number of tests is clearly reduced (solid vs. dashed lines). And so is the number of tests for periodicity (dotted lines from Fig. 5 vs dotted lines from Fig. 6).

MISTY. Next, we describe how we set up our automated search algorithm to find periodic functions for 4-round MISTY R-FK and 5-round MISTY L-FK. Based on our insights from the previous section, we choose gates

$$\mathcal{G} = \{\oplus, ENC_L, ENC_R, F, F^{-1}\}.$$

So, we split the encryption gate in the same manner as for our searches on Feistel structures. In terms of rules, we use r_{normal} and $r_\oplus$ and of course also ensure that F and F^{-1} only take a single input and do not uncompute each other. If we search for large circuits of size $k > 5$ we also restrict the number of encryption queries to one, again in the same way as we did for Feistel. For the input nodes X we either choose only a single input x or x and a constant α. For 5-round

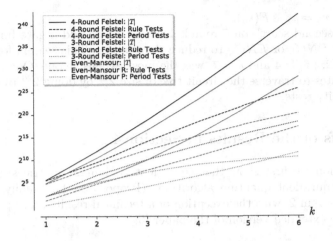

Fig. 6. Number of circuits and tests in practice.

MISTY L-FK, the search yields not only f_2 from Eq. (5) but also the following additional functions t_i with periods r_i.

$$t_1(x) = ENC_L(F^{-1}(x), \alpha) \oplus x \qquad\qquad r_1 = F(\alpha) \oplus k_1$$
$$t_2(x) = ENC_R(F^{-1}(F^{-1}(x)), F^{-1}(x)) \oplus x \qquad r_2 = F(k_0) \oplus k_2$$
$$t_3(x) = ENC_L(F^{-1}(F^{-1}(x)), F^{-1}(x)) \oplus F(x)$$
$$\qquad\qquad \oplus ENC_R(F^{-1}(F^{-1}(x)), F^{-1}(x)) \qquad r_3 = k_0 \oplus k_1 \oplus k_2 \oplus F(k_0)$$
$$t_4(x) = ENC_L(F^{-1}(F^{-1}(x)), F^{-1}(x)) \oplus F(x) \oplus x \quad r_4 = k_0 \oplus k_1$$

Here, $\alpha \in \mathbb{F}_2^n$ is an arbitrary constant. However, notice that these are of course our polished results. In reality, we might have encountered some variations first. For instance, if we choose the circuit size k for t_1 too large, we find circuits where α is permuted first. Furthermore, notice the close connection between t_2, t_3 and t_4 and their corresponding periods. We have $t_4(x) = t_2(x) \oplus t_3(x)$ and $r_4 = r_2 \oplus r_3$. This is of course due to the internal structure of MISTY and nothing we can exploit in general. E.g., consider t_1 and t_2. It is easy to verify that $t_1(x) \oplus t_2(x)$ is not periodic.

For MISTY, the search that yielded the circuit for t_3, for which we have $|X| = 1$, $|\mathscr{G}| = 5$ and $k = 7$, was the most expensive one. Our laptop took six minutes to traverse the circuit tree of size 2^{41} by doing 2^{25} rule tests and 2^{18} periodicity tests.

Feistel. For our search on Feistel, we use essentially the same setup as before. Furthermore, for 4-round Feistel-FK, our search yields not only f_3 from Eq. (6) but also

$$t_5(x) = ENC_L(F(x), x) \oplus F(x)$$

with period $r_5 = k_1 \oplus F(k_0)$.

For the second search on 5-rounds Feistel-FK, we add a gate function F^{-1} and remove ENC_L or ENC_R to reduce the runtime. This search, for which we have $|X| = 2$, $|\mathscr{G}| = 4$ and $k = 7$, was the most expensive one. Our laptop took twelve minutes to traverse the circuit tree of size 2^{44} by doing 2^{26} rule tests and 2^{19} periodicity tests.

6   Proofs of the Results in Section 4

In this section we first show that equivalent Hadamard matrices give rise to essentially equivalent quantum algorithms (Proposition 1). Finally, we give a proof of Theorem 2, with the exception of a technical result whose proof can be found in the extended version of the paper [5].

6.1   Equivalence of Hadamard Transformations

Let us now consider a Hadamard matrix $H \in \mathbb{R}^{2^n \times 2^n}$ and consider it given as

$$(H)_{x,y} = (-1)^{g(x,y)},$$

for a suitable choice of $g : \mathbb{F}_2^n \times \mathbb{F}_2^n \to \mathbb{F}_2$.

We define the Fourier-like transformation of H as follows

Definition 10. *For a Boolean function* $f : \mathbb{F}_2^n \to \mathbb{F}_2$, *we define*

$$\widehat{f}^H(x) := (H\phi)_x = \sum_{y \in \mathbb{F}_2^n} (-1)^{f(y)+g(x,y)},$$

where $(H\phi)_x$ *is the component* x *of the vector* $H_0\phi$, *and* ϕ *is the vector*

$$\phi = \left((-1)^{f(0)}, \ldots, (-1)^{f(2^n-1)} \right)^T.$$

Hadamard matrices are an interesting research topic on their own, with fundamental questions still being unsolved. In particular, it is not even clear for which dimension N Hadamard matrices exist. A famous conjecture states that there exists at least one Hadamard matrix if the dimension is divisible by four. This is still an open problem and, at the time of writing, the smallest such integer for which no Hadamard matrix is known is $N = 668$ [16].

However, since we work on vector spaces of dimension 2^n for some $n \in \mathbb{N}$, we know that there is at least one Hadamard matrix for each of these dimensions, and that is indeed H_0.

In fact, a related question that is more interesting for our context is understanding how many *different* Hadamard matrices exist in each dimension that could possibly result in meaningfully different routines $\texttt{Simon}(H)$. To this end, we consider the following – standard – notion of equivalence.

Definition 11. *Two Hadamard matrices H, H' are said to be equivalent if there exist diagonal matrices D_1, D_2 whose diagonals take entries in $\{-1,1\}$ and permutation matrices P_1, P_2 such that*

$$H' = P_1 D_1 H D_2 P_2.$$

Similarly, we will say that two transformations $\widehat{f}^H$ and $\widehat{f}^{H'}$ are equivalent if H and H' are equivalent.

As proved in [5], two equivalent matrices H and H' will result in the circuits $\texttt{Simon}(H)$ and $\texttt{Simon}(H')$ being the same, up to some classical pre- and post-processing, as we state in the following result.

Proposition 1. *Let H and H' be two equivalent Hadamard matrices. There exist functions $\texttt{PRE} : \mathcal{B}_n \to \mathcal{B}_n$ and $\texttt{POST} : \mathbb{F}_2^n \to \mathbb{F}_2^n$ such that, for any $f : \mathbb{F}_2^n \to \mathbb{F}_2$*

$$\Pr(x \leftarrow \texttt{Simon}(H')(f)) = \Pr(x \leftarrow \texttt{POST}(\texttt{Simon}(H)(\texttt{PRE}(f)))).$$

Thus $\texttt{Simon}(H)$, with some classical pre- and post-processing, perfectly simulates the routine $\texttt{Simon}(H')$ for any H' equivalent to H. It follows that we can indeed reduce ourselves to consider only non-equivalent Hadamard matrices.

6.2 Proof of Theorem 2

In this section we provide a proof of Theorem 2. First, we prove that we can reduce the problem to the simpler case where the matrix B is not arbitrary and simply consider $B = A^T$ (Proposition 2), thanks to a result on the structure of the group $\mathrm{GL}(n, \mathbb{F}_2)$. After that, we prove that the possibility for H are then limited (Proposition 3) and conclude the proof.

Let us consider a Hadamard matrix H and let $\widehat{f}^H : \mathbb{F}_2^n \to \mathbb{Z}$ be its transform $\widehat{f}^H(i) = (H\phi)_i$ as in Sect. 4.1. Let $g : \mathbb{F}_2^n \times \mathbb{F}_2^n \to \mathbb{F}_2$ be the (unique) Boolean function implicitly defined by $(-1)^{g(x,y)} = (H)_{x,y}$. We will make this relation explicit by indicating H as H_g. The idea of the proof of Theorem 2 is that, if $\widehat{f}^{H_g}$ satisfies the theorem, then the corresponding Boolean function g is (almost) the scalar product, and therefore H_g is equivalent to $H_0 = H_{\langle x,y \rangle}$.

Indeed, let for any Boolean function f we have:

$$\widehat{f \circ A}^{H_g}(x) = \sum_{y \in \mathbb{F}_2^n} (-1)^{(f \circ A)(y) + g(x,y)} = \sum_{y \in \mathbb{F}_2^n} (-1)^{f(y) + g(x, A^{-1}y)}$$

where we considered A^{-1} instead of A for ease of notation. On the other hand,

$$(\widehat{f}^{H_g} \circ B)(x) = \sum_{y \in \mathbb{F}_2^n} (-1)^{f(y) + g(Bx, y)}.$$

Given the arbitrary choice of f, the above quantities are equal for all $x \in \mathbb{F}_2^n$ if and only if

$$g(Bx, y) = g(x, A^{-1}y) \tag{12}$$

for all $x, y \in \mathbb{F}_2^n$. In fact, if there exist $\chi, \upsilon \in \mathbb{F}_2^n$ for which Eq. (13) does not hold, then if we consider the Boolean function $f_\chi(y) := g(\chi, A^{-1}y)$ for all $y \in \mathbb{F}_2^n$, it is clear that $\widehat{f_\chi \circ A}^{H_g}(\chi) \neq \widehat{f_\chi^{H_g}} \circ B(\chi)$. Furthermore, notice that for the arbitrary choice of A, Eq. (12) is equivalent to finding B such that

$$g(x, Ay) = g(B^{-1}x, y). \tag{13}$$

Therefore proving the theorem is equivalent to solving Eq. (13).

The main difficulty of the proof is the a priori freedom in choosing B for a given A. We therefore want to first understand what is the dependence of B on A. To do so, we define the function $F_g : \mathrm{GL}(n, \mathbb{F}_2) \to \mathrm{GL}(n, \mathbb{F}_2)$ such that

$$F_g(A) = B.$$

The key observation is that this mapping is actually an automorphism over $\mathrm{GL}(n, \mathbb{F}_2)$. Indeed, if g is a solution of Eq. (13), F_g is a well-defined function because if for $A \in \mathrm{GL}(n, \mathbb{F}_2)$ there existed two distinct $B, B' \in \mathrm{GL}(n, \mathbb{F}_2)$ such that Eq. (13) holds, then if we consider $z \in \mathbb{F}_2^n$ such that $B^{-1}z \neq (B')^{-1}z$, we would have that

$$g(B^{-1}z, x) = g(z, Ax) = g((B')^{-1}z, x)$$

for all $x \in \mathbb{F}_2^n$. But this contradicts the fact that $H_g H_g^T$ is the identity matrix.

The same reasoning shows that F_g is injective, and therefore bijective. Furthermore, it also holds that $F_g(A \cdot A') = F_g(A) \cdot F_g(A')$, from which it follows that F_g is an automorphism over $\mathrm{GL}(n, \mathbb{F}_2)$. Luckily for us, it is possible to characterize such automorphisms in a nice way, thanks to a result due to Dieudonné [9], which can be found in a more convenient formulation for our purposes in [19].

Lemma 2 ([9,19]). *For every automorphism F of $\mathrm{GL}(n, \mathbb{F}_2)$, there exists $G \in \mathrm{GL}(n, \mathbb{F}_2)$ such that either*

$$F(A) = G^{-1}AG \quad or \quad F(A) = G^{-1}(A^T)^{-1}G \tag{14}$$

for all $A \in \mathrm{GL}(n, \mathbb{F}_2)$.

This characterization, together with the considerations above, will allow us to reduce the proof to the case of Theorem 2 with $B = (A^T)^{-1}$, as is stated by the following proposition.

Proposition 2. *For any g such that H_g is Hadamard and that fulfils Eq. (13), there exists a matrix $G \in \mathrm{GL}(n, \mathbb{F}_2)$ such that $g(x, y) = \overline{g}(Gx, y)$, where $\overline{g}$ fulfils*

$$\overline{g}(x, Ay) = \overline{g}(A^T x, y). \tag{15}$$

Proof. The result is trivial for $n = 1, 2$ and thus we assume $n \geq 3$ from now on.

Let us suppose that F_g is of the first form, i.e. it exists $G \in \mathrm{GL}(n, \mathbb{F}_2)$ such that $F_g(A) = G^{-1}AG$ for all $A \in \mathrm{GL}(n, \mathbb{F}_2)$. Let us prove that this is not possible. Let $x \neq y \in \mathbb{F}_2^n \setminus \{0\}$. Then, since H_g is Hadamard, we have that $\sum_{z \in \mathbb{F}_2^n} (-1)^{g(x,z)+g(z,y)} = 0$, that is there are exactly 2^{n-1} values of z for which $g(x,z) \neq g(z,y)$. This means that for any $n \geq 3$ we can find z_1, z_2 such that $z_1 \notin \{0, Gx\}$ and $z_2 \notin \{0, G^{-1}y\}$ and $g(x, z_1) \neq g(x, z_2)$. Then, there exits $A \in \mathrm{GL}(n, \mathbb{F}_2)$ such that $y = Az_1$ and $x = G^{-1}A^{-1}Gz_2$ (that is, A is such that $z_1 \mapsto^A y$ and $Gx \mapsto^A Gz_2$), so that

$$g(z_2, y) = g(z_2, Az_1) = g(F_g(A)^{-1}z_2, z_1) = g(G^{-1}A^{-1}Gz_2, z_1) = g(x, z_1)$$

which leads to a contradiction.

Let us now suppose that F_g is of the second form, i.e. $F_g(A) = G^{-1}(A^T)^{-1}G$ for some $G \in \mathrm{GL}(n, \mathbb{F}_2)$. Consider $\bar{g}$ such that $\bar{g}(x, y) = g(x, (G^T)^{-1}y)$. Since $(G^T)^{-1}$ is a permutation, we have that H_g is Hadamard if and only if $H_{\bar{g}}$ is Hadamard and, furthermore, g satisfies Eq. (13) with $B = F_g(A)^{-1} = G^{-1}A^TG$ if and only if for all $x, y \in \mathbb{F}_2^n$ and $z = G^Ty$

$$\bar{g}(x, Az) = \bar{g}(x, AG^Ty) = g(x, (G^T)^{-1}AG^Ty) = g(F_g((G^T)^{-1}AG^T)^{-1}x, y)$$
$$= g(A^Tx, y) = \bar{g}(A^Tx, G^Ty) = \bar{g}(A^Tx, z),$$

i.e. $\bar{g}$ satisfies Eq. (13) with $B = A^T$. This is true for any $A \in \mathrm{GL}(n, \mathbb{F}_2)$ and concludes the proof. $\qquad \square$

In other words, for the proof of Theorem 2 we can consider without loss of generality the case $B = F_g(A) = (A^T)^{-1}$.

What is now left to conclude is that if $F_g(A)^{-1} = A^T$, then g is *almost* the scalar product $\langle x, y \rangle$. This is exactly what the following proposition states. The rather technical proof can be found in [5].

Proposition 3. *Let* $g : \mathbb{F}_2^n \times \mathbb{F}_2^n \to \mathbb{F}_2^n$ *such that for any* $A \in \mathrm{GL}(n, \mathbb{F}_2)$

$$g(x, Ay) = g(A^Tx, y) \tag{16}$$

for all $x, y \in \mathbb{F}_2^n$. *Then*

$$g(x, y) = \varepsilon_0 + \varepsilon_1 \delta_{\{0\}}(x) + \varepsilon_2 \delta_{\{0\}}(y) + \varepsilon_3 \langle x, y \rangle + \varepsilon_4 \delta_{\{(0,0)\}}(x, y)$$

where δ_M *is the indicator function of a set* M *and* $\varepsilon_0, \dots, \varepsilon_4 \in \mathbb{F}_2$.

Remark 1. The family of functions g of the proposition are the very natural solutions that are found by observing that we have

1. if g, h are solutions then $g + h$ is also a solution;
2. the scalar product $\langle x, y \rangle$ is a solution;
3. if $g(x, y) = \delta_M(x, y)$, where M is either $\{(0,0)\}$ or $\{0\} \times \mathbb{F}_2^n$ or $\mathbb{F}_2^n \times \{0\}$ or $\mathbb{F}_2^n \times \mathbb{F}_2^n$, then g is a solution because for any $A \in \mathrm{GL}(n, \mathbb{F}_2)$ and *any* $B \in \mathrm{GL}(n, \mathbb{F}_2)$, $g(x, Ay) = g(x, y) = g(Bx, y)$.

Now we can conclude the proof of Theorem 2.

Proof of Theorem 2. We restrict to the case of g such that H_g is Hadamard and fulfils Eq. (16). If g represents a Hadamard matrix H_g, then we know that

$$(H_g H_g^T)_{\alpha,\beta} = \sum_{x \in \mathbb{F}_2^n} (-1)^{g(x,\alpha)+g(x,\beta)}$$

is zero whenever $\alpha \neq \beta$. We can assume the form given in Proposition 3, that is

$$g(x,y) = \varepsilon_0 + \varepsilon_1 \delta_{\{0\}}(x) + \varepsilon_2 \delta_{\{0\}}(y) + \varepsilon_3 \langle x, y \rangle + \varepsilon_4 \delta_{\{(0,0)\}}(x,y).$$

Then we have

$$g(x,\alpha) + g(x,\beta) = \varepsilon_2(\delta_{\{0\}}(\alpha) + \delta_{\{0\}}(\beta)) + \varepsilon_3 \langle x, \alpha + \beta \rangle + \\ \varepsilon_4(\delta_{\{(0,0)\}}(x,\alpha) + \delta_{\{(0,0)\}}(x,\beta))$$

so that

$$\sum_{x \in \mathbb{F}_2^n} (-1)^{g(x,\alpha)+g(x,\beta)} = \sum_{x \in \mathbb{F}_2^n} (-1)^{\varepsilon_3 \langle x, \alpha+\beta \rangle + \varepsilon_4(\delta_{\{(0,0)\}}(x,\alpha) + \delta_{\{(0,0)\}}(x,\beta))}.$$

But if $\alpha = 0$ and $\beta \neq 0$, then we must have that

$$(H_g H_g^T)_{0,\beta} = \sum_{x \in \mathbb{F}_2^n} (-1)^{g(x,0)+g(x,\beta)} = \sum_{x \in \mathbb{F}_2^n} (-1)^{\varepsilon_3 \langle x, \beta \rangle + \varepsilon_4(\delta_0(x))} = 0$$

where we have used the fact that H_g is Hadamard. But $\sum_{x \in \mathbb{F}_2^n} (-1)^{\langle x, \beta \rangle} = 0$, as $\beta \neq 0$. Then, the above equality holds if and only if $\varepsilon_3 = 1$ and $\varepsilon_4 = 0$. It follows that if g is Hadamard and satisfies Eq. (16) then

$$g(x,y) = \varepsilon_0 + \varepsilon_1 \delta_{\{0\}}(x) + \varepsilon_2 \delta_{\{0\}}(y) + \langle Gx, y \rangle$$

which means that $H_g = (-1)^{\varepsilon_0} (D_{\delta_{\{0\}}})^{\varepsilon_1} H_0 (D_{\delta_{\{0\}}})^{\varepsilon_2}$, where D_h is the diagonal matrix such that $(D_{\delta_{\{0\}}})_{z,z} = \delta_{\{0\}}(z)$ for all $z \in \mathbb{F}_2^n$. Therefore, we conclude that H_g is indeed equivalent to H_0. Thus concludes the proof of our main result. $\square$

7   Conclusion

Motivated by the search for alternative ways to attack symmetric primitives, our goal was to find new applications of Simon's algorithm, as well as study possible generalizations.

On the one hand, we have seen that the standard Hadamard transformation is the only one that preserves linear equivalence. This result suggests that using alternative Hadamard transformations will not help in improving known attack vectors using the well studied linear-invariant cryptographic criteria. However, it does not exclude the possibility of new attacks based on non linear-invariant properties, that could profit from Simon(H). Moreover, for exploiting the standard criteria, our result shows that it is most promising to focus on the standard Hadamard-transform when searching for new quantum algorithms.

On the other hand, we have successfully automatized the search of periodic functions, resulting in new key-recovery attacks. However, our algorithm can be applied to other targets and can be still improved in order to search for larger circuits. We leave a more optimized and parallelized implementation or the use of a different representation of the functions, possibly allowing for the use of symbolic computation, as interesting future work.

Acknowledgments. This work was funded by the DFG (German Research Foundation), under Germany's Excellence Strategy - EXC 2092 CASA – 390781972. The authors would further like to thank Alessandro Ghigi and Philippe Langevin for fruitful discussions, particularly for pointing out the results of [9] and [19].

References

1. Bernstein, E., Vazirani, U.V.: Quantum complexity theory. SIAM J. Comput. **26**(5), 1411–1473 (1997)
2. Bonnetain, X., Hosoyamada, A., Naya-Plasencia, M., Sasaki, Yu., Schrottenloher, A.: Quantum attacks without superposition queries: the offline Simon's algorithm. In: Galbraith, S.D., Moriai, S. (eds.) ASIACRYPT 2019. LNCS, vol. 11921, pp. 552–583. Springer, Cham (2019). https://doi.org/10.1007/978-3-030-34578-5_20
3. Bonnetain, X., Jaques, S.: Quantum period finding against symmetric primitives in practice. IACR Cryptol. ePrint Arch. **2020**, 1418 (2020)
4. Bonnetain, X., Leurent, G., Naya-Plasencia, M., Schrottenloher, A.: Quantum linearization attacks. In: Tibouchi, M., Wang, H. (eds.) ASIACRYPT 2021, Part I. LNCS, vol. 13090, pp. 422–452. Springer, Cham (2021). https://doi.org/10.1007/978-3-030-92062-3_15
5. Canale, F., Leander, G., Stennes, L.: Simon's algorithm and symmetric crypto: Generalizations and automatized applications. Cryptology ePrint Archive, Paper 2022/782 (2022), https://eprint.iacr.org/2022/782
6. Carlet, C.: Boolean Functions for Cryptography and Coding Theory. Cambridge University Press, Cambridge (2021)
7. Chen, Y.L., Lambooij, E., Mennink, B.: How to build pseudorandom functions from public random permutations. In: Boldyreva, A., Micciancio, D. (eds.) CRYPTO 2019, Part I. LNCS, vol. 11692, pp. 266–293. Springer, Cham (2019). https://doi.org/10.1007/978-3-030-26948-7_10
8. Cui, J., Guo, J., Ding, S.: Applications of Simon's algorithm in quantum attacks on Feistel variants. Quantum Inf. Process. **20**(3), 117 (2021)
9. Dieudonné, J., Hua, L.: On the Automorphisms of the Classical Groups. Memoirs of the American Mathematical Society, American Mathematical Society (1951)
10. Dutta, A., Nandi, M., Talnikar, S.: Permutation based EDM: an inverse free BBB secure PRF. IACR Trans. Symmetric Cryptol. **2021**(2), 31–70 (2021)
11. Gouget, A., Patarin, J., Toulemonde, A.: (Quantum) cryptanalysis of Misty schemes. In: Hong, D. (ed.) ICISC 2020. LNCS, vol. 12593, pp. 43–57. Springer, Cham (2021). https://doi.org/10.1007/978-3-030-68890-5_3
12. Grover, L.K.: A fast quantum mechanical algorithm for database search. In: Miller, G.L. (ed.) Proceedings of the Twenty-Eighth Annual ACM Symposium on the Theory of Computing, pp. 212–219. ACM (1996)

13. Guo, T., Wang, P., Hu, L., Ye, D.: Attacks on beyond-birthday-bound MACs in the quantum setting. In: Cheon, J.H., Tillich, J.-P. (eds.) PQCrypto 2021 2021. LNCS, vol. 12841, pp. 421–441. Springer, Cham (2021). https://doi.org/10.1007/978-3-030-81293-5_22

14. Ito, G., Hosoyamada, A., Matsumoto, R., Sasaki, Y., Iwata, T.: Quantum chosen-ciphertext attacks against FEISTEL ciphers. In: Matsui, M. (ed.) CT-RSA 2019. LNCS, vol. 11405, pp. 391–411. Springer, Cham (2019). https://doi.org/10.1007/978-3-030-12612-4_20

15. Kaplan, M., Leurent, G., Leverrier, A., Naya-Plasencia, M.: Breaking symmetric cryptosystems using quantum period finding. In: Robshaw, M., Katz, J. (eds.) CRYPTO 2016, Part I. LNCS, vol. 9815, pp. 207–237. Springer, Heidelberg (2016). https://doi.org/10.1007/978-3-662-53008-5_8

16. Kharaghani, H., Tayfeh-Rezaie, B.: A Hadamard matrix of order 428. J. Comb. Des. **13**(6), 435–440 (2005)

17. Kuwakado, H., Morii, M.: Quantum distinguisher between the 3-round Feistel cipher and the random permutation. In: IEEE International Symposium on Information Theory, ISIT 2010, Proceedings, pp. 2682–2685. IEEE (2010)

18. Kuwakado, H., Morii, M.: Security on the quantum-type Even-Mansour cipher. In: Proceedings of the International Symposium on Information Theory and its Applications, ISITA 2012, pp. 312–316. IEEE (2012)

19. Landin, J., Reiner, I.: Automorphisms of the general linear group over a principal ideal domain. Ann. Math. **65**(3), 519–526 (1957)

20. Leander, G., May, A.: Grover meets SIMON – quantumly attacking the fx-construction. In: Takagi, T., Peyrin, T. (eds.) ASIACRYPT 2017, Part II. LNCS, vol. 10625, pp. 161–178. Springer, Cham (2017). https://doi.org/10.1007/978-3-319-70697-9_6

21. Matsui, M.: New structure of block ciphers with provable security against differential and linear cryptanalysis. In: Gollmann, D. (ed.) FSE 1996. LNCS, vol. 1039, pp. 205–218. Springer, Heidelberg (1996). https://doi.org/10.1007/3-540-60865-6_54

22. May, A., Schlieper, L.: Quantum period finding with a single output qubit - factoring n-bit RSA with n/2 qubits. CoRR abs/1905.10074 (2019)

23. May, A., Schlieper, L., Schwinger, J.: Practical period finding on IBM Q - quantum speedups in the presence of errors. CoRR abs/1910.00802 (2019)

24. Nielsen, M.A., Chuang, I.L.: Quantum Computation and Quantum Information (10th Anniversary edition). Cambridge University Press (2016)

25. Rahman, M., Paul, G.: Quantum attacks on HCTR and its variants. IACR Cryptol. ePrint Arch. **2020**, 802 (2020)

26. Santoli, T., Schaffner, C.: Using Simon's algorithm to attack symmetric-key cryptographic primitives. Quantum Inf. Comput. **17**(1&2), 65–78 (2017)

27. Xie, H., Yang, L.: Using Bernstein-Vazirani algorithm to attack block ciphers. CoRR abs/1711.00853 (2017)

28. Xie, H., Yang, L.: Using Bernstein-Vazirani algorithm to attack block ciphers. Des. Codes Cryptogr. **87**(5), 1161–1182 (2019)

Author Index

Printed in the United States
by Baker & Taylor Publisher Services